# Programming ColdFusion

# Programming ColdFusion

Rob Brooks-Bilson

O'REILLY®

*Beijing · Cambridge · Farnham · Köln · Paris · Sebastopol · Taipei · Tokyo*

**Programming ColdFusion**
by Rob Brooks-Bilson



Published by O'Reilly & Associates, Inc., 101 Morris Street, Sebastopol, CA 95472.

**Editors:** Paula Ferguson and Laura Lewin

**Production Editor:** Mary Anne Weeks Mayo

**Cover Designer:** Hanna Dyer

**Printing History:**

August 2001: First Edition.



*Library of Congress Cataloging-in-Publication Data*

Brooks-Bilson, Rob.
Programming ColdFusion/Rob Brooks-Bilson
p. cm.
ISBN 1-56592-698-6
1. Web databases 2. Database design. 3. Cold fusion (Computer file) I. Title.

QA76.9.W43 B76 2001
005.75'8--dc21 2001033093

[M]

# Table of Contents

# Preface

I first started using ColdFusion in early 1996. I had been hired by a company to build and manage both their external web site and their intranet. Both started as completely static sites, with a few Perl scripts thrown in to handle such tasks as emailing HTML form submissions. But it was only a matter of time before I was asked to add some dynamic content—the request was to "web enable" our corporate address book, which was stored in a Microsoft Access database. My first reaction was to develop the application in Perl. However, at the time, building an application like this in NT Perl (all of our web servers were NT-based) wasn't feasible, so I began looking for other solutions.

I first tried a product called DB Web, from a company named Aspect Software that had just been acquired by Microsoft. After a bit of experimentation, I realized that DB Web wasn't what I was looking for. It was more of a tool for querying data from Microsoft Access databases (it wrote VB code on the back end) than a real application development platform. (As a side note, Microsoft stopped supporting DB Web shortly after I evaluated it and rereleased it as Active Server Pages (ASP) a few months later.)

Frustrated, I decided to look into another product I had been hearing about on a web development discussion list. The product was Allaire's ColdFusion (Cold Fusion at the time), a rapid application development platform for creating and deploying dynamic server-based web applications.* Within hours of downloading

* Early in 2001, Allaire and Macromedia announced plans to merge, with the combined company using the Macromedia name. Although the merger closed before this book went to press, the Allaire name is still being used in conjunction with ColdFusion, so that's what I'm going to use throughout this book. Besides, I've been working with ColdFusion for so long now, calling it "Macromedia ColdFusion" is going to require breaking a longstanding habit!

the trial version of the software, I had created a proof-of-concept for the corporate address book application.

Looking back, it is almost funny to imagine that I fell in love with a language that had just over 30 language elements in the 1.5 release. At the time, though, ColdFusion had enough power to handle any web programming task thrown my way. And as the tasks have become more complex, ColdFusion has kept pace. Today, those initial 30 language elements have proliferated to over 335. Each new release of ColdFusion contains features and functionality that seem to show up just as I find myself needing or wanting them.

## Audience

This book is for anyone who is interested in learning more about ColdFusion, but it is especially aimed at web developers who are designing and building web applications with ColdFusion. I hope this book will help you become proficient with ColdFusion, and that you find it as powerful, easy to program with, and productive as I do.

If you are a beginning web developer, without any programming experience, you may find that the book moves quite quickly through the basics of ColdFusion. Before you start to learn ColdFusion, you should have some experience with web page creation, including a solid understanding of HTML. After that, if you focus on the examples provided in the early chapters and do a lot of experimenting with the code while you are reading, you should be able to learn ColdFusion with this book.

For intermediate developers who already have some web programming experience, this book is the perfect place to learn ColdFusion and get up to speed quickly. You'll learn about the ColdFusion Markup Language (CFML), which is ColdFusion's tag-based language for embedding dynamic content in web pages. This book provides examples that use CFML to implement all the standard web tasks, such as processing form data, performing database queries, and handling session data, so you should be up and running with ColdFusion in no time.

And if you are an advanced ColdFusion developer, you'll find this book loaded with strategies, hints, tips, and tricks that you can apply to your own projects. I've tried to include all the useful ColdFusion tidbits that I've discovered over the years, so that you can benefit from my experience. The book also includes reference material on all CFML tags and functions, so that you can have this information at your fingertips while you are programming.

## Organization

This book is divided into 24 chapters and 4 appendixes, as follows:

Chapter 1, *Introducing ColdFusion*
: Introduces the book and gives a high-level overview of the components that make up the ColdFusion development platform.

Chapter 2, *ColdFusion Basics*
: Gets you started using ColdFusion and covers such topics as datatypes, variables, expressions, conditional processing, and looping.

Chapter 3, *Passing Data Between Templates*
: Looks at passing data between templates using HTML forms and hyperlinks.

Chapter 4, *Database Basics*
: Gets you started using ColdFusion to query databases. Provides an overview of Structured Query Language (SQL) and demonstrates its use within ColdFusion applications.

Chapter 5, *Maintaining Database Records*
: Covers techniques for adding, updating, and deleting database records.

Chapter 6, *Complex Datatypes*
: Looks at the complex datatypes available in ColdFusion: lists, arrays, structures, and query objects.

Chapter 7, *Maintaining State*
: Investigates methods for maintaining state in ColdFusion applications.

Chapter 8, *Security*
: Covers the basics of application security and discusses several methods and models for securing your ColdFusion applications.

Chapter 9, *Error and Exception Handling*
: Explains several techniques for implementing error and exception handling within your ColdFusion applications.

Chapter 10, *Dynamic Form Controls*
: Gives an overview of the dynamic form controls provided by ColdFusion as an extension to standard HTML form controls.

Chapter 11, *Advanced Database Techniques*
: Covers several advanced techniques for querying and displaying data as well as advanced SQL topics.

Chapter 12, *Manipulating Files and Directories*
: Deals with techniques for manipulating files and directories on both local and remote servers.

Chapter 13, *Working With Email*
: Shows how to use ColdFusion to send email through SMTP servers and how to retrieve messages from POP3 servers. A working example of a web-based mail client is included.

Chapter 14, *Interacting with Other Web Servers Using HTTP*
: Demonstrates how to interact with other web servers via the HTTP GET and POST methods using ColdFusion.

Chapter 15, *Interfacing with LDAP-Enabled Directories*
: Gives a general overview of the Lightweight Directory Access Protocol (LDAP) and shows how to use ColdFusion to interface with LDAP-enabled directories.

Chapter 16, *Working with the Verity Search Interface*
: Explains how ColdFusion interacts with a bundled version of Verity's VDK, K2 Server, and Spider engines to index and search both file- and query-based content.

Chapter 17, *Regular Expressions in ColdFusion*
: Introduces regular expressions and demonstrates ways to integrate them into your ColdFusion applications.

Chapter 18, *Scripting*
: Provides an overview of CFScript, a server-side scripting language modeled after JavaScript that can be used in place of some of ColdFusion's tag-based language constructs. It also covers User Defined Functions (UDF), a new capability added in ColdFusion 5.0.

Chapter 19, *Creating Custom Tags*
: Shows how to extend the core capabilities of the ColdFusion language through reusable components called Custom Tags.

Chapter 20, *Sharing Data with WDDX*
: Covers the Web Distributed Data Exchange (WDDX), an XML-based technology for sharing data across disparate platforms and programming languages.

Chapter 21, *Working with the System Registry*
: Explains how ColdFusion can be used to read and write to the system registry. For non-Windows versions of ColdFusion (Unix/Linux), a miniversion of the registry is created when ColdFusion is installed.

Chapter 22, *Using the ColdFusion Scheduler*
: Explains how to schedule one-time and recurring tasks using ColdFusion's built-in scheduler.

Chapter 23, *Calling External Objects*
: Covers the basics of using ColdFusion to interact with COM-, CORBA-, and Java-based objects, as well as command-line programs.

Chapter 24, *Graphing and Charting*
: Shows how to use ColdFusion's built-in server-side graphing and charting capabilities to produce dynamic charts and graphs.

Appendix A, *Tag Reference*
: A complete CFML tag reference that includes several previously undocumented tags.

Appendix B, *Function Reference*
: A complete CFML function reference that contains numerous previously undocumented functions. The function reference includes a working example for each function wherever possible.

Appendix C, *Example Database Tables*
: Contains the schema and sample data for all database tables used in the book's examples.

Appendix D, *ColdFusion Resources*
: Provides a comprehensive listing of free ColdFusion resources available over the Internet. These resources include user groups, e-zines, support forums, and other community-minded resources.

# Conventions Used in This Book

The following typographical conventions are used throughout this book:

*Italic*
: Used for commands, URLs, filenames, file extensions, command-line utilities, directory and folder names, and UNC pathnames, as well as new terms where they are defined.

`Constant width`
: Used for anything that appears in a ColdFusion template, including CFML and HTML tags and attributes, variables, and functions. Also used for code listings.

*`Constant-width italic`*
: Used as general placeholders to indicate that an item should be replaced by some actual value in your own program.

# Comments and Questions

Please address comments and questions concerning this book to the publisher:

O'Reilly & Associates, Inc.
101 Morris Street
Sebastopol, CA 95472
(800) 998-9938 (in the United States or Canada)

(707) 829-0515 (international/local)
(707) 829-0104 (fax)

There is a web page for this book, which lists errata, examples, or any additional information. You can access this page at:

*http://www.oreilly.com/catalog/coldfusion/*

To comment or ask technical questions about this book, send email to:

*bookquestions@oreilly.com*

For more information about books, conferences, software, Resource Centers, and the O'Reilly Network, see the O'Reilly web site at:

*http://www.oreilly.com*

## Acknowledgments

While it is impossible to individually acknowledge everyone who had a hand in getting this book from an idea to the printed work you now hold in your hand, I would like to recognize and thank a few of these special people.

First and foremost, I'd like to thank my wife Persephone for putting up with my lack of participation in the day-to-day responsibilities of homeownership and maintaining a relationship. On more nights than I can remember, she remained pleasant and understanding while I stayed sequestered in my office until the wee hours of the morning. She also gets credit for giving me the idea for the first paragraph in the book's introduction. For some reason, I found the most difficult part of writing the book was coming up with the introduction *after* the rest of the book was finished.

Thanks also to my parents, Bob Bilson and Dianne Bilson. If it weren't for that Commodore Vic20, I wouldn't be where I am today. While I'm at it, this is also a good time to thank all of my friends and family who are probably tired of hearing "working on the book" in reply to the question "what are you doing tonight?"

I am forever indebted to Dr. Helen Munro for inspiring me when I was younger and showing me that applying creativity to problem solving can be as effective an approach as any scientific method. Good teachers rarely get the credit they deserve.

Three of my technical reviewers, Selene Bainum, Artur Bakhtriger, and Michael Dinowitz also deserve thanks for their hard work in ensuring the book was readable and accurate. I'd like to give special thanks to two additional technical reviewers, Elias Jo and Amy Wong. Their sharp eye for detail and ability to read and comment on virtually every section of the book was responsible for catching more errors and omissions than I care to admit. The feedback they provided, both from a development and a technical support perspective, was invaluable.

Thanks to J.J. and Jeremy Allaire and the rest of the team at Allaire for the hard work and vision that went into ColdFusion. I'd also like to thank Bushan Byragani, Tim Buntel, Chris Kintzing, Damon Cooper, Zane Kuchera, and Tom Harwood for helping me understand some of ColdFusion's finer technical points. Thanks especially to Jeremy Allaire for getting me excited about ColdFusion and the world of opportunity it has made possible for web development. Thanks also to the Allaire developer community for some of the great ideas and great people it has produced. Allaire can honestly claim one of the most tightly knit and supportive developer communities around.

I would like to thank everyone at Amkor Technology for providing me with the challenges that necessitated learning every facet of ColdFusion. I'd especially like to thank Scott Varga for some of his comments on early drafts of many of the chapters as well as readability and usability testing he provided while simultaneously learning ColdFusion.

My editors at O'Reilly, Paula Ferguson and Laura Lewin, also deserve recognition. Without their editorial skill and ability to help me focus in on the important aspects of the book, you wouldn't be reading this. Finally, I'd like to thank the production staff at O'Reilly for their hard work in getting the book to print.

*In this chapter:*
- *What Is Allaire's ColdFusion?*
- *ColdFusion Architecture*
- *Getting Started with ColdFusion*

# 1 Introducing ColdFusion

In 1989, two physicists, Martin Fleischmann and Stanley Pons, claimed that their research had uncovered a phenomenon that promised to solve the world's energy problems. What they claimed to have accomplished was nothing short of astonishing: that they had achieved nuclear fusion at room temperature. They called their discovery Cold Fusion. Unfortunately, the scientific community at large dismissed their findings because no one was ever able to reproduce the results claimed in the original experiment. Oh wait, wrong book...

## What Is Allaire's ColdFusion?

In 1995, J.J. and Jeremy Allaire introduced a product they believed would revolutionize application development for the Web. They too called their creation ColdFusion. Unlike its infamous namesake, Allaire's ColdFusion has delivered on the promises put forth by its creators.*

ColdFusion is a rapid application development platform for creating and deploying dynamic server-based web applications. Web applications exist as a collection of web pages, also known as templates, that work together to allow users to perform such tasks as reading email, buying books, or tracking packages. Web applications often act as the frontend to back-end services, such as legacy applications and databases. Some examples of web applications built using ColdFusion include Autobytel.com's application for researching and purchasing a car (*http://www.*

* Early in 2001, Allaire and Macromedia announced plans to merge, with the combined company using the Macromedia name. The merger closed before this book went to press, but the Allaire name is still being used to refer to ColdFusion, so that's what this book uses. In addition, as this book went to press, all the official ColdFusion web sites still use the *www.allaire.com* address, but that may change at any time. If you find that these URLs no longer work, please check the errata on the catalog page for this book (*http://www.oreilly.com/catalog/coldfusion/*) for the new addresses.

*autobytel.com/*) Williams-Sonoma's storefront application (*http://www.williams-sonoma.com/*), and Infonautics's Company Sleuth application for tracking publicly traded companies (*http://www.sleuth.com/*).

One key aspect of a web application is that it is dynamic; it is not just a static collection of web pages. The benefits of dynamically driven design are obvious. If you think of it in practical terms, which would you rather do each time a new press release has to be added to your web site? Would you rather the marketing department send you the text for the new press release so you can convert it to an HTML page, upload the page to your server, then go add a link to the menu of available press releases? Or, would you rather provide an HTML form to the marketing department so they can enter the text from the press release themselves and store it in a database that can then be queried to dynamically build the press release menu and associated pages? ColdFusion allows you to create just this kind of application.

Of course, there are a lot of different technologies you can use to create dynamic web applications, from open source technologies such as Perl/CGI scripts or PHP, to such commercial options as Java Server Pages and Java servlets or Microsoft's Active Server Pages. With all these choices, why use ColdFusion?

One reason has to do with ease of development. Unlike with most of the other technologies I mentioned, you don't have to be a hard-core programmer to get started with ColdFusion. This doesn't, however, mean that ColdFusion isn't powerful. Quite the contrary. ColdFusion makes it simple to do common tasks, such as processing form data and querying a database. But when you need to perform more complex operations, such as transaction processing and personalization, ColdFusion makes that possible too.

ColdFusion is also designed for rapid application development (RAD). ColdFusion abstracts complex, low-level programming tasks, such as establishing connectivity with a mail server or querying a database, with simple HTML-like tags. The result is an application development cycle that is second to none.

Another advantage of ColdFusion is that it is available for all the popular operating systems and web servers. ColdFusion is available for Windows 95/98/NT/2000, Solaris, Linux, and HP-UX. The application server can be configured to run in CGI mode or within the context of many popular web server APIs such as ISAPI, NSAPI, and WSAPI. Thus, ColdFusion runs on Netscape's Enterprise and iPlanet servers, Microsoft's Internet Information Server, Microsoft's Personal Web Server, O'Reilly's WebSite Pro, and Apache. In general, you can migrate ColdFusion applications between different operating systems web servers, and databases, for instance, when you upgrade your databases for scalability purposes. There are, however, some minor incompatibilities between platforms, i.e., there is no COM support in the Unix/Linux version of ColdFusion. Although minor for the most part, these differences are explained in relevant sections of this book.

ColdFusion is a mature, robust product; the current version as of this writing is ColdFusion 5.0. When ColdFusion was released in 1995, it provided simple database and SMTP mail connectivity and supported basic output formatting. Each successive release of ColdFusion has added features and functionality. Today, ColdFusion contains over 80 tags and 255 functions for handling almost any task imaginable. Add to that scalability features to handle high-traffic sites such as load balancing and failover, and it is easy to see why ColdFusion is so popular among developers and administrators alike.

There is a vibrant community of ColdFusion users who are active both in shaping the future direction of the product and in supporting others who use it. A number of ColdFusion-related conferences are held each year by both Allaire and members of the developer community. Allaire also runs several web-based forums, where developers can post and answer questions related to ColdFusion development (*http://forums.allaire.com*). The forums are monitored by Allaire support engineers as well as a volunteer group known as Team Allaire. In addition, Allaire sponsors a number of user groups around the world. Known as CFUGs (ColdFusion User Groups), these groups provide a place for ColdFusion developers to get together and share information on a variety of ColdFusion-related topics. Finally, there are a number of web sites devoted to furthering the ColdFusion community. For a complete list of community resources, see Appendix D.

# ColdFusion Architecture

There are several components that make up the ColdFusion environment, from which you can develop ColdFusion applications. As I mentioned earlier, a ColdFusion application is simply a collection of templates (web pages) that work together to allow a user to perform a task. These templates don't exist in a vacuum, however. To get a better idea of how a ColdFusion application is constructed, you need to understand the components that make up the ColdFusion environment:

*ColdFusion Application Server*

The ColdFusion Application Server processes all the CFML code in the templates passed to it by the web server. It then returns the dynamically generated results to the web server, so that the output can be sent to the user's browser. The ColdFusion Application Server integrates with a number of popular web servers via native APIs and is also capable of running in CGI mode. Once the ColdFusion Application Server is set up, it works silently in the background, so we won't be talking much about it in this book.

*ColdFusion Studio (or other text-editing software)*

ColdFusion Studio is the Integrated Development Environment (IDE) for the ColdFusion Application Server. Studio provides developers with a visual environment for developing, testing, debugging, and deploying ColdFusion applications. Although ColdFusion applications can be written using any text editor capable of saving ASCII output, ColdFusion Studio offers many advantages that make it worth considering. This book doesn't concern itself with how you create your ColdFusion applications, so ColdFusion Studio isn't covered.

*ColdFusion Markup Language (CFML) templates*

The ColdFusion Markup Language (CFML) is the language that you use to create ColdFusion applications. CFML is a tag-based language, just like HTML. You use it in conjunction with HTML and other client-side languages, such as JavaScript and VBScript, to create the templates that make up a ColdFusion application. CFML is used to determine *what* to display, while HTML specifies *how* to display it, an important distinction. This book covers all the CFML tags and functions supported by ColdFusion.

*Web server*

The web server funnels browser requests for CFML templates through the ColdFusion Application Server. The web server is also responsible for passing the output returned by the ColdFusion Application Server back to the browser. As I already mentioned, ColdFusion works the same way on all supported web servers, so your choice of web server isn't important and won't affect your programming.

*ColdFusion Administrator*

The ColdFusion Administrator is actually a ColdFusion application for configuring and administering the ColdFusion Application Server. The ColdFusion Administrator handles everything from registering and setting up data sources to logging and security. This is a book for programmers, so it doesn't cover configuration and administration. For more information on configuring and administering the ColdFusion Application Server, you need to consult the documentation that comes with your edition of ColdFusion.

*Data sources*

ColdFusion is capable of interacting with a number of external data sources, including databases (via ODBC, OLE-DB, and native drivers), Verity collections, LDAP directories, POP3 and SMTP mail servers, FTP servers, and other HTTP servers. This allows you to create ColdFusion applications that send and receive email, transfer files with FTP, query directory servers, and request content from other web servers. Because most web applications interact with databases, this book demonstrates using ColdFusion with databases. It also includes chapters that show how to use ColdFusion to interact with the other kinds of data sources I just mentioned.

*Objects*

ColdFusion can interact with various external objects, including COM/DCOM objects, CORBA objects, and Java objects (including Enterprise JavaBeans components). This allows your ColdFusion applications to interact with third-party components as well as back-end systems written in other languages, which makes ColdFusion an excellent choice for acting as the "glue" that ties together all sorts of disparate systems into a cohesive application. Using ColdFusion to interact with external objects is covered in Chapter 23.

*Extensions*

CFML is extensible via custom extensions written in a variety of languages, such as C++, Java, and Delphi, and even CFML. By writing an extension, you can include functionality not natively available in the core ColdFusion language. For example, ColdFusion can't natively connect to a NNTP news server, but if you are skilled in C++, Java, or Delphi, you can easily build a CFX extension to support such a connection. Creating custom tags using CFML is covered in Chapter 19. Custom extensions are beyond the scope of this book, however, so for more information on developing your own custom extensions using C++, Delphi, or Java, you need to consult the documentation that came with your edition of ColdFusion.

Now that you understand the components that comprise the ColdFusion environment, let's look at how ColdFusion processes requests:

1. A web browser makes a request to a web server for a template with a *.cfm* extension.
2. The web server receives the request and forwards it to the ColdFusion Application Server.
3. The ColdFusion Application Server parses the CFML template and processes the tags and functions accordingly, interacting with other services, such as data sources or mail servers, as necessary.
4. The ColdFusion Application Server combines its dynamic output with the static HTML (and JavaScript or VB Script, if any) in the template and passes the whole page back to the web server.
5. The web server passes the dynamically generated content back to the client machine's web browser.

This entire process is illustrated in Figure 1-1.

# *Getting Started with ColdFusion*

Obviously, to use this book, you need access to a ColdFusion server. If your company is already developing web applications with ColdFusion, the server should

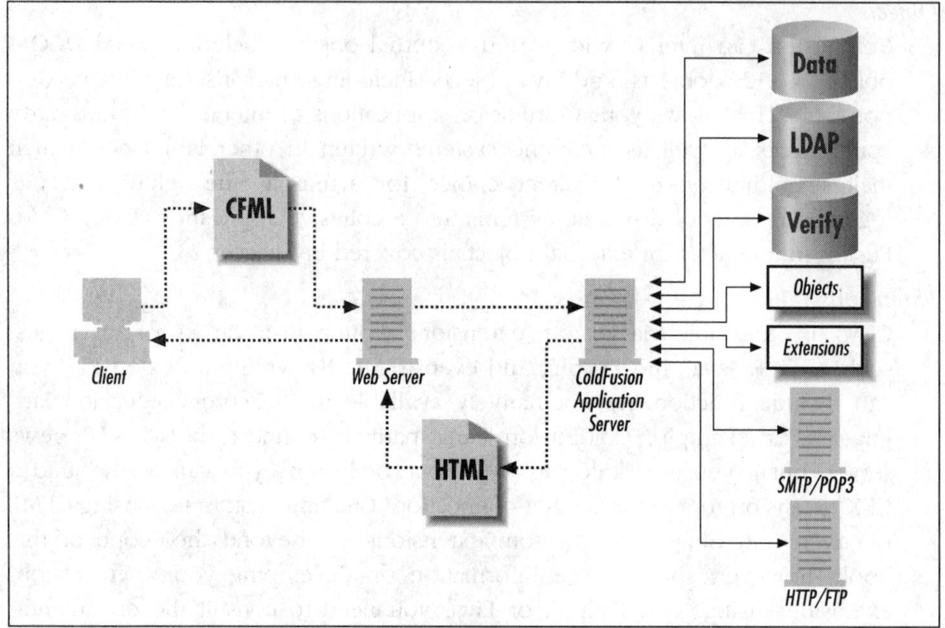


*Figure 1-1. How ColdFusion requests are processed*

already be available to you. Or, if you are developing for a remote server, you should be all set. In either case, you just need to know where to put your templates; check with your system administrator or webmaster.

If you don't have access to a ColdFusion server, your first step is to pick an edition of ColdFusion. There are currently four editions of ColdFusion available to support the needs of various sized projects and organizations; all of them are available at Allaire's web site, *http://www.allaire.com* (as of this writing, the latest release of ColdFusion is Version 5.0):

*ColdFusion Express (Windows and Linux only)*
: A free, bare bones edition of ColdFusion designed to introduce you to the ColdFusion development environment. ColdFusion Express supports only a subset of the full CFML language and provides limited database support and limited server administration. ColdFusion Express can be downloaded for free from Allaire's web site.

*ColdFusion Professional (Windows and Linux only)*
: The professional edition gives full access to the CFML language as well as full ODBC database support, administration, and advanced security services.

*ColdFusion Enterprise (Windows, Solaris, Linux, and HP-UX)*
: Contains all the functionality of ColdFusion Professional but adds server clustering, native database drivers for certain databases, upgraded Merant ODBC

drivers, and complete sandbox security for securing ColdFusion in multisite hosted environments.

*ColdFusion Single User (Windows only)*
: This is a single-user edition of ColdFusion Enterprise that comes bundled with ColdFusion Studio and limits access to one IP address per session. ColdFusion Single User allows you to build and test applications without having to purchase a full ColdFusion Enterprise license. As of ColdFusion 5.0, the trial version of ColdFusion Enterprise automatically becomes the single-user version once the 30-day trial period expires.

Hardware requirements for running ColdFusion vary depending on your platform and the edition of ColdFusion you want to run. You should make sure the machine on which you plan to run the ColdFusion Application Server can meet the demands you might place on it. ColdFusion generally requires a system with 100 to 400 MB of hard disk space and between 128 and 512 MB of RAM, depending on the platform. Memory requirements are only a guideline. In general, the more physical RAM available to ColdFusion, the better it will perform, because many tasks performed by web applications such as intensive database queries, Verity indexing/searching, and integration with other third-party resources are memory-intensive. For the most up-to-date system requirements, please refer to the documentation that came with your edition of ColdFusion or visit *http://www.allaire.com/products/ColdFusion/generalInformation/SystemReqs/*.

If you work in an organization with an IT department, you should be able to get them to install and configure ColdFusion. Otherwise, you'll have to perform these tasks yourself. Because ColdFusion is available for multiple platforms, installation procedures vary. For specific instructions on installing and configuring the ColdFusion Application Server, see the documentation provided with your edition of ColdFusion or visit the Allaire Installation Support web site at *http://www.allaire.com/support/installation/*.

Once you have a working ColdFusion installation, you're ready to start programming. In the next chapter, we'll dive in and learn about ColdFusion basics. For this material to make sense, though, you need to have some basic experience with web page creation and, in particular, HTML. If you don't have any experience with HTML, you should spend some time learning basic HTML before you try to learn ColdFusion. For this, I recommend *HTML: The Definitive Guide*, by Chuck Musciano and Bill Kennedy (O'Reilly & Associates). If you are planning to use ColdFusion to interact with a database, you may also find it helpful to have a general understanding of relational databases and SQL (Structured Query Language). For more information on SQL, see *SQL in a Nutshell*, by Kevin Kline with Daniel Kline, Ph.D (O'Reilly).

# 2

# ColdFusion Basics

*In this chapter:*
- *Getting Started*
- *Datatypes*
- *Variables*
- *Expressions*
- *Writing Output*
- *Conditional Processing*
- *Looping*
- *Including Other Templates*

Part of what makes developing web applications with ColdFusion so easy is the simplicity of the ColdFusion Markup Language (CFML). Because CFML is a tag-based language like HTML, it is simple to write and easy to understand. All ColdFusion code is written inside tags or within the boundaries of paired tags (just like HTML). There are over 80 tags and 255 functions in the CFML language that you can use to accomplish virtually any task. ColdFusion tags wrap complex functionality, such as database connectivity and data manipulation, into simple tags that can be invoked with a minimum of coding. CFML functions offer even more power, as they provide access to common operations, such as string manipulation and mathematical functions that aren't possible using HTML alone.

Because CFML is a programming language, we need to start with some basics about the language. In this chapter, I cover how to create and save ColdFusion applications as well as the major aspects of the language such as datatypes, variables, expressions, conditional processing, and more.

## Getting Started

To write a ColdFusion application, you can use virtually any text editor or an HTML authoring tool that allows you to directly edit the code. As we discussed in Chapter 1, a ColdFusion application is a collection of web pages, also called templates, that work together to allow a user to perform a task. When you create a CFML template, you typically embed the CFML code within standard HTML (although it is also possible to create files that contain only CFML, as you'll see later in the chapter). A ColdFusion application can be as simple as a single page. Consider the following example, which outputs the current date to the browser:

```
<HTML>
<HEAD>
  <TITLE>CFML Example</TITLE>
</HEAD>

<BODY>

<CFOUTPUT>
<H2>Today's date is #DateFormat(Now(),'mm/dd/yyyy')#</H2>
</CFOUTPUT>

</BODY>
</HTML>
```

At first glance, this template looks just like an HTML template. If you look closer, however, you'll see embedded CFML code right in the middle of the template. The code here uses a single tag (`<CFOUTPUT>`) and two functions (`DateFormat()` and `Now()`) to output the current date to the browser. We'll get to what this tag and the functions do in a bit. For now, we're just concerned with running the template and understanding how CFML and HTML coexist.

## Saving CFML Templates

To execute this template, you need to save the file on the machine that is running your web server and the ColdFusion Application Server. You can either type in this example and save it to a file or you can copy the file from the book's example archive (available at *http://www.oreilly.com/catalog/coldfusion*). You should put the file in a directory accessible under the root directory of your particular web server. For example, if the root directory for your web server is *c:\inetpub\wwwroot*, you can create a subdirectory two levels down such as *c:\inetpub\wwwroot\examples\chapter2* and save the template there as *2-1.cfm*. Now if you use your web browser to view this file (*http://127.0.0.1/examples/chapter2/2-1.cfm*), you'll see the web page displayed in Figure 2-1.

By default, CFML files need to have the extension *.cfm* in order for your web server to know to send the files to the ColdFusion engine for processing. It is possible to use an extension other than *.cfm*, as long as you configure your web server to associate the new extension with the ColdFusion engine.

When you save your CFML template, you should follow the conventions set forth by your web server for saving HTML templates. For example, in Windows environments, filenames are case-insensitive. On Unix, however, filenames are case-sensitive. These differences are important to remember when coding your applications, especially if you ever need to port your application from a Windows to a Unix environment.

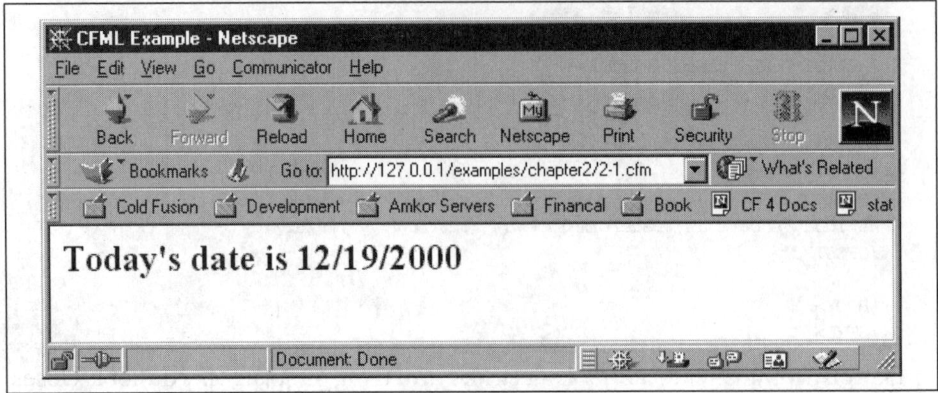


*Figure 2-1. Calling a CFML template from your web browser*

## Tag Syntax

CFML tags are written in the same manner as HTML tags. Most CFML tags have a start tag (written as `<CF`*`TagName`*`>`) and an end tag (written as `</CF`*`TagName`*`>`). All CFML tags begin with the letters "CF". In keeping with XML conventions, any CFML tag that doesn't have or require an end tag may optionally be written with a trailing forward slash, as in `<CF`*`TagName`*`/>`.

Most CFML tags accept one or more attributes that affect the tag's behavior, just like HTML tags. A tag's attributes allow you to pass values to the tag for processing. Tags can accept both required and optional attributes. To get a better idea of how attributes affect a tag's behavior, consider the following example, in which we call the `<CFMAIL>` tag (used to send email messages via SMTP):

```
<!--- call the CFMAIL tag --->
<CFMAIL FROM="webmaster@example.com"
        TO="you@example.com"
        SUBJECT="Text Message"
        SERVER="127.0.0.1">
This is a test message
</CFMAIL>

<H2>Message Sent</H2>
```

In this example, we pass four attributes to the `CFMAIL` tag. The `FROM`, `TO`, and `SUBJECT` attributes are all required attributes; they specify what you'd expect about the email message. `SERVER` is an optional attribute that specifies the server name or IP address of the mail server ColdFusion should use to send SMTP mail. Specifying a value here overrides any value set in the ColdFusion Administrator. Several other optional attributes can be passed to the `CFMAIL` tag to further affect its behavior. You need to pass optional parameters only if you wish to use a value other than the default. (The `CFMAIL` tag is discussed in detail in Chapter 12.)

Attributes can accept both literal values and expressions. Literal values are generally surrounded by double quotes, although this isn't necessary when referring to numeric values, Boolean values, or expressions. In the interest of style and consistency, however, I suggest that you surround all attribute values with double quotes.

Attributes aren't the only way for CFML tags to get data. Many CFML tags can act on any content that appears between its start and end tags. If you look at the previous example, you'll notice that the text "This is a test message" appears between the `<CFMAIL>` and `</CFMAIL>` tags. Any text appearing within the `CFMAIL` block is used by the tag as the message body.

## *Comments*

One final thing to note about the previous example is its use of comments. Commenting your code is an essential part of application development. Including quality comments in your code is important for a number of reasons:

- It allows you to remember what a particular section of code does long after you have forgotten about the application.
- It helps break up sections of code into more readable chunks.
- It helps other developers understand your development style in the event they inherit your application.

There are two types of comments that can be used in your CFML templates: HTML-style comments and CFML comments. The standard HTML-style comment takes the form:

```
<!--This is a comment-->

<!-- This is a comment too. -->

<!-- So is this
     it is just on two lines -->
```

Notice that each comment begins with `<!--` and ends with `-->`. HTML comments contain two dashes and may or may not have a space between the dash and the comment text.

CFML comments differ from HTML comments in three ways. First, CFML comments contain three dashes, as opposed to the two dashes in HTML comments:

```
<!--- This is a CFML comment --->

<!--- This is a multi-line
     CFML comment --->
```

The second difference is that CFML comments must have a space between the opening and closing comment marker and the comment text. Failure to include these spaces can result in incorrectly parsed code and produce undesirable results when a template is executed.

The third difference between CFML comments and regular HTML comments is that CFML comments aren't displayed in the HTML code generated by ColdFusion. If you display the HTML code generated by ColdFusion by using your browser's "View Source" function, you won't see any CFML comments you wrote in the source code. You will, however, see any HTML comments you made. For this reason, you should write your comments as CFML comments when you want to comment your code, but you don't want to let visitors to your site view the comments.

# Datatypes

ColdFusion supports a number of datatypes for use in building expressions. These datatypes can be broken into two categories, simple and complex. The simple datatypes are made up of Booleans, strings, numbers (both integer and floating point), and date/time objects:

*Boolean*

ColdFusion uses the Boolean datatype to store the value generated by a logical operation. Boolean values are stored as either `TRUE` or `FALSE`. In numeric operations, Boolean values evaluate to `1` for `TRUE` and `0` for `FALSE`. When dealing with strings, Boolean values are set to `Yes` for `TRUE` and `No` for `FALSE`. Note that no quotes are necessary to delimit Boolean values.

*Strings*

ColdFusion stores text values in strings delimited by a set of single or double quotes. For example, `"This is a string."` and `'So is this!'` are both strings. `"1000"` and `'1000'` are also strings so long as the numbers are delimited by a set of quotes. The empty string can be written as either `''` or `""`. There are certain special characters that must be escaped within strings. These special characters are the single quote (`'`), double quote (`"`), and pound sign (`#`). These characters may be escaped by doubling up on them as in the following examples:

```
<CFSET String1 = "This is a ""good"" use of escaped double quotes">
<CFSET String2 = "This is a ''good'' use of escaped single quotes">
<CFSET String3 = "What is the ##1 team in the league?">
```

As we'll discuss in the next section, `<CFSET>` is a CFML tag you use to set a variable to a particular value.

*Numbers*

ColdFusion supports both floating-point (decimal) and integer (whole number) values. Numbers don't need to be delimited by quotes when referenced within expressions. The range for floating-point values in ColdFusion is $\pm10^{300}$ (1 followed by 300 zeros). The range for integer values is –2,147,483,648 to 2,147,483,647. ColdFusion automatically converts numbers outside this range to floating-point values.

Most ColdFusion functions can perform calculations accurate to 12 decimal places. Numbers may be represented as either regular numbers or in scientific notation. ColdFusion formats numbers in scientific notation as *x*E*y* ($x*10^y$) where *x* is a positive real number in the range 1–10, and *y* is an integer. So, 100,000 equals 1.0E5 or $1*10^5$ while .001 equals 1.0E–2 or $1*10^{-2}$.

*Date/time objects*

ColdFusion allows you to specify date and time values separately or combined. Dates must range from 100 A.D. to 9999 A.D. and can be written as:

```
08/15/1998
1998-08-15
August 15, 1998
Aug 15, 1998
Aug. 15, 1998
```

ColdFusion handles two-digit years from 00 to 29 as 21st-century dates and two digit years from 30 to 99 as 20th-century dates.*

Times are accurate to the second and can be written as:

```
7pm
7:00p
7:00pm
19:00:00
```

Combined date/time objects can be written as any combination of the previous dates and times.

Complex datatypes include query objects, lists, arrays, structures, and component objects:

*Lists*

Lists are a special type of string that contains delimited elements. For example, `"a,b,c,d,e,f,g"` is a list where `"a"`, `"b"`, `"c"`, `"d"`, `"e"`, `"f"`, and `"g"` are considered the list elements while the comma (`,`) is considered the delimiter. Lists are covered in Chapter 6.

---

* If you are running ColdFusion on Unix and have Fast Date/Time Parsing enabled in the Server area of the ColdFusion Administrator, you must specify objects as month, day, and year. With the `DateFormat()` function, you must use a date mask that follows the required format (month, day, year) in order for ColdFusion to parse the date object.

*Arrays*

Arrays are objects that can store indexed values. Each value stored in an array is referred to as an element of the array. Each element has an integer assigned to it that marks its position within the array. This number is referred to as the element's index. Arrays elements can store any ColdFusion datatype including additional arrays.

ColdFusion supports one-dimensional (think of this as a single column of data or a list), two-dimensional (think of this as a spreadsheet with rows and columns), and three-dimensional arrays (think of this as a cube of data). Additional dimensions can be created dynamically by nesting multidimensional arrays (creating an array of arrays). Arrays are discussed in Chapter 6.

*Structures*

Structures are objects that allow you to store and manipulate key/value pairs. Structures are similar to one-dimensional arrays except elements are referenced via an alphanumeric "key" (string) as opposed to a numeric index within the array. Structures offer an advantage over arrays in certain situations by allowing you to reference groups of related information by key as opposed to by numeric index. This feature allows structures to also be used as associative arrays. Structures are covered in Chapter 6.

*Query objects*

Query objects are special ColdFusion data structures that hold record sets. Record sets are most often returned by database query operations. In addition, several CFML tags return query objects upon completion. Query objects are similar in structure to two-dimensional arrays and are made up of rows and columns (like a spreadsheet). Query objects are discussed in Chapter 4.

*Component objects*

ColdFusion allows you to interact with three distinct component types: COM objects (Windows 95, 98, NT, and 2000 only), CORBA objects, and Java objects. Regardless of the type of object invoked, component objects usually consist of methods and properties that can be accessed by ColdFusion. Component objects are a fairly advanced topic and are covered in Chapter 23.

CFML provides a number of functions for dynamically determining the datatype of a variable: `IsArray()`, `IsBinary()`, `IsBoolean()`, `IsDate()`, `IsNumeric()`, `IsQuery()`, `IsSimpleValue()`, and `IsStruct()`. Additionally, several functions exist specifically for manipulating data specific to each particular datatype. These functions are discussed throughout the book and can be found in Appendix B.

# *Variables*

A *variable* is a name associated with a data value; it is common to say that a variable stores or contains a value. Variables allow you to store and manipulate data in your applications; they are called variables because the values they represent can change throughout the life of an application. In ColdFusion, you don't have to explicitly declare your variables, as you do in a language such as C++. Additionally, ColdFusion variables are typeless, meaning that you can assign a value of any datatype (string, numeric, Boolean, object, etc.) to any variable.

## *Variable Names*

The following rules and guidelines apply to variable names in CFML:

- Variable names must begin with a letter and can contain only letters, numbers, and the underscore character. Variable names can't contain spaces. For example, `Test`, `MyVariable`, `My_variable`, `MyVariable1`, and `MyDescriptive_var2` are all valid ColdFusion variables, while `4C`, `My Variable`, `Phone#`, and `A/P` aren't.
- Avoid using variable names that may be reserved words in SQL, such as `Time`, `Date`, and `Order`.
- Avoid using variable names that are the same as ColdFusion variable scopes: `Application`, `Attribute`, `Caller`, `CGI`, `Client`, `Cookie`, `Form`, `Variable`, `Request`, `Server`, `Session`, `URL`, and `Query`.
- Avoid choosing variable names that end in `_date`, `_eurodate`, `_float`, `_integer`, `_range`, `_required`, or `_time`, as these are reserved suffixes for server-side form validation variables and can cause naming conflicts.
- ColdFusion variable names aren't case-sensitive. In the interest of good style and readability, however, you should keep the case of your variable names consistent.
- Always try to use descriptive terms for your variables. It might seem like a pain, but you will be grateful when it comes time to debug or add a new feature.
- If your application interacts with a database, you can make your code clearer by using ColdFusion variable names that match the corresponding fields in the database.

## Assigning Values to Variables

The <CFSET> tag assigns a value to a variable in ColdFusion. The variable name is followed by an equal sign and the value or expression you want to assign to the variable. For example:

```
<CFSET x = 1>
<CFSET y = x+2>
<CFSET Name = "Rob">
<CFSET x = Name>
<CFSET Authenticated = True>
<CFSET TheDate = DateFormat(Now(),'mm/dd/yyyy')>
```

You can set only one variable in each `CFSET` tag. Note that the `CFSET` tag doesn't have an end tag.

## Variable Scope

ColdFusion supports a number of different variable scopes, where *scope* refers to the context in which the variable exists within an application. The scope encompasses where the variable came from (such as a form field, a URL, etc.), how it can be used, and how long it persists. As we'll discuss shortly, when you refer to a variable in your code, you can use just the variable's simple name (*`MyVar`*) or it's fully scoped name (*`Scope.MyVar`*). The variable scopes available in ColdFusion are as follows:

*Local*
: By default, all variables created using the `CFSET` and `CFPARAM` tags are local variables. (We haven't discussed the `CFPARAM` tag yet; we'll get to it shortly.) Local variables are accessible only on the page on which they are created and can be referenced by their simple names or as `Variables.`*`variable_name`*.

*Form*
: Form variables are passed from HTML forms or ColdFusion Java forms to other ColdFusion templates. Data is passed when a user fills out a form and submits it. Both the form field name and associated data are passed from the form to the ColdFusion template specified in the form's `ACTION` attribute. Form field variables can be referenced as `Form.`*`field_name`*. By default, a variable called `Form.FieldNames` is always available within the form scope; it contains a comma-delimited list of all field names posted from a form.

*URL*
: URL variables contain parameters passed to ColdFusion templates via URLs. For example, consider the following hypertext link:

```
http://www.example.com/view_news.cfm?ArticleID=5&ViewMode=public
```

Clicking on this link causes a ColdFusion template named *view_news.cfm* to execute. Two variables, `ArticleID` and `ViewMode`, with the values 5 and `public`, respectively, are available to the *view_news.cfm* template. To refer to the variables in the *view_mode.cfm* template, you can use the syntax `URL.ArticleID` and `URL.ViewMode`.

*Query*

The query scope references variables within a ColdFusion query object. For example, to reference a field called `Name` from a query called `Employees`, you use the following syntax: `Employees.Name`. Three predefined variables are always available for any query object:

```
queryname.ColumnList
queryname.CurrentRow
queryname.RecordCount
```

The query scope is covered in detail in Chapter 4.

*File*

File variables are automatically created by ColdFusion when you use the `<CFFILE>` tag to upload a file. These variables are read-only and are referenced as `CFFILE.variable_name`. File variables are covered in detail in Chapter 15. For a complete list of available file variables, see the `<CFFILE>` tag in Appendix A.*

*CGI*

CGI variables are read-only variables that report specific information about the server and browser environments in use. CGI variables are accessible in all ColdFusion templates; the available variables vary depend on the combination of server and browser software being used. CGI variables take the form `CGI.`*`variable_name`*. A list of some of the most common CGI variables is shown in Table 2-1.

*Table 2-1. Common CGI Variables*

| | |
|---|---|
| AUTH_PASSWORD | HTTP_HOST |
| AUTH_TYPE | HTTP_USER_AGENT |
| AUTH_USER | HTTPS |
| CERT_COOKIE | HTTPS_KEYSIZE |
| CERT_FLAGS | HTTPS_SECRETKEYSIZE |
| CERT_ISSUER | HTTPS_SERVER_ISSUER |
| CERT_KEYSIZE | HTTPS_SERVER_SUBJECT |
| CERT_SECRETKEYSIZE | PATH_INFO |

* Prior to Version 4.5, the file scope was prefixed using the `File` prefix. While this prefix is still supported in ColdFusion 5.0, it has been deprecated.

*Table 2-1. Common CGI Variables (continued)*

| | |
|---|---|
| CERT_SERIALNUMBER | PATH_TRANSLATED |
| CERT_SERVER_ISSUER | QUERY_STRING |
| CERT_SERVER_SUBJECT | REMOTE_ADDR |
| CERT_SUBJECT | REMOTE_HOST |
| CF_TEMPLATE_PATH | REMOTE_USER |
| CONTENT_LENGTH | REQUEST_METHOD |
| CONTENT_TYPE | SCRIPT_NAME |
| GATEWAY_INTERFACE | SERVER_NAME |
| HTTP_ACCEPT | SERVER_PORT |
| HTTP_ACCEPT_CHARSET | SERVER_PORT_SECURE |
| HTTP_ACCEPT_ENCODING | SERVER_PROTOCOL |
| HTTP_ACCEPT_LANGUAGE | SERVER_SOFTWARE |
| HTTP_CONNECTION | WEB_SERVER_API |
| HTTP_COOKIE | |

It is also possible to obtain a list of the CGI variables available for your particular configuration by turning on debugging in the ColdFusion Administrator. Once you have done this (provided you have access to the ColdFusion Administrator), simply execute any CFML template on your server. A list of all accessible CGI variables should appear at the bottom of the page.

*Server*

Server variables store data associated with the server on which ColdFusion is running. Server variables are available to all ColdFusion applications and persist until the ColdFusion Application Server is stopped. You can create your own server variables or reference the following predefined ones:

```
Server.ColdFusion.ProductName
Server.ColdFusion.ProductVersion
Server.ColdFusion.ProductLevel
Server.ColdFusion.SerialNumber
Server.ColdFusion.SupportedLocales
Server.ColdFusion.Expiration (Version 5.0 only)
Server.OS.Name
Server.OS.AdditionalInformation
Server.OS.Version
Server.OS.BuildNumber
```

Server variables must always be referenced using the `Server` prefix as in `Server.`*`variable_name`*. Server variables are discussed in detail in Chapter 7.

*Cookie*

Cookie variables hold the values of HTTP cookies retrieved from a user's web browser. Cookies are a unique type of persistent variable that are stored on the client machine and sent to the ColdFusion server each time a page is requested. Cookies are covered in Chapter 7.

*Application*

Application variables define application-wide settings such as default directories and data source names. Application variables are usually defined in the *Application.cfm* file. Application variables are available to all clients, or users, accessing the named application and are often referred to as global variables. Application variables must always be referenced using the `Application` prefix, as in `Application.`*`variable_name`*. By default, a single predefined application variable is available:

```
Application.ApplicationName
```

Application variables and the `CFAPPLICATION` tag are discussed in detail in Chapter 7.

*Session*

Session variables are persistent variables that store information for a specific session. Session variables are held in the server's memory and persist for a finite amount of time. Each session is unique to a user and can be referenced across ColdFusion templates. Session variables are often used for shopping carts and user authentication systems. Session variables must be specifically set and referenced as `Session.`*`variable_name`*. In order to use session variables, they must be turned on in both the ColdFusion administrator and within an *Application.cfm* template for the application. By default, the following predefined session variables are available:

```
Session.CFID
Session.CFToken
Session.SessionID
Session.URLToken
```

Session variables as well as the *Application.cfm* template are discussed in detail in Chapter 7.

*Client*

Client variables store values associated with a particular user. Most often they are used to maintain state as a user navigates from page to page throughout an application. What makes client variables different from session variables is that they can persist across multiple sessions. That is, client variables are stored by the ColdFusion server and can be retrieved during subsequent visits. For example, an application might use a client variable to remember things such as the last time a user visited your site or their font size/color preferences. By default, client variables are stored in the system registry, but they can also be stored in a cookie or a database. When creating client variables, the variable name must always be referenced using the `Client` prefix, as in `Client.`*`variable_name`*. This is optional when writing client variables. In addition to the client variables you create in an application, there are several read-only client variables ColdFusion creates automatically:

```
Client.CFID
Client.CFToken
Client.HitCount
Client.LastVisit
Client.TimeCreated
Client.URLToken
```

Client variables are discussed in Chapter 7.

*Attribute*

The attribute scope is unique to ColdFusion custom tags. It allows you to refer to attributes passed from the calling template to the custom tag. Caller variables must always be referenced using the `Attributes` prefix as in `Attributes.`*`variable_name`*. Custom tags and attribute variables are discussed in detail in Chapter 19.

*Caller*

The caller scope is also unique to ColdFusion custom tags; it passes a value from a custom tag back to its calling template. Caller variables must always be referenced using the `Caller` prefix as in `Caller.`*`variable_name`*. Caller variables are discussed in Chapter 19.

*Request*

Request variables offer a way to store data in a structure that can be passed to nested custom tags. Data passed using the request scope is intended for one time use. Request variables must always be referenced using the `Request` prefix as in `Request.`*`variable_name`*. Request variables are discussed in Chapter 19.

As of ColdFusion 4.5, several variable scopes can be accessed via like-named ColdFusion structures. These scopes/structures are Application, Attributes, CGI, Cookie, Form, Request, Session, and URL. These structures contain all the variable names and associated values for the particular scope and can be manipulated using any of the structure functions listed in Appendix B.

Functions.In addition to the previously mentioned variable types, many CFML tags return variables known as *return values* or *return variables*. These variables are usually prefixed with the name of the tag generating them. For example, the `<CFHTTP>` tag returns several variables, such as `CFHTTP.FileContent` and `CFHTTP.MimeType`, depending on the action you have it perform.

The ColdFusion environment also defines some variables automatically in different scopes. For example, when form data is passed to a ColdFusion template, form variables are automatically created for all the form fields. The same holds true for URL parameters passed to a ColdFusion template.

To get a better understanding of how these variable scopes relate to one another, consider the relationships depicted in Figure 2-2.

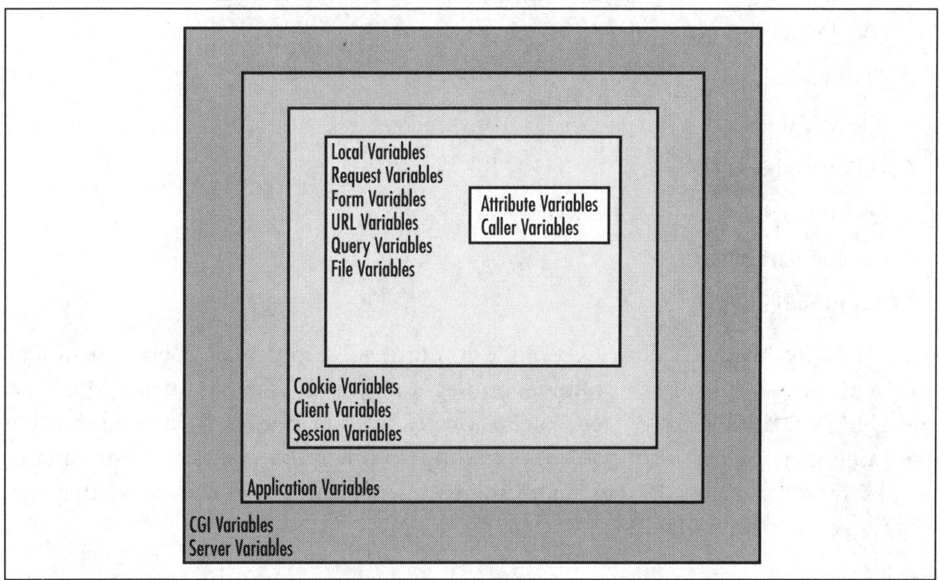


*Figure 2-2. Variable scope relationships*

When you refer to a variable in your code, you can refer to it using just the variable's simple name (*MyVar*) or its fully scoped name (*Scope.MyVar*). Referencing a variable using its fully scoped name is called *scoping* the variable. With application, server, session, attribute, caller, and request variables, you must always use the fully scoped name.

Because ColdFusion supports different variable scopes, the potential exists for having like-named variables of different scopes within an application. ColdFusion allows you to deal with this potential conflict in two ways.

One way to handle potential variable conflicts is to always provide the variable scope when referencing a variable. For example, a URL variable should be referenced as `URL.`*`MyVariable`*, while a form variable should be referenced as `Form.`*`MyVariable`*. Using the variable scope has two additional benefits. First, by identifying the variable scope right along with the variable, it makes your code more readable. When you look through your code, you know in exactly what context a particular variable is used. The second benefit has to do with performance. When ColdFusion encounters a scoped variable, it is able to process the code faster because it doesn't have to take time to determine the variable's scope.

The second way to deal with potential variable conflicts is to let ColdFusion handle them. When the ColdFusion server encounters an unscoped variable, it attempts to evaluate it in a specific order. Because application, server, session, attribute, caller, and request variables must always be scoped, they aren't included in the order of evaluation, which is as follows:

1. Local variables
2. CGI variables
3. File variables
4. URL variables
5. Form variables
6. Cookie variables
7. Client variables

As you might imagine, allowing ColdFusion to resolve potential conflicts can lead to unexpected results. For example, you might refer to a variable thinking that you are getting a URL variable, but ColdFusion resolves it to a local variable that has the same name. Of course, you can avoid this problem by choosing your variable names more carefully. But to make things even clearer, I recommend that you always scope your variables.

## *Specifying Default Values Using CFPARAM*

The `<CFPARAM>` tag allows you to define a variable and set a default value in the event that the variable doesn't already exist, such as when you expect a value to be passed into a template via a form or URL variable. The tag can also test for the existence of a variable as well as test its datatype. The `CFPARAM` tag is called using the following syntax:

```
<CFPARAM NAME="parameter_name"
         TYPE="data_type"
         DEFAULT="value">
```

The `NAME` attribute specifies the name of the variable to create. `TYPE` is optional and is used to specify the datatype the variable must be to be considered valid. Possible options are `Any`, `Array`, `Boolean`, `Date`, `Numeric`, `Query`, `String`, `Struct`, `UUID`, and `VariableName`. The default value for `TYPE` is `Any`. `VariableName` is a special option; it checks to make sure the variable you are checking contains a value that is a valid variable name according to the naming conventions we covered earlier. The final attribute, `DEFAULT`, assigns a default value or expression to the variable if it doesn't exist or has no value already assigned. The `CFPARAM` tag can be used in three ways:

*Test for a required variable*

Use the `NAME` attribute to specify the name of the variable to test for. If the variable doesn't exist, ColdFusion throws an error.

*Test for a required variable of a specific datatype*

Use the `NAME` attribute to specify the name of the variable and the `TYPE` attribute to specify the required datatype for the value assigned to the variable. If the variable doesn't exist or contains a value of the wrong datatype, ColdFusion throws an error.

*Test for an optional variable and assign a default value*

Use the `NAME` attribute to specify the name of the variable and the `DEFAULT` attribute to specify a value assigned to the variable in the event it doesn't exist.

The following example demonstrates how the `CFPARAM` tag can assign a default value to a variable in the event it doesn't already exist:

```
<CFPARAM NAME="URL.RecordID" DEFAULT="12">
```

In this case, the `CFPARAM` tag assigns a default value of 12 to a URL variable called `RecordID` in the event that the variable doesn't already exist in the template. Using `CFPARAM` lets you define a default value to use in the event that the URL variable isn't passed (for whatever reason) so that ColdFusion doesn't throw an error.

# Expressions

Expressions are the building blocks of the CFML language. In its most basic form, an expression is nothing more than a single element such as `1`, `test`, `MyVar`, or `CHR(54)`. Compound expressions let you to evaluate data that is acted upon by operators. For example, `1*10` is a mathematical expression that evaluates to `10`. The values `1` and `10` are both data, while the asterisk (*) is considered an operator. On the other end of the spectrum, expressions can be complex, consisting of one or more subexpressions:

```
<CFSET x = 1+(10 MOD (3 * (11 - ACOS(-1))))>
```

## Operators

Operators allow you to perform calculations and make comparisons between expressions. In other words, they allow you to combine simple expressions to form ones that are more complex. For example, `<CFSET x = 10*(3+2)>` uses the asterisk (*) as an operator to multiply 10 by the sum of another expression that uses the plus (+) operator to add 3 and 2. There are four types of operators available in ColdFusion:

*Arithmetic*
: Performs arithmetic operations such as sign changes, addition, subtraction, etc., on numeric values.

*Comparison*
: Compares two values and return a Boolean `True/False`.

*String*
: There is only one string operator in the CFML language. The ampersand (&) concatenates strings.

*Boolean*
: Also known as logical operators, Boolean operators perform connective and negation operations and return Boolean `True/False` values.

Table 2-2 lists the operators available in ColdFusion by order of precedence (P).

*Table 2-2. ColdFusion Operators*

| Operator | Operation | Type | P |
|---|---|---|---|
| Unary +, unary – | Sign change | Arithmetic | 1 |
| ^ | Raise to a power | Arithmetic | 2 |
| *, / | Multiplication, division | Arithmetic | 3 |
| \ | Integer division | Arithmetic | 4 |
| MOD | Remainder | Arithmetic | 5 |
| +, - | Addition, subtraction | Arithmetic | 6 |
| & | Concatenation | String | 7 |
| IS (EQUAL, EQ),<br>IS NOT (NOT EQUAL, NEQ),<br>CONTAINS,<br>DOES NOT CONTAIN,<br>GREATER THAN (GT),<br>GREATER THAN OR EQUAL TO (GTE),<br>LESS THAN (LT),<br>LESS THAN OR EQUAL TO (LTE) | Equality<br>Inequality<br>Contains substring<br>Doesn't contain substring<br>><br>>=<br><<br><= | Comparison | 8 |
| NOT | Logical NOT | Boolean | 9 |
| AND | Logical AND | Boolean | 10 |
| OR | Logical OR | Boolean | 11 |
| XOR | Logical XOR | Boolean | 12 |
| EQV | Equivalence | Boolean | 13 |
| IMP | Implication | Boolean | 14 |

## *Functions*

Functions are a type of operator that let you perform a predefined action on a piece of data. CFML functions encapsulate a set of operations that would otherwise require a substantial amount of programming. ColdFusion comes with several hundred predefined functions. In addition, as of ColdFusion 5.0, you can create your own user-defined functions. Most functions take input in the form of parameters. Functions can standalone or be nested.

Many functions accept a single argument:

```
<CFSET MyCharacter = CHR(76)>
```

String arguments may be delimited by single or double quotes:

```
<CFSET String1 = Reverse('Hello')>
<CFSET String2 = Reverse("Hello")>
```

Functions can also accept variables as arguments:

```
<CFSET x = -1>
<CFSET ABSx = ABS(x)>
```

There are a few functions that take no arguments:

```
<CFSET TheTime = Now()>
<CFSET x = CreateUUID()>
```

Some functions require more than one argument. Multiple arguments are separated with a comma:

```
<CFSET x = Compare(1234, 4321)>
```

Other functions contain both required and optional arguments. If no value is supplied for an optional argument, a default is used instead:

```
<CFSET MyList = "Monday;Tuesday;Wednesday;Thursday;Friday;Saturday;Sunday">
<CFSET Length = ListLen(MyList, ';')>
```

In this example, the second argument passed to the `ListLen()` function is optional. It specifies the delimiter that separates elements of the list. If no delimiter is specified, the function uses the default, a comma (,).

Function calls can also be nested within other function calls. Consider this example where the `Now()` function is nested within the `DateFormat()` function:

```
<CFSET TodaysDate = DateFormat(Now(),'mm/dd/yyyy')>
```

Regardless of an expression's complexity, they all have one thing in common: functions always return a value. This value can be of any ColdFusion datatype (Boolean, string, numeric, date/time, list, array, structure, query object, or component object), and can be output to the browser, or included as part of another expression. There are over 255 functions in the CFML language. For a complete list, see Appendix B. For more information on creating your own functions, see Chapter 18.

## Writing Output

To output the contents or results of a ColdFusion expression, you use the <CFOUTPUT> tag. CFOUTPUT is a paired tag, which means that it has both start and end tags. CFOUTPUT tells ColdFusion to parse any text found between the tag pairs for variables and expressions that need to be evaluated. We'll use the CFOUTPUT tag in a variety of ways throughout the book; it is one of the most commonly used CFML tag. For now, let's focus on how the CFOUTPUT tag outputs simple variable values.

The following example creates a number of variables using CFSET tags and then outputs the values of the variables within CFOUTPUT tags:

```
<!--- assign values to variables --->
<CFSET x = 1>
<CFSET y = x+2>
<CFSET Name = "Rob">
<CFSET z = Name>
<CFSET Authenticated = True>
<CFSET TheDate = DateFormat(Now(),'mm/dd/yyyy')>

<!--- output the variable values --->
<H2>Writing Output</H2>
<CFOUTPUT>
x = #x#<BR>
y = #y#<BR>
Name = #Name#<BR>
z = #z#<BR>
TheDate = #TheDate#<BR>
Authenticated = #Authenticated#<BR>
</CFOUTPUT>
```

Executing this template causes the value assigned to each variable to be output to the browser, as shown in Figure 2-3. Note the use of pound signs (#) in this example. ColdFusion uses pound signs to separate expressions from literal text. When ColdFusion encounters an expression surrounded by pound signs, it attempts to evaluate it.

The most common usage of pound signs occurs when evaluating expressions within CFOUTPUT tags. Use pound signs around variable names when you want to substitute the variable's value within your output:

```
<CFOUTPUT>
Hello #Name#, how are you today?
</CFOUTPUT>
```

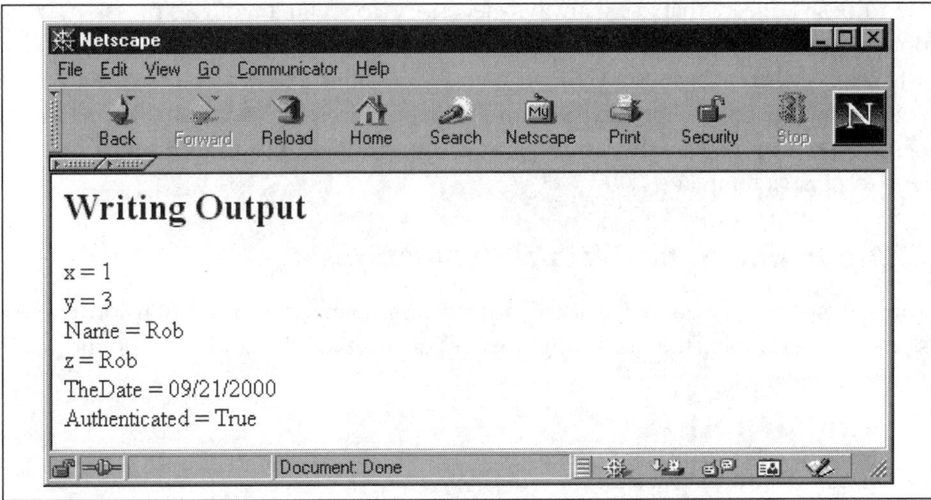


*Figure 2-3. Writing output using the CFOUTPUT tag*

When you have multiple variables, each variable should be delimited by its own set of pound signs:

```
<CFOUTPUT>
Hello #FirstName# #LastName#, how are you today?
</CFOUTPUT>
```

In addition, expressions also need to be delimited by pound signs:

```
<CFOUTPUT>
The absolute value of -1 is #ABS(-1)#.
</CFOUTPUT>
```

Be careful when trying to use compound expressions. The following example produces an error because ColdFusion doesn't allow you to evaluate compound expressions directly within `CFOUTPUT` tags:

```
<CFOUTPUT>
10*10 = #10*10#
</CFOUTPUT>
```

If you need to evaluate a compound expression, use the `CFSET` tag to perform the evaluation:

```
<CFSET x=10*10>

<CFOUTPUT>
10*10 = #x#
</ CFOUTPUT>
```

Or, use ColdFusion's `Evaluate()` function to perform the evaluation inline:

```
<CFOUTPUT>
10*10 = #Evaluate(10*10)#
</CFOUTPUT>
```

This doesn't mean that it is always necessary to delimit your expressions with pound signs, though. The following guidelines should help you understand when it is necessary to use pound signs in your expressions and when it isn't. As a rule, you should try to use pound signs only when necessary, for both aesthetic and performance reasons; unnecessary pound signs add to the time it takes ColdFusion to parse a template.

## *Using Pound Signs Within Expressions*

For the most part, you don't need to use pound signs within ColdFusion expressions. For example, the following expressions, although valid, use pound signs unnecessarily:

```
<CFSET #x# = 1>
<CFSET x = #abs(-1)#>
<CFSET x = #DateFormat(#Now()#,'mm/dd/yyyy')#>
```

Because the ColdFusion parser must take time to parse all text within a tag or function, it is much more efficient (not to mention readable) to write the expressions as:

```
<CFSET x = 1>
<CFSET x = abs(-1)>
<CFSET x = DateFormat(Now(),'mm/dd/yyyy')>
```

There are a few instances, however, where it is necessary to use pound signs within a ColdFusion function or tag.

### *Including an expression within a string*

You need to use pound signs when you include an expression within a string:

```
<CFSET MyNewString = "Hello #Name#, how are you today?">
```

Alternately, you can achieve the same results via concatenation:

```
<CFSET MyNewString = "Hello" & " " & Name & ", how are you today?">
```

In this case, you don't need to use pound signs around the variable name nor is it necessary to delimit the variable using quotation marks.

### *Including expressions within tag attributes*

You need to use pound signs within tag attributes when the value being passed is contained in a variable or expression:

```
<CFMAIL TO=#DistributionList#
        FROM="webmaster@mycompany.com"
        SUBJECT="Hello #Name#">
Greetings!
</CFMAIL>
```

It isn't necessary (although it is allowed) to delimit the variable name `DistributionList` with quotes. The same code can also be written as:

```
<CFMAIL TO="#DistributionList#"
        FROM="webmaster@mycompany.com"
        SUBJECT="Hello #Name#">
Greetings!
</CFMAIL>
```

It is worth noting that custom CFML tags can have complex datatypes, such as queries, arrays, and structures, passed to them via tag attributes. These datatypes are passed the same way as simple values—with their variable names escaped by pound signs. This example assumes that `#TheItems#` is a query object:

```
<CF_MYTAG NAME="orders"
          ITEMS="#TheItems#">
```

## Nested Pound Signs

There are rare occasions where it may appear necessary to nest pound signs within other pound signs. While there is never a situation where this is absolutely a requirement (there is always a workaround), certain complex expressions involving string manipulation can be created using nested pound signs:

```
<CFSET List1="a,b,c,d">
<CFSET List2="1,2,3,4">

<CFOUTPUT>
The combined list: #List1#,#List2#<BR>
The fourth element: #ListGetAt("#List1#,#List2#", 4)#
</CFOUTPUT>
```

While this code is allowable, it is preferable to write it as:

```
<CFSET List1="a,b,c,d">
<CFSET List2="1,2,3,4">
<CFSET CombinedList = ListAppend(List1, List2)>

<CFOUTPUT>
The combined list: #CombinedList#<BR>
The fourth element: #ListGetAt(CombinedList, 4)#
</CFOUTPUT>
```

### Escaping Pound Signs

There are occasions where you will find it necessary or desirable to use pound signs as plain text within your CFML. In these instances, pound signs can be escaped by doubling them up:

```
<CFOUTPUT>
<TR>
  <TD BGCOLOR="##FFFFCC">My phone ## is #MyPhoneNumber#</TD>
</TR>
</CFOUTPUT>
```

Notice that both the pound sign used for the color's hex value and the pound sign for the telephone number abbreviation are escaped. Using a single pound sign in either case results in ColdFusion throwing an exception.

## Conditional Processing

Conditional processing makes it possible to implement flow control and decision making within your ColdFusion templates. ColdFusion provides three techniques for applying conditional processing in your programs: if/elseif/else functionality with the <CFIF>, <CFELSEIF>, and <CFELSE> tags, a C-style switch statement with the <CFSWITCH>, <CFCASE>, and <CFDEFAULTCASE> tags, and the `IIF()` function for inline conditionals.

### CFIF, CFELSEIF, and CFELSE

If/elseif/else processing allows you to add logical decision-making and flow control to your ColdFusion applications, so you can evaluate an expression and take different actions based upon the results. Basic if/elseif/else processing takes the following form:

```
<CFIF expression>
   HTML and CFML...
<CFELSEIF expression>
   HTML and CFML...
<CFELSE>
   HTML and CFML...
</CFIF>
```

The `CFIF` statement can evaluate any expression capable of returning a Boolean value. If the statement evaluates `True`, ColdFusion processes the code associated with the `CFIF` statement. The `CFELSEIF` statement provides an alternate expression in the event that the expression in the `CFIF` statement evaluates `False`. Any number of `CFELSEIF` statements can provide additional decision-making options. The `CFELSE` statement provides a default option in the event that both the `CFIF` statement and any `CFELSEIF` statements all evaluate `False`. The following example uses if/elseif/else logic to evaluate a URL variable called `Action`:

```
<CFIF URL.Action IS "Add">
   <CFINCLUDE TEMPLATE="AddRecord.cfm">
<CFELSEIF URL.Action IS "Edit">
   <CFINCLUDE TEMPLATE="EditRecord.cfm">
<CFELSEIF URL.Action IS "Delete">
   <CFINCLUDE TEMPLATE="DeleteRecord.cfm">
<CFELSE>
   You have chosen an invalid action!
</CFIF>
```

Depending on the value of `Action`, one of three additional templates is called via a `<CFINCLUDE>` tag (which we'll discuss shortly). If the value of the URL variable doesn't match one of the values in the `CFIF` or `CFELSEIF` statements, a default message contained within the `CFELSE` tag is displayed.

The following rules can be applied to if/elseif/else statements:

- `CFIF/CFELSEIF/CFELSE` statements can be nested.
- Multiple `CFELSEIF` statements can be used within a single `CFIF` block.
- `CFIF` statements can contain more than one expression to evaluate as in:

  ```
  <CFIF IsDefined('MyVar') AND MyVar IS "a">
  ```

- Compound `CFIF` statements that contain multiple expressions separated by operators such as `AND` and `OR` are processed using short-circuit Boolean evaluation. This means that ColdFusion stops processing the `<CFIF>` statement once an expression evaluates `TRUE`.
- Consider using `CFSWITCH/CFCASE` to speed up performance when possible.

## *CFSWITCH, CFCASE, and CFDEFAULTCASE*

In addition to standard if/elseif/else decision-making using `CFIF`, `CFELSEIF`, and `CFELSE` tags, ColdFusion also supports switch/case processing. Switch/case is often used in place of lengthy if/elseif/else statements for both readability and performance reasons. Whenever possible, switch/case should be used in place of if/elseif/else processing as it provides better overall performance. The syntax used for switch/case processing is as follows:

```
<CFSWITCH EXPRESSION="expression">
     <CFCASE VALUE="value_or_list_of_values" DELIMITERS="delimiter">
          HTML and CFML...
     </CFCASE>
     <CFCASE VALUE="value_or_list_of_values" DELIMITERS="delimiter">
          HTML and CFML...
     </CFCASE>
     ...
     <CFDEFAULTCASE>
          HTML and CFML...
     </CFDEFAULTCASE>
</CFSWITCH>
```

The CFSWITCH tag sets the expression to be evaluated. CFCASE statements allow you to specify individual values or delimited lists of values that can result from the expression evaluated by the CFSWITCH statement. If the expression contained in the CFSWITCH statement evaluates to a value contained in one of the CFCASE statements, then the corresponding code is executed. The CFDEFAULTCASE tag allows you to specify a default action to take in the event that no CFCASE value matches the result of the expression from the CFSWITCH tag. The same example used in the section on if/elseif/else processing can be easily rewritten using switch/case logic as follows:

```
<CFSWITCH EXPRESSION="Url.Action">
<CFCASE VALUE="Add">
   <CFINCLUDE TEMPLATE="AddRecord.cfm">
</CFCASE>
<CFCASE VALUE="Edit">
   <CFINCLUDE TEMPLATE="EditRecord.cfm">
</CFCASE>
<CFCASE VALUE="Delete">
   <CFINCLUDE TEMPLATE="DeleteRecord.cfm">
</CFCASE>
<CFDEFAULTCASE>
   You have chosen an invalid action!
</CFDEFAULTCASE>
</CFSWITCH>
```

CFSWITCH/CFCASE can be used to reduce the amount of code necessary to evaluate certain types of conditions. Consider the following example in which a number of CFIF statements are used to evaluate the current month and determine the corresponding season:

```
<!--- sets TheMonth to the current month --->
<CFSET TheMonth=MonthAsString(Month(Now()))>

<CFOUTPUT>
<CFIF TheMonth IS "December">
  #TheMonth# is in the winter.
<CFELSEIF TheMonth IS "January">
  #TheMonth# is in the winter.
<CFELSEIF TheMonth IS "February">
  #TheMonth# is in the winter.
<CFELSEIF TheMonth IS "March">
  #TheMonth# is in the spring.
<CFELSEIF TheMonth IS "April">
  #TheMonth# is in the spring.
<CFELSEIF TheMonth IS "May">
  #TheMonth# is in the spring.
<CFELSEIF TheMonth IS "June">
  #TheMonth# is in the summer.
<CFELSEIF TheMonth IS "July">
  #TheMonth# is in the summer.
<CFELSEIF TheMonth IS "August">
```

```
  #TheMonth# is in the summer.
<CFELSEIF TheMonth IS "September">
  #TheMonth# is in the fall.
<CFELSEIF TheMonth IS "October">
  #TheMonth# is in the fall.
<CFELSEIF TheMonth IS "November">
  #TheMonth# is in the fall.
</CFIF>
</CFOUTPUT>
```

As you can see, each month of the year requires its own **CFIF** statement to determine whether it is the same as the current month. While this code is perfectly acceptable, it is redundant. We can use switch/case processing to handle the same task using considerably less code:

```
<!--- sets TheMonth to the current month --->
<CFSET TheMonth=MonthAsString(Month(Now()))>

<CFOUTPUT>
<CFSWITCH EXPRESSION="#TheMonth#">
   <CFCASE VALUE="December,January,February" DELIMITERS=",">
      #TheMonth# is in the winter.
   </CFCASE>
   <CFCASE VALUE="March,April,May" DELIMITERS=",">
      #TheMonth# is in the spring.
   </CFCASE>
   <CFCASE VALUE="June,July,August" DELIMITERS=",">
      #TheMonth# is in the summer.
   </CFCASE>
   <CFDEFAULTCASE>
      #TheMonth# is in the fall.
   </CFDEFAULTCASE>
</CFSWITCH>
</CFOUTPUT>
```

## *IIF*

`IIF()` is a ColdFusion function that evaluates a condition inline, and depending on the results, outputs one of two expressions. The function takes the form:

```
IIF(Condition, Expression_A, Expression_B)
```

If *`Condition`* evaluates `True`, *`Expression_A`* is processed and *`Expression_B`* is ignored. If, however, *`Condition`* evaluates `False`, *`Expression_B`* is processed, and *`Expression_A`* is ignored.

Consider the following example that uses `IIF()` to evaluate the current day of the week. If the day of the week is `Wednesday`, the message `Today is Wednesday!` is displayed. If the current day isn't `Wednesday`, the message `Today is not Wednesday, it is ___` is displayed:

```
<HTML>
<HEAD>
```

```
    <TITLE>IIF/DE Example</TITLE>
</HEAD>

<BODY>
<CFOUTPUT>
#IIF(DayOfWeek(Now()) IS 4, DE("Today is <B>Wednesday</B>!"), DE("Today is not
     Wednesday, it is <B>#DayOfWeekAsString(DayOfWeek(Now()))#</B>"))#
</CFOUTPUT>
</BODY>
</HTML>
```

The `DE()` function, which stands for delay evaluation, is used with the `IIF()` function to allow you to pass it a string without having the string evaluated. This is necessary in the case of the second expression in the `IIF()` function (the third parameter): it keeps ColdFusion from evaluating the third parameter when the `IIF()` function is initially evaluated.

# Looping

Looping allows you to repeat specific blocks of code (both HTML and CFML) within your CFML templates. ColdFusion supports a variety of looping constructs with the `<CFLOOP>` tag, including index (`for`) loops, conditional (`while`) loops, collection loops, list loops, and query loops. For now, we are just going to cover basic index and conditional loops. Query loops are covered in Chapter 4, while collection and list loops are covered in Chapter 6.

## Index Loops

Also known as a `for` loop, an index loop repeats a number of times specified as a range of values:

```
<CFLOOP INDEX="index_name"
        FROM="number"
        TO="number"
        STEP="increment">
   HTML and CFML...
</CFLOOP>
```

The `INDEX` attribute of the loop specifies a variable name to hold the value corresponding to the current iteration of the loop. The `FROM` attribute initializes the starting value for the loop. The `TO` attribute refers to the value at which iteration should stop. `STEP` specifies the increment value for each iteration of the loop. `STEP` may be either a positive or a negative number. Here is an example that uses an index loop to output all the numbers between `10` and `100` in increments of `10`, with each number on its own line:

```
<H2>Calling the loop...</H2>

<CFLOOP INDEX="i"
```

```
        FROM="10"
        TO="100"
        STEP="10">

<CFOUTPUT>
#i#<BR>
</CFOUTPUT>

</CFLOOP>

<H2>We are now outside of the loop</H2>
```

Here, `INDEX` is set to `i`. Since we want to begin the count at `10`, we assign that value to the `FROM` attribute. The `TO` attribute is set to `100` because that is where we want the loop to stop iterating. In order to get the loop to increment by multiples of `10`, the `STEP` attribute is set to `10`. Executing the template results in the output shown in Figure 2-4.

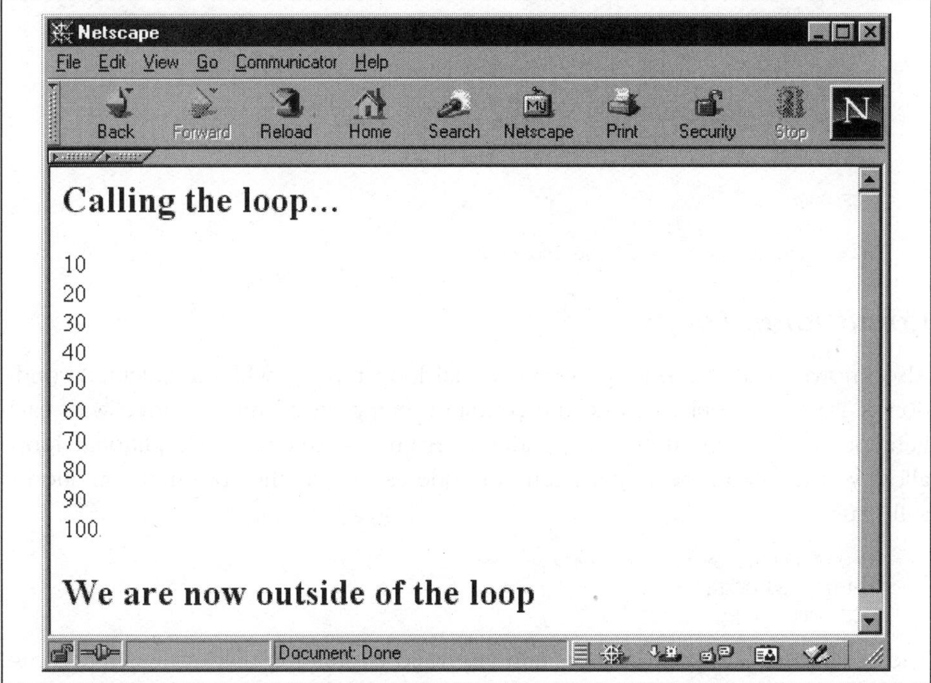


*Figure 2-4. Use an index loop to output the numbers between 10 and 100 in multiples of 10*

We can easily modify this example to output all of the numbers between `1` and `100` by changing the `FROM` attribute to `1` and the `TO` attribute to `100`:

```
<H2>Calling the loop...</H2>

<CFLOOP INDEX="i"
```

```
        FROM="1"
        TO="100">

<CFOUTPUT>
#i#<BR>
</CFOUTPUT>

</CFLOOP>

<H2>We are now outside of the loop</H2>
```

Likewise, we can output the numbers from `1` to `100` in reverse order (`100` to `1`) simply by changing the `FROM` attribute to `100`, the `TO` attribute to `1`, and the `STEP` attribute to `-1`:

```
<H2>Calling the loop...</H2>

<CFLOOP INDEX="i"
        FROM="100"
        TO="1"
        STEP="-1">

<CFOUTPUT>
#i#<BR>
</CFOUTPUT>

</CFLOOP>

<H2>We are now outside of the loop</H2>
```

## *Conditional Loops*

Also known as a `while` loop, a conditional loop repeats while a specified condition is `True`. In order to work, the condition being tested must change with each iteration of the loop until the condition evaluates to `False`. Conditional loops allow you to keep repeating a chunk of code as long as the specified condition is still `True`:

```
<CFLOOP CONDITION="expression">
   HTML and CFML...
</CFLOOP>
```

The `CONDITION` attribute may contain any valid expression that evaluates to `True`. The following example uses a conditional loop to update the value of `x` as long as `x` remains less than or equal to `10`:

```
<CFSET x=1>

<H2>Calling the loop...</H2>

<CFLOOP CONDITION="x LTE 10">
<CFOUTPUT>
```

```
#x#<BR>
</CFOUTPUT>
<CFSET x = IncrementValue(x)>
</CFLOOP>

<H2>We are now outside of the loop</H2>
```

In this example, `x` is set to `1` before the loop is executed. Next, a conditional loop is called to execute as long as `x` is less than or equal to `10`. With each iteration of the loop, the value of `x` is output to the browser then incremented by 1. As soon as the value of `x` is greater than `10`, the loop terminates at the beginning of the next iteration when `x` evaluates equal to `10`.

## *Including Other Templates*

ColdFusion allows you to embed references to other ColdFusion templates, HTML documents, and plain-text files in your ColdFusion applications via the `<CFINCLUDE>` tag. `CFINCLUDE` is the ColdFusion equivalent of Server Side Includes (SSI). `CFINCLUDE` takes a single attribute, `TEMPLATE`, which specifies a logical path to the file to be included. The logical path must be either a virtual directory or a directory that has been explicitly mapped in the ColdFusion Administrator:

```
<CFINCLUDE TEMPLATE="MyIncludedFile.cfm">
```

Or:

```
<CFINCLUDE TEMPLATE="/MyDirectory/MyIncludedFile.txt">
```

Including files allows you to use repetitive code without having to cut and paste it into your template every time you want to use it. A good example of this is header and footer files that contain things such as site navigation, legal notices, and copyright information. By including header and footer files with each of your templates, you can make changes to the header or footer once and have that change instantly available to every template that includes the files. To understand how this works, consider the following ColdFusion template that includes both a header and footer file:

```
<!--- set the title for the page --->
<CFSET Title="My Page">

<!--- include the header for the page --->
<CFINCLUDE TEMPLATE="_header.cfm">

<H2>Hello World!</H2>
I'm just some regular text.

<!--- include the footer --->
<CFINCLUDE TEMPLATE="_footer.cfm">
```

You can save this template under any name you want. For this example, I saved the template as *MyPage.cfm*. The template works by assigning a title for the page to a variable appropriately named `Title`. Next, a template called *_Header.cfm* is included using the `CFINCLUDE` tag. I use the underscore as the first character of any include files so that I can differentiate include files from other templates. The next part of the template constitutes the body of the page. In this example, we just output some simple text. The last line of code in the template uses another `CFINCLUDE` tag to include the footer for the page.

The code for the header template follows. The header sets the title for the page based on the value of the `Title` variable set in the *MyPage.cfm* template. The header also sets the background color for the page as well as other display characteristics for various page elements. Be sure to save the template as *_header.cfm* in the same directory as the previous template.

```
<HTML>
<HEAD>
  <CFOUTPUT><TITLE>#Title#</TITLE></CFOUTPUT>
  <STYLE>
    BODY {
      background: #C0C0C0;
      font-family: Arial;
      font-size: 10pt;
      text-align: center
      }
    H2 {
      font-family: Arial;
      font-size: 16pt
      }
  </STYLE>
</HEAD>

<BODY>
```

The footer file is even simpler. If contains a copyright notice to display at the end of each template that calls it. The footer template should be saved as *_footer.cfm* in the same directory as the previous two templates.

```
<HR WIDTH="400" NOSHADE>
<DIV ALIGN="center">Copyright 2000 My company, Inc. All Rights Reserved.</DIV>
</BODY>
</HTML>
```

When the *Mypage.cfm* template is requested by a web browser, ColdFusion dynamically assembles the page from the *MyPage.cfm*, *_header.cfm*, and *_footer.cfm* templates and returns it as a single page to the browser. This is shown in Figure 2-5.

Included CFML templates have access to all the variables available to the calling CFML template. Because of this, you should make sure your include templates don't unintentionally contain variable names that exist in your calling template as it is possible for one template to overwrite the variables referenced in the other.

*Figure 2-5. Using <CFINCLUDE> to include a header and footer*

# 3

*In this chapter:*
- *Passing Parameters via URL*
- *Passing Data Using Forms*
- *Dealing with Nonexistent Parameters*

# *Passing Data Between Templates*

While web applications might seem to be all about individual web pages, it is the passing of data between pages that is key to making an application work. You need to be able to pass data between ColdFusion templates for any form of interactivity. For example, if the user fills out an online form requesting additional information about a product, your application needs a mechanism for passing the data entered in the form fields to another page that is capable of taking that data and acting on it. Likewise, if the user clicks on a hyperlink that initiates a parameter-driven query, the application needs a way to pass the parameters that make up the choice to the next template in the application for processing.

There are three methods for passing data between application templates in ColdFusion. You can pass data in the form of URL parameters, by posting it as form-field variables, or you can pass data via persistent variables. This section covers the first two methods of passing data between application templates. The use of persistent variables is covered at length in Chapter 7.

## *Passing Parameters via URL*

One way to pass data from one template to the next is through hyperlinks containing special URL parameters. The HTTP specification allows you to append parameters to the end of a URL in the format:

```
filename.cfm?param1=value1&param2=value2&param3=value3
```

The question mark immediately following the extension of the template in the URL specifies the beginning point for appending URL parameters. Each URL parameter consists of a parameter name followed by an equal sign, then the value assigned to the parameter. You can append more than one URL parameter to a URL by delimiting them with ampersands. Note that no spaces may appear in the URL string.

When you click on a hyperlink containing one or more URL parameters, those parameters are automatically sent to the template specified in the URL of the link, and thus are available to the template as URL variables. The following example illustrates how URL variables are passed from template to template in ColdFusion. The first template, shown in Example 3-1, creates several ColdFusion variables and appends them and their associated values to a URL.

*Example 3-1. Creating URL Parameters*

```
<!--- set variables to be passed to another template --->
<CFSET x=1>
<CFSET color="green">
<CFSET Pass = True>

<H2>Passing Data via URL Parameters</H2>

<!--- Create a hyperlink containing URL parameters --->
<CFOUTPUT>
<A HREF="ReceiveURLParameters.cfm?x=#x#&color=#color#&pass=#pass#">Click this link to
pass the URL parameters</A>
</CFOUTPUT>
```

Executing this template results in a page that contains a single hyperlink. If you move your mouse over the hyperlink and look in the status window of your browser, you should see a URL that looks like this:

```
ReceiveURLParameters.cfm?x=1&color=green&Pass=True
```

As you can see, the URL contains the parameters you appended in the original code. Clicking on the hyperlink requests the template in Example 3-2, called *ReceiveURLParameters.cfm*, and passes along the URL parameters.

*Example 3-2. Receiving URL Parameters*

```
<H2>URL Parameters from the Previous Template</H2>
<CFOUTPUT>
x: #URL.x#<BR>
Color: #URL.Color#<BR>
Pass: #URL.Pass#
</CFOUTPUT>
```

*ReceiveURLParameters.cfm* does nothing more that output the value associated with each URL parameter; you can see the results in Figure 3-1. Notice that each reference to a URL parameter is scoped by the URL prefix. Although this isn't necessary, it is the preferred method for referring to variables passed to a template via a URL.

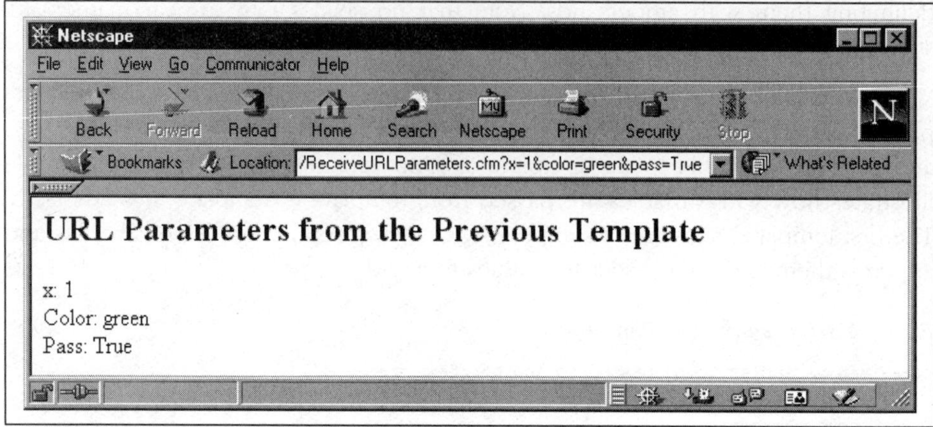


*Figure 3-1. Passing data via URL parameters*

## Dealing with Special Characters

There are certain special characters, such as spaces, symbols, and other nonalphanumeric characters, that don't lend themselves to being passed via URL. The `URLEncodedFormat()` function is used to encode strings that would otherwise cause errors or truncate the URL when passed as URL parameters. `URLEncodedFormat()` replaces nonalphanumeric characters with their equivalent hexadecimal escape sequences. When a URL-encoded parameter is passed to another template, ColdFusion automatically decodes any URL-escaped strings it encounters. The following template, called *EncodedURL.cfm*, illustrates this point. This template, shown in Example 3-3, takes three variables, encodes them using the `URLEncodedFormat()` function, and appends them to the URL of a hyperlink. Clicking on the hyperlink causes the template to call itself, passing the URL parameters to the template.

*Example 3-3. Special Characters in URL Parameters Using URLEncodedFormat()*

```
<CFIF IsDefined('URL.TheDate')>
<H2>Decoded URL Parameters</H2>

<CFOUTPUT>
TheDate: #URL.TheDate#<BR>
ItemID: #URL.ItemID#<BR>
Customer: #URL.Customer#
</CFOUTPUT>

<CFELSE>

<CFSET TheDate = "08/15/2000">
<CFSET ItemID = "123456">
<CFSET Customer = "Caroline Smith">
```

*Example 3-3. Special Characters in URL Parameters Using URLEncodedFormat() (continued)*

```
Click on the link below to check-out:<BR>
<P>
<CFOUTPUT>
<A HREF="EncodedURL.cfm?TheDate=#UrlEncodedFormat(TheDate)#&
ItemID=#UrlEncodedFormat(ItemID)#&Customer=#UrlEncodedFormat(Customer)#">
Check-out
</A>
</CFOUTPUT>
</CFIF>
```

If you execute this template and move your mouse over the hyperlink, you should see a URL that looks like this:

```
EncodedURL.cfm?TheDate=08%2F15%2F2000&ItemID=123456&Customer=Caroline%20Smith
```

Clicking on the link causes the template to call itself. The `CFIF` statement at the beginning of the template checks for the existence of a URL variable called `TheDate`. If it exists in the URL (which it should), all the URL variables passed in are output to the browser. The results of clicking on the hyperlink are shown in Figure 3-2.

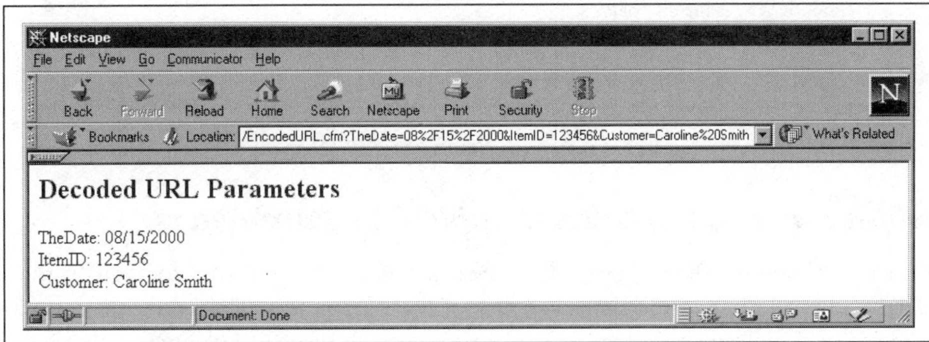


*Figure 3-2. Automatically decoding encoded URL parameters*

If for some reason you ever find yourself in the situation where you must manually decode an encoded URL parameter, ColdFusion has a `URLDecode()` function to handle the task. `URLDecode()` takes a single parameter, the encoded string to be decoded. Example 3-4 demonstrates how to use the `URLDecode()` function.

*Example 3-4. Manually Decoding an Encoded URL Parameter Using URLDecode*

```
<CFSET MyString="Why is the sky blue?">
<CFSET EncodedString=URLEncodedFormat(MyString)>
<CFSET DecodedString=URLDecode(EncodedString)>

<CFOUTPUT>
Original String: #MyString#<BR>
```

*Example 3-4. Manually Decoding an Encoded URL Parameter Using URLDecode (continued)*

```
URL Encoded: #EncodedString#<BR>
Decoded: #DecodedString#
</CFOUTPUT>
```

In this example, a variable called `MyString` is assigned a value, then encoded using the `URLEncodedFormat()` function. The resulting encoded value is assigned to a variable called `EncodedString`. Next, `EncodedString` is decoded using the `URLDecode()` function, and the resulting string is assigned to a variable called `DecodedString`. A `CFOUTPUT` block then outputs the original string, the encoded version, and the decoded version for comparison, as shown in Figure 3-3.

*Figure 3-3. Manually decoding an encoded string using URLDecode*

## Obtaining a List of All Available URL Parameters

You can obtain a list of all URL variables that have been passed to a given template without knowing the names of any of the parameters. This is useful in situations such as debugging where you want to view all the URL parameters that have been passed to a given page. As of Version 4.5, URL variables have a ColdFusion structure associated with them that contains a list of all URL variable names and values available to the current template. This structure is appropriately named `URL`. To obtain a list of all URL variables within a given template, you can use the code shown in Example 3-5.

*Example 3-5. Accessing the URL Structure to Obtain a List of URL Variables*

```
<!--- this simulates URL variables being passed into the template --->
<CFSET URL.x=1>
<CFSET URL.y=2>
<CFSET URL.Color="Yellow">

<TABLE>
<TR>
  <TH>Variable Name</TH>
```

*Example 3-5. Accessing the URL Structure to Obtain a List of URL Variables (continued)*

```
  <TH>Value</TH>
</TR>

<!--- loop over the URL structure and output all of the variable names
      and their associated valuess --->
<CFLOOP COLLECTION="#URL#" ITEM="VarName">
  <CFOUTPUT>
  <TR>
    <TD>#VarName#</TD>
    <TD>#URL[VarName]#</TD>
  </TR>
  </CFOUTPUT>
</CFLOOP>
</TABLE>
```

This template uses a collection loop to iterate over the URL structure. Each variable name and its associated value are output in an HTML table. Executing this template results in the output shown in Figure 3-4.

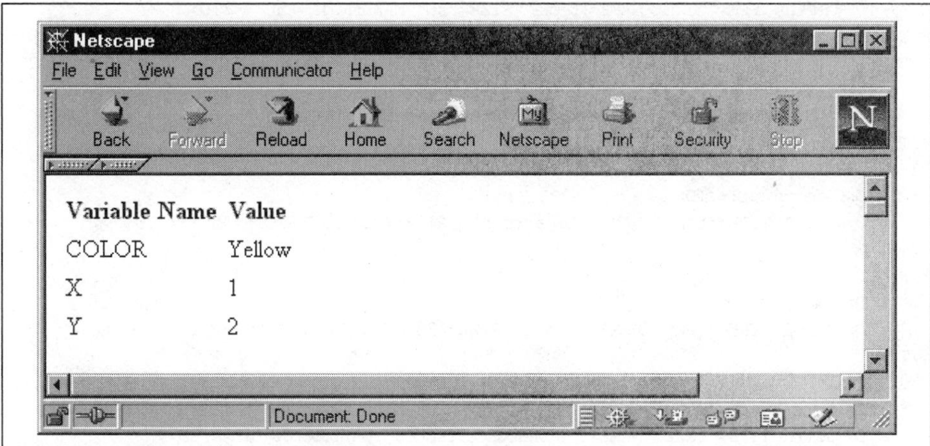


*Figure 3-4. Outputting the contents of the URL structure*

For more information about working with structures, including how to use a collection loop, see Chapter 6.

# Passing Data Using Forms

Another method for passing data from template to template involves sending the data via the HTTP Post method as form-field data. When you create an HTML form that posts to another ColdFusion template, each form field is automatically available as a form variable within the template specified in the `ACTION` attribute of the `FORM` tag. Within the receiving template, each form field can be referenced by prefixing the field name with `Form`, as in `Form.`*`MyField`*. To see just how this works, let's look at an example. The *ContactForm.cfm* template, shown in Example 3-6, creates a simple HTML form that collects basic contact information and posts it to the *DisplayContactInfo.cfm* template, shown in Example 3-7.

*Example 3-6. Template for Collecting and Posting Contact Information*

```
<HTML>
<HEAD>
  <TITLE>Passing Variables via Form Fields</TITLE>
</HEAD>

<BODY>

<H2>Employee Contact Information</H2>
<FORM ACTION="DisplayContactInfo.cfm" METHOD="post">

<TABLE>
<TR>
    <TD>Name:</TD>
    <TD><INPUT TYPE="text" NAME="Name" SIZE="25" MAXLENGTH="50"></TD>
</TR>
<TR>
    <TD>Title:</TD>
    <TD><INPUT TYPE="text" NAME="Title" SIZE="25" MAXLENGTH="50"></TD>
</TR>
<TR>
    <TD>Department:</TD>
    <TD><INPUT TYPE="text" NAME="Department" SIZE="25" MAXLENGTH="50"></TD>
</TR>
<TR>
    <TD>E-mail:</TD>
    <TD><INPUT TYPE="text" NAME="Email" SIZE="25" MAXLENGTH="255"></TD>
</TR>
<TR>
    <TD>Phone Ext.:</TD>
    <TD><INPUT TYPE="text" NAME="PhoneExt" SIZE="6" MAXLENGTH="4"></TD>
</TR>
<TR>
    <TD COLSPAN="2"><INPUT TYPE="submit" NAME="Submit" VALUE="submit"></TD>
</TR>
</TABLE>
</FORM>

</BODY>
</HTML>
```

Filling in the form fields (Figure 3-5) and clicking on the "submit" button posts the form-field information to the *DisplayContactInfo.cfm* template shown in Example 3-7.

*Example 3-7. Displaying Submitted Form-Field Values*

```
Name: #Form.Name#
Title: #Form.Title#
Department: #Form.Name#
E-mail: #Form.Email#
Phone Ext.: #Form.PhoneExt#
```

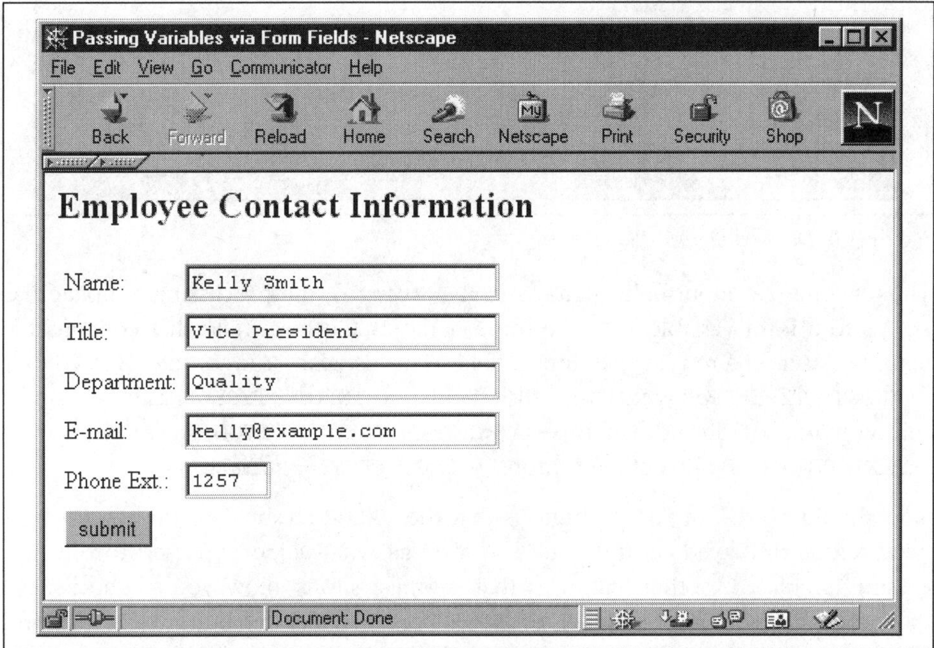


*Figure 3-5. HTML form for collecting employee contact information*

Once the form in Example 3-6 is submitted, the template in Example 3-8 outputs the contents of each form field in an HTML table. Each form variable name corresponds to the form-field name from the template in Example 3-6. Note that the output is wrapped in a set of `CFOUTPUT` tags, since we need to output the values of the form variables. The results are shown in Figure 3-6.

## *Handling Specific Types of Form Fields*

Most form fields in HTML are handled as you saw in the previous examples. One key aspect of this is that you have to define a `NAME` attribute for each field in your form. When the user submits the form, the value of each form field is available to the processing template in a form variable of the same name.

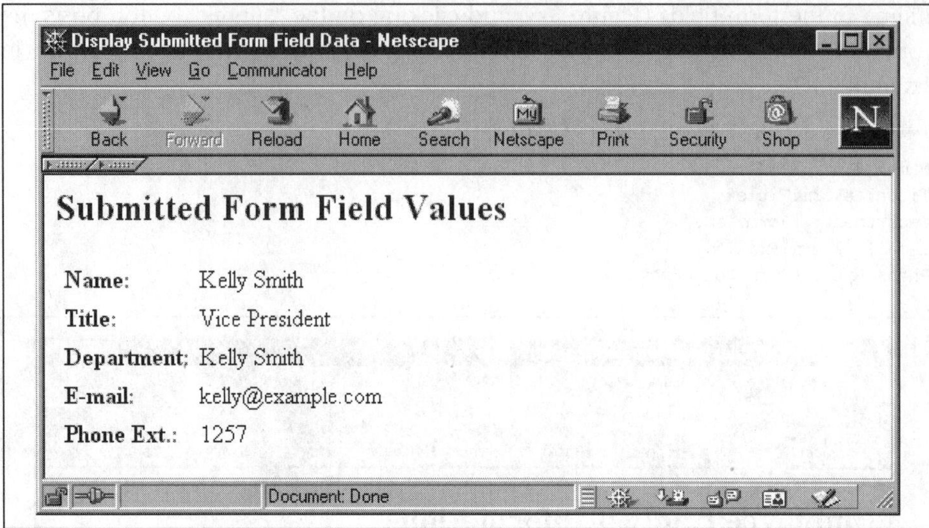


*Figure 3-6. Displaying form-field values*

Thus, with a text input field (`<INPUT TYPE="text>`), the processing template has access to a form variable with the same name as the form field that contains the text the user entered in the input field. This is also true of password fields (`<INPUT TYPE="Password">`), file fields (`<INPUT TYPE="File">`, single selection lists or drop-down boxes (`<SELECT>` and `<OPTION>` tags), text areas (`<TEXTAREA>` tags) and submit buttons (`<INPUT TYPE="submit">`).

You should note with submit buttons that the `VALUE` attribute of the tag controls what text is displayed on the button as well as what value is passed to the processing template. Another feature is that submit buttons allow you to check from the processing template whether or not a particular submit button was pressed. This allows you to build forms with more than one submit button for handling different tasks. For example, consider a form with the following submit buttons:

```
<INPUT TYPE="Submit" NAME="Add" VALUE="Add Record">
<INPUT TYPE="Submit" NAME="Edit" VALUE="Edit Record">
<INPUT TYPE="Submit" NAME="Edit" VALUE="Delete Record">
```

In your processing template, you can easily test to see what action the user wants to perform by checking for the existence of a form variable corresponding to a specific button name:

```
<CFIF IsDefined('Form.Add')>
  Add record code goes here...
<CFELSEIF IsDefined('Form.Edit')>
  Edit record code goes here...
<CFELSEIF IsDefined('Form.Delete')>
  Delete record code goes here...
<CFELSE>
```

```
    Default code goes here...
</CFIF>
```

Some form fields are a bit more complicated than the ones we just covered, so we'll discuss them in more detail.

### *Multiple selection lists*

A multiple selection list is a special type of form field that allows you to choose one or more options from a list of possible choices. They are actually the same as single selection lists (drop-down boxes) except they contain an additional attribute, `MULTIPLE`, that indicates the control should allow more than one item to be selected. Additionally, multiple selection lists generally display more than one item from the list within their window. The number of items to display is specified by the `SIZE` attribute.

Multiple items may be chosen by holding down the Control key and clicking on each item you wish to choose. When a form containing a multiple selection list is submitted, a single form-field parameter that matches the name given to the selection list is passed to the template specified by the form. This parameter contains a comma-delimited list of the values the user selected in the multiple selection box. The *MultipleSelect.cfm* template in Example 3-8 shows how a form passes values from a multiple select list. For simplicity, the form posts to itself.

*Example 3-8. Passing Form-Field Values from a Multiple Select List*

```
<H2>Multiple Selection List Example</H2>

<FORM ACTION="MultipleSelect.cfm" METHOD="post">
<TABLE>
<TR>
<TH>Colors:</TH>
<TD><SELECT NAME="Colors" SIZE="5" MULTIPLE>
        <OPTION VALUE="Red" SELECTED>Red</OPTION>
        <OPTION VALUE="Yellow">Yellow</OPTION>
        <OPTION VALUE="Pink">Pink</OPTION>
        <OPTION VALUE="Green">Green</OPTION>
        <OPTION VALUE="Purple">Purple</OPTION>
        <OPTION VALUE="Orange">Orange</OPTION>
        <OPTION VALUE="Blue">Blue</OPTION>
    </SELECT></TD>
<TD><INPUT TYPE="submit" NAME="Submit" VALUE="Submit"></TD>
</TR>
<TR>
<TD COLSPAN="3">Use the ctrl key to select multiple colors</TD>
</TR>
</TABLE>
</FORM>

<!--- if the page has been submitted to itself, output the values passed
    by the form --->
```

*Example 3-8. Passing Form-Field Values from a Multiple Select List (continued)*

```
<CFIF IsDefined('Form.Submit')>
<HR>
<CFOUTPUT>
You selected: <B>#Form.Colors#</B>
</CFOUTPUT>
</CFIF>
```

The template creates an HTML form that contains a multiple selection list and a submit button. The multiple selection list displays seven colors (anyone remember Captain Noah?) from which to select. As I mentioned, the form submits to itself. When this occurs, the last section of code in the template uses a `CFIF` statement to determine whether a variable called `Form.Submit` exists. If it does, we know that the template is calling itself, and the selected colors are output to the browser. Figure 3-7 shows both multiple selection lists, both before and after a selection is made. Since we are just outputting the values, we don't have to do anything special with the `Form.Colors` variable. But if we needed to get at the individual values, we could do that by manipulating the list, as described in Chapter 6.

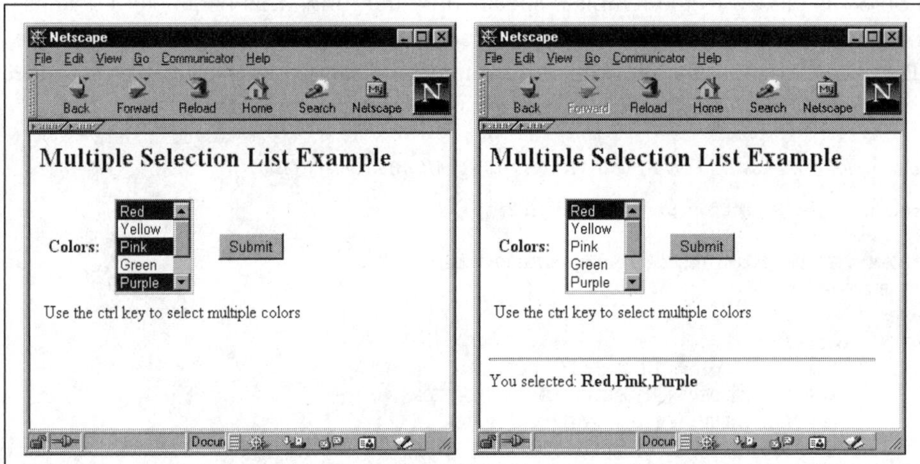


*Figure 3-7. Handling a multiple selection list*

### *Checkboxes and radio buttons*

Checkboxes (`<INPUT TYPE="checkbox">`) and radio buttons (`<INPUT TYPE="radio">`) differ from other form controls in how they pass data from one template to the next. Both checkboxes and radio buttons use the `NAME` attribute to specify the name of the form field to pass to the processing template. Additionally, a value for the form field must be specified using the `VALUE` attribute. Unlike the other types of form fields we've discussed, both radio buttons and checkboxes must be checked at the time the form is submitted for the form fields to be passed to the processing template. In other words, if a user doesn't check any boxes or buttons associated with a particular form-field name, that form field isn't passed to the processing template and is therefore not available as a form variable. This is an extremely important point because attempting to reference a variable that doesn't exist causes ColdFusion to throw an error. To get a better idea of how ColdFusion handles data passed by radio button and checkboxes, look at the *CheckboxRadio.cfm* template shown in Example 3-9.

*Example 3-9. Passing Form-Field Values from Radio Buttons and Checkboxes*

```
<HTML>
<HEAD>
  <TITLE>Passing Checkbox and Radio Button Values</TITLE>
</HEAD>

<BODY>

<H2>Checkbox and Radio Button Example</H2>

<FORM ACTION="CheckboxRadio.cfm" METHOD="post">

<B>How did you hear about us?</B> (check all that apply)<BR>
<TABLE>
<TR>
  <TD><INPUT TYPE="checkbox" NAME="Magazine" VALUE="Magazine">Magazine</TD>
  <TD><INPUT TYPE="checkbox" NAME="Internet" VALUE="Internet">Internet</TD>
  <TD><INPUT TYPE="checkbox" NAME="Other" VALUE="Other">Other</TD>
</TR>
</TABLE>

<P>
<B>Which product(s) would you like to receive additional information on?</B>
(check all that apply)<BR>
<TABLE>
<TR>
  <TD><INPUT TYPE="checkbox" NAME="Products" VALUE="Widgets">Widgets</TD>
  <TD><INPUT TYPE="checkbox" NAME="Products" VALUE="Thingies">Thingies</TD>
  <TD><INPUT TYPE="checkbox" NAME="Products" VALUE="Stuff">Stuff</TD>
</TR>
<TR>
  <TD><INPUT TYPE="checkbox" NAME="Products" VALUE="Gadgets">Gadgets</TD>
  <TD><INPUT TYPE="checkbox" NAME="Products"
          VALUE="Whatchamacallits">Whatchamacallits</TD>
  <TD><INPUT TYPE="checkbox" NAME="Products" VALUE="Junk">Junk</TD>
</TR>
</TABLE>

<P>
<B>Would you like to be added to our mailing list?</B>
<INPUT TYPE="radio" NAME="MailingList" VALUE="Yes" CHECKED>Yes
<INPUT TYPE="radio" NAME="MailingList" VALUE="No">No
```

*Example 3-9. Passing Form-Field Values from Radio Buttons and Checkboxes (continued)*

```
<P>
<INPUT TYPE="submit" NAME="Submit" VALUE="Submit">
</FORM>

<!--- if the page has been submitted to itself, output the values passed
      by the form --->

<!--- check to see if each of the "how did you hear about us" values was
      passed in.  This is an example of how NOT to code your
      checkboxes --->
<CFIF IsDefined('Form.Submit')>
<HR>
<CFOUTPUT>
<CFIF IsDefined('Form.Magazine') OR IsDefined('Form.Internet') OR
      IsDefined('Form.Other')>
<B>How you heard about us:</B>
    <CFIF IsDefined('Form.Magazine')>
    #Form.Magazine#
    </CFIF>
    <CFIF IsDefined('Form.Internet')>
    #Form.Internet#
    </CFIF>
    <CFIF IsDefined('Form.Other')>
    #Form.Other#
    </CFIF>
<BR>
</CFIF>

<!--- if any products were checked, output them.  This is the proper way to
      code a checkbox --->
<CFIF IsDefined('Form.Products')>
<B>Products:</B> #Products#<BR>
<CFELSE>
<B>Products:</B> No Products Selected<BR>
</CFIF>

<!--- output the mailing list value from the radio button --->
<B>Mailing List:</B> #MailingList#
</CFOUTPUT>
</CFIF>

</BODY>
</HTML>
```

This template creates an HTML form that contains three questions the user is asked to answer using both checkbox and radio button form controls. The form is shown in Figure 3-8.

The first section of the form asks how the user heard about the fictitious company providing the form. The user may check any boxes that apply. If you look at the code that created this section, you'll notice that each checkbox has its own name

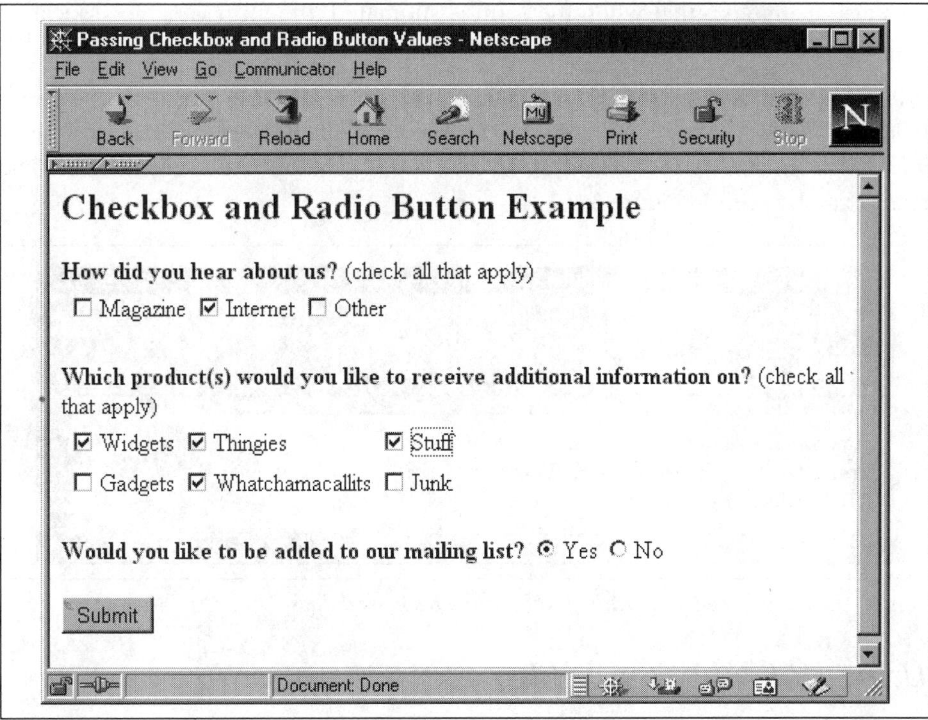


*Figure 3-8. HTML form containing checkboxes and radio buttons*

and associated value. When the form is submitted, a form-field variable is created only for each checkbox that was selected. This is an example of how *not* to code checkboxes. We'll talk about why in just a moment.

But first, let's look at the second section. Here we have another set of checkboxes that specify products the user is interested in receiving additional information about. If you look at the code here, you'll notice that each checkbox control has the same name but a different value. Using this technique for coding checkboxes is the preferred method, as it passes a single form variable that contains all the checked values in a comma-delimited list. Thus, simply by examining the list elements, it's easy to see if a particular checkbox was checked. This is in contrast to the first method I described, where you have no programmatic way of knowing which checkboxes are checked except by using an individual `IsDefined()` statement for each form-field variable that *could* be passed.

The third section of the form asks users to indicate whether they wish to subscribe to a mailing list. The yes/no choice is coded using two radio button controls. Each radio button has the same name but a different value (`Yes` and `No` respectively). This allows you to force a choice between one or the other option.

This also guarantees that when the form is submitted, the form variable associated with the radio button will exist and will contain a value.

When the user presses the submit button, the form template posts all the form-field data back to itself. The code in the second half of the template determines what form variables were passed in, so that you can output the user's choices. The results can be seen in Figure 3-9.

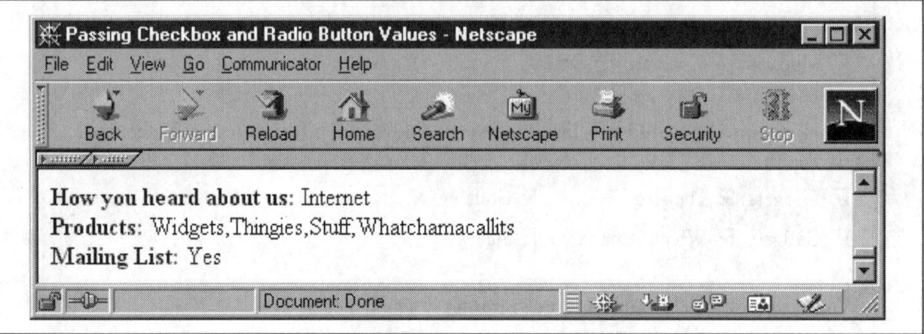


*Figure 3-9. Displaying posted radio button and checkbox values*

## Using Hidden Form Fields

Hidden form fields allow you to pass form-field parameters without having to create an associated input control. This lets you pass data from one template to another without having to display that data on the page containing your HTML form. Hidden form fields are often used to pass session information, such as a username, a primary key value, or client state information, between templates. As far as ColdFusion is concerned, data passed via hidden form fields is treated exactly the same as data passed using a text field. The processing template has a form variable with the same name and value as the hidden form field. Consider a scenario where a time stamp is generated when a user requests a particular form. In order to pass the value of the time stamp without having to display it as a visible form field, you use a hidden form field as in the following code:

```
<FORM NAME="MyForm" ACTION="Process.cfm" METHOD="Post">
<CFOUTPUT>
<INPUT TYPE="hidden" NAME="TimeStamp" VALUE="#Now()#">
</CFOUTPUT>

Name: <INPUT TYPE="text" NAME="Name"><BR>
Age: <INPUT TYPE="text" NAME="Age"><BR>
<INPUT TYPE="Submit" NAME="Submit" VALUE="Submit">
</FORM>
```

Note that although the data being passed via hidden form fields isn't immediately visible on the page containing the HTML form, all hidden form fields and their associated values can easily be seen by viewing the template source from within your web browser. Because hidden form-field data is stored as plain text, you should never use this mechanism to pass sensitive data such as passwords or credit-card numbers.

## *Automatically Validating Form-Field Data*

HTML forms don't contain a built-in mechanism for making fields required or for validating the data entered in form fields. ColdFusion allows you to make form fields required and perform certain data-validation checks by appending certain suffixes to the names of special hidden form fields in your HTML forms. Including these hidden form fields causes ColdFusion to perform a server-side check of the data after the form is submitted but before the data is processed by ColdFusion. To understand how ColdFusion's built-in data validation works, consider the *ValidationTest.cfm* template shown in Example 3-10.

*Example 3-10. Form-Field Validation Using Hidden Form Fields*

```
<HTML>
<HEAD>
  <TITLE>Form Field Validation Test Form</TITLE>
</HEAD>

<BODY>

<H2>Article Submission Form</H2>
<FORM ACTION="ValidationTest.cfm" METHOD="post">
<INPUT TYPE="hidden" NAME="ArticleDate_required"
       VALUE="You must enter an Article Date.">
<INPUT TYPE="hidden" NAME="ArticleDate_date"
       VALUE="Date must use a valid date format (e.g., 11/11/2000).">
<INPUT TYPE="hidden" NAME="Title_required"
       VALUE="You must enter a title for the article.">
<INPUT TYPE="hidden" NAME="Priority_required"
       VALUE="You must enter a priority for the article.">
<INPUT TYPE="hidden" NAME="Priority_range" VALUE="Min=1 Max=100">

<TABLE>
<TR>
    <TD>Date:</TD>
    <TD><INPUT TYPE="text" NAME="ArticleDate" SIZE="12"
               MAXLENGTH="10"></TD>
</TR>
<TR>
    <TD>Title:</TD>
    <TD><INPUT TYPE="text" NAME="Title" SIZE="50" MAXLENGTH="255"></TD>
</TR>
<TR>
    <TD>Article:</TD>
    <TD><TEXTAREA COLS="43" ROWS="5" NAME="Article"></TEXTAREA></TD>
```

*Example 3-10. Form-Field Validation Using Hidden Form Fields (continued)*

```
</TR>
<TR>
    <TD>Priority (1-100):</TD>
    <TD><INPUT TYPE="text" NAME="Priority" SIZE="4" MAXLENGTH="3"></TD>
</TR>
<TR>
    <TD COLSPAN="2"><INPUT TYPE="submit" NAME="Submit" VALUE="submit"></TD>
</TR>
</TABLE>
</FORM>

</BODY>
</HTML>
```

This HTML form contains four fields, named `ArticleDate`, `Title`, `Article`, and `Priority`. If you look at the code immediately following the `FORM` tag, you'll notice a number of hidden form fields. Each of these hidden form fields is responsible for a specific type of validation for a single form field. A suffix specifying what type of validation to perform is appended to the name of the form field specified in the `NAME` attribute. The supported validation suffixes are:

`_required`
: Makes the form field a required field.

`_date`
: Checks to see that the form field contains a date. Automatically converts the date to ODBC date format.

`_eurodate`
: Checks to see that the form field contains a European-formatted date. Automatically converts the date to ODBC date format.

`_time`
: Checks to see that the form field contains a time. Automatically converts the time to ODBC time format.

`_integer`
: Checks to see that the form field contains a number. If the number isn't an integer, it is automatically rounded to the nearest integer.

`_float`
: Checks to see that the form field contains a number.

`_range`
: Checks to see that the form field contains a numeric value in the range specified by the `VALUE="Min=x Max=y"` attribute of the `INPUT` tag.

The `VALUE` attribute of each hidden field specifies a message to display in the event that a validation rule is broken. To see how the validation violation messages are displayed, try submitting the form without filling in any form fields. You should see output similar to that shown in Figure 3-10.

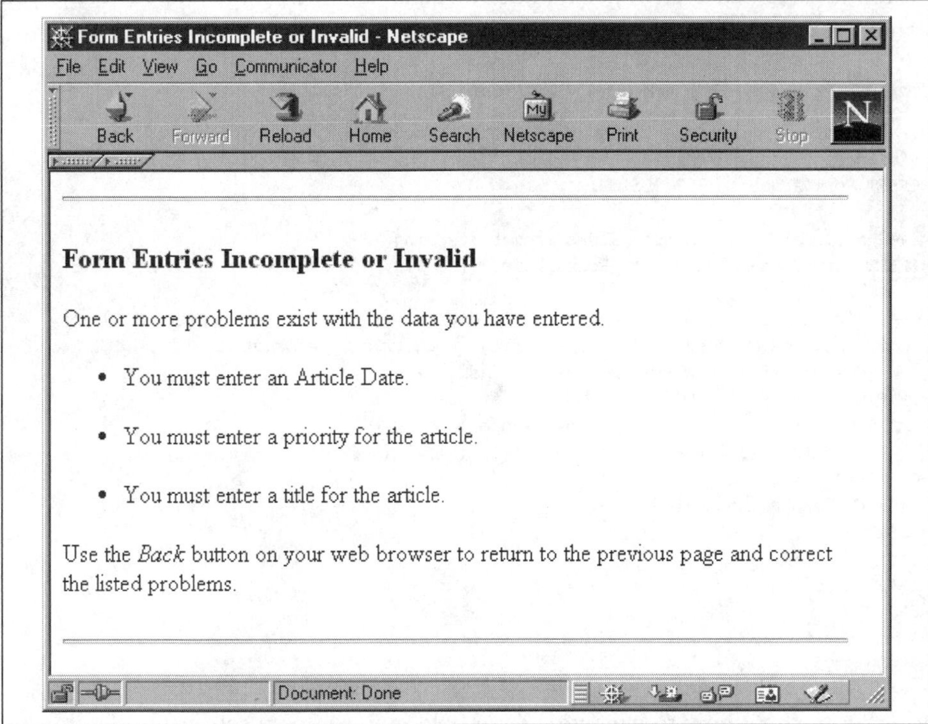


*Figure 3-10. Error messages displayed when validation rules are violated*

To see some of the other validation error messages, try entering bogus values in the form fields and submit the form. Notice that the validation screen is entirely generated by ColdFusion. The only aspect you have any control over is the bullet point message generated for each incomplete or invalid form-field entry. Each message may be set in the `VALUE` attribute of the hidden form field used to specify the validation rule.

To prevent variable name conflicts, you should avoid choosing variable names that end in `_date`, `_eurodate`, `_float`, `_integer`, `_range`, `_required`, or `_time` as they are reserved suffixes for server-side form validation.

## Manually Validating Form-Field Data

The automatic form-field validation provided by ColdFusion is nice, but it obviously doesn't cover every situation in which you might like to validate form data on the server side, such as ensuring a phone number has the correct number of digits and is formatted correctly. In cases like this, it is necessary to manually create a validation routine at the beginning of the template that accepts the form-field data. If you wanted to build a routine for validating a phone number to ensure it contained the proper number of digits and was formatted correctly, you could use code like that shown in Example 3-11.

*Example 3-11. Manual Form-Field Validation*

```
<!--- create a form field called Form.Phone.  Normally, this would be
      passed in by a form. --->
<CFSET Form.Phone = "302-555 1212">

<!--- strip all non numeric values from the string --->
<CFSET Form.Phone = ReReplace(Form.Phone, "[^0-9]", "", "ALL")>

<!--- a standard U.S. phone number has 10 digits.  If there are more or
      less, assign "invalid" to the string.  Otherwise, reformat the phone
      number using (xxx)xxx-xxxx as the mask.  --->
<CFIF Len(Form.Phone) EQ 10>
  <CFSET Form.Phone = ReReplace(Form.Phone,
         '([0-9]{3})([0-9]{3})([0-9]{4})','(\1)\2-\3')>
<CFELSE>
  <CFSET Form.Phone = "Invalid">
</CFIF>

<!--- output the phone number --->
<CFOUTPUT>
#Form.Phone#
</CFOUTPUT>
```

In order to show how to validate a form field, this example sets a form-field value called `Form.Phone` at the beginning of the template. Normally, all form fields are passed to the template by a submitted form. The validation is performed in two steps. First, the `ReReplace()` function is used to remove any nonnumeric values contained in `Form.Phone`. `ReReplace()` uses a regular expression to specify the data to be removed. Regular expressions are covered in Chapter 17.

The second step uses a bit of conditional logic along with the `Len()` function to check the number of characters remaining in the `Form.Phone` field. If there are exactly 10 digits in the field (the number of digits in a U.S. phone number), the `ReReplace()` function is used with a different regular expression to reformat the digits so they conform to the mask *(xxx)xxx-xxxx*. If the number of digits in `Form.Phone` isn't 10, we know the string contained in the form variable doesn't contain enough digits to be a valid phone number, so the value `Invalid` is assigned to `Form.Phone` instead. If this were an actual application, you could include additional code to act appropriately if the phone number was determined to be invalid.

## *Obtaining a List of All Available Form Variables*

There are two methods you can use to obtain a list of all form variables that have been passed to a given template. Just like with URL variables, form variables also have a special ColdFusion structure (as of ColdFusion 4.5), named `Form`, that contains each form-field name and its associated value. To obtain a list of all form variables within the `Form` structure, you can use the code shown in Example 3-12.

*Example 3-12. Obtaining a List of All Form Variables Passed to a Template*

```
<TABLE>
<TR>
  <TH>Variable Name</TH>
  <TH>Value</TH>
</TR>

<!--- loop over the Form structure and output all of the variable
      names and their associated values --->
<CFLOOP COLLECTION="#Form#" ITEM="VarName">
<CFOUTPUT>
<TR>
  <TD>#VarName#</TD>
  <TD>#Form[VarName]#</TD>
</TR>
</CFOUTPUT>
</CFLOOP>
</TABLE>
```

This template uses a collection loop to loop over the `Form` structure. Each variable name and its associated value are output in an HTML table. For more information about working with structures, see Chapter 6.

The second method for obtaining a list of every form variable passed to a template involves a special form variable called `Form.FieldNames`. This variable is automatically available to any ColdFusion template and contains a comma-delimited list of form-field names that have been posted to the current template. Example 3-13 shows how to access the `Form.FieldNames` variable and the value associated with each form field.

*Example 3-13. Obtaining a List of Form Fields Using Form.FieldNames*

```
<CFOUTPUT>
<B>Field Names:</B> #Form.FieldNames#
<P>
<B>Field Values:</B><BR>
<CFLOOP INDEX="TheField" list="#Form.FieldNames#">
#TheField# = #Evaluate(TheField)#<BR>
</CFLOOP>
</CFOUTPUT>
```

In this example, the list of field names is output on a single line. Next, a list loop loops over the list of field names and outputs each one along with its associated value. The value for each form field is obtained using the `Evaluate()` function. For more information on `Evaluate()`, see Appendix B.

Note that the special validation form fields (i.e., ones that have names that end with `_date`, `_time`, etc.) aren't present in the `Form.FieldNames` variable. They are, however, present in the `Form` structure.

# *Dealing with Nonexistent Parameters*

The final thing to consider when passing data between templates is how to check for and handle missing parameters. When dealing with data passed via URL or form field, it is entirely possible that an application template won't receive a parameter it is expecting. You should build mechanisms into your application templates to account for this possibility. As always, there are a few ways you can go about this.

The first method involves using the `CFPARAM` tag to assign a default value to any parameters expected by your application template. That way, if an expected parameter isn't passed, a default value is automatically assigned, and the application can continue processing. If you remember, the `CFPARAM` tag was covered earlier in Chapter 2. Additional information on the `CFPARAM` tag can be found in Appendix A.

The `CFPARAM` tag is great for assigning a default value if one doesn't exist, however, it doesn't allow you to display an error message or perform an alternate action if an expected variable doesn't exist. The next method uses the `IsDefined()` function to check for the existence of a variable before allowing processing of the template to continue. If the expected variable exists, the template is processed. If not, an error message is written to the browser. For example, if you have a template that is expecting a URL parameter named `ArticleID` to be passed in, you can use the following code to output an error message if the parameter isn't present:

```
<!--- if the parameter is present, output it to the screen --->
<CFIF IsDefined('URL.ArticleID')>
<CFOUTPUT>
The article ID is: #URL.ArticleID#
</CFOUTPUT>

Additional program code...
```

```
<!--- otherwise, output an error message --->
<CFELSE>
A required parameter, <B>ArticleID</B> was not supplied!
</CFIF>
```

In this example, the `IsDefined()` function checks for the existence of a URL parameter called `ArticleID`. If it is present, its value is output to the browser and any additional program code for the page is executed. If the parameter isn't present, an error message to that effect is written to the browser.

While this method works well in this situation, it isn't well suited for use in templates that contain a lot of code. It is generally not desirable to wrap the contents of an entire template inside of an if/else block for both performance and readability reasons. A better approach is to use the `NOT` operator in conjunction with the `IsDefined()` function as in the following example:

```
<CFIF NOT IsDefined('URL.ArticleID')>
A required parameter, <B>ArticleID</B> was not supplied!
<CFABORT>
</CFIF>

<!--- if the parameter is present, output it to the screen --->
<CFOUTPUT>
The article ID is: #URL.ArticleID#
</CFOUTPUT>

Additional program code...
```

In this example, the `IsDefined()` function is used in conjunction with the `NOT` operator to check for the existence of the URL parameter `ArticleID`. If the parameter hasn't been passed to the template via URL, an error message is written to the browser telling the user so, and all processing of the template is halted using the `CFABORT` tag. When ColdFusion encounters a `CFABORT` tag, it halts processing of the template at that position. Although this might sound drastic, what it allows you to do is separate the validation and error handling routines from the actual application code within a template.

This technique can be extended to check additional properties of a parameter. For example, say your application template expects a parameter called `ArticleID` as in our previous example. Now let's say that `ArticleID` must contain a value, and that value must be numeric. We can easily test for these conditions using the following code:

```
<CFIF NOT IsDefined('URL.ArticleID') OR NOT IsNumeric(URL.ArticleID)>
A required parameter, <B>ArticleID</B> was not supplied or the supplied value was
not numeric.
<CFABORT>
</CFIF>
```

```
<!--- if the parameter is present, output it to the screen --->
<CFOUTPUT>
The article ID is: #URL.ArticleID#
</CFOUTPUT>
```

This time, we added another condition to the initial `CFIF` statement to check to make sure that the value passed in is numeric. The `IsNumeric()` function determines whether the value associated with the `ArticleID` parameter is a numeric value. Note that single quotes aren't used around the variable name within the `IsNumeric()` function. If `ArticleID` doesn't contain a value, or the value is any datatype other than numeric, a message to that effect is output to the browser, and processing of the template is halted. If the `ArticleID` parameter does exist and it does contain a numeric value, processing of the template is allowed to continue, and the value of `ArticleID` is written to the browser.

# 4

# Database Basics

*In this chapter:*



Many people begin their relationship with ColdFusion out of a need to provide web-based access to data stored in a database. This might be as simple as wanting to output the contents of a single database table as an HTML table or as sophisticated as a multipage report generated from several related tables in a database. Whatever your requirements, the methods for querying the data from the database and outputting the results to a user's web browser using ColdFusion remain the same.

ColdFusion doesn't stop with allowing you to query data from a database. Using ColdFusion, you can perform a wide range of database operations including adding, updating, and deleting records; adding new columns to existing tables; and creating, altering, and dropping existing tables. In this chapter, we cover the basics you need to know in order to use ColdFusion to interact with a database. Included in the discussion are configuring data sources, an introduction to SQL, and techniques for retrieving and displaying data.

## Configuring Data Sources

In ColdFusion, the term *data source* refers to a connection between ColdFusion and an information source, such as a database, LDAP server, flat file, etc. This chapter focuses on connecting with one specific type of data source: databases.

Before you can use ColdFusion to interact with a database, the database has to be set up as a data source that the ColdFusion server can recognize. There are three types of database connections supported by ColdFusion:

*ODBC*
: Open Database Connectivity (ODBC) is arguably the most common format for accessing databases in both client-server and Internet-based applications. ODBC drivers are available for virtually every RDBMS in existence. If you already have ODBC data sources set up on the system you installed ColdFusion on, they are automatically available for use by ColdFusion. Depending on the platform you are running ColdFusion on, any number of ODBC drivers may be installed by default. For specifics, consult the documentation for your particular flavor of ColdFusion.

*OLE DB*
: OLE DB is a relatively new driver technology from Microsoft designed to replace ODBC as the preferred method for accessing a variety of data sources. OLE DB is available only with the Windows version of ColdFusion and requires a special set of drivers (called providers) to implement. ColdFusion comes with OLE DB providers for accessing MS Access and MS SQL Server. Other third-party OLE DB drivers are available from a number of vendors.

*Native drivers*
: The Enterprise version of ColdFusion comes with native driver support for DB2 5.0 and 6.1, Informix 7.x and 9.x, Oracle 7.3, 8.0, and 8i, and Sybase System 11 and 12 databases. Native drivers sometimes offer better performance than ODBC drivers and often include support for features not implemented in the ODBC version of the driver. In order to use a native driver, you must have client software from the particular database vendor installed on your ColdFusion server.

Regardless of the method you choose for connecting your data source to ColdFusion, one thing remains the same. You must register the data source with the ColdFusion Administrator in order to take advantage of ColdFusion's database management and security features. Registering the data-source name also tells ColdFusion which database to associate with a particular data-source name.

You should note that not all databases and connection methods are supported across all editions of ColdFusion. For the most up-to-date listing of supported database drivers, see the *Advanced ColdFusion Server Administration* book (part of the ColdFusion documentation) for your edition of ColdFusion.

## *Configuring a Data Source in the ColdFusion Administrator*

To add a new data source via the ColdFusion Administrator, follow these steps:

1. Open the ColdFusion Administrator in your browser.
2. Click on the ODBC, OLEDB, or Native Drivers link under the Data Sources section to set up the appropriate type of connection for your data source.
3. Enter a name for your data source. The name you choose is up to you, but it should be something meaningful. Names must begin with a letter and can contain only letters, numbers, and the underscore (_) character. Be sure not to use any ColdFusion tag, function, variable name, or other reserved word as your data-source name.
4. Choose your driver/provider type from the drop-down list of available types. If you are attempting to set up an ODBC connection for certain database types, such as DB2, you may not be able to add the data source through the ColdFusion Administrator. In such a case, you have to add the data source at the operating-system level and then use the ColdFusion Administrator to set any ColdFusion-specific parameters.
5. After you have provided a name for the data source and chosen the driver/provider type, click the Add button. This takes you to the Create Data Source page for the particular driver/provider you chose.
6. Depending on the driver/provider you chose, the Create Data Source page lets you enter information about the data source you want to add such as its name, location (if it is a file-based database such as MS Access), and hostname or IP address (if it is an enterprise-level database such as SQL Server, Oracle, or DB2). For more information on various configuration options, see the *Advanced ColdFusion Server Administration* book.
7. After you have finished entering the basic setup information, click on the CF Settings button in the lower right corner of the page. This takes you to a new page where you can enter information about how ColdFusion should access the database and the actions it should be allowed to perform.
8. Once you have finished configuring any ColdFusion specific settings, click the Create button at the bottom of the page. ColdFusion will attempt to register your data source and verify the connectivity. If verification fails, a message that lists likely causes for the problem is displayed. If you can connect to the data source successfully, you will be returned to the main data source configuration page. You should see the word "Verified" to the right of the data source you just created (under the Status column).

Once you have successfully created and verified the connection to your data source, you are ready to begin using it in your ColdFusion applications.

## Additional Resources

In the event you run into trouble trying to get a data source setup, consult the documentation that came with ColdFusion. Additionally, there are a number of Allaire Knowledge Base articles that may help you troubleshoot the problem. These can be found at *http://www.allaire.com/support/knowledgebase/SearchForm.cfm*. Some of the more common issues are included in the following list:

*Article 1397*
: "Troubleshooting Data Sources/Database Connectivity in Windows NT"

*Article 11328*
: "Troubleshooting Data Sources/Database Connectivity in Solaris"

*Article 14632*
: "Configuring OLE DB Data Sources in ColdFusion"

*Article 11426*
: "Solaris: How to Connect to SQLANYwhere

*Article 13104*
: "Solaris: Native Connection to Oracle 8i with CF 4.01"

*Article 16301*
: "Sybase OpenClient Problems with ColdFusion 4.5.1 and Redhat Linux"

*Article 16050*
: "Unknown Connection Error When Connecting to mySQL Databases Using myODBC on ColdFusion 4.5.x for Solaris"

*Article 4008*
: "Accessing a MS Access (or Other File System) Database on a Remote WIN32 System"

*Article 1150*
: "Connecting to Network Data Sources from Stand-alone Servers"

# Introducing CFQUERY

The `CFQUERY` tag is the main tag used by ColdFusion to interact with databases. Using `CFQUERY`, you can pass any Structured Query Language (SQL) statement to a data source registered with the ColdFusion Administrator. The content of your SQL statements determines what action is performed against the data source. The next section provides a quick primer on SQL.

The CFQUERY tag works by establishing a connection with the specified data source, passing a series of SQL commands, and returning query variables that contain information about the operation. The basic syntax for using the CFQUERY tag is as follows:

```
<CFQUERY NAME="query_name"
         DATASOURCE="datasource_name"
         DBTYPE="dbtype"
         CONNECTSTRING="connection_string">
SQL statements
</CFQUERY>
```

Each attribute in the opening CFQUERY tag specifies information about the data source and how ColdFusion should access it. The NAME attribute assigns a name to the query. Valid query names must begin with a letter and can contain only letters, numbers, and underscore characters. NAME is required when passing an SQL SELECT statement and is optional for all other SQL operations.* The DATASOURCE attribute is required in all circumstances except when DBTYPE is Query or Dynamic and specifies the name of the data source (as it appears in the ColdFusion Administrator) to connect to when executing the query. The DBTYPE attribute is optional and specifies the type of database driver to use when connecting to the data source. Possible entries are:

ODBC *(the default)*
: Connect to the data source using an ODBC driver.

OLEDB
: Make the connection using an OLEDB driver.

Oracle73
: Connect using the Oracle 7.3 native driver. This requires the 7.3.4.0.0 or later client libraries be installed on the ColdFusion server.

Oracle80
: Connect using the Oracle 8 native driver. This requires the 8.0 or later client libraries be installed on the ColdFusion server.

Sybase11
: Connect using the Sybase 11 native driver. This requires the 11.1.1 or later client libraries be installed on the ColdFusion server.

DB2
: Connect using the DB2 5.2 native driver.

* Although the NAME attribute is required only for SQL SELECT statements, you may wish to use it with all your queries. It makes debugging easier, especially for templates that contain multiple queries, because it allows you to identify each query by name in the debug output.

`Informix73`
: Connect using the Informix 7.3 native driver. This requires the Informix SDK 2.5 or later or Informix-Connect 2.5 (or later) for Windows.

`Query`
: Specifies the query should use an already existing query as the data source. If this option is used, you don't need to specify a value for `DATASOURCE`. The ability to query a query was introduced in ColdFusion 5.0 and is discussed in Chapter 11.

`Dynamic`
: Allows ColdFusion to make an ODBC connection to a data source without registering the data source in the ColdFusion Administrator. The ability to make a dynamic data source connection was added in ColdFusion 5.0. When making a dynamic connection, all information normally provided in the ColdFusion Administrator for the connection must be specified in the `CONNECTSTRING` attribute.

The `CONNECTSTRING` attribute was introduced in ColdFusion 5.0 and allows you to pass additional connection information to an ODBC data source that can't be passed via the ColdFusion Administrator. `CONNECTSTRING` can also override connection information set for a data source already registered in the ColdFusion Administrator. For example, if you use SQL Server as your database, there is no way to specify the name of the application connecting to the data source in the ColdFusion Administrator. Using `CONNECTSTRING`, however, it is possible to pass this additional bit of information:

```
<CFQUERY NAME="GetEmployeeInfo"
         DATASOURCE="MySQLServer"
         CONNECTSTRING="APP=MyCFApp">
```

For specific connection string options, you should consult the documentation for your particular database. There are a number of additional attributes that can be used with the `CFQUERY` tag. For a complete list, see its tag reference in Appendix A.

## *Connecting to a Data Source Dynamically*

A new feature in ColdFusion 5.0 is the ability to make a dynamic ODBC connection to a data source that isn't registered with the ColdFusion Administrator. You make a dynamic connection by setting the `DBTYPE` attribute of the `CFQUERY` tag to `Dynamic` and specifying all the information required to connect to the data source in the `CONNECTSTRING` attribute. For example, to make a dynamic connection to an Access database named *ProgrammingColdFusion.mdb*, you use the following:

```
<CFQUERY NAME="GetEmployeeInfo"
         DBTYPE="dynamic"
```

```
        CONNECTSTRING="DRIVER=Microsoft Access Driver (*.mdb);
                       DBQ=D:\databases\programmingcoldfusion.mdb;
                       FIL=MSAccess;
                       UID=myusername;
                       PWD=mypassword">
```

In this example, a connection is made using the Microsoft Access ODBC driver to a database named *ProgrammingColdFusion.mdb*, stored in *D:\databases*. The `UID` and `PWD` parameters specify the username and password, if any, for the database. Note that name/value pairs in the connection string are delimited by semicolons. Additionally, no spaces should be present between the parameter name, the equal sign, and the value associated with the parameter. If you find yourself encountering errors when trying to connect using a `CONNECTSTRING`, be sure each value is typed exactly as it is expected by your driver. For example, specifying "Microsoft Access Driver(*.mdb)" causes an error, as the correct driver name is "Microsoft Access Driver (*.mdb)" (note the space before the open parenthesis). Connecting to an enterprise level database is just as simple. For example, a connection to a SQL Server database looks something like this:

```
<CFQUERY NAME="GetEmployeeInfo"
         DBTYPE="dynamic"
         CONNECTSTRING="DRIVER={SQL SERVER};
                        SERVER=MySQLServer;
                        DATABASE=ProgrammingColdFusion;
                        UID=myusername;
                        PWD=mypassword">
```

By default, ColdFusion uses a special internally defined data source `__dynamic__` to pool all dynamic connections. Connection pooling improves query performance as additional requests to the same data source use the same connection. You can define additional connection pools for your dynamic connections in two ways:

- Specify a name for the `DATASOURCE` attribute of the `CFQUERY` tag. Doing this when `DBTYPE` is `Dynamic` causes ColdFusion to create a new connection pool, usable by any dynamic connections that use the same DATASOURCE name.
- Create a bogus data source in the ColdFusion Administrator and reference it using the `DATASOURCE` attribute of the `CFQUERY` tag. To create a bogus data source in the ColdFusion Administrator, you need to enter the name of a database file, hostname, or IP address. For consistency, I suggest you use "dynamic". This method allows you to set default values for your dynamic connections such as timeouts, passwords, restricted SQL operations, etc.

Due to the security risks of allowing developers (especially in hosted environments) to make dynamic data-source connections and to pass additional connection string parameters, both actions can be disabled in the Tag Restrictions section of the Security tab in the ColdFusion Administrator.

# *A Quick SQL Primer*

Before we go any further, a quick primer on SQL is in order. If you are already an SQL guru, feel free to skip this section. If, however, you are new to SQL, this section quickly covers the basic elements that go into creating an SQL statement. This primer is by no means a substitute for a thorough lesson on SQL. You may want to consult additional SQL references before proceeding, as a good understanding of SQL is an essential element in ColdFusion application design. One of the surest ways to bottleneck your applications is with poorly written SQL. Additionally, SQL is implemented in slightly different ways across various RDBMS platforms. For this reason, it is important to consult the documentation specific to your database to understand these differences.

With the disclaimer out of the way, let's move on and look at the elements that go into creating an SQL statement for use in a `CFQUERY` tag. If you don't completely understand everything we are about to cover, don't worry. Every aspect (and more) of the SQL we cover in the primer is covered in more detail throughout this and the next chapter.

Most database transactions in a web application can be grouped into one of four categories: selecting, inserting, updating, and deleting data. Not surprisingly, there are four commands in SQL that handle theses tasks. They are `SELECT`, `INSERT`, `UPDATE`, and `DELETE`, respectively:

`SELECT`
: Retrieves data from a data source

`INSERT`
: Inserts new data in a data source

`UPDATE`
: Updates existing data in a data source

`DELETE`
: Deletes data from a data source

Once you have determined the type of operation you want to perform, the next step is to refine the SQL statement by adding various clauses and operators. Depending on the action you want to perform, the syntax of the SQL statement varies. Here are some common SQL clauses:

`FROM`
: The table name or names you want to perform the `SELECT`, or `DELETE` action against

`INTO`
: Specifies the table name and column names you want to `INSERT` data into

`VALUES`
: The values to add to the columns specified in `INTO` when adding data with an `INSERT`

`SET`
: Specifies the column names you wish to `UPDATE` with new values

`WHERE`
: Specifies one or more conditions governing what data is returned by a `SELECT`, what data is changed by a `UPDATE`, or what data is deleted by a `DELETE`

`ORDER BY`
: Determines the sort order for records returned by a `SELECT`

`GROUP BY`
: Groups related data in a `SELECT`. Frequently used along with aggregate functions (discussed later in the chapter)

`HAVING`
: Generally used in place of a `WHERE` clause when using the `GROUP BY` clause

`JOIN`
: Used along with a `SELECT` statement to retrieve data from two or more related tables

`UNION`
: Combines the results of two record sets returned by a `SELECT` statement into a single record set, provided both record sets have the same number of columns, and those columns are of compatible or convertible datatypes

SQL provides a number of operators, such as `AND`, `=`, and `OR`, that can be used to construct compound, conditional, and comparison statements. Some of the more popular operators are shown in Table 4-1.

*Table 4-1. Common SQL Operators*

| Operator | Description |
|---|---|
| = | Equal to. |
| <> | Not equal to. |
| < | Less than. |
| > | Greater than. |
| <= | Less than or equal to. |
| >= | Greater than or equal to. |
| + | Plus (addition). |
| - | Minus (subtraction). |
| / | Divided by (division). |

*Table 4-1. Common SQL Operators (continued)*

| Operator | Description |
|---|---|
| * | Multiplied by (multiplication). |
| AND | Both conditions must be `True`. |
| OR | One or the other condition must be `True`. |
| NOT | Ignores a condition. |
| IS [NOT] NULL | Value is [not] null. |
| IN | Value is in a list of values. |
| BETWEEN | Value is in the range between one value and another. |
| LIKE | Value is like a wildcarded value. Wildcards are % (string) and _ (character). |
| EXISTS | Used only with subqueries. Tests for a nonempty record set. |

Now we can look at some SQL examples. Here's how to select all the fields from a database table:

```
SELECT *
FROM TableName
```

Here's how to select specific fields from a table where a certain field must meet a specific condition:

```
SELECT Field1, Field2
FROM TableName
WHERE Field = value
```

This example shows how to select fields from two different tables:

```
SELECT TableName1.Field1, TableName2.Field1
FROM TableName1, TableName2
```

This example selects two fields from a table and orders the result set by the value of ***`Field1`*** in ascending order:

```
SELECT Field1, Field2
FROM TableName
WHERE Field1 = Value1 AND Field2 = Value2
ORDER BY Field1 ASC
```

To perform the same query but have the result set ordered in descending order use this code:

```
SELECT Field1, Field2
FROM TableName
WHERE Field1 = Value1 OR Field1 = Value2
ORDER BY Field1 DESC
```

To insert a record into a table, use the `INSERT` clause with the `INTO` and `VALUES` operators:

```
INSERT INTO TableName(Field1, Field2, Field3)
VALUES('value1', value2, 'value3')
```

If you want to update an existing row, you can do so on a field-by-field basis using the `UPDATE` clause along with the `SET` and `WHERE` operators:

```
UPDATE TableName
SET Field1 = 'value1',
    Field2 = value2,
    Field3 = 'value3'
WHERE Fieldx = valuex
```

This code deletes a single row of data from a table:

```
DELETE FROM TableName
WHERE Field = value
```

If you want to delete multiple rows in one operation, use the `IN` operator like this:

```
DELETE FROM TableName
WHERE field IN (field1,field2,fieldx)
```

Now you should be primed and ready to jump into embedding SQL statements within the `CFQUERY` tag. The next section looks at using the `CFQUERY` tag in conjunction with SQL to retrieve data from a database and display the results in the browser.

# *Retrieving and Displaying Data*

When you query records from a database, the results (known as a record set) are returned in a special ColdFusion data type called a *query object*. A query object stores the records within it in rows and columns—just like a spreadsheet. Throughout this book, I'll use the terms record and row interchangeably. Column name and field are also used interchangeably. Before we get into the specifics of querying databases and working with query objects, we need to create a database with some sample data to work with.

## *Creating the Example Database*

The majority of examples in this chapter (and throughout the book) use a data source called `ProgrammingCF` that contains several database tables including one called `EmployeeDirectory`. The schema and sample data for this database are listed in Appendix C. For simplicity, I've chosen to use a Microsoft Access database for all the examples; you can download the sample Access database from O'Reilly's catalog page for this book (*http://www.oreilly.com/catalog/coldfusion/*). Of course, you can use any database you choose. To get started, you need to create a new database and save it as `ProgrammingCF`. Next, create a new table and add the fields shown in Table 4-2.

*Table 4-2. Employee Directory Table Within the ProgrammingCF Database*

| Field Name | Field Type | Max Length |
|---|---|---|
| ID (primary key) | AutoNumber | N/A |
| Name | Text | 255 |
| Title | Text | 255 |
| Department | Text | 255 |
| Email | Text | 255 |
| PhoneExt | Number (long int) | N/A |
| Salary | Number (double, two decimal places) | N/A |
| Picture | Memo | N/A |

In this example, `ID` is an AutoNumber field designated as the primary key for the table. A primary key is a single field or concatenation of fields that uniquely identifies a record. In Microsoft Access, AutoNumber is a special field type that automatically assigns a sequentially incremental number when a record is inserted into the table.* If you aren't using Access as your database, and your database doesn't have the equivalent of the AutoNumber field, consider using ColdFusion's `CreateUUID()` function to generate a universally unique identifier (UUID) to use as the primary key value for your record. UUIDs are 35-character representations of 128-bit strings where each character is a hexadecimal value in the range 0–9 and A–F. UUIDs are guaranteed to be unique:

```
<!--- create a UUID and output it to the browser --->
<CFSET MyPrimaryKeyValue = CreateUUID()>
<CFOUTPUT>
ID: #MyPrimaryKeyValue#
</CFOUTPUT>
```

When you finish adding the fields, go ahead and save the table as `EmployeeDirectory`. Now it is time to populate the `EmployeeDirectory` table with data. Table 4-3 contains a short listing of records. For the complete list, see Appendix C.

* Because portability from one database platform to another may be an issue, it's not desirable to use an AutoNumber field as a table's primary key value. The examples in this book use AutoNumber fields for primary key values as a matter of convenience.

*Table 4-3. Employee Directory Database Table Containing Employee Contact Information*

| ID | Name | Title | Department | Email | Phone-Ext | Salary |
|---|---|---|---|---|---|---|
| 1 | Pere Money | President | Executive Mgmt | *pere@example.com* | 1234 | 400K |
| 2 | Greg Corcoran | Director | Marketing | *greg@example.com* | 1237 | 960K |
| 3 | Mark Edward | VP | Sales | *mark@example.com* | 1208 | 155K |

Once you finish entering all the records, save the database to a directory on your ColdFusion server. If you have downloaded the sample Access database, you need to make sure that it resides on the same machine as your ColdFusion server or on a network share available to the server. Before you can begin using the database, you need to register it as a data source with the ColdFusion Administrator. Be sure to register the data-source name as `ProgrammingCF`.

## *Retrieving Data from a Data Source*

The `CFQUERY` tag can retrieve data from a data source by passing an SQL `SELECT` statement to the data source. The `SELECT` statement specifies what data to retrieve from the data source. For example, if you want to retrieve all records from the `EmployeeDirectory` table in the `ProgrammingCF` data source, you can use a `CFQUERY` tag with a `SELECT` statement like this:

```
<CFQUERY NAME="GetEmployeeInfo" DATASOURCE="ProgrammingCF">
         SELECT *
         FROM EmployeeDirectory
</CFQUERY>
```

This `SELECT` statement uses a wildcard (*) to retrieve all records from the `EmployeeDirectory` table in the `ProgrammingCF` data source.

Alternately, if you want to retrieve data from only a few columns as opposed to all columns (don't confuse this with all rows), you can modify the `SELECT` statement like this:

```
<CFQUERY NAME="GetEmployeeInfo" DATASOURCE="ProgrammingCF">
         SELECT Name, Title
         FROM EmployeeDirectory
</CFQUERY>
```

This query retrieves only the `Name` and `Title` columns from each row of the database. This type of query is used when you need only a subset of the data stored in a data source. Retrieving only the data you need as opposed to the entire table contents improves the overall performance of your queries. It is much more efficient for a database to send a small subset of data back to ColdFusion as opposed to an entire table, especially when you need only a small portion of the larger data set to begin with.

In general, it is not advisable to retrieve data using `SELECT *`. From a database standpoint, selecting all fields using a wildcard creates a performance hit, especially on larger record sets, because the database has to do extra work to determine what fields to return. If you really do need all the fields from a particular table returned in your result set, still consider specifying them individually by name, because it saves the database from having to construct the list.

You can further refine the `SELECT` statement to return only a limited number of rows of data based on a condition. This is done by including the condition using the `WHERE` keyword. The idea at work here is to return the smallest record set you need. The more specific the data returned by a query is to your needs, the less work you need to have the ColdFusion server do to process it. Executing the following `CFQUERY` returns just the names and email addresses of employees in the IT department:

```
<CFQUERY NAME="GetEmployeeInfo" DATASOURCE="ProgrammingCF">
         SELECT Name, Title
         FROM EmployeeDirectory
         WHERE Department = 'IT'
</CFQUERY>
```

Note the use of the single quotes around the value `'IT'` in the `WHERE` clause. String values must always be enclosed in single quotes. Numeric, Boolean, and date values may be specified without quotes.

You can extend this one step further, providing a dynamic value for the condition in the `WHERE` clause:

```
<CFQUERY NAME="GetEmployeeInfo" DATASOURCE="ProgrammingCF">
         SELECT Name, Title
         FROM EmployeeDirectory
         WHERE Department = '#Form.Department#'
</CFQUERY>
```

This example retrieves the name and title of each employee in the department specified by a form variable called `Department`. Using this type of technique allows you to build dynamic SQL statements that return different results depending on form or URL input. Dynamic SQL is discussed in Chapter 11.

## *Outputting Query Results*

Once you have data stored in a query object, the next step is to display it using the `CFOUTPUT` tag. The `CFOUTPUT` tag allows you to display data contained in a query object by referencing the query name in the `QUERY` attribute. Example 4-1 queries the `EmployeeDirectory` of the `ProgrammingCF` data source and outputs the results to the browser using `CFOUTPUT`.

*Example 4-1. Outputting the Results of a Query in an HTML Table*

```
<!--- retrieve all records from the database --->
<CFQUERY NAME="GetEmployeeInfo" DATASOURCE="ProgrammingCF">
        SELECT ID, Name, Title, Department, Email, PhoneExt, Salary
        FROM EmployeeDirectory
</CFQUERY>

<HTML>
<HEAD>
    <TITLE>Outputting Query Results</TITLE>
</HEAD>

<BODY>

<H2>Employee Records</H2>
<!--- create an HTML table for outputting the query results.  This section
      creates the first row of the table - used to hold the column
      headers --->
<TABLE CELLPADDING="3" CELLSPACING="0">
<TR BGCOLOR="#888888">
    <TH>ID</TH>
    <TH>Name</TH>
    <TH>Title</TH>
    <TH>Department</TH>
    <TH>E-mail</TH>
    <TH>Phone Extension</TH>
    <TH>Salary</TH>
</TR>

<!--- the CFOUTPUT tag is used in conjunction with the QUERY attribute to loop
      over each row of data in the result set.  During each iteration of the
      loop, a table row is dynamically created and populated with the query
      data from the current row. --->
<CFOUTPUT QUERY="GetEmployeeInfo">
<TR BGCOLOR="##C0C0C0">
    <TD>#ID#</TD>
    <TD>#Name#</TD>
    <TD>#Title#</TD>
    <TD>#Department#</TD>
    <TD><A HREF="Mailto:#Email#">#Email#</A></TD>
    <TD>#PhoneExt#</TD>
    <TD>#Salary#</TD>
</TR>
</CFOUTPUT>
</TABLE>

</BODY>
</HTML>
```

In this example, the `CFQUERY` tag executes a `SELECT` statement against the `EmployeeDirectory` table of the `ProgrammingCF` data source. The query retrieves all the columns for all the records stored in the table. The template then creates an HTML table and generates column headings using a series of HTML <TH> tags.

Next, the `CFOUTPUT` tag is used in conjunction with the `QUERY` attribute to loop over each row of data in the result set. With each iteration of the loop, a table row is dynamically created and populated with the query data from the current row. Note the double pound signs (`##`) before the hex color code in the <TR> tag. Because the color code is used within a `CFOUTPUT` block, the pound sign that comes before the hex code must be escaped. If is isn't escaped, ColdFusion tries to interpret the color as a variable and throws an error because no ending pound sign is found

## Obtaining Additional Query Information

Whenever you perform a query using ColdFusion, four variables are automatically created that contain information about the `CFQUERY` operation and the result set it returned, if any. Here are the four variables:

`CFQUERY.ExecutionTime`
: The amount of time in milliseconds it takes the query to execute

*`Queryname`*`.ColumnList`
: Comma-delimited list of the query column names from the database

*`Queryname`*`.CurrentRow`
: The current row of the query that is being processed by `CFOUTPUT`

*`Queryname`*`.RecordCount`
: The total number of records returned by the query

These variables can be used in countless ways and are used heavily throughout this book for such things as knowing how many records were returned by a particular query and breaking the display of query result sets into manageable chunks.

# Sorting Query Results

When you use a basic SQL `SELECT` statement to retrieve records from a database, those records are returned in the order in which they were originally entered. If you want to change the order in which the records are displayed, you need to use an `ORDER BY` clause, as shown in Example 4-2.

*Example 4-2. Sorting Query Results Using the SQL ORDER Clause*

```
<CFQUERY NAME="GetEmployeeInfo" DATASOURCE="ProgrammingCF">
         SELECT Name, Title, Department, Email, PhoneExt
         FROM EmployeeDirectory
         ORDER BY Name ASC
</CFQUERY>

<TABLE CELLPADDING="3" CELLSPACING="0">
<TR BGCOLOR="#888888">
   <TH>Name</TH>
   <TH>Title</TH>
   <TH>Department</TH>
   <TH>E-mail</TH>
   <TH>Phone Extension</TH>
</TR>
<CFOUTPUT QUERY="GetEmployeeInfo">
<TR BGCOLOR="##C0C0C0">
   <TD>#Name#</TD>
   <TD>#Title#</TD>
   <TD>#Department#</TD>
   <TD><A HREF="Mailto:#Email#">#Email#</A></TD>
   <TD>#PhoneExt#</TD>
</TR>
</CFOUTPUT>
</TABLE>
```

The `ORDER BY` clause specifies which column or columns to use in ordering the query results. Sorting can be either `ASC` (ascending) or `DESC` (descending). Example 4-2 sorts the result set by `NAME` column, in ascending order. The output is shown in Figure 4-1.

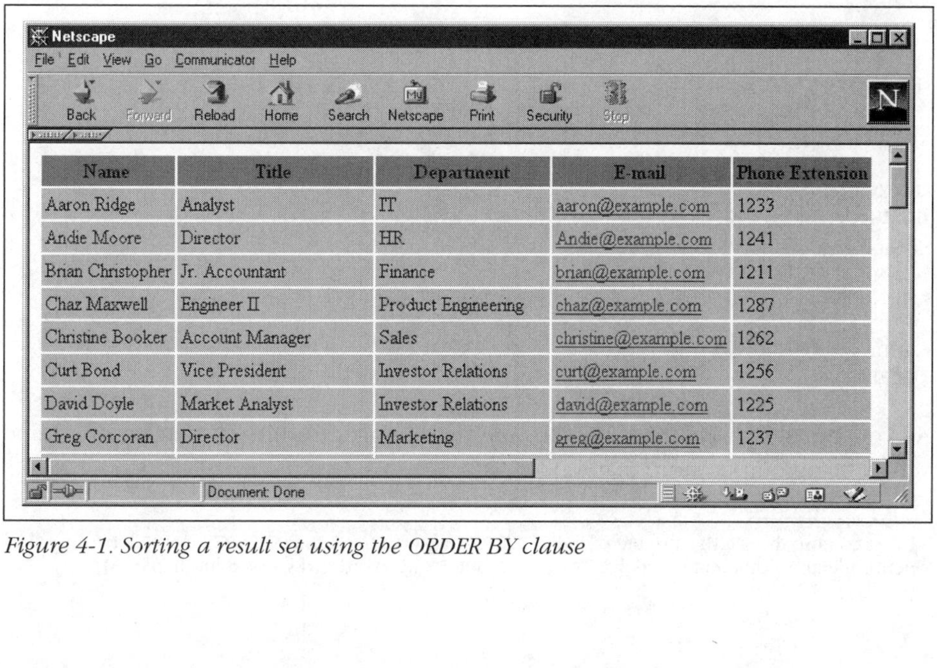
Netscape
File Edit View Go Communicator Help
Back Forward Reload Home Search Netscape Print Security Stop
Name Title Department E-mail Phone Extension
Aaron Ridge Analyst IT aaron@example.com 1233
Andie Moore Director HR Andie@example.com 1241
Brian Christopher Jr. Accountant Finance brian@example.com 1211
Chaz Maxwell Engineer II Product Engineering chaz@example.com 1287
Christine Booker Account Manager Sales christine@example.com 1262
Curt Bond Vice President Investor Relations curt@example.com 1256
David Doyle Market Analyst Investor Relations david@example.com 1225
Greg Corcoran Director Marketing greg@example.com 1237
Document: Done

*Figure 4-1. Sorting a result set using the ORDER BY clause*

Multicolumn sorts can be performed by specifying a comma-delimited list of column names and sort orders for the ORDER BY clause as in:

```
<CFQUERY NAME="GetEmployeeInfo" DATASOURCE="ProgrammingCF">
        SELECT Name, Title, Department, Email, PhoneExt
        FROM EmployeeDirectory
        ORDER BY Title ASC, Name ASC
</CFQUERY>
```

# *Grouping Output*

The CFOUTPUT tag has an attribute called GROUP that lets you to group output from your record sets before displaying it to the browser. There are two ways to use the GROUP attribute of the CFOUTPUT tag. The first method uses GROUP to remove any duplicate rows from the query result set.* This is useful in situations where the result set you return from a query contains duplicate rows of data but you want to display only unique records.

Example 4-3 demonstrates what happens when you query a table containing duplicate values and output the results without using the GROUP attribute of the CFOUTPUT tag.

*Example 4-3. Failing to Use the GROUP Attribute Results in Duplicate Values in the Output*

```
<CFQUERY NAME="GetDepartment" DATASOURCE="ProgrammingCF">
        SELECT Department
        FROM EmployeeDirectory
        ORDER BY Department
</CFQUERY>


<HTML>
<HEAD>
    <TITLE>Using GROUP to remove duplicate records</TITLE>
</HEAD>

<BODY>
<H2>Departments:</H2>
<CFOUTPUT QUERY="GetDepartment">
#Department#<BR>
</CFOUTPUT>

</BODY>
</HTML>
```

As you can see in Figure 4-2, executing the template results in many of the same values being output more than once.

* Don't confuse the GROUP attribute of the CFOUTPUT tag with the SQL GROUP BY keyword, because they perform entirely different functions. The SQL GROUP BY keyword is discussed in Chapter 11.

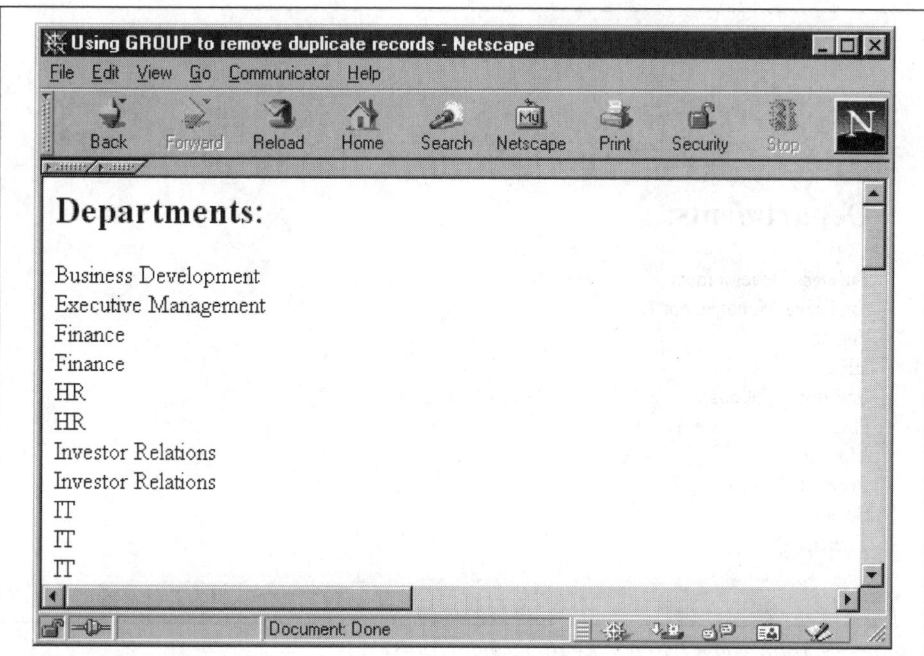


*Figure 4-2. Duplicate records are displayed because GROUP wasn't used*

This is easy enough to fix. To remove the duplicates from the output, all you have to do is modify the line of code containing the `CFOUTPUT` tag to read like this:

```
<CFOUTPUT QUERY="GetDepartment" GROUP="Department" GROUPCASESENSITIVE="No">
```

Adding `GROUP="Department"` to the `CFOUTPUT` tag tells ColdFusion to discard any duplicate values in the result set and output only unique values. The `GROUPCASESENSITIVE` attribute indicates whether grouping should be case-insensitive or case-sensitive. This attribute is optional and defaults to `Yes`. For our example, set `GROUPCASESENSITIVE` to `No` in case someone enters the name of a department using the wrong case. The difference in output is shown in Figure 4-3.

It is important to note that using `GROUP` to remove duplicates from the result set does so *after* the result set is returned from the database. You should consider how this might affect the performance of your application if you want to return only a few records from a large record set that contains numerous duplicate values. In such a case, you should use SQL to remove the duplicates.

If you look at the code in Example 4-3, you'll notice that we included `ORDER BY Department` in our SQL statement. It is necessary to sort the result set by the column being grouped. To see what happens if you don't include the `ORDER BY` clause, remove it from the query and execute the template.

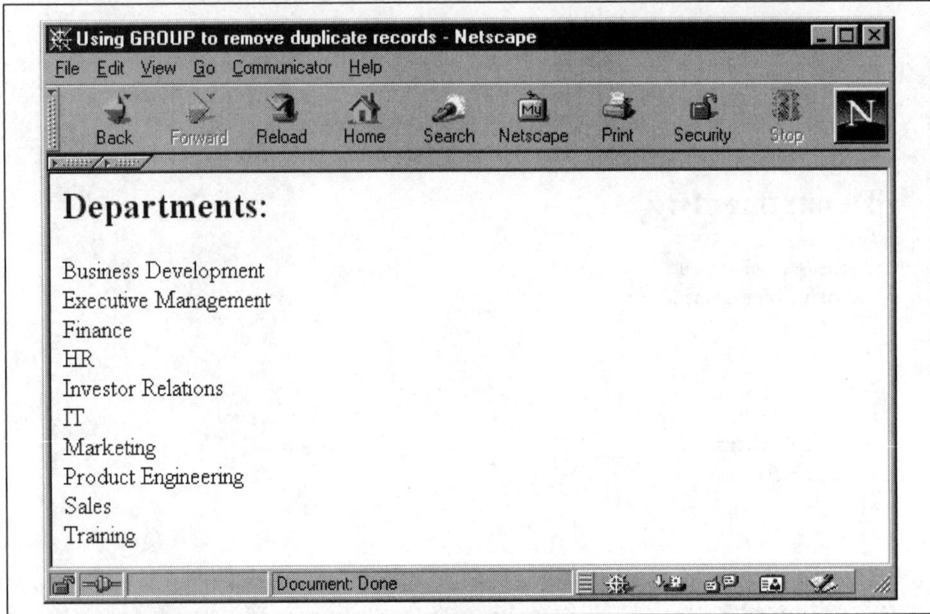


*Figure 4-3. Using GROUP to remove duplicate records*

As I mentioned in the beginning of this section, **GROUP** can be used in two ways. The second way the **GROUP** attribute can be used is to group like records for output. This allows you to do such things as group the output of a query by a certain field or fields such as age, gender, department, color, etc. This is done by including (nesting) a second set of **CFOUTPUT** tags without the **GROUP** attribute inside the first set. Example 4-4 shows how to use the **GROUP** attribute of the **CFOUTPUT** tag to group the results of a query by `Department`.

*Example 4-4. Using the GROUP Attribute of the CFOUTPUT Tag to Group Records by Department*

```
<CFQUERY NAME="GetEmployeeInfo" DATASOURCE="ProgrammingCF">
         SELECT Name, Title, Department, Email, PhoneExt
         FROM EmployeeDirectory
         ORDER BY Department
</CFQUERY>

<TABLE CELLPADDING="3" CELLSPACING="0">
<CFOUTPUT QUERY="GetEmployeeInfo" GROUP="Department" GROUPCASESENSITIVE="No">
<TR>
<TD COLSPAN="5" HEIGHT="30" VALIGN="bottom"><FONT SIZE="+1"><B>#Department#</B>
    </FONT></TD>
</TR>
<TR BGCOLOR="##888888">
   <TH>Name</TH>
   <TH>Title</TH>
   <TH>Department</TH>
```

*Example 4-4. Using the GROUP Attribute of the CFOUTPUT Tag to Group Records by Department (continued)*

```
    <TH>E-mail</TH>
    <TH>Phone Extension</TH>
</TR>
<CFOUTPUT>
<TR BGCOLOR="##C0C0C0">
    <TD>#Name#</TD>
    <TD>#Title#</TD>
    <TD>#Department#</TD>
    <TD><A HREF="Mailto:#Email#">#Email#</A></TD>
    <TD>#PhoneExt#</TD>
</TR>
</CFOUTPUT>
</CFOUTPUT>
</TABLE>
```

The **GROUP** attribute of the **CFQUERY** tag lets you group your query's result set by the specified column. In this case, we want to group the query results by Department. It is necessary to use the **ORDER BY** clause to order the result set by the column being grouped. Failing to do so results in unwanted output. Notice the second set of **CFOUTPUT** tags nested within the pair declaring the **GROUP**. This creates an outer and inner loop for looping over the result set and grouping the output appropriately. Nested **CFOUTPUT** tags may be used only when the outermost **CFOUTPUT** tag has a value specified for the **QUERY** and **GROUP** attributes. If you attempt to nest **CFOUTPUT** tags without using these attributes in the outermost tag, ColdFusion throws an error. Additionally, if you omit the nested **CFOUTPUT**, the nested grouping doesn't occur, and you end up removing any duplicate records from the result set (just like our previous example). Executing the template results in the output shown in Figure 4-4.

It is entirely possible to group data several levels deep. Doing so requires nesting several sets of **CFOUTPUT** tags using the following general syntax:

```
<CFOUTPUT QUERY="query_name" GROUP="column">
HTML and CFML...
<CFOUTPUT GROUP="different_column">
HTML and CFML...
<CFOUTPUT>
HTML and CFML...
</CFOUTPUT>
</CFOUTPUT>
</CFOUTPUT>
```

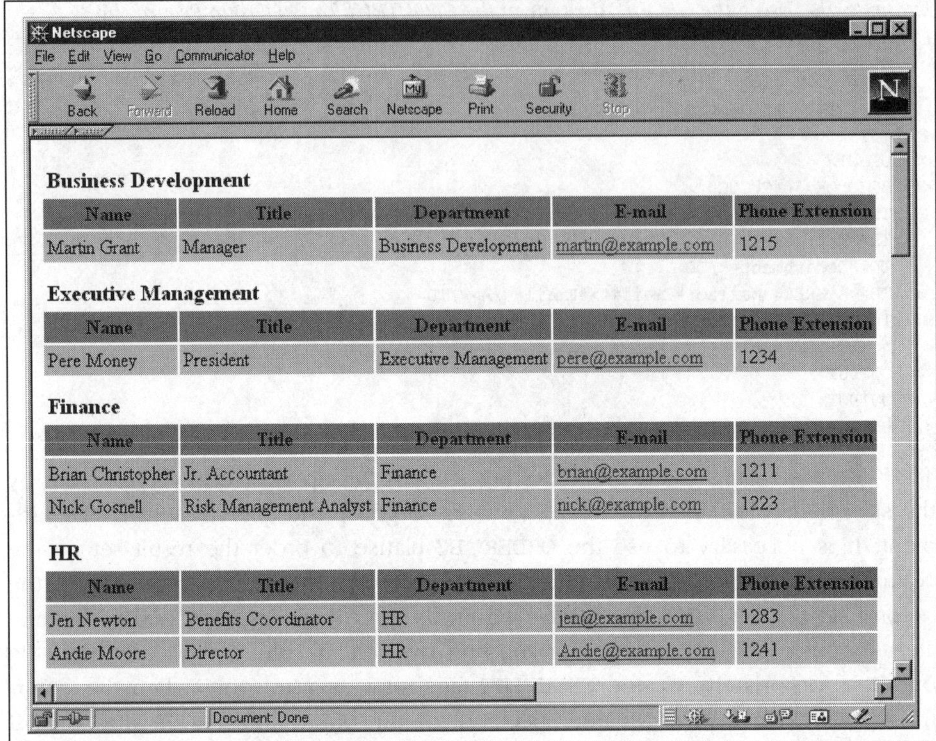


*Figure 4-4. Using CFOUTPUT to group query results*

When ColdFusion encounters nested CFOUTPUT tags, it executes successive levels of nested loops to group the query result set. In general, there are a few rules you need to keep in mind when working with nested CFOUTPUT tags:

- The outermost CFOUTPUT tag must have the QUERY and GROUP attributes defined.
- The innermost CFOUTPUT tag can't have any attributes specified.
- All other CFOUTPUT tags may have only the GROUP attribute specified.

## *Looping Over a Query Result Set*

As I mentioned briefly in Chapter 2, a query loop (CFLOOP tag with the QUERY attribute) performs essentially the same job as using a CFOUTPUT tag with the QUERY attribute. A query loop iterates over each row in a query object. Optionally, a start row and end row within the query may be specified:

```
<CFLOOP QUERY="query_name"
        STARTROW="row_number"
        ENDROW="row_number">
...
</CFLOOP>
```

The QUERY attribute specifies the name of a valid ColdFusion query object. STARTROW is optional and may be used to specify the row within the query object where the loop should begin. ENDROW is also optional and specifies the last row within a query object that should be included within the loop.

The query loop may be used instead of the QUERY attribute of the CFOUTPUT tag to display the contents of a query:

```
<CFQUERY NAME="GetEmployeeInfo" DATASOURCE="ProgrammingCF">
        SELECT Name, Title
        FROM EmployeeDirectory
</CFQUERY>

<CFLOOP QUERY="GetEmployeeInfo">
  <CFOUTPUT>#Name#, #Title#<BR></CFOUTPUT>
</CFLOOP>
```

Using a query loop allows you to work around limitations inherent in the CFOUTPUT tag such as the inability to nest additional output queries within a CFOUTPUT block. For example, the following code produces an error in ColdFusion because you can't nest CFOUTPUT tags without using the GROUP attribute:

```
<CFQUERY NAME="MyQuery1" DATASOURCE="MyDSN">
    SELECT *
    FROM MyTable
    WHERE Field = Value
</CFQUERY>

<CFOUTPUT QUERY="MyQuery1">
  <CFQUERY NAME="MyQuery2" DATASOURCE="MyDSN">
      SELECT *
      FROM MyTable
      WHERE Field = Value
  </CFQUERY>

  <CFOUTPUT QUERY="MyQuery2">
    Additional processing and output code here...
  </CFOUTPUT>
</CFOUTPUT>
```

You can get around this limitation by using a query loop within the CFOUTPUT block:

```
<CFQUERY NAME="MyQuery1" DATASOURCE="MyDSN">
    SELECT *
    FROM MyTable
```

```
    WHERE Field = Value
</CFQUERY>

<CFOUTPUT QUERY="MyQuery1">
  <CFQUERY NAME="MyQuery2" DATASOURCE="MyDSN">
      SELECT *
      FROM MyTable
      WHERE Field = Value
  </CFQUERY>

  <CFLOOP QUERY="MyQuery2">
    Additional processing and output code here...
  </CFLOOP>
</CFOUTPUT>
```

Additionally, you can use the query loop to output a section of a record set by dynamically defining the start row and end row of the query object to loop over:

```
<CFSET TheStart = 3>
<CFSET TheEnd = 5>

<CFQUERY NAME="GetEmployeeInfo" DATASOURCE="ProgrammingCF">
        SELECT Name, Title
        FROM EmployeeDirectory
</CFQUERY>

<CFLOOP QUERY="GetEmployeeInfo"
        STARTROW="#TheStart#"
        ENDROW="#TheEnd#">
  <CFOUTPUT>#Name#, #Title#<BR></CFOUTPUT>
</CFLOOP>
```

This technique can be used to create a next/previous record browser in which a predetermined number of rows from a query result set are displayed on the page. This allows users to browse a set number of records at a time while moving forward and backward through the record set. Next/previous browsing is discussed in detail in Chapter 11.

# Formatting Techniques

Once you have query data in the form of a result set, you might want to massage it a bit before outputting it to the browser or to a file. ColdFusion provides several built-in functions for formatting a variety of datatypes. This section covers some of the more popular functions for formatting strings, HTML code, numbers, currency, dates, times, and Boolean values. For more information on all the functions covered in this section, see Appendix B.

## *Formatting Plain-Text Strings*

ColdFusion provides functions for formatting text strings: `ParagraphFormat()`, `Ucase()`, `Lcase()`, `JSStringFormat()`, and `XMLFormat()`. Each function is covered in the sections that follow.

### *Using ParagraphFormat*

`ParagraphFormat()` takes a string and formats it so that single newline characters are replaced with a space, and double newline characters are replaced with HTML <P> tags. This function is most often used to display data that has been entered into a `Textarea` HTML form field. The following example shows how the `ParagraphFormat()` function handles single and double newline characters:

```
<CFSET MyText="This is my block of text.
It has both single newline characters in it like this paragraph, and double
newline characters like in the next paragraph.

This is the paragraph with the double newline characters.">

<FORM>
<CFOUTPUT>
<TEXTAREA COLS=50 ROWS=10 NAME="TheText" WRAP="virtual">
#ParagraphFormat(MyText)#
</TEXTAREA>
</CFOUTPUT>
</FORM>
```

### *Changing case*

You can change the case of an entire string using the `Ucase()` and `Lcase()` functions. `Ucase()` converts a string to all uppercase characters, while `Lcase()` converts a string to all lowercase characters. The following example demonstrates both functions:

```
<CFSET MyString = "This Is A Mixed Case String!">

<H3>UCase/LCase</H3>
<CFOUTPUT>
Original String: #MyString#<BR>
After UCase: #UCase(MyString)#<BR>
After LCase: #LCase(MyString)#
</CFOUTPUT>
```

### *Making strings JavaScript-safe*

On occasion, you may need to retrieve a string from a database for use in a JavaScript function within your application. The `JSStringFormat()` function can be used to make the string safe for use in JavaScript statements by automatically escaping special characters that normally cause a problem, such as double quotes, single quotes, and the newline character (\). The following example returns a string that has been formatted for use in a JavaScript statement:

```
<CFSET MyString="""Escape double quotes"". Escape the \ character. 'Escape
    single quotes'">

<CFSET SafeString=JSStringFormat(MyString)>

<CFOUTPUT>
<B>Original String:</B> #MyString#<BR>
<B>JavaScript Safe String:</B> #SafeString#
</CFOUTPUT>
```

### *Making strings safe for XML*

You can make a string safe to use with XML by using the `XMLFormat()` function. `XMLFormat()` takes a string as its only parameter and returns it in a format that is safe to use with XML by escaping the following special characters:

Ampersand (&)
Double quotation mark (")
Greater than sign (>)
Less than sign (<)
Single quotation mark (')

The following example takes a string and makes it safe to use with XML:

```
<CFSET MyString="Here's an example of the XMLFormat function: 5+5<20">

<CFOUTPUT>
#XMLFormat(MyString)#
</CFOUTPUT>

<P>
<I>View the page source to see the escaped text.</I>
```

## *Formatting HTML*

In order to display literal HTML or CFML code, it is necessary to escape certain special characters so that they don't cause the browser to interpret the code contained inside them. For example, if you have a string that contains `Hello <B> World!</B>`, and you want to display the HTML code contained in the string without having it execute, you need to escape the < and > characters. ColdFusion provides you with two functions to do this: `HTMLCodeFormat()` and `HTMLEditFormat()`.

### *HTMLCodeFormat*

The `HTMLCodeFormat()` function returns a string enclosed in `<PRE>` and `</PRE>` tags with all carriage returns removed and special characters (`< > " &`) escaped.

The function takes two parameters, a string to format and optionally, the HTML version to use for the character escape sequences. Valid entries for the HTML version are shown in Table 4-4.

*Table 4-4. HTML Versions*

| Value | Description |
|---|---|
| -1 | Current HTML version |
| 2.0 | HTML v2.0 (default) |
| 3.2 | HTML v3.0 |

The following example demonstrates the **HTMLCodeFormat()** function:

```
<CFSET MyString="<H3>This is an example of the HTMLCodeFormat function.</H3>
View the source of this document to see the escaping of the HTML characters.">

<CFOUTPUT>
#HTMLCodeFormat(MyString, "3.2")#
</CFOUTPUT>
```

### *HTMLEditFormat*

The **HTMLEditFormat()** function is almost identical in functionality to **HTMLCodeFormat()**. The only difference is that it doesn't add **<PRE></PRE>** tags to the output returned by the function. The following example demonstrates the **HTMLEditFormat()** function:

```
<CFSET MyString="<H3>This is an example of the HTMLEditFormat function.</H3>
View the source of this document to see the escaping of the HTML characters.">

<CFOUTPUT>
#HTMLEditFormat(MyString, "3.2")#
</CFOUTPUT>
```

## *Formatting Numbers*

ColdFusion provides three functions for formatting numbers: **DecimalFormat()**, **NumberFormat()**, and **LSNumberFormat()**. These functions can format numbers in a variety of ways, as described in the following sections.

### *Formatting decimal numbers*

The **DecimalFormat()** function takes a number and returns it formatted to two decimal places, with thousands separators. The following example formats a variety of numbers using **DecimalFormat()**:

```
<CFOUTPUT>
1:  #DecimalFormat(1)#<BR>
10: #DecimalFormat(10)#<BR>
100: #DecimalFormat(100)#<BR>
```

```
1000: #DecimalFormat(1000)#<BR>
10000: #DecimalFormat(10000)#<BR>
100000: #DecimalFormat(100000)#<BR>
1000000: #DecimalFormat(1000000)#<BR>
</CFOUTPUT>
```

### *General number formatting*

The `NumberFormat()` function handles general number formatting in ColdFusion. `NumberFormat()` allows you to format numbers using a variety of masks. The function accepts two parameters, the number you wish to format and a mask to specify the formatting, in the form `NumberFormat(`*`Number`*`, '`*`mask`*`')`. If no mask is supplied, `NumberFormat()` returns the number formatted with thousands separators. Valid entries for the mask are listed in Table 4-5.

*Table 4-5. Mask Values for NumberFormat()*

| Mask | Description |
|---|---|
| _ | Optional digit placeholder |
| 9 | Optional digit placeholder; same as _ but better for showing decimal places |
| . | Decimal point location |
| 0 | Forces padding with zeros |
| ( ) | Surrounds negative numbers in parentheses |
| + | Places a plus sign in front of positive numbers and a minus sign in front of negative numbers |
| - | Places a space in front of positive numbers and a minus sign in front of negative numbers |
| , | Separates thousands with commas |
| L | Left justifies the number within the width of the mask |
| C | Centers the number within the width of the mask |
| $ | Places a dollar sign in front of the number |
| ^ | Separates left from right formatting |

The following example shows the `NumberFormat()` function applied to various numbers:

```
<!--- Assign a number to a variable to be used throughout the example --->
<CFSET MyNumber = 1000.99>

<H3>Formatting Numeric Values using NumberFormat</H3>

<CFOUTPUT>
<B>MyNumber = #MyNumber#</B>
<P>
NumberFormat(MyNumber, '____'): #NumberFormat(MyNumber, '____')#<BR>
NumberFormat(MyNumber, '9999.99'): #NumberFormat(MyNumber, '9999.99')#<BR>
NumberFormat(MyNumber, '09999.9900'): #NumberFormat(MyNumber, '09999.9900')#<BR>
```

```
NumberFormat(-MyNumber, '(9999.99)'): #NumberFormat(-MyNumber, '(9999.99)')#<BR>
NumberFormat(MyNumber, '+9999.99'): #NumberFormat(MyNumber, '+9999.99')#<BR>
NumberFormat(-MyNumber, '+9999.99'): #NumberFormat(-MyNumber, '+9999.99')#<BR>
NumberFormat(MyNumber, '-9999.99'): #NumberFormat(MyNumber, '-9999.99')#<BR>
NumberFormat(-MyNumber, '-9999.99'): #NumberFormat(-MyNumber, '-9999.99')#<BR>
NumberFormat(MyNumber, '$9,999.99'): #NumberFormat(MyNumber, '$9,999.99')#<BR>
NumberFormat(MyNumber, 'L999,999.99'): #NumberFormat(MyNumber, 'L999,999.99')#<BR>
NumberFormat(MyNumber, 'C999,999.99'): #NumberFormat(MyNumber, 'C999,999.99')#<BR>
NumberFormat(MyNumber, 'C_____(^___)'): #NumberFormat(MyNumber, 'C_____(^___)')#
</CFOUTPUT>
```

### *Locale-specific number formatting*

In addition to general number formatting using the `NumberFormat()` function, ColdFusion provides another function for formatting numbers in a format that is locale-specific. Locale-specific formatting allows you to format numbers for a specific language or dialect (often country-specific). For example, in many European countries, the period (.) is used as a thousands separator instead of the comma (,) as in the United States. The `LSNumberFormat()` function behaves the same as the `NumberFormat()` function (using the same masks), but it takes into account the formatting used by the default locale. If no formatting mask is supplied, `LSNumberFormat()` returns the number as an integer.

The following example loops through each locale supported by ColdFusion and applies a variety of different number masks for each locale:

```
<H3>Formatting Locale Specific Numeric Values using LSNumberFormat</H3>

<!--- loop over each locale.  The list of locales is obtained from the server
      variable Server.ColdFusion.SupportedLocales --->
<CFLOOP INDEX="locale" LIST="#Server.Coldfusion.SupportedLocales#">
<!--- this causes the CF server to assume the locale specified by the current
      iteration of the loop --->
<CFSET temp = SetLocale(locale)>

<CFOUTPUT>
<P>
<B>#locale#</B><BR>
LSNumberFormat(1000.99, '____'): #LSNumberFormat(1000.99, '____')#<BR>
LSNumberFormat(1000.99, '9999.99'): #LSNumberFormat(1000.99, '9999.99')#<BR>
LSNumberFormat(1000.99, '09999.9900'): #LSNumberFormat(1000.99, '09999.9900')#<BR>
LSNumberFormat(-1000.99, '(9999.99)'): #LSNumberFormat(-1000.99, '(9999.99)')#<BR>
LSNumberFormat(1000.99, '+9999.99'): #LSNumberFormat(1000.99, '+9999.99')#<BR>
LSNumberFormat(-1000.99, '+9999.99'): #LSNumberFormat(-1000.99, '+9999.99')#<BR>
LSNumberFormat(1000.99, '-9999.99'): #LSNumberFormat(1000.99, '-9999.99')#<BR>
LSNumberFormat(-1000.99, '-9999.99'): #LSNumberFormat(-1000.99, '-9999.99')#<BR>
LSNumberFormat(1000.99, '$9,999.99'): #LSNumberFormat(1000.99, '$9,999.99')#<BR>
LSNumberFormat(1000.99, 'L999,999.99'): #LSNumberFormat(1000.99, 'L999,999.99')#<BR>
LSNumberFormat(1000.99, 'C999,999.99'): #LSNumberFormat(1000.99,'C999,999.99')#<BR>
LSNumberFormat(1000.99, 'C____(^___)'): #LSNumberFormat(1000.99, 'C____(^___)')#<BR>
</CFOUTPUT>
</CFLOOP>
```

## Formatting Currency Values

Numeric values can be automatically formatted as currency values with the help of three ColdFusion functions: `DollarFormat()`, `LSCurrencyFormat()`, and `LSEuroCurrencyFormat()`.

### Formatting dollars

The `DollarFormat()` function returns a number formatted as U.S. dollars. The returned number is formatted to two decimal places with a dollar sign and thousands separators. If the number is negative, it is returned in parentheses. The following example formats a variety of numbers using `DollarFormat()`:

```
<CFOUTPUT>
-1000: #DollarFormat(-1000)#<BR>
-100: #DollarFormat(-100)#<BR>
-10: #DollarFormat(-10)#<BR>
-1: #DollarFormat(-1)#<BR>
1:  #DollarFormat(1)#<BR>
10: #DollarFormat(10)#<BR>
100: #DollarFormat(100)#<BR>
1000: #DollarFormat(1000)#<BR>
10000: #DollarFormat(10000)#<BR>
100000: #DollarFormat(100000)#<BR>
1000000: #DollarFormat(1000000)#<BR>
</CFOUTPUT>
```

### Locale-specific currency formatting

In addition to U.S. dollar formatting using the `DollarFormat` function, ColdFusion provides another function for formatting currency values specific to a particular locale. The `LSCurrencyFormat()` function behaves the same as the `DollarFormat()` function, but it takes into account the currency conventions used by the default locale. The function takes two parameters, a numeric value and an optional locale-specific convention. Table 4-6 lists the valid values for the convention.

*Table 4-6. Locale-Specific Conventions for LSCurrencyFormat()*

| Value | Description |
|---|---|
| None | Returns the amount |
| Local | Returns the currency amount with locale-specific currency formatting; the default |
| International | Returns the currency value with its corresponding three-letter international currency prefix |

The following example loops through each locale supported by ColdFusion and applies each type of currency mask to a currency value for each locale:

```
<H3>Formatting Locale Specific Currency Values using LSCurrencyFormat</H3>

<!--- loop over each locale.  The list of locales is obtained from the server
      variable Server.ColdFusion.SupportedLocales --->
<CFLOOP INDEX="locale" LIST="#Server.Coldfusion.SupportedLocales#">
<!--- this causes the CF server to assume the locale specified by the current
      iteration of the loop --->
<CFSET temp = SetLocale(locale)>

<CFOUTPUT>
<P>
<B>#locale#</B><BR>
None: #LSCurrencyFormat(1000000.99, "None")#<BR>
Local: #LSCurrencyFormat(1000000.99, "Local")#<BR>
International: #LSCurrencyFormat(1000000.99, "International")#<BR>
</CFOUTPUT>
</CFLOOP>
```

### *Locale-specific currency formatting with the Euro*

The final currency formatting function, `LSEuroCurrencyFormat()`, is the same as the `LSCurrencyFormat()` function except it returns the formatted currency with the Euro symbol. The following example displays Euro currency formats for each locale:

```
<H3>Formatting Locale Specific Currency Values with the Euro using
   LSCurrencyFormat</H3>

<!--- loop over each locale.  The list of locales is obtained from the server
      variable Server.ColdFusion.SupportedLocales --->
<CFLOOP INDEX="locale" LIST="#Server.Coldfusion.SupportedLocales#">
<!--- this causes the CF server to assume the locale specified by the current
      iteration of the loop --->
<CFSET temp = SetLocale(locale)>

<CFOUTPUT>
<P>
<B>#locale#</B><BR>
None: #LSEuroCurrencyFormat(1000000.99, "None")#<BR>
Local: #LSEuroCurrencyFormat(1000000.99, "Local")#<BR>
International: #LSEuroCurrencyFormat(1000000.99, "International")#<BR>
</CFOUTPUT>
</CFLOOP>
```

## *Formatting Boolean Values*

ColdFusion uses the Boolean datatype to store the value generated by a logical operation. Boolean values are stored as either `TRUE` or `FALSE`. In numeric operations, Boolean values evaluate to `1` for `TRUE` and `0` for `FALSE`. When dealing with strings, Boolean values are set to `Yes` for `TRUE` and `No` for `FALSE`. Because most users are used to seeing the results of a Boolean operation as either `Yes` or `No`,

ColdFusion has a function called `YesNoFormat()` you can use to automatically convert any Boolean value to its equivalent `Yes/No` format (all non-zero values are returned as `Yes`, while a zero value is returned as `No`). The following example demonstrates this by applying the `YesNoFormat()` function to a variety of Boolean values:

```
<H3>Formatting Boolean Values using YesNoFormat</H3>

<CFOUTPUT>
-1: #YesNoFormat(-1)#<BR>
-1.123: #YesNoFormat(-1.123)#<BR>
-0.123: #YesNoFormat(-0.123)#<BR>
0: #YesNoFormat(0)#<BR>
0.123: #YesNoFormat(0.123)#<BR>
1: #YesNoFormat(1)#<BR>
1.123: #YesNoFormat(1.123)#
</CFOUTPUT>
```

Please note that Version 4.01 of ColdFusion contains a bug in the `YesNoFormat()` function that causes certain negative decimal values to evaluate incorrectly. This behavior was fixed in ColdFusion 4.5.

## Formatting Dates and Times

Depending on the database you use, date and time values returned as part of a query result set can come in a variety of formats. ColdFusion affords a lot of flexibility in formatting date and time values before you output them to the browser.

### General date formatting

General date formatting is handled by the `DateFormat()` function. `DateFormat()` allows you to format dates using a variety of masks.* The function accepts two parameters, the date you wish to format and a mask to specify the formatting in the format `DateFormat(`*`date`*`, "`*`mask`*`")`. If no mask is supplied, `DateFormat()` defaults to *dd-mmm-yy*. Valid entries for the date mask are shown in Table 4-7.

*Table 4-7. Mask Values for DateFormat()*

| Mask | Description |
|---|---|
| d | Day of the month as a number with no leading zero for single-digit days |
| dd | Day of the month as a number with a leading zero for single-digit days |

* If you are running ColdFusion on Unix and have Fast Date/Time Parsing enabled in the Server area of the ColdFusion Administrator, you must refer to date objects as month, day, year. When using the `DateFormat()` function, a date mask following the required format (month, day, year) must be used to parse the date object.

*Table 4-7. Mask Values for DateFormat() (continued)*

| Mask | Description |
|---|---|
| ddd | Three-letter abbreviation for day of the week |
| dddd | Full name of the day of the week |
| gg | Period/era; this mask is currently ignored |
| m | Month as a number with no leading zero for single-digit months |
| mm | Month as a number with a leading zero for single-digit months |
| mmm | Three-letter abbreviation for the month |
| mmmm | Full name of the month |
| y | Last two digits of year with no leading zero for years less than 10 |
| yy | Last two digits of year with a leading zero for years less than 10 |
| yyyy | Four-digit year |

You should note that `DateFormat()` supports U.S. date formats only. To use locale-specific date formats, see the `LSDateFormat()` function in the next section.

The following example demonstrates the `DateFormat()` function utilizing a variety of different date masks:

```
<!--- set TheDate to the current date --->
<CFSET TheDate = Now()>

<H3>Formatting US Date Values using DateFormat</H3>

<CFOUTPUT>
TheDate = #DateFormat(TheDate, "mm/dd/yyyy")#
<P>
DateFormat(TheDate, "m/d/yy"): #DateFormat(TheDate, "m/d/yy")#<BR>
DateFormat(TheDate, "mm/dd/yy"): #DateFormat(TheDate, "mm/dd/yy")#<BR>
DateFormat(TheDate, "mm/dd/yyyy"): #DateFormat(TheDate, "mm/dd/yyyy")#<BR>
DateFormat(TheDate, "dd/mm/yyyy"): #DateFormat(TheDate, "dd/mm/yyyy")#<BR>
DateFormat(TheDate, "dd mmm yy"): #DateFormat(TheDate, "dd mmm yy")#<BR>
DateFormat(TheDate, "dddd mmmm dd, yyyy"): #DateFormat(TheDate, "dddd mmmm dd
     Yyyy")#<BR>
</CFOUTPUT>
```

### *Locale-specific date formatting*

In addition to U.S. date formatting using the `DateFormat()` function, ColdFusion provides another function for formatting dates specific to a particular locale. The `LSDateFormat()` function behaves the same as the `DateFormat()` function, but it takes into account the formatting used by the default locale. If no formatting mask is supplied, `LSDateFormat()` uses the locale-specific default.

The following example loops through each locale supported by ColdFusion and applies a number of different date masks to the current date for each locale:

```
<H3>Formatting Locale Specific Date Values using LSDateFormat</H3>

<!--- loop over each locale.  The list of locales is obtained from the server
      variable Server.ColdFusion.SupportedLocales --->
<CFLOOP INDEX="locale" LIST="#Server.Coldfusion.SupportedLocales#">
<!--- this causes the CF server to assume the locale specified by the current
      iteration of the loop --->
<CFSET temp = SetLocale(locale)>

<!--- output formatted dates using a variety of masks --->
<CFOUTPUT>
<P>
<B>#locale#</B><BR>
#LSDateFormat(Now())#<BR>
#LSDateFormat(Now(), "d/m/yy")#<BR>
#LSDateFormat(Now(), "d-mmm-yyyy")#<BR>
#LSDateFormat(Now(), "dd mmm yy")#<BR>
#LSDateFormat(Now(), "dddd, mmmm dd, yyyy")#<BR>
#LSDateFormat(Now(), "mm/dd/yyyy")#<BR>
#LSDateFormat(Now(), "mmmm d, yyyy")#<BR>
#LSDateFormat(Now(), "mmm-dd-yyyy")#<BR>
</CFOUTPUT>
</CFLOOP>
```

### *Time formatting*

You can format times in ColdFusion using the `TimeFormat()` function. `TimeFormat()` is similar to the `DateFormat()` function in that it allows you to use a mask to control the formatting. The function accepts two parameters, the time you wish to format and a mask to specify the formatting in the format `TimeFormat(time, "mask")`. If no mask is specified, the default `hh:mm tt` is used. Valid mask values are shown in Table 4-8.

*Table 4-8. Mask Values for TimeFormat()*

| Mask | Description |
|---|---|
| h | Hours based on a 12-hour clock with no leading zeros for single-digit hours |
| hh | Hours based on a 12-hour clock with leading zeros for single-digit hours |
| H | Hours based on a 24-hour clock with no leading zeros for single-digit hours |
| HH | Hours based on a 24-hour clock with leading zeros for single-digit hours |
| m | Minutes with no leading zero for single-digit minutes |
| mm | Minutes with a leading zero for single-digit minutes |
| s | Seconds with no leading zero for single-digit seconds |
| ss | Seconds with a leading zero for single-digit seconds |

*Table 4-8. Mask Values for TimeFormat() (continued)*

| Mask | Description |
|---|---|
| t | Single character meridian, either A or P |
| tt | Multicharacter meridian, either AM or PM |

The following example demonstrates the **TimeFormat()** function using a number of time masks:

```
<!--- set a variable containing the current time using the Now function --->
<CFSET TheTime = Now()>

<H3>Formatting Time Values using TimeFormat</H3>

<CFOUTPUT>
TheTime = #TimeFormat(TheTime,"hh:mm:ss tt")#
<P>
TimeFormat(TheTime, "h:m:s"): #TimeFormat(TheTime, "h:m:s")#<BR>
TimeFormat(TheTime, "h:m:s t"): #TimeFormat(TheTime, "h:m:s t")#<BR>
TimeFormat(TheTime, "hh:mm:ss"): #TimeFormat(TheTime, "hh:mm:ss")#<BR>
TimeFormat(TheTime, "hh:mm:ss tt"): #TimeFormat(TheTime, "hh:mm:ss tt")#<BR>
TimeFormat(TheTime, "H:M:ss"): #TimeFormat(TheTime, "H:M:s")#<BR>
TimeFormat(TheTime, "HH:MM:ss"): #TimeFormat(TheTime, "HH:MM:ss")#<BR>
</CFOUTPUT>
```

# 5

*In this chapter:*
- *Inserting Records*
- *Updating Existing Records*
- *Deleting Records*

# *Maintaining Database Records*

Now that we've covered the basics of retrieving records from a database, let's focus our attention on techniques you can use to add new records, update existing records, and delete unwanted records from a database. These techniques come into play when your web application needs to go beyond simply displaying information from a database. For example, with our employee directory application, we can add the ability to insert new employees into the directory, update employee information, and delete employee records.

## *Inserting Records*

Inserting a new record into a database table is a two-step process. The first step involves creating a template with an input form that collects the information you want to insert. The second step in the process takes the form-field data and inserts it into the database table. The code for this process is generally broken up into two templates, but it is possible to use a single template (with conditional code, as described in Chapter 3) that posts to itself if you desire.

### *Inputting Data via Forms*

The most popular method for collecting data to insert into a database is via an HTML form. When creating your input form, you should name your form fields the same as their equivalent database fields. This avoids any confusion when writing SQL statements or code that manipulates data.

Example 5-1 shows the *InsertForm.cfm* template, which creates an HTML form for inputting a new employee record in the `EmployeeDirectory` table of the `ProgrammingCF` database.

*Example 5-1. HTML Input Form for Inserting a Record into a Database*

```
<HTML>
<HEAD>
    <TITLE>Data Input Form</TITLE>
</HEAD>

<BODY>

<H2>Add a New User</H2>
<FORM ACTION="Insert.cfm" METHOD="post">
<!--- data validation --->
<INPUT TYPE="hidden" NAME="Name_Required" VALUE="Name is a required field">
<INPUT TYPE="hidden" NAME="Title_Required"
       VALUE="Title is a required field">
<INPUT TYPE="hidden" NAME="Department_Required"
       VALUE="Department is a required field">
<INPUT TYPE="hidden" NAME="Email_Required"
       VALUE="E-mail is a required field">
<INPUT TYPE="hidden" NAME="PhoneExt_Required"
       VALUE="Phone Ext. is a required field">
<INPUT TYPE="hidden" NAME="Salary_Required"
       VALUE="Salary is a required field">
<INPUT TYPE="hidden" NAME="PhoneExt_Integer"
       VALUE="Phone Ext. is a numeric field">
<INPUT TYPE="hidden" NAME="Salary_Float" VALUE="Salary is a numeric field">

<TABLE>
<TR>
  <TD>Name:</TD>
  <TD><INPUT TYPE="text" NAME="Name" SIZE="20" MAXLENGTH="80"></TD>
</TR>
<TR>
  <TD>Title:</TD>
  <TD><INPUT TYPE="text" NAME="Title" SIZE="20" MAXLENGTH="80"></TD>
</TR>
<TR>
  <TD>Department:</TD>
  <TD><INPUT TYPE="text" NAME="Department" SIZE="20" MAXLENGTH="80"></TD>
</TR>
<TR>
  <TD>E-mail:</TD>
  <TD><INPUT TYPE="text" NAME="Email" SIZE="20" MAXLENGTH="80"></TD>
</TR>
<TR>
  <TD>Phone Ext::</TD>
  <TD><INPUT TYPE="text" NAME="PhoneExt" SIZE="5" MAXLENGTH="4"></TD>
</TR>
<TR>
  <TD>Salary:</TD>
  <TD><INPUT TYPE="text" NAME="Salary" SIZE="20" MAXLENGTH="12"></TD>
</TR>

</TABLE>
```

*Example 5-1. HTML Input Form for Inserting a Record into a Database (continued)*

```
<INPUT TYPE="submit" VALUE="Submit">
</FORM>
</FORM>

</BODY>
</HTML>
```

The input form uses the HTTP POST method to post the form-field data to a template called *Insert.cfm*. We're going to look at three different implementations of this template, in Example 5-2 to Example 5-4. The input form also uses several hidden fields to set up server-side validation rules for the form fields. The form itself is shown in Figure 5-1.

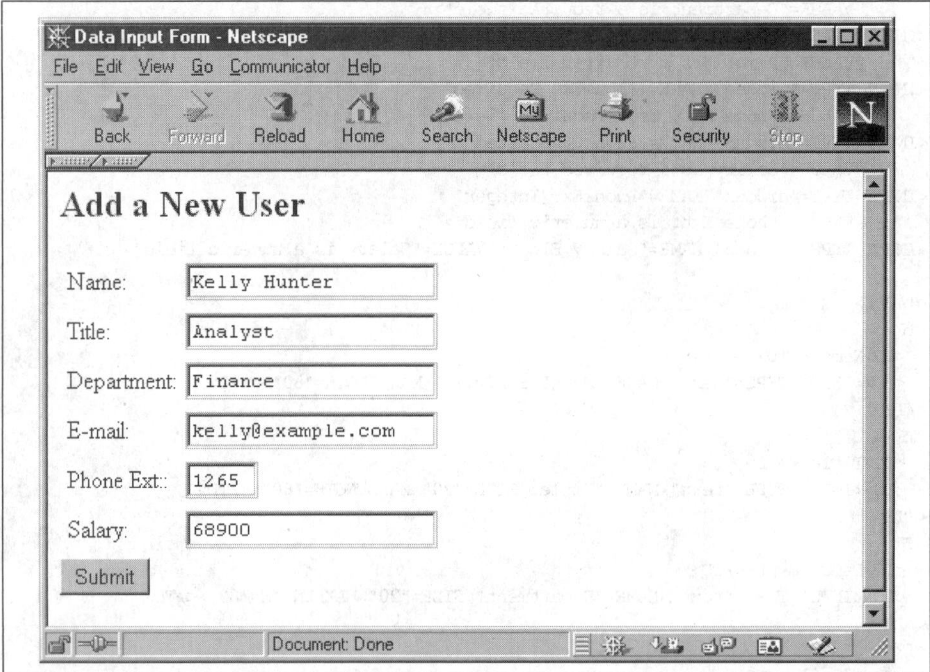


*Figure 5-1. HTML form for inserting a new employee record*

## *Inserting Form-Field Data*

When you have form-field data to be inserted into a database, you have two options for how to do the actual insert. You can use the `CFQUERY` tag and write your own SQL `INSERT` statement, or you can use the `CFINSERT` tag to handle the insert without writing a single line of SQL.

### *Inserting a record using CFQUERY*

The **CFQUERY** tag lets you insert a record into a table using an SQL **INSERT** statement. This method gives you the most flexibility and power in inserting records. Example 5-2 demonstrates using the **CFQUERY** tag to insert a new record into the database. The template receives its input from the form shown in Example 5-1. In order for the example to work, the template in Example 5-2 must be saved as *Insert.cfm* in the same directory as the template in Example 5-1.

*Example 5-2. Using CFQUERY to Insert Data into a Data Source*

```
<!--- Insert the record into the EmployeeDirectory table. --->

<CFLOCK NAME="InsertNewRecord" TYPE="EXCLUSIVE" TIMEOUT="30">
<CFTRANSACTION>
<CFQUERY NAME="AddRecord" DATASOURCE="ProgrammingCF">
         INSERT INTO EmployeeDirectory(Name, Title, Department, Email,
                     PhoneExt, Salary)
         VALUES('#Form.Name#', '#Form.Title#', '#Form.Department#',
                '#Form.Email#', #Form.PhoneExt#, #Form.Salary#)
</CFQUERY>

<!--- This query retrieves the primary key value of the record we
      just inserted. --->
<CFQUERY NAME="GetPK" DATASOURCE="ProgrammingCF">
         SELECT Max(ID) AS MaxID
         FROM EmployeeDirectory
</CFQUERY>
</CFTRANSACTION>
</CFLOCK>

<!--- This query uses the value returned by the GetPK query to lookup
      the full record we inserted. --->
<CFQUERY NAME="GetRecord" DATASOURCE="ProgrammingCF">
         SELECT ID, Name, Title, Department, Email, PhoneExt, Salary
         FROM EmployeeDirectory
         WHERE ID = #GetPK.MaxID#
</CFQUERY>

<HTML>
<HEAD>
    <TITLE>CFQUERY Insert</TITLE>
</HEAD>

<BODY>

<H2>Record Inserted!</H2>

<H3>Here are the record details...</H3>

<TABLE CELLPADDING="3" CELLSPACING="0">
<TR BGCOLOR="#888888">
    <TH>ID</TH>
```

*Example 5-2. Using CFQUERY to Insert Data into a Data Source (continued)*

```
    <TH>Name</TH>
    <TH>Title</TH>
    <TH>Department</TH>
    <TH>E-mail</TH>
    <TH>Phone Extension</TH>
    <TH>Salary</TH>
</TR>

<!--- output the record --->
<CFOUTPUT QUERY="GetRecord">
<TR BGCOLOR="##C0C0C0">
    <TD>#ID#</TD>
    <TD>#Name#</TD>
    <TD>#Title#</TD>
    <TD>#Department#</TD>
    <TD><A HREF="Mailto:#Email#">#Email#</A></TD>
    <TD>#PhoneExt#</TD>
    <TD>#DollarFormat(Salary)#</TD>
</TR>
</CFOUTPUT>
</TABLE>

</BODY>
</HTML>
```

If you fill out the form in Example 5-1 and submit it to this template, a new record containing all the information from the form is inserted into the `EmployeeDirectory` table. The `INSERT` statement is used within the `CFQUERY` tag to insert a record into the database. The `INTO` clause controls what fields to insert data into by specifying them as a comma-delimited list. `VALUES` specifies the data to insert into each field specified by the `INTO` clause. Note that numeric values aren't enclosed in single quotes in the `VALUES` clause.

Notice that we are inserting the employee name, title, etc., but not the ID. That's because the ID is specified as an AutoNumber field in our Access database. If you are using a database that doesn't support AutoNumber fields, you can use the `CreateUUID()` function here to generate a unique value on the fly. If you do this, be sure to include the ID field in the `INSERT INTO` clause and the UUID value in the `VALUES` clause.

After the record is inserted, another `CFQUERY` is run to extract the primary key value for the record we just inserted, so that we can look up the record we just inserted. This query uses a `SELECT` statement containing a special clause, known as an aggregate function, to obtain the maximum value in the `ID` column. (Aggregate functions are discussed in Chapter 11.) Because we use an AutoNumber field that automatically increments by one each time a new record is inserted into the database, the value returned by our query is the primary key value for the record we just inserted.

The `CFLOCK` tag ensures that the code it wraps is accessible by only one request at a time. The `CFTRANSACTION` tag groups the queries into a single transaction. The combination of these two techniques prevents you from retrieving the primary key value of another user's record in the event they insert a new record right after you do and before you retrieve the `MAX ID` value. The `CFLOCK` tag is covered in Chapter 7, while the `CFTRANSACTION` tag is covered in Chapter 11.

Once we know the primary key value for the record we inserted, we execute yet another `CFQUERY` tag to `SELECT` the record from the `EmployeeDirectory` table whose `ID` field contains the primary key value returned by our second query. The template finishes by outputting all the values stored in the record we just inserted in a neatly formatted HTML table. The results are can be seen in Figure 5-2.

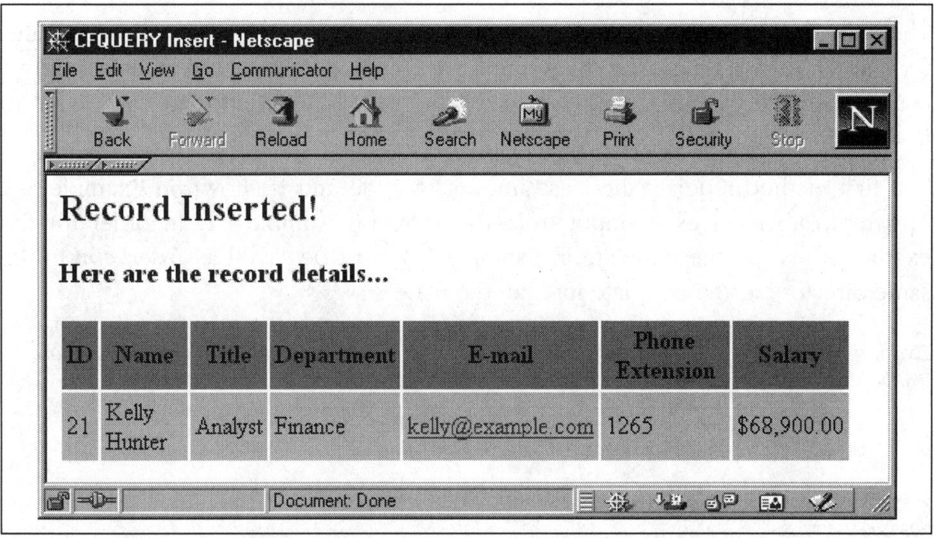


*Figure 5-2. Inserting a record into a table using CFQUERY*

### *Inserting a record using CFINSERT*

If you don't want to concern yourself with the SQL necessary to insert a record into a database, ColdFusion provides a tag called `CFINSERT` that does most of the work for you. The tag takes most of the parameters the `CFQUERY` tag takes, but doesn't require you to include any SQL inside the tag. The basic syntax for using the `CFINSERT` tag is as follows:

```
<CFINSERT DATASOURCE="datasource_name"
          TABLENAME="table_name"
          FORMFIELDS="formfield1, formfield2, ...">
```

The three attributes for the CFINSERT tag are:

DATASOURCE
: The name of the data source to connect to when performing the insert. Required.

TABLENAME
: The name of the table to insert the data into. Required. It should be noted that Oracle database drivers require the table name to be in all upper case. In addition, Sybase database drivers use a case-sensitive table name.

FORMFIELDS
: A comma-delimited list of form fields to insert. Optional. If no form fields are supplied, ColdFusion uses all the form fields passed from the form.

Several additional attributes are available for use with the **CFINSERT** tag. For a complete list, see Appendix A.

There are two ways to use the **CFINSERT** tag. You can use the tag to insert values for every form field passed to the template containing the tag, or you can supply a comma-delimited list of form fields (using the **FORMFIELDS** attribute) you want to insert.

The first method requires the least amount of code and is shown in Example 5-3. This template receives its input from the form in Example 5-1. In order for the example to work, the template in Example 5-3 must be saved as *Insert.cfm* in the same directory as the template in Example 5-1.

*Example 5-3. Using CFINSERT Without a List of Form Fields to Insert Data into a Database Table*

```
<!--- insert all of the form field data into the EmployeeDirectory
      table of the ProgrammingCF data source. --->

<CFLOCK NAME="InsertNewRecord" TYPE="EXCLUSIVE" TIMEOUT="30">
<CFTRANSACTION>
<CFINSERT DATASOURCE="ProgrammingCF"
          TABLENAME="EmployeeDirectory">

<!--- This query retrieves the primary key value of the record we
      just inserted. --->
<CFQUERY NAME="GetPK" DATASOURCE="ProgrammingCF">
        SELECT Max(ID) AS MaxID
        FROM EmployeeDirectory
</CFQUERY>
</CFTRANSACTION>
</CFLOCK>

<!--- This query uses the value returned by the GetPK query to lookup
      the full record we inserted. --->
<CFQUERY NAME="GetRecord" DATASOURCE="ProgrammingCF">
```

*Example 5-3. Using CFINSERT Without a List of Form Fields to Insert Data into a Database Table (continued)*

```
        SELECT ID, Name, Title, Department, Email, PhoneExt, Salary
        FROM EmployeeDirectory
        WHERE ID = #GetPK.MaxID#
</CFQUERY>

<HTML>
<HEAD>
    <TITLE>CFINSERT Insert</TITLE>
</HEAD>

<BODY>

<H2>Record Inserted using CFINSERT without Field Names!</H2>

<H3>Here are the record details...</H3>

<TABLE CELLPADDING="3" CELLSPACING="0">
<TR BGCOLOR="#888888">
    <TH>ID</TH>
    <TH>Name</TH>
    <TH>Title</TH>
    <TH>Department</TH>
    <TH>E-mail</TH>
    <TH>Phone Extension</TH>
    <TH>Salary</TH>
</TR>

<!--- output the record --->
<CFOUTPUT QUERY="GetRecord">
<TR BGCOLOR="##C0C0C0">
    <TD>#ID#</TD>
    <TD>#Name#</TD>
    <TD>#Title#</TD>
    <TD>#Department#</TD>
    <TD><A HREF="Mailto:#Email#">#Email#</A></TD>
    <TD>#PhoneExt#</TD>
    <TD>#DollarFormat(Salary)#</TD>
</TR>
</CFOUTPUT>
</TABLE>

</BODY>
</HTML>
```

When the form in Example 5-1 posts to this template, the `CFINSERT` tag attempts to take every form field passed in and inserts it into the `EmployeeDirectory` table. This method works well when you have a corresponding database field for each form field. If, however, there are form fields that don't have corresponding database fields, ColdFusion throws an error. Once the record has been inserted, the template uses the same code from Example 5-3 to retrieve the record we just inserted and display it in the browser. As with our first implementation of *Insert.cfm*, the value for the employee ID is inserted automatically by Access. This version also uses CFLOCK and CFTRANSACTION to protect against collisions between multiple requests. If you look at the output from this template, you should notice that it looks identical to that shown in Example 5-2 (minus the title, of course).

The second method for inserting a new record using the CFINSERT tag requires one more line of code but allows you to specify which form fields should be inserted into the database. This lets you make sure that only the form fields you want inserted into the table are inserted. The code for this template is shown in Example 5-4. As in the previous examples, this template receives its input from the form in Example 5-1. In order for the example to work, the template in Example 5-4 must be saved as *Insert.cfm* in the same directory as the template in Example 5-1.

*Example 5-4. Inserting a Record Using the CFINSERT Tag with Field Names Specified*

```
<!--- insert the data from the specified form fields into the
      EmployeeDirectory table of the ProgrammingCF data source. --->

<CFLOCK NAME="InsertNewRecord" TYPE="EXCLUSIVE" TIMEOUT="30">
<CFTRANSACTION>
<CFINSERT DATASOURCE="ProgrammingCF"
          TABLENAME="EmployeeDirectory"
          FORMFIELDS="Name,Title,Email">

<!--- This query retrieves the primary key value of the record we
      just inserted. --->
<CFQUERY NAME="GetPK" DATASOURCE="ProgrammingCF">
         SELECT Max(ID) AS MaxID
         FROM EmployeeDirectory
</CFQUERY>
</CFTRANSACTION>
</CFLOCK>

<!--- This query uses the value returned by the GetPK query to lookup
      the full record we inserted. --->
<CFQUERY NAME="GetRecord" DATASOURCE="ProgrammingCF">
         SELECT ID, Name, Title, Department, Email, PhoneExt, Salary
         FROM EmployeeDirectory
         WHERE ID = #GetPK.MaxID#
</CFQUERY>

<HTML>
<HEAD>
    <TITLE>CFINSERT Insert</TITLE>
</HEAD>

<BODY>
```

*Example 5-4. Inserting a Record Using the CFINSERT Tag with Field Names Specified (continued)*

```
<H2>Record Inserted using CFINSERT with Specific Field Names!</H2>

<H3>Here are the record details...</H3>

<TABLE CELLPADDING="3" CELLSPACING="0">
<TR BGCOLOR="#888888">
    <TH>ID</TH>
    <TH>Name</TH>
    <TH>Title</TH>
    <TH>Department</TH>
    <TH>E-mail</TH>
    <TH>Phone Extension</TH>
    <TH>Salary</TH>
</TR>

<!--- output the record --->
<CFOUTPUT QUERY="GetRecord">
<TR BGCOLOR="##C0C0C0">
    <TD>#ID#</TD>
    <TD>#Name#</TD>
    <TD>#Title#</TD>
    <TD>#Department#</TD>
    <TD><A HREF="Mailto:#Email#">#Email#</A></TD>
    <TD>#PhoneExt#</TD>
    <TD>#DollarFormat(Salary)#</TD>
</TR>
</CFOUTPUT>
</TABLE>

</BODY>
</HTML>
```

Using the form in Example 5-1 to post to this template, the `CFINSERT` tag inserts only the `Name`, `Title`, and `Email` form fields into the `EmployeeDirectory` table. Once the record has been inserted, the template uses the same code from Example 5-3 to retrieve the record we just inserted and display it in the browser. The results are shown in Figure 5-3. Notice that the `Department` and `PhoneExt` fields contain no values, and the `Salary` field contains a zero.

## Updating Existing Records

Updating a database record is a three-step process that involves a bit more work that just inserting a new record. The first step in the process is to identify the record to be updated; there are two ways to handle this task. Next, an HTML form containing the editable fields needs to be created. This form must be prepopulated with the data from the record to be edited. Finally, you need another

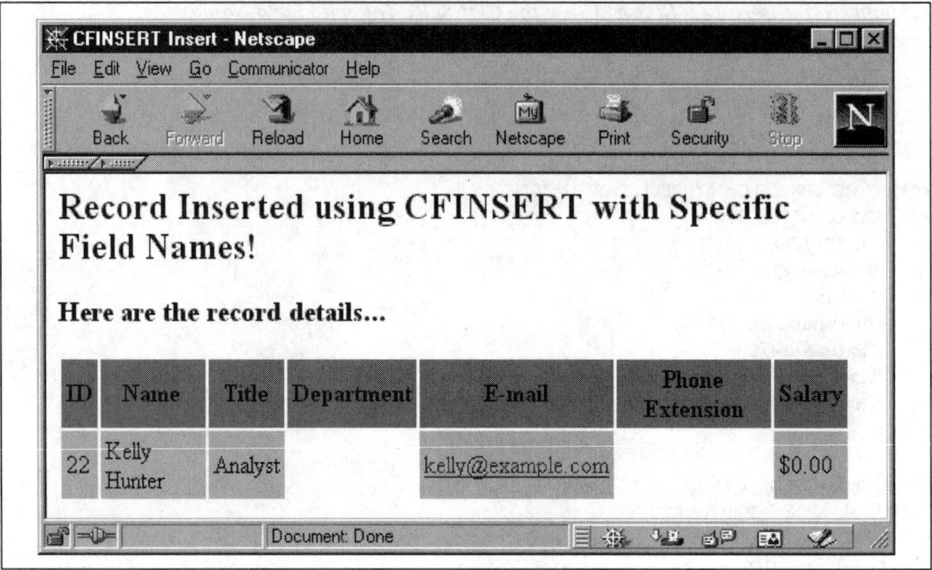


Figure 5-3. Inserting specific fields using CFINSERT

template to take the updated form-field data and update the appropriate record in the database.

## Choosing a Record to Update

Before you can make an update to a record, you need some sort of interface that allows you to choose the record you wish to modify. There are two general approaches to this interface. The first approach involves a URL-based technique for selecting the record to modify. The second approach utilizes a forms-based technique to achieve the same goal. Both approaches begin by querying a data source (in our case, the `EmployeeDirectory` table of the `ProgrammingCF` data source) to retrieve a list of all the records from the database. Usually, you need to retrieve only the primary key value and a distinguishing field or two. In our example, we retrieve the `ID` field (primary key) and the `Name` field from the `EmployeeDirectory` table. It is from this point forward that the two approaches differ.

The first approach uses the information returned by the query to generate an HTML table listing each employee from the database. The code for this template, *UpdateMenu_Hyperlink.cfm*, is shown in Example 5-5.

*Example 5-5. URL-Based Menu for Selecting a Record to Update*

```
<!--- query the database for all employee names and their associated
      IDs (the primary key value) --->
<CFQUERY NAME="GetEmployees" DATASOURCE="ProgrammingCF">
```

*Example 5-5. URL-Based Menu for Selecting a Record to Update (continued)*

```
        SELECT ID, Name
        FROM EmployeeDirectory
        ORDER BY Name
</CFQUERY>

<HTML>
<HEAD>
    <TITLE>Employee Update Menu</TITLE>
</HEAD>
<BODY>
<CENTER>
<H3>Employee Profiles</H3>
<TABLE BORDER="1">
<TR BGCOLOR="#C0C0C0">
    <TH>Employee</TH>
    <TH>Action</TH>
</TR>
<!--- output a table containing each employee's name.  Create dynamic
      links to edit and delete templates.  Pass the ID
      associated with each record in the URL of the link --->
<CFOUTPUT QUERY="GetEmployees">
  <TR BGCOLOR="##E7E7E7">
    <TD>#Name#</TD>
    <TD><A HREF="UpdateForm.cfm?ID=#ID#">Update</A> |
        <A HREF="UpdateForm.cfm?ID=#ID#&Action=Delete">Delete</A></TD>
  </TR>
</CFOUTPUT>
<TR BGCOLOR="#E7E7E7">
    <TD COLSPAN="2" ALIGN="center"><A HREF="InsertForm.cfm">Add</A> a
        new record</TD>
</TR>
</TABLE>
</CENTER>
</BODY>
</HTML>
```

Executing this template generates an HTML table that contains each employee's name in the left column, as shown in Figure 5-4. The right column contains two hyperlinks, one labeled Update and the other labeled Delete. Each of the Update hyperlinks contains a link to a template called *UpdateForm.cfm*. Appended to each URL is a URL parameter called `ID` that contains the `ID` associated with the employee as returned by the **`GetEmployees`** query. Clicking on any of the "Update" links calls the *UpdateForm.cfm* template, shown later in Example 5-7, and passes the `ID` associated with the employee so that the record can be retrieved for editing. If a "Delete" link is clicked on, the same *UpdateForm.cfm* template is called, but this time, a URL parameter called `Action` with a value of `Delete` is passed so that the *UpdateForm.cfm* template knows that the user want to delete a record and what record to delete. At the bottom of the template is a hyperlink that points to the *InsertForm.cfm* template from Example 5-1. Clicking on this link takes the user to the template for inserting a new record into the database.

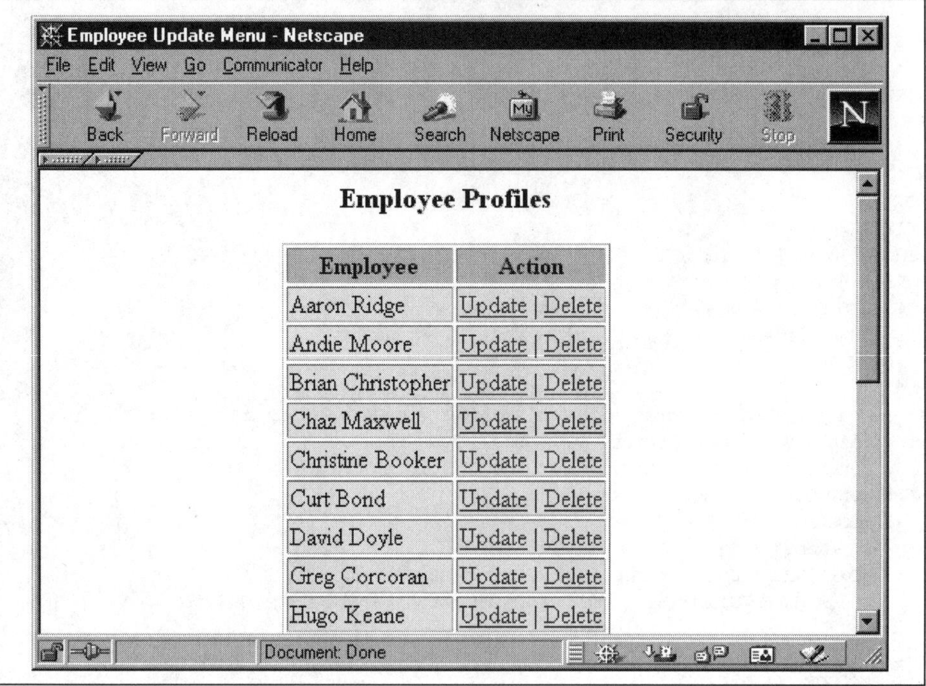


*Figure 5-4. Hyperlink-based menu for selecting a record to update/delete*

One drawback to the URL method becomes evident when the user needs to make a selection from a large number of records. It becomes highly inefficient to display hundreds or thousands of employees in an HTML table and realistically expect the user to scroll through all of them.

In this scenario, it is more efficient to use the second approach, which involves building a select list to display the names of all the employees. While the user still has to scroll through the list of names, the scrolling is confined to the select list, keeping the main body of the page in view at all times. Building the select list as opposed to an entire HTML table is also a lot easier on the client's machine, as it takes far less code and thus less system memory. Using a select list also changes the way the `ID` field associated with the user's record is passed to the next template. Instead of passing the `ID` value in a URL, the value is submitted as a form-field value. The code for the select box method, *UpdateMenu_Form.cfm*, is shown in Example 5-6.

*Example 5-6. Form-Based Menu for Selecting a Record to Update/Delete*

```
<!--- query the database for all employee names and their associated Ids
      (the primary key value --->
<CFQUERY NAME="GetEmployees" DATASOURCE="ProgrammingCF">
         SELECT ID, Name
         FROM EmployeeDirectory
         ORDER BY Name
</CFQUERY>

<HTML>
<HEAD>
  <TITLE>Employee Update Menu</TITLE>
</HEAD>

<BODY>

<CENTER>
<H3>Employee Profiles</H3>

<TABLE BORDER="3" CELLPADDING="5" CELLSPACING="0" BGCOLOR="#c0c0c0">
<FORM ACTION="UpdateForm.cfm" METHOD="post">
<TR>
  <TD ROWSPAN="3">
   <!--- generate a dynamic select list based on the GetEmployees
         query --->
   <SELECT NAME="ID" SIZE="5">
    <CFOUTPUT QUERY="GetEmployees">
      <OPTION VALUE="#ID#" <CFIF GetEmployees.CurrentRow EQ 1>SELECTED
      </CFIF>>#Name#</OPTION>
    </CFOUTPUT>
  </SELECT>
  </TD>
  <TD><INPUT TYPE="submit" NAME="Update" VALUE="Update Record"></TD>
</TR>
<TR>
  <TD><INPUT TYPE="submit" NAME="Delete" VALUE="Delete Record "></TD>
</TR>
</FORM>
<TR>
<FORM ACTION="InsertForm.cfm" METHOD="post">
  <TD><INPUT TYPE="Submit" Name="Insert" VALUE="  Add Record  "></TD>
</FORM>
</TR>
</TABLE>
</CENTER>

</BODY>
</HTML>
```

This template illustrates a new technique we haven't covered yet: how to generate a select box containing data pulled from a query. The technique works by querying a data source and retrieving a record set. In this case, we queried the

EmployeeDirectory table of the ProgrammingCF data source and returned a record set containing employee names (NAME) and their associated employee IDs (ID). The dynamic select box is generated within the form by using a CFOUTPUT statement to loop over the contents of the GetEmployees query, building the OPTION list for the SELECT statement from the record set. Each OPTION VALUE is populated with the value of an ID from the record set while the actual value displayed in the select box is derived from the corresponding NAME. The result is a menu of employee names the user can use to select an employee record to update, as shown in Figure 5-5.

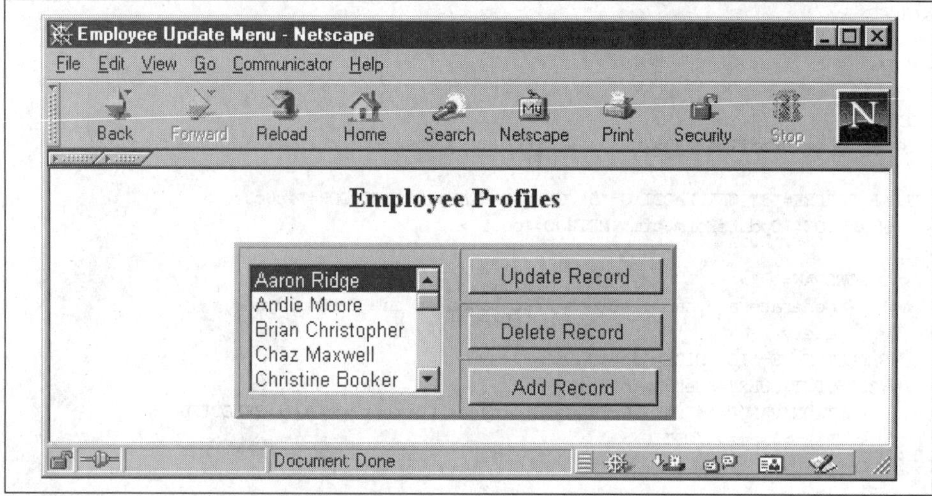


*Figure 5-5. Dynamically generated select box for choosing an employee record to update*

Note the CFIF statement that builds the OPTION tags for the SELECT statement. It makes sure the first option is always selected. This prevents a user from clicking the Update Record or Delete Record buttons without first choosing a record to update or delete. This piece of code eliminates the need for a hidden form field to make a selection from the menu required.

Highlighting an employee name and clicking on the Update Record or Delete Record button posts the ID value to a template called *UpdateForm.cfm* (Example 5-7). Clicking on the Add Record button calls the *InsertForm.cfm* template from Example 5-1.

## Dynamically Populating Update Forms

Once the user has selected a record to update, the next step for our application is to query the database and retrieve all the fields associated with the chosen record. This data is then used to populate the appropriate fields in an HTML form. As is often the case, our update form is identical to the form that inserts a new record. Our update template can also delete a record if the appropriate parameters are passed to the template by the record selection menu. Example 5-7 shows the *UpdateForm.cfm* template for populating the update form with the record information retrieved from the database.

*Example 5-7. Dynamically Populating the Update Form*

```
<!--- check to see if we're dealing with a delete operation --->
<CFIF (IsDefined('Form.Delete') AND Trim(Form.Delete) EQ "Delete Record")
   OR (IsDefined('URL.Action') AND URL.Action EQ "Delete")>
  <CFQUERY NAME="DeleteRecord" DATASOURCE="ProgrammingCF">
           DELETE FROM EmployeeDirectory
           WHERE ID = #ID#
  </CFQUERY>
  <H2>Record Deleted Successfully</H2>
  <!--- abort processing so that the template does not show the update
        form --->
  <CFABORT>
</CFIF>

<!--- retrieve the record specified by the ID value passed into the
      template by form or url variable --->
<CFQUERY NAME="GetRecord" DATASOURCE="ProgrammingCF">
         SELECT ID, Name, Title, Department, Email, PhoneExt, Salary
         FROM EmployeeDirectory
         WHERE ID = #ID#
</CFQUERY>

<HTML>
<HEAD>
    <TITLE>Record Update Form</TITLE>
</HEAD>

<BODY>

<H2>Edit an Existing User</H2>
<FORM ACTION="Update.cfm" METHOD="post">
<!--- include the primary key value for this record so we know which
      record to update without SQL UPDATE (or CFUPDATE) statement in
      the next template --->
<CFOUTPUT>
<INPUT TYPE="hidden" NAME="ID" VALUE="#GetRecord.ID#">
</CFOUTPUT>

<!--- data validation --->
<INPUT TYPE="hidden" NAME="Name_Required"
       VALUE="Name is a required field">
<INPUT TYPE="hidden" NAME="Title_Required"
       VALUE="Title is a required field">
<INPUT TYPE="hidden" NAME="Department_Required"
       VALUE="Department is a required field">
<INPUT TYPE="hidden" NAME="Email_Required"
```

*Example 5-7. Dynamically Populating the Update Form (continued)*

```
       VALUE="E-mail is a required field">
<INPUT TYPE="hidden" NAME="PhoneExt_Required"
       VALUE="Phone Ext. is a required field">
<INPUT TYPE="hidden" NAME="Salary_Required"
       VALUE="Salary is a required field">
<INPUT TYPE="hidden" NAME="PhoneExt_Integer"
       VALUE="Phone Ext. is a numeric field">
<INPUT TYPE="hidden" NAME="Salary_Float"
       VALUE="Salary is a numeric field">

<!--- populate the form with the user's record --->
<CFOUTPUT>
<TABLE>
<TR>
  <TD>Name:</TD>
  <TD><INPUT TYPE="text" NAME="Name" VALUE="#GetRecord.Name#"
           SIZE="20" MAXLENGTH="80"></TD>
</TR>
<TR>
  <TD>Title:</TD>
  <TD><INPUT TYPE="text" NAME="Title" VALUE="#GetRecord.Title#"
           SIZE="20" MAXLENGTH="80"></TD>
</TR>
<TR>
  <TD>Department:</TD>
  <TD><INPUT TYPE="text" NAME="Department" VALUE="#GetRecord.Department#"
           SIZE="20" MAXLENGTH="80"></TD>
</TR>
<TR>
  <TD>E-mail:</TD>
  <TD><INPUT TYPE="text" NAME="Email"
           VALUE="#GetRecord.Email#" SIZE="20" MAXLENGTH="80"></TD>
</TR>
<TR>
  <TD>Phone Ext::</TD>
  <TD><INPUT TYPE="text" NAME="PhoneExt" VALUE="#GetRecord.PhoneExt#"
           SIZE="5" MAXLENGTH="4"></TD>
</TR>
<TR>
  <TD>Salary:</TD>
  <TD><INPUT TYPE="text" NAME="Salary" VALUE="#GetRecord.Salary#"
           SIZE="20" MAXLENGTH="12"></TD>
</TR>
</TABLE>
</CFOUTPUT>

<INPUT TYPE="submit" VALUE="Submit">
</FORM>

</BODY>
</HTML>
```

As you can see, this template isn't all that different from the template we used to insert new employee profiles into our database. There are, however, a few important distinctions.

First, the template checks to see if a URL or form variable was passed to the template indicating a record should be deleted. If so, the appropriate record is deleted using an SQL DELETE statement. This code is included to show you how to create a template for adding, updating, and deleting records from a single administrative interface. We'll cover deleting records later in this chapter. For now, let's concentrate on updating an existing record.

Once we determine that we aren't dealing with a delete operation, we can proceed with the update operation. Because we are going to update a specific record, we need a way to tell ColdFusion exactly what record to update. This is done by specifying the primary key value for the record in a hidden form field. The hidden form field that passes the value must have the same name as the primary key field in the database. If the primary key field isn't specified, ColdFusion throws an error. In this case, we specify the value using the `ID` form field. Another difference is that in the case of our update form, we populate each HTML form field with data from the employee's record so that it can be modified. In this example, all the fields in our form are text boxes. All you need to do to populate a text box with a value from a query is include a `VALUE` attribute containing the variable name from the query in the `INPUT` tag:

```
<INPUT TYPE="text" NAME="Name" VALUE="#GetRecord.Name#>
```

It is important to note a couple of things here. First, populating form fields requires they be enclosed in a `CFOUTPUT` block. Second, because you aren't using the `QUERY` attribute of the `CFOUTPUT` tag, you must scope your variables with the name of the query that retrieves the record. In this example, all query variables are scoped with `GetRecord`:

```
<CFOUTPUT>
#GetRecord.Name#
</CFOUTPUT>
```

Figure 5-6 shows the form populated with an employee record from the database.

## *Performing the Database Update*

When the user submits the form for the record that is being updated in the database, you have two options for doing the actual update. You can use the `CFQUERY` tag and write your own SQL `UPDATE` statement, or you can use the `CFUPDATE` tag to handle the update without writing a single line of SQL. We'll use our update template (Example 5-7) to post the employee record to a template called *Update.*

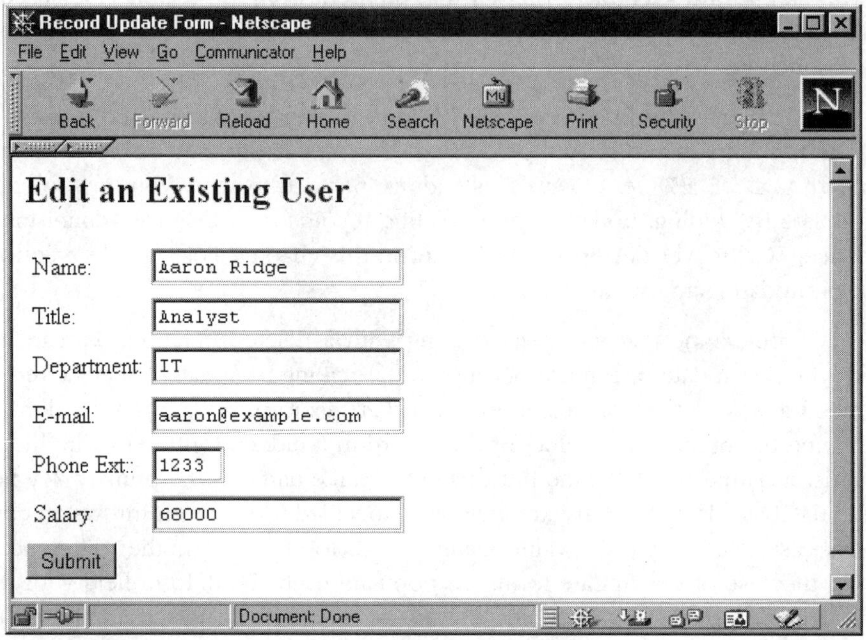

*Figure 5-6. The populated employee update form*

*cfm*. We're going to look at three different implementations of this template, in Examples 5-8 to 5-10.

### *Updating a record using CFQUERY*

The `CFQUERY` tag offers the most power and flexibility when it comes to updating a database record. The `CFQUERY` tag allows you to write your own SQL `UPDATE` statement, giving you full control over how the update takes place. Example 5-8 demonstrates using the `CFQUERY` tag to update an existing record with form-field data passed in by the template in Example 5-7. In order for the example to work, the template in Example 5-8 must be saved as *Update.cfm* in the same directory as the template in Example 5-7.

*Example 5-8. Using CFQUERY to Update a Database Record*

```
<!--- Update the record specified by the ID field.  Note that numeric
      values are not enclosed in single quotes in the SET clause. --->
<CFQUERY NAME="UpdateRecord" DATASOURCE="ProgrammingCF">
UPDATE EmployeeDirectory
SET Name = '#Form.Name#',
    Title = '#Form.Title#',
    Department = '#Form.Department#',
    Email = '#Form.Email#',
    PhoneExt = #Form.PhoneExt#,
```

*Example 5-8. Using CFQUERY to Update a Database Record (continued)*

```
    Salary = #Form.Salary#
WHERE ID = #Form.ID#
</CFQUERY>

<!--- retrieve the record we just updated --->
<CFQUERY NAME="GetRecord" DATASOURCE="ProgrammingCF">
         SELECT ID, Name, Title, Department, Email, PhoneExt, Salary
         FROM EmployeeDirectory
         WHERE ID = #Form.ID#
</CFQUERY>

<HTML>
<HEAD>
    <TITLE>CFQUERY Update</TITLE>
</HEAD>

<BODY>

<H2>Record updated using CFQUERY!</H2>

<H3>Here are the record details...</H3>

<TABLE CELLPADDING="3" CELLSPACING="0">
<TR BGCOLOR="#888888">
    <TH>ID</TH>
    <TH>Name</TH>
    <TH>Title</TH>
    <TH>Department</TH>
    <TH>E-mail</TH>
    <TH>Phone Extension</TH>
    <TH>Salary</TH>
</TR>

<!--- output the record --->
<CFOUTPUT QUERY="GetRecord">
<TR BGCOLOR="##C0C0C0">
    <TD>#ID#</TD>
    <TD>#Name#</TD>
    <TD>#Title#</TD>
    <TD>#Department#</TD>
    <TD><A HREF="Mailto:#Email#">#Email#</A></TD>
    <TD>#PhoneExt#</TD>
    <TD>#Salary#</TD>
</TR>
</CFOUTPUT>
</TABLE>

</BODY>
</HTML>
```

Submitting the form from Example 5-7 posts to the template in Example 5-8 and updates the record in the database using the SQL `UPDATE` statement. Each field to be updated is specified as part of the SET clause. Multiple fields are separated by a comma. Note that numeric fields don't need to be surrounded by single quotes. The WHERE clause specifies the ID of the record we want to update.

After the record is updated, another CFQUERY is run to retrieve the record we just updated. Because we already have the ID value for the record, it only takes a single query to retrieve the record. The template finishes by outputting all the values stored in the record we just updated in a neatly formatted HTML table. The results are can be seen in Figure 5-7.

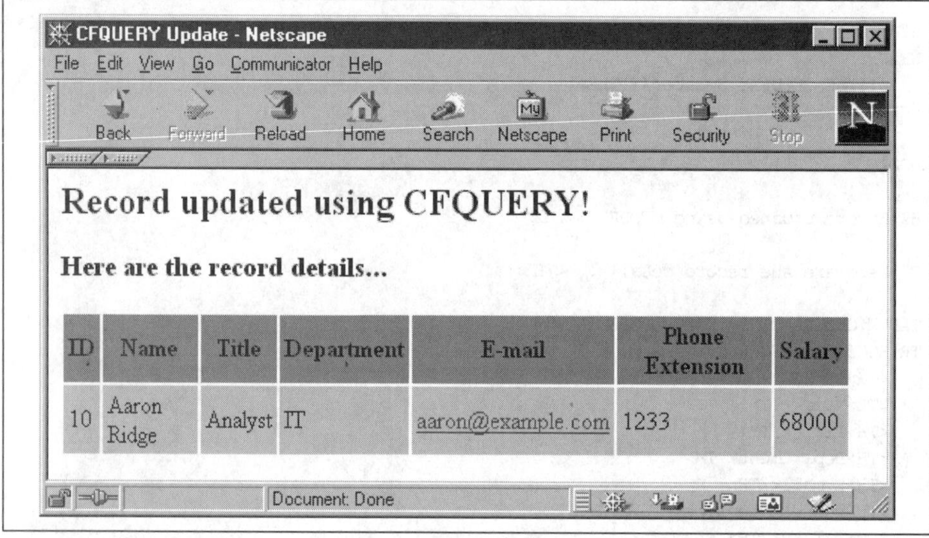


*Figure 5-7. Updating an existing record using CFQUERY*

### *Updating a record using CFUPDATE*

The CFUPDATE tag lets you update a record in a table without having to write an SQL UPDATE statement. The tag looks and functions almost identically to the CFINSERT tag and uses the following basic syntax:

```
<CFUPDATE DATASOURCE="datasource_name"
          TABLENAME="table_name"
          FORMFIELDS="field_names">
```

The attributes for the CFUPDATE tag are:

DATASOURCE
: The name of the data source to connect to when performing the update. Required.

`TABLENAME`

The name of the table to perform the update on. Required. It should be noted that Oracle database drivers require the table name to be in all uppercase. In addition, Sybase database drivers use a case-sensitive table name.

`FORMFIELDS`

A comma-delimited list of form fields to update. Optional. If no form fields are supplied, ColdFusion attempts to update the database using all the form fields passed from the form.

Several additional attributes are available for use with the **CFUPDATE** tag. For a complete list, see Appendix A.

Just as with the **CFINSERT** tag, there are two ways to use the **CFUPDATE** tag to update a record. You can use the tag to update values for every form field passed to the template containing the tag, or you can supply a comma-delimited list of form fields you want to update. Regardless of the method you use, it is important to make sure the primary key value for the record is passed to the **CFUPDATE** statement as a hidden form field. The hidden form field that passes the value must have the same name as the primary key field in the database. If the primary key field isn't specified, ColdFusion throws an error.

The first method requires only a few lines of code and is shown in Example 5-9. This template receives its input from the form in Example 5-7. In order for the example to work, the template in Example 5-9 must be saved as *Update.cfm* in the same directory as the template in Example 5-7.

*Example 5-9. Updating a Record with CFUPDATE*

```
<!--- update all of the form fields passed in the EmployeeDirectory
      table of the ProgrammingCF data source. --->
<CFUPDATE DATASOURCE="ProgrammingCF"
          TABLENAME="EmployeeDirectory">

<!--- This query uses the Form.ID value to lookup the full record
      we just updated. --->
<CFQUERY NAME="GetRecord" DATASOURCE="ProgrammingCF">
         SELECT ID, Name, Title, Department, Email, PhoneExt, Salary
         FROM EmployeeDirectory
         WHERE ID = #Form.ID#
</CFQUERY>

<HTML>
<HEAD>
    <TITLE>CFUPDATE Update</TITLE>
</HEAD>

<BODY>
```

*Example 5-9. Updating a Record with CFUPDATE (continued)*

```
<H2>Record updated using CFUPDATE without Field Names!</H2>

<H3>Here are the record details...</H3>

<TABLE CELLPADDING="3" CELLSPACING="0">
<TR BGCOLOR="#888888">
    <TH>ID</TH>
    <TH>Name</TH>
    <TH>Title</TH>
    <TH>Department</TH>
    <TH>E-mail</TH>
    <TH>Phone Extension</TH>
    <TH>Salary</TH>
</TR>

<!--- output the record --->
<CFOUTPUT QUERY="GetRecord">
<TR BGCOLOR="##C0C0C0">
    <TD>#ID#</TD>
    <TD>#Name#</TD>
    <TD>#Title#</TD>
    <TD>#Department#</TD>
    <TD><A HREF="Mailto:#Email#">#Email#</A></TD>
    <TD>#PhoneExt#</TD>
    <TD>#Salary#</TD>
</TR>
</CFOUTPUT>
</TABLE>

</BODY>
</HTML>
```

When the form in Example 5-7 posts to this template, the `CFUPDATE` tag attempts to take every form field passed and updates the equivalent field in the `EmployeeDirectory` table. This method works only when you have a corresponding database field for each form field. If, however, there are form field that don't have corresponding database fields, ColdFusion throws an error. Once the record has been updated, the template uses the same code from Example 5-8 to retrieve the record we just inserted and display it in the browser. If you look at the output from this template, you should notice that it looks identical to that shown in Example 5-8 (minus the title, of course).

The second method for using the `CFUPDATE` tag involves passing one additional attribute that allows you to specify which form fields should be updated in the database. This ensures that only the form fields you want are updated. The code for this template is shown in Example 5-10. As in the previous examples, this template receives its input from the form in Example 5-7. In order for the example to work, the template in Example 5-10 must be saved as *Update.cfm* in the same directory as the template in Example 5-7.

*Example 5-10. Updating Specific Form Fields Using CFUPDATE*

```
<!--- update the specified form fields in the EmployeeDirectory
      table of the ProgrammingCF data source. --->
<CFUPDATE DATASOURCE="ProgrammingCF"
          TABLENAME="EmployeeDirectory"
          FORMFIELDS="Name,Title,Email">

<!--- This query uses the Form.ID value to lookup the full record
      we just updated. --->
<CFQUERY NAME="GetRecord" DATASOURCE="ProgrammingCF">
         SELECT ID, Name, Title, Department, Email, PhoneExt, Salary
         FROM EmployeeDirectory
         WHERE ID = #Form.ID#
</CFQUERY>

<HTML>
<HEAD>
    <TITLE>CFUPDATE Update</TITLE>
</HEAD>

<BODY>

<H2>Record updated using CFUPDATE with Specific Field Names!</H2>

<H3>Here are the record details...</H3>

<TABLE CELLPADDING="3" CELLSPACING="0">
<TR BGCOLOR="#888888">
    <TH>ID</TH>
    <TH>Name</TH>
    <TH>Title</TH>
    <TH>Department</TH>
    <TH>E-mail</TH>
    <TH>Phone Extension</TH>
    <TH>Salary</TH>
</TR>

<!--- output the record --->
<CFOUTPUT QUERY="GetRecord">
<TR BGCOLOR="##C0C0C0">
    <TD>#ID#</TD>
    <TD>#Name#</TD>
    <TD>#Title#</TD>
    <TD>#Department#</TD>
    <TD><A HREF="Mailto:#Email#">#Email#</A></TD>
    <TD>#PhoneExt#</TD>
    <TD>#Salary#</TD>
</TR>
```

*Example 5-10. Updating Specific Form Fields Using CFUPDATE (continued)*

```
</CFOUTPUT>
</TABLE>

</BODY>
</HTML>
```

Using the form in Example 5-7 to post to this template, the `CFUPDATE` tag updates only the `Name`, `Title`, and `Email` fields in the `EmployeeDirectory` table with the data from `Form.Name`, `Form.Title`, and `Form.Email`. Once the record has been updated, the template uses the same code from Example 5-9 to retrieve the record we just updated and display it in the browser. Notice that even though we were able to make changes to all the fields in the update form, only the `Name`, `Title`, and `Email` fields contain updated values.

## Dynamically Populating Additional Form-Field Types

In Example 5-7, we dynamically populated several text boxes with data pulled from a query object. It is also possible to dynamically populate other form-field types using techniques that vary from form-field type to form-field type.

### Populating text areas

Populating a text area with data from a query is a little different from populating a text box. In the case of the text area, there is no `VALUE` attribute. Instead, the query variable is placed between the text area tags as shown in Example 5-11.

*Example 5-11. Dynamically Populating a Text Area*

```
<CFQUERY NAME="GetName" DATASOURCE="ProgrammingCF">
         SELECT Name
         FROM EmployeeDirectory
         Where ID=1
</CFQUERY>

<H2>Populating a Text Area</H2>
<FORM>
Name:<BR>

<!--- output the employee's name in a text area.  Generally, text areas are
      used to store large blocks of text. --->
<CFOUTPUT>
<TEXTAREA COLS="50" ROWS="5" NAME="Department"
          WRAP="virtual">#GetName.Name#</TEXTAREA>
</CFOUTPUT>
</FORM>
```

This example queries the `EmployeeDirectory` table of the `ProgrammingCF` database and returns the `Name` of the employee whose `ID` is `1`. This value is then output inside a text area. The results are shown in Figure 5-8. In general, text areas are used with large blocks of text. The `Name` column was used here for illustrative purposes only.

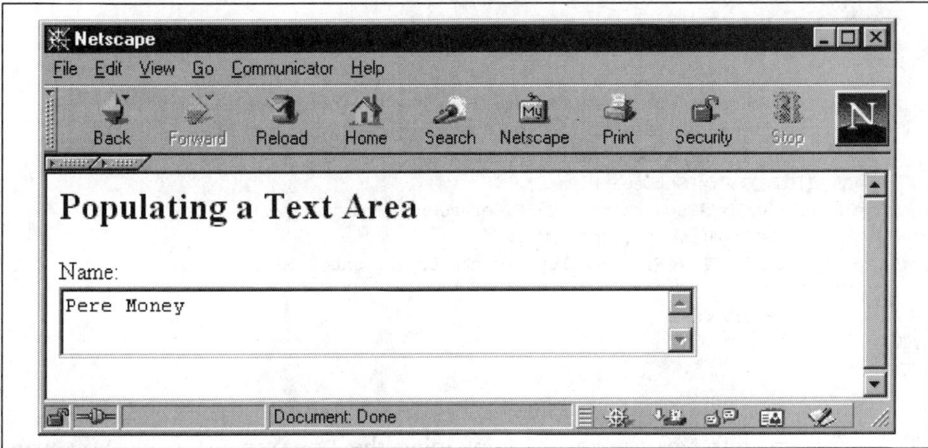


*Figure 5-8. Dynamically populating a text area*

### *Populating select lists*

Select lists are a bit trickier to handle than the other form-field types we have covered so far. In order to dynamically generate a simple select list and automatically select the option that matches a value from a database record, you need to run two queries, as shown in Example 5-12.

*Example 5-12. Dynamically Populating a Simple Select List*

```
<!--- retrieve a specific employee record --->
<CFQUERY NAME="GetRecord" DATASOURCE="ProgrammingCF">
        SELECT Name, Department
        FROM EmployeeDirectory
        WHERE ID=1
</CFQUERY>

<!--- retrieve a unique list of departments from the Department column
      of the EmployeeDirectory using the DISTINCT operator --->
<CFQUERY NAME="GetDepartments" DATASOURCE="ProgrammingCF">
        SELECT DISTINCT Department
        FROM EmployeeDirectory
        ORDER BY Department
</CFQUERY>

<H2>Populating a Select List</H2>
<FORM>
<TABLE>
```

*Example 5-12. Dynamically Populating a Simple Select List (continued)*

```
<TR>
  <TD>Name:</TD>
  <TD><CFOUTPUT>#GetRecord.Name#</CFOUTPUT></TD>
</TR>
<TR>
  <TD>Department:</TD>
  <TD><SELECT NAME="Department">
      <!--- dynamically generate the department list from the
            GetDepartments query.  Use a CFIF statement to determine if
            the current option tag is equal to the Department value
            retrieved as part of the employee record. If so, add the
            SELECTED attribute to the option tag --->
      <CFOUTPUT QUERY="GetDepartments">
      <OPTION VALUE="#Department#"<CFIF GetRecord.Department EQ
              GetDepartments.Department>
              SELECTED</CFIF>>#GetDepartments.Department#</OPTION>
      </CFOUTPUT>
      </SELECT></TD>
</TR>
</TABLE>
</FORM>
```

The first query retrieves the record containing the `Department` value you want preselected in the select list. In this example, we retrieve the `Name` and `Department` for the employee whose `ID` is `1`. The second query retrieves a list of unique department names from the database. The unique list is obtained by using the `DISTINCT` operator in the query. `DISTINCT` is discussed in Chapter 11. Once both queries have been run, the select list is dynamically generated using the `GetDepartments` query. With each `OPTION` tag generated, a check is made to see if the current `Department` (from the `GetDepartments` query) matches the `Department` from the `GetRecord` query. If a match is made, that `OPTION` tag has a `SELECTED` attribute added. The result is a select list with the option matching the database record preselected, as shown in Figure 5-9.

The technique for dynamically populating a multiple select list is a little different from the technique we used for the simple select list. In this scenario, we want to dynamically generate a select list but instead of having one option selected, we want to have multiple items selected based on a record retrieved from the database. Let's look at an example in which we want to build a prepopulated multiple select list that contains a list of all employees in our `EmployeeDirectory` table. To make things interesting, we'll preselect only those employees belonging to the IT department. Example 5-13 shows the code.

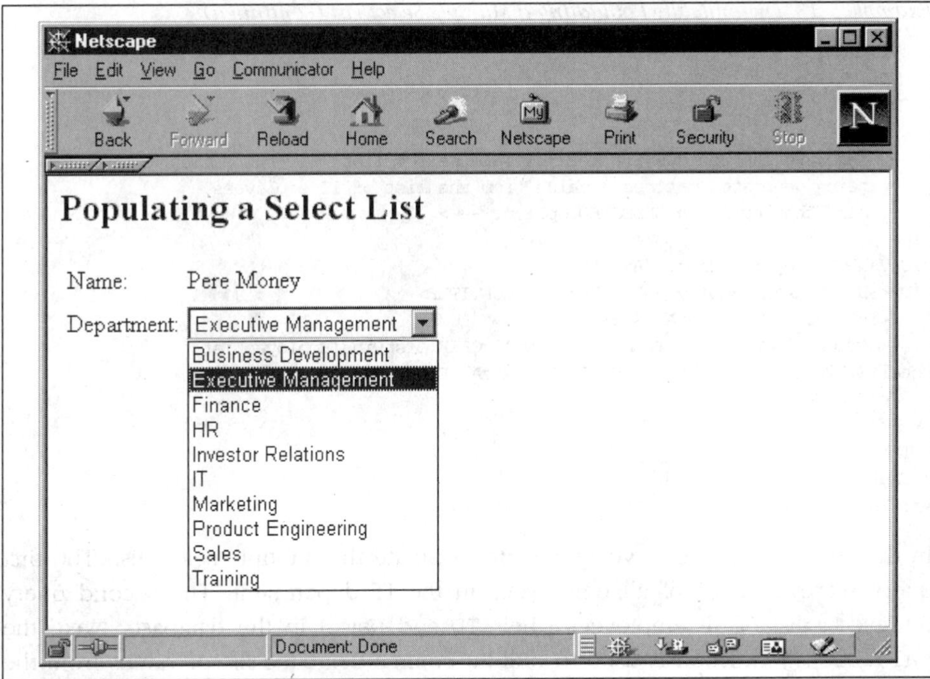


*Figure 5-9. Dynamically populating a select list*

*Example 5-13. Dynamically Populating a Multiple Select List*

```
<!--- retrieve a list of all employees who are in the IT department --->
<CFQUERY NAME="GetITEmployees" DATASOURCE="ProgrammingCF">
         SELECT Name
         FROM EmployeeDirectory
         WHERE Department = 'IT'
</CFQUERY>

<!--- retrieve all the employee from the EmployeeDirectory table --->
<CFQUERY NAME="GetAllEmployees" DATASOURCE="ProgrammingCF">
         SELECT ID, Name
         FROM EmployeeDirectory
         ORDER BY Name
</CFQUERY>

<!-- the ValueList function is used to build a comma-delimited list of
     values from a query column --->
<CFSET EmployeeList = ValueList(GetITEmployees.Name)>

<H2>Populating a Multiple Select Box</H2>
<FORM>
<TABLE>
<TR>
```

*Example 5-13. Dynamically Populating a Multiple Select List (continued)*

```
  <TD><B>Department:</B></TD>
  <TD>IT</TD>
</TR>

<!--- generate the options for the multiple select list.  If the option
      being generated matches a value from the list of IT employees,
      make that option a SELECTED option. --->
<TR>
<TD VALIGN="top"><B>Name:</B></TD>
<TD><SELECT NAME="Employees" SIZE="10" MULTIPLE>
    <CFOUTPUT QUERY="GetAllEmployees">
    <OPTION VALUE="#GetAllEmployees.ID#" <CFIF ListFind(EmployeeList,
GetAllEmployees.Name)>SELECTED</CFIF>>#GetAllEmployees.Name#
    </CFOUTPUT>
    </SELECT></TD>
</TR>
</TABLE>
</FORM>
```

In this example, we use two queries to populate the multiple select list. The first query retrieves a list of all employees in the IT department. The second query retrieves a list of all employees (their `ID` and `Name`) in the database. Next, the `ValueList()` function is used to build a comma-delimited list of values from the `Name` column of the `GetITEmployees` query. The list is assigned to a variable called `EmployeeList`. The next section of the template dynamically generates a multiple select list using the results of the `GetAllEmployees` query. With each `OPTION` tag generated, the `ListFind()` function is used to see if the current `Name` is in the `EmployeeList` list. If so, that `OPTION` tag has a `SELECTED` attribute added. The result is a multiple select list with the options matching the database record preselected, as shown in Figure 5-10.

### *Generating and selecting multiple checkboxes*

Checkboxes are similar to multiple select lists in that they are typically used to select one or more options from a list of choices. Dynamically generating checkboxes and automatically checking the ones that match entries in a database record is similar to the technique we used to generate the multiple select list. In fact, we'll use the same scenario to generate a checkbox for each employee in the `EmployeeDirectory` table and to automatically place a check in the box of each employee belonging to the IT department. The code to accomplish this is shown in Example 5-14.

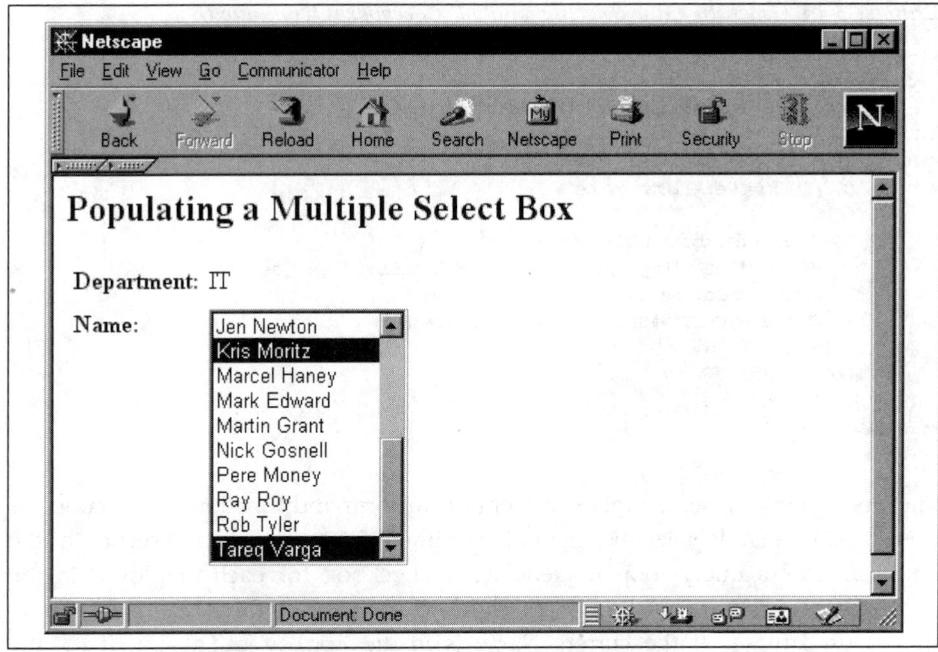


*Figure 5-10. Dynamically populating a multiple select list*

*Example 5-14. Generating and Selecting Multiple Checkboxes*

```
<!--- retrieve a list of all employees who are in the IT department --->
<CFQUERY NAME="GetITEmployees" DATASOURCE="ProgrammingCF">
         SELECT Name
         FROM EmployeeDirectory
         WHERE Department = 'IT'
</CFQUERY>

<!--- retrieve all the employee from the EmployeeDirectory table --->
<CFQUERY NAME="GetAllEmployees" DATASOURCE="ProgrammingCF">
         SELECT ID, Name
         FROM EmployeeDirectory
         ORDER BY Name
</CFQUERY>

<!-- the ValueList function is used to build a comma-delimited list of
     values from a query column --->
<CFSET EmployeeList = ValueList(GetITEmployees.Name)>

<H2>Populating Multiple Checkboxes</H2>
<FORM>
<TABLE>
<TR>
  <TD><B>Department:</B></TD>
  <TD>IT</TD>
</TR>
```

*Example 5-14. Generating and Selecting Multiple Checkboxes (continued)*

```
<!--- generate the individual checkboxes by looping over the query
      results and creating a check box for each record.  Check the
      appropriate boxes based on the CFIF statement. --->
<TR>
<TD VALIGN="top"><B>Name:</B></TD>
<TD><CFLOOP QUERY="GetAllEmployees">
    <CFOUTPUT>
    <INPUT TYPE="Checkbox" NAME="Employees"
           VALUE="#GetAllEmployees.ID#" <CFIF ListFind(EmployeeList,
           GetAllEmployees.Name)>
           CHECKED</CFIF>>#GetAllEmployees.Name#<BR>
    </CFOUTPUT>
    </CFLOOP></TD>
</TR>
</TABLE>
</FORM>
```

The first section of this template is identical in form and function to the code we used for the multiple select list example (Example 5-13). The second section of the template uses a query loop to generate a checkbox for each employee in the `GetAllEmployees` query. With each checkbox generated, the `ListFind()` function is used to see if the current Name is in the `EmployeeList` list. If so, the `INPUT` tag associated with the checkbox has a `CHECKED` attribute added. The result is a list of checkboxes with the checkboxes matching the database record checked. The results are shown in Figure 5-11.

Note that checkboxes are sometimes used to represent Boolean values such as `Yes/No`, `True/False`, or `On/Off`. Although you can code checkboxes in this manner, this type of option is better represented by radio buttons.

### *Generating and selecting radio buttons*

The final type of form field we need to cover is radio buttons. As you know, radio buttons are used to force a choice between several options. Dynamically generating radio buttons and automatically selecting the one that matches an entry in a database record is similar to the technique we used to generate the simple select list in Example 5-12.

Example 5-15 outputs the name of an employee from the `EmployeeDirectory` table and displays radio buttons that correspond to the distinct departments in the database, with the radio button that matches to the department in the database record selected.

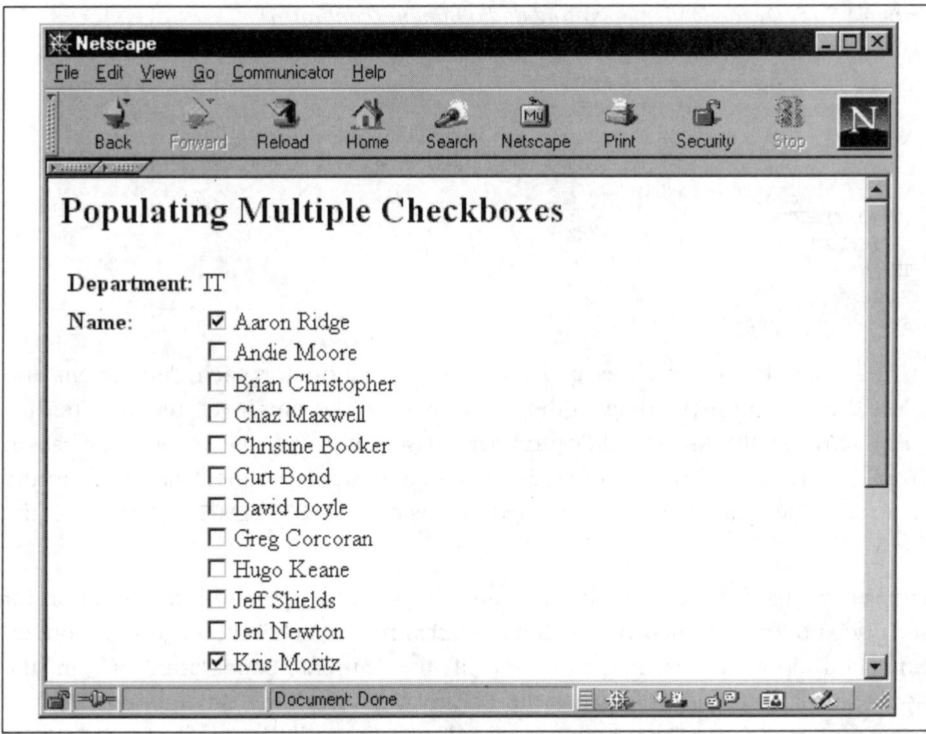


*Figure 5-11. Generating and selecting multiple checkboxes*

*Example 5-15. Dynamically Generating Radio Buttons*

```
<!--- retrieve a specific employee record --->
<CFQUERY NAME="GetRecord" DATASOURCE="ProgrammingCF">
         SELECT Name, Department
         FROM EmployeeDirectory
         WHERE ID=3
</CFQUERY>

<!--- retrieve a unique list of departments from the Department column of
      the EmployeeDirectory using the DISTINCT operator --->
<CFQUERY NAME="GetDepartments" DATASOURCE="ProgrammingCF">
         SELECT DISTINCT Department
         FROM EmployeeDirectory
         ORDER BY Department
</CFQUERY>

<H2>Populating Radio Buttons</H2>
<FORM>
<TABLE>
<TR>
  <TD><B>Name:</B></TD>
  <TD><CFOUTPUT>#GetRecord.Name#</CFOUTPUT></TD>
</TR>
<TR>
```

*Example 5-15. Dynamically Generating Radio Buttons (continued)*

```
<TD VALIGN="top"><B>Department:</B></TD>
<TD><CFLOOP QUERY="GetDepartments">
    <CFOUTPUT>
    <INPUT TYPE="Radio" NAME="Department" VALUE="#Department#" <CFIF
           GetRecord.Department EQ GetDepartments.Department>CHECKED</CFIF>
           >#Department#<BR>
    </CFOUTPUT>
    </CFLOOP></TD>
</TR>
</TABLE>
</FORM>
```

In this example, two queries generate a radio button for each department and select the one corresponding to the department in the employee record. The first query retrieves the `Name` and `Department` associated with the record that has an `ID` of 3. The second query retrieves a list of unique department names from the database. The unique list is obtained by using the `DISTINCT` operator in the query.

The second part of the template uses a query loop to generate a radio button for each department returned by the `GetDepartments` query. With each radio button generated, a check is made to see if the current `Department` (from the `GetDepartments` query) matches the `Department` from the `GetRecord` query. If a match is made, the `INPUT` tag associated with the radio button has a `SELECTED` attribute added. The result is a list of radio buttons, one for each department, with the radio button matching the `Department` from the database record selected, as is shown in Figure 5-12.

# *Deleting Records*

The `CFQUERY` tag can be used to delete records from a data source using the SQL `DELETE` clause. You can use `DELETE` to delete a single record or multiple records, depending on how you write the code. Once a record has been deleted, it can't be recovered, so be extremely careful when writing code that deletes records, as it is quite easy to accidentally delete the contents of an entire table. Because of this, I recommend testing your code against a test database or a temporary table before deploying it in a live application.

## *Deleting a Single Record*

Deleting a single record is as simple as it gets. The SQL for the delete looks something like this:

```
DELETE FROM tablename
WHERE primary_key = #primary_key#
```

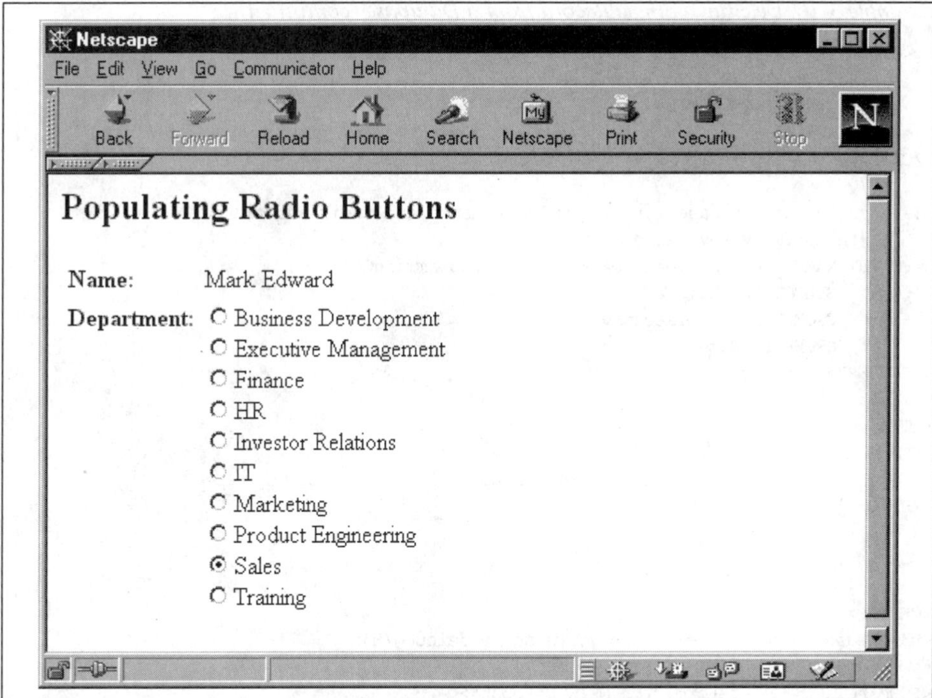


*Figure 5-12. Generating and selecting radio buttons*

We simply instruct the database to delete the record from the specified table where the primary key matches the one we supply. If there is such a record in the database, it is deleted. In this case, the primary key is a numeric value called `ID`. Primary keys don't have to be numeric values, but they do have to be unique.

If you look back at Example 5-7, you'll recall that it supports the ability to delete a record instead of populating the update form, if the appropriate parameter is passed from the record selection template. The code used to delete the record is quite simple:

```
<CFQUERY NAME="DeleteRecord" DATASOURCE="ProgrammingCF">
        DELETE FROM EmployeeDirectory
        WHERE ID = #ID#
```

To better illustrate the technique of deleting a record, let's look at a single template, *DeleteForm.cfm*, that allows a user to select a record from a database and then delete it. Example 5-16 shows the code.

*Example 5-16. Deleting a Single Record from a Database*

```
<!--- Check to see if the form is calling itself to delete a single record.
      Note that by NOT scoping the ID variable in the WHERE clause, we
      Allow the template to accept both Form and URL variables. --->
<CFIF IsDefined('Delete')>
```

*Example 5-16. Deleting a Single Record from a Database (continued)*

```
  <CFQUERY NAME="DeleteRecord" DATASOURCE="ProgrammingCF">
          DELETE FROM EmployeeDirectory
          WHERE ID = #ID#
  </CFQUERY>
</CFIF>

<!--- query the database for all employee names and their associated Ids
      (the primary key value --->
<CFQUERY NAME="GetEmployees" DATASOURCE="ProgrammingCF">
        SELECT ID, Name
        FROM EmployeeDirectory
        ORDER BY Name
</CFQUERY>

<HTML>
<HEAD>
    <TITLE>Deleting a Single Record</TITLE>
</HEAD>

<BODY>

<CENTER>
<H3>Please select the employee you wish to delete</H3>

<FORM ACTION="DeleteForm.cfm" METHOD="post">
<TABLE BORDER="0">
<TR>
  <TD>
  <SELECT NAME="ID" SIZE="5">
    <CFOUTPUT QUERY="GetEmployees">
      <OPTION VALUE="#ID#">#Name#</OPTION>
    </CFOUTPUT>
  </SELECT>
  </TD>
</TR>
<TR>
  <TD ALIGN="center">
    <INPUT TYPE="submit" NAME="Delete" VALUE="Delete">
  </TD>
</TR>
</TABLE>
</FORM>
</CENTER>

</BODY>
</HTML>
```

This template first checks to see if a variable called `Delete` has been passed in. This is done using the `IsDefined()` function. If `Delete` does exist, a **`CFQUERY`** statement deletes the record whose primary key value (`ID`) was also passed as a form or URL variable. By not scoping the `ID` variable in the **`WHERE`** clause, we allow the template to accept both form and URL variables. Because `ID` is a numeric value, no quotes are needed around the variable name in the `WHERE` clause.

The next part of the template performs a `SELECT` query to return all the employee names as well as their associated `IDs` from the database. An HTML form containing a select box and a submit button is then constructed. The query object then generates an `OPTION` tag for each record returned by the query. The `VALUE` attribute of each `OPTION` tag is dynamically populated with the `ID` of the corresponding record. The actual value displayed is determined by the `Name` field. The results are an HTML form with a select box containing a list of every employee from the database. A user can select a single employee from the select box and click on the submit button. The template then posts to itself. If an employee is selected, that record is deleted from the database. The form is then regenerated.

## *Deleting Multiple Records*

The `DELETE` clause can also be used to delete more than one record at a time. There are two basic techniques for implementing this. The first technique allows you to delete a group of records having one or more common values. For example, to delete the records for all employees who work in the marketing department, use the following:

```
<CFQUERY NAME="DeleteMarketing" DATASOURCE="ProgrammingCF">
        DELETE FROM EmployeeDirectory
        WHERE Department = 'Marketing'
</CFQUERY>
```

Here, we specify that all records with `Marketing` as the value for `Department` should be deleted.

The second technique involves passing a comma-delimited list of primary key values in the SQL statement. The syntax is similar to what we have already covered in Example 5-16. The main difference is that instead of using a `WHERE` clause like this:

```
WHERE ID = #ID#
```

we introduce a new operator, `IN`:

```
WHERE ID IN (#ID#)
```

In this case, the value of `#ID#` is either a single value or a comma-delimited list of values. The `IN` operator tells the database that `ID` must be `IN` (as opposed to equal to a single `ID`) a list of passed `IDs`. We can get a better idea of how this works by looking at an example. If you remember from Example 5-16, we created an HTML form that allowed a user to select a single employee from the database and subsequently deleted that employee's record. We can modify that example to allow a user to select more than one employee at a time. Example 5-17 shows the *MultipleDelete.cfm* template that implements this functionality.

*Example 5-17. Deleting Multiple Records from a Database*

```
<!--- Check to see if the form is calling itself to delete record(s) --->
<CFIF IsDefined('Form.Delete')>
  <CFQUERY NAME="DeleteRecord" DATASOURCE="ProgrammingCF">
         DELETE FROM EmployeeDirectory
         WHERE ID IN (#Form.ID#)
  </CFQUERY>
</CFIF>

<!--- query the database for all employee names and their associated Ids
      (the primary key value) --->
<CFQUERY NAME="GetEmployees" DATASOURCE="ProgrammingCF">
        SELECT ID, Name
        FROM EmployeeDirectory
        ORDER BY Name
</CFQUERY>

<HTML>
<HEAD>
    <TITLE>Deleting Multiple Records</TITLE>
</HEAD>

<BODY>

<CENTER>
<H3>Please select the employee(s) you wish to delete</H3>

<FORM ACTION="MultipleDelete.cfm" METHOD="post">
<TABLE BORDER="0">
<TR>
  <TD>
  <SELECT NAME="ID" SIZE="5" MULTIPLE>
    <CFOUTPUT QUERY="GetEmployees">
      <OPTION VALUE="#ID#">#Name#</OPTION>
    </CFOUTPUT>
  </SELECT>
  </TD>
</TR>
<TR>
  <TD ALIGN="center">
    <INPUT TYPE="submit" NAME="Delete" VALUE="Delete">
  </TD>
</TR>
</TABLE>
</FORM>
</CENTER>

</BODY>
</HTML>
```

There are only two areas where Example 5-16 differs from Example 5-17. The first is in the `CFQUERY` statement (the first one) that deletes the records selected in the form. Notice the `WHERE` clause is changed to read:

```
WHERE ID IN (#Form.ID#)
```

This is what allows us to delete either a single record or multiple records passed in from the select box.

The second difference is in the code that generates the select box. If you remember, Example 5-16 allowed only a single selection. We overcome this in Example 5-17 by adding the `MULTIPLE` attribute to the `SELECT` tag. This small change allows us to select multiple values within the select box. When the form is submitted, the values (in this case `IDs`) of the items selected are passed as a comma-delimited list. This list is stored as the form variable `Form.ID`.

## *Asking for Confirmation Before Deleting*

As you have seen, it is quite easy to delete records from a database table using a web-based frontend. This means that it is also easy to accidentally delete records with the click of a button. Because of this, you should consider including a confirmation mechanism in your application that warns users that the action they are about to take will permanently delete records from the database. This mechanism allows users to cancel the delete operation if they so desire.

You can easily make this functionality server-side and include it in the template that performs the SQL `DELETE`. However, this requires the use of several templates and actions on the part of users as they step screen by screen through the confirmation process. A better method is to use a single line of JavaScript in the same template as the HTML form you use to select the record(s) you want to delete. To include this functionality, change the `INPUT` statement that creates the Delete button in either Example 5-16 or Example 5-17 to use the following code:

```
<INPUT TYPE="submit" NAME="Delete" VALUE="Delete"
       onClick="return confirm('Are you sure you want to delete the
specified record(s)?')">
```

Including a JavaScript `onClick` event handler similar to the one we just described causes a JavaScript confirmation box to pop up whenever the Delete button is pressed. This confirmation box displays the message "Are you sure you want to delete the specified record(s)?" along with an Ok and a Cancel button. If the OK button is clicked, the form submits, and the records are deleted. If on the other hand, the Cancel button is clicked, the form isn't submitted, and the user is free to select another record.

# 6

*In this chapter:*
- *Lists*
- *Arrays*
- *Structures*
- *Query Objects*

# *Complex Datatypes*

Besides the simple datatypes covered in Chapter 2, ColdFusion supports several complex datatypes you can use to increase the complexity and functionality of your applications. These datatypes include lists, arrays, structures, query objects, and component objects. With the exception of component objects (these are covered later in Chapter 23), this chapter discusses each of these complex datatypes and provides numerous examples illustrating how they can further enhance your applications.

## *Lists*

A list is a special type of string that contains delimited elements. For example, "a,b,c,d,e,f,g" is a list where "a", "b", "c", "d", "e", "f", and "g" are considered the list elements while the comma (,) is considered the delimiter. Lists are commonly used to store related items in a single variable. For example, you might use a list to store all the primary key values for a group of database records you want to delete.

It should be noted that ColdFusion treats list elements containing null values as though they don't exist. For example, the list "1,2,,4" contains only three list elements (as far as ColdFusion is concerned) even though there is a null list element ",,". The concept of a null list element shouldn't be confused with a blank list element as in "1,2, ,4" which contains four list elements, the space occupying list element three being counted. To further illustrate the point, consider Example 6-1, which creates three lists using `CFSET` tags and then uses the `ListLen()` function to evaluate the number of elements in each list.

*Example 6-1. Creating Lists and Evaluating Their Length*

```
<CFSET List1 = "1,2,3,4">
<CFSET List2 = "1,2,,4">
<CFSET List3 = "1,2, ,4">

<CFOUTPUT>
List1 (#List1#) contains #ListLen(List1)# elements.<BR>
List2 (#List2#) contains #ListLen(List2)# elements.<BR>
List3 (#List3#) contains #ListLen(List3)# elements.
</CFOUTPUT>
```

Executing the template in Example 6-1 results in the output shown in Figure 6-1.

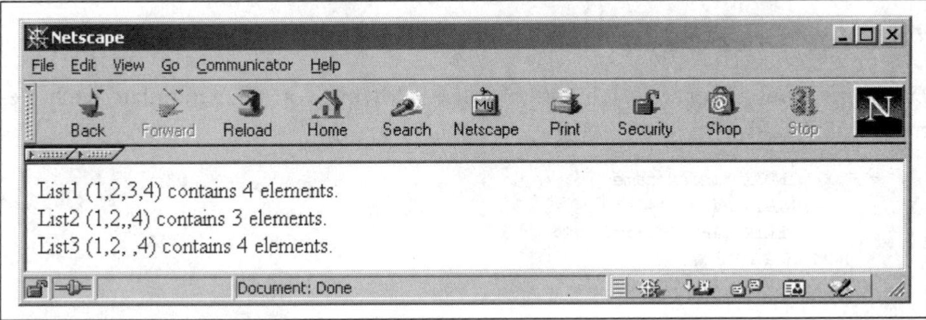


*Figure 6-1. Outputting the number of elements in various lists*

In the previous example, each element in the list was delimited by a comma. Although the comma is considered the default delimiter for lists in ColdFusion, it is possible to use any character or combination of characters as the delimiter. This is done by specifying the delimiter as an optional parameter in the appropriate list function:

```
<CFSET List1 = "a;b;c;d">
<CFSET List2 = "a|b|c|d">
<CFSET List3 = "a+|+b+|+c+|+d">

<CFOUTPUT>
List1 (#List1#) contains #ListLen(List1, ";")# elements.<BR>
List2 (#List2#) contains #ListLen(List2, "|")# elements.<BR>
List3 (#List3#) contains #ListLen(List3, "+|")# elements.
</CFOUTPUT>
```

In this example, the `ListLen()` function outputs the number of elements contained in each list. Note that each list uses a delimiter other than the comma. Because of this, it is necessary to specify the delimiter in the `ListLen()` function. If you omit the delimiter in any of these examples, the `ListLen()` function returns 1 for the length of the list because no commas are found.

It's also possible to use more than one delimiter within a list:

```
<CFSET List1 = "a,b;c,d;">
<CFSET List2 = "a,b,c|d">

<CFOUTPUT>
List1 (#List1#) contains #ListLen(List1, ",;")# elements.<BR>
List2 (#List2#) contains #ListLen(List2, ",|")# elements.
</CFOUTPUT>
```

In this case, each list has two different delimiters. In order to be recognized by the `ListLen()` function, each delimiter has to be specified. Note that the delimiters themselves aren't separated by a delimiter.

## Looping Over a List

List loops iterate over the elements of a list, allowing you to manipulate each element individually:

```
<CFLOOP INDEX="index_name"
        LIST="list_items"
        DELIMITERS="delimiter">
   HTML and CFML...
</CFLOOP>
```

The `INDEX` attribute of the loop specifies a variable name to hold the value corresponding to the current position in the list. `LIST` specifies a delimited list of values or variable name (including pound signs) over which to loop. The `DELIMITER` attribute specifies the delimiter that separates the elements of the list. The default is the comma. Example 6-2 uses a list loop to output each element of a list on a new line.

*Example 6-2. Looping Over a List Using a List Loop*

```
<CFSET MyList = "a,b,c,d,e,f,g,h,i,j,k,l,m,n,o,p,q,r,s,t,u,v,w,x,y,z">
<CFLOOP INDEX="i"
        LIST="#MyList#"
        DELIMITERS=",">

<CFOUTPUT>
#i#<BR>
</CFOUTPUT>

</CFLOOP>
```

## Manipulating Lists

A number of functions are available in ColdFusion to manipulate list elements. We've already looked at the `ListLen()` function. Other commonly used list functions enable you to manipulate lists in a number of ways.

To append an item to the end of an existing list, you can use the `ListAppend()` function:

```
<CFSET MyList = "1,2,3,4">
<CFSET MyList = ListAppend(MyList, 5)>
```

You can also prepend an item to the beginning of a list using the `ListPrepend()` function:

```
<CFSET MyList = "2,3,4,5">
<CFSET MyList = ListPrepend(MyList, 1)>
```

To insert an item into a specific position within a list, use the `ListInsertAt()` function:

```
<CFSET MyList = "Monday,Tuesday,Thursday,Friday">
<CFSET MyList = ListInsertAt(MyList, 3, "Wednesday")>
```

If you want to return the first item in a list, use the `ListFirst()` function:

```
<CFSET MyList = "1,2,3,4">
<CFOUTPUT>
#ListFirst(MyList)#
</CFOUTPUT>
```

Likewise, you can use the `ListLast()` function to return the last item in a list:

```
<CFSET MyList = "1,2,3,4">
<CFOUTPUT>
#ListLast(MyList)#
</CFOUTPUT>
```

You can output a list item occupying a specific position within a list using the `ListGetAt()` function:

```
<CFSET MyList = "1,2,3,4">
<CFOUTPUT>
#ListGetAt(MyList, 3)#
</CFOUTPUT>
```

For a complete listing as well as examples showing the usage of all list functions, see Appendix B.

# *Arrays*

An array is an object that stores indexed values. Each value stored in an array is referred to as an element of the array. Each element has an integer assigned to it that marks its position within the array. This number is referred to as the element's index. Arrays elements can store any ColdFusion datatype including additional arrays.

As previously discussed, ColdFusion supports one-dimensional (think of this as a single column of data or a list), two-dimensional (think of this as a spreadsheet with rows and columns), and three-dimensional arrays (think of this as a cube of data). Additional dimensions can be created dynamically by nesting multidimensional arrays (creating an array of arrays). ColdFusion arrays differ slightly from traditional arrays found in other programming languages. Whereas traditional arrays are fixed in size, ColdFusion arrays are dynamic. This means that a ColdFusion array can expand or contract as elements are added and removed from the array.

Arrays can store groups of related data such as the contents of a visitor's shopping cart, student test scores, or historic stock prices. Because array elements can store any ColdFusion datatype, they are ideal for storing complex objects such as an array of query result sets or an array of structures.

## *Initializing an Array*

Initializing an array in ColdFusion is accomplished using the **ArrayNew()** function. This function takes a single argument that determines the number of dimensions for the array (1, 2, or 3). The following code initializes a one-dimensional array called **grades**:

```
<CFSET Grades = ArrayNew(1)>
```

If you wanted to create a two-dimensional array called **grades**, use the following:

```
<CFSET Grades = ArrayNew(2)>
```

Similarly, a three-dimensional array called **grades** is created like this:

```
<CFSET Grades = ArrayNew(3)>
```

To create an array with more than three dimensions, you must nest multidimensional arrays:

```
<CFSET MyArray = ArrayNew(3)>
<CFSET NestedArray = ArrayNew(3)>
<CFSET MyArray[1][1][1] = NestedArray>
```

You can also initialize an array using the **CFPARAM** tag, as in the following:

```
<CFPARAM NAME="Grades" TYPE="Array" VALUE="#ArrayNew(1)#>
```

Note that you must surround the **ArrayNew()** function with pound signs. This tells ColdFusion to evaluate the **ArrayNew()** function as opposed to treating it as literal text.

## *Adding Data to an Array*

Once you have initialized an array, you can populate it with data. Because ColdFusion arrays are dynamic, there is no need to predefine the size of the array. Data is added to an array using the **CFSET** tag to specify the index position within the array where the data should be stored. The index position within each dimension is referenced with a set of brackets ([]). Unlike in many other programming languages, in ColdFusion, array indexes begin with 1. Consider the following example that populates elements in a one, two, and three dimensional array:

```
<!--- This populates an element in a one-dimensional array --->
<CFSET MyArray[1]  = "cat">

<!--- This populates an element in a two-dimensional array --->
<CFSET MyArray[1][1] = "dog">

<!--- This populates an element in a three-dimensional array --->
<CFSET MyArray[1][1][1] = "fish">
```

In a one-dimensional array, the index position refers to the element's linear position within the array (if you think of a one-dimensional array as a list of elements). In a two-dimensional array, the index positions refer to the element's x-y position (if you think of a two-dimensional array as a grid of data with an x and y axis). Because a three-dimensional array stores data in a three-dimensional cube configuration, the index position of any element is referred to by its x-y-z position within the cube.

To get a better idea of how data is stored in an array, consider Example 6-3 in which a one-dimensional array called **Grades** is initialized, populated with values, then output by looping over each element in the array.

*Example 6-3. Grades for a Single Student Stored in a One-Dimensional Array*

```
<CFSET Grades = ArrayNew(1)>

<CFSET Grades[1] = 95>
<CFSET Grades[2] = 93>
<CFSET Grades[3] = 87>
<CFSET Grades[4] = 100>
<CFSET Grades[5] = 74>

<CFLOOP INDEX="Element" FROM="1" TO="#ArrayLen(Grades)#">
  <CFOUTPUT>
  Grade #Element#: #Grades[Element]#<BR>
  </CFOUTPUT>
</CFLOOP>
```

In this example, an index loop is used to loop over the elements in the Grades array. This is accomplished by setting the TO attribute of the CFLOOP tag to the total number of elements in the array. This number is derived using the ArrayLen() function. Executing this template results in the output shown in Figure 6-2.

It's just as easy to create a two-dimensional array. The next example creates a two-dimensional array called Grades. This array also holds student grades, but instead of holding the grades for a single student, the array holds multiple grades for

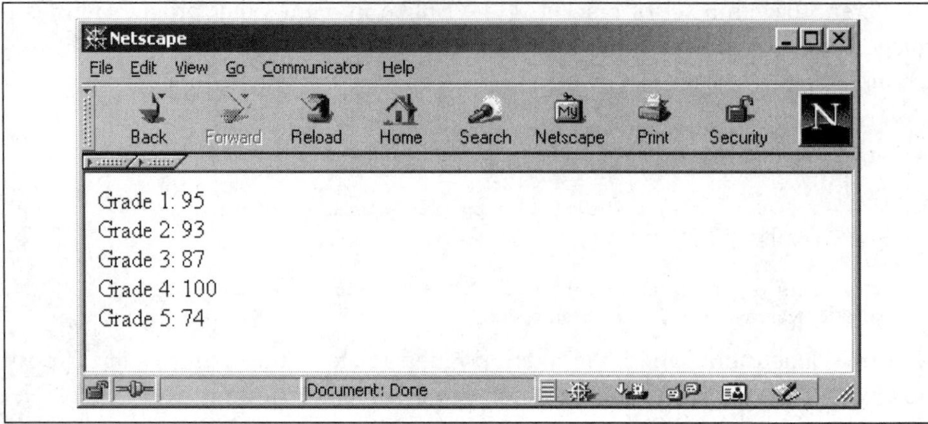


*Figure 6-2. Outputting the contents of the one-dimensional Grades array*

multiple students. Each student is represented by the first dimension of the array while each corresponding grade is represented by the second dimension. The code in Example 6-4 initializes the **Grades** array, populates it with data, and then uses a nested loop technique to output the contents to the browser.

*Example 6-4. Grades for More than One Student Stored in a Two-Dimensional Array*

```
<!--- create a two dimensional array of student grades.  Each student
     (represented by the first dimension) has grades for multiple tests
     (represented by the second dimension). --->
<CFSET Grades = ArrayNew(2)>

<CFSET Grades[1][1] = 95>
<CFSET Grades[1][2] = 93>
<CFSET Grades[1][3] = 87>
<CFSET Grades[2][1] = 100>
<CFSET Grades[2][2] = 74>
<CFSET Grades[2][3] = 86>
<CFSET Grades[3][1] = 90>
<CFSET Grades[3][2] = 94>
<CFSET Grades[3][3] = 96>


<!--- this looping technique utilizes an outer and an inner loop (designated
      o and i respectively) for looping through each element in each
      dimension of the array --->
<CFLOOP INDEX="o" FROM="1" TO="#ArrayLen(Grades)#">
  <CFLOOP INDEX="i" FROM="1" TO="#ArrayLen(Grades[o])#">
    <CFOUTPUT>
    Student #o#, Grade #i#: #Grades[o][i]#<BR>
    </CFOUTPUT>
  </CFLOOP>
</CFLOOP>
```

Executing this template results in the output shown in Figure 6-3.

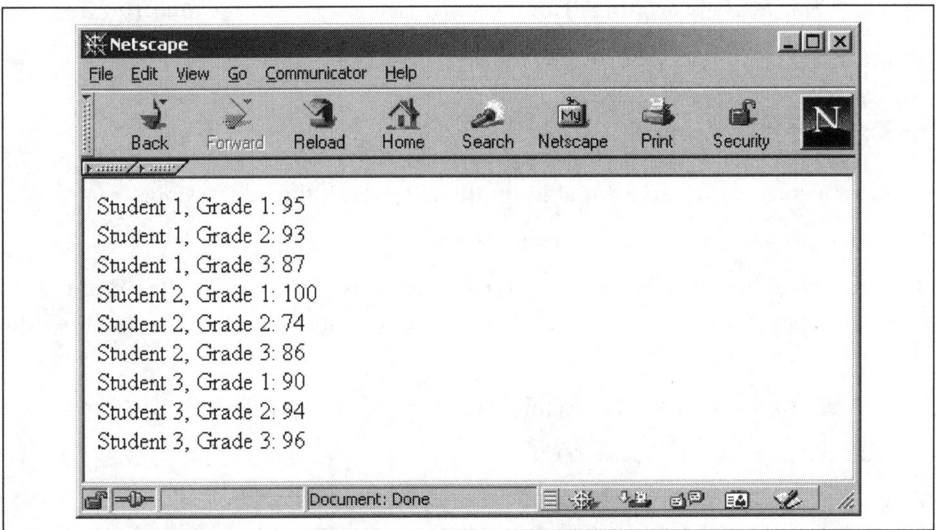


*Figure 6-3. Outputting the contents of the two-dimensional Grades array*

## *Manipulating Array Elements*

A number of functions are available in ColdFusion to manipulate arrays. We've already covered the `ArrayNew()` and `ArrayLen()` functions as well as how to create array elements. There are other common array functions worth mentioning.

To append an element to the end of an existing array use the `ArrayAppend()` function:

```
<CFSET ArrayAppend(Grades, "66")>
```

You may have noticed that the `CFSET` tag in the previous example doesn't assign a value to a variable:

```
<CFSET ArrayAppend(Grades, "66")>
```

This is a special circumstance in which the `CFSET` tag executes a function without assigning the results to a variable. There are only a handful of functions that allow you to execute them in this manner. These functions are shown in Table 6-1.

*Table 6-1. Functions Not Requiring Variable Assignment with CFSET*

| | | |
|---|---|---|
| `ArrayAppend()` | `CF_SetDataSourceUsername()` | `SetLocale()` |
| `ArrayClear()` | `CF_SetDataSourcePassword()` | `SetProfileString()` |
| `ArrayDeleteAt()` | `CFusion_Disable_DBConnections()` | `SetVariable()` |
| `ArrayInsertAt()` | `CFusion_SetODBCIni()` | `StructAppend()` |
| `ArrayPrepend()` | `CFusion_Settings_Refresh()` | `StructClear()` |
| `ArrayResize()` | `CFusion_DBConnections_Flush()` | `StructDelete()` |

*Table 6-1. Functions Not Requiring Variable Assignment with CFSET (continued)*

| | | |
|---|---|---|
| `ArraySet()` | `QueryAddColumn()` | `StructGet()` |
| `ArraySort()` | `QueryAddRow()` | `StructInsert()` |
| `ArraySwap()` | `QuerySetCell()` | `StructUpdate()` |

You can just as easily use a variable on the left side of the expression:

```
<CFSET temp = ArrayAppend(Grades, "66")>
```

Whichever method you use is a matter of personal choice and style. There is no noticeable performance gain (other than having to write less code) by omitting the variable assignment.

If you want to prepend a value to the beginning on an array, use `ArrayPrenend()`:

```
<CFSET ArrayPrepend(Grades, "66")>
```

You can also insert an element anywhere within an array using the `ArrayInsertAt()` function. For example, to insert the value 66 as the third element in an array named `Grades`, use the following syntax:

```
<CFSET ArrayInsertAt(Grades, 66, 3)>
```

Deleting an element is just as simple and is done using the `ArrayDeleteAt()` function. For example, to delete the third element in an array named `Grades`, use:

```
<CFSET ArrayDeleteAt(Grades, 3)>
```

Because ColdFusion arrays are dynamic, adding or deleting an element from the middle of an index results in a shift in the index position of other elements in the array.

You can remove all data from an array using `ArrayClear()`:

```
<CFSET ArrayClear(Grades)>
```

If you need to determine whether an array contains any data, use the `ArrayIsEmpty()` function:

```
<CFIF ArrayIsEmpty(Grades)>
  There are no grades to process
</CFELSE>
 Processing grades...
</CFIF>
```

Sorting an array is done using the `ArraySort()` function. You can specify a sort type (`Numeric`, `Text`, or `TextNoCase`) as well as a sort order (the default, `Asc`, or `Desc`):

```
<CFSET SortedGrades = ArraySort(Grades, 'Numeric', 'Asc')>
```

If you are dealing with numeric elements in an array, you can find the average value using the `ArrayAvg()` function:

```
<CFSET TheAverage = ArrayAvg(Scores)>
```

You can just as easily determine the minimum value or maximum value using `ArrayMin()` or `ArrayMax()`:

```
<CFSET MinValue = ArrayMin(Scores)>
<CFSET MaxValue = ArrayMax(Scores)>
```

If you want to add the numeric values in an array, use the `ArraySum()` function:

```
<CFSET TheSum = ArraySum(Scores)>
```

For a complete listing as well as examples showing the usage of each array function, see Appendix B.

# *Structures*

A structure is a ColdFusion datatype that allows you to store and manipulate key/value pairs. Structures are similar to one-dimensional arrays, except each element is referenced via an alphanumeric "key" (string) as opposed to a numeric index within the array. Structures are also commonly known as associative arrays or hashes. Structures offer an advantage over arrays in certain situations, by allowing you to reference groups of related information by key as opposed to by numeric index. Structures are useful for storing sets of related data in a single variable. For example, you can easily store an employee's contact information in a structure called `Employee`. That structure can contain keys such as `Name`, `Address`, `City`, `State`, and `Zip`. Additionally, a number of ColdFusion variable scopes are accessible as structures. For example, you can access all form variables available to a page by referencing a structure named `Form`. A similar structure is also available for several other variable scopes.

## *Creating a Structure*

Structures are created using the `StructNew()` function. Unlike with arrays, you don't have to pass any information to this function. To create a new structure called `Stock`, you use the following code:

```
<CFSET Stock = StructNew()>
```

Just like arrays, structures can also be created using the `CFPARAM` tag:

```
<CFPARAM NAME="Stock" TYPE="Struct" DEFAULT="#StructNew()#">
```

Be sure to wrap the `StructNew()` function with hash marks to avoid having ColdFusion treat the function as literal text.

## Populating a Structure with Data

Once you have created a structure with the `StructNew()` function, it is ready to be populated with key/value pairs. Structures are a unique datatype in that you can reference structure elements using three styles of notation:

*Function notation*

Elements within structures can be indirectly referenced using structure functions as opposed to directly using one of the other methods of notation:

```
<CFSET StructInsert(Stock, "company", "Allaire")>
```

*Object notation*

Structure values are referenced as ***`object.property`*** where ***`object`*** is the name of the structure, and ***`property`*** is the name of the key. All references using object notation are case-insensitive.

```
<CFSET Stock.Company = "Allaire">
```

*Associative array notation*

You can use associative array notation to refer to structure elements much as you refer to elements within an array. The difference is that in the case of associative arrays, the indexes are strings as opposed to numbers:

```
<CFSET Stock["company"] = "Allaire">
```

Example 6-5 uses function notation to create a structure called `Stock` and populate it with key/value pairs. Each key/value pair is added using the `StructInsert()` function.

*Example 6-5. Populating a Structure Using Function Notation*

```
<CFSET Stock = StructNew()>
<CFSET StructInsert(Stock, "company", "Allaire")>
<CFSET StructInsert(Stock, "ticker", "ALLR")>
<CFSET StructInsert(Stock, "exchange", "NASDAQ")>
<CFSET StructInsert(Stock, "price", "66.25")>
<CFSET StructInsert(Stock, "change", "+0.375")>
<CFSET StructInsert(Stock, "lasttradetime", "10:17AM")>
<CFSET StructInsert(Stock, "lasttradedate", "08/15/2000")>
<CFSET StructInsert(Stock, "volume", "8300")>

<CFSET MyKeyList = StructKeyList(Stock)>

<TABLE>
<TR>
  <TH>Key</TH><TH>Value</TH>
</TR>

<CFLOOP INDEX="Key" LIST="#MyKeyList#">
  <CFOUTPUT>
  <TR>
    <TD>#Key#</TD><TD>#StructFind(Stock,Key)#</TD>
```

*Example 6-5. Populating a Structure Using Function Notation (continued)*

```
  </TR>
  </CFOUTPUT>
</CFLOOP>

</TABLE>
```

In this example, once the structure has been populated, the `StructKeyList()` function generates a delimited list of all keys in the `Stock` structure. A `LIST` loop is then used to iterate over each key in the list. A table containing each key/value pair is dynamically generated by obtaining the key from the list and the value from the structure. The output from this template is shown in Figure 6-4.

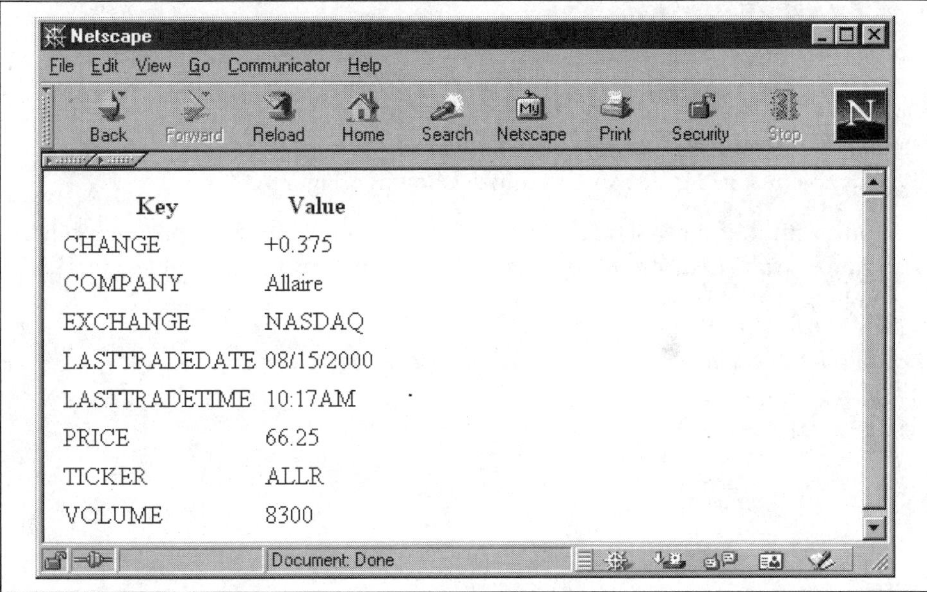


*Figure 6-4. Outputting the contents of a structure using a LIST loop and the StructFind function*

Example 6-6 shows how to populate the same `Stock` structure with object notation.

*Example 6-6. Populating a Structure Using Object Notation*

```
<CFSET Stock = StructNew()>
<CFSET Stock.Company = "Allaire">
<CFSET Stock.Ticker = "ALLR">
<CFSET Stock.Exchange = "NASDAQ">
<CFSET Stock.Price = "66.25">
<CFSET Stock.Change = "+0.375">
<CFSET Stock.LastTradeTime = "10:17AM">
<CFSET Stock.LastTradeDate = "08/15/2000">
<CFSET Stock.Volume = "8300">
```

*Example 6-6. Populating a Structure Using Object Notation (continued)*

```
<TABLE>
<TR>
    <TH>Key</TH><TH>Value</TH>
</TR>

<CFOUTPUT>
<TR><TD>COMPANY</TD><TD>#Stock.company#</TD></TR>
<TR><TD>TICKER</TD><TD>#Stock.ticker#</TD></TR>
<TR><TD>EXCHANGE</TD><TD>#Stock.exchange#</TD></TR>
<TR><TD>PRICE</TD><TD>#Stock.price#</TD></TR>
<TR><TD>CHANGE</TD><TD>#Stock.change#</TD></TR>
<TR><TD>LASTTRADETIME</TD><TD>#Stock.lasttradetime#</TD></TR>
<TR><TD>LASTTRADEDATE</TD><TD>#Stock.lasttradedate#</TD></TR>
<TR><TD>VOLUME</TD><TD>#Stock.volume#</TD></TR>
</CFOUTPUT>
</TABLE>
```

Once the `Stock` structure has been populated, the contents of the structure are output by referencing each element individually using object notation. Executing the example results in the same output as shown in Figure 6-4.

Working with the same `Stock` structure from our previous examples, we can use associative array notation to populate the structure with key/value pairs as in Example 6-7.

*Example 6-7. Populating a Structure Using Associative Array Notation*

```
<CFSET Stock = StructNew()>
<CFSET Stock["Company"] = "Allaire">
<CFSET Stock["Ticker"] = "ALLR">
<CFSET Stock["Exchange"] = "NASDAQ">
<CFSET Stock["Price"] = "66.25">
<CFSET Stock["Change"] = "+0.375">
<CFSET Stock["LastTradeTime"] = "10:17AM">
<CFSET Stock["LastTradeDate"] = "08/15/2000">
<CFSET Stock["Volume"] = "8300">

<CFSET MyKeyArray = StructKeyArray(Stock)>

<TABLE>
<TR>
  <TH>Key</TH><TH>Value</TH>
</TR>
<CFLOOP index="position" from="1" to="#ArrayLen(MyKeyArray)#">
  <CFOUTPUT>
  <TR>
    <TD>#MyKeyArray[position]#</TD>
    <TD>#Stock[MyKeyArray[position]]#</TD>
  </TR>
  </CFOUTPUT>
</CFLOOP>
</TABLE>
```

We use a third technique here to output the contents of the `Stock` structure. The `StructKeyArray()` function is used to create an array called `MyKeyArray()` that contains all the keys in the structure. An `index` loop is then used to iterate over each of the keys in the array. A table containing each key/value pair is dynamically generated by obtaining the key from the array and the value from the structure. The results are the same as those shown in Figure 6-4.

## *Using a Collection Loop to Loop Over the Contents of a Structure*

Collection loops can iterate over a COM collection object or a ColdFusion structure. To better understand how collection loops allow you to loop over structures, let's look at the general syntax that codes a collection loop:

```
<CFLOOP COLLECTION="COM_object_or_structure"
        ITEM="collection_or_key">
   HTML and CFML...
</CFLOOP>
```

The `COLLECTION` attribute specifies the name of a registered COM object or a ColdFusion structure object. `ITEM` specifies the name of the variable that holds each item in the COM collection or structure object that is referenced by the loop. Example 6-8 uses a collection loop to output each key/value pair contained in a structure object called `Stock`.

*Example 6-8. Using a Collection Loop to Loop Over a Structure*

```
<CFSET Stock = StructNew()>
<CFSET Stock.Company = "Allaire">
<CFSET Stock.Ticker = "ALLR">
<CFSET Stock.Exchange = "NASDAQ">
<CFSET Stock.Price = "66.25">
<CFSET Stock.Change = "+0.375">
<CFSET Stock.LastTradeTime = "10:17AM">
<CFSET Stock.LastTradeDate = "08/15/2000">
<CFSET Stock.Volume = "8300">

<TABLE>
<TR>
  <TH>Key</TH><TH>Value</TH>
</TR>

<CFLOOP COLLECTION="#Stock#" ITEM="Key">
  <CFOUTPUT>
  <TR>
    <TD>#Key#</TD><TD>#StructFind(Stock,Key)#</TD>
  </TR>
  </CFOUTPUT>
</CFLOOP>
</TABLE>
```

Here, a `collection` loop iterates over each of the keys in the structure. The values associated with the keys are obtained using the `StructFind()` function. This combination outputs all the key/value pairs within the structure. The output from this template is the same as shown in Figure 6-4.

## *Creating an Array of Structures*

If you look at all the structure examples we've created so far, you'll probably come to the conclusion that while structures appear to be a great way to store and reference data, their ability to store multiple sets of similar data seems limited. For example, while you can store all the information about a particular stock in a structure, you can't store information about additional stocks in the same structure. You can create a separate structure for each stock, but that could get unwieldy to manage, especially if you need to pass the data to another template. The solution is to create an array of structures to hold the information about each stock. Example 6-9 shows the code to do just this.

*Example 6-9. Creating an Array of Structures to Hold Stock Information*

```
<!--- create an array called MyArray --->
<CFSET MyArray = ArrayNew(1)>

<!--- create a structure as the first array element --->
<CFSET MyArray[1] = StructNew()>
<CFSET MyArray[1].Ticker = "ALLR">
<CFSET MyArray[1].Company = "Allaire">
<CFSET MyArray[1].Price = 47.75>

<!--- create a structure as the second array element --->
<CFSET MyArray[2] = StructNew()>
<CFSET MyArray[2].Ticker = "AMKR">
<CFSET MyArray[2].Company = "Amkor Technology">
<CFSET MyArray[2].Price = 31.75>

<!--- create a structure as the third array element --->
<CFSET MyArray[3] = StructNew()>
<CFSET MyArray[3].Ticker = "YHOO">
<CFSET MyArray[3].Company = "Yahoo">
<CFSET MyArray[3].Price = 140>

<H2>Stock Quotes in an Array of Structures</H2>
<TABLE>
<TR>
  <TH>Ticker</TH><TH>Company</TH><TH>Price</TH>
</TR>

<CFLOOP INDEX="i" FROM="1" TO="#ArrayLen(MyArray)#">
  <CFOUTPUT>
  <TR>
    <TD>#MyArray[i].Ticker#</TD>
```

*Example 6-9. Creating an Array of Structures to Hold Stock Information (continued)*

```
    <TD>#MyArray[i].Company#</TD>
    <TD>#MyArray[i].Price#</TD>
  </TR>
  </CFOUTPUT>
</CFLOOP>
</TABLE>
```

The template begins by initializing a one-dimensional array called `MyArray`. Next, `CFSET` tags are used to assign values to each index in the array. Instead of assigning string values, a new structure is created for each stock. The structure is then populated with the stock's ticker, company name, and price. Once the array of structures has been populated, an HTML table containing the information from each structure is constructed on the fly by looping over each array element. Executing the template results in the output shown in Figure 6-5.

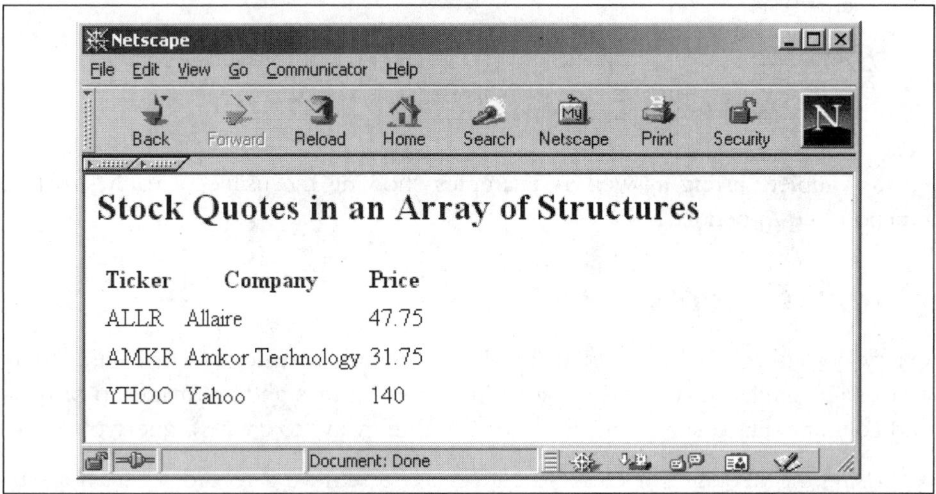


*Figure 6-5. Outputting stock information from an array of structures*

## *Manipulating Structures*

A number of functions are available in ColdFusion to manipulate structures. We've already seen the `StructInsert()`, `StructFind()`, `StructKeyList()`, and `StructKeyArray()` functions. There are a few others worth mentioning here.

Use the `StructClear()` function to remove all data from a structure named `Stock`:

```
<CFSET StructClear(Stock)>
```

To delete a specific key named `Price` (and its associated value) from a structure named `Stock`, use `StructDelete()`:

```
<CFSET StructDelete(Stock, "price")>
```

You can obtain a count of the number of key/value pairs in a structure using the `StructCount()` function:

```
<CFSET TheCount = StructCount(Stock)>
```

If you want to determine whether a given structure contains data, use `StructIsEmpty()`:

```
<CFIF StructIsEmpty(Stock)>
  The Stock structure doesn't contain any data.
<CFELSE>
  The Stock structure contains data
</CFIF>
```

You can determine whether a particular key exists within a structure using the `StructKeyExists()` function:

```
<CFIF StructKeyExists(Stock, Price)>
  <CFOUTPUT>
  The price is #Price#
  </CFOUTPUT>
<CFELSE>
  There is no price for this stock.
</CFIF>
```

For a complete listing as well as examples showing the usage of each structure function, see Appendix B.

# *Query Objects*

Query objects are special ColdFusion data structures that hold record sets. Query objects are similar in structure to two-dimensional arrays and are made up of rows and columns (like a spreadsheet). There are three ways to create a query object:

- Using the `CFQUERY` or `CFSTOREDPROC` tag to retrieve a record set from a data source. We haven't covered the `CFSTOREDPROC` tag yet; we'll get to it in Chapter 11. For now, just be aware that the tag can return a record set just like the `CFQUERY` tag.
- Certain CFML tags such as `CFFTP` and `CFHTTP` return information stored in a query object.
- Query objects can be manually created using `QueryNew()` and other associated query manipulation functions.

By this point, you should be quite familiar with the first method in which query objects are automatically returned by the `CFQUERY` tag. The second method has to do with certain CFML tags returning information stored as query objects. These tags are covered in detail later in the book. We're going to focus on the third method in this section, creating and manipulating query objects using

`QueryNew()` and several other CFML functions. Creating a query in this way is useful when you want to make application-generated data available as a query object. This technique is especially useful when used within custom tags to return a query result set. Custom tags are covered in Chapter 19. The query manipulation functions can also add additional data to an existing query.

To create a query object, you use the `QueryNew()` function. `QueryNew()` takes a single argument—a comma-delimited list of column names for the query object. If you want to create a query object called **`Products`** with column headers for the product name, color, price, and quantity on hand you can use the following code:

```
<CFSET Products = QueryNew(ProductName, Color, Price, Qty)>
```

Once you have created a query object, the next step is to populate it with data. This is done using various query-manipulation functions. Example 6-10 shows how to use the most popular query manipulation functions to manually create a query object, populate it with data, and output the contents to the browser.

*Example 6-10. Manually Creating a Query Object and Outputting to the Browser*

```
<!--- create a new query object called Products and add four column
      headers --->
<CFSET Products = QueryNew("ProductName, Color, Price, Qty")>

<!--- add three blank rows of data --->
<CFSET NewRows  = QueryAddRow(Products, 3)>

<!--- populate each blank row with data for each column --->
<CFSET temp = QuerySetCell(Products, "ProductName", "Widget", 1)>
<CFSET temp = QuerySetCell(Products, "Color", "Silver", 1)>
<CFSET temp = QuerySetCell(Products, "Price", "19.99", 1)>
<CFSET temp = QuerySetCell(Products, "Qty", "46", 1)>

<CFSET temp = QuerySetCell(Products, "ProductName", "Thingy", 2)>
<CFSET temp = QuerySetCell(Products, "Color", "Red", 2)>
<CFSET temp = QuerySetCell(Products, "Price", "34.99", 2)>
<CFSET temp = QuerySetCell(Products, "Qty", "12", 2)>

<CFSET temp = QuerySetCell(Products, "ProductName", "Sprocket", 3)>
<CFSET temp = QuerySetCell(Products, "Color", "Blue", 3)>
<CFSET temp = QuerySetCell(Products, "Price", "1.50", 3)>
<CFSET temp = QuerySetCell(Products, "Qty", "460", 3)>

<!--- create a one-dimensional array called ShippingArray to hold shipping
      prices to be appended to the query object --->
<CFSET ShippingArray = ArrayNew(1)>
<CFSET ShippingArray[1] = "1.99">
<CFSET ShippingArray[2] = "3.48">
<CFSET ShippingArray[3] = "5.00">

<!--- create a new column called Shipping and populate it with the data from
      the ShippingArray array --->
```

*Example 6-10. Manually Creating a Query Object and Outputting to the Browser (continued)*

```
<CFSET MyNewColumn = QueryAddColumn(Products, "Shipping", ShippingArray)>

<!--- create a table and output the contents of the query object --->
<TABLE>
<TR>
  <TH>Product</TH>
  <TH>Color</TH>
  <TH>Price</TH>
  <TH>Quantity</TH>
  <TH>Shipping</TH>
</TR>
<CFOUTPUT QUERY="Products">
<TR>
  <TD>#ProductName#</TD>
  <TD>#Color#</TD>
  <TD>#Price#</TD>
  <TD>#Qty#</TD>
  <TD>#DollarFormat(Shipping)#</TD>
</TR>
</CFOUTPUT>
</TABLE>
```

In this example, the `QueryNew()` function is used to create an empty query object named `Products` and gives it four column headers, `ProductName`, `Color`, `Price`, and `Qty`. Three empty rows are then added to the query object using `QueryAddRow()`, which takes the name of a query and an optional number of rows. If the number is omitted, one blank row is added.

Next, each row is populated with data using the `QuerySetCell()` function to populate each individual cell in the given row with data. This function takes the name of a query, a column name, a value, and an optional row number. The cell specified by the column name and row number is set to the given value. If no row number is specified, the last row in the query is used.

After this, a one-dimensional array called `ShippingArray` is created and populated with three prices. The `QueryAddColumn()` function is used to create a new column called `Shipping` and populate it with the contents of the `ShippingArray` array.

Finally, the `CFOUTPUT` tag is used to output the contents of the query object in a nicely formatted HTML table. You can see the results of the outputted query in Figure 6-6.

For more information on all of ColdFusion's query-manipulation functions, including the ones shown here, see Appendix B.

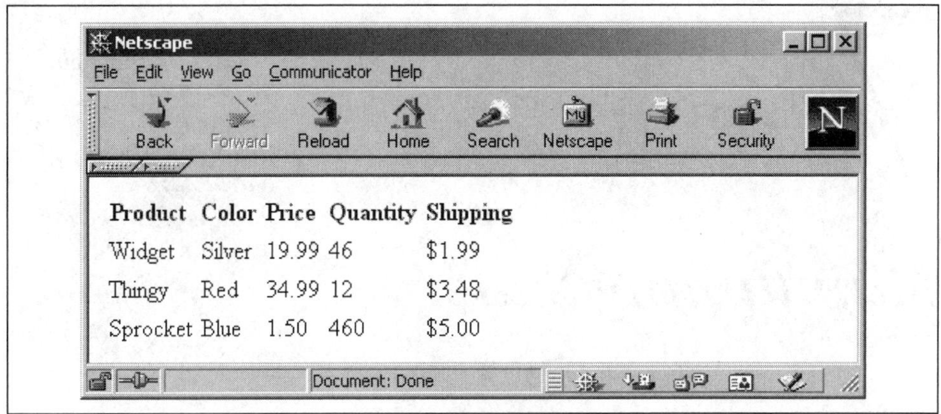


*Figure 6-6. Outputting the contents of a manually created query*

# 7

*In this chapter:*
- *Setting Up the Web Application Framework*
- *Using Persistent Variables*
- *Browser Redirection*
- *Portal Example*

# Maintaining State

By design, the Web is a stateless environment. This means that each request from a web browser to a web server is independent of every other request. While this might make for efficient use of bandwidth, it is the bane of web developers who must be able to keep track of users as they navigate their way through an application. Without the ability to maintain state, applications have no way of knowing what information belongs to which user. To borrow from the metaphor, this means that a shopping cart can't remember what items it contains, let alone which user is pushing the cart!

ColdFusion handles the stateless nature of the Web via a mechanism known as the Web Application Framework. The Web Application Framework enables you to build and manage virtually any type of application from a simple employee directory to amazingly complex business-to-business systems and everything in between. Specifically, the Web Application Framework was devised as a means for maintaining state, setting application constants, handling errors, and managing security.

In this chapter, we'll discuss the state maintenance features of the Web Application Framework. Chapter 8 covers the security features, and Chapter 9 explores exception and error handling.

## Setting Up the Web Application Framework

The first question you might be asking is "Why do I need an application framework in the first place"? The answer is simple: the Web Application Framework allows you to logically group your CFML templates into a cohesive application or group of applications capable of maintaining state, utilizing constants, handling errors and exceptions, and enforcing security. Sound complicated? It really isn't. As usual, ColdFusion abstracts the high level programming that would normally be required to accomplish all of the tasks I just mentioned by providing two templates that serve as the foundation for the Web Application Framework. These templates, named *Application.cfm* and *OnRequestEnd.cfm*, are responsible for setting up and controlling every aspect of the Web Application Framework.

## *The Application.cfm File*

In order to use the Web Application Framework, you have to create a template named *Application.cfm*, a special filename reserved by ColdFusion for use in the Web Application Framework. The *Application.cfm* template should be placed in the root directory of your ColdFusion application. Note that the filename is spelled with a capital "A". This is especially important if you are running ColdFusion for Unix or Linux, where filenames are case-sensitive.

When a CFML template is requested, ColdFusion checks to see if there is an *Application.cfm* file in the same directory as the requested template. If so, the application template is included at the beginning of the requested template. In other words, if ColdFusion finds an *Application.cfm* file, it essentially uses `CFINCLUDE` at the beginning of the page request to include this file. If no *Application.cfm* file is found, ColdFusion traverses up the directory tree looking for an *Application.cfm* file until it finds one.

This system allows you to specify a single *Application.cfm* file for all your ColdFusion code regardless of where it resides in your application's directory structure, as shown in Figure 7-1.

It also means that you can use different *Application.cfm* files to control different segments of your application within the directory structure, as shown in Figure 7-2, because ColdFusion uses the first *Application.cfm* file it finds. Regardless of where you place your *Application.cfm* file or how many you have in your application's directory structure, only one *Application.cfm* file is processed per page request. Thus, if your application template includes additional templates with `CFINCLUDE`, ColdFusion still performs just one search for an *Application.cfm* file as part of the initial request; it doesn't search for additional *Application.cfm* files for each included file.

*Figure 7-1. A single Application.cfm file placed in the application's root directory*

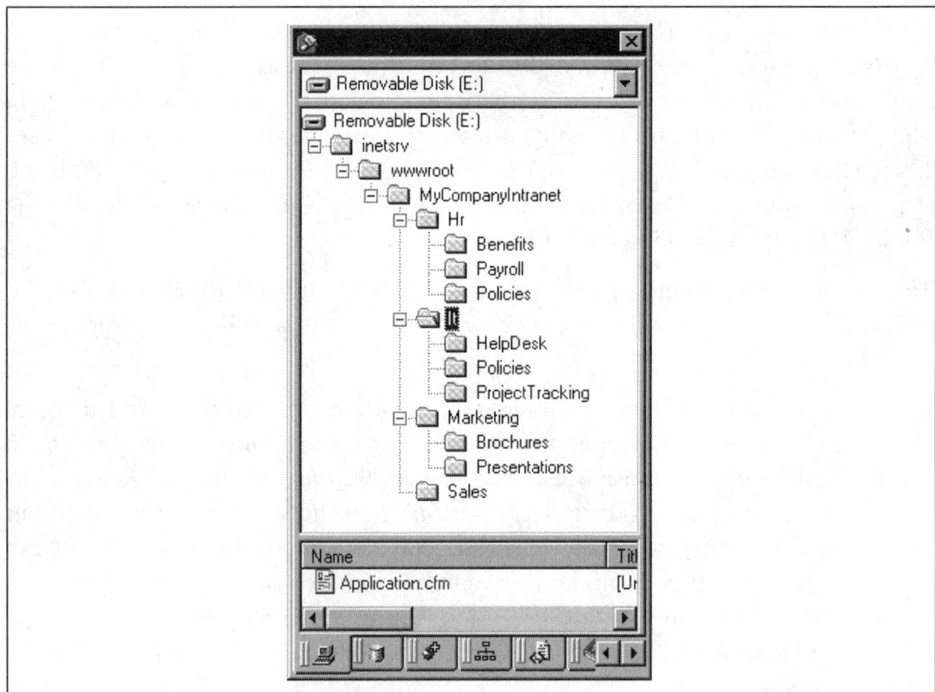


*Figure 7-2. Each directory has its own Application.cfm file*

Now that you understand how to create an *Application.cfm* file and where to save it, let's look at what it consists of. As I mentioned earlier, the *Application.cfm* template is used for a number of tasks within the Web Application Framework including:

- Maintaining state by providing a means for creating application, client, and session variables
- Setting application constants, such as data-source names, source directories, and style elements
- Handling errors that occur within your application
- Providing security services such as user authentication and entitlements

At the most basic level, every *Application.cfm* template must contain a `CFAPPLICATION` tag. The `CFAPPLICATION` tag names the application as well as sets state management options. Here's the syntax for the `CFAPPLICATION` tag:

```
<CFAPPLICATION NAME="application_name"
        CLIENTMANAGEMENT="Yes|No"
        CLIENTSTORAGE="client_storage_type"
        SESSIONMANAGEMENT="Yes|No"
        SESSIONTIMEOUT="#CreateTimeSpan(days, hours, minutes, seconds)#"
        APPLICATIONTIMEOUT="#CreateTimeSpan(days, hours, minutes, seconds)#"
        SETCLIENTCOOKIES="Yes|No"
        SETDOMAINCOOKIES="Yes|No">
```

The `NAME` attribute is the only required attribute. As you might expect, it specifies the name of the ColdFusion application. We'll be discussing the rest of the attributes of the `CFAPPLICATION` tag in more detail as we proceed through this chapter. Example 7-1 shows what a typical *Application.cfm* file looks like.

*Example 7-1. A Typical Application.cfm File*

```
<!--- suppress extraneous whitespace.  Note that the CFSETTING tag must be
      paired --->
<CFSETTING ENABLECFOUTPUTONLY="Yes">

<!--- set the app name, turn on session management, enable cookies, and set
      application and session variable timeouts of 30 minutes each --->
<CFAPPLICATION NAME="MyApplication" SESSIONMANAGEMENT="Yes" SETCLIENTCOOKIES="Yes"
     SESSIONTIMEOUT="#CREATETIMESPAN(0, 0, 30, 0)#"
     APPLICATIONTIMEOUT="#CREATETIMESPAN(0, 0, 30, 0)#">

<!--- check to see if the application has been initialized.  If not, set the
      necessary application variables and initialize the app --->
<CFLOCK TIMEOUT="30" THROWONTIMEOUT="No" TYPE="Exclusive" SCOPE="Application">
<CFIF NOT IsDefined('Application.Initialized')>
  <CFSET Application.TheDatasource = "MyDatasource">
  <CFSET Application.AdminEmail = "webmaster@mydomain.com">
  <CFSET Application.UploadDirectory = "D:\uploads\">
  <!--- Set the application.initialized variable to true so that this block
        of code does not execute every time the Application.cfm file is
        called --->
```

*Example 7-1. A Typical Application.cfm File (continued)*

```
  <CFSET Application.Initialized = TRUE>
</CFIF>
</CFLOCK>
<!--- this is the end tag for the first CFSETTING tag --->
<CFSETTING ENABLECFOUTPUTONLY="No">
```

## The OnRequestEnd.cfm File

The *OnRequestEnd.cfm* template is executed after every template request. The main purpose for this template is to allow you to include a common footer at the bottom of each requested page.

The *OnRequestEnd.cfm* template must be located in the same directory as the *Application.cfm* file used by ColdFusion. You may not have an *OnRequestEnd.cfm* template without a corresponding *Application.cfm*. It is also important to note that the "O," "R," and "E" in the filename must be capitalized. This is especially true on Linux- and Unix-based ColdFusion servers where filenames are case-sensitive. If a ColdFusion template throws an error during execution, the *OnRequestEnd.cfm* template doesn't execute. Likewise, if a `CFABORT` or `CFEXIT` tag is encountered in the calling template, the *OnRequestEnd.cfm* template isn't executed.

# Using Persistent Variables

As I mentioned in the introduction, the Web is a stateless environment. ColdFusion addresses this problem by providing five variable scopes you can use to maintain state within your application: application, client, cookie, session, and server. These are known as persistent variable scopes because the variables you set within them persist from template to template, in spite of the stateless nature of the Web. This allows you to build applications that can share data across multiple templates without having to pass the values via form fields or URL variables.

Here's an overview of the types of persistent variables you can use in your ColdFusion applications:

*Application*

Application variables define application-wide settings for your application, such as data-source names and other constants. Application variables are stored in the server's RAM and are most often defined in the *Application.cfm* template. Application variables are available to all users accessing the named application and are often referred to as global variables. Application variables must always be referenced using the `Application` prefix, as in `Application.`*`variable_name`*. By default, a single predefined application variable is available:

```
Application.ApplicationName
```

`Application.ApplicationName` returns the name of the application as defined in the `NAME` attribute of the `CFAPPLICATION` tag.

*Client*

Client variables store values associated with a particular user across multiple sessions. An application might use a client variable to remember things such as the last time a user visited a site, or their font size/color preferences. By default, client variables are stored in the system registry, but they can also be stored in a cookie or a database. When creating client variables, the variable name must always be referenced using the `Client` prefix, as in `Client.`*`variable_name`*. This is optional when writing client variables. In addition to the client variables you create in an application, there are several read-only client variables that ColdFusion creates automatically:

```
Client.CFID
Client.CFToken
Client.HitCount
Client.LastVisit
Client.TimeCreated
Client.URLToken
```

*Cookie*

Cookie variables hold the values of HTTP cookies retrieved from a user's web browser. Cookies are a unique type of persistent variable that are stored on the client machine and sent to the ColdFusion server each time a page is requested. By default, ColdFusion uses cookies to store the `CFID` and `CFToken` values associated with client and session variable management. Additional uses for cookies typically include storing a unique identifier (such as a user ID or UUID) for a particular user that is used by each page request to determine what content to deliver to the user.

*Session*

Session variables are persistent variables that store information for a specific user session. Session variables are held in the server's memory and persist for a finite amount of time (as specified in the *Application.cfm* template or in the ColdFusion Administrator). Each session is unique to a user and can be referenced across all ColdFusion templates in a given application. Session variables are often used for things like shopping carts and user authentication systems. Session variables must be specifically set and must be referenced as `Session.`*`variable_name`*. By default, the following predefined session variables are available:

```
Session.CFID
Session.CFToken
Session.SessionID
Session.URLToken
```

*Server*

Server variables, as their name implies, store data associated with the server on which ColdFusion is running. Server variables are stored in the server's RAM and are available to all ColdFusion applications and users. Additionally, server variables persist until the ColdFusion Application Server is stopped. Server variables are often used in multiplatform ColdFusion applications where the application behaves differently depending on what platform the code is running on. You can create your own server variables using `CFSET` or `CFPARAM`, or reference the following predefined ones:

```
Server.ColdFusion.ProductName
Server.ColdFusion.ProductVersion
Server.ColdFusion.ProductLevel
Server.ColdFusion.SerialNumber
Server.ColdFusion.SupportedLocales
Server.ColdFusion.Expiration (Version 5.0 only)
Server.OS.Name
Server.OS.AdditionalInformation
Server.OS.Version
Server.OS.BuildNumber
```

Server variables must always be referenced using the `Server` prefix as in `Server.`*`variable_name`*. Because server variables persist until the ColdFusion server is stopped, you should try to limit the number of server variables you create as the memory consumption required may negatively affect performance.

## Locking

Before we can discuss the details of the different kinds of persistent variables in ColdFusion, we need to spend a little time talking about a concept known as locking. Because ColdFusion is a multithreaded application server, it is possible for multiple threads to attempt to access the same variable at the same time. For application, session, and server variables, this is a problem. Because each of these persistent variable types is stored in the ColdFusion server's RAM, the potential exists for the memory to become corrupted as multiple threads attempt to access (read or write) the same variable concurrently and end up colliding. When a collision occurs, all sorts of problems can result. I've heard of everything from users receiving other users' data, to server instability, to crashing the ColdFusion application server. Because memory space is involved, the results of a collision are, at best, unpredictable.

Fortunately, ColdFusion has a mechanism for preventing collisions; it's known as *locking*. When I talk about locking, what I'm really referring to is ColdFusion's ability to manage concurrent access to specific variables or chunks of code. Locking can be broken down into two types, exclusive and read-only. *Exclusive locking* means that ColdFusion single-threads access to a particular variable or chunk of code; only one thread at a time is allowed to access code that has been exclusively locked. Any other threads that attempt to access an exclusively locked block of code are queued until the initial request completes. Exclusive locks must be used (notice I say must, and not should) when writing to application, session, and server variables. They should also be used when writing to nonthread-safe objects or when using file-manipulation tags such as `CFFILE`, `CFINDEX` and `CFCOLLECTION`. Because exclusive locks single-thread concurrent requests, they have a negative impact on performance. For this reason, it is important to use them sparingly.

The other type of lock you can use is a *read-only lock*. When you place a read-only lock around a particular piece of code, ColdFusion doesn't automatically single-thread access to that code. What it does do is prevent an exclusive lock from being placed on the code while it is being read from. In other words, if you have a read-only lock placed around a chunk of code that reads a shared persistent variable, multiple threads can read the variable's value, but a concurrent request to write to the variable isn't processed until the read operations complete. Conversely, if an exclusive lock is already in effect, a read-only lock waits until the exclusive lock is released before proceeding. Because of this, read-only locks don't generally result in degraded performance. Read-only locks should be used any time you read data from a shared persistent variable or perform a file-based operation in which the potential exists for concurrent write access by another thread.

Now that you understand the why of locking, let's discuss the how. ColdFusion allows you to deal with locking in two complimentary ways, via the ColdFusion Administrator (as of ColdFusion 4.5) and using a tag introduced in ColdFusion 4.0 called `CFLOCK`.

It is possible to control certain aspects of how ColdFusion handles locking from within the ColdFusion Administrator. As of ColdFusion 4.5, locking options are available via the ColdFusion Administrator under the Server section, as shown in Figure 7-3. These options allow you to determine how ColdFusion treats locking for all applications across the server. Performance can be significantly affected depending on the options you choose. The following choices are available:

*Single Threaded Sessions (session scope)*
: ColdFusion single-threads access to each session by session ID for the duration of a request. This means that only one request can be processed at a time, defeating the whole reason for having a multithreaded application server. While this eliminates all potential for variable corruption and conflict within a session, it can have a dramatically negative effect on performance as a single, long running request can tie up processing of all additional requests in the queue.

*No Automatic Checking or Locking (session, application, and server scopes)*
: ColdFusion performs no automatic checking or locking of persistent variables. All variables must be locked explicitly using the `CFLOCK` tag. No exceptions are thrown when nonlocked variables are encountered. This method is how ColdFusion handled locking prior to Version 4.5. This option offers the best overall performance and should be used within a production environment.

*Full Checking (session, application, and server scopes)*
: ColdFusion checks to make sure locks are placed around all reads and writes of the variable type specified. If an unlocked variable is encountered, an exception is thrown. This option should be used only in debug mode and is useful for locating unlocked persistent variables, but it should be used with care as it can have a negative impact on performance.

*Automatic Read Checking (session, application, and server scopes)*
: If this option is checked, ColdFusion automatically locks reading of the variable scope specified. All writes to the variable scope must be explicitly locked using `CFLOCK`. If a write occurs to an unlocked variable, an exception is thrown. This option should also be used with careful planning as it can have a negative impact on performance.

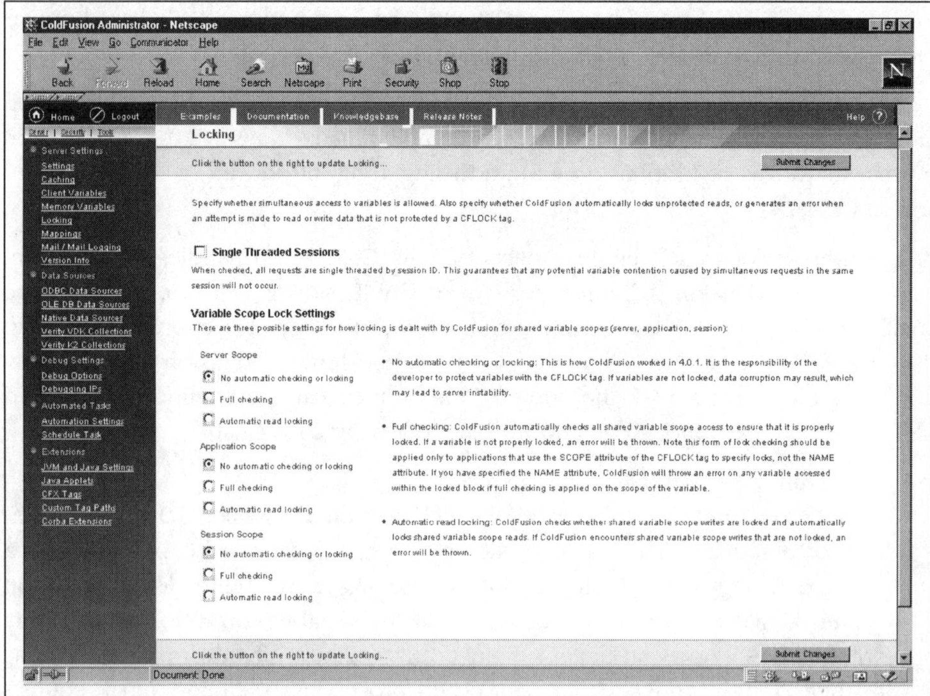


*Figure 7-3. ColdFusion Administrator page for managing variable locking*

Ideally, Full Checking and Single Threaded Sessions should be used only within a development or test environment to help you debug your application. In order to squeeze every bit of performance out of your production applications, it is advisable to enable No Automatic Checking or Locking and leave the variable locking up to your application as opposed to the ColdFusion server.

The `CFLOCK` tag provides a programmatic means for protecting access to shared persistent variables as well as other blocks of code. `CFLOCK` should be used when reading and writing application, session, and server variables within your ColdFusion applications. This must be done in order to eliminate the potential for data corruption and server instability caused by colliding read/writes of variables stored in the ColdFusion server's RAM. `CFLOCK` can also be used to lock access to non-thread-safe objects (such as CFX tags, covered in Chapter 19, and COM objects, covered in Chapter 23) and to file-manipulation operations (`CFFILE`, `CFDIRECTORY`, `CFCOLLECTION`, and `CFINDEX`) that could result in multiple threads attempting to access an already open file.

The `CFLOCK` tag uses different attribute combinations depending on the context it is used in and what version of ColdFusion is running on the server. The tag usage and syntax can be divided into three categories based on these combinations: locking shared persistent variables in ColdFusion 4.5 and beyond, locking shared persistent variables in ColdFusion 4.0/4.01, and locking access to blocks of code (such as file and object access) regardless of what version of ColdFusion you are running.

### *Locking shared persistent variables as of ColdFusion 4.5*

The most common use for the `CFLOCK` tag is for locking access to shared persistent scope variables (application, session, and server variables). As we already discussed, you need to lock access to all reads and writes of these types of variables. The following example demonstrates the correct way to lock application, session, or server variables as of Version 4.5:

```
<CFLOCK SCOPE="Session" TYPE="Exclusive" TIMEOUT="30" THROWONTIMEOUT="Yes">
  <CFSET Session.Username="pmoney">
  <CFSET Session.AccessLevel=5>
</CFLOCK>

<CFLOCK SCOPE="Session" TYPE="ReadOnly" TIMEOUT="30" THROWONTIMEOUT="Yes">
  <CFOUTPUT>
  Username: #Session.Username#<BR>
  Access Level: #Session.AccessLevel#
  </CFOUTPUT>
</CFLOCK>
```

The first thing you'll notice is that the example uses two sets of `CFLOCK` tags. We'll get to the reason for this in just a moment. For now, look at the first `CFLOCK` tag used. The `SCOPE` attribute references the scope of the variable you are attempting to lock access to. Possible values are `Application`, `Server`, and `Session`. In this case, we are locking access to a session variable, so we set `SCOPE` to `Session`. If you have used the `CFLOCK` tag prior to ColdFusion 4.5, you'll notice that the `SCOPE` attribute is used in place of the `NAME` attribute. While you may still use the `NAME` attribute for locking shared persistent variables in ColdFusion 4.5 (we'll talk about the `NAME` attribute in a few minutes), using the `SCOPE` attribute is the preferred method. You can't use both the `NAME` and `SCOPE` attributes in the same `CFLOCK` tag; doing so results in an error.

The next attribute, `TYPE`, specifies the type of lock to employ. Possible entries are `ReadOnly` or `Exclusive`. `ReadOnly` allows more than one read request to access the block of code within the `CFLOCK` tag at a time. This option should be used when reading application, session, and server variables. This is the faster of the two options. `Exclusive` allows only one request to access the block of code within the `CFLOCK` tag at a time. This option should be used when writing data to persistent variables, as the case with the second `CFLOCK` tag in our example.

The `TIMEOUT` attribute specifies the time in seconds that ColdFusion should wait when attempting to obtain an exclusive lock before timing out. It is a required attribute. `THROWONTIMEOUT` indicates how ColdFusion should behave in the event that a `CFLOCK` requests time out. If set to `Yes` and a time-out occurs, ColdFusion throws an error that can be caught with `CFTRY`/`CFCATCH` (which are discussed in more detail in Chapter 9). If `No`, the template continues execution after skipping the code within the `CFLOCK` tag. The `THROWONTIMEOUT` attribute is optional and defaults to `Yes`.

#### *Locking shared persistent variables in ColdFusion 4.0/4.01*

As I mentioned in the previous section, the `SCOPE` attribute was introduced in ColdFusion 4.5 to replace the `NAME` attribute when locking access to application, client, and server variables. If you are still developing applications for ColdFusion 4.0/4.01, you need to use the `NAME` attribute to lock access to application, session, and server variables. In order to ensure synchronization across sessions and applications using locks, `Session.SessionID` and `Application.ApplicationName` should be used for the `NAME` attribute when locking access to session and application variables, respectively. For server variable locks, you should be sure to use the same name for all locks in all templates on the server. If no `NAME` is specified, ColdFusion assigns a random name to the lock. You should note that as of ColdFusion 4.5, the `NAME` attribute works only if the No Automatic Checking or Locking option is set in the ColdFusion Administrator's Locking section for the variable scope you are attempting to lock. So, to code our previous example for older versions of ColdFusion, use the following:

```
<CFLOCK NAME="#Session.SessionID#" TYPE="Exclusive" TIMEOUT="30"
        THROWONTIMEOUT="Yes">
  <CFSET Session.Username="pmoney">
  <CFSET Session.AccessLevel=5>
</CFLOCK>

<CFLOCK NAME="#Session.SessionID#" TYPE="ReadOnly" TIMEOUT="30"
        THROWONTIMEOUT="Yes">
  <CFOUTPUT>
  Username: #Session.Username#<BR>
  Access Level: #Session.AccessLevel#
  </CFOUTPUT>
</CFLOCK>
```

Notice that the `NAME` attribute is used in place of the `SCOPE` attribute and that the name is set to the value of the automatically set session variable, `Session.SessionID`. Other than this change, the code remains the same.

### *Locking access to nonthread-safe objects and file operations*

Besides locking access to shared persistent variables, the `CFLOCK` tag can also be used to lock access to nonthread-safe objects and file-manipulation operations such as `CFFILE`, `CFCOLLECTION`, and `CFINDEX`. In each of these instances, the `NAME` attribute should specify a name for the lock. All locks for code accessing the same object or file should have the same name in order to be effective. Failure to use the same lock name opens the possibility for data corruption as locks to the same variable, object, or file without the same name aren't able to synchronize.

In the case of nonthread-safe objects, locking is important to guard against potential data corruption resulting from concurrent access. Since these objects aren't designed to handle concurrent access from multiple threads, all access to them should be exclusively locked. For example, to lock access to a nonthread-safe CFX tag called `CFX_MyTag`, use the following code:

```
<CFLOCK NAME="CFX_MyTag_Lock" TYPE="Exclusive" TIMEOUT="10" THROWONTIMEOUT="Yes">
  <CFX_MyTag SomeAttribute="Some value">
</CFLOCK>
```

File-manipulation operations should be locked to prevent multiple threads from concurrently trying to write to the same file because of the possibility of data corruption. If there is a possibility that a particular file can be written to by multiple threads concurrently, you need to place read locks around all code that reads the file and exclusive locks on all operations that write to the file. You should be sure to keep lock naming (both read-only and exclusive) consistent across your applications. The most common file-manipulation operations that require locking are `CFFILE`, `CFDIRECTORY`, `CFCOLLECTION`, and `CFINDEX`. Additionally, you may want to lock calls to `CFHTTP` and `CFFTP` depending on how you use these tags. Locking examples for each tag are given in the chapters dealing with the specific tags.

### *Additional locking considerations*

Now that we've talked about the basics of locking in ColdFusion, let's turn our attention to a few scenarios that developers inevitably run into. The first scenario involves a situation where you need to both read and write to a shared persistent variable in a block of code. Let's say we have a situation in which we need to evaluate whether or not an application variable called **Application. Initialized** exists. If the variable doesn't exist, two application variables are written to. For example:

```
<CFIF NOT IsDefined('Application.Initialized')>
  <CFSET Application.TheDatasource = "MyDatasource">
  <CFSET Application.DefaultDir = "c:\temp">
</CFIF>
```

Based on what we discussed earlier, it is obvious that you'll need to place a read-only lock on the code that evaluates **Application.Initialized** and an exclusive lock around the code that writes to the two other application variables. One way to do this is to place a single exclusive lock around the entire operation:

```
<CFLOCK SCOPE="Application" TYPE="Exclusive" TIMEOUT="30" THROWONTIMEOUT="No">
<CFIF NOT IsDefined('Application.Initialized')>
  <CFSET Application.TheDatasource = "MyDatasource">
  <CFSET Application.DefaultDir = "c:\temp">
</CFIF>
</CFLOCK>
```

Using an exclusive lock forces ColdFusion to single-thread access to this particular piece of code each time it is requested. Normally, you won't experience very much of a performance hit by single threading such a basic operation. However, in the case of a more complex operation, such as a long running query, you run a greater risk of queued requests timing out while waiting to obtain an exclusive lock. To get around this problem, you can use another technique that involves making a local copy of the shared persistent variable in the request scope, thus allowing you to avoid the excessive use of read locks:

```
<CFLOCK SCOPE="Application" TYPE="Readonly" TIMEOUT="30">
  <CFSET Request.Initialized = Application.Initialized>
</CFLOCK>

<CFIF NOT IsDefined(Request.Initialized')>
  <CFLOCK SCOPE="Application" TYPE="Exclusive" TIMEOUT="30">
    <CFSET Application.TheDatasource = "MyDatasource">
    <CFSET Application.DefaultDir = "c:\temp">
  </CFLOCK>
</CFIF>
```

Another situation where you can use this technique is with code that appears to need nested locks in order to lock differently scoped variables, such as:

```
<CFQUERY NAME="GetRecord" datasource="#Application.dsn#"
         USERNAME="#Application.dbusername#"
         PASSWORD="#Application.dbpassword#">
    SELECT * FROM MyTable WHERE Name = '#Session.Name#'
</CFQUERY>
```

As you can see, this example presents a bit of a challenge. Because the query uses both application and session variables, you can't place a single lock on the entire operation. The solution seems to call for nested locks, as follows:

```
<CFLOCK SCOPE="Session" TYPE="Readonly" TIMEOUT="10">
<CFLOCK SCOPE="Application" TYPE="Readonly" TIMEOUT="10">
  <CFQUERY NAME="GetRecord" datasource="#Application.dsn#"
 USERNAME="#Application.dbusername#"
 PASSWORD="#Application.dbpassword#">
    SELECT * FROM MyTable WHERE Name = '#Session.Name#'
  </CFQUERY>
</CFLOCK>
</CFLOCK>
```

While this solution does indeed work, it isn't recommended for a number of reasons. First, you really don't want to place a lock around an operation such as a query, as the time it takes to complete the query can be rather long compared to other typically locked operations such as variable reads and writes. Second, nesting locks can lead to a problem known as a *deadlock*, where no request can access a locked piece of code, resulting in a timeout. Deadlocks occur when you have inconsistencies in how nested locks are implemented. As a rule, it is recommended you always follow this sequence when nesting locks:

1. Lock the session scope
2. Lock the application scope
3. Lock the server scope

Strict adherence to these guidelines helps ensure you don't unintentionally create a potential deadlock in your application.

The preferred way to solve the problem from the previous example is to copy both the application and the session variables to the request scope, eliminating the need to place a lock around the query operation and eliminating the need for nested locks:

```
<CFLOCK TIMEOUT="30" THROWONTIMEOUT="No" TYPE="Readonly"
        SCOPE="Application">
  <CFSET Request.dsn = Application.dsn>
  <CFSET Request.dbUsername = Application.dbusername>
  <CFSET Request.dbPassword = Application.dbpassword>
</CFLOCK>

<CFLOCK TIMEOUT="30" THROWONTIMEOUT="No" TYPE="Readonly"
        SCOPE="Session">
```

```
    <CFSET Request.Name = Session.Name>
</CFLOCK>

<CFQUERY NAME="GetRecord" datasource="#Request.dsn#"
        USERNAME="#Request.dbusername#" PASSWORD="#Request.dbpassword#">
    SELECT * FROM MyTable WHERE Name = '#Request.Name#'
</CFQUERY>
```

There is one exception to these techniques you need to be aware of. If you want to copy a structure to a different variable scope such as the request scope, you can't do it using the **CFSET** tag alone. This is because structures aren't really copied to the new scope. Instead, a pointer is created in the new scope that points to the variable in the old scope. Because of this, any time you reference the variable in the new scope, you are actually referencing the original variable. This means you can't simply move a variable containing a structure to the request scope to avoid having to lock access to that variable.

In order to copy a structure without creating a pointer to it, you need to use the **Duplicate()** function. Consider a structure named **Grades** that is stored as a session variable. If you attempt to assign **Session.Grades** to the request scope using the **CFSET** tag, you end up with a pointer to the variable in the session scope:

```
<CFSET Request.Grades = Session.Grades>
```

Instead, to create a true copy of the **Grades** structure, you need to use the **Duplicate()** function:

```
<CFSET Request.Grades = Duplicate(Session.Grades)>
```

Copying a structure using the **Duplicate()** function ensures you have a true copy of the structure, not a pointer.

## Application Variables

You can think of application variables as global variables within a ColdFusion application because they are available to all templates within an application without regard to user sessions. Application variables typically define application-wide settings such as default directories and data-source names. Any ColdFusion datatype may be assigned to an application variable. Application variables are most often set in the *Application.cfm* file. Like session and server variables, application variables persist in the server's RAM and have a set timeout period. This timeout period can be set using the **APPLICATIONTIMEOUT** attribute of the **CFAPPLICATION** tag. The following example shows how to set application variables within the *Application.cfm* file:

```
<CFSETTING ENABLECFOUTPUTONLY="Yes">
<CFAPPLICATION NAME="MyApplication"
```

```
     APPLICATIONTIMEOUT="#CREATETIMESPAN(0, 2, 0, 0)#">
<CFLOCK SCOPE="Application" TYPE="Exclusive" TIMEOUT="60" THROWONTIMEOUT="No">
<CFIF NOT IsDefined('Application.Initialized')>
    <CFSET Application.TheDatasource = "MyDatasource">
    <CFSET Application.AdminEmail = "webmaster@mydomain.com">
    <CFSET Application.BGColor = "##FFFFCC">
    <!--- Set the application.initialized variable to true so that this block
of code does not execute every time the Application.cfm file is
called --->
    <CFSET Application.Initialized = TRUE>
</CFIF>
</CFLOCK>
<CFSETTING ENABLECFOUTPUTONLY="No">
```

In this example, the `CFSETTING` tag suppresses any whitespace that might be generated by the tags within the *Application.cfm* file. This is because ColdFusion has a tendency to generate unnecessary whitespace in the output returned to the browser, resulting in pages that take longer to download. Suppressing the whitespace results in smaller files that, in turn, translate into faster downloads. The `ENABLECFOUTPUTONLY` attribute is set to `Yes` to specify the beginning of the block of code that should allow only output from CFML tags. As we'll discuss in more detail in Chapter 11, the `CFSETTING` tag must always be used in pairs, so `ENABLECFOUTPUTONLY` is set to `No` at the end of the example to complete the tag pair. You should be aware that forgetting the closing `CFSETTING` tag results in no HTML output for any of your templates within the application controlled by the *Application.cfm* file. So if you see this kind of behavior, be sure that you've closed the `CFSETTING` tag.

The `CFAPPLICATION` tag simply sets the application name and a timeout for any application variables used in the application. In this case, we set the timeout for application variables to two hours. This is done using the `CreateTimeSpan()` function. `CreateTimeSpan()` allows us to specify a date/time object that can be added and subtracted from other date/time objects. The `CreateTimeSpan()` function creates the date/time object from a comma-delimited list of four values: *`days`*, *`hours`*, *`minutes`*, and *`seconds`*. The next block of code starts with a `CFIF` statement that checks to see if an application variable named `Application.Initialized` exists. If it does, the block of code is skipped. If the variable doesn't exist, the code within the `CFIF` tags is executed. You'll see the importance of this in just a second.

If `Application.Initialized` doesn't exist, four application variables are set using the `CFSET` tag. Before these variables can be set, however, write access must first be locked. This is accomplished using the `CFLOCK` tag. The `SCOPE` attribute is set to `Application` since we want to lock access while we set application variables. Because we are writing values to application variables, we set the `TYPE` attribute to `Exclusive`. This ensures that no one else can access these application variables while we assign them values. The `TIMEOUT` attribute is required and specifies the time in seconds that ColdFusion should wait when attempting to obtain an exclusive lock before timing out. Note that the `CFLOCK` tag is placed before the `CFIF` statement that checks to see if the `Application.Initialized` variable exists. Although we are reading this value, it is more efficient to use an exclusive lock around the entire block of code as opposed to trying to rewrite the code so that both a read-only and an exclusive lock can be used in the appropriate places.

The first application variable we set is called `Application.TheDatasource`; it contains the name of the data source used throughout the application. Setting the data-source name here allows us to insert the variable name into `CFQUERY` statements as opposed to the actual data-source name. This makes it easy to change the data source name at a later point. Instead of having to open every template within your application to change the hardcoded data-source name, all you have to do is open the *Application.cfm* file and change the name of the data source you assigned to the `Applicatrion.TheDatasource` variable.

The next two application variables, `Application.AdminEmail` and `Application.BGColor`, store an administrator's email address and a default background color for the web site. Again, the value here isn't in the one-to-one substitution but in the ability to change any of these values once and have the changes reflected across your application.

The final application variable we set, `Application.Initialized`, is used as a control variable to indicate whether the application variables within the *Application.cfm* file have already been set. Because the *Application.cfm* file is called with each request for a CFML template, it is important that we have a way to determine if application variables have already been set. Resetting the application variables every time the *Application.cfm* file is called is a waste of resources and processing time, as application variables need to be set only once within an application. The solution is to set an application variable called `Application.Initialized` to `True` the first time the *Application.cfm* file is called. Once this variable has been created, it is easy to check if it exists each time *Application.cfm* is executed. If the variable exists, there is no need to set the application variables. If the variable doesn't exist, we know that the application variables haven't been set yet and can execute the appropriate code to set them.

You should note that application variables shouldn't be used within a clustered environment, as they are stored in the RAM of a single ColdFusion server and may not be available to other servers within the cluster. The exception to this is in the case of session-aware or "sticky" clusters. We'll talk more about session-aware clusters later in the chapter.

Because application variables are stored in a structure object called `Application`, you can manipulate application variables using structure functions. For example, to delete an application variable (e.g., for debugging purposes) called `Application.Datasource`, you can use the `StructDelete()` function:

```
<CFLOCK SCOPE="Application" TYPE="Exclusive" TIMEOUT="60" THROWONTIMEOUT="No">
<CFSET StructDelete(Application,"Datasource")>
</CFLOCK>
```

## *Client Variables*

Client variables store values associated with a particular client or, to use the more common term, user. Most often, they are used to maintain state as a user navigates from page to page throughout an application. What makes client variables different from session variables is that they can persist across multiple sessions. That is, client variables are stored by the ColdFusion server and can be retrieved during subsequent visits by the user. By default, client variables are stored in the system registry, but they can also be stored in a cookie or a database. Client variables are commonly used to store things such as user preferences for highly personalized applications. These preferences often include background and text colors as well as font faces and sizes. Client variables can also be used in place of session variables in clustered environments where it is essential to maintain state in the event that a user is redirected from one server to another. In order to use client variables, you have to enable them using the `CFAPPLICATION` tag within your application's *Application.cfm* file:

```
<CFSETTING ENABLECFOUTPUTONLY="Yes">
  <CFAPPLICATION NAME="MyApplication" CLIENTMANAGEMENT="Yes"
       SETCLIENTCOOKIES="Yes" CLIENTSTORAGE="Registry">
<CFSETTING ENABLECFOUTPUTONLY="No">
```

In this example, there are four attributes for the `CFAPPLICATION` tag to consider. The `NAME` attribute specifies the name to associate with the application and all its persistent variables. The `CLIENTMANAGEMENT` attribute must be set to `Yes` in order to use client variables. `SETCLIENTCOOKIES` determines whether to save the `CFID` and `CFToken` values as HTTP cookies on the user's machine. If you set this attribute to `No`, you must be sure to manually pass the `CFID` and `CFToken` values from template to template. Techniques for doing this are described later in this section. The final attribute, `CLIENTSTORAGE`, determines which method to use for storing the client variables. Possible options include `Registry` (the default), `Database`, and `Cookie`. Each of these methods will be described in detail shortly.

Besides the client variables you create yourself, ColdFusion creates several client variables automatically:

`Client.CFID`
: An incremental ID number created by the ColdFusion Application Server for each client accessing the server.

`Client.CFToken`
: A random token that combines with the `CFID` to form a unique identifier for each client visiting your site. The range of possible values for `CFToken` is 1 to 2,147,483,647.

`Client.HitCount`
: An integer that represents the number of times a client has visited the web site.

`Client.LastVisit`
: The time and date of a client's last visit to the web site.

`Client.TimeCreated`
: The time and date that the `CFID` and `CFToken` were created.

`Client.URLToken`
: A concatenation of the `CFID` and `CFToken` values that can be appended to a URL when cookies aren't used for client variable storage.

By default, ColdFusion uses a random number for the value of `CFToken`. Although sufficient for most purposes, this method doesn't guarantee a unique `CFToken` value. It is possible to add a registry setting so that ColdFusion generates a guaranteed unique value for `CFToken`. This is done by adding the key `UuidToken (REG_SZ)` with a string value of "1" to the following registry branch:

```
HKEY_LOCAL_MACHINE\Software\Allaire\ColdFusion\CurrentVersion\Clients
```

Making this registry change causes ColdFusion to generate a `CFToken` consisting of a random number concatenated with a UUID. The random number makes it difficult to guess the next `CFToken` value. UUIDs alone are relatively easy to guess as they are assigned in a sequential order. To understand how this all looks, consider the following UUID generated by ColdFusion:

```
777A3190-6D65-11D4-BC6B00105A16C3AD
```

If the same UUID were used in generating a `CFToken` value, it might look something like this:

```
3cfcfd0-777a3190-6d65-11d4-bc6b-00105a16c3ad
```

For performance reasons, there is no structure object that contains a list of all available client variable names. However, you can obtain a list of all currently available client variables using the `GetClientVariablesList()` function:

```
<CFOUTPUT>
Client Variables available within this application: #GetClientVariablesList()#
</CFOUTPUT>
```

### *Client variable storage options*

ColdFusion offers three options for client variable storage: the system registry, browser cookies, or an external data source. These options must be set within the ColdFusion Administrator. Figure 7-4 shows the ColdFusion Administrator page for managing client variable storage options.

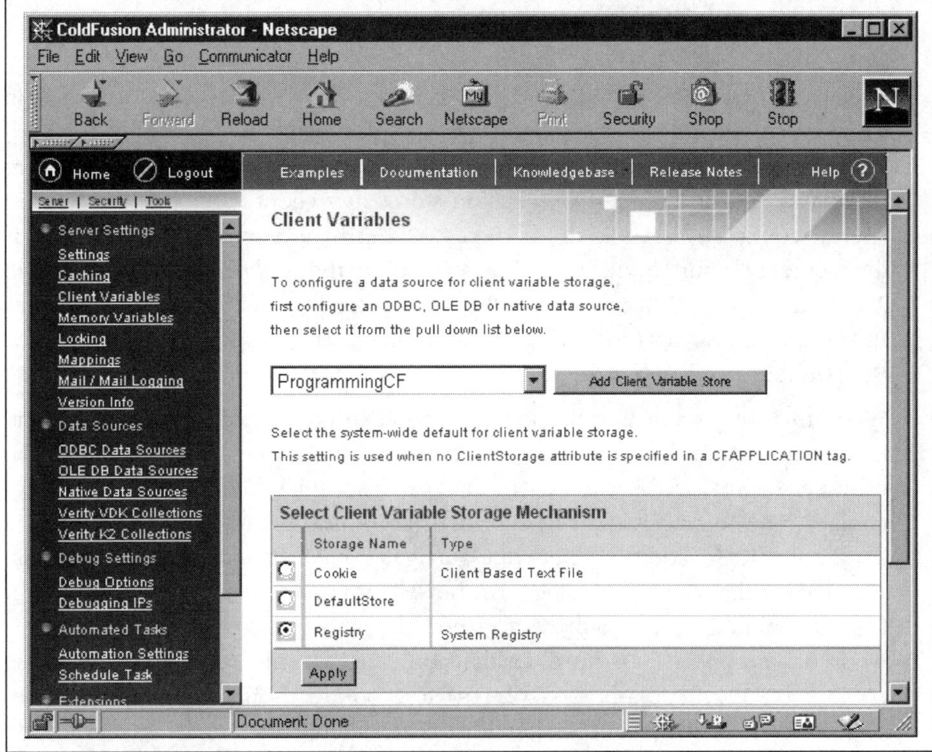


*Figure 7-4. Managing client variable storage options within the ColdFusion Administrator*

You can override the default client variable storage mechanism set in the ColdFusion Administrator by using the `CLIENTSTORAGE` attribute of the `CFAPPLICATION` tag to specify the method you wish to use. You should note that you can access client variables only for the storage method specified for a particular application, even if you have client variables stored in another storage type. To help you decide which client variable storage option is right for you, here are some pros and cons of each of the three storage methods:

*System registry (default)*
: Setting `CLIENTSTORAGE` to `Registry` stores all client variables in the system registry. This method is the easiest to implement and offers relatively good performance. However, size limitations of the system registry can affect scalability. In addition, client variables stored in the registry can't be used in a clustered environment. Client variables stored in the registry are automatically purged after 90 days of inactivity by the client. This 90-day period can be modified using the ColdFusion Administrator.

*Cookie*
: Specifying `Cookie` for `CLIENTSTORAGE` causes client variables to be stored in browser cookies. This storage mechanism places the responsibility for variable storage on the client as opposed to the server. If you choose to store client variables in cookies, ColdFusion stores any client variables you set in a special cookie. This cookie is named `CFCLIENT_`*`appname`* where *`appname`* is the name of your application as specified in the *Application.cfm* template. Additionally, ColdFusion stores the automatically created client variables `HitCount`, `LastVisited`, and `TimeCreated` in a special cookie called `CFGLOBALS`.

  While this may seem like the ideal situation from a performance standpoint, there are a number of potential problems with this storage method. First, you can't set client variables for users that can't accept or choose not to accept cookies. The second issue is that ColdFusion limits the amount of data set as a cookie to 4K. In addition, Netscape Navigator has a 20-cookie-per-host limit. This means that only 20 cookies can be set by your server at any one time. If the 20-cookie-limit is reached, any new cookies added automatically overwrite older cookies. Because ColdFusion automatically uses three of these cookies (`CFID`, `CFToken`, `CFGlobals`) to store read-only client information, only 17 cookies are available per host. The default timeout for cookies is 38 years.

*External data source*
: Setting `CLIENTSTORAGE` to `External` stores client variables in an external data source, which allows you to keep your client data in a platform-independent format. It also allows you to use client variables within a clustered environment. However, using an external data source to store client variables can negatively impact performance because each read or write of a client variable requires a database transaction. If you choose to use an external data source to store your client variables, ColdFusion can automatically create the necessary database tables for you. It is recommended that whatever data source you

use be dedicated to the storage and retrieval of client variables. The default timeout for client variables stored in an external database is 10 days. This timeout period can be modified using the ColdFusion Administrator.

### *Creating an external data source for client variable storage*

If you decide to use an external data source to store your client variables, you need to create the necessary database tables and register the data source with the ColdFusion Administrator. You may manually create the tables, or you can have ColdFusion create them for you. Regardless of which method you choose, the first step is to register the data source with the ColdFusion Administrator. To do this, you need to go to the ODBC Data Sources section of the ColdFusion Administrator and register the data source. The second step is to access the Client Variables section of the ColdFusion Administrator as shown in Figure 7-4. To add a new data source for storing client variables, highlight the data-source name in the drop-down box and click on the Add Client Variable Store button. You will then be presented with three options for configuring your data source. These choices can be seen in Figure 7-5.

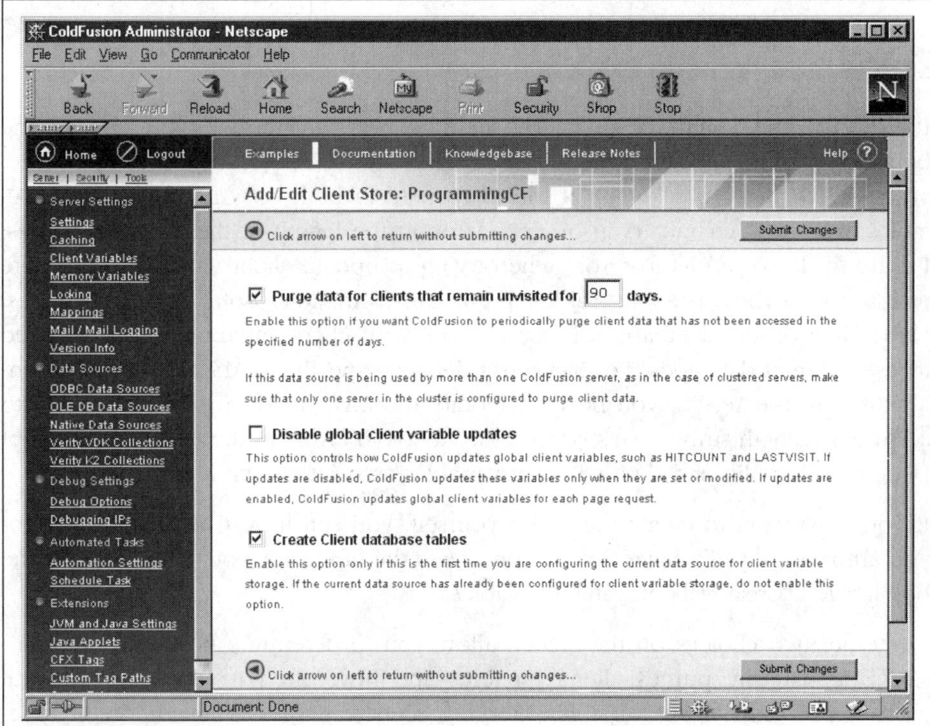


*Figure 7-5. Configuring an external data source to store client variables*

At this time, you need to decide whether you want to manually create the database tables necessary to store client variables or to let ColdFusion create the tables for you. The preferred method is to let ColdFusion create the tables for you. However, depending on your database platform or the level of database access you are allowed to the database, it may be necessary to manually create the necessary tables. If you choose to manually create the tables, you need to create two tables, as shown in Tables 7-1 and 7-2.

*Table 7-1. CDATA*

| Field Name | Datatype | Max Length |
|---|---|---|
| `CFID` | `Text` | 20 |
| `APP` | `Text` | 64 |
| `DATA` | `Memo` | N/A |

*Table 7-2. CGLOBAL*

| Field Name | Datatype | Max Length |
|---|---|---|
| `CFID` | `Text` | 20 |
| `DATA` | `Memo` | N/A |
| `LVISIT` | `Date` | N/A |

By default, the length of the `CFID` field is 20 characters. If you change the behavior of the ColdFusion to use a concatenated UUID as the `CFToken` value, you need to make the length of the `CFID` field in both the `CDATA` and `CGLOBAL` tables at least 50 characters in order to support the length of the `CFToken` values. Failure to do so results in errors when trying to update client variables. Also note that the datatypes listed in Tables 7-1 and 7-2 are Microsoft Access datatypes. Depending on the database you use to store your client variables, you may need to use different datatypes (i.e., `Memo` is a datatype specific to MS Access). Additionally, if you use Access, you need to modify the `DATA` field in the `CDATA` table to allow zero length strings. This is necessary to avoid errors in the event you attempt to delete all application defined client variables associated with a particular user.

If you don't want to create the tables yourself, you can have ColdFusion do it for you automatically. To have ColdFusion create the tables for you, simply check the box labeled "Create Client Database Tables".

The other two choices on the screen allow you to determine how often ColdFusion automatically purges client variables and how often it should update the global (read-only) client variables. Purging client variables is an important function for two reasons. First, it keeps your database from accumulating unnecessary and irrelevant data. The second reason is that you usually want to expire data associated with a particular client after some predetermined period of inactivity.

For example, say you run a public web site that allows users to customize certain aspects of the site to their own liking. If you use client variables to keep track of these preferences, you probably want to delete the preferences of visitors that haven't visited your site for a predetermined amount of time. You can specify the amount of time in days before ColdFusion purges inactive client variables by checking the box labeled "Purge data for clients that remain unvisited for x days" and specifying the number of days in the text box.

The "Disable Global Client Variable Updates" option allows you to indicate whether ColdFusion should update global client variables such as `HitCount`, `LastVisited`, and `TimeCreated` each time a ColdFusion template is requested or only when the variables are set or updated. If the box is checked (the default), global client variables are updated only when they are set or updated, not with each page request.

### *Using client variables without cookies*

By default, the `CFID` and `CFToken` variables for each user are stored as cookies on the user's hard drive. In order to make your application work with users who can't or don't accept cookies, you must pass the `CFID` and `CFToken` values via URL to each template within your application. To pass `CFID` and `CFToken` from template to template, all you need to do is append the `URLToken` variable to each URL that you use in your application. For example, to pass the `CFID` and `CFToken` along in a form, you can use the following code:

```
<CFOUTPUT>
<FORM NAME="MyForm" ACTION="MyTemplate.cfm?#Client.URLToken#" METHOD="Post">
</CFOUTPUT>
```

If you want to pass the `CFID` and `CFToken` using standard hyperlinks, the code looks like this:

```
<CFOUTPUT>
<A HREF="MyTemplate.cfm?#Client.URLToken#">MyTemplate</A>
</CFOUTPUT>
```

### *Storing complex datatypes in client variables*

Because client variables must be stored in a physical medium such as the system registry, database field, or cookie, it isn't possible to assign complex datatypes such as arrays, structures, or query objects to client variables. There is, however a workaround. Using the `CFWDDX` tag you can serialize a complex datatype and assign the resulting WDDX packet to a client variable. For more information on using WDDX to serialize and deserialize complex datatypes, see Chapter 20.

### *Client variables and clustering*

In order to effectively use client variables within a clustered environment, you need to have ColdFusion store client variables in an external data source or as cookies. By storing the client variables in either fashion, they become accessible from any server in your cluster.

If you choose to store your client variables in an external data source, you should be sure to set the `SETDOMAINCOOKIES` attribute to `Yes` in the `CFAPPLICATION` tag of your *Application.cfm* template. Setting this attribute to `Yes` causes ColdFusion to create a new cookie variable at the domain level called `CFMAGIC`. `CFMAGIC` tells ColdFusion that cookies have been set at the domain level and contains the values of the `CFID` and `CFToken` cookies. Existing host level cookies are automatically compared to the values stored in `CFMagic` and migrated to domain-level cookies if the values don't match.

There are a few additional considerations when configuring your clustered servers to use client variables. First, if you want to have ColdFusion automatically purge client variables stored in a data source after a set period of inactivity, you need to make sure that this option is set on only one of the ColdFusion servers in your cluster. To enable or disable this option, click on the name of the data source in the Variables section of the ColdFusion Administrator and check or uncheck the box labeled "Purge data for clients that remain unvisited for x days".

The second consideration has to do with setting up the external data source for each of your clustered servers. If you want ColdFusion to automatically create the database tables for you, you need to make sure to check this option in the ColdFusion Administrator during the setup of the first server only. If you attempt to have ColdFusion create tables for the same data source more than once, the ColdFusion Administrator generates an ODBC error.

### *Deleting client variables*

Several scenarios exist in which you might find it necessary to delete one or more client variables, such as a login application in a clustered environment. There are different techniques you can use to delete client variables depending on the number and type you want to delete. To delete a single client variable, use the `DeleteClientVariable()` function:

```
<CFSET Temp = DeleteClientVariable("MyClientVar")>
```

If you want to delete all client variables for the current user associated with your application, you can use a list loop to loop over the contents of the list of client variables returned by the `GetClientVariableList()` function, deleting each variable one at a time:

```
<!--- loop over the list of client variables, deleting them one by one --->
<CFLOOP INDEX="i" LIST="#GetClientVariablesList()#">
  <CFSET Temp = DeleteClientVariable(i)>
</CFLOOP>
```

Note that the `DeleteClientVariable()` function can't be used to delete any of the automatically created client variables such as `CFID`, `CFToken`, and `HitCount`.

You can delete all a user's client variables by expiring the `CFID`, `CFToken`, and `CFGlobals` cookies for that user. To do this, set the expiration for each cookie to `Now`:

```
<CFCOOKIE NAME="CFID" EXPIRES="Now">
<CFCOOKIE NAME="CFTOKEN" EXPIRES="Now">
<CFCOOKIE NAME="CFGLOBALS" EXPIRES="Now">
```

## *Cookies*

As I mentioned earlier in the chapter, cookies are a unique type of persistent variable in that they are stored on the client machine and sent to the ColdFusion server each time a page is requested. Cookies are available to every ColdFusion template provided they exist and provided they are set within the domain from which they are being requested. Cookies typically store identifying information about a user such as a user ID or other unique value. Because cookies exist as plain text on a user's system, they should never be used to store sensitive information, such as passwords or credit-card numbers. Cookies can be both set and read by ColdFusion. All cookie operations are performed using the `CFCOOKIE` tag.

### *Setting cookies*

ColdFusion allows you to set cookies via the `CFCOOKIE` tag. Before you decide to use cookies in your application, please keep in mind the following considerations:

- You can't set cookies for users that can't or choose not to accept them. This has the potential to limit the audience for your application.
- ColdFusion limits the amount of data set in a cookie to 4K.
- Netscape Navigator has a 20-cookie-per-host limit. As more cookies are added, older ones are pushed out.

The following example sets a cookie called `UserID` on the client's browser:

```
<CFCOOKIE NAME="UserID" VALUE="123456" PATH="/MyPath;/MyOtherPath"
DOMAIN=".example.com" EXPIRES="Never" SECURE="No">
```

The `NAME` attribute is required and specifies the name for the cookie. `VALUE` refers to the value you want to set for the cookie. The `PATH` attribute is also optional and specifies which URL(s) the cookie applies to. Multiple paths are separated by semicolons. If you specify values for `PATH`, you also have to use the `DOMAIN` attribute.

DOMAIN lists domains for which the cookie can be read or written. Entries must always start with a dot. Multiple domains can be specified provided they are separated by semicolons. The EXPIRES attribute allows you to set an expiration for the cookie. You have a lot of flexibility here. You can specify the expiration as an integer, specific date, Never, or Now. Specifying an integer for EXPIRES causes the cookie to expire in that number of days. For example, setting EXPIRES="14" causes the cookie to expire 14 days from when it is set. Likewise, setting EXPIRES="1/1/2099" causes the cookie to expire on January 1, 2099. Setting EXPIRES="Never" causes the cookie to persist forever, while setting EXPIRES="Now" causes the cookie to expire immediately. The final attribute, SECURE, indicates whether the cookie must be transmitted securely via SSL. This attribute is optional and defaults to No.

### *Retrieving cookies*

To retrieve a cookie, all you have to do is reference it by name using the cookie variable scope. The following example shows you how to retrieve the value of the UserID cookie that we set in the previous example:

```
<CFOUTPUT>
The Value of the UserID cookie is: #Cookie.UserID#
</CFOUTPUT>
```

You can see a list of all cookies and their associated values by turning on debugging for the current template and viewing the list of CGI variables available, or by referencing the cookie structure (as of Version 4.5).

### *Deleting cookies*

To delete a cookie, simply set the EXPIRES attribute of the CFCOOKIE tag to Now as in the following example:

```
<CFCOOKIE NAME="UserID"
EXPIRES="Now">
```

Setting the EXPIRES attribute to Now causes the cookie to expire and therefore deletes it from the user's system.

## *Session Variables*

Session variables are persistent variables that store information for a specific user session. Session variables are held in the server's memory and persist for a finite amount of time. Each session variable is unique to a user and can be referenced across all ColdFusion templates within an application. Session variables must be specifically set and are scoped as Session.*variable_name*. Any ColdFusion datatype may be assigned to a session variable. Session variables are commonly used in applications where information about a particular user needs to accompany the user from page to page for the duration of the visit to the site or application. Session variables are commonly used to store information such as authentication information, shopping cart contents, and other data specific to an individual user.

In order to use session variables, they must be enabled in both the ColdFusion Administrator and within an *Application.cfm* template for the application. This example shows how to enable session variables within the *Application.cfm* file:

```
<CFSETTING ENABLECFOUTPUTONLY="Yes">
  <CFAPPLICATION NAME="MyApplication" SESSIONMANAGEMENT="Yes"
       SETCLIENTCOOKIES="Yes"
       SESSIONTIMEOUT="#CREATETIMESPAN(0, 0, 30, 0)#">
<CFSETTING ENABLECFOUTPUTONLY="No">
```

In this case, the `CFAPPLICATION` tag turns on session variables by setting the `SESSIONMANAGEMENT` attribute to `Yes`. `SETCLIENTCOOKIES` determines whether to save the `CFID` and `CFToken` values as HTTP cookies on the user's machine. Since the `CFID` and `CFToken` values are used by both session and client variables, it is important to note that the value you specify for `SETCLIENTCOOKIES` affects both session and client management. If you set this attribute to `No`, you must be sure to manually pass the `CFID` and `CFToken` values from template to template. Techniques for doing this are described later in this section. The `SESSIONTIMEOUT` attribute sets the timeout for any application variables used in the application. In this case, the timeout for session variables is set to 30 minutes using the `CreateTimeSpan()` function.

Besides the session variables you create throughout your application, ColdFusion automatically creates the following session variables whenever session management is enabled:

`Session.CFID`
: An incremental ID number created by the ColdFusion Application Server for each client accessing the server.

`Session.CFToken`
: A random token that combines with the `CFID` to form a unique identifier for each client visiting your site.

`Session.SessionID`
: A concatenation of the application name (as specified in the Name attribute of the `CFAPPLICATION` tag), the `CFID`, and the `CFToken`. `SessionID` is used to uniquely identify each session within an application.

`Session.URLToken`
: A concatenation of the `CFID` and `CFToken` values that can be appended to a URL when cookies aren't used for session variable storage.

There is a structure object associated with session variables that contains a list of all available session variable names within a given application. This structure is appropriately named `Session`. To obtain a list of all session variables within an application, use the following code:

```
<CFLOCK SCOPE="Session" TYPE="ReadOnly" TIMEOUT="60" THROWONTIMEOUT="No" >
<TABLE>
<TR>
  <TH>Variable Name</TH><TH>Value</TH>
</TR>

<CFLOOP COLLECTION="#Session#" ITEM="VarName">
  <CFOUTPUT>
  <TR>
    <TD>#VarName#</TD><TD>#Session[VarName]#</TD>
  </TR>
  </CFOUTPUT>
</CFLOOP>
</CFLOCK>
</TABLE>
```

Note that the `CFLOCK` tag isn't necessary in this example if automatic read locking is enabled within the ColdFusion Administrator. This is true for any template that reads a session variable.

### *Using session variables without cookies*

As with client variables, by default the `CFID` and `CFToken` variables for each session are stored on the client's hard drive. In order to make your application work with users who can't or don't accept cookies, you must pass the `CFID` and `CFToken` values via URL to each template within your application. To pass `CFID` and `CFToken` from template to template, all you need to do is append the `URLToken` variable to each URL you use in your application. For example, to pass the `CFID` and `CFToken` along in a form, you can use the following code:

```
<CFLOCK SCOPE="Session" TYPE="ReadOnly" TIMEOUT="60">
<CFOUTPUT>
<FORM NAME="MyForm" ACTION="MyTemplate.cfm?#Session.URLToken#" METHOD="Post">
</CFOUTPUT>
...
</FORM>
</CFLOCK>
```

If you prefer, you can also pass the values of `CFID` and `CFToken` as hidden form fields as opposed to URL parameters:

```
<CFLOCK SCOPE="Session" TYPE="ReadOnly" TIMEOUT="60" THROWONTIMEOUT="No" >
<FORM NAME="MyForm" ACTION="MyTemplate.cfm" METHOD="Post">
<CFOUTPUT>
<INPUT TYPE="hidden" NAME="CFID" VALUE="#Session.CFID#">
<INPUT TYPE="hidden" NAME="CFTOKEN" VALUE="#Session.CFTOKEN#">
```

```
</CFOUTPUT>
...
</FORM>
</CFLOCK>
```

If you want to pass the `CFID` and `CFToken` using standard hyperlinks, the code looks like this:

```
<CFLOCK SCOPE="Session" TYPE="ReadOnly" TIMEOUT="60" THROWONTIMEOUT="No" >
<CFOUTPUT>
<A HREF="MyTemplate.cfm?#Session.URLToken#">MyTemplate</A>
</CFOUTPUT>
</CFLOCK>
```

### *Deleting session variables*

Sometimes, you may find it necessary to delete one or more session variables, such as when a user logs out of an application. Because session variables are stored in a structure object called `Session`, you can delete individual session variables using the structure function `StructDelete()`. For example, to delete a session variable called `Session.Username`, you can use the `StructDelete()` function as shown in the following example:

```
<CFLOCK SCOPE="Session" TYPE="Exclusive" TIMEOUT="60" THROWONTIMEOUT="No" >
<CFSET StructDelete(Session,"Username")>
</CFLOCK>
```

Remember that it is necessary to use `CFLOCK` whenever you read or write a session variable. In this example, we set the lock `TYPE` to `Exclusive` because we are writing to a session variable.

You can also delete all the session variables contained within the current session (without expiring the session) by looping through the session structure and individually deleting each variable. It is necessary to loop through the structure, excluding the preset session variables `CFID`, `CFToken`, `SessionID`, and `URLToken`, because ColdFusion sets these variables only at the start of the session:

```
<CFLOCK SCOPE="Session" TYPE="Exclusive" TIMEOUT="60" THROWONTIMEOUT="No" >
<CFLOOP COLLECTION="#Session#" ITEM="Key">
  <CFIF NOT ListFindNoCase('CFID,CFToken,SessionID,URLToken', Key)>
    <CFSET StructDelete(Session, Key)>
  </CFIF>
</CFLOOP>
</CFLOCK>
```

You can take things one step further and terminate a user's session using the `StructClear()` function:

```
<CFLOCK SCOPE="Session" TYPE="Exclusive" TIMEOUT="60" THROWONTIMEOUT="No" >
<CFSET StructClear(Session)>
</CFLOCK>
```

Using `StructClear()` deletes all session variables, including the `CFID` and `CFToken` variables, effectively terminating the user's session. You should note that while using `StructClear()` clears all session variables from the `Session` structure, it doesn't delete the `Session` structure itself.

### *Session variables and clustering*

Because session variables are stored in the ColdFusion server's RAM, they can't be shared across multiple servers in a clustered environment. Many clustering products (including Allaire's ClusterCATS, part of the ColdFusion Enterprise Server) offer "sticky" or session-aware load balancing options. This type of load balancing allows you to use memory-resident variables (session, application, and server) in your applications by ensuring that a user isn't bumped from the server they are originally routed to regardless of the amount of load on the server. In the event that a server fails in a session-aware cluster, all memory resident variables on that server are lost, resulting in a loss of all active user sessions. For more information on using ClusterCATS, see the Allaire documentation.

## *Server Variables*

Server variables are the final type of persistent variable in ColdFusion. Server variables store data associated with the server on which ColdFusion is running. Server variables are stored in the ColdFusion server's RAM and are available to all ColdFusion applications and users. Server variables persist until the ColdFusion Application Server is stopped. You can create your own server variables using the `CFSET` and `CFPARAM` tags or reference the following predefined ones:

`Server.ColdFusion.Expiration`
: Date (in ODBC date format) on which the ColdFusion server expires (applies only to trial versions of ColdFusion); new as of ColdFusion 5.0

`Server.ColdFusion.ProductLevel`
: The level of the ColdFusion product running on the server (Express, Professional, Enterprise, etc.)

`Server.ColdFusion.ProductName`
: The name of the ColdFusion product running on the server

`Server.ColdFusion.ProductVersion`
: The version number of the ColdFusion product running on the server

`Server.ColdFusion.SerialNumber`
: The serial number registered to the ColdFusion server

`Server.ColdFusion.SupportedLocales`
: A comma-delimited list of locales supported by the server

`Server.OS.AdditionalInformation`
: Any additional information specified by the operating system on the ColdFusion server such as service packs installed, etc.

`Server.OS.BuildNumber`
: The build number of the operating system installed on the ColdFusion server

`Server.OS.Name`
: The name of the operating system installed on the ColdFusion server

`Server.OS.Version`
: The version number of the operating system running on the ColdFusion server

Server variables are often used in multiplatform ColdFusion applications in which the applications behave differently depending on what platform the code is running on.

When you read or write a server variable, it is important to use the `CFLOCK` tag around it to prevent data corruption issues. Remember to set the `TYPE` of lock to `ReadOnly` when reading server variables and `Exclusive` when writing them. The following example writes several server variables, then displays them:

```
<CFLOCK SCOPE="Server" TYPE="Exclusive" TIMEOUT="60" THROWONTIMEOUT="No" >
  <CFSET Server.Location = "West Chester">
  <CFSET Server.Function = "B2B Applications">
</CFLOCK>

<CFLOCK SCOPE="Server" TYPE="ReadOnly" TIMEOUT="60" THROWONTIMEOUT="No" >
  <CFOUTPUT>
  This server is located in #Server.Location#<BR>
  This server is used for #Server.Function#
  </CFOUTPUT>
</CFLOCK>
```

For security reasons, there is no structure object that contains a list of all available server variable names. In addition, server variables shouldn't be used within a clustered environment (unless "sticky" or session-aware load balancing is used), because they are exclusive to the server on which they are created.

# *Browser Redirection*

At times, you may wish to redirect a user's browser to a location other than the current template. This is generally handled using the `CFLOCATION` tag. The following example creates a drop-down box listing several web sites. Choosing one of the sites and clicking on the Go button posts the form to itself and uses the `CFLOCATION` tag to redirect the user to the selected web site.

```
<CFIF IsDefined('Form.Go')>
  <CFLOCATION URL="http://#Goto#" ADDTOKEN="No">
</CFIF>

<B>Please choose a location:</B><BR>
<FORM ACTION="Go.cfm" METHOD="post">
  <SELECT NAME="Goto">
    <OPTION VALUE="www.allaire.com" Selected>Allaire</OPTION>
    <OPTION VALUE="www.yahoo.com">Yahoo</OPTION>
    <OPTION VALUE="www.amkor.com">Amkor</OPTION>
  </SELECT>
<INPUT TYPE="Submit" NAME="Go" VALUE="Go"></FONT></TD></FORM>
```

The `URL` attribute specifies an absolute or relative path to the page you want to redirect the user's browser to. `ADDTOKEN` is an optional attribute and indicates whether to append client variable information (`CFID` and `CFToken` values) to the end of the URL specified in the `URL` attribute. In order to use the `ADDTOKEN` attribute, `CLIENTMANAGEMENT` must be turned on in the *Application.cfm* file. The default value for `ADDTOKEN` is `Yes`.

Due to the way ColdFusion assembles dynamic pages, you shouldn't attempt to use the `CFLOCATION` tag within a template after a cookie variable has been set. Setting a cookie variable and using `CFLOCATION` afterward results in the cookie not being set. If you need to redirect to a different template after setting a cookie, consider using the `CFHEADER` tag instead as in:

```
<CFCOOKIE NAME="MyCookie" VALUE="Hey, look at me!">
<CFHEADER NAME="Refresh" VALUE="0; URL=http://www.example.com/mytemplate.cfm">
```

The `CFHEADER` tag generates a custom HTTP header with a Refresh element that contains the number of seconds to wait before refreshing the page as well as the URL of the page to retrieve when the refresh occurs.

## Portal Example

Because state management is such an important part of web application development, I think it's appropriate we end the chapter with an example application that showcases the material we've just covered. I've opted to create a portal application, that allows a registered visitor to create a personalized home page from a list of prebuilt components, as it is sufficiently complex to allow me to demonstrate a number of techniques. Figure 7-6 shows an overview of how the portal application is put together, including relationships between the various templates. The application uses all the persistent variable scopes we discussed with the exception of the server scope. We'll cover all of the templates used in the application except for *Login.cfm* and *Validate.cfm*. These templates are discussed in Chapter 8.

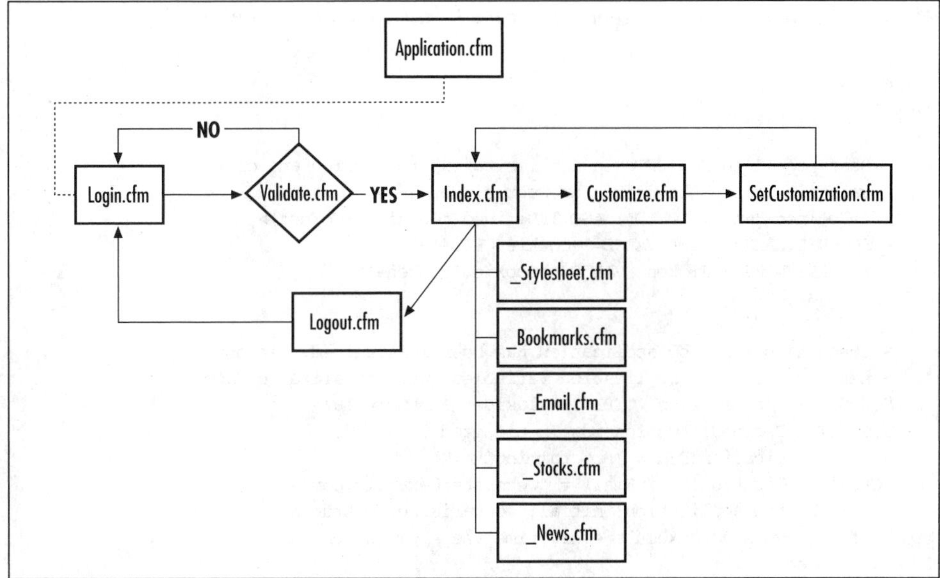


*Figure 7-6. Application flow for the portal example*

## Web Application Framework

The *Application.cfm* template shown in Example 7-2 has four functions in the portal application: it turns on client and session management, handles authentication, expires the session when appropriate, and sets application variables.

*Example 7-2. Application.cfm Template for the Portal Application*

```
<CFSETTING ENABLECFOUTPUTONLY="Yes">
<CFAPPLICATION NAME="MyApplication" CLIENTMANAGEMENT="Yes"
     SESSIONMANAGEMENT="Yes" SETCLIENTCOOKIES="Yes"
     SESSIONTIMEOUT="#CreateTimeSpan(0, 0, 30, 0)#"
     APPLICATIONTIMEOUT="#CreateTimeSpan(0, 0, 30, 0)#"
     CLIENTSTORAGE="Registry">
<!--- Set the default session state to false, meaning that by default,
      users are NOT logged into the application --->
<CFLOCK SCOPE="Session" TYPE="Exclusive" TIMEOUT="10">
  <CFPARAM NAME="Session.LoggedIn" DEFAULT="False">
</CFLOCK>

<!--- if the user isn't logged in or they aren't currently on the login
      page, send them to the login page --->
<CFLOCK SCOPE="Session" TYPE="ReadOnly" TIMEOUT="10">
  <CFIF NOT Session.LoggedIn>
    <CFIF (CGI.SCRIPT_NAME IS NOT "/examples/7/portal/Login.cfm")
      AND (CGI.SCRIPT_NAME IS NOT "/examples/7/portal/Validate.cfm")>
        <CFLOCATION URL="/examples/7/portal/Login.cfm" ADDTOKEN="No">
```

*Example 7-2. Application.cfm Template for the Portal Application (continued)*

```
    </CFIF>
  </CFIF>
</CFLOCK>

<!--- Reset the CFID and CFToken cookies to expire session and client
      variables after the user's browser closes --->
<CFIF IsDefined("Cookie.CFID") AND IsDefined("Cookie.CFToken")>
    <CFCOOKIE NAME="CFID" VALUE="#Cookie.CFID#">
    <CFCOOKIE NAME="CFToken" VALUE="#Cookie.CFToken#">
</CFIF>

<!--- check to see if the application has been initialized.  If not,
      set the necessary application variables and initialize the app --->
<CFLOCK SCOPE="Application" TYPE="Exclusive" TIMEOUT="10">
  <CFIF NOT IsDefined('Application.Initialized')>
    <CFSET Application.DSN = "ProgrammingCF">
    <CFSET Application.AdminEmail = "webmaster@example.com">
    <!--- Set the application.initialized variable to true so that this
block of code does not execute every time the Application.cfm
file is called --->
    <CFSET Application.Initialized = TRUE>
  </CFIF>
</CFLOCK>
<CFSETTING ENABLECFOUTPUTONLY="No">
```

The first task in *Application.cfm* is to turn on both client and session management for the application. The application uses the system registry to store client variables (for simplicity), but you can use any storage option you choose. Both application and session variables are set to time out after 30 minutes. Additionally, client cookies are enabled.

Because the *Application.cfm* template is invoked each time a template is requested, it is well suited to handle authentication for the portal. Although we'll be discussing the entire login process in Chapter 8, it is important to understand that the *Application.cfm* template prescreens all user requests to see if a user is logged into the application. It does this by checking for a session variable called `Session.LoggedIn`. If this variable exists and is set to `True`, the requested template is sent to the user. If the variable isn't present or is set to false (as it is by default), the user is rerouted to the *Login.cfm* template via a `CFLOCATION` tag.

The third function of this *Application.cfm* template is to expire a session in the event the browser is closed. This is done so that in a shared environment, another user can't simply open the previous user's browser and start using the application. The technique used to accomplish this involves resetting the `CFID` and `CFToken` cookies so that they are never written to the user's system. This in effect terminates a user's session. You should note that this technique works only if the `CFID` and `CFToken` values aren't passed via URL.

The final function of this *Application.cfm* template checks for the existence of an application variable called `Application.Initialized`. If it doesn't exist (which it won't the first time a CFML template is invoked), ColdFusion responds by setting a number of constants for the application. After the constants are set, `Application.Initialized` is set to `True` so the next time the *Application.cfm* template is called, it isn't necessary to set all the constants again (since you only need to set application variables once).

## Main Template

When a user successfully logs in to the application via the *Login.cfm* and *Validate.cfm* templates (discussed in Chapter 8), two session variables are set by the *Validate.cfm* template, `Session.LoggedIn` (set to `True`) and `Session.FullName` (set to the full name of the user who logged in). The user is then redirected to the *Index.cfm* template shown in Example 7-3. The *Index.cfm* template is the main template for the portal. It displays all the user's content and contains links to customize the portal, remove specific content modules, and log out of the portal.

*Example 7-3. The Main Application Template, Index.cfm*

```
<!--- set default values for client variables --->
<CFPARAM NAME="Client.Email" DEFAULT="Yes">
<CFPARAM NAME="Client.Stocks" DEFAULT="Yes">
<CFPARAM NAME="Client.News" DEFAULT="Yes">
<CFPARAM NAME="Client.Bookmarks" DEFAULT="Yes">
<CFPARAM NAME="Client.BGColor" DEFAULT="FFFFFF">
<CFPARAM NAME="Client.FontFace" DEFAULT="Arial">
<CFPARAM NAME="Client.HeaderFontColor" DEFAULT="000000">
<CFPARAM NAME="Client.HeaderBGColor" DEFAULT="6666FF">
<CFPARAM NAME="Client.FontColor" DEFAULT="000000">

<HTML>
  <HEAD>
    <TITLE>My Portal</TITLE>
    <CFINCLUDE TEMPLATE="_StyleSheet.cfm">
  </HEAD>
<BODY>
<CFOUTPUT><H1>Welcome #ListFirst(Session.FullName, " ")#</H1></CFOUTPUT>
<TABLE WIDTH="100%" BORDER="0" CELLPADDING="0" CELLSPACING="5">
  <TR>
    <CFOUTPUT>
    <TD CLASS="CustomizeLink"><A HREF="Customize.cfm">Customize</A></TD>
    <TD CLASS="CustomizeLink" ALIGN="right"><A
        HREF="Logout.cfm">Logout</A></TD>
    </CFOUTPUT>
  </TR>
  <TR>
    <TD WIDTH="19%" VALIGN="top">
      <TABLE WIDTH="100%" BORDER="0" CELLSPACING="0" CELLPADDING="5">
```

*Example 7-3. The Main Application Template, Index.cfm (continued)*

```
        <CFIF Client.Email>
<CFINCLUDE TEMPLATE="_Email.cfm">
        </CFIF>
        <CFIF Client.Stocks>
<CFINCLUDE TEMPLATE="_Stock.cfm">
        </CFIF>
      </TABLE>
    </TD>
    <TD WIDTH="81%" VALIGN="top">
      <TABLE WIDTH="100%" BORDER="0" CELLSPACING="0" CELLPADDING="5">
        <CFIF Client.News>
<CFINCLUDE TEMPLATE="_News.cfm">
        </CFIF>
        <CFIF Client.Bookmarks>
<CFINCLUDE TEMPLATE="_Bookmarks.cfm">
        </CFIF>
      </TABLE>
    </TD>
  </TR>
</TABLE>
<HR>
<CFLOCK SCOPE="Application" TYPE="Readonly" TIMEOUT="10">
  <CFOUTPUT>
  <DIV CLASS="Footer">Please email questions or concerns to <A HREF="mailto:
   #Application.AdminEmail#">#Application.AdminEmail#</A>.</DIV>
  </CFOUTPUT>
</CFLOCK>
</BODY>
</HTML>
```

The *Index.cfm* template begins by setting default values for several client variables. These client variables define the look and feel for the portal as well as specify what types of content should be displayed. Because these values are stored in client variables, they are specific to individual users. This allows you to provide a personalized portal experience for each user.

The next part of the template uses a **CFINCLUDE** tag to include an inline stylesheet for the application. The stylesheet defines such things as the font face and size for various sections of the portal. These attributes are dynamically populated based on values stored in the various client variables specified at the beginning of the template. The code for the stylesheet (*_Stylesheet.cfm*) is shown in Example 7-4.

*Example 7-4. Stylesheet.cfm Template for Defining the Stylesheet for the Portal*

```
<STYLE TYPE="text/css">
  <!--
  <CFOUTPUT>
  BODY {Background-color: ###Client.BGColor#; font-family: #Client.FontFace#;
         font-size: 10pt; color: ###Client.FontColor#}
```

*Example 7-4. Stylesheet.cfm Template for Defining the Stylesheet for the Portal (continued)*

```
  H1 {font-family: #Client.FontFace#; font-size: 16pt; font-weight: bold}
  .SectionHeader {font-family: #Client.FontFace#; font-size: 12pt;
        font-weight: bold;
        background-color: ###Client.HeaderBGColor#;
        color: ###Client.HeaderFontColor#}
  .LeftTableBody {font-family: #Client.FontFace#; font-size: 9pt;
        font-weight: normal; background-color: ##CCCCCC;
        color: ###Client.FontColor#}
  .TableRemove {font-family: #Client.FontFace#; font-size: 8pt;
      text-decoration: underline;
      background-color: ###Client.HeaderBGColor#;
      text-align: right;
      color: ###Client.FontColor#}
  .ListItems {font-family: #Client.FontFace#; font-size: 10pt;
    list-style-type: circle; color: ###Client.FontColor#}
  .CustomizeLink {font-family: #Client.FontFace#; font-size: 8pt;
        text-decoration: underline; color: ###Client.FontColor#}
  .Ticker {font-family: #Client.FontFace#; font-size: 9pt; font-weight: bold}
  .Quote {font-family: #Client.FontFace#; font-size: 9pt}
  .Footer {font-family: #Client.FontFace#; font-size: 8pt}
  </CFOUTPUT>
  -->
</STYLE>
```

The rest of the *Index.cfm* template displays the various types of content the user has specified for inclusion in the portal. By default, all content is displayed the first time the user logs into the application. This is accomplished by setting defaults for all the client variables in the beginning of the template. Each type of content (email, stock quotes, news, and bookmarks) is pulled into the template via `CFINCLUDE` tags. This allows the design of the portal to remain modular and makes editing any of the individual content modules easy. The code for the various content modules is shown in Example 7-5 (*_Email.cfm*), Example 7-6 (*_Stock.cfm*), Example 7-7 (*_News.cfm*), and Example 7-8 (*_Bookmarks.cfm*). Figure 7-7 shows how the portal looks the first time a user logs in

*Example 7-5. Email.cfm Template for the Email Module*

```
<TR>
  <TD CLASS="SectionHeader">E-mail</TD>
  <TD CLASS="TableRemove">
    <CFOUTPUT>
      <A HREF="SetCustomization.cfm?Section=Email&Action=Remove">Remove</A>
    </CFOUTPUT></TD>
</TR>
<TR>
  <TD CLASS="LeftTableBody" COLSPAN="2">Check Email (6 new)</TD>
</TR>
```

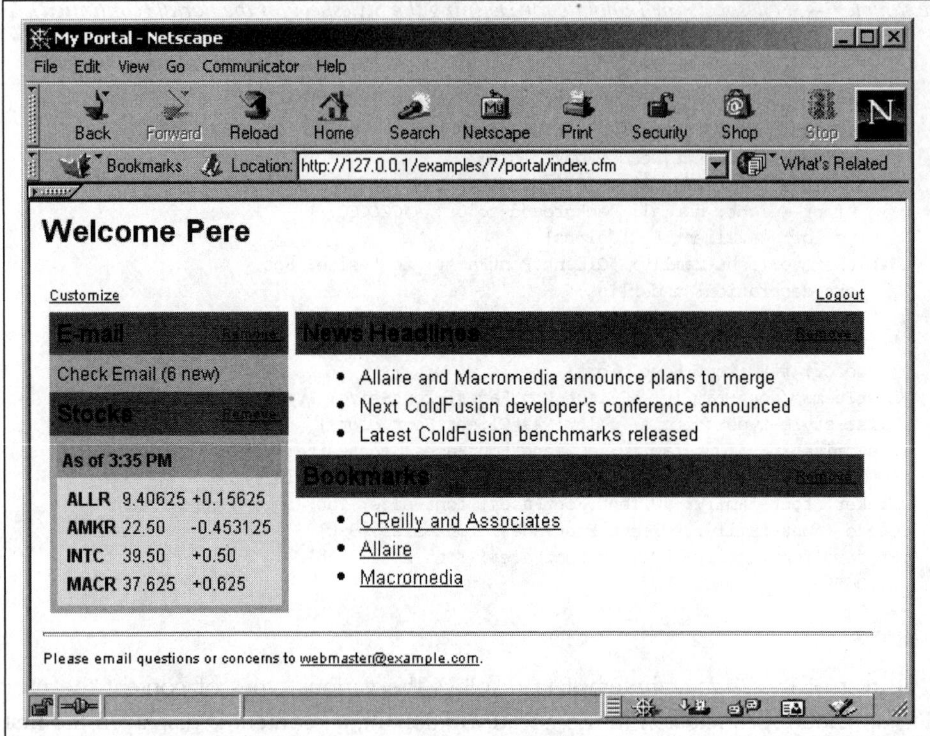


*Figure 7-7. Displaying the portal the first time a user logs in*

*Example 7-6. Stock.cfm Template for Displaying Stock Quotes*

```
<TR>
  <TD BGCOLOR="#CCCC66" CLASS="SectionHeader">Stocks</TD>
  <TD CLASS="TableRemove">
    <CFOUTPUT>
      <A HREF="SetCustomization.cfm?Section=Stocks&Action=Remove">Remove</A>
    </CFOUTPUT>
  </TD>
</TR>
<TR BGCOLOR="#CCCCCC">
  <TD CLASS="LeftTableBody" COLSPAN="2">
  <TABLE BORDER="0" CELLPADDING="4" CELLSPACING="0" WIDTH="100%"
         BGCOLOR="#EEEEEE">
  <TR BGCOLOR="#C0C0C0">
    <TD WIDTH="100%" CLASS="Ticker">As of 3:35 PM</TD>
  </TR>
  <TR>
    <TD>
    <TABLE WIDTH="100%" CELLSPACING="0" CELLPADDING="1">
      <TR>
        <TD CLASS="Ticker">ALLR</TD><TD CLASS="Quote">9.40625</TD>
        <TD CLASS="Quote">+0.15625</TD>
      </TR>
```

*Example 7-6. Stock.cfm Template for Displaying Stock Quotes (continued)*

```
      <TR>
        <TD CLASS="Ticker">AMKR</TD><TD CLASS="Quote">22.50</TD>
        <TD CLASS="Quote">-0.453125</TD>
      </TR>
      <TR>
        <TD CLASS="Ticker">INTC</TD><TD CLASS="Quote">39.50</TD>
        <TD CLASS="Quote">+0.50</TD>
      </TR>
      <TR>
        <TD CLASS="Ticker">MACR</TD><TD CLASS="Quote">37.625</TD>
        <TD CLASS="Quote">+0.625</TD>
      </TR>
    </TABLE>
    </TD>
  </TR>
  </TABLE>
  </TD>
</TR>
```

*Example 7-7. News.cfm Template for Displaying News Headlines*

```
<TR>
  <TD CLASS="SectionHeader">News Headlines</TD>
  <TD CLASS="TableRemove">
    <CFOUTPUT>
      <A HREF="SetCustomization.cfm?Section=News&Action=Remove">Remove</A>
    </CFOUTPUT>
  </TD>
</TR>
<TR>
  <TD COLSPAN="2">
    <UL>
      <LI><SPAN CLASS="ListItems">Allaire and Macromedia announce
          plans to merge</SPAN></LI>
      <LI><SPAN CLASS="ListItems">Next ColdFusion developer's
          conference announced</SPAN></LI>
      <LI><SPAN CLASS="ListItems">Latest ColdFusion benchmarks
          released</SPAN></LI>
    </UL>
  </TD>
</TR>
```

*Example 7-8. Bookmarks.cfm Template for Displaying Links to Other Sites*

```
<TR>
  <TD CLASS="SectionHeader">Bookmarks</TD>
  <TD CLASS="TableRemove">
    <CFOUTPUT>
      <A HREF="SetCustomization.cfm?Section=Bookmarks&Action=Remove">Remove</A>
    </CFOUTPUT>
  </TD>
</TR>
<TR>
```

*Example 7-8. Bookmarks.cfm Template for Displaying Links to Other Sites (continued)*

```
  <TD COLSPAN="2">
    <UL>
      <LI><SPAN CLASS="ListItems"><A
          HREF="http://www.oreilly.com">O'Reilly and Associates</A></SPAN></LI>
      <LI><SPAN CLASS="ListItems"><A
          HREF="http://www.allaire.com">Allaire</A></SPAN></LI>
      <LI><SPAN CLASS="ListItems"><A
          HREF="http://www.macromedia.com">Macromedia</A></SPAN></LI>
    </UL>
  </TD>
</TR>
```

## Customization

From the main page of the portal (*Index.cfm*), a user can customize the portal by clicking on the Customize link in the upper left corner of the screen. Clicking this link takes the user to the *Customize.cfm* template. Example 7-9 contains the code for the *Customize.cfm* template.

*Example 7-9. Customize.cfm Template Customizes the Portal's Look/Feel, Content*

```
<CFPARAM NAME="Client.Email" DEFAULT="No">
<CFPARAM NAME="Client.Stocks" DEFAULT="No">
<CFPARAM NAME="Client.News" DEFAULT="No">
<CFPARAM NAME="Client.Bookmarks" DEFAULT="No">

<H1>Customize Your Portal</H2>
<CFOUTPUT>
<FORM ACTION="SetCustomization.cfm" METHOD="Post">
</CFOUTPUT>
<TABLE>
<CFOUTPUT>
<TR>
  <TD>Background color:</TD>
  <TD><INPUT TYPE="text" NAME="BGColor" SIZE="6" MAXLENGTH="6"
   VALUE="#Client.BGColor#"></TD>
</TR>
<TR>
  <TD>Font face:</TD>
  <TD><SELECT NAME="FontFace">
        <OPTION VALUE="Arial" <CFIF Client.FontFace EQ
      "Arial">SELECTED</CFIF>>Arial</OPTION>
        <OPTION VALUE="Helvetica" <CFIF Client.FontFace EQ
      "Helvetica">SELECTED</CFIF>>Helvetica</OPTION>
        <OPTION VALUE="Sans-serif" <CFIF Client.FontFace EQ
      "Sans-serif">SELECTED</CFIF>>Sans-Serif</OPTION>
        <OPTION VALUE="Comic Sans MS" <CFIF Client.FontFace EQ
      "Comic Sans MS">SELECTED</CFIF>>Comic Sans MS</OPTION>
      </SELECT></TD>
</TR>
<TR>
```

*Example 7-9. Customize.cfm Template Customizes the Portal's Look/Feel, Content (continued)*

```
  <TD>Header font color:</TD>
  <TD><INPUT TYPE="text" NAME="HeaderFontColor" SIZE="6" MAXLENGTH="6"
   VALUE="#Client.HeaderFontColor#"></TD>
</TR>
<TR>
  <TD>Header background color:</TD>
  <TD><INPUT TYPE="text" NAME="HeaderBGColor" SIZE="6" MAXLENGTH="6"
   VALUE="#Client.HeaderBGColor#"></TD>
</TR>
<TR>
  <TD>Font color:</TD>
  <TD><INPUT TYPE="text" NAME="FontColor" SIZE="6" MAXLENGTH="6"
   VALUE="#Client.FontColor#"></TD>
</TR>
</CFOUTPUT>
<TR>
  <TD COLSPAN="2">Content:</TD>
</TR>
<TR>
  <TD COLSPAN="2">
  <TABLE>
    <TR>
      <TD><input type="checkbox" name="Email" value="Yes"
<CFIF Client.Email>CHECKED</CFIF>>Email</TD>
      <TD><input type="checkbox" name="News" value="Yes"
<CFIF Client.News>CHECKED</CFIF>>News</TD>
    </TR>
    <TR>
      <TD><input type="checkbox" name="Stocks" value="Yes"
<CFIF Client.Stocks>CHECKED</CFIF>>Stocks</TD>
      <TD><input type="checkbox" name="Bookmarks" value="Yes"
<CFIF Client.Bookmarks>CHECKED</CFIF>>Bookmarks</TD>
    </TR>
  </TABLE>
  </TD>
</TR>
<TR>
  <TD COLSPAN="2"><INPUT TYPE="submit" NAME="Customize" VALUE="Save"></TD>
</TR>
</TABLE>
</FORM>
```

This template, shown in Figure 7-8, contains an HTML form that lets the user change the background color, font face, font color, header background color, and header font color for the portal. Additionally, checkboxes are provided next to the name of each available content module. Unchecking a box removes the specified module from the user's portal display, while checking an unchecked box adds the specified module. All the values used to populate this page come from the client variables associated with the user. Clicking on the Save button at the bottom of the page submits the changes to the *SetCustomization.cfm* template shown in Example 7-10.

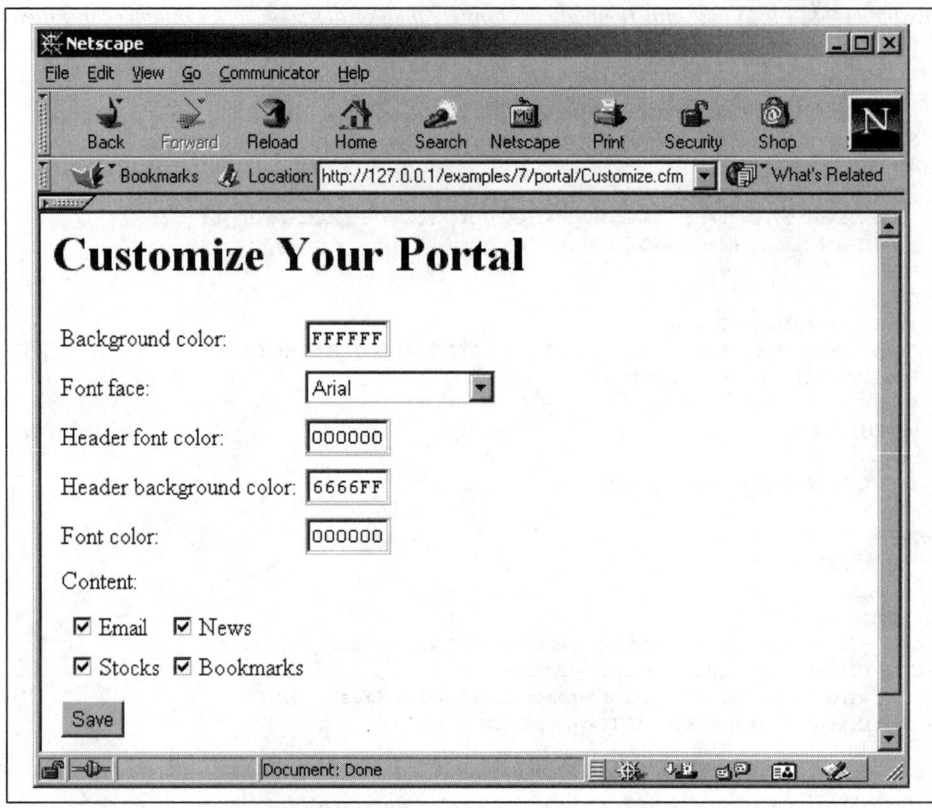


*Figure 7-8. Customizing the portal*

*Example 7-10. SetCustomization.cfm Handles Changes to Look/Feel, Content*

```
<H1>Saving Changes...</H1>
<CFIF IsDefined('Form.Customize')>
  <CFSET Client.BGColor = Form.BGColor>
  <CFSET Client.FontFace = Form.FontFace>
  <CFSET Client.FontColor = Form.FontColor>
  <CFSET Client.HeaderBGColor = Form.HeaderBGColor>
  <CFSET Client.HeaderFontColor = Form.HeaderFontColor>

  <CFPARAM NAME="Form.Email" DEFAULT="No">
  <CFPARAM NAME="Form.Stocks" DEFAULT="No">
  <CFPARAM NAME="Form.News" DEFAULT="No">
  <CFPARAM NAME="Form.Bookmarks" DEFAULT="No">

  <CFSET Client.Email = Form.Email>
  <CFSET Client.Stocks = Form.Stocks>
  <CFSET Client.News = Form.News>
  <CFSET Client.Bookmarks = Form.Bookmarks>
<CFELSEIF IsDefined('URL.Action') AND URL.Action EQ "Remove">
  <CFSWITCH EXPRESSION="#Section#">
```

*Example 7-10. SetCustomization.cfm Handles Changes to Look/Feel, Content (continued)*

```
    <CFCASE VALUE="Email">
      <CFSET Client.Email = "No">
    </CFCASE>
    <CFCASE VALUE="Stocks">
      <CFSET Client.Stocks = "No">
    </CFCASE>
    <CFCASE VALUE="News">
      <CFSET Client.News = "No">
    </CFCASE>
    <CFCASE VALUE="Bookmarks">
      <CFSET Client.Bookmarks = "No">
    </CFCASE>
  </CFSWITCH>
</CFIF>

<CFHEADER NAME="Refresh" VALUE="0; URL=Index.cfm">
```

This template first checks to see how the user arrived at the page. If the user arrived by submitting the form from the *Customize.cfm* template, the user's client variables are updated with the new values. If the user came in by clicking on one of the Remove links on the *Index.cfm* page, the client variable controlling the display of that particular content module is set to `No`, so that it is no longer displayed. Regardless of how the user arrived, once the template has finished executing, the user is sent back to the *Index.cfm* template via the `CFHEADER` tag. The `CFHEADER` tag is used instead of the `CFLOCATION` tag in case the application is set to store client variables as client cookies.

## Logging Out

Example 7-11 contains the code for the final template in our portal application, the *Logout.cfm* template. This template is called by clicking the Logout link in the upper right corner of the *Index.cfm* page.

*Example 7-11. Logout.cfm Template for Terminating a User's Session*

```
<!--- terminate the user's session by deleting all session variables --->
<CFLOCK SCOPE="Session" TYPE="Exclusive" TIMEOUT="10">
  <CFSET StructClear(Session)>
</CFLOCK>

<CFLOCATION URL="Login.cfm?Message=#URLEncodedFormat("Thank you for logging
out. Please visit again soon!")#">
```

This template uses the `StructClear()` function to clear all of the values stored in the entire session scope. Because this is where the `Session.CFID`, `Session.CFToken`, and `Session.LoggedIn` values associated with the user's session are stored, clearing these values terminates the user's session, forcing the user back to the *Login.cfm* template (covered in Chapter 8).

*In this chapter:*
- *Security Basics*
- *Implementing Security from Scratch*
- *Using ColdFusion's Built-in Advanced Security Services*

# 8

# *Security*

Security is a key part of any web application. As more and more aspects of daily life get conducted online, users want to be sure that the information they provide to web applications is taken care of properly. On the flip side, businesses want to make sure that the people who use their web applications are who they say they are. In this chapter, we'll cover two keys aspects of security: authentication and authorization. *Authentication* is the process of verifying the identity of a user, while *authorization* is the process of limiting access to resources to particular users.

In this chapter, we'll look at two approaches to application security. The first approach uses a combination of database tables and application code to manage authentication and user entitlements, in effect implementing security from scratch. Because the *Application.cfm* template is automatically invoked with each page request, it is the ideal place to handle security tasks in your ColdFusion applications. The second approach uses ColdFusion's new Advanced Security services for authenticating users and authorizing access to resources. Each method has its pros and cons, which will be discussed.

Note that there is Basic Security within ColdFusion, but it has a different purpose than the Advanced Security services. Basic Security is configurable only from within the ColdFusion Administrator and is used to specify usernames and passwords for the ColdFusion Administrator and ColdFusion Studio. It can also enable and disable access to the `CFCONTENT`, `CFDIRECTORY`, `CFFILE`, `CFOBJECT`, `CFREGISTRY`, `CFADMINSECURITY`, `CFEXECUTE`, `CFFTP`, `CFLOG`, and `CFMAIL` tags as well as the `DBTYPE=DYNAMIC` and `CONNECTSTRING` attributes of the `CFQUERY`, `CFINSERT`, `CFUPDATE`, `CFSTOREDPROC` and `CFGRIDUPDATE` tags. For more information on Basic Security, refer to the Allaire documentation specific to your flavor of ColdFusion.

# Security Basics

Before we dive into the different security techniques, let's look at some general do's and don'ts to consider when designing and implementing a security solution for your ColdFusion applications:

- Don't base security solely on a user's IP address. IP addresses are easily spoofed and can often change during a user's session (especially in the case of AOL users because of the way AOL's network works). Additionally, dialup users most likely won't have the same IP address the next time they dial in and use your application because most ISPs use DHCP.
- Do use SSL whenever possible to encrypt the session between the server and the browser. Because SSL is handled at the web-server level and not by ColdFusion, you need to consult the documentation for your particular web server to determine how to set it up.
- Do require users to choose passwords that aren't easily guessed or found in the dictionary. If possible, require users to choose a password that contains a combination of letters, numbers, and possibly symbols. One way to handle this is by automatically assigning passwords to users. There is a custom tag called `CF_RandomPassword`, described in Chapter 19, that can do this automatically for you. If you let users choose their own passwords, you can still ensure they contain certain characters by using ColdFusion's `ReFind()` function (described in Chapter 17).
- Do include error and exception handling in your applications to prevent users from receiving server and application information when an error or exception occurs. These concepts are covered in Chapter 9.
- Don't store passwords as clear text if you store them in a database or LDAP directory. Use the `Hash()` function or some other method to obfuscate the password before storing it.
- Don't pass usernames and passwords from template to template in URLs or as hidden form fields because this increases the potential for compromise. Use session variables to store and pass usernames and passwords from template to template, because they are stored in the ColdFusion server's memory and expire when a user's session expires.

# Implementing Security from Scratch

As I mentioned in the introduction, it is entirely possible and quite easy to build a robust security model using nothing more than a simple database table and a small bit of CFML code. Consider the portal example we created at the end of Chapter 7. This application is the perfect candidate for implementing security from scratch.

If you refer back to Chapter 7 for a moment, to Figure 7-6, you'll remember that we said security for the portal could be handled by three templates: *Application.cfm*, *Login.cfm*, and *Validate.cfm*. Both authentication and authorization functions are handled by these templates. If you look at Figure 8-1, you'll see the basic flow of the authentication/authorization process. Note that this view differs slightly from the one in Chapter 7 due to the addition of two new templates that handle user registration. Don't worry about them for the time being, we'll get to them soon enough.

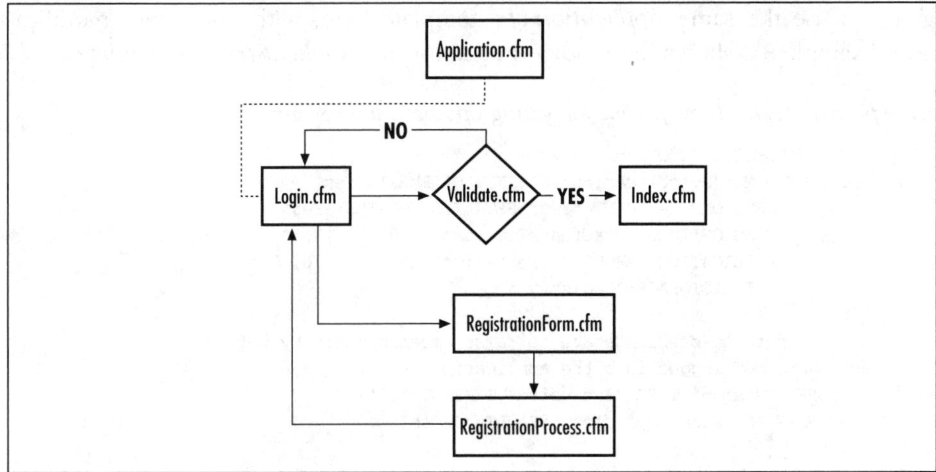


*Figure 8-1. Security scheme for the portal application*

## *Creating a Simple Security Table in the Database*

The first step to building security into the portal application is to create a database to store username and password information. Table 8-1 shows the schema for a single table called `Users` that will store our profile and security information.

*Table 8-1. Setup for the User Security Table*

| Field Name | Field Type | Max Length |
|---|---|---|
| Username (primary key) | Text | 50 |
| Password | Text | 50 |
| FullName | Text | 255 |

The field names should be self-descriptive. In our table, `Username` holds an individual's username, and the `Password` field stores the user's password. Because it isn't a good idea to store passwords as plain text in the database, we'll be storing hashes (a one-way encryption) of the passwords instead. Finally, we decided to include a field called `FullName` to store the full name of the user associated with the Username and Password. This table is about as barebones as you can get. You could easily expand it to include all sorts of additional profiling information such as the user's address, phone number, email address, etc.

## Setting Up the Application.cfm Template

Now that we have a security table, we need an *Application.cfm* template to serve as the foundation for our security model. In Chapter 7, we designed an *Application.cfm* template to handle security for our portal application. We are going to use the same *Application.cfm* template here, with one minor modification. Example 8-1 shows the modified code for our *Application.cfm* template.

*Example 8-1. Application.cfm File for Setting Up Application Security*

```
<CFSETTING ENABLECFOUTPUTONLY="Yes">
<CFAPPLICATION NAME="MyApplication" CLIENTMANAGEMENT="Yes"
               SESSIONMANAGEMENT="Yes" SETCLIENTCOOKIES="Yes"
               SESSIONTIMEOUT="#CreateTimeSpan(0, 0, 30, 0)#"
               APPLICATIONTIMEOUT="#CreateTimeSpan(0, 0, 30, 0)#"
               CLIENTSTORAGE="Registry">

<!--- Set the default session state to false, meaning that by default,
      users are NOT logged into the application --->
<CFLOCK SCOPE="Session" TYPE="Exclusive" TIMEOUT="10">
  <CFPARAM NAME="Session.LoggedIn" DEFAULT="False">
</CFLOCK>

<!--- if the user isn't logged in or they aren't currently on the login
      page, send them to the login page --->
<CFLOCK SCOPE="Session" TYPE="ReadOnly" TIMEOUT="10">
  <CFIF NOT Session.LoggedIn>
    <CFIF (CGI.SCRIPT_NAME IS NOT "/examples/7/portal/Login.cfm")
      AND (CGI.SCRIPT_NAME IS NOT "/examples/7/portal/Validate.cfm")
      AND (CGI.SCRIPT_NAME IS NOT
        "/examples/7/portal/RegistrationForm.cfm")
      AND (CGI.SCRIPT_NAME IS NOT
        "/examples/7/portal/RegistrationProcess.cfm")>
        <CFLOCATION URL="/examples/7/portal/login.cfm" ADDTOKEN="No">
    </CFIF>
  </CFIF>
</CFLOCK>

<!--- Reset the CFID and CFToken cookies to expire session and client
      variables after the user's browser closes --->
<CFIF IsDefined("Cookie.CFID") AND IsDefined("Cookie.CFToken")>
    <CFCOOKIE NAME="CFID" VALUE="#Cookie.CFID#">
    <CFCOOKIE NAME="CFToken" VALUE="#Cookie.CFToken#">
</CFIF>

<!--- check to see if the application has been initialized.  If not,
      set the necessary application variables and initialize the app --->
<CFLOCK SCOPE="Application" TYPE="Exclusive" TIMEOUT="10">
```

*Example 8-1. Application.cfm File for Setting Up Application Security (continued)*

```
  <CFIF NOT IsDefined('Application.Initialized')>
    <CFSET Application.DSN = "ProgrammingCF">
    <CFSET Application.AdminEmail = "webmaster@example.com">
    <!--- Set the application.initialized variable to true so that this
          block of code does not execute every time the Application.cfm
          file is called --->
    <CFSET Application.Initialized = TRUE>
  </CFIF>
</CFLOCK>
<CFSETTING ENABLECFOUTPUTONLY="No">
```

Once we name the application and set up session and application variable management, the next thing to do is make sure all users are logged out by default. This is accomplished by creating a session variable called `Session.LoggedIn` and setting it to `False`. This ensures that any user request to a template governed by the *Application.cfm* template from a user who isn't yet logged in will be treated as such. The next bit of code says that if `Session.LoggedIn` is `False`, and the user isn't currently in one of the login, validation, registration, or registration-processing templates, the user isn't logged in and should be redirected to the login screen. The addition of the registration form and registration-processing template to the list of templates exempt from the login requirement is the only difference between this *Application.cfm* template and the one from Chapter 7. This is the most important part of this type of security model, as it determines who is logged in and who isn't and responds appropriately. If `Session.LoggedIn` is `True`, we know that the user has successfully logged in.

The next action taken by the *Application.cfm* template is to take the `CFID` and `CFTOKEN` cookies set by ColdFusion and reset them to their current values. Doing this changes the expiration date of the cookies used by ColdFusion to maintain session state so they expire as soon as the user closes his or her browser. This prevents the potentially negative consequences of a user's session persisting after they have closed their browser.

The final section of this *Application.cfm* template checks for the existence of an application variable called `Application.Initialized`. If it doesn't exist (which it won't the first time a CFML template is invoked), ColdFusion responds by setting a number of constants for the application. After the constants are set, `Application.Initialized` is set to `True` so the next time the *Application.cfm* template is called, it isn't necessary to set all the constants again (since you only need to set application variables once).

## Creating Login and Registration Screens

The portal application is designed so that a nonauthenticated user attempting to access the portal is automatically redirected to a login screen, unless the user is already on the login screen or registering to become a user of the portal. The login process is handled by two CFML templates—one containing an HTML form for the user to enter a username and password and another template to process the form. Because this is a portal application, it's appropriate to allow users who aren't yet registered with the site to enroll themselves. To do this, a link to a registration form (*RegistrationForm.cfm*) is provided. Example 8-2 shows the code for the *Login.cfm* template.

*Example 8-2. Login.cfm Template for Authenticating Users*

```
<CFPARAM NAME="Username" DEFAULT="">

<CFIF IsDefined('Cookie.Username')>
  <CFSET Username = Cookie.Username>
</CFIF>

<CENTER>
<H2>Portal Login</H2>
<CFIF IsDefined('URL.Message')>
<CFOUTPUT>
<FONT COLOR="Red">#URL.Message#</FONT>
</CFOUTPUT>
<P>
</CFIF>

<FORM NAME="ValidateUser" ACTION="Validate.cfm" METHOD="POST">
<INPUT TYPE="hidden" NAME="Username_required" VALUE="You must supply a username">
<INPUT TYPE="hidden" NAME="Password_required" VALUE="You must supply a password">
<TABLE BORDER="0">
<TR>
  <TD>Username:</TD>
  <TD>
    <CFOUTPUT>
      <INPUT TYPE="text" NAME="Username" SIZE="15"
             MAXLENGTH="255" VALUE="#Username#">
    </CFOUTPUT>
  </TD>
</TR>
<TR>
  <TD>Password:</TD>
  <TD><INPUT TYPE="password" NAME="Password" SIZE="15" "MAXLENGTH="255"></TD>
</TR>
<TR>
  <TD COLSPAN="2">
    <INPUT TYPE="checkbox" NAME="SaveUsername"
           VALUE="Yes">Remember my username for future logins</TD>
</TR>
<TR>
```

*Example 8-2. Login.cfm Template for Authenticating Users (continued)*

```
  <TD COLSPAN="2" ALIGN="center">
    <INPUT TYPE="SUBMIT" NAME="Submit" VALUE="Submit">
  </TD>
</TR>
</TABLE>
</FORM>
*This site is for registered users.  If you are not currently a member,
you may <A HREF="RegistrationForm.cfm">register here</A>.
</CENTER>
```

This template creates a simple login screen that allows the user to enter a username and password (Figure 8-2). The password field uses the HTML password form control so that the user's password is obfuscated as it is typed.

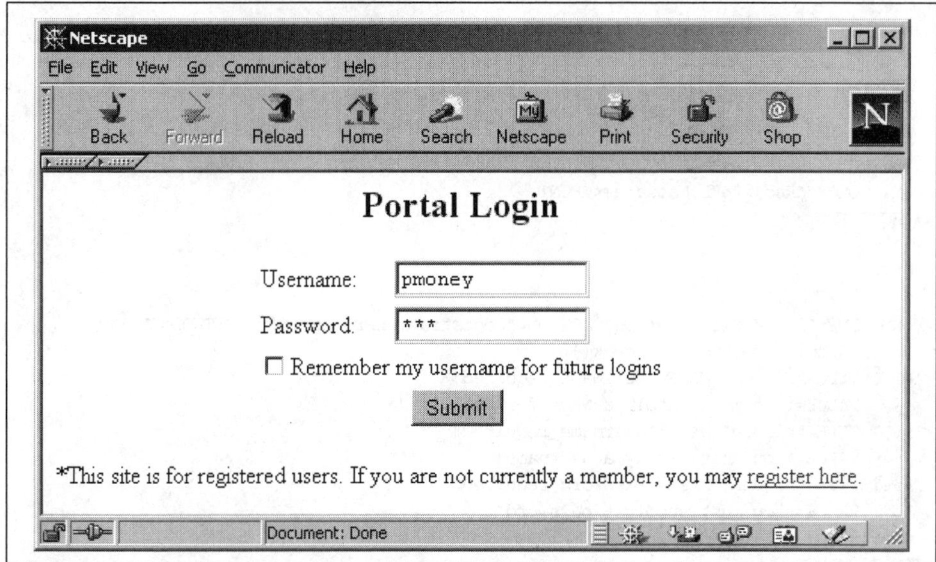


*Figure 8-2. Login.cfm template for logging in to the portal*

When this form is submitted, the information is posted to the *Validate.cfm* template shown in Example 8-5 for processing (we'll discuss this template in the next section, when we discuss authenticating users). If the user doesn't yet have an account, however, and wishes to register for one, he may do so by clicking on the "register here" link at the bottom of the page. Doing so takes the user to the registration form, *Registration.cfm*, shown in Example 8-3.

*Example 8-3. Registration.cfm template for Enrolling Users*

```
<CFPARAM NAME="FullName" DEFAULT="">

<!--- Function that ensures passwords match and that they aren't blank --->
<SCRIPT LANGUAGE="JavaScript">
```

*Example 8-3. Registration.cfm template for Enrolling Users (continued)*

```
function formCheck()
{
  if (document.PortalRegistration.Password.value !=
    document.PortalRegistration.Password2.value) {
      alert("The passwords you entered do not match.  Please reenter them.");
      document.PortalRegistration.Password.value = '';
      document.PortalRegistration.Password2.value = '';
      return false;
  }
  if (document.PortalRegistration.Password.value == "" ||
    document.PortalRegistration.Password2.value == "") {
      alert("You can not leave either password field blank.");
      return false;
  }
}
</SCRIPT>

<CENTER>
<H2>Portal Account Registration</H2>
<CFIF IsDefined('URL.Message')>
<CFOUTPUT>
<FONT COLOR="Red">#URL.Message#</FONT>
</CFOUTPUT>
<P>
</CFIF>

<FORM NAME="PortalRegistration" ACTION="RegistrationProcess.cfm" METHOD="POST"
      onSubmit="return formCheck()">
<INPUT TYPE="hidden" NAME="FullName_required"
      VALUE="You must supply a Name for the user">
<INPUT TYPE="hidden" NAME="Username_required"
      VALUE="You must supply a username">
<INPUT TYPE="hidden" NAME="Password_required"
      VALUE="You must supply a password">

<TABLE BORDER=0>
<TR>
  <TD>Full Name:</TD>
  <TD>
  <CFOUTPUT>
    <INPUT TYPE="text" NAME="FullName" SIZE="15" MAXLENGTH="255"
         VALUE="#FullName#">
  </CFOUTPUT>
  </TD>
</TR>
<TR>
  <TD>Username:</TD>
  <TD>
    <INPUT TYPE="text" NAME="Username" SIZE="15" MAXLENGTH="50">
  </TD>
</TR>
<TR>
```

*Example 8-3. Registration.cfm template for Enrolling Users (continued)*

```
  <TD>Password:</TD>
  <TD>
    <INPUT TYPE="password" NAME="Password" SIZE="15" MAXLENGTH="50">
  </TD>
</TR>
<TR>
  <TD>Confirm Password:</TD>
  <TD>
    <INPUT TYPE="password" NAME="Password2" SIZE="15" MAXLENGTH="50">
  </TD>
</TR>
<TR>
  <TD COLSPAN="2" ALIGN="center">
    <INPUT TYPE="SUBMIT" NAME="Submit" VALUE="Submit">
  </TD>
</TR>
</TABLE>
</FORM>
</CENTER>
```

This template creates a form that takes four inputs: Full Name, Username, Password and Confirm Password (Figure 8-3). The reason for two password fields is to ensure that the person entering the password gets it right (since the password is obfuscated by asterisks when it is typed).

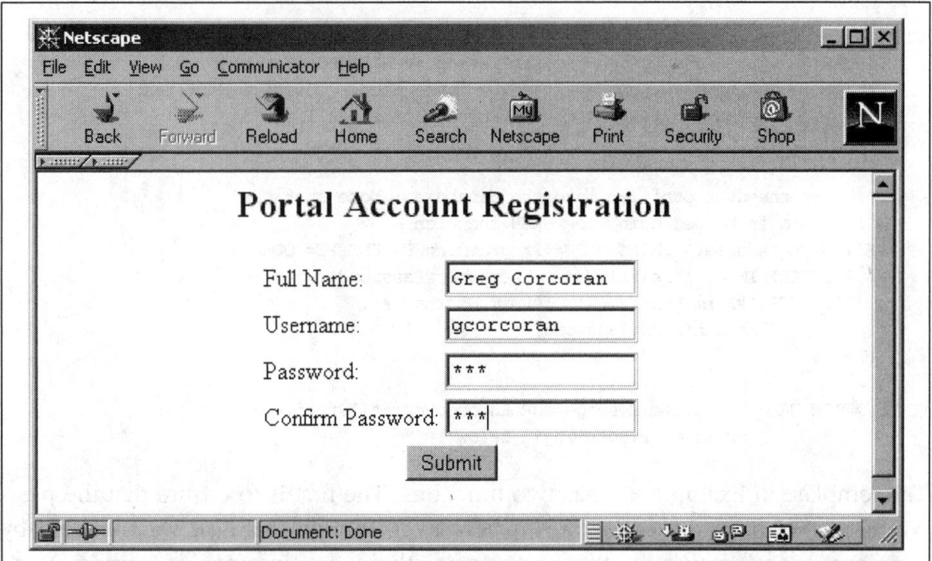


*Figure 8-3. RegistrationForm.cfm template for the portal application*

When the form is submitted, a JavaScript `onSubmit` event handler is invoked from the `FORM` tag. This event handler calls a short JavaScript function called

**formCheck()** at the beginning of our template. Note that JavaScript is case-sensitive, so it is important to reference field names and other functions with the proper case. The **formCheck()** function checks to see that the values entered for **Password** and Confirm Password (**Password2**) are the same, and that they aren't blank. If either test fails, a JavaScript alert box pops up letting the user know. After the user clicks the OK button, the function clears the Password and Confirm Password fields and returns the user to the form so that he can reenter the password. If both passwords match, the form is submitted to the *RegistrationProcess.cfm* template shown in Example 8-4.

*Example 8-4. Accepting User Profile Information*

```
<!--- check to see that passwords match in case the user had JavaScript
      disabled --->
<CFIF Form.Password NEQ Form.Password2>
  The passwords you entered on the login screen do not match.  Please
  hit your browser's back button and try again.
  <CFABORT>
</CFIF>

<!--- check to make sure the username (the primary key) doesn't already
      exist. If it does, make the user go back and enter a different
      username --->
<CFQUERY NAME="CheckPK" DATASOURCE="ProgrammingCF" DBTYPE="ODBC">
    SELECT Username FROM Users WHERE Username = '#Form.Username#'
</CFQUERY>
<CFIF CheckPK.RecordCount GT 0>
  <CFLOCATION URL="RegistrationForm.cfm?Message=#URLEncodedFormat("The
             username you chose already exists, please choose a different
             username.")#&FullName=#URLEncodedFormat(FullName)#">
</CFIF>

<!--- insert the user profile, into the database.  Note that the
      password is hashed using the HASH function --->
<CFQUERY NAME="AddUser" DATASOURCE="ProgrammingCF" DBTYPE="ODBC">
        INSERT INTO Users(FullName, Username, Password)
        VALUES('#Form.FullName#', '#Form.Username#',
               '#Hash(Form.Password)#')
</CFQUERY>

<CFLOCATION URL="login.cfm?Message=#URLEncodedFormat("Profile successfully
               created. Please login below")#">
```

The template in Example 8-4 has two functions. The first is to ensure that the passwords passed from the entry form match. Even though this task was handled by our JavaScript function in the entry form, there are instances where a user's browser doesn't support JavaScript or has it disabled. In case of this, we provide a server-side check by checking to see if **Form.Password** and **Form.Password2** are the same. If they aren't, a message is displayed to the user telling him to hit the back button on his browser and reenter the passwords, and processing of the template is halted. If the passwords do match, a **CFQUERY** is executed to insert the information from the form into the database. Before the password is inserted, it is hashed using ColdFusion's **Hash()** function. The **Hash()** function encrypts a string one way using the MD5 hash algorithm. The resulting string is a 32-character hexadecimal representation of the original string. Because the MD5 algorithm is a one-way hash, there is no way to decrypt the encrypted string. This makes it ideal for storing passwords in database tables, where you wouldn't want anyone to be able to open a table and view a list of user passwords.

Let's go ahead and add two records to the database using the form we just created. Use the data supplied in Table 8-2.

*Table 8-2. User Profile Information to Enter for Security Table*

| Username | Password | FullName |
|---|---|---|
| Gcorcoran | Dog | Greg Corcoran |
| Pmoney | Cat | Pere Money |

Once you have entered the data, open up your database and look at the data you just entered. Notice that each password field is populated with a 32-character string (as shown in Table 8-3). These strings are the hashed versions of the passwords you initially entered. We'll cover how to validate a password entered by a user on the login screen against the hashed value stored in the database in a few moments.

*Table 8-3. User Profile as It Appears in the Database After Having the Passwords Hashed*

| Username | Password | FullName |
|---|---|---|
| Gcorcoran | 06D80EB0C50B49A509B49F2424E8C805 | Greg Corcoran |
| Pmoney | D077F244DEF8A70E5EA758BD8352FCD8 | Pere Money |

## *Authenticating Users*

Once a user is registered for our portal, the next step is to allow him to log in to the system. You've already seen the login form from Example 8-2. When a user enters a username and password in the login form and clicks the submit button, the information from the form is posted to the *Validate.cfm* template in Example 8-5.

*Example 8-5. Validate.cfm Template for Handling User Validation*

```
<CFQUERY NAME="ValidateUser" DATASOURCE="ProgrammingCF">
    SELECT FullName FROM Users WHERE Username = '#Form.Username#'
    AND Password = '#Hash(Form.Password)#'
</CFQUERY>
```

*Example 8-5. Validate.cfm Template for Handling User Validation (continued)*

```
<!--- if the login is successful, log the user in.  Otherwise, redirect
      them back to the login.cfm page --->
<CFIF ValidateUser.RecordCount EQ 1>
   <!--- set Session.LoggedIn to True, logging the user in --->
   <CFLOCK TIMEOUT="30"  THROWONTIMEOUT="No" TYPE="EXCLUSIVE" SCOPE="SESSION">
     <CFSET Session.LoggedIn = TRUE>
   </CFLOCK>
   <!--- assign the user's fullname to a session variable so we can
         reference it anywhere in our application --->
   <CFLOCK TIMEOUT="30" THROWONTIMEOUT="No" TYPE="EXCLUSIVE" SCOPE="SESSION">
     <CFSET Session.FullName = ValidateUser.FullName>
   </CFLOCK>
   <!--- redirect the user to the index.cfm page of our application  --->
   <CFLOCATION URL="index.cfm" ADDTOKEN="no">
<CFELSE>
   <!--- redirect the user back to the login page and display the error
         message --->
   <CFLOCATION URL="Login.cfm?Message=#UrlEncodedFormat("Invalid Login.
                  Please Try Again")#&Username=#Username#" ADDTOKEN="no">
</CFIF>
```

The template shown in Example 8-5 queries the `Users` table of the database using the username and password posted by the login form in Example 8-2 as parameters for the `WHERE` clause. Note that the `Hash()` function is used on the `Form.Password` variable. This allows us to compare the hashed value of the password entered by the user against the hashed password stored in the database. If both the username and hashed password match those of a record in the database, `ValidateUser.RecordCount` evaluates to `1`. We consider this a valid login and set the session variable `Session.LoggedIn` to `True`. The user is then redirected to our portal's *Index.cfm* template (Example 7-3 in Chapter 7). If no records are found, `ValidateUser.RecordCount` evaluates to `0`. At this point, we know that the username/password combination is invalid, so we redirect the user back to the login page where the message "Invalid Login. Please Try Again" is displayed along with the login form. As a courtesy to users, the `Username` box is populated with the username originally submitted by the form. This is accomplished by passing the `Username` back as a URL variable.

As you can see, it really wasn't much work to add basic security features to our portal application. We simply made a database table to hold our user profiles and created a few simple CFML templates to handle the authentication and authorization functions required for the application.

## Securing Non-CFML Files

The security model we used in our portal application works well for controlling access to CFML templates, but what about other types of files, such as HTML templates, Microsoft Word documents, or Adobe PDF files? The problem is that if you place any file type other than a CFML template in a directory under the control of the security model, the user can still access the file by entering its URL because the *Application.cfm* template is included only for CFML templates. Because these files aren't parsed by ColdFusion, they aren't subject to the control of our security model. So, how can you secure non-CFML files while still using the security model?

The trick is to store the files you want to secure in a directory above your web root directory where they can't be accessed by a URL. For example, if your web root directory is *c:\inetsrv\wwwroot*, you can store the files you wish to secure in *c:\inetsrv*, *c:\inetsrv\securedfiles*, *c:\securedfiles*, or any other directory above *c:\inetsrv\wwwroot*, keeping the files inaccessible via URL provided you don't create a virtual directory to any of those directories.

Since files stored above the web root are inaccessible via URL, you need to use another method to retrieve them. This is where the `CFCONTENT` tag comes in. The `CFCONTENT` tag sends content (in this case a file) of a specified MIME type to the browser. This allows you to grab the file from its location above the web root and send it to the user's browser. The `CFCONTENT` tag accepts the following attributes:

```
<CFCONTENT TYPE="MIME_type"
           FILE="filename"
           RESET="Yes|No"
           DELETEFILE="Yes|No">
```

The `TYPE` attribute is required and specifies the MIME type of the content to be sent to the browser. `FILE` is optional and specifies the name of the file being sent to the browser. The `RESET` attribute is another optional attribute and accepts a `Yes/No` value. Specifying `Yes` results in the suppression of any output preceding the call to the `CFCONTENT` tag while `No` preserves the output. The `RESET` attribute is ignored if a value is specified for `FILE`. The default is `Yes`. The final attribute, `DELETEFILE`, is also optional and determines whether to delete the file after it has been sent to the browser. `DELETEFILE` is valid only if a file is specified in the `FILE` attribute. The default is `No`.

To demonstrate how the `CFCONTENT` tag can retrieve secured files, look at the code in Example 8-6. The template creates three hyperlinks, one for a Word document, one for a PDF file, and one for an HTML file.

*Example 8-6. Displaying a Menu of Secured Files*

```
<!--- You may use other files here.  Simply change the file name and MIME
      type to match the file you wish to use --->
<CFSET File1 = "MyDocument.doc">
<CFSET MIME1 = "application/msword">
<CFSET File2 = "MyPDF.pdf">
```

*Example 8-6. Displaying a Menu of Secured Files (continued)*

```
<CFSET MIME2 = "application/pdf">
<CFSET File3 = "MyHTML.htm">
<CFSET MIME3 = "text/html">

<H2>Secure File Download</H2>
<CFOUTPUT>
<TABLE>
<TR>
  <TD><A HREF="display.cfm?Filename=#URLEncodedFormat(File1)#&
MIMEType=#URLEncodedFormat(MIME1)#">Word Document</A></TD>
</TR>
<TR>
  <TD><A HREF="display.cfm?Filename=#URLEncodedFormat(File2)#&
MIMEType=#URLEncodedFormat(MIME2)#">PDF Document</A></TD>
</TR>
<TR>
  <TD><A HREF="display.cfm?Filename=#URLEncodedFormat(File3)#&
MIMEType=#URLEncodedFormat(MIME3)#">HTML File</A></TD>
</TR>
</TABLE>
</CFOUTPUT>
```

Although the list in this example is static, you can imagine how to easily pull the information used to construct the list from a database. This allows you to basically control who sees what file. Each link points to a template called *Display.cfm*, shown in Example 8-8. Two URL parameters are appended to each link. The first parameter, `Filename`, specifies the filename (including extension) of the file you want to download or display. The second URL parameter is `MIMEType` and specifies the MIME type of the file. You'll see why this is important in a moment. For now, look at the output generated by the template, shown in Figure 8-4.

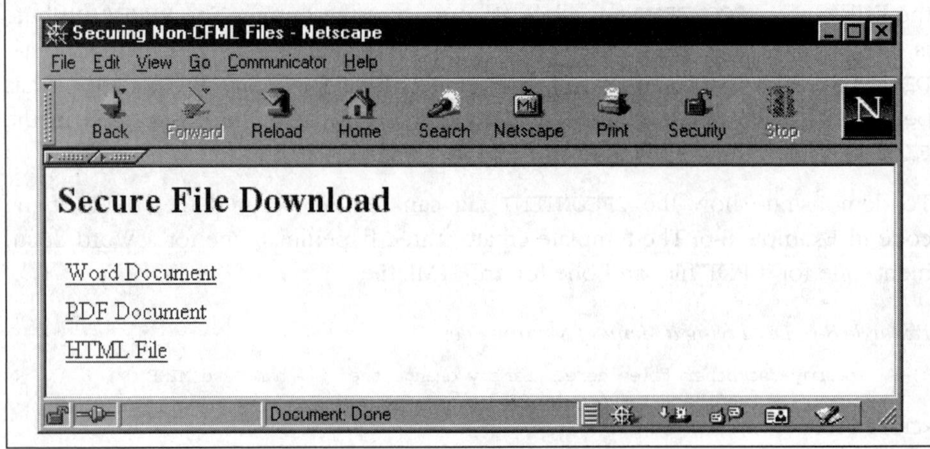


*Figure 8-4. Displaying links to secured files*

Clicking on any of the links generated by Example 8-6 passes the associated URL parameters to the *Display.cfm* template in Example 8-7.

*Example 8-7. Displaying Secured Files Using CFCONTENT*

```
<!--- Check to make sure the filename and mime type were passed in
      before processing --->
<CFIF IsDefined('URL.MIMEType') AND IsDefined('URL.FileName')>
  <!--- send the specified file to the browser.  You will need to store
        your files in a directory called c:\SecuredFiles for this
        example to work.  If you wish to use a different directory,
        change the directory name In the FILE attribute of the CFCONTENT
        tag. --->
  <CFCONTENT TYPE="#URL.MIMEType#"
             FILE="c:\SecuredFiles\#URL.Filename#">
<CFELSE>
  <H2>The specified file does not exist</H2>
</CFIF>
```

When the *Display.cfm* template receives the `Filename` and `MIMEType` URL parameters, it uses them to dynamically populate the `TYPE` and `FILE` attributes of the `CFCONTENT` tag. If the user clicks on the hyperlink to the Word document, the `CFCONTENT` tag retrieves the Word document and returns it to the browser. If the user has Word associated with the web browser, Word should launch automatically and display the document. If not, a Save As dialog box should pop up, allowing the user to save the Word document to his system. If the user clicks on the hyperlink to the Adobe PDF document and has the Adobe Acrobat reader installed on the system, the PDF file should automatically display in the browser. If Acrobat reader isn't installed, the same Save As dialog box appears. Finally, if the user clicks on the link to the HTML file, the `CFCONTENT` tag retrieves it and displays it directly in the browser.

The technique presented here isn't the only way to use the `CFCONTENT` tag to serve secured files. Instead of passing the filename and mime type in the URL, you could pass a file ID (such as a UUID) and use it to look up a database record containing the filename and MIME type as well as any additional information such as the directory on the server where the file is stored. Regardless of the technique you use, it is important to make sure you control access to the template(s) used to retrieve the secured files.

## *Levels of Access*

The security model we've been discussing is great for granting and denying access to an application based on a user login. If a user is granted access, they are given access to the entire application and all its functionality. There are instances, however, where you might want to grant different levels of access to an application depending on who the user is. This can be handled easily with the security model we just described with the introduction of a few additional lines of code and a new database field. If you add an additional field to the database called `SecurityLevel`, you could use this field to assign a numeric security level for each of your users. When a user logs in, retrieve their `SecurityLevel` using the same query used to get their `Username` and assign it to a session variable. In each template of your application, include a bit of logic to check the user's `Session.SecurityLevel` against the level required for access to the page. If it is equal to or greater than the level required, grant them access. If not, redirect them to a page telling them their `SecurityLevel` isn't high enough for access to the page.

# Using ColdFusion's Built-in Advanced Security Services

Now that we've looked at implementing security from scratch, let's talk about the built-in Advanced Security services in ColdFusion. ColdFusion supports a set of Advanced Security services that integrate with an OEM version of Netegrity's popular SiteMinder (Version 3.51 for ColdFusion 4.5.x and Version 4.11 for ColdFusion 5.0) security product for providing granular control within your ColdFusion applications. In order to use ColdFusion's Advanced Security services, you must be running either the Windows NT or Unix version of ColdFusion Professional or Enterprise edition. Advanced security on Linux is planned for a future release.

From a developer's perspective, there are two pieces that make up ColdFusion's Advanced Security services: security contexts and application code that validates against the security contexts. Security contexts are created in the ColdFusion Administrator and provide the framework for authenticating and authorizing users. Security contexts consist of policies that govern users' access to resources such as files, CFML tags, and data sources within an application. Security administration is handled via the ColdFusion Administrator.

## Administering Advanced Security

Although a full discussion of the ins and outs of setting up and administering ColdFusion's Advanced Security services is beyond the scope of this book, it is useful to briefly cover the basic steps involved in creating a security context for authenticating users and controlling access to resources.

### Enable Advanced Security

The first step you need to take is to enable Advanced Security. To do this, click the Security tab in the ColdFusion Administrator. Next, click the Security Configuration link under the Advanced Security section. Check the Use Advanced Server

Security box on the Security Configuration page, and click the Submit Changes Button.

On the Advanced Security page (Figure 8-5), change the value in the Shared Secret field to any arbitrary value. By default, all ColdFusion servers install with the same encryption key. When you have finished, click the Submit Changes button.

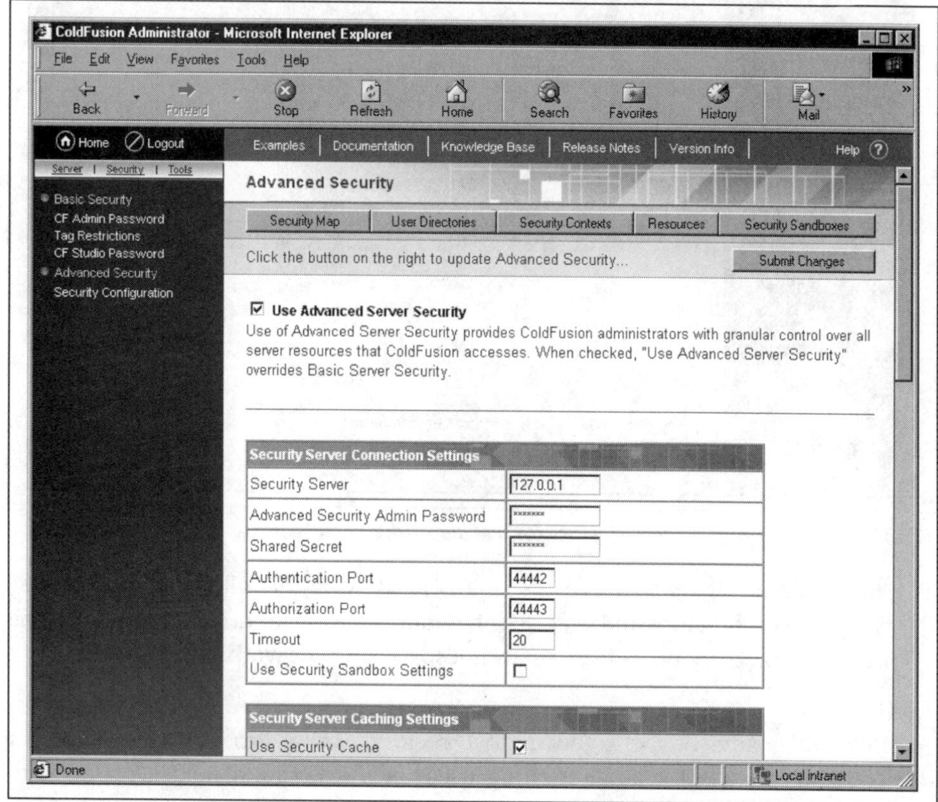


*Figure 8-5. Advanced Security page in the ColdFusion Administrator*

### *Set up a user directory*

Once you have enabled Advanced Security, the next step is to set up a user directory for authenticating users. You set up a user directory by clicking on the User Directories button at the top or bottom of the Advanced Security page. At this point, you will be taken to a screen (Figure 8-6) where you can choose to add a new user directory or edit an existing one. Enter the name for your new user directory here, and click on the Connect Directory button.

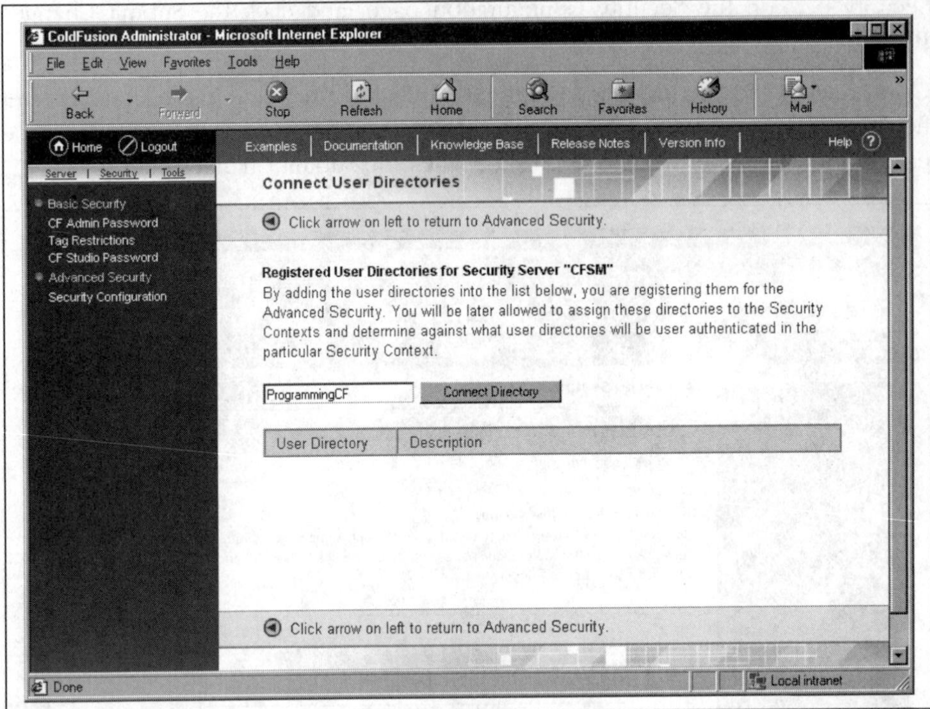


*Figure 8-6. Registering a user directory for use with Advanced Security*

The next screen (Figure 8-7) consists of an HTML form that allows you to choose the type of user directory and enter configuration information. You can select one of three user directory types from the Namespace drop-down box:

*LDAP*
: Enter the name of the Lightweight Directory Access Protocol (LDAP) server you want to use for authenticating users in the Location field. You need to specify additional options under the LDAP Settings section of the form. Basic LDAP concepts are covered in Chapter 15. This is the only valid option for the Unix version of ColdFusion.

*ODBC*
: In order to use a database structure other than the Microsoft Access database *SmSampleUsers.mdb* included with ColdFusion, you must modify the contents of the fields under the ODBC Settings heading to match the schema used by your security database. Once you have done that, enter the name of the database as defined in your ODBC settings in the Location field. It is recommended that you use an enterprise-level database (i.e., not Access) for storing user directory information in a production environment. The following Knowledge Base articles (available at *http://www.allaire.com/support/KnowledgeBase/*

*SearchForm.cfm)* explain how to upsize the database from Access to Microsoft SQL Server and Oracle respectively:

*Article 14566*

"Migrating the Advanced Security Policy Store and User Directory from Access to Microsoft SQL Server"

*Article 15891*

"Advanced Security: Migrating Policy Store from Access to Oracle"

*Windows NT*

To use a Windows NT user directory, enter the domain name of the server in the Location box. If required by the domain, you may also need to enter a username and password in the appropriate fields. When you have finished, click the Apply button. Note that Microsoft Active Directory is supported only in ColdFusion 5.0.

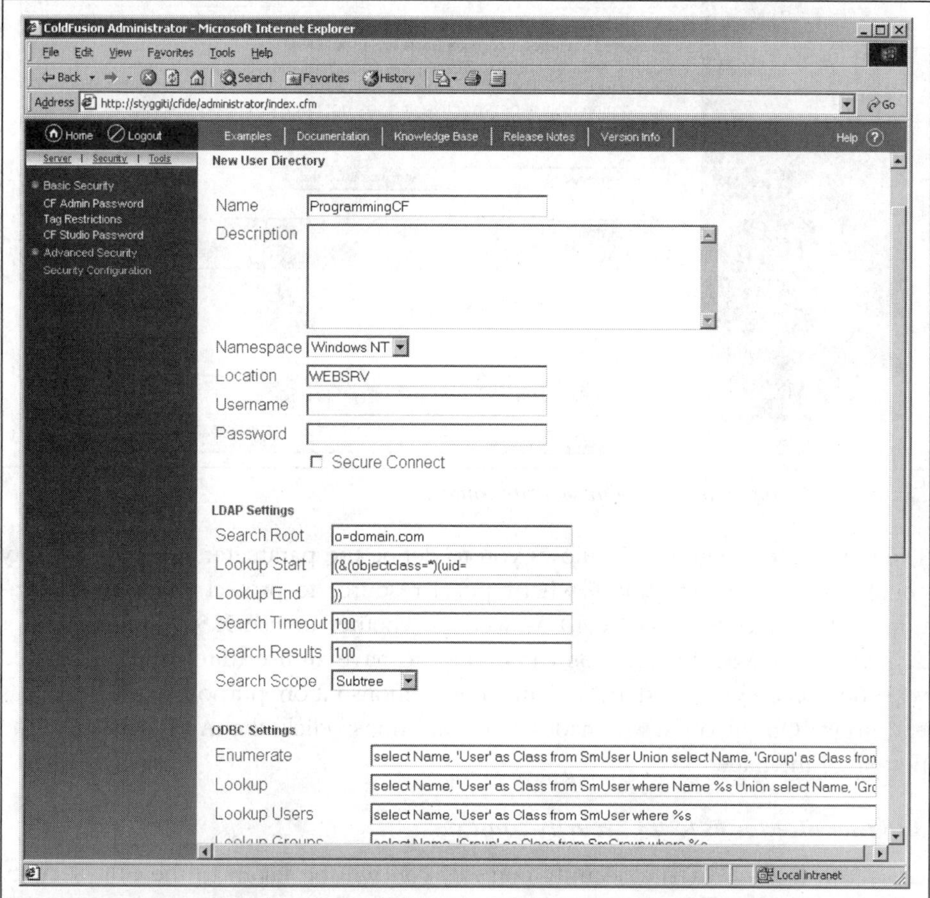


*Figure 8-7. Configuring a user directory*

For additional information on configuring user directories, consult the Allaire documentation that came with your version of ColdFusion.

### *Create a security context*

The next step is to create a security context. To get started, click on the button at the top or bottom of the Advanced Security page labeled Security Contexts. On the next page (Figure 8-8), enter a name for your security context and click on the Add Security Context button.

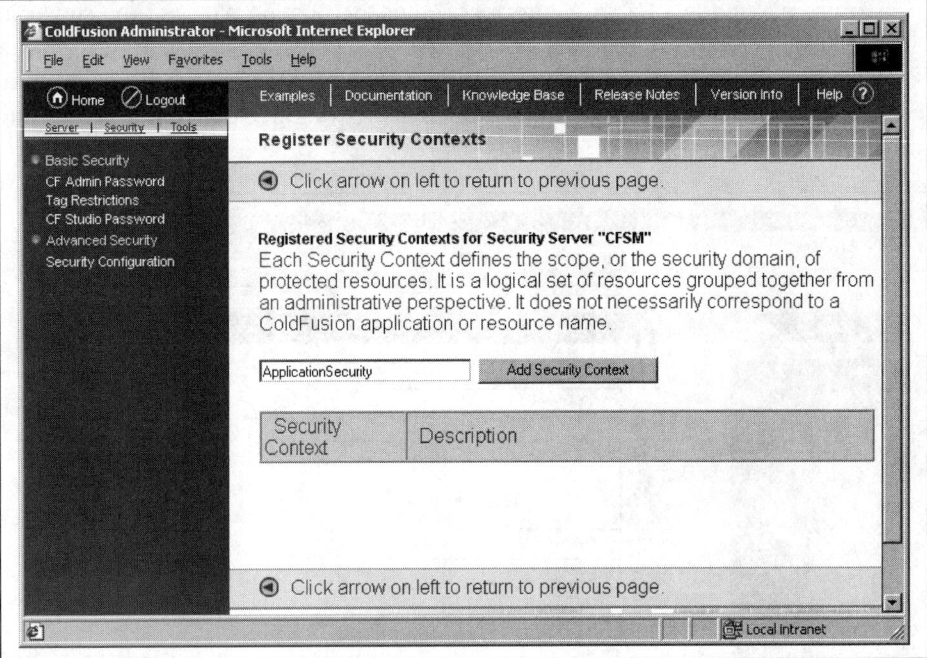


*Figure 8-8. Giving a name to your security context*

The next screen (Figure 8-9) allows you to define the parameters for your security context. Here you can choose what type of resource to protect (such as Application, DataSource, Function, etc.) as well as whether to use X.509 certificates for authentication. Additionally, you can choose to have all user directories associated with this security context by default. For demonstration purposes, uncheck this checkbox. Once you have made your selections, click the Add button at the bottom of the page.

### *Add user directories to the security context*

Once you have created a security context, you will be taken to the Edit Security Context page. Here you can make any changes to the information you just added.

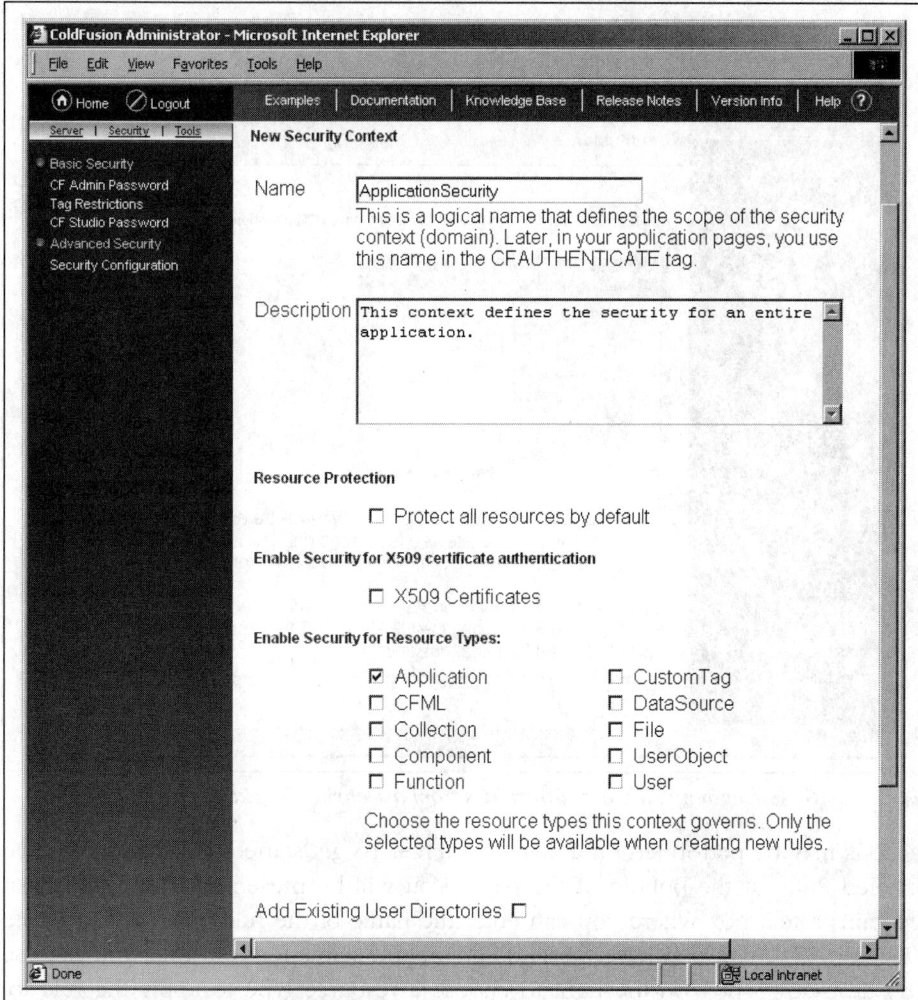


*Figure 8-9. Editing security context parameters*

If you didn't check the Add Existing User Directories box when you created your security context, you need to associate at least one user directory with your context now. To do this, scroll to the bottom of the page and click on the button labeled User Directories. This takes you to a page where you can choose what user directories you want to associate with your security context (Figure 8-10). When you are finished, click on the Back button to continue.

### *Establish rules for resources within the security context*

After associating user directories with your security context, you need to go ahead and create one or more rules for the context. Rules are used to control what

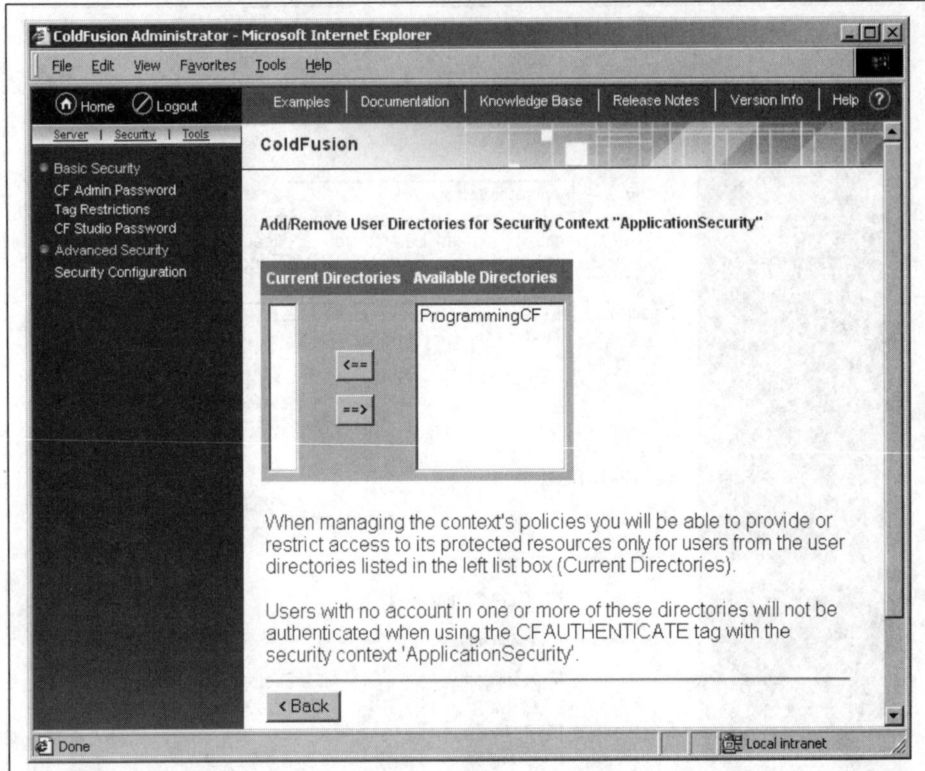


*Figure 8-10. Adding/removing user directories from a security context*

actions may be performed on a given resource. To get started, click on the button labeled Rules at the bottom of the page. You will be presented with a page that contains a text box where you can enter the name of the rule you want to create (Figure 8-11). After you have finished entering the name for your rule, you can use the drop-down box on the right to choose a resource type to apply the rule to. The list of resource types varies depending on the resource types you selected when setting up your security context. Once you have named your rule and associated it with a resource type, click on the Add button.

The next page you come to allows you to set the parameters for your rule (Figure 8-12). Your options will vary depending on the type of resource you chose to protect. Once you have established the parameters for your rule, click on the Add button at the bottom of the page. At this point, you can choose to add more rules to your security context, or you can click on the Back button to continue.

#### *Create policies for associating users with rules*

The final step in creating a security context is to match the rules you created to specific users or groups of users. This is done by creating one or more policies

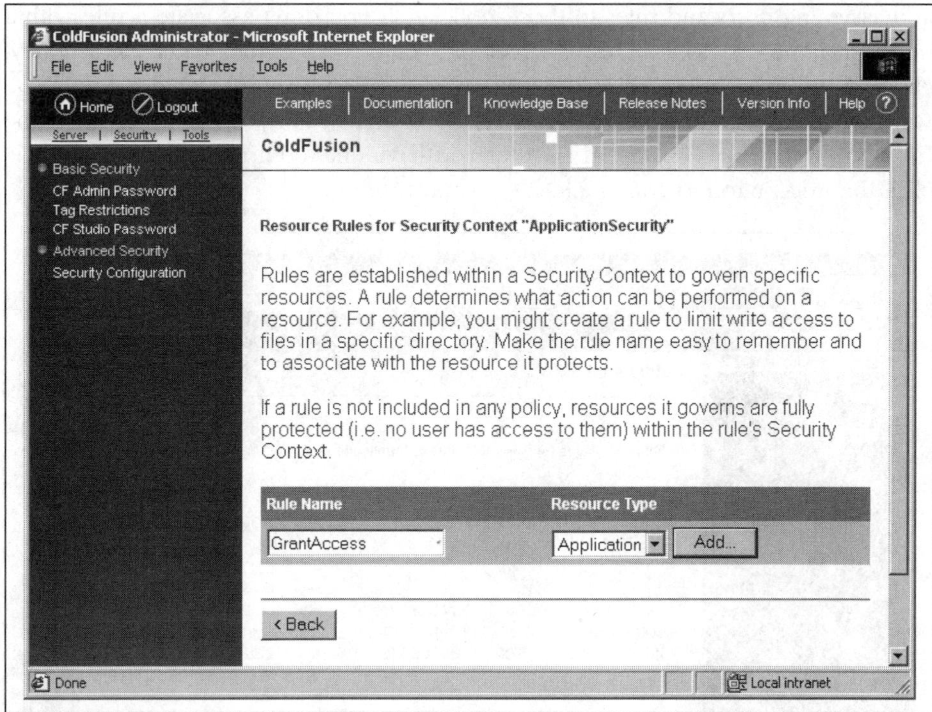


*Figure 8-11. Naming a rule and choosing a resource type*

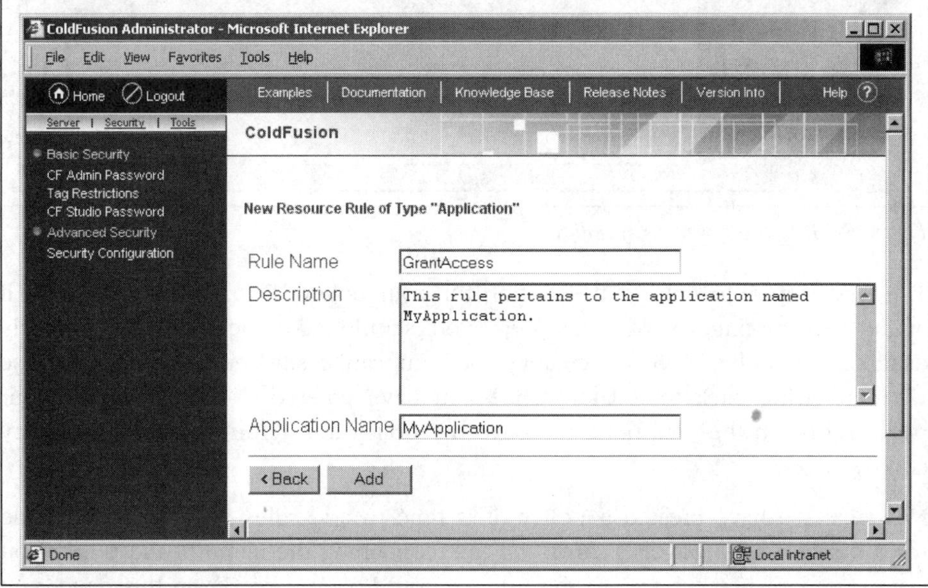


*Figure 8-12. Setting the parameters for a rule*

and assigning users and rules to those policies. If you don't associate a rule with a policy, no one can access the resources protected by that rule. To create a policy, click on the Policies button at the bottom of the Edit Security Context page. You will be presented with a page containing a text box where you can enter the name for your new policy (Figure 8-13). After you have entered a name for your policy, click the Add button to continue.

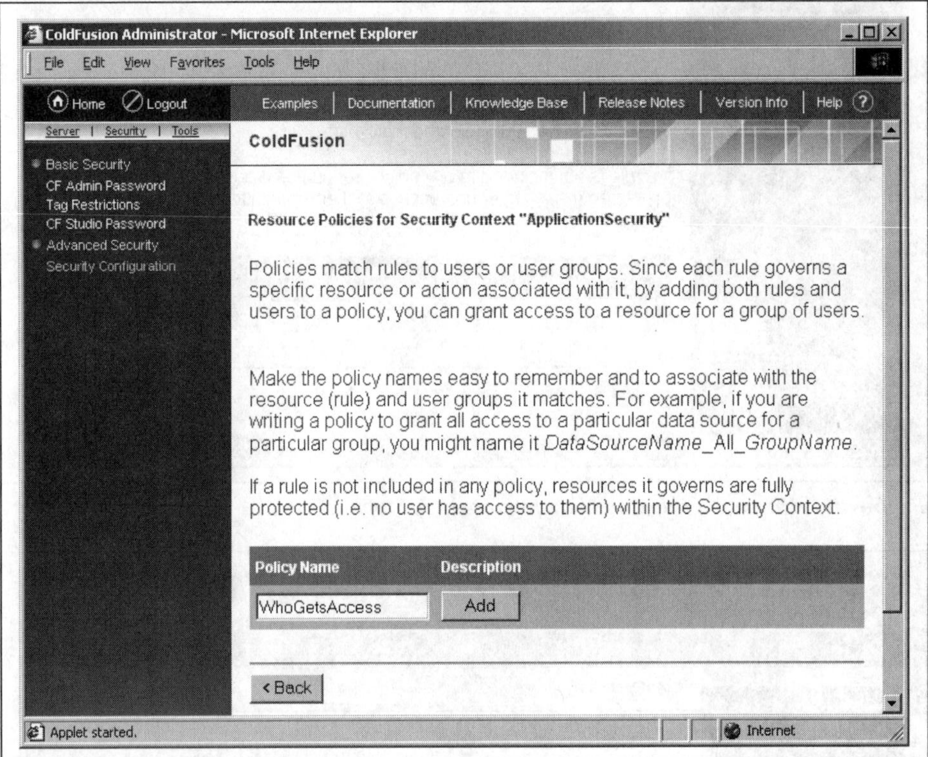


*Figure 8-13. Naming a security policy*

The next step is to enter a description for your policy (Figure 8-14). Although it might be tempting to skip this step, you should take the time to accurately describe the policy you are creating, so you can easily remember its purpose when referring back to it later. Once you have entered a description for your policy, click on the Add button to save the policy and return to the main policy editing page.

Now that we have created a policy, it is time to add rules and users. From the main policy-editing page, click on the link containing the name of the policy you just created. This takes you to the Edit Security Policy page. From this page, you can edit your policy as well as add users and rules. To add rules, click on the

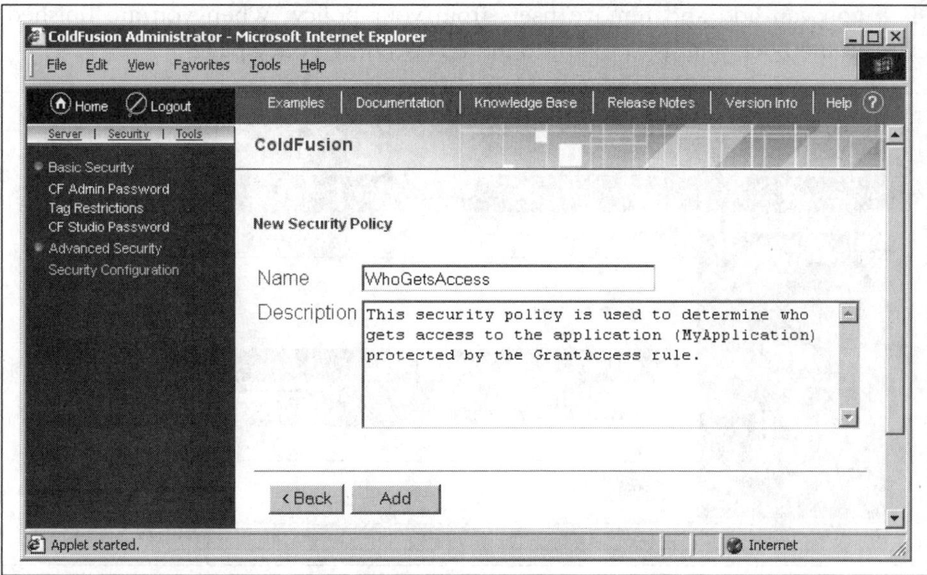


*Figure 8-14. Adding a description to your security policy*

Rules button at the bottom of the page. This takes you to the Resource Rules for Policy page (Figure 8-15) where you can choose to add and remove rules from your policy. Once you have finished adding rules to your policy, click on the Back button to return to the Edit Security Policy page.

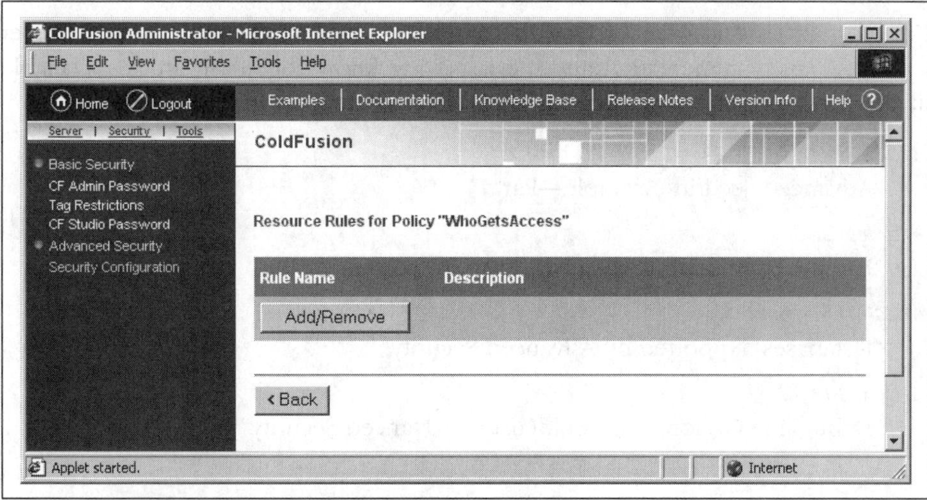


*Figure 8-15. Adding rules to your security policy*

To add users to your policy, click on the Users button at the bottom of the Edit Security Policy page. This takes you to the Users for Policy page (Figure 8-16).

Here you can add and remove users from your policy. When you are finished, click on the Back button to return to the Edit Security Policy page.

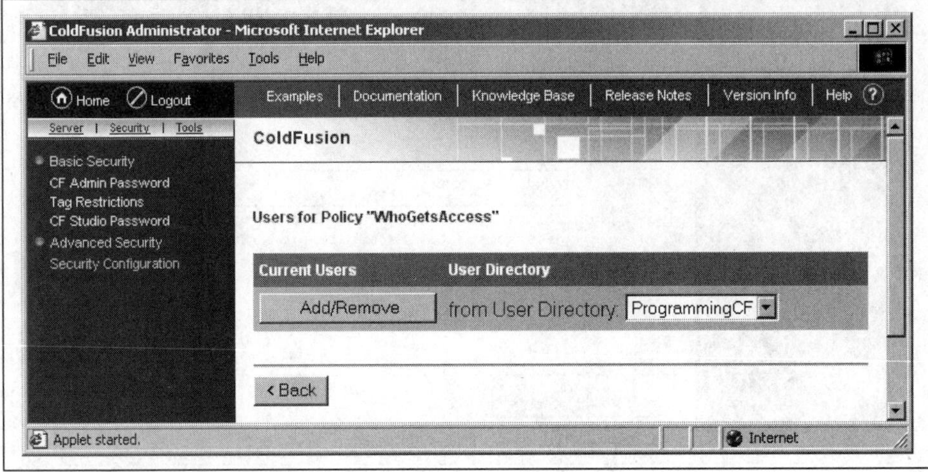


*Figure 8-16. Adding users to your security policy*

Once you have finished adding users and rules to your policy, you can begin using your security context within your applications to authenticate users and authorize them access to specific resources.

### *Additional resources*

For more information on working with users, policies and security contexts, refer to the Allaire documentation and the following knowledge-base articles available at *http://www.allaire.com/support/knowledgebase/SearchForm.cfm*:

*Article 12385*
: "Advanced Security Example—Part I"

*Article 12250*
: "Using CFAuthenticate to Secure your Templates"

*Article 15746*
: "Databases Supported by Advanced Security"

*Article 11432*
: "Debugging Options with ColdFusion Advanced Security"

*Article 14566*
: "Advanced Security—Migrating Policy Store from Access to MS SQL Server"

*Article 13335*
: "Converting the SiteMinder Policy Server to an LDAP Database"

*Article 12561*

"Advanced Security: Configuring LDAP as a User Directory"

*Article 15670*

"Advanced Security Installation with Netscape LDAP 411"

## *Authenticating Users*

The first programmatic step in implementing security using Advanced Security is to authenticate users. Just as in our previous security examples, we need to create an *Application.cfm* template to serve as the foundation for this security model. In this case, however, the *Application.cfm* file is going to handle all the authentication tasks in a single template. The code for our *Application.cfm* template can be seen in Example 8-8.

*Example 8-8. Application.cfm Template for Implementing Advanced Security*

```
<CFAPPLICATION NAME="MyApplication" SESSIONMANAGEMENT="Yes"
               CLIENTMANAGEMENT="No" SETCLIENTCOOKIES="Yes"
               SESSIONTIMEOUT="#CreateTimeSpan(0, 0, 30, 0)#"
               APPLICATIONTIMEOUT="#CreateTimeSpan(0, 0, 30, 0)#">

<!--- set the default value for username to blank --->
<CFPARAM NAME="Username" DEFAULT="">

<!--- if username and password exist, and the user is not already
      authenticated, we know that the login form was used to call the
      page, so we attempt to authenticate the user --->
<CFIF IsDefined('Form.Username') AND IsDefined('Form.Password')
      AND NOT IsAuthenticated()>
  <CFTRY>
    <CFAUTHENTICATE SecurityContext="ApplicationSecurity"
                    Username="#form.username#" Password="#form.password#"
                    SetCookie="Yes" ThrowOnFailure="Yes">

    <!-- if the authentication attempt fails, present the user with a
         message telling them the login is invalid and to please try
         again --->
    <CFCATCH TYPE="Security">
      <CENTER>
      <H2>Invalid Login.  Please Try Again</H2>
      </CENTER>
    </CFCATCH>
  </CFTRY>
</CFIF>

<!--- if the user is not authenticated, present them with the login
      form.  Note that the login form posts to your Index.cfm page --->
<CFIF not IsAuthenticated()>
  <CENTER>
  <FORM ACTION="index.cfm" METHOD="POST">
```

*Example 8-8. Application.cfm Template for Implementing Advanced Security (continued)*

```
  <INPUT TYPE="hidden" NAME="Username_required" VALUE="You must supply
         a username">
  <INPUT TYPE="hidden" NAME="Password_required" VALUE="You must supply
         a password">

  <TABLE BORDER=0>
  <TR>
    <TD>Username:</TD>
    <TD>
      <CFOUTPUT>
          <INPUT TYPE="text" NAME="Username" SIZE="15" MAXLENGTH="255"
              VALUE="#Username#">
      </CFOUTPUT>
    </TD>
  </TR>

  <TR>
    <TD>Password:</TD>
    <TD>
      <INPUT TYPE="password" NAME="Password" SIZE="15" "MAXLENGTH=255">
    </TD>
  </TR>

  <TR>
    <TD COLSPAN="2" ALIGN="center">
      <INPUT TYPE="SUBMIT" NAME="Submit" VALUE="Submit">
    </TD>
  </TR>
</TABLE>
</FORM>
</CENTER>
<!--- this CFABORT keeps the requesting page from executing and
      including its content on the same page as our form --->
<CFABORT>
</CFIF>
```

This *Application.cfm* template differs from the one we created for our portal application (Example 8-1). Instead of using three templates to handle the authentication process, everything is wrapped up inside the *Application.cfm* template. Additionally, authentication is now handled via the `CFAUTHENTICATE` tag as opposed to by a `CFQUERY`.

The `CFAPPLICATION` tag establishes an application called `MyApplication`. Session management is enabled, and session and application timeouts of 30 minutes are set. Next, a variable called `Username` is set using the `CFPARAM` tag with a default of `""`. This is significant in that if the *Application.cfm* template is called, and `Username` doesn't already exist, it is created and assigned a value of `""`. We'll get to the importance of this in just a moment.

Next, we check to see if the form variables `Username` and `Password` exist. If they do, we know that the *Application.cfm* template is being called from our login form. In the same `CFIF` statement, we also use the `IsAuthenticated()` function to make sure that the user accessing the page isn't already authenticated. This step allows us to keep a person from logging in as more than one user at a time. If the user isn't already authenticated, and we have values for both `Username` and `Password`, we use the `CFAUTHENTICATE` tag to try to authenticate the user using the information provided. The `CFAUTHENTICATE` tag can be used only when Advanced Security is enabled within the ColdFusion Administrator. The `CFAUTHENTICATE` tag takes the following attributes:

`SECURITYCONTEXT`
: The name of the security context to authenticate the user within. Required. Security contexts are defined in the ColdFusion Administrator.

`USERNAME`
: The name of the user being authenticated. Required.

`PASSWORD`
: The password of the user being authenticated. Required.

`SETCOOKIE`
: If set to `Yes`, ColdFusion sets an encrypted cookie on the users browser containing the username, security context, browser's remote address, and HTTP user agent. Optional. The default is `Yes`.

`THROWONFAILURE`
: Determines if ColdFusion should throw an exception if authentication fails. Optional. The default is `Yes`.

The authentication code is wrapped in a `CFTRY/CFCATCH` to catch invalid logins and other errors. If an invalid login is given, a message alerting the user to the error is displayed to the browser along with a login form containing the `Username` field already filled out with the username previously provided by the user. If authentication is successful, the user is sent to the template specified in the `ACTION` attribute of the `FORM` tag used for the login form.

If `Username` and `Password` aren't already defined when the *Application.cfm* template is called, a login form is created. Note that the `CFABORT` tag is used after the form is created in order to keep the template calling the *Application.cfm* from displaying. Submitting the login form results in the *Application.cfm* template being called again before the *Index.cfm* template specified in the `ACTION` attribute of the `FORM` tag. If authentication is successful, the *Application.cfm* template relinquishes control to the *Index.cfm* template.

One of the main reasons for placing all login functionality within the *Application.cfm* template has to do with the way ColdFusion deals with setting cookies and using the CFLOCATION tag in the same template. Because using CFLOCATION after setting a cookie in a template results in the cookie not being set, you can't use the CFAUTHENTICATE tag with the SETCOOKIE attribute set to Yes on the same page you have a CFLOCATION tag.

## *Authorizing Access to Specific Resources*

Besides authenticating users, ColdFusion's Advanced Security services allow you to grant and deny access to individual resources within a given security context. This means that with very little application code, you can grant individual users of your applications different levels of access based on who they are. For example, you can implement a security context that has several rules determining what users have access to various file-manipulation features (such as upload, write, delete, etc.) within an application that uses the CFFILE tag. Using two functions, IsProtected() and IsAuthorized(), it is possible to programmatically determine what resources are protected and whether a user is authorized to access them. The granularity of the Advanced Security services lets you be as relaxed or as strict with security as you need to be.

### *Using IsProtected()*

IsProtected() lets you check to see if a resource is protected before you try to determine if a user is authorized to use it. IsProtected() is called in the following manner:

```
IsProtected(ResourceType, ResourceName [, Action])
```

The function returns True if the specified resource is a protected resource within the security context of the currently authenticated user. The parameter *ResourceType* specifies the type of resource to check while *ResourceName* specifies the actual name of the resource (i.e. tag name, function name, collection name, etc.). The possible resource types are listed in Table 8-4, along with the possible values for *Action*. *Action* is required for all resource types except Compontent, CustomTag, Function, and User and specifies the action of the resource we are trying to check.

*Table 8-4. Resource Types and Associated Actions for the IsProtected() Function*

| ResourceType | Possible Values for Action |
|---|---|
| Application | All, UseClientVariables |
| CFML | Any valid action of the CFML tag specified in *ResourceType* |
| Collection | Delete, Optimize, Purge, Search, Update |
| Component | N/A |
| CustomTag | N/A |

*Table 8-4. Resource Types and Associated Actions for the IsProtected() Function (continued)*

| ResourceType | Possible Values for Action |
|---|---|
| `Datasource` | `All`, `Connect`, `Delete`, `Insert`, `Select`, `SP` (stored procedure), `Update` |
| `File` | `Read`, `Write` |
| `Function` | N/A |
| `User` | N/A |
| `UserObject` | *`Action`* as specified in the ColdFusion Administrator |

In order to use the `IsProtected()` function, Advanced Security needs to be enabled within the ColdFusion Administrator, and a valid security context must already be defined.

The following bit of code uses the `IsProtected()` function to determine if file uploading via `CFFILE` is a protected resource:

```
<CFIF IsProtected('CFML', 'CFFILE', 'Upload')>
  File uploading using CFFILE is a protected resource!
<CFELSE>
  File uploading using CFFILE is not a protected resource!
</CFIF>
```

### *Using IsAuthorized()*

Once you have authenticated a user within your application and determined that a resource is protected, you can check to see if the user is authorized access to a specific resource within the current security context. This is accomplished using the `IsAuthorized()` function. Note that it isn't necessary to check whether a resource is protected before you see if a user is authorized to access it. `IsAuthorized()` is called like this:

```
IsAuthorized(ResourceType, ResourceName [, Action])
```

The function returns `True` if the user is authorized to perform the *`Action`* specified against a particular ColdFusion resource. The parameter *`ResourceType`* specifies the type of resource to check while *`ResourceName`* specifies the actual name of the resource. The possible resource types are listed in Table 8-4, along with possible values for *`Action`*. *`Action`* is required for all resource types except `Compontent` and `CustomTag` and specifies the action we are checking authorization for.

In order to use the `IsAuthorized()` function, Advanced Security needs to be enabled within the ColdFusion Administrator, and a valid security context must already be defined.

The following snippet of code checks to see if file uploading is a protected resource, and if so, uses the `IsAuthorized()` function to determine if a user is authorized to use the `CFFILE` tag to perform the file upload:

```
<CFIF IsProtected('CFML', 'CFFILE', 'Upload')>
   <CFIF IsAuthorized('CFML', 'CFFILE', 'Upload')>
     perform file upload...
   <CFELSE>
     You are not authorized to upload files!
   </CFIF>
</CFIF>
```

Note that the `IsProtected()` and `IsAuthorized()` functions are a lot less strict than many other ColdFusion functions. If you accidentally specify a resource type, name, or action that doesn't exist, an error will not be thrown in most cases, and the function will evaluate to `False`. Because of this, you should pay close attention when coding with the `IsProtected()` and `IsAuthorized()` functions.

## Impersonating Users

At times, you may need to let users access resources they aren't normally authorized to use. The `CFIMPERSONATE` tag was created for just this purpose. It lets you temporarily impersonate a user within a security context previously set up within the ColdFusion Administrator. The syntax for using `CFIMPERSONATE` is as follows:

```
<CFIMPERSONATE SECURITYCONTEXT="security_context"
               USERNAME="username"
               PASSWORD="password"
               TYPE="CF|OS">
...
</CFIMPERSONATE>
```

The `CFIMPERSONATE` tag takes the following attributes:

`SECURITYCONTEXT`
: The name of the security context to authenticate the user within. Required. Security contexts are defined in the ColdFusion Administrator.

`USERNAME`
: The name of the user you want to impersonate for authentication. Required.

`PASSWORD`
: The password of the user you want to impersonate. Required.

`TYPE`
: Specifies the type of impersonation to use. Possible values are `CF` and `OS`. `CF` specifies impersonation at the application level. `OS` specifies impersonation at the operating system level—where the user specified is a valid user on the system. `OS` is available only on the Windows NT version of ColdFusion. The operating-system user being impersonated must be assigned the user right to

"Logon as a Batch Job". While OS impersonation processes faster than CF impersonation, it is limited in the types of resources the operating system can grant or deny access to. Required.

To better understand how CFIMPERSONATE works, consider the following example. Suppose your ISP has the CFREGISTRY tag disabled on their server for security reasons. Say your ISP also wants to allow you to programmatically retrieve a list of all available Verity collections on their server for use in a new search engine you are building. You have a dilemma. You need to use the CFREGISTRY tag in order to get the list of Verity collections from the server's registry, but your ISP has the CFREGISTRY tag disabled. Don't worry, there is a solution. Your ISP can use CFIMPERSONATE wrapped in a shared custom tag to allow you to get the Verity collection names without having to code the CFREGISTRY piece yourself. That way, you get access to the information you need, and your ISP is able to maintain full control over a potentially problematic CFML tag. The template for calling such a tag and using the results can be seen in Example 8-9.

*Example 8-9. Calling the GetVerityCollections Custom Tag and Displaying the Results*

```
<!--- call the GetVerityCollections custom tag --->
<CF_GETVERITYCOLLECTIONS RETURNQUERY="CollectionNames">

<!--- build a search form with a select box containing the names of the
      Verity collections we retrieved from the registry.  Note that the
      name of the query used to build the select box is the name we
      passed the custom tag.  ENTRY is a column name returned with the
      query --->
<H3>Collection Search</H3>
<FORM ACTION="searchresults.cfm" METHOD="post">
Search for: <INPUT TYPE="text" NAME="SearchString" SIZE="15" MAXLENGTH="255"
<BR>
Collection: <SELECT NAME="CollectionNames">
               <OPTION VALUE="">ALL Collections</OPTION>
               <CFOUTPUT QUERY="CollectionNames">
               <OPTION VALUE="#Entry#">#Entry#</OPTION>
               </CFOUTPUT>
            </SELECT>
<BR>
<INPUT TYPE="Submit" NAME="Submit" VALUE="Search">
</FORM>
```

This template makes a call to a custom tag called CF_GetVerityCollections (Example 8-10) and passes a single attribute containing a name for the query object to be returned by the tag. In this case, we named the return query CollectionNames. The next part of the template creates a search form containing a text box where users can input their search criteria and a drop-down box they can use to select a Verity collection to search. This drop-down box is dynamically populated from the query object returned by the CF_Get-

VerityCollections custom tag. The code for the CF_GetVerityCollections tag can be seen in Example 8-10. The template needs to be saved as *GetVerityCollections.cfm* in the CustomTags directory or in the same directory as Example 8-9. Custom tags are covered in detail in Chapter 19.

*Example 8-10. Wrapping CFIMPERSONATE Functionality in a Custom Tag*

```
<!--- assign a default value to ReturnQuery in the event the variable
      does not exist --->
<CFPARAM NAME="ReturnQuery" DEFAULT="GetcollectionNames">

<!--- check to see that an attribute called ReturnQuery was passed to
      the tag and that it is not blank.  If either condition is False,
      use the default set by the CFPARAM tag at the beginning of the
      template --->
<CFIF IsDefined('Attributes.ReturnQuery') AND Attributes.ReturnQuery
      NEQ "">
   <CFSET ReturnQuery = Attributes.ReturnQuery>
</CFIF>

<!--- impersonate a valid user for the SharedTags context. --->
<CFIMPERSONATE SECURITYCONTEXT="SharedTags" USERNAME="SharedTag"
               PASSWORD="Free4All" TYPE="CF">

<!--- get a list of Verity collections from the registry --->
<CFREGISTRY ACTION="GetAll"
          BRANCH= "HKEY_LOCAL_MACHINE\SOFTWARE\Allaire\ColdFusion\CurrentVersion\
Collections"
          TYPE="Key" NAME="TheRegistryQuery">

</CFIMPERSONATE>

<!--- return the query object containing the names of the Verity
      collections obtained from the registry.  Use the value passed in
      to the custom tag as the name of the query object --->
<CFSET 'Caller.#ReturnQuery#' = TheRegistryQuery>
```

The first thing the custom tag does is check to set a default value for ReturnQuery to CollectionNames. Next, we check to see that an attribute called Attributes.ReturnQuery was passed to the tag and that it isn't blank. If these conditions are both True, we set a local variable called ReturnQuery equal to the value of Attributes.ReturnQuery. If either condition is False, we use the value already assigned to ReturnQuery at the beginning of the template.

The next part of the custom tag uses the CFIMPERSONATE tag to impersonate a valid user for the SharedTags security context. This allows a developer/user who normally isn't allowed access to the CFREGISTRY tag to use it in a specific manner without having to grant them absolute access within a security context. Note that the SharedTags security context must be set up in the ColdFusion Administrator and Advanced Security enabled before this tag will work. Once the user has been impersonated, the custom tag calls the `CFREGISTRY` tag and retrieves a list of Verity collections from the server. This list is stored in a query object named `TheRegistryQuery`. For more information on using `CFREGISTRY`, see Chapter 21.

Once the list of Verity collections has been retrieved, the custom tag passes the contents of the query object `TheRegistryQuery` back to the calling template as the query object named in the variable `ReturnQuery`. This allows the calling template to reference the query object using the name they originally passed to the custom tag.

# 9

# Error and Exception Handling

*In this chapter:*
- *Basic Exception Handling*
- *Custom Exception Handling*
- *Rethrowing Exceptions*
- *Error Handling Within the Web-Application Framework*
- *Server-wide Error Handling*

Structured exception handling lets you gracefully catch and handle exceptions that occur in your ColdFusion applications. Exceptions can include anything from a page timeout or a missing file to a database error or a problem with an external object. Using the techniques discussed in this chapter, you can build extremely robust exception-handling capabilities into your ColdFusion applications.

There are a number of different levels at which you can handle exceptions and errors in a ColdFusion application. At the most basic level, you can use the `CFTRY` and `CFCATCH` tags in a template, to test for and trap exceptions right where they occur. With the `CFTHROW` tag, you can also define, throw, and catch custom exceptions in your application.

Of course, catching every exception when it occurs can become quite tedious, so ColdFusion provides a couple of different mechanisms for handling exceptions at a higher level. With the `CFERROR` tag, you can define generic error handlers for different kinds of errors. The `CFERROR` tag is normally used in the *Application.cfm* template, so that error handling occurs in the context of the Web Application Framework. This ability to provide "catch all" error handling for an application is quite convenient and powerful.

In addition, as of ColdFusion 4.5, a site administrator can set up error and exception handling at the server level, using the ColdFusion Administrator. We'll cover all these different techniques for error and exception handling in this chapter.

# *Basic Exception Handling*

Exception handling allows you to test for and trap exceptions when they happen, so that your applications can respond to problems appropriately, as opposed to just throwing an error or invoking a separate error-handling template. With exception handling, it is usually possible to allow your application to continue functioning despite the fact that an exception has occurred.

Basic exception handling in ColdFusion uses two tags, CFTRY and CFCATCH. These tags allow you to identify potentially problematic areas of your application code and deal with anticipated exceptions where they are most likely to occur. The basic syntax for using CFTRY/CFCATCH is:

```
<CFTRY>
Potentially problematic code...

<CFCATCH TYPE="exception_type">
Code to implement in the event the exception is caught...
</CFCATCH>

<CFCATCH TYPE="exception_type">
...
</CFCATCH>

</CFTRY>
```

The CFTRY/CFCATCH syntax is straightforward. First, you wrap the section of code for which you wish to provide exception handling by a set of CFTRY tags. Immediately following the potentially problematic code, you use one or more CFCATCH blocks to test for various types of exceptions. This means that you can protect individual sections of your code from more than one exception at a time. Within a CFCATCH block, you can include any HTML and CFML you want, including CFCATCH variables (which we'll cover in just a few moments). It is also possible to nest additional CFTRY/CFCATCH tags within a CFCATCH block for.

Let's consider an example. Say you have an application that uses the CFHTTP tag to retrieve data from a text file that is generated and stored on your server on a regular basis. There is a chance that your application might attempt to access the text file at the same time that the file is being updated, resulting in an error. To prevent this, you can wrap your CFHTTP call with CFTRY/CFCATCH tags to catch any problems that might come up when trying to access the text file. If an exception does occur, you can handle it by displaying a page that tells the user that the file is in the process of being updated and to try back again in a few minutes. Example 9-1 illustrates this technique.

*Example 9-1. CFTRY/CFCATCH Block for Handling Any Exception Generated by a CFHTTP Call*

```
<!--- Attempt to use the CFHTTP tag to retrieve the stock quotes file --->
<CFTRY>

<CFHTTP URL="http://www.example.com/myfile.txt" METHOD="GET"
        COLUMNS="Ticker, Time, Price" DELIMITER=","
        RESOLVEURL="false" THROWONERROR="yes">

<!--- catch any exceptions and let the user know the file is being updated --->
<CFCATCH TYPE="Any">
<CENTER>
<H2>Stock quotes are currently being updated.  Please check back again in a few
minutes...</H2>
</CENTER>
</CFCATCH>

</CFTRY>
```

The `CFCATCH` tag takes a single attribute called `TYPE`, which specifies the type of exception to watch for. Possible values for `TYPE` include the following:

`Any` *(default)*
: Catches any unexpected exceptions. This exception type should be coded as the last `CFCATCH` within a `CFTRY` block if more than one `CFCATCH` is used.

`Application`
: Catches application-level exceptions, which are defined using the `Application` type in the `CFTHROW` tag. This `TYPE` is covered in detail in the next section.

*`CustomType`*
: Catches developer-specified exceptions as defined with the `CFTHROW` tag. This `TYPE` is covered in detail in the next section.

`Database`
: Catches exceptions raised when interacting with data sources.

`Expression`
: Catches exceptions that occur when the evaluation of an expression results in an error.

`Lock`
: Catches exceptions associated with the `CFLOCK` tag, such as timeouts, etc.

`MissingInclude`
: Catches exceptions that occur when an included template isn't found. This exception type covers exceptions thrown by the `CFINCLUDE`, `CFMODULE` and `CFERROR` tags.

`Object`
: Catches exceptions associated with external objects, such as COM/DCOM, CORBA, and Java objects.

`Security`
: Catches exceptions that result when authentication fails within the ColdFusion security framework.

`Template`
: Catches general application errors associated with ColdFusion templates.

In addition to the values already listed for the `TYPE` attribute, ColdFusion also supports a number of additional structured exception types. These exception types are generated by very specific conditions, such as request timeouts or by exceptions encountered as the result of a call to various ColdFusion tags. These exceptions types are listed under `CFTRY` in Appendix A.

As I already mentioned, you can refer to several `CFCATCH` variables inside a `CFCATCH` block. These variables are automatically generated whenever an exception is trapped by a `CFCATCH` block; they are stored in the `CFCATCH` structure. The `CFCATCH` variables are available to use within the trapping `CFCATCH` block only and can perform any number of tasks, such as evaluating additional processing options, writing log entries, and providing custom error or informational messages to users. Additionally, any valid HTML, CFML, or JavaScript can be used within a `CFCATCH` block in conjunction with the `CFCATCH` return variables. The following variables are available regardless of the exception type raised:

`CFCATCH.Type`
: The type of exception that occurred.

`CFCATCH.Message`
: The error message generated by the exception, if any.

`CFCATCH.Detail`
: A detailed error message generated by the CFML interpreter.

`CFCATCH.TagContext`
: The name and position of each tag in the tag stack, as well as the full path names of the files containing the tags as an array of structures. Each structure in the `TagContext` array contains the following:

  `ID` The name of the tag within the stack

  `TEMPLATE`
  : The full path to the template containing the tag

  `LINE`
  : The line number within the template where the tag was found

`COLUMN`
The column number within the template where the tag was found

CFML Stack Trace must be enabled in the Debugging section of the ColdFusion Administrator in order to populate this variable. If this option isn't enabled, ColdFusion returns a zero-length array for `CFCATCH.TagContext`.

In addition to these variables, there are some `CFCATCH` variables that are available only for specific exception types. These variables are detailed under `CFTRY` in Appendix A.

The next three examples step through the process of trapping different types of exceptions and offer different strategies for handling them. Example 9-2 generates an exception by attempting to use an undefined variable (`y`) in an expression. Because the `TYPE` of exception it's set to catch is `Any`, the `CFCATCH` tag that handles the exception is an example of a general exception handler.

*Example 9-2. Using CFTRY/CFCATCH to Catch Unexpected Exceptions*

```
<CFTRY>
<CFSET x=y+1>

<CFCATCH TYPE="Any">
<H2>An unknown exception has occurred!  Diagnostic information is shown
below:</H2>

<BR>
<H3>CFCATCH Exception Information</H3>

<TABLE BORDER="0">
<TR BGCOLOR="#0000FF">
  <TH><FONT COLOR="#FFFFFF">Variable</FONT></TH>
  <TH><FONT COLOR="#FFFFFF">Value</FONT></TH>
</TR>

<CFOUTPUT>
<TR BGCOLOR="##C0C0C0">
  <TD>CFCATCH.Type</TD><TD>#CFCATCH.Type#</TD>
</TR>
<TR BGCOLOR="##C0C0C0">
  <TD>CFCATCH.Message</TD><TD>#CFCATCH.Message#</TD>
</TR>
<TR BGCOLOR="##C0C0C0">
  <TD>CFCATCH.Detail</TD><TD>#CFCATCH.Detail#</TD>
</TR>
<TR BGCOLOR="##C0C0C0">
  <TD>CFCATCH.TagContext</TD>
  <TD>
    <TABLE BORDER="0">
    <TR>
      <TH COLSPAN="3">Tag Stack</TH>
    </TR>
```

*Example 9-2. Using CFTRY/CFCATCH to Catch Unexpected Exceptions (continued)*

```
    <TR BGCOLOR="##0000FF">
      <TH><FONT COLOR="##FFFFFF">Tag</FONT></TH>
      <TH><FONT COLOR="##FFFFFF">Position</FONT></TH>
      <TH><FONT COLOR="##FFFFFF">Template</FONT></TH>
    </TR>
    <CFLOOP index="element" from="1" TO="#ArrayLen(CFCATCH.TagContext)#">
    <CFSET TheStack = #CFCATCH.TagContext[element]#>
    <TR BGCOLOR="##D3D3D3">
      <TD>#TheStack["ID"]#</TD>
      <TD>(#TheStack["Line"]#:#TheStack["Column"]#)</TD>
      <TD>#TheStack["Template"]#</TD>
    </TR>
    </CFLOOP>
    </TABLE>
  </TD>
</TR>
<TR BGCOLOR="##C0C0C0">
  <TD>CFCATCH.ErrNumber </TD><TD>#CFCATCH.ErrNumber #</TD>
</TR>
</CFOUTPUT>
</TABLE>

</CFCATCH>
</CFTRY>
```

The CFCATCH block in this template is set to catch any type of exception that occurs (TYPE is Any). Generally, you should trap for specific types of exceptions before implementing a CFCATCH tag to handle Any exceptions. As a rule, setting TYPE to Any should be done as the last CFCATCH tag in a multi CFCATCH scenario. I've used it alone in this example mainly for illustrative purposes.

If we execute the template in Example 9-2, it generates a table that contains all the CFCATCH error variables and their associated values. The table is created by looping over each key/value in the CFCATCH structure (remember that the CFCATCH variables are all stored in a special ColdFusion structure called CFCATCH). First, each of the keys in the structure is returned as an array using the StructKeyArray() function. Next, each array element is looped over, and the name of the error variable and associated value are output. Because the CFCATCH structure contains a complex variable called CFCATCH.TagContext (it is actually an array of structures), we need a way to handle this variable when we come across it (otherwise it will cause an error as ColdFusion won't be able to output the array as a simple value). We deal with this by using the IsSimpleValue() function to evaluate every CFCATCH variable value being output. If the function returns False, we know that the value isn't a simple value and can't be directly output. The variable CFCATCH.TagContext (the array) is looped over and a nested table is built containing the tag, position, and template of each item in the tag stack. If IsSimpleValue() returns True, the value for the associated error variable is output directly.

Example 9-3 takes a different approach to exception handling. It attempts to include a template called *MyBogusHeader.cfm* at the beginning of the template via `CFINCLUDE`. The `CFINCLUDE` tag is wrapped in a `CFTRY` block. A `CFCATCH` tag with `TYPE` set to `MissingInclude` is used to deal with the exception generated in the event that the included file doesn't exist (which it doesn't).

*Example 9-3. Handling a Missing Include and Notifying the Site Administrator of the Problem*

```
<CFTRY>
<CFINCLUDE TEMPLATE="MyBogusHeader.cfm">

<CFCATCH TYPE="MissingInclude">
Error loading header template.  Notifying site administrator...

<CFMAIL TO="siteadministrator@example.com"
        FROM="webmaster@example.com"
        SUBJECT="Missing Header Template">
Site Administrator,

The following template: #CFCATCH.MissingFileName# seems to be missing from the
Web site.  Please investigate as soon as possible,

Regards,

The Webmaster
</CFMAIL>
</CFCATCH>
</CFTRY>

<CENTER>
<H2>Hello World!</H2>
</CENTER>
```

When this template is invoked, the `CFCATCH` is triggered, and an email message is automatically generated (via `CFMAIL`) and sent to the site administrator informing her of the error. The name of the missing template is included in the email. Although executing the template in Example 9-3 generates an exception, the template can still continue processing (thanks to the `CFTRY`/`CFCATCH` handlers).

As I mentioned earlier, it is possible to use more than one `CFCATCH` tag within a single `CFTRY` block. Example 9-4 illustrates this point by providing two different types of exception handling for the same piece of code.

*Example 9-4. Anticipating Multiple Exception Types with CFTRY/CFCATCH*

```
<CFTRY>

<!--- set the default log file write status to successful --->
<CFPARAM NAME="LogFileStatus" DEFAULT="Log entry successful.">

<H2>Attempting to write a log file entry...</H2>
```

*Example 9-4. Anticipating Multiple Exception Types with CFTRY/CFCATCH (continued)*

```
<!--- lock the cffile call so that only one call can be attempted at a time.
      If you want to purposely generate an exception for the second CFCATCH
      tag to catch, change the directory in the FILE attribute of the CFFILE
      tag to a directory that does not exist on your server. --->
<CFLOCK TIMEOUT="30" THROWONTIMEOUT="Yes" TYPE="EXCLUSIVE">

<!--- write an entry to the log file --->
<CFFILE ACTION="Append" FILE="c:\temp\logfile.txt"
        OUTPUT="This is a test entry" ADDNEWLINE="Yes">
</CFLOCK>

<!--- catch lock exceptions --->
<CFCATCH TYPE="Lock">
  <CFSET LogFileStatus = "There was a problem obtaining a file lock.  Log
         entry <B>NOT</B> written.">
</CFCATCH>

<!-- catch any other type of exception that might occur --->
<CFCATCH TYPE="Any">
  <CFSET LogFileStatus = "An unknown exception occurred.  Log entry <B>NOT</B>
         written.">
</CFCATCH>
</CFTRY>

<P>
<CFOUTPUT>
Processing Complete:  #LogFileStatus#
</CFOUTPUT>
```

This template uses the `CFFILE` tag to attempt to write a simple log file entry. The `CFFILE` tag is wrapped by a `CFLOCK` tag so that the log file can be accessed only one process at a time. Failing to use the `CFLOCK` tag can result in a file-access error or corruption of the log file. The call to the `CFFILE` tag is also wrapped by a `CFTRY` tag and two `CFCATCH` tags. The first `CFCATCH` tag catches exceptions related to the `CFLOCK` tag we used around our `CFFILE` call. This is done by specifying `Lock` for the `TYPE` attribute of this `CFCATCH` tag. Any exceptions resulting from the lock (such as a timeout) are handled by this tag. If an exception is generated, the value of `LogFileStatus` is set to "There was a problem obtaining a file lock. Log entry NOT written".

A second `CFCATCH` tag is used as a backup to catch any unforeseen exceptions. This is facilitated by setting the `TYPE` attribute of the second `CFCATCH` tag to `Any`. If any exception not caught by the first `CFCATCH` tag is thrown, this `CFCATCH` tag handles it by setting the value of `LogFileStatus` to "An unknown exception occurred. Log entry NOT written". Once the `CFTRY/CFCATCH` section has completed, a message containing the value of `LogFileStatus` is output to the browser.

# Custom Exception Handling

In the previous section, we covered the basics of using CFTRY/CFCATCH to handle predefined types of exceptions that might occur within a ColdFusion application. While these general exception types can handle any type of exception, they do so in a generic, one-size-fits-all manner. Fortunately, ColdFusion also allows you to specify custom exception types that can be caught with the same CFTRY/CFCATCH techniques we already covered.

As I mentioned in the previous section, the CFCATCH tag can accept a custom exception type for its TYPE attribute. That custom exception type is defined using the CFTHROW tag. The CFTHROW tag generates a custom exception type that can be caught by a CFCATCH tag when the TYPE attribute is set to Application, Any, or the custom type you specified in the CFTHROW tag. In other words, when something goes wrong in your application, and you need to generate a custom exception, use CFTHROW. The general syntax for using CFTHROW is as follows:

```
<CFTHROW TYPE="custom_exception_type"
         MESSAGE="error_message"
         DETAIL="detailed_event_description"
         ERRORCODE="error_code"
         EXTENDEDINFO="extended_information">
```

The CFTHROW tag accepts the following optional attributes:

TYPE
: Specifies a name for the exception type. You may give the exception type a custom name or use the predefined type Application.

MESSAGE
: Message describing the event that triggered the exception.

DETAIL
: Specifies additional information about the exception.

ERRORCODE
: A custom error code (numeric) you want to make available.

EXTENDEDINFO
: Specifies additional information regarding the error you want made available.

When you have CFML code that can possibly generate a custom exception with the CFTHROW tag, you obviously want to use a CFCATCH block to test for the custom exception. This is done by setting the TYPE attribute of the CFCATCH tag to the name specified in the TYPE attribute of the CFTHROW tag or by setting it to Application (the default).

As of ColdFusion 4.5, you can name custom exception types in a hierarchical manner, so that you can reference groups of custom exception types with a single

CFCATCH tag. ColdFusion uses pattern matching to search from the most specific to the least specific name. Consider the following CFTHROW tag:

```
<CFTHROW TYPE="MyApp.RequiredParameters.MyVar">
```

Any of the three following CFCATCH tags can catch the exception:

```
<CFCATCH TYPE="MyApp.RequiredParameters.MyVar ">
<CFCATCH TYPE="MyApp.RequiredParameters">
<CFCATCH TYPE="MyApp">
```

Note that this new behavior in CF 4.5 (and later) results in a potential backward compatibility problem with version 4.01 of ColdFusion. In Version 4.01, a custom exception coded as:

```
<CFTHROW TYPE="MyApp.RequiredParameters.MyVar">
```

can be caught only by an identically named CFCATCH tag, as in:

```
<CFCATCH TYPE="MyApp.RequiredParameters.MyVar">
```

but not by these:

```
<CFCATCH TYPE="MyApp.RequiredParameters">
<CFCATCH TYPE="MyApp">
```

The pattern matching behavior in ColdFusion 4.5 (and later) can be manually overridden by including the CFSETTING tag in your *Application.cfm* template with the CATCHEXCEPTIONSBYPATTERN attribute set to No, as in:

```
<CFAPPLICATION NAME="MyApplication">
<CFSETTING CATCHEXCEPTIONSBYPATTERN="No">
```

Now that we've covered the basics of how the CFTHROW tag works in conjunction with CFTRY/CFCATCH, let's look at an example that ties everything together. Example 9-5 uses the CFTHROW tag to define a custom exception to throw in the event that a variable called Form.MyVar doesn't exist.

*Example 9-5. Trapping a Custom Exception Type Using CFTHROW*

```
<CFTRY>

<!--- see if the form variable MyVar exists.  If not, throw a custom
      exception --->
<CFIF NOT IsDefined('Form.MyVar')>
    <CFTHROW TYPE="MyApp.RequiredParameters.MissingMyVar"
             MESSAGE="The form variable MyVar does not exist!"
             DETAIL="This variable must be present for this template to
                    function"
             ERRORCODE="10"
             EXTENDEDINFO="This is all the information available.">
</CFIF>

<!--- catch the custom exception --->
<CFCATCH TYPE="MyApp.RequiredParameters.MissingMyVar">
```

*Example 9-5. Trapping a Custom Exception Type Using CFTHROW (continued)*

```
<H2>Ooops - your variable (Form.MyVar) was not found!  Diagnostic
    information is shown below:</H2>

<BR>
<H3>CFCATCH Exception Information</H3>

<TABLE BORDER="0">
<TR BGCOLOR="#0000FF">
  <TH><FONT COLOR="#FFFFFF">Variable</FONT></TH>
  <TH><FONT COLOR="#FFFFFF">Value</FONT></TH>
</TR>

<CFOUTPUT>
<TR BGCOLOR="##C0C0C0">
  <TD>CFCATCH.Type</TD><TD>#CFCATCH.Type#</TD>
</TR>
<TR BGCOLOR="##C0C0C0">
  <TD>CFCATCH.Message</TD><TD>#CFCATCH.Message#</TD>
</TR>
<TR BGCOLOR="##C0C0C0">
  <TD>CFCATCH.Detail</TD>
  <TD>#CFCATCH.Detail#</TD>
</TR>
<TR BGCOLOR="##C0C0C0">
  <TD>CFCATCH.TagContext</TD>
  <TD>
  <TABLE BORDER="0">
  <TR>
    <TH COLSPAN="3">Tag Stack</TH>
  </TR>
  <TR BGCOLOR="##0000FF">
    <TH><FONT COLOR="##FFFFFF">Tag</FONT></TH>
    <TH><FONT COLOR="##FFFFFF">Position</FONT></TH>
    <TH><FONT COLOR="##FFFFFF">Template</FONT></TH>
  </TR>
  <CFLOOP index="element" from="1" TO="#ArrayLen(CFCATCH.TagContext)#">
    <CFSET TheStack = #CFCATCH.TagContext[element]#>
    <TR BGCOLOR="##D3D3D3">
      <TD>#TheStack["ID"]#</TD>
      <TD>(#TheStack["Line"]#:#TheStack["Column"]#)</TD>
      <TD>#TheStack["Template"]#</TD>
    </TR>
  </CFLOOP>
  </TABLE>
</TD>
</TR>
<TR BGCOLOR="##C0C0C0">
  <TD>CFCATCH.ErrorCode</TD><TD>#CFCATCH.ErrorCode#</TD>
</TR>
<TR BGCOLOR="##C0C0C0">
  <TD>CFCATCH.ExtendedInfo</TD><TD>#CFCATCH.ExtendedInfo#</TD>
</TR>
```

*Example 9-5. Trapping a Custom Exception Type Using CFTHROW (continued)*

```
  </TABLE>
  </CFOUTPUT>
</CFCATCH>

</CFTRY>
```

In this example, a `CFIF` statement is used within a `CFTRY` block to check for the existence of a form variable called `Form.MyVar`. If the form variable doesn't exist (which it doesn't), a `CFTHROW` tag generates a custom exception. The tag uses several attributes to identify the exception and provide detailed error information. After the exception has been defined with the `CFTHROW` tag, a `CFCATCH` block tests for the custom exception. Notice the `TYPE` attribute of the `CFCATCH` tag is set to the same name as specified in the `TYPE` attribute of the `CFTHROW` tag. The `CFCATCH` block catches the error and writes a table out to the browser containing the information related to the exception.

When `CFTHROW` is used in conjunction with the `CFTRY` and `CFCATCH` tags, a number of variables are made available when an exception is thrown. If these variables look familiar, it is because they are. The variables are the same as those available for a regular `CFCATCH` tag, except that most of the values are provided by the `CFTHROW` tag as opposed to the CFML interpreter:

`CFCATCH.Type`
: The type of exception that occurred.

`CFCATCH.Message`
: The error message specified in the `MESSAGE` attribute of the `CFTHROW` tag, if any.

`CFCATCH.Detail`
: A detailed error message generated by the CFML interpreter.

`CFCATCH.TagContext`
: The name and position of each tag in the tag stack as well as the full pathnames of the files containing the tags. CFML Stack Trace must be enabled in the Debugging section of the ColdFusion Administrator in order to populate this variable.

`CFCATCH.ErrorCode`
: The contents of the `ErrorCode` attribute, if any, from the `CFTHROW` tag.

`CFCATCH.ExtendedInfo`
: The contents of the `ExtendedInfo` attribute, if any, from the `CFTHROW` tag.

# Rethrowing Exceptions

Now that we've discussed the framework for building robust error- and exception-handling capabilities into your ColdFusion applications, let's look at a technique you can use to create more advanced exception handling systems for your applications. On occasion, it may be desirable to rethrow an exception that can't be handled adequately by a CFCATCH tag. For example, you may have a CFCATCH block that catches an error that it isn't explicitly designed to handle. In this case, it's desirable to rethrow the exception so that a more qualified error handler can deal with the exception. This can be accomplished using the CFRETHROW tag. The CFRETHROW tag is used within a CFCATCH block to rethrow the active exception while preserving the CFCATCH.Type and CFCATCH.TagContext return variables. This lets you build an additional level of decision making into your exception-handling routines.

To get a better idea of how the CFRETHROW tag can be used, consider an example in which you want to provide a backup data source to use in the event that a query to your main data source fails. This type of functionality is highly desirable in cases where your entire database is refreshed (i.e., in the case of an extract file) or when you use a file-based database such as MS Access or FoxPro where updating the database often means overwriting the production version with a new version. It is also a good idea when you just want to provide redundancy as you would in any sort of e-commerce or mission-critical application that requires 100% uptime.

Example 9-6 shows how to create this type of functionality using nested CFTRY/CFCATCH tags and the CFRETHROW tag.

*Example 9-6. Using CFRETHROW*

```
<CFTRY>

<!--- Try to query the first database.  Note that the query points to a bogus
      table, so it will fail. --->
<CFTRY>
<CFQUERY NAME="GetData" DATASOURCE="ProgrammingCF">
   SELECT * FROM BogusTable
</CFQUERY>

<!--- Catch any database errors resulting from the attempt to query the first
      database. --->
<CFCATCH TYPE="database">
  <H3>First data source failed.  Attempting to use alternate...</H3>

  <!--- Write out a table containing all CFCATCH variables --->
  <CFSET MYKEYARRAY = STRUCTKEYARRAY(CFCATCH)>
  <TABLE BORDER="0">
  <TR BGCOLOR="#0000FF">
```

*Example 9-6. Using CFRETHROW (continued)*

```
    <TH>Name</TH><TH>Value</TH>
  </TR>
  <CFLOOP INDEX="position" FROM="1" TO="#ArrayLen(MyKeyArray)#">
    <CFOUTPUT>
    <TR BGCOLOR="##C0C0C0">
      <TD>#MyKeyArray[position]#</TD>
      <TD><CFIF ISSIMPLEVALUE(CFCATCH[MYKEYARRAY[POSITION]])>
            #CFCATCH[MyKeyArray[position]]# </TD>
          <CFELSE>
            <TABLE BORDER="0">
            <TR>
              <TH COLSPAN="3">Tag Stack</TH>
            </TR>
            <TR BGCOLOR="##0000FF">
              <TH><FONT COLOR="##FFFFFF">Tag</FONT></TH>
              <TH><FONT COLOR="##FFFFFF">Position</FONT></TH>
              <TH><FONT COLOR="##FFFFFF">Template</FONT></TH>
            </TR>
            <CFLOOP INDEX="element" FROM="1"
                    TO="#ArrayLen(CFCATCH.TagContext)#">
              <CFSET THESTACK = #CFCATCH.TAGCONTEXT[ELEMENT]#>
              <TR BGCOLOR="##D3D3D3">
                <TD>#TheStack["ID"]#</TD>
                <TD>(#TheStack["Line"]#:#TheStack["Column"]#)</TD>
                <TD>#TheStack["Template"]#</TD>
              </TR>
            </CFLOOP>
            </TABLE></TD>
          </CFIF>
    </TR>
    </CFOUTPUT>
  </CFLOOP>
  </TABLE>

  <CFTRY>
  <!--- Try querying the second database.  Note that this also points to a
        bogus data source, so it will fail.  We do this to illustrate the use
        of the CFRETHROW tag. --->
  <CFQUERY NAME="GetData" DATASOURCE="ProgrammidngCF">
     SELECT * FROM EmployeeDirectory
  </CFQUERY>

  <!--- If there is a problem with the second database, rethrow the exception
        so that it can be handled by the general cfcatch handler --->
  <CFCATCH TYPE="database">
    <H3>Alternate data source failed.  Rethrowing exception...</H3>

    <CFSET MYKEYARRAY = STRUCTKEYARRAY(CFCATCH)>
    <TABLE BORDER="0">
    <TR BGCOLOR="#0000FF">
      <TH>Name</TH><TH>Value</TH>
    </TR>
```

*Example 9-6. Using CFRETHROW (continued)*

```
    <CFLOOP INDEX="position" FROM="1" TO="#ArrayLen(MyKeyArray)#">
      <CFOUTPUT>
      <TR BGCOLOR="##C0C0C0">
        <TD>#MyKeyArray[position]#</TD>
        <TD><CFIF ISSIMPLEVALUE(CFCATCH[MYKEYARRAY[POSITION]])>
              #CFCATCH[MyKeyArray[position]]# </TD>
            <CFELSE>
              <TABLE BORDER="0">
              <TR>
                <TH COLSPAN="3">Tag Stack</TH>
              </TR>
              <TR BGCOLOR="##0000FF">
                <TH><FONT COLOR="##FFFFFF">Tag</FONT></TH>
                <TH><FONT COLOR="##FFFFFF">Position</FONT></TH>
                <TH><FONT COLOR="##FFFFFF">Template</FONT></TH>
              </TR>
              <CFLOOP INDEX="element" FROM="1"
                      TO="#ArrayLen(CFCATCH.TagContext)#">
                <CFSET THESTACK = #CFCATCH.TAGCONTEXT[ELEMENT]#>
                <TR BGCOLOR="##D3D3D3">
                  <TD>#TheStack["ID"]#</TD>
                  <TD>(#TheStack["Line"]#:#TheStack["Column"]#)</TD>
                  <TD>#TheStack["Template"]#</TD>
                </TR>
              </CFLOOP>
              </TABLE></TD>
            </CFIF>
      </TR>
      </CFOUTPUT>
    </CFLOOP>
    </TABLE>

    <!--- This is where the exception is rethrown --->
    <CFRETHROW>
  </CFCATCH>
  </CFTRY>
</CFCATCH>
</CFTRY>

<!--- Catch any exception not already planned for.  Output all of the
      information returned by the CFCATCH variables. --->
<CFCATCH TYPE="Any">
  <H3>Unexpected exception caught.  Detailed information follows:</H3>

  <CFSET MYKEYARRAY = STRUCTKEYARRAY(CFCATCH)>
  <TABLE BORDER="0">
  <TR BGCOLOR="#0000FF">
    <TH>Name</TH>
    <TH>Value</TH>
  </TR>
  <CFLOOP INDEX="position" FROM="1" TO="#ArrayLen(MyKeyArray)#">
    <CFOUTPUT>
```

*Example 9-6. Using CFRETHROW (continued)*

```
    <TR BGCOLOR="##C0C0C0">
      <TD>#MyKeyArray[position]#</TD>
      <TD><CFIF ISSIMPLEVALUE(CFCATCH[MYKEYARRAY[POSITION]])>
            #CFCATCH[MyKeyArray[position]]# </TD>
          <CFELSE>
            <TABLE BORDER="0">
            <TR>
              <TH COLSPAN="3">Tag Stack</TH>
            </TR>
            <TR BGCOLOR="##0000FF">
              <TH><FONT COLOR="##FFFFFF">Tag</FONT></TH>
              <TH><FONT COLOR="##FFFFFF">Position</FONT></TH>
              <TH><FONT COLOR="##FFFFFF">Template</FONT></TH>
            </TR>
            <CFLOOP INDEX="element" FROM="1"
                    TO="#ArrayLen(CFCATCH.TagContext)#">
              <CFSET THESTACK = #CFCATCH.TAGCONTEXT[ELEMENT]#>
              <TR BGCOLOR="##D3D3D3">
                <TD>#TheStack["ID"]#</TD>
                <TD>(#TheStack["Line"]#:#TheStack["Column"]#)</TD>
                <TD>#TheStack["Template"]#</TD>
              </TR>
            </CFLOOP>
            </TABLE></TD>
          </CFIF>
    </TR>
    </CFOUTPUT>
  </CFLOOP>
  </TABLE>
</CFCATCH>
</CFTRY>
```

The template works by attempting to query the primary data source. If an exception is thrown, an attempt is made to query a backup data source. If an exception occurs while trying to query the backup data source, the CFRETHROW tag rethrows the exception, which can then be caught by a general CFCATCH tag with TYPE set to Any. To get a better idea of what is happening, consider the following pseudocode:

```
try {
   query database
}
catch(database){
  output exception information
  try{
      query alternate database
  }
  catch(database){
    output exception information
    rethrow exception
```

```
    }
  }
  catch(any){
    output exception information
  }
```

For illustrative purposes, each time an exception is detected in Example 9-6, all the associated CFCATCH variables are written to the browser so that you can see what is happening.

# Error Handling Within the Web-Application Framework

While CFTRY and CFCATCH provide a granular means of handling errors and exceptions within your applications, they can be cumbersome to code. Trying to identify all the potential trouble spots in your applications where CFTRY/CFCATCH code should be placed only compounds the problem. Fortunately, ColdFusion provides a way to handle errors at a more general level. By including ColdFusion's CFERROR tag within your application's *Application.cfm* template, you can implement application-specific "catch all" error handlers.

Although the CFERROR tag can be used in other templates besides *Application.cfm*, it makes the most sense to use it in this template. The CFERROR tag is generally placed directly below the CFAPPLICATION tag:

```
<CFAPPLICATION NAME="MyApplication">

<!--- implement error handling --->
<CFERROR TYPE="Exception" TEMPLATE="MyRequestHandler.cfm"
         EXCEPTION="Any" MAILTO="webmaster@example.com">
```

The CFERROR tag can implement one of four types of error handling, depending on the value specified in the TYPE attribute. The TEMPLATE attribute is also required; it specifies the relative path to a custom error template to execute in the event that an error or exception occurs. Depending on the value specified in the TYPE attribute, different options are available to the error-handling template. Here are the values for TYPE and the corresponding options that are available in the error template:

`Exception`
: Handles a specific exception type as specified in the EXCEPTION attribute of the CFERROR tag. Any ColdFusion tags may be used in the exception-handling template. Exception-handling templates may also be invoked by specifying a Site-wide Error Handler within the Server Settings section of the ColdFusion Administrator.

`Monitor`
: Sets up an exception monitor for the exception type specified in the `EXCEPTION` attribute of the `CFERROR` tag. Used to monitor and debug ColdFusion applications. With this type of exception handling, ColdFusion invokes the specified error-handling template before processing any `CFTRY`/`CFCATCH` error handling that may be in the executing template.

`Request` *(default)*
: Handles any errors generated during a template request. Only certain error variables are available to the error-handling page. No other CFML tags may be used in the template.

`Validation`
: Handles form-field validation errors that occur when a form is submitted. This `TYPE` is useful only when the `CFERROR` tag is included within an *Appplication.cfm* template. Only certain error variables are available to the error-handling page. No other CFML tags or functions may be used in the template.

If you set the `TYPE` attribute to `Exception` or `Monitor`, you should specify the type of exception that the `CFERROR` tag should watch for in the `EXCEPTION` attribute. You may specify the same exception types as for the `CFCATCH` tag: `Any` (the default), `Application`, *`CustomTag`*, `Database`, `Expression`, `Lock`, `MissingInclude`, `Object`, `Security`, and `Template`. And just as with the `CFCATCH` tag, the `CFERROR` tag also supports a number of additional structured exception types. These exception types are listed under `CFTRY` in Appendix A.

The final attribute, `MAILTO`, is optional and provides the email address of the person who should be notified if an error occurs. The value of `MAILTO` is available to the custom error handler specified in the `TEMPLATE` attribute.

Depending on the `TYPE` of error handling you implement in your application, ColdFusion makes several variables available to the template specified in the `TEMPLATE` attribute that can be referenced within a `CFOUTPUT` block. These variables can be referenced individually or as key/value pairs within a ColdFusion structure called `Error`. For `Exception`, `Monitor`, and `Request` error handling, the available variables are:

`Error.Browser`
: The browser in use when the error occurred

`Error.DateTime`
: The date and time when the error occurred

`Error.Diagnostics`
: A detailed error message provided by the ColdFusion server

`Error.HTTPReferer`
The page that contains the link to the template where the error occurred

`Error.MailTo`
The email address specified in the `MAILTO` attribute of the `CFERROR` tag

`Error.RemoteAddress`
The IP address of the remote client

`Error.QueryString`
The URL query string, if any, from the client's request

`Error.Template`
The page that was in the process of executing when the error occurred

Additionally, if `TYPE` is set to `Monitor` or `Exception`, the following variable is available:

`Error.GeneratedContent`
The content generated by the failed request

You can also use any of the `CFCATCH` return variables available to the exception specified in the `EXCEPTION` attribute of the `CFERROR` tag. These variables are: `Error.Type`, `Error.Message`, `Error.Detail`, `Error.TagContext`, `Error.ErrorCode`, `Error.NativeErrorCode`, `Error.SQLState`, `Error.ErrNumber`, `Error.LockName`, `Error.LockOperation`, `Error.MissingFileName`, and `Error.ExtendedInfo`.*

When `TYPE` is set to `Validation`the following variables are available:

`Error.ValidationHeader`
Predefined header text for the validation error page

`Error.InvalidFields`
An HTML unordered (`<UL>`) list of validation errors

`Error.ValidationFooter`
Predefined footer text for the validation error page

`Error.MailTo`
The email address specified in the `MAILTO` attribute of the `CFERROR` tag

Now that we've covered what the `CFERROR` tag can do, let's look at some specific examples of how it can be used. We'll discuss each type of exception handling and provide examples.

---

* You can use `CFError` instead of the `Error` prefix if you have `TYPE` set to `MonitororException` as in `CFError.Browser` or `CFError.Template`. Just as with `Error` variables, `CFError` variables can be referenced individually or as key/value pairs within a ColdFusion structure named `CFError`.

## *Form Validation Errors*

Validation errors occur when you use ColdFusion's built-in form-field validation routines to handle form submissions. As you may recall from Chapter 3, ColdFusion allows you to embed special hidden form fields within your HTML forms for validating user input. To refresh your memory, here are the built-in validation suffixes: `_required`, `_date`, `_eurodate`, `_time`, `_integer`, `_float`, and `_range`.

Under normal circumstances, if a validation rule is violated, ColdFusion displays a generic error page that lets the user know that the input violated a validation rule. While this is a handy feature, the generic page displayed by ColdFusion leaves something to be desired. There is no way to customize the generic error page displayed when a validation rule is violated. By using the `CFERROR` tag with `TYPE` set to `Validation`, however, you can overcome this limitation (to a degree). Although you can place the `CFERROR` tag directly in the page responsible for processing the form post, it makes more sense to place it in your *Application.cfm* template as you generally want to apply this type of error handling to an entire application as opposed to a single form. The following examples show how to set up a custom validation handler for your application. To begin, we need to create an *Application.cfm* template with the code for calling the validation error handler. This code is shown in Example 9-7.

*Example 9-7. Application.cfm File with CFERROR Tag Set to Handle Validation Errors*

```
<CFAPPLICATION NAME="MyApplication">

<!--- handle any form field validation errors --->
<CFERROR TYPE="Validation" TEMPLATE="ValidationHandler.cfm"
         MAILTO="webmaster@example.com">
```

All that's necessary to set up the custom validation handler is a single `CFERROR` tag. `TYPE` is set to `Validation` so that any validation errors are handled by the template specified by the tag. The `TEMPLATE` attribute specifies the relative path to a ColdFusion template to invoke in the event a validation error occurs. In this case, we want to invoke a template called *ValidationHandler.cfm* that resides in the same directory as our *Application.cfm* template. The final attribute, `MAILTO`, is optional and provides the email address of the person who should be notified if an error occurs. The value of `MAILTO` is available to the custom error handler specified in the `TEMPLATE` attribute.

With the *Application.cfm* template all set up, let's look at the *ValidationHandler.cfm* template our `CFERROR` tag calls when a validation error occurs. The code for this template is shown in Example 9-8.

*Example 9-8. ValidationHandler.cfm Template for Custom Handling of Validation Errors*

```
<BODY BGCOLOR="#FFFFCC">

<CENTER>
<H2>Validation Handler</H2>

<TABLE BORDER="1" CELLPADDING="10">
<TR>
  <TD>
  #Error.ValidationHeader#<BR>
  #Error.InvalidFields#<BR>
  #Error.ValidationFooter#
  <P>
  Please send any questions or comments to
  <A HREF="mailto:#Error.Mailto#">#Error.Mailto#</A>
  </TD>
</TR>
</TABLE>
</CENTER>

</BODY>
```

As I already mentioned, only the variables passed by the `CFERROR` tag can be referenced in the *ValidationHandler.cfm* template. It isn't necessary to use a `CFOUTPUT` tag. No additional CFML tags or functions may be used. For our template, I chose to add a background color and create a centered table for holding the rest of our content. A header displaying "Form Entries Incomplete or Invalid. One or more problems exist with the data you have entered" is automatically placed on the page by the `Error.ValidationHeader` variable. If you want to preset a different header, simply omit this variable and supply your own text. Next, an unordered (bulleted) list of validation errors is presented within the table using the `Error.InvalidFields` variable. The bullets are automatically created by ColdFusion and can't be modified. The footer "Use the Back button on your web browser to return to the previous page and correct the listed problems" is automatically included by referencing `Error.ValidationFooter`. Finally, a line providing a contact email address is presented using `Error.MailTo`. As you may recall, this value is obtained from the `MAILTO` attribute of the `CFERROR` tag.

Now that we have our *Application.cfm* and *ValidationHandler.cfm* templates set up, we need to create a template to test them. The code for the form that tests the validation error handler is shown in Example 9-9. This template should be called *ValidationTest.cfm* and placed in the same directory as the other templates for this example.

*Example 9-9. HTML Form for Testing Custom Validation Error Handling*

```
<H2>Article Submission Form</H2>
<FORM ACTION="ValidationTest.cfm" METHOD="post">
```

*Example 9-9. HTML Form for Testing Custom Validation Error Handling (continued)*

```
<INPUT TYPE="hidden" NAME="ArticleDate_date" VALUE="You must supply a valid date
       format (ex. 11/11/2000).">
<INPUT TYPE="hidden" NAME="Title_required" VALUE="You must enter a title for the
       article.">
<INPUT TYPE="hidden" NAME="Priority_required" VALUE="You must enter a priority
       for the article.">
<INPUT TYPE="hidden" NAME="Priority_range" VALUE="Min=1 Max=100">

<TABLE>
<TR>
    <TD>Date:</TD>
    <TD><INPUT TYPE="text" NAME="ArticleDate" SIZE="12" MAXLENGTH="10"></TD>
</TR>
<TR>
    <TD>Title:</TD>
    <TD><INPUT TYPE="text" NAME="Title" SIZE="50" MAXLENGTH="255"></TD>
</TR>
<TR>
    <TD>Article:</TD>
    <TD><TEXTAREA COLS="43" ROWS="5" NAME="Article"></TEXTAREA></TD>
</TR>
<TR>
    <TD>Priority (1-100):</TD>
    <TD><INPUT TYPE="text" NAME="Priority" SIZE="4" MAXLENGTH="3"></TD>
</TR>
<TR>
    <TD COLSPAN="2"><INPUT TYPE="submit" NAME="Submit" VALUE="submit"></TD>
</TR>
</TABLE>
</FORM>
```

Note the four hidden form fields declared after the `FORM` tag. These form fields use some of the built-in form validation suffixes. These suffixes apply validation rules to the form fields listed in each `NAME` attribute. When the form is submitted, ColdFusion checks the values supplied for each form field against the validation rules defined by each hidden form field. If any rules are violated, the `CFERROR` tag in the *Application.cfm* template invokes the *ValidationHandler.cfm* template, displaying the custom error message to the user. An example of this can be seen in Figure 9-1.

## Request Errors

Setting `TYPE` to `Request` allows you to handle any application-related errors that occur during a page request. If you are going to use the `CFERROR` tag to catch `Request` errors, you have two options. First, you can include the `CFERROR` tag at the beginning of every template for which you want to provide error handling. While this option works fine, it is a pain to have to put the code (or a `CFINCLUDE` to the code) at the beginning of each CFML template. A more logical solution is to

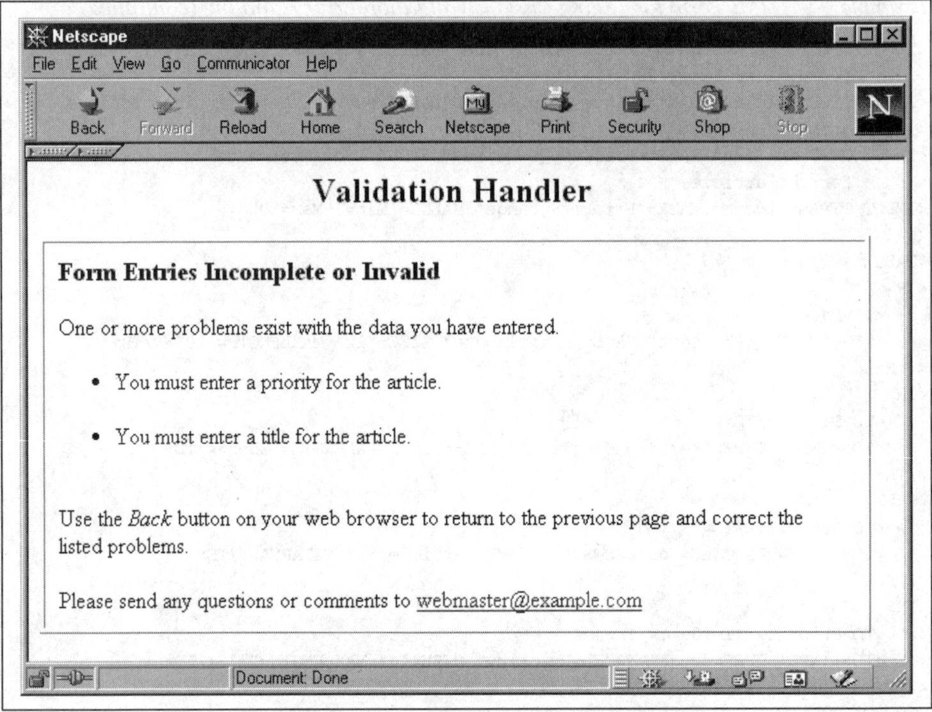


*Figure 9-1. Custom validation error page invoked when a validation rule is violated*

place the CFERROR tag in your *Application.cfm* template to provide error checking for your entire application. Example 9-10 shows the fragment of an *Application.cfm* template that sets up Request error handling.

*Example 9-10. CFERROR Tag Set to Handle Request Errors*

```
<CFAPPLICATION NAME="MyApplication">

<!--- Handle Request Errors --->
<CFERROR TYPE="Request" TEMPLATE="RequestHandler.cfm"
        MAILTO="webmaster@example.com">
```

All you have to do to set up a custom-request error handler is place a single CFERROR tag inside your *Application.cfm* template. TYPE is set to Request so that any application errors are handled by the *RequestHandler.cfm* template specified by the TEMPLATE attribute. As before, specify the MAILTO attribute to set an email address for notification about any errors.

With the *Application.cfm* template taken care of, let's focus our attention on the *RequestHandler.cfm* template our CFERROR tag calls when a request error occurs. The code for this template is shown in Example 9-11.

*Example 9-11. RequestHandler.cfm Template for Custom Handling of Request Errors*

```
<BODY BGCOLOR="#FFFFCC">

<CENTER>
<H3>An error has occurred while requesting a CFML template</H3>
<H4>Diagnostic information is shown below</H4>

<TABLE BORDER="0">
<TR BGCOLOR="#0000FF">
  <TH><FONT COLOR="white">Error Variable</FONT></TH>
  <TH><FONT COLOR="white">Value</FONT></TH>
</TR>
<TR BGCOLOR="#C0C0C0">
  <TD>Browser</TD><TD>#Error.Browser# </TD>
</TR>
<TR BGCOLOR="#C0C0C0">
  <TD>Date/Time</TD><TD>#Error.DateTime# </TD>
</TR>
<TR BGCOLOR="#C0C0C0">
  <TD>Diagnostics</TD><TD>#Error.Diagnostics# </TD>
</TR>
<TR BGCOLOR="#C0C0C0">
  <TD>HTTP Referer</TD><TD>#Error.HTTPReferer# </TD>
</TR>
<TR BGCOLOR="#C0C0C0">
  <TD>Mailto</TD><TD>#Error.MailTo# </TD>
</TR>
<TR BGCOLOR="#C0C0C0">
  <TD>Remote Address</TD><TD>#Error.RemoteAddress# </TD>
</TR>
<TR BGCOLOR="#C0C0C0">
  <TD>Query String</TD><TD>#Error.QueryString# </TD>
</TR>
<TR BGCOLOR="#C0C0C0">
  <TD>Template</TD><TD>#Error.Template# </TD>
</TR>
</TABLE>
</CENTER>

</BODY>
```

The *RequestHandler.cfm* template creates a custom page for reporting details of the request error to the user. Only the variables passed by the `CFERROR` tag can be referenced in the *RequestHandler.cfm* template. It isn't necessary to reference the error variables within a `CFOUTPUT` block. Just like `Validation` handling, no additional CFML tags or functions may be used within the template. The actual details of the error are output in a nicely formatted table with the error variables in the left column and their values in the right column.

Now that we've created our *Application.cfm* and *RequestHandler.cfm* templates, let's test them. Here's some code that tests our templates:

```
<!--- try to CFINCLUDE a template that does not exist --->
<CFINCLUDE TEMPLATE="nonexistanttemplate.cfm?ID=123">
```

Executing this template causes the `CFERROR` tag in our *Application.cfm* template to invoke the *RequestHandler.cfm* template (because of the `CFINCLUDE` call to a non-existent template). The results of this can be seen in Figure 9-2.

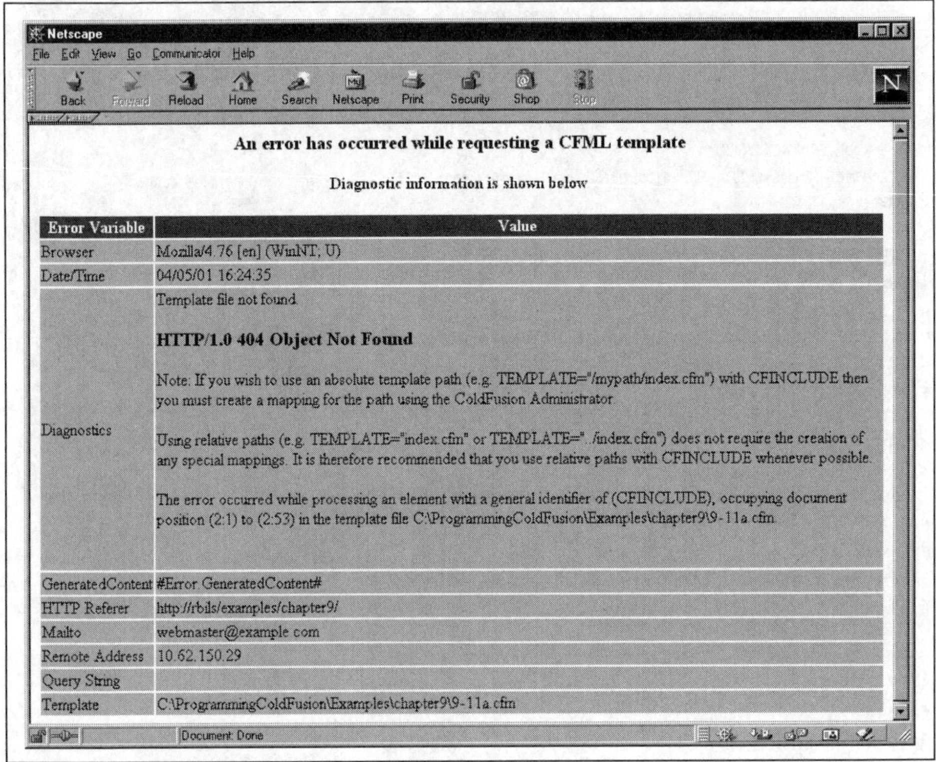


*Figure 9-2. Custom request error handler*

## *Specific Exceptions*

As of ColdFusion 4.5, the `CFERROR` tag can catch specific exceptions at either the application or template level, when `TYPE` is set to `Exception`. `Exception` handling differs from `Request` handling in three important ways. First, using `Exception` allows you to specify an exception to trigger the `CFERROR` response. If `TYPE` is set to `Request`, ColdFusion responds to *any* error or exception by invoking the `CFERROR` tag.

The second difference has to do with the information the CFERROR tag makes available to the error-handling template specified in the TEMPLATE attribute. In addition to the error variables available to a Request handler, an Exception handler also has access to all the error variables available to the CFCATCH tag.

The third difference is perhaps the most significant. Unlike the template specified by the CFERROR tag when TYPE is Request, the template specified when TYPE is Exception has access to all CFML tags and functions. This gives you the ability to code much more sophisticated and customized error handlers than using the Request type because you can include any ColdFusion tags (such as CFMAIL) or functions you wish.

The next series of examples demonstrate how to set up multiple exception handlers for your application. The first step is to create an *Application.cfm* template to define the types of exceptions to catch, as shown in Example 9-12.

*Example 9-12. Application.cfm Template with Multiple CFERROR Tags for Handling Various Exceptions*

```
<CFAPPLICATION NAME="MyApplication">

<!--- Catch POP authentication exceptions --->
<CFERROR TYPE="Exception" TEMPLATE="ExceptionHandler.cfm"
         EXCEPTION="COM.Allaire.ColdFusion.POPAuthFailure"
         MAILTO="webmaster@example.com">

<!--- Catch a custom exception called MyApp.MyException defined by a CFTHROW
      tag.  Call a more advanced error handler --->
<CFERROR TYPE="Exception" TEMPLATE="CustomExceptionHandler.cfm"
         EXCEPTION="MyApp.MyException" MAILTO="webmaster@example.com">

<!--- Catch any exception not previously covered --->
<CFERROR TYPE="Exception" TEMPLATE="ExceptionHandler.cfm"
         EXCEPTION="Any" MAILTO="webmaster@example.com">
```

This *Application.cfm* template differs from the ones we have previously created in this chapter in that it contains not one but three CFERROR tags. You can include as many CFERROR tags in your *Application.cfm* template as necessary to handle the exceptions you expect to encounter. In this example, we set three. The first CFERROR tag catches the exception COM.Allaire.ColdFusion.POPAuthFailure. This exception occurs when the CFPOP tag can't successfully authenticate a user with a POP server. If our *Application.cfm* template detects this error, it invokes a template called *ExceptionHandler.cfm*, shown in Example 9-13.

The second CFERROR tag catches a custom exception called MyApp.MyException that is defined using the CFTHROW tag. If the exception is detected, a template called *CustomExceptionHandler.cfm* is invoked to handle the error, as shown in Example 9-14.

The third and final CFERROR tag catches any exceptions not handled by our other two CFERROR tags. By setting the TYPE attribute to Any, we effectively create a backup exception handler for dealing with unforeseen exceptions. This type of error handler should always be included as the last CFERROR tag in your *Application.cfm* template. If an exception occurs that isn't caught by either specific exception handler, the *ExceptionHandler.cfm* template (the same template used by our first CFERROR tag) is invoked to deal with the exception.

Let's turn our attention now to the two exception-handling templates we just mentioned, *ExceptionHandler.cfm* and *CustomExceptionHandler.cfm*. The *ExceptionHandler.cfm* template is used by both the first and third CFERROR tags in our *Application.cfm* template to handle a COM.Allaire.ColdFusion.POPAuthFailure exception as well as any exception other than a custom one called MyApp.MyException (the second CFERROR tag). The code for the *ExceptionHandler.cfm* template is shown in Example 9-13.

*Example 9-13. Displaying Exception Error Variables*

```
<H3>Generic Exception Handler</H3>

<CFSET MyKeyArray = StructKeyArray(Error)>

<TABLE BORDER="0">
<TR BGCOLOR="#0000FF">
  <TH>Key #</TH><TH>Name</TH><TH>Value</TH>
</TR>
<CFLOOP index="position" from="1" to="#ArrayLen(MyKeyArray)#">
 <CFOUTPUT>
 <TR BGCOLOR="##C0C0C0">
   <TD>#position#:</TD><TD>#MyKeyArray[position]#</TD>
   <TD><CFIF IsSimpleValue(Error[MyKeyArray[position]])>
                                    #Error[MyKeyArray[position]]# </TD>
    <CFELSE>
     <TABLE BORDER="0">
     <TR>
      <TH COLSPAN="3">Tag Stack</TH>
     </TR>
     <TR BGCOLOR="##0000FF">
       <TH><FONT COLOR="##FFFFFF">Tag</FONT></TH>
       <TH><FONT COLOR="##FFFFFF">Position</FONT></TH>
       <TH><FONT COLOR="##FFFFFF">Template</FONT></TH>
     </TR>
     <CFLOOP index="element" from="1" TO="#ArrayLen(ERROR.TagContext)#">
     <CFSET TheStack = #ERROR.TagContext[element]#>
     <TR BGCOLOR="##D3D3D3">
       <TD>#TheStack["ID"]#</TD>
       <TD>(#TheStack["Line"]#:#TheStack["Column"]#)</TD>
       <TD>#TheStack["Template"]#</TD>
     </TR>
     </CFLOOP>
     </TABLE>
```

*Example 9-13. Displaying Exception Error Variables (continued)*

```
    </TD>
</CFIF>
</TR>
</CFOUTPUT>
</CFLOOP>
</TABLE>
```

The *ExceptionHandler.cfm* template generates a table containing all the error variables and their associated values by looping over each key/value in the `Error` structure (remember that the error variables are stored in a special ColdFusion structure called `Error`). First, each key in the structure is returned as an array using the `StructKeyArray()` function. Next, each array element is looped over, and the name of the error variable and associated value are output. Because the `Error` structure contains a complex error variable called `Error.TagContext` (it is actually an array of structures), we need to use special handling for this variable, just as we did with the `CFCATCH.TagContext` variable previously. The output of this template is in Figure 9-3.

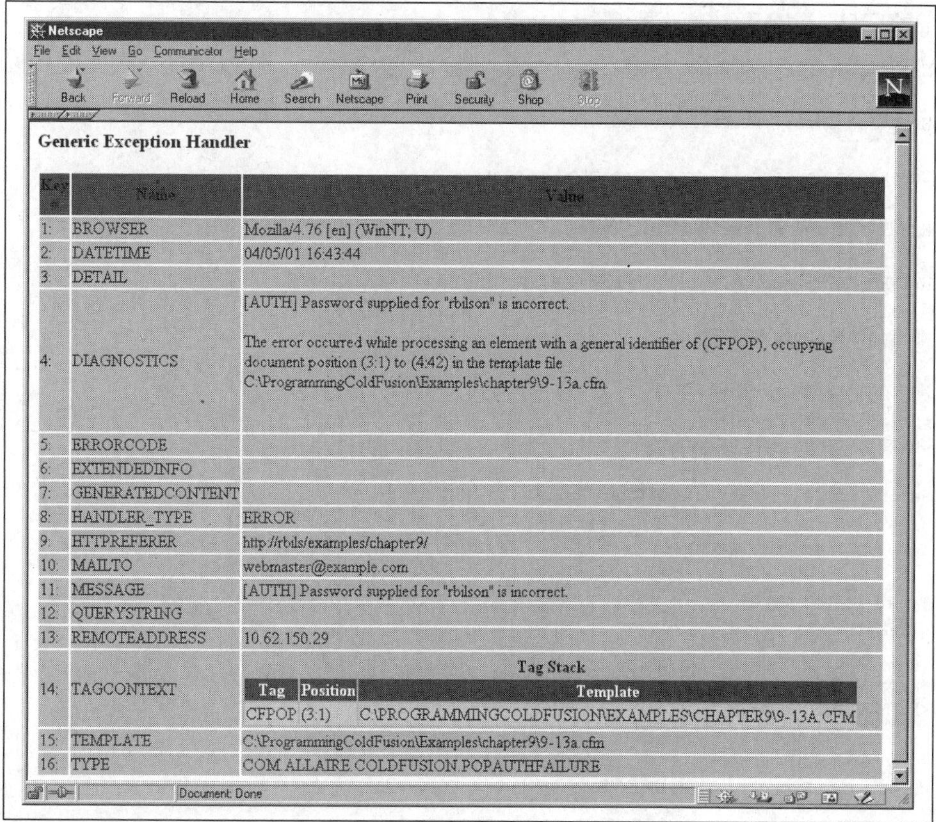


**Generic Exception Handler**

| Key # | Name | Value |
|---|---|---|
| 1: | BROWSER | Mozilla/4.76 [en] (WinNT; U) |
| 2: | DATETIME | 04/05/01 16:43:44 |
| 3: | DETAIL | |
| 4: | DIAGNOSTICS | [AUTH] Password supplied for "rbilson" is incorrect.<br><br>The error occurred while processing an element with a general identifier of (CFPOP), occupying document position (3:1) to (4:42) in the template file C:\ProgrammingColdFusion\Examples\chapter9\9-13a.cfm. |
| 5: | ERRORCODE | |
| 6: | EXTENDEDINFO | |
| 7: | GENERATEDCONTENT | |
| 8: | HANDLER_TYPE | ERROR |
| 9: | HTTPREFERER | http://rbils/examples/chapter9/ |
| 10: | MAILTO | webmaster@example.com |
| 11: | MESSAGE | [AUTH] Password supplied for "rbilson" is incorrect. |
| 12: | QUERYSTRING | |
| 13: | REMOTEADDRESS | 10.62.150.29 |
| 14: | TAGCONTEXT | **Tag Stack**<br>Tag: CFPOP; Position: (3:1); Template: C:\PROGRAMMINGCOLDFUSION\EXAMPLES\CHAPTER9\9-13A.CFM |
| 15: | TEMPLATE | C:\ProgrammingColdFusion\Examples\chapter9\9-13a.cfm |
| 16: | TYPE | COM.ALLAIRE.COLDFUSION.POPAUTHFAILURE |

*Figure 9-3. Handling a POP authentication exception with CFERROR*

The next example we have to look at is the *CustomExceptionHandler.cfm* template. This template highlights the level of customization you can achieve using the CFERROR tag. Unlike the Request and Validation examples given earlier, this type of exception handler has access to the full range of CFML tags and functions. The code for the *CustomExceptionHandler.cfm* template is shown in Example 9-14.

*Example 9-14. Emailing Error Information to the Site Administrator*

```
<!--- E-mail the administrative contact and let them know that an exception
     occurred.  Include the details in the message. --->
<CFMAIL TO="#Error.MailTo#" FROM="webmaster@example.com"
       SUBJECT="Application Exception Encountered">
An exception occurred with one of our applications.  Details follow:

Browser: #Error.Browser#

DateTime: #Error.DateTime#

Detail: #Error.Detail#

Diagnostics: #Error.Diagnostics#

Error Code: #Error.ErrorCode#

Extended Info: #Error.ExtendedInfo#

Generated Content: #Error.GeneratedContent#

Handler Type: #Error.Handler_Type#

HTTPREFERER: #Error.HTTPREFERER#

Mailto: #Error.MAILTO#

Message: #Error.MESSAGE#

Query String: #Error.QUERYSTRING#

Remote Address: #Error.REMOTEADDRESS#

Template: #Error.TEMPLATE#

Type: #Error.Type#
</CFMAIL>

<!--- display an error page to the user --->
<BODY BGCOLOR="#FFFFCC">

<CENTER>
<H2>Custom Exception Handler</H2>

<TABLE BORDER="1" WIDTH="400" CELLPADDING="10">
```

*Example 9-14. Emailing Error Information to the Site Administrator (continued)*

```
<TR>
<TD>An error has occurred while trying to process your request.  The error has
been logged and an e-mail notifying the system administrator has automatically
been sent.
<P>
Please e-mail questions or comments to <CFOUTPUT><A HREF="#Error.Mailto#">#Error.
Mailto#</A></CFOUTPUT>.</TD>
</TR>
</TABLE>
</CENTER>

</BODY>
```

The *CustomExceptionHandler.cfm* template uses the exception information it receives from the `CFERROR` tag to generate an email (using `CFMAIL`) that is automatically sent to the contact specified in the `MAILTO` attribute of the `CFERROR` tag. This email contains information about the exception (from the `Error` variables) such as the time and date the error occurred, diagnostic information, and the template executing when the exception happened. A message is also displayed to the user telling him that an error has occurred and that an email message has been sent to the site administrator.

Now let's look at some templates for generating exceptions that can be caught by the `CFERROR` tags in our *Application.cfm* template. Here's some code that generates a POP authentication exception; in order to use this example, you must change the `SERVER` attribute to the name of a valid POP server:

```
<!--- make sure to change the SERVER attribute to a valid POP server.  Be sure
      to use a username and password you know to be invalid --->
<CFPOP ACTION="GETHEADERONLY" NAME="test" SERVER="my.popserver.com"
       USERNAME="test" PASSWORD="test">
```

Executing this template causes the first `CFERROR` tag in our *Application.cfm* template to invoke the *ExceptionHandler.cfm* template (Example 9-13). The results can be seen in Figure 9-3.

Here's a template that generates a custom exception called `MyApp.MyException` (defined using the `CFTHROW` tag) if a variable called `Form.MyVar` doesn't exist:

```
<CFIF NOT ISDEFINED('Form.MyVar')>
<CFTHROW MESSAGE="<H2>My variable does not exist!</H2>"
          TYPE="MyApp.MyException" DETAIL="Here are the details:"
          ERRORCODE="100"
          EXTENDEDINFO="No extended information is available.">
</CFIF>
```

When this template is executed, ColdFusion checks for the existence of a form variable called `Form.MyVar`. If the variable doesn't exist (which it doesn't in this example), a custom exception named `MyApp.MyException` is generated using the

CFTHROW tag. Once the exception is thrown, the CFERROR tag in our *Application.cfm* template invokes the *CustomExceptionHandler.cfm* template from Example 9-14.

Our final example causes a database exception to occur, triggering the third CFERROR tag in our *Application.cfm* template:

```
<!--- perform a bogus query --->
<CFQUERY NAME="test" DATASOURCE="ProgrammingCF">
  SELECT * FROM bogustable
</CFQUERY>
```

As you may recall, the third CFERROR tag has its TYPE attribute set to Any so it can handle any exceptions not caught by the first two CFERROR tags. Since our database exception isn't handled by either of the first two CFERROR tags, it is automatically caught by the final one.

## Monitors

When ColdFusion's CFML interpreter first detects an exception, it searches for an exception monitor to invoke before it starts looking for CFCATCH blocks or other CFERROR tags to handle the exception. Exception monitors are useful for monitoring and debugging exception handling within ColdFusion applications. To create a monitor, you simply place a CFERROR tag with the TYPE attribute set to Monitor in your *Application.cfm* template. If an exception occurs, and a monitor is found, the template specified in the TEMPLATE attribute of the CFERROR tag is executed. Once the template has finished executing, the exception is rethrown to allow any additional error and exception handling code to deal with the exception. Because of this, it is necessary to have additional CFTRY/CFCATCH or CFERROR tags in place to handle the rethrown exception. Exception monitors are most often used to log errors to a log file, while still allowing other CFERROR tags or CFCATCH blocks to deal with the actual exception.

Example 9-15 shows an *Application.cfm* template that creates a basic exception monitor to write all available exception information to a log file in the event an exception occurs.

*Example 9-15. Application.cfm Template Containing CFERROR Code for Invoking an Exception Monitor*

```
<CFAPPLICATION NAME="MyApplication">

<!--- call an exception monitor for any type of exception --->
<CFERROR TYPE="Monitor" TEMPLATE="MonitorHandler.cfm" EXCEPTION="Any"
      MAILTO="webmaster@example.com">

<!--- after the exception monitor has finished executing, this CFERROR tag will
      execute.  It calls the ExceptionHandler.cfm template from Example 9-13 --->
```

*Example 9-15. Application.cfm Template Containing CFERROR Code for Invoking an Exception Monitor (continued)*

```
<CFERROR TYPE="Exception" TEMPLATE="ExceptionHandler.cfm" EXCEPTION="Any"
        MAILTO="webmaster@example.com">
```

This *Application.cfm* template contains two `CFERROR` tags. The first `CFERROR` tag makes the call to the *MonitorHandler.cfm* template in the event that any exception occurs. This is done by setting the `TYPE` attribute to `Monitor` and the `EXCEPTION` attribute to `Any`.

Because of the way that the `Monitor` exception type works, it is necessary to include a second `CFERROR` tag with the `TYPE` attribute set to `Exception` and the `EXCEPTION` attribute set to `Any`. This is because ColdFusion automatically rethrows the original exception after the *MonitorHandler.cfm* template has finished executing. Because of this, we need a second `CFERROR` tag to handle the rethrown exception. If the second `CFERROR` isn't there, the exception is rethrown, an error is written out to the browser, and all processing halts.

With the *Application.cfm* template set up, it's time to move to the *MonitorHandler.cfm* template we specified in the `TEMPLATE` attribute of our first `CFERROR` tag. This template is used to write an entry in a log file called *Monitor_log.txt* each time it is invoked by the `CFERROR` tag. The code for *MonitorHandler.cfm* is shown in Example 9-16.

*Example 9-16. Writing Exception Information to a Log File with CFFILE*

```
<!--- Basic exception monitor for writing a log file with CFFILE --->

<!--- Initialize a variable to hold the log entry --->
<CFSET TheException = "">

<!--- Loop over the error structure and build the log entry --->
<CFLOOP COLLECTION=#Error# ITEM="Message">
  <CFIF IsSimpleValue(Error[Message])>
    <CFSET TheException = ListAppend(TheException, Error[message], "|")>
  </CFIF>
</CFLOOP>

<!--- Write the exception info in the log file --->
<CFLOCK TIMEOUT="60" THROWONTIMEOUT="Yes" TYPE="EXCLUSIVE">
<CFFILE ACTION="append" FILE="c:\temp\Monitor_log.txt"
       OUTPUT="#TheException#" ADDNEWLINE="Yes">
</CFLOCK>
```

Once invoked, the *MonitorHandler.cfm* template initializes a variable called `TheException`. The template then loops over the `Error` structure appending each value to `TheException` and delimiting them with the pipe (|) character. The pipe is used as a delimiter because we know that it is unlikely to show up as a character in any of the error variable values. Each value is tested with the

IsSimpleValue() function before it is appended to the list. If the value isn't a simple value, we know it is part of the Error.TagContext variable, and we omit it from the log file (for simplicity's sake). Finally, the CFFILE tag is used to write the contents of our exception string (TheException) to a file called *Monitor_log.txt*. A new line character is added at the end of each entry so that the next time an entry is written, it begins on a new line. The CFLOCK tag is used around the CFFILE tag so that no two exceptions can write to the *Monitor_log.txt* file at the same time.

If you are running a ColdFusion 5.0 server, you can write your log file entry using the CFLOG tag instead of CFFILE. CFLOG allows you to log messages to ColdFusion's default *Application.log*, *Scheduler.log* or to a custom log file that you specify. Example 9-17 shows the code from Example 9-14 modified to use the CFLOG tag.

*Example 9-17. Writing Exception Information to a Log File with CFLOG*

```
<!--- Basic exception monitor for writing a log file with CFLOG --->

<!--- Initialize a variable to hold the log message --->
<CFSET TheException = "">

<!--- Loop over the error structure and build the log entry --->
<CFLOOP COLLECTION=#Error# ITEM="Message">
  <CFIF IsSimpleValue(Error[Message])>
    <CFSET TheException = ListAppend(TheException, Error[message], "|")>
  </CFIF>
</CFLOOP>

<!--- Write the exception info in the log file --->
<CFLOG TEXT = "#TheException#"
       FILE = "MonitorLog"
       TYPE = "Error"
       THREAD = "Yes"
       DATE = "Yes"
       TIME = "Yes"
       APPLICATION = "Yes">
```

When this exception monitor is invoked, it builds the message to add to the log file in the same way as Example 9-16. The process of logging the error, however, is somewhat different. In this case, the CFLOG tag is used to write the message to a log file. The log files generated by CFLOG follow a standard format. The first line of each log file contains a comma-delimited list of column headers qualified with double quotes that looks like this:

```
"Severity","ThreadID","Date","Time","Application","Message"
```

When an entry is made to the log file, the values that are written to each column are also qualified with double quotes and delimited with commas. Column values are based on the values specified for the various attributes of the CFLOG tag. TEXT is the only required attribute and specifies the message to be written to the file. Here, we use the exception string (TheException). The FILE attribute specifies the name of the log file (without the extension) you want to write the log entry to. You must specify the name of a file with a *.log* extension. If the file doesn't exist, ColdFusion automatically creates it in the default log file directory specified in the Logging section of the ColdFusion Administrator. In this case, we are going to write our log entry to a log file called *MonitorLog.log*.

If you don't want to write your entry to a custom log file, you may omit the FILE attribute and use the LOG attribute instead (not shown in the example). The LOG attribute specifies one of two standard ColdFusion log files to write the entry to:

`Application`
: The entry is written to the *Application.log* file. This file is automatically created by ColdFusion and is used to log application-specific messages.

`Scheduler`
: The entry is written to the *Scheduler.log file*. This file is used by ColdFusion to log execution information concerning scheduled tasks.

The TYPE attribute lets you assign a severity level to the log entry. Possible entries are Information (the default), Warning, Error, and Fatal. THREADID accepts a Yes/No value and indicates whether to include the ID of the service thread responsible for logging the message in the log entry. Service threads typically handle a particular page request from request through completion before moving to the next queued request. Logging thread IDs can be useful (especially to Allaire technical support) for identifying server activity patterns. The default is Yes. The DATE and TIME attributes are used to specify whether to include the system date and time, respectively, in the log file. The default for both of these attributes is Yes. Specifying Yes (the default) for the APPLICATION attribute writes the application name to the log file if a name is specified in a CFAPPLICATION tag for the application. For more information on the CFLOG tag, see Appendix A.

Our exception monitor example wouldn't be complete without a template to test everything out. The following code causes a database exception by attempting to query a nonexistent data source:

```
<CFQUERY NAME="test" DATASOURCE="asd">
         SELECT * FROM Test
</CFQUERY>
```

Executing this template causes the first CFERROR tag to invoke the *MonitorHandler.cfm* template and write the exception information to the log file. After that is complete, the exception is rethrown and caught by the second

CFERROR tag in our *Application.cfm* template. That CFERROR tag calls the *ExceptionHandler.cfm* template from Example 9-13.

# *Server-wide Error Handling*

As of Version 4.5, ColdFusion provides site administrators with a way to handle errors and exceptions at the server level. Via the ColdFusion Administrator, you can designate a template to handle requests for CFML templates that don't exist on the server. You can also specify an additional template that is invoked when an error or exception occurs anywhere within your ColdFusion application.

## *Missing Template Handler*

Within the Settings section of the ColdFusion Administrator, there is a place for you to specify a Missing Template Handler. This template is called if a requested ColdFusion template can't be found on the server, allowing you to avoid the dreaded "404 Object Not Found" error that otherwise results. Note that the Missing Template Handler isn't invoked for template types other than CFML. In other words, requests for missing HTML templates are handled by the web server, not ColdFusion. When setting the Missing Template Handler, you should provide the physical path (not the URL) to the template's location on your ColdFusion server.

If the template you are calling attempts to call another template that doesn't exist, like as a custom tag call, CFMODULE, or CFINCLUDE, ColdFusion generates a MissingInclude exception but doesn't invoke the Missing Template Handler. This exception can be trapped by placing the following code in the *Application.cfm* template of your application:

```
<CFERROR TYPE="Exception" EXCEPTION="MissingInclude"
         TEMPLATE="MissingIncludeHandler.cfm">
```

## *Site-wide Error Handler*

There are times when you might want to display a generic error page in the event that an unforeseen error occurs somewhere in your application. The Site-wide Error Handler setting, again in the Settings section of the ColdFusion Administrator, lets you specify a ColdFusion template to invoke in the event that an error occurs within any of your ColdFusion applications. This feature is useful in situations where you have applications that don't contain their own internal error and exception handling or where you want to provide a backup error handler.

Using the Site-wide Error Handler is equivalent to placing the following code in your *Application.cfm* file:

```
<CFERROR TYPE="Exception" EXCEPTION="Any" TEMPLATE="ErrorHandler.cfm">
```

Note, however, that using a Site-wide Error Handler overrides the use of any instances of the `CFERROR` tag when the `TYPE` attribute of `CFERROR` is set to `Exception`.

When setting the Site-wide Error Handler, you should provide the physical path (not the URL) to the template's location on your ColdFusion server.

# 10

# *Dynamic Form Controls*

*In this chapter:*
- *Combining HTML and CFML Form Controls*
- *Data Validation*
- *Basic Input Controls*
- *Textual Input*
- *A Selection Control*
- *Sliders*
- *Grids*
- *Trees*
- *Custom Controls*
- *Form Controls in Version 5.0*

Anyone who has ever worked with HTML forms knows their importance. Forms are the basis for much of the interaction between users and web applications. Yet, for all of their benefits, HTML forms leave a lot to be desired from a development standpoint. For starters, HTML forms are all alike—from a data gathering perspective and from a user interface perspective. A text box is a text box is a text box. Nothing you can do can change that. With regular HTML forms, you are limited to a standard set of input types, each identical in style and function to those used by every other HTML developer. Sure you can make your forms unique, but the form controls themselves are completely void of customization. The second limitation (if you want to call it that) of HTML form controls is the lack of data-validation capabilities. HTML form controls do nothing more than gather data and POST it to another template for processing. Sure, you can write JavaScript routines to validate each form field individually, but do you really want to? This is where ColdFusion comes in.

ColdFusion includes a set of tags for extending the capabilities of regular HTML forms. These tags provide additional functionality to forms such as data validation, new data views, and new input types. Not only can you customize the appearance of many of the form controls, but there are several additional ColdFusion form controls, including Java applet-based tree, grid, and slider controls. The following list details the form controls available under `CFFORM`:

`CFINPUT`
: Creates text boxes, password entry boxes, radio buttons, and checkboxes with optional JavaScript validation routines. Not a Java applet.

`CFTEXTINPUT`
: Java applet-based text box. Allows more formatting options than a standard text box.

`CFSELECT`
: Creates drop-down lists from query results with optional JavaScript validation routines. Not a Java applet.

`CFSLIDER`
: Java applet-based slider control for selecting a value from a range of numeric values.

`CFGRID`
: Java applet-based grid control for displaying, entering, and editing tabular data.

`CFTREE`
: Java applet-based tree control for displaying and selecting hierarchical data.

`CFAPPLET`
: Allows you to use custom Java controls within your `CFFORM`s as if they were native ColdFusion tags.

# *Combining HTML and CFML Form Controls*

The `CFFORM` tag enables you to create dynamic forms using controls that include such HTML controls as input boxes, drop-down boxes, and radio buttons, as well as a number of specialized Java applet-based controls, such as trees, grids, and sliders. Forms created using the `CFFORM` tag are coded in the same manner as regular HTML forms. In fact, the `CFFORM` tag allows you to mix standard HTML and CFML form controls in the same form.

The following example creates a form using `CFFORM` and places a standard HTML submit button on the page:

```
<CFFORM ACTION="MyFormProcessor.cfm" NAME="MyForm" ENABLECAB="Yes"
        ENCTYPE="application/x-www-form-urlencoded">

<INPUT TYPE="submit" NAME="Submit" VALUE="Submit">

</CFFORM>
```

The `CFFORM` tag has many of the same attributes as the HTML `FORM` tag. The `ACTION` attribute is required and specifies where the form should be submitted upon completion. `NAME` is optional and specifies a name for the form. You should specify a value for `NAME` if you plan to reference the form later in your application.

`ENABLECAB` is another optional attribute and allows you to specify whether or not Java controls associated with other `CFFORM` elements should be made available to Microsoft Internet Explorer users as Microsoft cabinet files. This attribute has been deprecated and is nonfunctional in Version 5.0. For more information, see the last section in this chapter "Form Controls in Version 5.0." The `ENCTYPE` attribute is also optional and specifies the MIME type for data being submitted via the `POST` method. The default `ENCTYPE` is `application/x-www-form-urlencoded`. If, however, you plan to allow file uploads via your form, you must specify `multipart/form-data` for the `ENCTYPE`. For more information on uploading files via forms, see Chapter 12.

Three additional attributes, all optional and available to the `CFFORM` tag, aren't shown in the example. The `TARGET` attribute allows you to specify the name of a frame or window for the target template to be opened in. The second attribute, `ONSUBMIT`, allows you to designate a JavaScript function that should be executed after validation occurs but before the form is submitted. This is useful in situations where you want to use JavaScript to clean up or reformat data before submitting it. The third attribute, `PASSTHROUGH`, allows you to pass any additional HTML attributes that aren't directly supported by the `CFFORM` tag. For example, you can pass an additional parameter called `MyParameter` with a value of `Yes` by adding the following code to your `CFFORM` tag:

```
PASSTHROUGH="MyParameter=""Yes"""
```

Note that in order to pass quoted values through `CFFORM`, you must escape the quotation marks by doubling up on them.

# *Data Validation*

One of the big benefits of using `CFFORM` over standard HTML forms is the built-in data validation that is available. Both the `CFINPUT` and `CFTEXTINPUT` tags have an attribute called `VALIDATE` that accepts any of the following values:

`CreditCard`
: Validates the form field data using the mod10 algorithm. Credit-card numbers can be entered as a single number or with dashes or spaces. ColdFusion automatically strips dashes and spaces before validating.

`Date`
: Requires the form-field value to be in the U.S. date format *mm/dd/yyyy*.

`EuroDate`
: Requires the form-field value to be in the European date format *dd/mm/yyyy*.

`Float`
: Requires the form-field value to be a floating-point number.

`Integer`
: Requires the form-field value to be an integer.

`Social_Security_Number`
: Requires the form-field value to be a U.S. social security number in the format *xxx-xx-xxxx* or *xxx xx xxxx*.

`Telephone`
: Requires the form-field value to be a U.S. telephone number formatted either *xxx-xxx-xxxx* or *xxx xxx xxxx*. The area code and exchange are required to begin with a number in the range of 1–9.

`Time`
: Requires that the form-field value be entered as a valid time using the format *hh:mm:ss*.

`ZipCode`
: Requires that the form-field value be entered as either a five- or nine-digit U.S. ZIP code using the format *xxxxx*, *xxxxx-xxxx*, or *xxxxx xxxx*.

In addition to the `VALIDATE` attribute, the `CFINPUT` and `CFTEXTINPUT` tags as well as the `CFGRID`, `CFSLIDER`, and `CFTREE` tags support an additional attribute for data validation. The `ONVALIDATE` attribute allows you to designate your own JavaScript validation function that should be executed before the form is submitted. You don't need to know all the ins and outs of JavaScript to use the `ONVALIDATE` function (although it sure helps!) Example 10-1 demonstrates how to use `ONVALIDATE` to call a custom JavaScript function.

*Example 10-1. Using ONVALIDATE*

```
<SCRIPT LANGUAGE="JavaScript">
  <!--
      function PasswordCheck() {
         if (document.MyForm.Password.value !=
              document.MyForm.Password2.value) {
            return false;
         }
         else
            return true;
      }
  //-->
</SCRIPT>

<CFIF IsDefined('Form.Fieldnames')>
  <H3>You submitted:</H3>
  <CFLOOP INDEX="Field" LIST="#Form.Fieldnames#">
    <CFOUTPUT><B>#Field#</B>: #Evaluate(Field)#<BR></CFOUTPUT>
  </CFLOOP>
  <HR NOSHADE>
</CFIF>
```

*Example 10-1. Using ONVALIDATE (continued)*

```
<CFFORM ACTION="Example10-1.cfm" ENABLECAB="Yes" NAME="MyForm"
        ENCTYPE="application/x-www-form-urlencoded">
<TABLE>
<TR>
  <TD>User Name:</TD>
  <TD><CFINPUT TYPE="Text" NAME="MyTime" REQUIRED="Yes" MESSAGE="You must enter a
      User Name." SIZE="10" MAXLENGTH="10"></TD>
</TR>

<TR>
  <TD>Password:</TD>
  <TD><CFINPUT TYPE="Password" NAME="Password" REQUIRED="Yes" MESSAGE="You must
      enter a Password." SIZE="10" MAXLENGTH="10"></TD>
</TR>
<TR>
  <TD>Confirm:</TD>
  <TD><CFINPUT TYPE="Password" NAME="Password2" MESSAGE="The
      passwords you entered don't match, please re-enter them and submit the form
      again." ONVALIDATE="PasswordCheck" SIZE="10" MAXLENGTH="10"></TD>
</TR>
</TABLE>

<P>
<INPUT TYPE="submit" NAME="Submit" VALUE="Submit">
</CFFORM>
```

What happens in Example 10-1 is straightforward. We define a JavaScript function called `PasswordCheck` at the beginning of the template. It contains the JavaScript code to be called by the password confirmation field (the last `CFINPUT` statement in the template). The second section of the code is a conditional block of code that executes only if the template is called via a POST operation. The code loops through any form fields passed to the template and outputs them along with their corresponding values.

The third section of code is the `CFFORM` section. This section of code creates a form with three text-input fields and a submit button. The fields allow a user to enter a username, a password of his choice and a confirmation of that password. When the user submits the form, the first `CFINPUT` tag automatically checks to see that a value has been entered. If not, a JavaScript alert box is displayed along with the text in the `MESSAGE` attribute of the tag. Next, the `Password` field is evaluated to ensure that a value has been entered. If one hasn't, a similar JavaScript alert box is displayed. Finally, the `CFINPUT` tag containing the `Password2` field calls the `PasswordCheck` JavaScript function via the `ONVALIDATE` attribute. The `PasswordCheck` function evaluates the value of `Password1` against `Password2`. If they are equal, the form is submitted. If, however, the values aren't equal, a JavaScript alert is displayed along with the text from the MESSAGE attribute of the CFINPUT tag. The form can't successfully be submitted until all the validation conditions have been met.

When ColdFusion calls out to a custom JavaScript function via the ONVALIDATE attribute, the form object, input object, and input object value are all automatically passed to the specified JavaScript function. The JavaScript function should return True if the validation is successful and False if it fails. Using the ONVALIDATE attribute overrides any options specified in the VALIDATE attribute.

# Basic Input Controls

The CFINPUT tag closely resembles the HTML INPUT tag and can be used for creating text boxes, password entry boxes, radio buttons, and checkboxes. At the most basic level, the CFINPUT tag behaves exactly like the HTML INPUT tag. Consider the following HTML INPUT tags:

```
<INPUT TYPE="Text" NAME="MyText" SIZE="10" MAXLENGTH="10" VALUE="MyValue">
<INPUT TYPE="Password" NAME="MyPassword" SIZE="10" MAXLENGTH="10">
<INPUT TYPE="Radio" NAME="MyRadioButton" VALUE="MyValue" CHECKED>
<INPUT TYPE="Checkbox" NAME="MyCheckbox" VALUE="MyValue" CHECKED>
```

Here are the equivalent CFINPUT tags:

```
<CFINPUT TYPE="Text" NAME="MyText" SIZE="10" MAXLENGTH="10" VALUE="MyValue">
<CFINPUT TYPE="Password" NAME="MyPassword" SIZE="10" MAXLENGTH="10">
<CFINPUT TYPE="Radio" NAME="MyRadioButton" VALUE="MyValue" CHECKED>
<CFINPUT TYPE="Checkbox" NAME="MyCheckbox" VALUE="MyValue" CHECKED>
```

As you can see, the tags are virtually identical. What sets a CFINPUT tag apart from its HTML counterpart is built-in data validation. The CFINPUT tag can require input for a given form field as well as validate the data against a predefined or custom validation routine. Example 10-2 demonstrates how to use the CFINPUT tag to require data entry for various input types.

*Example 10-2. Creating a Form with CFFORM and CFINPUT*

```
<CFIF ISDEFINED('FORM.FIELDNAMES')>
  <H3>You submitted:</H3>
  <CFLOOP INDEX="Field" LIST="#Form.Fieldnames#">
    <CFOUTPUT><B>#Field#</B>: #Evaluate(Field)#<BR></CFOUTPUT>
  </CFLOOP>
  <HR NOSHADE>
</CFIF>

<CFFORM ACTION="Example10-2.cfm" ENABLECAB="Yes" NAME="MyForm"
        ENCTYPE="application/x-www-form-urlencoded">
<TABLE>
<TR>
  <TD>Name:</TD>
```

*Example 10-2. Creating a Form with CFFORM and CFINPUT (continued)*

```
  <TD><CFINPUT TYPE="Text" NAME="Name" REQUIRED="yes" MESSAGE="You must enter
      your name." SIZE="10" MAXLENGTH="10">
  </TD>
</TR>
<TR>
  <TD>Password:</TD>
  <TD><CFINPUT TYPE="Password" NAME="Password" REQUIRED="yes" MESSAGE="You must
      enter your password." SIZE="10" MAXLENGTH="10">
  </TD>
</TR>
</TABLE>

<TABLE>
<TR>
  <TD>Do you like programming with ColdFusion?</TD>
  <TD><CFINPUT TYPE="Radio" NAME="LikeCF" VALUE="Yes" CHECKED="Yes">Yes <CFINPUT
      TYPE="Radio" NAME="LikeCF" VALUE="No">No
  </TD>
</TR>
<TR>
  <TD COLSPAN="2">Which database(s) do you use?</TD>
</TR>
<TR>
  <TD COLSPAN="2"><CFINPUT TYPE="Checkbox" NAME="Access" VALUE="Yes">Access<BR>
          <CFINPUT TYPE="Checkbox" NAME="DB2" VALUE="Yes">DB2<BR>
          <CFINPUT TYPE="Checkbox" NAME="Informix" VALUE="Yes">Informix<BR>
          <CFINPUT TYPE="Checkbox" NAME="Oracle" VALUE="Yes">Oracle<BR>
          <CFINPUT TYPE="Checkbox" NAME="SQL_Server" VALUE="Yes">SQL Server
  </TD>
</TR>
</TABLE>

<P>
<INPUT TYPE="submit" NAME="Submit" VALUE="Submit">
</CFFORM>
```

Example 10-2 starts by using a `CFIF` statement to see if a `Form` variable called `FieldNames` was passed to the template. `Form.FieldNames` is a special ColdFusion variable that is automatically created whenever a ColdFusion template receives information via an HTTP POST operation. `Form.FieldNames` contains a comma-delimited list of all the field names passed from the form making the POST to the ColdFusion template. If the variable `Form.FieldNames` exists, the template loops through the list of field names and outputs each field name from the list as well as the value it contains. This technique allows you to submit the form to itself and display the results without knowing what form fields were passed.

The form itself is set up using the `CFFORM` tag. The first `CFINPUT` tag collects a user's name. The `REQUIRED` attribute indicates whether or not to require that data be entered before the form can be successfully submitted. In this case, we set

REQUIRED to Yes. The MESSAGE attribute contains the text to display in a JavaScript alert box in the event that a user submits the form without filling in a required field. You can use the REQUIRED and MESSAGE attributes with any of the CFINPUT controls.

In addition to making form fields required, the CFINPUT tag can also validate form fields against several predefined datatypes. Example 10-3 demonstrates the CFINPUT tag along with some of the predefined data validation settings discussed in the previous section on data validation.

*Example 10-3. Using Predefined Data Validation with CFINPUT*

```
<CFIF ISDEFINED('Form.FieldNames')>
  <H3>You submitted:</H3>
  <CFLOOP INDEX="Field" LIST="#Form.FieldNames#">
    <CFOUTPUT><B>#Field#</B>: #Evaluate(Field)#<BR></CFOUTPUT>
  </CFLOOP>
  <HR NOSHADE>
</CFIF>

<CFFORM ACTION="Example10-3.cfm" ENABLECAB="Yes" NAME="MyForm"
        ENCTYPE="application/x-www-form-urlencoded">
<TABLE>
<TR>
  <TD>Date:</TD>
  <TD><CFINPUT TYPE="Text" NAME="MyDate" VALIDATE="date" REQUIRED="Yes"
      MESSAGE="You must enter a valid Date."  SIZE="10" MAXLENGTH="10"></TD>
</TR>
<TR>
  <TD>EuroDate:</TD>
  <TD><CFINPUT TYPE="Text" NAME="MyEuroDate" VALIDATE="eurodate"
      MESSAGE="You must enter a valid EuroDate." SIZE="10" MAXLENGTH="10"></TD>
</TR>
<TR>
  <TD>Time:</TD>
  <TD><CFINPUT TYPE="Text" NAME="MyTime" VALIDATE="time"
      MESSAGE="You must enter a valid Time." SIZE="10" MAXLENGTH="10"></TD>
</TR>
<TR>
  <TD>Float:</TD>
  <TD><CFINPUT TYPE="Text" NAME="MyFloat" VALIDATE="float"
      MESSAGE="You must enter a valid floating point number." SIZE="10"
      MAXLENGTH="255"></TD>
</TR>
<TR>
  <TD>Integer (range 1-100):</TD>
  <TD><CFINPUT TYPE="Text" NAME="MyInteger" VALIDATE="integer" RANGE="1,100"
      MESSAGE="You must enter a valid integer between 1 and 100."  SIZE="10"
      MAXLENGTH="255"></TD>
</TR>
<TR>
```

*Example 10-3. Using Predefined Data Validation with CFINPUT (continued)*

```
  <TD>Phone Number:</TD>
  <TD><CFINPUT TYPE="Text" NAME="MyPhone" VALIDATE="telephone"
      MESSAGE="You must enter a valid phone number (xxx-xxx-xxxx, xxx xxx xxxx)."
      SIZE="15" MAXLENGTH="25"></TD>
</TR>
<TR>
  <TD>Zip code:</TD>
  <TD><CFINPUT TYPE="Text" NAME="MyZip" VALIDATE="zipcode"
      MESSAGE="You must enter a valid zip code (xxxxx, xxxxx-xxxx, xxxxx xxxx)."
      SIZE="15" MAXLENGTH="15"></TD>
</TR>
<TR>
  <TD>Credit Card Number:</TD>
  <TD><CFINPUT TYPE="Text" NAME="MyCreditCard" VALIDATE="creditcard"
      MESSAGE="You must enter a valid credit card number." SIZE="10"
      MAXLENGTH="255"></TD>
</TR>
<TR>
  <TD>Social Security Number:</TD>
  <TD><CFINPUT TYPE="Text" NAME="MySSN" VALIDATE="social_security_number"
     MESSAGE="You must enter a valid Social Security Number  (xxx-xx-xxxx, xxx xx
     xxxx)." SIZE="13" MAXLENGTH="11"></TD>
</TR>
</TABLE>

<P>
<INPUT TYPE="submit" NAME="Submit" VALUE="Submit">
</CFFORM>
```

Each `CFINPUT` tag in Example 10-3 performs a different type of validation against the data it accepts. The type of validation performed is determined by the value specified by the `VALIDATE` attribute. `MESSAGE` specifies a message to display in a JavaScript alert box in the event that validation for a particular field fails. You can set an additional attribute, `RANGE` with the Integer validation type. `RANGE` allows you to specify a range of acceptable values for the form field. `RANGE` is specified as `RANGE(`*`m`*`,`*`n`*`)` where *`m`* is the beginning value in the range, and *`n`* is the ending value.

Besides the attributes already mentioned, there are three additional attributes available to the `CFINPUT` tag. These attributes are `ONVALIDATE`, `ONERROR`, and `PASSTHROUGH`. The `ONVALIDATE` attribute allows you to specify a JavaScript function to execute in lieu of the default function associated with the form field. `ONERROR` allows you to designate the name of a JavaScript function that is executed if validation fails for any reason. Finally, you can use `PASSTHROUGH` to pass any additional HTML attributes that aren't directly supported by the `CFINPUT` tag.

# *Textual Input*

The CFTEXTINPUT tag offers a Java control for accepting basic text input. Although it provides the same basic functionality as the CFINPUT and HTML INPUT tags, CFTEXTINPUT differs in that it allows you to specify a number of attributes affecting the look of both the text box and the data entered into it. Consider Example 10-4, in which two CFTEXTINPUT tags are used to solicit information from a user.

*Example 10-4. Creating a Form Using CFFORM and CFTEXTINPUT*

```
<!--- check to see if form field data is being passed and if so, display it --->
<CFIF IsDefined('Form.Fieldnames')>
  <H3>You submitted:</H3>
  <CFOUTPUT>
  MyName:  #MyName#<BR>
  PhoneNumber: #PhoneNumber#
  </CFOUTPUT>
  <HR NOSHADE>
</CFIF>

<CFFORM ACTION="Example10-4.cfm" ENABLECAB="Yes" NAME="MyForm"
ENCTYPE="application/x-www-form-urlencoded">
<TABLE>
<TR>
  <TD>Name:</TD>
  <TD><CFTEXTINPUT NAME="MyName" ALIGN="ABSMIDDLE"
                HEIGHT="25" WIDTH="250" BGCOLOR="##C0C0C0"
                FONT="Arial" FONTSIZE="14" BOLD="Yes" ITALIC="No"
                TEXTCOLOR="##000000" MAXLENGTH="255" REQUIRED="Yes"
                MESSAGE="You must enter your name"></TD>
</TR>
<TR>
  <TD>Phone Number:</TD>
  <TD><CFTEXTINPUT NAME="PhoneNumber" VALUE="xxx-xxx-xxxx"
                ALIGN="ABSMIDDLE" HEIGHT="25" WIDTH="100"
                BGCOLOR="##C0C0C0" FONT="Arial" FONTSIZE="14" BOLD="Yes"
                ITALIC="Yes" TEXTCOLOR="##000000" MAXLENGTH="12"
                REQUIRED="Yes" VALIDATE="telephone"
                MESSAGE="You must enter your phone number as xxx-xxx-xxxx">
  </TD>
</TR>
<TR>
  <TD COLSPAN="2"><INPUT TYPE="submit" NAME="Submit" VALUE="Submit"></TD>
</TR>
</TABLE>
</CFFORM>
```

Example 10-4 uses two CFTEXTINPUT tags that solicit information from a user, as shown in Figure 10-1. The first tag creates a text box for a user to enter his name. The second collects a user's phone number. In both cases, the NAME attribute is required to name the form field. The `VALUE` attribute is optional, and you can use it to specify a default value to appear in the text box. In the case of the text box called `PhoneNumber`, a default `VALUE` of *xxx-xxx-xxxx* is used. You can specify the positioning of the text-input box by using the `ALIGN` attribute. Possible values are `top`, `texttop`, `bottom`, `absbottom`, `baseline`, `middle`, `absmiddle`, `left`, and `right`. The height and width of the text boxes is set using the `HEIGHT` and `WIDTH` attributes, respectively. You can specify a background color for the control by entering the color name or appropriate hex color code in the `BGCOLOR` attribute. If you specify a hex value, you must escape the pound sign, or ColdFusion will throw an error.

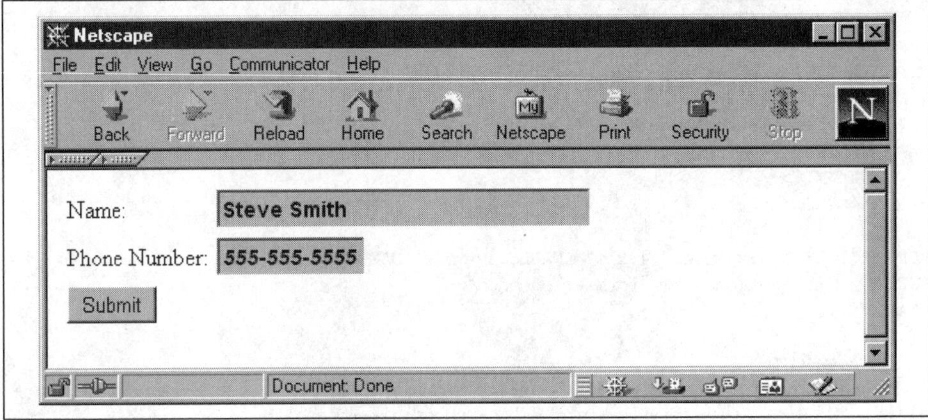


*Figure 10-1. CFFORM using CFTEXTINPUT*

One nice feature of the `CFTEXTINPUT` control that isn't available in regular HTML forms is the ability to control font characteristics with the form control itself. The `FONT` attribute specifies the font to use when representing the text entered in the form control. The size of the font is controlled by the `FONTSIZE` attribute. Bold and italic effects may be used by indicating `Yes` or `No` within the `BOLD` and `ITALIC` attributes. Text color is specified using the `TEXTCOLOR` attribute and may be entered as the color name or as a valid hex color value.

You can specify a maximum number of characters that can be entered in the text control with the `MAXLENGTH` attribute. This prevents users from entering more data in the form than your corresponding database field allows. Setting the `REQUIRED` attribute to `Yes` makes the text-box field a required form field. As shown in Figure 10-1, in the case of the `PhoneNumber` field, additional validation is performed by setting the `VALIDATE` field to `"Telephone"`. This requires any value entered for `PhoneNumber` to follow the U.S. telephone format before the form can be submitted. The `MESSAGE` attribute is used when the `REQUIRED` attribute is set to `Yes`; the `VALIDATE` attribute is used to require a specific type of validation be performed. You specify a text message to display in the event that validation fails for the given field.

## A Selection Control

The `CFSELECT` tag extends the functionality provided by the HTML `SELECT` tag by including data validation as well as a mechanism for quickly and easily building dynamic drop-down boxes from query results. Example 10-5 shows a simple use of `CFSELECT` with static option values.

*Example 10-5. Using CFSELECT with Static Option Values*

```
<CFIF IsDefined('Form.Selectbox')>
  <CFOUTPUT>You submitted <B>#Form.Selectbox#</B>.</CFOUTPUT>
  <HR NOSHADE>
</CFIF>

<CFFORM ACTION="Example10-5.cfm" ENABLECAB="Yes" NAME="MyForm"
ENCTYPE="application/x-www-form-urlencoded">

<CFSELECT NAME="Selectbox" SIZE="5"
          MESSAGE="You must select at least one item from the selection box."
          REQUIRED="Yes" MULTIPLE="Yes">
   <OPTION VALUE="January">January
   <OPTION VALUE="February">February
   <OPTION VALUE="March">March
   <OPTION VALUE="April">April
   <OPTION VALUE="May">May
   <OPTION VALUE="June">June
   <OPTION VALUE="July">July
   <OPTION VALUE="August">August
   <OPTION VALUE="September">September
   <OPTION VALUE="October">October
   <OPTION VALUE="November">November
   <OPTION VALUE="December">December
</CFSELECT>
<P>
<INPUT TYPE="submit" NAME="Submit" VALUE="Submit Form">
</CFFORM>
```

In Example 10-5, a drop-down box is created within a `CFFORM` using the `CFSELECT` tag. We specify the name of the select-box field using the `NAME` attribute. Setting the `SIZE` to `5` creates a select box five rows high. Note that `SIZE` must be set to at least two (2) for the `REQUIRED` validation to work. The `MULTIPLE` attribute allows the user to select multiple values from the select box. By setting the `REQUIRED` attribute to `Yes`, we can require the user to select at least one value from the list. The `MESSAGE` attribute specifies a message to appear in a JavaScript alert box should the user fail to choose at least one option. In the case of this example, all `OPTION` values for the select box are hardcoded.

While the data-validation capabilities of CFSELECT are a good reason to use the tag, the real benefit of CFSELECT becomes evident when you use it to dynamically populate the options of a select box with the results of a query. By adding a few additional attributes to the CFSELECT tag, it is possible to generate all the OPTION tags necessary for the select list dynamically. Example 10-6 shows the basic syntax for populating the CFSELECT tag with the results of a query.

*Example 10-6. Populating a CFSELECT Box with Dynamic Values from a Query*

```
<CFIF IsDefined('Form.Selectbox')>
  <CFOUTPUT>You submitted <B>#Form.Selectbox#</B>.</CFOUTPUT>
  <HR NOSHADE>
</CFIF>

<CFQUERY NAME="GetPeople" DATASOURCE="ProgrammingCF">
        SELECT ID,Name FROM EmployeeDirectory
</CFQUERY>

<CFFORM ACTION="Example10-6.cfm" ENABLECAB="Yes" NAME="MyForm"
       ENCTYPE="application/x-www-form-urlencoded">

<CFSELECT NAME="Selectbox" SIZE="5"
         MESSAGE="You must select at least one item from the selection box."
         QUERY="GetPeople" VALUE="ID" DISPLAY="Name"
         SELECTED="Pere Money" REQUIRED="Yes" MULTIPLE="Yes">
</CFSELECT>
<P>
<INPUT TYPE="submit" NAME="Submit" VALUE="Submit Form">
</CFFORM>
```

In Example 10-6, the CFSELECT tag takes on four additional attributes: QUERY, VALUE, DISPLAY, and SELECTED. The QUERY attribute specifies the name of the query to use to populate the tag. In this case, we used GetPeople. The VALUE attribute determines which field from the query to use to fill in the option values. For this example, we use the ID field, which happens to be the primary key for the table. The next attribute, DISPLAY, allows us to choose an alternate field from the query to display in the select box itself. We chose the NAME field in this case. The final new attribute, SELECTED, allows us to supply a value that is selected automatically when the template is called. In this example, we chose Pere Money, a value known to be in the database under the NAME column.

## Sliders

The CFSLIDER tag is a Java slider control you can embed in your applications. It offers an efficient and user-friendly way to select a value from a range of numeric values. Possible uses include volume controls, time lines, and dollar amounts. The control works by allowing users to drag the slider bar to the left to decrease the value or to the right to increase the value. The slider control is shown in Figure 10-2.

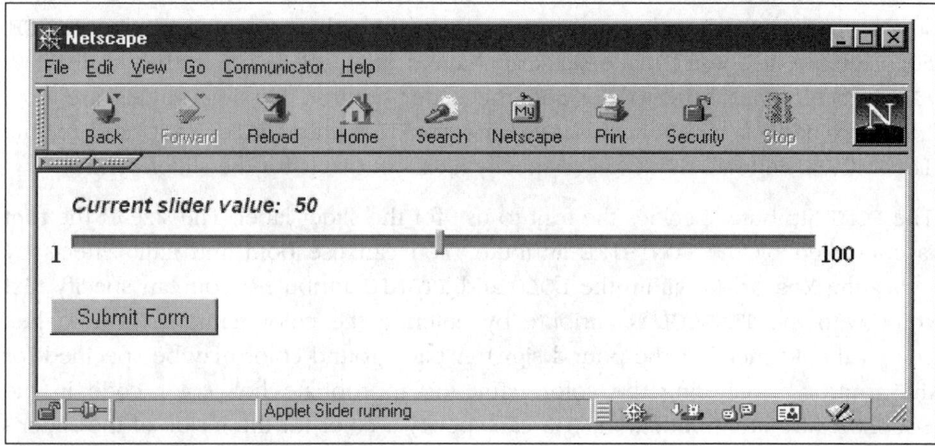


*Figure 10-2. A typical slider control*

To better illustrate how the CFSLIDER control works, consider Example 10-7.

*Example 10-7. Using the CFSLIDER Control with No Background*

```
<CFIF IsDefined('Form.Slider')>
  <CFOUTPUT>You submitted a slider value of <B>#Form.Slider#</B>.</CFOUTPUT>
  <HR NOSHADE>
</CFIF>

<CFFORM ACTION="Example10-7.cfm" METHOD="POST" ENABLECAB="Yes" NAME="MyForm"
        ENCTYPE="application/x-www-form-urlencoded">
<B>1</B> <CFSLIDER NAME="Slider" LABEL="Current slider value:  %value%"
                   REFRESHLABEL="Yes" RANGE="1,100" VALUE="50" SCALE="1"
                   ALIGN="baseline" HEIGHT="50" WIDTH="500"
                   FONT="Arial" FONTSIZE="14" BOLD="Yes" ITALIC="Yes"
                   TEXTCOLOR="##000000" BGCOLOR="##FFFFFF" GROOVECOLOR="gray"
                   NOTSUPPORTED="<B>Your web browser must support Java to view
                   ColdFusion Java Applets</B>"><B>100</B>
<P>
<INPUT TYPE="submit" NAME="Submit" VALUE="Submit Form">
</CFFORM>
```

The CFSLIDER tag accepts several parameters that determine how to display the slider control. The NAME attribute specifies a name for the form field. LABEL is used to display a label for the slider control as well as the current value associated with the slider's position. By default, the value associated with the slider's current position is shown to the right of the LABEL text. REFRESHLABEL indicates whether the value specified in LABEL should be refreshed as the slider control is moved from one side to the other. You can specify the beginning and ending values for the slider control by the RANGE attribute. A default value for the slider control can be specified with the VALUE attribute. The SCALE attribute allows you to specify an increment value for the slider control. When choosing a SCALE, be sure to pick a number that corresponds with the values you specified in RANGE. For example, it doesn't make sense to have a range of 1-100 with a scale of 7. ALIGN determines how to position the slider control. Possible values are top, texttop, bottom, absbottom, baseline, middle, absmiddle, left, and right. The HEIGHT and WIDTH attributes specify a size in pixels for the slider control.

The FONT attribute specifies the font to use for the slider label. The size of the font is controlled by the FONTSIZE attribute. You can use bold and italic effects by indicating Yes or No within the BOLD and ITALIC attributes. You can specify text color with the TEXTCOLOR attribute by entering the color name or a valid hex color value (remember the pound sign). A background color may be specified for the control by entering the color name or appropriate hex color code in the BGCOLOR attribute. In addition, you can specify a color for the inside of the slider's groove by providing a color name or hex code for the GROOVECOLOR attribute. The final attribute, NOTSUPPORTED, specifies a text message to display in the event that the browser accessing the form containing the slider control doesn't support Java.

You can further customize the slider control by adding other optional attributes. As Example 10-8 and Figure 10-3 show, it is possible to add a background image to the slider bar.

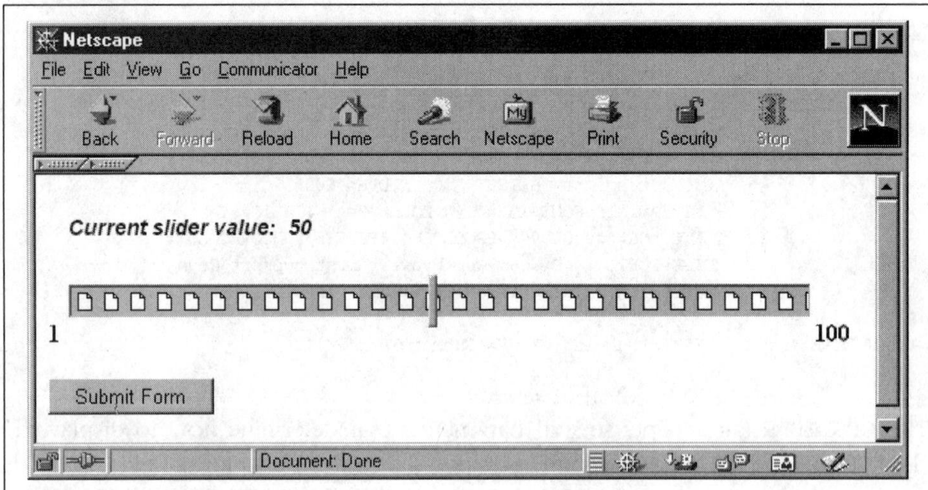


*Figure 10-3. A CFSLIDER control with a tiled background image*

*Example 10-8. Using the CFSLIDER Control with a Background Image*

```
<CFIF IsDefined('Form.Slider')>
   <CFOUTPUT>You submitted a slider value of <B>#Form.Slider#</B>.</CFOUTPUT>
   <HR NOSHADE>
</CFIF>

<CFFORM ACTION="Example10-8.cfm" METHOD="POST" ENABLECAB="Yes" NAME="MyForm"
        ENCTYPE="application/x-www-form-urlencoded">
<B>1</B> <CFSLIDER NAME="Slider" LABEL="Current slider value:  %value%"
                   RANGE="1,100" VALUE="50" ALIGN="baseline"
                   MESSAGE="This is the message"
                   SCALE="1" HEIGHT="100" WIDTH="500" FONT="Arial"
                   FONTSIZE="14" BGCOLOR="##FFFFFF" TEXTCOLOR="##000000"
                   IMG="newfile.gif" IMGSTYLE="tiled" BOLD="Yes" ITALIC="Yes"
                   REFRESHLABEL="Yes"
                   NOTSUPPORTED="<B>Your web browser must support Java to view
                   ColdFusion Java Applets</B>"><B>100</B>
<P>
<INPUT TYPE="submit" NAME="Submit" VALUE="Submit Form">
</CFFORM>
```

In Example 10-8, we removed the `GROOVECOLOR` attribute and replaced it with two new attributes, `IMG` and `IMGSTYLE`. The `IMG` attribute specifies the name of an image file to be placed within the groove of the slider control. By default, ColdFusion looks for the image file in the */cfide/classes/images* directory. You may specify an alternate location using a relative reference such as *../../../myimage.gif*. The `IMGSTYLE` attribute specifies the method for placing the image within the groove. Possible values for this attribute are `Centered`, `Tiled`, and `Scaled`. Choosing `Centered` results in the image being centered within the groove space. A `Tiled` `IMGSTYLE` results in the image being tiled across the entire length of the slider groove. `Scaled` images are stretched or shrunk to fit within the slider groove. In Example 10-8, the image is tiled within the image groove.

# Grids

The `CFGRID` tag provides a Java-based grid control for displaying and editing tabular data. `CFGRID` allows you to display data sets in a familiar spreadsheet format that makes scrolling through and updating multiple records easy. A sample `CFGRID` control for displaying data can be seen in Figure 10-4.

Example 10-9 queries a database and subsequently populates a `CFGRID` control with the record set data.

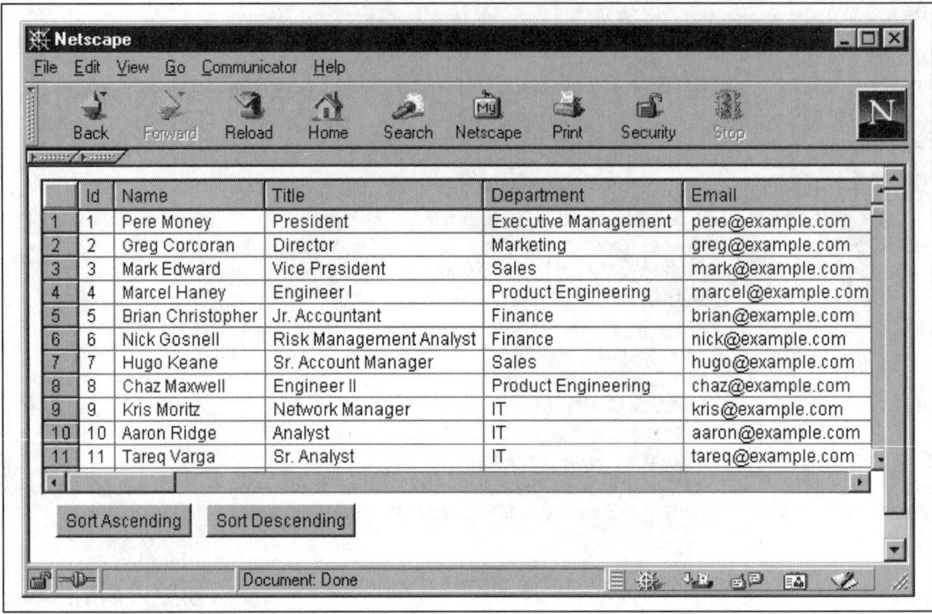


| | Id | Name | Title | Department | Email |
|---|---|---|---|---|---|
| 1 | 1 | Pere Money | President | Executive Management | pere@example.com |
| 2 | 2 | Greg Corcoran | Director | Marketing | greg@example.com |
| 3 | 3 | Mark Edward | Vice President | Sales | mark@example.com |
| 4 | 4 | Marcel Haney | Engineer I | Product Engineering | marcel@example.com |
| 5 | 5 | Brian Christopher | Jr. Accountant | Finance | brian@example.com |
| 6 | 6 | Nick Gosnell | Risk Management Analyst | Finance | nick@example.com |
| 7 | 7 | Hugo Keane | Sr. Account Manager | Sales | hugo@example.com |
| 8 | 8 | Chaz Maxwell | Engineer II | Product Engineering | chaz@example.com |
| 9 | 9 | Kris Moritz | Network Manager | IT | kris@example.com |
| 10 | 10 | Aaron Ridge | Analyst | IT | aaron@example.com |
| 11 | 11 | Tareq Varga | Sr. Analyst | IT | tareq@example.com |

*Figure 10-4. The CFGRID control*

*Example 10-9. Creating a Basic Grid Control*

```
<CFQUERY NAME="GetPeople" DATASOURCE="ProgrammingCF">
         SELECT * FROM EmployeeDirectory
</CFQUERY>

<CFFORM ACTION="Example10-9.cfm" ENABLECAB="Yes" NAME="MyForm"
        ENCTYPE="application/x-www-form-urlencoded">

<CFGRID NAME="MyGrid" WIDTH="600" HEIGHT="250" QUERY="GetPeople"
        SORT="yes" SELECTMODE="browse" PICTUREBAR="no"
        SORTASCENDINGBUTTON="Sort Ascending"
        SORTDESCENDINGBUTTON="Sort Descending"
        NOTSUPPORTED="<B>Your web browser must support Java to view
                      ColdFusion Java Applets</B>">
</CFGRID>

</CFFORM>
```

The `NAME` attribute specifies the name of the grid control. `HEIGHT` and `WIDTH` specify the height and width (in pixels) for the grid's display area. `HSPACE` and `VSPACE` specify the amount of padding (in pixels above, below, to the left, and to the right of the grid control; we're allowing the grid to use its default values of 0 pixels for both. The `ALIGN` attribute determines the grid's alignment on the page. Possible values are `Left`, `Right`, `Top`, `TextTop`, `Bottom`, `AbsBottom`, `Baseline`,

`Middle`, and `AbsMiddle`. We're relying on the default value of `Baseline`. The `QUERY` attribute specifies the name of a query that should be used to populate the grid with data. `SORT` indicates whether users should be allowed to sort the data displayed in the grid. Data is sorted using a simple text sort. `SELECTMODE` determines the selection mode to use for items in the grid. Valid entries are:

`Browse` *(default)*
: Allows browsing of data only

`Edit`
: Allows editing of data

`Single`
: Confines selections to a single cell

`Column`
: Selections automatically include the entire column

`Row`
: Selections automatically include the entire row

In Example 10-8, we set the selection mode to `Browse`, preventing users from selecting or editing data displayed in the grid. The next attribute, `PICTUREBAR`, is optional and determines whether or not to display images for the `Insert`, `Delete`, and `Sort` buttons. We set this attribute to `No` (the default), indicating that the buttons should display text as opposed to images. Because we have opted for text buttons rather than images, our next task is to set the messages to display on the buttons, which is done using the `SORTASCENDINGBUTTON` and `SORTDESCENDINGBUTTON` attributes, respectively. The last attribute in this example, `NOTSUPPORTED`, specifies a text message to display in the event that the browser accessing the grid control doesn't support Java.

Now that you see how simple it is to display query data using the grid control, let's look at some formatting options that are available to the grid control. These formatting options allow you to tailor the display of text within the grid and include both font and positioning options. Example 10-10 takes the same grid we built in Example 10-9 and adds formatting. You can see the results in Figure 10-5.

*Example 10-10. Using the CFGRID Control to Present Query Data*

```
<CFQUERY NAME="GetPeople" DATASOURCE="ProgrammingCF">
         SELECT * FROM EmployeeDirectory
</CFQUERY>

<CFFORM ACTION="Example10-10.cfm" ENABLECAB="Yes" NAME="MyForm"
        ENCTYPE="application/x-www-form-urlencoded">

<CFGRID NAME="MyGrid" HEIGHT="250" WIDTH="600" HSPACE="10" VSPACE="10"
        QUERY="GetPeople" SORT="yes" FONT="Arial" FONTSIZE="12" BOLD="no"
```

*Example 10-10. Using the CFGRID Control to Present Query Data (continued)*

```
        ITALIC="no" GRIDDATAALIGN="left" GRIDLINES="yes" ROWHEIGHT="12"
        ROWHEADERS="yes" ROWHEADERALIGN="left" ROWHEADERITALIC="yes"
        ROWHEADERBOLD="yes" ROWHEADERFONT="Courier" ROWHEADERFONTSIZE="12"
        COLHEADERS="yes" COLHEADERALIGN="left" COLHEADERITALIC="no"
        COLHEADERBOLD="yes" COLHEADERFONT="Courier" COLHEADERFONTSIZE="16"
        BGCOLOR="##FFFFCC" SELECTMODE="browse"  PICTUREBAR="no"
        SORTASCENDINGBUTTON="Sort Ascending"
        SORTDESCENDINGBUTTON="Sort Descending"
        NOTSUPPORTED="<B>Your web browser must support Java to view
        ColdFusion Java Applets.</B>">
</CFGRID>

</CFFORM>
```

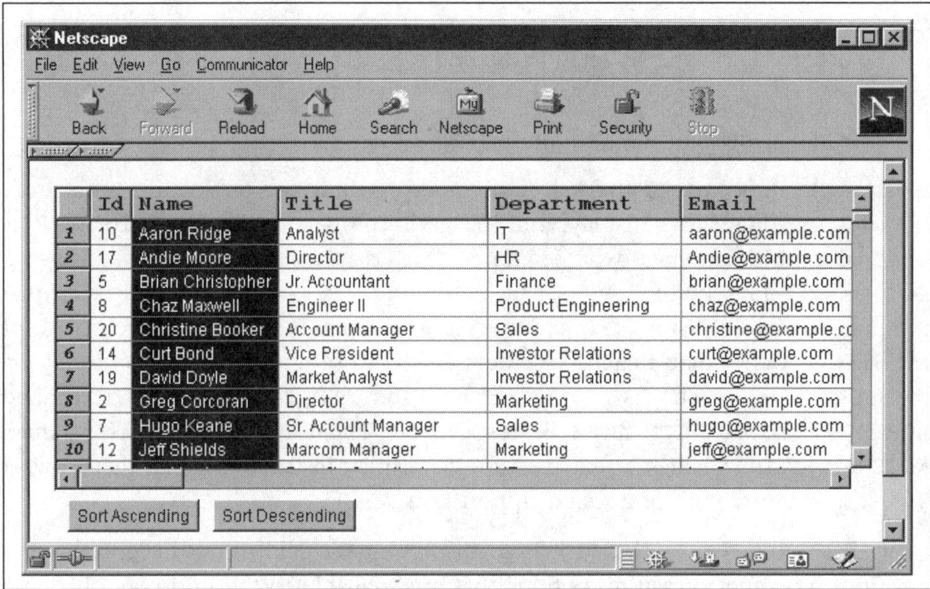


*Figure 10-5. Result of adding additional formatting to a CFGRID*

As you can see, we have introduced several new attributes to the `CFGRID` tag. Each attribute controls a different aspect of the grid's display properties. Many attributes have names that are fairly self-explanatory, so I'm not going to explain each one. One group of attributes control how row headings appear, while another group controls the column headings. The `GRIDDATAALIGN` attribute specifies alignment for the grid data. Choices are `Left`, `Right`, or `Center`. The default value is `Left`. The `GRIDLINES` attribute indicates whether or not to add row and column lines to the grid. The default value is `Yes`. For a complete listing of all attributes available to the `CFGRID` tag, see Appendix A.

## *Customizing Column Data*

You can get even more control of the data displayed within the grid by using a child tag of `CFGRID` called `CFGRIDCOLUMN`. `CFGRIDCOLUMN` allows you to specify individual column data and formatting options. Example 10-11 shows `CFGRIDCOLUMN` used in the most basic context.

*Example 10-11. Populating a CFGRID Using CFGRIDCOLUMN*

```
<CFQUERY NAME="GetPeople" DATASOURCE="ProgrammingCF">
        SELECT Name, Title, Department FROM EmployeeDirectory
</CFQUERY>

<CFFORM ACTION="Example10-11.cfm" ENABLECAB="Yes" NAME="MyForm"
       ENCTYPE="application/x-www-form-urlencoded">

<CFGRID NAME="MyGrid" WIDTH="600" HEIGHT="250" QUERY="GetPeople"
       SORT="yes" GRIDDATAALIGN="left" GRIDLINES="yes"
       ROWHEIGHT="12" ROWHEADERS="yes" COLHEADERS="Yes"
       BGCOLOR="##FFFFCC" SELECTMODE="browse" PICTUREBAR="yes"
       NOTSUPPORTED="<B>Your web browser must support Java to view
                     ColdFusion Java Applets.</B>">

   <CFGRIDCOLUMN NAME="Name" HEADER="Full Name">
   <CFGRIDCOLUMN NAME="Title" HEADER="Title">
   <CFGRIDCOLUMN NAME="Department" HEADER="Department">

</CFGRID>
</CFFORM>
```

In Example 10-11, rather than let the `CFGRID` tag determine which columns of data to display, we leave that task up to the `CFGRIDCOLUMN` tag. In Example 10-10, all the columns present in the database were displayed in the grid. In Example 10-11, only the `Name`, `Title`, and `Department` columns are present. The `NAME` attribute of each `CFGRIDCOLUMN` tag determines which query column to display. The actual column header that appears in the grid is specified in the `HEADER` attribute. If `HEADER` is omitted, ColdFusion uses the column name from the database.

We can specify additional formatting options for each grid column by including other attributes within the `CFGRIDCOLUMN` tags. Example 10-12 shows how to apply this additional formatting.

*Example 10-12. Formatting Individual Columns with CFGRIDCOLUMN*

```
<CFQUERY NAME="GetPeople" DATASOURCE="ProgrammingCF">
        SELECT Name, Title, Department FROM EmployeeDirectory
</CFQUERY>

<CFFORM ACTION="Example10-12.cfm" ENABLECAB="Yes" NAME="MyForm"
       ENCTYPE="application/x-www-form-urlencoded">
```

*Example 10-12. Formatting Individual Columns with CFGRIDCOLUMN (continued)*

```
<CFGRID NAME="MyGrid" WIDTH="600" HEIGHT="250" QUERY="GetPeople"
        SORT="yes" GRIDDATAALIGN="left" GRIDLINES="yes"
        ROWHEIGHT="12" ROWHEADERS="yes" COLHEADERS="Yes"
        BGCOLOR="##FFFFCC" SELECTMODE="browse" PICTUREBAR="yes"
        NOTSUPPORTED="<B>Your web browser must support Java to view ColdFusion
        Java Applets</B>">

  <CFGRIDCOLUMN NAME="Name" HEADER="Full Name" HEADERFONT="Arial"
                HEADERFONTSIZE="14" HEADERITALIC="Yes" HEADERBOLD="Yes"
                HEADERALIGN="left" WIDTH="125" FONT="Arial" FONTSIZE="12"
                ITALIC="No" BOLD="No" DATAALIGN="left" SELECT="No" DISPLAY="Yes"
                TYPE="String_NoCase">

  <CFGRIDCOLUMN NAME="Title" HEADER="Title" HEADERFONT="Arial"
                HEADERFONTSIZE="14" HEADERITALIC="Yes" HEADERBOLD="Yes"
                HEADERALIGN="left" FONT="Arial" FONTSIZE="12" ITALIC="No"
                BOLD="No" DATAALIGN="left" SELECT="No" DISPLAY="Yes"
                TYPE="String_NoCase">

  <CFGRIDCOLUMN NAME="Department" HEADER="Department" HEADERFONT="Arial"
                HEADERFONTSIZE="14" HEADERITALIC="Yes" HEADERBOLD="Yes"
                HEADERALIGN="left" FONT="Arial" FONTSIZE="12" ITALIC="No"
                BOLD="No" DATAALIGN="left" SELECT="No" DISPLAY="Yes"
                TYPE="String_NoCase">

</CFGRID>
</CFFORM>
```

Note that all the formatting attributes used with the `CFGRIDCOLUMN` tag are optional. Most of these attributes do exactly what their names imply and are used to control the appearance of column headers and column data. A few attributes require further explanation. `SELECT` indicates whether or not to allow users to select column data to be edited. `SELECT` is ignored when the `SELECTMODE` attribute of the `CFGRID` tag is set to `Row` or `Browse`. The `SELECT` attribute indicates whether or not to display the column in the grid. The default is `Yes`. Finally, the `TYPE` attribute specifies the type of column data to display. Choices for this attribute are:

`Image`
: Specifies an image corresponding to the column value to display. You may specify a path to your own image or use one of the images supplied with ColdFusion by referencing the image name. Valid options are `CD`, `Computer`, `Document`, `Element`, `Folder`, `Floppy`, `Fixed`, and `Remote`. If the image is larger than the cell in which it is being displayed, the image is automatically cropped to fit within the cell.

`Numeric`
: Allows data in the grid to be sorted by the user as numeric data, rather than as text.

`String_NoCase`
: Allows data in the grid to be sorted by the user as case-insensitive text rather than case-sensitive, which is the default.

A few additional attributes aren't used in Example 10-12 but are worth mentioning here. The `HREF` attribute specifies a URL to associate with the grid item. The URL can be absolute or relative. You can specify the name of a frame or window in which the template specified in the `HREF` attribute should be opened using the `TARGET` attribute. You may apply a mask to numeric values using the `NUMBERFORMAT` attribute. For valid options, see the `NumberFormat()` function in Appendix B. `HREFKEY` specifies the name of a query column to use as the `Key` when a query is used to populate the grid. For a complete list of all attributes associated with the `CFGRIDCOLUMN` tag, see Appendix A.

Figure 10-6 shows some of the different effects you can achieve using the `CFGRID` control.

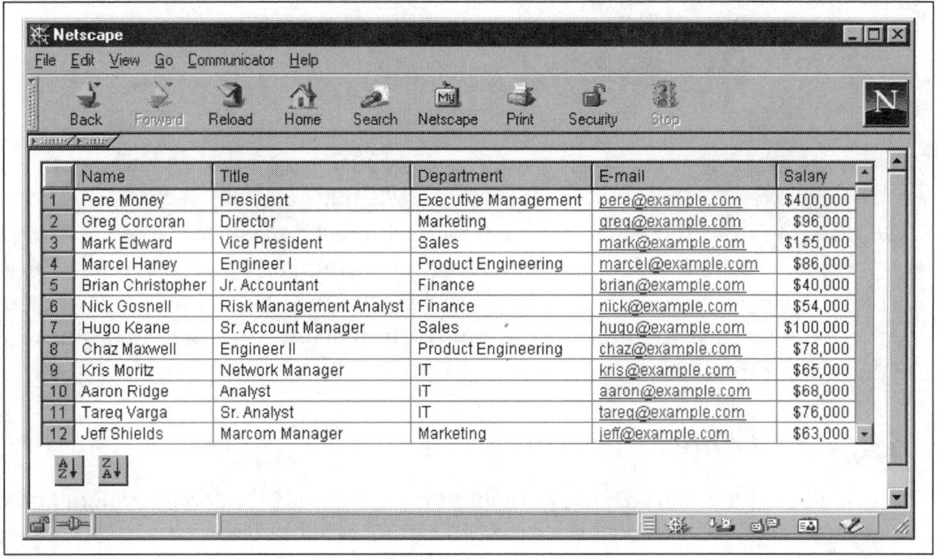

Netscape
File Edit View Go Communicator Help
Back Forward Reload Home Search Netscape Print Security Stop
Name Title Department E-mail Salary
1 Pere Money President Executive Management pere@example.com $400,000
2 Greg Corcoran Director Marketing greg@example.com $96,000
3 Mark Edward Vice President Sales mark@example.com $155,000
4 Marcel Haney Engineer I Product Engineering marcel@example.com $86,000
5 Brian Christopher Jr. Accountant Finance brian@example.com $40,000
6 Nick Gosnell Risk Management Analyst Finance nick@example.com $54,000
7 Hugo Keane Sr. Account Manager Sales hugo@example.com $100,000
8 Chaz Maxwell Engineer II Product Engineering chaz@example.com $78,000
9 Kris Moritz Network Manager IT kris@example.com $65,000
10 Aaron Ridge Analyst IT aaron@example.com $68,000
11 Tareq Varga Sr. Analyst IT tareq@example.com $76,000
12 Jeff Shields Marcom Manager Marketing jeff@example.com $63,000


*Figure 10-6. CFGRID with embedded hyperlinks and a NUMBERFORMAT mask*

## *Specifying Row Data*

`CFGRIDROW` is another child tag of `CFGRID` you can use to populate a grid with query data. You can opt for `CFGRIDROW` instead of the `QUERY` attribute in the

CFGRID tag. When you do use the QUERY attribute in the CFGRID tag, the CFGRIDROW tag is ignored. Example 10-13 illustrates this technique.

*Example 10-13. Using CFGRIDROW*

```
<CFQUERY NAME="GetPeople" DATASOURCE="ProgrammingCF">
        SELECT * FROM EmployeeDirectory
</CFQUERY>

<CFFORM ACTION="Example10-13.cfm" ENABLECAB="Yes" NAME="MyForm"
       ENCTYPE="application/x-www-form-urlencoded">

<CFGRID NAME="MyGrid" WIDTH="600" HEIGHT="250" SORT="yes" GRIDDATAALIGN="left"
       GRIDLINES="yes" ROWHEIGHT="12" ROWHEADERS="yes" COLHEADERS="Yes"
       BGCOLOR="##FFFFCC" SELECTMODE="browse" PICTUREBAR="yes"
       NOTSUPPORTED="<B>Your web browser must support Java to view
                    ColdFusion Java Applets.</B>">

   <CFGRIDCOLUMN NAME="Name" HEADER="Name">
   <CFGRIDCOLUMN NAME="Title" HEADER="Title">
   <CFGRIDCOLUMN NAME="Department" HEADER="Department">
   <CFGRIDCOLUMN NAME="Email" HEADER="E-mail">
   <CFGRIDCOLUMN NAME="PhoneExt" HEADER="Extension">

<CFLOOP query="GetPeople">
  <CFGRIDROW DATA="#Name#,#Title#,#Department#,#Email#,#PhoneExt#">
</CFLOOP>
</CFGRID>
</CFFORM>
```

Example 10-13 differs only slightly from our previous examples. In this example, we leave out the QUERY attribute in the CFGRID tag, and we make use of the CFGRIDROW tag instead. Column headers are still defined using the CFGRIDCOLUMN tag. The actual column data is output using the CFGRIDROW tag. The query must be looped over so that each row of data from the query can be output. If you want to perform any additional formatting or further massage the data, you can use this method of populating the grid.

## Creating Updateable Grids

You can also use the CFGRID tag to build updateable grids for adding, editing, and deleting individual cells and records. Creating an editable grid is an easy way to allow your users to quickly make database additions and updates. Making a grid editable is simply a matter of setting the SELECTMODE attribute of the CFGRID tag to Edit.

### *Updating a grid using CFGRIDUPDATE*

The simplest way to update the data contained in a data source is via the CFGRIDUPDATE tag. This tag takes all the data posted from a CFGRID control and automatically makes the necessary updates to the data source. Example 10-14 demonstrates how to create an editable grid that updates the data source using the CFGRIDUPDATE tag.

*Example 10-14. Creating an Updateable Grid Using CFGRIDUPDATE*

```
<!--- if the grid has been changed, update it --->
<CFIF IsDefined('form.MyGrid.rowstatus.action')>
   <CFGRIDUPDATE GRID="MyGrid" DATASOURCE="ProgrammingCF"
                 TABLENAME="EmployeeDirectory" KEYONLY="No">
</CFIF>

<CFQUERY NAME="GetPeople" DATASOURCE="ProgrammingCF">
   SELECT * FROM EmployeeDirectory
</CFQUERY>

<CFFORM ACTION="Example10-14.cfm" ENABLECAB="Yes" NAME="MyForm"
        ENCTYPE="application/x-www-form-urlencoded">

<CFGRID NAME="MyGrid" WIDTH="600" HEIGHT="250" QUERY="GetPeople"
        INSERT="Yes" DELETE="Yes" SORT="Yes" FONT="Arial" BOLD="No" ITALIC="No"
        APPENDKEY="No" HIGHLIGHTHREF="No" GRIDDATAALIGN="LEFT" GRIDLINES="Yes"
        ROWHEADERS="Yes" ROWHEADERALIGN="LEFT" ROWHEADERITALIC="No"
        ROWHEADERBOLD="No" COLHEADERS="Yes" COLHEADERALIGN="LEFT"
        COLHEADERITALIC="No" COLHEADERBOLD="No" SELECTCOLOR="Red"
        SELECTMODE="EDIT" PICTUREBAR="No" INSERTBUTTON="Add New Record"
        DELETEBUTTON="Delete" SORTASCENDINGBUTTON="Sort ASC"
        SORTDESCENDINGBUTTON="Sort DESC">

<CFGRIDCOLUMN NAME="ID" HEADER="ID" DATAALIGN="LEFT" BOLD="No" ITALIC="No"
              SELECT="Yes" DISPLAY="Yes" HEADERBOLD="No" HEADERITALIC="No">

<CFGRIDCOLUMN NAME="Name" HEADER="Name" HEADERALIGN="LEFT" DATAALIGN="LEFT"
              BOLD="Yes" ITALIC="No" SELECT="Yes" DISPLAY="Yes" HEADERBOLD="No"
              HEADERITALIC="Yes">

<CFGRIDCOLUMN NAME="Title" HEADER="Title" HEADERALIGN="LEFT" DATAALIGN="LEFT"
              BOLD="No" ITALIC="No" SELECT="Yes" DISPLAY="Yes" HEADERBOLD="No"
              HEADERITALIC="No">

<CFGRIDCOLUMN NAME="Department" HEADER="Department" HEADERALIGN="LEFT"
              DATAALIGN="LEFT" FONT="Times" BOLD="No" ITALIC="No" SELECT="Yes"
              DISPLAY="Yes" HEADERBOLD="No" HEADERITALIC="No">

<CFGRIDCOLUMN NAME="Email" HEADER="E-mail" HEADERALIGN="LEFT" DATAALIGN="LEFT"
              BOLD="No" ITALIC="No" SELECT="Yes" DISPLAY="Yes" HEADERBOLD="No"
              HEADERITALIC="No">
```

*Example 10-14. Creating an Updateable Grid Using CFGRIDUPDATE (continued)*

```
<CFGRIDCOLUMN NAME="PhoneExt" HEADER="Phone ext." HEADERALIGN="LEFT"
              DATAALIGN="LEFT" BOLD="No" ITALIC="No" SELECT="Yes" DISPLAY="Yes"
              HEADERBOLD="No" HEADERITALIC="No">
</CFGRID>
<BR>

<INPUT TYPE="Submit" NAME="submit" VALUE="Submit Changes">
<INPUT type="hidden" NAME="GridChanged" VALUE="yes">
</CFFORM>
```

In Example 10-14, the `CFGRIDUPDATE` tag takes the information submitted by the form and makes the necessary updates to the data source. The `GRID` attribute specifies the name of the `CFGRID` control supplying the data for the update. The data source to update is specified using the `DATASOURCE` attribute. The database table within the data source that is to be updated is specified using the `TABLENAME` attribute. Setting `KEYONLY` to `No` causes the `WHERE` clause of the SQL statement that ColdFusion generates to contain both the key values as well as the original values from any changed cells within the grid.

In addition to the attributes already mentioned, the `CFGRIDUPDATE` tag also accepts a number of optional attributes that allow you to specify more detailed information about the database being used. See Appendix A for more details.

### *Updating a grid using CFQUERY*

Using `CFGRIDUPDATE` isn't the only way to update your data source with data from a `CFGRID` control. You can also use the `CFQUERY` tag to handle updates. When an editable grid (with `SELECTMODE` set to `Edit`) is submitted, three one-dimensional arrays are returned containing information about the changes to the data:

`Form.`*`gridname`*`.`*`columnname`*`[`*`RowIndex`*`]`
: Contains the new value of an edited grid cell

`Form.`*`gridname`*`.Original.`*`columnname`*`[`*`RowIndex`*`]`
: Contains the original value of the edited grid cell

`Form.`*`gridname`*`.RowStatus.Action[`*`RowIndex`*`]`
: Contains the type of edit made to the grid cell: `I` for insert, `U` for update, and `D` for delete

To update your data source using `CFQUERY`, you can loop through the arrays passed by the `CFGRID` tag and generate the necessary `CFQUERY` tags to insert, update, and delete data as necessary. This technique is shown in Example 10-15.

*Example 10-15. Updating a Grid Using CFQUERY*

```
<!--- check to see if data was added, updated, or deleted from the grid --->
<CFIF IsDefined('form.MyGrid.rowstatus.action')>
```

*Example 10-15. Updating a Grid Using CFQUERY (continued)*

```
<!--- loop over each instance of a grid action --->
<CFLOOP INDEX = "i" FROM = "1" TO ="#ArrayLen(form.MyGrid.rowstatus.action)#">

  <!--- If the action is Insert, insert a new record --->
  <CFIF form.MyGrid.rowstatus.action[i] IS "I">
    <CFQUERY NAME="InsertNewEmployee" DATASOURCE="ProgrammingCF">
             INSERT into EmployeeDirectory
                        (Name, Title, Department, Email, PhoneExt)
             VALUES ('#form.MyGrid.Name[i]#', '#form.MyGrid.Title[i]#',
                     '#form.MyGrid.Department[i]#', '#form.MyGrid.Email[i]#',
                      #form.MyGrid.PhoneExt[i]#)
    </CFQUERY>

    <!--- If the action is Update, update the record --->
  <CFELSEIF form.MyGrid.rowstatus.action[i] IS "U">
    <CFQUERY NAME="UpdateExistingEmployee" DATASOURCE="ProgrammingCF">
             UPDATE EmployeeDirectory
             SET Name='#form.MyGrid.Name[i]#',
                 Title='#form.MyGrid.Title[i]#',
                 Department='#form.MyGrid.Department[i]#',
                 Email='#form.MyGrid.Email[i]#',
                 PhoneExt=#form.MyGrid.PhoneExt[i]#
             WHERE ID=#form.MyGrid.original.ID[i]#
    </CFQUERY>

  <!--- If the action is Delete, Delete the record --->
  <CFELSEIF form.MyGrid.rowstatus.action[i] IS "D">
    <CFQUERY NAME="DeleteExistingEmployee" DATASOURCE="ProgrammingCF">
             DELETE FROM EmployeeDirectory
             WHERE ID=#form.MyGrid.original.ID[i]#
    </CFQUERY>
  </CFIF>
</CFLOOP>
</CFIF>

<!--- create/recreate the grid from a query --->
<CFQUERY NAME="GetPeople" DATASOURCE="ProgrammingCF">
   SELECT * FROM EmployeeDirectory
</CFQUERY>

<CFFORM ACTION="Example10-15.cfm" ENABLECAB="Yes" NAME="MyForm"
        ENCTYPE="application/x-www-form-urlencoded">

<CFGRID NAME="MyGrid" WIDTH="600" HEIGHT="250" QUERY="GetPeople"
        INSERT="Yes" DELETE="Yes" SORT="Yes" FONT="Arial" BOLD="No" ITALIC="No"
        APPENDKEY="No" HIGHLIGHTHREF="No" GRIDDATAALIGN="LEFT" GRIDLINES="Yes"
        ROWHEADERS="Yes" ROWHEADERALIGN="LEFT" ROWHEADERITALIC="No"
        ROWHEADERBOLD="No" COLHEADERS="Yes" COLHEADERALIGN="LEFT"
        COLHEADERITALIC="No" COLHEADERBOLD="No" SELECTCOLOR="Red"
        SELECTMODE="EDIT" PICTUREBAR="No"
        INSERTBUTTON="Add New Record" DELETEBUTTON="Delete"
        SORTASCENDINGBUTTON="Sort ASC" SORTDESCENDINGBUTTON="Sort DESC">
```

*Example 10-15. Updating a Grid Using CFQUERY (continued)*

```
<!--- hide the ID (primary key) field, but make the value available for
      updates and deletes. --->
<CFGRIDCOLUMN NAME="ID" DISPLAY="No" HEADERITALIC="No">

<CFGRIDCOLUMN NAME="Name" HEADER="Name" HEADERALIGN="LEFT" DATAALIGN="LEFT"
              BOLD="Yes" ITALIC="No" SELECT="Yes" DISPLAY="Yes" HEADERBOLD="No"
              HEADERITALIC="Yes">

<CFGRIDCOLUMN NAME="Title" HEADER="Title" HEADERALIGN="LEFT" DATAALIGN="LEFT"
              BOLD="No" ITALIC="No" SELECT="Yes" DISPLAY="Yes" HEADERBOLD="No"
              HEADERITALIC="No">

<CFGRIDCOLUMN NAME="Department" HEADER="Department" HEADERALIGN="LEFT"
              DATAALIGN="LEFT" FONT="Times" BOLD="No" ITALIC="No" SELECT="Yes"
              DISPLAY="Yes" HEADERBOLD="No" HEADERITALIC="No">

<CFGRIDCOLUMN NAME="Email" HEADER="E-mail" HEADERALIGN="LEFT" DATAALIGN="LEFT"
              BOLD="No" ITALIC="No" SELECT="Yes" DISPLAY="Yes" HEADERBOLD="No"
              HEADERITALIC="No">

<CFGRIDCOLUMN NAME="PhoneExt" HEADER="Phone ext." HEADERALIGN="LEFT"
              DATAALIGN="LEFT" BOLD="No" ITALIC="No" SELECT="Yes" DISPLAY="Yes"
              HEADERBOLD="No" HEADERITALIC="No">
</CFGRID>
<BR>
<INPUT TYPE="Submit" NAME="submit" VALUE="Submit Changes">
<INPUT type="hidden" NAME="GridChanged" VALUE="yes">
</CFFORM>
```

In Example 10-15, the form data submitted by the `CFGRID` control comes across in three one-dimensional arrays:

```
Form.MyGrid.RowStatus.Action[i]

Form.MyGrid.ID[i]
Form.MyGrid.Name[i]
Form.MyGrid.Title[i]
Form.MyGrid.Department[i]
Form.MyGrid.Email[i]
Form.MyGrid.PhoneExt[i]

Form.MyGrid.Original.ID[i]
Form.MyGrid.Original.Name[i]
Form.MyGrid.Original.Title[i]
Form.MyGrid.Original.Department[i]
Form.MyGrid.Original.Email[i]
Form.MyGrid.Original.PhoneExt[i]
```

Each cell's data from the grid is represented in an index of the array, specified by *`i`* in the code. The arrays then dynamically generate the SQL necessary to update the database. The template loops over each element in the `Form.MyGrid.RowStatus.Action` array. For each iteration of the loop, ColdFusion checks to see if the `Action` is set to `I` for insert, `U` for Update, or `D` for delete. Depending on the `Action` value, ColdFusion performs the corresponding query action (add, update, or delete) using the value stored in the appropriate array index of the other two arrays. When all of the query actions have been performed, the grid control is redrawn using the updated data from the database.

# *Trees*

You can use the `CFTREE` tag to create a Java-based tree control within your `CFFORM`. Tree controls are useful in a number of data display and selection scenarios. Because they allow the user to expand and collapse branches, tree controls are particularly well-suited for displaying large amounts of hierarchical data in a relatively small amount of screen space. You can build tree controls using the `CFTREE` tag, plus multiple `CFTREEITEM` tags for defining the individual branches. The following example uses the `CFTREE` tag to create the display area for a tree control:

```
<CFFORM ACTION="tree1.cfm" ENABLECAB="Yes" NAME="MyForm">
<CFTREE NAME="MyTree" HEIGHT="200" WIDTH="300" BORDER="Yes"
        HSCROLL="Yes" VSCROLL="Yes"
        NOTSUPPORTED="<B>Your web browser must support Java to view
                      ColdFusion Java Applets</B>">
</CFTREE>
</CFFORM>
```

This example does nothing more than create an empty shell for the tree control. The `NAME` attribute specifies a name for the tree control. The `HEIGHT` and `WIDTH` attributes specify the height and width in pixels for the tree control. `BORDER` indicates whether to include a border around the tree control. The default is `Yes`. `HSCROLL` and `VSCROLL` each indicate whether or not to allow users to scroll horizontally and vertically, respectively, in the event the tree takes up more space than the boundaries of the control. Finally, the `NOTSUPPORTED` attribute specifies a text message to display in the event the user's browser doesn't support Java. By itself, the `CFTREE` tag doesn't do a whole lot. It must be combined with one or more `CFTREEITEM` tags to build a useable tree control.

## *Populating a Tree Control*

Individual `CFTREEITEM` tags are used within the `<CFTREE>` and `</CFTREE>` tags to populate a tree control. `CFTREEITEM` tags may have their values hardcoded, or they may obtain them from query data.

### *Creating a static tree*

Example 10-16 hardcodes several CFTREEITEM tags within a CFTREE tag to create a tree control containing several branches of nested values. This method of building a tree allows you to control exactly what goes into the tree as well as how to display it. The results can be seen in Figure 10-7.

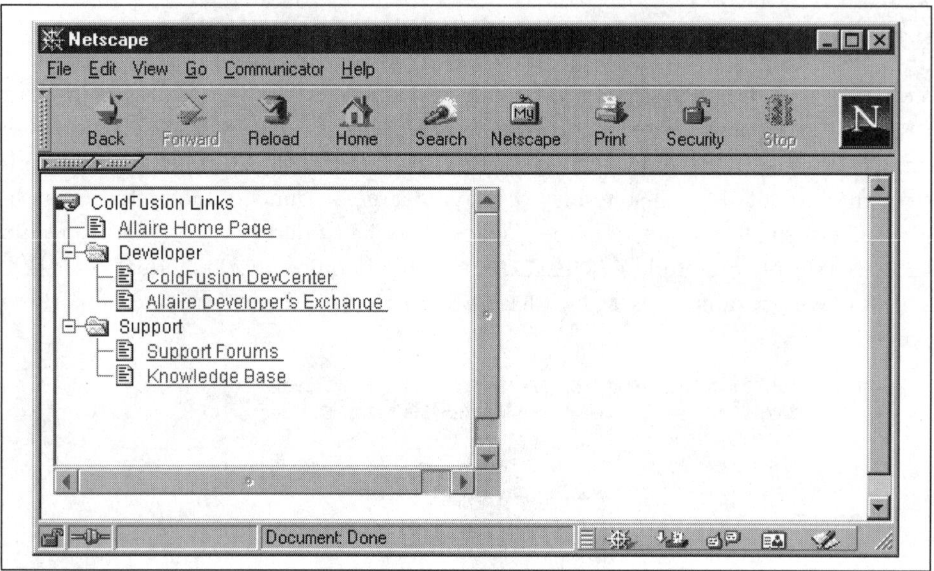


*Figure 10-7. CFTREE control built with hardcoded CFTREEITEM tags*

*Example 10-16. Populating a Tree Control with Static Values*

```
<CFFORM ACTION="Example10-16.cfm" ENABLECAB="Yes" NAME="MyForm"
        ENCTYPE="application/x-www-form-urlencoded">
<CFTREE NAME="MyTree" HEIGHT="200" WIDTH="300" FONT="Arial" FONTSIZE="12"
        BOLD="No" ITALIC="No" BORDER="Yes" HSCROLL="Yes" VSCROLL="Yes"
        REQUIRED="Yes" MESSAGE="You must select an item from the tree."
        HIGHLIGHTHREF="Yes" COMPLETEPATH="Yes" APPENDKEY="Yes"
        NOTSUPPORTED="<B>Your web browser must support Java to view ColdFusion
        Java Applets</B>">

 <CFTREEITEM VALUE="ColdFusion Links" PARENT="MyTree" EXPAND="Yes" IMG="fixed">

   <CFTREEITEM VALUE="Allaire Home Page" PARENT="ColdFusion Links"
               HREF="http://www.allaire.com" EXPAND="No" IMG="document">

   <CFTREEITEM VALUE="Developer" PARENT="ColdFusion Links" EXPAND="no">

      <CFTREEITEM VALUE="ColdFusion DevCenter" PARENT="Developer"
                  HREF="http://www.allaire.com/developer/referenceDesk/index.cfm"
                  EXPAND="No" IMG="document">

      <CFTREEITEM VALUE="Allaire Developer's Exchange" PARENT="Developer"
```

*Example 10-16. Populating a Tree Control with Static Values (continued)*

```
                HREF="http://www.allaire.com/developer/gallery.cfm"
                EXPAND="No" IMG="document">

   <CFTREEITEM VALUE="Support" PARENT="ColdFusion Links" EXPAND="no">

      <CFTREEITEM VALUE="Support Forums" PARENT="Support"
                HREF="http://forums.allaire.com/DevConf/index.cfm"
                EXPAND="No" IMG="document">

      <CFTREEITEM VALUE="Knowledge Base" PARENT="Support"
             HREF="http://www.allaire.com/Support/KnowledgeBase/SearchForm.cfm"
             EXPAND="No" IMG="document">
</CFTREE>
</CFFORM>
```

In Example 10-16, we added a few optional attributes to the `CFTREE` tag. You can set data displayed within the tree to any font residing on the ColdFusion server if you specify the font name in the`FONT` attribute. Likewise, the size of the font can be set with the `FONTSIZE` attribute. Bold and italic text effects can be applied to all data displayed within the tree by setting the `BOLD` and `ITALIC` attributes to `Yes`. The `REQUIRED` attribute requires a user to make a selection from the tree before being allowed to submit the form to the ColdFusion server. `MESSAGE` specifies the text message to display if the form is submitted without making a selection from the tree. The `HIGHLIGHTHREF` attribute indicates whether to highlight URLs specified in the `HREF` attribute of associated `CFTREEITEM` tags. Setting the `COMPLETEPATH` attribute to `Yes` tells ColdFusion to pass the root level of the `Path` form variable (`Form.TreeName.Path`) when the `CFFORM` containing the `CFTREE` is submitted. The final new attribute in the `CFTREE` tag, `APPENDKEY,` indicates whether to append the `CFTREEITEMKEY` variable to the end of the value of a selected `CFTREEITEM`.

You can build the tree itself by nesting a series of `CFTREEITEM` tags. The `CFTREEITEM` tag accepts several attributes for defining its position within the tree. The `VALUE` attribute specifies a value to be associated with the tree item. The `PARENT` attribute allows you to specify the name of another tree item to use as the parent for the current tree item. The value you specify for `PARENT` should match the `VALUE` attribute of the tree item you wish to use as the parent. The `HREF` attribute allows you to specify a hyperlink (URL or mailto) to associate with the tree item. You can indicate whether to expand a particular tree branch via the `EXPAND` attribute. If `EXPAND` is omitted, it is automatically set to `Yes`. Another optional attribute, `IMG` allows you to specify an image to display alongside the tree item. You may specify a path to your own image or use one of the images supplied with ColdFusion by referencing the image name. Valid options for `IMG` are `CD`, `Computer`, `Document`, `Element`, `Folder`, `Floppy`, `Fixed`, and `Remote`. The default image is `Folder`.

### *Dynamically populating a tree control with query data*

The CFTREE control can also be populated dynamically from a database query. The big advantage to populating a tree from a query instead of hardcoding it is in the amount of code you use. Using a query to populate the tree requires a minimum amount of CFML to get the job done. Example 10-17 shows how to populate a CFTREE control using the results of a CFQUERY. The results can be seen in Figure 10-8.

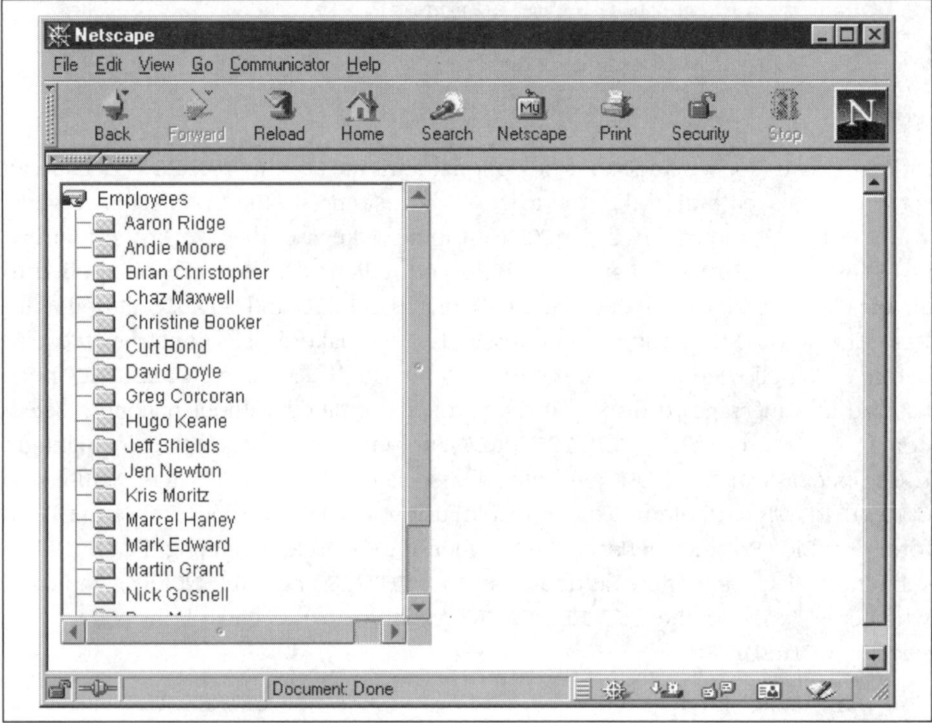


*Figure 10-8. Dynamically populating a tree with query data*

*Example 10-17. Populating CFTREE with Dynamic Values from a Query*

```
<CFQUERY NAME="GetEmployeeInfo" DATASOURCE="ProgrammingCF">
   SELECT Name FROM EmployeeDirectory ORDER BY Name
</CFQUERY>

<CFFORM ACTION="Example10-17.cfm" ENABLECAB="Yes" NAME="MyForm"
        ENCTYPE="application/x-www-form-urlencoded">

<CFTREE NAME="MyTree" HEIGHT="300" WIDTH="300" BORDER="Yes"
        HSCROLL="Yes" VSCROLL="Yes"
        NOTSUPPORTED="<B>Your web browser must support Java to view ColdFusion
                    Java Applets</B>">
```

*Example 10-17. Populating CFTREE with Dynamic Values from a Query (continued)*

```
   <CFTREEITEM QUERY="GetEmployeeInfo" VALUE="name" QUERYASROOT="Employees"
               IMG="Fixed, Folder" EXPAND="Yes">
</CFTREE>
</CFFORM>
```

Example 10-17 creates a tree control with the `CFTREE` tag and then populates the tree with a single `CFTREEITEM` tag. The `QUERY` attribute allows us to specify the name of a query to use to populate the tree. In this case, we used `GetEmployeeInfo`, referring to the query we executed at the top of the template. Setting `VALUE` to `Name` populates the tree with the name of each employee. `QUERYASROOT` lets us specify a title to appear as the root of the tree. The Allaire documentation on the `QUERYASROOT` attribute states that it accepts `Yes` or `No` as possible values—indicating whether or not to use the value specified in `QUERY` as the title for the root. This isn't entirely true. Besides `Yes/No`, `QUERYASROOT` allows you to specify any title you wish as the query root. Therefore, in Example 10-17, we set `QUERYASROOT` to `Employees` as it is a little more aesthetically pleasing than using `GetEmployeeInfo`. The next attribute, `IMG`, lets us specify a comma-delimited list of image types to use when building our tree. Setting `IMG` equal to `Fixed, Folder` results in the `Fixed` image being used for the root level and the `Folder` image being used for all branches off the root. Finally, `EXPAND` is set to `Yes`, resulting in every level of the tree (all two of them in this case) being fully expanded in the display.

There is another technique for generating a tree from a query that uses `CFLOOP` to let you specify additional sublevels within your tree. Let's say you want to take the tree we built in Example 10-17 and expand it to include each employee's title, department, hyperlinked email address, and phone extension as subbranches below each employee within the tree. The most obvious way to do this is to pull the data used to populate the `CFTREEITEM` tags from a query. What isn't so obvious, however, is the fact that you can't use the same technique we used in Example 10-17 to build the tree. This is because the technique used in that example is only capable of producing a tree with a single parent/child relationship. The way around this is to use `CFLOOP` to loop over the query data and build the appropriate `CFTREEITEM` tags with each iteration of the loop. This technique is shown in Example 10-18.

*Example 10-18. Populating a CFTREE Using CFLOOP*

```
<CFQUERY NAME="GetEmployeeInfo" DATASOURCE="ProgrammingCF">
   SELECT * FROM EmployeeDirectory
</CFQUERY>

<CFFORM ACTION="Example10-18.cfm" ENABLECAB="Yes" NAME="MyForm"
        ENCTYPE="application/x-www-form-urlencoded">
```

*Example 10-18. Populating a CFTREE Using CFLOOP (continued)*

```
<CFTREE NAME="MyTree" HEIGHT="300" WIDTH="300" BORDER="Yes" HSCROLL="Yes"
        VSCROLL="Yes" HIGHLIGHTHREF="Yes"
        NOTSUPPORTED="<B>Your web browser must support Java to view ColdFusion
                      Java Applets</B>">

<CFTREEITEM VALUE="Employees" EXPAND="yes" IMG="fixed">

<CFLOOP QUERY="GetEmployeeInfo">

   <CFTREEITEM VALUE="#name#" PARENT="Employees" EXPAND="no">

   <CFTREEITEM VALUE="#title#" PARENT="#name#" IMG="document" EXPAND="no">

   <CFTREEITEM VALUE="#department#" PARENT="#name#" IMG="document" EXPAND="no">

   <CFTREEITEM VALUE="#email#" DISPLAY="#email#" PARENT="#name#" IMG="document"
               HREF="mailto:#email#" EXPAND="no">

   <CFTREEITEM VALUE="ext: #phoneext#" PARENT="#name#" IMG="document">

</CFLOOP>
</CFTREE>
</CFFORM>
```

After the query is run, the shell for the tree is built with the `CFTREE` tag. Next, we specify the root level for the tree using a static `CFTREEITEM` tag. For this example, we set the root to `Employees`. The next step involves using a `CFLOOP` to loop over the query results from the `GetEmployeeInfo` query. For each record in the query, a series of `CFTREEITEM` tags are created. The first `CFTREEITEM` tag anchors the tree item to the root of the tree. This is done by setting the `PARENT` attribute to `Employees`—the name of our root tree item. Each of the rest of the `CFTREEITEM` tags are populated with values from the current query row. The second to last `CFTREEITEM` uses a new attribute, `HREF`, to specify a hyperlink to display within the tree control. In order to use this feature, the `HIGHLIGHTHREF` attribute of the `CFTREE` tag must be set to `Yes`. In our example, we want to use this tree item to display the employee's email address as a mailto link. We do this by setting `HREF` to `mailto:#Email#`. The output of this template can be seen in Figure 10-9.

Another method for populating the `CFTREE` control is to specify the tree items as a comma-delimited list of values. In this scenario, the information that populates the tree is queried from a database. A `CFTREEITEM` tag then populates the tree control. Instead of coding a `CFTREEITEM` tag for each sublevel in the tree, multiple values are specified within the `VALUE`, `EXPAND`, and `IMG` attributes. This technique is shown in Example 10-19.

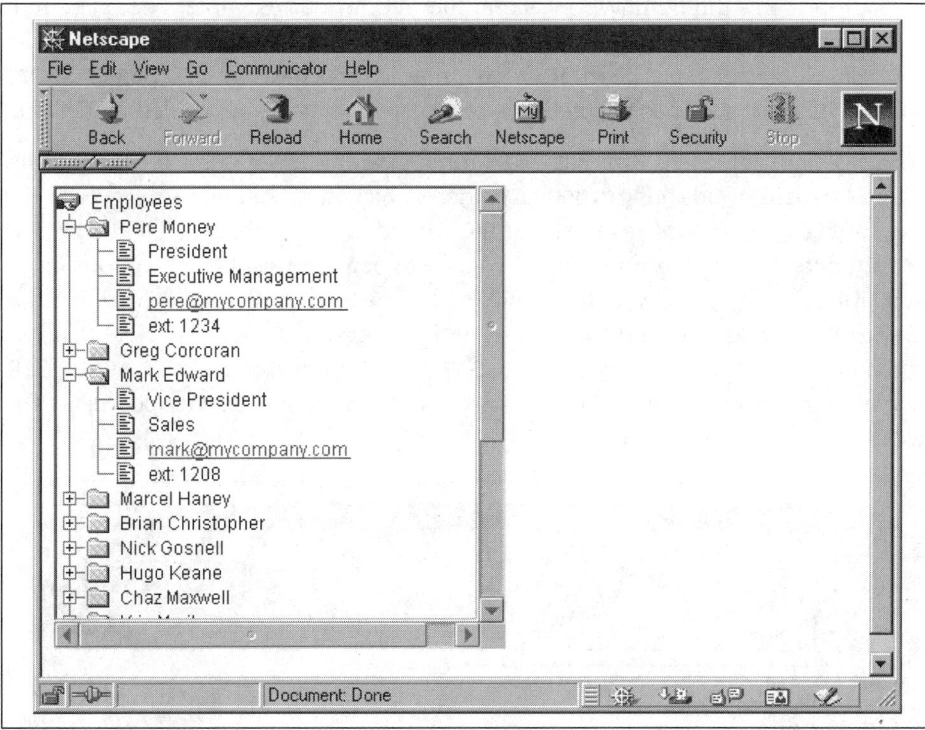


*Figure 10-9. Populating a tree control from query data*

*Example 10-19. Specifying Multiple Tree Items Using a Comma-Delimited List*

```
<CFQUERY NAME="GetEmployeeInfo" DATASOURCE="ProgrammingCF">
         SELECT Department, Name, Title FROM EmployeeDirectory
         ORDER BY Department
</CFQUERY>

<CFFORM ACTION="Example10-19.cfm" NAME="MyForm">

<CFTREE NAME="MyTree" HEIGHT="300" WIDTH="300" FONT="Arial" BOLD="No"
        ITALIC="No" BORDER="Yes" HSCROLL="Yes" VSCROLL="Yes" HIGHLIGHTHREF="Yes">

<CFTREEITEM QUERY="GetEmployeeInfo" VALUE="Department,Name,Title"
            QUERYASROOT="Org Chart" EXPAND="Yes,No"
            IMG="fixed,folder,folder,document">

</CFTREE>
</CFFORM>
```

In Example 10-19, we create the shell for the tree control using the `CFTREE` tag. The tree is then populated using a single `CFTREEITEM` tag. The `QUERY` attribute specifies the name of the query to use to populate the tree. In `VALUE`, we specify a comma-delimited list of query columns to use in building the tree. Each value in the list represents a different level within the tree. In our example, `Department` is the first branch from the main root. `Name` is a sublevel of `Department`, and `Title` is a sublevel of `Name`. The root of the tree is specified in the `QUERYASROOT` attribute. `EXPAND` specifies which levels of the tree should be expanded by default.

Although undocumented, the `EXPAND` attribute can accept a comma-delimited list of `Yes/No` values indicating whether or not to expand additional sublevels in the tree. In this case, we opted to expand the root level but nothing beyond that. The `IMG` attribute accepts a comma-delimited list of images to display the various levels and sublevels within the tree. In Example 10-19, we set the root to `Fixed`, the first level to `Folder`, the second to `Folder`, and the third to `Document`. Note that it is extremely important to include the `ORDER BY Department` clause in the SQL statement in this example. Failing to do so results in incorrectly grouped data. The results can be seen in Figure 10-10.

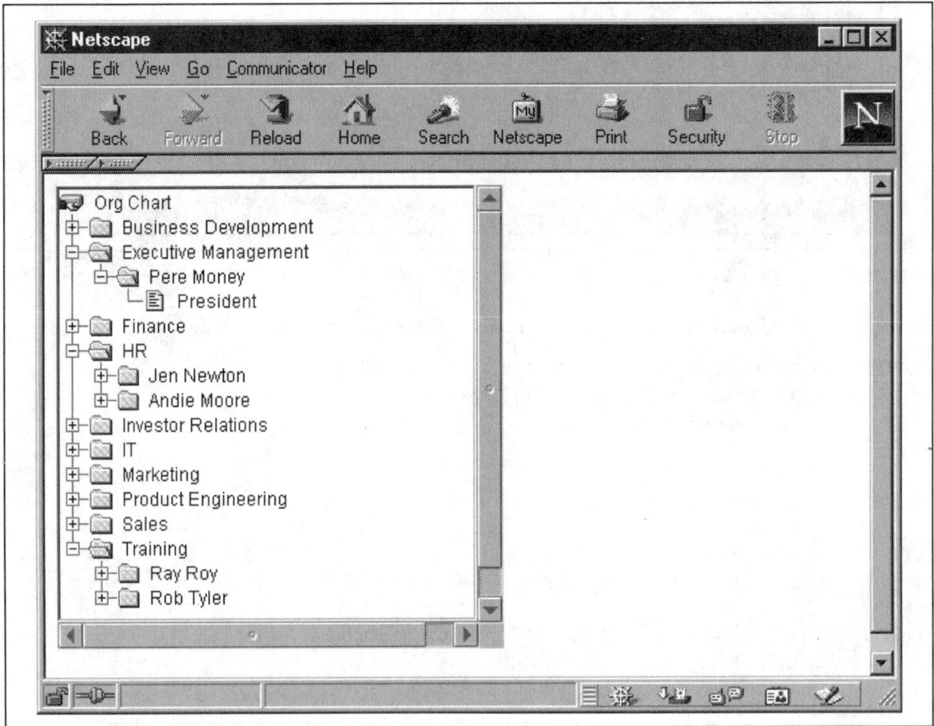


*Figure 10-10. Building a multilevel tree using delimited data*

## *Submitting a Tree Selection*

Up to this point in the chapter, we have built tree controls that only display data. Because the `CFTREE` tag is used within the context of `CFFORM`, the tree control can also select and submit data. When you submit a CFFORM containing a CFTREE control, two variables are made available to the template being POSTED to:

`Form.`*`TreeName`*`.Node`
: Returns the node selected by the user from the tree.

`Form.`*`TreeName`*`.Path`
: If the COMPLETEPATH attribute of the CFTREE tag is set to Yes, `Form.`*`TreeName`*`.Path` returns the user's selection specified as root\node1\noden\value. Otherwise, `Form.`*`TreeName`*`.Path` returns the path from the first node. The delimiter can be changed by specifying a value for the DELIMITER attribute.

An example demonstrating what happens when you submit a form containing a CFTREE is shown in Example 10-20.

*Example 10-20. Submitting a Tree Selection*

```
<CFIF IsDefined('Form.Submit')>
  <CFOUTPUT>
  <H3>You chose:</H3>
  Node: #MyTree.Node#<BR>
  Path: #MyTree.Path#<BR>
  </CFOUTPUT>
</CFIF>

<CFQUERY NAME="GetEmployeeInfo" DATASOURCE="ProgrammingCF">
         SELECT Department, Name, Title FROM EmployeeDirectory
         ORDER BY Department
</CFQUERY>

<CFFORM ACTION="Example10-20.cfm" NAME="MyForm">

<CFTREE NAME="MyTree" HEIGHT="300" WIDTH="300" FONT="Arial" BOLD="No"
        ITALIC="No" BORDER="Yes" HSCROLL="Yes" VSCROLL="Yes" HIGHLIGHTHREF="Yes">

  <CFTREEITEM VALUE="Department,Name,Title" QUERY="GetEmployeeInfo"
              QUERYASROOT="Org Chart" EXPAND="Yes,No"
              IMG="fixed,folder,folder,document" PARENT="Org Chart">

</CFTREE>
<INPUT TYPE="Submit" NAME="Submit" VALUE="Submit">
</CFFORM>
```

Example 10-20 is essentially the same as Example 10-19 with two small additions. At the bottom of the template, we added a standard submit button for the form. At the top of the template, we added a short bit of code wrapped within a CFIF statement that checks to see if the template is being called as a result of being submitted to itself. If so, the Node and Path of the user's selection from the tree are written to the browser. The results can be seen in Figure 10-11.

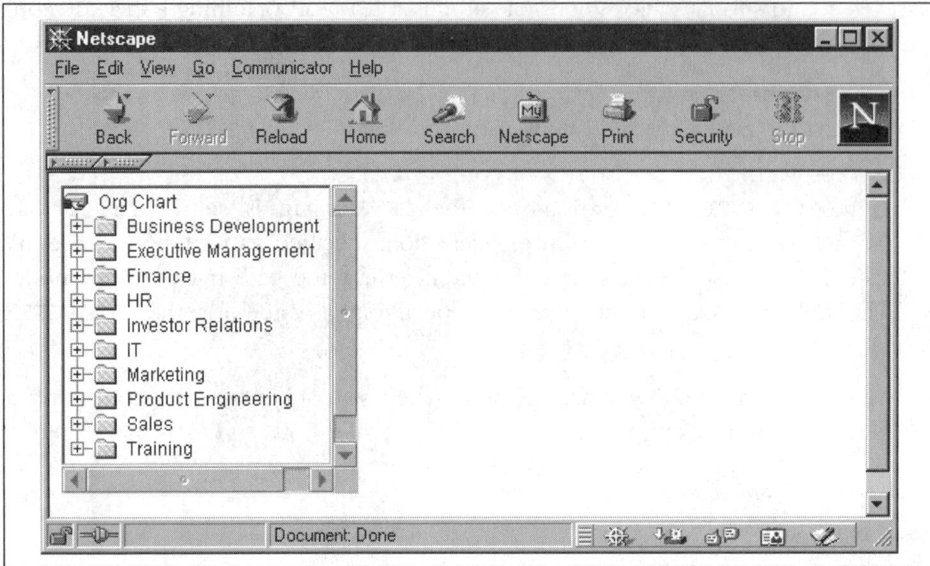


*Figure 10-11. Processing the results of a CFTREE form submission*

## Creating a Tree via Recursion

Tree controls are the perfect way to represent nested levels of data. In many cases, you might not know in advance how many subbranches the tree contains. The key to handling this in your applications is a technique known as recursion. *Recursion* is the ability to traverse all the relationships within a tree. All trees can be represented as a series of parent/child relationships. If you start at the root of the tree, each branch off of the main branch can be thought of as a child of the root. Conversely, the root is the parent to all the main branches. Now, if you look at each of the branches growing off of the root, they may or may not have child branches. This pattern can potentially repeat itself for any number of sub-branches within a tree.

Modeling this pattern in a database is a straightforward process that can be accomplished with a single table. Table 10-1 shows the structure necessary to build a database table for storing all data required to build a tree of infinite sublevels.

*Table 10-1. Database Design for a Parent/Child Tree*

| Field Name | Field Type | Max Length |
|---|---|---|
| ItemID (primary key) | AutoNumber | N/A |
| ParentItemID | Numeric | N/A |
| ItemName | Text | 255 |
| LinkURL | Text | 255 |

The model shown in Table 10-1 is generic enough that it can be used to build a tree for practically any type of data that can be grouped in multiple levels. Let's populate the database with categories and hyperlinks so that we can build a tree containing categorized hyperlinks—similar to the bookmarks concept seen in web browsers (See Table C-6 in Appendix C).

Each record in the database has a unique number assigned to it in the `ItemID` field, which ensures that no two items are identical. The parent-child relationship is established using the `ParentItemID` field. You can create a top-level tree branch by setting `ParentItemID` to `0`. You can then create child branches off these top-level branches by setting their `ParentItemID` values to an appropriate `ItemID`. This process is repeated for *n* number of branches and subbranches within the tree.

Now that we have described the setup and expected output of the application, let's look at the actual code necessary to build it. The code consists of two templates. The first template (shown in Example 10-21) displays any selected items from the tree as well as creates the shell for the tree control and calls the custom tag (shown in Example 10-22) that populates it.

*Example 10-21. Setting Up the Tree Control and Calling the Recursion Custom Tag*

```
<!--- If the form is submitting to itself, display the node and path from the
      selected tree item --->
<CFIF IsDefined('Form.Submit')>
  <CFOUTPUT>
  <H3>You chose:</H3>
  Node: #Links.Node#<BR>
  Path: #Links.Path#<BR>
  </CFOUTPUT>
</CFIF>

<!--- create the form --->
<CFFORM ACTION="Example10-21.cfm" NAME="Links" METHOD="Post"
        ENCTYPE="multipart/form-data">
<!--- add a tree control --->
<CFTREE NAME="Links" HEIGHT="350" WIDTH="300"HSPACE="0" VSPACE="6" HSCROLL="yes"
        VSCROLL="yes" BORDER="yes" REQUIRED="yes" APPENDKEY="no"
        MESSAGE="You must choose a category or item from the tree.">

<!--- insert the root level tree item --->
<CFTREEITEM VALUE="0" PARENT="0" DISPLAY="Links" EXPAND="Yes" IMG="computer">

<!--- call the recursion tag to generate the rest of the tree --->
<CF_Recurse>

<!--- close the tree control --->
</CFTREE>
<BR>
```

*Example 10-21. Setting Up the Tree Control and Calling the Recursion Custom Tag (continued)*

```
<INPUT TYPE="Submit" NAME="Submit" VALUE="Submit">
</CFFORM>
```

Example 10-21 begins with a `CFIF` statement that checks to see if the form is submitting data to itself. If so, the user's tree selection is written to the browser. Next, a tree control is created with the `CFTREE` tag. The root level of the tree is then created using a static `CFTREEITEM` tag. The value of the node is set to `0`. The actual value displayed is configured by setting `VALUE` to `Links`. Once the root level has been established, a call to the `CF_Recurse` custom tag is made. We'll cover the specifics of building custom tags later in Chapter 19. For now, all you need to know is that the custom tag is responsible for the recursion algorithms necessary to build the rest of the tree.

The custom tag should be named *Recurse.cfm* and saved in the same directory as Example 10-21 or in the Custom Tags directory (usually *c:\cfusion\custom tags*). The code for the `CF_Recurse` tag is shown in Example 10-22.

*Example 10-22. Recursion Custom Tag for Creating Individual Tree Items*

```
<!--- check to see if a ParentItemID was passed in.  If so, this is a recursive
      call to this tag, so we set the ParentItemID to the value passed in.  If
      ParentItemID does not exist, this is a request for a top level tree item,
      so we set the ParentItemID to 0. --->
<CFIF ISDEFINED("Attributes.ParentItemID")>
  <CFSET ParentItemID = Attributes.ParentItemID>
<CFELSE>
  <CFSET ParentItemID = 0>
</CFIF>

<!--- get the info for each parent item for the current level.  Items directly
     under the root have a ParentItemID of 0.  This info is passed in with each
     iteration of this tag.  By default, the ParentItemID is set to 0. --->
<CFQUERY NAME="GetParents" DATASOURCE="ProgrammingCF">
        SELECT ItemID, ParentItemID, ItemName, LinkURL
        FROM Links WHERE ParentItemID = #ParentItemID# ORDER BY ItemName
</CFQUERY>

<!--- loop through the GetParents query and create a tree item for each
      parent --->
<CFLOOP QUERY="GetParents">
<!--- if the parent is a category, set image to folder.  If it is a link, set the
      image to document --->
<CFIF LINKURL IS "">
  <CFSET IMAGE="folder">
<CFELSE>
  <CFSET IMAGE="Document">
</CFIF>

<!--- create the tree item --->
<CFTREEITEM VALUE="#ItemID#" PARENT="#ParentItemID#" DISPLAY="#ItemName#"
```

*Example 10-22. Recursion Custom Tag for Creating Individual Tree Items (continued)*

```
          HREF="#LinkURL#" IMG="#Image#" EXPAND="No">

<!--- find children of the current parent --->
<CFQUERY NAME="GetChildren" DATASOURCE="ProgrammingCF">
        SELECT ItemID, ParentItemID, ItemName, LinkURL
        FROM links WHERE ParentItemID = #GetParents.ItemID#
</CFQUERY>

<!---  If there is a child for the parent, call the recurse tag again, but this
       time make the parentitemid equal to the itemid of the current child item.
       This is what recursion is all about. --->
<CFIF GETCHILDREN.RECORDCOUNT GT 0 >
  <CF_RECURSE
      PARENTITEMID="#GetParents.ItemID#">
</CFIF>
</CFLOOP>
```

Example 10-22 begins by checking to see if an attribute called `attributes.ParentItemID` was passed to the custom tag. If so, the tag sets a local variable called `ParentItemID` equal to the value passed into the tag. If `attributes.ParentItemID` doesn't exist, we know that this is the first time the tag is being called. Therefore, we set the local copy of `ParentItemID` equal to zero (0)—the value we assigned to the root level of the tree. The next action taken by the tag is to kick off a query that gets all items in the database associated with the level specified by the `ParentItemID` value. Items directly under the root have a `ParentItemID` of zero (0). Once this is accomplished, the query results are looped over using a `CFLOOP`, which allows us to work with the query data one row at a time. First the `LinkURL` field from each row of the query is checked to see if it is empty. If so, we know that the item in question isn't a hyperlink. We thus set a local variable called `IMAGE` to `Folder`. If `LinkURL` isn't empty, we know that the item is a hyperlink, and we set the `IMAGE` to `Document`. Next, a `CFTREEITEM` tag is created for each record. The `IMG` attribute is populated with the image specified in the `IMAGE` variable we set a moment ago. After the initial `CFTREEITEM` tag is created, another query is run to determine if the current item (parent) has any child items. If there are child items associated with the parent, the custom tag calls itself and passes the child item's `ItemID` as the `PARENTITEMID` attribute and the process of setting up the parent tree item and stepping through all its child items begins again. This is what recursion is all about. The pattern continues until there are no more parent/child relationships in the database. The results of this example are shown in Figure 10-12.

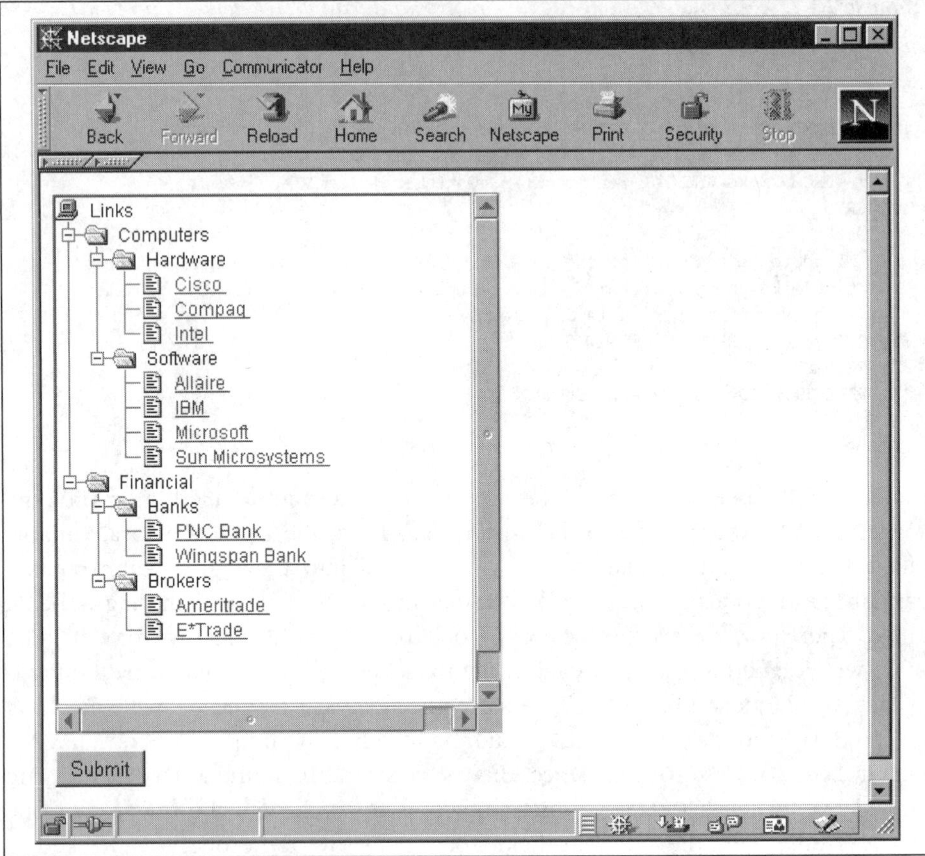


*Figure 10-12. Using recursion to display hyperlinks*

# Custom Controls

The `CFAPPLET` tag allows you to use custom Java controls within your `CFFORMs` as if they were native ColdFusion tags, like `CFTREE` and `CFGRID`. For example, you might have a Java applet called Menu that acts as an expandable/collapsible menu you'd like to use in a ColdFusion application. In order to call a custom Java applet, it first has to be registered with the ColdFusion Administrator (Figure 10-13).

To register a custom Java applet, you need to complete the following steps:

1. Open the ColdFusion Administrator, and click on the Java Applets link.
2. Click the Register New Applet button.

   Enter information into the applet registration page, which is shown in Figure 10-14. When you are finished filling in the form, click the Submit Changes button to save your selection.

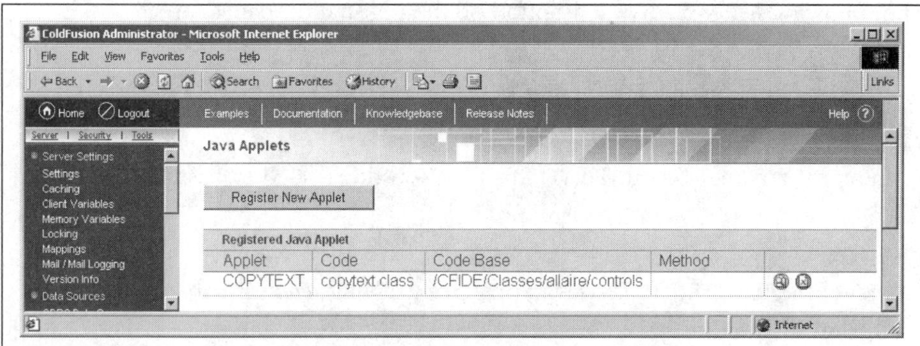


*Figure 10-13. The Applets section of the ColdFusion Administrator*

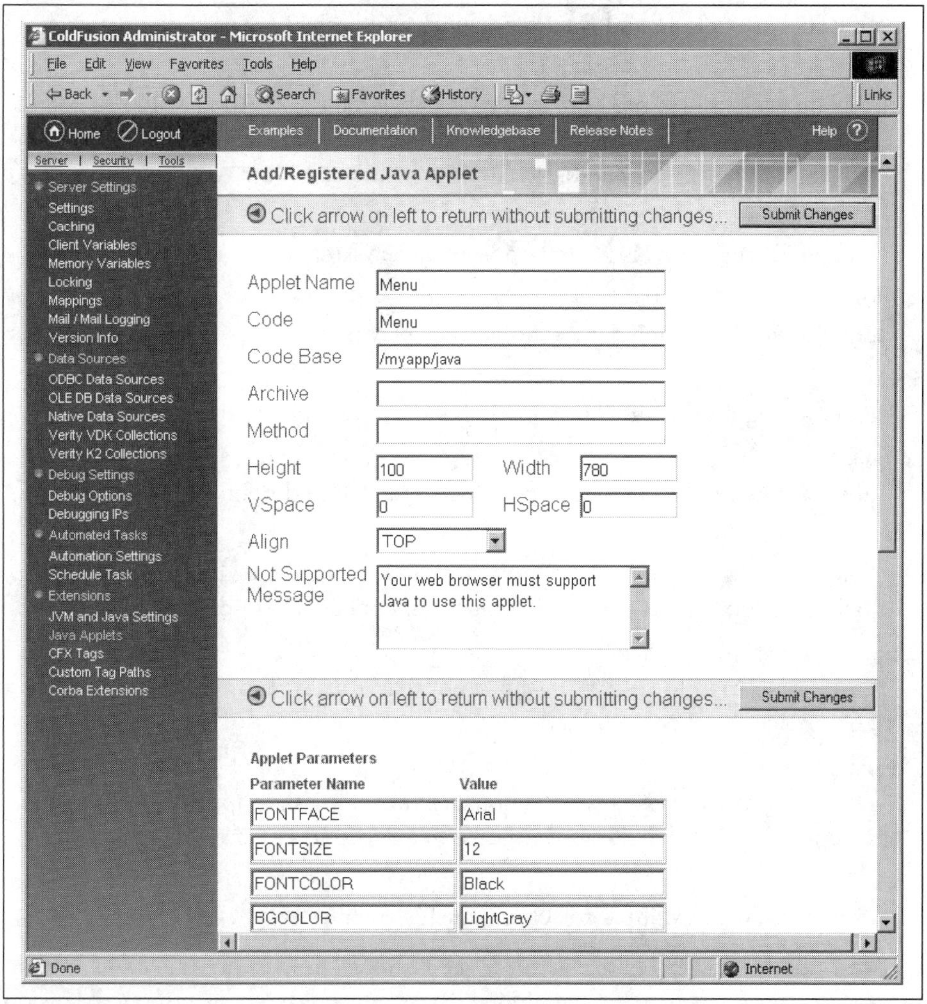

*Figure 10-14. The Applet Registration page of the ColdFusion Administrator*

The following list explains each option on the registration page:

*Applet Name*
: Enter a name for your Java control.

*Code*
: Enter the name of your Java *.class* file. You don't need to list the *.class* extension. (e.g., *myapplet*).

*Codebase*
: Enter the base URL to the Java applet. (e.g., *http://www.myserver.com/java* or */java*).

*Archive*
: Enter the location of a compressed file (*.jar*) relative to the `Codebase`. This is an optional attribute and is currently supported only by Netscape browsers.

*Method*
: If your Java applet provides a method that returns a string value, enter the name of that method here. The value you specify for Method is also the value you should specify for the `NAME` attribute of the `CFAPPLET` tag.

*Height*
: Enter a height in pixels for the applet's display area.

*Width*
: Enter a width in pixels for the applet's display area.

*VSpace*
: Enter a height in pixels for the padding above and below the applet.

*HSpace*
: Enter a width in pixels for the padding to the left and right of the applet.

*Align*
: Enter an alignment for the applet. Valid entries are `Left`, `Right`, `Top`, `TextTop`, `Bottom`, `AbsBottom`, `Baseline`, `Middle`, and `AbsMiddle`.

*Java Not Supported Message*
: Enter a message to display in the event that a user's browser doesn't support Java or Java has been disabled.

*Parameter*
: Enter the names of any additional parameters the applet is capable of accepting. Enter each parameter name in a separate `Parameter` box.

*Value*
: Provide a default value for each parameter entered.

Once an applet has been registered, it is a simple process to call it. As default values for each parameter have already been registered in the ColdFusion

Administrator, it's possible to call the tag with nothing more than the following code line:

```
<CFAPPLET APPLETSOURCE="Menu" NAME="MyFormFieldName">
```

The `CFAPPLET` tag has only two required attributes: `APPLETSOURCE` and `NAME`. `APPLETSOURCE` refers to the applet's registered name as entered in the ColdFusion Administrator, while `NAME` specifies the name to use for the form field. If a `METHOD` was specified for the applet in the ColdFusion Administrator, it should match the value specified for `NAME` in the `CFAPPLET` tag.

Besides the two required attributes, the `CFAPPLET` tag also accepts a number of optional attributes. These optional attributes correspond to the information entered in the ColdFusion Administrator. Because default values have already been specified for each attribute, if you include any of the optional attributes in the `CFAPPLET` tag, you will overwrite the default value listed in the ColdFusion Administrator. For example, if you registered the Menu applet we previously described, you can call the applet and specify values for all the default parameters using a single `CFAPPLET` tag:

```
<CFAPPLET APPLETSOURCE="vslider" NAME="MySlider"
          HEIGHT="250" WIDTH="100" HSPACE="10" VSPACE="10"
          ALIGN="middle" NOTSUPPORTED="You need Java to see my applet!"
          FONTFACE="Arial" FONTSIZE="12" FONTCOLOR="Black" BGCOLOR="LightGray">
```

For more information on the `CFAPPLET` tag, see Appendix A.

# *Form Controls in Version 5.0*

Version 5.0 of ColdFusion introduces a number of significant architectural, behavioral, functional, and cosmetic changes to the various `CFFORM` controls. The most significant change has to do with the architecture of the controls themselves. Different versions of different web browsers each have a different Java Runtime Environment (JRE), making it impossible to guarantee that the pre-CF 5.0 applets will run as intended on all browser version/JRE combinations. Because of this, all the Java applet-based `CFFORM` controls (`CFTEXTINPUT`, `CFGRID`, `CFSLIDER`, and `CFTREE`) were rewritten for ColdFusion 5.0. The new versions of the controls require the Sun Java web browser plugin, which allows the applets to function across the widest possible spectrum of browsers. When a user requests a page containing any of the new applet controls, ColdFusion automatically attempts to send and install the Java plugin if it isn't already present on the user's system. Depending on what browser the user has and the version they are running, installation can be completely seamless, or it can require a few additional steps on the part of the user.

The requirement that users download and install a plugin in order to use Java based CFFORM controls is worth considering when designing your applications. While this may not be a concern for intranet applications, where a company may have strict control over what software users have installed, it may present a barrier to Internet/extranet users unwilling or unable to download and install the plugin.

In previous versions of ColdFusion, the CFFORM tag used the ENABLECAB attribute to make Java-based form controls available to Microsoft Internet Explorer users as Microsoft cabinet files. In Version 5.0, the ENABLECAB attribute is deprecated and nonfunctional. Instead, two new optional attributes have been added to the CFFORM tag to enhance performance of the Java-based CFFORM controls:

CODEBASE="url"
: Specifies the URL to a downloadable JRE plugin for MS Internet Explorer. The default URL is */CFIDE/classes/cf-j2re-win.cab.*

ARCHIVE="url"
: Specifies the URL to a downloadable Java archive file containing Java-based CFFORM controls. The default URL is */CFIDE/classes/CFJava2.jar.*

## *Preserving Input*

A new attribute called PRESERVEDATA has been added to the CFFORM tag in ColdFusion 5.0. Setting PRESERVEDATA to Yes causes ColdFusion to retain and display data submitted from a CFINPUT (excluding checkbox and radio button controls), CFTEXTINPUT, CFSLIDER, or CFTREE control when a form is submitted to itself or to another page with like-named CFFORM controls. The exact effect of the PRESERVEDATA attribute depends on the type of form control you use in your CFFORM. For CFINPUT and CFTEXTINPUT controls, setting PRESERVEDATA to Yes allows you to display the data entered by the user after the form has been submitted without any additional coding. For CFSLIDER controls, the slider is set automatically to the position from the previous form post. For CFTREE controls, the tree expands automatically to the branch containing the previously selected item. For PRESERVEDATA to work with a tree control, the COMPLETEPATH attribute of the CFTREE tag must be set to Yes. Example 10-23 shows the code for a template named *PreserveData.cfm* that shows how the PRESERVEDATA attribute works with each type of form control it is compatible with.

*Example 10-23. Using the PRESERVEDATA Attribute of CFFORM*

```
<CFFORM ACTION="PreserveData.cfm" NAME="MyForm" PRESERVEDATA="Yes">
<TABLE>
<TR>
  <TD>CFINPUT (text):</TD>
  <TD><CFINPUT TYPE="Text" NAME="teex" SIZE="10" MAXLENGTH="10"></TD>
```

*Example 10-23. Using the PRESERVEDATA Attribute of CFFORM (continued)*

```
</TR>
<TR>
  <TD>CFINPUT (password):</TD>
  <TD><CFINPUT TYPE="Password" NAME="password" SIZE="10" MAXLENGTH="10"></TD>
</TR>
<TR>
  <TD>CFINPUT (radio)</TD>
  <TD><CFINPUT TYPE="Radio" NAME="radio" VALUE="Yes" CHECKED="Yes">Yes
      <CFINPUT TYPE="Radio" NAME="radio" VALUE="No">No</TD>
</TR>
<TR>
  <TD>CFINPUT (checkbox)</TD>
  <TD><CFINPUT TYPE="Checkbox" NAME="checkbox" VALUE="1">One<BR>
      <CFINPUT TYPE="Checkbox" NAME="checkbox" VALUE="2">Two<BR>
      <CFINPUT TYPE="Checkbox" NAME="checkbox" VALUE="3">Three</TD>
</TR>
<TR>
  <TD>CFTEXTINPUT:</TD>
  <TD><CFTEXTINPUT NAME="textinput" HEIGHT="25" BGCOLOR="##C0C0C0"
                   TEXTCOLOR="##000000" MAXLENGTH="255"></TD>
</TR>
<TR>
  <TD>CFSLIDER</TD>
  <TD><B>1</B> <CFSLIDER NAME="Slider" LABEL="Current slider value:  %value%"
                         REFRESHLABEL="Yes" RANGE="1,100" VALUE="50"
                         SCALE="1" ALIGN="Absmiddle" HEIGHT="50"
                         WIDTH="200"><B>100</B></TD>
</TR>
<TR>
  <TD>CFTREE</TD>
  <TD><CFTREE NAME="Tree" HEIGHT="150" WIDTH="250" COMPLETEPATH="Yes">
        <CFTREEITEM VALUE="ColdFusion Links" PARENT="MyTree" IMG="fixed"
                    EXPAND="Yes">
          <CFTREEITEM VALUE="Executive" PARENT="ColdFusion Links" EXPAND="No">
            <CFTREEITEM VALUE="Allaire Home Page" PARENT="Executive"
                        IMG="document">
          <CFTREEITEM VALUE="Developer" PARENT="ColdFusion Links" EXPAND="No">
            <CFTREEITEM VALUE="ColdFusion DevCenter" PARENT="Developer"
                        IMG="document">
            <CFTREEITEM VALUE="Allaire Developer's Exchange"
                        PARENT="Developer" IMG="document">
      </CFTREE></TD>
</TR>
<TR>
  <TD COLSPAN="2"><input type="submit" name="Submit"></TD>
</TR>
</TABLE>
</CFFORM>
```

## Data Validation with JavaScript Regular Expressions

Another new feature in ColdFusion 5.0 is the addition of JavaScript regular expressions as a means for validating data entered in CFINPUT and CFTEXTINPUT tags. Regular expressions allow you to specify patterns to match data input against. For example, you can write regular expressions to validate things such as valid email address formats, string lengths, file-naming conventions, and anything else that follows a pattern. To use a JavaScript regular expression as a validation mechanism in your CFINPUT or CFTEXTINPUT tags, you need to do two things. First, you must specify `Regular_Expression` in the VALIDATE attribute of your tag. `Regular_Expression` is a new value in ColdFusion 5.0 and lets ColdFusion know you want to use a JavaScript regular expression to validate the input for the form control.

The second thing you need to do is specify the JavaScript regular expression you want to validate against. This done using a new attribute called PATTERN. The PATTERN attribute accepts any combination of characters comprising a valid JavaScript regular expression. There are, however, a few rules that you need to be aware of:

- You shouldn't enter the forward slashes (/) normally used to surround a JavaScript regular expression as ColdFusion does this behind the scenes for you.
- ColdFusion variables and expressions can dynamically construct the regular expression as they are evaluated before the regular expression validates the form-field input.

Although there are similarities between JavaScript regular expressions and those native to ColdFusion (covered in Chapter 17), enough of a difference exists to warrant separate coverage. However, a thorough discussion of JavaScript regular expressions is beyond the scope of this book, so I recommend consulting the following resources to learn more:

*JavaScript: The Definitive Guide by David Flanagan (O'Reilly & Associates)*
Chapter 10, Pattern Matching with Regular Expressions

*Developing ColdFusion Applications (ColdFusion documentation)*
Chapter 9, Building Dynamic Forms

*Netscape JavaScript Guide*
*http://developer.netscape.com/docs/manuals/communicator/jsguide/regexp.htm*

*CNet's Builder.com*
*http://www.builder.com/Programming/Kahn/050698/*

For those already familiar with JavaScript regular expressions, Example 10-24 shows how to use this new feature to perform a few simple validation tasks.

*Example 10-24. Using JavaScript Regular Expressions to Validate Form Input*

```
<CFFORM ACTION="10-24.cfm" ENABLECAB="Yes" NAME="MyForm" PRESERVEDATA="Yes">
<TABLE>
<TR>
  <TD>Employee ID:</TD>
  <TD><CFINPUT TYPE="Text" NAME="Name" REQUIRED="yes"
              MESSAGE="You must enter your 5 digit employee ID."
              VALIDATE="Regular_Expression" PATTERN="^\d{5}$"></TD>
</TR>
<TR>
  <TD>Password:</TD>
  <TD><CFINPUT TYPE="Password" NAME="Passwrod" REQUIRED="yes"
        MESSAGE="You must enter at least 8 characters, consisting of letters,
                numbers, and underscores only."
        VALIDATE="Regular_Expression" PATTERN="^\w{8,}$"></TD>
</TR>
<TR>
  <TD>E-mail:</TD>
  <TD><CFINPUT TYPE="Text" NAME="Email" REQUIRED="yes"
        MESSAGE="You must enter your e-mail address."
        VALIDATE="Regular_Expression"
        PATTERN="^[A-Za-z0-9_\.\-]+@([A-Za-z0-9_\.\-]+\.)+[A-Za-z]{2,4}$">
  </TD>
</TR>
</TABLE>
<P>
<INPUT TYPE="submit" NAME="Submit" VALUE="Submit">
</CFFORM>
```

The form in this example expects three inputs: a five-digit employee number, a password at least eight characters long that is made up of letters, numbers, and underscores only, and a correctly formatted (notice I didn't say valid) email address.

To validate that the user has entered exactly five digits and nothing else, the first `CFINPUT` tag uses this regular expression:

```
^\d{5}$
```

The `^` character anchors the expression to the beginning of the string while `\d` matches any single digit from 0–9. The `{5}` tells the regular expression to match the last group of characters (in this case, a single digit) five times. Finally, the `$` character anchors the regular expression to the end of the string.

The next `CFINPUT` tag uses a similar regular expression to make sure the form input is at least eight characters long and contains only letters, digits, and underscores:

```
^\w{8,}$
```

In this case, the ^ and $ characters perform the same job as in the previous example. The \w tells the regular expression to match any single letter, digit, or underscore character. Adding the comma to the repetition character makes the regular expression match eight *or more* occurrences of the last group of characters.

The final CFINPUT tag uses a slightly more complicated regular expression to ensure that a correctly formatted email address is entered:

```
^[A-Za-z0-9_\.\-]+@([A-Za-z0-9_\.\-]+\.)+[A-Za-z]{2,4}$
```

This regular expression also uses the ^ and $ characters for the same purpose as the previous two regular expressions. The [A-Za-z0-9_\.\-]+@ means that the regular expression should match one or more letters (regardless of case), digits, underscores, periods, or dashes followed by an @ character. The next part, ([A-Za-z0-9_\.\-]+\.)+ matches one or more sets of letters (again, regardless of case), digits, underscores, periods, or dashes followed by a period. The final part of the regular expression matches a string containing at least two letters (regardless of case) but not more than four. This allows you to enter email addresses such as *me@example.com* and *me.oh.my@my.example.ru*. While this regular expression doesn't prevent people from entering invalid email addresses, it does cut down on the number of accidental formatting mistakes.

## Grids

In ColdFusion 5.0, the grid produced by the CFGRID and CFGRIDCOLUMN tags looks and functions differently than it did in previous versions. Many of the same attributes apply to these tags, however, some work differently, and some attributes are completely new. One thing you'll notice right away if you run any of the previous CFGRID examples from this chapter is a completely new look and feel for the grid control. Figure 10-15 shows how the grid created by Example 10-9 looks in ColdFusion 5.0. Compare it to the grid in Figure 10-4 to see the contrast.

Besides the obvious visual differences, there are several new behaviors in the ColdFusion 5.0 grid control:

- The user may rearrange the order in which columns are displayed by clicking on a column header and dragging it left or right.
- The user may sort the grid data by double-clicking the column header of the column you wish to sort by. The first time the user sorts, the data is sorted in ascending order. Double-clicking again resorts the data in descending order.
- When SELECTMODE is EDIT, ROW, COLUMN, or SINGLE, clicking once on a non-editable cell causes the background color of that cell (or row or column) to turn pink with a yellow border. Clicking once on an editable cell turns the background color of the cell white with a yellow border.

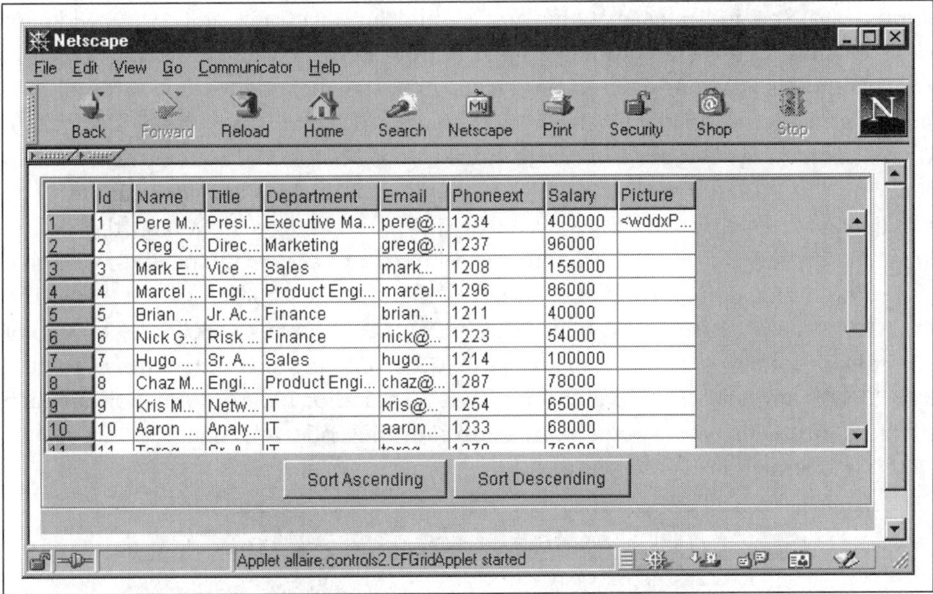


*Figure 10-15. CFGRID's new look in ColdFusion 5.0*

- To edit the contents of an editable cell, the user can double click on it. Pressing the Enter key or clicking on a different cell finishes the editing.

In addition to the cosmetic and behavioral changes, the `CFGRID` and `CFGRIDCOLUMN` tags have several new optional attributes you can use to enhance the grid control. This section outlines these additions and provides examples of how to use these new features in your applications.

Four new attributes have been added to the `CFGRID` tag. These attributes are `AUTOWIDTH`, `TEXTCOLOR`, `COLHEADERTEXTCOLOR`, and `ROWHEADERTEXTCOLOR`. Example 10-25 creates a simple grid that illustrates their use.

*Example 10-25. New CFGRID Attributes in ColdFusion 5.0*

```
<CFQUERY NAME="GetPeople" DATASOURCE="ProgrammingCF">
   SELECT Name, Department, Email, PhoneExt FROM EmployeeDirectory
</CFQUERY>

<CFFORM ACTION="10-25.cfm" ENABLECAB="Yes" NAME="MyForm">

<CFGRID NAME="MyGrid" QUERY="GetPeople" WIDTH="400" AUTOWIDTH="Yes"
        TEXTCOLOR="blue" COLHEADERTEXTCOLOR="##000000"
        ROWHEADERTEXTCOLOR="FF0000"/>
</CFFORM>
```

This example creates a grid 400 pixels wide containing four columns of data from the `EmployeeDirectory` table of our example database. Setting the `AUTOWIDTH` attribute to `Yes` indicates that the grid should automatically adjust the width of each column so that all columns appear within the grid without having to scroll. By default, this attribute is set to `No`. `TEXTCOLOR` specifies the text color for all data in the grid. Colors may be specified by name (`Black`, `Blue`, `Cyan`, `Darkgray`, `Gray`, `Lightgray`, `Magenta`, `Orange`, `Pink`, `Red`, `White`, `Yellow`) or hex code in the form `TEXTCOLOR="##FFFFCC"`. The double pound signs are necessary to keep ColdFusion from throwing a syntax error. If you wish, you may omit the pound signs altogether. By using the appropriate hex code, you may specify colors that can't be specified by name. The default text color is `Black`. The `COLHEADERTEXTCOLOR` and `ROWHEADERTEXTCOLOR` attributes specify the text color for column and row headers in the grid. Color choices are the same as for the `TEXTCOLOR` attribute. The default for both is `Black`. For more information on each of these attributes, see Appendix A. Executing the code in Example 10-25 results in the grid shown in Figure 10-16.

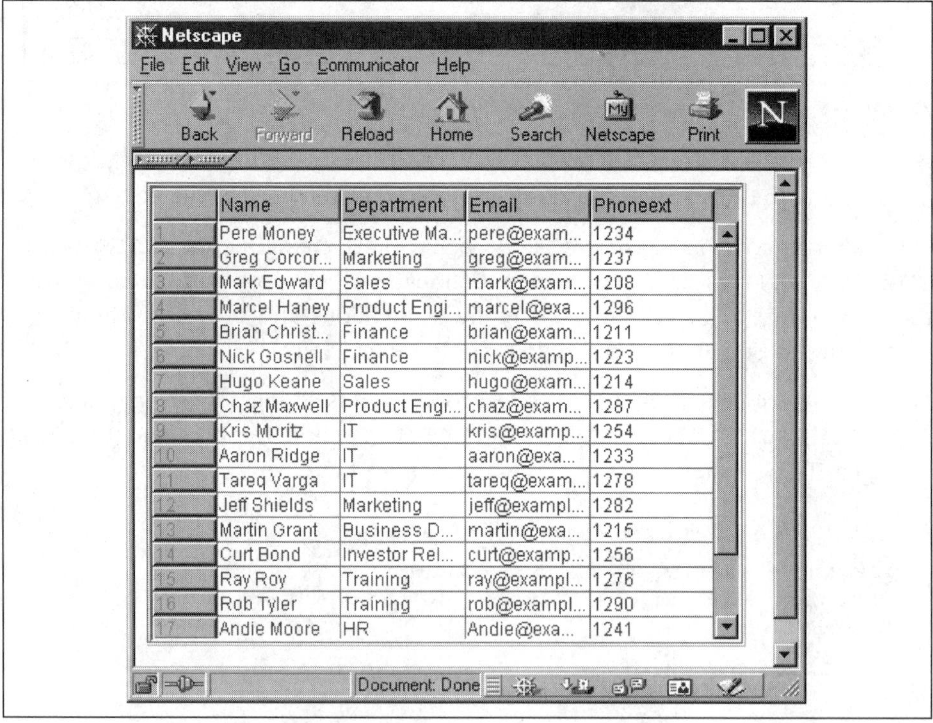


*Figure 10-16. New CFGRID display controls in ColdFusion 5.0*

The `CFGRIDCOLUMN` tag has several new attributes you can use to enhance individual columns of data within your grids. These new attributes are `TEXTCOLOR`, `BGCOLOR`, `HEADERTEXTCOLOR`, `VALUES`, `VALUESDISPLAY`, and `VALUESDELIMITER`. In addition to these new attributes, the `TYPE` attribute now accepts an additional value called Boolean. Rather than explain each new attribute and value individually, let's look at an example that utilizes them all. Example 10-26 creates a grid that provides just such an example.

*Example 10-26. Grid Showing New CFGRIDCOLUMN Attributes and Values*

```
<!--- if the grid has been changed, update it --->
<CFIF IsDefined('form.MyGrid.rowstatus.action')>
   <CFGRIDUPDATE GRID="MyGrid" DATASOURCE="ProgrammingCF"
                 TABLENAME="EmployeeDirectory" KEYONLY="No">
</CFIF>

<CFQUERY NAME="GetPeople" DATASOURCE="ProgrammingCF">
   SELECT * FROM EmployeeDirectory ORDER BY Name
</CFQUERY>

<CFQUERY NAME="GetDepartments" DATASOURCE="ProgrammingCF">
   SELECT DISTINCT Department FROM EmployeeDirectory
</CFQUERY>

<CFFORM ACTION="10-26.cfm" ENABLECAB="Yes" NAME="MyForm"
        ENCTYPE="application/x-www-form-urlencoded">

<CFGRID NAME="MyGrid" WIDTH="600" HEIGHT="250" AUTOWIDTH="Yes" QUERY="GetPeople"
        SELECTMODE="EDIT" INSERT="Yes" DELETE="Yes" INSERTBUTTON="Add New Record"
        DELETEBUTTON="Delete">

  <CFGRIDCOLUMN NAME="ID" DISPLAY="No">
  <!--- if the employee is the president, change the
        text color to blue. Otherwise, leave it alone --->
  <CFGRIDCOLUMN NAME="Name" BOLD="Yes" HEADERTEXTCOLOR="Blue"
                TEXTCOLOR="(C2 EQ President ? blue : black)" BGCOLOR="LightGray">

  <CFGRIDCOLUMN NAME="Title" TEXTCOLOR="(CX EQ President ? blue : black)"
                HEADERTEXTCOLOR="Blue">

  <!--- here's where we create a dropdown list of departments --->
  <CFGRIDCOLUMN NAME="Department" HEADERTEXTCOLOR="Blue"
                VALUES="#ValueList(GetDepartments.Department)#"
                VALUESDISPLAY="Off" VALUESDELIMITER=",">

  <CFGRIDCOLUMN NAME="Email" HEADER="E-mail" HEADERTEXTCOLOR="Blue">
  <CFGRIDCOLUMN NAME="PhoneExt" HEADER="Phone ext." HEADERTEXTCOLOR="Blue">

   <!--- use a checkbox to represent Boolean values --->
  <CFGRIDCOLUMN NAME="Exempt" HEADERTEXTCOLOR="Blue" TYPE="Boolean">
</CFGRID>
<BR>
<INPUT TYPE="Submit" NAME="submit" VALUE="Submit Changes">
<INPUT type="hidden" NAME="GridChanged" VALUE="yes">
</CFFORM>
```

This example creates an updateable grid loosely based on the one we created in Example 10-14. There are, however, some significant differences. Before you run this template, you'll have to add a new field to the `EmployeeDirectory` table in the `ProgrammingCF` database. Call the new field `Exempt`, and make it a `Yes/No` (Boolean) datatype. This new field is necessary to demonstrate one of the new features of `CFGRIDCOLUMN`. Don't worry about populating the new column with data just yet; we'll get to that in just a moment.

If you turn your attention back to the template in Example 10-26, you'll see that things are pretty straightforward right up until the second `CFGRIDCOLUMN` tag. The first thing you should notice is a new `HEADERTEXTCOLOR` attribute. `HEADERTEXTCOLOR` works exactly the same as the `COLHEADERTEXTCOLOR` attribute in the `CFGRID` tag, except that it allows you to specify the text color of a column header on a column-by-column basis.

The next new attribute you should see in the first `CFGRIDCOLUMN` tag is `TEXTCOLOR`. This attribute lets you specify the text color for all data in the column. It follows the same color-name rules as the `HEADERTEXTCOLOR` attribute. Instead of a color, you can specify an expression that returns a color based on its evaluation, as we do in this example. The expression uses the following format:

```
( CX|Cn GT|LT|EQ string ? color_true : color_false )
```

`CX` represents the current column while `Cn` specifies a specific column where *n* is the index position of the column (only displayed columns are available). Operator can be `GT`, `LT`, or `EQ` for both string and numeric comparisons. The `?` separates the expression from the values you wish to return. *`color_true`* is the color to return in the event the expression evaluates `True` while *`color_false`* is the color to return if the expression evaluates `False`. Colors are specified using a color name or hex code (without the pound signs). The two return values are separated with a colon. Note that whitespace is ignored within the expression except for within string. In our example, we use the expression `(C2 EQ President ? blue : black)`. What this says is if the value in the corresponding row in column 2 (`Title`) equals `President`, make the text color for this item blue; otherwise, leave it as black.

The final attribute in our first `CFGRIDCOLUMN` tag is `BGCOLOR`. `BGCOLOR` specifies a background color for all the cells in the column or, like `TEXTCOLOR`, an expression that returns a color based on its evaluation. For color choices, see the `TEXTCOLOR` attribute.

If you look at the fourth `CFGRIDCOLUMN` tag, the one for the Department column, you'll notice three new attributes, `VALUES`, `VALUESDISPLAY`, and `VALUESDELIMITER`. These attributes place a drop-down box for each cell in the column provided the grid is an editable grid (which ours is). The `VALUES` attribute accepts a delimited list of values, a range of numeric values, or `Off`. It determines the actual value to pass when the form containing the grid is submitted. For a delimited list of values, the default delimiter is the comma. To specify a range of numeric values, use the format *`n-m`* where *`n`* is the minimum value in the range, and *`m`* is the maximum value. The default is `Off`. In our example, we use the results of the `GetDepartments` query to generate a list of unique department names. The `ValueList()` function converts the values in the query to a comma-delimited list of values. The `VALUESDISPLAY` attribute allows you to provide a delimited list or range of values to display in lieu of the values specified in `VALUES`. This works like the HTML `SELECT` control in that it allows you to display one set of values in the drop-down box while associating them with different values behind the scenes. The `VALUESDISPLAY` attribute may also be set to `Off`. If you want to use a delimiter other than the default comma with the `VALUES` and `VALUESDISPLAY` lists, you can specify it using the `VALUESDELIMITER` attribute.

The final new feature of the `CFGRIDCOLUMN` tag is demonstrated in the tag that displays the new `Exempt` field we created. Setting the `TYPE` attribute to `Boolean` causes the grid to display a checkbox representing the Boolean value in the grid column. Because the grid ID editable, you can check and uncheck the box. If the grid isn't editable, the checkbox is read-only. Figure 10-17 shows the grid with all of the new features visible. Changing any values in the grid and clicking the Submit Changes button updates the database with the edited data. For more information on any of the attributes covered in this example, see Appendix A.

## Sliders

The `CFSLIDER` control has been completely overhauled in ColdFusion 5.0. There are a few important changes to be aware of with the new control. First, both the `IMGSTYLE` and `GROOVECOLOR` attributes have been deprecated and are no longer functional in ColdFusion 5.0. Having these attributes present in your code won't cause an error, as they are simply ignored.

Several new attributes have been added to `CFSLIDER` that affect both the look and feel of the control and its functionality. One of the most significant additions is an attribute named `VERTICAL` that allows you to specify whether the control should slide vertically as opposed to horizontally. The default is `No`. Example 10-27 shows the code to generate a vertical slider control. The slider is shown in Figure 10-18.

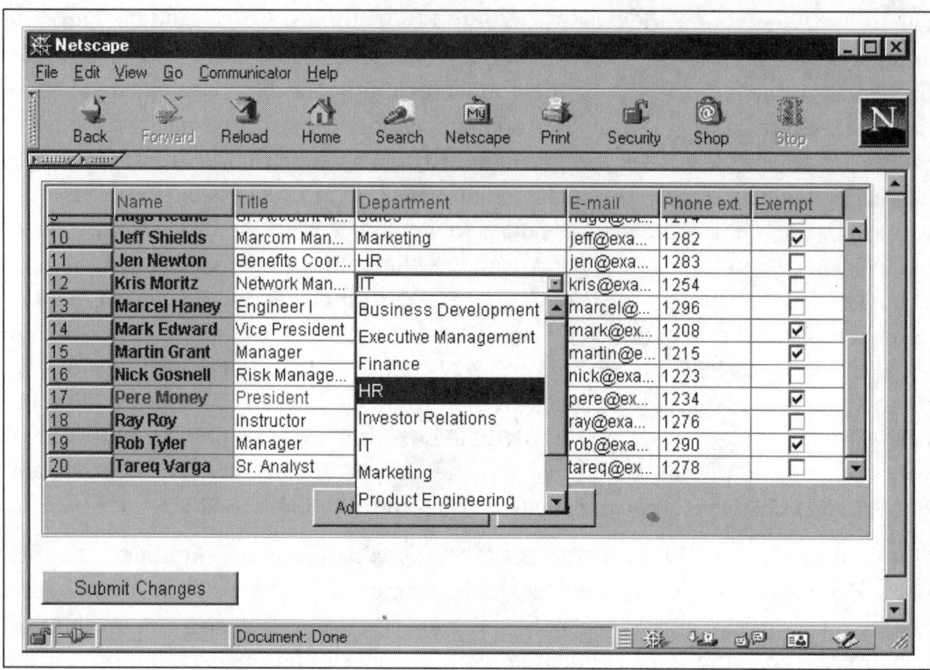


*Figure 10-17. New CFGRIDCOLUMN display controls in ColdFusion 5.0*

*Example 10-27. Creating a Vertical Slider*

```
<CFFORM ACTION="10-27.cfm" METHOD="POST" ENABLECAB="Yes" NAME="MyForm"
        PRESERVEDATA="Yes">
     <CFSLIDER NAME="Slider" LABEL="Current value:  %value%"
               REFRESHLABEL="Yes" RANGE="0,100" SCALE="10"
               VALUE="50" ALIGN="top" HEIGHT="250" WIDTH="115"
               VERTICAL="Yes" LOOKANDFEEL="Motif" TICKMARKMAJOR="Yes"
               TICKMARKMINOR="Yes" TICKMARKLABELS="Yes">
<P>
<INPUT TYPE="submit" NAME="Submit" VALUE="Submit Form">
</CFFORM>
```

In this example, the `VERTICAL` attribute tells ColdFusion to create a vertical slider. The `LOOKANDFEEL` attribute specifies an overall look and feel for the slider control. Options are `Windows` (the default), `Metal`, and `Motif`. For this example, the `CFSLIDER` control is sporting a `Motif` look. Setting `TICKMARKMAJOR` to `Yes` causes a large tick mark to display at every increment value along the axis of the slider control. In this case, the major tick marks are at every 10 places along the slider. The `TICKMARKMINOR` attribute determines whether to display smaller tick marks between the major tick marks along the slider control. For this example, we set it to `Yes`. The final attribute is `TICKMARKLABELS`. It indicates whether to display labels next to each major tick mark. If `Yes`, the numeric value corresponding to the tick mark is displayed. Instead of numeric values, you may choose to display

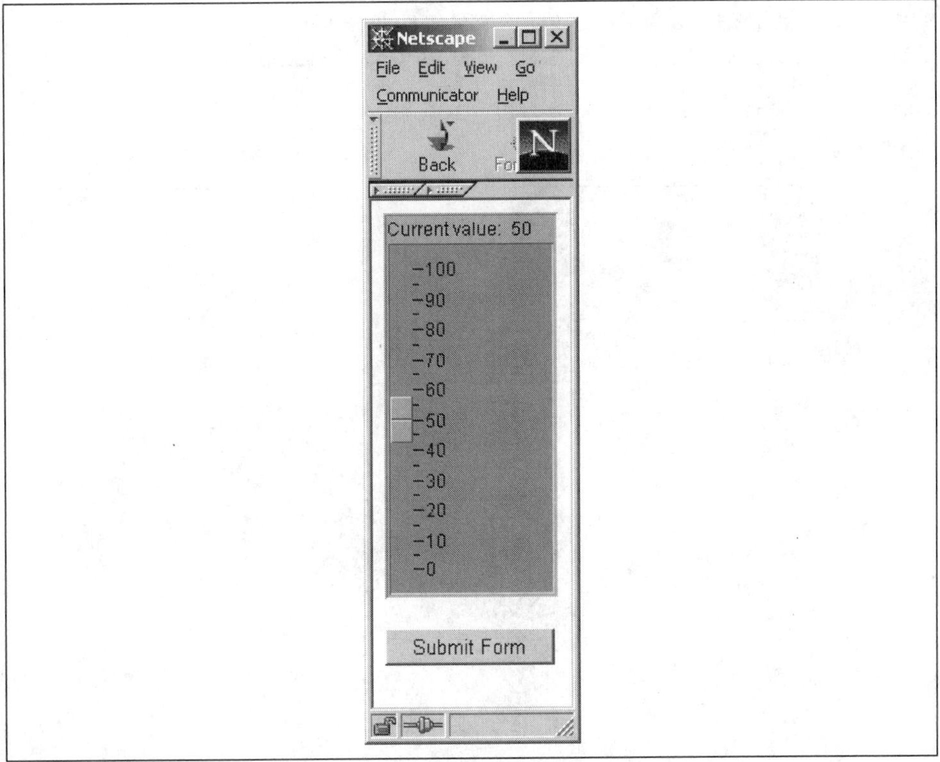


*Figure 10-18. Vertical slider control with major and minor tick marks and tick mark labels.*

string values instead. This is done by specifying a string or comma delimited list of string values, one for each major tick mark between the minimum value and the maximum value for the slider. If you don't provide enough tick mark strings, the CFSLIDER control repeats the last value until enough have been displayed.

Instead of (or in addition to) using the standard tick marks that come standard with the CFSLIDER tag, you can use custom images. This is accomplished with the new TICKMARKIMAGES attribute, which accepts a single URL or comma-delimited list of URLs (absolute or relative) to images you want to use as tick marks for the slider control. Figure 10-19 shows another vertical slider control that uses an image from the ColdFusion Administrator as the tick mark image. The code is shown in Example 10-28.

*Example 10-28. Specifying an Image to Use as a Tick Mark*

```
<CFFORM ACTION="10-28.cfm" METHOD="POST" ENABLECAB="Yes" NAME="MyForm"
        PRESERVEDATA="Yes">
  <CFSLIDER NAME="Slider" LABEL="Current value:  %value%"
            REFRESHLABEL="Yes" RANGE="0,100" SCALE="10" VALUE="50"
            ALIGN="top" HEIGHT="250" WIDTH="115" VERTICAL="Yes"
            LOOKANDFEEL="Metal" TICKMARKLABELS="Yes"
```

*Example 10-28. Specifying an Image to Use as a Tick Mark (continued)*

```
          TICKMARKIMAGES="/cfide/administrator/images/back.gif">
<P>
<INPUT TYPE="submit" NAME="Submit" VALUE="Submit Form">
</CFFORM>
```

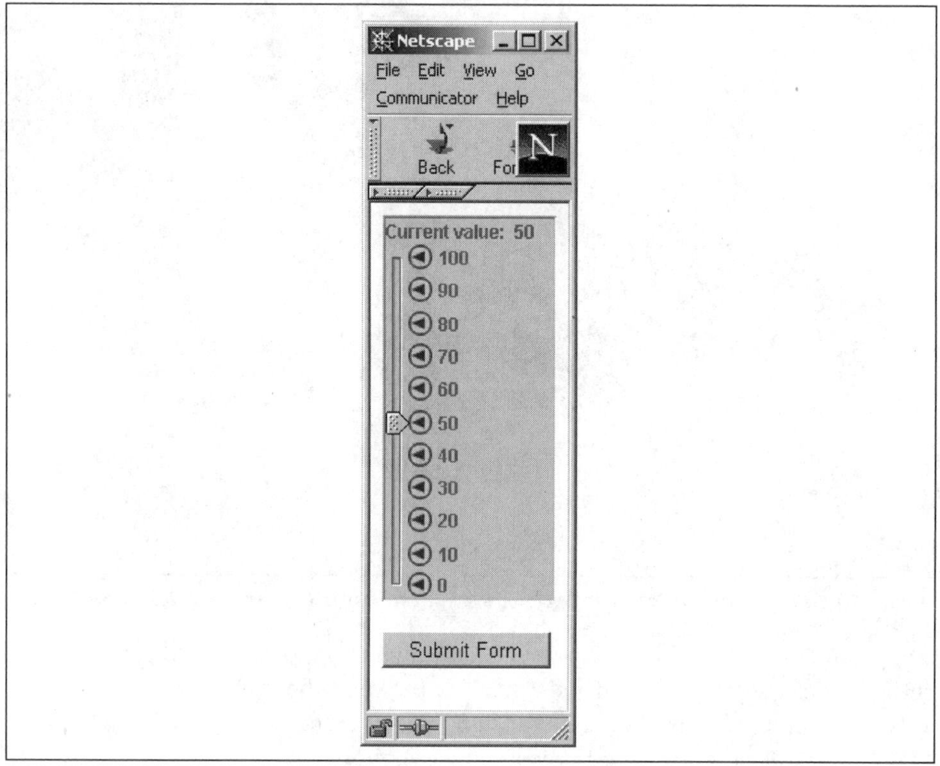


*Figure 10-19. Using an image as a tick mark*

Here you'll notice that we still include the `TICKMARKLABELS` attribute, giving us the numeric value corresponding to each of our custom tick-mark images. The images are specified by providing the URL, to the image in the `TICKMARKIMAGES` attribute. For this example, I chose an image from the ColdFusion Administrator that just happens to line up nicely on the slider control.

## Trees

The `CFTREE` control contains only one new attribute in ColdFusion 5.0, `LOOKANDFEEL`. Just as with the `CFSLIDER` tag, `LOOKANDFEEL` controls the overall appearance of the tree control. Choices are `Windows`, `Motif`, and `Metal`. If no value is specified, ColdFusion first tries `Windows`, then uses the platform default.

Figure 10-20 shows the tree control from Example 10-16 with the addition of the `LOOKANDFEEL` attribute set to `Metal`.

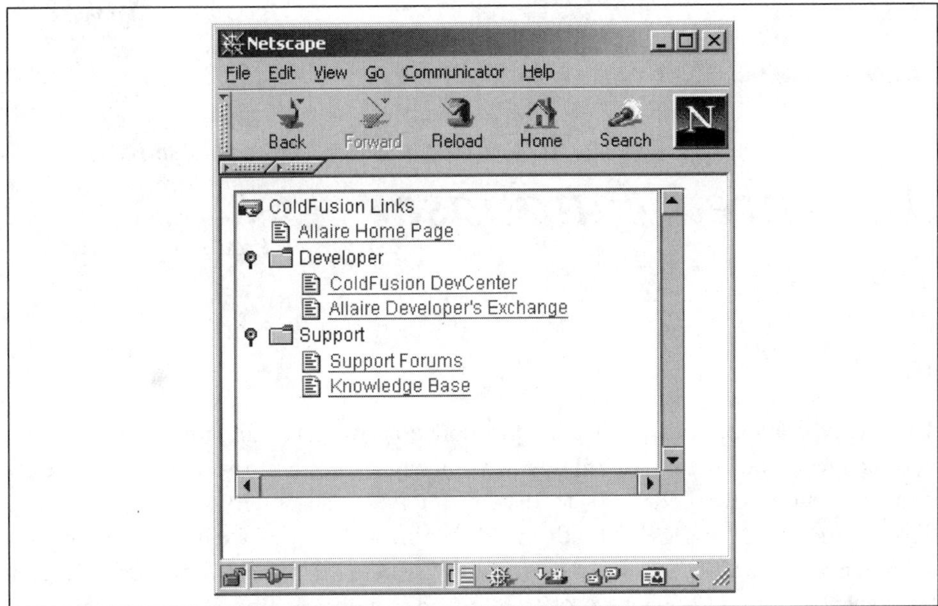


*Figure 10-20. Tree control with a Metal appearance*

# 11

# *Advanced Database Techniques*

*In this chapter:*
- *Display Techniques*
- *Drill-Down Queries*
- *Query Caching*
- *Advanced SQL*
- *CFSQL*
- *Calling Stored Procedures*
- *Transaction Processing*

This chapter attempts to strengthen the concepts we have already covered while adding several advanced techniques to your bag of ColdFusion tricks. These techniques include advanced ways to display query results, query-caching strategies, and advanced SQL topics. The advanced display techniques we'll cover allow you to enhance the way you display dynamically generated data beyond simple HTML table dumps. Taking advantage of ColdFusion's query-caching abilities allows you to shave precious processing time off your frequently run queries. The advanced SQL topics cover the essentials necessary for building dynamic, highly scalable applications.

## *Display Techniques*

This section focuses on techniques you can use to enhance the display of dynamic data. Some of these techniques include displaying limited record sets, creating dynamic HTML tables with alternating row colors, working with various multi-column output displays, and browsing records with next/previous. You will also learn several methods for controlling whitespace in dynamic pages in order to optimize page-download times.

### *Flushing Page Output*

A complaint often heard regarding web applications is the amount of time it takes to return data to a user once a page is requested, be it by a form submission or a URL the user clicks on. Often this is due to the large amount of data a particular operation must sift through and return to the user. In situations such as this, it is often desirable to present the user with a "Please Wait" message while their request processes or to provide incremental amounts of data as results from a large query result set become available. ColdFusion lets you handle these tasks with a new tag introduced in Version 5.0 called CFFLUSH. The CFFLUSH tag provides a means to send incremental amounts of data from your ColdFusion server to a user's browser as they become available.

The first time a CFFLUSH tag is encountered on a page, it sends all the HTTP headers for the request along with any generated content up to the position in the template where the tag is encountered. Successive CFFLUSH tags return any content generated since the previous flush. Because of this, CFFLUSH is usually used within loops or output queries to send results back to the browser in incremental chunks. The following example shows the CFFLUSH tag used to incrementally return the results of a database query:

```
<H1>Outputting Query Results</H1>
Please be patient as this may take a few moments...
<P>
<!--- flush the output up to this point --->
<CFFLUSH>

<CFQUERY NAME="GetEmployees" DATASOURCE="ProgrammingCF">
SELECT *
FROM EmployeeDirectory
</CFQUERY>

<CFSET Stall=0>
<CFLOOP QUERY="GetEmployees">
  <!--- flush the rest of the output as it is generated in chunks of 100
        bytes --->
  <CFFLUSH INTERVAL="100">
  <!--- use this loop to exaggerate the processing time --->
  <CFLOOP INDEX="i" FROM="1" TO="3500">
    <CFSET Stall = Stall+1>
  </CFLOOP>

  <CFOUTPUT>
  #Name#<BR>
  </CFOUTPUT>
</CFLOOP>
```

If you run this example, you'll notice all of the content before the first CFFLUSH tag is output almost immediately. After that, the next CFFLUSH tag is used in a loop and specifies that the rest of the content generated by the page should be sent to the browser in chunks of 100 bytes. This is achieved by setting the INTERVAL attribute of CFFLUSH to 100. The code in the example contains an index loop that essentially ties up processing time for 3,500 iterations between the output of each name returned by the query. This results in an artificially inflated amount of time required to output the query results, which is perfect to demonstrate how the CFFLUSH tag incrementally sends data back to the browser in chunks as it becomes available. This is done because the **EmployeeDirectory** table doesn't contain enough records to effectively demonstrate the **CFFLUSH** tag.

Once a **CFFLUSH** tag has been used in a template, you can't use any other CFML tags that write to the HTTP header; doing so causes ColdFusion to throw an error because the header has already been sent to the browser. These tags include **CFCONTENT**, **CFCOOKIE**, **CFFORM**, **CFHEADER**, **CFHTMLHEAD**, and **CFCONTENT**. In addition, attempting to set a variable in the cookie scope with the **CFSET** tag results in an error. This is because cookies are passed from the server to the browser in the HTTP header.

## *Displaying Limited Record Sets*

You may decide that for a given application, it's more effective not to display the contents of an entire record set. For these applications, you can use two additional optional attributes of the **CFOUTPUT** tag to display a subset of the full record set returned by a query:

STARTROW
: Specifies what query row to begin outputting from

MAXROWS
: Specifies the maximum number of rows to output

Example 11-1 uses the **STARTROW** and **MAXROWS** attributes of the **CFOUTPUT** tag to output a subset of a full record set.

*Example 11-1. Displaying a Limited Record Set Using CFOUTPUT*

```
<CFQUERY NAME="GetEmployeeInfo" DATASOURCE="ProgrammingCF">
         SELECT Name, Title, Department, Email, PhoneExt
         FROM EmployeeDirectory
</CFQUERY>

<!--- display the total number of records returned by the query --->
<H2>Displaying a Limited Record Set</H2>
<CFOUTPUT>
<H3>#GetEmployeeInfo.RecordCount# total records - Displaying records 6-10</H3>
</CFOUTPUT>

<!--- output rows 6-10 of the query result set --->
<TABLE CELLPADDING="3" CELLSPACING="0">
<TR BGCOLOR="#888888">
  <TH>Record Number</TH>
  <TH>Name</TH>
  <TH>Title</TH>
  <TH>Department</TH>
  <TH>E-mail</TH>
  <TH>Phone Extension</TH>
</TR>
```

*Example 11-1. Displaying a Limited Record Set Using CFOUTPUT (continued)*

```
<CFOUTPUT QUERY="GetEmployeeInfo" STARTROW="6" MAXROWS="5">
<TR BGCOLOR="##C0C0C0">
  <TD>#CurrentRow#</TD>
  <TD>#Name#</TD>
  <TD>#Title#</TD>
  <TD>#Department#</TD>
  <TD><A HREF="Mailto:#Email#">#Email#</A></TD>
  <TD>#PhoneExt#</TD>
</TR>
</CFOUTPUT>
</TABLE>
```

In Example 11-1, a query is performed against the `EmployeeDirectory` table. Setting the `STARTROW` attribute to 6 and the `MAXROWS` attribute to 5 results in records 6 to 10 of the query result set getting output to the browser.

## *Alternating Row Color in HTML Tables*

Another popular way to display tabular data is to alternate the background color of the rows being displayed. The technique is easy to implement and offers an attractive way to display tabular data, so that it stands out. Example 11-2 generates an HTML table of alternating row color from a database query. The results can be seen in Figure 11-1.

*Example 11-2. Alternating Row Color in HTML Tables*

```
<CFQUERY NAME="GetEmployeeInfo" DATASOURCE="ProgrammingCF">
         SELECT Name, Title, Department, Email, PhoneExt
         FROM EmployeeDirectory
</CFQUERY>

<TABLE CELLPADDING="3" CELLSPACING="0">
<TR BGCOLOR="#888888">
   <TH>Name</TH>
   <TH>Title</TH>
   <TH>Department</TH>
   <TH>E-mail</TH>
   <TH>Phone Extension</TH>
</TR>

<CFOUTPUT QUERY="GetEmployeeInfo">
<TR BGCOLOR="###IIF(GetEmployeeInfo.currentrow MOD 2, DE('E6E6E6'),
DE('C0C0C0'))#">
   <TD>#Name#</TD>
   <TD>#Title#</TD>
   <TD>#Department#</TD>
   <TD><A HREF="Mailto:#Email#">#Email#</A></TD>
   <TD>#PhoneExt#</TD>
</TR>
```

*Example 11-2. Alternating Row Color in HTML Tables (continued)*

```
</CFOUTPUT>
</TABLE>
```

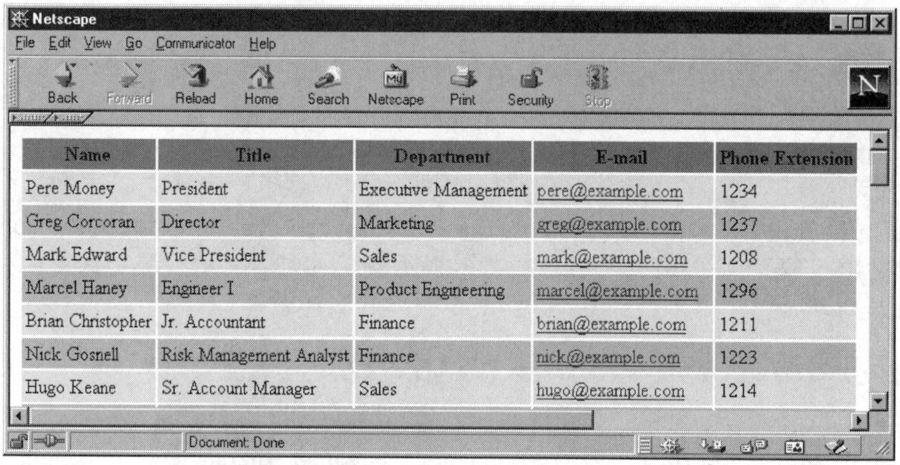

| Name | Title | Department | E-mail | Phone Extension |
|---|---|---|---|---|
| Pere Money | President | Executive Management | pere@example.com | 1234 |
| Greg Corcoran | Director | Marketing | greg@example.com | 1237 |
| Mark Edward | Vice President | Sales | mark@example.com | 1208 |
| Marcel Haney | Engineer I | Product Engineering | marcel@example.com | 1296 |
| Brian Christopher | Jr. Accountant | Finance | brian@example.com | 1211 |
| Nick Gosnell | Risk Management Analyst | Finance | nick@example.com | 1223 |
| Hugo Keane | Sr. Account Manager | Sales | hugo@example.com | 1214 |

*Figure 11-1. A dynamically generated table with alternating row colors*

We alternate the row color by using the `IIF()` and `DE()` functions along with the `MOD` operator to determine whether or not the row number for the current record is odd or even. Depending on the outcome of the evaluation, one color or the other is used as the background color for the current row. Because hex color codes are supposed to begin with a pound sign (#), we have to create an escape sequence before we call the `IIF()` function. This is done by doubling up on the first pound sign.

## Multicolumn Output

Another popular formatting technique involves outputting a query result set in more than one column, similar to how a newspaper story is printed. There are several techniques you can use to achieve multicolumn output. Two of the more popular methods are covered in the following sections.

### *Sorting multicolumn output from left to right*

One technique for outputting a result set in more than one column involves sorting the results from left to right, then top to bottom. You can see the technique for sorting multicolumn output from left to right in Example 11-3.

*Example 11-3. Sorting Multicolumn Output from Left to Right*

```
<!--- retrieve a list of employee names from the employeedirectory table --->
<CFQUERY NAME="GetEmployeeInfo" DATASOURCE="ProgrammingCF">
```

*Example 11-3. Sorting Multicolumn Output from Left to Right (continued)*

```
        SELECT Name
        FROM EmployeeDirectory
        ORDER BY Name
</CFQUERY>

<H2>Two column output sorted left to right</H2>
<!--- initialize the STARTNEWROW variable as True --->
<CFSET StartNewRow = True>

<!--- The CFPROCESSING tag suppresses extra whitespace as much as possible.
      To remove the max amount of whitespace, remove these comments as
      well. --->
<TABLE>
<CFPROCESSINGDIRECTIVE SUPPRESSWHITESPACE="Yes">
<CFOUTPUT QUERY="GetEmployeeInfo">
<!--- Add a TR if we are supposed to start a new row.  Otherwise, continue
      adding TDs --->
<CFIF StartNewRow IS True><TR></CFIF>
  <TD>#Name#</TD>
<!--- set STARTNEWROW to the opposite of its currnet True/False value --->
<CFSET StartNewRow = NOT(StartNewRow)>
<!--- if STARTNEWROW is True, add a /TR to close the row --->
<CFIF StartNewRow IS True>
  </TR>
</CFIF>
</CFOUTPUT>
</CFPROCESSINGDIRECTIVE>
</TABLE>
```

After the query is performed, a variable called `StartNewRow` is initialized and set to `True`. `CFPROCESSINGDIRECTIVE` helps limit the amount of whitespace created by ColdFusion during the generation of the table. Using this tag helps reduce the overall size of the file generated by ColdFusion and sent to the browser. The `CFOUTPUT` tag loops over the result set specified in the `QUERY` attribute. If the value of `StartNewRow` is still `True`, a `<TR>` tag is dynamically inserted, beginning a new row in the table. Next, we output an employee name in a table cell using `<TD>#Name#</TD>`. The value of `StartNewRow` is then set to the opposite of its current value (either `False` or `True`). A `CFIF` statement determines the value of `StartNewRow`. If `StartNewRow` evaluates `True`, a `</TR>` tag is dynamically inserted into the table, ending the current row. If `StartNewRow` is `False`, another `<TD>#Name#</TD>` is inserted into the table, adding another employee name to the current row. This process continues until there are no more rows of data in the result set for the `CFOUTPUT` tag to loop over. The two-column output generated by this example is shown in Figure 11-2.

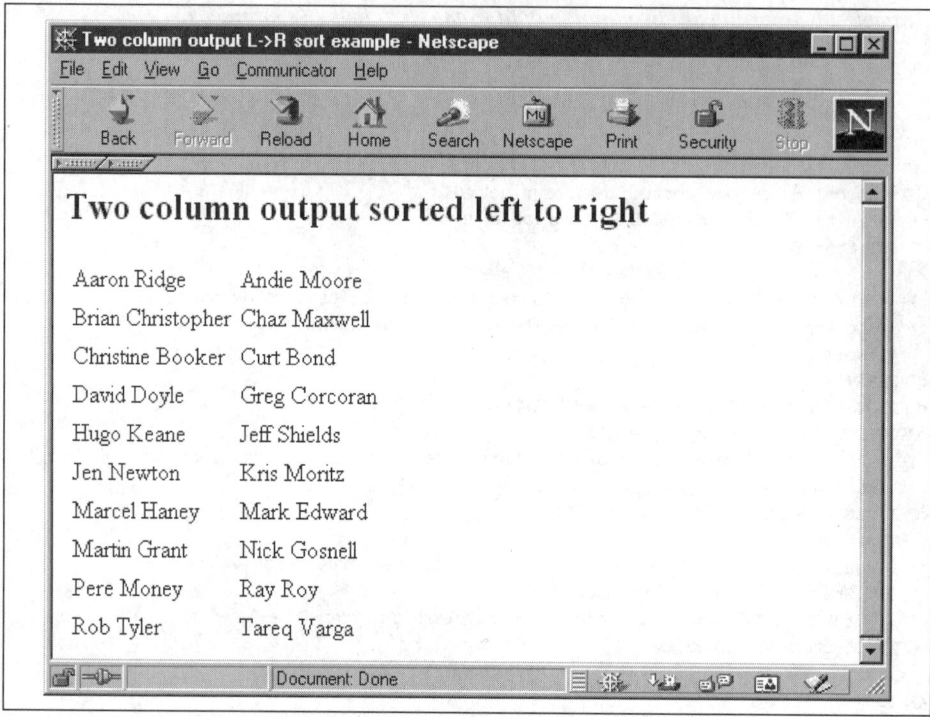


*Figure 11-2. Multicolumn result set display sorted left to right*

### *Sorting multicolumn output from top to bottom*

It is also possible to sort multicolumn output from top to bottom, then left to right, as opposed to the sequence in the previous section. In this example, we also specify the number of columns to display on the page. Example 11-4 shows how to sort multicolumn output from top to bottom.

*Example 11-4. Sorting Multicolumn Output from Top to Bottom*

```
<!--- Thanks to Sean Clairmont of Team Allaire for helping to refine the
      original code --->
<!--- query the employeedirectory table for a list of employee names --->
<CFQUERY NAME="GetEmployeeInfo" DATASOURCE="ProgrammingCF">
         SELECT Name,Email
         FROM EmployeeDirectory
         ORDER BY Name
</CFQUERY>

<!--- Columns sets the total number of output columns. --->
<CFSET Columns = 3>
<CFSET CurrentColumn = 0>
<CFSET RowCompleted = 0>
<!--- Set the total number of rows equal to the number of records divided by
      the number of columns. --->
<CFSET Rows=Int(GetEmployeeInfo.RecordCount/Columns)>
```

*Example 11-4. Sorting Multicolumn Output from Top to Bottom (continued)*

```
<!--- Set a variable to hold the number of columns with extra records --->
<CFSET OddColumns = GetEmployeeInfo.RecordCount MOD Columns>
<!--- if there are columns with extra records, increase the number of rows by
      one --->
<CFIF OddColumns NEQ 0>
   <CFSET Rows = IncrementValue(Rows)>
</CFIF>
<CFSET Increment = IncrementValue(Int(GetEmployeeInfo.RecordCount/Columns))>

<H2>Multicolumn Query Output Sorted Top to Bottom</H2>

<TABLE BORDER=0>
<CFPROCESSINGDIRECTIVE SUPPRESSWHITESPACE="Yes">
<!--- create a loop that iterates a number of times equal to the total number
      of output rows needed --->
<CFLOOP FROM="1" TO="#rows#" INDEX="Row">
   <CFSET LeftOverIncrement = 0>
   <TR>
   <!--- create an inner loop for handling each column --->
   <CFLOOP INDEX="Column" FROM="1" TO="#Columns#">
     <CFIF Column GT (OddColumns + 1) >
       <CFSET LeftOverIncrement = IncrementValue(LeftOverIncrement)>
     </CFIF>
     <!--- Set the current row and column --->
         <CFSET CurrentRow = (Row + (Increment * (CurrentColumn) )  -
LeftOverIncrement) >
         <CFSET CurrentColumn = IIf(CurrentColumn is (columns - 1),0
,IncrementValue(CurrentColumn))>
     <!--- Output the current row --->
     <CFOUTPUT>
     <TD><CFIF (Row lt Increment or OddColumns gt 0) AND (CurrentRow LTE
GetEmployeeInfo.Recordcount)>
                              #GetEmployeeInfo.name[CurrentRow]#
         <CFELSE>
             
                </CFIF></TD>
     </CFOUTPUT>

                <CFIF Row is Increment>
                        <CFSET RowCompleted = IncrementValue(RowCompleted)>
                </CFIF>
                <CFIF RowCompleted is OddColumns>
                        <CFSET OddColumns = 0>
                </CFIF>
   </CFLOOP>
   </TR>
</CFLOOP>
</CFPROCESSINGDIRECTIVE>
</TABLE>
```

Before the individual columns are created and populated with data, a number of variables are initialized. You specify the number of columns to display the result set using the `Columns` variable. You may display the result set using any number of columns you desire, up to the total number of records returned. If you specify a number greater than the total number of records returned by the query, ColdFusion throws an exception. In Example 11-4, we display the result set in three columns.

We set the next variable, `CurrentColumn`, to specify a starting point for our output. `RowCompleted` is created and assigned an initial value of 0. We'll get back to the purpose for this variable in a moment. `Rows` is set to the total number of rows containing a record for each column. This is calculated by taking the total number of records and dividing it by the number of columns we want to use to display the output. The next variable we initialize is `OddColumns`. If a remainder is present when we calculate `Rows`, we use `OddColumns` to store the value. The value is important in determining how many cells need to be populated with data in the last row of the table. The final variable we initialize is `Increment`. `Increment` is used in the calculation that determines the index position of the next record to be output. It's initial value is set by adding 1 to the integer value of the total number of records divided by the number of columns to be output.

Once all of the variables have been initialized, an HTML table is started. A loop generates the appropriate number of rows for the table based on the value of the `Rows` variable. A second loop iterates over each column in the current row and populates it with the appropriate value from the query. After each table cell is built, the index position in the `Rows` loop is compared to the `Increment` value. If they are the same, the value of the `RowCompleted` variable is incremented by 1. This only happens in the last row of data generated for the table. Next, the value of `RowCompleted` is compared to the value of `OddColumns`. If they are the same, we set the value of `OddColumns` to 0. When the number of records is evenly divisible by the number of desired columns, `OddColumns` is always 0. Otherwise, it is 0 only for odd cells within the last row.

## *Next/Previous Record Browsing*

One question of great concern to most CF developers is how to implement next/previous record browsing in ColdFusion. When building web applications with ColdFusion, you will inevitably create an application that queries a database and returns a record set with too many rows to display in a single browser window. To display thousands of rows of data in the browser at once is an unrealistic task, for a number of reasons. Sending thousands of rows of data to the browser eats up a lot of bandwidth. And no one likes to sit around waiting for a browser to download and render a 1-MB web page when the probability of the end user reading through thousands of rows of data is slim. So, what are our options? The solution is to break up the record sets returned to the browser into manageable chunks that allow the user to browse through the query results one chunk at a time. This type of interface is known as next/previous record browsing.

Implementing next/previous record browsing in ColdFusion might seem tricky at first glance. However, thanks to ColdFusion's query caching and the partial record set display capabilities we just covered, implementing a next/previous solution is a lot simpler than you might think.

The *NextPrevious.cfm* template in Example 11-5 shows how to build a next/previous record browser that can easily be modified to work with any query. The larger the query, the more benefit to this type of interface.

*Example 11-5. Creating a Next/Previous Record Browser*

```
<!--- StartRow is the default starting row for the output.
      DisplayRows determines how many records to display at a time --->
<CFPARAM NAME="StartRow" DEFAULT="1">
<CFPARAM NAME="DisplayRows" DEFAULT="4">

<!--- query the EmployeeDirectory table. Cache the result set for 15
      minutes. --->
<CFQUERY NAME="GetEmployeeInfo" DATASOURCE="ProgrammingCF"
         CACHEDWITHIN="#CreateTimeSpan(0,0,15,0)#">
         SELECT Name,  Title, Department, Email, PhoneExt
         FROM EmployeeDirectory
</CFQUERY>

<!--- Set a variable to hold the record number of the last
      record to output on the current page. --->
<CFSET ToRow = StartRow + (DisplayRows - 1)>
<CFIF ToRow GT GetEmployeeInfo.RecordCount>
    <CFSET ToRow = GetEmployeeInfo.RecordCount>
</CFIF>

<HTML>
<HEAD>
    <TITLE>Next/Previous Record Browsing</TITLE>
</HEAD>

<BODY>

<!--- Output the range of records displayed on the page as well as the total
      number of records in the result set --->
<CFOUTPUT>
<H4>Displaying records #StartRow# - #ToRow# from the
#GetEmployeeInfo.RecordCount# total records in the database.</H4>
</CFOUTPUT>

<!--- create the header for the table --->
<TABLE CELLPADDING="3" CELLSPACING="0">
<TR BGCOLOR="#888888">
  <TH>Name</TH>
  <TH>Title</TH>
```

*Example 11-5. Creating a Next/Previous Record Browser (continued)*

```
  <TH>Department</TH>
  <TH>E-mail</TH>
  <TH>Phone Extension</TH>
</TR>
<!--- dynamically create the rest of the table and output the number of
      records specified in the DisplayRows variable --->
<CFOUTPUT QUERY="GetEmployeeInfo" STARTROW="#StartRow#"
          MAXROWS="#DisplayRows#">
<TR BGCOLOR="##C0C0C0">
  <TD>#Name#</TD>
  <TD>#Title#</TD>
  <TD>#Department#</TD>
  <TD><A HREF="Mailto:#Email#">#Email#</A></TD>
  <TD>#PhoneExt#</TD>
</TR>
</CFOUTPUT>
</TABLE>

<!--- update the values for the next and previous rows to be returned --->
<CFSET Next = StartRow + DisplayRows>
<CFSET Previous = StartRow - DisplayRows>

<!--- Create a previous records link if the records being displayed aren't the
      first set --->
<CFOUTPUT>
<CFIF Previous GTE 1>
   <A HREF="NextPrevious.cfm?StartRow=#Previous#"><B>Previous #DisplayRows#
      Records</B></A>
<CFELSE>
Previous Records
</CFIF>

<B>|</B>

<!--- Create a next records link if there are more records in the record set
      that haven't yet been displayed. --->
<CFIF Next LTE GetEmployeeInfo.RecordCount>
    <A HREF="NextPrevious.cfm?StartRow=#Next#"><B>Next
    <CFIF (GetEmployeeInfo.RecordCount - Next) LT DisplayRows>
      #Evaluate((GetEmployeeInfo.RecordCount - Next)+1)#
    <CFELSE>
      #DisplayRows#
    </CFIF>  Records</B></A>
<CFELSE>
Next Records
</CFIF>
</CFOUTPUT>

</BODY>
</HTML>
```

The first thing Example 11-5 does is initialize two variables. `StartRow` specifies the starting row for the record set being displayed. The default value is set to `1`. `DisplayRows` specifies the number of rows of data to display per page. We set `DisplayRows` to `4`. Next, a query is run to retrieve all the records from the `EmployeeDirectory` table. The query is then cached for 15 minutes using the `CACHEDWITHIN` attribute of the `CFQUERY` tag. If you feel your users will use the record browser for more or less than 15 minutes on average, feel free to change this value.

Note that every cached query in ColdFusion takes up some of the server's memory. Depending on the amount of RAM on your server and the number of cached queries you allow (configurable in the ColdFusion Administrator), you may run into memory issues when dealing with cached queries. If you plan to use cached queries extensively, you should add additional RAM to your server so it can handle the anticipated load.

Next we set a variable called `ToRow` to hold the record number of the last record to be output on the current page. If `ToRow` is greater than the total number of records in the result set, it is set equal to the total number of records.

The next part of the template uses the `CFOUTPUT` tag to output the first chunk of records to the browser. The `STARTROW` and `MAXROWS` attributes determine the starting row and number of rows to output, respectively. These values are dynamically populated by the `StartRow` and `DisplayRows` variables we set in the beginning of the template. The results are shown in Figure 11-3. If you turn on debugging in the ColdFusion Administrator, you should be able to see that the query is being cached.

The final section of Example 11-5 calculates the starting and previous row number for the next or previous batch of records to output. Depending on how many records have already been displayed, appropriate `Next` and `Previous` links are created for the user to click on to retrieve the next or previous set of records.* Clicking on one of the `Next` or `Previous` links causes the template to call itself and pass the starting row number for the next/previous chunk of records as a URL variable. When the template calls itself, instead of performing a fresh query and potentially wasting a lot of time waiting for the database to generate and return a record set, the template uses the cached query and returns the next set of records almost instantaneously! If it weren't for the cached query, you would have to query the database for the full record set every time you clicked on a `Next` or `Previous` link. It doesn't take much to imagine the enormous amount of wasted overhead just to display a few records at a time.

* This example can easily be modified to use HTML Form buttons. If you prefer to use buttons instead of links, simply pass the `StartRow` value as a hidden form field and have the form post to itself.

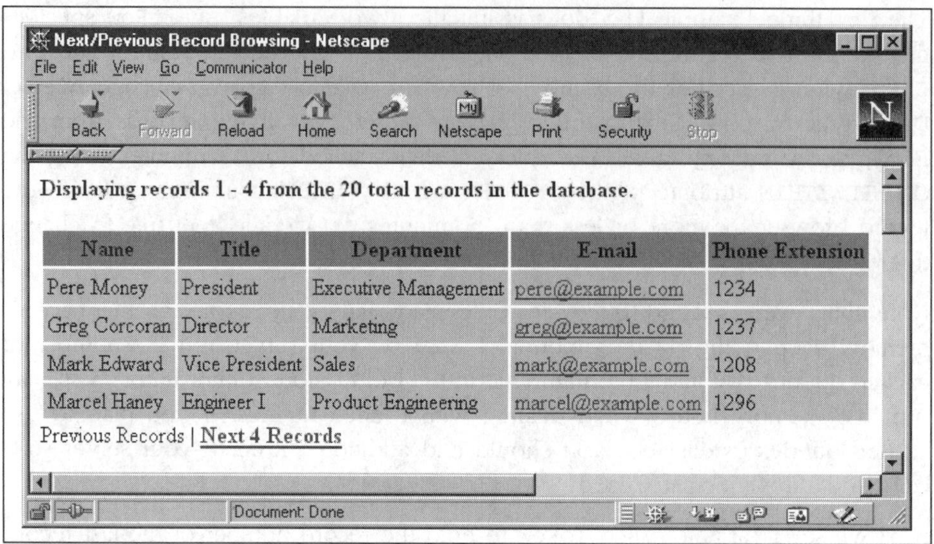


*Figure 11-3. Implementing a next/previous record browser*

## Controlling Whitespace

If you have ever looked at the HTML generated by a ColdFusion template (by viewing the source within your web browser), you may have noticed a lot of extraneous whitespace. Though whitespace in the HTML won't affect the display of your page, it can affect the overall file size of the page that is sent to the browser. File size can have a considerable impact on the time it takes for a page generated by ColdFusion to download.

When a CFML template is requested by a web browser, the web server that fulfills the request first passes the CFML template to the ColdFusion Application Server. Before the ColdFusion Application Server can process the instructions in the CFML template, the language processor within the application server must parse the CFML template into a special "language" called p-code that can be executed by the application server. It is during the conversion of CFML and HTML code into p-code that the extraneous whitespace is generated. The specifics of how this all happens aren't important for our purposes. What is important is realizing that there are several techniques you can use to suppress whitespace in the pages generated by your ColdFusion application.

### *Optimizing output*

The `CFSETTING` tag is a sort of "catch-all" tag when it comes to optimizing output. There are three different functions currently handled by the tag: controlling whitespace, enabling/disabling the display of debug information, and overriding

ColdFusion's default error and exception-handling mechanism. To accomplish these tasks, the `CFSETTING` tag has three attributes:

```
<CFSETTING ENABLECFOUTPUTONLY="yes/no"
           SHOWDEBUGOUTPUT="yes/no"
           CATCHEXCEPTIONSBYPATTERN="yes/no>
```

The first attribute, `ENABLECFOUTPUTONLY`, suppresses all HTML output, including whitespace, within a `CFSETTING` block. When `ENABLECFOUTPUTONLY` is set to `Yes`, only HTML code generated within a `CFOUTPUT` block is output to the browser:

```
<CFSETTING ENABLECFOUTPUTONLY="Yes">




<CFOUTPUT>
You should be able to see this...
</CFOUTPUT>
But not this...
<CFSETTING ENABLECFOUTPUTONLY="No">
Of course you can see this!
```

When the `ENABLECFOUTPUTONLY` attribute is used, `CFSETTING` tags must occur in matched pairs, where the first tag turns on the output suppression (`Yes`) and the second tag turns it off (`No`). `CFSETTING` tags may be nested any number of levels as long as there are always matching tag pairs.

The second attribute you can use with the `CFSETTING` tag is `SHOWDEBUGOUTPUT`. This optional attribute takes a `Yes/No` value that indicates whether to suppress debugging information normally output to ColdFusion templates when debugging is turned on in the ColdFusion Administrator. The default value for `SHOWDEBUGOUTPUT` is `Yes`. You don't need to use paired `CFSETTING` tags with the `SHOWDEBUGOUTPUT` attribute unless you are using it in combination with an `ENABLECFOUTPUTONLY` attribute.

The final attribute, `CATCHEXCEPTIONSBYPATTERN`, is also optional. This attribute takes a `Yes/No` value and indicates whether to override structured exception handling. This attribute was introduced in ColdFusion 4.5 to handle incompatibility issues arising from changes to ColdFusion's structured exception handling in Version 4.5. In Version 4.0.x of ColdFusion, exceptions caught with `CFTRY` and `CFCATCH` were handled by the first `CFCATCH` block capable of dealing with the type of exception generated. In ColdFusion 4.5, exceptions are handled by the `CFCATCH` block that is best able to deal with the exception. The default value is `No`. Structured exception handling is discussed in Chapter 9. You don't need to use paired `CFSETTING` tags with the `CATCHEXCEPTIONBYPATTERN` attribute unless it is used in combination with an `ENABLECFOUTPUTONLY` attribute.

### *Suppressing output*

The CFSILENT tag suppresses all output produced between CFSILENT tag pairs. CFSILENT can suppress generated whitespace in *Application.cfm* templates as well as in instances where your template does a lot of looping but doesn't produce any output. CFSILENT is similar to the CFSETTING tag except that it doesn't allow any content to be generated. The following code shows how the tag can be used with a typical loop to suppress whitespace:

```
<CFSILENT>
<CFLOOP INDEX="i" FROM="1" TO="1000">
  <CFSET i = i+1>
</CFLOOP>
</CFSILENT>

<CFOUTPUT>
#i#
</CFOUTPUT>
```

If you execute this template and view the source in your web browser, notice that the number 1001 appears at the top of the page. If you remove the CFSILENT tags, rerun the template, and view the source again, notice that an awful lot of whitespace appears at the top of the page, resulting in the need to scroll considerably to reach the number 1001 in the source code.

Although it may appear to make more sense to use the CFSETTING tag instead of CFSILENT, the CFSILENT tag is better at eliminating whitespace than CFSETTING and should be used when output generation isn't a factor.

### *Suppressing whitespace*

The CFPROCESSINGDIRECTIVE tag specifies a p-code compiler processing option to suppress all whitespace produced by the ColdFusion server (spaces, tabs, carriage returns, and linefeeds) within an executing CFML template. CFPROCESSINGDIRECTIVE tags must always occur in matched pairs and may be nested. CFPROCESSINGDIRECTIVE settings don't apply to templates called via CFINCLUDE, CFMODULE, or as custom tags. The syntax for using the CFPROCESSINGDIRECTIVE tag is as follows:

```
<CFPROCESSINGDIRECTIVE SUPPRESSWHITESPACE="yes/no">
CFML...
</CFPROCESSINGDIRECTIVE>
```

The SUPPRESSWHITESPACE attribute is required and indicates whether ColdFusion should suppress all whitespace between CFPROCESSINGDIRECTIVE tag pairs. The ColdFusion Administrator contains an option in the Settings section that allows you to enable this suppression of whitespace by default. If this option is enabled, it may be overridden by setting a `CFPROCESSINGDIRECTIVE` tag pair to `No` within a CFML template.

# *Drill-Down Queries*

A drill-down query is one that starts by retrieving and displaying a relatively broad or general result set. Then, hyperlinks from one or more columns in the result set are used to call another template that performs a query based on URL parameters passed by the hyperlinks. This process is designed to narrow the number of records returned until a desired level of granularity is achieved, hence the name drill-down query.

For drill-down queries, you usually need two templates, but it is possible to use as many as you want to achieve the level of granularity you need. In a two-template drill-down application, the first template queries a data source and displays a summary (usually just a few fields) of every record in the data source meeting the user's criteria. Hyperlinks from some of the fields in these results pass the primary key values of records to the second template. The second template then performs a query using the primary key value passed in via URL in the `WHERE` clause of the `SELECT` statement. The results (usually the full record) are then output to the browser. Example 11-6 demonstrates how a two-template drill-down query works by querying the `EmployeeDirectory` table and generating an HTML table containing the `Name`, `Title`, and `Department` of each employee.

*Example 11-6. Initial Screen Listing Partial Information About Each Record*

```
<!--- retrieve a list of all employees in the EmployeeDirectory table --->
<CFQUERY NAME="GetEmployeeList" DATASOURCE="ProgrammingCF">
         SELECT ID, Name, Title, Department
         FROM EmployeeDirectory
</CFQUERY>

<HTML>
<HEAD>
    <TITLE>Drilldown Example</TITLE>
</HEAD>

<BODY>

<H2>Drilldown Query Example</H2>
<B>Click on an employee's name to retrieve the full employee record as well
as a list of all incentive awards granted to the employee<B>
<P>
<TABLE CELLPADDING="3" CELLSPACING="0">
<TR BGCOLOR="#888888">
  <TH>Name</TH>
  <TH>Title</TH>
  <TH>Department</TH>
```

*Example 11-6. Initial Screen Listing Partial Information About Each Record (continued)*

```
</TR>

<!--- dynamically build an HTML table containing the list of employees from
      the GetEmployeeList query.  Create a hyperlink for the Name field
      that points to a template called DrillDown.cfm and pass the value
      of the ID field as a query parameter, identifying the record --->
<CFOUTPUT QUERY="GetEmployeeList">
<TR BGCOLOR="##C0C0C0">
  <TD><A HREF="Drilldown.cfm?ID=#ID#">#Name#</A></TD>
  <TD>#Title#</TD>
  <TD>#Department#</TD>
</TR>
</CFOUTPUT>
</TABLE>

</BODY>
</HTML>
```

Example 11-6 queries the `EmployeeDirectory` table and returns a result set containing the `Name`, `Title`, and `Department` of every employee in the table. The result set dynamically generates an HTML table with a row for each record. Each name is displayed as a hyperlink that points to a template called *Drilldown.cfm* (shown in Example 11-7). Clicking on any one of the names calls the *Drilldown.cfm* template and passes the `ID` value (the primary key) associated with the name as a URL parameter so that the *Drilldown.cfm* template knows which record to drill down on. The initial results screen is shown in Figure 11-4.

When the *Drilldown.cfm* template in Example 11-7 is called, the first thing it does is execute a query to retrieve all the fields in the record whose `ID` matches the value specified by the `URL.ID` parameter. These values can also have been passed by form field, but for our example we'll do it this way. Just for fun, a second query is made to the `IncentiveAwards` table to retrieve any awards the employee has been granted.

*Example 11-7. Drill-Down Screen for Displaying Detail Information*

```
<!--- retrieve the full record of the employee whose ID was passed in
      as a URL parameter. --->
<CFQUERY NAME="GetEmployeeRecord" DATASOURCE="ProgrammingCF">
         SELECT Name, Title, Department, Email, PhoneExt, Salary
         FROM EmployeeDirectory
         WHERE ID = #URL.ID#
</CFQUERY>

<!--- query the IncentiveAwards table and retrieve all records for
      for the ID passed in as a URL parameter.  This query can return
      0 or more records --->
<CFQUERY NAME="GetIncentiveAwards" DATASOURCE="ProgrammingCF">
         SELECT DateAwarded, Category, Amount
```

*Example 11-7. Drill-Down Screen for Displaying Detail Information (continued)*

```
        FROM IncentiveAwards
        WHERE ID = #URL.ID#
</CFQUERY>

<HTML>
<HEAD>
     <TITLE>Drilldown Example</TITLE>
</HEAD>

<BODY>

<H2>Employee Profile</H2>

<TABLE CELLPADDING="3" CELLSPACING="0">
<TR BGCOLOR="#888888">
  <TH>Name</TH>
  <TH>Title</TH>
  <TH>Department</TH>
  <TH>E-mail</TH>
  <TH>Phone Extension</TH>
  <TH>Salary</TH>
</TR>
<!--- generate an HTLML table containing the employee record from the
      GetEmployeeRecord query. --->
<CFOUTPUT>
<TR BGCOLOR="##C0C0C0">
  <TD>#GetEmployeeRecord.Name#</TD>
  <TD>#GetEmployeeRecord.Title#</TD>
  <TD>#GetEmployeeRecord.Department#</TD>
  <TD><A HREF="Mailto:#GetEmployeeRecord.Email#">
      #GetEmployeeRecord.Email#</A></TD>
  <TD>#GetEmployeeRecord.PhoneExt#</TD>
  <TD>#GetEmployeeRecord.Salary#</TD>
</TR>
</CFOUTPUT>
</TABLE>

<H3>Incentive Awards</H3>

<!--- only display the table if 1 or more awards are found in the database --->
<CFIF GetIncentiveAwards.RecordCount GT 0>
<TABLE CELLPADDING="3" CELLSPACING="0">
<TR BGCOLOR="#888888">
    <TH>Date Awarded</TH>
    <TH>Incentive Type</TH>
    <TH>Amount</TH>
</TR>

<!--- generate an HTML table listing the awards granted the employee --->
<CFOUTPUT QUERY="GetIncentiveAwards">
<TR BGCOLOR="##C0C0C0">
    <TD>#DateFormat(DateAwarded, 'mm/dd/yyyy')#</TD>
```

*Example 11-7. Drill-Down Screen for Displaying Detail Information (continued)*

```
    <TD>#Category#</TD>
    <TD>#DollarFormat(Amount)#</TD>
</TR>
</CFOUTPUT>
</TABLE>

<CFELSE>
<B>No incentive awards granted.</B>
</CFIF>

</BODY>
</HTML>
```

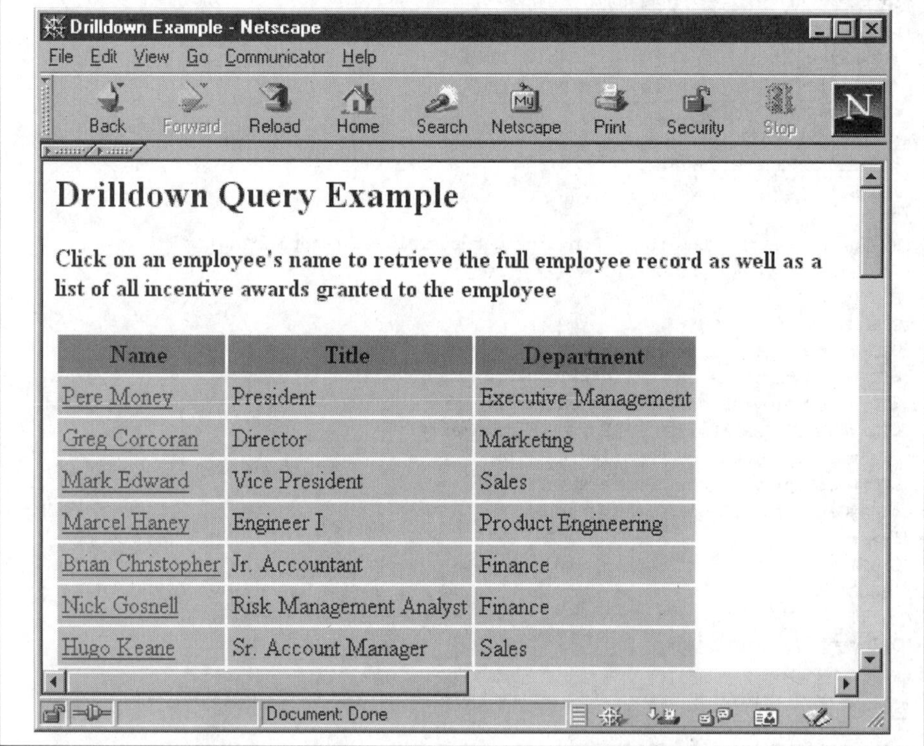


*Figure 11-4. Initial results screen with hyperlink to drill-down template*

Next, two HTML tables are generated from the query results. The first table contains all the information about the employee stored in the `EmployeeDirectory` table. The second table lists any awards the employee has earned. If no awards are found for the employee, a message to that effect is output in lieu of the table. The results of the *Drilldown.cfm* template are shown in Figure 11-5.

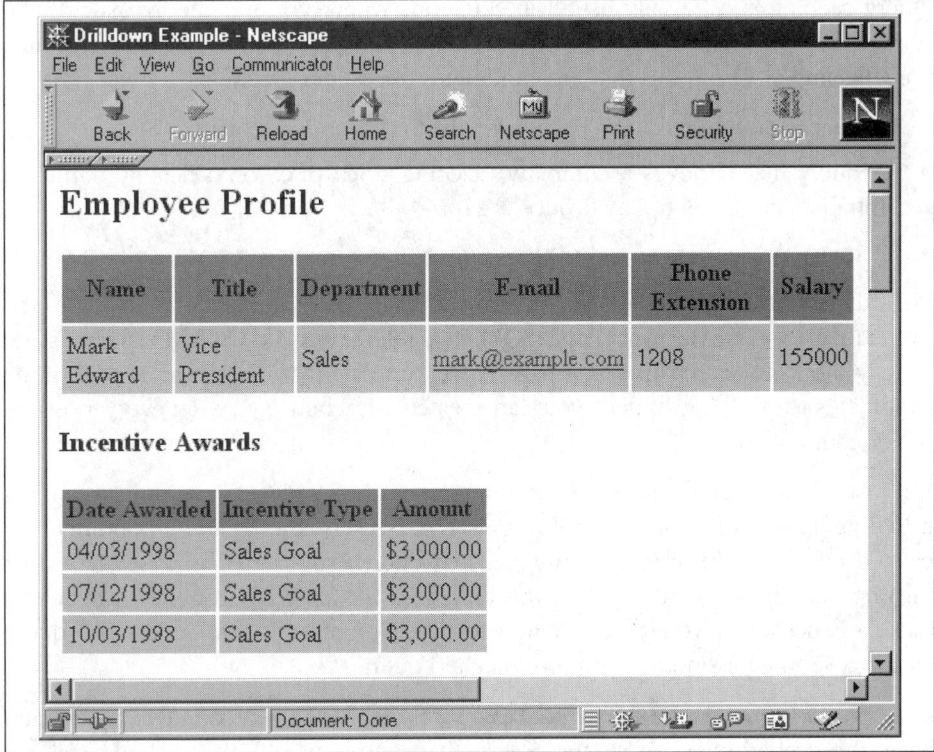


*Figure 11-5. Drill-down template displaying entire employee record*

# Query Caching

If you want to squeeze every last bit of performance out of your ColdFusion applications (and who doesn't?), you might want to consider query caching. Query caching allows you to retrieve query result sets from memory as opposed to requiring a round trip to the database. This can significantly reduce the amount of time it takes to return a result set in your application. Query caching is implemented using the `CFQUERY` tag and one of two optional attributes:

`CACHEDAFTER`
: Specifies a date for using cached query data. Cached query data is used only if the date of the original query is after the date specified in `CACHEDAFTER`.

`CACHEDWITHIN`
: Specifies a time span (using the `CreateTimeSpan()` function) for using cached query data.

Query caching is especially useful in situations where you repeatedly execute the same query to obtain a result set that remains static for a known period of time. Some examples of queries that are candidates for caching include:

- A query that retrieves a "what's new" list that is updated once a day
- A query that retrieves a company's closing stock price on a heavily trafficked Intranet site that is updated once a day
- A query that retrieves a list of users to use in an administration application

Regardless of the type of query you want to cache, one guideline is absolute: the `CFQUERY` statement (including the SQL) that references the cached data must be exactly the same every time. For this reason, queries that use dynamic SQL aren't candidates for caching, unless you can created a cached query for every possible query combination.

Because cached queries take up server memory, the ColdFusion Administrator has a setting under Caching that allows you to specify the maximum number of cached queries to keep in memory. Cached queries are managed in a FIFO (first in, first out) manor so that when the threshold for allowable queries is reached, older queries are pushed out as newer ones are brought in. To disable query caching, set the maximum number of cached queries to `0`.

Example 11-8 queries the `EmployeeDirectory` table of the `ProgrammingCF` database. If a cached query exists that is less than one hour old, the cached result set is used. If not, a live query is performed, and the result set is then cached.

*Example 11-8. Using CACHEDWITHIN to Cache a Query*

```
<!--- query the employeedirectory table.  If a cached result set that is less
      than 1 hour old, use it.  Otherwise, perform a new query and cache the
      result set. --->
<CFQUERY NAME="GetEmployeeInfo" DATASOURCE="ProgrammingCF"
         CACHEDWITHIN="#CreateTimeSpan(0,1,0,0)#">
         SELECT Name, Title, Department, Email, PhoneExt
         FROM EmployeeDirectory
</CFQUERY>

<HTML>
<HEAD>
    <TITLE>Cachedwithin Example</TITLE>
</HEAD>

<BODY>

<!--- output the result set.  If you have debugging turned on, you will be able
      to see whether the query was live or cached --->
<TABLE CELLPADDING="3" CELLSPACING="0">
<TR BGCOLOR="#888888">
  <TH>Name</TH>
```

*Example 11-8. Using CACHEDWITHIN to Cache a Query (continued)*

```
  <TH>Title</TH>
  <TH>Department</TH>
  <TH>E-mail</TH>
  <TH>Phone Extension</TH>
</TR>
<CFOUTPUT QUERY="GetEmployeeInfo">
<TR BGCOLOR="##C0C0C0">
  <TD>#Name#</TD>
  <TD>#Title#</TD>
  <TD>#Department#</TD>
  <TD><A HREF="Mailto:#Email#">#Email#</A></TD>
  <TD>#PhoneExt#</TD>
</TR>
</CFOUTPUT>
</TABLE>

</BODY>
</HTML>
```

The CACHEDWITHIN attribute of the CFQUERY tag handles all the caching. Use the CreateTimeSpan() function to specify the amount of time the cached query should persist. In our example, we set the cached query to persist for one hour. Every time the query is called, the ColdFusion checks to see if the time associated with the cached query is more than one hour older than the time associated with the current request. If not, the cached data is used. If, however, it is older, a new query is run, the results are cached, and the timer refreshed.

We can easily rewrite this example to use CACHEDAFTER instead of CACHEDWITHIN. Instead of providing a time span for the cached query, CACHEDAFTER provides a date after which all queries should be cached:

```
<CFQUERY NAME="GetEmployeeInfo" DATASOURCE="ProgrammingCF"
         CACHEDAFTER="06/15/2000">
```

Persistent queries created with CACHEDAFTER don't expire automatically as do those created with CACHEDWITHIN.

To see the difference between a normal query and a cached query, run the template in Example 11-8 (make sure debugging is turned on in the ColdFusion Administrator). The first time you run the template, you will see a processing time associated with the query of approximately 30 milliseconds. This is to be expected, as the query wasn't actually cached until after you executed it for the first time. If you hit the reload button on your browser and refresh the page, you should see something different (as shown in Figure 11-6).

This time, the words "Cached Query" should appear where the processing time for the query was previously displayed. This lets you know that the query you just ran came from the cache and not from the data source.

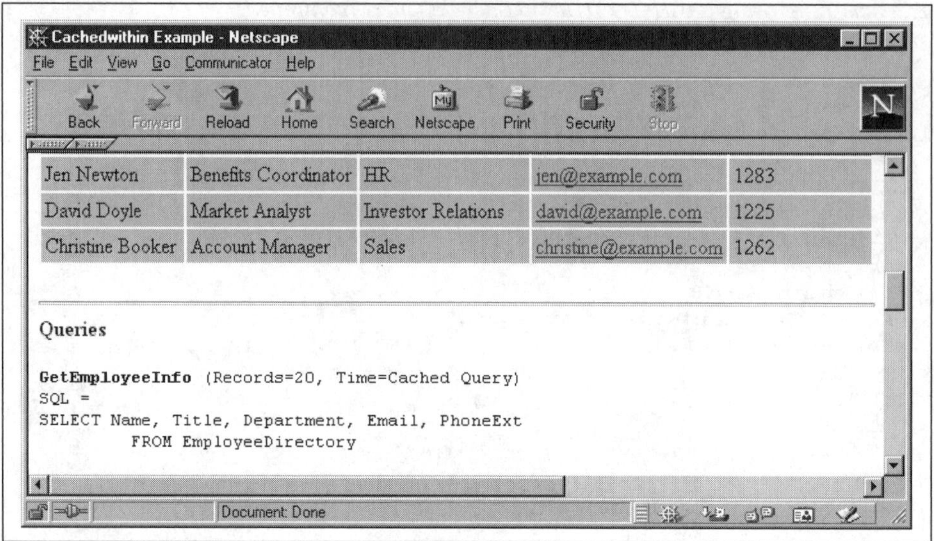


*Figure 11-6. Reloading the template retrieves cached data*

# Advanced SQL

This section moves beyond the basic database manipulation techniques we discussed in earlier chapters. Here, we'll cover methods for creating dynamic SQL, creating and modifying database tables using SQL, using aggregate and scalar functions, performing table unions and joins, and several other database-manipulation techniques. These are the kinds of operations that allow you to interact with databases at a higher level. Most advanced applications such as shopping carts, threaded discussion lists, and business-to-business applications use one or more of the techniques described in this section.

## Dynamic SQL

An extremely powerful feature of ColdFusion is the ability to generate dynamic SQL queries based on a variety of inputs. In Chapter 3, you learned how to pass a single dynamic value in an SQL statement:

```
SELECT Name, Title, Department
FROM EmployeeDirectory
WHERE ID = #ID#
```

We extend this concept a bit in Example 11-9 to allow for completely dynamic SQL in the `WHERE` clause of a SQL statement.

*Example 11-9. HTML Form for Searching Database Records*

```
<!--- query the EmployeeDirectory table for a list of departments --->
<CFQUERY NAME="GetDepartments" DATASOURCE="ProgrammingCF">
         SELECT DISTINCT Department
         FROM EmployeeDirectory
         ORDER BY Department
</CFQUERY>

<H2>Locate a User</H2>
<FORM ACTION="Search.cfm" METHOD="post">

<TABLE>
<TR>
  <TD>Name:</TD>
  <TD><INPUT TYPE="text" NAME="Name" SIZE="20" MAXLENGTH="80"></TD>
</TR>
<TR>
  <TD>Title:</TD>
  <TD><INPUT TYPE="text" NAME="Title" SIZE="20" MAXLENGTH="80"></TD>
</TR>
<TR>
  <TD>Department:</TD>
  <TD><SELECT NAME="Department" SIZE="5" MULTIPLE>
      <CFOUTPUT QUERY="GetDepartments">
        <OPTION VALUE="#Department#">#Department#</OPTION>
      </CFOUTPUT>
      </SELECT>
</TR>
</TABLE>
<INPUT TYPE="submit" VALUE="Submit">
</FORM>
```

Example 11-9 generates an HTML form for the user to specify search criteria when constructing a dynamic SQL statement to retrieve matching records from the `EmployeeDirectory` table. The form contains a field where the user can enter a name, another for title, and a multiple select list where he can choose one or more departments to narrow down the search. The list of department names in the multiple select list is obtained by performing a query using the `DISTINCT` keyword against the `Department` column in the `EmployeeDirectory` table. The `DISTINCT` keyword is covered in more detail later in this chapter. Note that the variable name in the `VALUE` attribute of the `OPTION` tag is enclosed in a set of single quotes. Because we'll be passing the values from the `Department` field as a delimited list of text values, it is necessary to enclose each value in the list in single quotes. If the values were numeric, this wouldn't be necessary.

Once you fill out and submit the search form, the search criteria are posted to the *Search.cfm* template shown in Example 11-10.

*Example 11-10. Searching Database Records Using Dynamically Generated SQL*

```
<!--- set a default of "" for Form.Department since the parameter isn't passed
      if no department is selected --->
<CFPARAM NAME="Form.Department" DEFAULT="">

<!--- query the EmployeeDirectory table with an SQL statement dynamically
      generated by the parameters passed in as form field values. --->
<CFQUERY NAME="GetRecords" DATASOURCE="ProgrammingCF">
         SELECT Name, Title, Department, Email, PhoneExt, Salary
         FROM EmployeeDirectory
         WHERE 0=0
<!--- if a value is passed for Name, use the SQL LIKE command and the %
      wildcard to include a wildcarded search for the Name, including it
      in the SQL statement using the AND operator. --->
<CFIF Form.Name NEQ "">
    AND Name LIKE '%#Form.Name#%'
</CFIF>

<!--- if a value is passed for Title, use the SQL LIKE command and the %
      wildcard to include a wildcarded search for the Title, including it
      in the SQL statement using the AND operator. --->
<CFIF Form.Title NEQ "">
    AND Title LIKE '%#Form.Title#%'
</CFIF>

<!--- if the value passed for Department is "", omit the AND statement
      for Department, removing Department as a criteria.  If Department
      contains any values other than "", use those values to construct
      the dynamic AND for Department. --->
<CFIF Form.Department NEQ "">
    AND Department IN (#ListQualify(Form.Department, "'")#)
</CFIF>
</CFQUERY>

<CFOUTPUT>
<B>#GetRecords.RecordCount# records matched your search criteria:</B><BR>
Name like: #Form.Name#<BR>
Title like: #Form.Title#<BR>
Department: #Form.Department#
</CFOUTPUT>

<P>
<TABLE CELLPADDING="3" CELLSPACING="0">
<TR BGCOLOR="#888888">
    <TH>Name</TH>
    <TH>Title</TH>
    <TH>Department</TH>
    <TH>E-mail</TH>
    <TH>Phone Extension</TH>
    <TH>Salary</TH>
</TR>
<!--- generate an HTML table containing all of the records matching the
      search criteria --->
```

*Example 11-10. Searching Database Records Using Dynamically Generated SQL (continued)*

```
<CFOUTPUT QUERY="GetRecords">
<TR BGCOLOR="##C0C0C0">
    <TD>#Name#</TD>
    <TD>#Title#</TD>
    <TD>#Department#</TD>
    <TD><A HREF="Mailto:#Email#">#Email#</A></TD>
    <TD>#PhoneExt#</TD>
    <TD>#Salary#</TD>
</TR>
</CFOUTPUT>
</TABLE>
```

Example 11-10 queries the `EmployeeDirectory` table with a dynamically generated SQL statement. The exact contents of the SQL statement may vary depending on the form-field values passed into the template. Note that the `WHERE 0=0` clause is necessary in the `CFQUERY` tag, in order to build the dynamic `WHERE` statement. `0=0` is another way of saying `True`, and provides the initial condition to which to attach any dynamically generated `AND` statements. If no search parameters are passed, the `0=0` prevents ColdFusion from throwing an error.

`CFIF` statements evaluate the form-field values and generate the necessary SQL. If values are passed for `Name` and `Title`, the SQL `LIKE` clause adds wildcarded searches to the `WHERE` statement. Finally, we have to deal with the `Department`. Because the `Department` form control is a multiple selection list, we have to use the `PreserveSingleQuotes()` function to keep the single quotes around the values we passed in, so they can be used in the `IN` statement. Once we've built up the query, it is a simple matter to output the results to the browser.

Note that in general, it is preferable not to use the SQL `LIKE` operator to perform wildcard searches because of the amount of database overhead associated with full-text searching. SQL (as a query language) was never meant to handle full-text searching (there are very few operators that facilitate text searches). For serious full-text indexing and searching, consider the Verity search interface included with ColdFusion and discussed in more detail in Chapter 16. Additionally, some databases such as MS SQL Server 7.0 contain extensions to the database to facilitate full-text searching. Consult your database documentation for more information on how full-text searching is handled by your database.

## Creating and Modifying Tables

It is possible to use SQL to handle such tasks as creating a new table, creating a new table and populating it with data from an existing table, modifying the design of a table, and deleting a table. These options are especially useful for developers working remotely without physical access to their data sources. Four SQL commands are available to facilitate these tasks: `CREATE TABLE`, `SELECT INTO`, `ALTER`

TABLE, and DROP TABLE. The descriptions and examples given in this section are meant to provide a general overview of each function. Actual implementation and syntax varies from database to database. Consult your database documentation for specific information on how your particular database handles each function.

### *Creating new tables*

The CREATE TABLE statement creates a new database table in the specified data source. Example 11-11 creates a new table called EmployeeDirectory2 with the same structure as the EmployeeDirectory table referred to throughout this book.

*Example 11-11. Creating a New Table Using CREATE TABLE*

```
<!--- create the EmployeeDirectory table --->
<CFQUERY NAME="CreateTable" DATASOURCE="ProgrammingCF">
CREATE TABLE EmployeeDirectory2 (
             ID counter,
             Name varchar(255),
             Title varchar(255),
             Department varchar(255),
             Email varchar(255),
             PhoneExt integer,
             Salary numeric,
       CONSTRAINT ID PRIMARY KEY (ID)
)

</CFQUERY>

Employee Directory table created.
```

Each column you wish to add to the newly created table takes the syntax:

```
column_name data_type[(length)] [constraint]
```

Datatypes vary depending on the database you are using. Some of the more common datatypes are: Bit, Byte, Char, Character, Dec, Date, DateTime, Decimal, Float, Int, Integer, Long, Memo, Numeric, Real, Short, SmallInt, Text, Time, TimeStamp, TinyInt, and Varchar. Constraints also vary from database to database. Some common constraints are: CHECK, DEFAULT, FOREIGN KEY, IDENTITY, INDEX, PRIMARY KEY, [NOT] NULL, and UNIQUE.

### *Populating new tables with existing data*

The SELECT INTO statement creates a new database table and populates it with data from an existing table. Example 11-12 demonstrates the SELECT INTO statement by selecting the name, title, email address, and phone extension for each employee in the EmployeeDirectory table who belongs to the IT department. The resulting record set is then used to populate a new table called ITDirectory.

*Example 11-12. Using SELECT INTO to Create a Copy of a Table*

```
<!--- Select the name, title, email, and phone ext for each employee in
      the EmployeeDirectory table that belongs to the IT department and
      use it to populate a new table called ITDirectory --->
<CFQUERY NAME="MakeITDirectory" DATASOURCE="ProgrammingCF">
         SELECT Name, Title, Email, PhoneExt
         INTO ITDirectory
         FROM EmployeeDirectory
         WHERE Department = 'IT'
</CFQUERY>

<!--- retrieve all of the records from the ITDirectory table we just
      created --->
<CFQUERY NAME="GetEmployees" DATASOURCE="ProgrammingCF">
         SELECT Name, Title, Email, PhoneExt
         FROM ITDirectory
         ORDER BY Name
</CFQUERY>

<H2>ITDirectorty table successfully created and populated with data:</H2>

<TABLE CELLPADDING="3" CELLSPACING="0">
<TR BGCOLOR="#888888">
  <TH>Name</TH>
  <TH>Title</TH>
  <TH>E-mail</TH>
  <TH>Phone Ext.</TH>
</TR>

<!--- dynamically generate a table containing all of the records returned
      by the query --->
<CFOUTPUT QUERY="GetEmployees">
<TR BGCOLOR="##C0C0C0">
  <TD>#Name#</TD>
  <TD>#Title#</TD>
  <TD>#Email#</TD>
  <TD>#PhoneExt#</TD>
</TR>
</CFOUTPUT>
</TABLE>
```

### *Altering table design*

The ALTER TABLE statement alters the design of an existing database table. You can use ALTER TABLE to add, modify the properties of, or delete a column from a specified table. The syntax for using ALTER TABLE is similar to the syntax used by CREATE TABLE as shown in the following code fragments:

```
<!--- add new column called DateHired to the Employee Directory Table --->
<CFQUERY NAME="Add" DATASOURCE="ProgrammingCF">
        ALTER TABLE EmployeeDirectory
              ADD COLUMN DateHired Varchar(8)
</CFQUERY>
```

```
<!--- modify the datatype of the DateHired column from varchar to date --->
<CFQUERY NAME="Alter" DATASOURCE="ProgrammingCF">
         ALTER TABLE EmployeeDirectory
               ALTER COLUMN DateHired Date
</CFQUERY>

<!--- drop (remove) the DateHired column from the table --->
<CFQUERY NAME="AddDateHired" DATASOURCE="ProgrammingCF">
         ALTER TABLE EmployeeDirectory
               DROP COLUMN DateHired
</CFQUERY>

Column added, altered, and deleted!
```

As you can see, you can perform three different actions with `ALTER TABLE`. You can choose to `ADD`, `ALTER`, or `DROP` a particular column to/from your table. Some databases let you use an additional clause called `DROP CONSTRAINT` to remove a named constraint from your schema.

### *Deleting tables*

The `DROP TABLE` statement deletes an existing table (including all data) from a database:

```
<CFQUERY NAME="DropITDirectory" DATASOURCE="ProgrammingCF">
         DROP TABLE ITDirectory
</CFQUERY>
```

You should exercise caution when using the `DROP TABLE` statement. Once a table has been dropped, it is permanently deleted from the database. Before we go on, you should also note that `DROP TABLE`, `ALTER TABLE`, and `CREATE TABLE` can be used with stored procedures, triggers, views, and any other objects supported by your database.

## *Retrieving Unique Values*

The `DISTINCT` keyword is used in a `SELECT` statement to retrieve all unique values stored in a specified column. Any duplicate values in the specified column are discarded. For example, if you want to retrieve all the unique department names stored in the `Departments` column of the `EmployeeDirectory` table, you can use the `DISTINCT` keyword:

```
<!--- query the employeedirectory table for a list of departments --->
<CFQUERY NAME="GetDepartment" DATASOURCE="ProgrammingCF">
         SELECT DISTINCT Department
         FROM EmployeeDirectory
         ORDER BY Department
</CFQUERY>
```

## *Using Column Aliases*

Aliases allow you to provide an alternate name to reference a particular query column. Aliases have three general uses:

- In situations where the field names used in a database aren't descriptive
- To deal with nonsupported column names, such as those that contain spaces or special characters
- With scalar and aggregate functions (covered later in this chapter)

To create an alias for a field name you use the `AS` operator in a `SELECT` statement:

```
SELECT ItmN AS ItemNumber
FROM MyTable
```

You specify the original name of the column to retrieve, in this case `ItmN`, followed by the AS operator and the alias name, `ItemNumber`.

To get a better idea of how an alias works, consider the code in Example 11-13.

*Example 11-13. Creating Aliases for Query Column Names*

```
<!--- retrieve all records from the database.  Provide aliases for some of the
      field names.  Note that the Name field (not the alias) is used in the SORT
      BY clause. --->
<CFQUERY NAME="GetEmployeeInfo" DATASOURCE="ProgrammingCF">
        SELECT Name AS EmployeeName, Title, Department,
               Email AS EmailAddress, PhoneExt AS PhoneExtension
        FROM EmployeeDirectory
        ORDER BY Name
</CFQUERY>

<H3>Using Column Aliases</H3>
<!--- create an HTML table for outputting the query results.  This section
      creates the first row of the table - used to hold the column
      headers --->
<TABLE CELLPADDING="3" CELLSPACING="0">
<TR BGCOLOR="#888888">
    <TH>Employee Name</TH>
    <TH>Title</TH>
    <TH>Department</TH>
    <TH>E-mail Address</TH>
    <TH>Phone Extension</TH>
</TR>

<!--- Output the query results. Use the new field names to refer to the
      aliases column names. --->
<CFOUTPUT QUERY="GetEmployeeInfo">
<TR BGCOLOR="##C0C0C0">
   <TD>#EmployeeName#</TD>
   <TD>#Title#</TD>
   <TD>#Department#</TD>
```

*Example 11-13. Creating Aliases for Query Column Names (continued)*

```
   <TD><A HREF="Mailto:#EmailAddress#">#EmailAddress#</A></TD>
   <TD>#PhoneExtension#</TD>
</TR>
</CFOUTPUT>
</TABLE>
```

Example 11-13 queries the `EmployeeDirectory` table of the `ProgrammingCF` data source and assigns aliases for the `Name`, `Email`, and `PhoneExt` fields. Next, an HTML table is dynamically generated from the query results. The aliased column names are used in place of the original column names to generate the output.

To escape nonsupported column names (such as those containing spaces, characters, and especially pound signs), you can use the back quote (`) character. In this case, the SQL `AS` keyword is used to alias column name as in the following example:

```
SELECT `Item Number` AS ItemNumber
FROM MyTable
```

You can also use the back quote (`) character to escape field names containing pound signs. To keep ColdFusion from throwing an error, be sure to escape the pound sign by doubling it up as in this example:

```
SELECT `Item ##` AS ItemNumber
FROM MyTable
```

Depending on the database you are working with, you may need to use a character or characters other than the back quote to identify special fields. If you get an error using the back quote, try surrounding the field name in square brackets as in `[Item Number]` or in parentheses with double quotation marks, `("Item Number")`.

## Scalar Functions

Scalar functions let you format record-set data at the database level before it is returned to your ColdFusion application. Many scalar functions have equivalent functions in ColdFusion (even identical names for some). For example, the scalar function `Left()` is the same as the `Left()` function in ColdFusion.

The ODBC specification (as outlined in the Microsoft ODBC SDK Programmer's Reference, available online at *http://msdn.microsoft.com/downloads/sdks/platform/database.asp*) contains a list of driver-independent ODBC scalar functions for use with SQL. Because support for these functions varies from driver to driver, it is important that you consult your database driver's documentation for a list of supported scalar functions.

At this point, you may be asking yourself why bother using scalar functions in your SQL statements when you can just code the functions in CFML. There is an inherent advantage to using scalar functions on the database side, as opposed to waiting until the data has been transferred. If you think in terms of performance, it makes sense to let the database handle any data manipulation and formatting so that ColdFusion is free to process other tasks. To illustrate the point, let's consider two examples.

The following example retrieves all the article titles from a table called **News**, then outputs the first 50 characters using the CFML **Left()** function:

```
<CFQUERY NAME="GetTitles" DATASOURCE="ProgrammingCF">
        SELECT Title
        FROM News
</CFQUERY>

<CFOUTPUT QUERY="GetTitles">
#Left(Title, 50)#<BR>
</CFOUTPUT>
```

Now look at the same example using the scalar function **Left()** instead:

```
<CFQUERY NAME="GetTitle" DATASOURCE="ProgrammingCF">
        SELECT {fn Left(Title, 50)} As ShortTitle
        FROM News
</CFQUERY>

<CFOUTPUT QUERY="GetTitle">
#ShortTitle#<BR>
</CFOUTPUT>
```

In this case, using the **Left()** scalar function saves processing time and memory on the ColdFusion server, since the result set returned by the query contains only the first 50 characters of each title as opposed to the entire title as in the previous example. Note the use of **{fn ...}** around the ODBC **Left()** function. While this notation isn't always necessary (it depends on your ODBC driver), I recommend you use it to help visually separate ODBC functions from CFML functions in your code and avoid any confusion. This scenario obviously shows just a simple example of how to use scalar functions to improve performance. It all comes down to one thing—returning the minimum amount of data possible in the most useful format.

## *Aggregate Functions*

You can use aggregate functions to summarize data within a database. Aggregate functions are most often used to create reports that answer such questions as the following. How many employees are in each department? How many widgets were sold in the month of March? Can you break down widget sales by region?

What was the date of the first press release issued by the company? What is the average employee salary?

Here are the aggregate functions commonly associated with most databases:

`MIN(Fieldname)`
: Returns the minimum value (numeric, date, or character) in a column

`MAX(fieldname)`
: Returns the maximum value (numeric, date, or character) in a column

`AVG(Fieldname)`
: Returns the average value in a column of numeric values

`SUM(Fieldname)`
: Returns the sum of all values in a column of numeric values

`COUNT(Fieldname)`
: Returns the number of rows for a given column name that don't contain null values. To count the number of unique row values for a given column, use the `DISTINCT` keyword as in `COUNT(DISTINCT Fieldname)`

`COUNT(*)`
: Returns the total number of rows in a table. If you use a `WHERE` clause, this function provides the number of rows returned in the result set

Although ColdFusion has its own functions that can provide the same functionality as the aggregate functions, you should let the database handle calculations whenever possible. From a performance standpoint, databases are optimized to manipulate data whereas ColdFusion is less so. For this reason alone, it makes sense to offload as much processing as you can from ColdFusion to your database. To see how simple aggregate functions can make life easier, consider the following code, which uses the `COUNT(*)` function to retrieve the total number of records in the `EmployeeDirectory` table:

```
<!--- Retrieve a count of the total number of records in the EmployeeDirectory
      table of the database.  You should use COUNT(*) as opposed to COUNT for
      this operation as it is faster.  --->
<CFQUERY NAME="GetTotalRecords" DATASOURCE="ProgrammingCF">
         SELECT Count(*) AS TotalRecords
         FROM EmployeeDirectory
</CFQUERY>

<H3>Using COUNT(*)</H3>
<CFOUTPUT>
Total Records in the EmployeeDirectory Table: #GetTotalRecords.TotalRecords#
</CFOUTPUT>
```

Of course, you can do the same thing by querying an arbitrary column using the `CFQUERY` tag, then using the *`queryname`*`.RecordCount` variable to output the total number of records retrieved by the query. As simple as this seems, it actually wastes a fair amount of resources. Using the CFQUERY tag to query a single field returns all the data associated with that field. So, if you query a table that happens to have one million rows of data in it, you are going to get a result set back that contains one million records. From a performance standpoint, not only will the process take forever, but your server will most likely run out of memory as ColdFusion attempts to store the entire result set. By using the COUNT(*) method instead, the database does all the work and returns only a single record back to ColdFusion that contains the total number of rows in the table.

You can also use aggregate functions to provide summarization on groups of related data. For example, if you want to know how many employees are in each department, you could use the COUNT (not COUNT(*)) function along with the GROUP BY clause to find out, as shown in Example 11-14.

*Example 11-14. Counting Employees in Each Department*

```
<!--- Retrieve a count of the number of employees for each department in
      the EmployeeDirectory table of the database --->
<CFQUERY NAME="GetDepartment" DATASOURCE="ProgrammingCF">
         SELECT COUNT(Name) AS TotalEmployees,
                Department
         FROM EmployeeDirectory
         GROUP BY Department
</CFQUERY>

<H3>Using COUNT and GROUP BY to return the Total Number of Employees for
    each Department</H3>
<TABLE BORDER="0" CELLPADDING="3">
<TR BGCOLOR="#C0C0C0">
  <TH>Department</TH>
  <TH>Total Employees</TH>
</TR>

<CFOUTPUT QUERY="GetDepartment">
<TR BGCOLOR="##E3E3E3">
  <TD>#Department#</TD>
  <TD>#TotalEmployees#</TD>
</TR>
</CFOUTPUT>
</TABLE>
```

You can provide additional filtering of grouped data with a HAVING clause. HAVING works just like the WHERE clause except the filtering takes place after the data has been grouped. In addition, HAVING allows you to specify an aggregate function, whereas the WHERE statement doesn't. Example 11-15 modifies the code in from Example 11-14 so that only departments that have two or more employees are returned by the query.

*Example 11-15. Displaying Departments That Have Two or More Employees*

```
<!--- Retrieve a count of the number of employees for each department in
      the EmployeeDirectory table of the database where the total number
      of employees is greater than or equal to two. --->
<CFQUERY NAME="GetDepartment" DATASOURCE="ProgrammingCF">
         SELECT COUNT(Name) AS TotalEmployees,
                Department
         FROM EmployeeDirectory
         GROUP BY Department
         HAVING COUNT(Name) >= 2
</CFQUERY>

<H3>Using COUNT, GROUP BY, and HAVING to return the Total Number of Employees
    for each Department where the total number of employees is greater than or
    equal to two </H3>
<TABLE BORDER="0" CELLPADDING="3">
<TR BGCOLOR="#C0C0C0">
  <TH>Department</TH>
  <TH>Total Employees</TH>
</TR>

<CFOUTPUT QUERY="GetDepartment">
<TR BGCOLOR="##E3E3E3">
  <TD>#Department#</TD>
  <TD>#TotalEmployees#</TD>
</TR>
</CFOUTPUT>
</TABLE>
```

## Subqueries

As the name implies, a subquery is a query that exists within another query. Subqueries can be used inside the **SELECT**, **INSERT**, **UPDATE**, and **DELETE** queries. In the case of **SELECT** queries, subqueries are often used along with aggregate functions to create a summarized column from data contained in the other columns. Subqueries can also associate data from different tables (much like a join, which we'll cover shortly).

Example 11-16 uses a subquery along with an aggregate function to calculate the average salary of all employees in the `EmployeeDirectory` table.

*Example 11-16. Using a Subquery Along with an Aggregate Function*

```
<!--- Retrieve employee records from the EmpoloyeeDirectory.  Employ a
      subquery to obtain the average salary of all employees  --->
<CFQUERY NAME="GetSalaries" DATASOURCE="ProgrammingCF">
         SELECT Name, Title, Department,
                Salary, (SELECT AVG(Salary)
                         FROM EmployeeDirectory) AS AverageSalary
         FROM EmployeeDirectory
         ORDER BY Name
```

*Example 11-16. Using a Subquery Along with an Aggregate Function (continued)*

```
</CFQUERY>

<H3>Average Salary Report</H3>

<TABLE CELLPADDING="3" CELLSPACING="0">
<TR BGCOLOR="#888888">
  <TH>Name</TH>
  <TH>Title</TH>
  <TH>Department</TH>
  <TH>Salary</TH>
</TR>
<!--- output the employee records --->
<CFOUTPUT QUERY="GetSalaries">
<TR BGCOLOR="##C0C0C0">
  <TD>#Name#</TD>
  <TD>#Title#</TD>
  <TD>#Department#</TD>
  <TD ALIGN="Right">#DollarFormat(Salary)#</TD>
</TR>
</CFOUTPUT>

<!--- output the average employee salary.  Note that the QUERY attribute of
      the CFOUTPUT tag was not used.  The query name is prepended to the
      AverageSalary salary variable --->
<CFOUTPUT>
<TR BGCOLOR="##808080">
  <TD>Average Salary</TD>
  <TD COLSPAN="3" ALIGN="Right">#DollarFormat(GetSalaries.AverageSalary)#</TD>
</TR>
</CFOUTPUT>
</TABLE>
```

In Example 11-16, a query is run to retrieve the `Name`, `Title`, `Department`, and `Salary` of each employee in the `EmployeeDirectory` table. A subquery is used within the `SELECT` statement to obtain the average of all salaries using the `AVG` aggregate function. Subqueries returning more than one record can be used only in the `WHERE` clause. The results are written to the browser in an HTML table that contains a listing of all the employees in the table along with their salaries. The average salary is given at the bottom of the table.

You can also include subqueries in the `WHERE` clause of a query. One way to do this is with the `EXISTS` keyword. `EXISTS` is used only with subqueries and tests for a nonempty record set (you can test for an empty record set by using `NOT EXISTS`). To see how this is useful, consider Example 11-17, in which we retrieve a list of all employees from the `EmployeeDirectory` table who have received individual incentive awards of less than $5,000 each in 2000.

*Example 11-17. Using EXISTS with a Subquery*

```
<!--- Retrieve a list of employees who received individual incentive awards
      of less than $5000 each in 2000 --->
<CFQUERY NAME="GetSalaries" DATASOURCE="ProgrammingCF">
         SELECT ID, Name, Title, Department
         FROM EmployeeDirectory
         WHERE EXISTS
           (SELECT ID
            FROM IncentiveAwards
            WHERE IncentiveAwards.ID = EmployeeDirectory.ID
            AND Amount < 5000
            AND {fn YEAR(DateAwarded)} = 2000)
         ORDER BY Name
</CFQUERY>

<H3>Incentive Awards under $5000 Granted in 1998</H3>

<TABLE CELLPADDING="3" CELLSPACING="0">
<TR BGCOLOR="#888888">
  <TH>Name</TH>
  <TH>Title</TH>
  <TH>Department</TH>
</TR>

<!--- output the employee records --->
<CFOUTPUT QUERY="GetSalaries">
<TR BGCOLOR="##C0C0C0">
  <TD>#Name#</TD>
  <TD>#Title#</TD>
  <TD>#Department#</TD>
</TR>
</CFOUTPUT>
</TABLE>
```

Example 11-17 uses a few of the advanced techniques we covered so far. In plain English, the query works by saying "select the employees from the `EmployeeDirectory` table where a matching record exists in the `IncentiveAwards` table that meets the criteria set in the subquery".

Subqueries can also be used in the `WHERE` clause of a `SELECT` query by using the equal sign (=) or the `[NOT] IN` operator. Use the equal sign when only one record will be returned by the subquery. If more than one record can be returned, use `IN`. Here are some example `WHERE` clauses:

```
WHERE MyField = (SELECT SomeField
                 FROM SomeTable
                 WHERE OtherField = Value)

WHERE MyField IN (SELECT SomeField
                  FROM SomeTable
                  WHERE OtherField = Value)
```

```
WHERE MyField NOT IN (SELECT SomeField
                      FROM SomeTable
                      WHERE OtherField = Value)
```

## Unions

The `UNION` clause is used with a `SELECT` statement to merge result sets from two or more queries into a single result set. In order to use the `UNION` clause, each result set must contain the same number of columns, with each matching column being of the same datatype. Additionally, each column must have been `SELECT`'ed in the same order during the formation of the original result sets. Example 11-18 demonstrates how this works.

*Example 11-18. Using the UNION Clause to Merge Two Result Sets*

```
<!--- retrieve records from both the ITDirectory and HRDirectory tables
      and merge them using the UNION clause.  This example is somewhat
      impractical as the user's department is not stored in the
      database --->
<CFQUERY NAME="GetEmployees" DATASOURCE="ProgrammingCF">
         SELECT Name, Title, Email, PhoneExt
         FROM ITDirectory
         UNION
         SELECT Name, Title, Email, PhoneExt
         FROM HRDirectory
</CFQUERY>

<H2>Combined IT Directory and HR Directory:</H2>

<TABLE CELLPADDING="3" CELLSPACING="0">
<TR BGCOLOR="#888888">
  <TH>Name</TH>
  <TH>Title</TH>
  <TH>E-mail</TH>
  <TH>Phone Ext.</TH>
</TR>

<!--- dynamically generate a table containing all of the records returned
      by the query --->
<CFOUTPUT QUERY="GetEmployees">
<TR BGCOLOR="##C0C0C0">
  <TD>#Name#</TD>
  <TD>#Title#</TD>
  <TD>#Email#</TD>
  <TD>#PhoneExt#</TD>
</TR>
</CFOUTPUT>
</TABLE>
```

In order to get Example 11-18 to work, you need to go back to the code in Example 11-12 and modify it to create a new table called `HRDirectory`. Simply substitute HRDirectory for ITDirectory in the FROM clause and 'HR' for 'IT' in the WHERE clause and execute the template. You should now have an ITDirectory and an HRDirectory table containing IT employees and HR employees respectively.

Once you have these two tables in your database, go ahead and execute Example 11-18. The template retrieves a list of all employees from both tables and merges the result sets using the UNION clause. An HTML table containing the records from the merged result set is dynamically generated.

## Joins

Relational database design allows you to create database tables that maintain relationships. These relationships are usually defined in terms of primary and foreign key values. For example, in our EmployeeDirectory table, the ID value for each employee is the primary key value. The IncentiveAwards table contains a field named ID as well. The ID field in the IncentiveAwards table is known as a foreign key. Records in the IncentiveAwards table are related to records in the EmployeeDirectory table by their ID values. Each record in the IncentiveAwards table should have a corresponding record in the EmployeeDirectory table.

A join operation lets you select records from two or more tables where a relationship between primary key and foreign key values exists. Most joins fall into one of two categories: inner or outer joins.

### Inner joins

Inner joins are the most common type of join and are used to retrieve records from two or more tables where values in the joined columns match. There are many ways to implement inner joins in SQL, and support for these methods varies from database to database. Consult your database documentation to find out which methods are supported by your database.

One common method involves using the equal sign (=) in the WHERE statement to join the tables by a related column, as shown in Example 11-19.

*Example 11-19. Inner Join Performed in the WHERE Statement*

```
<!--- query the EmployeeDirectory and IncentiveAwards tables and only return
      records where the ID from the EmployeeDirectory table matches the ID in
      the IncentiveAwards table,  The inner join is performed by the equal
      sign. --->
<CFQUERY NAME="GetEmployeeInfo" DATASOURCE="ProgrammingCF">
        SELECT EmployeeDirectory.ID, EmployeeDirectory.Name,
               IncentiveAwards.ID, IncentiveAwards.Category,
               IncentiveAwards.DateAwarded, IncentiveAwards.Amount
```

*Example 11-19. Inner Join Performed in the WHERE Statement (continued)*

```
        FROM EmployeeDirectory, IncentiveAwards
        WHERE EmployeeDirectory.ID = IncentiveAwards.ID
</CFQUERY>

<H3>Incentive Awards</H3>

<TABLE CELLPADDING="3" CELLSPACING="0">
<TR BGCOLOR="#888888">
  <TH>Name</TH>
  <TH>Award Type</TH>
  <TH>Date Awarded</TH>
  <TH>Amount</TH>
</TR>

<!--- dynamically generate a table containing all of the records returned
      by the query --->
<CFOUTPUT QUERY="GetEmployeeInfo">
<TR BGCOLOR="##C0C0C0">
  <TD>#Name#</TD>
  <TD>#Category#</TD>
  <TD>#DateFormat(DateAwarded, 'mm/dd/yyyy')#</TD>
  <TD>#DollarFormat(Amount)#</TD>
</TR>
</CFOUTPUT>
</TABLE>
```

Example 11-19 queries the `EmployeeDirectory` and `IncentiveAwards` tables and returns only records in which the `ID` value from the `EmployeeDirectory` table matches the `ID` value in the `IncentiveAwards` table. The inner join is performed using the equal sign in the `WHERE` clause. Executing this template results in the output shown in Figure 11-7.

You can also perform an inner join using `INNER JOIN` in the `FROM` clause of the `SELECT` statement, as shown in Example 11-20. The results of this query will mimic the results of Example 11-19 (shown in Figure 11-7).

*Example 11-20. Inner Join Performed in the FROM Statement*

```
<!--- query the EmployeeDirectory and IncentiveAwards tables and only return
      records where the ID from the EmployeeDirectory table matches the ID in
      the IncentiveAwards table.  The inner join is performed by the INNER
      JOIN operator. --->
<CFQUERY NAME="GetEmployeeInfo" DATASOURCE="ProgrammingCF">
        SELECT employee.ID, employee.Name, incentive.ID,
               incentive.Category, incentive.DateAwarded, incentive.Amount
        FROM EmployeeDirectory employee
        INNER JOIN IncentiveAwards incentive
        ON employee.ID = incentive.ID
</CFQUERY>

<H3>Incentive Awards</H3>
```

*Example 11-20. Inner Join Performed in the FROM Statement (continued)*

```
<TABLE CELLPADDING="3" CELLSPACING="0">
<TR BGCOLOR="#888888">
  <TH>Name</TH>
  <TH>Award Type</TH>
  <TH>Date Awarded</TH>
  <TH>Amount</TH>
</TR>

<!--- dynamically generate a table containing all of the records returned
      by the query --->
<CFOUTPUT QUERY="GetEmployeeInfo">
<TR BGCOLOR="##C0C0C0">
  <TD>#Name#</TD>
  <TD>#Category#</TD>
  <TD>#DateFormat(DateAwarded, 'mm/dd/yyyy')#</TD>
  <TD>#DollarFormat(Amount)#</TD>
</TR>
</CFOUTPUT>
</TABLE>
```

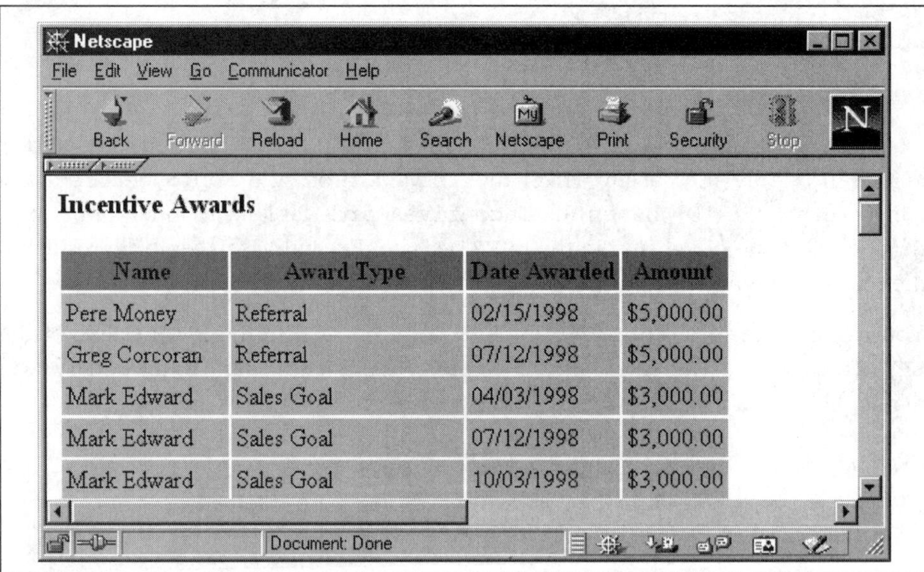


*Figure 11-7. Inner join performed using the equal sign in the WHERE clause*

Example 11-20 introduces another technique known as table aliasing. If you look at the first query, you'll notice that we refer to the `EmployeeDirectory` table as `employee` and the `IncentiveAwards` table as `incentive`:

```
SELECT employee.ID, employee.Name, incentive.ID,
               incentive.Category, incentive.DateAwarded, incentive.Amount
FROM EmployeeDirectory employee
```

```
INNER JOIN IncentiveAwards incentive
ON employee.ID = incentive.ID
```

SQL lets us alias table names when working with multiple tables. To create an alias for a table name, simply specify the alias immediately following the table name in the `FROM` clause.

### *Outer joins*

Outer joins differ from inner joins in that they let you query all the records from one table even if corresponding records don't exist in the other table. There are two types of outer joins: left and right.

As its name implies, a left outer join returns all the records from the left table (as specified in the `WHERE` or `FROM` clause) and only the records from the right table where the values in the joined fields match. All empty rows from the right table are assigned `NULL` values.

Example 11-21 uses a left outer join in the `FROM` clause to query the `EmployeeDirectory` and `IncentiveAwards` tables and return all records from the left table (`EmployeeDirectory`) and only those from the right table (`IncentiveAwards`) that match `ID` values.

*Example 11-21. Using LEFT OUTER JOIN in the FROM Clause*

```
<!--- query the EmployeeDirectory and IncentiveAwards tables and return all
      records from the left table (EmployeeDirectory) and only those from
      the right table (IncentiveAwards) where the ID values are equal.  The
      left outer join is performed by the LEFT OUTER JOIN operator. --->
<CFQUERY NAME="GetEmployeeInfo" DATASOURCE="ProgrammingCF">
        SELECT employee.ID, employee.Name, incentive.ID,
               incentive.Category, incentive.DateAwarded, incentive.Amount
        FROM EmployeeDirectory employee
        LEFT OUTER JOIN IncentiveAwards incentive
        ON employee.ID = incentive.ID
</CFQUERY>

<H3>Incentive Awards</H3>

<TABLE CELLPADDING="3" CELLSPACING="0">
<TR BGCOLOR="#888888">
    <TH>Name</TH>
    <TH>Award Type</TH>
    <TH>Date Awarded</TH>
    <TH>Amount</TH>
</TR>

<!--- dynamically generate a table containing all of the records returned
      by the query.  Substitute NULL for any blanks (NULLs) returned by
      the Left Outer Join --->
<CFOUTPUT QUERY="GetEmployeeInfo">
<TR BGCOLOR="##C0C0C0">
```

*Example 11-21. Using LEFT OUTER JOIN in the FROM Clause (continued)*

```
    <TD>#Name#</TD>
    <TD><CFIF Category EQ "">NULL<CFELSE>#Category#</CFIF></TD>
    <TD><CFIF DateAwarded EQ "">NULL<CFELSE>
        #DateFormat(DateAwarded, 'mm/dd/yyyy')#</CFIF></TD>
    <TD><CFIF Amount EQ "">NULL<CFELSE>#DollarFormat(Amount)#</CFIF></TD>
</TR>
</CFOUTPUT>
</TABLE>
```

Executing the template in Example 11-21 results in the output shown in Figure 11-8.

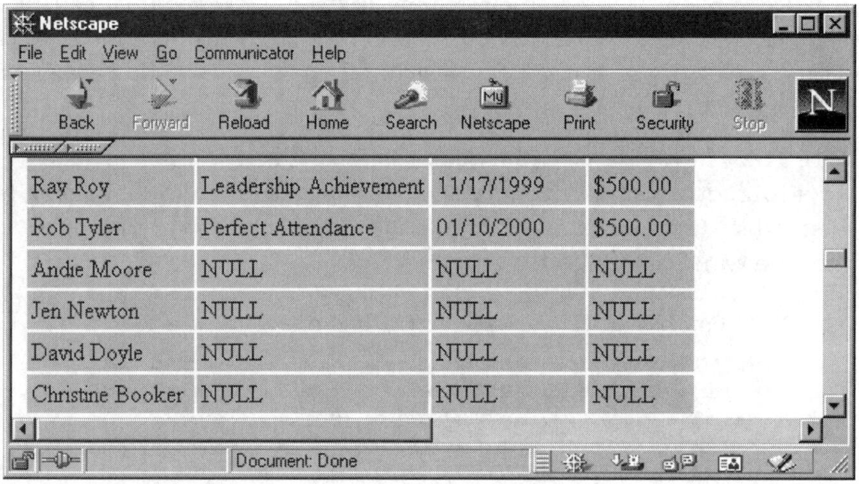
Netscape
File Edit View Go Communicator Help
Back Forward Reload Home Search Netscape Print Security Stop
Ray Roy | Leadership Achievement | 11/17/1999 | $500.00
Rob Tyler | Perfect Attendance | 01/10/2000 | $500.00
Andie Moore | NULL | NULL | NULL
Jen Newton | NULL | NULL | NULL
David Doyle | NULL | NULL | NULL
Christine Booker | NULL | NULL | NULL
Document: Done

*Figure 11-8. Results of using a left outer join in the FROM clause*

A right outer join is the exact opposite of a left outer join. Right outer joins return all records from the right table and only the records from the left table where the values in the joined fields match. All empty rows from the left table are assigned `NULL` values.

Example 11-22 uses a right outer join to query the `EmployeeDirectory` and `IncentiveAwards` tables. A result set containing all records from the right table (`IncentiveAwards`) and only those from the left table (`EmployeeDirectory`) where the `ID` values are equal is returned.

*Example 11-22. Using RIGHT OUTER JOIN in the FROM Clause*

```
<!--- query the EmployeeDirectory and IncentiveAwards tables and return all
      records from the Right table (IncentiveAwards) and only those from
      the left table (EmployeeDirectory) where the ID values are equal.  The
      right outer join is performed by the RIGHT OUTER JOIN operator. --->
<CFQUERY NAME="GetEmployeeInfo" DATASOURCE="ProgrammingCF">
```

*Example 11-22. Using RIGHT OUTER JOIN in the FROM Clause (continued)*

```
        SELECT employee.ID, employee.Name, incentive.ID,
               incentive.Category, incentive.DateAwarded, incentive.Amount
        FROM EmployeeDirectory employee
        RIGHT OUTER JOIN IncentiveAwards incentive
        ON employee.ID = incentive.ID
</CFQUERY>

<H3>Incentive Awards</H3>

<TABLE CELLPADDING="3" CELLSPACING="0">
<TR BGCOLOR="#888888">
    <TH>Name</TH>
    <TH>Award Type</TH>
    <TH>Date Awarded</TH>
    <TH>Amount</TH>
</TR>

<!--- dynamically generate a table containing all of the records returned
      by the query.  Substitute NULL for any blanks (NULLs) returned by
      the Right Outer Join --->
<CFOUTPUT QUERY="GetEmployeeInfo">
<TR BGCOLOR="##C0C0C0">
    <TD><CFIF Name EQ "">NULL<CFELSE>#Name#</CFIF></TD>
    <TD><CFIF Category EQ "">NULL<CFELSE>#Category#</CFIF></TD>
    <TD><CFIF DateAwarded EQ "">NULL<CFELSE>#DateFormat(DateAwarded,
        'mm/dd/yyyy')#</CFIF></TD>
    <TD><CFIF Amount EQ "">NULL<CFELSE>#DollarFormat(Amount)#</CFIF></TD>
</TR>
</CFOUTPUT>
</TABLE>
```

Executing the template in Example 11-22 results in the output shown in Figure 11-9.

Note that there are various shorthand techniques you can use to specify left outer joins and right outer joins in the `WHERE` clause. The syntax varies from database to database. Refer to your specific database's documentation for guidelines on specific syntax for outer joins.

There are several other types of joins that can be performed in SQL. Most of these are variations on the joins we already covered. Many are highly specialized and rarely employed. Some are exclusive to specific database platforms. For more information on joins, see your database documentation or pick up a good SQL reference book, such as O'Reilly & Associates' *SQL in a Nutshell.*

## Data Binding

You can use the `CFQUERYPARAM` tag to check the datatype of a query parameter and optionally validate it against a specific SQL type. You can also use the

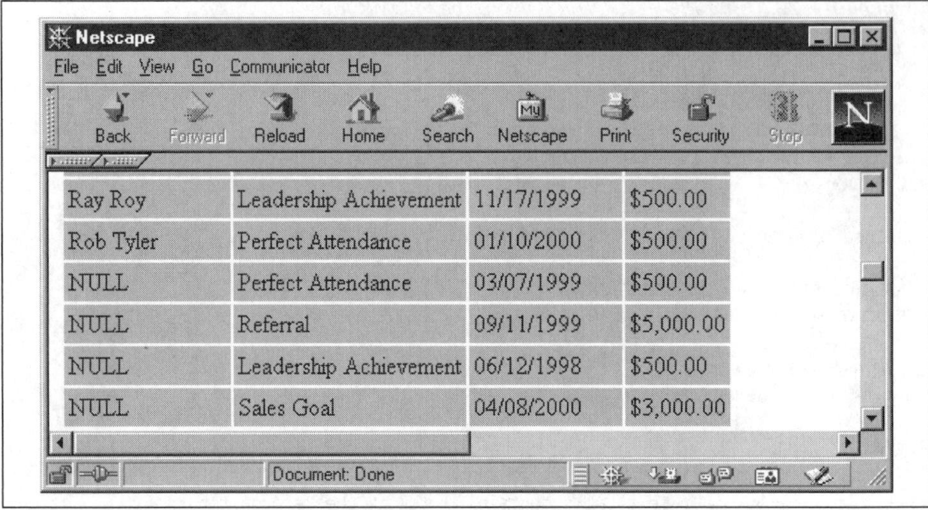


*Figure 11-9. Using a Right Outer Join in the FROM clause*

`CFQUERYPARAM` tag to update long text fields. The `CFQUERYPARAM` tag must be nested within a `CFQUERY` tag and appears on the right side of the = sign in the `WHERE` clause:

```
<CFQUERY NAME="MyQUERY" DATASOURCE="MyDatasource">
        SELECT *
        FROM MyTable
        WHERE MyValue =
              <CFQUERYPARAM VALUE="parameter_value"
                            CFSQLTYPE="parameter_data_type"
                            MAXLENGTH="number"
                            SCALE="number_of_decimal_places"
                            SEPARATOR="seperator_character"
                            LIST="yes/no"
                            NULL="Yes/No">
</CFQUERY>
```

The `VALUE` attribute is required and specifies the value that ColdFusion should pass to the right of the comparison operator in the `WHERE` clause. `CFSQLTYPE` is also required and specifies the SQL type the parameter should be bound to. Possible entries are listed in Table 11-1. The default value for `CFSQLTYPE` is `CF_SQL_CHAR`.

*Table 11-1. Values for CFSQLTYPE*

| | | |
|---|---|---|
| CF_SQL_BIGINT | CF_SQL_IDSTAMP | CF_SQL_REFCURSOR |
| CF_SQL_BIT | CF_SQL_INTEGER | CF_SQL_SMALLINT |
| CF_SQL_CHAR | CF_SQL_LONGVARCHAR | CF_SQL_TIME |
| CF_SQL_DATE | CF_SQL_MONEY | CF_SQL_TIMESTAMP |

*Table 11-1. Values for CFSQLTYPE (continued)*

| | | |
|---|---|---|
| CF_SQL_DECIMAL | CF_SQL_MONEY4 | CF_SQL_TINYINT |
| CF_SQL_DOUBLE | CF_SQL_NUMERIC | CF_SQL_VARCHAR |
| CF_SQL_FLOAT | CF_SQL_REAL | |

The MAXLENGTH attribute specifies the maximum length of the parameter being passed and is an optional attribute. SCALE is also optional and, if you use a numeric datatype, specifies the number of decimal places for the parameter. The SEPARATOR attribute is optional and specifies the character used to delimit the list of values when the LIST attribute is set to Yes. The default is the comma (,). The LIST attribute is optional and accepts a Yes/No value indicating whether the VALUE attribute of the CFQUERYPARAM tag should be treated as a list of values separated by the character specified in the SEPARATOR attribute. If set to Yes, a SQL parameter is generated for each value in the list. Each list item is validated separately. If a value is specified for the MAXLENGTH attribute, the MAXLENGTH applies to each item in the list as opposed to the list as a whole. If the value passed is NULL, it is treated as a single NULL value. The default is No.

The final attribute is NULL. NULL is optional and specifies a Yes/No value indicating whether the value passed is a NULL. If Yes, ColdFusion ignores the VALUE attribute. The default value for NULL is No.

If the database being used doesn't support the binding of parameters (such as the Sybase 11 native driver), validation is still performed with the validated parameter being written back to the string. If for any reason validation fails, ColdFusion throws an exception. The following rules determine the validation performed:

- CF_SQL_SMALLINT, CF_SQL_INTEGER, CF_SQL_REAL, CF_SQL_FLOAT, CF_SQL_DOUBLE, CF_SQL_TINYINT, CF_SQL_MONEY, CF_SQL_MONEY4, CF_SQL_DECIMAL, CF_SQL_NUMERIC, and CF_SQL_BIGINT can be converted to numbers.
- CF_SQL_DATE, CF_SQL_TIME and CF_SQL_TIMESTAMP can be converted to a valid date format.
- If the MAXLENGTH attribute is used, the length of the value for the specified parameter can't exceed the specified length.

The actual SQL that is generated by the CFQUERYPARAM tag is dependent on the database used. Example 11-23 uses the CFQUERYPARAM tag to validate the value of a variable called ID. Changing the value of ID from numeric to a text character causes ColdFusion to throw an error.

*Example 11-23. Using CFQUERYPARAM for Data Binding and Validation*

```
<!--- set ID = 1.  Normally, this value would come from a form post or as
      a URL parameter --->
<CFSET ID = 1>

<!--- retrieve the full record of the employee whose ID is specified.
      Use the CFQUERYPARAM tag to bind ID to a numeric value. --->
<CFQUERY NAME="GetEmployeeRecord" DATASOURCE="ProgrammingCF">
         SELECT Name, Title, Department, Email, PhoneExt, Salary
         FROM EmployeeDirectory
         WHERE ID = <CFQUERYPARAM VALUE="#ID#"
                                  CFSQLTYPE="CF_SQL_INTEGER">
</CFQUERY>

<H2>Employee Profile</H2>

<TABLE CELLPADDING="3" CELLSPACING="0">
<TR BGCOLOR="#888888">
  <TH>Name</TH>
  <TH>Title</TH>
  <TH>Department</TH>
  <TH>E-mail</TH>
  <TH>Phone Extension</TH>
  <TH>Salary</TH>
</TR>
<!--- generate an HTLML table containing the employee record from the
      GetEmployeeRecord query. --->
<CFOUTPUT>
<TR BGCOLOR="##C0C0C0">
  <TD>#GetEmployeeRecord.Name#</TD>
  <TD>#GetEmployeeRecord.Title#</TD>
  <TD>#GetEmployeeRecord.Department#</TD>
  <TD><A
      HREF="Mailto:#GetEmployeeRecord.Email#">#GetEmployeeRecord.Email#</A></TD>
  <TD>#GetEmployeeRecord.PhoneExt#</TD>
  <TD>#GetEmployeeRecord.Salary#</TD>
</TR>
</CFOUTPUT>
</TABLE>
```

# *CFSQL*

Now that you have an understanding of advanced SQL, it's time to introduce a new concept known as "query of a query" or CFSQL (ColdFusion SQL). Introduced in ColdFusion 5.0, CFSQL allows you to use the `CFQUERY` tag to query an already existing query using a subset of ANSI SQL 92. This feature makes it easy to program functionality previously difficult or impossible to implement in ColdFusion. Some potential uses for CFSQL include:

- Manipulate query objects (sort, summarize, group, etc.) returned by other ColdFusion tags such as CFHTTP, CFFTP, CFLDAP, CFPOP, CFSEARCH, or CFSTROEDPROC as well as the various query functions
- Perform joins and unions between tables from different data sources
- Resorting a query result set without having to go back to the data source
- Moving entire tables into memory (Macromedia recommends no more than 10,000 rows), effectively speeding up query times because ColdFusion no longer has to make a round trip to the database for each query performed

Regardless of what you decide to use CFSQL for, you need to know what SQL constructs are available. For starters, you can perform only an SQL SELECT in CFSQL. This means that CFSQL can be used only to select records, not INSERT, UPDATE, or DELETE them. This makes sense, as the purpose of CFSQL is to allow you to perform a query against an already existing query. When you perform your SELECT, a number of SQL keywords are available to help you construct your query. These keywords are FROM, WHERE, ORDER BY, GROUP BY, HAVING, JOIN, and UNION. A number of comparison and Boolean operators are also available: =, <>, <, >, <=, >=, AND, OR, NOT, IN, BETWEEN, LIKE, and EXISTS. In addition, CFSQL supports several aggregate functions including COUNT, SUM, AVG, MAX, and MIN. You should note that CFSQL doesn't support nested aggregate functions nor does it support ODBC dates in comparison operations.

To perform a query of a query, you set the DBTYPE attribute of the CFQUERY tag to Query and reference the name of one or more existing queries in the FROM clause of your SQL statement. The DATASOURCE attribute isn't used when performing a query of a query. Example 11-24 shows a simple query of a query.

*Example 11-24. Using CFSQL to Perform a Query of a Query*

```
<!--- put the entire EmployeeDirectory table into memory --->
<CFQUERY NAME="GetAll" DATASOURCE="ProgrammingCF">
SELECT *
FROM EmployeeDirectory
</CFQUERY>


<!--- Use CFSQL to retrieve a count of the number of employees for each
      department in the EmployeeDirectory table of the database --->
<CFQUERY NAME="GetDepartmentSummary" DBTYPE="query">
         SELECT COUNT(Name) AS TotalEmployees,
                Department
         FROM GetAll
         GROUP BY Department
         ORDER BY Department
</CFQUERY>

<H3>Total Number of Employees for
```

*Example 11-24. Using CFSQL to Perform a Query of a Query (continued)*

```
    each Department</H3>
<TABLE BORDER="0" CELLPADDING="3">
<TR BGCOLOR="#C0C0C0">
  <TH>Department</TH>
  <TH>Total Employees</TH>
</TR>

<CFOUTPUT QUERY="GetDepartmentSummary">
<TR BGCOLOR="##E3E3E3">
  <TD>#Department#</TD>
  <TD>#TotalEmployees#</TD>
</TR>
</CFOUTPUT>
</TABLE>
```

In this example, the first `CFQUERY` retrieves all the records in the `EmployeeDirectory` table in a query called `GetAll`. In the second `CFQUERY`, the `DBTYPE` is set to `Query`, indicating that the query should use an existing query as its data source. The SQL used is the same aggregate function from Example 11-14. It retrieves a count of the number of employees in each department. However, instead of going to the database for this information, the query is performed against the `GetAll` query, as specified in the `FROM` clause. While you probably wouldn't use ColdFusion's query of a query for such a trivial task in a real application, this example shows how simple it is to implement this technique.

## Calling Stored Procedures

Most enterprise-level databases (MS SQL Server, DB2, Oracle, Informix, Sybase) support creating special programs within the database called stored procedures. Stored procedures allow you to encapsulate SQL and other database-specific functions in a wrapper that can be called from external applications. There are several reasons to use stored procedures whenever possible in your applications:

- Stored procedures execute faster than identical code passed using the `CFQUERY` tag because they are precompiled on the database server.
- Stored procedures support code reuse. A single procedure needs to be created only once and can be accessed by any number of templates, even different applications and those written in other languages.
- Stored procedures allow you to encapsulate complex database manipulation routines, often utilizing database-specific functions.
- Security is enhanced by keeping all database operations encapsulated within the stored procedure. Because ColdFusion passes parameters only to the stored procedure, there is no way to execute arbitrary SQL commands.

There are two ways to call stored procedures in ColdFusion. You can use the CFQUERY tag (which is now outdated) or the CFSTOREDPROC tag (which is new as of ColdFusion Version 4.0). Unfortunately, material on writing stored procedures is beyond the scope of this book. For more information on creating stored procedures, consult the documentation for your specific database.

## *Using CFSTOREDPROC*

The preferred method for calling stored procedures in ColdFusion is via the CFSTOREDPROC tag. This tag takes several attributes that allow you to specify information about the data source on which you want to execute the stored procedure, as well as the stored procedure itself. The three most commonly used attributes are:

```
<CFSTOREDPROC PROCEDURE="procedure_name"
              DATASOURCE="datasource_name"
              RETURNCODE="Yes/No">
</CFSTOREDPROC>
```

PROCEDURE is a required attribute and specifies the name of the stored procedure on the database server that you want to execute. The DATASOURCE attribute is also required and specifies the data source that contains the stored procedure. The final attribute, RETURNCODE is optional and accepts a Yes/No value. If set to Yes, populates CFSTOREDPROC.STATUSCODE with the status code returned by the stored procedure. The default value for RETURNCODE is No. There are a number of additional attributes that can be used with the CFSTOREDPROC tag. For a complete list, see Appendix A.

The CFSTOREDPROC tag calls only the stored procedure you want to execute. You still need a way to pass values in and receive data back from the stored procedure. These functions are handled by two child tags of the CFSTOREDPROC tag, the CFPROCPARAM and CFPROCRESULT tags respectively.

When a stored procedure is executed using the CFSTOREDPROC tag, two return values are automatically created by ColdFusion. These variables are:

CFSTOREDPROC.STATUSCODE
: Returned when RETURNCODE is set to Yes; contains the status code returned by the stored procedure

CFSTOREDPROC.EXECUTIONTIME
: The number of milliseconds it took for the stored procedure to execute

### *Passing parameters using CFPROCPARAM*

The CFPROCPARAM tag specifies parameter information to send to the stored procedure named in the CFSTOREDPROC tag. You may specify multiple CFPROCPARAM tags within a single CFSTOREDPROC tag. CFPROCPARAM tags must be nested within the CFSTOREDPROC tag and use the following syntax:

```
<CFPROCPARAM TYPE="In/Out/InOut"
             VARIABLE="variable_name"
             DBVARNAME="database_variable_name"
             VALUE="parameter_value"
             CFSQLTYPE="parameter_data_type"
             MAXLENGTH="length"
             SCALE="decimal_places"
             NULL="yes/no">
```

The TYPE attribute is optional and specifies whether the variable being passed is an input (In), output (Out), or input/output (InOut) variable. The default TYPE is input (In). VARIABLE is required when TYPE is Out or InOut and specifies the name of the ColdFusion variable used to reference the value returned by the output parameter after the stored procedure is called. DBVARNAME is required if named notation is used and specifies the name of the parameter within the stored procedure. If you are using positional notation in your stored procedure, you must pass the CFPROCPARAM tags in the order expected by the stored procedure. The VALUE attribute is required when TYPE is In or InOut. It specifies the value to pass to the stored procedure.

The next attribute, CFSQLTYPE, is required and specifies the SQL type of the parameter being passed to the stored procedure. Possible values are listed back in Table 11-1.The default value for CFSQLTYPE is CF_SQL_CHAR. The MAXLENGTH attribute specifies the maximum length of the parameter being passed and is an optional attribute. SCALE is also optional and specifies the number of decimal places for the parameter should it be a numeric datatype. The final attribute is NULL. NULL is optional and specifies a Yes/No value indicating whether the value passed is a NULL. If Yes, ColdFusion ignores the VALUE attribute. The default value for NULL is No.

### *Specifying result sets using CFPROCRESULT*

The CFPROCRESULT tag specifies the name for a given result set returned by the CFSTOREDPROC tag. This allows other ColdFusion tags to reference the result set returned by the stored procedure. Because stored procedures can return more than one result set, the CFPROCRESULT tag allows you to specify which result set to use. Because of this feature, it is possible to nest multiple CFPROCRESULT tags within a CFSTOREDPROC tag, provided you assign a different NAME for each CFPROCRESULT set:

```
<CFPROCRESULT NAME="query_name"
              RESULTSET="1-n"
              MAXROWS="number">
```

The `NAME` attribute is required and specifies a name for the query result set returned by the stored procedure. `RESULTSET` is an optional attribute and specifies the result set to use if the stored procedure returns more than one result set. The default value for `RESULTSET` is `1`. The final attribute is `MAXROWS`. `MAXROWS` is also optional and specifies the maximum number of rows to return with the result set. By default, all rows are returned.

Example 11-25 uses the `CFSTOREDPROC` tag, several `CFPROCPARAM` tags, and the `CFPROCRESULT` tag to execute a stored procedure called `sp_AddEmployee` that adds a new employee record to a database.

*Example 11-25. Executing a Stored Procedure Using CFSTOREDPROC*

```
<!--- assign blank default values for any fields not passed in --->
<CFPARAM NAME="Form.Name" DEFAULT="">
<CFPARAM NAME="Form.Title" DEFAULT="">
<CFPARAM NAME="Form.Department" DEFAULT="">
<CFPARAM NAME="Form.Email" DEFAULT="">
<CFPARAM NAME="Form.PhoneExt" DEFAULT="">
<CFPARAM NAME="Form.Salary" DEFAULT="">

<!--- call the sp_AddEmployee stored procedure --->
<CFSTOREDPROC PROCEDURE="sp_AddEmployee"
              DATASOURCE="ProgrammingCF"
              RETURNCODE="Yes">
<!--- pass each parameter.  If the field being passed contains a blank value,
      make it NULL --->
<CFPROCPARAM TYPE="In" CFSQLTYPE="CF_SQL_VARCHAR" DBVARNAME="Name"
             VALUE="#Form.Name#" MAXLENGTH="255"
             NULL=#IIF(Form.Name IS "", 1, 0)#>
<CFPROCPARAM TYPE="In" CFSQLTYPE="CF_SQL_VARCHAR" DBVARNAME="Title"
             VALUE="#Form.Title#" MAXLENGTH="255"
             NULL=#IIF(Form.Title IS "", 1, 0)#>
<CFPROCPARAM TYPE="In" CFSQLTYPE="CF_SQL_VARCHAR" DBVARNAME="Department"
             VALUE="#Form.Department#" MAXLENGTH="255"
             NULL=#IIF(Form.Department IS "", 1, 0)#>
<CFPROCPARAM TYPE="In" CFSQLTYPE="CF_SQL_VARCHAR" DBVARNAME="Email"
             VALUE="#Form.Email#" MAXLENGTH="255"
             NULL=#IIF(Form.Email IS "", 1, 0)#>
<CFPROCPARAM TYPE="In" CFSQLTYPE="CF_SQL_DECIMAL" DBVARNAME="PhoneExt"
             VALUE="#Form.PhoneExt#" NULL=#IIF(Form.PhoneExt IS "", 1, 0)#>
<CFPROCPARAM TYPE="In" CFSQLTYPE="CF_SQL_DECIMAL" DBVARNAME="Salary"
             VALUE="#Form.Salary#" NULL=#IIF(Form.Salary IS "", 1, 0)#>

<!--- assign a query object named InsertRecord to the first result set
      returned --->
<CFPROCRESULT NAME="InsertRecord" RESULTSET="1">
</CFSTOREDPROC>


<!--- Output status information --->
<CFIF CFSTOREDPROC.StatusCode IS 1>
```

*Example 11-25. Executing a Stored Procedure Using CFSTOREDPROC (continued)*

```
  <CFOUTPUT>
  Record inserted successfully.  The employee ID assigned is: #InsertRecord.ID#
  <BR>
  The stored procedure executed in #CFSTOREDPROC.ExecutionTime# milliseconds.
  </CFOUTPUT>
<CFELSE>
  There was an error inserting the record!
</CFIF>

</BODY>
</HTML>
```

In Example 11-25, if the stored procedure returns a `StatusCode` of 1, the record was inserted successfully, and you can output the ID value assigned to the newly inserted record. Returning this value is part of the stored procedure. If it returns any other `StatusCode`, an error occurred. The value of `StatusCode` is set inside of the stored procedure, allowing you to assign any status codes you intend.

The following Allaire Knowledge Base articles (*http://www.allaire.com/support/knowledgebase/SearchForm.cfm*) provide additional information on using stored procedures with ColdFusion:

*Article 13754*
: "New Features and Enhancements in ColdFusion Server 4.5" (Page 2)

*Article 8622*
: "How to Execute a DB2 Stored Procedure in ColdFusion"

## Using CFQUERY

Prior to the introduction of the `CFSTOREDPROC` tag in ColdFusion 4.0, the only way to call a stored procedure from ColdFusion was with the `CFQUERY` tag. The syntax for calling a stored procedure using `CFQUERY` is:

```
<CFQUERY NAME="MyQuery" DATASOURCE="MyDataSource">
{Call MyDB.dbo.sp_mysp (#var1#, '#Var2#')}
</CFQUERY>
```

There are several drawbacks to using the `Call` statement with `CFQUERY` to call stored procedures. For example, parameters must be passed in the order in which they appear in the stored procedure, and you can't specify input parameters by name or bind parameters to datatypes. There is no way to explicitly pass a `NULL`, and you can't specify the length for a given parameter. There is also no way to access return codes or output parameters created by the stored procedure.

Depending on your database, you may be able to use a native function to call a stored procedure with the `CFQUERY` tag. Several databases allow you to call stored procedures using the `Execute` or `Exec` keyword instead of `Call` as in:

```
<CFQUERY NAME="MyQuery" DATASOURCE="MyDataSource">
{Execute MyDB.dbo.sp_mysp
 @Var = #var#,
 @Var2 = '#Var2#'}
</CFQUERY>
```

Using a native database function for calling a stored procedure allows you to overcome some of the problems associated with using the Call method such as referring to input parameters by name. However, this in and of itself isn't justification for using the `CFQUERY` tag to call stored procedures. Unless you are running a version of ColdFusion prior to Version 4.0, you should call your stored procedures using the `CFSTOREDPROC` tag.

# *Transaction Processing*

ColdFusion provides support for database transaction processing using the `CFTRANSACTION` tag. The `CFTRANSACTION` tag lets you treat all query operations with the `<CFTRANSACTION>` and `</CFTRANSACTION>` tags as a single transaction. Changes to the database aren't committed until all queries in the transaction have executed successfully. In the event a query within the transaction fails, all previous queries are automatically rolled back. The exception to this occurs when the database itself is changed, as in the case when a table or column is created or deleted.

The `CFTRANSACTION` tag accepts two optional attributes for controlling how transactions are processed, `ACTION` and `ISOLATION`:

`ACTION`
: Specifies the transaction action to take. Valid options include:

  `Begin (default)`
  : Specifies the beginning of the block of code to execute

  `Commit`
  : Commits a pending transaction

  `Rollback`
  : Rolls back a pending transaction

`ISOLATION`
: Specifies the ODBC lock type to use for the transaction. The following ODBC lock types are supported: `Read_Uncommitted`, `Read_Committed`, `Repeatable_Read`, and `Serializable`.

Note that not all databases and/or database drivers support isolation levels. Many support only a subset of those listed. Refer to your particular database/driver's documentation for more information on the isolation levels supported.

Example 11-26 shows how to use the CFTRANSACTION tag with two queries that delete records from different tables within the same data source. You need to use the CFTRANSACTION tag to ensure that both queries are treated as a single transaction. If either query fails, any changes made are automatically rolled back.

*Example 11-26. Simple CFTRANSACTION Usage*

```
<!--- use the CFTRANSACTION tag to ensure that both queries are treated
      as a single transaction.  If either query fails, any changes made
      are automatically rolled back --->
<CFTRANSACTION>
<!--- delete an employee from the EmployeeDirectory table where the
      employee's ID is equal to the ID value passed in as a form var --->
<CFQUERY NAME="DeleteEmployee" DATASOURCE="ProgrammingCF">
       DELETE FROM EmployeeDirectory
       WHERE ID = #Form.ID#
</CFQUERY>

<!--- delete any entries for the employee from the IncentiveAwards table.
      This table is described later in the chapter. --->
<CFQUERY NAME="DeleteBonusRecords" DATASOURCE="ProgrammingCF">
       DELETE FROM IncentiveAwards
       WHERE ID = #Form.ID#
</CFQUERY>
</CFTRANSACTION>
```

In Example 11-25, the CFTRANSACTION tag ensures that both DELETE queries are treated as a single transaction. If either query fails, any changes made are automatically rolled back. Note that both queries are made to the same data source, but not to the same table.

A particularly useful feature of the CFTRANSACTION tag is that it can be nested to allow portions of a transaction to be committed or rolled back within the main CFTRANSACTION block as the code executes. The syntax for a nested transaction differs slightly from the syntax used to call most other tags. To commit a transaction within a nested CFTRANSACTION tag, use the following syntax:

```
<CFTRANSACTION ACTION="Commit"/>
```

Note the trailing forward slash at the end of the tag. This lets ColdFusion know you have nested the CFTRANSACTION tag and no end tag is necessary. Rolling back a transaction uses similar syntax:

```
<CFTRANSACTION ACTION="Rollback"/>
```

Using nested CFTRANSACTION tags and exception handling with CFTRY/CFCATCH gives you full control over how queries are committed and rolled back within CFTRANSACTION blocks. This technique also lets you write to more than one database within a single CFTRANSACTION block, if each transaction is committed or rolled back prior to writing a query to the next database. Example 11-27 demonstrates how to use nested **CFTRANSACTION** tags to create a new table populated with data from an existing table (using **SELECT INTO**) and then add another record to the table.

*Example 11-27. Using Nested CFTRANSACTION Tags with Multiple Queries*

```
<!--- Initialize a variable called Continue to control the transaction --->
<CFSET Continue = "Yes">

<!--- begin transaction --->
<CFTRANSACTION ACTION="BEGIN">

<!--- wrap the INSERT INTO in a CFTRY block --->
<CFTRY>
<!--- Select the name, title, email, and phone ext for each employee in
      the EmployeeDirectory table that belongs to the Sales department
      and use it to populate a new table called SalesDirectory --->
<CFQUERY NAME="MakeSalesDirectory" DATASOURCE="ProgrammingCF">
         SELECT Name, Title, Email, PhoneExt
         INTO SalesDirectory
         FROM EmployeeDirectory
         WHERE Department = 'Sales'
</CFQUERY>

<!--- if a database error occurs, rollback the transaction and set the
      Continue variable to No. --->
<CFCATCH TYPE="Database">
    <CFTRANSACTION ACTION="ROLLBACK"/>
    <CFSET ProblemQuery = "MakeSalesDirectory">
    <CFSET Continue = "No">
</CFCATCH>
</CFTRY>

<!--- if the INSERT INTO was successful, commit the transaction and
      execute another query to insert a new record into the table we
      created with the last query. --->
<CFIF Continue EQ "Yes">
<CFTRY>
<CFTRANSACTION ACTION="COMMIT"/>
<CFQUERY NAME="InsertRecord" DATASOURCE="ProgrammingCF">
         INSERT INTO SalesDirectory(Name, Title, Email, PhoneExt)
         VALUES('Lynda Newton', 'Account Manager', 'lynda@example.com', 1261)
</CFQUERY>

<!--- if a database error occurs, rollback the transaction and set the
      Continue variable to No. --->
<CFCATCH TYPE="DATABASE">
    <CFTRANSACTION ACTION="ROLLBACK"/>
    <CFSET ProblemQuery = "InsertRecord">
    <CFSET Continue = "No">
</CFCATCH>
</CFTRY>
</CFIF>
```

*Example 11-27. Using Nested CFTRANSACTION Tags with Multiple Queries (continued)*

```
<!--- if the record was successfully added, commit the transaction --->
<CFIF Continue EQ "Yes">
    <CFTRANSACTION ACTION="COMMIT"/>
</CFIF>
</CFTRANSACTION>

<!--- if both transactions were successful, generate a table containing all
      of the records from the new table.  If not display a message letting
      the user know there was a problem. --->
<CFIF Continue EQ "Yes">

<!--- retrieve all of the records from the Sales Directory table we just
      created --->
<CFQUERY NAME="GetEmployees" DATASOURCE="ProgrammingCF">
         SELECT Name, Title, Email, PhoneExt
         FROM SalesDirectory
         ORDER BY Name
</CFQUERY>

<H2>All queries in the transaction executed successfully</H2>
<H3>Below is the data from the new table:</H3>

<TABLE CELLPADDING="3" CELLSPACING="0">
<TR BGCOLOR="#888888">
  <TH>Name</TH>
  <TH>Title</TH>
  <TH>E-mail</TH>
  <TH>Phone Ext.</TH>
</TR>

<!--- dynamically generate a table containing all of the records returned
      by the query --->
<CFOUTPUT QUERY="GetEmployees">
<TR BGCOLOR="##C0C0C0">
  <TD>#Name#</TD>
  <TD>#Title#</TD>
  <TD>#Email#</TD>
  <TD>#PhoneExt#</TD>
</TR>
</CFOUTPUT>
</TABLE>

<CFELSE>
<CFOUTPUT>
<H2>An Error has occurred.  All queries have been rolled back</H2>
<B>The query that caused the error is: <I>#ProblemQuery#</I>.</B>
</CFOUTPUT>
</CFIF>
```

In Example 11-27, the `Continue` variable controls the transaction. At the start of the template, this variable is initialized to `Yes`. As long as queries within the `CFTRANSACTION` block execute successfully, `Continue` keeps the value of `Yes`.

Each subsequent query checks the status of this variable before executing. If at any point `Continue` is `No`, the transaction is rolled back, and no other queries with the `CFTRANSACTION` block are executed.

Executing the template in Example 11-27 results in the output shown in Figure 11-10. If you execute the template a second time, however, you should see the error message generated by the template.

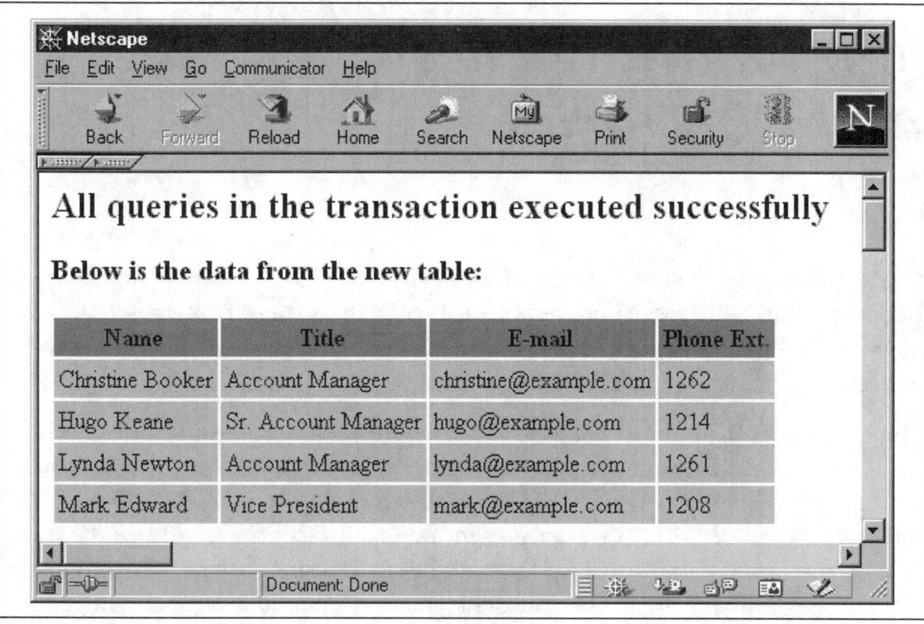


*Figure 11-10. Successful completion of queries within a nested CFTRANSACTION block*

# 12

*In this chapter:*
- *Working with Directories*
- *Dealing with Files*
- *Performing FTP Operations*

# *Manipulating Files and Directories*

ColdFusion comes with three tags that make it possible to manipulate files and directories on both local and remote servers. These tags enable you to build sophisticated applications such as document management systems, forms capable of accepting file uploads, FTP clients, and more.

The `CFDIRECTORY` and `CFFILE` tags allow you to manipulate directories and files on your local ColdFusion server, while the `CFFTP` tag makes it possible to conduct file transfers between your ColdFusion server and remote FTP servers. Both the `CFFILE` and `CFDIRECTORY` tag present potential security hazards, as these tags have direct access to the filesystem of the ColdFusion server. Therefore care should be taken with their use and deployment. Depending on the configuration of your web server and operating system, it may also be possible to upload executable code via the `CFFILE` tag and execute it on your server. The consequences can be potentially devastating to a system as a user could easily upload malicious code to the server and subsequently execute it. Therefore, both tags can be disabled from the ColdFusion administrator, should you decide not to make them available to developers on your server.

## *Working with Directories*

The `CFDIRECTORY` tag lists directory contents as well as creates, renames, and deletes directories on your ColdFusion application server. In an application such as a document management system, the `CFDIRECTORY` tag allows you to do such tasks as list all the documents stored in a particular folder or build a Windows Explorer-style view of files and folders on your server. Because the `CFDIRECTORY` tag provides direct access to your ColdFusion server's filesystem, the tag can be disabled from the basic security tab in the ColdFusion Administrator.

## *Listing Directory Contents*

As just noted, the CFDIRECTORY tag lists the contents of any directory on the ColdFusion server. Example 12-1 uses the CFDIRECTORY tag to list the contents of the root directory on the C drive of the ColdFusion server.

*Example 12-1. Listing a Directory with CFDIRECTORY*

```
<CFLOCK NAME="CLock" TYPE="ReadOnly" TIMEOUT="30">
<CFDIRECTORY ACTION="LIST"
             DIRECTORY="c:\"
             NAME="MyQuery"
             FILTER="*.*"
             SORT="Type ASC, NAME ASC">
</CFLOCK>

<TABLE BORDER="1">
<TR>
   <TH>Name</TH><TH>Size</TH><TH>Type</TH><TH>Last Modified</TH>
   <TH>Attributes</TH><TH>Mode</TH>
</TR>

<CFOUTPUT QUERY="MyQuery">
<TR>
   <TD>#Name#</TD><TD>#Size#</TD><TD>#Type#</TD><TD>#DateLastModified#</TD>
   <TD>#Attributes#</TD><TD>#Mode#</TD>
</TR>
</CFOUTPUT>
</TABLE>
```

The first attribute, ACTION, tells ColdFusion what CFDIRECTORY operation to perform. In this case, we want to LIST the contents of a particular directory on our ColdFusion server. Valid entries for ACTION are LIST, CREATE, RENAME, and DELETE. The DIRECTORY attribute specifies the full path (including drive letter) to the directory that we want to list the contents of. In this case, we want to list the contents of the root directory on drive C. The NAME attribute specifies the name assigned to the query object returned by the CFDIRECTORY operation. The FILTER attribute is optional and allows us to specify a file extension to filter the results returned. Only one file extension can be used with the FILTER attribute. For our example, we set the FILTER attribute to *.* so that all files and directories are listed. The final attribute in our example is the SORT attribute. SORT is an optional attribute that allows us to specify how we want to sort each query column returned by the operation. Note that the SORT attribute can take a single query column or a comma-separated list. The actual direction for the sort is specified as ASC for ascending and DESC for descending.

The CFLOCK tag places a read-only lock on the CFDIRECTORY operation. Each individual directory you read from or write to via CFDIRECTORY should have a unique NAME assigned for it in the CFLOCK tag to keep locking consistent. This means that all read/write operations to the same directory should use the same name.

When the tag executes, a number of query columns are returned as part of the ColdFusion query object specified in the NAME attribute of the CFDIRECTORY tag:

`Attributes`
: The attributes, if any, for the given object.

`DateLastModified`
: The time/date stamp that the object was last modified.

`Mode`
: This column applies only to the Unix version of ColdFusion and specifies the permissions set for the file or directory. The `Mode` is the same as the permissions set by the Unix *chmod* command.

`Name`
: The name of the directory or file.

`Size`
: The size in bytes of the directory or file.

`Type`
: `Dir` if the object is a directory or `File` if it is a file.

## *Creating a Directory*

Creating a directory using the CFDIRECTORY tag is quick and easy to do. The following example shows the syntax for creating a directory on your ColdFusion application server:

```
<CFLOCK NAME="Lock_Name" TYPE="EXCLUSIVE" TIMEOUT="30">
  <CFDIRECTORY ACTION="CREATE"
               DIRECTORY="d:\MyCreatedDirectory"
               MODE="777">
</CFLOCK>
```

Setting the ACTION attribute to CREATE tells ColdFusion that you want to create a new directory. The directory to be created is referenced in the DIRECTORY attribute. Note that you must specify the full path to the directory you want to create. The MODE attribute is optional and is used only with the Unix version of ColdFusion. The MODE attribute allows you to set permissions the way you would with the Unix *chmod* command. For example, setting the MODE equal to 777 as in our example assigns read, write, and execute permissions to the directory for everyone.

As shown in this example, we use an exclusive CFLOCK so that only one process can access the directory at a time. This ensures that multiple operations don't step on each others' toes, potentially resulting in an error or corrupted directory.

## *Renaming a Directory*

The CFDIRECTORY tag can also rename an existing directory on the ColdFusion server. For example, to change the name of the directory *d:\MyOldDirectoryName* to *d:\MyNewDirectoryName*, use the CFDIRECTORY tag as follows:

```
<CFLOCK NAME=" Lock_Name" TYPE="EXCLUSIVE" TIMEOUT="30">
  <CFDIRECTORY ACTION="RENAME"
               DIRECTORY="d:\MyOldDirectoryName"
               NEWDIRECTORY="MyNewDirectoryName">
</CFLOCK>
```

Setting the ACTION attribute to RENAME lets ColdFusion know that we want to change the name of the directory specified in the DIRECTORY attribute. Note that the full path, including the drive letter, is required in the DIRECTORY attribute. The NEWDIRECTORY parameter specifies the new name we want to use for the directory being changed. The name for the new directory doesn't require a full path. Again, note the use of CFLOCK to exclusively lock access to the directory while it is renamed.

## *Deleting a Directory*

The CFDIRECTORY tag can also delete directories. The following is an example of a typical delete operation using the CFDIRECTORY tag.

```
<CFLOCK NAME="Lock_Name" TYPE="EXCLUSIVE" TIMEOUT="30">
  <CFDIRECTORY ACTION="DELETE"
               DIRECTORY="c:\MyDirectory">
</CFLOCK>
```

Setting the ACTION attribute to Delete lets ColdFusion know we want to use the CFDIRECTORY tag to delete a directory. The actual directory to delete is specified in the DIRECTORY attribute. In this case, we are using the tag to delete *c:\MyDirectory*. As with the other operations that change the directory structure, we use CFLOCK here.

Before a directory can be deleted, it must be completely empty. If you try to delete a directory that isn't empty, ColdFusion throws an error and halts processing. Therefore, it is a good idea to include code to check if a particular directory is empty before you attempt to delete it. One technique for checking to see if a directory is empty is shown here:

```
<!--- get a list of the directory contents --->
<CFLOCK NAME="TestLock" TYPE="ReadOnly" TIMEOUT="30">
```

```
  <CFDIRECTORY ACTION="List"
               NAME="MyDirectory"
               DIRECTORY="D:\test">
</CFLOCK>

<!--- Check the record count for the query object. --->
<CFIF MyDirectory.RecordCount IS 2>
  <CFLOCK NAME="TestLock" TYPE="EXCLUSIVE" TIMEOUT="30">
    <CFDIRECTORY ACTION="Delete"
                 DIRECTORY="d:\test">
  </CFLOCK>
   Directory deleted!
<CFELSE>
  The directory wasn't empty!
</CFIF>
```

The first `CFDIRECTORY` tag gets a list of the contents of *d:\test*. Next, we check to see if the directory list operation returned exactly two objects. This is done by using a `CFIF` statement to evaluate the value stored in the `RecordCount` query column. If the value of `RecordCount` is two, we know that the directory is empty, and we use the `CFDIRECTORY` tag to delete the directory by setting the `ACTION` attribute to `Delete`. If any number other than two is returned for the `RecordCount`, the directory isn't deleted, and a message is sent back to the user letting them know that the directory wasn't empty. At first, this fact might seem strange. You would think that a count of two means that the directory isn't empty because there are two files in it, but this isn't the case. All directories contain two objects by default (.) and (..). These two objects serve no purpose as far as ColdFusion is concerned, but they are still present in any listing returned by the `CFDIRECTORY` tag. Because of this, a `RecordCount` greater than two means that the directory isn't empty.

# *Dealing with Files*

The `CFFILE` tag handles all file manipulation that takes place on the local ColdFusion server. The `CFFILE` tag has three purposes. First, it makes it possible to upload files to the ColdFusion server via an HTML form. This means you can design forms that allow users to upload files from their machines directly to your ColdFusion server. This lets you create things such as web-based email clients, document management systems, and other applications that require users to upload files to your server. The second purpose of the `CFFILE` tag is to allow you to manipulate files located on your ColdFusion server. The `CFFILE` tag allows you to rename, move, copy, and delete files on the ColdFusion server. The final purpose of the `CFFILE` tag is to allow you to read, write, and append both text and binary files.

## *Uploading Files*

Enabling file uploads is one of the more popular uses for the CFFILE tag. To do this, you first have to include a file input type in an HTML form. This allows a user to select a file from their system and post it along with the other form fields. When the form is submitted, the file is posted to the server/template specified in the ACTION attribute of the FORM tag. The receiving template then uses a CFFILE tag to process the uploaded file.

You should exercise extreme caution when implementing the CFFILE tag's Upload action within your ColdFusion applications. Because the tag allows users to upload files directly to your ColdFusion server, you need to make sure that the security of your server is given the proper attention. Files uploaded via the CFFILE tag should be written only to directories that aren't accessible via a URL. In addition, execute permissions should be turned off in the directory where files are being uploaded. These two steps help to keep executable files from being uploaded to the server and subsequently run.

Example 12-2 shows how to build a simple two-template application for uploading a file from your machine to your ColdFusion server. The first template consists of an HTML form for choosing the file to be uploaded. It can be saved as a ColdFusion template or a regular HTML file.

*Example 12-2. HTML Form for Uploading a File*

```
<HTML>
<HEAD>
    <TITLE>HTML File Upload Form</TITLE>
</HEAD>

<BODY>
<FORM ACTION="Example12-2.cfm" METHOD="POST" ENCTYPE="multipart/form-data">
<TABLE>
<TR>
    <TD>File:</TD>
    <TD><INPUT TYPE="File" NAME="FileToUpload" SIZE="25" MAXLENGTH="255"></TD>
</TR>
<TR>
    <TD COLSPAN="2"><INPUT TYPE="Submit" NAME="Submit" VALUE="Upload"></TD>
</TR>
</TABLE>
</FORM>

</BODY>
</HTML>
```

In Example 12-2, one thing you might notice right away is the use of the ENCTYPE attribute in the <FORM> tag. In order to upload files via HTML forms, it is necessary to specify ENCTYPE="multipart/form-data". Another feature unique to file uploads is the use of `File` as the input type. This input type tells the browser to allow the user to select a file from her system. You should note that not all web browsers support `File` as an input type. While Netscape browsers have supported file uploading since Version 2.0, Microsoft Internet Explorer didn't begin full support until Version 4.0. Other browsers may or may not support file uploading. There is no programmatic way to determine whether a particular browser supports file uploading. You need to keep this in mind when implementing file uploading in your applications.

Once the user selects a file and clicks on the submit button, the form data is passed to the ColdFusion template specified in the `ACTION` attribute of the `<FORM>` tag. You should be aware that there are limitations on the size of a file that can be uploaded. File size is limited by the amount of physical memory that you have installed on the server running ColdFusion. Although there isn't an exact formula for determining the amount of memory necessary to handle file uploads, it is necessary to have more physical RAM available than the largest file size that you intend to upload. Attempting to upload a file with a file size greater than the available amount of physical RAM results in an error and causes ColdFusion to halt processing of the template. For more information on file-size limitations of the `CFFILE` tag, see Allaire Knowledge Base Article 280, available online at *http://www.allaire.com/Support/KnowledgeBase/SearchForm.cfm*.

It is possible to check the file size of a file after it has been uploaded to the web server and before it is permanently written to the filesystem, by checking the CGI environment variable `CGI.CONTENT_LENGTH`. In a file upload scenario such as ours, the `CGI.CONTENT_LENGTH` variable contains the length of the file being passed from the form template. By using a `CFIF` statement, we can evaluate the length of the file after it has been uploaded to the web server, before it is written to the specified directory by ColdFusion. Because ColdFusion is a server-side language, there is no way to know the size of an uploaded file before it reaches the server. The only way to assess file size on the client machine before an upload is via a signed Java applet or ActiveX control. Another workaround would be to write a filter (ISAPI, NSAPI, or WSAPI) at the web-server level to filter incoming HTTP uploads based on file size. The technique shown here is still useful, however, as it allows you to limit the size of files accepted by your application. Example 12-3 illustrates the ColdFusion template for processing an uploaded file with code to ensure that no files over 100K in size are committed to the server.

*Example 12-3. Uploading a File Using CFFILE*

```
<!--- check the CGI environment variable Content_Length to make sure the file
      being uploaded is less than 100k in size.  If it is not, halt
      processing --->
<CFIF Val(CGI.CONTENT_LENGTH) GT 100000>
The file you are attempting to upload exceeds the maximum allowable size of
```

*Example 12-3. Uploading a File Using CFFILE (continued)*

```
100k and cannot be uploaded to this server!  Please choose a smaller file and
try again.
<CFABORT>
</CFIF>

<!--- use the CFFILE tag to upload the file passed from the form to our
      ColdFusion server --->
<CFFILE ACTION="UPLOAD"
        FILEFIELD="FileToUpload"
        DESTINATION="c:\temp"
        NAMECONFLICT="Overwrite"
        ACCEPT="text/html,text/plain"
        ATTRIBUTES="Archive">

<!--- Output the results in a HTML table --->
<CENTER>
<H2>CFFILE Upload Results:</H2>

<CFOUTPUT>
<TABLE>
<TR>
  <TD>AttemptedServerFile</TD><TD>#CFFILE.AttemptedServerFile#</TD>
  <TD>FileWasAppended</TD><TD>#CFFILE.FileWasAppended#</TD>
</TR>
<TR>
  <TD>ClientDirectory</TD><TD>#CFFILE.ClientDirectory#</TD>
  <TD>FileWasOverwritten</TD><TD>#CFFILE.FileWasOverwritten#</TD>
</TR>
<TR>
  <TD>ClientFile</TD><TD>#CFFILE.ClientFile#</TD>
  <TD>FileWasRenamed</TD><TD>#CFFILE.FileWasRenamed#</TD>
</TR>
<TR>
  <TD>ClientFileExt</TD>TD>#CFFILE.ClientFileExt#</TD>
  <TD>FileWasSaved</TD><TD>#CFFILE.FileWasSaved#</TD>
</TR>
<TR>
  <TD>ClientFileName</TD><TD>#CFFILE.ClientFileName#</TD>
  <TD>OldFileSize</TD><TD>#CFFILE.OldFileSize#</TD>
</TR>
<TR>
  <TD>ContentSubType</TD><TD>#CFFILE.ContentSubType#</TD>
  <TD>ServerDirectory</TD><TD>#CFFILE.ServerDirectory#</TD>
</TR>
<TR>
  <TD>ContentType</TD><TD>#CFFILE.ContentType#</TD>
  <TD>ServerFile</TD><TD>#CFFILE.ServerFile#</TD>
</TR>
<TR>
  <TD>DateLastAccessed</TD><TD>#CFFILE.DateLastAccessed#</TD>
  <TD>ServerFileExt</TD><TD>#CFFILE.ServerFileExt#</TD>
</TR>
```

*Example 12-3. Uploading a File Using CFFILE (continued)*

```
<TR>
  <TD>FileExisted</TD><TD>#CFFILE.FileExisted#</TD>
  <TD>ServerFileName</TD><TD>#CFFILE.ServerFileName#</TD>
</TR>
<TR>
  <TD>FileSize</TD><TD>#CFFILE.FileSize#</TD>
  <TD>TimeCreated</TD><TD>#CFFILE.TimeCreated#</TD>
</TR>
</TABLE>
</CFOUTPUT>
</CENTER>
```

The first part of Example 12-3 uses a `CFIF` statement to compare the number stored in the `CGI.CONTENT_LENGTH` variable to 100,000. `Val()` is a ColdFusion function that returns a number that a particular string can be converted to. In this case, `Val(CGI.CONTENT_LENGTH)` returns the length in bytes of the file being uploaded via the form in Example 12-2. If the length in bytes is greater than 100,000, we know that the file is over 100K and don't want to save to our ColdFusion server. A message is written back to the browser letting the user know that the file was too big to upload and processing of the ColdFusion template is halted before the file can be uploaded. If, however, the value of `CGI.CONTENT_LENGTH` is less than or equal to 100,000, the template continues processing uninterrupted.

In the next part of Example 12-3, we use the `CFFILE` tag to actually perform the file upload from the client's machine to our ColdFusion server. We set the `ACTION` attribute in the `CFFILE` tag to `Upload` to begin the operation. In the `FILEFIELD` attribute, we specify the name we gave to the file upload form field from Example 12-2. The `DESTINATION` attribute specifies the full directory path to the location to which we want to store the uploaded file. `NAMECONFLICT` is used to specify how ColdFusion should proceed if the file being uploaded has the same name as a file already existing in the `DESTINATION` directory. There are four possible values for the `NAMECONFLICT` attribute:

`ERROR`
: Generates a ColdFusion error if the file already exists on the server.

`MAKEUNIQUE`
: Assigns a unique name to the file being uploaded if the file already exists on the server.

`OVERWRITE`
: Overwrites the file already on the server with the file being uploaded.

`SKIP`
: Results in the uploaded file not being saved to the server. No error message is returned, however.

The ACCEPT attribute specifies a comma-separated list of MIME types the ColdFusion server should be allowed to accept. This attribute is optional and set to allow all MIME types by default. For our example, we set the ACCEPT attribute to `text/html,text/plain` to allow both HTML and plain-text files to be uploaded. The final attribute, ATTRIBUTES is also optional and is used to specify a comma-separated list of attributes for the file. Valid entries are `Archive`, `Hidden`, `Normal`, `ReadOnly`, `System`, and `Temporary`. If the ATTRIBUTES attribute isn't specified, the file's original attributes are used.

One thing you'll notice here is that we didn't include a CFLOCK tag around the CFFILE operation. In the case of file uploads, it isn't necessary to lock the CFFILE tag, as you aren't reading or writing to a file already on the ColdFusion server. ColdFusion handles the possibility of uploading a file with the same name as a file already on the server with the NAMECONFLICT attribute of the CFFILE tag.

Once the file has been uploaded to the server, the template in Example 12-3 displays the results of the file upload transaction, which can be seen in Figure 12-1.

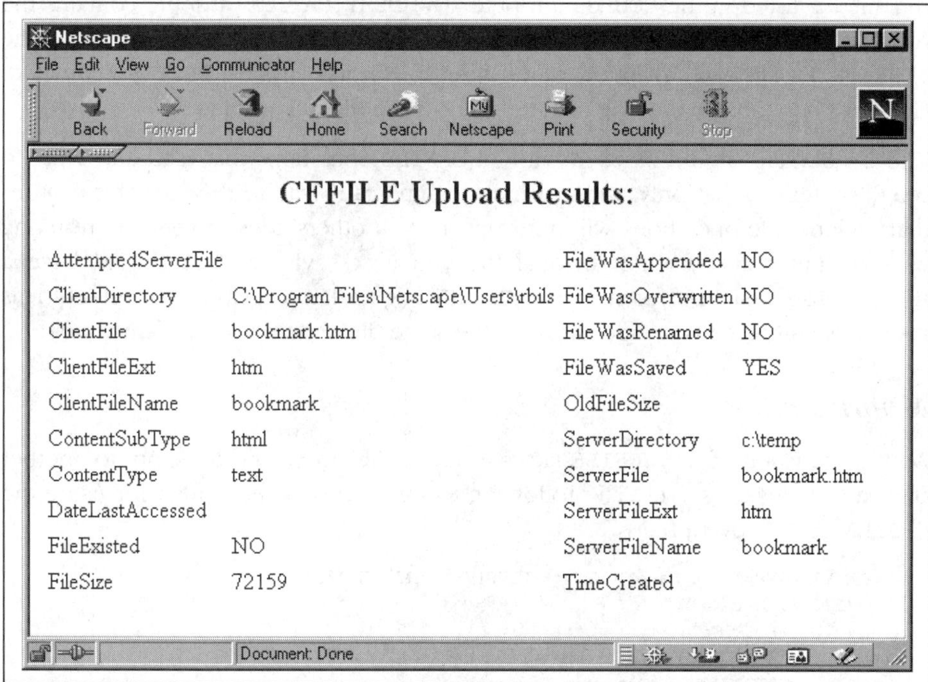


*Figure 12-1. Sample output from a CFFILE upload operation*

When the CFFILE tag is executed, a number of ColdFusion variables are created to hold information about the transaction. These variables are read-only and can be referenced using the file scope as in `CFFILE.VariableName`.* Most of these variables have self-explanatory names, as you can see from Example 12-3 and Figure 12-1. For more information on these variables, see the `CFFILE` entry in Appendix A.

## Renaming Files

The `CFFILE` tag can also rename files already on the server. The syntax for renaming a file is as follows:

```
<CFLOCK NAME="Lock_Name" TYPE="EXCLUSIVE" TIMEOUT="30">
  <CFFILE ACTION="Rename"
          SOURCE="D:\myoldfilename.txt"
          DESTINATION="D:\mynewfilename.txt"
          ATTRIBUTES="Normal">
</CFLOCK>
```

Setting the `ACTION` attribute to `Rename` lets the ColdFusion server know that we want to use the `CFFILE` tag to rename a file. The full path to the file being renamed is listed in the `SOURCE` attribute. The `DESTINATION` attribute contains the full path including the new filename that we want to use for the file. The `ATTRIBUTES` attribute is optional and is set to `Normal`. If `ATTRIBUTES` is omitted, ColdFusion maintains the original attributes of the file being renamed.

The `CFLOCK` tag should be used with all `CFFILE` operations that read and write to the filesystem so that only one process at a time can write to the file. This ensures that multiple file operations will not step on each others' toes, potentially resulting in a corrupted file. Each individual file you access via `CFFILE` should have a unique `NAME` assigned for it in the `CFLOCK` tag to keep locking consistent. This means that all read/write operations to the same file should use the same name.

## Moving Files

Another function of the `CFFILE` tag is to move files from one directory to another on the ColdFusion server. The following example shows the syntax for using the `CFFILE` tag to move a file:

```
<CFLOCK NAME="Lock_Name" TYPE="EXCLUSIVE" TIMEOUT="30">
  <CFFILE ACTION="Move"
          SOURCE="d:\myfile.txt"
          DESTINATION="d:\temp\myfile.txt"
          ATTRIBUTES="ReadOnly,Hidden">
</CFLOCK>
```

* Prior to Version 4.5, the file scope was prefixed using the `File` prefix. While this prefix is still supported in ColdFusion 5.0, it has been deprecated.

This time, the `ACTION` attribute is set to `Move`. The `SOURCE` attribute includes the full path to the current location of the file that we want to move. The `DESTINATION` attribute contains the full path including the filename to the destination where we want to move the file. The `ATTRIBUTES` attribute is optional and is set to `ReadOnly` and `Hidden`. If `ATTRIBUTES` is omitted, ColdFusion maintains the original attributes of the file being renamed. Again, note the use of the `CFLOCK` tag to exclusively lock access to the file while we move it.

## *Copying Files*

The `CFFILE` tag is also capable of copying files from one directory to another. For example, to copy the file *d:\myfile.txt* to *d:\temp\myfile.txt*, you can use the following syntax within your `CFFILE` tag:

```
<CFLOCK NAME="Lock_Name" TYPE="EXCLUSIVE" TIMEOUT="30">
  <CFFILE ACTION="Copy"
          SOURCE="d:\myfile.txt"
          DESTINATION="d:\temp\myfile.txt">
</CFLOCK>
```

In this case, we set the `ACTION` attribute to `Copy`. The `SOURCE` attribute specifies the full path to the file we want a copy of. The `DESTINATION` attribute contains the full path to the directory where the file will be saved. The filename here is optional. If no filename is used, the trailing backslash (Unix slash) must be used. `ATTRIBUTES` is optional and set to `Normal` for our example. If `ATTRIBUTES` is omitted, ColdFusion maintains the original attributes of the file being copied.

## *Deleting Files*

The `CFFILE` tag can delete a tag from the server by setting the `ACTION` attribute to `Delete` and the `FILE` attribute to the full path of the file you want to delete. For example, to delete the file *d:\myfile.txt*, use the following `CFFILE` statement:

```
<CFLOCK NAME="Lock_Name" TYPE="EXCLUSIVE" TIMEOUT="30">
  <CFFILE ACTION="DELETE"
          FILE="D:\myfile.txt">
</CFLOCK>
```

You should exercise caution when using the `CFFILE` tag with the `ACTION` attribute set to `Delete`, as the tag has direct access to the entire filesystem of the server. Care should also be taken to secure from unauthorized use all ColdFusion templates that perform delete functions.

## *Reading Text Files*

The `CFFILE` tag can read the contents of a text file and store the data in a variable that is accessible to ColdFusion. The following example shows how to read and store the contents of a text file called *MyFile.txt* inside a ColdFusion variable called **TheFileContents**. The contents of **TheFileContents** are then output to the screen.

```
<CFLOCK NAME="Lock_Name" TYPE="ReadOnly" TIMEOUT="30">

<CFFILE ACTION="READ"
        FILE="D:\temp\MyFile.txt"
        VARIABLE="TheFileContents">
</CFLOCK>

<CFOUTPUT>
#TheFileContents#
</CFOUTPUT>
```

The **ACTION** attribute is set to **Read** so that ColdFusion knows to use the **CFFILE** tag to read the contents of a text file. The actual text file we want to read gets specified in the **FILE** attribute. For this example, we want to read the contents of a file called *MyFile.txt* that is located in *d:\temp*. Setting the **VARIABLE** attribute to **TheFileContents** causes ColdFusion to read the contents of *MyFile.txt* and store them in a variable called **TheFileContents**. The **CFOUTPUT** section simply writes the contents of **TheFileContents** to the screen. Note the use of the read-only **CFLOCK** to ensure we don't try to read the file at the same moment another process is writing to it.

## Reading Binary Files

ColdFusion also can read a binary file and store its contents in a variable that can be manipulated by ColdFusion. Reading a binary file in and of itself is a trivial operation, as the file must be converted to a base64 representation before ColdFusion can perform any additional functions on it. *Base64* is a method of encoding that takes a binary string and converts the binary data to printable characters. This is useful in situations where you want to store a binary file in a database or send it via email. The following example reads a binary file and converts the object to a base64 representation, which is then output to the screen:

```
<CFLOCK NAME="Lock_Name" TYPE="ReadOnly" TIMEOUT="30">
  <CFFILE ACTION="ReadBinary"
          FILE="D:/Inetsrv/cf/e/dot.gif"
          VARIABLE="MyBinaryFile">
</CFLOCK>
<CFSET MyBase64 = ToBase64(MyBinaryFile)>

Base64 encoded binary file:<BR>
<FORM>
<CFOUTPUT>
<TEXTAREA COLS="50" ROWS="25" WRAP="virtual">#MyBase64#</TEXTAREA>
</CFOUTPUT>
</FORM>
```

The binary file is read by setting the `ACTION` attribute of the `CFFILE` tag to `ReadBinary`. The `FILE` attribute specifies the full path to the file to be read. The file object is stored in the ColdFusion variable specified in the `VARIABLE` attribute. Once the file has been read into memory by ColdFusion, it is converted to its base64 representation using the `ToBase64()` function. The results are then written out to the browser.

## *Writing Text Files*

In addition to reading files, the `CFFILE` tag can also write files to the server. This is useful for a number of purposes including writing log files for your applications and creating static HTML files from dynamic content. Example 12-4 shows how to create a static HTML file from the results of a `CFHTTP` operation that returns the contents of a dynamically generated page.

*Example 12-4. Writing a Text File with CFFILE*

```
<!--- Execute the remote cfm file via CFHTTP --->
<CFHTTP METHOD="GET"
        URL="http://www.example.com/dir/file.cfm">
</CFHTTP>

<!--- Write the output of the CFHTTP operation to a static html file on
      the server --->
<CFLOCK NAME="MyFileLock" TYPE="EXCLUSIVE" TIMEOUT="30">
  <CFFILE ACTION="write"
          FILE="d:\inetpub\wwwroot\myfile.htm"
          OUTPUT="#CFHTTP.FileContent#"
          ATTRIBUTES="Temporary"
          MODE="777"
          ADDNEWLINE="Yes">
</CFLOCK>
```

The `CFHTTP` operation executes a ColdFusion template called *file.cfm* and stores the resulting page in the `CFHTTP.FileContent` variable. `CFHTTP.FileContent` is automatically created by the `CFHTTP` operation. This is all you need to understand about `CFHTTP` for now; we'll cover this tag in more detail in Chapter 14.

The `CFFILE` tag then creates a text file by setting the `ACTION` attribute to `Write`. The `FILE` attribute contains the filename and directory where we want to write our new text file. In this case, we are creating a text file called *myfile.htm*. The actual content to be written to the file is specified in the `OUTPUT` attribute. Because we want to create a static web page from the results of the ColdFusion template we accessed with `CFHTTP`, we assign `#CFHTTP.FileContent#` to the `OUTPUT` attribute. It is important to include the pound signs around the `CFHTTP.FileContent` variable so that ColdFusion knows to treat it as a variable as opposed to literal text.

`ATTRIBUTES` is optional and can specify a comma-delimited list of attributes for the newly created text file. In this case, we are making the file a temporary file. The `MODE` attribute can define file permissions on a Unix server. In this example, the `MODE` attribute is set to 777, so that everyone has read, write, and execute permissions for the file. Setting `ADDNEWLINE` to `Yes` causes ColdFusion to add a trailing new line character to the end of the `OUTPUT` string. `ADDNEWLINE` is an optional attribute and is set to `Yes` by default.

## *Writing Binary Files*

The `CFFILE` tag can also write binary files to the server. There is only one difference between writing a text file to the server and writing a binary file. The contents making up a binary file must be converted to a binary object in order to be written as a binary file. Example 12-5 illustrates the point by creating a GIF image of the letter "R" from its base64 equivalent.

*Example 12-5. Writing a Binary File with CFFILE*

```
<CFSET MyBase64="R0lGODlhGQAZAPcAAP////v7+/Pz8+7u7uLi4t3d3dnZ2dXV1cTExLe3t6qqqp6e
npGRkYmJiYiIiH9/f3t7e25ubmZmZllZWVZWVlFRUURERDw8PDQ0NC8vLyIiIhUVFREREQwMDAQEBAAAA
AAAAAAAAAAAAAAAAAAAAAAAAAAAAAAAAAAAAAAAAAAAAAAAAAAAAAAAAAAAAAAAAAAAAAAAAAAAAAAAAAAA
AAAAAAAAAAAAAAAAAAAAAAAAAAAAAAAAAAAAAAAAAAAAAAAAAAAAAAAAAAAAAAAAAAAAAAAAAAAAAAAAAAA
AAAAAAAAAAAAAAAAAAAAAAAAAAAAAAAAAAAAAAAAAAAAAAAAAAAAAAAAAAAAAAAAAAAAAAAAAAAAAAAAAAA
AAAAAAAAAAAAAAAAAAAAAAAAAAAAAAAAAAAAAAAAAAAAAAAAAAAAAAAAAAAAAAAAAAAAAAAAAAAAAAAAAAA
AAAAAAAAAAAAAAAAAAAAAAAAAAAAAAAAAAAAAAAAAAAAAAAAAAAAAAAAAAAAAAAAAAAAAAAAAAAAAAAAAAA
AAAAAAAAAAAAAAAAAAAAAAAAAAAAAAAAAAAAAAAAAAAAAAAAAAAAAAAAAAAAAAAAAAAAAAAAAAAAAAAAAAA
AAAAAAAAAAAAAAAAAAAAAAAAAAAAAAAAAAAAAAAAAAAAAAAAAAAAAAAAAAAAAAAAAAAAAAAAAAAAAAAAAAA
AAAAAAAAAAAAAAAAAAAAAAAAAAAAAAAAAAAAAAAAAAAAAAAAAAAAAAAAAAAAAAAAAAAAAAAAAAAAAAAAAAA
AAAAAAAAAAAAAAAAAAAAAAAAAAAAAAAAAAAAAAAAAAAAAAAAAAAAAAAAAAAAAAAAAAAAAAAAAAAAAAAAAAA
AAAAAAAAAAAAAAAAAAAAAAAAAAAAAAAAAAAAAAAAAAAAAAAAAAAAAAAAAAAAAAAAAAAAAAAAAAAAAAAAAAA
AAAAAAAAAAAAAAAAAAAAAAAAAAAAAAAAAAAAAAAAAAAAAAAAAAAAAAAAAAAAAAAAAAAAAAAAAAAAAAAAAAA
AAAAACwAAAAAGQAZAEcIiwABCBxIsKDBgwQffPigAIHDBh4+YEBoUOGHAgMlLHRAsaPHjyApWlxI8sMEA
SFTqlwpkIGGlzAxUECQ0iLGgRc+cAhpE4CBDR86HKi58KbABQsrsFzKtKlTkCNLfvCQgGdRghUWWv0Q4c
EDCBYWRthaoQKHoFWJXhSYYGGGAFuNDgDagcDTu3gpBgQAOw==">

<CFSET MyBinary=ToBinary(MyBase64)>

<CFLOCK NAME="MyBinaryLock" TYPE="EXCLUSIVE" TIMEOUT="30">
  <CFFILE ACTION="write"
          FILE="c:\temp\mybinary.gif"
          OUTPUT=#MyBinary#>
</CFLOCK>

<CFLOCK NAME="MyBinaryLock" TYPE="EXCLUSIVE" TIMEOUT="30">
  <CFCONTENT TYPE="image/gif"
            FILE="c:\temp\mybinary.gif"
            DELETEFILE="Yes">
</CFLOCK>
```

The first section of this example sets a variable called `MyBase64` to the base64 representation of a binary object (in this case, a GIF image of the letter "R"). This information could have been pulled from a database or read directly from a file. The second section of the example converts the base64 string to a binary object using the `ToBinary()` function. Once that is done, the binary object is written out to a file using the `CFFILE` tag with the `OUTPUT` attribute set to the value of the binary object we created. Finally, the `CFCONTENT` tag takes the file specified in the `FILE` attribute and sends it to the browser using the MIME type specified in the `TYPE` attribute. Setting `DELETEFILE` to `Yes` tells ColdFusion to delete the GIF file from the server once it has been sent to the browser. Note that a `CFLOCK` tag is placed around the `CFCONTENT` tag. This is done because in this particular case, the `CFCONTENT` tag deletes the file it grabs after sending it to the browser.

## *Appending Text Files*

Data can be appended to the end of an existing text file by setting the `ACTION` attribute of the `CFFILE` tag to `Append`. The following example shows how to use the `CFFILE` tag to append additional information to a file called *MyFile.txt*:

```
<CFSET MyString="This is the line to be added!">

<CFLOCK NAME=" Lock_Name" TYPE="EXCLUSIVE" TIMEOUT="30">
  <CFFILE ACTION="APPEND"
          FILE="d:\temp\MyFile.txt"
          OUTPUT="#MyString#"
          ADDNEWLINE="Yes">
</CFLOCK>
```

The `FILE` attribute specifies the file we want to append additional information to. We use the `OUTPUT` attribute to specify the data that we want to append to the end of the text file. The `OUTPUT` attribute can contain text or a previously defined ColdFusion variable. In our example, we use a ColdFusion variable that has been previously defined with a `CFSET` statement. Note the use of pound signs around the ColdFusion variable name; they are necessary in this case, to differentiate between a variable and literal text. To finish the operation off, we use the optional `ADDNEWLINE` attribute. Setting `ADDNEWLINE` to `Yes` causes ColdFusion to add a trailing new line character to the end of the `OUTPUT` string.

# *Performing FTP Operations*

As we've already discussed, the `CFFILE` tag allows you to upload files from a client machine to the ColdFusion server and perform file and directory operations on your ColdFusion server. When you need to work with files and directories on a remote server, however, you need to use the `CFFTP` tag instead.

## Connecting to a Remote Server

FTP operations using the CFFTP tag begin by opening a connection to the remote FTP server. The following example shows how to connect to an anonymous FTP server using the CFFTP tag:

```
<CFFTP ACTION="Open"
       SERVER="ftp.microsoft.com"
       PORT="21"
       USERNAME="anonymous"
       PASSWORD="YourEmailAddress@yourdomain.com"
       CONNECTION="MyConnection"
       AGENTNAME="MyFTPClient"
       PROXYSERVER="MyProxyServer"
       PROXYBYPASS="127.0.0.1"
       RETRYCOUNT="3"
       TIMEOUT="60"
       STOPONERROR="No"
       PASSIVE="No">
```

To open the connection to the remote FTP server, we set the ACTION parameter of the CFFTP tag to Open. There are several additional parameters available for the ACTION attribute that will be discussed later in this section. The SERVER attribute specifies the hostname or IP address of the remote server with which to open an FTP session. In this case, we want to connect to Microsoft's public FTP server at *ftp.microsoft.com*. The PORT attribute specifies what port the CFFTP tag should try to connect to. This attribute is optional and defaults to the standard FTP port 21. Because Microsoft allows anonymous access to their FTP server, we set the USERNAME attribute to Anonymous. As a matter of convention and netiquette, your email address should be entered in the PASSWORD attribute for anonymous FTP connections. We could just as easily connect to a non-anonymous FTP site by specifying an actual username and password in the USERNAME and PASSWORD attributes, respectively.

The CONNECTION attribute is optional and set to MyConnection. CONNECTION is used to let the ColdFusion server know that the FTP connection should be cached so that we can perform batch operations without having to reestablish a new connection for each task. AGENTNAME is an optional attribute that allows us to declare a name for the application or entity making the FTP connection. The PROXYSERVER attribute is also optional and allows us to list the IP address or hostname of a proxy server if it is required. If this attribute is NULL, ColdFusion attempts to obtain proxy server information from the registry. PROXYBYPASS is another optional attribute and provides a list of IP addresses or hostnames that don't need to be routed through the proxy server. If the PROXYBYPASS attribute is NULL, ColdFusion attempts to obtain the proxy bypass list from the registry.

The next several attributes deal with how ColdFusion should behave if there is trouble connecting to the remote server. The `RETRYCOUNT` is an optional attribute that determines the number of times the FTP operation should be attempted before an error is reported. The default number of retries is 1. The `TIMEOUT` attribute is also an optional attribute and defaults to 30 seconds. It determines the length in seconds that an operation has to execute before the request is timed out. The `STOPONERROR` attribute is optional and set to `No` (the default) so that the application continues to process in the event an error in the FTP operation occurs. If you set the `STOPONERROR` attribute to `Yes`, ColdFusion throws an error and ceases processing if an FTP operation fails. The final attribute, `PASSIVE`, specifies whether ColdFusion should initiate a passive transfer with the remote FTP server. This is an optional attribute and set to `No` by default.

If you plan to utilize the same FTP connection across multiple ColdFusion templates, you should store the connection caching information in a session variable. To do this, all you need to do is modify the `CONNECTION` attribute in your `CFFTP` statement to reflect the assignment to the session variable. It is also necessary to make sure that session management is enabled for your application. Here's how we can modify our previous example to accomplish this:

```
<CFLOCK SCOPE="Session" TYPE="Exclusive" TIMEOUT="60" THROWONTIMEOUT="Yes">

<CFFTP ACTION="open"
       SERVER="ftp.microsoft.com"
       USERNAME="anonymous"
       PASSWORD="YourEmailAddress@yourdomain.com"
       CONNECTION="Session.MyConnection"
       STOPONERROR="No">
</CFLOCK>
```

By establishing the cached connection as a session variable, it is possible to maintain the FTP connection across multiple ColdFusion templates. The use of `CFLOCK` around the `CFFTP` tag is necessary when reading and writing session variables, to ensure the integrity of the session. Setting the `TYPE` attribute to `Exclusive` ensures single-threaded access when writing the session variable.

## *Closing the Connection*

Before we can talk about doing anything interesting with an FTP connection, I want to discuss how you close a connection. When you are finished with all your `CFFTP` operations for a cached connection, it is a good idea to close the FTP connection. You can do this by setting the `ACTION` attribute of the `CFFTP` tag to `Close`. Failing to explicitly close a cached FTP connection causes the connection to remain open until the connection times out. Depending on the server your `CFFTP` operation connects to, this can take quite a while. It isn't necessary to close noncached FTP operations as the connection is automatically dropped after each operation. The following example shows how to close a cached FTP connection:

```
<CFLOCK SCOPE="Session" TYPE="ReadOnly" TIMEOUT="60" THROWONTIMEOUT="Yes">

<CFFTP ACTION="Close"
       CONNECTION="Session.MyConnection"
       STOPONERROR="Yes">
</CFLOCK>
```

Once again, the CFFTP operation is wrapped within a CFLOCK tag to ensure exclusive reading of the session variable used to cache the FTP connection. In this case, the TYPE attribute of the CFLOCK tag is set to ReadOnly, so that more than one request can access the locked code at a time.

Setting the ACTION to Close tells ColdFusion to close the FTP connection. The CONNECTION attribute specifies the exact connection we want to close. In this case, we are closing the connection from our previous example, so we use Session.MyConnection as the parameter. Finally, we set STOPONERROR to Yes. Setting this attribute to Yes causes ColdFusion to throw an error and halt processing in the event that an error occurs while closing the connection.

## *Performing File and Directory Operations*

Now that we know how to open and close FTP sessions with the CFFTP tag, it is time to move on to file and directory operations. Once a connection to a remote FTP server has been made, the CFFTP tag can perform a variety of file and directory operations on the remote server. In the previous example, we opened a cached FTP session called Session.MyConnection by setting the ACTION attribute to Open. To perform directory and file operations, all we need to do is change the value of the ACTION attribute to reflect the operation we want the CFFTP tag to perform. The following list describes the ACTION parameters you have available for working with remote files and directories using the CFFTP tag:

ChangeDir
: Changes the directory the CFFTP tag has access to on the remote FTP server. Requires that you specify the directory in the DIRECTORY attribute.

CreateDir
: Creates a new directory on the remote server. The CreateDir parameter requires the use of the DIRECTORY attribute.

Exists
: Returns Yes if the value specified in the ITEM attribute exists or No if it doesn't. The value for the ITEM attribute can be any file, directory, or object.

`ExistsDir`
: Returns `Yes` if the value specified in the `DIRECTORY` attribute exists or `No` if it doesn't.

`ExistsFile`
: Returns `Yes` if the value specified in the `REMOTEFILE` attribute exists or `No` if it doesn't.

`GetCurrentDir`
: Returns the current directory being accessed by the `CFFTP` tag.

`GetCurrentURL`
: Returns the URL to the current location being accessed by the `CFFTP` tag.

`GetFile`
: Gets a file from the remote server and downloads it to the ColdFusion server. Using this `ACTION` requires that you also specify values for the `REMOTEFILE` and `LOCALFILE` attributes.

`ListDir`
: Lists the directories specified in the `NAME` and `DIRECTORY` attributes.

`PutFile`
: Takes a file from the ColdFusion server and uploads it to the remote FTP server. Using this `ACTION` requires that you also specify values for the `LOCALFILE` and `REMOTEFILE` attributes.

`Remove`
: Deletes a file on the remote FTP server. Using this `ACTION` requires that you also specify values for the `SERVER` and `ITEM` attributes.

`Removedir`
: Deletes a directory on the remote FTP server. Using this `ACTION` requires that you also specify a value for the `DIRECTORY` attribute.

`Rename`
: Renames a file on the remote FTP server. Using this `ACTION` requires that you also specify values for the `EXISTING` and `NEW` attributes.

### *Obtaining a directory listing*

Example 12-6 uses everything we have learned so far about the `CFFTP` tag to open a connection to a remote FTP server, cache the connection, obtain a directory listing, and close the connection. Before you execute Example 12-6, make sure you have an *Application.cfm* template that enables session management in the directory in which you saved the example template.

*Example 12-6. Obtaining a File and Directory Listing from a Remote FTP Server*

```
<!--- open the FTP connection --->
<CFLOCK SCOPE="Session" TYPE="Exclusive" TIMEOUT="60" THROWONTIMEOUT="Yes">

<CFFTP ACTION="Open"
       SERVER="ftp.microsoft.com"
       USERNAME="anonymous"
       PASSWORD="YourEmailAddress@yourdomain.com"
       CONNECTION="Session.MyConnection"
       STOPONERROR="No">
</CFLOCK>

<!--- if there is an error, display it to the user and stop processing the
      template --->
<CFIF NOT CFFTP.Succeeded>
   Connection aborted!<BR>
   <CFOUTPUT>
      Error number #CFFTP.ErrorCode#: #CFFTP.ErrorText#
   </CFOUTPUT>
   <CFABORT>
</CFIF>
<B>Connection opened successfully!</B><BR>
<B><I>Directories and files at:  ftp.microsoft.com</I></B>

<!--- get a list of the files and directories in the current directory --->
<CFLOCK SCOPE="Session" TYPE="ReadOnly" TIMEOUT="60" THROWONTIMEOUT="Yes">

<CFFTP ACTION="ListDir"
       STOPONERROR="No"
       NAME="ListFiles"
       DIRECTORY="/"
       CONNECTION="Session.MyConnection">
</CFLOCK>

<!--- if there is an error, display it to the user and stop processing --->
<CFIF NOT CFFTP.Succeeded>
   Connection aborted!<BR>
   <CFOUTPUT>
      Error number #CFFTP.ErrorCode#: #CFFTP.ErrorText#
   </CFOUTPUT>
   <CFABORT>
</CFIF>

<!--- build a table of the directory contents --->
<P>
<TABLE BORDER="0" CELLSPACING="1" CELLPADDING="3">
<TR BGCOLOR="#0000FF">
   <TH><FONT COLOR="#FFFFFF">Name</FONT></TH>
   <TH><FONT COLOR="#FFFFFF">Path</FONT></TH>
   <TH><FONT COLOR="#FFFFFF">URL</FONT></TH>
   <TH><FONT COLOR="#FFFFFF">Length</FONT></TH>
   <TH><FONT COLOR="#FFFFFF">Last Modified</FONT></TH>
   <TH><FONT COLOR="#FFFFFF">Directory or File</FONT></TH>
```

*Example 12-6. Obtaining a File and Directory Listing from a Remote FTP Server (continued)*

```
   <TH><FONT COLOR="#FFFFFF">Attributes</FONT></TH>
</TR>

<CFOUTPUT QUERY="ListFiles">
<TR BGCOLOR="##c0c0c0">
   <TD>#name#</TD>
   <TD>#path#</TD>
   <TD>#url#</TD>
   <TD>#length#</TD>
   <TD>#DateFormat(lastmodified,'mm/dd/yyyy')#</TD>
   <TD><CFIF #isdirectory#>Directory<CFELSE>File</CFIF></TD>
   <TD>#Attributes#</TD>
</TR>
</CFOUTPUT>
</TABLE>

<!--- close the ftp connection --->
<CFLOCK SCOPE="Session" TYPE="ReadOnly" TIMEOUT="60" THROWONTIMEOUT="Yes">

<CFFTP ACTION="Close"
       CONNECTION="Session.MyConnection"
       STOPONERROR="No">
</CFLOCK>

<!--- if there is an error, display it to the user and stop processing --->
<CFIF NOT CFFTP.Succeeded>
   Connection aborted!<BR>
   <CFOUTPUT>
      Error number #CFFTP.ErrorCode#: #CFFTP.ErrorText#
   </CFOUTPUT>
   <CFABORT>
<CFELSE>
   <B>Connection closed successfully!</B>
</CFIF>
```

Example 12-6 begins by opening the connection to the anonymous FTP server at *ftp.microsoft.com* and caching the connection in a session variable called `Session.MyConnection`. This code follows the guidelines that were used in our previous example on opening a connection. Once the attempt to open the FTP connection has been made, we check to see if the connection was successful by checking for the existence of a special variable called `CFFTP.Succeeded`. `CFFTP.Succeeded` is automatically created each time a `CFFTP` action is performed; it contains `True` if the operation was successful. In our case, if the FTP session is opened successfully, we allow the application to continue processing. If, however, the FTP session isn't opened successfully, an error is generated and reported back to the user in the variables `CFFTP.ErrorCode` and `CFFTP.ErrorText`, and processing is aborted with a `CFABORT` tag. The values for `CFFTP.ErrorCode` and `CFFTP.ErrorText` are listed under the `CFFTP` tag in Appendix A.

Now Example 12-6 uses the CFFTP tag to get a list of the files and directories from *ftp.microsoft.com.* This is done by setting the ACTION attribute to ListDir. Because we are using connection caching, there is no need to respecify the SERVER, USERNAME, or PASSWORD attributes. We set the STOPONERROR attribute to No so that processing of the template continues in the event an error occurs. The NAME attribute is required when the ACTION attribute is set to ListDir and specifies a name for the ColdFusion query object created by the ListDir ACTION. Another attribute that is required for ListDir operations is the DIRECTORY attribute. The DIRECTORY attribute specifies the directory from which to obtain the file and directory listing. In our case, we set the DIRECTORY attribute to / to obtain a listing for the root directory at *ftp.microsoft.com.* The final attribute, CONNECTION is set to MyConnection and specifies the name of the cached connection to use for the action.

Next comes another bit of error-checking code that is identical to the code we used earlier. It is important to build in error checking like this since we set the STOPONERROR attribute to No to allow ColdFusion to continue processing our template in the event of an error. If the FTP operation fails for any reason, the error-checking code gives us a way to handle the error gracefully.

Now we build an HTML table that contains a list of the files and directories found in the directory specified in the DIRECTORY attribute of the CFFTP tag. Each row of the table is dynamically populated with information from the ColdFusion query object created by the CFFTP operation. Query objects created by the CFFTP tag contain the following query columns:

Attributes
: Returns the attributes, if any, for the given object

IsDirectory
: Returns True if the object is a directory; False if it isn't

LastModified
: Date that the file or directory was last modified

Length
: Length in bytes of the file or directory

Name
: The name of the file or directory

Path
: Path without drive-letter designation to the file or directory

URL
: URL to the file or directory

Example 12-6 uses a `CFIF` statement to evaluate the contents of the variable `IsDirectory()` for each row returned by the query. If `IsDirectory()` evaluates to `True`, we know the object is a directory and list it as such. If `IsDirectory()` evaluates to `False`, the object is a file and is listed that way instead. Figure 12-2 shows the directory listing from Microsoft's FTP site as returned by Example 12-6.

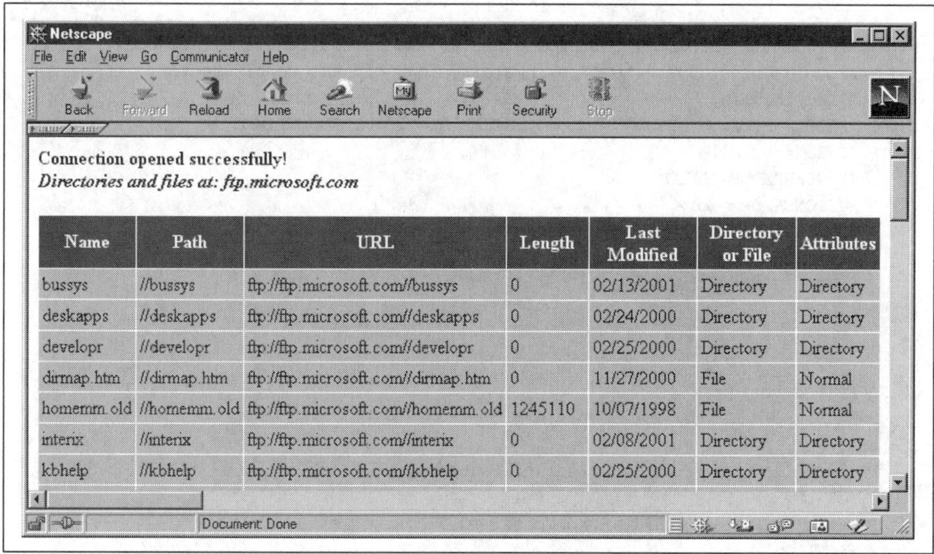


*Figure 12-2. Directory listing from ftp.microsoft.com using CFFTP tag*

The rest of the code in Example 12-6 closes our cached FTP connection the same way we did in our earlier example on closing connections. As with our other FTP operations, we also perform some error checking after closing the connection.

### *Uploading files*

Example 12-7 shows how to upload a file to a remote FTP server using the `CFFTP` tag. For this example to work, it is necessary to have access to an FTP server that is capable of accepting file uploads. Although the example uses 127.0.0.1 (the local host) as the FTP server, you can change this attribute to any FTP server you have write access to.

*Example 12-7. Uploading a File to a Remote Server with CFFTP*

```
<!--- open the FTP connection --->
<CFLOCK SCOPE="Session" TYPE="Exclusive" TIMEOUT="60" THROWONTIMEOUT="Yes">

<CFFTP ACTION="Open"
       USERNAME="myusername"
       CONNECTION="MyConnection"
```

*Example 12-7. Uploading a File to a Remote Server with CFFTP (continued)*

```
        PASSWORD="mypassword"
        SERVER="127.0.0.1"
        STOPONERROR="Yes">
</CFLOCK>

<P>
<B>Connection opened</B>

<!--- take the file from the ColdFusion server and upload it via FTP to the
      remote machine.  put the file in a directory off the root directory
      called incoming. --->
<CFLOCK SCOPE="Session" TYPE="ReadOnly" TIMEOUT="60" THROWONTIMEOUT="Yes">
<CFFTP ACTION="PutFile"
        TRANSFERMODE="AUTO"
        STOPONERROR="No"
        REMOTEFILE="\incoming\myfile.txt"
        LOCALFILE="d:\temp\myfile.txt"
        CONNECTION="MyConnection">
</CFLOCK>

<P>
<CFIF CFFTP.Succeeded>
    <B>File successfully uploaded!</B>
<CFELSE>
    <B>The following error occurred while attempting to upload your file:</B><BR>
    <CFOUTPUT>
    <B><I>Error number #CFFTP.ErrorCode#: #CFFTP.ErrorText#</I></B>
    </CFOUTPUT>
</CFIF>


<!--- close the ftp connection --->
<CFLOCK SCOPE="Session" TYPE="ReadOnly" TIMEOUT="60" THROWONTIMEOUT="Yes">

<CFFTP ACTION="Close"
        CONNECTION="MyConnection"
        STOPONERROR="Yes">
</CFLOCK>

<P>
<B>Connection closed.</B>
```

As you would expect, this example uses a `CFFTP` tag to open an FTP session and caches the connection as `MyConnection`. Once the connection is opened, we use another `CFFTP` tag to carry out the file upload from the ColdFusion server to the FTP server. This is done by setting the `ACTION` attribute of the `CFFTP` tag to `PutFile`. `TRANSFERMODE` specifies the FTP transfer mode to use when retrieving the file from the FTP server. Valid options are `Text`, `Binary`, and `Auto`. In this case, we set `TRANSFERMODE` to `Auto`. `STOPONERROR` is set to `No` so that ColdFusion continues to process the template in the event an error occurs.

`REMOTEFILE` is a required attribute for a `PutFile` operation and specifies the file on the FTP server we want to download to our ColdFusion server. The full path to the file on the FTP server should be used. In this case, the file we want to download gets referenced as *\incoming\myfile.txt.* The next attribute, `LOCALFILE` is also a required attribute for a `PutFile` operation and determines the location to save the downloaded file on the ColdFusion server. Setting the `LOCALFILE` attribute to *d:\temp\myfile.txt* results in ColdFusion saving the file as *myfile.txt* in *d:\temp*. The `CONNECTION` attribute is set to `MyConnection`, the cached connection we defined at the beginning of the code.

After the `CFFTP` download completes, a `CFIF` tag evaluates the status of the download. If it is successful, a message is written to the browser informing the user. If the download isn't successful, an error code and error message are written back to the browser. Finally, another `CFFTP` tag closes the cached FTP connection.

### *Downloading files*

The `CFFTP` tag can also download files from remote servers to your ColdFusion server. Example 12-8 uses the `CFFTP` tag to download a file called *disclaimer.txt* from Microsoft's anonymous FTP server. This is a powerful feature in that it allows your ColdFusion applications to download data files from remote FTP servers that would otherwise require a manual download using a standard FTP client.

*Example 12-8. Downloading a File from a Remote Server with CFFTP*

```
<!--- open the FTP connection --->
<CFLOCK SCOPE="Session" TYPE="Exclusive" TIMEOUT="60" THROWONTIMEOUT="Yes">

<CFFTP ACTION="Open"
       USERNAME="anonymous"
       CONNECTION="MyConnection"
       PASSWORD="username@domain.com"
       SERVER="ftp.microsoft.com"
       STOPONERROR="Yes">
</CFLOCK>

<P>
<B>Connection opened</B>

<!--- Get the file called DISCLAIMER.txt from the root directory of the
      Microsoft FTP site and download it to a temp directory on the
      ColdFusion server --->
<CFLOCK SCOPE="Session" TYPE="ReadOnly" TIMEOUT="60" THROWONTIMEOUT="Yes">

<CFFTP ACTION="GetFile"
       TRANSFERMODE="Auto"
       STOPONERROR="No"
       REMOTEFILE="DISCLAIMER.TXT"
       LOCALFILE="d:\temp\disclaimer.txt"
       CONNECTION="MyConnection">
```

*Example 12-8. Downloading a File from a Remote Server with CFFTP (continued)*

```
</CFLOCK>

<P>
<CFIF CFFTP.Succeeded>
   <B>File successfully downloaded!</B>
<CFELSE>
   <B>The following error occurred while attempting to download the file:</B><BR>
   <CFOUTPUT>
   <B><I>Error number #CFFTP.ErrorCode#: #CFFTP.ErrorText#</I></B>
   </CFOUTPUT>
</CFIF>


<!--- close the ftp connection --->
<CFLOCK SCOPE="Session" TYPE="ReadOnly" TIMEOUT="60" THROWONTIMEOUT="Yes">

<CFFTP ACTION="Close"
       CONNECTION="MyConnection"
       STOPONERROR="Yes">
</CFLOCK>

<P>
<B>Connection closed.</B>
```

As before, this example uses the `CFFTP` tag to open an FTP connection to Microsoft's FTP server and caches the connection. Once the connection has been opened and verified, we perform the actual file transfer from Microsoft's FTP server to our local ColdFusion server. This is done by setting the `ACTION` attribute of the `CFFTP` tag to `GetFile`. `TRANSFERMODE` specifies the FTP transfer mode to use when retrieving the file from the FTP server. Valid options are `Text`, `Binary`, and `Auto`. In this case, we set `TRANSFERMODE` to `Auto`. We also set the `STOPONERROR` attribute to `No` so that ColdFusion continues to process the template in the event that an error occurs.

The `REMOTEFILE` attribute specifies the filename, including the path, of the file we want to download from the remote FTP server. In our case, we want the *disclaimer.txt* file located in the root directory of Microsoft's FTP server. If we wanted to download a file from a different directory other than the root directory, we would have to specify the path to the file as part of the `REMOTEFILE` attribute. The `LOCALFILE` attribute specifies the filename, including the path, where you want to save the downloaded file on your ColdFusion server. For our example, we'll save the file as *disclaimer.txt* to a directory on our *D* drive called *temp*. The final attribute for our `CFFTP` operation is the `CONNECTION` attribute. The connection attribute is set to `MyConnection`, the name we assigned to our cached connection in the previous `CFFTP` operation.

### *Deleting files*

Another common task that can be performed with the **CFFTP** tag is deleting files that exist on a remote FTP server. To do this, you first have to make sure that you have write access to the files you want to delete on the remote FTP server. Assuming that you have write access, you can use **CFFTP** to perform the delete, as shown in Example 12-9.

*Example 12-9. Using CFFTP to Delete a File on a Remote Server*

```
<!--- open the FTP connection --->
<CFLOCK SCOPE="Session" TYPE="Exclusive" TIMEOUT="60" THROWONTIMEOUT="Yes">

<CFFTP ACTION="Open"
       USERNAME="myusername"
       CONNECTION="MyConnection"
       PASSWORD="mypassword"
       SERVER="127.0.0.1"
       STOPONERROR="Yes">
</CFLOCK>

<P>
<B>Connection opened</B>

<!--- Remove the file called myfile.txt from the incoming directory on the
      remote FTP server --->
<CFLOCK SCOPE="Session" TYPE="ReadOnly" TIMEOUT="60" THROWONTIMEOUT="Yes">

<CFFTP ACTION="Remove"
       STOPONERROR="No"
       ITEM="/incoming/myfile.txt"
       CONNECTION="MyConnection">
</CFLOCK>

<P>
<CFIF CFFTP.Succeeded>
    <B>File successfully removed!</B>
<CFELSE>
    <B>The following error occurred while attempting to remove your file:</B><BR>
    <CFOUTPUT>
    <B><I>Error number #CFFTP.ErrorCode#: #CFFTP.ErrorText#</I></B>
    </CFOUTPUT>
</CFIF>


<!--- close the ftp connection --->
<CFLOCK SCOPE="Session" TYPE="ReadOnly" TIMEOUT="60" THROWONTIMEOUT="Yes">

<CFFTP ACTION="Close"
       CONNECTION="MyConnection"
       STOPONERROR="Yes">
</CFLOCK>
```

*Example 12-9. Using CFFTP to Delete a File on a Remote Server (continued)*

```
<P>
<B>Connection closed.</B>
```

This template starts by opening the FTP session with the remote server and caching the connection. Since the `STOPONERROR` attribute of the `CFFTP` tag is set to `Yes`, ColdFusion throws an error and halts processing if the connection fails.

Next comes the `CFFTP` tag that deletes the remote file. This is accomplished by setting the `ACTION` attribute to `Delete`. The file we want to delete is specified in the `ITEM` attribute by referencing the full path and filename. We set the `CONNECTION` attribute to `MyConnection` because we are using a cached FTP connection. Once the `CFFTP` tag has executed, we use a `CFIF` statement to evaluate whether or not the file was deleted successfully. If it wasn't, an error code and message are output to the screen before the FTP connection is closed in section three.

You should note that the `CFFTP` tag can delete both files and directories. To delete a directory instead of a file, specify `Removedir` for the `ACTION` parameter and provide the directory you want to delete using the `DIRECTORY` attribute. You don't need to use the `ITEM` attribute when deleting a directory.

*In this chapter:*
- *Sending Email*
- *Dealing with Undeliverable Email*
- *Retrieving Messages*
- *Building a Web-Based Email Client*

# 13

# *Working With Email*

It's no wonder that email is considered the Internet's "killer application." The ability to send and receive text messages as well as binary file attachments to locations around the globe has revolutionized the way we communicate. ColdFusion wouldn't be a complete development platform without a way to tap the power of email. As such, two tags are provided for working with email, one for sending messages (CFMAIL) and another for retrieving messages (CFPOP).

There are lots of ways to integrate email into your ColdFusion applications. For example, you can allow users to enter feedback about your web site via an HTML form and have the feedback automatically emailed to the appropriate people. You can send email confirmation message to users, such as a registration confirmation when the user signs up for an account or an order confirmation after the user places an order with your e-commerce application. You can also allow users to sign up to receive periodic information via email, such as announcements of new products.

## *Sending Email*

ColdFusion uses the CFMAIL tag to send email messages using an Internet standard known as Simple Mail Transport Protocol (SMTP). In order for ColdFusion to send email, an SMTP server must be specified in the ColdFusion Administrator under the Mail option. If you don't have access to the ColdFusion Administrator, the CFMAIL tag provides an optional attribute, SERVER, where you can provide a hostname or IP address to your SMTP server. The following example shows how to use the CFMAIL tag to send a simple email message. The example assumes that you are using the SMTP server specified in the ColdFusion Administrator.

```
<CFMAIL TO="postmaster@example.com"
        FROM="webmaster@example.com"
        CC="administrator@example.com"
        BCC="postmaster@example.com"
        SUBJECT="ColdFusion can send email!"
        MAILERID="My E-mail Engine"
        TIMEOUT="900">
I just wanted to let you know that ColdFusion is now sending email!

-Webmaster
</CFMAIL>
```

The first attribute in the `CFMAIL` tag is `TO`, which you use to specify the addressee of the email. The `TO` attribute is required and can accept a single email address or a comma-separated list of email addresses. The `FROM` attribute is also required and contains the sender's email address. The `CC` attribute is optional and can add additional email recipients. Like the `TO` attribute, the `CC` attribute can also accept a comma-separated list of email addresses. `BCC` stands for blind carbon copy and specifies an optional comma-delimited list of recipients that should also receive the email but whose email addresses shouldn't appear in the email's header. The `SUBJECT` attribute is required and contains the subject for our email message. The `MAILERID` attribute specifies a mailer ID to pass along in the X-Mailer SMTP header. The X-Mailer header identifies the program generating the SMTP message. The X-Mailer header is only passed if a value is specified for `MAILERID`.

The final attribute in this example is `TIMEOUT`. The `TIMEOUT` attribute provides an optional number of seconds that ColdFusion should wait for the `CFMAIL` operation to execute before timing out the connection to the SMTP server. Specifying a value for `TIMEOUT` overrides the default timeout value you set in the ColdFusion Administrator.

The space between the start and end `CFMAIL` tags is where the email message goes. Unlike the space between most HTML and CFML tags, the area between the start and end `CFMAIL` tags is sensitive to whitespace. This means that ColdFusion interprets carriage returns and spaces between text as they are typed.

If you don't have access to the SMTP mail server specified in the ColdFusion Administrator or just want to send the email via a different SMTP server than the default, you can specify the server and associated port within the `CFMAIL` tag as shown here:

```
<CFMAIL TO="postmaster@example.com"
        FROM="webmaster@example.com"
        CC="administrator@example.com"
        BCC="postmaster@example.com"
        SUBJECT="ColdFusion can send e-mail!"
        TIMEOUT="900"
        SERVER="127.0.0.1"
        PORT="25">
```

```
I just wanted to let you know that ColdFusion is now sending e-mail!

-Webmaster
</CFMAIL>
```

In this example, the SERVER attribute is set to the IP address of the SMTP server we want to use to send our message. The value for SERVER can be either the IP address or the hostname of the SMTP server. The PORT attribute is optional and tells the CFMAIL tag what port the SMTP server is listening on for incoming requests. The default port is 25.

Note that when a ColdFusion application creates an email message using the CFMAIL tag, the ColdFusion server doesn't send it right away. Instead, a temporary file is created and stored in a spool directory on the ColdFusion server. ColdFusion then pipes the messages from the spool directory to the SMTP server as a background process. ColdFusion looks for new messages in the spool directory at an interval that can be set in the Mail section of the ColdFusion Administrator. The default is every 60 seconds.

## *Sending HTML Mail*

In addition to the standard text based email messages, ColdFusion can also send HTML formatted email messages. HTML formatted messages are readable by many popular email clients and allow you to embed HTML formatting tags within the body of the message, as shown in the following example:

```
<CFMAIL TO="postmaster@example.com"
        FROM="webmaster@example.com"
        SUBJECT="ColdFusion can send HTML e-mail too!"
        TYPE="HTML">
<CENTER>
   <H2>This is an HTML formatted e-mail message</H2>
</CENTER>
<HR>

I just wanted to let you know that
<A HREF="http://www.example.com">ColdFusion</A> is now sending HTML
Formatted e-mail!

-Webmaster
</CFMAIL>
```

In this example, setting the TYPE attribute to HTML tells ColdFusion to format the email message using HTML. An entry is made in the header of the email to let email clients know that the incoming message is formatted using HTML. In order to view the email message correctly, the recipient of the message must be using an email client capable of reading HTML email. Some such clients are Netscape Communicator or Microsoft Outlook. HTML is the only value currently supported by the TYPE attribute.

## Emailing Form Contents

One of the most popular uses of the CFMAIL tag is for emailing the contents of an HTML form once it has been submitted. Although the practical applications of this feature are virtually unlimited, the technique for sending the message is simple. A typical scenario involves emailing the contents of a feedback form to the appropriate department or person within a company. The following example shows how this is accomplished using two templates. The first template, shown in Example 13-1, contains the feedback form.

*Example 13-1. HTML Feedback Form*

```
<HTML>
<HEAD>
  <TITLE>Feedback Form</TITLE>
</HEAD>

<BODY>
<H2>Feedback Form</H2>
<FORM ACTION="Example13-2.cfm" METHOD="post">
Name: <INPUT TYPE="text" NAME="Name" SIZE="15" MAXLENGTH="255"><BR>
E-mail: <INPUT TYPE="text" NAME="Email" SIZE="15" MAXLENGTH="255">
<P>
Who should recieve this feedback?<BR>
<SELECT NAME="SendTo">
   <OPTION VALUE="marketing@example.com" SELECTED>Marketing</OPTION>
   <OPTION VALUE="sales@example.com">Sales</OPTION>
   <OPTION VALUE="customerservice@example.com">Customer Service</OPTION>
</SELECT>
<P>
Comments:<BR>
<TEXTAREA COLS="40" ROWS="4" NAME="Comments" WRAP="Virtual"></TEXTAREA>
<BR>
<INPUT TYPE="submit" NAME="Submit" VALUE="Send">
</FORM>

</BODY>
</HTML>
```

The template in Example 13-1 is a basic HTML form that collects a user's name, email address, comments, and the department they would like the email sent to. Once the information is collected and the form is submitted, the template shown in Example 13-2 takes over.

*Example 13-2. Generating an Email from an HTML Form Submission*

```
<CFMAIL FROM="webmaster@example.com"
        TO="#Form.SendTo#"
        SUBJECT="Feedback Form">
The following information was submitted via our feedback form:
```

*Example 13-2. Generating an Email from an HTML Form Submission (continued)*

```
Name: #Form.Name#
E-mail: #Form.Email#
Comments:
#Form.Comments#
</CFMAIL>

<HTML>
<HEAD>
  <TITLE>Feedback Form Processor</TITLE>
</HEAD>

<BODY>
<H2>The feedback form has been processed successfully!</H2>
The following information was submitted:<BR>
<CFOUTPUT>
To:  #Form.SendTo#<BR>
Name: #Form.Name#<BR>
E-mail: #Form.Email#<BR>
Comments:<BR>
#Form.Comments#
</CFOUTPUT>

</BODY>
</HTML>
```

Example 13-2 takes the information posted from the form in Example 13-1 and uses it to generate an email. The `CFMAIL TO` attribute is populated with the `SendTo` form field value passed from the feedback form. The body of the message is created by referencing the rest of the form fields from the feedback form. The values entered in the feedback form are also output to the browser so that you can see what values were passed.

## Adding Query Results to Email

Another feature of the `CFMAIL` tag is the ability to include query results in `CFMAIL` generated email messages. Say you want to send an email to your HR department that contains a listing of the contact information for each employee in the company. You can use ColdFusion to query the database and then use the `CFMAIL` tag to generate an email message containing the query results in the body of the message, as shown in Example 13-3.

*Example 13-3. Including Query Results in an Email Message*

```
<CFQUERY NAME="GetMailingList" DATASOURCE="ProgrammingCF">
         SELECT Name, Title, Email, PhoneExt, Department
         FROM EmployeeDirectory Order BY Name
</CFQUERY>

<CFMAIL QUERY="GetMailingList"
```

*Example 13-3. Including Query Results in an Email Message (continued)*

```
        TO="hr@example.com"
        FROM="webmaster@example.com"
        SUBJECT="Employee Contact Listings"
        TIMEOUT="900"
        TYPE="HTML">
Here is the employee contact information you requested:
<P>
<TABLE BORDER="1">
<TR>
  <TH>Name</TH><TH>Title</TH><TH>Department</TH><TH>E-mail</TH>
  <TH>Phone Ext.</TH>
</TR>
<CFOUTPUT>
<TR>
  <TD>#Name#</TD><TD>#Title#</TD><TD>#Department#</TD><TD>#Email#</TD>
  <TD>#PhoneExt#</TD>
</TR>
</CFOUTPUT>
</TABLE>
<P>
Best regards,
<P>
The Webmaster
</CFMAIL>
```

As you can see in Example 13-3, including the query results in the message body is simple. The only real difference between using a query result set in an email message and outputting the result set to a browser is that you don't have to specify a `QUERY` attribute in the `CFOUTPUT` tag because it is already specified within the `CFMAIL` tag.

## Including Grouped Query Results

On occasion, you may want to group query results in the body of your email message. For example, you need to send an email message to a contact in your human-resources department listing every employee in your employee database. You can list them in alphabetical order by creating a simple `CFQUERY` that orders the results by the employee's name. But you may want to list all the current employees grouped by department. This process gets a little more complicated.

Example 13-4 demonstrates how to query the `EmployeeDirectory` table of the database and then output each employee record to the browser. The query results are grouped by department using the `GROUP` attribute of the `CFOUTPUT` tag. Notice the nesting of the second `CFOUTPUT` tag within the `CFOUTPUT` tag that accompanies the `QUERY` attribute.

*Example 13-4. Grouping Data Using CFOUTPUT*

```
<CFQUERY NAME="GetMailingList" DATASOURCE="ProgrammingCF">
        SELECT Department, Name, Title, Email, PhoneExt
        FROM EmployeeDirectory Order BY Department
</CFQUERY>

<CFOUTPUT QUERY="GetMAilingList" GROUP="Department">
<H3>#Department#</h3>

<CFOUTPUT>
#Name#<BR>
#Title#<BR>
#Email#<BR>
x#PhoneExt#<P>
</CFOUTPUT>
</CFOUTPUT>
```

Now that you see how to group the query results using the `GROUP` attribute of the `CFOUTPUT` tag, let's apply the same logic to an email message generated by the `CFMAIL` tag. The syntax for grouping within a `CFMAIL` message is slightly different from the syntax used in the previous example. Before we get into Example 13-5, let me say that the example isn't going to work as you would expect it to. Because of a "bug" in the way the `GROUP` attribute is handled in the `CFMAIL` tag, you can't group output correctly. Example 13-5 shows the syntax that *should* work for grouping within a `CFMAIL` generated message. There is a workaround to this problem that we'll get to shortly.

*Example 13-5. Grouping Query Results Within a CFMAIL Message Should Work, but Doesn't*

```
<CFQUERY NAME="GetMailingList" DATASOURCE="ProgrammingCF">
        SELECT Department, Name, Title, Email, PhoneExt
        FROM EmployeeDirectory Order BY Department
</CFQUERY>

<CFMAIL QUERY="GetMailingList"
       GROUP="Department"
       TO="you@example.com"
       FROM="me@example.com"
       SUBJECT="Employees grouped by department">
#Department#
====================
<CFOUTPUT>
#Name#
#Title#
#Email#
x#PhoneExt#

</CFOUTPUT>
</CFMAIL>

<H2>The message has been sent...</H2>
```

The problem here is that instead of generating the expected single email message, the **CFMAIL** tag generates a unique message for each grouping of data within the query. Therefore, instead of receiving a single message containing all employees grouped by department, your human-resources contact receives a different message for each department containing a list of employees for that department. Have no fear, there is a workaround.

The workaround for the **CFMAIL** grouping problem involves creating the grouped output and storing the results in a single variable that can then populate the body of the message, as shown in Example 13-6.

*Example 13-6. Workaround to Include Grouped Query Results in a Single Email*

```
<CFQUERY NAME="GetMailingList" DATASOURCE="ProgrammingCF">
        SELECT Department, Name, Title, Email, PhoneExt
        FROM EmployeeDirectory Order BY Department
</CFQUERY>

<!--- initialize a variable --->
<CFSET x="">

<!--- group the output and append it to x for each query record --->
<CFOUTPUT QUERY="GetMAilingList" GROUP="Department">
<CFSET x=x&"
#Department#
============================
">
<CFOUTPUT>
<CFSET x=x&"
#Name#
#Title#
#Email#
x#PhoneExt#
">
</CFOUTPUT>
</CFOUTPUT>

<!--- send out a message with the contents of x as the body --->
<CFMAIL TO="you@example.com"
        FROM="me@example.com"
        SUBJECT="Employees grouped by department">
#x#
</CFMAIL>

<H2>The message has been sent...</H2>
```

The first part of the template in Example 13-6 simply queries the `EmployeeDirectory` table and stores the results in a query object called `GetMailingList`. Next, a variable called **x** is initialized and set to **""**. This is necessary because we want to append data to this variable as opposed to assign a single value to it. Once **x** has been initialized, the next step is to write the grouped data to `x`. The first `CFOUTPUT` tag sets the outermost loop for the output. This loop iterates for each unique value contained in the column specified in `GROUP`. In this case, the loop iterates for each unique department. The second step sets the innermost loop for the output. This loop iterates for each employee within the current group. The results are appended to the variable x until the entire query object has been output.

The final part of the template in Example 13-6 creates the actual mail message using the `CFMAIL` tag. Notice that the `QUERY` attribute isn't used in this case, because we aren't going to use the query to populate the mail message. Instead, the variable `x` outputs the grouped records within the body of the message.

## *Sending Customized Email to Multiple Recipients*

The real power of the `CFMAIL` tag lies in its ability to send email to multiple recipients based on information from a ColdFusion query object, which in effect allows you to send customized email messages to multiple recipients using very few lines of code. With this technique, you can perform such tasks as mail merges and mass emailings (not spam, of course!). Example 13-7 shows the basic method for sending out multiple emails with information pulled from a query.

*Example 13-7. Sending Email to Multiple Recipients Based on a Query*

```
<!--- query the sample database for all of the names and email addresses of
      people stored in the recipients table --->
<CFQUERY NAME="GetMailingList" DATASOURCE="ProgrammingCF">
         SELECT Email, Name FROM EmployeeDirectory
</CFQUERY>

<!--- Use the CFMAIL tag in conjunction with the above query to email a
      personalized message to each person in the database --->
<CFMAIL QUERY="GetMailingList"
        TO="#email#"
        FROM="webmaster@example.com"
        SUBJECT="Hello!"
        TIMEOUT="900">
#Name#,

We just wanted to let you know that a new page on the wonderful widget has
been added to our web site.  To visit the new page, point your browser here:

http://www.example.com/widget.cfm


Best regards,

The Webmaster
</CFMAIL>
```

Example 13-7 uses a standard CFQUERY to select the Name and Email fields from the database. The name of the query is then specified in the QUERY attribute of the CFMAIL tag. By specifying the Email variable from the query in the TO attribute of the CFMAIL tag, ColdFusion sends a message to the email address listed in each row of the record set returned by the query. Each recipient receives a copy of the message addressed specifically to that recipient, with no other recipients appearing in the TO header. The body for each email message can be personalized with the name of the recipient if you reference the Name variable from the query. Additional fields from the database can also be added depending on your requirements.

## *Sending File Attachments*

ColdFusion can send file attachments via email. Files are attached to a message using the CFMAILPARAM tag nested within the CFMAIL tag. The following example shows the proper syntax to get this done:

```
<CFMAIL TO="webmaster@example.com"
        FROM="rbils@example.com"
        SUBJECT="Test CFMAIL 4.5 file attachments">
This is a test.  There should be two file attachments included in this e-mail.

-Rob

<CFMAILPARAM FILE="d:\inetsrv\cf\graph.cfm">
<CFMAILPARAM FILE="d:\inetsrv\cf\getpath.cfm">
</CFMAIL>
```

The CFMAILPARAM tag uses the FILE attribute to specify the full path (on your CF server) to the file you'd like to attach to your email message. You can also select multiple file attachments using the CFMAILPARAM tag for each file you want to attach. You should note that to attach a file to a CFMAIL-generated message, the file must reside on the local ColdFusion server or on a network drive accessible from that server. If you are building an application such as a web-based email client that allows users to attach files to their messages, the attachment must first be uploaded to the ColdFusion server with the CFFILE tag before it can be included as an attachment. There will be more on this technique later on in this chapter.

Prior to Version 4.5 of ColdFusion, attachments were handled via the MIMEATTACH attribute of the CFMAIL tag. The MIMEATTACH attribute specified the full path to a single file to be MIME-encoded and attached to the message being sent. MIMEATTACH performed the same function as the CFMAILPARAM tag but allowed only a single file to be attached to the mail message. The MIMEATTACH attribute is still valid, but you can see why the preferred method for attaching files to email messages is via the CFMAILPARAM tag. The following example uses the

MIMEATTACH attribute to include an attachment with an email generated using CFMAIL:

```
<CFMAIL FROM="webmaster@example.com"
        TO="you@example.com"
        SUBJECT="Sending an attachment with MIMEATTACH"
        MIMEATTACH="c:\temp\myfile.zip">
Here is your attachment!
</CFMAIL>
```

### *Specifying Additional Header Information*

The CFMAILPARAM tag also lets you specify additional SMTP header information not natively supplied by the CFMAIL tag. The following example uses the CFMAILPARAM tag to append a Reply-To value to the message header generated by the CFMAIL tag:

```
<CFMAIL TO="webmaster@example.com"
        FROM="rbils@example.com"
        SUBJECT="Test CFMAIL 4.5">
<CFMAILPARAM NAME="Reply-To" VALUE="rbils@example.com">
This e-mail specifies additional header information!

-Rob
</CFMAIL>
```

In this case, the CFMAILPARAM tag uses the NAME attribute to specify the name for the header entry. The VALUE attribute passes the actual value for the header entry. Multiple header entries can be made using multiple CFMAILPARAM tags.

## *Dealing with Undeliverable Email*

Every now and then, something goes wrong when ColdFusion attempts to send an email. Problems can range from a missing email address in the TO attribute, to a problem connecting to the SMTP server. Regardless of the cause of the problem, ColdFusion deals with undeliverable email in a consistent and simple manner. All undeliverable email messages are written to temporary files and saved to a folder on the ColdFusion server called *Undelivr*. The *Undelivr* folder is usually located in *c:\cfusion\mail\undelivr*. The exact location can be determined by looking at the following value in the system registry:

```
HKEY_LOCAL_MACHINE/Software/Allaire/ColdFusion/CurrentVersion/Mail/BaseDirectory
```

To resend a message that has been moved to the *Undelivr* folder, the temporary file must be moved back to the *Spool* folder, which is usually located in *c:\cfusion\mail\spool*. This can be done manually or via ColdFusion. Obviously, using ColdFusion to monitor the *Undelivr* directory for undelivered mail is more convenient than manually checking the directory every time an email is generated. To do this, you need to create a template that scans the *Undelivr* folder and schedule it to run at set intervals. Example 13-8 contains a template you can use to scan your *Undelivr* folder and move any files found back to the *Spool* folder so that attempts can be made to resend them. Using the Scheduler within the ColdFusion Administrator, the template can be set to run at predetermined intervals.

*Example 13-8. CFML Template for Dealing with Undeliverable Mail*

```
<!--- Get the mail root directory from the registry.  The CFREGISTRY tag is
      discussed in Chapter 21, Working with the System Registry --->
<CFREGISTRY ACTION="GET"
      BRANCH="HKEY_LOCAL_MACHINE\SOFTWARE\Allaire\ColdFusion\CurrentVersion\Mail"
      ENTRY="BaseDirectory"
      VARIABLE="MailRoot"
      TYPE="String">

<!--- set the date trigger to 7, one week --->
<CFSET DateTrigger=7>

<!--- Read all of the files from the undeliverable directory for processing --->
<CFDIRECTORY Directory="#MailRoot#\undelivr"
             Name="Undeliverables">

<!--- Because of the . and .. listing in the directory, an empty directory
      actually returns 2 for the record count.  Taking this into account, if the
      record count is equal to 2, we know there are no files in the directory to
      be moved.  If there are more than 2 records returned, we know that there
      are files that either need to be moved or deleted. --->
<CFIF Undeliverables.RecordCount IS 2>
  <CFSET FilesMoved=0>
  <CFSET FilesDeleted=0>
  <CFSET MyQuery=QueryNew("FileName, FileSize, LastMod")>
  <CFSET Temp=QueryAddRow(MyQuery)>
  <CFSET Temp=QuerySetCell(MyQuery, "FileName", "N/A", 1)>
  <CFSET Temp=QuerySetCell(MyQuery, "FileSize", "N/A", 1)>
  <CFSET Temp=QuerySetCell(MyQuery, "LastMod", "N/A", 1)>
<CFELSE>
  <!--- Set Constants --->
  <CFSET FilesMoved=0>
  <CFSET FilesDeleted=0>
  <CFSET FileName="">
  <CFSET FileSize="">
  <CFSET LastMod="">

  <!--- exclude . and .. as files --->
  <CFLOOP Query="Undeliverables">
    <CFIF Name is not "." and Name is not ".." and Type is "File">

      <!--- Check to see if the last modified date of the file in the
            undeliverable directory is older than the number of days specified in
            the date trigger.  If it is, delete the file.  If the file is not
            older, move it to the spool directory to be resent. --->
```

*Example 13-8. CFML Template for Dealing with Undeliverable Mail (continued)*

```
      <CFIF DateDiff("y", DateLastModified, Now()) GT DateTrigger>

        <CFFILE ACTION="Delete"
                FILE="#MailRoot#\undelivr\#NAME#">
        <CFSET FilesDeleted=FilesDeleted+1>
      <CFELSE>
        <CFFILE ACTION="move"
                SOURCE="#MailRoot#\undelivr\#NAME#"
                DESTINATION="#MailRoot#\spool\">
        <CFSET FilesMoved=FilesMoved+1>

        <CFOUTPUT>
        <CFSET FileName=ListAppend(FileName, Name, ",")>
        <CFSET FileSize=ListAppend(FileSize, Size, ",")>
        <CFSET LastMod=ListAppend(LastMod, DateLastModified, ",")>
        </CFOUTPUT>
      </CFIF>
    </CFIF>
  </CFLOOP>

  <!--- build the query to return  --->
  <CFSET #LenOfString#=#FilesMoved#>

  <CFIF #LenOfString# GTE 1>
    <CFSET MyQuery=QueryNew("FileName, FileSize, LastMod")>
    <CFSET Temp=QueryAddRow(MyQuery, #LenOfString#)>
    <CFLOOP INDEX="ThisCol" FROM="1" TO="#LenOfString#">
      <CFSET Temp=QuerySetCell(MyQuery, "FileName", ListGetAt(FileName,
      ThisCol), ThisCol)>
      <CFSET Temp=QuerySetCell(MyQuery, "FileSize", ListGetAt(FileSize,
      ThisCol), ThisCol)>
      <CFSET Temp=QuerySetCell(MyQuery, "LastMod", ListGetAt(LastMod,
      ThisCol), ThisCol)>
    </CFLOOP>

  <CFELSE>

    <CFSET MyQuery=QueryNew("FileName, FileSize, LastMod")>
    <CFSET Temp=QueryAddRow(MyQuery)>
    <CFSET Temp=QuerySetCell(MyQuery, "FileName", "N/A", 1)>
    <CFSET Temp=QuerySetCell(MyQuery, "FileSize", "N/A", 1)>
    <CFSET Temp=QuerySetCell(MyQuery, "LastMod", "N/A", 1)>
  </CFIF>
</CFIF>

<CFIF FilesMoved GTE 1 OR FilesDeleted GTE 1>

<CFMAIL QUERY="MyQuery"
        TO="you@yourdomain.com"
        FROM="webmaster@mydomain.com"
        SUBJECT="Undeliverable Mail Report">
Total Files Moved: #FilesMoved#
```

*Example 13-8. CFML Template for Dealing with Undeliverable Mail (continued)*

```
Total Files Deleted: #FilesDeleted#

These are the files affected:
<CFOUTPUT>
#FileName# (#filesize# bytes, #DateFormat(LastMod,'mm/dd/yyyy')#)
</CFOUTPUT>
</CFMAIL>

</CFIF>
```

This template works by reading the location of the mail root directory from the registry using the `CFREGISTRY` tag. A variable called `DateTrigger` is then set to specify the number of days ColdFusion should attempt to move the file back into the *spool* directory before deleting it. Next, the `CFDIRECTORY` tag obtains a list of all files in the *undelivr* directory. If files exist in the directory, their last modified date is compared to the number of days specified in the `DateTrigger`. If the file is older than the specified number of days, it is deleted. If not, the file is moved back to the *spool* directory so ColdFusion can attempt to send it again. Finally, an email is sent out listing the number of files deleted and the number moved as well as the names of the files affected.

# Retrieving Messages

You have seen that ColdFusion can send email via the `CFMAIL` tag. In addition to sending email, ColdFusion can also retrieve email messages using the Post Office Protocol (POP3) via the `CFPOP` tag. Using this tag, ColdFusion can retrieve message headers, message contents and file attachments. In essence, this allows you to use ColdFusion to create a web-based email system, like Yahoo! Mail or Hotmail. The `CFPOP` tag can also create applications such as auto-responders and mailing-list managers.

## Retrieving Message Headers

The `CFPOP` tag can retrieve just the header portion of email messages stored on a POP server. This is useful when you want to retrieve summary information such as the message title for more than one message. Retrieving just the message headers allows you to avoid the overhead associated with retrieving the entire contents of each message you retrieve. In the context of a web-based email client, this technique is used to build a list of messages in a user's mailbox. You can retrieve the headers for a group of messages by setting the `ACTION` attribute of the `CFPOP` tag to `GetHeaderOnly` as shown in Example 13-9.

*Example 13-9. Retrieving Message Headers*

```
<CFPOP ACTION="GETHEADERONLY" NAME="GetMessageHeaders"
       SERVER="popserver.example.com"
       TIMEOUT="600" USERNAME="username" PASSWORD="password">

<CFOUTPUT>
   <H3>#GetMessageHeaders.RecordCount# messages on the server</H3>
</CFOUTPUT>

<TABLE BORDER="0" CELLPADDING="3" CELLSPACING="0">
<TR>
   <TD><B>From<B></TD><TD>  </TD><TD><B>Date</B></TD>
   <TD>  </TD><TD><B>Subject</B></TD>
</TR>

<!--- output the message header contents --->
<CFOUTPUT QUERY="GetMessageHeaders">
<TR>
   <TD><FONT SIZE="-1">#FROM#</FONT></TD><TD>  </TD>
   <TD><FONT SIZE="-1">#DateFormat(ParseDateTime(DATE),'mm/dd/yyyy')#
    #TimeFormat(ParseDateTime(DATE),'hh:mm:ss tt')#</FONT></TD>
   <TD>  </TD><TD><FONT SIZE="-1">#HTMLCodeFormat(SUBJECT)#</FONT></TD>
</TR>
</CFOUTPUT>
</TABLE>
```

Example 13-9 calls the `CFPOP` tag and sets the `ACTION` attribute to `GetHeaderOnly`. This tells ColdFusion to retrieve only message headers from the POP server. Message headers contain information such as who the message is from, the time and date it was sent, and the subject of the message. The `NAME` attribute specifies the name to give the query object created to hold the header information. In this example, we'll call our query `GetMessageHeaders`. The `SERVER` attribute is set to the hostname or IP address of the POP server you want to retrieve messages from. `TIMEOUT` specifies an amount of time in seconds that you want ColdFusion to wait while processing a request before timing out the connection to the POP server. This attribute is optional and defaults to 60 seconds. The `USERNAME` and `PASSWORD` attributes send the username and password to the POP server you want to retrieve messages from. The remote POP server authenticates access and determines which messages should be returned to the ColdFusion application.

After the `CFPOP` tag executes (assuming no errors occur), the message headers retrieved from the POP server are output to the browser as a simple HTML table. Only a subset of the available return variables are used in our example. See the CFPOP tag in Appendix A for the complete list of variables returned when retrieving message headers.

## Retrieving Message Contents

Besides retrieving message headers, the CFPOP tag can also retrieve the rest of a message's content such as the body text and any attachments included with the message. In the context of a web-based email system, this functionality allows you to display an email message and build links to any file attachments. To retrieve everything associated with a particular message, set the ACTION attribute of the CFPOP tag to GetAll as in Example 13-10.

*Example 13-10. Retrieving a Complete Message*

```
<CFPOP ACTION="GetAll" NAME="GetMessage" MESSAGENUMBER="1"
       SERVER="popserver.example.com"
       TIMEOUT="600" USERNAME="username" PASSWORD="password">

<CFOUTPUT QUERY="GetMessage">
<FONT COLOR="blue">From:</FONT> #HTMLCodeFormat(FROM)#
  on #HTMLCodeFormat(DATE)#<BR>
<FONT COLOR="blue">To:</FONT> #HTMLCodeFormat(TO)# <BR>
<FONT COLOR="blue">Cc:</FONT> #HTMLCodeFormat(CC)# <BR>
<FONT COLOR="blue">Subject:</FONT> #HTMLCodeFormat(SUBJECT)#
<P>
#HTMLCodeFormat(BODY)# <BR>
</CFOUTPUT>
```

In Example 13-10, the ACTION attribute of the CFPOP tag is set to GetAll, which lets ColdFusion know that we want to retrieve an entire message as opposed to just the message header. The NAME attribute lets us specify a name for the query object that will hold the contents of the retrieved message. Because we are retrieving the full contents of a single message, we need to specify the actual message to retrieve using the MESSAGENUMBER attribute.* In Example 13-10, we hard-code the value for MESSAGENUMBER, setting it to 1, so that it retrieves the first message stored in the user's account. If you wish to retrieve a full message in an application, the value assigned to MESSAGENUMBER is dynamic, most likely passed in via URL. We'll look at how this is done at the end of the chapter when we cover how to build a web-based mail client.

If you look at the output section in Example 13-10, you can see that we used the same output variables as were used in our previous example with one exception. In this case, we displayed the body of the message using the variable Body. The HTMLCodeFormat() function escapes any HTML that might be contained in the message body. This is generally a good idea if you want to keep HTML tags

* As an alternative to the MESSAGENUMBER attribute, ColdFusion now offers an optional attribute (as of Service Pack 2 (SP2) for ColdFusion 4.5.1) called UID. The UID attribute allows you to specify the unique identifier (UID) assigned to a mail message (or comma-delimited list of UIDs) as opposed to the message number. UID can be used instead of the MESSAGENUMBER attribute in cases where the specified POP server doesn't support message numbers (as in the case of the Mercury POP server).

embedded in the message body from being rendered by the browser. It is also a good way to avoid potential security exploits from malicious code embedded within a message.

## *Dealing with Attachments*

When you retrieve the contents of a message with the `ACTION` attribute set to `GetAll`, ColdFusion allows you to use an optional attribute, `ATTACHMENTPATH`, to specify a path where any attachments retrieved should be stored. ColdFusion creates two additional variables to store the filenames as they are retrieved from the POP server and written to the ColdFusion server, respectively:

*`queryname`*`.Attachments`
: Returns a tab-delimited list of the original filenames of all attached files

*`queryname`*`.AttachmentFiles`
: Returns a tab-delimited list of the names of the attachment files as they were written to the directory specified in the `ATTACHMENTPATH` attribute of the `CFPOP` tag

Now that you know what variables are offered for dealing with file attachments, let's look at how to use them. Example 13-11 uses the `CFPOP` tag to retrieve an email message along with any attached files.

*Example 13-11. Retrieving Multiple Attachments with CFPOP*

```
<!--- set a variable called tab to the chr value of tab --->
<CFSET TAB = CHR(9)>

<!--- set the message number to retrieve to 1.  This is used as an example only.
      in an actual application, the message number to retrieve would most likely
      be passed in as a URL variable from a hyperlinked message header  --->
<CFSET Message = 1>

<!--- set the attachment path for the retrieved attachments.  --->
<CFSET AttachmentPath = "d:\inetsrv\cf\13">

<!--- retrieve the message from the POP server --->
<CFPOP ACTION="GetAll" NAME="GetMessage" MESSAGENUMBER="#Message#"
       SERVER="popserver.example.com"
       TIMEOUT="600" USERNAME="username" PASSWORD="password"
       ATTACHMENTPATH="#AttachmentPath#"
       GENERATEUNIQUEFILENAMES="yes">

<!--- Output the message header info as well as the body --->
<CFOUTPUT QUERY="GetMessage">
<HR NOSHADE>
<P>
<FONT COLOR="blue">From:</FONT> #HTMLEditFormat(FROM)# on
#HTMLEditFormat(DATE)#<BR>
```

*Example 13-11. Retrieving Multiple Attachments with CFPOP (continued)*

```
<FONT COLOR="blue">To:</FONT> #HTMLEditFormat(TO)# <BR>
<FONT COLOR="blue">Cc:</FONT> #HTMLEditFormat(CC)# <BR>
<FONT COLOR="blue">Subject:</FONT> #HTMLEditFormat(SUBJECT)#
<P>
#HTMLEditFormat(BODY)# <BR>

<!--- If there are file attachments, display them and provide links to the
      attachments --->
<CFIF Attachments IS NOT "">
<P>
Attachments:<BR>
<CFLOOP FROM="1" TO="#ListLen(Attachments,Tab)#" INDEX="TheAttachment">
<A HREF="#URLEncodedFormat(GetFileFromPath(ListGetAt(AttachmentFiles,
TheAttachment,tab)))#">#ListGetAt(Attachments, TheAttachment,tab)#</A><BR>
</CFLOOP>
</CFIF>
</CFOUTPUT>
```

The first thing we do in Example 13-11 is create a variable called `Tab` and set it equal to `CHR(9)`, the ASCII value for the tab character. This allows us to represent the tab as a delimiter without having to actually include a hard tab in our code. This might seem like a trivial step, but it solves a problem that often occurs when trying to include tabs in programming code. Depending on the editor you use to write your code and the platform you develop on, the tab character may not be preserved when you save your code. Using `CHR(9)` instead of a hard tab eliminates the possibility of this occurring. The next step involves creating a variable called `Message` that holds the message number to be retrieved. Please note that this is used as an example only. In an actual application, the message number to retrieve would most likely be passed in as a URL variable from a hyperlinked message header. We'll cover this technique later in the chapter when we build a complete POP mail client.

The third step is to create a variable called `AttachmentPath`, to specify the location on your ColdFusion server where file attachments should be stored after they are retrieved from the POP server. It is important that this path be within your web server's root directory, so that it can be viewed/downloaded without having to call a separate template to retrieve the file(s).

Once all the constants have been defined, the next step is to use the `CFPOP` tag to retrieve the message, including attachments, from the POP server. To do this, you need to include a new attribute within the tag. The `ATTACHMENTPATH` attribute specifies a location on the ColdFusion server where any attachments retrieved from the POP server should be stored. In our example, we set this attribute to the value of the `AttachmentPath` variable we defined at the beginning of the template. A second new attribute, `GENERATEUNIQUEFILENAMES` is set to `Yes`, causing ColdFusion to automatically generate unique filenames for any attachment retrieved from the POP server so that any name conflicts can be avoided. Generated names are guaranteed to be unique within the directory specified in ATTACHMENTPATH.

Once the message and associated attachments have been retrieved, the message header and body are output to the browser. Next, a CFIF statement determines if there are any attachments associated with the message. If there are, the Attachments variable is looped over, and a link to each file attachment in the list is provided.

### *Deleting Messages*

The CFPOP tag can delete unwanted messages from the POP server. Deleting messages is a simple process and takes only a few short lines of code:

```
<CFPOP ACTION="Delete"
       MESSAGENUMBER="1,2,6,9"
       SERVER="popserver.example.com"
       TIMEOUT="600"
       USERNAME="username"
       PASSWORD="password">
```

In this case, we set the ACTION attribute of the CFPOP tag to Delete. MESSAGENUMBER specifies the message number or comma-delimited list of message numbers to delete.* Message numbers are usually passed to the tag via a URL or form variable. We'll cover this technique in more detail in the next section. The POP server to delete the message from is specified using the SERVER attribute. An optional timeout value for the operation can be set with the TIMEOUT attribute. The USERNAME and PASSWORD attributes are required and specify which account on the POP server the message(s) should be deleted from. You should note that once a message has been deleted from the POP server, message numbers are automatically reassigned. This isn't true of UIDs, which are unique and persist for the life of each message.

## *Building a Web-Based Email Client*

Now that you have a feel for how the CFMAIL and CFPOP tags work, let's take a look at a more complex example that showcases most features of both tags. In our example, we shall build a basic web-based email client. Before beginning, let's

---

* As of ColdFusion 4.5.1 SP2, you can use the UID attribute in place of the MESSAGENUMBER attribute to specify message(s) to delete.

outline the functionality and features we'll need for the application. Remember, this is a *basic* email client with bare-bones functionality. We'll need:

- A login screen for users to enter POP server, SMTP server, email address, username, and password
- A method for passing login information from template to template (in a relatively secure manner) without using persistent variables
- An "Inbox" for listing all emails belonging to the user on the POP server with next/previous functionality
- The ability to read a message and download any associated file attachments
- The ability to forward a message to other recipients, including file attachments
- The ability to reply to a message
- The ability to create a new message and attach a file to that message
- The ability to delete messages from the POP server

With the list of requirements for the application defined, let's map out exactly how the application should flow. The application consists of three templates for handling all POP client functions. The first template, named *PopForm.cfm*, gathers login information for the POP server and posts to the *Inbox.cfm* template. The *Inbox.cfm* template creates the user's inbox. The inbox consists of a list of the email messages in the user's mailbox. It is here that a user can choose what message to read, delete a message, or create a new message. The *Action.cfm* template handles the bulk of the mail client's functionality. It is responsible for reading, creating, forwarding, replying to, and deleting messages.

Now that we have the basic flow of the application, let's look at the templates. Example 13-12 shows *PopForm.cfm*, the user login screen for the application.

*Example 13-12. Email Client Login Screen*

```
<HTML>
  <HEAD>
    <TITLE>CF Pop Mail Client - Login</TITLE>
  </HEAD>
<BODY>

<FORM ACTION="Inbox.cfm" METHOD="post">
<TABLE>
  <TR>
    <TD>Your e-mail address:</TD>
    <TD><INPUT TYPE="text" NAME="EmailAddress" SIZE="30" MAXLENGTH="255"></TD>
  </TR>
  <TR>
    <TD>POP server:</TD>
    <TD><INPUT TYPE="text" NAME="POPServer" SIZE="30" MAXLENGTH="255"></TD>
  </TR>
```

*Example 13-12. Email Client Login Screen (continued)*

```
  <TR>
    <TD>SMTP Server:</TD>
    <TD><INPUT TYPE="text" NAME="SMTPServer" SIZE="30" MAXLENGTH="255"></TD>
  </TR>
  <TR>
    <TD>Username:</TD>
    <TD><INPUT TYPE="text" NAME="UserName" SIZE="30" MAXLENGTH="255"></TD>
  </TR>
  <TR>
    <TD>Password:</TD>
    <TD><INPUT TYPE="password" NAME="Password" SIZE="30" MAXLENGTH="255"></TD>
  </TR>
  <TR>
    <TD COLSPAN="2"><INPUT TYPE="submit" NAME="Submit" VALUE="Submit"></TD>
  </TR>
</TABLE>
</FORM>

</BODY>
</HTML>
```

There isn't much to the login screen. It is just a simple HTML form that gathers the user's email address, POP and SMTP server addresses, username, and password. The results are then sent to the next template, *Inbox.cfm*, shown in Example 13-13.

*Example 13-13. Inbox.cfm for the Mail Client*

```
<!--- initialize constants --->
<CFPARAM NAME="URL.action" DEFAULT="">
<CFSET NumDisplayMessages=10> <!--- number of messages to display in inbox --->
<CFPARAM NAME="CurrentMessageNumber" DEFAULT="1">

<!--- If the Password is sent encrypted by URL, decrypt it --->
<CFIF ISDEFINED('URL.PASSWORD')>
<CFSET PASSWORD = DECRYPT(URL.PASSWORD,815)>
</CFIF>

<!--- create a url parameter string. Encrypt the password.  This is NOT strong
      encryption --->
<CFSET PARAMETERS = "EmailAddress=#URLEncodedFormat(EmailAddress)#&PopServer=
#URLEncodedFormat(PopServer)#&SMTPServer=#URLEncodedFormat(SMTPServer)#&Username=
#URLEncodedFormat(Username)#&Password=#URLEncodedFormat(Encrypt(Password,815))#">

<!--- retrieve and display all message headers, 10 at a time.  The number
      displayed per screen can be increased here by increasing the value of the
      NumDisplayMessages variable --->
<CFPOP ACTION="GetHeaderOnly" NAME="GetMessageHeaders" SERVER="#popserver#"
       TIMEOUT="600" USERNAME="#username#" PASSWORD="#password#"
       STARTROW="#CurrentMessageNumber#" MAXROWS="#NumDisplayMessages#">
```

*Example 13-13. Inbox.cfm for the Mail Client (continued)*

```
<HTML>
<HEAD>
<TITLE>E-mail Client - Inbox</TITLE>
</HEAD>
<BODY BGCOLOR="#C0C0C0">

<CENTER>
<TABLE BORDER="1" WIDTH="600" CELLPADDING="5">
<TR>
  <TD BGCOLOR="#FFFFFF">
  <TABLE BORDER="1" CELLPADDING="5" CELLSPACING="0">
  <TR BGCOLOR="#C0C0C0">
  <!--- allow the user to refresh the page or create a new message --->
    <CFOUTPUT>
    <TD><A HREF="Inbox.cfm?#Parameters#">Refresh</A></TD>
    <TD><A HREF="Action.cfm?action=create&#Parameters#">Create Message</A></TD>
    </CFOUTPUT>
  </TR>
  </TABLE>

  <CENTER>
  <H2>E-mail Client - Inbox</H2>
  </CENTER>

  <!--- Create next/previous buttons as necessary for the messages displayed in
        the inbox.  If you want to display more than 10 messages at a time, you
        need to increase the value in the constants section. --->
  <CFOUTPUT>
  <CFIF Evaluate(CurrentMessageNumber - NumDisplayMessages) GTE 0>
  <A HREF="Inbox.cfm?CurrentMessageNumber=#Evaluate(CurrentMessageNumber
  - 10)#&#Parameters#">Previous</A> |
  </CFIF>

  <CFIF GetMessageHeaders.RecordCount EQ NumDisplayMessages>
  <A HREF="Inbox.cfm?CurrentMessageNumber=#Evaluate(CurrentMessageNumber
  + NumDisplayMessages)#&#Parameters#">Next</A>
  </CFIF>
  </CFOUTPUT>
  <P>

  <!--- if there are messages to be displayed, do so and make the page a form so
        that multiple messages can be deleted. --->

  <CFIF GetMessageHeaders.RecordCount GT 0>
  <CFOUTPUT>
  <FORM ACTION="Action.cfm?action=delete&#Parameters#" METHOD="post">
  </CFOUTPUT>

  <TABLE BORDER="0" CELLPADDING="3" CELLSPACING="0">
  <TR>
    <TD> </TD><TD><B>From<B></TD><TD>  </TD><TD><B>Date</B></TD>
    <TD>  </TD><TD><B>Subject</B></TD>
```

*Example 13-13. Inbox.cfm for the Mail Client (continued)*

```
  </TR>

  <!--- output the message headers --->
  <CFOUTPUT QUERY="GetMessageHeaders">
  <TR>
    <TD><INPUT TYPE="checkbox" NAME="Message" VALUE="#MessageNumber#"></TD>
        <!--- link the message to the action.cfm page where the full message can
              be retrieved --->
    <TD><FONT SIZE="-1">
        <A HREF="Action.cfm?action=read&#Parameters#&message=#MessageNumber#">
        #FROM#</A></FONT></TD>
    <TD>  </TD>
        <!--- This date is not formatted because some mail messages contain non
              standard date formats that cause ColdFusion to throw an error when
              attempting to format them --->
    <TD><FONT SIZE="-1">#Date#</FONT></TD>
    <TD>  </TD>
    <TD><FONT SIZE="-1">#SUBJECT#</FONT></TD>
  </TR>
  </CFOUTPUT>
  </TABLE>
  <INPUT TYPE="submit" VALUE="Delete">
  </FORM>

  <!--- If no messages are found, let the user know --->
  <CFELSE>
  <H3>No messages found...</H3>
  </CFIF>
  </TD>
</TR>
</TABLE>
</CENTER>
</BODY>
</HTML>
```

The first thing that Example 13-13 does is initialize a few constants to be used throughout the template. These constants make it easy to customize the application without having to replace multiple instances of the same value. After the constants are initialized, the template checks to see if a user's POP account password has been passed in via an encrypted URL variable. If it has, ColdFusion decrypts the password using the key `815` (this is arbitrary and can be changed to anything you want provided it is used consistently throughout the application) so that it can be used by the application. Next, a variable called `Parameters` is created to hold all the URL parameters that will be passed from template to template throughout the application. The URL parameters contain the user's email address, POP server, SMTP server, username, and encrypted password.

The next section of Example 13-13 retrieves a list of the message headers from the user's POP account using the `CFPOP` tag with the `ACTION` attribute set to

`GetHeaderOnly`. Only the first 10 message headers are retrieved by setting the `STARTROW` and `MAXROWS` attributes to 1 and 10, respectively. These values are set in the constants section of the template. This is also how next/previous functionality is enabled. After the first 10 message headers are retrieved, next/previous links are automatically created that recalculate the values for `STARTROW` and `MAXROWS`. Clicking on one of the next/previous links causes the *Inbox.cfm* template to be reloaded with the attribute values necessary to grab the next/previous set of message headers.

Once the messages have been retrieved, the inbox page is dynamically assembled and output to the browser, as shown in Figure 13-1. The message headers are listed in table format with the "From" part of the header displayed as a hyperlink. The "From" addresses are linked to the next template in the application, *Action.cfm*, shown in Example 13-14. The links pass several variables as URL parameters. These variables contain all the user's login information, as well as the message number to be retrieved and the action to be performed by the *Action.cfm* template. The inbox template also adds a checkbox next to each message header displayed, which allows users to select multiple messages to be deleted at one time, a very useful feature for web-based mail clients.

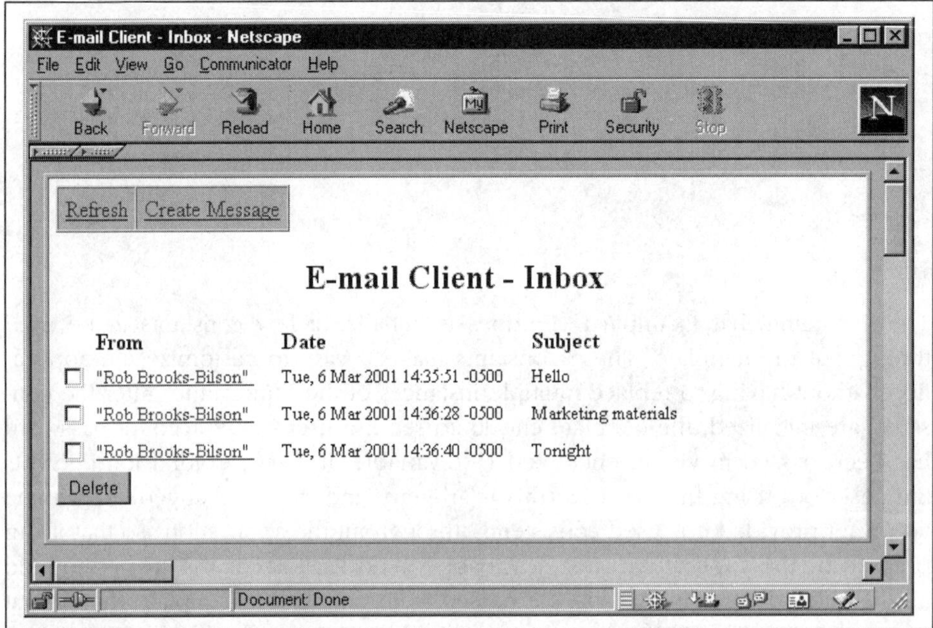


*Figure 13-1. Inbox page generated by Inbox.cfm*

The *Action.cfm* template (shown in Example 13-14) performs the majority of the tasks available in the application. This template is responsible for displaying message contents, creating, forwarding, replying to, and deleting messages.

*Example 13-14. Action.cfm File for the POP Mail Client*

```
<!--- initialize constants --->
<CFPARAM NAME="URL.action" DEFAULT=""> <!--- sets default action --->
<CFPARAM NAME="ReSubject" DEFAULT=""> <!--- default Re: subject --->
<!--- set the attachment path to the same directory the application resides
      in. --->
<CFSET TheAttachmentPath = GetDirectoryFromPath(GetCurrentTemplatePath())>
<CFSET TAB=CHR(9)> <!--- sets a tab character --->

<!--- If the Password is sent encrypted by URL, decrypt it --->
<CFIF IsDefined('URL.Password')>
   <CFSET Password = Decrypt(URL.Password,815)>
</CFIF>

<!--- create a url parameter string containing the user's e-mail address, POP
      server, SMTP server, username, and password. Encrypt the password using
      the cfencrypt function.  This is NOT strong encryption --->
<CFSET Parameters = "EmailAddress=#URLEncodedFormat(EmailAddress)#&PopServer=
#URLEncodedFormat(PopServer)#&SMTPServer=#URLEncodedFormat(SMTPServer)#&Username=
#URLEncodedFormat(Username)#&Password=#URLEncodedFormat(Encrypt(Password,815))#">

<HTML>
<HEAD>
<TITLE>Pop Client</TITLE>
</HEAD>
<BODY BGCOLOR="#C0C0C0">

<CENTER>
<TABLE BORDER="1" WIDTH="600" CELLPADDING="5">
<TR>
<TD BGCOLOR="#FFFFFF">

<!--- read a message --->
<CFIF URL.Action IS "Read">
<CFPOP ACTION="GetAll" NAME="GetMessages" MESSAGENUMBER="#Message#"
       SERVER="#popserver#" TIMEOUT="600" USERNAME="#username#"
       PASSWORD="#password#" ATTACHMENTPATH="#TheAttachmentPath#"
       GENERATEUNIQUEFILENAMES="yes">

<!--- Output action options --->
<TABLE BORDER="1" CELLPADDING="5" CELLSPACING="0">
<TR BGCOLOR="#C0C0C0">
<CFOUTPUT>
<TD><A HREF="Inbox.cfm?#Parameters#">Inbox</A></TD>
<TD><A HREF="Action.cfm?action=create&#Parameters#">Create Message</A></TD>
<TD>
<A HREF="Action.cfm?action=reply&message=#URL.Message#&#Parameters#">Reply</A>
</TD>
<TD>
```

*Example 13-14. Action.cfm File for the POP Mail Client (continued)*

```
<A HREF="Action.cfm?action=forward&message=#URL.Message#&#Parameters#">Forward</A>
</TD>
<TD>
<A HREF="Action.cfm?action=delete&message=#URL.Message#&#Parameters#">Delete</A>
</TD>
</CFOUTPUT>
</TR>
</TABLE>

<CFOUTPUT QUERY="GetMessages">
<HR NOSHADE>
<P>
<FONT COLOR="blue">From:</FONT> #HTMLEditFormat(FROM)# on #HTMLEditFormat(Date)#
<BR>
<FONT COLOR="blue">To:</FONT> #HTMLEditFormat(TO)# <BR>
<FONT COLOR="blue">Cc:</FONT> #HTMLEditFormat(CC)# <BR>
<FONT COLOR="blue">Subject:</FONT> #HTMLEditFormat(SUBJECT)#
<P>
#BODY# <BR>
<!--- If there are attachments, display links to them --->
<CFIF Attachments IS NOT "">
Attachments:<BR>
<CFLOOP FROM="1" TO="#ListLen(Attachments, Tab)#" INDEX="TheAttachment">
<A HREF="#URLEncodedFormat(GetFileFromPath(ListGetAt(AttachmentFiles,
   TheAttachment, Tab)))#">#ListGetAt(Attachments, TheAttachment, Tab)#</A><BR>
</CFLOOP>
</CFIF>
</CFOUTPUT>

<!--- reply to, forward, or create a message --->
<CFELSEIF URL.Action IS "Reply" OR URL.Action IS "Forward" OR URL.Action IS
          "create">
<TABLE BORDER="1" CELLPADDING="5" CELLSPACING="0">
<TR BGCOLOR="#C0C0C0">
    <CFOUTPUT>
    <TD><A HREF="inbox.cfm?#Parameters#">Inbox</A></TD>
    </CFOUTPUT>
</TR>
</TABLE>
<CFIF URL.Action IS "Reply" OR URL.Action IS "Forward">

<CFPOP ACTION="GETALL" NAME="GetMessage" MESSAGENUMBER="#Message#"
       SERVER="#popserver#" TIMEOUT="600" USERNAME="#username#"
       PASSWORD="#password#" ATTACHMENTPATH="#TheAttachmentPath#"
       GENERATEUNIQUEFILENAMES="yes">

<!--- Preface the subject with Re: --->
<CFIF FindNoCase("Re:", Left(Trim(GetMessage.Subject), 3)) IS 0>
    <CFSET ReSubject = "Re: " & Trim(GetMessage.Subject)>
<CFELSE>
    <CFSET ReSubject = Trim(GetMessage.Subject)>
</CFIF>
```

*Example 13-14. Action.cfm File for the POP Mail Client (continued)*

```
</CFIF>

<CFOUTPUT>
<FORM ACTION="action.cfm?action=send&#Parameters#" METHOD="POST"
      ENCTYPE="multipart/form-data">
<CFIF IsDefined('GetMessage.Attachments')>
<!--- Include the attachment info --->
<INPUT TYPE="hidden" NAME="ForwardedAttachmentFiles"
       VALUE="#GetMessage.AttachmentFiles#">
<INPUT TYPE="hidden" NAME="ForwardedAttachments" VALUE="#GetMessage.Attachments#">
</CFIF>
</CFOUTPUT>
<INPUT TYPE="SUBMIT" VALUE="Send">
<CFOUTPUT>
<TABLE>
<TR>
    <TD ALIGN="RIGHT"><FONT COLOR="blue"><B>To:</B></FONT></TD>
    <TD><INPUT TYPE="TEXT" NAME="To" VALUE="<CFIF URL.Action IS "Reply">
#HTMLEditFormat(Trim(GetMessage.From))#</CFIF>" SIZE="50"></TD>
</TR>
<TR>
    <TD ALIGN="RIGHT"><FONT COLOR="blue"><B>cc:</B></FONT></TD>
    <TD><INPUT TYPE="TEXT" NAME="cc" SIZE="50"></TD>
</TR>
<TR>
    <TD ALIGN="RIGHT"><FONT COLOR="blue"><B>bcc:</B></FONT></TD>
    <TD><INPUT TYPE="TEXT" NAME="bcc" SIZE="50"></TD>
</TR>
<TR>
    <TD ALIGN="RIGHT"><FONT COLOR="blue"><B>Subject:</B></FONT></TD>
    <TD><INPUT TYPE="TEXT" NAME="Subject" VALUE="<CFIF URL.Action IS NOT
       "Create">#HTMLEditFormat(ReSubject)#</CFIF>" SIZE="50"></TD>
</TR>
</TABLE>

<P>
<TEXTAREA NAME="Body" COLS="70" ROWS="15" WRAP="VIRTUAL"><CFIF URL.Action IS NOT
 "Create">>>#GetMessage.Body#</CFIF></TEXTAREA></P>
</CFOUTPUT>

<!--- If forwarding, include attachments --->
<CFIF Action IS "Forward">
File Attachments:<BR>
<CFOUTPUT>
<FONT COLOR="Blue">
<CFLOOP FROM="1"
        TO="#ListLen(GetMessage.Attachments, Tab)#"
        INDEX="TheAttachment">
#ListGetAt(GetMessage.Attachments, TheAttachment, Tab)#<BR>
</CFLOOP></FONT>
</CFOUTPUT>
</CFIF>
```

*Example 13-14. Action.cfm File for the POP Mail Client (continued)*

```
<P>
<FONT COLOR="blue"><B>File Attachment:</B></FONT><BR>
<INPUT TYPE="FILE" NAME="Attachment">
<P>
<INPUT TYPE="SUBMIT" VALUE="Send">
</FORM>

<!--- delete a message.  --->
<CFELSEIF URL.Action IS "Delete" OR (IsDefined('Form.Action') AND Form.Action
 IS "Delete")>
<CFPOP ACTION="Delete" MESSAGENUMBER="#Message#" SERVER="#popserver#"
      TIMEOUT="600" USERNAME="#username#" PASSWORD="#password#">
<CFLOCATION URL="inbox.cfm?#Parameters#">

<!--- send the message --->
<CFELSEIF URL.Action IS "Send">

<!--- Check to see if there is an attachment to upload before sending --->
<CFIF IsDefined('Form.Attachment') AND Form.Attachment IS NOT "">
<CFFILE ACTION="UPLOAD" FILEFIELD="Attachment"
        DESTINATION="#TheAttachmentPath#"
        NAMECONFLICT="MAKEUNIQUE">
</CFIF>

<!--- send the message --->
<CFMAIL TO="#Form.To#"
        FROM="#EmailAddress#"
        SUBJECT="#Form.Subject#"
        CC="#Form.cc#"
        BCC="#Form.bcc#"
        SERVER="#SMTPServer#"
        TIMEOUT="600">
#Form.Body#
<!--- Include the new attachment if necessary --->
<CFIF IsDefined('Form.Attachment') AND Form.Attachment IS NOT "">
<CFMAILPARAM FILE="#TheAttachmentPath#\#File.ServerFile#">
</CFIF>

<!--- Include any forwarded attachments if necessary --->
<CFIF IsDefined('ForwardedAttachments')>
<CFLOOP FROM="1" TO="#ListLen(ForwardedAttachments, Tab)#" INDEX="TheAttachment">
<CFMAILPARAM FILE="#ListGetAt(ForwardedAttachmentFiles, TheAttachment, Tab)#">
</CFLOOP>
</CFIF>
</CFMAIL>
<CFLOCATION URL="inbox.cfm?#Parameters#">

<!--- No Action selected.  Redirect back to inbox --->
<CFELSE>
<CFLOCATION URL="inbox.cfm?#Parameters#">
</CFIF>
```

*Example 13-14. Action.cfm File for the POP Mail Client (continued)*

```
</TD>
</TR>
</TABLE>
</CENTER>
</BODY>
</HTML>
```

Example 13-14 begins in much the same way as Example 13-13. First, constants are assigned for the entire template. If an encrypted password is received, it is unencrypted. Next, a variable called `Parameters` is created to hold all the URL parameters that will be passed from template to template throughout the application. The URL parameters contain the user's email address, POP server, SMTP server, username, and encrypted password.

After these preliminary steps, the template evaluates the `URL.Action` variable passed from the previous template (either *Inbox.cfm* or the *Action.cfm* template calling itself) and performs the appropriate action. Possible actions for the *Action.cfm* template are:

`URL.Action="Read"`
: If `Action` is set to `Read`, the `CFPOP` tag retrieves the entire message including attachments. The message number to retrieve is supplied from the *Inbox.cfm* template as a URL variable. If there are file attachments associated with the message, they are displayed by looping through the contents of the `Attachments` and `AttachmentFiles` variables and creating hyperlinks to the actual files. A menu is generated at the top of the page allowing the user to create a new message, reply to, forward, or delete the message being read, or return to the inbox.

`URL.Action="Create"`
: When the `Action` is set to `Create`, the template displays a form for creating a mail message. The form allows you to specify values for `To`, `Cc`, `Bcc`, `Subject`, `Body`, and a single file attachment.

`URL.Action="Reply"`
: If `Action` is set to `Reply`, the template displays a form for creating a new message with the `To` field already populated with the email address of the sender of the original message. In addition, the body of the original message is included in the body of the new message.

`URL.Action="Forward"`
: Forwarding a message works exactly like replying to a message, except that the `To` field isn't automatically populated. Additionally, any file attachments included with the original message are automatically sent along when the message that is forwarded.

`URL.Action="Delete"`
: If `Action` is set to `Delete`, the template permanently deletes one or more messages from the POP server. Messages are selected for deletion from the inbox page (one message or multiple messages) or from the "Read Message" page.

`URL.Action="Send"`
: If `Action` is set to `Send`, ColdFusion physically sends the message that was created, replied to, or forwarded. If a file attachment is specified, it is uploaded from the client machine to the ColdFusion server, so that it can be sent along with the message. File attachments associated with forwarded messages are also included.

*In this chapter:*
- *Retrieving Information*
- *Parsing Data*
- *Generating Static HTML Pages*
- *Posting Information*
- *CFHTTP Considerations*

# 14
# *Interacting with Other Web Servers Using HTTP*

One of ColdFusion's most powerful features is its ability to interact with other web servers via the CFHTTP tag. CFHTTP allows a ColdFusion application to perform standard HTTP GET and POST operations on remote servers. Using CFHTTP, you can perform a wide range of functions, such as retrieving text and binary files, reading the contents of delimited text files into query objects, and posting information to forms and applications on remote servers. Some of the more common uses include generating static HTML pages from dynamic data, gathering content such as news articles and press releases from remote sites, automatic form submissions, and intelligent agents capable of interacting with remote services such as stock quote and news feeds. For example, you can use CFHTTP to write an agent that can gather information related to a particular company from various services including news sources, search engines, and financial service providers. The information gathered by the agent can be presented to users in any number of ways such as in an email, on a personalized web page, or even in an alphanumeric message sent to a pager. The uses for the CFHTTP tag are limited only by your imagination.

Because CFHTTP has the ability to "grab" content from remote sites, questions of copyright, trademark, and intellectual property infringement can come up. It is important to remember that much of what is out on the Internet is protected by copyright. When using CFHTTP to gather information from remote sites, you should have a clear understanding of what is protected and what is considered to be under public domain. When in doubt, consider contacting the publisher of the information for permission.

# Retrieving Information

CFHTTP uses the HTTP GET method to initiate a one-way request for information from a remote server. The transaction mimics the one that a standard web browser uses to request a web page. The only difference is that in the case of CFHTTP, the requested page is stored in a ColdFusion variable or in a query object, as opposed to being displayed in the user's browser. Let's look at the different ways in which you can use CFHTTP to request information from a remote server.

## Saving Information to a Variable

In its most simplistic form, CFHTTP can grab an entire file (either plain text or HTML) and store it in a single variable called CFHTTP.FileContent. You can access and manipulate the information stored in CFHTTP.FileContent as you can with any other ColdFusion variable. The following example illustrates how to use CFHTTP to retrieve a remote web page and store it as a variable:

```
<CFHTTP METHOD="GET"
        PROXYSERVER="myproxy.example.com"
        URL="http://www.yahoo.com/"
        PORT="80"
        RESOLVEURL="Yes"
        PROXYPORT="80"
        REDIRECT="Yes"
        USERAGENT="Mozilla/4.5 [en] (WinNT; U)"
        TIMEOUT="180"
        THROWONERROR="Yes">
</CFHTTP>

<CFOUTPUT>
   #CFHTTP.FileContent#
</CFOUTPUT>
```

The first CFHTTP attribute you see is the required METHOD attribute. This specifies whether CFHTTP uses the HTTP GET or POST method. If you must pass through a proxy server for Internet access, the hostname or IP address of that server may be specified in the PROXYSERVER attribute. If you don't use a proxy server, don't include this attribute. The next attribute, URL is also required; it specifies the full URL of the remote web page you are accessing. Additionally, you may append a port number to the URL (e.g., *http://www.myserver.com:8080/*). In this case, we've used CFHTTP to retrieve the home page from Yahoo's web site. The PORT attribute specifies what port the CFHTTP tag should try to connect to. This attribute is optional and defaults to the standard HTTP port 80. If used in conjunction with the RESOLVEURL attribute, the port number is automatically appended to all resolved URLs. The PORT attribute is ignored if a port number is specified in the URL attribute.

Setting the RESOLVEURL attribute to Yes specifies that any partial or relative URLs embedded in the retrieved document are fully resolved, so that all links in the document remain valid. If you want to resolve a URL that doesn't end in a filename (such as *http://www.example.com*), and you set the RESOLVEURL attribute to Yes, you need to supply a trailing forward slash (*http://www.example.com/*) for the URL attribute in order for certain URLs (such as those in IMG tags) to resolve properly. Since we are outputting the retrieved page to the screen using CFOUTPUT, it is important that all the links function properly. If the page you are trying to retrieve sits behind a proxy server, you can specify the port number used by the proxy server in the PROXYPORT attribute. If a value is specified for PROXYPORT, it is automatically appended to resolved URLs when the RESOLVEURL attribute is set to Yes.

REDIRECT is an optional attribute that indicates whether or not to allow a CFHTTP request to be automatically redirected. If set to No, the CFHTTP request fails upon encountering a redirect. The CFHTTP tag can follow as many as five redirections per request. If this limit is exceeded, ColdFusion treats the next redirect as if the REDIRECT is set to No. The USERAGENT attribute specifies the user agent to pass in the HTTP request header when CFHTTP makes a request to a remote web server. In this example, we set USERAGENT to Mozilla/4.5 [en] (WinNT; U) so that the request appears to the remote web server as if it originated from a Netscape 4.5 browser. This feature is especially useful when the information you are trying to receive varies, depending on the browser making the request.

Another optional attribute, TIMEOUT, specifies a timeout in seconds for the CFHTTP operation. If a URL timeout parameter is used in conjunction with the template employing the CFHTTP tag, and the TIMEOUT attribute of the CFHTTP tag is used, ColdFusion uses the lesser of the two values. If, however, no URL timeout value is passed, no CFHTTP TIMEOUT attribute is used, and no default timeout value is set in the ColdFusion Administrator, ColdFusion will wait indefinitely for the CFHTTP tag to process. Because each instance of the CFHTTP tag being processed requires a thread of its own, this can have serious performance consequences. Depending on your server and ColdFusion configuration, the potential to hang the server exists if the CFHTTP tag utilizes all available threads on the system.

Finally, the THROWONERROR attribute specifies whether ColdFusion should generate an exception that can be caught with CFTRY/CFCATCH tags should an error occur when executing the CFHTTP request. THROWONERROR is optional and defaults to No. If the THROWONERROR attribute is set to No, an HTTP 1.1 status code and message are written to the CFHTTP.StatusCode return variable. There are 37 status codes detailed in the HTTP 1.1 specification outlined in RFC-2068. For a list of the status codes, see the listing for the CFHTTP tag in Appendix A. The complete text of RFC-2068 is available at *http://www.w3.org/Protocols/rfc2068/rfc2068*. In order to get detailed information in the event the CFHTTP tag throws an exception, THROWONERROR must be set to Yes. More information on error and exception handling can be found in Chapter 9.

The use of the closing </CFHTTP> tag is optional for GET operations. In the interest of good style and to be compatible with XML standards, however, it is a good idea to include the closing tag regardless of the METHOD invoked.

## *Saving Information to a File*

You may opt to save a retrieved file directly to the local filesystem. By adding the PATH and FILE attributes to the previous example, we can store the page we retrieved from Yahoo's web site right on the hard drive of our ColdFusion server:

```
<CFHTTP METHOD="Get" URL="http://www.yahoo.com/"
    FILE="index.htm" PATH="c:\temp">
</CFHTTP>
```

Note that the RESOLVEURL attribute is intentionally left out. Setting the FILE and PATH attributes causes the RESOLVEURL attribute to be ignored. When retrieving a file, ColdFusion uses an additional variable, CFHTTP.MimeType, to contain the MIME type of the downloaded file. This is especially useful when downloading a file with an unknown MIME type.

You can also use CFHTTP to retrieve binary files from a remote server. Here's how to use CFHTTP to retrieve a binary file, in this case a GIF file from Allaire's web site:

```
<CFHTTP METHOD="Get"
    URL="http://www.allaire.com/Image2/GlobalPageFormatting/newhomepage/home.gif"
    PATH="c:\temp\">
</CFHTTP>

<CFOUTPUT>
The MIME type of the downloaded file is #CFHTTP.MimeType#
</CFOUTPUT>
```

After the file is downloaded, its MIME type is returned to the screen via CFOUTPUT. Note that the FILE attribute has been left out this time. By default, CFHTTP uses the filename from the URL if no FILE attribute is specified. To save the file under a different name from the default, simply add the new name using the FILE attribute.

## *Retrieving HTTP Header Information*

In addition to retrieving the file specified in the URL attribute, the CFHTTP tag also returns the response header associated with the HTTP GET operation. The HTTP response header is returned as a ColdFusion structure called CFHTTP.ResponseHeader. The exact contents of the CFHTTP.ResponseHeader structure vary depending on the web server in use where the page is requested. If a particular key appears only once in the header, it is stored as a simple value within the structure. If a key appears more than once, it is stored as an array within the structure. Another variable, `CFHTTP.Header` is also returned and contains the raw HTTP response header as a string as opposed to a structure. The following example illustrates a method for requesting a remote web page and outputting all the data in the HTTP response header without knowing the specific keys in the `CFHTTP.ResponseHeader` structure:

```
<CFHTTP URL="http://www.allaire.com" METHOD="GET">

<TABLE BORDER="1" CELLSPACING="0" CELLPADDING="5">
<TR>
  <TH>Key</TH><TH>Value</TH>
</TR>

<CFLOOP COLLECTION=#CFHTTP.ResponseHeader# ITEM="Key">
  <CFSET Value = CFHTTP.ResponseHeader[Key]>

<CFIF IsArray(Value)>
  <CFLOOP INDEX="i" FROM=1 TO=#ArrayLen(Value)#>
    <CFOUTPUT>
    <TR>
      <TD>#key#</TD><TD>#value[i]#</TD>
    </TR>
    </CFOUTPUT>
  </CFLOOP>

<CFELSE>

<CFOUTPUT>
<TR>
  <TD>#Key#</TD><TD>#value#</TD>
</TR>
</CFOUTPUT>

</CFIF>
</CFLOOP>
</TABLE>
```

In this example, the `CFHTTP` retrieves the home page from Allaire's web site. The `CFHTTP.ResponseHeader` is then looped over using the `CFLOOP` tag. Each value in the structure is then evaluated to determine whether it is a string or an array. If the value is a string, it is output directly to the browser. If, however, the value is an array (as is the case for several values in the response header obtained from Allaire's web site), the elements of the array must be looped over individually and output one at a time.

## Creating Query Objects from Text Files

One of the most useful features of the CFHTTP tag is its ability to construct a query object from data contained in a delimited text file. This essentially allows you to use any delimited text file accessible via a URL as a "pseudo" ColdFusion data source; in other words, you don't need an ODBC driver. I say a "pseudo" data source because although a query object can be built from a delimited text file using CFHTTP, the CFHTTP tag itself can't execute a ColdFusion query against the text file.

There are a number of different scenarios for having CFHTTP import the contents of a delimited text file into a query object. Some of the more common ones include working with flat files, interfacing with legacy systems, and handling news and stock feeds. For instance, say that the Human Resources department of a particular company uses an outdated personnel program that stores personnel data as a comma-delimited text file on the server. As your company is serious about web-enabling all your legacy data, your boss decides that a contact list application needs to be built that queries the Human Resources personnel database and displays the results as a web page. Using CFHTTP, you can construct a small program to read in the contents of that file and dynamically generate a nicely formatted web page listing all the employees and their contact information, as shown in the following example.

Here's a typical comma-delimited text file with column headers:

```
Name,Title,Department,Extension
Joe Smith,Lead Salesperson,Sales,5515
Nancy Jones,Liaison,Marketing,5596
Tom White,Mechanical Engineer I,Engineering,5525
Jen Brown,Collection Specialist,Billing,5543
```

Getting CFHTTP to import the contents of such a delimited text file into a query object is easy. The following example shows the proper syntax for building a query object from the data:

```
<CFHTTP URL="http://127.0.0.1/examples/chapter14/MyFile.txt"
    METHOD="get" NAME="MyQuery" DELIMITER="," TEXTQUALIFIER=" ">
</CFHTTP>

<TABLE>
<TR>
    <TH>Name</TH><TH>Title</TH><TH>Department</TH><TH>Extension</TH>
</TR>
<CFOUTPUT QUERY="MyQuery">
<TR>
    <TD>#Name#</TD><TD>#Title#</TD><TD>#Department#</TD><TD>#Extension#</TD>
</TR>
</CFOUTPUT>
</TABLE>
```

We use the NAME attribute to specify the name of the query. Note that this attribute tells CFHTTP to construct a query object. We set the DELIMITER attribute to a comma, since we are dealing with a comma-delimited text file. Because no text qualifier is used in the text file, the TEXTQUALIFIER attribute is set to " ". A text qualifier is sometimes used in a delimited text file to mark the beginning and end of a column. The default value for the TEXTQUALIFIER attribute is the quotation mark ("). Because the quotation mark is a reserved character, it must be escaped as ("").

CFHTTP uses the values found in the first row of a delimited text file as column headers. These headers are used as column names (i.e., variables) for the query unless alternate names are specified with the COLUMNS attribute. To ensure that all column headers remain unique within a given query, ColdFusion automatically adds an underscore character (_) to any duplicate column header it finds in the delimited text file. For example, if two column headers called Name are found, ColdFusion leaves the first one alone and adds an underscore to the second one, making it Name_.

Once we have the data stored as a query object, displaying the data is only a matter of using the variables in a CFOUTPUT tag. Our example displays the data stored in the query as an HTML table. Note that the column headers used in the <TH> tags are arbitrary and must be created manually.

In addition to creating a ColdFusion query, the CFHTTP operation creates a number of other variables that give information about the query object itself:

ColumnList
: A comma-delimited list of column headers for the query

CurrentRow
: The current row of the query that is being processed by CFOUTPUT

RecordCount
: The total number of records returned by the query

If for some reason you decide you don't like the column headers that accompany the delimited text file, you can change them with the COLUMNS attribute. You can use any value as a column header, provided it begins with a letter and contain only letters, numbers, and the underscore character. You must be careful to use the same number of column headers because there are columns in the delimited text file. Failure to do so causes CFHTTP to return an error.

Because you may not always know the column names being used in a text file, ColdFusion provides a variable called ColumnList that holds all the column headers contained in a specified query. As always, you access this variable through the query name:

```
#queryname.ColumnList#
```

With access to the column names, it is fairly easy to construct a single ColdFusion template that can use `CFHTTP` to retrieve the contents of any delimited text file that contains column headers and output the results to the screen. All this can be accomplished without knowing anything other than the location of the text file and the delimiter used, as illustrated in Example 14-1.

*Example 14-1. Displaying the Contents of Any Comma-Delimited Text File with CFHTTP*

```
<!--- Use CFHTTP GET to grab the delimited text file.  Assume that the comma
      is the delimiter and there is no text qualifier --->
<CFHTTP METHOD="GET"
    URL="http://127.0.0.1/examples/chapter14/textfile.txt"
    NAME="MyQuery" DELIMITER="," TEXTQUALIFIER=" ">

<!--- build an HTML table with the column headers parsed from the first line
      of the delimited text file --->
<TABLE BORDER="0" CELLPADDING="3">
<TR>
<!--- Dynamically build the column headers by looping through the column
      headers returned in the MyQuery.ColumnList variable --->
<CFLOOP INDEX="ThePosition" FROM="1" TO="#ListLen(MyQuery.ColumnList)#">
  <CFOUTPUT>
    <TH BGCOLOR="##8A8A8A">#ListGetAt(MyQuery.ColumnList, ThePosition)#</TH>
  </CFOUTPUT>
</CFLOOP>
</TR>

<!--- Dynamically build the columns and rows to be output by looping over the
      column names listed in the MyQuery.ColumnList variable.  The values
      contained in the column headers are extracted using the evaluate
      function --->
<CFLOOP QUERY="MyQuery">
     <TR>
    <CFLOOP INDEX="ListElement" LIST="#MyQuery.ColumnList#">
        <CFSET ColumnName = "MyQuery.#ListElement#">
        <CFSET ColumnValue = #Evaluate(ColumnName)#>
        <TD BGCOLOR="#C0C0C0"><CFOUTPUT>#ColumnValue#</CFOUTPUT></TD>
    </CFLOOP>
    </TR>
</CFLOOP>
</TABLE>
```

This template uses the `CFHTTP` tag to grab a text file called *textfile.txt* and store its contents in a query called `MyQuery`. To obtain the column names, we use a list loop to loop over `MyQuery.ColumnList` and output each column name as a cell in the first row of an HTML table. Remember that `ColumnList` is a special variable created by ColdFusion that contains a list of all columns in a given query object. Once we have the column names, all that is left is to dump the contents of the query object into the HTML table. This is done by looping over the column names listed in the `MyQuery.ColumnList` variable. The values contained in the column headers are extracted using the evaluate function. Executing the template in Example 14-1 results in the output shown in Figure 14-1.

*Figure 14-1. Using CFHTTP to display the contents of a comma-delimited text file*

## Passing Parameters

With a **CFHTTP GET** operation, you can pass URL parameters to a remote page that you are attempting to retrieve. This means you can retrieve a page that is dynamically generated from a script based on the parameters passed to it, such as a search page. Here's an example that shows the use of **CFHTTP** to retrieve the results page from a search for "ColdFusion" on Yahoo's web site:

```
<CFHTTP URL="http://search.yahoo.com/bin/search?p=ColdFusion"
   METHOD="GET" RESOLVEURL="Yes">
</CFHTTP>

<CFOUTPUT>
#CFHTTP.FileContent#
</CFOUTPUT>
```

Note the URL we are using. It contains the parameters needed to perform the search. Normally, searches on the Yahoo web site are performed by filling out and submitting an HTML form. The HTML form uses an HTTP **GET** operation to pass the search criteria as URL parameters to a CGI script. The script returns a dynamically generated HTML page that contains the search results. By passing the search criteria in the URL for our **CFHTTP** operation, we can completely bypass the search form. Of course, to do this, you need to understand exactly what parameters a remote page is expecting and in what form.

# Parsing Data

As shown in the previous examples, CFHTTP is great for importing the contents of a text file into a query object and allowing for output of results to the screen. This process is useful if you want to dump the results of the file into another database or output the results to a simple HTML table. But what if the data you import requires a little cleaning up beforehand? Take, for example, the following delimited text file containing employee information for a fictitious company:

```
Name,Title,Department,Extension,JobCode
Joe Smith,Lead Salesperson,Sales,5515,A:001
Nancy Jones,Liaison,Marketing,5596,B:003
Tom White,Mechanical Engineer I,Engineering,5525,A:002
Jen Brown,Collection Specialist,Billing,5543,C:004
Mike Johnson,Security Guard,Security,5512,E:012
```

Note that this text file is very similar to the one we used earlier, but there is an added field called JobCode. This new field is used for a number of purposes within the company, including classifying an employee's position. Suppose that we want to use CFHTTP to put the contents of this text file into a query object. Nothing tricky needed, it's just a simple CFHTTP GET operation.

Once we have the contents of the file in a query object, however, we will want to append an additional column of data called Status and populate it based on each employee's job code. Because the data is already contained within a query, there is no simple way to make the additions. We can wait until the results are output and make the additions inside the CFOUTPUT section, but that will work only if the data is output to the screen and not if you want to save the results of the query to another database. Making additions or changes within the query is the most efficient method. Example 14-2 details a method for inserting additional information into an existing query. In this case, we append an additional column, Status, to the query. This column is populated with data based on the value of the JobCode column.

*Example 14-2. Parsing the Contents of a CFHTTP Query*

```
<!--- Use CFHTTP GET to grab the delimited text file --->
<CFHTTP METHOD="GET"
    URL="http://127.0.0.1/examples/chapter14/hrdata.txt"
    NAME="MyQuery"
    COLUMNS="Name,Title,Department,Extension,JobCode"
    DELIMITER=","
    TEXTQUALIFIER="">
</CFHTTP>
```

*Example 14-2. Parsing the Contents of a CFHTTP Query (continued)*

```
<!--- create a one-dimensional array called StatusArray to hold the
      status value to be appended to the query object --->
<CFSET StatusArray = ArrayNew(1)>

<!--- loop over the query object checking the first letter of the jobcode.
      Assign a value for Stat depending on the jobcode. --->
<cfloop query="MyQuery">
        <CFIF Left(MyQuery.JobCode, 1) IS "A">
            <CFSET Stat="Exempt">
        <CFELSEIF Left(MyQuery.JobCode, 1) IS "B">
            <CFSET Stat="Exempt">
        <CFELSEIF Left(MyQuery.JobCode, 1) IS "C">
            <CFSET Stat="Non-exempt">
        <CFELSEIF Left(MyQuery.JobCode, 1) IS "D">
            <CFSET Stat="Temporary">
        <CFELSE>
            <CFSET Stat="Other">
        </CFIF>
        <!--- add the value of stat to the StatusArray --->
        <CFSET StatusArray[CurrentRow] = stat>
</CFLOOP>

<!--- create a new column called Shipping and populate it with the data from
      the ShippingArray array --->
<CFSET MyNewColumn = QueryAddColumn(MyQuery, "Status", StatusArray)>

<!--- Output the results of the modified query to an HTML table. --->
<TABLE BORDER="0" CELLPADDING="3">
<TR BGCOLOR="#8A8A8A">
    <TH>Name</TH>
    <TH>Title</TH>
    <TH>Department</TH>
    <TH>Extension</TH>
    <TH>Job Code</TH>
    <TH>Status</TH>
</TR>
<CFOUTPUT QUERY="MyQuery">
<TR BGCOLOR="##C0C0C0">
    <TD>#Name#</TD>
    <TD>#Title#</TD>
    <TD>#Department#</TD>
    <TD>#Extension#</TD>
    <TD>#JobCode#</TD>
    <TD>#Status#</TD>
</TR>
</CFOUTPUT>
</TABLE>
```

This template uses `CFHTTP` to grab a delimited text file and store its contents in a query object called `MyQuery`. Next a one-dimensional array called `StatusArray` is created to hold the status value we are going to append to each record in the query. The actual status value is assigned by looping over `MyQuery` and evaluating the first character of the JobCode column for each row. A status is then assigned for each row based on JobCode and written to the StatusArray array. Once the loop has completed, the values in the array are appended to the MyQuery query object using the QueryAddColumn() function. Finally, an HTML table containing the appended Status column is produced.

# *Generating Static HTML Pages*

Another popular use for CFHTTP is to generate static HTML pages from dynamic content. As useful as dynamically generated pages are, there are still times when using static HTML pages makes more sense, because static pages load faster than dynamic pages. Dynamic pages require more processing overhead, because each request must be passed to the ColdFusion Application Server, in addition to the web server. This doesn't include the added time it takes to process all the CFML code contained in each template. The differences in load time between static and dynamic pages becomes clear.

Yet, it isn't practical or even desirable to convert every page in a site to a static page. There are some amazing things that can be done with dynamic pages that just can't be recreated with static HTML pages. How do you decide which pages in a site or application should be static and which dynamic? There is no simple answer, but there are some useful guidelines to help you decide:

- Data that is infrequently refreshed is a prime candidate for static page material. For instance, if you have a ColdFusion template that outputs a table of sales figures that change only once per month, it makes more sense to have the page exist as a static page. Why tie up your server with the additional overhead of running the exact same query over and over only to return the same result set each time. It's much simpler to write a small ColdFusion template that performs the query and outputs the results to a static page. The template can even be scheduled to run on an automated basis via the ColdFusion Administrator. This completely eliminates the need for any further administrator involvement.
- Queries that take a long time to process are another candidate for static page generation. If there is one thing that drives users nuts, it is having to wait for long periods of time while a query executes or a page loads. Creating static pages from ColdFusion templates that contain unusually long queries, long execution times, or complex CFML code, is a service to your users that should definitely be considered.
- Making your site more visible to search engines is the third reason to consider generating static pages from your ColdFusion templates. While many of the popular search engines on the Web can now index ColdFusion pages, some

still have problems following links that contain URL parameters. If search engine exposure is a high priority for your site, you should consider making at least some of your pages static.

Creating a static HTML page from dynamic content is easy. Say your company web site has a dynamically generated press release page that gets its data from a small database residing on the server (in this case, Microsoft Access). The CFML template shown in Example 14-3 is used to query the database for a list of press release titles for the current year. Note that `ArticleID` is the primary key for the table. The other two field names are self-explanatory. Example 14-3 also queries the database for a list of previous years' press releases. Each time a user on the Internet requests this page with their web browser, both queries must be run against the database, and a results page must be dynamically constructed before it can be sent back to the user. This process has the potential to tie up a lot of the server's processing time. Because the query is the same each and every time this page is accessed, it is a perfect candidate for a static page.

*Example 14-3. Listing Press Release Headers in a Database*

```
<!--- assign the current year to the variable whichyear --->
<CFPARAM NAME="WhichYear" DEFAULT="#Year(Now())#">

<!--- query the database for all articles from the current year --->
<CFQUERY NAME="GetTitles" DATASOURCE="ProgrammingCF">
        SELECT ArticleID,Title,DatePosted FROM News
        WHERE {fn YEAR(DatePosted)} = #CreateODBCDate(WhichYear)#
        ORDER BY DatePosted
</CFQUERY>

<!--- query the database for all years besides the current year --->
<CFQUERY NAME="GetArchiveDates" DATASOURCE="ProgrammingCF">
        SELECT DISTINCT {fn YEAR(DatePosted)} AS PreviousYears FROM News
        WHERE {fn YEAR(DatePosted)} <> #CreateODBCDate(WhichYear)#
</CFQUERY>

<HTML>
<HEAD>
    <TITLE>Company Press Releases</TITLE>
</HEAD>
<BODY>
<CENTER>

<P>
<CFOUTPUT>
    <B><FONT FACE="Arial" SIZE="3">Press Releases for #WhichYear#</FONT></B>
</CFOUTPUT>
<P>
```

*Example 14-3. Listing Press Release Headers in a Database (continued)*

```
<!--- output all of the article headers from the selected year.  Make the
      headers links to another template which displays the entire article from
      the database --->
<TABLE CELLSPACING="0" CELLPADDING="3" BORDER="0">
<CFOUTPUT QUERY="GetTitles">
<TR>
  <TD VALIGN="center">#DateFormat(DatePosted,'mm/dd/yyyy')#  </TD>
  <TD VALIGN="top"><A HREF="shownews.cfm?ArticleID=#ArticleID#">#Title#</A></TD>
</TR>
</CFOUTPUT>
</TABLE>

<!--- list other years available for display.  If another year is chosen, it
      reloads the page with the press releases from that particular year --->
<P>
<B>Other Years</B>
<BR>
<CFOUTPUT QUERY="GetArchiveDates">
   <A HREF="Example14-3.cfm?WhichYear=#PreviousYears#">#PreviousYears#</A>
</CFOUTPUT>

</BODY>
</HTML>
```

The actual process of creating a static page from the output of a CFML template is easily achieved using CFHTTP. Example 14-4 shows the code necessary to create a static HTML page from the output of any CFML page. This template can be manually run once a day, included as part of an application for adding new press releases to the database, or scheduled to run via the Scheduler in the ColdFusion Administrator.

*Example 14-4. Creating A Static HTML Page from the Content*

```
<!--- plug variable values into cfhttp and execute the remote cfm file --->
<CFHTTP METHOD="GET"
        URL="http://127.0.0.1/examples/chapter14/Example14-3.cfm"
        RESOLVEURL="yes">
</CFHTTP>

<!--- write the file grabbed by cfhttp to a new html file on the server --->
<CFFILE ACTION="write"
        FILE="c:\inetsrv\wwwroot\press_releases\index.htm"
        OUTPUT="#CFHTTP.FileContent#">
```

It is worth noting that you need to turn off debugging options before attempting to create static pages from ColdFusion templates residing on your local server. Having debug information turned on will cause your static pages to contain all the debug information at the bottom of every page—not a pretty sight. The option to display debug information can be turned off in the ColdFusion Administrator.

# *Posting Information*

Besides allowing you to retrieve information, you can also post information to remote web sites with CFHTTP. By setting the METHOD attribute to POST, you can use CFHTTP to pass information such as files, URLs, CGI variables, cookies, and form fields to other web applications, such as a ColdFusion page or CGI program, on a remote server. CFHTTP POST operations are considered two-way transactions because they pass variables to remote applications, which usually process the input and return data.

When performing CFHTTP POST operations, you have to specify an additional tag, CFHTTPPARAM, for each value you are passing in the transaction. In other words, if you are using CFHTTP to post two form-field variables to a remote form, you need to use two CFHTTPPARAM tags in conjunction with the CFHTTP tag. By specifying the variable type in each CFHTTPPARAM tag, ColdFusion allows you to interact with applications that require multipart form data such as cookies, text, and file fields in the same operation. Note that CFHTTPPARAM tags are always nested within a CFHTTP tag. Here is the syntax for using the CFHTTPPARAM tag:

```
<CFHTTPPARAM NAME="name"
             TYPE="transaction_type"
             VALUE="variable_value"
             FILE="filename">
```

The TYPE attribute specifies the type of information you are passing to the remote application. Possible values are:

URL
: Posts URL variables to applications that get parameters from information passed in URLs

FormField
: Posts form-field data to applications that accept input from HTML forms

CGI
: Posts CGI environment variables to remote applications

Cookie
: Posts cookies to applications that use them to maintain state information

File
: Posts files to remote applications for processing

## *Posting Form-Field Data*

Probably the widest use for the CFHTTP POST method is posting form-field information to remote applications and scripts. CFHTTP allows you to pass variables to an application that takes its input from an HTML form. In Example 14-5, we use CFHTTP to pass information to a ColdFusion application on the Allaire web site.

*Example 14-5. Using CFHTTP POST to Obtain Knowledge Base Articles*

```
<CFHTTP URL="http://www.allaire.com/Support/KnowledgeBase/Search.cfm"
      METHOD="Post" RESOLVEURL="Yes">
   <CFHTTPPARAM TYPE="FORMFIELD" NAME="SearchString" VALUE="cfhttp">
   <CFHTTPPARAM TYPE="FORMFIELD" NAME="FilterKeywords" VALUE="330">
</CFHTTP>

<CFOUTPUT>
#CFHTTP.FileContent#
</CFOUTPUT>
```

This application takes the information posted by CFHTTP and uses it to find all articles in the Allaire Knowledge Base pertaining to the CFHTTP tag. The application then dynamically constructs an HTML page that contains the results of the search and passes it back to CFHTTP. CFHTTP stores the HTML file in the CFHTTP.FileContent variable, as always, so we can use CFOUTPUT to display the results.

## Posting URL Variables

Using a TYPE of URL allows you to post URL variables to an application that resides on a remote server. Passing a TYPE="URL" also allows you to exploit CFHTTP GET functionality in CFHTTP POST operations. This is done by passing URL variables in conjunction with form fields, cookies, CGI environment variables, or file variables. This technique is useful for interacting with applications that require multipart form data such as cookies and URL parameters in the same operation. Example 14-6 demonstrates how to pass URL parameters along with a cookie to a remote application. You will find here that we make a CFHTTP request to Allaire's Knowledge Base application and pass it two URL parameters as well as two cookie parameters.

*Example 14-6. Posting URL and Cookie Variables to Allaire's Knowledge Base*

```
<!--- Use CFHTTP to retrieve knowledge base article 1096 from Allaire's web
      site.  Also pass two cookies, CFID and CFTOKEN so the web site knows
      who the user is --->
<CFHTTP URL="http://www.allaire.com/Handlers/index.cfm"
       METHOD="Post" RESOLVEURL="yes">
    <CFHTTPPARAM TYPE="URL" NAME="ID" VALUE="1608">
    <CFHTTPPARAM TYPE="URL" NAME="method" VALUE="full">
    <CFHTTPPARAM TYPE="COOKIE" NAME="CFID" VALUE="1181774">
    <CFHTTPPARAM TYPE="COOKIE" NAME="CFTOKEN" VALUE="2159">
</CFHTTP>
```

*Example 14-6. Posting URL and Cookie Variables to Allaire's Knowledge Base (continued)*

```
<CFOUTPUT>
#CFHTTP.FileContent#
</CFOUTPUT>
```

Note that attempting to post URL variables as parameters in the URL itself causes an error unless at least one `CFHTTPPARAM` tag is declared within the `CFHTTP` operation (of course, you can pass parameters in the URL itself if you are using the `GET` method, as we discussed earlier). Likewise, attempting to pass URL variables in both the URL and in a `CFHTTPPARAM` tag causes an error.

## *Posting CGI Variables*

Most CGI applications don't require that actual CGI environment variables be passed to them (although there are some that do). The CGI variables that are available to an application depend on the server and browser software being used for the request. As a result, the `CFHTTP` tag provides a method for passing user-defined CGI environment variables to remote applications regardless of the browser or server software being used. It should be noted, however, that the CGI environment variables are read-only and thus can't be overwritten. This means that if a CGI environment variable already exists in your particular environment, its value can't be changed. A common mistake is to attempt to pass variables to a remote CGI application such as a Perl script in the form of CGI variables. More often than not, the application requires form-field variables, not CGI environment variables. You should use only a `TYPE` of CGI when you need to pass CGI environment variables to a remote application. For example, an application might need the value of the `HTTP_USER_AGENT` variable to check what browser is being used, so that it can determine what browser-specific features to include in its output. The following example shows how to pass two CGI environment variables `HTTP_USER_AGENT` and `REMOTE_HOST` to a remote template for processing. While you can pass the `HTTP_USER_AGENT` value with the `USERAGENT` attribute of the `CFHTTP` tag, it can also be passed via the `CFHTTPPARAM` tag, as shown here:

```
<CFHTTP URL="http://127.0.0.1/examples/cgiexample.cfm"
        METHOD="Post" RESOLVEURL="yes">
    <CFHTTPPARAM TYPE="CGI" NAME="HTTP_USER_AGENT" VALUE="ColdFusion 4.5.1">
    <CFHTTPPARAM TYPE="CGI" NAME="REMOTE_HOST" VALUE="127.0.0.1">
</CFHTTP>

<CFOUTPUT>
#CFHTTP.FileContent#
</CFOUTPUT>
```

## Posting Cookies

CFHTTP can also post cookies to remote sites, which is a useful feature in situations where you want your CFHTTP operations to mimic those of an actual user. For example, if you have an application that uses cookies to track users, you can have your CFHTTP POST operation pass the value of the cookie to the remote application each time it posts information there. This enables your application to differentiate hits caused by your CFHTTP operation from hits made by actual users. CFHTTP can only send cookies to remote servers; there's currently no mechanism for CFHTTP to receive cookies from remote servers (except in the HTTP header returned by a CFHTTP request). Example 14-7 demonstrates the method for passing cookies via CFHTTP and CFHTTPPARAM.

*Example 14-7. Passing Cookies via CFHTTP and CFHTTPPARAM*

```
<!--- use CFHTTP to retrieve the login page from the Allaire Forums site --->
<CFHTTP URL="http://forums.allaire.com/DevConf/Conf_ThreadList.cfm"
    METHOD="post"
    RESOLVEURL="yes">

    <!--- Pass two cookies so the site knows who you are.  Substitute the
          values found in your cookies.txt file or cookies directory for
          the values listed below --->
    <CFHTTPPARAM TYPE="COOKIE" NAME="CFTOKEN" VALUE="12345678">
    <CFHTTPPARAM TYPE="COOKIE" NAME="CFID" VALUE="123456">
</CFHTTP>

<!--- display the login screen to the user --->
<CFOUTPUT>
#CFHTTP.FileContent#
</CFOUTPUT>
```

Example 14-7 uses two cookie variables, CFTOKEN and CFID, to retrieve the login screen from the Allaire Forums web site. If the values specified for the two cookie parameters are valid, a personalized login screen should be displayed. You can see the example in action by first going to the Allaire Forums and registering as a user. The URL for the web site is *http://forums.allaire.com/*. Once registered, open your *cookies.txt* file (Netscape browsers) or look in your *cookies* directory (Internet Explorer users) and find the references to *forums.allaire.com*. To make the example work, cut the values for CFTOKEN and CFID from the cookie file and paste them into the example.

## Posting Files

You can also use CFHTTP to post files to remote web servers using the HTTP protocol. You should use this functionality when you want to send a file from your local ColdFusion server to an application located on a remote server for processing. In other words, a `TYPE` of `FILE` supports moving files only from your local ColdFusion server to a remote applications. Once the file has been posted, it is up to the remote program to handle the actual processing of the file. `CFHTTP` can't upload files from client browsers or to send files to FTP servers; those operations are handled by the `CFFILE` and `CFFTP` tags, respectively. Consider the following scenario. Imagine you have a ColdFusion application that uses an HTML form to allow users to upload files to a particular directory on the ColdFusion server. Now imagine that every week the same file must be manually uploaded to the ColdFusion server from the local development server. This menial process can easily be automated using `CFHTTP` to send the file from the local development server to the remote ColdFusion server. The following template can be called manually or scheduled via the Scheduler in the ColdFusion Administrator:

```
<!--- Post the file to the application that processes the HTML form on the remote
      ColdFusion server --->
<CFHTTP URL="http://127.0.0.1/examples/14/TemplateThatProcessesFile.cfm"
        METHOD="Post">

<!--- Picks the file from the specified directory on the server hosting this
      Template --->
<CFHTTPPARAM TYPE="File" NAME="File_Variable"
             FILE="c:\programmingColdFusion\examples\14\myfile.txt">
</CFHTTP>
```

# *CFHTTP Considerations*

While `CFHTTP` is extremely powerful, there are a few limitations in the current version that are worth mentioning. These issues include problems with `CFHTTP` parsing text files that don't contain column headers and methods for interacting with pages that require authentication. If you plan to make heavy use of `CFHTTP`, you should carefully consider the issues discussed here.

## *Column Headers and Delimited Text Files*

There is a problem with the current implementation of `CFHTTP` regarding the parsing of text files (that don't contain column headers) into query objects. Using `CFHTTP` to get a delimited text file (that doesn't contain column headers in the first row of data) causes `CFHTTP` to ignore the first row of the file. This results in the first row of data in the text file being left out of any subsequent operations. This occurs even if alternate column headers are specified in the `COLUMNS` attribute. There is currently no workaround for this problem other than ensuring that the first row of the delimited file contains column headers or a dummy record. Example 14-8 illustrates this point, by showing how `CFHTTP` retrieves a text file (that contains stock quote information) from Yahoo's web site. The text file doesn't contain any column headers. In this case, it is possible to get a dummy record by having the CGI program that generates the file include a duplicate record for the first record. In this example, passing the ticker symbol "YHOO" twice in the URL does the trick.

*Example 14-8. Handling Delimited Text Files Without Column Headers*

```
<!--- use CFHTTP to get the delimited text file from Yahoo's web site.  Note the
      use of the "" for the text qualifier --->
<CFHTTP METHOD="GET"
    URL="http://quote.yahoo.com/download/quotes.csv?Symbols=yhoo+yhoo+amzn&
format=sl1d1t1c1ohgv&ext=.csv"
    NAME="MyQuery"
    COLUMNS="Symbol,Last_Traded_Price,Last_Traded_Date,Last_Traded_Time,Change,
            Opening_Price,Days_High,Days_Low,Volume"
    DELIMITER="," TEXTQUALIFIER="""">

<!--- build an HTML table with the results from the query --->
<CENTER>
<H2>Stock Quotes From Yahoo</H2>
<TABLE BORDER=1>
<TR BGCOLOR="#FFCC99">
    <TH>Symbol</TH><TH>Price</TH><TH>Change</TH><TH>Time</TH><TH>Date</TH>
    <TH>Open</TH><TH>High</TH><TH>Low</TH><TH>Volume</TH>
</TR>
<CFOUTPUT QUERY="MyQuery">
<TR BGCOLOR="##EFD6C6">
    <TD>#Symbol#</TD><TD>#Last_Traded_Price#</TD><TD>#Change#</TD>
    <TD>#Last_Traded_Time#</TD><TD>#Last_Traded_Date#</TD><TD>#Opening_Price#</TD>
    <TD>#Days_High#</TD><TD>#Days_Low#</TD><TD>#Volume#</TD>
</TR>
</CFOUTPUT>
</TABLE>
</CENTER>
```

The code in this example works by calling a special CGI program on Yahoo's web site via URL that returns a delimited text file containing stock quotes. The quotes returned are determined by the ticker symbols that are passes in the URL. The delimited text file returned by the CGI program is converted to a query object by the `CFHTTP` tag. Because the first line of the text file doesn't contain any column headers, we specify some using the `COLUMNS` attribute. Additionally, because the text file uses double quotes to distinguish text from numeric values, we specify a set of double quotes for the `TEXTQUALIFIER` attribute. Once the contents of the text file are stored in a query object, an HTML table is dynamically constructed by outputting the contents of the query.

## *Authentication*

On Windows NT web servers, `CFHTTP` supports basic (plain-text) authentication for both `GET` and `POST` operations. This means you can use `CFHTTP` to access password-protected pages and files residing on remote servers. Basic authentication is performed by entering a valid username and password in the **USERNAME** and **PASSWORD** attributes of the **CFHTTP** tag, as shown here:

```
<CFHTTP METHOD="method"
        URL="url_to_server"
        USERNAME="username"
        PASSWORD="password">
```

Please note, however, that basic authentication doesn't work on Microsoft IIS servers with Windows Challenge/Response Authentication enabled. This is because Windows NT Challenge/Response is a proprietary protocol and is specific to sessions between Microsoft servers and Microsoft's Internet Explorer browser.

# 15

*In this chapter:*
- *LDAP Basics*
- *Querying an LDAP Directory*
- *Modifying LDAP Entries*
- *Modifying the Distinguished Name*

# *Interfacing with LDAP-Enabled Directories*

This chapter covers techniques for accessing both public and private LDAP servers and provides examples of searching directories; displaying results; and adding, editing, and deleting entries. You can use Cold Fusion's `CFLDAP` tag to access information stored in LDAP (Lightweight Directory Access Protocol) enabled directories (including X.500 directories). LDAP is quickly becoming a standard for delivering directory-based information over the Internet. Popular uses for the `CFLDAP` tag include creating search interfaces for public and private user directories and creating administrative interfaces for managing LDAP directories.

## *LDAP Basics*

The Lightweight Directory Access Protocol (LDAP), currently at Version 3, originated at the University of Michigan. LDAP is a specification that defines a standardized way for organizations to store and access directory information over TCP/IP. Information stored in an LDAP directory is arranged in a hierarchal manner as depicted in Figure 15-1.

LDAP makes it possible to create complex directories of information that can quickly and easily be searched. LDAP directories are most commonly (although by no means exclusively) used to maintain "white-page" type information such as names, addresses and telephone numbers, or organizational structures and contact information. Regardless of the information contained in an LDAP directory, the structure defined by LDAP makes finding the information within simple.

The ColdFusion CD contains a specially licensed version of Netscape's popular Directory Server 3.1 you can use to set up and maintain your own LDAP server. For clarity and consistency, all the examples used in this chapter assume you are

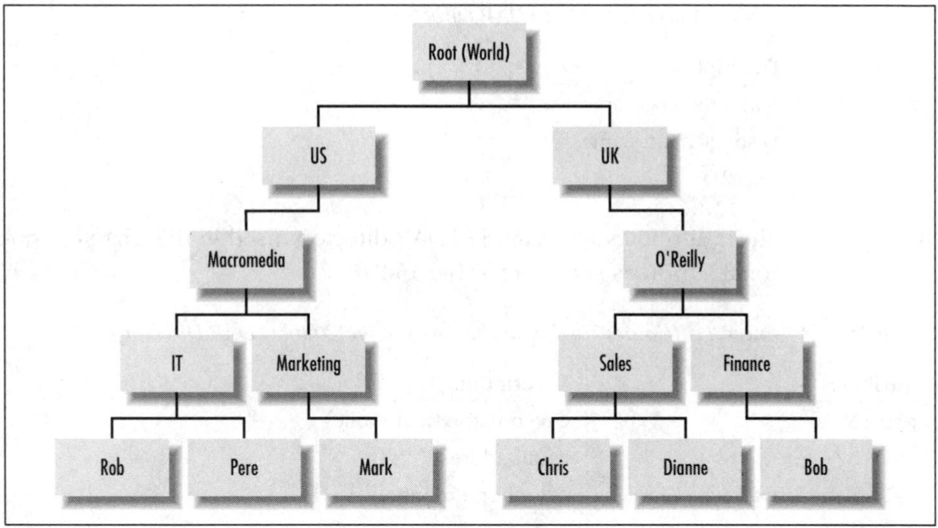


*Figure 15-1. A typical LDAP structure*

using the Netscape Directory Server included with ColdFusion and that you've installed the included sample LDAP directory for the fictitious company, *airius.com*. The examples can be modified easily to work with other directory servers such as those from Lotus, Microsoft, and Novell. For more information on installing and configuring Netscape Directory Server, consult the documentation included with the program.

## LDAP Attributes

To understand how an LDAP server stores information, you can think of it in database terms. The common descriptive element in a database is a field. In an LDAP directory, fields are called attributes. Although an LDAP server can be configured with any number of custom attributes, several common attributes can be found on most servers being used to store white-page information. Table 15-1 lists the common attributes along with their descriptions.

*Table 15-1. Attributes Common to Most LDAP Directories*

| Attribute | Description |
|---|---|
| `c` | Country |
| `st` | State/province |
| `l` | Locality/state |
| `o` | Organization |
| `ou` | Organizational unit |
| `cn` | Common name (full name) |

*Table 15-1. Attributes Common to Most LDAP Directories (continued)*

| Attribute | Description |
|---|---|
| `sn` | Surname (last name) |
| `dn` | Distinguished name |
| `uid` | User ID |

In addition to these attributes, the sample LDAP directory used in this chapter contains the additional attributes shown in Table 15-2.

*Table 15-2. Additional Attributes Used with the Airius.com Sample LDAP Directory*

| Attribute | Description |
|---|---|
| `givenName` | Given name (first name) |
| `Mail` | Email address |
| `telephonenumber` | Telephone number |
| `facsimiletelephonenumber` | Fax number |
| `roomnumber` | Room number |

## *Public LDAP Servers*

There are a number of public LDAP servers on the Internet that can be queried with the `CFLDAP` tag. Available attributes vary from server to server. Some of the more popular public LDAP servers include:

- Bigfoot *(http://ldap.bigfoot.com)*
- Four11 (*http://ldap.four11.com*)
- InfoSpace (*http://ldap.infospace.com*)
- WhoWhere (*http://ldap.whowhere.com*)

Before continuing, you should be thoroughly familiar with the ins and outs of LDAPv3. For more information on the protocol, check out the following web sites:

University of Michigan's LDAP site
*http://www.umich.edu/~dirsvcs/ldap/index.html*

Stanford University's LDAP Tutorial and FAQ
*http://www.stanford.edu/group/networking/directory/x500ldapfaq.html*

Dave Kosiur's "LDAP: The Next Generation Directory" from *SunWorld*
*http://www.sunworld.com/swol-10-1996/swol-10-ldap.html*

The Internet Engineering Task Force's (IETF) LDAP Extension (ldapext) charter and related information
*http://www.ietf.org/html.charters/ldapext-charter.html*

Innosoft's *LDAP World*
*http://www.innosoft.com/ldapworld/*

# *Querying an LDAP Directory*

The CFLDAP tag can query an LDAP directory and return the results as a ColdFusion query object. This gives you tremendous flexibility in how you use the data. The query object can be output to the browser using CFOUTPUT or used to feed directory information to other functions or templates.

## *Performing an LDAP Query*

Once you know the available attributes of a given LDAP server, you can easily perform a basic query against the directory and output the results to the browser. Example 15-1 shows how to perform a simple query against the *airius.com* sample directory included with the Netscape Directory Server.

*Example 15-1. Querying an LDAP Directory*

```
<!--- query the LDAP server for all entries under the airius.com organization
      where the surname of the person begins with 's' and their location is
      'Santa Clara'.  Sort the results by surname and given name. --->
<CFLDAP ACTION="QUERY" NAME="MyLDAPQuery" SERVER="localhost" PORT="389"
        ATTRIBUTES="cn,sn,givenName,ou,l" MAXROWS="100"
        START="o=airius.com" SCOPE="Subtree" FILTER="(&(sn=s*)(l=Santa Clara))"
        SORT="SN, givenName" SORTCONTROL="nocase, ASC" TIMEOUT="90">

<!--- output the query results --->
<TABLE CELLPADDING="3" CELLSPACING="1">
<TR bgcolor="#CoCoCo">
  <TH>Common Name (cn)</TH><TH>Surname (sn)</TH><TH>Given Name (givenName)</TH>
  <TH>Organizational Unit (ou)</TH><TH>Locality (l)</TH>
</TR>

<CFOUTPUT QUERY="MyLDAPQuery">
<TR bgcolor="##9999FF">
  <TD><CFIF cn IS ""> <CFELSE>#cn#</CFIF></TD>
  <TD><CFIF sn IS ""> <CFELSE>#sn#</CFIF></TD>
  <TD<CFIF givenName IS ""> <CFELSE>#givenName#</CFIF></TD>
  <TD><CFIF ou IS ""> <CFELSE>#ou#</CFIF></TD>
  <TD><CFIF l IS ""> <CFELSE>#l#</CFIF></TD>
</TR>
</CFOUTPUT>
</TABLE>
```

In Example 15-1, the first attribute, ACTION is required to specify what action the CFLDAP tag should perform. In this case, we want to use the tag to query an LDAP server, so we set ACTION to Query. Other possible values for the ACTION attribute are Add, Modify, ModifyDN, and Delete. Each action is covered later in this chapter. The NAME is another required attribute and specifies the name of the query ColdFusion should create to hold the results of the LDAP query. The hostname or IP address of the LDAP server you want to perform the search against is specified in the SERVER attribute. This attribute is also required. Our LDAP server resides on the same machine as our ColdFusion server, so we set SERVER to localhost. If the LDAP server you are trying to query listens on a port other than the default 389, you enter that value in the PORT attribute. If PORT isn't specified, the CFLDAP tag defaults to port 389.

ATTRIBUTES specifies a comma-delimited list of attributes to be returned by the query. Specifying a wildcard (*) returns all the attributes associated with the query. In this case, we want to retrieve the common name (cn), surname, (sn), organizational unit (ou), and locality (l), for each person listed in the directory. The maximum number of results returned by the query is set using the MAXROWS attribute. We set a limit of 100 records for our query. FILTER specifies the search criteria to use when performing the query. FILTER entries are referenced as:

```
(attribute operator value)
```

The default value for FILTER is (objectclass=*). In our example, we set the FILTER attribute so that only entries having a surname (sn) beginning with smi and a locality (l) of Santa Clara are returned. A list of all filter operators is shown in Table 15-3.

*Table 15-3. Filter Operators*

| Operator | Usage |
|---|---|
| = | Returns entries where the attribute equals the specified value. For example, searching for sn=smith returns entries where the surname of the person is smith. |
| ~= | Returns entries where the attribute approximating the specified value. For example, searching for sn~=smith returns entries where the surname of the person approximates smith. |
| <= | Returns entries where the entry is equal to or comes before the value specified by the attribute. For example, searching for st<=de returns entries where the state equals or comes before de. |
| >= | Returns entries where the entry is equal to or comes after the value specified by the attribute. For example, searching for st>=de returns entries where the state equals or comes after de. |
| * | Acts as a wildcard. For example, searching for sn=sm* returns entries that have a surname beginning with the letters sm while searching for sn=*ith returns entries that have a surname ending with the letters ith. |
| & | Returns entries only when all attributes are found. For example, searching for (&(sn=smith) (st=de)) returns only entries that contain both the surname smith and the state de. |

*Table 15-3. Filter Operators (continued)*

| Operator | Usage |
|---|---|
| \| | Returns entries when any one attribute is found. For example, searching for `(|(sn=smith) (st=de))` returns entries containing only the surname `smith`, only the state `de`, or both the surname `smith` and the state `de`. |
| ! | Returns entries that don't contain the value specified in the attribute. For example, searching for `(!(email=*))` returns all entries that don't have an email address. |

The next attribute, `START`, specifies the distinguished name to use as the start of the search. In Example 15-1, we use `o=airius.com` to begin the search at the organization level in our sample LDAP directory where the entry is `airius.com`. We use the `SCOPE` attribute to specify the scope of the search in relation to the value listed in `START`. Possible entries for `SCOPE` include:

`OneLevel` *(default)*
: Searches one level below the entry specified in the `START` attribute

`Base`
: Searches just the entry specified in the `START` attribute

`Subtree`
: Searches the entry specified in the `START` attribute and all entries below it

`SORT` is optional and specifies the attribute or comma-delimited list of attributes to use when sorting query results. In this example, the query results are sorted by the surname (`sn`) then given name (`givenName`) attributes. The `SORTCONTROL` attribute is also optional and specifies how the results should be sorted. If you wish to perform a case-insensitive sort, `SORTCONTROL` should be set to `Nocase`. Additionally, sort order may be specified as `ASC` (ascending, the default) or `DESC` (descending). Case sensitivity and sort order may be combined as in our example `SORTCONTROL="Nocase, ASC"`. Sorting is case-sensitive by default.

The final attribute, `TIMEOUT` is also optional and specifies the maximum amount of time in seconds that ColdFusion should wait when processing the query. If no `TIMEOUT` is specified, ColdFusion defaults to 60 seconds.

There are several additional attributes available in the CFLDAP tag that aren't covered in this example. For a complete list, see Appendix A.

Once the `CFLDAP` tag has finished querying the LDAP server, the results are returned in a ColdFusion query object that is subsequently output in an HTML table. The results can be seen in Figure 15-2.

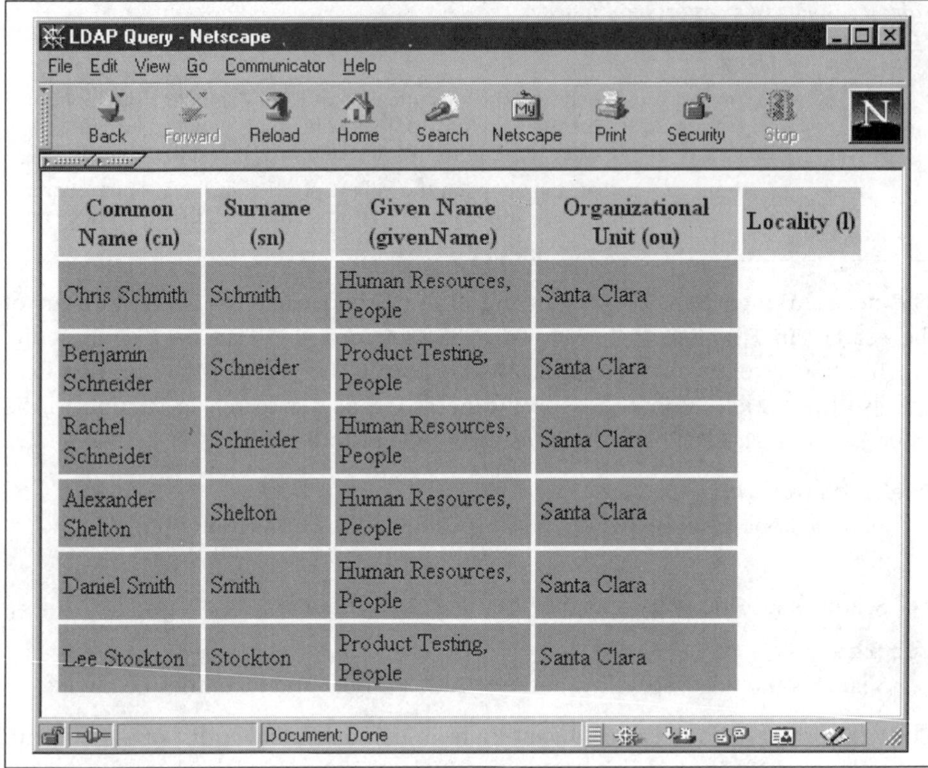


*Figure 15-2. Outputting the results of a CFLDAP query*

## *Obtaining the LDAP Server Schema*

In the previous example, we knew ahead of time what attributes were available on our LDAP server. This isn't always the case. If you aren't fortunate enough to have an LDAP server administrator who can provide you with a list of available attributes, you have to query the LDAP server directly and request its schema. LDAP v3 provides a mechanism for obtaining a directory's schema via a special entry in the root `DN`. Example 15-2 shows how to obtain the schema from an LDAP v3-compliant server.

*Example 15-2. Retrieving the Schema from a LDAP v3-Compliant Server*

```
<CFLDAP NAME="GetEntries" ACTION="QUERY"
        SERVER="ldap.example.com"
        ATTRIBUTES="dn, subschemasubentry"
        SCOPE="Base" FILTER="objectclass=*" START="">

<CFLDAP NAME="GetSubEntries" ACTION="Query"
        SERVER="ldap.example.com"
        ATTRIBUTES="dn, objectclasses, attributetypes"
        SCOPE="Base" FILTER="objectclass=*"
```

*Example 15-2. Retrieving the Schema from a LDAP v3-Compliant Server (continued)*

```
        START=#GetEntries.subschemasubentry#>

<TABLE BORDER="1">
<TR>
   <TH>DN</TH><TH>Object Classes</TH><TH>Attribute Types</TH>
</TR>

<CFOUTPUT QUERY="GetSubEntries">
<TR>
   <TD VALIGN="top">#dn#</TD><TD VALIGN="top">#objectclasses#</TD>
   <TD VALIGN="top">#attributetypes#</TD>
</TR>
</CFOUTPUT>
</TABLE>
```

In Example 15-2, the `CFLDAP` query queries the LDAP server specified in the `SERVER` attribute. `SERVER` is required and accepts the IP address or hostname of the LDAP server you want to connect to. We set the `ACTION` attribute to `Query`, letting ColdFusion know we want to use the tag to query an LDAP server. The `NAME` attribute sets up a query object to hold the result set of the query. In `ATTRIBUTES`, we specify `dn, subschemasubentry` as they are the attributes we want to retrieve. The `SCOPE` attribute is set to `Base` so that the query searches just the entry specified by the `START` attribute. `FILTER` is set to the default `objectclass=*`, resulting in all entries for the attribute being returned. The final attribute, `START` specifies the distinguished name (DN) to use as the start of the search. In Example 15-2, we set `START` to `" "`.

We use the second instance of the `CFLDAP` tag to query the actual attribute values returned by the first `CFLDAP` call. We do this by setting the `START` attribute of the second `CFLDAP` tag to `#GetEntries.SubSchemaSubEntry#`. Note that in this instance, we set `ATTRIBUTES` to `dn, objectclass, attributetypes`.

Once the schema has been queried from the LDAP server, it is output using the results of the second `CFLDAP` call. The results are written to the browser as an HTML table containing the distinguished name (DN), object classes, and attribute types.

## *Modifying LDAP Entries*

The best way to illustrate adding, updating, and deleting LDAP entries is to build an example administrative interface that can perform all the aforementioned tasks. The main template of the application is a template named *Index.cfm*, which is shown in Example 15-3. This template contains an HTML form with a single select box control containing the common names (first and last names) of each entry in the LDAP server. Below the select box are three buttons—one for adding a new entry, one for modifying an existing entry, and one for deleting an entry.

*Example 15-3. Main LDAP Administration Template*

```
<!--- query the ldap server for all entries --->
<CFLDAP ACTION="Query" NAME="GetEntries" SERVER="localhost"
        ATTRIBUTES="dn,cn,sn.givenName" FILTER="(sn>=A)"
        START="o=airius.com" SCOPE="subtree" SORT="sn, givenName">

<HTML>
<HEAD>
  <TITLE>LDAP Administration</TITLE>
</HEAD>

<CENTER>
<H2>LDAP Administration</H2>

<!--- if a message was passed from the action form, display it --->
<CFIF IsDefined('URL.Message')>
  <CFOUTPUT>
  <H3>#Message#</H3>
  </CFOUTPUT>
</CFIF>

<!--- display the common name for each entry in a multi-select box.  Assign
      the DN to each option value --->
<FORM NAME="MyForm" ACTION="action.cfm" METHOD="post">

<SELECT NAME="dn" SIZE="5">
    <CFOUTPUT QUERY="GetEntries">
    <OPTION NAME="DN" VALUE="#DN#">#CN#</OPTION>
    </CFOUTPUT>
</SELECT>
<BR>
<INPUT NAME="Add" TYPE="Submit" VALUE="Add">
<INPUT NAME="Update" TYPE="Submit" VALUE="Update">
<INPUT NAME="Delete" TYPE="Submit" VALUE="Delete">
</FORM>
</CENTER>

</BODY>
</HTML>
```

The *Index.cfm* template dynamically populates the select box form control by using the `CFLDAP` tag to query the LDAP server specified in the `SERVER` attribute. The query object designated to hold the results of the LDAP query is specified in the `NAME` attribute. Here we set `NAME` to `GetEntries`.

`ATTRIBUTES` takes a comma-delimited list of attributes to be returned with the query. In this case, we want to get the distinguished name (`dn`), common name (`cn`), surname (`sn`) and given name (`givenName`) for each entry. The `FILTER` attribute specifies the search criteria to use for the query. Because we want to return only names (and not blanks and groups), we set the `FILTER` to `(sn>=A)` so that only entries containing a surname (`sn`) are returned. `START` specifies the distinguished name to use as the beginning of the search. We set `START` to `o=airius.com` because we want to search entries that fall under the `airius.com` organization (`o`). The `SCOPE` attribute determines the scope of the search in relation to the value we set in `SCOPE`. We set `SCOPE` to `SubTree` because we want our search to encompass the entry specified in `START` as well as all the entries below it. The final attribute, `SORT`, specifies the list of attributes to use when sorting the query results. We chose to sort our results by surname (`sn`), then given name (`givenName`) in ascending order.

When an administrator opens the *index.cfm* template in a browser window, highlights a user in the select box, or adds a new user by clicking one of the buttons at the bottom of the page, the form posts to the *Action.cfm* template shown in Example 15-4.

*Example 15-4. Taking the Appropriate Action*

```
<CFIF IsDefined('Form.Add')>
   <!--- if the Add button was pressed, create a form for the administrator to
         create a new entry --->
   <CFINCLUDE TEMPLATE="_Add.cfm">
<CFELSEIF IsDefined('Form.AddEntry')>
   <!--- if the Add Entry button was pressed from the add user form, add the
         entry to the LDAP server --->
   <CFINCLUDE TEMPLATE="_AddEntry.cfm">
<CFELSEIF IsDefined('Form.Update') AND IsDefined('Form.DN')>
   <!--- if the Update button was pressed, create a form populated with the
         data from the selected entry --->
   <CFINCLUDE TEMPLATE="_Update.cfm">
<CFELSEIF IsDefined('Form.UpdateEntry')>
   <!--- if the Update Entry button was pressed from the Update user form,
         update the entry in the LDAP server --->
   <CFINCLUDE TEMPLATE="_UpdateEntry.cfm">
<CFELSEIF IsDefined('Form.Delete') AND IsDefined('Form.DN')>
   <!--- if the delete button was pressed, remove the entry --->
   <CFINCLUDE TEMPLATE="_Delete.cfm">
<CFELSE>
   <!--- if no valid action was selected or a button was pressed without
         selecting an entry to modify/delete display a message --->
   No Action Selected.
</CFIF>
```

The *Action.cfm* template in Example 15-4, uses a series of `CFIF`/`CFELSEIF` statements to evaluate the values of the form fields passed to the template. Depending on the value(s) passed in, the template includes an appropriate CFML template to handle the requested function. If no passed parameters meet the `CFIF`/`CFELSEIF` criteria, a final `CFELSE` statement displays a message to the administrator stating `No`

`Action Selected`. This message also displays if an administrator clicks on the Modify or Delete buttons on the *Index.cfm* template, in Example 15-3, without choosing an entry from the select box.

## Adding Entries

If the user clicks on the Add button in the administration template, the *Action.cfm* template includes the *_Add.cfm* template, as shown in Example 15-5.

*Example 15-5. Add.cfm Template*

```
<!--- create a form for adding an entry --->
<H2>Add LDAP Entry</H2>
<FORM ACTION="action.cfm" METHOD="post">
<TABLE>
<TR>
  <TD>First Name:</TD>
  <TD><INPUT TYPE="text" NAME="givenName" SIZE="15" MAXLENGTH="50"></TD>
</TR>
<TR>
  <TD>Last Name:</TD>
  <TD><INPUT TYPE="text" NAME="sn" SIZE="15" MAXLENGTH="50"></TD>
</TR>
<TR>
  <TD>Organizational Unit (ou):</TD>
  <TD><INPUT TYPE="text" NAME="ou" SIZE="15" MAXLENGTH="50"><TD>
</TR>
<TR>
  <TD>Locality:</TD>
  <TD><INPUT TYPE="text" NAME="l" SIZE="15" MAXLENGTH="50"><TD>
</TR>
<TR>
<TR>
  <TD>Phone</TD>
  <TD><INPUT TYPE="text" NAME="telephonenumber" SIZE="15" MAXLENGTH="50"><TD>
</TR>
<TR>
  <TD>E-mail:</TD>
  <TD><INPUT TYPE="text" NAME="mail" SIZE="25" MAXLENGTH="50"><TD>
</TR>
<TR>
  <TD COLSPAN="2"><INPUT TYPE="submit" NAME="AddEntry" VALUE="Add Entry"></TD>
</TR>
</TABLE>
</FORM>
```

The *_Add.cfm* template in Example 15-5 does nothing more than create an HTML form that allows an administrator to enter information to submit to the LDAP server as a new entry. The form contains fields for an entrant's given name, surname, organizational unit, locality, phone number, and email address. The sample directory included with Netscape's LDAP server contains many more attributes than we use here, but I have decided to keep our application simple. Clicking on the Add Entry button at the bottom of the page posts the form information back to the *Action.cfm* template in Example 15-4.

The *Action.cfm* template then includes a template called *_AddEntry.cfm*. This template takes the information posted by the *_Add.cfm* template and adds the entry to the LDAP directory, as shown in Example 15-6. Please note that Netscape's sample LDAP directory creates the UID as a concatenation of the first letter of the user's given name and their last name. This obviously causes problems when there are multiple users whose given names begin with the same letter. To account for this, we assign a UUID for each added user's `uid`. Depending on your organization, it might be more appropriate to utilize something else such as a username.

*Example 15-6. AddEntry.cfm Template*

```
<CFLDAP ACTION="Add" SERVER="localhost"
        USERNAME="cn=Directory Manager" PASSWORD="mypassword"
        ATTRIBUTES="objectclass=top, person, organizationalPerson,
                    inetOrgPerson; cn=#Form.givenName# #Form.sn#;
                    givenName = #Form.givenName#;
                    sn=#Form.sn#; mail=#Form.mail#;
                    telephonenumber=#Form.Telephonenumber#; ou=#Form.OU#;
                    l=#Form.l#"
        DN="uid=#CreateUUID()#, ou=People, o=airius.com">

<CFSET Message=UrlEncodedFormat('Entry Successfully Added')>

<!--- send the user back to the index page and display a message that the
      entry was Added --->
<CFLOCATION URL="index.cfm?Message=#Message#">
```

The template in Example 15-6 uses the `CFLDAP` tag with the `ACTION` set to `Add` to add the new entry to the LDAP directory. Because our LDAP server is set up on the same machine as our ColdFusion server, we set `SERVER` to `localhost`. If your LDAP server is on another machine, enter the hostname or IP address of that machine instead. The `USERNAME` attribute specifies the common name (`cn`) of a user with authority to delete entries. The user's password is specified with the `PASSWORD` attribute.

The attributes to be added are specified as a semicolon-delimited list in `ATTRIBUTES`. `DN` is required and specifies the distinguished name of the entry to be added. For the sample LDAP directory, the distinguished name consists of three attribute/value pairs: `uid`, `ou`, and `o`. For new entries in this example, only user id (`uid`) is a dynamic value. `uid` is used as a unique identifier for each individual entry. You can think of the `uid` attribute as the same as a database's primary key. Netscape's sample LDAP directory creates the `uid` as a concatenation of the first letter of the user's given name and their last name. This obviously causes problems when there are multiple users whose given names begin with the same letter. To account for this, we assign a UUID for each added user's `uid` using ColdFusion's `CreateUUID()` function to guarantee a unique value for each entry that is added. Once the entry is added, the administrator is sent back to the *Index.cfm* template, and the message `Entry Successfully Added` is displayed.

## Updating Entries

If an administrator selects an entry on the *Index.cfm* page and clicks on the Update button, the *Action.cfm* template includes the *_Update.cfm* template. The *_Update.cfm* template uses the `CFLDAP` tag to query the directory server for the entry matching the one the administrator selected from the select list and is shown in Example 15-7. In order to retrieve just the record the administrator selected, the `FILTER` attribute is set to `uid=x` where `x` is a unique identifier for the entry similar to a database's primary key. The `uid=x` string is extracted from the `Form.DN` field passed from the *Index.cfm* template. Because the `dn` contains three values delimited by commas, we use the `ListFirst()` function to retrieve just the first list item, which we know to be the `uid`.

*Example 15-7. Update.cfm Template*

```
<!--- query the ldap server for the user --->
<CFLDAP NAME="GetEntry" ACTION="Query" SERVER="localhost"
        ATTRIBUTES="dn,cn,sn,givenName,ou,l,telephonenumber,mail"
        SCOPE="subtree" START="o=airius.com" FILTER="(#ListFirst(Form.DN)#)">

<H2>Modify LDAP Entry</H2>
<FORM ACTION="action.cfm" METHOD="post">
<CFOUTPUT>
<INPUT TYPE="hidden" NAME="dn" VALUE="#GetEntry.dn#">

<TABLE>
<TR>
  <TD>First Name:</TD>
  <TD><INPUT TYPE="text" NAME="givenName" VALUE="#GetEntry.givenName#" SIZE="15"
       MAXLENGTH="50"></TD>
</TR>
<TR>
  <TD>Last Name:</TD>
  <TD><INPUT TYPE="text" NAME="sn" SIZE="15" VALUE="#GetEntry.sn#"
       MAXLENGTH="50"></TD>
</TR>
<TR>
  <TD>Organizational Unit (ou):</TD>
  <TD><INPUT TYPE="text" NAME="ou" SIZE="15" VALUE="#GetEntry.ou#"
       MAXLENGTH="50"><TD>
</TR>
<TR>
  <TD>Locality:</TD>
```

*Example 15-7. Update.cfm Template (continued)*

```
  <TD><INPUT TYPE="text" NAME="l" VALUE="#GetEntry.l#" SIZE="15"
       MAXLENGTH="50"><TD>
</TR>
<TR>
  <TD>Phone</TD>
  <TD><INPUT TYPE="text" NAME="telephonenumber"
       VALUE="#GetEntry.telephonenumber#" SIZE="15" MAXLENGTH="50"><TD>
</TR>
<TR>
  <TD>E-mail:</TD>
  <TD><INPUT TYPE="text" NAME="mail" VALUE="#GetEntry.mail#" SIZE="25"
       MAXLENGTH="50"><TD>
</TR>
<TR>
  <TD COLSPAN="2"><INPUT TYPE="submit" NAME="UpdateEntry" VALUE="Update
                  Entry"></TD>
</TR>
</TABLE>
</CFOUTPUT>
</FORM>
```

After the CFLDAP tag has finished retrieving the entry from the LDAP directory, an HTML form (identical to the form created by the *_Add.cfm* template in Example 15-5) is created and prepopulated with the values from the query object.

The DN from the selected entry is assigned to a hidden form field so that it can be passed to the *_UpdateEntry.cfm* template (shown in Example 15-8) and identifies the entry to be updated in the database. Clicking on the Update Entry button at the bottom of the page posts the form information back to the *Action.cfm* template in Example 15-4. The *Action.cfm* template then includes the *_UpdateEntry.cfm* template. The *_UpdateEntry.cfm* template takes the information posted by the *_Update.cfm* template and updates the entry in the LDAP directory with the new information.

*Example 15-8. UpdateEntry.cfm Template*

```
<!--- Update the entry in the LDAP server --->
<CFLDAP SERVER="localhost" ACTION="MODIFY"
        USERNAME="cn=Directory Manager" PASSWORD="mypassword"
        ATTRIBUTES="objectclass=top, person, organizationalPerson,
                    inetOrgPerson; cn=#Form.givenName# #Form.sn#;
                    givenName = #Form.givenName#;
                    sn=#Form.sn#; mail=#Form.mail#;
                    telephonenumber=#Form.Telephonenumber#; ou=#Form.OU#;
                    l=#Form.l#"
        DN=#Form.dn#>

<CFSET Message=UrlEncodedFormat('Entry Successfully Updated')>
```

*Example 15-8. UpdateEntry.cfm Template (continued)*

```
<!--- send the user back to the index page and display a message that the
      entry was updated --->
<CFLOCATION URL="index.cfm?Message=#Message#">
```

Example 15-8 uses the `CFLDAP` tag with the `ACTION` set to `Modify` to update the selected entry in the LDAP directory specified in `SERVER`. The `USERNAME` attribute specifies the common name (`cn`) of a user with authority to update entries. The user's password is specified with the `PASSWORD` attribute. The attributes to be updated are specified as a semicolon-delimited list in `ATTRIBUTES`. `DN` is required and specifies the distinguished name of the entry to be updated. Once the entry is updated, the administrator is sent back to the *Index.cfm* template, and the message `Entry Successfully Updated` is displayed.

## *Deleting Entries*

If an administrator selects an entry on the *Index.cfm* page and clicks on the Delete button, the *Action.cfm* template includes the *_Delete.cfm* template. Deleting an entry is simple once you have its `DN`. The template shown in Example 15-9 deletes the entry selected by the administrator by setting the `ACTION` attribute to `Delete`and passing the `DN` of the entry to be deleted.

*Example 15-9. Delete.cfm Template*

```
<!--- delete the entry from the LDAP server.  Use the DN passed from the form
      on the index.cfm page --->
<CFLDAP ACTION="DELETE" SERVER="localhost" USERNAME="cn=Directory Manager"
        PASSWORD="mypassword" DN="#Form.DN#">

<CFSET Message=UrlEncodedFormat('Entry Successfully Deleted')>

<!--- send the user back to the index page and display a message that the
      entry was deleted --->
<CFLOCATION URL="index.cfm?Message=#Message#">
```

In Example 15-9, setting `ACTION` to delete lets ColdFusion know to pass the `DELETE` command to the LDAP server specified in the `SERVER` attribute. The distinguished name of the entry to be deleted is specified in `DN`. We take the form variable `Form.DN` passed to this template from the *index.cfm* template. Once the entry is deleted, the user is sent back to the *Index.cfm* template, and the message `Entry Successfully Deleted` is displayed.

You should note that you can delete only one entry at a time with the `CFLDAP` tag. In order to delete more than one entry (if you allow administrators to select more than one user from the main user administration screen), you have to loop over each `DN` and perform a separate delete.

# *Modifying the Distinguished Name*

The CFLDAP tag can modify the distinguished name (DN) for a given entry by setting the ACTION attribute to ModifyDN. Our example LDAP directory uses a distinguished name (DN) consisting of three parts:

```
uid=x, ou=people, o=arius.com
```

The uid portion of the dn is known as the leaf relative distinguished name (RDN). The LDAP protocol specifies that when modifying the dn, only the leaf RDN may be modified. This means that you can only change the value of uid using the CFLDAP tag with the action set to ModifyDN. If you need to change any of the non-leaf RDN values (effectively moving the location of the entry in the directory), you have to delete the entry and recreate it under the correct branch.

To better understand how this works, consider the Example 15-10 where we modify the distinguished name by changing each entry's current user id (uid) to a unique one created with ColdFusion's CreateUUID() function. This method of generating a uid guarantees a unique identifier (unlike concatenating strings like the user's given name and surname).

*Example 15-10. Modifying the DN for Each Entry with a New UID*

```
<!--- Query the LDAP directory for all of the user entries --->
<CFLDAP ACTION="QUERY" NAME="GetUsers" ATTRIBUTES="dn,cn"
        START="o=airius.com" SCOPE="SUBTREE" FILTER="sn>=a"
        SERVER="localhost" TIMEOUT="90">

<!--- Output before changing the DN --->
<H3>Original list of user entries</H3>
<CFOUTPUT QUERY="GetUsers">
#cn#: #dn#<BR>
</CFOUTPUT>

<!--- loop over each entry and attempt to change the DN so that the current uid
      is replaced with a UUID created by ColdFusion.  Write an error message to
      the screen for any entries that can not be updated for whatever reason --->
<H3>Modifying the DN for each entry to update the UID</H3>
<CFLOOP QUERY="GetUsers">
  <CFTRY>
   <CFLDAP ACTION="ModifyDN" SERVER="localhost" USERNAME="cn=Directory Manager"
          PASSWORD="mypassword" ATTRIBUTES="uid=#CreateUUID()#"
          DN="#GetUsers.DN#" TIMEOUT="90">
   <CFCATCH TYPE="any">
    <CFOUTPUT>
    <B>Error:</B>  Couldn't modify DN for entry: #GetUsers.DN#<BR>
    </CFOUTPUT>
   </CFCATCH>
  </CFTRY>
</CFLOOP>
```

*Example 15-10. Modifying the DN for Each Entry with a New UID (continued)*

```
<!--- Query the LDAP directory for all of the user entries --->
<CFLDAP ACTION="QUERY" NAME="GetModifiedUsers" ATTRIBUTES="dn,cn"
        START="o=airius.com" SCOPE="SUBTREE" FILTER="sn>=a"
        SERVER="localhost" TIMEOUT="90">

<!--- Output the modified entries --->
<H3>Modified list of user entries</H3>
<CFOUTPUT QUERY="GetModifiedUsers">
#cn#: #dn#<BR>
</CFOUTPUT>
```

The template in Example 15-10 works by first querying the LDAP server for all entries under the `airius.com` organization (`o`). A table containing each entry's common name (`cn`) and distinguished name (`DN`) is output so you can see the original value for each `DN`.

Next, `CFLOOP` loops over each entry in the query object returned by the first call to the `CFLDAP` tag. With each iteration of the loop, another call is made to the `CFLDAP` tag with the action set to `ModifyDN`, so that an attempt can be made to change the `DN` for each entry. We want to modify the `DN` such that the current user id (`uid`) is replaced with a UUID created by ColdFusion. The `CFTRY/CFCATCH` tags can trap any errors that occur and allow processing to continue in case of an error or exception.

Finally, a third call to `CFLDAP` is made to query the directory for all entries under the *airius.com* organization (`o`). Another table is generated containing each entries common name (`cn`) and distinguished name (`DN`), so you can see the changes that were made to each `DN`.

*In this chapter:*

- *Creating Collections*
- *Populating Collections*
- *Searching Collections*
- *The Verity Search Language*
- *Updating Collections*
- *Maintaining Collections*
- *Advanced Techniques*

# 16

# *Working with the Verity Search Interface*

There is hardly a useful web site out there that doesn't contain a mechanism for allowing users to search through the site for information they are interested in. Not to be left out, ColdFusion comes bundled with a set of tags that leverage Verity Developer's Kit (VDK) 2.6.1 technology* to allow you to build powerful search interfaces into your own ColdFusion applications.

This chapter covers methods for setting up and indexing searchable collections using the ColdFusion Administrator and various CFML tags. Once you are familiar with these operations, we will explore techniques for searching collections and returning search results. Additional techniques for maintaining and optimizing collections are also discussed. The chapter concludes with several advanced techniques including methods for synchronizing database and document collections and scheduling automatic indexing of your data.

In addition to the VDK 2.6.1 engine, ColdFusion 5.0 comes with a restricted version of Verity's enterprise-level K2 server. The K2 server offers features that appeal to large scale and clustered sites such as simultaneous searching of distributed collections, concurrent queries, and an overall performance gain over VDK 2.6.1 of approximately ten-fold. The version of K2 server that comes with ColdFusion is limited to searching 250,000 documents for ColdFusion Enterprise and 125,000 documents for ColdFusion professional. Users of Allaire's Spectra product have a search limit of 750,000 documents. Procedures for searching collections on the K2 server are the same as for the VDK engine. There is no difference in the implementation of the CFSEARCH tag. ColdFusion uses the VDK server to search

* Prior to Version 5.0, ColdFusion shipped with an older version of the VDK.

collections unless they have been specifically configured to use the K2 server. Setting up, configuring, and running the Verity K2 server is a completely separate process and beyond the scope of this chapter. For more information on administering the K2 server, consult the Advanced ColdFusion Server Administration book that comes with the Allaire documentation for your version of ColdFusion.

Also new in ColdFusion 5.0 are several command-line utilities for creating, indexing, maintaining, and troubleshooting Verity collections. Although a through examination of each of these tools is well beyond the scope of this chapter, they are listed here as a reference. For complete documentation, see the *Advanced ColdFusion Server Administration* book that comes with the documentation for your version of ColdFusion.

*mkvdk (also available in previous versions of ColdFusion)*
: Utility for creating, indexing, and maintaining collections from the command line.

*rcvdk*
: Performs command-line searching of collections using the VDK engine.

*rck2*
: Performs command-line searching of collections using the K2 engine.

*didump*
: Utility for viewing collection word lists.

*browse*
: Utility for browsing the contents of document tables.

*merge*
: Utility for combining multiple collections into a single collection or for splitting a single collection into smaller collections. In order to merge collections, all the smaller collections must have been created with the same schema.

*Verity Spider*
: Creates and indexes collections by crawling filesystems. Spidering is limited to the same domain the ColdFusion server is installed on.

# Creating Collections

The first step in creating a search interface for your ColdFusion application is to define a *Verity collection* and register it with ColdFusion. A Verity collection is actually a specialized database that stores metadata about a group of documents or a ColdFusion query object that you specify. Instead of searching through each of your documents or query objects every time a search is performed, Verity searches through the metadata stored in the collection you created. Because the metadata is highly optimized, Verity can quickly and efficiently locate your search criteria.

Collections can be created and subsequently registered via the ColdFusion Administrator or created programmatically with the `CFCOLLECTION` tag or via command-line utilities such as Verity's *mkvdk* or Spider tools. Consult your ColdFusion documentation for more information on creating and indexing collections with Verity's command-line tools.

## *Creating Collections with the ColdFusion Administrator*

Creating a Verity collection using the ColdFusion Administrator is a quick and painless process. The steps for creating a new collection in the ColdFusion Administrator are as follows:

1. Type a unique name for the new collection in the Name text box under the Add a Collection section. Names should contain only letters, numbers, and underscores.
2. Enter a path on the server for the new Verity collection to be stored in. The default path for Verity collections is *\Cfusion\Verity\Collections*.
3. Choose the language for the new collection. English is the default language. To create an index in a language other than English requires the Verity International Language Search Pack. This add-on product is available for purchase from Allaire.
4. Click the Apply button to create the new collection. Your new collection should appear in the select box under the Verity Collections section.

The ColdFusion Administrator also allows you to register a Verity collection that resides on another ColdFusion server (as in a clustered environment) or a collection that was created with a tool other than ColdFusion. The steps for mapping an existing Verity collection are similar to those for creating an entirely new collection:

1. Enter an alias for the mapped collection in the Name text box under the Add a Collection section.
2. In the Path box, enter the full path to the Verity collection on the server.
3. Choose the language for the collection. Again, support for languages other than English requires the Verity International Language Search Pack.
4. Click on the radio button that is labeled Map an Existing Collection.
5. Click on the Apply button to register the collection. The collection alias should now appear in the select box under the Verity Collections section.

Note that collections created using the retail version of Verity can't be mapped and searched using the VDK engine, regardless of whether you own a license for the retail version of Verity. To search these types of collections, you need to use the K2 server engine.

## Creating Collections with the CFCOLLECTION Tag

The CFCOLLECTION tag allows you to create or map a Verity collection programmatically without having to use the ColdFusion Administrator. This method offers the advantage of allowing your ColdFusion applications to register their own Verity collections. It also allows developers without access to the ColdFusion Administrator to exploit all the administrative functions from within CFML templates.

To create a Verity collection using the CFCOLLECTION tag, all you have to do is specify a name for the collection, the path to the collection on the ColdFusion server, and the language that the information is in. The following example shows how to create a Verity collection using the CFCOLLECTION tag:

```
<CFLOCK NAME="CFCOLLECTION_Lock" TYPE="EXCLUSIVE" TIMEOUT="30">
  <CFCOLLECTION ACTION="create"
                COLLECTION="MyVerityCollection"
                PATH="c:\cfusion\verity\collections"
                LANGUAGE="English">
</CFLOCK>
```

It is a good idea to use the CFLOCK tag with all CFCOLLECTION operations so that only one process can access the collection at a time. This ensures that multiple operations don't step on each others' toes, potentially resulting in a corrupted Verity collection. Each collection you access via CFCOLLECTION should have a unique NAME assigned to it in the CFLOCK tag

The first attribute, ACTION, is required and tells the CFCOLLECTION tag what action to perform on the specified Verity collection. In this case, we are telling the CFCOLLECTION tag we want to create a new collection. Other values for the ACTION attribute are discussed later in the chapter. The COLLECTION attribute is also required and specifies a name for the collection being created. PATH, another required attribute, specifies the path to the Verity collection on the server. This must be a physical path accessible by the ColdFusion server. The LANGUAGE attribute is optional. It determines the language to be used when creating the collection. As noted above, to specify a language other than English (the default), you must purchase the ColdFusion International Search Pack from Allaire.

The CFCOLLECTION tag also lets you register an already existing Verity collection by setting the ACTION attribute to MAP. To map an already existing Verity collection, that collection must be available to the ColdFusion server via the local filesystem. The following example demonstrates how to map an existing Verity collection using the CFCOLLECTION tag:

```
<CFLOCK NAME="CFCOLLECTION_Lock" TYPE="EXCLUSIVE" TIMEOUT="30">
  <CFCOLLECTION ACTION="map"
                COLLECTION="MyVerityCollection"
                PATH="c:\cfusion\verity\collections"
                LANGUAGE="English">
</CFLOCK>
```

# Populating Collections

The next step after creating a Verity collection is to populate it with indexed data. Populating a Verity collection is accomplished with the `CFINDEX` tag. With the `CFINDEX` tag, ColdFusion can index data from a number of sources including numerous file types and query results from any ColdFusion query. What this means is that you can use the `CFINDEX` tag to index everything from HTML files and word-processed documents, to relational databases, LDAP directories, and POP mail accounts.

## Indexing Files

The great thing about bundling Verity's search technology with ColdFusion is that you can build applications capable of searching a wide range of document types including both text and binary formats. Here are the file types capable of being indexed by `CFINDEX`:

*Text files*
: HTML, CFML, ANSI, ASCII, SGML, XML, and plain text

*Word processing documents*
: Adobe PDF; Applix Words 4.2, 4.3, 4.4; Corel WordPerfect for Windows 5.x, 6, 7, and 8; Corel WordPerfect for Macintosh 2 and 3; Lotus AMI Pro 2 and 3; Lotus AMI Pro Write Plus; Lotus Word Pro 96 and 97; Microsoft Rich Text Format (RTF); Microsoft Word for Windows 2, 6, 95, 97, and 2000; Microsoft Word for DOS 4, 5 and 6; Microsoft Word for Macintosh 4, 5, and 6; Microsoft Works; Microsoft Write; and XYWrite 4.12.

*Spreadsheets*
: Applix Spreadsheets 4.3 and 4.4, Corel QuattroPro 7 and 8; Lotus 1-2-3 for DOS/Windows 2, 3, 4, 5, 96, and 97; Microsoft Excel 3, 4, 5, 95, 97, and 2000; and Microsoft Works.

*Presentations*
: Corel Presentations 7 and 8; Lotus Freelance 96 and 97; and Microsoft PowerPoint 4, 95, 97, and 2000.

Note that versions of ColdFusion through 4.5.1 contain the VDK 2.4.1 engine. Because VDK 2.4.1 is an older technology, Microsoft Office 2000 documents aren't supported. ColdFusion 5.0 includes the newer VDK 2.6.1 as well as the Verity K2 Server. These versions of the Verity engine include support for MS Office 2000 documents. You should also be aware that, due to a limitation in the Verity engine, the Linux version of ColdFusion through 5.0 can't index Adobe PDF documents.

### *Indexing files with the ColdFusion Administrator*

The ColdFusion Administrator provides an interface for indexing files. To follow is a quick and easy way to index a single file or group of files without having to write any code to do it:

1. Highlight the collection to be populated under the Verity Collections heading and click the Index button.
2. Enter a comma-delimited list of file extensions for the Verity engine to index.
3. Enter the full directory path for the directory in which you would like the indexing to take place.
4. If you want Verity to recursively index documents below the directory you specified in the Directory Path field, check the box. Otherwise, Verity indexes only the documents contained in the Directory Path field.
5. You can add a URL to be appended to the beginning of all files indexed by the Verity server. This is useful because it allows you to easily create links to the files indexed by the Verity engine. This technique will be discussed later in this chapter.
6. If you have installed the Verity International Language Search Pack, you can specify an alternate language for the indexing process.
7. Click on the update button to begin indexing your new collection. The indexing time varies depending on the number, type, and size of the files being indexed.

### *Indexing Files Programmatically with CFINDEX*

Indexing files programmatically with the `CFINDEX` tag allows you to exert more fine-grained control over your Verity collections. Suppose you have a web site consisting of nothing but HTML pages that you want to index. The following bit of code is all that is necessary to populate a Verity collection from all your HTML pages:

```
<CFLOCK NAME="CFINDEX_Lock" TYPE="EXCLUSIVE" TIMEOUT="30">
  <CFINDEX COLLECTION="MyWebsite" TYPE="Path" ACTION="Update"
           KEY="c:\inetsrv\wwwroot\" URLPATH="http://127.0.0.1/"
           EXTENSIONS=".htm, .html" RECURSE="Yes">
</CFLOCK>

<CENTER>
```

```
<H2>Finished Indexing The Web Site...</H2>
</CENTER>
```

Again, note the use of CFLOCK around the CFINDEX tag to allow only one thread to access the collection at a time. The COLLECTION attribute specifies the name of the collection (as created with the ColdFusion Administrator or the CFCOLLECTION tag) we want to populate. We set the TYPE attribute equal to Path to let ColdFusion know we want to index a group of files located in a particular path. The TYPE attribute is optional and defaults to Custom if none is specified. The second attribute, ACTION, is also optional and is set to Update in our example. Setting the ACTION attribute to Update updates the collection and adds the key specified in the KEY attribute. Updating the collection essentially appends new information to the end of a collection.

We set the KEY attribute to the path where the files that we are indexing are located. In the previous example, we set KEY equal to the root directory of our web site. URLPATH is also optional and is set to the URL path for the files on our fictitious web site. When this collection is searched using the CFSEARCH tag, the value specified in the URLPATH attribute is added to the beginning of all filenames and returned as the URL attribute. The EXTENSIONS attribute is optional and should be used when TYPE="Path". It specifies a comma-delimited list of file extensions to be included in the indexing operation. In our example, we set the EXTENSIONS attribute to *.htm* and *.html* so that only HTML files on our web site get indexed. Setting EXTENSIONS="*." indexes all files without extensions. Finally, RECURSE is set to Yes so that our indexing operation indexes all HTML files below the path specified in the KEY attribute.

Note that the CFINDEX tag can populate only an existing Verity collection. If the collection you want to populate doesn't exist, you have to create it using the ColdFusion Administrator or the CFCOLLECTION tag. The examples throughout this chapter assume you have already created a Verity collection with the name specified in the COLLECTION attribute of the CFINDEX tag.

Sometimes you may need to index only a single file contained in a particular directory as opposed to the whole directory. The CFINDEX tag can accommodate this by setting the TYPE attribute to File as opposed to Path. This lets ColdFusion know to index only a single file as opposed to every file in the designated path. The following example shows how to index a single file:

```
<CFLOCK NAME="CFINDEX_Lock" TYPE="EXCLUSIVE" TIMEOUT="30">
  <CFINDEX ACTION="UPDATE" COLLECTION="MyCollection"
           KEY="D:\inetsrv\wwwroot\myfile.htm"
           TYPE="FILE" URLPATH="http://127.0.0.1">
</CFLOCK>
```

As you can see from the example, the value assigned to the KEY attribute now contains the filename to index as well as the path to it on the server. Because the filename is specified as part of the KEY attribute, the EXTENSIONS attribute can be omitted from the operation.

## Indexing Query Results

Besides being able to index files, the Verity engine can also index the contents of any ColdFusion query object. This means that you can create collections from databases, LDAP directories, and POP mail accounts. Query objects can be indexed programmatically only via the CFINDEX tag. There is no means for indexing them through the ColdFusion Administrator.

### *Indexing database query results*

Why would you want to index the contents of a relational database when you can use SQL to perform searches of the database? The answer is simple. SQL just wasn't designed to efficiently handle full-text searching. Searching for text-based information using the Verity search interface is more powerful and faster than using standard SQL queries.

Suppose we have a Microsoft Access database that stores news related-articles. The database consists of a single table called News that contains the fields shown in Table 16-1.

*Table 16-1. News Table Schema*

| Field Name | Field Type | Max Length |
|---|---|---|
| ArticleID (primary key) | AutoNumber | N/A |
| ArticleType | Text | 255 |
| Title | Text | 255 |
| Article | Memo | N/A |
| DatePosted | Date/Time | N/A |

The article titles are stored in the Title field while the actual text of the articles is stored in the Article field. Let's say that we want to make the database searchable by either the Title field or the Article field. Creating a Verity collection that contains the contents of both the Title and Article fields is easy.

There are some differences between indexing files and indexing the contents of a relational database. For starters, you aren't actually indexing the database itself but rather a subset of the data existing as a query object. In other words, you are creating your Verity collection from the results of a ColdFusion query against a data source. Example 16-1 demonstrates the method for indexing the contents of a database query object.

*Example 16-1. Indexing the Contents of a Database Query Result Set Using CFINDEX*

```
<!--- Query the database for each of the news items to get the ArticleID, Title,
      and Article body --->
<CFQUERY NAME="IndexNews" DATASOURCE="ProgrammingCF">
    SELECT ArticleID, Title, Article FROM News
</CFQUERY>

<!--- Index the contents of the query object using CFINDEX --->
<CFLOCK NAME="CFINDEX_Lock" TYPE="EXCLUSIVE" TIMEOUT="30">
  <CFINDEX COLLECTION="News" ACTION="Update" TYPE="Custom" BODY="Title,Article"
      KEY="ArticleID" TITLE="Title" QUERY="IndexNews">
</CFLOCK>

<CENTER>
  <H2>Finished Indexing The News Database</H2>
</CENTER>
```

The first part of the template in Example 16-1 creates a query object containing the `ArticleID`, `Title`, and `Article` for each news item in the database. The second part of the template in Example 16-1 is the actual `CFINDEX` operation. This time, we change the `TYPE` attribute to `Custom`. This lets ColdFusion know we want to index the contents of a query object as opposed to a group of files. The `BODY` attribute contains the column names from the query that we want to index and is a required attribute when `TYPE` is set to `Custom`. In our case, we want to index both the `Title` and `Article` fields so we define them in the `BODY` attribute as a comma-delimited list. When indexing query objects, the `KEY` attribute should be set to a unique identifier, usually the primary key for the table. The `KEY` attribute differentiates records found during a `CFSEARCH`. In our example, we set the `KEY` attribute equal to the `ArticleID` field (primary key) from our database.

### *Indexing CFLDAP query results*

LDAP directories are another candidate for indexing using ColdFusion and the Verity engine. ColdFusion can index the results of `CFLDAP` queries against both public and private LDAP directories. Although most public LDAP servers provide a web page for browser-based searching, the Verity search interface offers a more powerful and flexible way of finding and presenting the information you need for your applications. The `CFINDEX` tag makes it easy to index the results of a query performed with the `CFLDAP` tag. Example 16-2 shows how to populate a collection with the results of a `CFLDAP` query. Because the contents of LDAP directories are subject to frequent change, it may be necessary to update the collection on a regular basis to avoid inaccurate searches. Example 16-2 shows how to use

CFLDAP in conjunction with CFINDEX to create a small collection from the LDAP server at *Bigfoot.com*.

*Example 16-2. Creating a Collection from the Results of a CFLDAP Query*

```
<!--- Use CFLDAP to query bigfoot.com for people named Tom Jones --->
<CFLDAP
    SERVER="ldap.bigfoot.com" ACTION="QUERY" NAME="MyQuery"
    START="cn=tom jones,c=US" FILTER="(cn=tom jones),(c=US)"
    ATTRIBUTES="dn,cn,o,mail" SORT="cn ASC">

<!--- populate the ldap_test collection with the results of the CFLDAP
      query --->
<CFLOCK NAME="CFINDEX_Lock" TYPE="EXCLUSIVE" TIMEOUT="30">
  <CFINDEX ACTION="refresh" COLLECTION="LDAP_Test" KEY="dn"
      TYPE="custom" TITLE="cn" BODY="cn,o,mail" QUERY="MyQuery">
</CFLOCK>

<CENTER>
  <H2>Done Indexing the LDAP Query</H2>
</CENTER>
```

In this case, we use CFLDAP to query a public LDAP server, *Bigfoot.com* for all people named Tom Jones. The results of the query are then added to a Verity collection. In the CFINDEX operation, we set the ACTION attribute to Refresh. This causes ColdFusion to clear out the contents of the entire collection before repopulating it with the data from the query. Setting the ACTION to Refresh is a good idea in situations where the data being indexed changes frequently.

### *Indexing CFPOP query results*

The CFINDEX tag can also index the contents of a POP mailbox. This is useful in situations where you want to allow users to search through the contents of a particular POP mailbox such as a mailing list or customer service request archive. Example 16-3 shows a simple template for querying and indexing the contents of a POP mailbox. To get the template to work with your POP server, all you have to do is change the values of the SERVER, USERNAME, and PASSWORD attributes to those of your choosing.

*Example 16-3. Populating an Index Based on the Results of a CFPOP Query*

```
<!--- Query the POP server --->
<CFPOP ACTION="getall" NAME="GetMessages" SERVER="127.0.0.1"
      USERNAME="username" PASSWORD="password">

<!--- populate the pop_test collection with the results of the CFPOP query --->
<CFLOCK NAME="CFINDEX_Lock" TYPE="EXCLUSIVE" TIMEOUT="30">
  <CFINDEX ACTION="refresh" COLLECTION="pop_test" KEY="messagenumber"
          TYPE="custom" TITLE="subject" QUERY="GetMessages" BODY="body">
```

*Example 16-3. Populating an Index Based on the Results of a CFPOP Query (continued)*

```
</CFLOCK>

<CENTER>
  <H2>Done Indexing the POP Query</H2>
</CENTER>
```

Because of the way POP servers work, message numbers tend to change frequently as messages are added or deleted from the server. In order to avoid searching through a collection that is out of synch with the data residing on the POP server, you should probably reindex your POP collection before performing each search operation against it.

# *Searching Collections*

Once you have created and populated a Verity collection, you will naturally want to provide a means for users to search its contents. The `CFSEARCH` tag provides just such capability. Using the `CFSEARCH` tag, ColdFusion allows you to build sophisticated searching into your applications. In its simplest form, `CFSEARCH` can perform the searching operation directly against a Verity collection without the user having to enter anything for the search criteria. A popular use for this technique is in the creation of "top ten" lists of search terms. This technique is covered later in the Advanced Techniques section of this chapter. For now, let's take a look at a basic example that demonstrates how to use the `CFSEARCH` tag to search a Verity collection without the user having to enter the search criteria:

```
<CFSEARCH COLLECTION="cfdocumentation" NAME="MySearchQuery" TYPE="simple"
          CRITERIA="verity" LANGUAGE="English" EXTERNAL="No">

<CFOUTPUT QUERY="MySearchQuery">
   <A HREF="/cfdocs/#MySearchQuery.url#">#MySearchQuery.Title#</A><BR>
</CFOUTPUT>
```

The `COLLECTION` attribute is required and specifies the name of the collection you wish to search or in the case of externally generated collections, the full path to the collection directory. Multiple collections may be searched provided the collection names or paths are separated by commas. When specifying multiple collections, you can't mix internal and external collections in the same search operation. Entering the name of a Verity collection that doesn't exist causes ColdFusion to throw an error. `NAME` is also a required attribute and assigns a name to the query object created by the search operation.

The `TYPE` attribute is optional and defines the type of search to be performed against the Verity collection. Valid types are `Simple` (the default) and `Explicit`. In this case, we set the `TYPE` to `Simple`, which means that the search returns matches for the word the user specifies and any stemmed variations. (You will find more information on different types of searches later in this chapter.) We define exactly what we want to search for with the `CRITERIA` attribute. In this example, we want to find all documents that contain the word "verity". The `CRITERIA` attribute can contain single words or expressions. This attribute is explained in full detail later in the chapter. Leaving the `CRITERIA` attribute blank causes all records in the Verity collection to be returned.

The `LANGUAGE` attribute is optional and requires the use of the Verity International Language Search Pack for languages other than English. It specifies which language to use in searching a particular Verity collection. The final attribute used in our example is the optional `EXTERNAL` attribute. Setting this attribute to `Yes` lets ColdFusion know that the collection being searched was created with a tool other than ColdFusion, such as the Verity Spider or *mkvdk* tool. `EXTERNAL` must be set to `Yes` when searching collections specified by `Path` in the `COLLECTION` attribute.

Every `CFSEARCH` operation returns a number of variables that can build various types of search result templates, as listed in Appendix A. We'll use some of these variables in upcoming examples.

## *Building a Search Interface*

Creating a search interface for your Verity collections is most often a two- or three-template process. The first template usually contains an HTML or ColdFusion Java form that allows a user to specify their search criteria. The second template takes the search criteria from the first template, uses it to search the Verity collection, and returns the results to the user in a meaningful way. In the case of a search against a file collection, the second template typically displays the filename or title of the file, the score assigned to the file, and possibly a short summary of the files contents. For searches against database collections, the second template usually displays the value placed in the `TITLE` attribute, with a hyperlink to a third template that drills down to a database record identified by the `KEY` value in the hyperlink.

### *Searching file collections*

Examples 16-4 and 16-5 illustrate the two-template approach with a search interface that searches the ColdFusion documentation that is installed as part of the standard ColdFusion installation. This Verity collection, named `cfdocumentation`, is created automatically the first time you search the documentation from the ColdFusion Documentation home page (*http://127.0.0.1/cfdocs/dochome.htm*). You can see if this collection already exists by looking for it in the Verity section of the ColdFusion Administrator. If the `cfdocumentation` collection doesn't exist, you can make ColdFusion create it by clicking on the search icon in the upper right corner of the ColdFusion Documentation home page. Clicking on the search icon causes a pop-up window to appear. To create and populate the `cfdocumentation` collection, simply click on the Index button.

The template in Example 16-4 creates a simple HTML form that allows the user to specify a string they want to search for. A checkbox is provided to allow them to optionally have the summary for each document displayed on the search results page.

*Example 16-4. Verity Search Form for Searching a Document Collection*

```
<CENTER>
<H2>ColdFusion Documentation Search</H2>

<FORM ACTION="Example16-5.cfm" METHOD="post">
<TABLE BORDER="0">
<TR>
   <TD>Search For:</TD>
   <TD><INPUT TYPE="Text" NAME="Criteria" SIZE="25" MAXLENGTH="255"></TD>
</TR>

<TR>
   <TD>Include Summary:</TD>
   <TD><INPUT TYPE="Checkbox" NAME="Summary" VALUE="Yes"></TD>
</TR>

<TR>
   <TD COLSPAN="2" ALIGN="center">
   <INPUT TYPE="Submit" NAME="Search" VALUE="Search">
   </TD>
</TR>
</TABLE>
</FORM>
</CENTER>
```

The second template in our scenario (Example 16-5) receives the form-field data from the template in Example 16-4. It performs the actual search and outputs any matches that it finds.

*Example 16-5. Verity Document Collection Search Results Template*

```
<!--- If no search criteria is passed, assume user wants all documents in the
      collection, so assign a wildcard (*) to the search criteria --->
<CFIF Form.Criteria IS "">
   <CFSET Form.Criteria = "*">
</CFIF>

<!--- Perform the search of the Verity collection(s) based on the parameters
      passed from the search criteria form.  In this case, we are searching
      the Verity collection created by ColdFusion the first time you attempt
      to search the ColdFusion documentation using the interface that ships
      with ColdFusion. --->
<CFSEARCH COLLECTION="cfdocumentation" NAME="MySearchQuery"
```

*Example 16-5. Verity Document Collection Search Results Template (continued)*

```
        TYPE="simple" CRITERIA="#Form.Criteria#">

<BODY>
<H2>Search Results</H2>

<CFOUTPUT>
Your search for: <B><FONT COLOR="##ff0000">#Form.Criteria#</FONT></B> turned up
#MySearchQuery.RecordCount# documents out of #MySearchQuery.RecordsSearched#
documents searched.
</CFOUTPUT>

<!--- If no records match the search criteria, inform the user --->
<CFIF MySearchQuery.RecordCount LTE 0>
  <CFOUTPUT>
  <P>Sorry.  No instances of #Form.Criteria# were found in the specified
  collection(s).  Please hit the back button on your browser and try again.
  </CFOUTPUT>

<!--- Otherwise, output the search results including linbks to the
      documents --->
<CFELSE>
  <TABLE BORDER="0" CELLPADDING="3" CELLSPACING="3" WIDTH="75%">
  <TR>
    <TD><B>Document Title</B></TD>
    <TD><B>Score</B></TD>
  </TR>

  <TR>
    <TD COLSPAN="2"><HR></TD>
  </TR>

  <CFOUTPUT QUERY="MySearchQuery">
  <TR>
    <TD><A HREF="http://127.0.0.1/cfdocs/#MySearchQuery.URL#">
    <CFIF MySearchQuery.Title IS "">
      <B>Untitled</B>
    <CFELSE>
      <B>#Title#</B>
    </CFIF>
    </A></TD>
    <TD><FONT COLOR="##ff0000"><B><CFIF MySearchQuery.Score IS NOT "">
       #Evaluate(MySearchQuery.Score * 100)#%</CFIF></B></FONT>
    </TD>
  </TR>

  <CFIF IsDefined('Form.Summary')>
  <TR>
    <TD><P ALIGN="justify">#Summary#</TD>
    <TD> </TD>
  </TR>
  </CFIF>
  </CFOUTPUT>
```

*Example 16-5. Verity Document Collection Search Results Template (continued)*

```
    <TR>
      <TD COLSPAN="2"><HR></TD>
    </TR>
    </TABLE>
</CFIF>
```

The template in Example 16-5 takes the search string from the form in Example 16-4 and uses it as the `CRITERIA` in the `CFSEARCH` routine. Once the search has been performed, the template checks to see if there were any matches and if so, presents them to the user. The template presents the results as a table containing the document's title as a hyperlink to the actual document as well and a score for the document. The score is calculated based on Verity's internal set of rules and is returned as a number between 0 and 1. The search results are automatically sorted by score. If you wish to change the sort order, you can do so as of ColdFusion 5.0 by writing a query of a query to resort the results based on a different sort criteria. The template checks to make sure a score was returned, and if so it uses the `Evaluate()` function to multiply the number returned by 100, which results in a percentage score for each match. Finally, if the user checks the summary box in the search template, a short summary of each document is included in the table. The output from Example 16-5 can be seen in Figure 16-1.

### *Searching database collections*

Searching a database collection is just as simple as searching a file collection with a few notable differences. Since we are now searching the contents of a query as opposed to a file collection, we need to change the way the search results are displayed and subsequently acted upon. This is relatively easy to do. Example 16-6 to Example 16-18 show a common three-template method for displaying the results of a search against a query collection. The examples use the same sample database we have been using throughout the chapter.

*Example 16-6. Specifying Database Search Criteria*

```
<FORM ACTION="example16-7.cfm" METHOD="post">
<TABLE BORDER="0">
<TR>
  <TD>Search For:</TD>
  <TD><INPUT TYPE="Text" NAME="Criteria" SIZE="25" MAXLENGTH="255"></TD>
</TR>

<TR>
  <TD COLSPAN="2" ALIGN="center"><INPUT TYPE="Submit" NAME="Search"
      VALUE="Search"></TD>
</TR>
</TABLE>
</FORM>
```

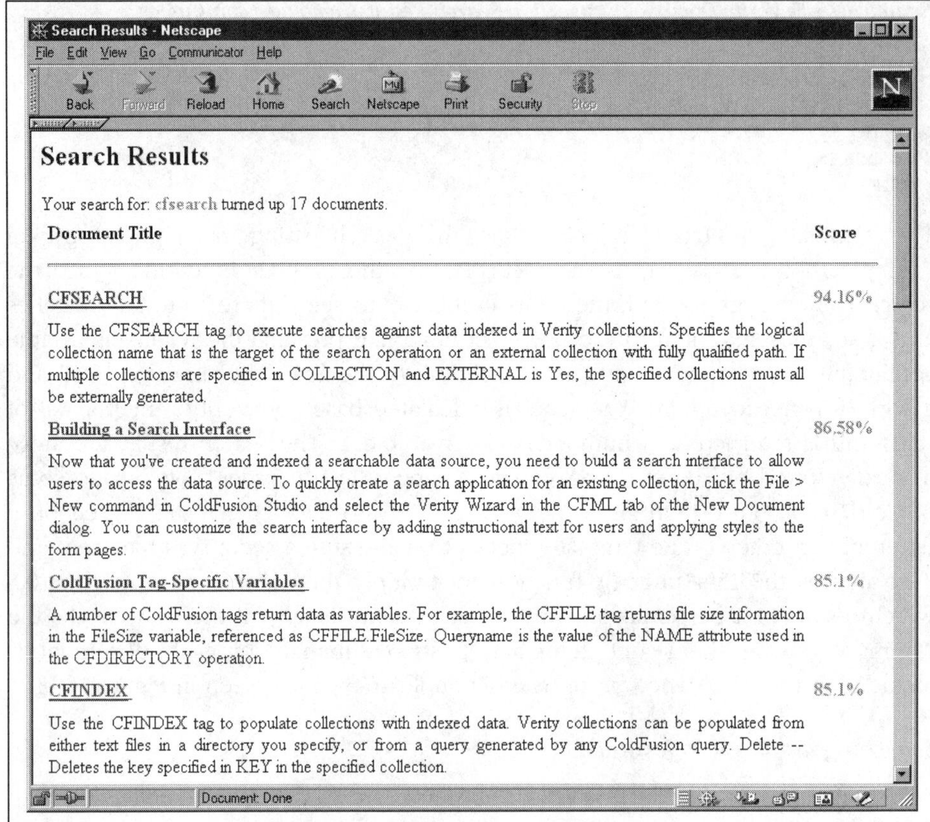


*Figure 16-1. Output from a CFSEARCH of a document collection*

The template in Example 16-6 creates the search screen that the user sees in his browser. The search screen is simply an HTML form that contains a single text-input box for entering a search string. Once the user enters a search string and clicks on the submit button, the form data is passed on to the template shown in Example 16-7.

*Example 16-7. Displaying the Results of a Query Collection Search*

```
<!--- If no search criteria is passed, assume user wants all documents in the
      collection, so assign a wildcard (*) to the search criteria --->
<CFIF Form.Criteria IS "">
  <CFSET Form.Criteria = "*">
</CFIF>

<CFSEARCH COLLECTION="News" NAME="MySearchQuery"
          TYPE="simple" CRITERIA="#Form.Criteria#">
<H2>Search Results</H2>

<CFOUTPUT>
```

*Example 16-7. Displaying the Results of a Query Collection Search (continued)*

```
Your search for: <B><FONT COLOR="##ff0000">#Form.Criteria#</FONT></B> turned up
#MySearchQuery.RecordCount# records out of #MySearchQuery.RecordsSearched# records
searched.
</CFOUTPUT>

<!--- If no records match the search criteria, inform the user --->
<CFIF MySearchQuery.RecordCount LTE 0>
  <CFOUTPUT>
  <P>Sorry.  No instances of #Form.Criteria# were found in the specified
  collection(s).  Please hit the back button on your browser and try
  again.
  </CFOUTPUT>

<!--- Otherwise, output the search results including links to the
      documents --->
<CFELSEIF MySearchQuery.RecordCount GT 0>
  <TABLE BORDER="0" CELLPADDING="3" CELLSPACING="3" WIDTH="75%">
  <TR>
    <TD><B>Title</B></TD><TD><B>Score</B></TD>
  </TR>

  <TR>
    <TD COLSPAN="2"><HR></TD>
  </TR>

  <CFOUTPUT QUERY="MySearchQuery">
  <TR>
    <TD><A HREF="example16-8.cfm?ID=#Key#">#Title#</A></TD>
    <TD><FONT COLOR="##ff0000">
        <B><CFIF MySearchQuery.Score IS NOT "">
        #Evaluate(MySearchQuery.Score * 100)#%</CFIF></B></FONT>
    </TD>
  </TR>
  </CFOUTPUT>

  <TR>
    <TD COLSPAN="2"><HR></TD>
  </TR>
  </TABLE>
</CFIF>
```

The template in Example 16-7 works the same way as the search and results template from Example 16-5 with one notable difference. Instead of returning the title of the document as a link to the actual document, the template returns the value placed in the `TITLE` attribute as a hyperlink to the template in Example 16-8. A parameter called `ID` is appended to the URL in the link so that the template in Example 16-8 knows which record to drill down to.

*Example 16-8. Displaying Database Record from Search Results Page*

```
<!--- Query the news table for the record specified by the ID
      parameter passed in the URL from the previous template --->
<CFQUERY NAME="GetRecord" DATASOURCE="ProgrammingCF">
        SELECT Title,Article FROM News WHERE ArticleID=#URL.ID#
</CFQUERY>

<CFOUTPUT QUERY="GetRecord">
<B>#Title#</B>
<P>
#Article#
</CFOUTPUT>
```

Example 16-8 takes the value in the URL parameter (the primary key value for the record) passed to it from the template in Example 16-7 and uses it to look up the actual news article in the example database. The article itself is retrieved from the database via a CFQUERY and output to the browser using a corresponding CFOUTPUT statement.

# The Verity Search Language

When you search a Verity collection using the CFSEARCH tag, you can specify the type of search to be performed using the TYPE attribute. As discussed earlier in this chapter, the TYPE attribute can be set to either `Simple` (the default) or `Explicit`. `Simple` searches consist of a word or words. `Explicit` searches make use of operators and modifiers and must specifically invoke each one in order to fine-tune the search. In the case of a `Simple` search, operators and modifiers are employed by default.

It should be noted that Verity handles case sensitivity in the following way:

- If your search string is in all lowercase characters or all uppercase characters, the search is treated as a case-insensitive search.
- If your search string consists of mixed-case characters, the search is treated as a case-sensitive search.

This default behavior can be changed via the <CASE> modifier (which is addressed in the following section) to specify the case for the search.

## Simple Searches

`Simple` searches allow you to use single words, comma-delimited lists of words, and phrases as the CRITERIA for a CFSEARCH. For example, if you want to return all documents containing the word "fish," specify the word "fish" in the CRITERIA attribute of the CFSEARCH tag. Similarly, entering a comma-delimited list such as "trout, bass, carp" returns all documents containing either "trout," "bass," or "carp."

Simple searches treat the comma as a Boolean OR. Phrases can also be used as CRITERIA in a CFSEARCH. Phrases are searched for by entering the phrase as it appears in the CRITERIA attribute. For example, entering the phrase "I like fishing" returns only documents that contain that complete phrase.

By default, Simple searches employ the STEM operator and the MANY modifier. This means that searching for the word "fish" returns all documents containing "fish" as well as "fishes" and "fishing." STEM is considered an evidence operator and causes the Verity engine to return documents containing derivatives of the word or words in the CRITERIA attribute. The MANY modifier counts the number of times a particular search term is encountered within a record being searched. A score is then calculated based on the number of times it appears and the density of the search term within the record.

Simple searches can also use wildcards. For example, entering con* as the CRITERIA returns all words beginning with "con" such as "construction," "condominium," and "conundrum."

## *Explicit Searches*

Explicit searches differ from Simple searches in that the Verity search engine interprets each search term as a literal. So, a search for the word "test" returns only records containing the word "test," not "tests" or "testing." In an Explicit search, operators must be called explicitly.

### *Operators*

Operators apply logic and rules to a Verity search. Operators determine the criteria a record must meet before it can be considered a match. Operators can be invoked by the user when using a form-based search interface or behind the scenes when hardcoded into the application. Operators are most often used in Explicit searches.

With the exception of AND, OR, and NOT, all operators must be enclosed in angle brackets. Enclosing operators in angle brackets keeps the Verity engine from treating the operator as a literal search term. For example, to search for the word TEST in uppercase, it is necessary to enter the search criteria as <CASE> as opposed to CASE. The latter causes Verity to look for the word "case" as opposed to interpreting it is an operator. Operators themselves aren't case-sensitive.

***Order of evaluation.*** Like expressions, the use of operators is also governed by a set of rules for establishing an order of evaluation. By default, certain operators are given more weight when evaluating search criteria. For instance, the AND operator is evaluated before an OR operator. Like the order of evaluation in math, parentheses take precedence over all other factors. When nested parentheses are encountered, evaluation begins with the innermost set.

***Prefix and infix notation.*** Excluding evidence operators, any search string that contains operators can be represented using either prefix or infix notation.

*Prefix notation* means that the operator being used gets specified before the search string. For example, setting the search criteria to `AND (test, exam, final)` returns records only if they contain the words "test," "exam," and "final."

*Infix notation* requires that an operator be placed between each search term. Using the previous search criteria of "test," "exam," and "final," if you want to search for them using infix notation, you would specify `test AND exam AND final` as the search criteria.

***Double quotation marks.*** Double quotation marks are used to search for operators as literal words. For example, to search for the word "not," it needs to be surrounded in double quotes to avoid having the Verity engine interpret it as an operator.

***Special characters.*** There are several characters considered "special" by the Verity engine and must be escaped to be searched as literals. The backslash (\) is used to escape all special characters. To specify a backslash as a literal search character, it must be escaped by another backslash (\\). The following is a list of special characters that require escaping:

- At/for sign (@)
- Backslash (\)
- Backquote (`)
- Comma (,)
- Double quotation mark (")
- Left and right angle bracket (<>)
- Left and right bracket ([])
- Left and right curly bracket ({})
- Left and right parentheses ()

In addition to the backslash character, special characters can also be searched as literals if they are included within backquotes. For example, to search for "webmaster@example.com," you specify the search criteria as "`webmaster@example.com`". To search for the backquote as a literal, it must be escaped with another backquote.

***Concept operators.*** Concept operators identify a concept in a document by linking a group of search terms using criteria specified by the operator. Records retrieved using concept operators are ranked by relevance. The following concept operators are available for use in your search criteria:

`ACCRUE`
: Causes records to be returned when they contain at least one of the search terms specified. `ACCRUE` differs from `OR` in that ranking is based on the number of times each search term is found.

`ALL`
: Causes records to be returned only when all search terms are found. Same as the `AND` operator except a score of 1.00 is always returned for matches.

`AND`
: Causes records to be returned only when all search terms are found. For example, searching for "dog AND cat" returns only records that contain both the word "dog" and the word "cat."

`ANY`
: Causes records to be returned when any of the search terms are found. Same as the `OR` operator except a score of 1.00 is always returned for matches.

`OR`
: Causes records to be returned when any one word is found. For example, searching for "cat OR dog" returns records containing only "cat," only "dog," or both "cat" and "dog."

***Evidence operators.*** Evidence operators differentiate between basic and intelligent word searches. Basic word searches look only for the particular word specified. Intelligent word searches look for additional words related to the search term based on derivatives and wildcards. Here are the evidence operators:

`SOUNDEX`
: Finds words that sound alike or have a similar structure to the specified word. SOUNDEX uses the AT&T standard soundex algorithm. For example, searching for "<SOUNDEX> there" typically returns records containing words such as "their" and, "they're." In order to use `SOUNDEX`, you must edit the *style.prm* file located in *c:\cfusion\verity\common\style\custom* or *c:\cfusion\verity\common\style\file* depending on the type of collection that you are working with. Change the line that reads:

```
$define WORD-IDXOPTS  "Stemdex Casedex"
```

to:

```
$define WORD-IDXOPTS  "Stemdex Casedex Soundex"
```

Once you have done this, purge and reindex the collection. You can now perform soundex searches using the `SOUNDEX` operator.

`STEM`

Finds words that derive from the search term(s). Searching for "<STEM>list" returns records containing the words "list," "lists," and "listing," etc. Simple searches employ the `STEM` operator by default.

`THESAURUS`

Allows you to search for synonyms of search terms. For example, searching for "<THESAURUS>run" returns records containing the word "run" as well as synonyms such as "sprint," "jog," and "dash."

`TYPO/N`

Searches for words that are spelled similarly. For example, searching for "<TYPO>special" finds all documents with words spelled similarly to the word "special." The `/N` is optional and specifes the maximum number of spelling errors to allow between the search word and any matched words. If no value is specified, a default of two errors is used.

`WILDCARD`

Returns all records matching wildcard characters used in the search criteria. The search string used with the `WILDCARD` operator should be enclosed in backquotes (`). For example, searching for "<WILDCARD>`test*`" returns all records containing words such as "test," "testing," and "tested." Table 16-2 shows a list of all wildcard characters that can be used in your Verity searches.

*Table 16-2. Wildcards*

| Wildcard | Description |
|---|---|
| * | The asterisk specifies zero or more alphanumeric characters in a particular search string. Asterisks are ignored inside [ ] and { } wildcard searches. |
| ? | A question mark specifies a single alphanumeric character. For example, searching for "<WILDCARD>`test?`" returns records containing "test" and "tests", but not "testing". |
| [ ] | Square brackets specify one of any characters appearing in a set. For example, searching for "<WILDCARD>`st[a,i,o]ck`" returns records containing "stack," "stick," and "stock." |
| { } | Curly brackets specify one of a group of characters appearing in a set. For example, searching for "<WILDCARD>`stock{s,ed,ing}` returns any records containing the word "stocks," "stocked," and "stocking." |
| ^ | The carat is used with the square brackets to specify one of any character that isn't listed in the set so that a search for "<WILDCARD> `st[^io]ck`" matches records containing "stack" or "stuck" but not "stick" or "stock." The carat must be the first character following the left bracket; otherwise it is matched as a literal character. |
| - | A hyphen is used in conjunction with square brackets and specifies a range of characters such that a search for "<WILDCARD>`b[a-z]d`" returns "bad," "bed," "bid," and "bud." |

It should be noted that in order to search for a wildcard character as a literal, it must be escaped. To escape a wildcard character, it must be preceded with a backslash. For example, to search for the sentence "What?", you need to escape it as "What\?". Asterisks must be escaped by two backslashes as in "test*".

`WORD`

Used when you want to have Verity match a specific word without resorting to wildcards or stemming. For example, if you want to search for the word "why?" including the question mark (Normally a wildcard), you enter your search criteria as "<WORD>why?"

***Proximity operators.*** Proximity operators are used to specify the proximal location of words within a record. Using proximity operators allows you to search for records that contain search terms within the same phrase, sentence, or paragraph. Retrieved records are ranked according to the proximity of the words specified in the search criteria. Here's a list of the proximity operators that can be used by the Verity search engine:

`IN`

Finds documents that contain the search term in a specified document zone. Document zones are specially defined areas within a document such as the title or body and are internally defined by Verity. For more information on customizing document zones, see the "Advanced Verity Tools" chapter in the *Advanced ColdFusion Administration* documentation.

`NEAR`

Causes the Verity engine to retrieve records containing the specified search terms. Records are scored based on the proximity of the search terms. The closer the terms are the higher the score. Records with search terms more than 1,000 words apart aren't counted in the scoring process.

`NEAR/N`

Finds documents that contain two or more search terms within *N* number of words of each other where *N* is an integer between 1 and 1024. Retrieved records are scored based on their proximity. The closer the words are, the higher the assigned score. Multiple search terms can be specified as long as the same value is used for *N*. For example, to search for the words "fish" and "carp" and "bass" within 10 words of each other, set the search criteria to "fish <NEARN/10> carp <NEARN/10> bass <NEARN/10>".

`PARAGRAPH`

Tells the Verity search engine to select records that contain all the specified search terms within the same paragraph. For example, to search for records containing the words "exam" and "professor" in the same paragraph, you specify "exam <PARAGRAPH> professor" as the search criteria. You may use the PARAGRAPH operator to search for three or more terms provided you separate each term with a PARAGRAPH operator.

PHRASE
: Selects records that contain the phrase specified in the search criteria. A phrase is defined as two or more words that occur in a specific order. For instance, to search for the phrase "open standards", you would use "open <PHRASE> standards" as the search criteria.

SENTENCE
: Selects records that contain all the words specified within the same sentence. So, to look for the words "ColdFusion" and "Allaire" in the same sentence, you use "<SENTENCE><ColdFusion, Allaire> as the search criteria.

***Relational operators.*** Relational operators search specific document fields within Verity collections. The five Verity document fields, TITLE, KEY, URL, CUSTOM1, and CUSTOM2 are referenced as CF_TITLE, CF_KEY, CF_URL, CF_CUSTOM1, and CF_CUSTOM2, respectively. The MANY modifier can't be used with relational operators. Records retrieved using relational operators aren't ranked by relevance. Relational operators can be broken down into two categories, text comparison operators and numeric/date relational operators.

The following operators are used for text comparisons:

CONTAINS
: Finds records by matching a word or phrase within a specific document field. For example, to find records that contain the word "pickle" anywhere in the TITLE field of a Verity collection, you use "CF_TITLE <CONTAINS> pickle".

ENDS
: Similar to the STARTS operator except that it returns only records that have values stored in the specified document field that end in the same values specified in the search criteria. For example, searching for "CF_TITLE <ENDS> ime" returns only records that have words like "time," "grime," and "lime" as the last word in the TITLE field.

MATCHES
: Finds records by matching the search criteria with values stored in the specified document field. In order for a record to be a match, the search term must exactly match the contents of the document field. For example, using "CF_TITLE <MATCHES> untitled" finds records that contain only "untitled" in the TITLE field.

STARTS

Finds records by matching the characters in your search criteria with records that have the same characters as the starting values in a specified document field. For example, searching for "CF_TITLE <STARTS> el" turns up records with titles beginning with "elephant" and "elevator."

SUBSTRING

Finds documents that contain the search criteria as a substring of a word or phrase within a document field. For example, searching for "CF_TITLE <SUB-STRING> exam" returns records with "exams," "examination," or "I have an exam today" as the `TITLE`.

Table 16-3 shows the operators can make numeric and date comparisons.

*Table 16-3. Comparison Operators*

| Operator | Description |
|---|---|
| < | Less than |
| > | Greater than |
| = | Equals |
| <= | Less than or equal to |
| >= | Greater than or equal to |

For example, to search for records that have a value stored in the `KEY` field greater than 77, use "CF_KEY > 77" as the search criteria.

***Score operators.*** Score operators determine how the Verity engine calculates the score it assigns to records that match the search criteria. Documents are assigned a score as a decimal percentage between 0 and 1.000 (100%) based on the operators and modifiers applied to the search criteria. Optionally, the score can be set to display the value to four decimal places. The following is a list of the score operators available to the Verity search engine:

COMPLEMENT

Causes the Verity engine to return the complement value for the score of a matching record. The complement value is arrived at by subtracting 1 from the matched record's original score. For example, if a search for "tea" resulted in a score of .25 being assigned to a matching document, a search for "<COMPLE-MENT> tea" results in a score of .75. It is worth noting that the `COMPLEMENT` operator causes all records with a score of 0 (all records NOT matching the search criteria) to have a recalculated score of 1 (a perfect match!). At the same time, all documents originally having a score of 1 get their score recalculated to 0. Why exactly you would want to use this feature is beyond me, but Verity makes it available nonetheless!

`PRODUCT`
: Multiplies the scores of each term found in a particular Verity record. Records with higher scoring matches score significantly higher than records with lower scoring matches. For example, a document with two terms that scored .5 and .75 respectively receives an overall score of .375, while a record with two terms scoring .25 and .5, respectively, receives an overall score of .125. Use of the `PRODUCT` operator has a tendency to result in fewer overall matches being returned. This can be useful in reducing the number of matches returned when searching large collections that tend to result in a high number of matches regardless of the search terms used.

`SUM`
: Adds the scores together for records matching the search criteria. For example, specifying "<SUM>(tea, coffee)" results in the scores for both search terms being added together. The maximum value a score can reach using the `SUM` operator is 1. Use of `SUM` operator has a tendency to return more "100 percent" matches.

`YESNO`
: Forces the score of a matching search term to 1 if the term's calculated score isn't zero. For example, using the search term "<YESNO> test" where a search for the term "test" normally results in a score of .50, causes Verity to force the score to 1. This means that if your search term appears anywhere in a document that is being searched, it will receive a score of 1 regardless of how many times the search term appears. The `YESNO` operator can return search results without ranking them by relevance.

***Modifiers.*** Modifiers are always combined with operators to change the behavior of operators in a predetermined way. For instance, you can use the `CASE` modifier with an operator to specify the case for the particular term to be matched. The following modifiers, commonly referred to as search modifiers, are available for use in your searches:

`CASE`
: Specifies a case-sensitive search. For example, to search for the word "Bill" in the Title field of a collection, you set the `CRITERIA` attribute in `CFSEARCH` to "CF_Title <CONTAINS> <CASE>Bill".

`MANY`
: Causes the Verity engine to rank results by relevance (score) based on the frequency and density of the search terms found. The `MANY` modifier is employed by default whenever a `SIMPLE` search is performed. It should be noted that the `MANY` modifier can't be used with the following concept operators: `AND`, `OR`, and `ACCRUE`, nor can it be used with relational operators.

`NOT`

Causes the Verity engine to ignore records that contain the specified search terms. For example, searching for "space NOT shuttle" causes Verity to return records containing the word "space" but not the word "shuttle."

`ORDER`

Specifies that your search criteria be found in a specified order to be considered a match. The `ORDER` modifier is usually used in conjunction with the `PARAGRAPH`, `SENTENCE`, `NEAR`, and `NEAR/N` operators. For example, to search for records containing the words "space" and "exploration," in order and in the same paragraph, you set your search criteria to "<ORDER> <PARAGRAPH> (space, exploration)".

## *Building an Advanced Search Interface*

Now that we have covered all the operators and modifiers used in the Verity search language, let's look at an example that puts some of these techniques to work. To show you how easy it is to use operators and modifiers in your search interfaces, we are going to build an advanced search interface for the documentation that installs with the ColdFusion application server. In order to do this, you first have to make sure that the Verity collection for the ColdFusion documentation exists on your server. This collection is created the first time you attempt to search the documentation from the "ColdFusion Documentation" page located in *http://127.0.0.1/cfdocs/dochome.htm* by default.

Once you have determined that you have the necessary Verity collection on your server, it is time to build the actual search interface. In Example 16-9, we build an interface that allows a user to enter a search string. It also allows users to choose case sensitivity and decide whether to search document titles only or both document titles and contents. Example 16-9 shows the template for specifying the search criteria.

*Example 16-9. Advanced Search Form*

```
<CENTER>
<H2>ColdFusion Documentation Advanced Search</H2>

<FORM ACTION="16-10.cfm" METHOD="POST">
<TABLE>
<TR>
   <TD>Search Criteria:</TD>
   <TD><INPUT TYPE="text" NAME="SearchString" SIZE="20"></TD>
</TR>
<TR>
   <TD>Search What?</TD>
   <TD><SELECT NAME="SearchIn">
         <OPTION VALUE="Title" SELECTED>Title Only
```

*Example 16-9. Advanced Search Form (continued)*

```
            <OPTION VALUE="Both">Title and Body
        </SELECT>
    </TD>
</TR>
<TR>
    <TD>Case Sensitive?</TD>
    <TD><INPUT TYPE="radio" NAME="CaseSensitive" VALUE="Yes">Yes<BR>
        <INPUT TYPE="radio" NAME="CaseSensitive" VALUE="No" CHECKED>No
    </TD>
</TR>
<TR>
    <TD COLSPAN="2"><INPUT TYPE=SUBMIT NAME=SEARCH1 VALUE="Search"></TD>
</TR>
</TABLE>
</FORM>
</CENTER>
```

Now that we have the search form created, we need to pass the parameters to another template so that the actual search can be performed. This is done by posting the form-field entries from Example 16-9 to the template shown in Example 16-10 for processing.

*Example 16-10. Advanced Search Using Operators and Modifiers*

```
<!--- If no search string is passed, assume user wants all documents in the
      collection, so assign a wildcard (*) to the search string --->
<CFIF Form.SearchString IS "">
    <CFSET Form.SearchString = "*">
</CFIF>

<!--- Check to see if search is for titles only --->
<CFIF Form.SearchIn IS "Title">
    <CFSET SearchString="CF_Title <CONTAINS> " & "#SearchString#">
</CFIF>

<!--- Check to see if search is to be case sensitive --->
<CFIF NOT Form.CaseSensitive>
    <CFSET SearchString=LCASE(SearchString)>
<CFELSE>
    <CFSET SearchString ="<CASE>" & "#SearchString#">
</CFIF>

<CFSEARCH
    NAME="MySearch" TYPE="Explicit" COLLECTION="cfdocumentation"
    CRITERIA = "#SearchString#">
<CENTER>
<H2>Search Results</H2>

<CFIF MySearch.RecordCount IS 0>
    <CFOUTPUT>
    <P>Sorry.  No instances of #Form.SearchString# were found in the specified
    collection(s).  Please hit the back button on your browser and try again.
```

*Example 16-10. Advanced Search Using Operators and Modifiers (continued)*

```
   </CFOUTPUT>
   <CFABORT>
</CFIF>

<TABLE>
<TR>
   <TD COLSPAN="2">
      <CFOUTPUT>
      Your search for <FONT COLOR="##0000FF">#Form.SearchString#</FONT> turned
      up #MySearch.RecordCount# matches out of #MySearch.RecordsSearched# records
      searched.
      </CFOUTPUT>
   </TD>
<TR>
   <TD><B>Title</B></TD><TD><B>Score</B></TD>
</TR>
<TR>
   <TD COLSPAN="2"><HR></TD>
</TR>

<CFOUTPUT QUERY="MySearch">
<TR>
   <TD><A HREF="/cfdocs/#URL#">#Title#</A></TD>
   <TD><CFIF Score IS NOT ""> #Evaluate(Score * 100)#%</CFIF></TD>
</TR>
</CFOUTPUT>
</TABLE>
</CENTER>
```

Example 16-10 first ensures that the user enters a value for the `SearchString` form variable. This is done using a `CFIF` statement to check that `SearchString` isn't blank. If it is, a `CFSET` statement assigns an asterisk (*) to `SearchString`. The asterisk is a wildcard character that causes the Verity engine to return all records contained in the collection being searched. Next, we need to see if the user wants to search only the document titles or both the titles and the actual contents of the files. The ColdFusion documentation is in HTML, so the titles being searched are the actual HTML titles of the files. If the user chooses to search only the document titles, a `CFSET` statement adds the `<CONTAINS>` operator to `SearchString`:

```
<CFSET SEARCHSTRING="CF_Title <CONTAINS> " & "#SearchString#">
```

Earlier in the chapter, you learned that `CF_TITLE` is a special document field in a Verity collection that contains the title of the document being indexed. In this case, `CF_TITLE` contains the HTML title of each document in the ColdFusion documentation collection.

The third `CFIF` statement checks the value of `Form.CaseSensitive`. If the value is `No`, `SearchString` is converted to lowercase using the `LCase` function inside a `CFSET` statement. If the value of `Form.CaseSensitive` is `Yes`, a `CFSET` statement inserts the `<CASE>` operator before the search term, making the search case-sensitive.

The next part of the template in Example 16-10 performs the actual search of the Verity collection using our modified `SearchString` as the search criteria. Note that the `TYPE` attribute of the `CFSEARCH` tag is set to `Explicit`. This tells the Verity engine that we want to perform an `Explicit` search using the operators and modifiers contained in the `CRITERIA` attribute. After the search is run, the results are output to the user's web browser in an HTML table containing a hyperlinked title and a percentage score for each matching document.

# Updating Collections

Unless your Verity collection is indexed from data that never changes, at some point in time you will need to make updates to it. Whether it is to add a new record to the collection or delete one, updating a Verity collection is an important part of keeping your searchable content current.

## Adding New Records to a Collection

New records can easily be added to an existing Verity collection using one of two methods. The first method consists of purging the Verity collection of all records and repopulating it. This is done by setting the `ACTION` attribute of the `CFINDEX` tag to `Refresh`. This method ensures that your Verity collections always contain the most up-to-date information. The disadvantage to this method is that it can be relatively time-consuming for larger collections because it has to completely reindex a collection just to add a single record. The following syntax shows how to use the `CFINDEX` tag to purge and reindex a collection:

```
<!--- Purge and repopulate a collection using the refresh property of the
      ACTION attribute --->
<CFQUERY NAME="IndexNews" DATASOURCE="ProgrammingCF">
    SELECT ArticleID, Title, Article FROM News
</CFQUERY>

<CFLOCK NAME="CFINDEX_Lock" TYPE="EXCLUSIVE" TIMEOUT="30">
  <CFINDEX COLLECTION="News" ACTION="Refresh" TYPE="Custom"
           BODY="Title,Article" KEY="ArticleID" TITLE="Title" QUERY="IndexNews">
</CFLOCK>
```

The second method is to add the new record by appending it to the end of the collection. This is simple to do using the `CFINDEX` tag and offers the advantage of a relatively quick update time. By setting the `ACTION` attribute to `Update`, ColdFusion appends the referenced record to the end of the Verity collection. The disadvantages to this technique include the possibility of duplicate entries in the collection and collection information that becomes "out of synch" with the actual information being indexed because of changes made to the database from other templates or applications. The following example illustrates the technique for appending a record to the end of a Verity collection:

```
<!--- Update the Verity collection by appending the queried record to the end
      of the collection --->
<CFQUERY NAME="IndexNews" DATASOURCE="ProgrammingCF">
    SELECT ArticleID, Title, Article FROM News
    WHERE ArticleID = #URL.ArticleID#
</CFQUERY>

<CFLOCK NAME="CFINDEX_Lock" TYPE="EXCLUSIVE" TIMEOUT="30">
  <CFINDEX COLLECTION="News" ACTION="Update" TYPE="CUSTOM" BODY="Title,Article"
           KEY="ArticleID" TITLE="Title" QUERY="IndexNews">
</CFLOCK>
```

## *Deleting Records from a Collection*

You can delete an individual record from a collection using the `CFINDEX` tag in conjunction with a `CFQUERY`. The following example demonstrates a method for deleting a single record from a Verity collection that was created from a database query:

```
<!---This query deletes the Article from the database where ArticleID equals the
     ArticleID value passed in as a URL parameter --->
<CFQUERY NAME="RemoveArticle" DATASOURCE="ProgrammingCF">
    DELETE * FROM News WHERE ArticleID = #URL.ArticleID#
</CFQUERY>

<!--- remove the reference from the verity collection --->
<CFLOCK NAME="CFINDEX_Lock" TYPE="EXCLUSIVE" TIMEOUT="30">
  <CFINDEX COLLECTION="News" ACTION="Delete" KEY="#ArticleID#">
</CFLOCK>
```

Setting the `ACTION="Delete"` for the `CFINDEX` operation tells ColdFusion that we want to delete a record from the Verity collection. The actual record is specified by setting the `KEY` attribute to the value that was stored during the indexing of the collection. In this case, we use `ArticleID` as the `KEY` value. The code can easily be modified to delete more than one record from the collection simply by modifying the `WHERE` clause in the `CFQUERY` to return more than one record.

# *Maintaining Collections*

Once you have your Verity collection up and running, you may be tempted to sit back and leave well enough alone. However, as with any collection of information, Verity collections require periodic maintenance to keep them running in top form. ColdFusion provides several tools for accomplishing these tasks.

## Optimizing Collections

Like relational databases, the contents of a Verity collection require periodic optimization for efficiency and streamlining. Because the data in a Verity collection is updated incrementally, over time the collection can become fragmented, which can result in bloated file sizes and slow search performance. Optimization compresses the data stored in a Verity collection, reducing the overall footprint of the collection and providing for more efficient searching. ColdFusion gives you two options for optimizing your Verity collections.

The first method for optimizing a Verity collection is through the ColdFusion Administrator. To optimize a Verity collection via the ColdFusion Administrator, all you need to do is highlight the desired Verity collection and click the Optimize button. A JavaScript confirmation box asks you if you are sure you want to do this. If you choose to continue, ColdFusion carries out the optimization. The optimization process can last from a few seconds to several minutes depending on the size and type of data being optimized.

The second method for optimizing a Verity collection is to do it programmatically with the `CFCOLLECTION` tag. To optimize a collection called `MyCollection` located in the default Verity collection location, you create a template containing the following:

```
<CFLOCK NAME="CFCOLLECTION_Lock" TYPE="EXCLUSIVE" TIMEOUT="30">
  <CFCOLLECTION ACTION="Optimize" COLLECTION="MyCollection">
</CFLOCK>
```

As you can see from the example, the only thing that differs in this `CFCOLLECTION` operation is that we set the `ACTION` attribute to `Optimize`. Programmatic optimization can easily be scheduled in the ColdFusion administrator for automatic and consistent results.

## Repairing Collections

Occasionally, Verity collections may become corrupt. This can happen for any number of reasons, such as an interrupted indexing or optimizing operation, and the problems are often fixable. To repair a corrupted collection using the ColdFusion Administrator, all you need to do is highlight the desired Verity collection and click the Repair button. A JavaScript confirmation box asks you if you are sure you want to do this. If you choose to continue, ColdFusion attempts to repair the collection. The repair process can last from a few seconds to several minutes depending on the size and type of the collection being repaired.

Repairs to corrupted Verity collections can also be made programmatically by setting the `ACTION` attribute of the `CFCOLLECTION` tag to `Repair`, as shown in the following example:

```
<CFLOCK NAME="CFCOLLECTION_Lock" TYPE="EXCLUSIVE" TIMEOUT="30">
  <CFCOLLECTION ACTION="REPAIR" COLLECTION="MyCollection">
</CFLOCK>
```

You should note that although ColdFusion is often able to repair a corrupted collection, it is usually better to delete a questionable collection and recreate it. Doing this ensures that the quality and integrity of the data in your Verity collection is up to par.

## *Purging Collections*

Purging a Verity collection results in the removal of all data stored within a particular collection without deleting the collection itself. This is useful when you want to clear out a collection and repopulate it without having to create the collection all over again. Purging a collection before repopulating it is the best way to ensure that the contents remain as up to date as possible.

Collections can be purged from the ColdFusion Administrator or programmatically. To purge a collection from the Cold Fusion Administrator, all you have to do is highlight the collection name and click on the Purge button. A JavaScript confirmation box will ask if you are sure you want to purge the collection. If you choose to continue, ColdFusion executes the purge.

To purge a collection from within a CFML template, you need to use the `CFINDEX` tag with the `ACTION` attribute set to `Purge`. Setting the `ACTION` attribute to `Purge` causes ColdFusion to clear all data in the specified collection without deleting. The following example illustrates using the `CFINDEX` tag to purge a collection:

```
<CFLOCK NAME="CFCOLLECTION_Lock" TYPE="EXCLUSIVE" TIMEOUT="30">
  <CFINDEX ACTION="purge" COLLECTION="MyCollection">
</CFLOCK>
```

## *Deleting Collections*

Deleting a Verity collection is a simple task and can be done from the ColdFusion Administrator or programmatically. To delete a Verity collection from inside the ColdFusion Administrator, simply highlight the collection in the Verity section and click on the Delete button. A JavaScript confirmation box will ask you to confirm the operation. If you choose to continue, the Verity collection is permanently deleted from the system.

Verity collections can also be deleted programmatically using the `CFCOLLECTION` tag. To delete a collection using `CFCOLLECTION`, you need to set the `ACTION` attribute to Delete and specify the collection name in the COLLECTION attribute like so:

```
<CFLOCK NAME="CFCOLLECTION_Lock" TYPE="EXCLUSIVE" TIMEOUT="30">
  <CFCOLLECTION ACTION="DELETE" COLLECTION="MyCollection">
</CFLOCK>
```

# Advanced Techniques

Now that you understand the basics of using the Verity search engine with ColdFusion, it is time to take a look at a couple of advanced techniques to help you get the most out of the technology. This section covers several advanced topics including how to build top-ten lists for your Internet or Intranet site, custom attributes, modifying the Verity SUMMARY attribute and searching database and document collections simultaneously.

## Creating a Top-Ten List

A cool feature that you can add to your Internet or Intranet site to help your visitors find information fast is a top-ten list. Top-ten lists are nothing more than a list of the ten most frequently searched terms on your site. The list appears as a series of links that execute a Verity search when clicked. The user need not enter a search criteria as the CFSEARCH tag is automatically populated based on the link clicked from the top-ten list.

Before you can actually start using a top-ten list on your site, you have to compile a list of the most frequently searched for terms on the site. This is a relatively easy task requiring a simple database table, a small bit of coding and time to allow users to add terms to the list.

The first step in creating a top-ten list is to create a database table to store all the search terms that users enter as search criteria in your search page. Start by creating a table in your database called Keywords. For this example, I used Microsoft Access, but feel free to use the database of your choice. In the Keywords table, create a field called SearchString and make it a text field with a maximum length of 255 characters. You may optionally create a primary key field if you wish to, though it isn't necessary. Once you have the table created, save it and exit from your database program.

The second step towards creating a top-ten list is to add a snippet of code to your search page that captures and saves the terms users enter as search criteria. Add the following snippet of code to the beginning of your search template. It is important to add it before your CFSEARCH code:

```
<CFIF IsDefined('SearchString') AND Searchstring IS NOT "">
<CFQUERY NAME="AddKeyWords" DATASOURCE="ProgrammingCF">
```

```
        INSERT INTO Keywords (SearchString)
        VALUES('#SearchString#')
    </CFQUERY>
    </CFIF>
```

The snippet works by first checking to make sure that a search string is passed from the search form and that it isn't blank. If these two conditions are met, the search string is saved to the **Keywords** table using **CFQUERY** to add the information.

Depending on how much traffic your site gets and how often users search, it may take anywhere from a few hours to a few weeks before your table contains enough keywords to make the top-ten list useable. Once you feel that you have a sufficient number of search strings in your database, you can implement the top-ten list, as shown in Example 16-11.

*Example 16-11. Creating a Top-Ten List of Commonly Used Search Terms*

```
<!--- query the keywords table in the database and use aggregate functions to
      get the n most frequently used words or phrases --->
<CFQUERY NAME="GetTopTen" DATASOURCE="ProgrammingCF" MAXROWS="10">
        SELECT SearchString, COUNT(SearchString) AS TheCount
        FROM keywords GROUP BY SearchString ORDER BY COUNT(SearchString) DESC
</CFQUERY>

<!--- Present the output to the user.  The search terms are hyperlinks that
      run the search template and automatically pass the search criteria --->
Top 10 Search terms:
<P>
<TABLE BORDER="1">
<TR>
    <TH>Search term</TH><TH>Number of times</TH>
</TR>
<CFOUTPUT QUERY="GetTopTen">
<TR>
    <TD><A HREF="Search.cfm?SearchString=#UrlEncodedFormat(SearchString)#">
        #SearchString#</A></TD>
    <TD>#TheCount#</TD>
</TR>
</CFOUTPUT>
</TABLE>
```

The first part of the template in Example 16-11 uses **CFQUERY** to select the search strings from the keywords table. **COUNT** is an aggregate function in SQL that allows us to count the number of times a particular string appears in a given field. In this case, we want to get a **COUNT** for each string in our **SearchString** field. The results are then ordered by the count from highest to lowest. Using the **MAXROWS** attribute of the **CFQUERY** tag allows us to limit the result set to the top-ten records.

The second part of the template displays the results to the browser. It takes the output of the query and displays it as an HTML table containing the search string in the left column and the number of times the string was searched in the right column.

The search string itself appears as a hyperlink. Clicking on the link results in SearchString being passed to your Verity search template via a URL parameter. Because SearchString can contain spaces, it is important to use the URLEncodedFormat() function when appending its value to the URL. This allows visitors to your site to search for the most popular terms without having to know how to spell them or having to enter them correctly in a search form.

## Custom Attributes

ColdFusion provides two additional user-defined attributes that can be populated with data during a CFINDEX operation and subsequently searched using CFSEARCH. These two attributes, CUSTOM1 and CUSTOM2 can be populated with any data you desire provided you are indexing query-based data. The value in using the CUSTOM1 and CUSTOM2 attributes comes in being able to store additional information about a particular query object that would otherwise have to be lumped in with the BODY attribute. For instance, when indexing a collection of database records, you might want to expose each record's creation date to the CFSEARCH tag so that you can search for records that were created within a certain time frame. The CUSTOM1 and CUSTOM2 attributes allow you to gain fine-grained control over your Verity searches.

### Populating the custom attributes

Populating the CUSTOM1 and CUSTOM2 attributes with data is done during a CFINDEX operation. Table 16-4 shows the sample database we described earlier in this chapter, populated with a few records.

*Table 16-4. Populating the News Table with Data*

| ArticleID | ArticleType | Title | Article | DatePosted |
|---|---|---|---|---|
| 1 | HTML | Article 1 | Body of Article 1 | 12/31/1997 |
| 2 | TEXT | Article 2 | Body of Article 2 | 06/12/1998 |
| 3 | XML | Article 3 | Body of Article 3 | 08/22/1999 |
| 4 | HTML | Article 4 | Body of Article 4 | 10/10/2000 |
| 5 | HTML | Article 5 | Body of Article 5 | 11/07/2000 |
| 6 | HTML | Article 6 | Body of Article 6 | 12/23/2000 |

In a typical CFINDEX operation, we use the ArticleID as the KEY attribute, the Title as the TITLE attribute, and the Article as the BODY attribute. This exposes the TITLE and BODY fields to searching, but what if we also want to search the collection based on ArticleType or DatePosted? Here is where the custom attributes come in. By populating `CUSTOM1` with the `ArticleType` and `CUSTOM2` with the `DatePosted`, we make both of those fields searchable in our Verity collection. Example 16-12 shows how to populate the `CUSTOM1` and `CUSTOM2` attributes based on our example database.

*Example 16-12. Populating the CUSTOM1 and CUSTOM2 Attributes*

```
<!--- Query the news table for all articles --->
<CFQUERY NAME="MyQuery" DATASOURCE="ProgrammingCF">
   SELECT ArticleID,ArticleType,Title,Article,DatePosted FROM News
</CFQUERY>

<!--- Purge and populate the Verity collection with the data from the above
      query --->
<CFLOCK NAME="CFINDEX_Lock" TYPE="EXCLUSIVE" TIMEOUT="30">
<CFINDEX ACTION="Refresh" COLLECTION="News" KEY="ArticleID" TYPE="CUSTOM"
         TITLE="Title" QUERY="MyQuery" BODY="Article" CUSTOM1="ArticleType"
         CUSTOM2="DatePosted">
</CFLOCK>

<CENTER>
  <H2>Done Indexing the Collection</H2>
</CENTER>
```

Note that it isn't necessary to use pound signs to enclose variable names inside the `CUSTOM1` and `CUSTOM2` attributes.

### *Searching the custom attributes*

Both the `CUSTOM1` and `CUSTOM2` attributes are searchable via the `CFSEARCH` tag. To reference either custom attribute in a `CFSEARCH` operation, you need to include them in the `CRITERIA` attribute. Because they are special attributes, they need to be referenced as `CF_CUSTOM1` and `CF_CUSTOM2`, respectively. Example 16-13 demonstrates the use of the `CUSTOM1` and `CUSTOM2` attributes by searching the news collection for articles that have HTML stored in the `CUSTOM1` attribute. The example outputs a table of all matching records and includes the values stored in the `CUSTOM1` and `CUSTOM2` fields in the table.

*Example 16-13. Searching the Values of CUSTOM1 and CUSTOM2*

```
<!--- Search the collection for articles that are in HTML --->
<CFSEARCH COLLECTION="News" NAME="MyQuery" TYPE="SIMPLE"
          CRITERIA="CF_Custom1=HTML" LANGUAGE="English">

<!--- Output the results --->
<TABLE>
<TR>
   <TH>Key</TH><TH>Title</TH><TH>Custom1</TH><TH>Custom2</TH>
</TR>
<CFOUTPUT QUERY="MyQuery">
<TR>
```

*Example 16-13. Searching the Values of CUSTOM1 and CUSTOM2 (continued)*

```
    <TD>#Key#</TD><TD>#Title#</TD><TD>#Custom1#</TD>
    <TD>#DateFormat(Custom2,'mm/dd/yyyy')#</TD>
</TR>
</CFOUTPUT>
</TABLE>
```

### *Extending the usefulness of custom attributes*

In case you haven't noticed, there are only two custom attributes available for you to populate with additional information. What if you have three, four, or more additional bits of information that you want to make available to your search operation? The answer lies in lists. Although you have only the `CUSTOM1` and `CUSTOM2` attributes at your disposal, you can squeeze quite a few additional pieces of information into these attributes by creating delimited lists of values and subsequently parsing them out when necessary.

Take our previous example in which we populated the `Custom1` attribute with `ArticleType` and `Custom2` with `DatePosted`. Now, suppose we add one more field to our sample database called `Status`. `Status` is a text field that contains "Public" if the article is for public viewing or "Private" if the article is for private distribution. Because there are only two `CUSTOM` attributes, if we want to put the value of `Status` as well as the values of `ArticleType` and `DatePosted` in the `CUSTOM` attributes, we are going to have to concatenate two of the fields into a list, as shown in Example 16-14.

*Example 16-14. Template for Populating a Collection and Including Custom Attributes*

```
<!--- Query the News table for all articles and create a new field called
      MultipleValues as a comma delimited concatenation of ArticleType and
      Status --->
<CFQUERY NAME="MyQuery" DATASOURCE="ProgrammingCF">
   SELECT *, ArticleType & ',' & Status AS MultipleValues FROM News
</CFQUERY>

<!--- Purge and populate the Verity collection with the data from the above
      query --->
<CFLOCK NAME="CFINDEX_Lock" TYPE="EXCLUSIVE" TIMEOUT="30">
<CFINDEX ACTION="Refresh" COLLECTION="News" KEY="ArticleID" TYPE="CUSTOM"
         TITLE="Title" QUERY="MyQuery" BODY="Article" CUSTOM1="MultipleValues"
         CUSTOM2="DatePosted">
</CFLOCK>

<CENTER>
  <H2>Done Indexing the Collection</H2>
</CENTER>
```

Example 16-14 populates the collection with data from the query. It also populates the `CUSTOM1` and `CUSTOM2` fields with the values contained in the

MultipleValues and DatePosted variables, respectively. Concatenating the ArticleType and Status fields from the database into a comma-separated list creates the MultipleValues variable.

The next template, shown in Example 16-15 searches the collection for any news article that has "HTML" as the ArticleType and "Public" as the Status. All articles matching those criteria are then displayed to the user. Although this template is being run as a standalone search that doesn't require any user input to run, you can easily build a frontend search form to allow users to enter their own search criteria.

*Example 16-15. Searching a Collection*

```
<!--- Search the collection based on the criteria that custom1 must contain
      HTML and Public --->
<CFSEARCH COLLECTION="News" NAME="MyQuery" TYPE="Explicit"
    CRITERIA="(CF_Custom1 <CONTAINS> 'HTML' AND CF_CUSTOM1 <CONTAINS> 'Public')"
    LANGUAGE="English">

<!--- Output the results --->
<TABLE>
<TR>
   <TH>Key</TH><TH>Title</TH><TH>Custom1</TH><TH>Custom2</TH>
</TR>
<CFOUTPUT QUERY="MyQuery">
<TR>
   <TD>#Key#</TD><TD>#Title#</TD><TD>#Custom1#</TD>
   <TD>#DateFormat(Custom2,'mm/dd/yyyy')#</TD>
</TR>
</CFOUTPUT>
</TABLE>
```

In Example 16-15, the CRITERIA attribute in the CFSEARCH tag contains the following line:

```
CRITERIA="(CF_Custom1 <CONTAINS> 'HTML' AND CF_CUSTOM1 <CONTAINS> 'Public')"
```

This line tells the CFSEARCH tag to look for records that contain both "HTML" and "Public" in the CUSTOM1 field.

## *Modifying the Verity Summary Attribute*

By default, the SUMMARY variable returned during a CFSEARCH of a Verity collection contains the best three sentences determined by score, up to 500 characters in length. Although this is acceptable for many applications, there are times when you might wish the summary feature behaved differently. For example, you might have a collection of files that contains a short two-sentence description followed by numerous tables of data. Chances are that the SUMMARY values returned after a search of those files may contain a useless bunch of text as the SUMMARY that is built from a sampling of all the data contained in the file. In this case, it would be much more beneficial if Verity would return the first two sentences in the document as opposed to the best three sentences.

Although there is no way to accomplish this using CFML, it is possible to modify a specific Verity configuration file named *style.prm* to achieve the desired results. By default, the *style.prm* file can be found under *c:\cfusion\verity\common\style\custom* or *c:\cfusion\verity\common\style\file* depending on the type of collection that you are attempting to modify. By changing the contents of the *style.prm* file in either of these directories, all subsequent indexing operations will take into account the modifications. If you want to modify the settings for a single collection as opposed to all collections, you need to make the changes to the *style.prm* file located in the individual collection directory: either *c:\cfusion\verity\collections\MyCollectionName\File\Style for file collections* or under *c:\cfusion\verity\collections\MyCollectionName\Custom\Style* for database collections.

Regardless of the type of collection you have indexed, you need to open the *style.prm* file for editing. Once you have the file opened, scroll to the bottom and find the block of code that matches the following:

```
# ------------------------------------------------------------------
# Document Summarization is enabled by uncommenting one of
# the DOC-SUMMARIES lines below.  The summarization data is
# stored in the documents table so that it might easily be
# shown when displaying the results of a search.
# See the discussions on Document Summarization in the
# Collection Building Guide for more information.

# The example below stores the best three sentences of
# the document, but not more than 500 bytes.
$define DOC-SUMMARIES    "XS MaxSents 3 MaxBytes 500"

# The example below stores the first four sentences of
# the document, but not more than 500 bytes.
#$define DOC-SUMMARIES    "LS MaxSents 4 MaxBytes 500"

# The example below stores the first 150 bytes of
# the document, with whitespace compressed.
#$define DOC-SUMMARIES    "LB MaxBytes 150"
```

As I stated earlier, by default, Verity is set to create a summary for each item indexed based on the best three sentences not to exceed 500 characters. That parameter can be modified by commenting out the line using a pound sign and uncommenting one of the other configurations listed in the example. Further combinations can be created by changing the values for `MaxSents` and `MaxBytes`.

## *Tweaking Verity's XML Filter*

The version of the Verity engine bundled with ColdFusion has been able to index and search XML documents for some time now. However, because XML is a completely flexible tag-based markup language that lets users define their own tags, there is no standard "Title" field returned when a search is performed against a collection containing XML documents. Fortunately, it is possible to tweak Verity's XML filter a bit to allow you to make any XML tag in a well-formed XML document populate the `CF_TITLE` or any other variable returned by the `CFSEARCH` tag.

To make Verity populate the `CF_TITLE` variable with the value of an XML tag, there are a few things you need to do. First, you need to decide what tag in your XML document you want to use to populate the `CF_TITLE` variable. For this example, let's assume your XML document (*MyXML.xml*) has a tag called `<title>` and looks something like this:

```
<?xml version="1.0"?>
 <book>
   <title>Programming ColdFusion</title>
   <author>Rob Brooks-Bilson</author>
   <publisher>O'Reilly</publisher>
 </book>
```

If you index this file, Verity is smart enough to index the content and leave out the tags, but it isn't smart enough (without a little help) to take the contents of the `<title>` tag and use it to populate the `CF_TITLE` variable. To do this, you need to create a special text file called *style.xml* and save it in your style directory: either *c:\cfusion\verity\common\style\file* for all file-based collections or *c:\cfusion\verity\collections\MyCollectionName\File\Style* where `MyCollectionName` is the name of the Verity collection containing the index for your XML files. The *style.xml* file should look like this:

```
## Place this in a file called style.xml in your style directory:
<field xmltag = "title" fieldname = "CF_TITLE" index = "override"/>
```

The file tells Verity to index the contents of XML tags named `<title>` and place the contents in the ColdFusion variable CF_TITLE, overriding the default value that is supposed to go there (in the case of XML, nothing goes there by default). Using this syntax, it is very easy to change both the XML tag that Verity indexes as well as the ColdFusion variable it places the content in. It is important to note that you must use an existing ColdFusion return variable for `CFSEARCH`. In other words, you can't go and make up your own variables; ColdFusion won't recognize them.

Once you save the file, you need to stop and restart your ColdFusion server and reindex your collection in order for the changes to take effect. The newly indexed collection should now return the title field from an XML document in the `CF_TITLE` variable.

## Searching Database and Document Collections Simultaneously

Chances are, sooner or later you are going to run into a situation where you want to search the contents of both a database collection and a document collection. A common scenario involves a web site that contains dynamic pages as well as static files. On the surface, it appears as though ColdFusion and the Verity engine won't provide a way to index both types of information in a single operation. The truth is, there is an easy way to get around this apparent problem using a little creative programming.

The first step in creating an interface capable of searching both database and document collections simultaneously is to create a separate collection for each group of data to be searched. That is, you need to create one collection for your database information and another collection for your documents. Example 16-16 shows how to do this in a single template. The example uses the same database used in previous examples, and assumes that you have already created two collections, `Database` and `Documents`, using the techniques described earlier.

*Example 16-16. Indexing a Database Query and a Group of Documents at the Same Time*

```
<!--- Query the news table for all articles --->
<CFQUERY NAME="IndexArticle" DATASOURCE="ProgrammingCF">
        SELECT ArticleID,Title,Article FROM News
</CFQUERY>

<!--- Populate the database collection from the indexarticle query --->
<CFLOCK NAME="CFINDEX_Database_Lock" TYPE="EXCLUSIVE" TIMEOUT="30">
<CFINDEX COLLECTION="Database" ACTION="refresh" TYPE="CUSTOM"
        BODY="Title,Article" KEY="ArticleID" TITLE="Title" QUERY="IndexArticle">
</CFLOCK>

<!--- Populate the documents collection --->
<CFLOCK NAME="CFINDEX_Documents_Lock" TYPE="EXCLUSIVE" TIMEOUT="30">
<CFINDEX ACTION="refresh" COLLECTION="Documents"
        KEY="D:\inetsrv\examples\16\dual\" TYPE="path"
        URLPATH="http://127.0.0.1/examples/16/dual"
        EXTENSIONS=".htm, .html, .doc, .pdf" RECURSE="no">
</CFLOCK>

<CENTER>
  <H2>Finished Indexing the Collections</H2>
</CENTER>
```

Once you have created and populated the collections, you need to build a search interface that can search through both collections at the same time. The trick here is to conditionally output different results to the user depending on which collection each match comes from. Example 16-17 and Example 16-18 show the technique for searching database and document collections simultaneously.

*Example 16-17. Searching Database and Document Collections Simultaneously*

```
<FORM ACTION="searchdual.cfm" METHOD="post">

<TABLE BORDER="0" CELLPADDING="3">

<TR>
  <TD>Search for:</TD>
  <TD>
    <INPUT TYPE="Text" NAME="SearchFor" SIZE="31" MAXLENGTH="255">
  </TD>
</TR>

<TR>
  <TD COLSPAN="2" ALIGN="center">
    <INPUT TYPE="Submit" NAME="Submit" VALUE="Search">
  </TD>
</TR>
</TABLE>
</FORM>
```

Example 16-17 creates a basic search form for passing a search string to the template in Example 16-18. The search performed in Example 16-18 differs from all of the other searches we have performed so far in that it searches both a database collection and a document collection at the same time. This is accomplished by specifying both Verity collections to be searched in the COLLECTION attribute of the CFSEARCH tag.

*Example 16-18. Simultaneous Search of a Database and a Document Collection*

```
<!--- If no search criteria is passed, assume user wants all records in the
collection, so assign a wildcard (*) to the search criteria --->
<CFIF Form.SearchFor IS "">
  <CFSET Form.SearchFor = "*">
</CFIF>

<!--- search the collections --->
<CFSEARCH NAME="test1" COLLECTION="database,documents" TYPE="SIMPLE"
          CRITERIA="#form.searchfor#">

<--- IF NO RECORDS MATCH, ABORT PROCESSING --->
<CFIF Test1.RecordCount IS 0>
  No records found matching your search criteria.
  <CFABORT>
</CFIF>
```

*Example 16-18. Simultaneous Search of a Database and a Document Collection (continued)*

```
<!--- Output matches to the user --->
<CFOUTPUT>
  #Test1.RecordCount# records found out of #test1.RecordsSearched# records
  searched.
</CFOUTPUT>

<P>
<TABLE BORDER="0" WIDTH="500">
<TR>
  <TH>Title</TH><TH>Score</TH>
</TR>

<CFOUTPUT QUERY="test1">
<TR>
  <TD><CFIF IsNumric(KEY)>
        <A HREF="Showrecord.cfm?ID=#Key#">#Title#</A>
      <CFELSE>
        <A HREF="#URL#">#Title#</A>
      </CFIF>
      <BR>
      #Summary#
  </TD>
  <TD>
    <CFIF Score IS NOT "">
      #Evaluate(Score * 100)#%
    </CFIF>
  </TD>
</TR>
</CFOUTPUT>
</TABLE>
```

As you can see, the technique used for searching both types of collections at the same time is fairly straightforward. Example 16-18 uses conditional logic to determine if the value of the **KEY** attribute is numeric or not. If the value of **KEY** is numeric, the template knows that the record comes from a database collection because the value of **KEY** in the database collection is always a number. If the value of **KEY** isn't numeric, the template knows that they record comes from the document collection. The value of **KEY** in the document collection is always the path to the file on the server.

*In this chapter:*
- *Regular-Expression Syntax*
- *Finding Strings*
- *Replacing Strings*
- *Back References*
- *Useful Regular Expressions*
- *Input Considerations*
- *Regular Expression Builder*

# 17
# *Regular Expressions in ColdFusion*

Anyone who has ever worked with regular expressions knows what an indispensable tool they can be for parsing and manipulating text. Without them, text-processing operations such as search and replace can be very difficult to say the least. Those with experience in Unix-based languages such as Perl, awk, or Tcl are probably already familiar with regular expressions as they are used extensively in those languages. For those new to the world of regular expressions, don't worry. This chapter shows you everything you need to know to start using regular expressions in your ColdFusion applications.

ColdFusion provides you with two sets of ColdFusion functions for finding and replacing strings. `REFind()` and `REFindNoCase()` search for strings within blocks of text, while `REReplace()` and `REReplaceNoCase()` perform search and replace operations. Both sets of functions are extremely powerful and allow you to add a whole host of useful text-manipulation features to your ColdFusion applications.

Before we get into the mechanics of regular expressions, it is important for you to gain a basic understanding of the regular expression language and how it is used by ColdFusion.

## *Regular-Expression Syntax*

In their most basic form, regular expressions match characters on a one-for-one basis. Thus, you can match the first occurrence of the letter "a" in a search string as follows:

```
REFind("abcdefg", "a")
```

Likewise, you can search for the letters "can" in succession with:

```
REFind("Watch the candle burn", "can")
```

Using “can” as your regular expression matches “can,” “candle,” and “scan.” Regular expressions that look for individual characters in this manor are said to be single-character regular expressions.

Single-character regular expressions are great when you know the exact series of characters that you want to match. But, what if you don't know? What if you need to find and remove all the HTML tags in a particular block of text? You certainly don't want to have to code a regular expression for every single HTML tag. What you can do is use what is known as a multicharacter regular expression. Multicharacter regular expressions use special characters (covered in a moment) to define ranges of characters to be matched. The following example takes the contents of a form variable (`Form.MyString`) and removes all HTML from it:

```
<CFSET NoHTML = REReplace(Form.MyString, "<[^>]*>", "", "All")>
```

At first glance, the regular expression looks like a string of unrelated and meaningless characters. If you take the regular expression and break it down, it is easier to see what is happening. In this case, the first part of the expression “<” matches the open angle bracket used to denote the beginning of an HTML tag. Adding “[^>]*” after the open angle bracket tells ColdFusion to match zero or more occurrences of any character other than the closed angle bracket “>”. The square brackets denote a range of characters. In this case, they are used in conjunction with the carat followed by the closed angle bracket. This tells ColdFusion to exclude the closed angle bracket from the match criteria. The asterisk tells ColdFusion to match zero or more occurrences of the expression contained inside the square angle brackets. The final part of the regular expression matches the closing angle bracket of an HTML tag.

## Special Characters

There are several “special” characters in the regular-expression language. These special characters perform functions within the regular-expression language and therefore must be escaped if you wish to search for them as literals. The following is a list of the special characters along with their functions:

*Dollar sign* ($)

: The dollar sign matches a newline character within a given string or anchors a regular expression to the end of a string. For example, searching for “[abc$]” matches the first occurrence of “abc” followed by a new line character. Likewise, searching for “[abc]$” matches the first occurrence of “abc” when it is at the end of a string. In order for the dollar sign to work within a set, it must be used as the last character in the set or range of characters.

*Carat* (^)

The carat excludes characters from being matched or to anchor a regular expression to the beginning of a string. Searching for "[^abc]" matches any characters in a string except for "a", "b", and "c". Similarly, searching for "[^0-9]" matches any characters in a string except for numbers. Searching for "^[abc]" matches only "abc" when it appears at the beginning of a string. In order for the carat to work within a set, it must be used as the first character in the set or range of characters.

*Question mark* (?)

The question mark signifies zero or one matches of a regular expression within a given string. For example, searching for "ab?c" matches "ac" as well as "abc". Likewise, searching for "[ab]?c" matches "c" as well as "abc". Using the question mark in your regular expressions essentially makes the expression optional.

*Asterisk* (*)

The asterisk is used to signify zero or more matches of a regular expression within a given string. For example, searching for "[a-z]*" matches zero or more lowercase characters in a string. Like the question mark, the asterisk effectively makes the expression optional.

*Plus* (+)

The plus sign signifies one or more matches of a regular expression within a given string. For example, searching for "[a-z]+" matches one or more lowercase characters in a string.

*Parentheses* ( ( ) )

Parentheses group segments of regular expressions together. These groups are known as subexpressions. Grouping subexpressions extends the capabilities of regular expressions by allowing you to apply special characters to the subexpressions as opposed to single characters. For example, searching for "(ab)+" matches one or more occurrences of "ab" within a string. Using parentheses to create subexpressions also enables you to take advantage of back referencing, which is covered later on in the chapter.

*Curly braces* ( { } )

Curly braces specify the number of times, as a range, that a regular expression should be matched within a string. The use of curly braces follows the syntax {m,n} where m is an integer greater than or equal to zero that specifies the start of the range, and n is a positive integer greater than or equal to m that specifies the end of the range. For example, searching for "(ab){1,4}" matches from one to four occurrences of "ab".

*Open square bracket* ([)

The open square bracket is used in conjunction with the closed square bracket (not a special character) to define a set of characters to be matched. For example, searching for "[abc]" matches any "a", "b", or "c" in a string. A hyphen (-) can also be used in conjunction with the square brackets to signify a range of characters to be matched such that searching for "[a-z]" matches any lowercase letter.

*Pipe* (|)

The pipe represents a logical OR such that searching for "tra(in|iner)" matches both "train" or "trainer".

*Backslash* (\)

A backslash escapes special characters so they can be searched as literal characters. For example, "\+12" finds the string "+12". To search for the backslash character, it must also be escaped. For example, "c:\\" finds the string "c:\".

*Period* (.)

A period matches any single character. For example, ".am" matches both "cam" and "ham".

To escape any special character, simply place a backslash (\) before the character. When a regular expression encounters an escaped special character, it is treated as a literal search value.

## POSIX Character Classes

Rather than having to use multicharacter classes such as "[A-Za-z]" in your regular expressions, ColdFusion allows you to use Portable Operating System Interface (POSIX) character classes to make coding and reading your regular expressions easier. POSIX character classes are referenced within ColdFusion regular expressions by enclosing them inside two sets of square brackets as in the following example.

```
<CFSET NewFilename = REReplace("My Filename.doc","[[:space:]]","_","ALL")>
```

This example replaces all spaces in the filename with underscores and creates a variable called `NewFilename` that contains "My_Filename.doc". Here's another example:

```
<CFSET NewString = REReplace("T8h3i53s 8a3 t3e2s9t.", "[[:digit:]]", "", "ALL")>
```

This example takes the string "T8h3i53s 8a3 t3e2s9t." and replaces all digits with a blank. The result is the string "This is a test."

The following POSIX character classes are supported by ColdFusion:

`alpha`
: Matches any letter regardless of the case used. Using `alpha` is the same as specifying "[A-Za-z]".

`alnum`
: Matches any letter or number regardless of the case used. Using `alnum` is the same as specifying "[A-Za-z0-9]".

`cntrl`
: Matches any character that isn't included in any of the other POSIX character classes (`alpha`, `alnum`, `digit`, `graph`, `lower`, `print`, `punct`, `space`, `upper`, `xdigit`).

`digit`
: Matches any digit. Using `digit` is the same as specifying "[0-9]".

`graph`
: Matches any printable character except for those listed in the `space` control set (carriage return, formfeed, newline, space, tab, or vertical tab).

`lower`
: Matches any lowercase letter. Using `lower` is the same as specifying "[a-z]".

`print`
: Matches any printable character.

`punct`
: Matches any punctuation character in the following set: ! ` # $ % & ` ( ) * + , - . / : ; < = > ? @ [ / ] ^ _ { | } ~

`space`
: Matches any carriage return, formfeed, newline, space, tab, or vertical tab.

`upper`
: Matches any uppercase letter. Using `upper` is the same as specifying "[A-Z]".

`xdigit`
: Matches any hexadecimal digit. Using `xdigit` is the same as specifying "[0-9A-Fa-f]".

# *Finding Strings*

To find a string in a block of text, you use the `REFind()` or `REFindNoCase()` functions. `REFind()` and `REFindNoCase()` are used when you want to know the position of the expression being searched for within a string. `REFind()` performs a case-insensitive search; **REFindNoCase()** performs a case-sensitive search. Regardless of the function used, they both use the same syntax:

```
REFind(RegularExpression, String [, StartPosition] [, ReturnSubExpressions])
REFindNoCase(RegularExpression, String [, StartPosition] [, ReturnSubExpressions])
```

Both the **REFind()** and **REFindNoCase()** functions accept the same parameters. The following example finds the first occurrence of "tom" regardless of case:

```
<CFSET MyString="This is a red tomato.">
<CFSET ThePosition= REFindNoCase("tom", MyString)>

<CFOUTPUT>
The Position:  #ThePosition#
</CFOUTPUT>
```

In this example, we use **REFindNoCase()** to find the starting position of "tom" within the string "This is a red tomato". This is done by assigning the result of the regular expression to a variable—in this case, **ThePosition**. The actual regular expression is embedded within the **REFindNoCase()** function. In it's basic form, **REFindNoCase()** accepts two parameters, the regular expression and the string. In this example, the regular expression is simply the three characters "tom", and the string is "This is a red tomato". Upon execution, the value returned for **ThePositon** should be 15 as the first occurrence of "tom" begins at position 15 of the string.

Now that you see how the **REFindNoCase()** function is used, let's take a look at another example that uses **REFind()** to perform a case-sensitive search. This code finds the first case-sensitive occurrence of "Tom":

```
<CFSET MyString="This is Tom's red tomato.">
<CFSET ThePosition= ReFind("Tom", MyString)>

<CFOUTPUT>
The Position:  #ThePosition#
</CFOUTPUT>
```

The syntax for **REFind()** is the same as that for **REFindNoCase()**. The only difference between the two tags is **REFind()** is case-sensitive. This time, the value of **ThePosition** is 9 as that is the position at which "Tom" first occurs in **MyString**. If we modify the example a bit so that the regular expression is "tom" instead of "Tom", **ThePosition** returns 19 as the first case-sensitive occurrence of "tom" is found at position 19 (the "tom" in "tomato").

Now that you've seen the mechanics of both tags, let's take a look at some additional examples that utilize the **REFind()** and **REFindNoCase()** tags:

- Find the first occurrence of the letter "a" in the string:

  ```
  ReFind("a", "zzxxyaabbccdd")
  ```

  Returns 6 as the first occurrence of "a" is in the sixth position of the string.

- Use a case-sensitive search to find the first occurrence of any character followed by "ar":

  ```
  ReFind(".ar", "There are a lot of aardvarks around here.")
  ```

  Returns 6 because the first occurrence of any character followed by the letters "ar" is in the sixth position of the string where a space precedes the word "are."

- Find the first case-sensitive occurrence of one or more "a" followed by one or more "b":

  ```
  ReFind("a+b+", "zzxxyaabbccdd")
  ```

  Returns 6 as "aabb" starts in the sixth position of the string.

- Find the first letter regardless of case:

  ```
  ReFind("[A-Za-z]", "1234567890asdfghjkl")
  ```

  Returns 11 as the first letter, "a", occurs in the eleventh position of the string.

- Find the first case-sensitive occurrence of "a" followed by one or more lowercase letters:

  ```
  ReFind("a[a-z]+", "Is there a doctor around here?")
  ```

  Returns 19 because the word "around," which begins in the nineteenth position, is the first occurrence of the letter "a" followed by one or more occurrences of another lowercase letter.

- Find the first occurrence of "to," "two," or "too," regardless of case:

  ```
  ReFindNoCase("(to|two|too)", "She said that he likes to rock climb.")
  ```

  Returns 24 because the word "to" occurs in the twenty-fourth position of the string.

- Find the first character in the string, regardless of case, that isn't a number:

  ```
  ReFindNoCase("[^0-9]", "50 miles to the beach!")
  ```

  Returns 3 because the first non-number (a space) is encountered at the third position of the string.

Both the **REFind()** and **REFindNoCase()** functions can accept two optional parameters besides the regular expression and the string. The first optional parameter allows you to specify a start position for the regular expression to begin its evaluation of the string. For example, to search the string "This cat is fat" for the first occurrence of "is" beginning at the fifth position, your regular expression would look like this:

```
<CFSET ThePosition = ReFindNoCase("is", "This cat is fat", 5)>
```

In this case, the value returned for ThePosition is 10. What happens here is the regular expression begins searching for the first occurrence of "is" at the fifth position in the string, which happens to be the blank space after "This" in our example.

The second optional parameter available to the REFind() and REFindNoCase() functions allows you to specify whether or not to return matched subexpressions if any are found during the search. This means that if a match for your regular expression is found, ColdFusion returns a structure containing the position of the first occurrence of the match as well as its length in characters. These values are stored in the keys Pos and Len, respectively. Here is an example to help illustrate the point:

```
<CFSET MyString="This cat is a fat cat">
<CFSET matches= ReFind("cat", MyString, 1, "TRUE")>

<CFOUTPUT>
<B>String:</B>  #MyString#<BR>
<B>Regex:</B>  Refind(&quot;cat&quot;, MyString, 1, &quot;TRUE&quot;)<BR>
<B>Position:</B> #matches.pos[1]#<BR>
<B>Length:</B> #matches.len[1]#
</CFOUTPUT>
```

This example uses the REFind() function to perform a case-sensitive search for "cat" in the string "This cat is a fat cat". The search begins at the first position in the string. Setting the optional ReturnSubExpressions parameter to TRUE causes the value of Matches to be returned as a structure containing the keys Pos and Len. The values contained in the structure are output by referencing them within a CFOUTPUT section. In this example, the values output for Pos[1] and Len[1] are 6 and 3, respectively.

## Replacing Strings

String replacement is performed with the REReplace() and REReplaceNoCase() functions. REReplace() performs case-sensitive search and replace functions, while REReplaceNoCase() is used for case-insensitive search and replace. Regardless of which tag you use, they have the same syntax:

```
REReplace(String, RegularExpression, Substring [, Scope])
REReplaceNoCase(String, RegularExpression, Substring [, Scope])
```

Both functions take three required parameters and one optional parameter. The first required parameter is the string to perform the regular expression on. The string can be either block of text enclosed in single or double quotes or a variable that contains the text that you want to search. The second required parameter is the regular expression you want to use for your search. Any valid ColdFusion regular expression can be used. The third required parameter is the substring. The substring contains the string to replace any matches made by the regular expression. The final parameter is optional and determines the scope of the search and replace operation. The scope can either be set to `ONE` or `ALL`. Setting the scope to `ONE` replaces only the first occurrence of the substring. Setting the scope to `ALL` (the default) replaces all occurrences of the substring. The following two examples show the use of the `ReReplace()` and `ReReplaceNoCase()` functions:

- Replace all occurrences of the number "7" with the word "seven":

```
REReplace("There are 7 words in this string.", "7", "Seven", "ALL")
```

- Replace all numbers with an asterisk character:

```
REReplace("My Social Security number is 999-99-9999.", "[0-9]", "*", "All")
```

# *Back References*

Back references allow your regular expressions to refer to previously matched subexpressions. This is useful in situations where you want your regular expression to use a match as part of the criteria for an additional regular-expression function. A commonly used scenario to illustrate back referencing involves using a regular expression to remove doubled words within a sentence. For example, suppose you have the string "I would like to go to to the park." The word "to" appears twice in a row—a common typing mistake. The regular expression to remove any doubled words from the sentence looks like this:

```
<CFSET NoDupes = ReReplaceNoCase("I would like to go to to the park.",
"([A-Z]+)[ ]+\1", "\1", "All")>
```

Let's break this example down so that we can get a better understanding of what is going on. We use the `REReplaceNoCase()` function to perform the search and replace without regard to case. The first parameter of the function is the string we want to perform the search and replace on. The second parameter is the actual regular expression. The "([A-Z]+)" tells ColdFusion to look for any word. Notice that this part of the regular expression is enclosed in parentheses, making it a subexpression. The next part of the regular expression "[ ]+" tells ColdFusion to look for one or more spaces. The third part of the regular expression, `\1`, is the back reference and tells ColdFusion to refer back to the first subexpression and use it as part of the search criteria. In this case, the regular expression is looking for any word followed by a space followed by the word from the first subexpression. The third parameter is the substring to replace the match made by the regular expression. Using `\1` as the substring tells ColdFusion to replace any doubled words with the corresponding subexpression. Using ALL as the fourth parameter tells ColdFusion to apply the search and replace to all repeated words in the string.*

Let's take a look at another example of back-referencing:

```
<CFSET NewString = REReplaceNoCase("<!-- This is a comment -->",
"<!--([[:print:]]*) -->", "<!--- \1 --->", "ALL")>
```

In this case, we use the REReplaceNoCase() function to search for the opening of an HTML comment tag, followed by any number of printable characters, followed by a closing HTML comment tag. Any matches are replaced by the opening of a ColdFusion comment tag, followed by the text matched by the first parenthesized subexpression (in this case "This is a comment"), followed by a closing ColdFusion comment tag. The \1 allows us to refer to all the text matched between the <!-- and --> tags.

In the previous examples, we used a single parenthesized subexpression along with a matching back reference to find and refer back to a particular string. If your regular expression contains more than one parenthesized subexpression, you can back-reference the additional subexpressions by referring to them as \2, \3, etc. To determine the numbering for your parenthesized subexpressions, simply number them from left to right across your regular expression.

It is important to note that back references can only refer back to parenthesized subexpressions. Attempting to refer to subexpressions not enclosed by parenthesis results in an error.

## Useful Regular Expressions

Now that you have a better idea of how regular expressions work, let's take a look at how you can actually use them in your own ColdFusion applications. Here are some regular expressions that perform common search-and-replace tasks:

- Replace all characters in a string that aren't numbers, letters, or underscores with an underscore:

  ```
  <CFSET NewString = REReplaceNoCase(MyString, "[^0-9A-Z_]", "_", "All")>
  ```

- Replace all spaces in a filename with the underscore character; useful in situations where you allow users to upload files to your ColdFusion server via their web browsers:

  ```
  <CFSET NewFilename = REReplace(MyFileName, "( )", "_", "ALL")>
  ```

* There is currently a bug in ColdFusion's regular-expression engine that causes the example we just covered to fail in certain instances. If you change the search string to "I want to go to to the park.", ColdFusion incorrectly parses the string and returns "I wanto go to the park."

- Return the full directory name from a string containing a full path including filename:

```
<CFSET TheDirectory =
  REReplaceNoCase(MyPath, "[A-Z0-9_]+\.[A-Z0-9_]+", "All")>
```

- Return the filename from a string containing a full path including filename:

```
<CFSET TheFileName =
  REReplaceNoCase(MyPath, "([A-Z]:\\)|[A-Z0-9_]+\\+", "", "All")>
```

- Remove all doubled words in a string:

```
<CFSET NoRepeates = REReplaceNoCase(MyString, "([A-Z]+)[ ]+\1","\1","All")>
```

- Strip all HTML tags from a string; useful for removing HTML from form-field submissions:

```
<CFSET NoHTML = REReplace(MyString, "<[^>]*>", "", "All")>
```

- Remove all HTML from links in a string, leaving just the URL:

```
<CFSET NoHTMLLinks =
  REReplaceNoCase(MyString, "<a *href[^>]+>([^(</a>)]*)</a>","\1",'All')>
```

- Format all email addresses in a string as HTML mailto links:

```
<CFSET MailtoLinks = REReplace(MyString,
  "([[:alnum:]_\.\-]+@([[:alnum:]_\.\-]+\.)+[[:alpha:]]{2,4})",
  "<A HREF=""mailto:\1"">\1</A>", "ALL")>
```

- Remove all ASCII character codes such as " and • and so on:

```
<CFSET NoASCIICodes = REReplace(MyString, "&(##[[:digit:]]+|[[:alpha:]]+);",
"", "ALL")>
```

- Escape all special characters in the Verity search language:

```
<CFSET EscapedSearchString =
  REReplace(SearchString, '([]<>\\@\`\,\(\)"\{}\[])',"\\1", "All")>
```

# *Input Considerations*

Because of a peculiarity in ColdFusion's implementation of regular expressions, certain regular expressions may cause a "Bad regular expression" error when applied to certain strings longer than 20,000 characters. If your application deals with strings longer than 20,000 characters, you should break the string into several smaller pieces, each 20,000 characters or less to avoid the possibility of encountering this behavior. In cases where you don't know or can't limit the maximum string length ahead of time, this is especially important. Example 17-1 shows one way to handle this dynamically, regardless of the string length.

*Example 17-1. Dynamically Handling Large Strings*

```
<CFSET Cutoff = 20000>
<CFSET Start = 1>
<CFSET Output = "">
```

*Example 17-1. Dynamically Handling Large Strings (continued)*

```
<CFLOCK NAME="FileLock" TYPE="ReadOnly" TIMEOUT="30">
  <CFFILE ACTION="Read" FILE="c:\test_in.txt" VARIABLE="Input">
</CFLOCK>

<!--- if the string is greater than the cutoff length, break it up and apply
      the regular expression to each chunk.  Then, create a new string by
      combining all of the chunks. --->
<CFIF Len(Input) GT Cutoff>
  <CFLOOP INDEX="i" FROM="1" TO="#Ceiling(Len(Input)/Cutoff)#">
    <CFSET Finish = (Cutoff + Start)-1>
    <CFIF Finish GT Len(Input)>
        <CFSET Cutoff = (Len(Input)-Start)+1>
    </CFIF>
    <CFSET temp = Mid(Input, Start, Cutoff)>
    <CFSET "Part#i#" = ReReplace(temp, "<[^>]*>", "", "All")>
    <CFSET Output = Output & Evaluate("Part#i#")>
    <CFSET Start = Finish+1>
  </CFLOOP>
<CFELSE>
  <CFSET Output = ReReplaceNoCase(Input, "<[^>]*>", "", "All")>
</CFIF>

<CFLOCK NAME="FileLock" TYPE="Exclusive" TIMEOUT="30">
  <CFFILE ACTION="WRITE" FILE="c:\test_out.txt" OUTPUT="#Output#" ADDNEWLINE="No">
</CFLOCK>

Finished...
```

In this example, a text file is read in using the `CFFILE` tag, and the contents assigned to a variable named Input. Next, the length of `Input` is evaluated. If it is greater than the `Cutoff` value we assigned (20,000 characters), a loop is used to break the input up into smaller pieces equal to or under 20,000 characters each. Then, the regular expression is used on each of the smaller pieces, avoiding the error that can result from parsing too large a string. In this example, the regular expression strips any HTML in the file. At the end of each iteration of the loop, the parsed string is added to a variable called `Output`. When the last iteration of the loop completes, `Output` contains the completely parsed and reassembled input string. If the value of `Input` is less than the value of `Cutoff` (20,000 characters), we know that the string length poses no issues, so our regular expression is applied directly to the string.

Once we have our finalized `Output` string, it is written out to a file called *test_out.txt*. This example can just as easily be modified to use any regular expression. You could also use an existing string as opposed to a file as your input source. The important point is that the length of the input string be limited to 20,000 characters or less.

# *Regular Expression Builder*

Writing a regular expression is usually a trial-and-error process. The process typically goes something like this:

1. Create a ColdFusion template that contains a string as well as a regular expression to perform the task you want.
2. Save the ColdFusion template.
3. Open your web browser, point it to the ColdFusion template, and see if the regular expression behaves as intended.
4. If the regular expression is successful, great! If not, you have to then modify the regular expression in the template and repeat Steps 2 through 4.

Some regular expressions are simple and can be worked out relatively quickly. Others, however, are more complicated and require you to repeat the trial-and-error process over and over. Constantly having to switch from the browser to the development environment can be a real pain.

With this in mind, let's look at a ColdFusion-based solution for building regular expressions. The template in Example 17-2, called *EvaluatorForm.cfm*, creates a form for collecting information about the regular expression you want to test.

*Example 17-2. Regular Expression Builder Input Screen*

```
<CENTER>
   <H2>Regular Expression Builder</H2>
</CENTER>

<FORM ACTION="Evaluator.cfm" METHOD="POST">
<TABLE>
<TR>
   <TD>String</TD>
   <TD><TEXTAREA NAME="MyString" COLS="50" ROWS="3"></TEXTAREA></TD>
</TR>
<TR>
   <TD>Operation</TD>
   <TD><SELECT NAME="Operation">
       <OPTION VALUE="ReReplace">ReReplace</OPTION>
       <OPTION VALUE="ReReplaceNoCase">ReReplaceNoCase</OPTION>
        </SELECT>
   </TD>
<TR>
   <TD>Regex</TD>
   <TD><INPUT TYPE="Text" NAME="MyRegex" SIZE="52" MAXLENGTH="255"></TD>
</TR>
<TR>
   <TD>Substring</TD>
   <TD><INPUT TYPE="Text" NAME="MySubstring" SIZE="52" MAXLENGTH="255"></TD>
```

*Example 17-2. Regular Expression Builder Input Screen (continued)*

```
</TR>
<TR>
   <TD>Scope</TD>
   <TD><SELECT NAME="MyScope">
       <OPTION VALUE="One">One</OPTION>
       <OPTION VALUE="All">All</OPTION>
       </SELECT>
   </TD>
</TR>
<TR>
   <TD COLSPAN="2"><INPUT TYPE="Submit" NAME="Submit" VALUE="Submit"></TD>
</TR>
</TABLE>
</FORM>
```

The template in Example 17-2 creates the user interface for the regular expression builder and can be seen in Figure 17-1. The program uses an HTML form to allow the user to enter a string to perform the regular expression on. The template also contains a text box for entering a subexpression as well as the regular expression to test out. Finally, a drop-down box is used to select the SCOPE attribute for the regular expression.

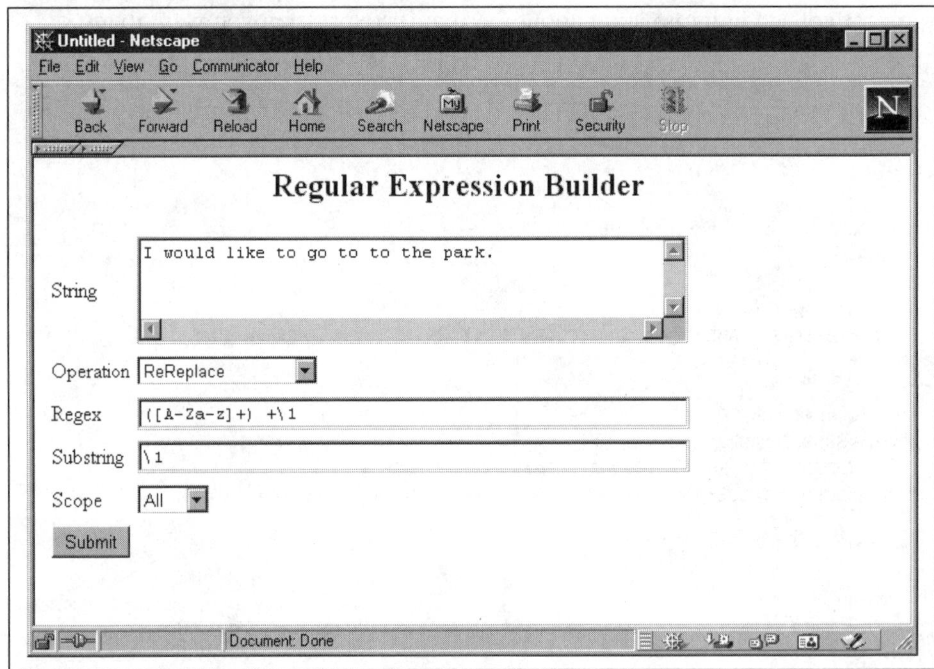


*Figure 17-1. Regular Expression Builder wizard*

Upon submission, the data entered in the form is passed to the *Evaluator.cfm* template shown in Example 17-3. The template takes the parameters from the form in Example 17-2 and uses them to evaluate the regular expression. The resulting output can be seen in Figure 17-2.

*Example 17-3. Regular Expression Builder Result Screen*

```
<!--- determine if replace operation is to be case-sensitive or case-insensitive
      and evaluate the regular expression accordingly --->
<CFIF Form.Operation IS "REReplace">
   <CFSET MyOutput= ReReplace(Form.MyString, Form.MyRegex, Form.MySubString,
    Form.MyScope)>
<CFELSE>
   <CFSET MyOutput= REReplaceNoCase(Form.MyString, Form.MyRegex,
    Form.MySubString, MyScope)>
</CFIF>

<CENTER>
   <H2>Regular Expression Builder - Results</H2>
</CENTER>

<CFOUTPUT>
<FORM METHOD="post" ACTION="EvaluatorForm.cfm">
<TABLE WIDTH="600">
<TR>
   <TD><B>Original string:</B></TD>
</TR>
<TR>
   <TD>#Form.MyString#</TD>
</TR>
<TR>
   <TD> </TD>
</TR>
<TR>
   <TD><B>After Regex:</B></TD>
</TR>
<TR>
   <TD>#MyOutput#</TD>
</TR>
<TR>
   <TD> </TD>
</TR>
<TR>
   <TD><B>Your Regex:</B></TD>
</TR>
<TR>
   <TD><TEXTAREA NAME="Text" COLS="75" ROWS="3" WRAP="Virtual">
       #Form.Operation#("#Form.MyString#", "#Form.MyRegex#",
       "#Form.MySubstring#", "#Form.MyScope#")</TEXTAREA>
   </TD>
</TR>
<TR>
   <TD><INPUT TYPE="Button" NAME="Modify" VALUE="Modify Regex"
```

*Example 17-3. Regular Expression Builder Result Screen (continued)*

```
        onClick="history.go(-1)">
      <INPUT TYPE="Submit" NAME="TryAgain" VALUE="Try Another Regex">
   </TD>
</TR>
</TABLE>
</FORM>
</CFOUTPUT>
```

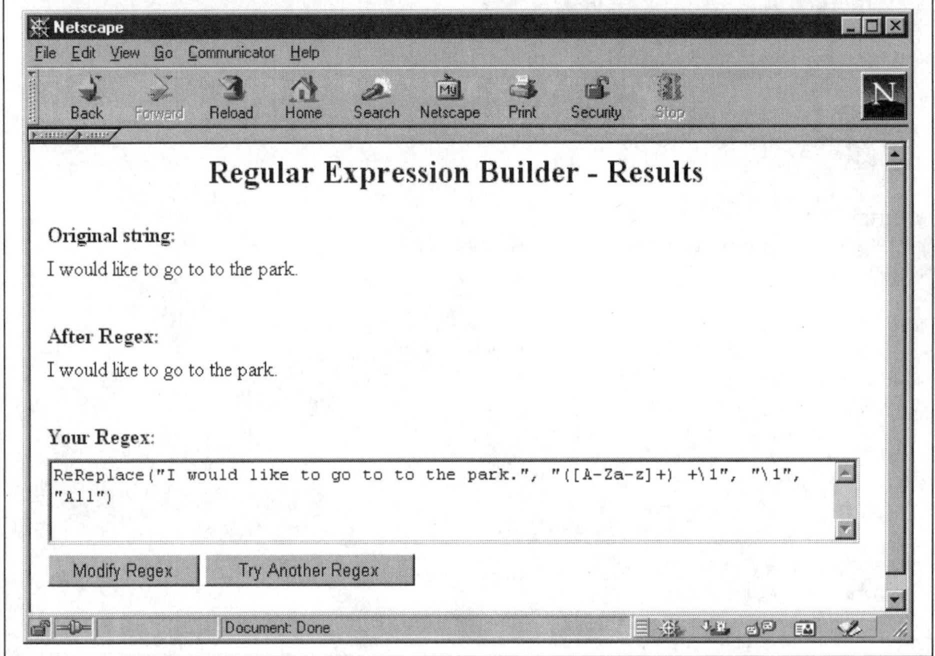


*Figure 17-2. Regular Expression Builder result screen*

The first part of the template uses `CFIF` statements to determine whether the replace operation should be case-sensitive or -insensitive. It then performs the replace operation using the parameters passed from the data-entry form and stores the results in a variable called `MyOutput`. The template finishes by outputting the string both before and after the regular expression. The regular expression is also presented in a text box so that it can be cut and pasted into your application.

*In this chapter:*
- *Scripting Syntax*
- *Writing Output*
- *CFScript Statements*
- *User-Defined Functions*

# 18

# *Scripting*

When Allaire released ColdFusion 4.0, they introduced a new server-side scripting language called CFScript. CFScript is similar in appearance to JavaScript and allows you to write sections of code in your templates using a more concise format than tag-based CFML. CFScript isn't meant to replace the CFML language; it just provides you with a choice for coding your pages. Additionally, with the introduction of ColdFusion 5.0, CFScript includes the ability to create user-defined functions. Those used to programming in JavaScript will find the CFScript constructs quite familiar.

This chapter covers everything you need to know about the CFScript language, along with examples.

## *Scripting Syntax*

The `<CFSCRIPT>` and `</CFSCRIPT>` tags are at the heart of the CFScript language. All CFScripting in a template takes place between these tags. There are a few general guidelines that will help you write your CFScripts:

- `CFSCRIPT` tag pairs can be placed anywhere in your template.
- More than one set of `CFSCRIPT` tags can be placed in your template.
- `CFSCRIPT` tags may not be nested.
- Code (including variable names) placed between `CFSCRIPT` tag pairs is case-insensitive.
- CFML tags may not be used within a `CFSCRIPT` tag block.
- CFML functions may be used within a `CFSCRIPT` block.

- CFML variables created outside a `CFSCRIPT` block are automatically available within the block.
- Not all CFML variables created inside the `CFSCRIPT` block are automatically available outside of the block.
- CFScript statements end in a semicolon.
- Curly braces {} are used to group related statements.

## Working with Variables

Assigning values to variables in CFScript is simple. Assignment statements take the following form:

```
variable = expression;
```

Here, *`variable`* is the name of the variable, and *`expression`* is the value you wish to assign to the variable. The semicolon marks the end of the statement. For comparison sake, consider the following example in which we assign values to a number of variables using the `CFSET` tag:

```
<CFSET x = 1>
<CFSET y = 1+2>
<CFSET MyMessage = "Hello World">
<CFSET MyStructure = structNew()>
```

The same functionality can be rewritten using CFScript syntax like so:

```
<CFSCRIPT>
 x = 1;
 y = 1+2;
 MyMessage = "Hello World";
 MyStructure = structNew();
</CFSCRIPT>
```

As you can see, setting values within a `CFSCRIPT` block takes less code and is generally easier to read than the equivalent code done using `CFSET`. Also, notice that you can use any ColdFusion functions (but not tags) that you want within a `CFSCRIPT` block.

## Commenting Your Code

ColdFusion provides two conventions for commenting code within a `CFSCRIPT` block that mimic JavaScript's commenting syntax. Comments can be single-line:

```
// this is a single line comment
x = 1;
x = 1+2; //This is a comment too
```

Comments that need to span multiple lines can be written using the // syntax:

```
// This is the first line of the comment
// This is the second
```

Alternately, multiline comments can be written using paired notation like this:

```
/* This is the first line of the comment
   This is the second line
   This is the third line */
```

To keep things more readable, an asterisk is typically used at the beginning of each line between the open and close comment markers:

```
/* This is the first line of the comment
 * This is the second line
 * This is the third line
 */
```

# Writing Output

You can't directly output text or variable values to the browser within a **CFSCRIPT** block. There is, however a function called **WriteOutput()** that you can use to write directly to the page output stream. This technique can output both variable values and plain text from within a **CFSCRIPT** block. Example 18-1 demonstrates the **WriteOutput()** function.

*Example 18-1. Using the WriteOutput Function Within a CFSCRIPT Block*

```
<H2>Using WriteOutput Within CFSCRIPT</H2>

<CFSCRIPT>
 x = 1;
 y = 2;
 MyMessage = "Hello World";

 WriteOutput("x = #x# <BR>");
 WriteOutput("MyMessage = #MyMessage# <BR>");
 WriteOutput(x+y);
</CFSCRIPT>
```

In this case, because there is no way to embed HTML directly within the **CFSCRIPT** block, all formatting is done by embedding the HTML code within the **WriteOutput()** function. Executing Example 18-1 results in the output shown in Figure 18-1.

It is also possible to output the value of variables set within a **CFSCRIPT** block outside of the **CFSCRIPT** tags. This is accomplished by using a **CFOUTPUT** block outside the **CFSCRIPT** block to handle the actual output, as shown in Example 18-2.

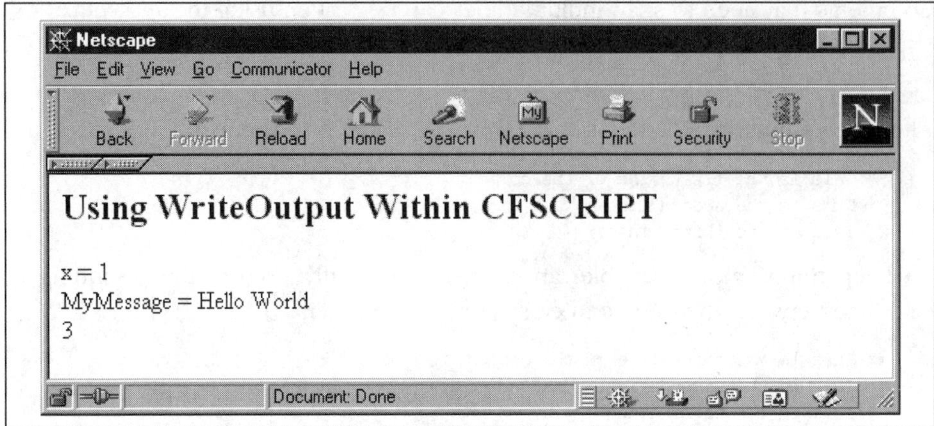


*Figure 18-1. Using WriteOutput within a CFScript block to write to the page output stream*

*Example 18-2. Outputting CFScript Variables Outside the CFSCRIPT Block*

```
<H2>Using CFOUTPUT To Output Variables Created Within CFSCRIPT</H2>
<CFSCRIPT>
 x = 1;
 y = 2;
 MyMessage = "Hello World";
</CFSCRIPT>

<CFOUTPUT>
x = #x#<BR>
MyMessage = #MyMessage#<BR>
#Evaluate(x+y)#
</CFOUTPUT>
```

The template in Example 18-2 generates the same output shown in Figure 18-1.

# *CFScript Statements*

CFScript contains a number of statements to handle flow control and looping, as we'll discuss in this section. Note that you can't use any CFML tags within a `CFSCRIPT` block.

## *if/else*

The `if/else` statement has the same functionality as the `CFIF` and `CFELSE` (and by extension, `CFELSEIF`) tags in regular CFML. The `if` statement can be used alone, as in:

```
if (expression)
  statement;
```

Or it can be used with the `else` statement, as in:

```
if(expression)
  statement;
else
  statement;
```

You can also use the `else` and `if` statements in combination to achieve the same results as the `CFELSEIF` tag:

```
if (expression)
  statement;
else if (expression)
  statement;
else
  statement;
```

To understand the differences between the `CFIF/CFELSE` tags and the `if/else` statement, let's first consider an example that uses the `CFIF` and `CFELSE` tags. Example 18-3 assigns the current year to a variable called `TheYear`. The `CFIF` and `CFELSE` tags are then used to determine whether the current year is a leap year. The results are then written to the browser.

*Example 18-3. Determining if the Current Year Is a Leap Year Using CFIF/CFELSE*

```
<!--- set a variable equal to the current year --->
<CFSET TheYear=Year(Now())>

<!--- Check to see if the current year is a leap year. --->
<CFIF IsLeapYear(TheYear)>
    <CFSET ReturnOutput="is a leap year.">
<CFELSE>
    <CFSET ReturnOutput="is not a leap year.">
</CFIF>

<CFOUTPUT>
#TheYear# #ReturnOutput#
</CFOUTPUT>
```

The same code can easily be rewritten using CFScript. Example 18-4 shows the ported code.

*Example 18-4. Using if/else to Determine if the Current Year Is a Leap Year*

```
<CFSCRIPT>
// set a variable equal to the current year
TheYear=Year(Now());

// Check to see if the current year is a leap year.
if (IsLeapYear(TheYear)){
    ReturnOutput="is a leap year.";
    }
else {
    ReturnOutput="is not a leap year.";
    }
```

*Example 18-4. Using if/else to Determine if the Current Year Is a Leap Year (continued)*

```
</CFSCRIPT>

<CFOUTPUT>
#TheYear# #ReturnOutput#
</CFOUTPUT>
```

As you can see, the code is almost identical. The only noticeable difference is that the CFScript version uses slightly less code and may be a bit easier to read.

Note that in Example 18-4 curly braces surround the code that gets executed in the event the `if` or `else` statement evaluates `True`. Although not necessary in this example (because we are executing only a single statement in our `if` and `else` statements), it is recommended you always use the curly braces as they do become necessary when you wish to execute more than one statement within an `if` or `else` statement.

## *switch/case*

The `switch/case` statement has the same basic functionality as do the `CFSWITCH`, `CFCASE`, and `CFDEFAULTCASE` tags in regular CFML. `switch/case` can simplify the coding process in situations where you would otherwise have to use multiple `if/else` statements. To get a better idea of how `switch/case` is implemented in CFScript, let's see how it is handled in regular CFML. Example 18-5 shows how the `CFSWITCH`, `CFCASE`, and `CFDEFAULTCASE` tags are used.

*Example 18-5. Determining What Quarter of the Year the Current Month Is in*

```
<!--- assign the quarter associated with the current month to
      TheQuarter --->
<CFSET TheQuarter = Quarter(Now())>

<!--- evaluate the current quarter --->
<CFSWITCH EXPRESSION="#TheQuarter#">

<!--- write output if the current month is in the first quarter --->
<CFCASE VALUE="1">
    <CFOUTPUT>
    #MonthAsString(Month(Now()))# is in the 1st quarter of the year.
    </CFOUTPUT>
</CFCASE>

<!--- write output if the current month is in the second quarter --->
<CFCASE VALUE="2">
    <CFOUTPUT>
    #MonthAsString(Month(Now()))# is in the 2nd quarter of the year.
    </CFOUTPUT>
</CFCASE>

<!--- write output if the current month is in the third quarter --->
<CFCASE VALUE="3">
```

*Example 18-5. Determining What Quarter of the Year the Current Month Is in (continued)*

```
    <CFOUTPUT>
    #MonthAsString(Month(Now()))# is in the 3rd quarter of the year.
    </CFOUTPUT>
</CFCASE>

<!--- this is the default case statement to use in the event the
      quarter's number is other than 1,2, or 3 --->
<CFDEFAULTCASE>
    <CFOUTPUT>
    #MonthAsString(Month(Now()))# is in the 4th quarter of the year.
    </CFOUTPUT>
</CFDEFAULTCASE>
</CFSWITCH>
```

Example 18-6 shows the same code written using CFScript syntax.

*Example 18-6. Implementing switch/case in CFScript*

```
<CFSCRIPT>
// assign the quarter associated with the current month to TheQuarter
TheQuarter = Quarter(Now());

//evaluate the current quarter
switch(TheQuarter)
{
    case 1: //write output if the current month is in the first quarter
    {
        WriteOutput(MonthAsString(Month(Now()))&" is in the 1st quarter
                    of the year.");
        break;
    }
    case 2: //write output if the current month is in the second quarter
    {
        WriteOutput(MonthAsString(Month(Now()))&" is in the 2nd quarter
                    of the year.");
        break;
     }
    case 3: //write output if the current month is in the third quarter
    {
        WriteOutput(MonthAsString(Month(Now()))&" is in the 3rd quarter
                    of the year.");
        break;
    }
    default: //this is the default case statement to use in the event the
            //quarter's number is other than 1,2, or 3
    {
        WriteOutput(MonthAsString(Month(Now()))&" is in the 4th quarter
                    of the year.");
        break;
    }
}
</CFSCRIPT>
```

In Example 18-6, the `switch` statement evaluates the value of `TheQuarter`. `TheQuarter` contains the quarter of the year that the current month belongs to (1, 2, 3, or 4). Each `case` statement allows you to specify an individual value that can result from the expression evaluated by the `switch` statement. Case values must be static values and can't be variables or expressions. If the expression contained in the `switch` statement evaluates to a value contained in one of the `case` statements, the corresponding code is executed. In this case, a message stating what quarter the current month is in is written to the browser using the `WriteOutput()` function.

The `default` statement allows you to specify a default action to take in the event that no `case` value matches the result of the expression from the `switch` statement. In our example, because we didn't provide a `case` statement for the number 4, the `default` statement is invoked only if the current month falls in the fourth quarter of the year.

Note that in Example 18-3, each `case` statement tests for a numeric value. You can also test for a string by enclosing it in quotation marks, such as:

```
case "myval":
```

You can also test for a Boolean value, such as

```
case True:
```

You can't, however, test for both a Boolean and a numeric value in the same `switch` statement.

The `break` statement at the end of each `case` statement is used to exit the `switch/case` statement. If you omit the `break` statements from the code, each `case` statement after the intended one will execute.

Unlike the `CFCASE` tag, it isn't possible to specify a delimited list of values for a single `case` statement in CFScript. This was done to keep the behavior and syntax of the `switch/case` statement inline with its JavaScript equivalent.

## *for Loops*

A `for` loop in CFScript is the equivalent of an index loop created by the `CFLOOP` tag and is used to repeat a block of code a specific number of times. Although `for` loops and index loops function identically, the syntax is a bit different. To understand the difference, look at the following index loop shown in Example 18-7.

*Example 18-7. Index Loop Created with CFLOOP*

```
<H2>Index Loop Using Regular CFML</H2>
<CFLOOP INDEX="i" FROM="10" TO="100" STEP="10">
```

*Example 18-7. Index Loop Created with CFLOOP (continued)*

```
<CFOUTPUT>
#i#<BR>
</CFOUTPUT>
</CFLOOP>
```

This loop loops from 10 to 100 by increments of 10. The results of each iteration are output to the browser.

Example 18-8 shows the same loop written within CFScript as a `for` loop.

*Example 18-8. Creating a for Loop in CFScript*

```
<H2>For (Index) Loop Using CFSCRIPT</H2>
<CFSCRIPT>
for (i=10; i LTE 100; i=i+10) {
    WriteOutput(i & "<BR>");
    }
</CFSCRIPT>
```

In Example 18-8, the `for` statement takes three arguments, an initial expression that determines the starting value for the loop, a test expression that determines what condition is necessary for the loop to continue iterating, and an increment expression that specifies how the value in the initial expression of the loop should be incremented. In this case, the initial expression within the `for` loop sets `i=10`. The initial expression can be a variable assignment, any valid ColdFusion expression, or blank. The test expression causes the loop to iterate as long as `i` is less than or equal to `100`. The test expression can be any valid ColdFusion expression or blank. The increment expression sets an increment value of `10` for the loop by setting `i=i+10`. The increment expression can be any variable assignment, valid ColdFusion expression, or blank. A `for` loop containing blanks for all three arguments it expects is shown in Example 18-9.

*Example 18-9. for Loop with Blank Arguments*

```
<CFSCRIPT>
i=10;

for( ; ; ){
    WriteOutput(i & "<BR>");
    i=i+10;
    if(i GT 100)
        break;
}
</CFSCRIPT>
```

In Example 18-9, a `break` statement is used to exit the loop when the value of `i` is greater than `100`. The `break` statement is covered later in this chapter.

## *for/in Loops*

`for/in` loops allow you to loop over ColdFusion structures and offer similar functionality to collection loops in regular CFML.* Example 18-10 uses the `CFLOOP` tag to loop over the contents of a structure.

*Example 18-10. Looping Over a Structure Using CFLOOP*

```
<CFSET Stock = StructNew()>

<CFSET Stock.ALLR = 135>
<CFSET Stock.AMKR = 35>
<CFSET Stock.YHOO = 238>

<H2>Collection Loop Using Regular CFML</H2>
<TABLE>
<TR>
  <TH>Ticker</TH>
  <TH>Price</TH>
</TR>

<CFLOOP COLLECTION="#Stock#" ITEM="Ticker">
<CFOUTPUT>
<TR>
  <TD>#Ticker#</TD>
  <TD>#StructFind(Stock,Ticker)#</TD>
</TR>
</CFOUTPUT>
</CFLOOP>
</TABLE>
```

Example 18-11 shows the same functionality rewritten using a `for/in` loop in `CFScript`.

*Example 18-11. Looping Over a Structure Using a for/in Loop in CFScript*

```
<H2>For-In (Collection) Loop Using CFSCRIPT</H2>
<CFSCRIPT>
Stock = StructNew();
Stock.ALLR = 135;
Stock.AMKR = 35;
Stock.YHOO = 238;

WriteOutput("<TABLE><TR><TH>Ticker</TH><TH>Price</TH></TR>");

for (Ticker in Stock) {
    WriteOutput("<TR><TD>#Ticker#</TD>
```

* Collection loops in regular CFML (`CFLOOP TYPE="Collection"`) can loop over ColdFusion structures and COM collections. The inability to loop over a COM collection is an unfortunate limitation in the current implementation of CFScript.

*Example 18-11. Looping Over a Structure Using a for/in Loop in CFScript (continued)*

```
                    <TD>#StructFind(Stock,Ticker)#</TD></TR>");
   }
WriteOutput('</TABLE>');
</CFSCRIPT>
```

Notice that in Example 18-11, the HTML table is created within the `CFSCRIPT` block by including the HTML code inside `WriteOutput()` statements.

## *while Loops*

A `while` loop offers the same functionality as a conditional `CFLOOP`. In a `while` loop, the loop repeats while a specified condition is `True`. In order to work, the condition being tested must change with each iteration of the loop until the condition evaluates to `False`. Example 18-12 demonstrates a conditional loop written using the `CFLOOP` tag.

*Example 18-12. Conditional Loop Using CFLOOP*

```
<CFSET x = 1>

<H2>Conditional (While) Loop Using Regular CFML</H2>
<CFLOOP CONDITION="x LTE 10">
<CFOUTPUT>
#x#<BR>
</CFOUTPUT>
<CFSET x = IncrementValue(x)>
</CFLOOP>
```

Example 18-13 shows the same code rewritten using a `while` loop in CFScript.

*Example 18-13. Creating a while Loop Using CFScript*

```
<H2>While Loop Using CFSCRIPT</H2>
<CFSCRIPT>
x = 1;
while (x LTE 10) {
    writeoutput(x & "<br>");
    x = IncrementValue(x);
    }
</CFSCRIPT>
```

In Example 18-13, while `x` is less than or equal to `10`, the loop continues to iterate. With each iteration, the value of `x` is output to the browser. Once `x` is equal to `11`, the loop stops iterating.

## *do/while Loops*

`do/while` loops are similar in appearance to `while` loops, but the conditional statement appears at the end of the loop as opposed to the beginning. While at first glance, there appears to be no functional difference between a do/while loop and a plain while loop, a subtle difference does exist. In the case of a while loop, that loop may never iterate if the expression being tested evaluates False before the first iteration occurs. A do/while loop, on the other hand, is guaranteed to iterate at least once because the condition being tested appears at the end of the loop. Example 18-14 demonstrates how a do/while loop is guaranteed to iterate at least once even when the condition being tested for is False before the loop begins iterating.

*Example 18-14. A do/while Loop in CFScript*

```
<H2>Do-While Loop Using CFSCRIPT</H2>

<CFSCRIPT>
x = 11;
do {
    WriteOutput(x & "<BR>");
    x = IncrementValue(x);
    } while (x LTE 10);
</CFSCRIPT>
```

In this case, the loop iterates once because the condition that checks to see if x is less than or equal to 10 appears at the end of the loop.

## Using break Within a Loop

The break statement is used within a loop to exit the loop if a certain condition is met. It has the same functionality as the CFBREAK tag.

Example 18-15 uses an index (for) loop to output the numbers between 10 and 100 in increments of 10. As soon as the loop gets to 50, the CFBREAK tag causes the program to exit the loop before the number 50 can be output. (continued)

*Example 18-15. Breaking Out of a Loop Using the CFBREAK Tag*

```
<H2>Using CFBREAK Within Regular CFML</H2>
<CFLOOP INDEX="i" FROM="10" TO="100" STEP="10">
<CFIF i EQ 50>
<CFBREAK>
</CFIF>

<CFOUTPUT>
#i#<BR>
</CFOUTPUT>
</CFLOOP>
```

The equivalent code written in CFScript is shown in Example 18-16.

*Example 18-16. Using the break Statement Within a for Loop in CFScript*

```
<H2>Using Break Within CFSCRIPT</H2>
<CFSCRIPT>
for (i=10; i LTE 100; i=i+10) {
    // this line breaks out of the loop before "50" can be output to the
    // browser
    if (i eq 50) {
        break;
    }
    WriteOutput(i & "<BR>");
}
</CFSCRIPT>
```

## *Using continue*

The `continue` statement resembles the `break` statement, but instead of breaking out of the loop altogether, `continue` allows the loop to skip over the code associated with the current iteration of the loop and pick back up with the next iteration. There is no CFML tag with equivalent functionality to the `continue` statement. Example 18-17 shows how the `continue` statement is used.

*Example 18-17. Using continue Within a Loop to Skip an Iteration*

```
<H2>Using Continue Within CFSCRIPT</H2>
<CFSCRIPT>
for (i=10; i LTE 100; i=i+10) {
    /* this line skips the iteration of the loop that would produce "50",
     * then continues iterating.  Notice the output contains 10,20,30,40,
     * 60,70,80,90,100.
     */
    if (i eq 50) {
        continue;
    }
    WriteOutput(i & "<BR>");
}
</CFSCRIPT>
```

In Example 18-17, a `for` loop outputs the number from `10` to `100` in increments of `10`. An `if` statement is used within the loop to test if the number produced by the current iteration of the loop is `50`. If `50` is encountered, the `continue` statement is executed, and that iteration of the loop is skipped.

# *User-Defined Functions*

In ColdFusion 5.0, you now have the ability to create user-defined functions (UDFs) that can be called inline, just like other ColdFusion functions. The premise behind UDFs is to allow you to extend ColdFusion's core set of functions with custom ones that encapsulate programming tasks not currently addressed by the language. For example, there is no CFML function for calculating the mean (average value) of a delimited list of numeric values. Rather than writing code that uses multiple functions each time you want to calculate the mean for a given list of numbers, you can create a UDF that can be called inline as often as you want in your template.

Before we get into the specifics of defining and calling UDFs, you should be aware of a few rules related to their use:

- UDFs can be used anywhere you use a normal CFML function: within a CFOUTPUT block, within CFSET tags, in any tag attributes, and within CFScript code.
- UDFs can be called recursively, which means that a UDF can call itself.
- UDFs can call other UDFs.
- Because UDFs are written using CFScript, they can't contain any CFML tags.
- Although it's possible to assign a UDF to a variable, it's generally not advisable to do so. This is especially true in the case of persistent variables (session, application, server) due to the locking issues this presents.

## *Defining Custom Functions*

All UDFs are defined within a CFSCRIPT block and follow the same basic format. You can define as many functions as you wish within a single CFSCRIPT block. The basic syntax for a UDF is as follows:

```
<CFSCRIPT>
function function_name([param1][,param2]...)
{
  CFScript statements
}
</CFSCRIPT>
```

All UDFs begin with the `function` statement. The name of the function is defined by *`function_name`*. Function names must begin with a letter and can contain only letters, numbers, and underscores. UDFs can't have the same name as already existing CFML functions. You also can't have more than one UDF with a given name available on the same template.

Functions can be written to accept zero or more required parameters and any number of optional parameters. You can think of parameters as variables. Each required parameter must be given a name and explicitly declared in the function statement. Like the function name, parameter names must begin with a letter and can contain only letters, numbers, and underscores. For example, to declare a function called **Mean** that accepts a single parameter called **Values**, you would code it like this:

```
function Mean(values)
```

Within the body of the function, you may use any CFScript statements you wish. Parameters are treated as variables and can be manipulated as such within the function scope. There are two additional CFScript statements exclusive to UDF that you may use in the body of your functions, **Var** and **Return**. **Var** is used to declare variables that are local to the function. This means that any variables declared with the **Var** statement are only available within the UDF in which they are defined. Variables declared with **Var** must be defined at the top of the function, before any other CFScript statements, and take precedence over any other variable with the same name, regardless of the variable's scope. Variables declared with **Var** follow the same naming rules as other variables. Additionally, they may not be compound variable names such as **My.Var.Name**. The syntax for declaring a variable using **Var** is:

```
Var variable = expression;
```

The **Return** statement is required and determines what value(s) to return when the function has finished executing. You may specify any valid expression in the **Return** statement. If no expression is given in the **Return** statement, ColdFusion returns the last value encountered before the **Return** statement:

```
Return;
Return x;
Return x-y;
Return DateFormat(MyVar, 'mm/dd/yyyy');
```

UDFs can return any ColdFusion datatype, including complex types such as arrays, structures, and queries.

At a minimum, you must provide at least one CFScript statement (the **Return** statement). Failure to do so results in an error. This is the simplest form of UDF, one in which all the functionality is contained in a single **Return** statement. To demonstrate this, consider a simple UDF for calculating the mean (average) of a comma-delimited list of numeric values:

```
<CFSCRIPT>
// Mean(values)
// Returns the mean (average) value of a list of comma delimited values
function Mean(values)
{
  Return ArrayAvg(ListToArray(values));
}
</CFSCRIPT>
```

In this example, the first line uses the **function** statement to declare a function named **Mean** that accepts a single parameter called **values**. The body of the UDF contains a single statement. In this case, it is a Return statement that converts the list of values to an array using the ListToArray() function and subsequently obtains the average value using the ArrayAvg() function.

## Calling User-Defined Functions

You call a UDF the same way you do any other CFML function—within a CFOUTPUT block, within a CFSET tag, in any tag attribute, and within CFScript code:

```
<CFOUTPUT>
  #MyFunction("test", 12)#
</CFOUTPUT>

<CFSET x=MyFunction()>

<CFMYTAG VALUE="#MyFunction('test')#">

<CFSCRIPT>
  x=MyFunction(MyOtherFunction());
</CFSCRIPT>
```

Before you can call a UDF, you need to decide where you want to locate it. You have two options: you can define the function in the template in which it is called, or you can use a CFINCLUDE tag to call another template containing your UDF.

A function defined in the template in which it is called may be defined anywhere on the page, including after it has already been referenced (this works because ColdFusion parses the entire page before processing the instructions). If you use this method, you should define all functions at the top of the page for readability and consistency. Using the Mean() function we just created, you define it inline and call it like this:

```
<CFSCRIPT>
// Mean(values)
// Returns the mean (average) value of a list of comma delimited values
function Mean(values)
{
  Return ArrayAvg(ListToArray(values));
}
</CFSCRIPT>

<CFSET MyValues="1,2,3,4,5,6,7,8,9,10">

<CFOUTPUT>
The mean is: #Mean(MyValues)#
</CFOUTPUT>
```

Functions defined in a separate template must be included via a CFINCLUDE tag. This method generally makes the most sense as it allows you to save your functions in a commonly accessible directory, so that they may be shared among multiple applications. If you find yourself repeatedly using the same functions over and over in your applications, it might make sense to **CFINCLUDE** a template containing all your UDFs from within your application's *Application.cfm* template. If you save the **Mean()** function in a template called *_Mean.cfm*, you call it like this:

```
<CFINCLUDE TEMPLATE="_mean.cfm">

<CFSET MyValues="1,2,3,4,5,6,7,8,9,10">

<CFOUTPUT>
The mean is: #Mean(MyValues)#
</CFOUTPUT>
```

## *Passing Optional Parameters*

UDFs would be of little use if they didn't allow you to pass optional parameters when calling them. Optional parameters are handled by a special one-dimensional array local to the UDF called **Arguments**. When a UDF is defined, the **Arguments** array is populated with the values of all the required and optional parameters passed to the function. The minimum number of elements in the **Arguments** array is always equal to the number of required parameters for a given function. For example, if a UDF takes three required parameters, the **Arguments** array contains three elements. Any number of optional parameters may be passed to a UDF. Each optional parameter's value is added to the **Arguments** array in the order in which it is passed in. When referencing a required parameter within a UDF, you may refer to it by name or by its index position within the **Arguments** array. Optional attributes can only be referred to by their index position. Example 18-18 demonstrates these concepts with a modified version of the **Mean()** function we created previously.

*Example 18-18. Passing Optional Arguments to a UDF*

```
<CFSCRIPT>
// Mean(values [, delimiter])
// Returns the mean (average) for an array or list of delimited values
function Mean(Values)
{
  Var TheDelimiter = ",";
  if (ArrayLen(Arguments) GT 1){
    TheDelimiter = Arguments[2];
  }
  if (IsArray(Values)){
    Return ArrayAvg(Values);
  }
  else{
```

*Example 18-18. Passing Optional Arguments to a UDF (continued)*

```
    Return ArrayAvg(ListToArray(Values, TheDelimiter));
  }
}
</CFSCRIPT>
```

In this example, we've modified our `Mean()` UDF to accept a one-dimensional array of numeric values or a delimited list of numeric values as well an optional parameter called `delimiter`. `delimiter` allows an optional delimiter to be passed to the function in the event the list of values is separated with a delimiter other than the comma. The parameter name `delimiter` isn't actually relevant, because all optional arguments are referred to by their index position within the `Arguments` array. I use it here just as a placeholder to make it easier to describe.

The first part of the function uses a `Var` statement to define a variable called `TheDelimiter`. The comma "," serves as the default delimiter. Remember that because we used the `Var` statement, `TheDelimiter` is available only within the `Mean()` UDF.

Since we are expecting only one required argument and one optional one, we use an `if` statement to check if there is more than one element in the `Arguments` array. If there is, we know the optional `delimiter` argument is present, so we assign the value of `Arguments[2]` (the delimiter) to the function variable `TheDelimiter`.

Next, another `if` statement is used to check whether `Values` is an array. If it is, we know that an array of values as opposed to a list of values was passed in, so we use the `ArrayAvg()` function to calculate the mean for the values and return it using the `Return` statement. If `Values` isn't an array, we assume it is a list and use the `ListToArray()` function to convert it to an array before using the `ArrayAvg()` function to calculate the mean and return it. The value of `TheDelimiter` is used in the `ListToArray()` function to specify the delimiter for the list.

## The Function Scope

A special variable scope called the function scope exists for variables that are local to UDFs. This scope differs slightly from the other variable scopes in ColdFusion in that there is no special prefix such as `variables.` or `client.` to identify the function scope. Variables within the function scope are accessible only within the UDF and can't be referenced by the template in which the UDF is called. The function scope consists of parameters passed to the function, variables created with the `Var` statement, and the `Arguments` array. We'll cover each of these shortly.

Any variables available in the template calling the UDF are automatically available (and can be modified) inside the UDF. Likewise, variables created or modified* within the UDF (except for those in the function scope) are available to the calling template after the function has been called. If a particular variable name exists in both the function scope and in another scope within the calling template, the function scope takes precedence within a UDF. Because of this, it's important to always scope variables outside the function scope when referencing them within a UDF.

## *Error and Exception Handling*

A custom function framework wouldn't be complete without a means to handle errors and exceptions that may occur both when calling and within the functions. There are several techniques you can use to deal with potential issues that may arise with custom functions.

First, there is a new function called `IsCustomFunction()` you can use to determine whether a particular name is that of a UDF. `IsCustomFunction()` takes a single parameter, the name you want to check. Note that the name isn't surrounded by quotes.

```
<CFSCRIPT>
if(IsDefined('Mean') AND IsCustomFunction(Mean)){
  WriteOutput("Mean is a custom function!");
  }
else{
  WriteOutput("Mean is not a custom function!");
  }
</CFSCRIPT>
```

The `IsDefined()` function makes sure the name exists before testing it with `IsCustomFunction()`. If you attempt to evaluate a name that doesn't exist with `IsCustomFunction()`, ColdFusion throws an error.

Second, you can use `if` statements within your custom functions to deal with errors inside the function and return an error code and/or error message in the event an error occurs. For example, if your UDF takes a single parameter and expects it to be an array, you can return an error message if the value of the parameter is anything other than an array:

* Different datatypes are passed to UDFs in different ways. Strings, numbers, date/time values, and arrays are passed by value. This means that any values passed to the UDF are actually copies of the original value. Any changes made to the value inside the UDF don't result in changes to the original value in the calling template. Queries and structures on the other hand are passed to UDFs by reference. In this case, the value passed to the UDF isn't actually the value, but rather a reference to the original value outside of the function. Because of this, any change made to a value passed by reference results in a change to the original value back in the calling template.

```
<CFSCRIPT>
function MyFunction(MyArray)
{
  var ErrMsg="Error!  You must supply an array.";
  if (IsArray(MyArray)){
    Return True;
  }
  else{
    Return ErrMsg;
  }
}
</CFSCRIPT>

<CFOUTPUT>
#MyFunction("test")#
</CFOUTPUT>
```

A third method is to use the CFTRY/CFCATCH tags to handle potential exceptions, as shown in Example 18-19. A good way to do this is to use one CFCATCH tag to handle Expression exceptions and a second CFCATCH tag as a backup (TYPE="Any") to catch any exceptions not caught by the first CFCATCH tag.

*Example 18-19. Providing Exception Handling for a UDF Using CFTRY/CFCATCH*

```
<CFTRY>
  <CFOUTPUT>
  #Mean()#
  </CFOUTPUT>

  <CFCATCH TYPE="Expression">
    Caught an exception using TYPE="Expression"
    <CFABORT>
  </CFCATCH>

  <CFCATCH TYPE="Any">
    Caught an exception using TYPE="Any"
    <CFABORT>
  </CFCATCH>
</CFTRY>
```

This is the method I prefer when working with regular CFML as it gives you more control over how you deal with an exception. This method tends to require less code than inline error handling and therefore offers (generally) better performance. It is also inline with the way errors and exceptions are handled within native CFML functions. Of course, you can't use this method within CFScript because CFML tags aren't allowed. This also prevents you from using the CFTHROW tag to generate custom exception types.

## *Function Libraries*

One exciting development to come out of ColdFusion's new UDF capabilities is the idea of function libraries. Function libraries are collections of UDFs that contain groups of related functions. For example, you might have a library for math functions, another one for string functions, and yet another library for data-manipulation functions. Several collaborative function library projects are underway as of this writing. One project in particular that is worth mentioning is the Common Function Library Project (CFLP), coordinated by Raymond Camden (a Spectra engineer for Allaire) and myself. The CFLP is a collaborative project, consisting of several open-source UDF libraries currently grouped into such functional areas as math functions, string functions, and data-manipulation functions. The idea behind the project is to involve the ColdFusion community in expanding the number and quality of UDFs available for ColdFusion. The libraries are available for download free of charge, and submissions of new functions are welcome. For more information on the project or to download the libraries, visit *http://www.cflib.org*.

# 19

# *Creating Custom Tags*

*In this chapter:*
- *Getting Started*
- *Custom Tags Versus User-Defined Functions*
- *Passing Data*
- *Returning Data*
- *Attribute Validation and Error Handling*
- *Advanced Techniques*
- *Protecting Your Tags*
- *CFX Tags*

One of the most powerful features of ColdFusion is the ability to extend the core capabilities of the platform through components known as custom tags. Custom tags allow you to encapsulate code in a neat wrapper that can then be invoked from within any CFML template. Those familiar with other programming languages can think of custom tags as similar to subroutines or procedures.

There are two varieties of custom tags: custom CFML tags (referred to as custom tags) and CFX tags. Because developing CFX tags requires C++, Java, or Delphi experience, this chapter focuses on the development and use of custom tags, since they are written in CFML. A brief section at the end of the chapter discusses installing and calling CFX tags.

## *Getting Started*

Custom tags are just like regular CFML templates and can contain any combination of CFML, HTML, and JavaScript code. What makes them different is how they are called and how they interact with the template that calls them. Custom tags allow you to pass attributes to them (just like other CFML and HTML tags), perform some sort of processing based on the attributes passed in, and can return data in the form of variables that can be used by the calling template in any number of ways. Let's first look at the benefits of custom tags.

### *Why Custom Tags?*

Right now, you are probably wondering about the specific types of situations that might warrant the use of custom tags. Here are four reasons to use custom tags in your ColdFusion applications:

*Code reuse*
: Custom tags give you a way to reuse frequently used code. You can create a single custom tag that can be called by any application residing on your server whenever the functionality it provides is needed. This allows you to develop your applications more quickly by reducing the amount of redundancy in your coding. It also improves development time in shared development environments where multiple developers have access to the same code base. Using custom tags, you can create a shared library of tags for handling various programming tasks that can be used by any developer on a given project.

*Abstraction*
: Using a custom tag allows you to abstract complex code and programming logic. To understand what we mean by abstraction, consider the `CFMAIL` tag. The `CFMAIL` tag provides a simple, tag-based interface for creating and sending SMTP messages. The tag abstracts the low-level programming that is typically required to create and send an SMPT message. Like the `CFMAIL` tag, custom tags allow you to abstract functionality (albeit written in CFML) using the same sort of tag-based interface.

*Code distribution*
: Custom tags provide a way to distribute your code to others. Because custom tags are self-contained, they provide an ideal framework for distributing functional code to other developers with a minimum of additional support.

*Security*
: Custom tags can also be used to keep developers away from back-end systems and processes you might not want them to have full access to. It is possible to secure access to these back-end systems and processes by providing developers with an encrypted version of a custom tag that accesses them.

If you need any more incentive to use custom tags in your applications, consider this. As of this writing, there are over 1,100 custom tags, many of them free of charge with source code that can be downloaded from an area of Allaire's web site called the Developer's Exchange. For example, a couple of my favorite tags are ones that handle complex user interface tasks that usually require JavaScript coding such as relating select boxes (Nate Weiss's CF_TwoselectsRelated), or moving items from one list box to another (Shlomy Gantz's CF_DoubleBox). The Developer's Exchange is a central resource for collecting and distributing custom tags and other ColdFusion-based applications. The Developer's Exchange can be found at *http://devex.allaire.com/developer/gallery/index.cfm.*

## *Custom Tags Versus CFINCLUDE*

At this point, you may be wondering why not just use the `CFINCLUDE` tag instead of going through the process of creating and using a custom tag. If you'll recall, you can reuse snippets of code stored in other files by embedding references to them in your template with the `CFINCLUDE` tag. There are times when this appropriate, and there are times when using a custom tag makes more sense. To help you decide which technique to use for which situation, consider the uses outlined in Table 19-1.

*Table 19-1. Custom Tags Versus CFINCLUDE*

| Situation | Technique |
|---|---|
| Headers and footers | `CFINCLUDE` |
| Porting a server-side include (SSI) | `CFINCLUDE` |
| Segmenting large templates into more logical and/or manageable chunks | `CFINCLUDE` |
| Including code that doesn't require parameters | `CFINCLUDE` |
| Reusing code | `CFINCLUDE` or custom tag |
| Encapsulating complex functionality | Custom tag |
| Nesting and recursion | Custom tag |
| Data needs to be passed in and out of the included code | Custom tag |
| Shared development | Custom tag |
| Securing code where it can't be accessed via URL | Custom tag |
| Parent/child relationships | Custom tag |
| End tags | Custom tag |

As you can, there are many issues to consider when trying to decide whether to use a custom tag or `CFINCLUDE`. From the standpoint of performance, using `CFINCLUDE` is generally faster than calling a custom tag, because there is practically no overhead on ColdFusion's part when including a file. Custom tags, on the other hand, have a significant amount of overhead associated with calling them.

Unlike code included using `CFINCLUDE`, custom tags execute in their own scope (not in the scope of the calling page). This means that certain types of variables you create in a custom tag aren't automatically available to the calling template; they must be explicitly passed. Likewise, certain types of variables created in the calling template must be explicitly passed to the custom tag. Certain variable types are automatically available to both the calling template and the custom tags. We'll cover this in detail later in the chapter. For now, just recognize that there are some major differences between using custom tags and included code.

## *Custom Tags Versus User-Defined Functions*

With the introduction of user-defined functions in ColdFusion 5.0, you now have an additional consideration when deciding how to develop reusable code. While your first reaction might be that custom tags and user-defined functions are basically the same, each has its place in ColdFusion application development.*

Table 19-2 contains some general guidelines to help you determine which technique makes the most sense in various situations.

*Table 19-2. Custom Tags vs. User-Defined Functions*

| Situation | Technique |
|---|---|
| You are using a version of ColdFusion prior to Version 5.0 | Custom tag |
| You need to include CFML tags in your code | Custom tag |
| You need to loop over COM collections within your code | Custom tag |
| You need to return more than one variable from your code | Custom tag |
| You want to be able to call your code inline | UDF |
| Performance is your biggest concern | UDF |
| You want to return a value inline | UDF |

# Calling Custom Tags

There is no real installation process for custom tags other than to save them on your ColdFusion server. There are, however, different locations on the server where you can save the tags that affect whether they can be called locally by a single application or shared across all applications.

To call a custom tag from within a CFML template, you simply prefix the template name of the tag with `CF_`. Therefore, if you have a custom tag saved on your server as *MyTag.cfm*, you call it like this:

```
<CF_MyTag>
```

When you call a custom tag from an application template, ColdFusion looks for the tag in the same directory as the calling template. For example, if your template resides in *c:\inetsrv\wwwroot\myapp* and tries to call a custom tag called `CF_MyTag`, ColdFusion looks for the tag in the *\myapp* directory first. Saving a custom tag in the same directory as its calling template makes the tag a local tag. That is, the tag is available only to templates residing in the same directory as the application. Using the local-tag technique allows you to use custom tags in hosted environments where you might not have access to the shared custom tags directory.

The very nature of custom tags makes them ideal for sharing among multiple applications on the server. In order to facilitate this, a default custom tags directory

* With this in mind, some of the example custom tags discussed in this chapter could easily be rewritten as user-defined functions. The examples included here are meant to show common techniques used in writing custom tags.

is automatically created when you install ColdFusion on your server. This directory is *c:\cfusion\customtags* by default. Any custom tags saved in this directory or any of its subdirectories are automatically available to any applications you create on the entire server.

In ColdFusion 5.0, the ability to specify additional custom tag paths was added to the ColdFusion Administrator. This allows you to use directories other than the default for making your tags available to multiple applications. To add a new custom tag path in the ColdFusion Administrator, follow these simple steps:

1. Click the Custom Tag Paths link under Extensions on the main ColdFusion Administrator page.
2. Enter the full path to your directory in the text box labeled Register Custom Tag Paths or use the Browse button to select a path from your ColdFusion server's filesystem.
3. Click the Add Path button when you are finished.

Note that you must start and stop the ColdFusion Application Server before the changes will take effect.

As I mentioned earlier, when a template calls a custom tag, ColdFusion starts its search for the custom tag in the same directory as the calling template. If ColdFusion can't find a tag with the name you specified, it moves its search to the default custom tags directory, and then any subdirectories. If the tag isn't found in the default custom tags directory, the search is extended to additional custom tag directories registered in the ColdFusion Administrator. These directories (and their subdirectories) are searched in the order they appear in the ColdFusion Administrator until a tag with the name you specified is found. In the event no tag is found during any of these searches, an exception is thrown.

The fact that the custom tag framework lets you store your custom tags in different locations suggests that you can have two or more different tags with the same name on your server. In the event that this happens, the order of evaluation states that ColdFusion use the first tag it encounters in its search. A method for using the `CFMODULE` tag to give you greater control over invoking custom tags is discussed in the "Advanced Techniques" section later in this chapter.

# *Passing Data*

Just like HTML and CFML tags, custom tags receive parameters via tag attributes. When you call a custom tag, you can pass parameters that automatically become available as variables within the custom tag. ColdFusion has a special variable scope called the `Attributes` scope that refers to reference attributes that have been passed to a custom tag. For example, you can call a custom tag named CF_MYTAG like this:

```
<CF_MYTAG NAME="Pere Money"
          TITLE="President">
```

Both NAME and TITLE are tag attributes. Once the tag is called, these attributes and their associated values are available within the custom tag as Attributes.Name and Attributes.Title, respectively. Because the custom tag exists within its own scope, you must scope any variables with the Attributes prefix in order to access them. Any ColdFusion datatype may be passed to a custom tag as an attribute. This allows you to create custom tags that can manipulate data from a variety of sources including query objects, arrays, and structures as well as such simple values as strings and numbers.

Let's look at a simple example that demonstrates how to pass a few attributes to a custom tag. Example 19-1 calls a custom tag called CF_DisplayEmployeeInfo (Example 19-2). A number of attributes are passed to the tag: Name, Title, Department, Email, and PhoneExt.

*Example 19-1. Passing Attributes to the CF_DisplayEmployeeInfo Custom Tag*

```
<CF_DisplayEmployeeInfo
    Name="Pere Money"
    Title="President"
    Department="Executive Management"
    Email="pere@example.com"
    PhoneExt="1234">
```

Once the CF_DisplayEmployeeInfo tag is called, the attributes passed to it are automatically available as attributes variables within the tag. These variables can be manipulated, in the same way that ColdFusion variables can be manipulated. In this case, they are used to populate an HTML table that is then output to the browser. Note that the variables are always referenced using the Attributes scope. Failing to scope the variables results in an error. The CFML code for the CF_DisplayEmployeeInfo tag is shown in Example 19-2. Be sure to save the template as *DisplayEmployeeInfo.cfm.*

*Example 19-2. Formatting and Displaying an Employee Record*

```
<!--- display the contents of each attribute passed into the custom tag --->
<H2>Employee Detail</H2>
<CFOUTPUT>
<TABLE>
<TR>
  <TD>Name:</TD><TD>#Attributes.Name#</TD>
</TR>
<TR>
  <TD>Title:</TD><TD>#Attributes.Title#</TD>
```

*Example 19-2. Formatting and Displaying an Employee Record (continued)*

```
</TR>
<TR>
  <TD>Department:</TD><TD>#Attributes.Department#</TD>
</TR>
<TR>
  <TD>E-mail:</TD><TD>#Attributes.Email#</TD>
</TR>
<TR>
  <TD>Phone Ext:</TD><TD>#Attributes.PhoneExt#</TD>
</TR>
</TABLE>
</CFOUTPUT>
```

Figure 19-1 shows the results of calling the custom tag. Note that in Example 19-2, the custom tag (as opposed to the calling template) created the table that is output to the browser.

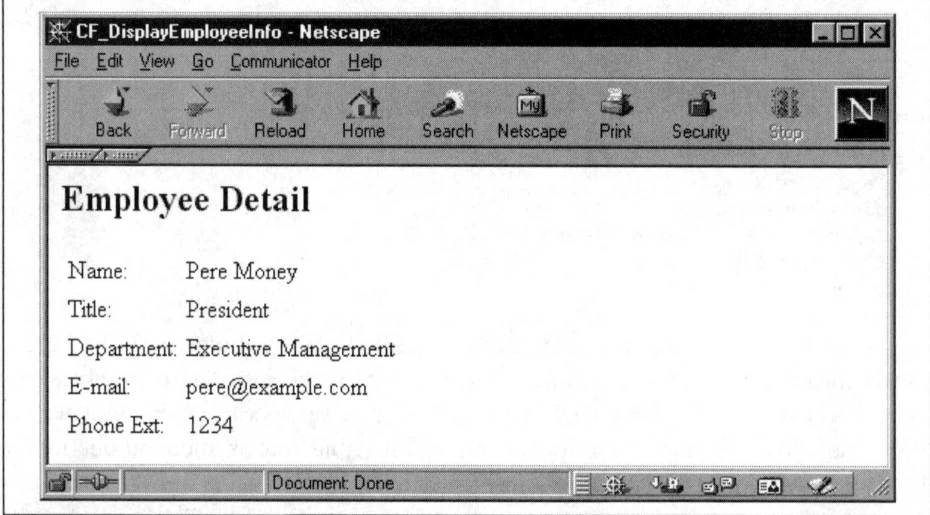


*Figure 19-1. Outputting attribute values in a custom tag*

# Returning Data

The caller scope passes data from inside a custom tag back to the calling template. Because custom tags exist within their own scope, you must use the caller scope if you want to make variables you create within your custom tag available to the calling template.

Setting a caller variable is just like setting any other type of ColdFusion variable. You may assign any datatype to a variable in the caller scope. This means that you can pass both simple and complex datatypes from inside a custom tag back to the template that called it.

Let's create a quick example that demonstrates passing an attribute to a custom tag, acting on that attribute, and passing a variable back using the **Caller** scope. In Example 19-3, you will find a custom tag called **CF_CountWords** (save the template as *CountWords.cfm* on your server). The tag is designed to accept a single attribute called **String**, count the number of words in the string, and return a caller variable back to the calling template with the number of words in the string. The number of words in the string is calculated by treating the string as a list and using the space character as the delimiter. The **ListLen()** function performs the calculation. Once the number of words is calculated, it is passed back to the calling template as a variable named **NumberOfWords**.

*Example 19-3. Counting the Number of Words in a Block of Text*

```
<CFSETTING ENABLECFOUTPUTONLY="Yes">
<!---------------------------------------------------------------------------
NAME:           CF_CountWords
FILE:           CountWords.cfm
CREATED:        04/24/1998
LAST MODIFIED:  04/24/1998
VERSION:        1.0
AUTHOR:         Rob Brooks-Bilson (rbils@amkor.com)
DESCRIPTION:    CF_CountWords is a custom CFML tag that counts the total
                number of words passed in a text string.  This tag is
                similar to the CFX tag CFX_WordCount but was written in
                CFML as opposed to C++.
ATTRIBUTES:     REQUIRED
                String(string) = Block of text to get a word count for.
KNOWN ISSUES:   None
---------------------------------------------------------------------------->

<!--- set a local variable to the passed attribute.  This isn't absolutely
      necessary, but it is a good idea as it allows you to reference the
      original value again if you ever need to. --->
<CFSET Local_String = Attributes.String>

<!--- Get the number of words in the string by treating the string as a list
      and using the space character as the delimiter. --->
<CFSET WordsInString = ListLen(Local_String, " ")>

<!--- return the count back to the calling template as a variable called
      NumberOfWords. --->
<CFSET Caller.NumberOfWords = WordsInString>
<CFSETTING ENABLECFOUTPUTONLY="No">
```

The **CFSETTING** tag is used at the beginning and end of the custom tag. This suppresses any whitespace generated by the tag during its execution. If the tag produced any output within its body (such as error messages), the output would have to be surrounded by CFOUTPUT tags to avoid being suppressed.

One other thing here is worth noting. Every custom tag you write (save a few of the smaller examples in this book) should have a header section that explains what the tag does, who created it, when it was last updated, what attributes it takes, and what caller variables it returns. Taking the time to add this information to your custom tags in the beginning will save you (and potentially others) a lot of time down the road when you need to look at the code behind the tag.

To test the CF_CountWords custom tag, create the template shown in Example 19-4 and save it to the same directory you saved the *CountWords.cfm* template to. You may name the template anything you desire.

*Example 19-4. Calling the Custom Tag CF_CountWords and Outputting the Results*

```
<!--- set a variable equal to a simple string value --->
<CFSET MyText = "How many words are in this sentence?">

<!--- call the custom tag CF_CountWords (CountWords.cfm) and pass in an
      attribute called String with the variable we set earlier --->
<CF_CountWords String="#MyText#">

<!--- output the value of NumberOfWords, the variable returned by the tag --->
<H2>Simple Custom Tag Example</H2>
<CFOUTPUT>
<I>#MyText#</I><BR>
There are #NumberOfWords# words in the sentence.
</CFOUTPUT>
```

Now that you've got a general idea how the attribute and caller scopes work, let's take things one step further and examine the separation between the variables created in a calling template and those created within a custom tag. As always, an example helps illustrate the concepts.

Example 19-5 shows a template that calls a custom tag called CF_VariableDemo, then passes it some attributes, and outputs the results returned by the tag. We include the CFAPPLICATION tag because this example makes use of session, client, and application variables. Normally, this tag would go in the *Application.cfm* template, but I've included it here in order to keep things simple. You also need to make sure that client and session management are enabled in the ColdFusion administrator.

*Example 19-5. Calling the CF_VariableDemo Tag and Outputting the Results*

```
<CFAPPLICATION NAME="MyApp"
               CLIENTMANAGEMENT="Yes"
               SESSIONMANAGEMENT="Yes"
               SETCLIENTCOOKIES="Yes"
```

*Example 19-5. Calling the CF_VariableDemo Tag and Outputting the Results (continued)*

```
            SESSIONTIMEOUT="#CreateTimeSpan(0,0,10,0)#"
            APPLICATIONTIMEOUT="#CreateTimeSpan(0,0,10,0)#">

<!--- create a variable to hold a query object --->
<CFSET QueryVariable = QueryNew("Text")>
<CFSET NewRows  = QueryAddRow(QueryVariable, 1)>
<CFSET temp = QuerySetCell(QueryVariable, "Text", "I am a Query variable", 1)>

<!--- assign values to all other variable types with the exception of CGI as
      CGI variables are read only --->
<CFSET Application.ApplicationVariable = "I am an Application variable">
<CFSET Session.SesssionVariable = "I am a Session variable">
<CFSET Client.ClientVariable = "I am a Client variable">
<CFSET Server.ServerVariable = "I am a Server variable">
<CFSET Variables.LocalVariable = "I am a Local variable">
<CFSET Form.FormVariable = "I am a Form variable">
<CFSET URL.URLVariable = "I am a URL variable">
<CFCOOKIE NAME="CookieVariable" VALUE="I am a Cookie variable">
<CFSET Request.RequestVariable = "I am a Request variable">

<HTML>
<HEAD>
    <TITLE>Untitled</TITLE>
</HEAD>

<BODY>

<!--- display all of the variable/values from the calling (this) template --->
<H2>Set in the calling template...</H2>
<CFOUTPUT>
<TABLE BORDER="1">
<TR>
  <TH>Variable</TH><TH>Value</TH>
</TR>
<TR>
  <TD>Application.ApplicationVariable</TD><TD>#Application.ApplicationVariable#</TD>
</TR>
<TR>
  <TD>QueryVariable.Text</TD><TD>#QueryVariable.Text#</TD>
</TR>
<TR>
  <TD>Session.SesssionVariable</TD><TD>#Session.SesssionVariable#</TD>
</TR>
<TR>
  <TD>Client.ClientVariable</TD><TD>#Client.ClientVariable#</TD>
</TR>
<TR>
  <TD>Server.ServerVariable</TD><TD>#Server.ServerVariable#</TD>
</TR>
<TR>
  <TD>Variables.LocalVariable</TD><TD>#Variables.LocalVariable#</TD>
</TR>
```

*Example 19-5. Calling the CF_VariableDemo Tag and Outputting the Results (continued)*

```
<TR>
  <TD>Form.FormVariable</TD><TD>#Form.FormVariable#</TD>
</TR>
<TR>
  <TD>Cookie.CookieVariable</TD><TD>#Cookie.CookieVariable#</TD>
</TR>
<TR>
  <TD>CGI.HTTP_USER_AGENT</TD><TD>#CGI.HTTP_USER_AGENT#</TD>
</TR>
<TR>
  <TD>Request.RequestVariable</TD><TD>#Request.RequestVariable#</TD>
</TR>
</TABLE>
</CFOUTPUT>

<!--- call the VariableDemo custom tag and pass two attributes in.  The custom
      tag will generate some output on its own in this example. --->
<CF_VariableDemo AttributeVariable="I am an Attribue variable"
                 OutVar="CallerVariable">

<!--- display all variables set inside of the custom tag as well as the caller
      variable returned by the tag --->
<H2>Set inside the custom tag..</H2>
<CFOUTPUT>
<TABLE BORDER="1">
<TR>
  <TH>Variable</TH><TH>Value</TH>
</TR>
<TR>
  <TD>Application Variable:</TD>
  <TD><CFIF IsDefined('Application.Tag_ApplicationVariable')>
        #Application.Tag_ApplicationVariable#
      <CFELSE><B>Not Available</B></CFIF>
  </TD>
</TR>
<TR>
  <TD>Query Variable:</TD>
  <TD><CFIF IsDefined('Tag_QueryVariable.Text')>#Tag_QueryVariable.Text#
      <CFELSE><B>Not Available</B></CFIF>
  </TD>
</TR>
<TR>
  <TD>Session Variable:</TD>
  <TD><CFIF IsDefined('Session.Tag_SesssionVariable')>
        #Session.Tag_SesssionVariable#
      <CFELSE><B>Not Available</B></CFIF>
  </TD>
</TR>
<TR>
  <TD>Client Variable:</TD>
  <TD><CFIF IsDefined('Client.Tag_ClientVariable')>#Client.Tag_ClientVariable#
      <CFELSE><B>Not Available</B></CFIF>
```

*Example 19-5. Calling the CF_VariableDemo Tag and Outputting the Results (continued)*

```
  </TD>
</TR>
<TR>
  <TD>Server Variable:</TD>
  <TD><CFIF IsDefined('Server.Tag_ServerVariable')>#Server.Tag_ServerVariable#
      <CFELSE><B>Not Available</B></CFIF>
  </TD>
</TR>
<TR>
  <TD>Local Variable:</TD>
  <TD><CFIF IsDefined('Variables.Tag_LocalVariable')>
        #Variables.Tag_LocalVariable#
      <CFELSE><B>Not Available</B></CFIF>
  </TD>
</TR>
<TR>
  <TD>Form Variable:</TD>
  <TD><CFIF IsDefined('Form.Tag_FormVariable')>#Form.Tag_FormVariable#
      <CFELSE><B>Not Available</B></CFIF>
  </TD>
</TR>
<TR>
  <TD>Cookie Variable:</TD>
  <TD><CFIF IsDefined('Cookie.Tag_CookieVariable')>#Cookie.Tag_CookieVariable#
      <CFELSE><B>Not Available</B></CFIF>
  </TD>
</TR>
<TR>
  <TD>CGI Variable:</TD>
  <TD><CFIF IsDefined('CGI.HTTP_USER_AGENT')>#CGI.HTTP_USER_AGENT#
      <CFELSE><B>Not Available</B></CFIF>
</TD>
</TR>
<TR>
  <TD>Request Variable:</TD>
  <TD><CFIF IsDefined('Request.Tag_RequestVariable')>
        #Request.Tag_RequestVariable#
      <CFELSE><B>Not Available</B></CFIF>
  </TD>
</TR>
<TR>
  <TD>CallerVariable</TD>
  <TD><CFIF IsDefined('CallerVariable')>#CallerVariable#
      <CFELSE><B>Not Available</B></CFIF>
  </TD>
</TR>
</TABLE>
</CFOUTPUT>
</BODY>
</HTML>
```

Before the custom tag is invoked, the calling template creates a number of differently scoped variables. A table is then output (shown in Figure 19-2) containing all the values associated with these variables while in the calling template.

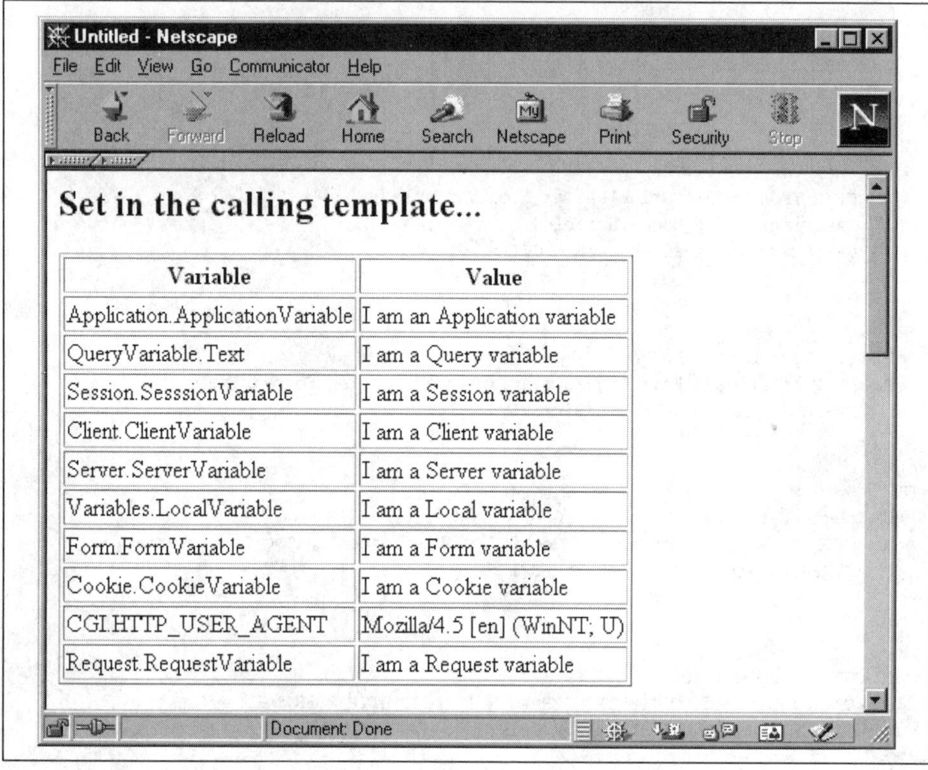

Set in the calling template...

| Variable | Value |
|---|---|
| Application.ApplicationVariable | I am an Application variable |
| QueryVariable.Text | I am a Query variable |
| Session.SesssionVariable | I am a Session variable |
| Client.ClientVariable | I am a Client variable |
| Server.ServerVariable | I am a Server variable |
| Variables.LocalVariable | I am a Local variable |
| Form.FormVariable | I am a Form variable |
| Cookie.CookieVariable | I am a Cookie variable |
| CGI.HTTP_USER_AGENT | Mozilla/4.5 [en] (WinNT; U) |
| Request.RequestVariable | I am a Request variable |

*Figure 19-2. Variables set and viewable in the calling template*

Next, the `CF_VariableDemo` tag is called, and two attributes, `AttributeVariable` and `OutVar` are passed to it from the calling template. The `CF_VariableDemo` tag, shown in Example 19-6, evaluates each variable that is set in the calling template and generates a table (shown in Figure 19-3) demonstrating which variables from the calling tag can be "seen" inside the custom tag.

The `CF_VariableDemo` tag then creates all the previous variable types (with the exception of an attribute variable) within the space of the custom tag. A caller variable is also created and automatically passed back to the calling template. Example 19-6 shows the CFML code for `CF_VariableDemo`; be sure this file is saved as *VariableDemo.cfm*.

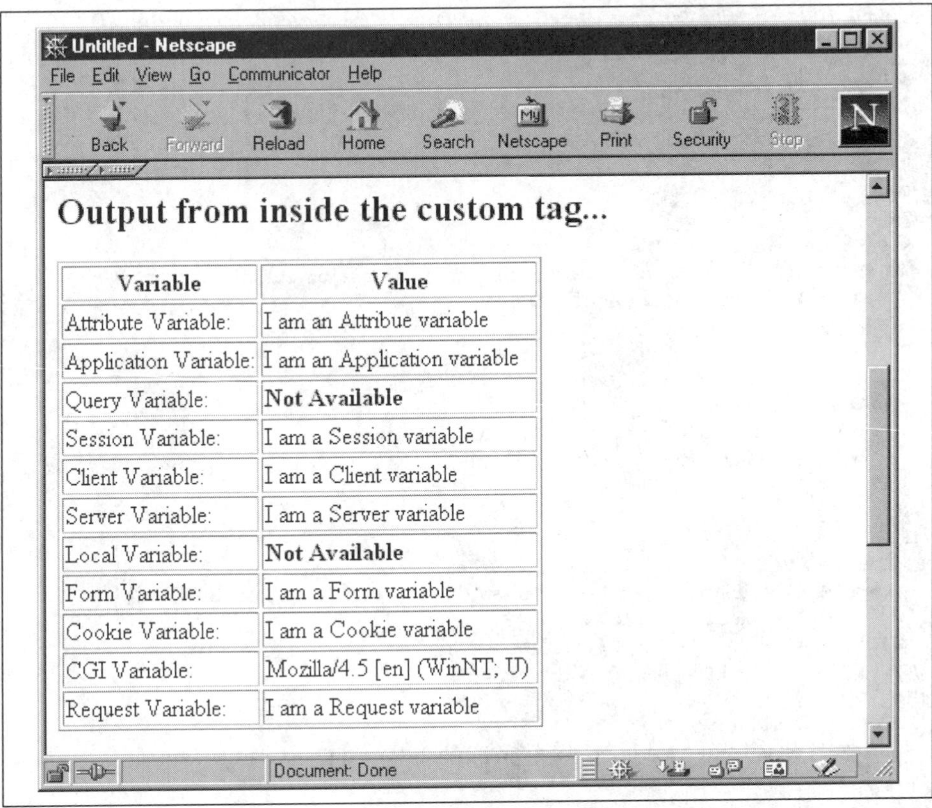

Untitled - Netscape
File Edit View Go Communicator Help
Back Forward Reload Home Search Netscape Print Security Stop
Output from inside the custom tag...
Variable
Value
Attribute Variable:
I am an Attribue variable
Application Variable:
I am an Application variable
Query Variable:
Not Available
Session Variable:
I am a Session variable
Client Variable:
I am a Client variable
Server Variable:
I am a Server variable
Local Variable:
Not Available
Form Variable:
I am a Form variable
Cookie Variable:
I am a Cookie variable
CGI Variable:
Mozilla/4.5 [en] (WinNT; U)
Request Variable:
I am a Request variable
Document: Done


*Figure 19-3. Variables set in the calling template and available for use by the custom tag*

*Example 19-6. The CF_VariableDemo (VariableDemo.cfm) Custom Tag*

```
<!--- attempt to output all of the variables set in the calling template.  If a
      variable is not accessible to the custom tag, note it.  In addition,
      output the attribute variable and set a caller and another request
      variable --->
<H2>Output from inside the custom tag...</H2>
<CFOUTPUT>
<TABLE BORDER="1">
<TR>
  <TH>Variable</TH><TH>Value</TH>
</TR>
<TR>
  <TD>Attribute Variable:</TD><TD>#Attributes.AttributeVariable#</TD>
</TR>
<TR>
  <TD>Application Variable:</TD>
  <TD><CFIF IsDefined('Application.ApplicationVariable')>
        #Application.ApplicationVariable#
      <CFELSE><B>Not Available</B></CFIF>
  </TD>
</TR>
```

*Example 19-6. The CF_VariableDemo (VariableDemo.cfm) Custom Tag (continued)*

```
<TR>
  <TD>Query Variable:</TD>
  <TD><CFIF IsDefined('QueryVariable.Text')>#QueryVariable.Text#
      <CFELSE><B>Not Available</B></CFIF>
  </TD>
</TR>
<TR>
  <TD>Session Variable:</TD>
  <TD><CFIF IsDefined('Session.SesssionVariable')>#Session.SesssionVariable#
      <CFELSE><B>Not Available</B></CFIF>
  </TD>
</TR>
<TR>
  <TD>Client Variable:</TD>
  <TD><CFIF IsDefined('Client.ClientVariable')>#Client.ClientVariable#
      <CFELSE><B>Not Available</B></CFIF>
  </TD>
</TR>
<TR>
  <TD>Server Variable:</TD>
  <TD><CFIF IsDefined('Server.ServerVariable')>#Server.ServerVariable#
      <CFELSE><B>Not Available</B></CFIF>
  </TD>
</TR>
<TR>
  <TD>Local Variable:</TD>
  <TD><CFIF IsDefined('Variables.LocalVariable')>#Variables.LocalVariable#
      <CFELSE><B>Not Available</B></CFIF>
  </TD>
</TR>
<TR>
  <TD>Form Variable:</TD>
  <TD><CFIF IsDefined('Form.FormVariable')>#Form.FormVariable#
      <CFELSE><B>Not Available</B></CFIF>
  </TD>
</TR>
<TR>
  <TD>Cookie Variable:</TD>
  <TD><CFIF IsDefined('Cookie.CookieVariable')>#Cookie.CookieVariable#
      <CFELSE><B>Not Available</B></CFIF>
  </TD>
</TR>
<TR>
  <TD>CGI Variable:</TD>
  <TD><CFIF IsDefined('CGI.HTTP_USER_AGENT')>#CGI.HTTP_USER_AGENT#
      <CFELSE><B>Not Available</B></CFIF>
</TD>
</TR>
<TR>
  <TD>Request Variable:</TD>
  <TD><CFIF IsDefined('Request.RequestVariable')>#Request.RequestVariable#
      <CFELSE><B>Not Available</B></CFIF>
```

*Example 19-6. The CF_VariableDemo (VariableDemo.cfm) Custom Tag (continued)*

```
  </TD>
</TR>
</TABLE>
</CFOUTPUT>

<!--- create a variable to hold a query object --->
<CFSET Tag_QueryVariable = QueryNew("Text")>
<CFSET NewRows  = QueryAddRow(Tag_QueryVariable, 1)>
<CFSET temp = QuerySetCell(Tag_QueryVariable, "Text", "I am a Query
              variable", 1)>

<!--- create variables within the scope of the custom tag to see which ones
      are available back in the calling template --->
<CFSET Application.Tag_ApplicationVariable = "I am an Application variable">
<CFSET Session.Tag_SesssionVariable = "I am a Session variable">
<CFSET Client.Tag_ClientVariable = "I am a Client variable">
<CFSET Server.Tag_ServerVariable = "I am a Server variable">
<CFSET Variables.Tag_LocalVariable = "I am a Local variable">
<CFSET Form.Tag_FormVariable = "I am a Form variable">
<CFSET URL.Tag_URLVariable = "I am a URL variable">
<CFCOOKIE NAME="Tag_CookieVariable" VALUE="I am a Cookie variable">
<CFSET Request.Tag_RequestVariable = "I am a Request variable">

<!--- create a Caller variable --->
<CFSET "Caller.#Attributes.OutVar#" = "I am a Caller variable">
```

Once the tag has finished processing, the calling template (shown in Example 19-5) resumes. An attempt is made to see if each of the variables set within the custom tag is now available to the calling template. Another HTML table (shown in Figure 19-4) is then generated to reveal the results.

As you can see from the results, all variables created within the calling template are available to the custom tag, with the exception of local and query variables. Conversely, the same holds true for variables created within the custom tag (with the exception of attribute variables that can't be set in the custom tag). Our examples have demonstrated the following:

- Persistent variables (application, client, session, server, cookie) are available to both regular templates and custom tags, regardless of where they are created.
- CGI variables are available to all templates and tags because they are read-only variables created by the system.
- Form and URL variables are available to both templates and custom tags regardless of where they are created. This is because as of ColdFusion 4.5, Form and URL variables are available via special structures called `Form` and `URL`, respectively.
- Attribute variables are created in a calling template and explicitly passed to a custom tag and are available only within the custom tag.

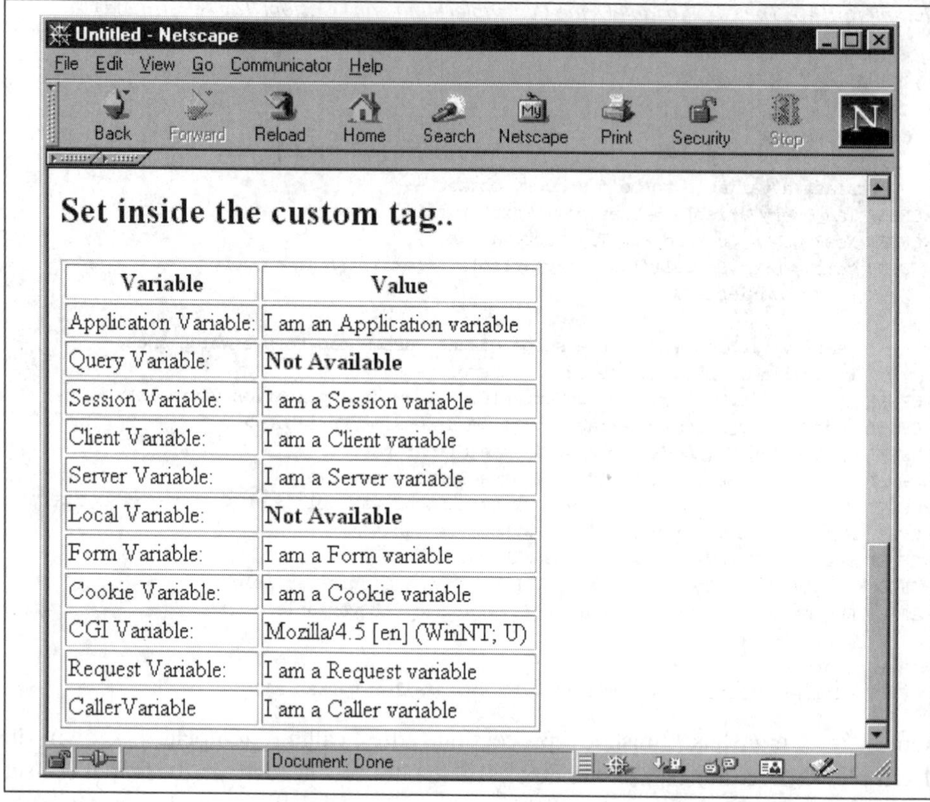

Set inside the custom tag..

| Variable | Value |
|---|---|
| Application Variable: | I am an Application variable |
| Query Variable: | **Not Available** |
| Session Variable: | I am a Session variable |
| Client Variable: | I am a Client variable |
| Server Variable: | I am a Server variable |
| Local Variable: | **Not Available** |
| Form Variable: | I am a Form variable |
| Cookie Variable: | I am a Cookie variable |
| CGI Variable: | Mozilla/4.5 [en] (WinNT; U) |
| Request Variable: | I am a Request variable |
| CallerVariable | I am a Caller variable |

*Figure 19-4. Variables set in the CF_VariableDemo custom tag*

- Caller variables are created in custom tags and are available only to the template that calls the custom tag.
- The request scope is a special variable scope that is shared by both the calling template and any custom tags for the duration of a single request.
- Local variables and query variables are available only within the templates or tags they are created in unless they are explicitly passed using a variable scope accessible to both calling templates and custom tags.

## Avoiding Potential Variable-Name Conflicts

It is a good idea to get in the habit of allowing developers to specify the name of the caller variable returned by the custom tag as an attribute that can be passed into the tag. This helps avoid any potential variable-name conflicts between variables in the calling template and hardcoded caller variables returned by a custom tag. If a variable with the same name as a caller variable returned by a custom tag already exists in the calling template, its value is overwritten by the value in the caller variable with the same name.

To invoke the tag more than one time in the calling template, you can also specify a name for the caller variable returned by your custom tag. For example, if you want to use the **CF_CountWords** tag more than once in a single template, you need to be able to specify different caller variable names for each instance of the tag call, or the variable returned by the second call overwrites the value of the first call.

We can modify the code in Example 19-3 so that the **CF_CountWords** tag can accept a new attribute called **OutVar** (as shown in Example 19-7) The **OutVar** attribute lets us specify a variable name to use as the caller variable for returning the number of words in the string.

*Example 19-7. Allowing a Developer-Specified Caller Variable*

```
<CFSETTING ENABLECFOUTPUTONLY="Yes">
<!------------------------------------------------------------------------
NAME:           CF_CountWords
FILE:           CountWords.cfm
CREATED:        04/24/1998
LAST MODIFIED:  06/29/2000
VERSION:        1.0
AUTHOR:         Rob Brooks-Bilson (rbils@amkor.com)
DESCRIPTION:    CF_CountWords is a custom CFML tag that counts the total
                number of words passed in a text string.  This tag is
                similar to the CFX tag CFX_WordCount but was written in
                CFML as opposed to C++.
ATTRIBUTES:     REQUIRED
                OutVar(string) = Name to assign to the variable returned by
                                 The Tag.
                String(string) = Block of text to get a word count for.

KNOWN ISSUES:   None
------------------------------------------------------------------------->
<!--- set local variables to the passed attributes.  This isn't absolutely
      necessary, but it is a good idea as it allows you to reference the
      original values again if you ever need to. --->
<CFSET Local_String = Attributes.String>
<CFSET Local_OutVar = Attributes.OutVar>

<!--- Get the number of words in the string by treating the string as a list
      and using the space character as the delimiter. --->
<CFSET WordsInString = ListLen(Local_String, " ")>

<!--- return the count back to the calling template.  The name of the caller
      variable is dynamically created using the OutVar value passed in as an
      attribute.  This allows the developer calling the template to use any
      variable name for the output that they want.  This avoids potential
      variable name conflicts within the calling template. --->
```

*Example 19-7. Allowing a Developer-Specified Caller Variable (continued)*

```
<CFSET "Caller.#Local_OutVar#" = WordsInString>
<CFSETTING ENABLECFOUTPUTONLY="No">
```

As you can see in Example 19-7, we created a new local variable called `Local_OutVar`. Instead of returning a hardcoded caller-variable name back to the calling template, we dynamically create the caller variable with the variable name in `Local_OutVar`:

```
<CFSET "Caller.#Local_OutVar#" = WordsInString>
```

Note that it is also possible to set the value of the caller variable using the `SetVariable()` function:

```
<CFSET Temp = SetVariable("#Caller.Local_OutVar#", WordsInString)>
```

You can test the new version of the tag by creating a template, as shown in Example 19-8. Be sure to save the template you create in the same directory as the *CountWords.cfm* template. Feel free to change the variable name specified in the `OutVar` attribute. Just be sure to use the same name in the `CFOUTPUT` section at the bottom of the template.

*Example 19-8. Calling the Modified CF_CountWords Tag*

```
<!--- set a variable equal to a simple string value --->
<CFSET MyText = "How many words are in this sentence?">

<!--- call the custom tag CF_CountWords (CountWords.cfm) and pass in an
      attribute called String with the variable we set earlier.  Pass in a
      second attribute called OutVar.  The value of OutVar is the name of the
      variable the custom tag will return containing the number of words in
      the string. --->
<CF_CountWords String = "#MyText#"
               OutVar = "TotalWords">

<!--- output the value of the variable returned by the tag --->
<H2>Simple Custom Tag Example</H2>
<CFOUTPUT>
<I>#MyText#</I><BR>
There are #TotalWords# words in the sentence.
</CFOUTPUT>
```

## Returning Multiple Values from a Custom Tag

If your tag is designed to return multiple caller variables, you might consider returning them as a structure rather than individual variables. Returning a single structure lets you keep everything in a neat package and lets you specify the name of the caller variable (the structure) to return while still letting the tag return multiple values.

Let's look at another custom tag called **CF_Range** (which is shown in Example 19-9). **CF_Range** takes two attributes, **Values** and **OutVar**. **Values** allows you to pass in a comma-delimited list of numeric values to determine the range for. In statistics, range is the distance between the lowest and highest (minimum and maximum) value in a given distribution. **OutVar** specifies a name for the caller variable generated by the tag. In the case of this tag, the caller variable is actually a structure that contains three different key/value pairs.

*Example 19-9. The CF_Range (Range.cfm) Custom Tag*

```
<CFSETTING ENABLECFOUTPUTONLY="Yes">
<!-------------------------------------------------------------------------
NAME:           CF_Range
FILE:           range.cfm
CREATED:        04/09/1998
LAST MODIFIED:  06/29/2000
VERSION:        1.0
AUTHOR:         Rob Brooks-Bilson (rbils@amkor.com)
DESCRIPTION:    CF_Range is a custom CFML tag that calculates the Range
                for a comma delimited list (distribution) of numeric values.
                The Range for a given distribution is determined by calculating
                the distance between the lowest and highest value in the list.
                Range is used to give an idea of how spread out data in a given
                set is.
ATTRIBUTES:     REQUIRED
                Values = Comma delimited list of numeric values
                OutVar = name to give the structure that is returned as a caller
                         var
RETURN VALUES:  This tag returns a structure (named by the OutVar attribute) that
                contains three key value pairs:
                MinValue = Minimum value in the list of values
                MaxValue = Maximum value in the list of values
                Range = Range calculate by subtracting the MinValue from MaxValue
KNOWN ISSUES:   None
-------------------------------------------------------------------------->
<!--- set local variables to the passed attributes.  This isn't absolutely
      necessary, but it is a good idea as it allows you to reference the
      original values again if you ever need to. --->
<CFIF IsDefined('Attributes.Values') AND Attributes.Values NEQ "">
  <CFSET Local_Values = Attributes.Values>
<CFELSE>
  <CFOUTPUT>
  You failed to pass a required attribute: <B>Values</B>
  </CFOUTPUT>
  <CFABORT>
</CFIF>


<CFIF IsDefined('Attributes.OutVar') AND Attributes.OutVar NEQ "">
  <CFSET Local_OutVar = Attributes.OutVar>
<CFELSE>
  <CFOUTPUT>
```

*Example 19-9. The CF_Range (Range.cfm) Custom Tag (continued)*

```
  You failed to pass a required attribute: <B>OutVar</B>
  </CFOUTPUT>
  <CFABORT>
</CFIF>

<!--- Make sure numeric values were passed --->
<CFLOOP INDEX="i" FROM="1" TO="#ListLen(Local_Values)#">
  <CFIF NOT IsNumeric(ListGetAt(Local_Values, i, ","))>
    <CFOUTPUT>
    <H3>You attempted to pass a non-numeric value to this tag.  All values must
        be numeric.</H3>
    </CFOUTPUT>
    <CFABORT>
  </CFIF>
</CFLOOP>

<!--- get the number of elements in the List --->
<CFSET NumberOfElements = ListLen(Local_Values)>

<!--- Build an array from the list --->
<CFSET MyArray = ArrayNew(1)>

<CFLOOP INDEX="n" FROM="1" TO="#NumberOfElements#">
    <CFSET MyArray[n] = ListGetAt(Local_Values, n, ",")>
</CFLOOP>

<!--- Create a structure called MyStruct and populate it with the minimum
      and maximum values from MyArray.  This is a temporary structure that
      will be renamed before it is sent back to the calling template.
      Also calculate the range and assign it to a third structure key. --->
<CFSET MyStruct = StructNew()>
<CFSET MyStruct.MinValue = ArrayMin(MyArray)>
<CFSET MyStruct.MaxValue = ArrayMax(MyArray)>
<CFSET MyStruct.Range = MyStruct.MaxValue - MyStruct.MinValue>


<!--- Copy MyStruct to the caller variable name passed into the tag by the
      OutVar attribute. --->
<CFSET "Caller.#Local_OutVar#" = MyStruct>
<CFSETTING ENABLECFOUTPUTONLY="No">
```

When the `CF_Range` tag is called, the first thing it does is check to see that both the `Values` and `OutVar` attributes were passed. If so, both attributes are assigned to local variables. If either of the attributes is missing, the `CFABORT` tag aborts all processing, including that of the calling template. The next part of the template in Example 19-9 loops through the list of values in the `Values` attribute and makes sure they are all numeric. If any of the values in the list aren't numeric, processing is aborted using the `CFABORT` tag. Attribute validation and error handling is covered in more detail in the next section of this chapter.

If everything checks out up to this point, the template converts the list of numeric values to a one-dimensional array by looping over each value in the list and assigning it to an array index using `CFSET`. Once the list is in an array, a structure called `MyStruct` is created. Three keys are added to `MyStruct`, `MinValue`, `MaxValue`, and `Range`. `MinValue` and `MaxValue` are calculated using the `ArrayMin()` and `ArrayMax()` functions, respectively. `Range` is calculated by subtracting he `MinValue` from the `MaxValue`. Once all the values are stored in the structure, it is renamed to the value of `OutVar` and sent back to the calling template as a caller variable.

You can test the `CF_Range` tag by executing the template shown in Example 19-10. Make sure you save the template to the same directory you saved the *Range.cfm* template before you execute it.

*Example 19-10. Calling the CF_Range Tag and Outputting the Results*

```
<!--- create a list of numbers to pass to the tag --->
<CFSET NumberList="1,2,3,4,5,6,7,8,9,10">

<!--- call the CF_Range tag and pass the list of numbers we created.  Also pass
      TheResults as the name of the caller variable we want to use to hold the
      structure returned by the tag. --->
<CF_Range Values="#NumberList#"
          OutVar="TheResults">

<HTML>
<HEAD>
    <TITLE>CF_Range Example</TITLE>
</HEAD>

<BODY>

<!--- output the min value, max value, and range as returned from the tag --->
<CFOUTPUT>
Values: #NumberList#<BR>
Min Value: #TheResults.MinValue#<BR>
Max Value: #TheResults.MaxValue#<BR>
Range: #TheResults.Range#
</CFOUTPUT>

</BODY>
</HTML>
```

The key/value pairs contained in the structure returned by the `CF_Range` tag are referenced individually in the output.

# Attribute Validation and Error Handling

In the previous section, we touched briefly on the idea of attribute validation when we used the `IsDefined()` function to check for the existence of an attribute before allowing processing within the custom tag to continue. This section takes things a step further by demonstrating various techniques you can use to create both required and optional attributes for your tags. Additionally, we'll look at error- and exception-handling strategies you can use to deal with problems that occur in your custom tags.

## Handling Required Attributes

Depending on the type of custom tag you create, you may want or need to require certain attributes to be passed in order for the tag to do its job. Making a tag attribute required is as simple as using a `CFIF` statement inside the custom tag to evaluate whether the tag exists. This is usually handled by the `IsDefined` function:

```
<CFIF IsDefined('Attributes.MyRequiredAttrib')>
```

If the required attribute exists, `IsDefined()` returns `True`, and your tag can continue processing. If, however, `IsDefined()` returns `False`, the required attribute hasn't been passed to the tag. At this point, you have a few choices:

- Assign a default value for the missing attribute and allow processing to continue. This is one of the approaches we have used in some of the examples up to this point.
- Return a message to the browser letting the user know that a required attribute wasn't passed and abort all processing using the `CFABORT` tag. This is an approach we used in some previous examples.
- Use the `CFEXIT` tag to exit the custom tag and continue processing the calling template. The `CFEXIT` tag is discussed in detail later on in this chapter.
- Throw an exception using `CFTHROW` and let the calling template handle the exception based on the exception information provided by the tag.

The `CFPARAM` tag can also handle a required attribute that isn't passed into the custom tag by assigning a default value for the attribute:

```
<CFPARAM NAME="Attributes.MyRequiredAttrib" DEFAULT="MYValue">
```

If the attribute is passed to the custom tag, the `CFPARAM` tag does nothing. However, if the attribute isn't passed to the custom tag, the `CFPARAM` tag assigns the `DEFAULT` value to the variable specified in `NAME`. The disadvantage to using the `CFPARAM` method is that you can't really take any additional action if the required attribute isn't present.

## *Handling Optional Attributes*

In some instances, you may want to allow optional attributes to be sent to your custom tags. Optional attributes are generally handled by checking to see if they were passed in using the `IsDefined()` function and then executing the appropriate code if they were found to exist:

```
<CFIF IsDefined('Attributes.MyOptionalAttrib')>
HTML and CFML...
</CFIF>
```

Using this technique, if the optional attribute is passed in, it is detected, and a block of code is run related to the processing of the optional attribute. If the attribute isn't passed in, the tag ignores the code specific to the optional attribute and continues processing.

You can also handle an optional attribute by assigning a default value if it doesn't exist. This is usually handled either using the `CFPARAM` tag or using `CFIF` along with the `IsDefined()` function to check for the attributes existence

## *Validating Datatypes*

Just because a value is passed in for a particular attribute doesn't mean it is the type of value your custom tag is expecting. For example, if you have a custom tag that expects a particular attributes value to be numeric, passing a string full of text may cause the tag to throw an error. ColdFusion provides several built-in functions you can use to evaluate the type of value contained in a particular variable. Some of the more common functions include the following:

`IsArray(`*`value`*` [, `*`dimension`*`])`
: Returns `True` if the *`value`* specified is an array or `False` if it isn't. In addition, `IsArray` can check to see if the array is of a specified ***`dimension`*** (1, 2, or 3).

`IsBinary(`*`value`*`)`
: Returns `True` if the specified value is binary or `False` if it isn't.

`IsBoolean(`*`value`*`)`
: Returns `TRUE` if the specified value can be converted to a Boolean or `FALSE` if it can't.

`IsDate(`*`string`*`)`
: Returns `TRUE` if the specified string can be converted to a valid date/time object or `FALSE` if it can't.

`IsNumeric(`*`string`*`)`
: Returns `TRUE` if the specified string can be converted to a number or `FALSE` if it can't.

`IsQuery(value)`
: Returns `True` if the specified *value* is a valid ColdFusion query or `False` if it isn't.

`IsSimpleValue(value)`
: Returns `TRUE` if the specified value is a number, string, Boolean, or date/time object or `FALSE` if it isn't.

`IsStruct(variable)`
: Returns `TRUE` if the specified variable is a ColdFusion structure or `FALSE` if it isn't.

These functions are most effective when used with the `IsDefined()` function. For example, suppose you have a custom tag that is expecting the value of an attribute named `Quantity` to be numeric. You can use the following code to make sure the `Quantity` attribute exists and its value is numeric:

```
<CFIF IsDefined('Attributes.Quantity') AND IsNumeric(Attributes.Quantity)>
Continue processing...
<CFELSE>
You attempted to pass a non-numeric value for the attribute <B>Quantity</B>.
<CFABORT>
</CFIF>
```

In order for processing to continue, `Attributes.Quantity` must exist, and it must be numeric. If either condition is `False`, a message is written to the browser, and all processing (of both the custom tag and the calling template) is aborted.

## *Error and Exception Handling*

It is generally a good idea to use some form of error- and exception-handling both when you build and when you call custom tags. Using the `CFTRY`, `CFCATCH`, and `CFTHROW` tags discussed in Chapter 9, makes it possible to include robust error- and exception-handling capabilities in your custom tags and the templates that call them.

Typically, a `CFTHROW` tag is used inside a custom tag in an area where an error or exception is likely to occur. For example:

```
<CFIF NOT IsDefined('Attributes.MyAttrib')>
<CFTHROW MESSAGE="You failed to pass a required attribute: <B>MyAttrib</B>"
         TYPE="Custom.Tag.MyTag">
</CFIF>
```

Any template that calls the custom tag can then use `CFTRY/CFCATCH` to trap the error generated by the `CFTHROW` tag:

```
<CFTRY>

<CF_MyTag>
```

```
<CFCATCH TYPE="Custom.Tag.MyTag">
<CFOUTPUT>
#CFCATCH.Message#
</CFOUTPUT>
</CFCATCH>

</CFTRY>
```

## Merging Validation and Error-Handling Concepts

Let's close out our discussion of attribute validation and error handling with a working example that demonstrates the concepts we covered. The `CF_RandomPassword` tag generates random passwords you can use in your applications. The parameters that govern the creation of the password are fully customizable. Generated passwords can be of any length and can contain numbers, symbols, and upper- and lowercase letters in any combination. The tag is well suited for use in registration modules that need to generate random passwords for users. Example 19-11 shows the *RandomPassword.cfm* template.

*Example 19-11. Generating Customizable Random Passwords*

```
<CFSETTING ENABLECFOUTPUTONLY="Yes">
<!---------------------------------------------------------------------------
NAME:           CF_RandomPassword
FILE:           RandomPassword.cfm
VERSION:        1.2
CREATED:        02/23/1998
LAST MODIFIED:  06/30/2000
AUTHOR:         Rob Brooks-Bilson (rbils@amkor.com)
DESCRIPTION:    CF_RandomPassword is a custom CFML tag that allows a user
                to generate random passwords for use in their applications.
                The parameters governing the creation of the password are
                fully customizable.  Passwords can be of any length and
                can contain numbers, symbols, uppercase, and lowercase
                letters in any combination.  This tag can easily be
                incorporated into registration modules to allow for the
                automatic generation of random passwords.
ATTRIBUTES:     REQUIRED
                OutVar = name to give the structure that is returned as a
                         caller var
                OPTIONAL
                NumberOfCharacters(numeric) = The length in characters of the
                                              password
                UseSymbols(Yes/No) = Indicates whether to include symbols in
                                     the password
                UseNumbers(Yes/No) = Indicates whether to include numbers in
                                     the password
                UseUppercaseLetters(Yes/No) = Indicates whether to include
                                              upper-case letters in the
                                              password
                UseLowercaseLetters(Yes/No) = Indicates whether to include
```

*Example 19-11. Generating Customizable Random Passwords (continued)*

```
                                        lower-case letters in the
                                        password
KNOWN ISSUES: None
------------------------------------------------------------------------------->

<!--- Check to see if OutVar was passed in.  If so, check to make
      sure that it is not a blank value.  If any of these
      checks return False, throw an exception. --->
<CFIF IsDefined('Attributes.OutVar') AND Attributes.OutVar NEQ "">
    <CFSET OutVar = Attributes.OutVar>
<CFELSE>
    <CFTHROW MESSAGE="You failed to pass a required attribute: <B>OutVar</B>"
             TYPE="Custom.Tag.RandomPassword">
</CFIF>

<!--- Check to see if NumberOfCharacters was passed in.  If so, check to make
      sure it is numeric.  If any of these checks return False, set a default
      length of 7 for the password.  --->
<CFIF IsDefined('Attributes.NumberOfCharacters') AND
                IsNumeric(Attributes.NumberOfCharacters)>
    <CFSET NumberOfCharacters = Int(Attributes.NumberOfCharacters)>
<CFELSE>
    <CFSET NumberOfCharacters = 7>
</CFIF>

<!--- Check to see if UseSymbols was passed in.  If so, check to make
      sure it is a Boolean.  If any of these checks return False, default
      UseSymbols to No. --->
<CFIF IsDefined('Attributes.UseSymbols') AND IsBoolean(Attributes.UseSymbols)>
    <CFSET UseSymbols=attributes.UseSymbols>
<CFELSE>
    <CFSET UseSymbols="No">
</CFIF>

<!--- Check to see if UseNumbers was passed in.  If so, check to make
      sure it is a Boolean.  If any of these checks return False, default
      UseNumbers to Yes. --->
<CFIF IsDefined('Attributes.UseNumbers') AND IsBoolean(Attributes.UseNumbers)>
    <CFSET UseNumbers=Attributes.UseNumbers>
<CFELSE>
    <CFSET UseNumbers="Yes">
</CFIF>

<!--- Check to see if UseUppercaseLetters was passed in.  If so, check to make
      sure it is a Boolean.  If any of these checks return False, default
      UseUppercaseLetters to Yes. --->
<CFIF IsDefined('Attributes.UseUppercaseLetters') AND
      IsBoolean(Attributes.UseUppercaseLetters)>
    <CFSET UseUppercaseLetters = Attributes.UseUppercaseLetters>
<CFELSE>
    <CFSET UseUppercaseLetters="Yes">
```

*Example 19-11. Generating Customizable Random Passwords (continued)*

```
</CFIF>

<!--- Check to see if UseLowercaseLetters was passed in.  If so, check to make
      sure it is a Boolean.  If any of these checks return False, default
      UseLowercaseLetters to Yes. --->
<CFIF IsDefined('Attributes.UseLowercaseLetters') AND
                IsBoolean(Attributes.UseLowercaseLetters)>
    <CFSET UseLowercaseLetters = Attributes.UseLowercaseLetters>
<CFELSE>
    <CFSET UseLowercaseLetters="Yes">
</CFIF>

<!--- make sure all attributes are NOT set to No.  If they are, send back an
      error message and abort processing.  This is an example of a required
      attribute. --->
<CFIF UseSymbols IS "No" AND UseNumbers IS "No" AND UseUpperCaseLetters IS "No"
      AND UseLowerCaseLetters IS "No">
     <CFTHROW MESSAGE="No random password can be generated because all
                        attributes have a <B>""No""</B> Value."
              TYPE="Custom.Tag.RandomPassword">
<CFELSE>

<!--- initialize variables. CharacterList holds the ASCII codes for each character
      and CharacterString holds the actual characters after they are generated --->
<CFSET CharacterList = "">
<CFSET CharacterString = "">

<!--- This next section builds the total available character list with values
      based on the parameters passed to the tag.  Each character is determined
      by its ASCII character code.  If you don't want to use certain characters
      (like the lowercase l and the number 1 and the <, ", and > characters),
      simply remove their corresponding ASCII character code from the
      appropriate list.  I'll leave that up to you. --->
<CFIF UseSymbols>
  <CFSET Symbols="33,34,35,36,37,38,39,40,41,42,43,44,45,46,47,58,59,60,61,62,63,
                64,91,92,93,94,95,96,123,124,125,126">
  <CFSET CharacterList=ListAppend(CharacterList, Symbols, ",")>
</CFIF>

<CFIF UseNumbers>
  <CFSET Numbers="48,49,50,51,52,53,54,55,56,57">
  <CFSET CharacterList=ListAppend(CharacterList, Numbers, ",")>
</CFIF>

<CFIF UseUppercaseLetters>
  <CFSET UppercaseLetters="65,66,67,68,69,70,71,72,73,74,75,76,77,78,79,80,81,82,
                          83,84,85,86,87,88,89,90">
  <CFSET CharacterList=ListAppend(CharacterList, UppercaseLetters, ",")>
</CFIF>

<CFIF UseLowercaseLetters>
  <CFSET LowercaseLetters="97,98,99,100,101,102,103,104,105,106,107,108,109,110,
```

*Example 19-11. Generating Customizable Random Passwords (continued)*

```
                          111,112,113,114,115,116,117,118,119,120,121,122">
  <CFSET CharacterList=ListAppend(CharacterList, LowercaseLetters, ",")>
</CFIF>

<!--- get the length of the character list --->
<CFSET TheLength=ListLen(CharacterList)>

<!--- Create a loop that iterates the same number of times as the length of the
      password.  For each iteration of the loop, one character is randomly
      chosen from the character list and added to the character string.  When
      the loop has finished iterating, you have a finished password  --->
<CFLOOP INDEX="CharacterPlaces" FROM="1" TO="#NumberOfCharacters#">

<CFSET GetPosition=RandRange(1,TheLength)>
<CFSET Character=ListGetAt(CharacterList, GetPosition, ",")>
<CFSET CharacterString=ListAppend(CharacterString, CHR(Character), ",")>
</CFLOOP>

<!--- return the random password back to the calling template with the
      caller variable name specified by the OutVar value --->
<CFSET "caller.#OutVar#" = ListChangeDelims(CharacterString, "")>
</CFIF>
<CFSETTING ENABLECFOUTPUTONLY="No">
```

In Example 19-11, the first part of the `CF_RandomPassword` tag checks to see that an attribute called `OutVar` is passed. `OutVar` is the only attribute explicitly required by the tag. If `OutVar` isn't passed in, the `CFTHROW` tag generates an exception, execution of the tag stops, and processing reverts to the calling template. If `OutVar` is passed in, processing of the custom tag continues.

The next section of the tag checks to see if an attribute called `NumberOfCharacters` exists and then checks to make sure its value is numeric using the `IsNumeric()` function. `NumberOfCharacters` determines the length of the password. If the attribute doesn't exist, or its value isn't numeric, a default value of 7 is set for the password length.

The next several `CFIF` statements are used to see if any of the remaining attributes the tag can accept were passed in. These attributes all take `Yes` or `No` as their values and indicate whether a particular type of character should be used when generating of the random password. The `IsBoolean()` function is used to see if each value passed in as a Boolean or not. If not, a default value is assigned.

The last `CFIF` statement makes sure all the character type attributes aren't set to `No` as this causes the tag to generate a password with no characters! If all the character type attributes are set to `No`, the `CFTHROW` tag throws an exception, processing of the tag is aborted, and processing reverts to the calling template.

The tag then creates a variable called `CharacterList`. `CharacterList` is used to hold the total available character list for the random password. The character list is a list of ASCII character codes belonging to each character type that was specified for inclusion by the character type attributes. Using the ASCII codes instead of the characters themselves keeps from having to escape any characters when building the list.

Once the character list has been built, the next step is to generate the random password from the list of available characters. This is done by creating a loop that iterates the same number of times as the length of the password. During each iteration of the loop, one character code is randomly chosen from the character list, converted to the actual character it represents using the `CHR()` function, and added to the character string. When the loop has finished iterating, you have a finished password. The password is then sent back to the calling template using a `Caller` variable named with the value specified by `OutVar`.

To examine how to call the `CF_RandomPassword` tag, see Example 19-12. The template is coded with a `CFTRY` block and two different `CFCATCH` blocks to handle any errors that could result from calling the tag. The first `CFCATCH` block catches either of the two validation exceptions thrown inside the custom tag (the ones set with the `CFTHROW` tag. The second `CFCATCH` block is used to catch any other errors that were not planned for, such as a missing custom tag template.

*Example 19-12. Calling CF_RandomPassword and Using CFTRY/CFCATCH*

```
<CFTRY>
<CF_RandomPassword NumberOfCharacters="7"
                   UseSymbols="No"
                   UseNumbers="Yes"
                   UseUppercaseLetters="Yes"
                   UseLowercaseLetters="Yes"
                   OutVar="RandomPassword">

<H2>Random Password Generator</H2>
<CFOUTPUT>
Your random password is: <B>#RandomPassword#</B>
</CFOUTPUT>
<P>
<I>Hit your browser's Reload button to generate a different password</I>

<!--- catch errors thrown by the CFTHROW tag inside of the custom tag --->
<CFCATCH TYPE="Custom.Tag.RandomPassword">
<CFOUTPUT>
#CFCATCH.Message#
</CFOUTPUT>
</CFCATCH>

<!--- catch any unplanned errors --->
<CFCATCH TYPE="Any">
```

*Example 19-12. Calling CF_RandomPassword and Using CFTRY/CFCATCH (continued)*

```
<CFOUTPUT>
#CFCATCH.Message#
</CFOUTPUT>
</CFCATCH>
</CFTRY>
```

Executing the template in Example 19-12 results in the output shown in Figure 19-5. If you want to see how error and exception handling works, set all the attributes to `No`, and don't pass the `OutVar` attribute or misspell the tag name.

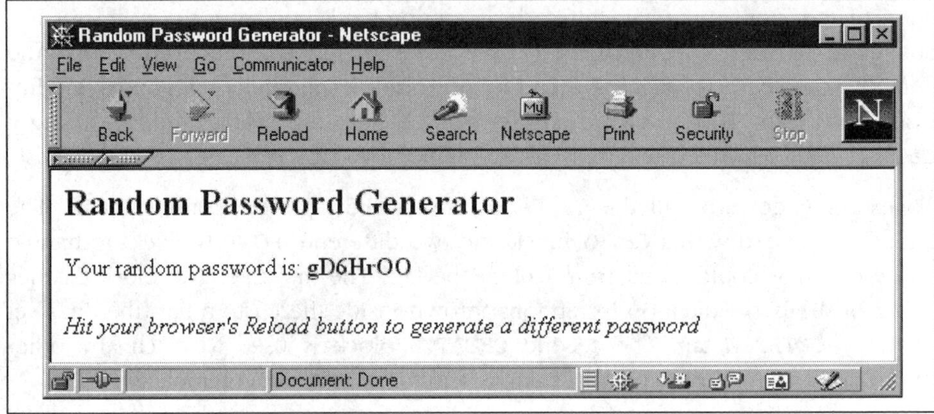


*Figure 19-5. Generating a random password with CF_RandomPassword*

# *Advanced Techniques*

There are several advanced features of the custom tag framework you can use to greatly expand the power of custom tags. You can:

- Use a new method to call custom tags
- Pass multiple attributes to a custom tag via a single attribute
- Create tag pairs
- Create a framework for creating nested tags
- Devise a method to halt the processing of custom tags without halting the processing of the calling template

This section covers each advanced technique and gives examples of how you can use them to extend the power of your ColdFusion applications.

## *Calling Custom Tags via CFMODULE*

As we mentioned earlier in the chapter, the CFMODULE tag provides another way to invoke custom tags. Using CFMODULE to call your custom tags allows you to call tags located in directories other than the *\cfusion\customtags* directory or the directory the calling template resides in. CFMODULE also enables you to resolve potential name conflicts among custom tags by allowing you to reference different custom tags that might have the same name but reside in different directories. The syntax for using CFMODULE follows:

```
<CFMODULE TEMPLATE="template"
          NAME="name"
          ATTRIBUTECOLLECTION="structure_containing_attributes"
          ATTRIBUTE1="value"
          ATTRIBUTE2="value"
          ...
          ATTRIBUTEn="value">
```

The following attributes are available to the CFMODULE tag:

TEMPLATE
: Specifies the path to the ColdFusion template to use as a custom tag. Relative paths are automatically expanded from the current page while absolute paths are expanded using the mappings defined in the ColdFusion Administrator. Optional. If a value is specified for TEMPLATE, the NAME attribute isn't used.

NAME
: Specifies the name of the custom tag you want to use. The default location for custom tag storage is *\cfusion\customtags.* Custom tags residing in this location may be referenced using dotted notation. For example, a custom tag called MyCustomTag (*MyCustomTag.cfm*) residing in the default custom tags directory (*\cfusion\customtags*) is referenced as MyCustomTag. The same tag residing under a subdirectory of the customtags directory called SpecialTags is referenced as SpecialTags.MyCustomTag. This dotted notation may be used to reference custom tags residing in or any number of levels below the default customtags directory. Optional. If a value is specified for NAME, the TEMPLATE attribute isn't used.

ATTRIBUTECOLLECTION
: Specifies the name of a ColdFusion structure containing attribute names and their associated values. Optional.

ATTRIBUTE*n*
: Additional attributes and their associated values as required by the custom tag. Optional. We'll talk more about custom tag attributes in just a few moments.

Now that you know the syntax for the CFMODULE tag, let's look at a few examples of how to use it to call custom tags. Suppose for a moment that we have a custom tag called CF_MyTag (*MyTag.cfm*) that is located in *c:\cfusion\customtags\subtags\subsubtags*. To call this tag using CFMODULE, we use the following code:

```
<CFMODULE NAME="SubTags.SubSubTags.MyTag">
```

In this scenario, the NAME attribute is used with the CFMODULE tag to specify a subdirectory under the *\cfusion\customtags* directory where the custom tag resides. The path to the custom tag is specified using a special dot notation to separate the directories.

However, what if CF_MyTag isn't stored under the *\cfusion\customtags* directory? This is where the TEMPLATE attribute comes in. Instead of invoking the custom tag with the NAME attribute, it is possible to use the TEMPLATE attribute to reference the tag no matter where it is located on the local filesystem. If the custom tag is located in the same directory as the calling template, it can be invoked directly as in the following example:

```
<CFMODULE TEMPLATE="MyTag.cfm">
```

If, however, the custom tag is located outside the current directory, it can be referenced using a relative path to the tag (the same way the CFINCLUDE tag works). For example, the following CFMODULE tag would call the *MyTag.cfm* custom tag located two directories above the location of the calling template:

```
<CFMODULE TEMPLATE="../../MyTag.cfm">
```

## *Passing Attributes via Structures*

The custom tag scope provides an advanced way to pass attribute information from a calling template to the custom tag using both the standard CF_MyTag format or via CFMODULE. Instead of passing attributes individually, you can use a special attribute named ATTRIBUTECOLLECTION to pass in a structure containing attribute/value pairs. Example 19-13 demonstrates this by creating a structure containing an employee record called Employee and passing the structure to a custom tag called CF_DisplayEmployee via the ATTRIBUTECOLLECTION attribute.

*Example 19-13. Passing Attributes Using ATTRIBUTECOLLECTION*

```
<!--- create a structure called Employee and populate it with the contact
      info for a single employee --->
<CFSET Employee = StructNew()>
<CFSET Employee.Name = "Pere Money">
<CFSET Employee.Title = "President">
<CFSET Employee.Department = "Executive Management">
<CFSET Employee.Email = "pere@mycompany.com">
<CFSET Employee.PhoneExt = "1234">
```

*Example 19-13. Passing Attributes Using ATTRIBUTECOLLECTION (continued)*

```
<!--- call the DisplayEmployee custom tag.  Pass the Employee structure to
      the tag as a list of attribute/value pairs using the ATTRIBUTECOLLECTION
      attribute. --->
<CF_DisplayEmployee AttributeCollection = "#Employee#">
```

Alternately, you can make the same tag call using the **CFMODULE** tag in place of **CF_DisplayEmployee**:

```
<CFMODULE TEMPLATE="DisplayEmployee.cfm"
          ATTRIBUTECOLLECTION="#Employee#">
```

Regardless of the method you use to call the custom tag, once the structure containing the attributes is passed to the custom tag, it is available inside the tag individually. The **CF_DisplayEmployee** tag is shown in Example 19-14. Note that we don't have to reference the attribute names as part of the structure, it's what makes the **ATTRIBUTECOLLECTION** attribute so convenient.

*Example 19-14. The CF_DisplayEmployee (DisplayEmployee.cfm) Custom Tag*

```
<!--- display the contents of the ATTRIBUTECOLLECTION attribute.  --->
<H2>Employee Detail</H2>
<CFOUTPUT>
<TABLE>
<TR>
  <TD>Name</TD><TD>#Attributes.Name#</TD>
</TR>
<TR>
  <TD>Title</TD><TD>#Attributes.Title#</TD>
</TR>
<TR>
  <TD>Department</TD><TD>#Attributes.Department#</TD>
</TR>
<TR>
  <TD>E-mail</TD><TD>#Attributes.Email#</TD>
</TR>
<TR>
  <TD>Phone Ext.</TD><TD>#Attributes.PhoneExt#</TD>
</TR>
</TABLE>
</CFOUTPUT>
```

Note that an explicitly named attribute takes precedence over a like-named attribute contained in the structure passed by the **ATTRIBUTECOLLECTION** attribute, resulting in the value from the structure being overwritten.

## Creating Tag Pairs

The next advanced feature of the custom tag framework is the idea of tag pairs. Up until now, every custom tag you have created has been called something like:

```
<CF_MyTag Attribute="Value">
```

If you look at HTML and CFML, both languages use end tags to allow you to wrap the functionality of the tag around some sort of arbitrary content. For example, in HTML almost every tag comes in pairs. That is, each tag has a begin tag and an end tag. Take any of the heading-level tags for example:

```
<H1>This is a heading level 1</H1>
```

Each heading-level tag contains a begin tag `<H1>` and an end tag `</H1>`. Whatever content appears between the tag pairs is available to be marked up by the tags. The same holds true for many CFML tags. Take the `CFMAIL` tag for example:

```
<CFMAIL FROM="me@example.com"
        TO="you@example.com"
        SUBJECT="Tag Pairs">
All of this content falls between the CFMAIL tag pairs!
</CFMAIL>
```

In this case, all the content between the `<CFMAIL>` and `</CFMAIL>` tags is available to the tag to be used as the body of an email message.

The custom tag framework gives you the means to create tags like these by providing a special structure called `ThisTag` that contains four key/value pairs that can be used with any custom tag to establish a tag pair:

`ThisTag.AssocAttribs`
: Returns an array of structures containing all the attributes of all nested tags associated with the base tag as long as the subtags were associated using `CFASSOCIATE`. This variable is returned only if the `CFASSOCIATE` tag is used to associate a nested tag with the base tag (this is covered later in the chapter).

`ThisTag.ExecutionMode`
: Returns the current execution mode of the tag. `ThisTag.ExecutionMode` returns `Start` when the tag is opened, `End` when the tag is closed, and `Inactive` if subtags of the base tag are being processed.

`ThisTag.GeneratedContent`
: Returns any content between the start and end tags. `ThisTag.GeneratedContent` is a read/write variable and can therefore be written to by your application.

`ThisTag.HasEndTag`
: Returns `True` if the tag has an associated end tag and `False` if it doesn't.

The best way to understand how tag pairs work within the context of custom tags is to look at an example. Say you want to create a custom tag that can strip all HTML from a block of text. You can write the tag the way we have so far and pass all the marked-up text via a single attribute. You could, but that would be awkward to code and even more awkward to read. What makes more sense is to surround the text from which you want to remove the HTML in a pair of tags:

```
<CF_HTMLbGone>
Text to have HTML removed goes here...
</CF_HTMLbGone>
```

As you can imagine, this type of tag layout is extremely flexible as it allows you to specify any text or variable containing the text between the tag pairs. The `CF_HTMLbGone` tag can take the text, remove any HTML code from it and return text right back to the calling template. The code for the `CF_HTMLbGone` tag (*HTMLbGone.cfm*) is shown in Example 19-15.

*Example 19-15. CF_HTMLbGone (HTMLbGone.cfm) Custom Tag*

```
<CFSETTING ENABLECFOUTPUTONLY="Yes">
<!----------------------------------------------------------------------------
NAME:           CF_HTMLbGone
FILE:           HTMLbGOne.cfm
CREATED:        04/23/1999
LAST MODIFIED:  06/29/2000
VERSION:        1.0
AUTHOR:         Rob Brooks-Bilson (rbils@amkor.com)
DESCRIPTION:    CF_HTMLbGone is a custom CFML tag that strips HTML tags
                from blocks of text using a regular expression.
ATTRIBUTES:     OPTIONAL
                OutVar(string) = Name to assign to the variable returned by the
                                 tag containing the HTML free text.  If no
                                 OUTVAR is specified, the stripped output is
                               written back to ThisTag.GeneratedContent.
                PreText(Yes/No) = If Yes, surrounds returned text in <PRE></PRE>
                                  tags so that some amount of formatting from
                                  the original page is preserved.  The default
                                  is No.
KNOWN ISSUES:   None
---------------------------------------------------------------------------->
<CFSWITCH EXPRESSION = "#ThisTag.ExecutionMode#">

<!--- begin processing when ThisTag.ExecutionMode is Start (when the tag is
      opened) --->
<CFCASE VALUE="Start">
<!--- Check to make sure an end tag is present.  If not, output a message and
      abort processing --->
<CFIF NOT ThisTag.HasEndTag>
    <CFOUTPUT>
    <B>This tag requires a matching end tag.  Please review your code and make
       sure the tag is paired: &lt;CF_HTMLbGone&gt;&lt;/CF_HTMLbGone&GT;</B>
```

*Example 19-15. CF_HTMLbGone (HTMLbGone.cfm) Custom Tag (continued)*

```
    </CFOUTPUT>
    <CFABORT>
</CFIF>
</CFCASE>

<!--- process this part of the tag when ThisTag.ExecutionMode is End (after the
      tag is closed) --->
<CFCASE VALUE="End">
<!--- strip all HTML from between the tags.  Assign the results to a local
      variable --->
<CFSET Local_GeneratedContent = REReplace(ThisTag.GeneratedContent, "<[^>]*>",
       "", "All")>

<!--- Clear the contents of ThisTag.GeneratedContent --->
<CFSET ThisTag.GeneratedContent = "">

<!--- see if the optional attribute PreText was passed and if so, assign
      it to a local variable --->
<CFIF IsDefined('Attributes.PreText') AND Attributes.PreText EQ "Yes">
  <CFSET Local_GeneratedContent = "<Pre>#Local_GeneratedContent#</PRE>">
</CFIF>

<!--- Send the string back with all HTML removed.  --->
<CFIF IsDefined('Attributes.OutVar') AND Attributes.OutVar NEQ "">
    <CFSET "Caller.#Attributes.OutVar#" = Local_GeneratedContent>
<CFELSE>
    <CFSET ThisTag.GeneratedContent = Local_GeneratedContent>
</CFIF>
</CFCASE>
</CFSWITCH>
<CFSETTING ENABLECFOUTPUTONLY="No">
```

As soon as the tag in Example 19-15 is called, `ThisTag.ExecutionMode` is set to `Start`, and the code in the first `CFSWITCH` statement executes. This code takes the variable `ThisTag.HasEndTag` and evaluates it using a `CFIF` statement. If the value is `No`, we know that no end tag is present so a message is written to the browser, and all processing is halted. If the value is `Yes`, we know that an end tag is present, and processing continues.

The second `CFSWITCH` statement detects when the `CF_HTMLbGone` tag is closed. As soon as this is detected, the tag proceeds to strip all the HTML tags from the contents of `ThisTag.GeneratedContent` and write the results to a variable called `Local_GeneratedContent`. `ThisTag.GeneratedContent` holds all the content between the start and end tags. The HTML is removed using a very simple regular expression.

Next, `ThisTag.GeneratedContent` is cleared by writing a blank string to the structure key. Once this is done, a check is made to see if an optional attribute named `PreText` was passed in. If so, the value of `Local_GeneratedContent` is wrapped with HTML `<PRE></PRE>` tags and written back to itself. The **PRE** tags allow any whitespace within the content of the variable to be preserved. We'll get to the reason for this attribute in just a moment.

The final section of code in the tag is used to send the content of **Local_GeneratedContent** back to the calling template with all HTML removed. The way the content is sent back depends on what attributes were passed to the tag. If an **OutVar** is passed, the string goes back as a caller variable of the same name. If an **OutVar** isn't passed, the text goes back as **ThisTag.GeneratedContent**, overwriting the content between the tag pair that called the custom tag to begin with. This gives you some flexibility in how you deal with the returned text.

To test the **CF_HTMLbGone** tag, create the template shown in Example 19-16 and save it to the same directory you saved the custom tag in.

*Example 19-16. Template for Calling the CF_HTMLbGone Tag*

```
<!--- call the HTMLbGone tag.  The HTML that appears between the tag pairs will
      be removed by the tag, leaving only the text --->
<CF_HTMLbGone>
<CENTER>
<H3>Today is Thursday June 29, 2000</H3>
<TABLE>
<TR>
  <TD><A HREF="/briefcase/cf/">Programming ColdFusion</A></TD>
</TR>
<TR>
  <TD><A HREF="/cfdocs/">ColdFusion Documentation</A></TD>
</TR>
<TR>
  <TD><A HREF="/cfide/administrator/">ColdFusion Administrator</A></TD>
</TR>
<TR>
  <TD><A HREF="/wddx_sdk/joust_files/index.htm">WDDX SDK 1.0</A></TD>
</TR>
</TABLE>
</CENTER>
</CF_HTMLbGone>
```

Executing the template in Example 19-16 results in the output shown in Figure 19-6. Note that the text that is output to the browser is all run together.

If you view the source of the HTML page in your browser, you'll notice that the text appears to be structured, but because HTML has no concept of whitespace, the spacing can't be displayed.

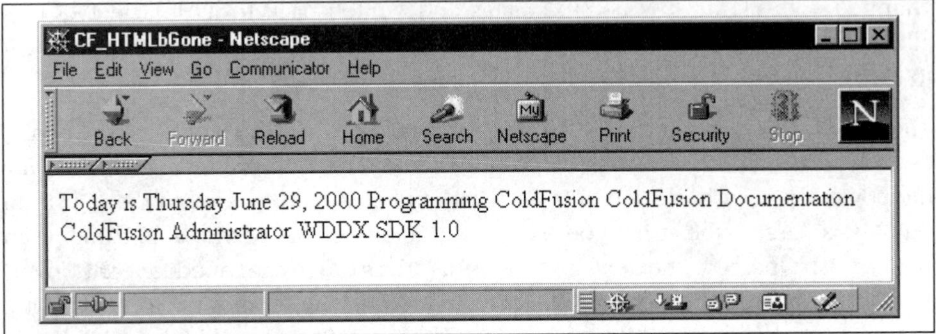


*Figure 19-6. Using CF_HTMLbGone to remove HTML code from a block of text*

We can make a small change to the code that calls the custom tag in Example 19-15 to change the way the HTML stripped output is sent back to the calling template and subsequently displayed in the browser:

```
<CF_HTMLbGone OutVar="CleanText" PreText="Yes">
```

One more change is required before you can see how adding the two optional attributes to the tag changes the behavior and output. This time, you need to append the following code to the end of the code shown in Example 19-16.

```
<CENTER>
<CFOUTPUT>
#CleanText#
</CFOUTPUT>
</CENTER>
```

Once you have finished modifying the templates go ahead and save them. Executing the template that calls the custom tag should result in output like that shown in Figure 19-7.

As you can see, passing the `PreText="Yes"` attribute results in the custom tag wrapping the stripped text in HTML `PRE` tags, which preserves the original whitespace around the text. In addition, sending the `OutVar` attribute causes the custom tag to return the stripped text as a caller variable that can be output with the `CFOUTPUT` tag. If `OutVar` isn't specified, the text replaces the original content between the start and ending `CF_HTMLbGone` tags.

## Nesting Custom Tags

Another benefit to creating tag pairs is the ability to create nested custom tags. Nested custom tags allow you to create sets of tags that can share data with one

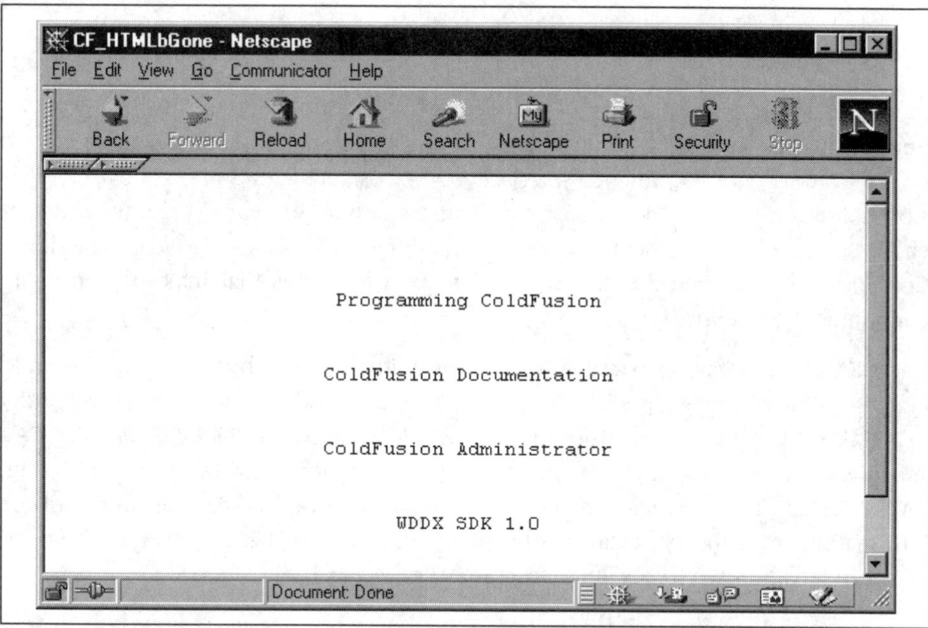


*Figure 19-7. Calling the CF_HTMLbGone custom tag with optional output parameters*

another. In CFML, a good example is the CFHTTP and CFHTTPPARAM tags. The tags can be nested as in the following example:

```
<CFHTTP URL="http://127.0.0.1/foo.cfm"
        METHOD="Post">

     <CFHTTPPARAM TYPE="Formfield" NAME="Name" VALUE="Pere Money">

     <CFHTTPPARAM TYPE="Formfield" NAME="Title" VALUE="President">
</CFHTTP>
```

In this case, the CFHTTP tag is the parent tag while the two CFHTTPPARAM tags are considered the children. The CFHTTPPARAM tags can pass the information contained in their attributes to the CFHTTP tag so that it can be posted to another template specified by the CFHTTP tag.

There are several metaphors that describe the relationships between nested custom tags. The most commonly used terms to describe the nesting relationship are: ancestor/descendant, base/sub, and parent/child tags. These terms are used interchangeably throughout this section.

Another important concept to understand in ancestor/descendant tag relationships is that a single tag can be both an ancestor and a descendant. Consider the following example:

```
<CF_BaseTag>
    <CF_SubTag>
```

```
        <CF_SubSubTag>
    </CF_SubTag>
</CF_BaseTag>
```

In this example, CF_BaseTag is a parent tag. CF_SubTag is a child tag of CF_BaseTag, but it is also a parent tag of CF_SubSubTag. CF_SubSubTag is a child tag of both CF_SubTag and CF_BaseTag. What is interesting about how ColdFusion handles nested-tag communication is the fact that you can have any parent or child tag pass information to any of its parent or child tags. How is this done? ColdFusion provides you with one tag and two functions that make the inter-tag communication possible.

The CFASSOCIATE tag associates a child tag with a parent by saving all the child tag's attributes to a special structure that is available to the parent tag. CFASSOCIATE takes two attributes, BASETAG and DATACOLLECTION. BASETAG specifies the name of the parent tag to associate with the child tag. DATACOLLECTION specifies a name for the structure used to pass all the attribute information from the child tag to the parent tag. If DATACOLLECTION isn't specified, ColdFusion uses the default structure AssocAttribs.

It is also possible for a child tag to request information about its ancestors. There are two functions that facilitate this:

GetBaseTagList()
: Returns a comma-delimited list (in uppercase) of ancestor tag names. GetBaseTagList is meant for use in custom CFML tags for inter-tag data exchange. The first element in the returned list of ancestor tags is always the top-level parent tag.

GetBaseTagData(*tag* [, *instance*])
: Returns an object containing data from the specified ancestor *tag*. An optional *instance* number may be set to specify the number of ancestor tag levels to skip through before returning data. The default value for *instance* is 1.

As always, the best way to explain the interaction between nested tags is with an example. In this case, we'll need to create three templates to accomplish the task. Examples 19-17 through 19-19 show how to create a simple demonstration of how nested tags communicate and how you can use the functions and tags we just discussed to abstract the underlying complexity.

Example 19-17 shows the caller template used to call our nested tags. Executing the template in Example 19-17 results in the output shown in Figure 19-8.

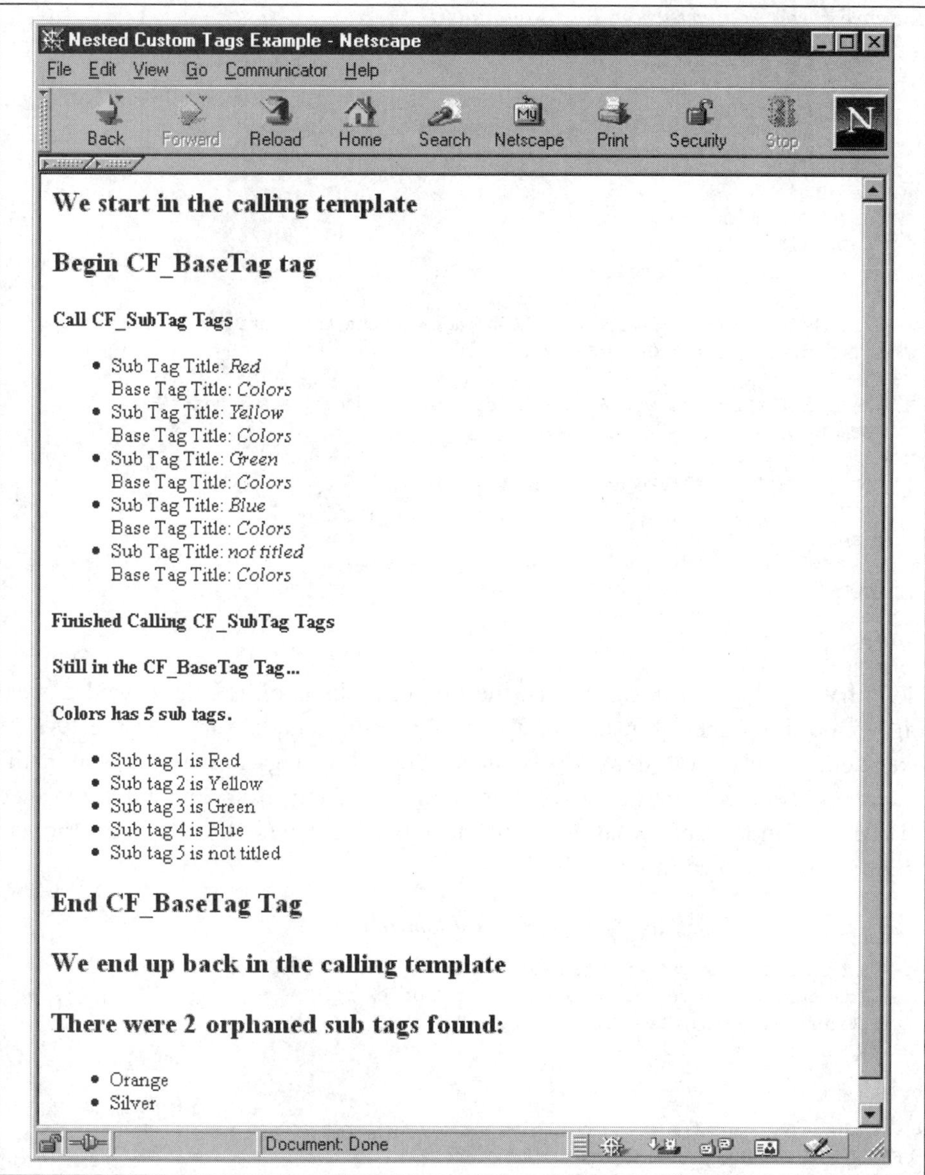


*Figure 19-8. Demonstrating communication between nested custom tags*

*Example 19-17. Nesting Custom Tags*

```
<H3>We start in the calling template</H3>

<!--- call the CF_BaseTag custom tag and nest a number of CF_SubTag tags.  Also
      call two CF_SubTag tags outside the CF_BaseTag to demonstrate how to
      handle orphaned CF_SubTag tags --->
<CF_BaseTag Title="Colors">
```

*Example 19-17. Nesting Custom Tags (continued)*

```
    <CF_SubTag Title="Red">
    <CF_SubTag Title="Yellow">
    <CF_SubTag Title="Green">
    <CF_SubTag Title="Blue">
    <CF_SubTag>
</CF_BaseTag>
<CF_SubTag Title="Orange">
<CF_SubTag Title="Silver">
<H3>We end up back in the calling template</H3>

<!--- If there are any orphaned CF_SubTag tags, output their attributes here --->
<CFIF IsDefined('Request.OrphanList')>
<CFOUTPUT>
<H3>There were #ListLen(Request.OrphanList)# orphaned sub tags found:</H3>
</CFOUTPUT>
<UL>
<CFLOOP INDEX="i" LIST="#Request.OrphanList#">
<CFOUTPUT>
<LI>#i#</LI>
</CFOUTPUT>
</CFLOOP>
</UL>
</CFIF>
```

Now that you have an idea of what the output looks like, let's discuss what went on behind the scenes to make it happen. Once the template in Example 19-17 is executed, a call to **CF_BaseTag** is made. Five child tags are nested within the parent tag. Each tag (with the exception of one child tag) passes an attribute called `Title`. To understand what happens next, let's examine the **CF_BaseTag** tag (*BaseTag.cfm*) shown in Example 19-18.

*Example 19-18. CF_BaseTag (BaseTag.cfm) Custom Tag*

```
<!--- if an attribute called Title exists, create a local copy of it.  Title is
      the only attribute used by the tags in this example. --->
<CFIF IsDefined('Attributes.Title')>
    <CFSET Title = Attributes.Title>
</CFIF>

<!--- this code executes when the CF_Parent tag is first opened --->
<CFSWITCH EXPRESSION = "#ThisTag.ExecutionMode#">
<CFCASE VALUE="Start">

<!--- check to make sure an end tag for CF_BaseTag is present.  If not, write a
      message out to the browser and abort processing.  This is necessary
      because you can't nest tags without using an end tag. --->
<CFIF NOT ThisTag.HasEndTag>
    <B>No end tag for the CF_BaseTag tag was found.  This tag can only be invoked
    when both a &lt;CF_BaseTag&gt; and a &lt;/CF_BaseTag&gt; are present.</B>
    <P>
    <B>Processing Aborted...</B>
```

*Example 19-18. CF_BaseTag (BaseTag.cfm) Custom Tag (continued)*

```
    <CFABORT>
</CFIF>

<H3>Begin CF_BaseTag tag</H3>
<b>Call CF_SubTag Tags</b>
<UL>
</CFCASE>


<!--- when the CF_Parent end tag is detected, this code executes --->
<CFCASE VALUE="End">
</UL>
<b>Finished Calling CF_SubTag Tags</b>
<P>

<!--- check to see if any attributes were passed back from a sub tag
      associated with this base tag --->
<CFIF IsDefined('ThisTag.AssocAttribs')>
<b>Still in the CF_BaseTag Tag...</b>
<P>

<!--- output the total number of sub tags associated with this tag --->
<CFOUTPUT>
<b>#Title# has #ArrayLen(ThisTag.AssocAttribs)# sub tags.</b>
</CFOUTPUT>

<!--- output the TITLE attribute of each sub tag associated with this tag --->
<UL>
<CFLOOP INDEX="i" FROM="1" TO="#ArrayLen(ThisTag.AssocAttribs)#">
  <CFOUTPUT>
    <LI>Sub tag #i# is #ThisTag.AssocAttribs[i].Title#</LI>
  </CFOUTPUT>
</CFLOOP>
</UL>
</CFIF>

<H3>End CF_BaseTag Tag</H3>
</CFCASE>
</CFSWITCH>
```

The tag starts by checking to see if an attribute called `Title` is passed in. If so, a local variable called `Title` is set. Next, `ThisTag.ExecutionMode` is checked to see if the value is `Start`. If so, the template checks to make sure an end tag for `CF_BaseTag` is present by evaluating the value of `ThisTag.HasEndTag`. If no end tag is found, a message is written out to the browser, and all processing of both the custom tag and the calling template is aborted. This is necessary because you can't nest tags without using an end tag. If everything up through here is okay, a message that processing of the custom tag has begun and that the sub tags are being called is output to the browser.

At this point, any sub tags located between the start and end tags of CF_BaseTag are processed. Let's examine what happens inside the sub tags in Example 19-19. Then we'll come back to the rest of the code in CF_BaseTag.

*Example 19-19. CF_SubTag (SubTag.cfm) Custom Tag*

```
<!--- if no Title attribute is passed with a sub tag, specify "not titled" for
      the title.  If you wanted to make Title a required attribute, you could
      use IsDefined to check for its existence here.  If Title wasn't passed,
      processing could be aborted or exited --->
<CFPARAM NAME="Attributes.Title" DEFAULT="not titled">

<!--- initialize a Request variable called OrphanList.  This variable is used
      to hold a comma delimited list of orphaned CF_SubTag Titles  in the event
      that there are any.  The Request scope is used so that the list can be
      available to the calling template (or any other template) within the
      scope of this page request --->
<CFPARAM NAME="Request.OrphanList" DEFAULT="">

<!--- retrieve a list of all ancestor tags --->
<CFSET AncestorTags = GetBaseTagList()>
<!--- look for CF_BaseTag in the list of retrieved ancestor tags.  If it is
      found, get all of the base tag's information and assign it to a variable
      called ParentTagData.  Then, output the Title for each CF_SubTag as
      well as the sub tag's base tag name --->
<CFIF ListFindNoCase(AncestorTags, "CF_BaseTag")>
    <CFOUTPUT>
    <CFSET BaseTagData = GetBaseTagData("CF_BaseTag")>
    <LI>Sub Tag Title: <I>#Attributes.Title#</I><BR>
        Base Tag Title: <I>#BaseTagData.Title#</I></LI>
    </CFOUTPUT>
    <!--- associate this tag with the base tag (CF_BaseTag) --->
    <CFASSOCIATE BASETAG="CF_BaseTag">
<CFELSE>
    <!--- if there are any orphaned sub tags, append their names to the
          Request.OrphanList variable we initialized earlier.  This variable
          is automatically available to any template within the scope of this
          request, including the calling template --->
    <CFOUTPUT>
    <CFSET Request.OrphanList = ListAppend(Request.OrphanList,
           Attributes.Title)>
    </CFOUTPUT>
</CFIF>
```

In Example 19-19, the first thing each CF_SubTag does is to assign a default value for the Title attribute that can be passed to the tag. If no Title exists, no title is assigned as the default.

Next, a default value of "" is assigned to a request variable called Request.OrphanList. This variable holds a comma-delimited list of the Title attributes of any CF_SubTag tags that are called outside the CF_BaseTag tag. Child tags called outside the scope of their parent tag are more commonly known as orphaned tags.

The request scope is used so that the list of orphaned tags is available to any template (including and especially the calling template) within the scope of this page request.

The next part of the template calls the `GetBaseTagList()` function. The function returns a comma-delimited list of ancestor tag names for the subtag. The list is written to a variable called `AncestorTags`.

The `ListFindNoCase()` function looks for `CF_BaseTag` in the list of ancestor tags stored in the `AncestorTags` variable. If it is found, all the base tag's information is assigned to a variable called `BaseTagData`. Next, the `Title` for each `CF_SubTag` as well as the subtag's parent tag `Title` is output to the browser. Finally, the subtag is associated with `CF_BaseTag` using the `CFASSOCIATE` tag. This lets the subtag share all of its information with the parent tag.

If `CF_BaseTag` isn't found in the list of ancestor tags, we know that the subtag is an orphaned tag, so we write its `Title` to the `Request.OrphanList` variable so that it can be passed back to the calling template.

When the last `CF_SubTag` has finished processing, control is returned back to the `CF_BaseTag` tag. At that point, evaluating `ThisTag.GeneratedContent` returns `End`. A message is written to the browser that we have finished calling all the subtags. Next, the total number of child tags associated with the `CF_BaseTag` tag is output by evaluating the length of the variable `ThisTag.AssocAttribs`. If you remember from earlier, `ThisTag.AssocAttribs` is an array of structures that contain all the attribute values from each child tag. The `ArrayLen()` function returns the length of the array, which represents the number of structures returned (one for each subtag).

Next, the `Title` of each subtag is output to the browser by looping over each structure in the `ThisTag.AssocAttribs` array. When the loop is finished, a message is output to the browser letting you know that the `CF_BaseTag` has finished processing. At this point, processing reverts to the calling template.

The calling template in Example 19-17 finishes up by outputting a message that processing has been passed back to it. Finally, a check is made to see if the variable `Request.OrphanList` exists. If it does, we know that there were some orphaned tags encountered. The list is looped over, and the title from each orphaned tag is output to the browser.

## *Aborting Tag Processing*

Sometimes, it is desirable to halt processing within a custom tag. There are many reasons why you might opt to do that, including error handling, attribute validation, and conditional processing. You can use the `CFABORT` tag inside a custom tag to halt processing, but doing that terminates the processing of the calling template or tag as well. There is, however, a tag you can use that allows you to halt processing of a custom tag, exit the tag gracefully, and resume processing of the template or tag that made the original call to the custom tag. That tag is `CFEXIT`.

The `CFEXIT` tag is similar in functionality to the `CFABORT` tag except it is intended for use within custom tags. If the `CFEXIT` tag is used outside a custom tag, it behaves the same as the `CFABORT` tag. The syntax for calling the `CFEXIT` tag is:

```
<CFEXIT METHOD="method">
```

The tag takes a single attribute, `METHOD` that specifies the method to use in exiting the custom tag. Each method produces different results depending on where you locate the `CFEXIT` tag within your custom tag. Possible entries for `METHOD` are:

`ExitTag` *(default)*
: When placed in the base tag, processing of the custom tag is halted, and control returns to the calling template. If placed within a block of code where `ThisTag.ExecutionMode` is `Start` or `ThisTag.ExecutionMode` is `End`, processing continues after the end tag.

`ExitTemplate`
: When placed in the base tag, processing of the custom tag is halted, and control returns to the calling template. If placed within a block of code where `ThisTag.ExecutionMode` is `Start`, processing continues from the first child tag of the calling tag. If `ThisTag.ExecutionMode` is `End`, processing continues after the end tag.

`Loop`
: Reexecutes a block of code in the currently executing custom tag (emulates a `CFLOOP`). This method can be used only when `ThisTag.ExecutionMode` is `End`. Using it in any other location results in an error.

The `CFEXIT` tag is most commonly used to halt the processing of a custom tag, exit the custom tag, and then resume processing of the calling template. Example 19-20 creates a custom tag called `CF_ExitTagTest`. Make sure to save the template as *ExitTagTest.cfm* in the directory you intend to call it from.

*Example 19-20. CF_ExitTagTest Custom Tag*

```
<CFIF IsDefined('Attributes.Name')>
    <CFSET Local_Name = Attributes.Name>
<CFELSE>
You failed to pass a required attribute: <B>Name</B>
<CFEXIT METHOD="ExitTag">
</CFIF>

<CFOUTPUT>
Hello #Attributes.Name#!
```

*Example 19-20. CF_ExitTagTest Custom Tag (continued)*

```
</CFOUTPUT>
<!--- the rest of your tag goes here --->
```

The `CF_ExitTagRequest` tag checks to see if an attribute called `Name` was passed in by the tag call. If it exists, the custom tag simply outputs the value of the attribute. If, however, the `Name` attribute doesn't exist, execution of the tag is halted, the tag is exited, and processing of the calling template resumes.

You can test `CF_ExitTagTest` by creating the template shown in Example 19-21. Be sure to save it in the same directory you saved the *ExitTagTest.cfm* template in.

*Example 19-21. Template for Calling the CF_ExitTagTest Custom Tag*

```
<H2>Exiting a custom tag using &lt;CFEXIT METHOD="Tag"&gt;</H2>
<B>This is in the Calling Template</B>
<P>
<!--- call the ExitTagTest custom tag. --->
<CF_ExitTagTest>
<P>
<B>We're back to the Calling Template again</B>
```

You can also use `CFEXIT` to emulate the behavior of a conditional `CFLOOP` within the context of a custom tag. By setting the `METHOD` attribute of the `CFEXIT` tag to `Loop`, you can have ColdFusion iterate over the same block of code in the custom tag until a specific condition is met. The template shown in Example 19-22 creates a custom tag called `CF_ExitLoopTest` (save it as *ExitLoopTest.cfm*) that demonstrates using the `CFEXIT` tag with the `METHOD` set to `Loop`.

*Example 19-22. CF_ExitLoopTest Custom Tag*

```
<CFSWITCH EXPRESSION = "#ThisTag.ExecutionMode#">

<CFCASE VALUE="Start">
<CFSET Count=1>
<B>Start Tag Execution...</B><BR>
</CFCASE>

<CFCASE VALUE="End">
 <CFIF Count LTE 10>
  <CFOUTPUT>Iteration #Count#<BR></CFOUTPUT>
  <CFSET Count = IncrementValue(Count)>
  <!--- this CFEXIT tag causes the body of the End ExecutionMode to execute
        again and again until Count=10.  When Count = 10, the tag is exited and
        processing is returned to the calling template. --->
  <CFEXIT METHOD="LOOP">
 </CFIF>
<B>End Tag Execution.</B>
</CFCASE>
</CFSWITCH>
```

The custom tag in Example 19-22 begins by checking the value of `ThisTag.ExecutionMode`. If it is `Start`, a counter variable called `Count` is set to `1`, and a message is written back to the calling template that reads "Start Tag Execution".

If `ThisTag.ExecutionMode` is `End`, a `CFIF` statement evaluates the value of `Count`. If `Count` is less than or equal to `10`, its value is output to the browser. The value of `Count` is then incremented by `1` using the `Increment()` function. Setting `METHOD` to `Loop` reprocesses the contents of the `CFCASE` statement, effectively creating a conditional loop until the value of `Count` is equal to 10. Once Count is greater than `10`, the `CFIF` statement evaluates `False`, and the custom tag returns processing control back over to the calling template.

To call the `CF_ExitLoopTest` tag, create the template shown in Example 19-23 and save it to the same directory you saved the *ExitLoopTest.cfm* template to. Note the tag is called using the syntax `<CF_ExitLoopTest/>`. The trailing forward slash indicates an end tag without actually having to code the opening and closing `<CF_ExitLoopTest>` and `</CF_ExitLoopTest>` tags.

*Example 19-23. Template for Calling the CF_ExitLoopTest Custom Tag*

```
<H2>Exiting a custom tag using &lt;CFEXIT METHOD="Loop"&gt;</H2>
<B>This is in the Calling Template</B>
<P>
<!--- call the ExitLoopTest custom tag.  Note the trailing forward slash used to
      call the tag.  This indicates a start and end tag without having to write
      two lines of code --->
<CF_ExitLoopTest/>
<P>
<B>We're back to the Calling Template again</B>
```

# Protecting Your Tags

ColdFusion comes with a command-line utility called CFEncode you can use to obfuscate the source code in your CFML templates so that it can't be easily viewed. The obfuscation process is designed to be one-way, so you should make sure you have a backup copy of any templates you wish to encode before proceeding. You should also be aware that the mechanism used to encode tags is relatively weak and has been broken in the past. For this reason, you shouldn't rely on the encoding mechanism as the sole means for protecting your source code.

To run the CFEncode utility (located in *\cfusion\bin* by default), simply execute it using the following syntax:

```
cfencode infile outfile [/r /q] [/h "header"] /v"2"
```

The following list explains each parameter and switch:

`infile`
: Specifies the name of the CFML template to be encoded. Optionally, you may specify a wildcarded filename if you wish to encode more than one template at a time.

`outfile`
: Specifies the full path to the output file for the encoded file. If you fail to specify an output file, the CFEncode utility overwrites the original file with the encoded version. For this reason, it is important that you always keep a backup copy of any templates you wish to encode.

`/r` Specifies that encoding should be recursive. This switch is used when you use a wildcard as the *`infile`* parameter, and you wish to have the CFEncode utility recurse subdirectories.

`/q` Specifying this optional switch turns off any warning messages usually generated by the utility.

`/h` Specifies a custom header to include at the beginning of the encoded file. This is an optional switch.

`/v` This switch allows you to use version-specific encoding. Possible values are `1` and `2`. Specifying `1` sets the encoding level at ColdFusion 3.x. Specifying `2` sets the encoding level at ColdFusion 4.0 or later. Unless you are encoding the tag to be used exclusively with ColdFusion 3.x, you should set this switch to `2`.

Note that prior to ColdFusion 4.5 the CFEncode utility was called CFCrypt. The name was changed to CFEncode in ColdFusion 4.5 to better reinforce the idea that encoded tags are obfuscated but not strongly encrypted.

# *CFX Tags*

As I mentioned in the beginning of the chapter, ColdFusion can be extended through another type of custom tag called a CFX tag. CFX tags differ from CFML custom tags in a number of ways:

- They are created in Visual C++, Delphi, or Java.
- They are compiled (*.dll* for Visual C++/Delphi, *.class* for Java).
- They must be registered in the ColdFusion Administrator before they can be used.
- They may or may not be cross-platform.

- They can extend the capabilities of the ColdFusion Application Server in ways that CFML tags can't by performing tasks not native to ColdFusion.
- They generally execute faster than CFML tags (because they are compiled).

## Registering CFX Tags

Before a CFX tag can be used, it must be registered in the ColdFusion Administrator. The following steps outline the procedure for ColdFusion 5.0. If you use an earlier version, the actual registration process and screens may vary slightly. Save the tag to your ColdFusion server. The default directory for custom tags is *\cfusion\customtags*.

1. Under the Extensions section of the ColdFusion Administrator, click on the CFX Tags link. This takes you to the Registered CFX Tags page (shown in Figure 19-9).
2. Click the button corresponding to the type of CFX tag you wish to register. Choose C++ for tags written in C++ or Delphi, or choose Java for tags written in Java.
3. Depending on whether you are registering a C++/Delphi CFX tag or a Java CFX tag, follow the additional steps outlined in the appropriate section.

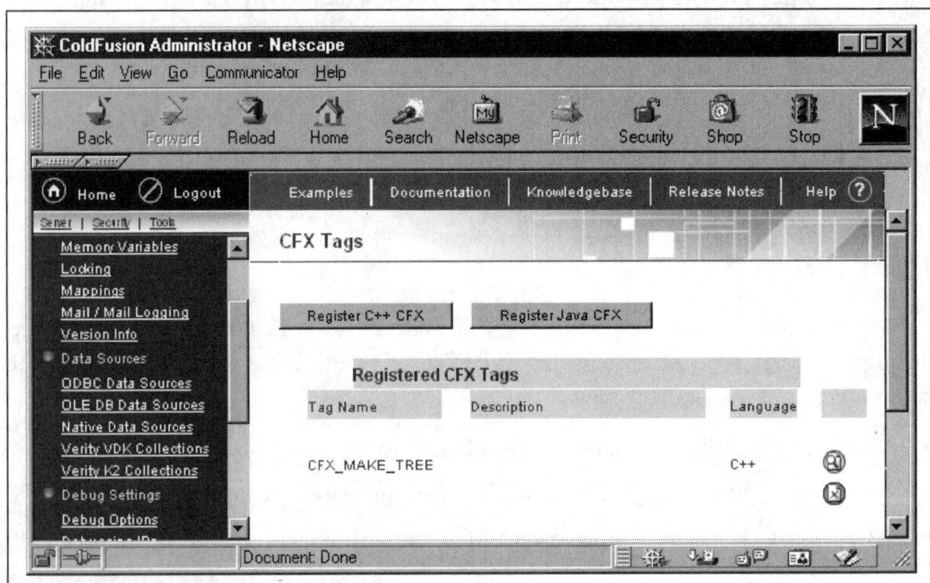


*Figure 19-9. Registering a CFX tag in the ColdFusion Administrator*

Note that Delphi isn't explicitly listed as a supported CFX tag type. However, because Delphi can create windows *.dll* files, it can create CFX tags. When registering a tag created in Delphi, treat it the same way you would a CFX tag created using C++.

### *Registering C++/Delphi CFX tags*

After clicking the Register C++ CFX button on the Registered CFX Tags page, you are taken to Add/Edit C++ CFX Tag (Figure 19-10). Here you must fill in a few details about your CFX tag before it can be registered:

1. Choose a name to register for your CFX tag. The name can be anything you want as long as it begins with `CFX_` and contains only letters, numbers, and underscores.
2. Enter the location to the CFX tag's *.dll* file on your server in the Server Library (DLL) field. If you don't know the location, you can click the Browse button to search through the local filesystem.
3. Make sure the Keep Library Loaded checkbox is checked; otherwise ColdFusion has to reload the tag into memory each time the tag is requested
4. You may enter an optional description for the tag in the Description field. The description is viewable only within the ColdFusion Administrator and generally serves as a reminder so you don't later forget what the tag is used for.
5. When you have finished adding all the setup information about the tag, click on the Submit Changes button to complete the registration process and to return to the Registered CFX Tags page.

### *Registering Java CFX tags*

If you choose to register a Java CFX tag from the Registered CFX Tags, you do so from the Add/Edit Java CFX Tag page shown in Figure 19-11. Here's what you need to do to register:

1. Choose a name to register for your CFX tag. The name can be anything you want as long as it begins with `CFX_` and contains only letters, numbers, and underscores.
2. In the Class Name field, enter the name of the CFX tag's Java class file. The Class Path for Java CFX tags is defined in the Java section of the ColdFusion Administrator.

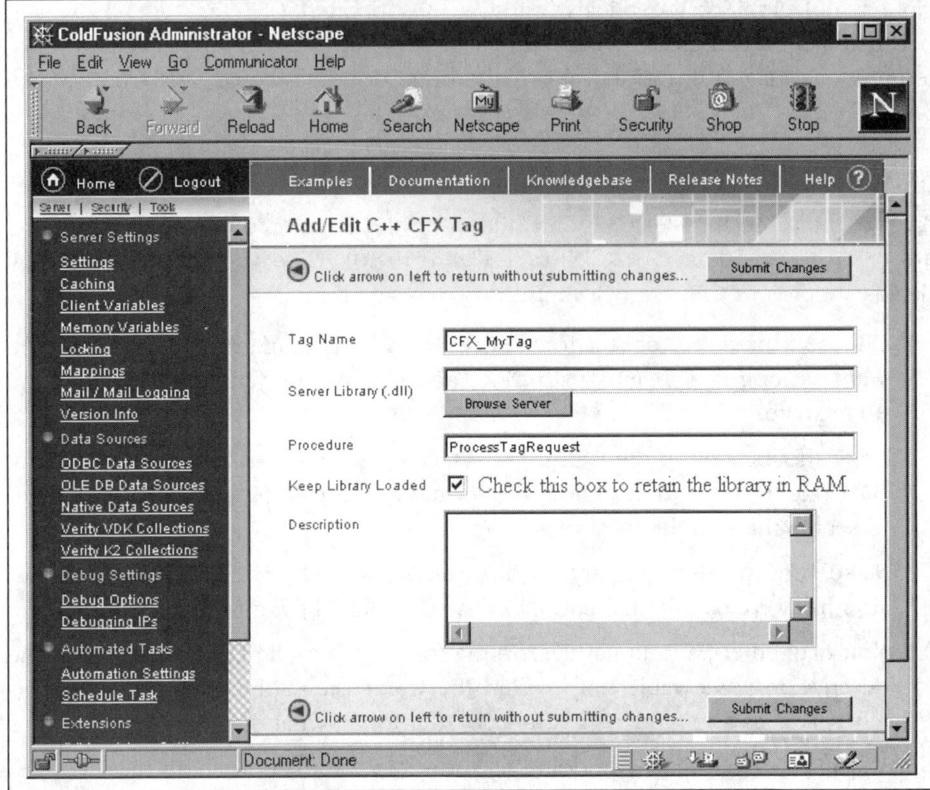


Figure 19-10. Registering a C++/Delphi CFX Tag

3. You may enter an optional description for the tag in the Description field. The description is viewable only within the ColdFusion Administrator and generally serves as a reminder so you don't later forget what the tag is used for.
4. When you have finished adding all the setup information about the tag, click on the Submit Changes button to complete the registration process and to return to the Registered CFX Tags page.

## Calling CFX Tags

Calling a CFX tag is simple and follows the same basic syntax used to call a custom CFML tag:

```
<CFX_MYCUSTOMTAG ATTRIBUTE1="value"
                 ATTRIBUTEn="value">
```

In this example, the CFX tag is named `CFX_MYCUSTOMTAG` (*mycustomtag.dll*). We differentiate calling a CFX tag from calling a regular custom tag by prefixing the call with `CFX_`.

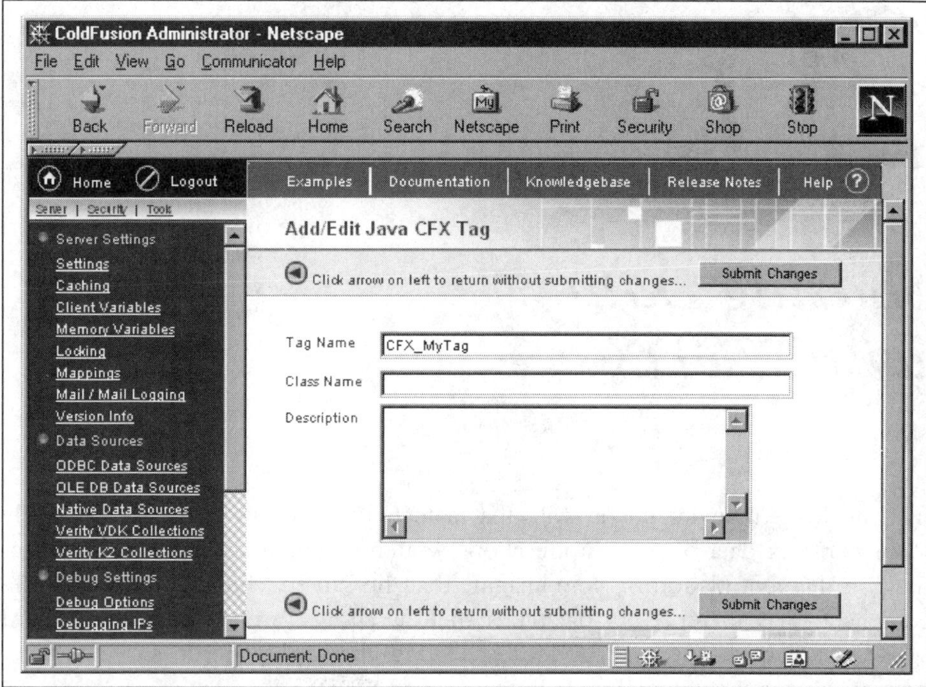


*Figure 19-11. Registering a Java CFX tag*

## *Additional Resources*

A thorough discussion on building CFX tags is well beyond the scope of this book. For more information on how you can create your own CFX tags, see the ColdFusion documentation from Allaire.

The Allaire Developer's Exchange (*http://devex.allaire.com/developer/gallery/index.cfm*) is a good place to look for preexisting CFX tags. At last count, there were several dozen CFX tags that were available for download free of charge as well as links to several other commercial tags.

# 20

# *Sharing Data with WDDX*

*In this chapter:*
- *WDDX Basics*
- *Serializing and Deserializing Data*
- *Storing WDDX Packets*
- *Server-to-Server WDDX*
- *Server-to-Browser WDDX Using JavaScript*

Imagine for a moment if you will, that a technology exists that lets you easily share complex data between applications written in different languages and running on different platforms. Now imagine that the same technology uses an XML-compliant DTD to represent datatypes such as strings, arrays, structures, record sets, and binary data as plain ASCII text. Sound like vaporware? It isn't. The technology exists, it is open and free, and it is called WDDX.

## *WDDX Basics*

In 1998, Allaire created a new XML-based technology called the Web Distributed Data Exchange, or WDDX. WDDX is an open technology for exchanging both simple and complex datatypes using a language-independent representation of the data based on an XML 1.0-compliant DTD. It is designed to be used by any number of programming languages without regard to the platforms they are running on. A number of serialization/deserialization modules have been written for a variety of popular programming and scripting languages and are freely available. For the most up-to-date information on WDDX or to obtain the SDK, please visit *http://www.openwddx.org*.

### *What Can You Do with WDDX?*

The first question you are probably asking is "what the heck can I do with WDDX?" Well, to put it simply, you can do a hell of a lot with it. Because WDDX allows you to represent data in a completely neutral and open format, WDDX is the perfect vehicle for sharing data between applications written in different languages. Imagine that you have an application written in Perl that performs some heavy-duty massaging on a large record set. Now suppose that you want to make the cleaned up data available to another application within your company that is built in ColdFusion. How are you going to do that? You could write the data to a database and then query the database in ColdFusion, but what if the database isn't accessible to your ColdFusion application, say because it is behind a firewall? What then? You can save the record set as a delimited text file, then allow the ColdFusion application to grab it using `CFHTTP` or `CFFTP`, but that won't work because you need the datatypes of each field in the database to be preserved. Using WDDX, you can take the record set you created in your Perl application, convert it to the WDDX format, and send it to your ColdFusion application while preserving the datatypes of all of the data. Your ColdFusion application can then easily convert the data from the WDDX format into a query object that can be used in any way the application needs.

Along the same lines, WDDX can enable content syndication between web sites. Syndication allows one site to make selected content available to other sites. Syndication can be open and public, or a closed endeavor between trading partners, clients, vendors, etc. Via syndication, a content aggregator (such as Yahoo, Excite, CNN, etc.) can provide other web sites with content such as news, weather, stock quotes, or sports scores using WDDX (an open format). The sites receiving the syndicated content can then use it in their applications and web sites regardless of what tools they use to build them. We'll give an actual example of content syndication later on in the chapter.

So far, we've mentioned two important ways in which you can use WDDX for server-to-server communication. But WDDX can be used for server-to-browser communication as well. If you use WDDX in conjunction with JavaScript, it is possible to create sophisticated user interfaces for browsing and manipulating data stored as WDDX.

Now that you have a better idea of what you can do with WDDX, let's look at how it works and how you can start using it within your own applications.

## How Does It Work?

As we mentioned in the introduction, WDDX itself is nothing more than an XML representation of data. As such, you are probably wondering how to convert data to and from the WDDX format. The process looks something like this:

Data → Serialization → WDDX Packet → Deserialization → Data

You'll notice three new terms: serialization, WDDX packet, and deserialization. *Serialization* consists of taking a chunk of data and converting it into the WDDX format. Data that has been converted to WDDX is referred to as a *WDDX packet*. A WDDX packet can represent a range of both simple and complex datatypes. The simple datatypes are made up of string, numeric, Boolean, null, and date/time values. Complex datatypes consist of arrays, structures, record sets (query objects in CFML), and binary data. The process of converting the contents of a WDDX packet back to their native datatype(s) is known as *deserialization*.

While this chapter primarily deals with WDDX within the context of the ColdFusion Markup Language (which has native support for WDDX), there are components available for several other languages. A COM component is available that can be used by any COM-enabled language, such as ASP, Visual Basic, Delphi, Visual C++, and PowerBuilder. Additionally, native modules now exist for Java, Perl, and PHP. Within each of these implementations (CFML, COM, Java, and Perl), support for client-side JavaScript objects capable of working with WDDX is provided. Server-side JavaScript is also supported via the COM implementation. Development is currently underway on several additional language modules, including one for Python.

## Show Me the WDDX!

Now that we've covered the how and why of WDDX, let's take a moment to examine the syntax of a WDDX packet. Because WDDX uses an XML DTD, a WDDX packet is just a collection of tags and data elements. The following is a WDDX packet containing a single string value:

```
<wddxPacket version='1.0'>
  <header></header>
  <data>
    <string>Programming ColdFusion</string>
  </data>
</wddxPacket>
```

All WDDX packets are considered well-formed XML in the sense that their syntax conforms to the XML 1.0 specification. Every WDDX packet must be enclosed in the `<wddxPacket></wddxPacket>` tags. The current version of the WDDX DTD is 1.0a and is specified along with the `<wddxPacket>` tag. The full WDDX DTD may be obtained by visiting *http://www.openwddx.org* and downloading the WDDX SDK. The next tag pair, `<header></header>` isn't currently used in WDDX, but they have been included in case a need for them arises in the future. The `<data></data>` tag pair marks the start and end of all serialized data within the WDDX packet. In this example, only a single string, `Programming ColdFusion`, is serialized within the packet. It is delimited appropriately using the `<string></string>` tags. Other datatypes include `<number>`, `<null>`, `<Boolean>`, `<dateTime>`, `<recordset>`, `<array>`, `<struct>`, and `<binary>`. These are covered later in the chapter.

There is no concept of whitespace in WDDX. The prior example in which we neatly indented the tag pairs of the WDDX packet and separated them with new lines is just as valid as a WDDX packet containing no whitespace at all. In fact, most WDDX packets that are created using the **CFWDDX** tag contain no whitespace between the pairs of tags. Although more difficult to read, this is actually a desirable format for transporting WDDX packets, as whitespace can add to the overall bulk of the packet (eating up precious bandwidth and additional storage space).*

One of the great things about using WDDX with ColdFusion is that you don't really have to do much work to serialize and deserialize WDDX packets. ColdFusion uses the **CFWDDX** tag to handle the serialization and deserialization of the data for you according to the WDDX XML DTD. The **CFWDDX** tag can also be used to create JavaScript statements that instantiate equivalent JavaScript objects (more on this later). The general syntax for using the **CFWDDX** tag is as follows:

```
<CFWDDX ACTION="action"
        INPUT="data_to_be_serialized/de-serialized"
        OUTPUT="variable_name_for_results"
        TOPLEVELVARIABLE="top_level_variable_name_for_javascript_object"
        USETIMEZONEINFO="Yes/No">
```

The `ACTION` attribute is required and specifies the action to be performed by the tag. Possible values include the following:

`CFML2WDDX`
: Serializes CFML to WDDX

`WDDX2CFML`
: Deserializes WDDX to CFML

`CFML2JS`
: Serializes CFML to WDDX, then automatically deserializes it to JavaScript in a single step

`WDDX2JS`
: Deserializes WDDX to JavaScript

The `INPUT` attribute specifies the data to be serialized/deserialized. As you might expect, `OUTPUT` specifies a variable to hold the serialized/deserialized data. `OUTPUT` is required when `ACTION` is `WDDX2CFML`. For all other actions, if no value is specified for `OUTPUT`, the results of the serialization/deserialization are output directly to the browser in the HTML stream. The `TOPLEVELVARIABLE` attribute is required when `ACTION` is set to `CFML2JS` or `WDDX2JS`. It specifies the name of the top-level JavaScript object created when deserialization occurs.

---

* If you use ColdFusion Studio as your development environment, you can open any WDDX packet residing in a file and apply the WDDX CodeSweeper (located under Tools→CodeSweeper→WDDX Sweeper) to it. The WDDX Sweeper takes an unformatted (all whitespace-stripped) WDDX packet and formats it for easy readability.

The final attribute is USETIMEZONEINFO. This attribute is optional, can be set to Yes or No, and indicates whether to use time-zone information when serializing CFML to WDDX. If this attribute is set to Yes, ColdFusion calculates the hour/minute offset for all date/time objects in the WDDX packet. If USETIMEZONEINFO is set to No, local time is used for all date/time objects. The default value for USETIMEZONEINFO is Yes.

# Serializing and Deserializing Data

In CFML, the process of serializing and deserializing data is handled by the CFWDDX tag. The following sections step through the process of using the tag to serialize and deserialize various simple and complex datatypes. Numerous examples are provided to make the concepts as clear as possible.

## Serializing and Deserializing Simple Values

The easiest types of values to work with are simple values, as simple values only consist of numbers, strings, Boolean, date/time values, and null datatypes. The process of serializing and deserializing simple values then is straightforward. Example 20-1 serializes an example of each simple datatype (boolean, dateTime, null, number, and string) and displays the resulting WDDX packets in an HTML table so that you can see how the structure of each packet varies depending on the datatype represented.

*Example 20-1. Serializing Simple Datatypes to WDDX*

```
<!--- serialize a boolean --->
<CFWDDX ACTION="CFML2WDDX" INPUT="#IsDefined('y')#" OUTPUT="WDDX_boolean">

<!--- serialize a dateTime --->
<CFWDDX ACTION="CFML2WDDX" INPUT="#now()#"
        OUTPUT="WDDX_dateTime" USETIMEZONEINFO="Yes">

<!--- serialize a number --->
<CFWDDX ACTION="CFML2WDDX" INPUT="#Val(123.456)#" OUTPUT="WDDX_Number">

<!--- serialize a null ColdFusion style (an empty string) --->
<CFWDDX ACTION="CFML2WDDX" INPUT="" OUTPUT="WDDX_Null">

<!--- serialize a string --->
<CFWDDX ACTION="CFML2WDDX" INPUT="I am a string!" OUTPUT="WDDX_String1">

<!--- serialize a string with a newline character --->
<CFWDDX ACTION="CFML2WDDX" INPUT="I am a string! So am I."
        OUTPUT="WDDX_String2">
```

*Example 20-1. Serializing Simple Datatypes to WDDX (continued)*

```
<!--- serialize a string with a tab --->
<CFWDDX ACTION="CFML2WDDX" INPUT="I am a string!#CHR(9)#So am I."
        OUTPUT="WDDX_String3">

<H2>Simple datatypes serialized as WDDX packets</H2>

<!--- output all of the wddx packets for the simple datatypes --->
<CFOUTPUT>
<TABLE BORDER="0" CELLPADDING="3" BGCOLOR="##C0C0C0">
<TR>
  <TH>Data Type</TH><TH>WDDX Packet</TH>
<TR>
<TR>
  <TD>boolean:</TD><TD>#HTMLEditFormat(WDDX_boolean)#</TD>
</TR>
<TR>
  <TD>dateTime:</TD><TD>#HTMLEditFormat(WDDX_dateTime)#</TD>
</TR>
<TR>
  <TD>null (CFML) as an empty string</TD><TD>#HTMLEditFormat(WDDX_null)#</TD>
</TR>
<TR>
  <TD>null (COM, Java and JavaScript)</TD>
  <TD>&lt;wddxPacket version='1.0'&gt;&lt;header&gt;&lt;/header&gt;&lt;data&gt;
    &lt;null/&gt;&lt;/data&gt;&lt;/wddxPacket&gt;</TD>
</TR>
<TR>
  <TD>number</TD><TD>#HTMLEditFormat(WDDX_number)#</TD>
</TR>
<TR>
  <TD>string</TD><TD>#HTMLEditFormat(WDDX_String1)#</TD>
</TR>
<TR>
  <TD>string with newline character encoded</TD>
  <TD>#HTMLEditFormat(WDDX_String2)#</TD>
</TR>
<TR>
  <TD>string with tab encoded</TD><TD>#HTMLEditFormat(WDDX_String3)#</TD>
</TR>
</TABLE>
</CFOUTPUT>
```

Figure 20-1 shows how the various simple datatypes are represented in WDDX. Each chunk of data is delimited by a set of tags declaring the datatype. Strings are delimited by `<string></string>`, numbers by `<number></number>`, and date/time objects by `<dateTime></dateTime>`. Null and Boolean values are handled slightly differently. Instead of tag pairs, null values are represented by `<null/>`

while Boolean values are represented by `<boolean value='false'/>` or `<boolean value='true'/>`.*

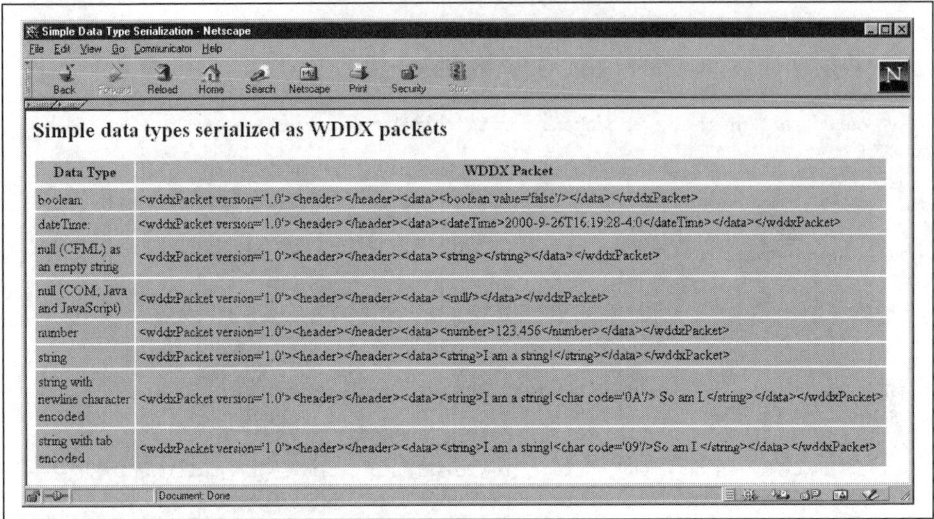


Simple data types serialized as WDDX packets

| Data Type | WDDX Packet |
|---|---|
| boolean: | <wddxPacket version='1.0'> <header> </header><data><boolean value='false'/></data> </wddxPacket> |
| dateTime: | <wddxPacket version='1.0'> <header> </header><data><dateTime>2000-9-26T16:19:28-4:0</dateTime></data></wddxPacket> |
| null (CFML) as an empty string | <wddxPacket version='1.0'><header></header><data><string></string></data></wddxPacket> |
| null (COM, Java and JavaScript) | <wddxPacket version='1.0'><header></header><data> <null/></data></wddxPacket> |
| number | <wddxPacket version='1.0'><header></header><data><number>123.456</number></data></wddxPacket> |
| string | <wddxPacket version='1.0'><header></header><data><string>I am a string!</string></data></wddxPacket> |
| string with newline character encoded | <wddxPacket version='1.0'> <header> </header><data><string>I am a string!<char code='0A'/> So am I. </string> </data></wddxPacket> |
| string with tab encoded | <wddxPacket version='1.0'><header></header><data><string>I am a string!<char code='09'/>So am I </string></data> </wddxPacket> |

*Figure 20-1. Simple values as represented by WDDX packets*

Note that the `HTMLEditFormat()` is used with each output variable that is written to the browser. It is necessary to do this because the WDDX packets contain special characters such as < and > that must be escaped before they can be displayed by a browser. The `HTMLEditFormat()` function ensures that all special characters are escaped before the WDDX packet is displayed. This technique is especially important if you plan to pass WDDX packets between templates as `FORM` variables.

Now that you understand the basics of serializing simple datatypes, let's turn our attention to the deserialization process. As I mentioned earlier, deserialization is the process of taking the data stored in a WDDX packet and converting it back to its native format. Thanks to the `CFWDDX` tag, deserialization involves only a single tag call. Example 20-2 demonstrates deserialization of a string stored in a WDDX packet.

*Example 20-2. Deserializing a WWDX Packet with a Single String Value*

```
<!--- first we need to serialize the string into a wddx packet --->
<CFWDDX ACTION="CFML2WDDX" INPUT="I am a string!" OUTPUT="MyWDDXPacket">

<!--- output the wddx packet in a text area so you can see the entire packet --->
<H3>WDDX Packet Containing A Simple Value (string)</H3>
<FORM>
```

* Because some programming languages (including CFML) have no concept of null, deserialized null values are automatically converted to blank strings where appropriate.

*Example 20-2. Deserializing a WWDX Packet with a Single String Value (continued)*

```
<CFOUTPUT>
<TEXTAREA ROWS="6" COLS="50" WRAP="virtual">#HTMLEditFormat(MyWDDXPacket)#
</TEXTAREA>
</CFOUTPUT>
</FORM>

<!--- deserialize the wddx packet containing the string.  The entire
      deserialization process is performed with this single tag call. --->
<CFWDDX ACTION="WDDX2CFML" INPUT="#MyWDDXPacket#"
        OUTPUT="DeserializedSimpleValue">

<H3>Here Is The Deserialized Simple Value:</H3>
<CFOUTPUT>
#DeserializedSimpleValue#
</CFOUTPUT>
```

In Example 20-2, the string "I am a string!" is serialized to a WDDX packet and output to the browser so you can see what it looks like. The `CFWDDX` tag is then called a second time, but the `ACTION` attribute is set to `WDDX2CFML`. This tells ColdFusion that we want to use the WDDX tag to deserialize a WDDX packet. The packet to deserialize is specified using the `INPUT` attribute. In our example, the packet is contained in a variable called `MyWDDXPacket`. The `OUTPUT` attribute specifies a variable to hold the deserialized value. We set `OUTPUT` to `DeserializedSimpleValue`. The template ends by outputting the value of `DeserializedSimpleValue` to the browser so we can see that the deserialization was successful.

#### *Datatype conversion issues*

Because CFML is considered a typeless language, you can run into problems with certain datatypes not serializing as you would expect them to. In these cases, you may need to "convert" certain values before having them properly serialized as the intended datatype by the `CFWDDX` tag. For example, both the `CFWDDX` calls shown in the following example serialize the date as a `<string>` as opposed to a `<dateTime>` value:

```
<CFWDDX ACTION="CFML2WDDX" INPUT="03/03/2000"
        OUTPUT="MyWDDXPacket1" USETIMEZONEINFO="Yes">

<CFOUTPUT>
#HTMLEditFormat(MyWDDXPacket1)#
</CFOUTPUT>

<CFWDDX ACTION="CFML2WDDX" INPUT="#DateFormat('03/03/2000','mm/dd/yyyy')#"
        OUTPUT="MyWDDXPacket2" USETIMEZONEINFO="Yes">
```

```
<CFOUTPUT>
#HTMLEditFormat(MyWDDXPacket2)#
</CFOUTPUT>
```

In order to get the date to serialize as a <dateTime> as opposed to a <string>, it is necessary to use a date function such as CreateDate(), ParseDateTime(), or Now() (but not CreateODBCDate() or DateFormat()) before serializing the date. It is also possible to use the Now() function as in the following examples:

```
<!--- use the CreateDate function to create a dateTime datatype --->
<CFWDDX ACTION="CFML2WDDX" INPUT="#CreateDate(1998,08,15)#"
        OUTPUT="MyWDDXPacket1" USETIMEZONEINFO="Yes">

<CFOUTPUT>
#HTMLEditFormat(MyWDDXPacket1)#
</CFOUTPUT>

<!--- use the Now function to create a dateTime datatype --->
<CFWDDX ACTION="CFML2WDDX" INPUT="#Now()#"
        OUTPUT="MyWDDXPacket2" USETIMEZONEINFO="Yes">

<P>
<CFOUTPUT>
#HTMLEditFormat(MyWDDXPacket2)#
</CFOUTPUT>

<!--- use the ParseDateTime function to create a dateTime datatype --->
<CFWDDX ACTION="CFML2WDDX"
        INPUT="#ParseDateTime('Sat, 15 Aug 1998 19:00:00 +0400', 'POP')#"
        OUTPUT="MyWDDXPacket3" USETIMEZONEINFO="Yes">

<P>
<CFOUTPUT>
#HTMLEditFormat(MyWDDXPacket3)#
</CFOUTPUT>
```

Because CFML is typeless, issues like this do arise with <boolean> and <number> datatypes. The following example shows one way to overcome this problem using a Boolean function (IsDefined()) and the Val() function, respectively:

```
<!--- using a boolean function such as IsDefined ensures a boolean datatype
      during serialization. Simply specifying "yes" or "No" for the INPUT
      attribute will result in the value being serialized as a string. --->
<CFWDDX ACTION="CFML2WDDX" INPUT="#IsDefined('y')#" OUTPUT="MyWDDXPacket1">

<CFOUTPUT>
#HTMLEditFormat(MyWDDXPacket1)#
</CFOUTPUT>


<!--- use the val function to ensure that a number is serialized as a numeric
      type and not as a string --->
```

```
<CFWDDX ACTION="CFML2WDDX" INPUT="#Val(123.456)#" OUTPUT="MyWDDXPacket2">

<P>
<CFOUTPUT>
#HTMLEditFormat(MyWDDXPacket2)#
</CFOUTPUT>
```

### *Testing for well-formed WDDX*

The `CFWDDX` tag is capable of deserializing only well-formed WDDX packets. If you attempt to deserialize a non well-formed WDDX packet, ColdFusion throws an error. Because of this, you need a way to test whether a WDDX packet is well-formed. This is especially true in the case of WDDX packets retrieved from other servers over which you have no control. There are two methods for determining whether a value is a well-formed WDDX packet. The first method uses a function introduced in ColdFusion 4.5.1 SP2 called `IsWDDX()`:

```
<CFIF IsWDDX(MyWDDXPacket)>
  <B>Is</B> a well-formed WDDX packet!
<CFELSE>
  <B>Is not</B> a well-formed WDDX packet!
</CFIF>
```

The `IsWDDX()` function uses a validating XML parser with the WDDX DTD to determine whether a specified value is a well-formed WDDX packet. It returns `TRUE` if the value is a well-formed WDDX packet; `FALSE` if it isn't. For more information on `IsWDDX()`, see Appendix B.

The second method involves an optional attribute added to the `CFWDDX` tag in ColdFusion 4.5.1 SP2:

```
<CFWDDX ACTION="WDDX2CFML" INPUT="#MyWDDXPacket#"
        OUTPUT="DeserializedSimpleValue" VALIDATE="Yes">
```

`VALIDATE`, can be set to either `Yes` or `No` and indicates whether to use a validating XML parser with the WDDX DTD to determine whether the value specified in `INPUT` is a well-formed WDDX packet when `ACTION` is `WDDX2CFML` or `WDDDX2JS`. If the value is a well-formed WDDX packet, deserialization takes place. If the value isn't well-formed WDDX, an exception is thrown. The `VALIDATE` parameter performs the same job as the `IsWDDX` function.

## *Serializing and Deserializing Complex Datatypes*

WDDX can also represent more complex datatypes than the ones we've covered so far. As such, it is possible to serialize and deserialize complex datatypes such as record sets (query objects), arrays, structures, and binary objects. Part of what makes WDDX so attractive to developers is that the process for serializing and deserializing complex datatypes is the same as it is for serializing simple values.

The difference lies in how each datatype is represented within the WDDX packet. Throughout this section, we'll look at serializing and deserializing complex datatypes.

### *Serializing/deserializing record sets*

The first complex datatype we'll cover is the record set. In ColdFusion terms, a record set is synonymous with a query object. Throughout the rest of this chapter, we'll use the terms interchangeably. With the `CFWDDX` tag, it is easy to take a ColdFusion query object and serialize it to a WDDX packet. Deserializing the packet is just as simple. Example 20-3 shows just how easy it is to deserialize a packet.

*Example 20-3. Serializing and Deserializing a Query Object (Record Set) Using CFWDDX*

```
<!--- get all employee records --->
<CFQUERY NAME="GetEmployeeInfo" DATASOURCE="ProgrammingCF">
   SELECT * FROM EmployeeDirectory
</CFQUERY>

<!--- serialize the employee records to a wddx packet --->
<CFWDDX ACTION="CFML2WDDX" INPUT="#GetEmployeeInfo#"
        OUTPUT="QueryObject" USETIMEZONEINFO="Yes">

<!--- output the wddx packet in a text area so you can see the entire packet --->
<H3>WDDX Packet Containing a Query Object</H3>
<FORM>
<CFOUTPUT>
<TEXTAREA ROWS="15" COLS="80" WRAP="virtual">#HTMLEditFormat(QueryObject)#
</TEXTAREA>
</CFOUTPUT>
</FORM>

<!--- deserialize the wddx packet containing the query object --->
<CFWDDX ACTION="WDDX2CFML" INPUT="#QueryObject#"
        OUTPUT="DeserializedQueryObject">

<H3>Here Is The Deserialized Query Object:</H3>
<TABLE CELLPADDING="3" CELLSPACING="0">
<TR BGCOLOR="#888888">
  <TH>Name</TH><TH>Title</TH><TH>Department</TH><TH>E-mail</TH>
  <TH>Phone Extension</TH>
</TR>
<CFOUTPUT QUERY="DeserializedQueryObject">
<TR BGCOLOR="##C0C0C0">
  <TD>#Name#</TD><TD>#Title#</TD><TD>#Department#</TD>
  <TD><A HREF="Mailto:#Email#">#Email#</A></TD><TD>#PhoneExt#</TD>
</TR>
</CFOUTPUT>
</TABLE>
```

In Example 20-3, the `EmployeeDirectory` table of the `ProgrammingCF` data source is queried. The resulting record set is serialized to a WDDX packet by setting the `ACTION` attribute of the `CFWDDX` tag to `CFML2WDDX`. Setting `INPUT` to `#GetEmployeeRecords#` tells the `CFWDDX` tag to serialize the record set contained in the `GetEmployeeRecords` variable. The `OUTPUT` attribute allows us to specify a variable to hold the WDDX packet created by the serialization process. We set our output variable to `QueryObject`

Once we have the WDDX packet, it is displayed to the browser in a `TEXTAREA` form element so we can see the packet in its entirety, as shown in Figure 20-2.

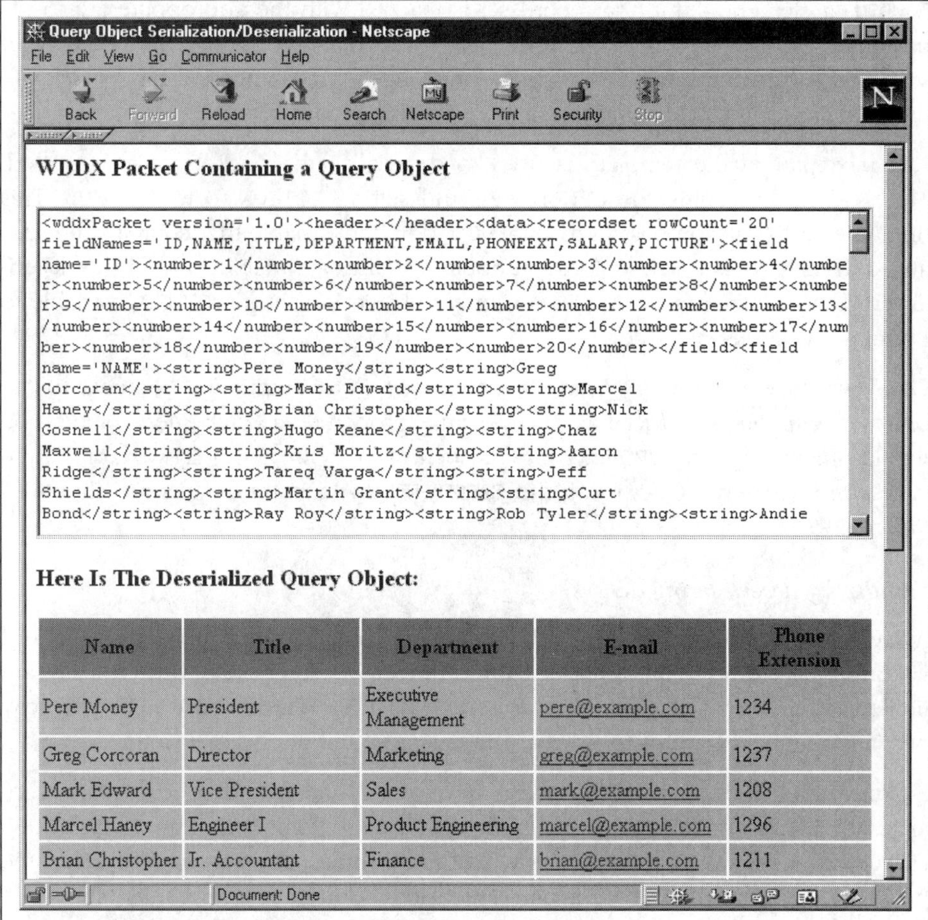


*Figure 20-2. Serialization and deserialization of a record set*

In Figure 20-2, you'll notice this tag in the WDDX packet:

```
<recordset rowCount='12' fieldNames='ID,NAME,TITLE,DEPARTMENT,EMAIL,PHONEEXT'>
```

This line (it ends with the `</recordset>` tag) identifies the data that follows as a record set. The `rowCount` attribute defines the record set consisting of twelve records (rows). The field names (column headers) for the record set are specified by the rowCount attribute. The data from the record set is then included in the WDDX packet, within the <recordset></recordset> tags, one column at a time:

```
<field name='ID'><number>1</number><number>2</number><number>3</number>
<number>4</number><number>5</number><number>6</number><number>7</number>
<number>8</number><number>9</number><number>10</number><number>11</number>
<number>18</number></field>
```

Each data element within the record set is marked with the appropriate tag for its datatype. Strings are marked up with <string></string>, numbers with <number></number>, etc. Only strings (including base64-encoded binary strings), numbers, and data/time values are allowed within record sets.

The next part of the template is used to deserialize the packet we just created. This is done by calling the CFWDDX tag and setting ACTION to WDDX2CFML. This time, the INPUT attribute is set to QueryObject, the variable that contains the serialized WDDX packet. The OUTPUT attribute specifies a variable to hold the deserialized data—in this case a ColdFusion query object. We set our OUTPUT variable to DeserializedQueryObject.

Once we have our query object, the next step is to output the contents to the browser. Our query object has all the same properties as any query object you would obtain using the CFQUERY tag. As such, we can create an HTML table of the values in the query object using the CFOUTPUT tag, and the results are shown in Figure 20-2.

### *Serializing/deserializing arrays*

Arrays are a complex datatype that use numeric (integer) indexes to store data of varying types. Arrays can consist of any number of dimensions, but typically are limited to one, two, or three. As far as the WDDX DTD is concerned, you may nest any number of arrays to achieve the desired number of dimensions.

Example 20-4 takes a one-dimensional array that contains student grades and serializes them into a WDDX packet. The results are then output in a TEXTAREA HTML form element so you can see what the resulting packet looks like. Next, the packet is deserialized back to a one-dimensional array and the results (shown in Figure 20-3) are output to the browser.

*Example 20-4. Serializing and Deserializing a One-Dimensional Array*

```
<!--- create a one-dimensional array of student grades --->
<CFSET GRADES = ARRAYNEW(1)>

<CFSET GRADES[1] = 95>
<CFSET GRADES[2] = 93>
```

*Example 20-4. Serializing and Deserializing a One-Dimensional Array (continued)*

```
<CFSET GRADES[3] = 87>
<CFSET GRADES[4] = 100>
<CFSET GRADES[5] = 74>

<!--- serialize the grades array to a wddx packet --->
<CFWDDX ACTION="CFML2WDDX" INPUT="#Grades#" OUTPUT="GradesArray">

<!--- output the wddx packet in a text area so you can see the entire packet --->
<H3>WDDX Packet Containing A One-dimensional Array</H3>
<FORM>
<CFOUTPUT>
<TEXTAREA ROWS="6" COLS="80" WRAP="virtual">#HTMLEditFormat(GradesArray)#
</TEXTAREA>
</CFOUTPUT>
</FORM>

<!--- deserialize the gradesarray wddx packet back to an array --->
<CFWDDX ACTION="WDDX2CFML" INPUT="#GradesArray#" OUTPUT="DeserializedArray">

<H3>Here Are The Deserialized Grades:</H3>
<CFLOOP INDEX="i" FROM="1" TO="#ArrayLen(DeserializedArray)#">
<CFOUTPUT>
Grade #i#: #DeserializedArray[i]#<BR>
</CFOUTPUT>
</CFLOOP>
```

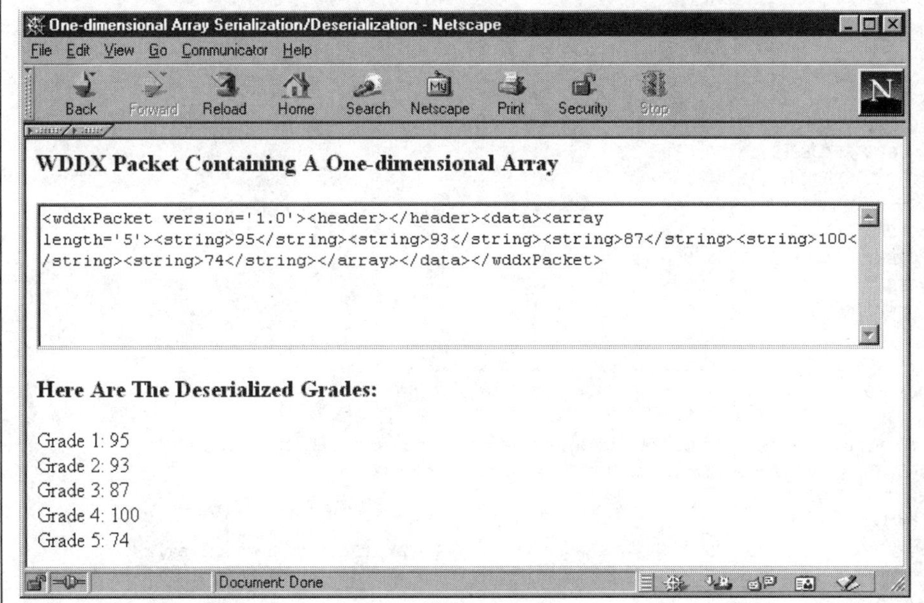


*Figure 20-3. WDDX packet containing a one-dimensional array*

Looking at the WDDX packet shown in Figure 20-3, it is easy to see how a one-dimensional array is represented within the packet. The line:

```
<array length='5'><string>95</string><string>93</string><string>87</string>
<string>100</string><string>74</string></array>
```

defines a one-dimensional array that is five elements in length. Each element in the array (in this case, all strings) is marked up by <string></string> tags. One of the advantages to using an array is that its elements can be made up of any datatype, simple or complex, that can be represented by WDDX.

Multidimensional arrays differ only slightly from their one-dimensional siblings in how they are represented within a WDDX packet. Consider Example 20-5 in which we create a two-dimensional array of student grades. Each student, represented by the elements in the first dimension of the array, has grades for three different tests, represented by the elements in the second dimension of the array. The array is serialized to a WDDX packet and output in a TEXTAREA element of an HTML form so that you can study the packet. After the packet is displayed, it is deserialized back into a two-dimensional array that is in turn presented to the browser, as shown in Figure 20-4.

*Example 20-5. Serializing and Deserializing a Two-Dimensional Array*

```
<!--- create a two dimensional array of student grades.  Each student
     (represented by the first dimension has grades for more than one test
     (represented by the second dimension). --->
<CFSET GRADES = ARRAYNEW(2)>

<CFSET GRADES[1][1] = 95>
<CFSET GRADES[1][2] = 93>
<CFSET GRADES[1][3] = 87>
<CFSET GRADES[2][1] = 100>
<CFSET GRADES[2][2] = 74>
<CFSET GRADES[2][3] = 86>
<CFSET GRADES[3][1] = 90>
<CFSET GRADES[3][2] = 94>
<CFSET GRADES[3][3] = 96>

<!--- serialize the grades array to a wddx packet --->
<CFWDDX ACTION="CFML2WDDX" INPUT="#Grades#" OUTPUT="GradesArray">

<!--- output the wddx packet in a text area so you can see the entire packet --->
<H3>WDDX Packet Containing A Two-dimensional Array</H3>
<FORM>
<CFOUTPUT>
<TEXTAREA ROWS="8" COLS="80" WRAP="virtual">#HTMLEditFormat(GradesArray)#
</TEXTAREA>
</CFOUTPUT>
</FORM>

<!--- deserialize the gradesarray wddx packet back to an array --->
```

*Example 20-5. Serializing and Deserializing a Two-Dimensional Array (continued)*

```
<CFWDDX ACTION="WDDX2CFML" INPUT="#GradesArray#" OUTPUT="DeserializedArray">

<H3>Here Are The Deserialized Grades:</H3>

<!--- this looping technique utilizes an outer and an inner loop (designated o
      and i respectively) for looping through each element in each dimension of
      the array --->
<CFLOOP INDEX="o" FROM="1" TO="#ArrayLen(DeserializedArray)#">
<CFLOOP INDEX="i" FROM="1" TO="#ArrayLen(DeserializedArray[o])#">
<CFOUTPUT>
Student #o#, Grade #i#: #DeserializedArray[o][i]#<BR>
</CFOUTPUT>
</CFLOOP>
</CFLOOP>
```

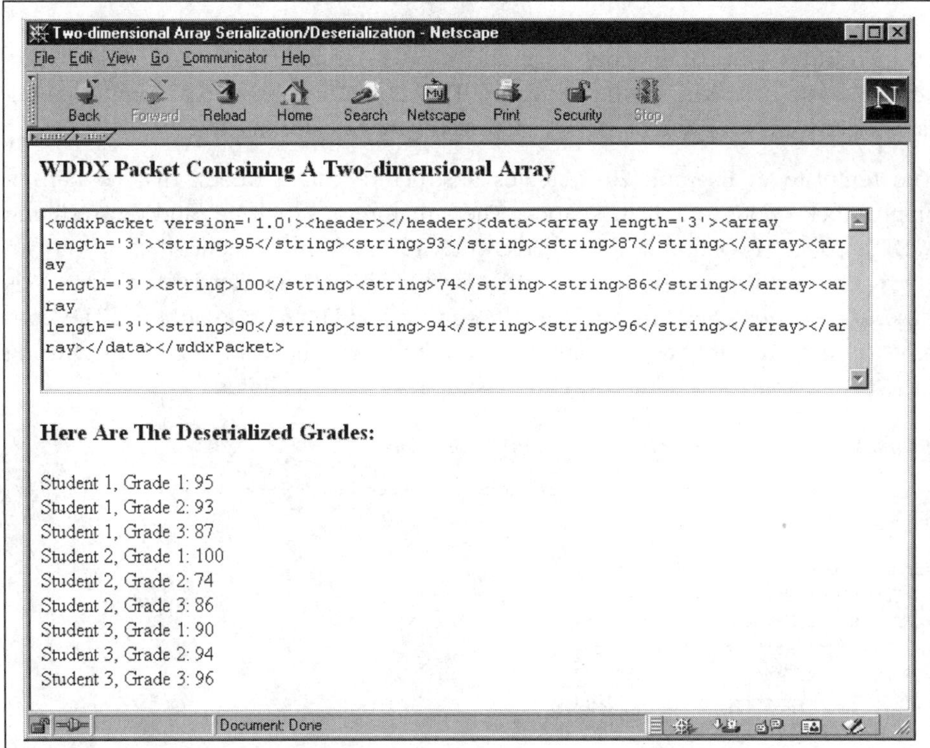


*Figure 20-4. Serializing and deserializing a multidimensional array*

If you look at the resulting WDDX packet shown in Figure 20-4, paying particular attention to the part that reads:

```
<array length='3'><array length='3'><string>95</string><string>93</string>
<string>87</string></array><array length='3'><string>100</string>
<string>74</string><string>86</string></array><array length='3'>
<string>90</string><string>94</string><string>96</string></array></array>
```

you will notice that the WDDX packet represents multidimensional arrays as an array of arrays! This allows you to create arrays of as many dimensions as you want.

Once the WDDX packet is deserialized, outputting the contents of the two-dimensional array is just a matter of performing an outer and inner loop over the array.

### *Structures*

Structures are similar to arrays in their architecture except that they are indexed by strings known as keys instead of integer values. Structures are also known as associative arrays, dictionaries, or maps depending on the programming language being used.

You should be careful when serializing and deserializing structures as WDDX handles them without regard to case. Because of this, if your structure contains two or more keys with the same name (regardless of case), only the last value is set when serializing or deserializing the structure. This is necessary as some programming languages with WDDX serializers/deserializers are case insensitive.

The template in Example 20-6 creates a structure called `Stock` that contains a single stock quote for Allaire's stock. The structure is serialized, and the resulting WDDX packet is output within a `TEXTAREA` HTML form element so that you can study its structure (no pun intended). After the WDDX packet is displayed, it is deserialized back to a structure called `DeserializedStockStructure`. The contents of that structure are then output to the browser (shown in Figure 20-5) using the `StructKeyArray()` function and a simple looping technique.

*Example 20-6. Serializing and Deserializing a Structure*

```
<!--- create a structure called stock to hold a stock quote --->
<CFSET STOCK = STRUCTNEW()>

<CFSET Stock.Company = "Allaire">
<CFSET Stock.Ticker = "ALLR">
<CFSET Stock.Exchange = "NASDAQ">
<CFSET Stock.Price = "66.25">
<CFSET Stock.Change = "+0.375">
<CFSET Stock.LastTradeTime = "10:17AM">
<CFSET Stock.LastTradeDate = "02/02/2001">
<CFSET Stock.Volume = "8300">

<!--- serialize the stock structure to a wddx packet --->
<CFWDDX ACTION="CFML2WDDX" INPUT="#Stock#" OUTPUT="StockStructure">

<!--- output the wddx packet in a text area so you can see the entire packet --->
<H3>WDDX Packet Containing a Structure</H3>
<FORM>
<CFOUTPUT>
```

*Example 20-6. Serializing and Deserializing a Structure (continued)*

```
<TEXTAREA ROWS="10" COLS="80" WRAP="virtual">#HTMLEditFormat(StockStructure)#
</TEXTAREA>
</CFOUTPUT>
</FORM>

<!--- deserialize the wddx packet containing the structure --->
<CFWDDX ACTION="WDDX2CFML" INPUT="#StockStructure#"
        OUTPUT="DeserializedStockStructure">

<CFSET MyKeyArray = StructKeyArray(DeserializedStockStructure)>

<H3>Here Is The Deserialized Structure:</H3>
<TABLE>
<TR>
  <TH>Key</TH><TH>Value</TH>
</TR>
<CFLOOP index="position" from="1" to="#ArrayLen(MyKeyArray)#">
<CFOUTPUT>
<TR>
  <TD>#MyKeyArray[position]#</TD>
  <TD>#DeserializedStockStructure[MyKeyArray[position]]#</TD>
</TR>
</CFOUTPUT>
</CFLOOP>
</TABLE>
```

Looking at the WDDX packet shown in Figure 20-5, you'll notice that the structure is marked up using `<struct></struct>`:

```
<struct><var name='CHANGE'><string>+0.375</string></var>
<var name='COMPANY'><string>Allaire</string></var>
<var name='EXCHANGE'><string>NASDAQ</string></var>
<var name='LASTTRADEDATE'><string>02/02/2001</string></var>
<var name='LASTTRADETIME'><string>10:17AM</string></var>
<var name='PRICE'><string>66.25</string></var>
<var name='TICKER'><string>ALLR</string></var>
<var name='VOLUME'><string>8300</string></var></struct>
```

Each key within the structure is defined by a set of `<var></var>` tags. The value for each key is marked up within the `<var></var>` tags using the tags appropriate for the datatype. Just like arrays, you can nest structures as well as store any datatype available in WDDX.

### *Serializing/deserializing binary data*

The ability to serialize and deserialize binary data was added to the **CFWDDX** tag in ColdFusion 4.5. This capability allows you to send and receive binary files as WDDX packets. As far as the WDDX DTD goes, the binary datatype was made available as of the 1.0 release.

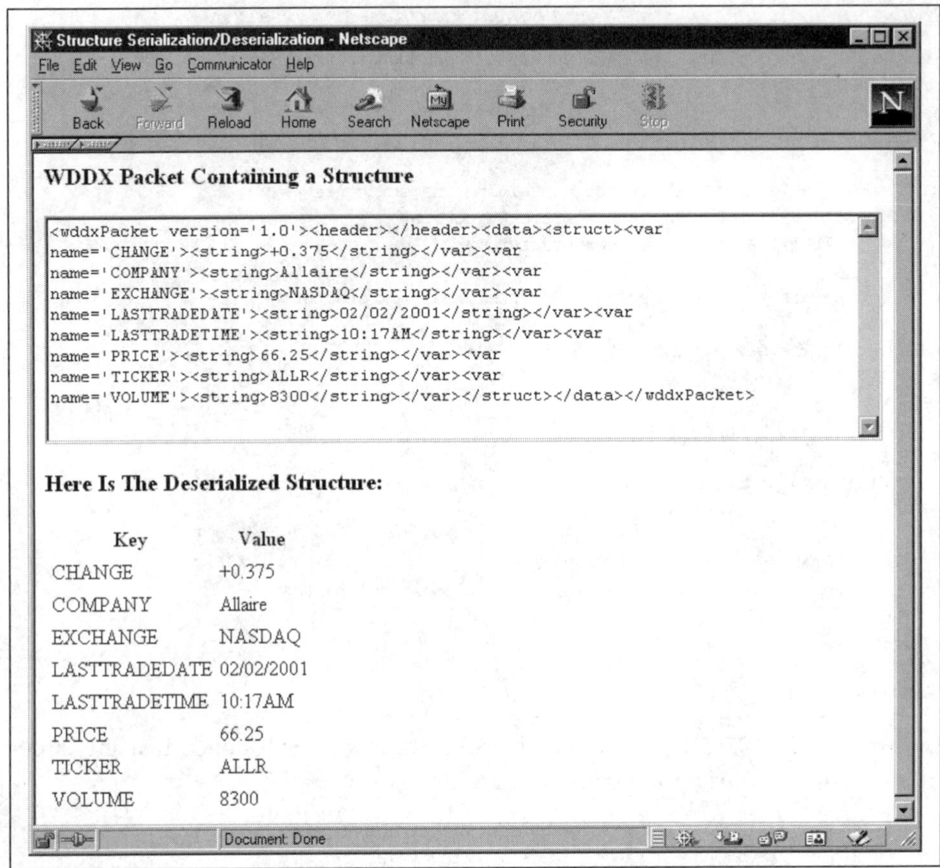


*Figure 20-5. Serialization and deserialization of a structure*

The WDDX DTD specifies that all binary data included in a WDDX packet must be base64-encoded. All the serializers/deserializers included with the WDDX SDK as well as the `CFWDDX` tag handle the encoding automatically. Future versions of WDDX may allow additional encoding schemes, but for now, only base64 encoding is supported.

Example 20-7 demonstrates serializing and deserializing a binary file. To keep things simple, we use a GIF file, which is installed by default when you install the ColdFusion server. Realistically, sending just a binary file as a WDDX packet makes little sense as the deserializer has no way of knowing anything else about the binary data other than its length (we'll talk about this in a few moments). When sending binary data, you'll probably want to include more descriptive information about the data such as a filename, MIME type, creation date, etc. All this information and more (as much as you want to include) can be included in the WDDX packet. To do this, all you need to do is create a structure to hold both the descriptive information and the base64 representation of the binary file as name/value pairs within the structure. The structure, including the binary data, can then be serialized into a WDDX packet. Example 20-7 shows a simple way to create the structure.

*Example 20-7. Serializing and Deserializing a Binary File*

```
<!--- read in the binary file using CFFILE --->
<CFFILE ACTION="ReadBinary"
        FILE="c:/inetsrv/wwwroot/cfide/administrator/images/coldfusion.gif"
        VARIABLE="MyBinaryFile">

<!--- create a structure to hold descriptive information about the file as well
      as the base64 encoded binary file --->
<CFSET FileInfo = StructNew()>

<CFSET FileInfo.MyBinaryFile = MyBinaryFile>
<CFSET FileInfo.FileName = "coldfusion.gif">
<CFSET FileInfo.MIMEType = "image/gif">

<!--- convert the structure to wddx.  The binary is automatically base64
      encoded --->
<CFWDDX ACTION="CFML2WDDX" INPUT="#FileInfo#" OUTPUT="MyWDDX">

<!--- output the wddx packet in a text area so you can see the entire packet --->
<H3>WDDX Packet Containing Binary Representation of a GIF File</H3>
<FORM>
<CFOUTPUT>
<TEXTAREA ROWS="15" COLS="80" WRAP="virtual">#HTMLEditFormat(MyWDDX)#</TEXTAREA>
</CFOUTPUT>
</FORM>

<!--- deserialize the wddx packet back to a structure --->
<CFWDDX ACTION="WDDX2CFML" INPUT="#MyWDDX#" OUTPUT="DeserializedBinaryFile">

<!--- write the binary object out to a file --->
<CFFILE ACTION="WRITE"
        FILE="c:/inetsrv/wwwroot/cfide/administrator/images/         new_
#DeserializedBinaryFile.FileName#"
        OUTPUT="#DeserializedBinaryFile.MyBinaryFile#">

<H3>Here Is The Deserialized Binary:</H3>
<!--- display the file to to browser.  This could be done using CFCONTENT as
      well, but then you wouldn't be able to see the rest of the content that
      was displayed prior to the CFCONTENT call --->
<CFOUTPUT>
FileName: #DeserializedBinaryFile.FileName#<BR>
MIME Type: #DeserializedBinaryFile.MIMEType#<BR>
<IMG SRC="/cfide/administrator/images/new_#DeserializedBinaryFile.FileName#">
</CFOUTPUT>
```

The first task that the template in Example 20-7 performs is to read the GIF file into a binary object using the `CFFILE` tag's `ReadBinary` `ACTION`. Next, a structure is created to hold the binary object, the file's name, and its MIME type. After that is accomplished, the CFWDDX tag serializes the structure into a WDDX packet. During serialization, the binary object within the structure is automatically base64-encoded. Once the WDDX packet has been created, it is displayed in the browser (Figure 20-6) so that you can see how the packet is constructed.

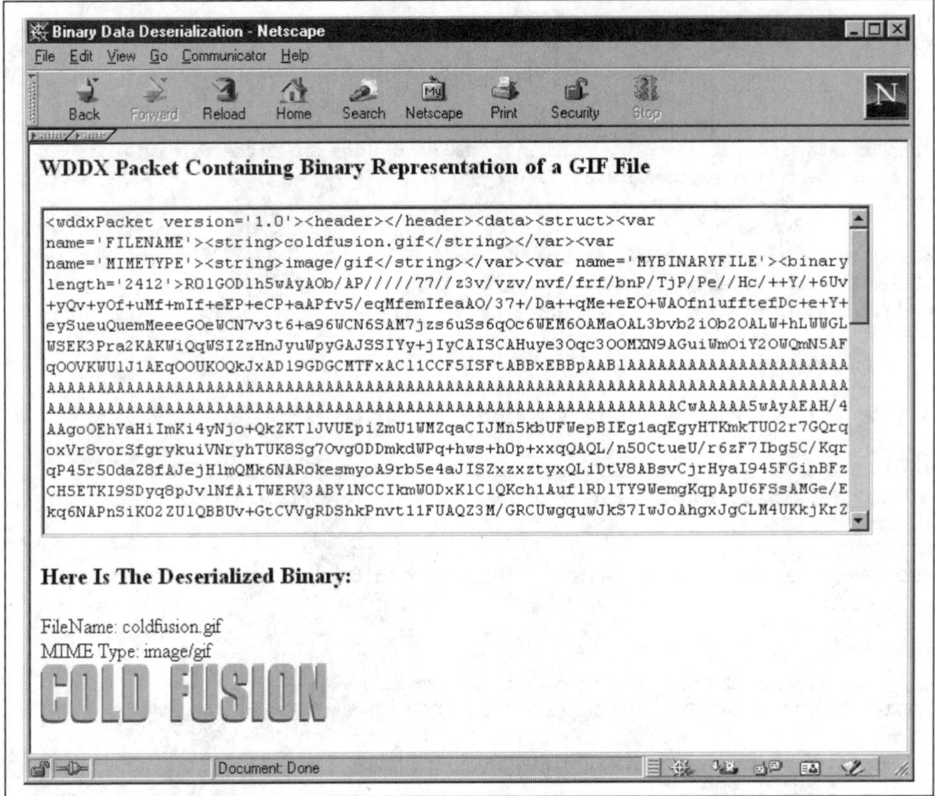


*Figure 20-6. Serializing and deserializing a structure containing a binary file*

There are two things worth mentioning here. The first is the `<binary length='2412'>` tag that appears near the beginning of the packet. This tag provides the deserializer with the length of the binary value being deserialized. The second important thing to notice here is that the `<binary>` datatype is nested within the `<var>` tag of a `<struct>`. As mentioned previously, complex datatypes such as arrays and structures afford a lot of flexibility and power in an incredibly simple and easy-to-use way.

After the WDDX packet has been displayed, it is deserialized back into a structure. Next, the CFFILE tag writes a copy of the GIF image back to the ColdFusion server. Finally, the filename and MIME type stored in the structure are both output along with the image itself.

If you want to include more than one binary file in your WDDX packet, all you need to do is create an array of structures with each array element containing a single structure holding the binary file and its descriptive information.

# *Storing WDDX Packets*

So far, in this chapter, we have covered all sorts of techniques for serializing and deserializing WDDX packets. All our examples have shown the serialization and deserialization process occurring on the same page. While great for illustrative purposes, the examples have little practical application. After all, why would you want to serialize and then deserialize a packet on the same page? This leads us to the topic for this section—storing your WDDX packets so that you can refer to them later. There are two ways you can store WDDX packets: in a text file or in a database (including LDAP directories). The next two sections discuss these two methods and provide examples of both storing and retrieving packets.

## *Storing Packets in a Text File*

One of the most interesting things about WDDX is you can use it to store for data without having to write the data to a database. For example, record-set data stored in a WDDX packet is much more useful than it is when it's stored in a delimited text file. Example 20-8 takes a query object and serializes it to a WDDX packet. The resulting WDDX pack is then written to a text file using the `CFFILE` tag.

*Example 20-8. Storing a WDDX Packet Containing a Record Set in a Text File*

```
<!--- get all employee records --->
<CFQUERY NAME="GetEmployeeInfo" DATASOURCE="ProgrammingCF" DBTYPE="ODBC">
         SELECT * From EmployeeDirectory
</CFQUERY>

<!--- serialize the employee records to a wddx packet --->
<CFWDDX ACTION="CFML2WDDX" INPUT="#GetEmployeeInfo#"
        OUTPUT="QueryObject" USETIMEZONEINFO="Yes">

<!--- store the wddx packet in a text file on the server --->
<CFFILE ACTION="WRITE" FILE="c:\temp\QueryObject.txt"
        OUTPUT="#QueryObject#" ADDNEWLINE="No">


<!--- Let the user know the file has been written --->
<H3>The WDDX packet has been written to a text file</H3>
```

Once you have the WDDX packet saved in the text file, you need a way to retrieve the packet and deserialize it. Example 20-9 uses the `CFFILE` tag to read the contents of the text file into a variable that is then fed to the `CFWDDX` tag and deserialized. The results are then output to the browser.

*Example 20-9. Retrieving and Deserializing a WDDX Packet from a Text File*

```
<!--- store the wddx packet in a text file on the server --->
<CFFILE ACTION="READ" FILE="c:\temp\QueryObject.txt" VARIABLE="MyWDDX">

<!--- deserialize the wddx packet containing the query object --->
<CFWDDX ACTION="WDDX2CFML" INPUT="#MyWDDX#" OUTPUT="DeserializedQueryObject">


<!--- output the results of the deserailized query object --->
<H3>Here Is The Deserialized Query Object Read From A Text File:</H3>
<TABLE CELLPADDING="3" CELLSPACING="0">
<TR BGCOLOR="#888888">
  <TH>Name</TH><TH>Title</TH><TH>Department</TH><TH>E-mail</TH>
  <TH>Phone Extension</TH>
</TR>
<CFOUTPUT QUERY="DeserializedQueryObject">
<TR BGCOLOR="##C0C0C0">
  <TD>#Name#</TD><TD>#Title#</TD><TD>#Department#</TD>
  <TD><A HREF="Mailto:#Email#">#Email#</A></TD><TD>#PhoneExt#</TD>
</TR>
</CFOUTPUT>
</TABLE>
```

## Storing Packets in a Database

There may be times when you want to store WDDX packets in a database. A classic example involves using a long text field (a memo field in MS Access) to store a WDDX packet for each record in the database, which allows you to add additional data to the database without modifying its original structure. This provides you with a mechanism for storing complex datatypes (such as arrays and structures) inside a database. Another possibility includes using WDDX to store binary files (such as GIF and JPEG images) inside a database.

Example 20-10 takes a GIF image (obtained from the sample applications that you can choose to have installed when you install ColdFusion) and stores it in a ColdFusion structure along with the filename and the file's MIME type. The structure is then serialized, and the resulting WDDX packet is saved in the `Picture` field in the `EmployeeDirectory` table used in many of our previous examples. The `Picture` field is set up as a Memo field (since our example database is an MS Access database).

*Example 20-10. Serializing a Binary File and Storing It in a Database*

```
<!--- read in the binary file using CFFILE --->
<CFFILE ACTION="ReadBinary"
        FILE="c:\inetsrv\wwwroot\cfdocs\exampleapps\employee\images\people\
              ls003081_comp.jpg"
        VARIABLE="MyBinaryFile">

<!--- create a structure to hold descriptive information about the file as well
      as the base64 encoded binary file --->
<CFSET FileInfo = StructNew()>

<CFSET FileInfo.MyBinaryFile = MyBinaryFile>
<CFSET FileInfo.FileName = "coldfusion.gif">
<CFSET FileInfo.MIMEType = "image/gif">

<!--- convert the structure to wddx.  The binary is automatically base64
      encoded --->
<CFWDDX ACTION="CFML2WDDX" INPUT="#FileInfo#" OUTPUT="MyWDDX">

<CFQUERY NAME="SaveImage" DATASOURCE="ProgrammingCF">
         UPDATE EmployeeDirectory SET Picture = '#MyWDDX#'
         WHERE Name = 'Pere Money'
</CFQUERY>

<H3>Finished updating the database</H3>
```

If you look at the CFQUERY statement in Example 20-10, you'll notice that we use an UPDATE statement to add the picture to an already existing database record. In this case, we add a picture for the employee named "Pere Money," so we include:

```
WHERE Name = 'Pere Money'
```

Once we have a WDDX packet stored in our database, we need a way to retrieve it and deserialize it. Example 20-11 shows how to do this.

*Example 20-11. Retrieving a WDDX Packet from a Database and Deserializing It*

```
<!--- query the database and retrieve the WDDX packet --->
<CFQUERY NAME="GetEmployee" DATASOURCE="ProgrammingCF">
         SELECT * FROM EmployeeDirectory WHERE Name = 'Pere Money'
</CFQUERY>

<!--- deserialize the wddx packet back to a structure --->
<CFWDDX ACTION="WDDX2CFML" INPUT="#GetEmployee.Picture#"
        OUTPUT="DeserializedImage">

<!--- write the image out to a file --->
<CFFILE ACTION="WRITE"
        FILE="c:/inetsrv/wwwroot/cfdocs/images/#DeserializedImage.FileName#"
        OUTPUT="#DeserializedImage.MyBinaryFile#">
```

*Example 20-11. Retrieving a WDDX Packet from a Database and Deserializing It (continued)*

```
<H3>From our employee directory:</H3>
<!--- display the file to to browser.  This could be done using CFCONTENT as
      well, but then you wouldn't be able to see the rest of the content that
      was displayed prior to the CFCONTENT call --->
<CFOUTPUT QUERY="GetEmployee">
<IMG SRC="/cfdocs/images/#DeserializedImage.FileName#" ALIGN="left">
#Name#<BR>
#Title#<BR>
<A HREF="mailto:#Email#">#Email#</A>
</CFOUTPUT>
```

The template in Example 20-11 works by retrieving the entire record from the database using `CFQUERY`. Next, the WDDX packet contained in the Picture field is deserialized using the `CFWDDX` tag. Because the deserialized packet contains a structure holding the binary image, the `CFFILE` tag is used to write the image to a file. After this step is complete, an HTML page is constructed, and the contents of the query are output to the browser. Using the information stored in the deserialized structure, an `IMG` tag is dynamically constructed to retrieve the saved image from the database. The image is output along with the rest of the record.

# *Server-to-Server WDDX*

One of the most exciting uses for WDDX is in the area of server-to-server data sharing. As we mentioned in the beginning of the chapter, WDDX can be used by applications to share data regardless of the source of the data or the programming/scripting language the application is written in. Many times disparate applications live on different servers. Because WDDX is text-based, it makes for an ideal format for transporting over HTTP.

Along the same lines, WDDX is the perfect technology to serve as a wrapper for *content syndication*, which is the process of making content from one web site (or Intranet or Extranet) available to others. Syndication (using WDDX) is a two-part process. The site containing the content to be syndicated creates a special template (or series of templates) the affiliate can access via URL. This special template acts as a go-between with the affiliate's request and the content provider's back-end system. When an affiliate makes a request for content, the template retrieves and serializes the requested content into a WDDX packet that can be taken by the affiliate and used for whatever purpose desired. In most cases, retrieving syndicated content using ColdFusion is handled by the `CFHTTP` tag. The `CFHTTP` tag lets you retrieve the content from remote sites and bring the data (in this case a WDDX packet) back as a variable that can then be deserialized.

## *Syndicating ColdFusion Tips and Tutorials*

The best way to demonstrate the power and potential of WDDX for syndication is with a real-world example. Hal Helms (a fellow Team Allaire member) runs the unofficial TeamAllaire web site at *http://www.teamallaire.com*. The site contains a section listing short tutorials on programming in ColdFusion.

Hal recently created an open repository for the collection and syndication of ColdFusion tips and tutorials. With more and more sites devoted to ColdFusion springing up all the time, it made sense for him to create a central repository for aggregating and sharing content. As a result, the TeamAllaire site allows any site to openly share ColdFusion tips and tutorials while at the same time allowing these sites to maintain control over the tips and tutorials themselves. Two interfaces to the repository are provided. One for affiliate sites to register their own tutorials with the repository and a second for retrieving a WDDX packet containing information about the tips and tutorials.

For our purposes, we'll stick to the syndication aspect of the site, covering how you can retrieve the tutorials and use them within your own sites using WDDX. For more information on how the repository works as well as instructions on how to add your own tutorials see *http://www.teamallaire.com/hal/halsMenu.cfm*. Note that for simplicity, the terms "tips" and "tutorials" are used interchangeably.

### *Retrieving and displaying tips and tutorials*

Hal has made retrieving the WDDX packet containing the tips and tutorials a straightforward process. The site contains a special template that returns a WDDX packet containing all the tutorials in the repository. The template can be accessed at *http://www.teamallaire.com/tutorials/tipsregistry.cfm*.

Retrieving the WDDX packet from your server using ColdFusion is just a matter of pointing the `CFHTTP` tag to the URL we just mentioned. The `CFHTTP` tag goes out to the URL and retrieves the WDDX packet, which it stores in a variable called `CFHTTP.FileContent`. The template and process is shown in Example 20-12.

*Example 20-12. Retrieving a WDDX Packet Containing Tutorials*

```
<!--- Retrieve the WDDX packet containing the tips from Hal Helms's TeamAllaire
      site. --->
 <CFHTTP URL="http://www.teamallaire.com/tutorials/tipsregistry.cfm"
         METHOD="GET">

<!--- Deserialize the wddx packet. --->
<CFWDDX ACTION="WDDX2CFML" INPUT="#CFHTTP.FileContent#" OUTPUT="MyTips">

<TABLE WIDTH="400">
<TR>
  <TD>
```

*Example 20-12. Retrieving a WDDX Packet Containing Tutorials (continued)*

```
  <!--- loop through the array and output the contents of each structure --->
  <CFOUTPUT>
  <CFLOOP INDEX="i" FROM="1" TO="#ArrayLen(MyTips)#">
    <B><FONT SIZE="+1">#MyTips[i].Title#</FONT></B><BR>
    <FONT SIZE="-1">Last updated: #MyTips[i].LastUpdate#</FONT><BR>
    <FONT SIZE="-1"><A HREF="mailto:#MyTips[i].Author#">#MyTips[i].Author#</A>
    </FONT>
    <BR>
    #MyTips[i].Synopsis#<BR>
    (<A HREF="http://#MyTips[i].URL#">Full tip...)</A>
    <P>
  </CFLOOP>
  </CFOUTPUT>
  </TD>
</TR>
</TABLE>
```

Once you retrieve the packet, you can deserialize it using the `CFWDDX` tag. The packet contains an array of structures. Each structure contains the following key/value pairs:

`TipID`
: This structure key contains a UUID that acts as a unique identifier for the tip.

`URL`
: The URL to the full version of the tutorial. This key can build a link to the full version of the tutorial wherever it may reside.

`Title`
: The title of the tutorial.

`Synopsis`
: A short summary of the tutorial.

`LastUpdate`
: The date the tutorial was last updated.

`Keywords`
: Comma-delimited list of keywords relating to the tutorial.

`Author`
: The author (email address) of the tutorial

Once the WDDX packet is deserialized, the array of structures is looped over, and the contents of each structure are output in a nicely formatted table (shown in Figure 20-7).

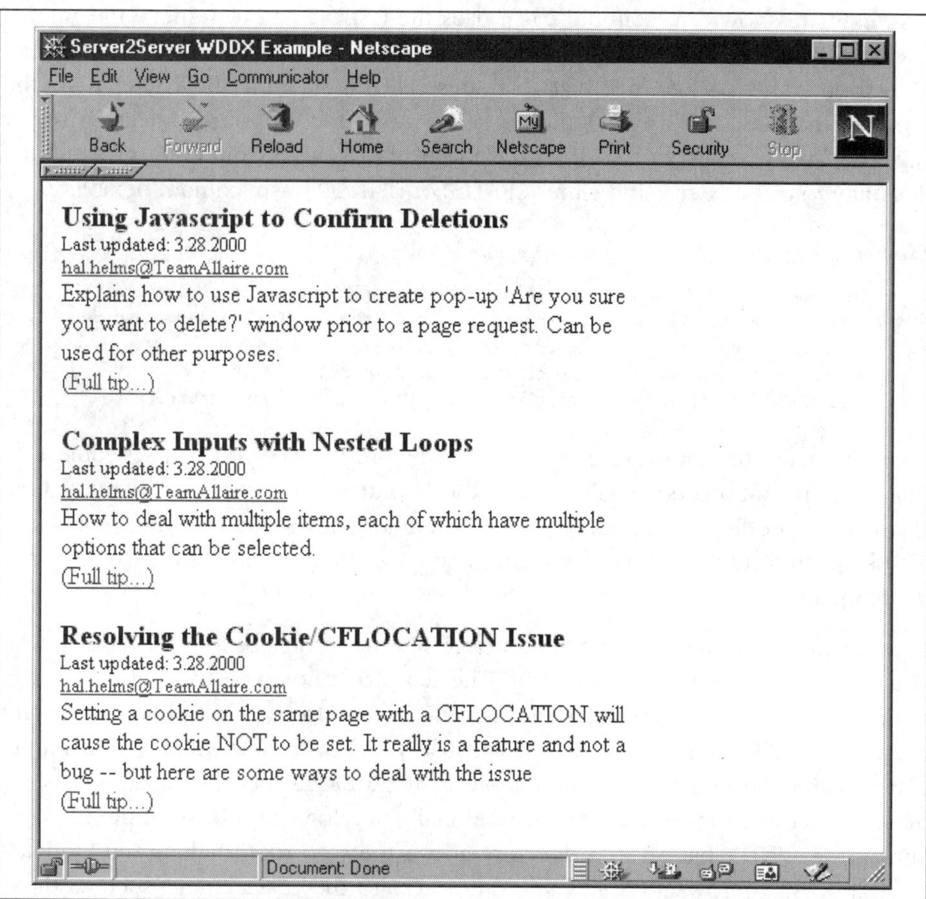


*Figure 20-7. Building a custom tutorial list using syndicated content*

### *Automating tip retrieval*

In Example 20-12, you saw how to retrieve the WDDX packet containing the tutorials using the `CFHTTP` tag and then display the tutorials to the user's browser. While this is certainly the easiest way to include tutorials on a site, it isn't necessarily the best or most reliable method. Because Example 20-12 makes a separate `CFHTTP` call every time someone requests the template to display the tips, there can be problems if, say, the TeamAllaire site goes down at the time of your request. Also, it's not very prudent to send a request to the TeamAllaire server every time a visitor to your site wants to see a tip. From a performance standpoint, it makes more sense to serve the list of tutorials from your page. It is much faster to display a local copy of the list than to have to make a request to another server somewhere out on the Internet.

The template shown in Example 20-13 uses the CFHTTP tag to retrieve the WDDX packet containing the tutorials just as in our previous example. This time, instead of grabbing the packet to a variable, deserializing it, and displaying it to the browser, the CFHTTP tag writes the packet to a text file on your ColdFusion server called *wddx_tipsregistry.txt*. Storing the file in the *wwwroot* directory gives us the flexibility to call it later using either CFFILE or CFHTTP for maximum flexibility.

*Example 20-13. Agent for Saving to a Text File*

```
<!--- Retrieve the WDDX packet containing the tips from Hal Helms's TeamAllaire
      site.  Save the WDDX packet as a text file on the ColdFusion server so we
      can call it up locally whenever we need it. --->
<CFHTTP URL="http://www.teamallaire.com/tutorials/tipsregistry.cfm"
        METHOD="GET" PATH="e:\inetsrv\wwwroot\" FILE="wddx_tipsregistry.txt">
```

To really make the template in Example 20-13 productive, you can schedule it to run on an automated basis using the ColdFusion Scheduler (covered in Chapter 22). Adding the template to the scheduler allows you to retrieve the latest list of tips and tutorials from the TeamAllaire site without having to manually run the template.

In order to retrieve the *wddx_tipsregistry.txt* file from your local ColdFusion server, you need to create another template. The template shown in Example 20-14 can retrieve the text file containing the WDDX packet from our ColdFusion server using either CFHTTP or CFFILE. You can use whichever method suits your particular situation. In general, it is preferable to use CFFILE because it is the fastest, most direct route to the filesystem. Additionally, it allows you to store the file containing the WDDX packet in a directory above the web root, making the file inaccessible to web browsers. Users without access to the CFFILE tag (such as those in a hosted environment where CFFILE is disabled for security reasons) can use the CFHTTP tag to retrieve the file via HTTP. Once the WDDX packet has been read and stored in a variable, it is deserialized using the CFWDDX tag and the resulting structure stored in a variable called MyTips. Next, the structure containing all the information about the tutorial is looped over and each key/value pair is output in an HTML table identical to that which is shown in Figure 20-7.

*Example 20-14. Retrieving the Tips WDDX Packet from the Local Server*

```
<!--- Retrieve the WDDX packet containing the tips from the wddx_tipsregistry.txt
      file we have saved on our CF server. --->
<CFHTTP URL="http://127.0.0.1/wddx_tipsregistry.txt " METHOD="GET">

<!--- This is the code you would use if you wanted to use CFFILE instead of
      CFHTTP.  It is commented out.
<CFFILE ACTION="Read"
        FILE="e:\inetsrv\wwwroot\wddx_tipsregistry.txt"
        VARIABLE="MyTips">
--->
```

*Example 20-14. Retrieving the Tips WDDX Packet from the Local Server (continued)*

```
<!--- Deserialize the wddx packet.  The packet contains an array of structures
      that contain the full URL to the tip as well as the title, a synopsis,
      and the author's e-mail address.  If you used CFFILE, change the INPUT
      value to MyTips --->
<CFWDDX ACTION="WDDX2CFML" INPUT="#CFHTTP.FileContent#" OUTPUT="MyTips">

<TABLE WIDTH="400">
<TR>
  <TD>
  <!--- loop through the array and output the contents of each structure --->
  <CFOUTPUT>
  <CFLOOP INDEX="i" FROM="1" TO="#ArrayLen(MyTips)#">
  <B><FONT SIZE="+1">#MyTips[i].Title#</FONT></B><BR>
  <FONT SIZE="-1">Last updated: #MyTips[i].LastUpdate#</FONT><BR>
  <FONT SIZE="-1"><A HREF="mailto:#MyTips[i].Author#">#MyTips[i].Author#</A>
  </FONT><BR>
  #MyTips[i].Synopsis#<BR>
  (<A HREF="http://#MyTips[i].URL#">Full tip...)</A>
  <P>
  </CFLOOP>
  </CFOUTPUT>
  </TD>
</TR>
</TABLE>
```

This is only one small example of what is possible using WDDX for syndication and server-to-server communication. Hopefully, by the time you have finished reading this chapter, a whole new range of possibilities for distributed web application development will have entered your mind.

## *Server-to-Browser WDDX Using JavaScript*

WDDX has fantastic possibilities that extend well beyond server-to-server data sharing. If you use WDDX along with client-side JavaScript, it becomes possible to offload data processing of complex datatypes to a historically underused resource—the browser. What does this mean for you as a web developer? For starters, it means that you now have the ability to easily convert complex datatypes, such as arrays, structures, and record sets from CFML, to JavaScript objects that can then be manipulated by the browser. This opens a whole range of possibilities for building more sophisticated and dynamic user interfaces to your application data. It also means you can potentially improve the performance of applications that involve heavy data browsing and editing by moving the records to the browser and using JavaScript to let the user scroll through and edit as necessary. Once all changes have been made, the data can be serialized (using JavaScript) back to a WDDX packet and then posted back to the server using a hidden form field.

## Passing Data to JavaScript on the Browser

The `CFWDDX` tag provides two mechanisms for passing data to JavaScript on the browser. The first mechanism involves using `CFWDDX` to serialize CFML data into a WDDX packet, then using the `CFWDDX` tag to deserialize the WDDX packet to an equivalent JavaScript object. Example 20-15 shows how to do this by serializing a structure containing a stock quote to WDDX, then deserializing the WDDX packet containing the structure to a JavaScript `struct`. The JavaScript code that creates the `struct` object is created dynamically using the `CFWDDX` tag. The JavaScript `struct` is then looped over and the contents output to the browser.

*Example 20-15. Generating Dynamic JavaScript Using the CFWDDX Tag*

```
<!--- create a structure called stock to hold a stock quote --->
<CFSET STOCK = STRUCTNEW()>
<CFSET STOCK.COMPANY = "Allaire">
<CFSET STOCK.TICKER = "ALLR">
<CFSET STOCK.EXCHANGE = "NASDAQ">
<CFSET STOCK.PRICE = "66.25">
<CFSET STOCK.CHANGE = "+0.375">
<CFSET STOCK.LASTTRADETIME = "10:17AM">
<CFSET STOCK.LASTTRADEDATE = "02/02/2001">
<CFSET STOCK.VOLUME = "8300">

<!--- first we need to serialize the structure into a wddx packet --->
<CFWDDX ACTION="CFML2WDDX" INPUT="#Stock#" OUTPUT="MyWDDXPacket">

<!--- output the wddx packet in a text area so you can see the entire packet --->
<H3>WDDX Packet Containing A Simple Value (string)</H3>
<FORM>
<CFOUTPUT>
<TEXTAREA ROWS="6" COLS="50" WRAP="virtual">#HTMLEditFormat(MyWDDXPacket)#
</TEXTAREA>
</CFOUTPUT>
</FORM>

<H3>Deserialize it to a JavaScript variable (view the source)</H3>
<!--- deserialize the wddx packet containing the string to a JAvaScript
    variable --->
<CFWDDX ACTION="WDDX2JS" INPUT="#MyWDDXPacket#"
      OUTPUT="MyJavaScript" TOPLEVELVARIABLE="MyStock">

<!--- use JavaScript to output the contents of the WDDX packet containing the
    serialized stock structure.  Note that the JavaScript code that creates
    the stock struct is created dynamically --->
<SCRIPT LANGUAGE="JavaScript">
```

*Example 20-15. Generating Dynamic JavaScript Using the CFWDDX Tag (continued)*

```
/** This line generates the dynamic JavaScript
  * necessary to create our "struct" object.
  */
<CFOUTPUT>#MyJavaScript#</CFOUTPUT>

// Loop through the stock "struct" and output each key/value
 for (i in MyStock) {
   document.write([i] + ': ' + MyStock[i] + '<br>');
     }
</SCRIPT>
```

Looking at Example 20-15, you'll notice that the first call to the `CFWDDX` tag converts the `Stock` structure to a WDDX packet. This is done by setting `ACTION` to `CFML2WDDX`. At this point, nothing has happened that involves any JavaScript or anything else we haven't covered so far. That all changes, however, with the next call to the `CFWDDX` tag. This time, we set `ACTION` to `WDDX2JS`. The `INPUT` attribute specifies the WDDX packet we just created. `OUTPUT` holds the dynamic JavaScript that is created automatically by the `CFWDDX` tag. If we were to leave out the `OUTPUT` attribute, the JavaScript is output in place automatically as part of the HTML stream. Specifying a variable name for `OUTPUT` allows us to decide exactly where in our template to output the dynamic JavaScript code. The final attribute, `TOPLEVELVARIABLE` names the top-level JavaScript object created when the WDDX packet is deserialized to JavaScript. In Example 20-15, we set our `TOPLEVELVARIABLE` to `MyStock`.

The final section of the template in Example 20-15 creates the JavaScript necessary to output the contents of the WDDX packet. First, we output the dynamic JavaScript we created in the previous section. This is done by putting the `MyJavaScript` variable (specified in the `OUTPUT` attribute) containing the JavaScript code within a set of `CFOUTPUT` tags. Next, we use a simple `for` loop to loop over the contents of the `struct` object and write each key/value pair to the browser.

If you choose View Source in your browser, you will see the dynamic JavaScript code that is generated by the `CFWDDX` tag. It should look something like this:

```
<SCRIPT LANGUAGE="JavaScript">
/** This line generates the dynamic JavaScript
  * necessary to create our "struct" object.
  */
MyStock=new Object();
MyStock["change"]="+0.375";
MyStock["company"]="Allaire";
MyStock["exchange"]="NASDAQ";
MyStock["lasttradedate"]="05/17/2000";
MyStock["lasttradetime"]="10:17AM";
MyStock["price"]="66.25";
```

```
MyStock["ticker"]="ALLR";
MyStock["volume"]="8300";

// Loop through the stock "struct" and output each key/value
 for (i in MyStock) {
   document.write([i] + ': ' + MyStock[i] + '<br>');
     }
</SCRIPT>
```

Note that the JavaScript code might not be visible in all browser versions.

### *Simplifying the process*

As we mentioned at the beginning of this section, the **CFWDDX** tag provides two mechanisms for passing data to JavaScript on the browser. In Example 20-15 we used a two-step process to convert a CFML structure to an equivalent JavaScript `struct` object. First, we used the **CFWDDX** tag to serialize the CFML structure to a WDDX packet. Then, we used the **CFWDDX** tag a second time to deserialize the WDDX packet to a JavaScript `struct` object. There is a more effective way to do this. The **CFWDDX** tag can serialize data directly from CFML to WDDX then automatically deserialize it to JavaScript in a single step by setting `ACTION` to `CFML2JS`, as shown in Example 20-16, which modifies the code we used in Example 20-15.

*Example 20-16. Going from CFML to JavaScript in a Single Step*

```
<!--- create a structure called stock to hold a stock quote --->
<CFSET STOCK = STRUCTNEW()>
<CFSET STOCK.COMPANY = "Allaire">
<CFSET STOCK.TICKER = "ALLR">
<CFSET STOCK.EXCHANGE = "NASDAQ">
<CFSET STOCK.PRICE = "66.25">
<CFSET STOCK.CHANGE = "+0.375">
<CFSET STOCK.LASTTRADETIME = "10:17AM">
<CFSET STOCK.LASTTRADEDATE = "02/02/2001">
<CFSET STOCK.VOLUME = "8300">

<!--- Serialize the CFML structure to WDDX then automatically deserialize it to
      a JavaScript object.  This is all done in the background, so the WDDX
      packet is never available for viewing or use. --->
<CFWDDX ACTION="CFML2JS" INPUT="#Stock#" OUTPUT="MyJavaScript"
        TOPLEVELVARIABLE="MyStock">

<H3>Create a JavaScript struct object from a CFML structure (view the source)</H3>

<!--- use JavaScript to output the contents of the WDDX packet containing the
      serialized stock structure.  Note that the JavaScript code that creates
      the stock struct is created dynamically --->
<SCRIPT LANGUAGE="JavaScript">
/** This line generates the dynamic JavaScript
  * necessary to create our "struct" object.
  */
```

*Example 20-16. Going from CFML to JavaScript in a Single Step (continued)*

```
<CFOUTPUT>#MyJavaScript#</CFOUTPUT>

// Loop through the stock "struct" and output each key/value
 for (i in MyStock) {
   document.write([i] + ': ' + MyStock[i] + '<br>');
     }
</SCRIPT>
```

The template in Example 20-16 produces the same output as the template in Example 20-15. The difference here is that we can accomplish the task using less code. Let's hear it for efficiency!

## Passing Data from JavaScript to ColdFusion

In the previous section, we discussed methods for getting simple and complex datatypes from ColdFusion to JavaScript using WDDX so that the data could be manipulated from within the browser. Now we need to look at how we can get that data back to ColdFusion from JavaScript once it is finished being manipulated. As always, the solution is close at hand.

A file called *wddx.js* is automatically installed into *\cfide\scripts* when you install the ColdFusion Application server. The *wddx.js* file contains two JavaScript objects (each with numerous functions) that can be used to manipulate WDDX data within JavaScript:

`WddxSerializer`
: The `WddxSerializer` object contains a single function, `serialize()`, that can serialize any JavaScript datatype into WDDX. Once a value or object has been serialized, the resulting WDDX is available as a JavaScript string value.

`WddxRecordset`
: The `WddxRecordset` object contains functions that can construct and manipulate WDDX record sets. Think of a record set as the same thing as a CFML query object.

To use the objects contained in the *wddx.js* template, you need to include the file from within your application code:

```
<SCRIPT LANGUAGE="JavaScript" SRC="/cfide/scripts/wddx.js"></SCRIPT>
```

A detailed discussion of the objects contained in the *wddx.js* file and their related functions is beyond the scope of this book. For more information, you can open the *wddx.js* file (located in *\cfide\scripts* be default when the ColdFusion server is installed) and read the detailed comments included with each function. Additional information can be found in Chapter 3 of "WDDX JavaScript Objects" from the *CFML Language Reference* that comes with the ColdFusion documentation or by visiting *http://wwwopenwddx.org*.

Let's look at Example 20-17, in which we use the `WddxRecordset` object to convert form-field data to a WDDX record set object. The form allows you to enter information about a new employee. Once the information has been entered, you can serialize it without having to refresh the current template by clicking on the button labeled Serialize, which is shown in Figure 20-8.

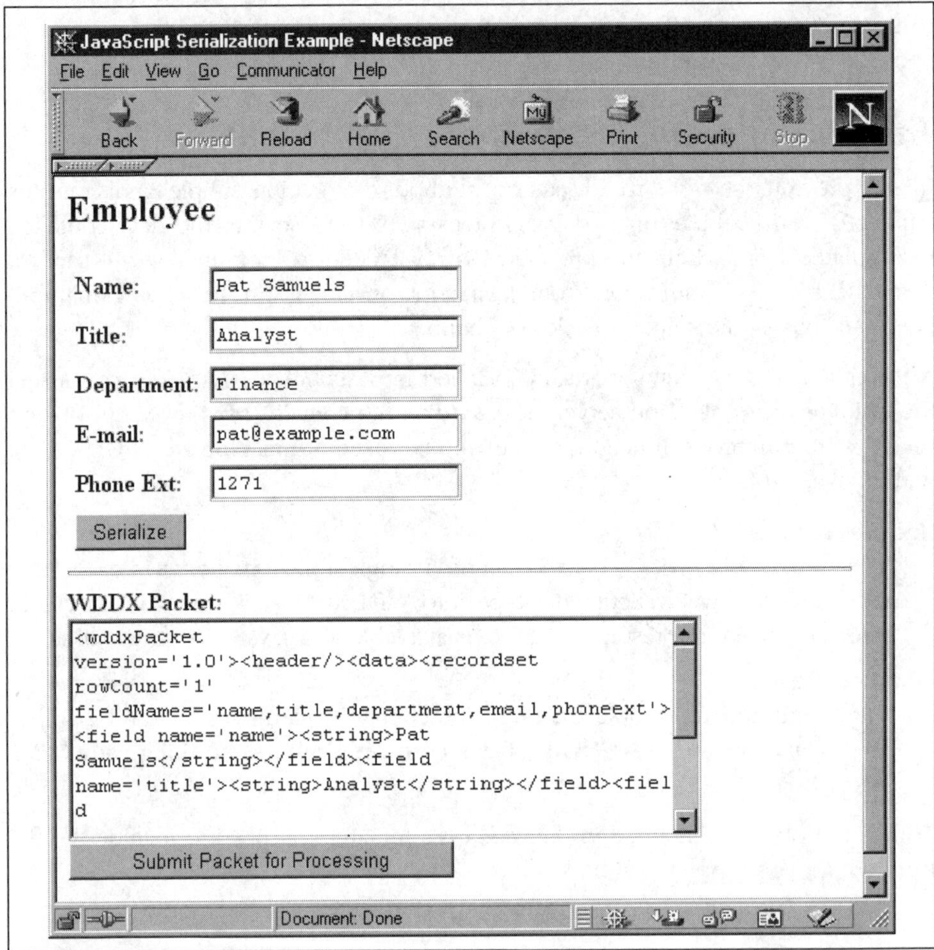


*Figure 20-8. Serializing form data to WDDX using JavaScript*

Once the Serialize button is clicked, the form-field information is converted to a WDDX record set object using the `WddxRecordset` object from the *wddx.js* file. The record set object is then serialized to a WDDX packet using the `WddxSerializer` object from the same file. Once the record set has been serialized, the resulting packet is placed in a **Textarea** form field called WDDX packet (shown in Figure 20-8).

*Example 20-17. Serializing a Record Set to a WDDX Packet Using JavaScript*

```
<H2>Employee</H2>

<!--- Include the wddx.js file containing the serialize function --->
<SCRIPT LANGUAGE="JavaScript" SRC="/cfide/scripts/Wddx.js"></SCRIPT>

<!--- serialize the contents of the form to a WDDX packet --->
<SCRIPT LANGUAGE="JavaScript">
    /** this function calls the wddxSerializer object from
      * the wddx.js file to serialize the Recordset object
      * after it is created
      */
    function SerializeEmployee() {
        var MySerializer = new WddxSerializer;
        /** create a recordset using the wddxRecordset object
          * in the wddx.js file.  Normally, if you were only
          * going to serialize a single record, you would be
          * better off using s structure.  However, we wanted
          * to demonstrate the use of the wddxRecordset object
          */
        var Employee = new WddxRecordset;
        Employee.addColumn("Name");
        Employee.addColumn("Title");
        Employee.addColumn("Department");
        Employee.addColumn("Email");
        Employee.addColumn("PhoneExt");
        Employee.addRows(1);
        Employee.setField(0, "Name", document.forms[0].Name.value);
        Employee.setField(0, "Title", document.forms[0].Title.value);
      Employee.setField(0, "Department", document.forms[0].Department.value);
        Employee.setField(0, "Email", document.forms[0].Email.value);
        Employee.setField(0, "PhoneExt", document.forms[0].PhoneExt.value);
        var WDDXPacket = MySerializer.serialize(Employee);

        // return the newly created WDDX packet to the form
        return WDDXPacket;
    }
</SCRIPT>


<!--- Form for inputting a new employee --->
<FORM ACTION="DeserializeFormPost.cfm" METHOD="POST">
<TABLE>
<TR>
  <TD><B>Name:</B></TD><TD><INPUT TYPE="TEXT" NAME="Name"></TD>
</TR>
<TR>
  <TD><B>Title:</B></TD><TD><INPUT TYPE="TEXT" NAME="Title"></TD>
</TR>
```

*Example 20-17. Serializing a Record Set to a WDDX Packet Using JavaScript (continued)*

```
<TR>
  <TD><B>Department:</B></TD><TD><INPUT TYPE="TEXT" NAME="Department"></TD>
</TR>
<TR>
  <TD><B>E-mail:</B></TD><TD><INPUT TYPE="TEXT" NAME="Email"></TD>
</TR>
<TR>
  <TD><B>Phone Ext:</B></TD><TD><INPUT TYPE="TEXT" NAME="PhoneExt"></TD>
</TR>
<TR>
  <!--- clicking on the button calls the SerializeEmployee function that
        serializes the form contents to a WDDX packet --->
  <TD COLSPAN="2"><INPUT TYPE="BUTTON" VALUE="Serialize"
               onClick="this.form.WDDXPacket.value = SerializeEmployee()"></TD>
</TR>
</TABLE>

<!--- display the WDDX packet and provide a submit button for the user to submit
      the packet to be deserialized --->
<HR>
<B>WDDX Packet:</B>
<BR>
<TEXTAREA NAME="WDDXPacket" ROWS="8" COLS="50" WRAP="virtual"></TEXTAREA>
<BR>
<INPUT TYPE="SUBMIT" VALUE="Submit Packet for Processing">
</FORM>
```

Submitting the form posts the WDDX packet to a template called *DeserializeFormPost.cfm*, shown in Example 20-18, where it is deserialized and the resulting record set output to the browser. The results are shown in Figure 20-9.

*Example 20-18. Deserializing a Posted WDDX Packet with a Record Set*

```
<FORM>
<H3>Your posted packet:</H3>
<CFOUTPUT>
<TEXTAREA NAME="WDDXPacket" ROWS="8" COLS="50" WRAP="virtual">#HTMLEditFormat(Form.
WDDXPacket)#</TEXTAREA>
</CFOUTPUT>
</FORM>

<CFWDDX ACTION="WDDX2CFML" INPUT="#Form.WDDXPacket#" OUTPUT="DeserializedPost">

<H3>Deserialized:</H3>

<!--- loop over the deserialized record set.  This technique allows you to output
      the contents of the record set without knowing any of the field names --->
<CFLOOP LIST="#DeserializedPost.ColumnList#" INDEX="ThisField">
<CFOUTPUT>
#ThisField#: #Evaluate("DeserializedPost." & ThisField)#<BR>
</CFOUTPUT>
</CFLOOP>
```

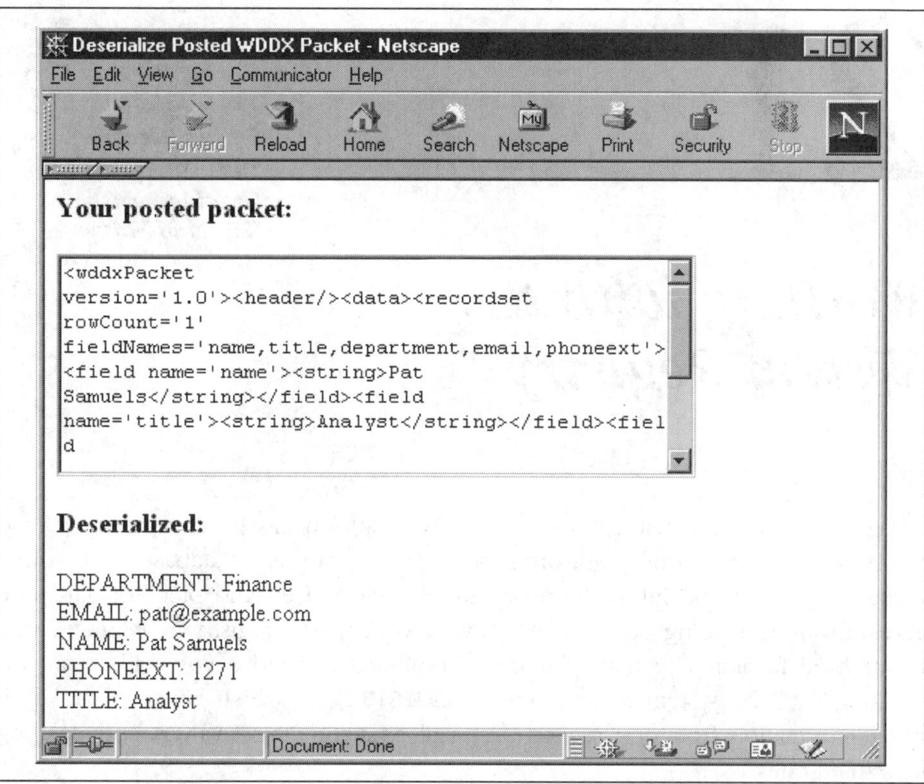


*Figure 20-9. Deserializing a WDDX packet received from a form post*

# 21

*In this chapter:*
- *Getting Registry Keys and Values*
- *Setting Registry Keys and Values*
- *Deleting Registry Keys and Values*

# *Working with the System Registry*

Anyone running ColdFusion on the Windows platform has probably encountered the system registry at one point or another. The registry is a database of sorts that contains configuration information on virtually every user, and piece of hardware and software (including ColdFusion) on your system. The registry is organized in a hierarchical fashion like that of a tree. ColdFusion provides you with a tag for working with the system registry, the **CFREGISTRY** tag, which is capable of querying information from the registry, as well as setting new values and deleting unwanted ones.

Before we get into the specifics of manipulating registry data, let's look at how the registry is organized. There are two basic units that make up the registry, keys and values. A *key* is a logical container similar to a filesystem's directory. Like a directory that contains files and additional subdirectories, keys can contain values and/or subkeys. A registry key and the subkeys and values below it are referred to as a branch. If we were to write out the structure of a typical registry branch, it might look something like this:

```
HKEY_LOCAL_MACHINE\Software\Allaire\ColdFusion\CurrentVersion\Mail
```

This branch stores values used by ColdFusion to interface with mail servers. As you can see, the key/subkey relationship looks exactly like a directory structure might (in DOS anyway).

*Values* (like files) are actually a representation for name/value pairs. Values are also known as entries. The following registry branch:

```
HKEY_LOCAL_MACHINE\Software\Allaire\ColdFusion\CurrentVersion\Mail
```

contains several entries such as `BaseDirectory`, `LogEntries`, and `MailServer`. In turn, each of these entries contains a value. If you are running ColdFusion on

Windows NT, you can use a GUI tool called the Registry Editor (which has a Windows Explorer-like interface) to view and manipulate registry keys and values.

Because the system registry contains configuration information on critical system resources, you need to be extremely careful when using the `CFREGISTRY` tag to change or delete registry information. Always keep a current backup of your registry and limit access to the tag when possible. This is especially important for administrators using ColdFusion in a multihost environment (such as an ISP). In general, it is recommended that you disable the `CFREGISTRY` tag from the Basic Security section of the ColdFusion Administrator if you don't plan to use it. If you use ColdFusion's Advanced Security Services, you can enable/disable `CFREGISTRY` on a per user basis. If you find that the examples in this chapter don't seem to be working, you should check to make sure the `CFREGISTRY` tag is enabled in the Basic Security section of the ColdFusion Administrator.

If you are running ColdFusion on a non-Windows operating system such as Unix or Linux, an abbreviated version of the system registry is automatically created when you first install ColdFusion. This scaled-down registry stores information about the configuration of your ColdFusion application server and is accessible via the `CFREGISTRY` tag.

# *Getting Registry Keys and Values*

The `CFREGISTRY` tag gives you two methods for retrieving keys and values from the registry. You can set the `ACTION` attribute to `GetAll` to retrieve all the particular keys/values associated with a particular branch, or you can set `ACTION="Get"` to retrieve the value associated with a specific entry.

Let's consider a scenario where we want to look up information about the ODBC connections setup on the same machine as ColdFusion. There is a registry branch we can access that contains this information. The branch is:

```
HKEY_LOCAL_MACHINE\Software\ODBC\ODBC.INI
```

It contains a list of every ODBC data source registered on the system. Each key contains several other subkeys relating to the ODBC connection. Example 21-1 shows how to perform the registry lookup.

*Example 21-1. Retrieving a List of Registry Keys*

```
<CFREGISTRY ACTION="GETALL" BRANCH="HKEY_LOCAL_MACHINE\Software\ODBC\ODBC.INI"
          NAME="GetODBC" TYPE="Any" SORT="Entry ASC">

<H3>HKEY_LOCAL_MACHINE\Software\ODBC\ODBC.INI</H3>

<TABLE BORDER="1">
<TR>
```

*Example 21-1. Retrieving a List of Registry Keys (continued)*

```
  <TH>Entry</TH><TH>Type</TH><TH>Value</TH>
</TR>

<CFOUTPUT QUERY="GetODBC">
<TR>
  <TD>#Entry#</TD><TD>#Type#</TD><TD>#Value#</TD>
</TR>
</CFOUTPUT>
</TABLE>
```

In Example 21-1, we set the `ACTION` attribute of the `CFREGISTRY` tag to `GetAll`. This action results in ColdFusion retrieving all the registry keys and values that fall under the branch specified in `BRANCH`. The `NAME` attribute allows us to specify a name for the query object that holds all the information we retrieve from the registry. `TYPE` is an optional attribute and specifies the type of registry entry to be accessed. Possibilities include `Key`, `DWord`, `String` (the default), and `Any`. In this case, we set `TYPE` to `Any` because we want to include any type of registry entry in our results. You should note that ColdFusion doesn't currently support the retrieval of binary values using the `CFREGISRTY` tag.

The final attribute, `SORT`, is also optional and determines the sort order for the results returned from the registry. Results may be ordered by `Entry`, `Type`, and `Value`. Multiple sort criteria can be entered as a comma-delimited list. In addition, the sort type may be specified after each column name as either `ASC` (ascending) or `DESC` (descending). In Example 21-1, we sort the results by `Entry`, in ascending order.

Executing the template results in an HTML table (shown in Figure 21-1), which contains all the subkeys contained in the specified registry branch. Note that the table contains three columns, `Entry`, `Type`, and `Value`. These column headers match up with the three query columns returned by the `CFREGISTRY` tag:

*`queryname`*`.Entry`
: Returns the name of the registry entry

*`queryname`*`.Type`
: The type of registry entry returned

*`queryname`*`.Value`
: The value of the registry entry if `TYPE` is set to `String` or `DWord`

Building on our previous example, let's delve one level deeper in the registry. Let's look at what you get if you use `ACTION="GetAll"` to retrieve all the subkeys from one of the keys (branches) we originally returned. We'll use the exact same code as in Example 21-1, except this time, we'll plug in the values for the `BRANCH` attribute:

```
HKEY_LOCAL_MACHINE\Software\ODBC\ODBC.INI\CFExamples
```

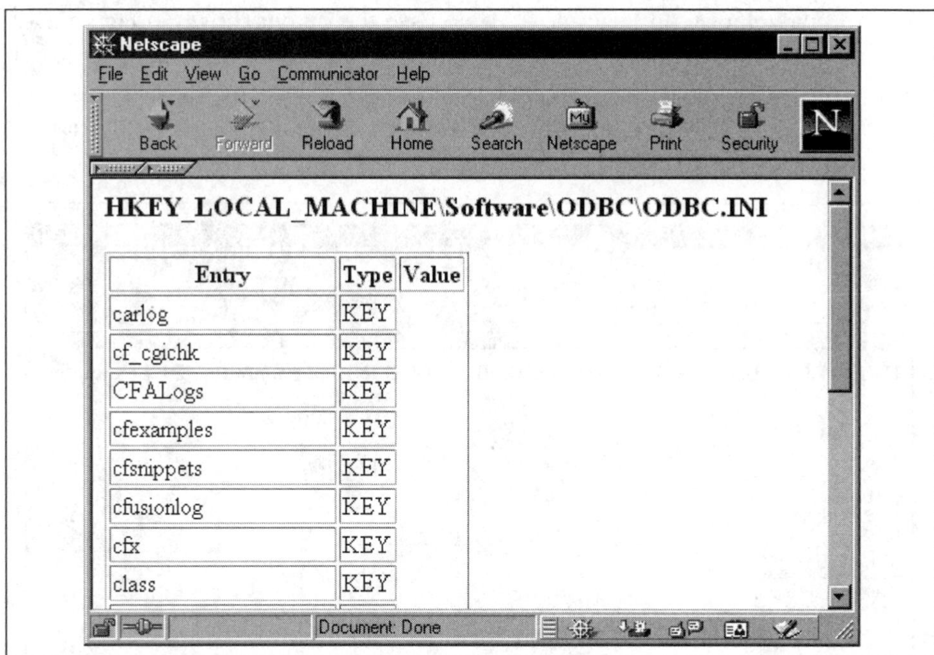


*Figure 21-1. Retrieving a list of entries from the registry*

**CFExamples** is the name of the sample database that installs by default when you install ColdFusion. If you don't have the **CFExamples** database installed on your machine, don't worry. You can reference any valid ODBC data source you have installed on your server. The complete template for retrieving a list of registry values can be seen in Example 21-2.

*Example 21-2. Retrieving a List of Registry Values*

```
<CFREGISTRY ACTION="GetAll"
            BRANCH="HKEY_LOCAL_MACHINE\Software\ODBC\ODBC.INI\CFExamples"
            NAME="GetODBC" TYPE="Any" SORT="Entry ASC">

<H3>HKEY_LOCAL_MACHINE\Software\ODBC\ODBC.INI\ProgrammingCF\CFExamples</H3>

<TABLE BORDER="1">
<TR>
  <TH>Entry</TH><TH>Type</TH><TH>Value</TH>
</TR>

<CFOUTPUT QUERY="GetODBC">
<TR>
  <TD>#Entry#</TD><TD>#Type#</TD><TD>#Value#</TD>
</TR>
</CFOUTPUT>
</TABLE>
```

If you run the template in Example 21-1, you see the output shown in Figure 21-2. Note that the table that is generated is similar to the one we created earlier in Figure 21-1, except that this time, there are other values in the `TYPE` column besides `Key`. Also, notice that the `VALUE` column now contains data for some of the entries we retrieved.

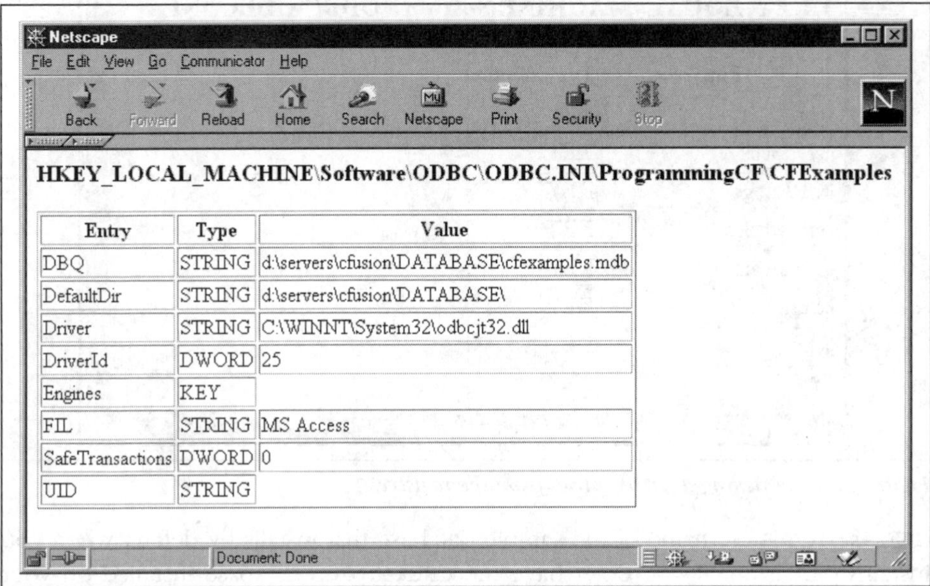


| Entry | Type | Value |
|---|---|---|
| DBQ | STRING | d:\servers\cfusion\DATABASE\cfexamples.mdb |
| DefaultDir | STRING | d:\servers\cfusion\DATABASE\ |
| Driver | STRING | C:\WINNT\System32\odbcjt32.dll |
| DriverId | DWORD | 25 |
| Engines | KEY | |
| FIL | STRING | MS Access |
| SafeTransactions | DWORD | 0 |
| UID | STRING | |

*Figure 21-2. Retrieving a list of entries containing values*

As I mentioned earlier, `CFREGISTRY` can also retrieve values for specific registry keys. For example, say you want your application to retrieve the location (IP address or hostname) of the mail server ColdFusion uses to send SMTP mail. You know the information is stored in the registry key:

```
HKEY_LOCAL_MACHINE\Software\Allaire\ColdFusion\CurrentVersion\Mail
```

By setting the `ACTION` attribute to `Get`, you can retrieve the value associated with the key, as shown in Example 21-3.

*Example 21-3. Retrieving a Specific Registry Value*

```
<CFREGISTRY ACTION="GET"
      BRANCH="HKEY_LOCAL_MACHINE\Software\Allaire\ColdFusion\CurrentVersion\Mail"
      ENTRY="MailServer" VARIABLE="TheMailServer" TYPE="String">

<H3>HKEY_LOCAL_MACHINE\Software\Allaire\ColdFusion\CurrentVersion\Mail</H3>

<CFOUTPUT>
The value of MailServer is: #TheMailServer#
</CFOUTPUT>
```

In Example 21-3, we set `ACTION` to `Get` so that ColdFusion knows we want to retrieve a single value. The name of the registry branch containing the entry to be accessed is specified in `BRANCH`. `ENTRY` is required and specifies the entry in the registry we want to look up the value for. In this instance, we want to look up the value for `MailServer`. The `VARIABLE` attribute allows us to specify a variable name to hold the value we retrieve from the registry. We set our `VARIABLE` to `TheMailServer`. The final attribute, `TYPE` is optional and specifies the type of registry data being retrieved. Valid options include `String` (the default), `DWord`, and `Key`. We set `TYPE` equal to `String`. Once the `CFREGISTRY` tag has executed, we output the value to the browser using the `TheMailServer` variable.

# *Setting Registry Keys and Values*

Besides retrieving registry keys and values, the `CFREGISTRY` tag can also create new registry keys as well as set and update registry values. This allows you, for example, to store application-specific information in the system registry as opposed to in a database. It also allows you to add/update ODBC data sources and Verity collections that normally must be added/updated through the ColdFusion Administrator. As a matter of fact, this is exactly how the ColdFusion Administrator handles these tasks behind the scenes. Example 21-4 shows how to add a key called `Test` to the registry.

*Example 21-4. Creating a Registry Key*

```
<!--- this creates a new key called Test under CurrentVersion --->
<CFREGISTRY ACTION="Set"
          BRANCH="HKEY_LOCAL_MACHINE\Software\Allaire\ColdFusion\CurrentVersion"
          TYPE="Key" ENTRY="Test">

<!--- Query the CurrentVersion key so that we can show it was added --->
<CFREGISTRY ACTION="GETALL"
          BRANCH="HKEY_LOCAL_MACHINE\Software\Allaire\ColdFusion\CurrentVersion"
          NAME="GetCurrent" TYPE="Any" SORT="ASC">

<H3>HKEY_LOCAL_MACHINE\Software\Allaire\ColdFusion\CurrentVersion</H3>

<TABLE BORDER="1">
<TR>
  <TH>Entry</TH><TH>Type</TH><TH>Value</TH>
</TR>

<CFOUTPUT QUERY="GetCurrent">
<TR>
  <TD>#Entry#</TD><TD>#Type#</TD><TD>#Value#</TD>
</TR>
</CFOUTPUT>
</TABLE>
```

Example 21-4 uses the CFREGISTRY tag to create a new registry key called Test by setting the ACTION attribute to Set. BRANCH specifies the registry branch to create the new key under. We decide to create our new key under the registry branch:

```
HKEY_LOCAL_MACHINE\Software\Allaire\ColdFusion\CurrentVersion
```

The TYPE attribute is optional and specifies the type of registry data to be set. Possible entries are Key, DWord, and String (the default). In Example 21-4, we set TYPE to Key. The name of the key to create is specified by the ENTRY attribute. Once the registry key has been created, we use another CFREGISTRY tag to get a list of all the subkeys (including the one we just created) under CurrentVersion.

As I mentioned, the CFREGISTRY tag can also set registry values. Example 21-5 creates an entry called Test and populates it with the string value "This is a test."

*Example 21-5. Setting a Registry Value*

```
<!--- Set a string value for the Test key --->
<CFREGISTRY ACTION="Set"
          BRANCH="HKEY_LOCAL_MACHINE\Software\Allaire\ColdFusion\CurrentVersion"
          ENTRY="Test" TYPE="String" VALUE="This is a test">

<!--- Query the Test key so that we can show a value was set --->
<CFREGISTRY ACTION="GET"
          BRANCH="HKEY_LOCAL_MACHINE\Software\Allaire\ColdFusion\CurrentVersion"
          ENTRY="Test" VARIABLE="GetTest" TYPE="String">

<H3>HKEY_LOCAL_MACHINE\Software\Allaire\ColdFusion\CurrentVersion</H3>

<CFOUTPUT>
The value of <B>Test</B> is: <I>#GetTest#</I>
</CFOUTPUT>
```

In Example 21-5, the ACTION is still Set. BRANCH specifies the registry branch where we want to create our new key/value pair. The ENTRY attribute is required and specifies the key or value in the registry to be set. We set ENTRY to Test, telling ColdFusion that we want to set an entry called Test. TYPE is an optional attribute and specifies the type of registry data to be set. Possible entries are Key, DWord, and String (the default). In this example, we set TYPE to String. The actual value we want to set is specified by the VALUE attribute. The second CFREGISTRY call gets the value we just set and outputs it to the browser.

If you use CFREGISTRY to set a value for an entry that already exists, ColdFusion overwrites the old value with the one you supply. Example 21-6 updates an already existing registry entry with a new value and outputs the results to the browser.

*Example 21-6. Updating a Registry Value*

```
<!--- Query the Test key so that we can show the original value --->
<CFREGISTRY ACTION="GET"
          BRANCH="HKEY_LOCAL_MACHINE\Software\Allaire\ColdFusion\CurrentVersion"
          ENTRY="Test" VARIABLE="GetOriginalTest" TYPE="String">

<H3>HKEY_LOCAL_MACHINE\Software\Allaire\ColdFusion\CurrentVersion</H3>

<CFOUTPUT>
The original value of Test: <I>#GetOriginalTest#</I><BR>
</CFOUTPUT>
Change the value...<BR>

<!--- Set a string value for the Test key --->
<CFREGISTRY ACTION="Set"
          BRANCH="HKEY_LOCAL_MACHINE\Software\Allaire\ColdFusion\CurrentVersion"
          ENTRY="test" TYPE="String" VALUE="This is another test">

<!--- Query the Test key so that we can show the new value --->
<CFREGISTRY ACTION="GET"
          BRANCH="HKEY_LOCAL_MACHINE\Software\Allaire\ColdFusion\CurrentVersion"
          ENTRY="Test" VARIABLE="GetTest" TYPE="String">

<CFOUTPUT>
The new value of Test: <I>#GetTest#</I>
</CFOUTPUT>
```

# Deleting Registry Keys and Values

There are times when you might find it desirable to delete information from the system registry, for example, if you want to delete a data source without having to go through the ColdFusion Administrator. The `CFREGISTRY` tag can delete a registry value, a single registry key or an entire registry branch by setting the `ACTION` attribute to `Delete`. But it is extremely important to know what you are doing with regards to the registry before you use this action. You should also have a current backup of your registry before using the `CFREGISTRY` tag to delete registry entries. Example 21-7 deletes an entry from the registry.

*Example 21-7. Deleting a Registry Value*

```
<CFREGISTRY ACTION="Delete"
          BRANCH="HKEY_LOCAL_MACHINE\Software\Allaire\ColdFusion\CurrentVersion"
          ENTRY="Test">
```

*Example 21-7. Deleting a Registry Value (continued)*

```
<CFREGISTRY ACTION="GETALL"
         BRANCH="HKEY_LOCAL_MACHINE\Software\Allaire\ColdFusion\CurrentVersion"
         NAME="GetCurrent" TYPE="Any" SORT="ASC">

<H3>HKEY_LOCAL_MACHINE\Software\Allaire\ColdFusion\CurrentVersion</H3>

<TABLE BORDER="1">
<TR>
  <TH>Entry</TH><TH>Type</TH><TH>Value</TH>
</TR>

<CFOUTPUT QUERY="GetCurrent">
<TR>
  <TD>#Entry#</TD><TD>#Type#</TD><TD>#Value#</TD>
</TR>
</CFOUTPUT>
</TABLE>
```

In Example 21-7, we set the `ACTION` attribute of the `CFREGISTRY` tag to `Delete`. `BRANCH` specifies the branch containing the entry we want to delete. The `ENTRY` attribute specifies the name of the entry we want to delete; in this case, an entry named `Test`. Note that if the entry specified in `Entry` doesn't exist, ColdFusion returns an error.

`CFREGISTRY` can also delete a single registry key or an entire registry branch, including all subbranches and their associated keys and values. Example 21-8 deletes all the subbranches and key/value pairs below the key:

```
HKEY_LOCAL_MACHINE\Software\Allaire\ColdFusion\CurrentVersion\test
```

*Example 21-8. Deleting an Entire Registry Branch*

```
<CFREGISTRY ACTION="Delete"
     BRANCH="HKEY_LOCAL_MACHINE\Software\Allaire\ColdFusion\CurrentVersion\test">

<CFREGISTRY ACTION="GETALL"
     BRANCH="HKEY_LOCAL_MACHINE\Software\Allaire\ColdFusion\CurrentVersion"
     NAME="GetCurrent" TYPE="Any" SORT="ASC">

<H3>HKEY_LOCAL_MACHINE\Software\Allaire\ColdFusion\CurrentVersion</H3>

<TABLE BORDER="1">
<TR>
  <TH>Entry</TH><TH>Type</TH><TH>Value</TH>
</TR>

<CFOUTPUT QUERY="GetCurrent">
<TR>
  <TD>#Entry#</TD><TD>#Type#</TD><TD>#Value#</TD>
</TR>
```

*Example 21-8. Deleting an Entire Registry Branch (continued)*

```
</CFOUTPUT>
</TABLE>
```

In Example 21-8, the `CFREGISTRY` tag needs only two attributes, `ACTION` and `BRANCH`. As in Example 21-7, we set `ACTION` to `Delete` to let ColdFusion know we want to delete information from the registry. The key to begin recursively deleting from is specified by `BRANCH`. All keys, subkeys, and values in or below the specified branch are deleted. If the branch doesn't exist, ColdFusion throws an error.

# 22

*In this chapter:*
- *Scheduling Tasks with the ColdFusion Administrator*
- *Scheduling Tasks with CFSCHEDULE*
- *Additional Considerations*

# *Using the ColdFusion Scheduler*

The ColdFusion Scheduler allows you to incorporate a whole new level of functionality into your CFML applications. With the Scheduler, you can set up various templates to run automatically on a recurring basis. Scheduled template execution has numerous uses including automatic report generation, maintenance, and system monitoring. You can also automate so-called intelligent agents—templates that are capable of retrieving information from other sites and applications without user intervention.

The Scheduler comes standard as part of the ColdFusion Application Server and can be accessed via the ColdFusion Administrator or programmatically. Using the Scheduler, it is possible to schedule the execution of templates on a recurring basis, e.g., daily, weekly, or monthly. In addition, tasks can be set to execute at a particular time or interval, or can be set to run only a single time. Additionally, the Scheduler can automatically generate static HTML files from dynamic content.

## *Scheduling Tasks with the ColdFusion Administrator*

The fastest way to schedule the execution of a template is through the ColdFusion Administrator. The ColdFusion Administrator provides a clean and intuitive interface for managing scheduled tasks. Using the ColdFusion Administrator interface, you can specify general settings for the Scheduler as well as add, update, and delete scheduled tasks. Scheduled tasks can also be run directly from within the ColdFusion Administrator, which makes it possible to test your scheduled tasks or execute them manually.

## *Scheduler Settings*

Before you begin to use the Scheduler, it is important to take note of a couple of administrative settings that impact how the Scheduler runs. If you open the ColdFusion Administrator in your browser and click on the Automation Settings link under the Automated Tasks section, you will see a screen that allows you to set the Scheduler Refresh Interval and enable logging of ColdFusion Executive Task Scheduling. This configuration screen is shown in Figure 22-1.

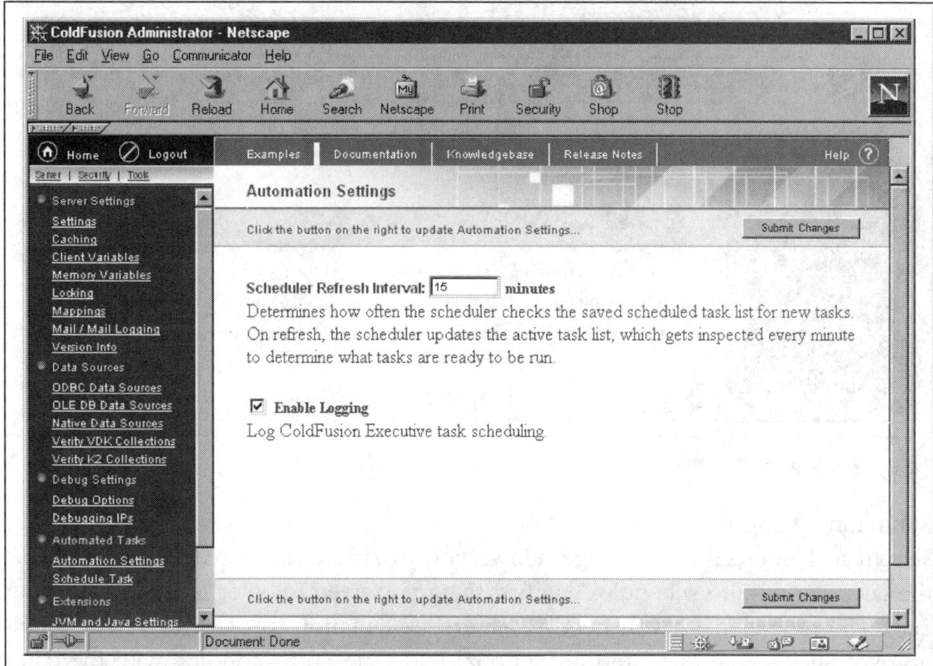


*Figure 22-1. Configuring automated task settings*

The Scheduler Refresh Interval allows you to specify how often (in minutes) the ColdFusion Scheduler should check for newly scheduled tasks. When a task is added to the Scheduler, it isn't included as an actively scheduled task until the list is refreshed. The actively scheduled task list is scanned by the Scheduler once every minute for tasks to execute.

Checking the box to Enable ColdFusion Executive Task Scheduling causes the ColdFusion Executive service to write a log entry to the *scheduler.log* file each time a new task is added to the list or an existing task is modified.

## Adding a Task

To add a new task to the Scheduler, click on the Schedule Task link under the Automated Tasks section of the ColdFusion Administrator. You are then presented with a page listing all currently scheduled tasks (shown in Figure 22-2). To add a new task, click the Schedule New Task button.

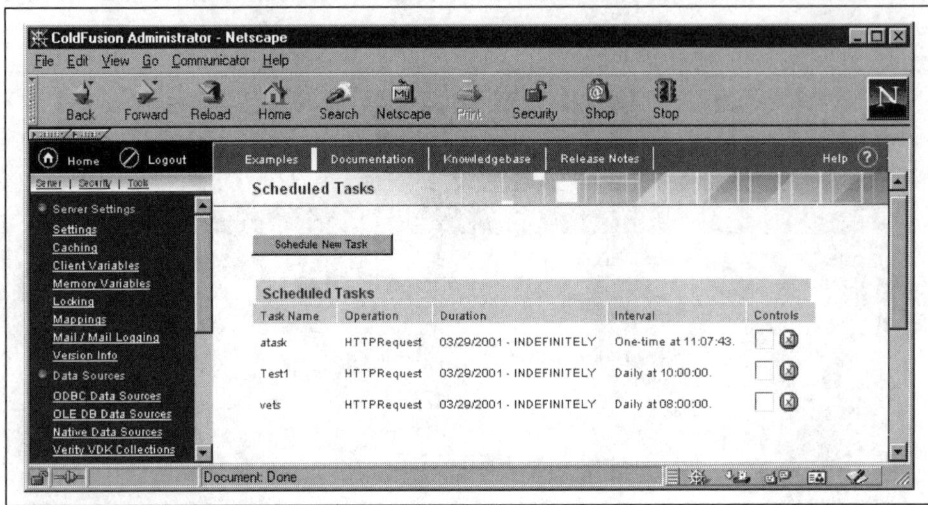


*Figure 22-2. Adding a new task name to the Scheduled Tasks Menu*

Submitting the form in Figure 22-2 takes you to the Add/Edit Scheduled Task page shown in Figure 22-3. This page allows you to specify all the details concerning the task you wish to schedule. The first thing you need to enter is a name for your task. The next element you need to enter is a Duration for your task. The Duration specifies a Start Date and an optional End Date corresponding with the dates you want the scheduled execution to begin and optionally end. If you want the task to remain scheduled indefinitely, omit the End Date.

The next section of the form in Figure 22-3 lets you specify an interval for your scheduled task. This interval determines how often the task is to be scheduled. You have three options:

*One Time*
: The scheduled task executes a single time on the Start Date you specified. The time you wish the task to execute can be specified here. After the task executes, it remains in the list of scheduled tasks, although it doesn't execute again.

*Recurring*
: This option allows you to specify how frequently the scheduled task should execute. Possibilities include Daily, Weekly, and Monthly). Execution begins

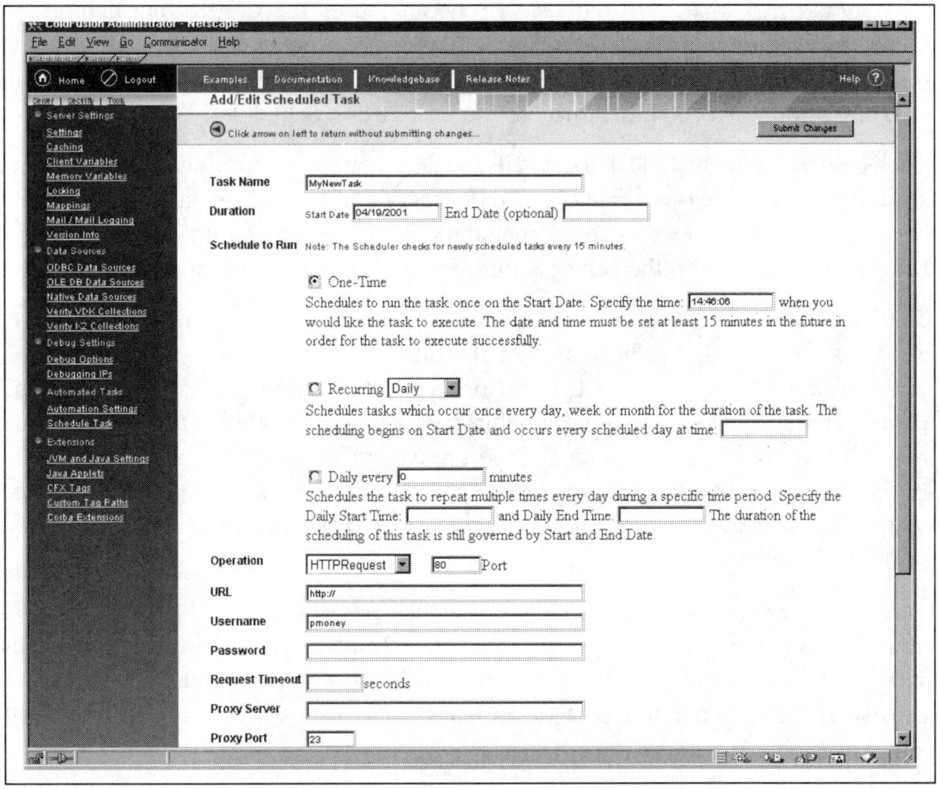

*Figure 22-3. Adding a new task to the Scheduler*

on the Start Date with the task executing at the time specified in the Daily Start Time field.

*Daily every n minutes*
With this option, you can schedule your task to repeat every *n* minutes beginning on the Start Date. Optionally, you can specify a Daily Start Time and a Daily End Time for the task so that it executes only within the given time period each day.

The next option you can specify is Port. Port allows you to specify the port number on a remote (or local) server to listen for HTTP requests. This option is used in conjunction with the next field—URL. The value you enter for URL should be the absolute URL (*http://* or *https://*) to the template you want the scheduled task to execute. If you are attempting to execute a template over SSL, make sure to specify the SSL port in the Port attribute. The default port for SSL is 403. The template can reside on any server accessible by URL. If the remote template requires authentication, you can specify a Username and Password in the appropriate fields.

You should note that the ColdFusion Scheduler uses the `CFHTTP` tag behind the scenes to execute the template you specify. As such, the same issues that apply to the `CFHTTP` tag (such as no support for NT Challenge/Response Authentication) also apply to tasks scheduled through the ColdFusion Scheduler.

The Request Timeout field is optional and lets you specify an amount of time in seconds to wait before timing out the scheduled task. This field is important because it allows you to extend the amount of time a request has to execute beyond the value set in the Server Settings section of the ColdFusion Administrator.

The next two fields, Proxy Server and Proxy Port are both optional. Proxy Server allows you to specify the hostname or IP address of a proxy server you must pass your request through if your ColdFusion server is behind a firewall. If the template you are trying to execute sits behind a proxy server, you can specify the port number used by the proxy server in the Proxy Port field. If a value is specified for Proxy Port, it is automatically appended to any resolved URLs within the executed template. This allows you to preserve links within a template that resolve to a port other than 80.

The last section of the Add/Edit Scheduled Task page (shown in Figure 22-4) gives you the option to have the output from the template you request automatically saved as a file on your ColdFusion server. This allows you to schedule tasks that call dynamically generated content and have the results saved as a static HTML template.

In order to save the output of your scheduled task, you must check the box labeled "Save output to a file". Next, enter the full path (i.e., *c:\inetsrv\wwwroot*) to the directory where you want to save the file in the Path field. The File field lets you specify a name for the file you want to save. You can give the file any extension you want. Checking the box next to Resolve URL results in any relative links in the output file being converted to absolute URLs. This ensures that no broken links appear in the file you create. This is especially useful when you schedule a task to retrieve dynamic content from a remote server.

Once you have finished setting up the options for your scheduled task, click the Submit Changes button at the bottom of the page to create the task. If you decide for some reason that you don't want to create the task, click the arrow to the left of the Submit Changes button to return to the main Scheduled Tasks menu.

## Manually Executing a Task

As of ColdFusion 4.5, you can now manually execute a scheduled task from within the ColdFusion Administrator. This is useful when you need to execute a scheduled task at a time other than originally scheduled, or when you want to execute a task for troubleshooting purposes. To manually execute a task from the

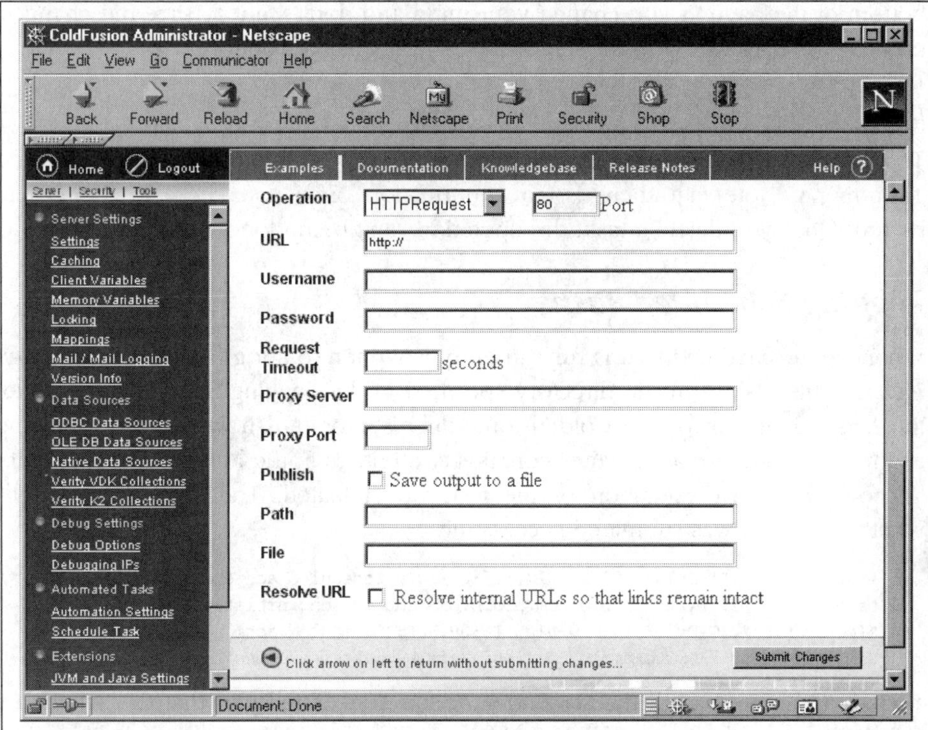


*Figure 22-4. Specifying that Scheduler output should be saved as a file*

ColdFusion Administrator, click on the Schedule Task link, then on the run icon (under the controls column.) If the task can be executed, a page displaying a message to that effect is displayed.

## Updating and Deleting Tasks

The ColdFusion Administrator provides you with a way to update existing tasks with new information and to delete tasks you no longer want or need. All editing and deleting of scheduled tasks starts by choosing a task from the Scheduled Tasks menu in the ColdFusion Administrator.

### Updating a task

To edit an existing task, click on the task name link from the Scheduled Task menu. This action takes you to a page labeled Add/Edit Scheduled Task. This is the same as the page shown in Figure 22-3, except all the information about the task is already filled in the form fields. And you can now make changes to the task information. When you are finished, click on the Submit Changes button at the bottom of the page. If you change your mind and don't want to save the changes, click on the back arrow to the left of the Submit Changes button.

#### *Deleting a task*

To delete a task, click on the delete icon next to the task name on the Scheduled Task menu. Note that there is no confirmation once you click on the Delete button. Once you delete a task, the operation can't be undone.

## *Logging Scheduled Tasks*

Whenever a scheduled task is run, an entry is written to a log file called *scheduler.log*. This file resides in the directory specified in the Logging Settings page under the Logging section of the ColdFusion Administrator. As shown in the following example, each task that executes contains two entries in the log file. The first entry acknowledges that execution of the task was initiated. The second entry tells whether the task was submitted successfully.

```
"Information","TID=75","03/19/01","16:09:50","Scheduled action TestHttps,
template https://www.example.com/login.cfm submission initiated."
"Information","TID=75","03/19/01","16:09:50","Scheduled action TestHttps,
template https://www.example.com/login.cfm submitted successfully."
```

You should note that all the *scheduler.log* file does is tell you that the scheduled task was submitted successfully. It doesn't tell you whether or not the template you called has executed successfully. This is an important distinction to remember when troubleshooting failed scheduled tasks.

You can view the *scheduler.log* file from the Log Files section of the ColdFusion Administrator, under Logging.

# *Scheduling Tasks with CFSCHEDULE*

Besides being able to schedule tasks with the ColdFusion Administrator, you can use the `CFSCHEDULE` tag to do it programmatically. With the `CFSCHEDULE` tag, you can add, update, delete, and run scheduled tasks. Scheduling tasks programmatically let's you add a whole new level of functionality to your applications. For example, you can create a reporting application that allows users to have automatic email delivery of their reports on a scheduled basis. With the `CFSCHEDULE` tag, it is easy to set things up so that your application automatically schedules a task for each user. And each task can automatically generate a report and email it to the user at a chosen interval.

The attributes used by the `CFSCHEDULE` tag roughly coincide with the form fields from the Add Scheduler Task page in the ColdFusion Administrator, as you can see in Appendix A.

## *Adding Tasks*

Adding a task to the Scheduler using `CFSCHEDULE` is a lot like adding a task via the ColdFusion Administrator. The information you enter in the ColdFusion Administrator is the same information you specify for the `CFSCHEDULE` tag attributes. For example, to schedule a task called `MyTask` that calls the template located at *http://www.example.com/myscript.cfm* once a day at 1:30 p.m., you can use the following code:

```
<CFSCHEDULE ACTION="Update" TASK="MyTask" OPERATION="HTTPRequest"
            URL="http://www.example.com/myscript.cfm"
            STARTDATE="#DateFormat(Now(),'mm/dd/yyyy')#"
            STARTTIME="13:30:00" INTERVAL="Daily" REQUESTTIMEOUT="60">

<H2>Task scheduled successfully</H2>
```

The `ACTION` attribute is required and specifies the action you want the Scheduler to perform. Possible actions are `Update`, `Delete`, and `Run`. `Update` can be used to create a new task or update an existing task. In this case, we use `Update` to create a new task. When `ACTION` attribute is set to `Update`, several required attributes are expected. These attributes are `TASK`, `OPERATION`, `URL`, `STARTDATE`, `STARTTIME`, and `INTERVAL`. The `TASK` attribute allows you to specify a name for the task. The name you assign to the task is used by the ColdFusion Scheduler to uniquely identify the task—similar to how a database uses a primary key. Before adding a task using `CFSCHEDULE`, it is a good idea to see if a task by the same name already exists. If it does, and you try to add a new task with the same name, you will overwrite the original task. To look up a task name, use the `CFREGISTRY` tag. Scheduled tasks can be found under the branch:

```
HKEY_LOCAL_MACHINE\Software\Allaire\ColdFusion\CurrentVersion\Schedule
```

For more information on using the `CFREGISTRY` tag, see Chapter 21.

The `OPERATON` attribute specifies the operation the Scheduler should perform when `ACTION` is `Update`. The only `OPERATION` currently supported is `HTTPRequest`. URL points to the absolute URL (*http://* or *https://*) of the template to be executed when the scheduled task runs. The starting date for the scheduled task is specified by `STARTDATE`. In this case, we use `#DateFormat(Now( ),'mm/dd/yyyy')#` to indicate that the scheduled task should start on the current day. The time that the scheduled task gets executed is governed by the `STARTTIME`. `INTERVAL` indicates how often a scheduled task should be executed. Intervals can be set in seconds or as `Once`, `Daily`, `Weekly`, or `Monthly`. The default interval is one hour (3,600 seconds). The minimum `INTERVAL` allowed is 60 seconds. `REQUESTTIMEOUT` is an optional attribute and specifies a value for the `REQUESTTIMEOUT` URL parameter. This attribute can extend the time allowed for execution of the scheduled task beyond the default set in the ColdFusion Administrator.

There are several additional optional attributes available to the CFSCHEDULE tag. For more information, see Appendix A.

Let's look at a more advanced example that demonstrates the power of using the CFSCHEDULE tag to let your applications schedule tasks on their own. Consider a scenario in which you want to allow an administrator to schedule the automatic delivery of reports to various users within your organization. These reports can contain any sort of information. In Example 22-1, we'll send the employee a copy of their contact information.

The first step is to create a form for the administrator to select an employee and enter information on when the report should run, and how it should be delivered (either via email or published to a static HTML page).

*Example 22-1. Choosing an Employee and Scheduling Delivery of a Report*

```
<!--- get all of the employees from the EmployeeDirectory table.  This query
      is used to populate the employee drop down box --->
<CFQUERY NAME="GetEmployees" DATASOURCE="ProgrammingCF">
        SELECT ID, Name FROM EmployeeDirectory
</CFQUERY>

<!--- retrieve the refresh interval (in seconds) for the scheduler from the
      registry --->
<CFREGISTRY ACTION="GET"
   BRANCH="HKEY_LOCAL_MACHINE\Software\Allaire\ColdFusion\CurrentVersion\Schedule"
   ENTRY="CheckInterval" VARIABLE="TheInterval" TYPE="String">

<H2>Schedule Report</H2>

<FORM ACTION="ScheduleTheTask.cfm" METHOD="POST">
<TABLE BORDER=0 >
<TR>
  <!--- Populate the employee drop down with the query results from earlier --->
  <TD><B>Employee:</B></TD>
  <TD><SELECT NAME="Employee">
        <CFOUTPUT QUERY="GetEmployees">
        <OPTION VALUE="#ID#">#Name#</OPTION>
        </CFOUTPUT>
      </SELECT>
  </TD>
</TR>
<TR>
  <TD><B>Task Name:</B></TD>
  <TD><INPUT NAME="TaskName" TYPE="Text" SIZE="20" MAXLENGTH="255"></TD>
</TR>
<TR>
  <!--- specifies the type of report to schedule --->
  <TD><B>Delivery Format:</B></TD>
```

*Example 22-1. Choosing an Employee and Scheduling Delivery of a Report (continued)*

```
  <TD><SELECT NAME="DeliveryFormat">
        <OPTION VALUE="Email" SELECTED>E-mail
        <OPTION VALUE="HTMLPage">HTML Page</SELECT>
  </TD>
</TR>
<TR>
  <TD><B>Start Date:</B></TD>
  <TD><CFOUTPUT><INPUT NAME="StartDate" TYPE="TEXT" VALUE="#DateFormat(Now(),
      'mm/dd/yy')#" SIZE=10></CFOUTPUT></TD>
</TR>
<TR>
  <TD><B>Schedule to run </B></TD>
  <TD><SELECT NAME="Interval">
        <OPTION VALUE="Daily">Daily
        <OPTION VALUE="Weekly">Weekly
        <OPTION VALUE="Monthly">Monthly
      </SELECT> at
      <CFOUTPUT>
      <!--- output the refresh interval in minutes --->
      <INPUT NAME="StartTime" TYPE="TEXT" VALUE="#TimeFormat(DateAdd("N", 15,
             Now()),'HH:mm:ss')#" SIZE=10> (EST)
      </CFOUTPUT>
  </TD>
</TR>
<TR>
  <CFOUTPUT>
  <TD COLSPAN="2"><B>Note: Our scheduler checks for newly scheduled tasks every
#Evaluate(TheInterval/60)# minutes.</B></TD>
  </CFOUTPUT>
</TR>
<TR>
  <TD COLSPAN="2" ALIGN="center"><INPUT NAME="Create" TYPE="SUBMIT"
      VALUE="Schedule">
  </TD>
</TR>
</TABLE>
</FORM>
```

The template in Example 22-1 creates a form for the administrator to set up the scheduled task (shown in Figure 22-5). A query is performed to obtain a list of the employee names. The names are then used to dynamically populate a drop-down box in the form. The next field in the form allows the administrator to choose a delivery format for the report. Valid options here are `Email` and `HTML Page`. The rest of the fields specify a name for the scheduled task as well as the start date and frequency with which the task should run.

Once the administrator finishes filling out the form, she can click the Schedule button at the bottom of the form to schedule the task. Clicking on the button posts the form-field information to a template called *ScheduleTheTask.cfm,* shown in Example 22-2.

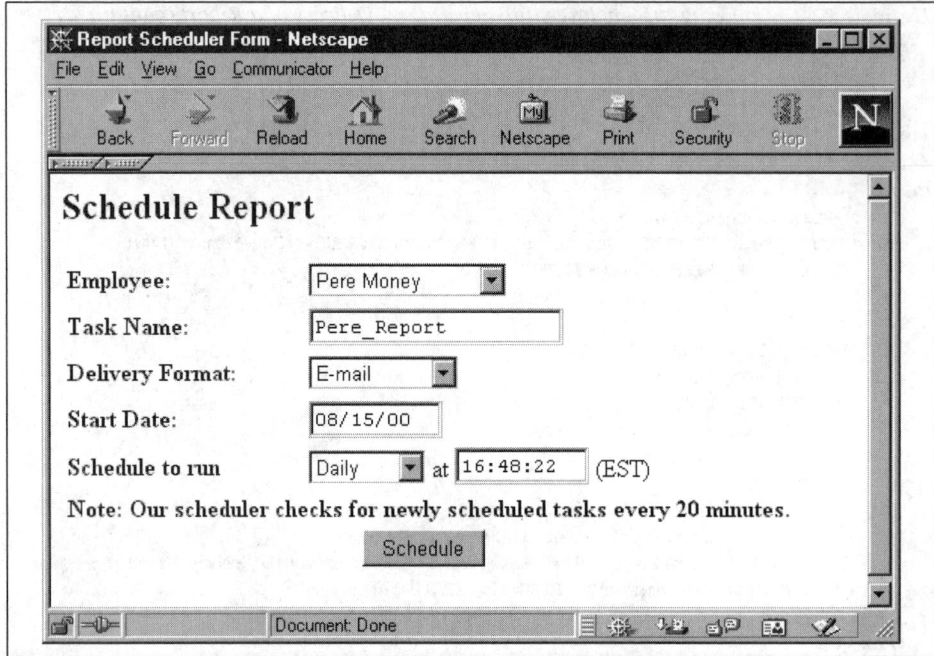


*Figure 22-5. Choosing an employee and scheduling delivery of a report*

*Example 22-2. Scheduling the Report Delivery Using CFSCHEDULE*

```
<!--- Get the employee name associated with the ID we passed in --->
<CFQUERY NAME="GetEmployee" DATASOURCE="ProgrammingCF">
        SELECT Name
        FROM EmployeeDirectory
        WHERE ID = #Form.Employee#
</CFQUERY>

<!--- assign defaults in case of blanks --->
<CFPARAM NAME="Form.TaskName" DEFAULT="#CreateUUID()#">
<CFPARAM NAME="Form.StartDate" DEFAULT="#DateFormat(Now(),'mm/dd/yyyy')#">
<CFPARAM NAME="Form.StartTime" DEFAULT="#TimeFormat(Now(),'HH:mm:ss')#">

<!--- if the delivery format is Email, schedule the task --->
<CFIF FORM.DELIVERYFORMAT IS "Email">
  <CFSCHEDULE ACTION="Update" TASK="#Form.TaskName#" OPERATION="HTTPRequest"
     STARTDATE="#DateFormat(Form.StartDate,'mm/dd/yyyy')#"
     STARTTIME="#TimeFormat(Form.StartTime,'HH:mm:ss')#"
     URL="http://127.0.0.1/RunScheduledReport.cfm?ID=#Form.Employee#&
          DeliveryFormat=#Form.DeliveryFormat#"
     INTERVAL="#Form.interval#" REQUESTTIMEOUT="3600">
<!--- if the delivery format is HTML, schedule the generation of the static
     HTML file --->
<CFELSE>
  <CFSCHEDULE ACTION="Update" TASK="#Form.TaskName#" OPERATION="HTTPRequest"
     STARTDATE="#DateFormat(Form.StartDate,'mm/dd/yyyy')#"
```

*Example 22-2. Scheduling the Report Delivery Using CFSCHEDULE (continued)*

```
    STARTTIME="#TimeFormat(Form.StartTime,'HH:mm:ss')#"
    URL="http://127.0.0.1/RunScheduledReport.cfm?ID=#Form.Employee#&
         DeliveryFormat=#Form.DeliveryFormat#"
    INTERVAL="#Form.interval#" REQUESTTIMEOUT="3600"
    RESOLVEURL="Yes" PUBLISH="Yes"
    FILE="#Replace(GetEmployee.Name, ' ', '_', 'All')#.htm"
    PATH="e:\inetsrv\wwwroot\#Replace(GetEmployee.Name, ' ', '_', 'All')#">
</CFIF>

<H2>Report Successfully Scheduled</H2>
```

The template in Example 22-2 takes the form-field data posted to it and uses it to create the scheduled task. A `CFQUERY` is run at the beginning of the template to look up the name of the employee the task is being scheduled for. This is done because the value passed with `Form.Employee` is the `ID` number (primary key from the database) of the employee as opposed to her name. (I'll show you why I did this in just a moment.)

The next part of the template assigns default values for any of the required form fields in case they are left blank. This prevents the template from throwing an error or scheduling a task that can never be executed because it is missing a start time and date. If a name for the task isn't passed, a UUID is created to serve as the name. A UUID is used because it is guaranteed to be unique.

The third part of the template uses a `CFIF` statement to determine whether or not the delivery format for the report generated by the scheduled task should be an email or an HTML file. Regardless of the format, a task is scheduled using the `CFSCHEDULE` tag that runs a template called *RunScheduledReport.cfm*. Note that two URL variables are appended to the end of the URL. The first URL variable, `ID`, specifies the `ID` of the employee (see, I told you I would get to this) for whom the report should be generated. The second URL variable, `DeliveryFormat`, specifies the delivery format for the report. If `Form.DeliveryFormat` is `HTMLPage`, a few additional attributes are used with the `CFSCHEDULE` tag to specify that the output generated by the *RunScheduledReport.cfm* template should be saved as a static HTML file. The filename and path for the generated file are both dynamically created using the name of the employee (with spaces stripped out). Once the task has been created, a message is output to the browser letting the administrator know that the task has been successfully added.

The template in Example 22-3 is the *RunScheduledReport.cfm* template, which is the template that is called by any scheduled task created by the two previous templates. The template takes the `ID` URL variable passed in by the scheduled task and uses it to look up the employee for whom the report is supposed to be run. It then checks the value of the `DeliveryFormat` URL variable to determine the delivery format for the report. If the delivery format is email, the `CFMAIL` tag sends the report to the appropriate employee. If, however, the report format is an HTML page, a table is output to the "browser". The CFHTTP tag then writes the contents of the page to a static HTML file on the server. Note that the directory the Scheduler is supposed to write to must already exist. You could get sophisticated and have this template check to make sure the directory exists using the CFDIRECTORY tag, and if not create it first, but for the purposes of this example, let's keep it simple. Once the static file has been created, an email is then sent using CFMAIL to notify the employee that her report is ready. The email contains a link to the newly created report. The *RunScheduledReport.cfm* template is shown in Example 22-3.

*Example 22-3. RunScheduledReport.cfm for Creating and Delivering Reports*

```
<!--- get the employee record based on the info passed in by the scheduler --->
<CFQUERY NAME="GetRecord" DATASOURCE="ProgrammingCF" DBTYPE="ODBC">
         SELECT Name, Title, Department, Email, PhoneExt
         FROM EmployeeDirectory WHERE ID = #Url.ID#
</CFQUERY>

<!--- check the desired delivery format from URL.DeliveryFortmat and act
      accordingly --->
<CFIF URL.DELIVERYFORMAT IS "HTMLPage">
<!--- create the page to be written as a static page. --->
<HTML>
<HEAD>
 <CFOUTPUT>
 <TITLE>Report for #GetRecord.Name#</TITLE>
 </CFOUTPUT>
</HEAD>

<BODY>

<CFOUTPUT>
<H2>Employee Information for #GetRecord.Name#</H2>
</CFOUTPUT>

<TABLE CELLPADDING="3" CELLSPACING="0">
<TR BGCOLOR="#888888">
  <TH>Name</TH><TH>Title</TH><TH>Department</TH><TH>E-mail</TH>
  <TH>Phone Extension</TH>
</TR>
<CFOUTPUT QUERY="GetRecord">
<TR BGCOLOR="##C0C0C0">
  <TD>#Name#</TD><TD>#Title#</TD><TD>#Department#</TD>
  <TD><A HREF="Mailto:#Email#">#Email#</A></TD><TD>#PhoneExt#</TD>
</TR>
</CFOUTPUT>
</TABLE>
</BODY>
</HTML>
```

*Example 22-3. RunScheduledReport.cfm for Creating and Delivering Reports (continued)*

```
<!--- now send an e-mail to the employee letting them know where their page
      is --->
<CFMAIL TO="#GetRecord.Email#" FROM="webmaster@example.com"
        SUBJECT="Your scheduled report is ready">
#GetRecord.Name#,

Your scheduled report is now ready for viewing.  You may see it by pointing your
browser to:

http://127.0.0.1/#Replace(GetRecord.Name, ' ', '_',
'All')#/#Replace(GetRecord.Name, ', '_', 'All')#.htm

Best regards,

The Webmaster
</CFMAIL>

<!--- otherwise, send an e-mail report to the employee --->
<CFELSE>
<CFMAIL TO="#GetRecord.Email#" FROM="webmaster@example.com"
        SUBJECT="Your scheduled report" QUERY="GetRecord">
#Name#,

Here is your employee report:

Name: #Name#
Title: #Title#
Department: #Department#
E-mail: #Email#
Phone Ext: #PhoneExt#

Best regards,

The Webmaster
</CFMAIL>
</CFIF>
```

## Updating Tasks

As far as the `CFSCHEDULE` tag is concerned, updating an existing task and adding a new task are the same operation. Both operations are performed by setting `ACTION` to `Update`. To successfully update an existing task, make sure to provide the exact task name in the `TASK` attribute of the `CFSCHEDULE` tag. For example, if you want to take an existing task named `MyTask` and update the `INTERVAL` for the task from `Daily` to `Weekly`, all you need is the following code:

```
<CFSCHEDULE ACTION="Update" TASK="MyTask" INTERVAL="Weekly">
```

The only two attributes required for an update are `ACTION` and `TASK`. Beyond that, you may choose to update as few or as many attributes as you like. If you wish to change the name of the task, you have to delete it first, then recreate it under the new task name.

It is possible to pull up all the existing attributes for a record so that it is easier for a user to edit them. This can be done with the CFREGISTRY tag, which retrieves the information about the scheduled task from the system registry. Examples 22-4 and 22-5 show how to update tasks programmatically.

*Example 22-4. Obtaining Information about a Scheduled Task*

```
<!--- retrieve all of the scheduled tasks from the registry --->
<CFREGISTRY ACTION="GETALL"
   BRANCH="HKEY_LOCAL_MACHINE\Software\Allaire\ColdFusion\CurrentVersion\Schedule"
   NAME="GetScheduledTasks" TYPE="Key" SORT="Entry ASC">


<H2>Scheduled Tasks</H2>
<H3>Please choose a task to edit</H3>

<TABLE BORDER="0" CELLSPACING="1">
<TR>
<TH BGCOLOR="#0000FF"><FONT COLOR="#FFFFFF">Task Name</FONT></TH>
</TR>

<!--- output the scheduled tasks.  Create a link to the EditTask.cfm template
      and pass the name of the entry to retrieve from the registry --->
<CFOUTPUT QUERY="GetScheduledTasks">
<TR>
<TD BGCOLOR="##C0C0C0"><A HREF="EditTask.cfm?Task=#URLEncodedFormat(Entry)#">
                    #Entry#</A></TD>
</TR>
</CFOUTPUT>
</TABLE>
```

The template in Example 22-4 uses the CFREGISTRY tag to retrieve a list of registry keys from the registry branch:

```
HKEY_LOCAL_MACHINE\Software\Allaire\ColdFusion\CurrentVersion\Schedule
```

Each key in the branch represents the name of a task in the ColdFusion Scheduler. Once a list of all the tasks is obtained, a table containing each task name is output to the browser. Each task name is then displayed as a hypertext link with the name of the task appended to the URL as a parameter named Task. Clicking on the link passes the task name to the *EditTask.cfm* template shown in Example 22-5.

*Example 22-5. EditTask.cfm Template for Editing a Scheduled Task*

```
<!--- retrieve all of the information from the entry passed in via URL --->
<CFREGISTRY ACTION="GETALL"
         BRANCH="HKEY_LOCAL_MACHINE\Software\Allaire\ColdFusion\CurrentVersion\
                 Schedule\#URL.Task#"
```

*Example 22-5. EditTask.cfm Template for Editing a Scheduled Task (continued)*

```
          NAME="GetTaskInfo" TYPE="Any">

<CFOUTPUT>
<H2>Edit Task: #URL.Task#</H2>
</CFOUTPUT>

<FORM ACTION="UpdateTask.cfm" METHOD="Post">
<CFOUTPUT>
<!--- need to pass the task name along to the next template --->
<INPUT TYPE="hidden" NAME="Task" VALUE="#URL.Task#">
</CFOUTPUT>

<TABLE BORDER="0" CELLSPACING="1">
<!--- dynamically create the edit form by looping over all of the entry/value
      pairs from the registry --->
<CFOUTPUT QUERY="GetTaskInfo">
<TR>
<TD BGCOLOR="##C0C0C0">#Entry#</TD>
<TD BGCOLOR="##C0C0C0"><INPUT TYPE="text" NAME="#Entry#" VALUE="#Value#"
SIZE="#Evaluate(Len(Value) + 8)#"></TD>
</TR>
</CFOUTPUT>
<TR>
<TD COLSPAN="2"><INPUT TYPE="submit" NAME="Submit" VALUE="Submit Changes"></TD>
</TR>
</TABLE>
</FORM>
```

The *EditTask.cfm* template then takes the **Task** URL parameter passed from the *GetScheduledTasks.cfm* template in Example 22-4 and uses it to retrieve the specific registry entry for the scheduled task that requires editing. The registry entry contains the name of each Scheduler attribute along with its value. An HTML form containing all the Scheduler attribute names and their associated values is dynamically constructed by looping over the result set returned by the **CFREGISTRY** tag. At this point, the user can make any edits to the scheduled task they desire.

Submitting the form created by Example 22-5 posts all the task information to the *UpdateTask.cfm* template shown in Example 22-6. The *UpdateTask.cfm* template takes the information posted to it and uses it to update the scheduled task using the **CFSCHEDULE** tag.

*Example 22-6. Updating a Scheduled Task Using CFSCHEDULE*

```
<!--- set defaults so NULLS don't cause errors --->
<CFPARAM NAME="Form.Task" DEFAULT="">
<CFPARAM NAME="Form.URL" DEFAULT="">
<CFPARAM NAME="Form.StartDate" DEFAULT="">
<CFPARAM NAME="Form.StartTime" DEFAULT="">
<CFPARAM NAME="Form.EndDate" DEFAULT="">
<CFPARAM NAME="Form.EndTime" DEFAULT="">
```

*Example 22-6. Updating a Scheduled Task Using CFSCHEDULE (continued)*

```
<CFPARAM NAME="Form.Username" DEFAULT="">
<CFPARAM NAME="Form.Password" DEFAULT="">
<CFPARAM NAME="Form.Interval" DEFAULT="">
<CFPARAM NAME="Form.RequestTimeOut" DEFAULT="">
<CFPARAM NAME="Form.ProxyServer" DEFAULT="">
<CFPARAM NAME="Form.ResolveURL" DEFAULT="No">
<CFPARAM NAME="Form.Publish" DEFAULT="No">
<CFPARAM NAME="Form.File" DEFAULT="">
<CFPARAM NAME="Form.Path" DEFAULT="">
<CFPARAM NAME="Form.HTTPPort" DEFAULT="80">
<CFPARAM NAME="Form.HTTPProxyPort" DEFAULT="80">

<!--- update the scheduled task posted by the edit form.  If this were a
      production application, we would add code before this call to validate
      that appropriate values were passed before attempting to update the
      task. --->
<CFSCHEDULE ACTION="UPDATE" TASK="#Form.Task#" OPERATION="HTTPRequest"
            URL="#Form.URL#" STARTDATE="#DateFormat(Form.StartDate,'mm/dd/yyyy')#"
            STARTTIME="#TimeFormat(Form.StartTime,'HH:mm:ss')#"
            ENDDATE="#DateFormat(Form.EndDate,'mm/dd/yyyy')#"
            ENDTIME="#TimeFormat(Form.EndTime,'HH:mm:ss')#"
            USERNAME="#Form.Username#" PASSWORD="#Form.Password#"
            INTERVAL="#Form.Interval#" REQUESTTIMEOUT="#Form.RequestTimeOut#"
            PROXYSERVER="#Form.ProxyServer#" RESOLVEURL="#Form.ResolveURL#"
            PUBLISH="#Form.Publish#" FILE="#Form.File#" PATH="#Form.Path#"
            PORT="#Form.HTTPPort#" PROXYPORT="#Form.HTTPProxyPort#">

<H3>Task successfully updated</H3>
```

## Deleting a Task

Deleting a task using CFSCHEDULE requires only two attributes, ACTION and TASK. The ACTION attribute should be set to Delete, and the TASK attribute should be set to the task name you wish to delete:

```
<!--- delete a task named MyTask from the task list --->
<CFSCHEDULE ACTION="Delete" TASK="MyTask">
```

Once you delete a task using CFSCHEDULE, it is permanently removed from the task list.

## Running Tasks

The CFSCHEDULE tag can execute any scheduled task independent of the Scheduler in the ColdFusion Administrator. To do this, set the ACTION attribute in the CFSCHEDULE tag to Run. Provide the name of the task to run using the TASK attribute:

```
<!--- run a task named MyTask from the task list --->
<CFSCHEDULE ACTION="Run"  TASK="MyTask">
```

When you run a task using `CFSCHEDULE` any additional attributes specified for the task in the ColdFusion Administrator (such as Time Out, Publish, etc.) are automatically applied.

## *Additional Considerations*

As useful as the ColdFusion Scheduler is, it does have its limitations. One of the most notable limitations of the Scheduler is that there is no built-in redundancy. That is, if a scheduled task fails to execute for whatever reason (say the server is down) the Scheduler has no way of knowing this condition, and only attempts to execute the task again the next time it is scheduled for execution.

It is possible to build redundancy into your scheduled tasks, but it takes work. One solution involves creating a small database that contains a record for each entry in the Scheduler. Each time you execute a scheduled task, you `CFINCLUDE` a file or call a custom tag that updates a field in the database with the time and date that the task should be executed next. A second template scans the database of scheduled tasks and checks to make sure none of the tasks have a time/date for next execution that is older than the current time/date. If so, you know that the task didn't execute for some reason, and you can call the `CFSCHEDULE` tag to immediately try to run that task again. The template that performs the scan should itself be scheduled to run at an interval that is appropriate for your particular needs (i.e., every 15 minutes, every 30 minutes, etc.).

# 23

*In this chapter:*
- *Connecting to External Objects*
- *Executing Programs*
- *Invoking Java Servlets*

# *Calling External Objects*

If you had to choose a single word to describe ColdFusion, it just might be connectivity. So far, we've talked about using ColdFusion to talk to databases, LDAP servers, FTP servers, HTTP servers, SMTP servers, POP servers, custom tags, and the local filesystem. Well, you'll be happy to know that the list doesn't stop there. ColdFusion can also communicate with a number of other technologies including command-line programs, COM/DCOM objects, CORBA objects, Java classes, Enterprise JavaBeans, and Java servlets. All this connectivity is handled via three tags, `CFOBJECT`, `CFEXECUTE`, and `CFSERVLET`. This chapter discusses how to use these tags to communicate with several types of external objects and programs to expand the functionality of ColdFusion to unlimited heights.

## *Connecting to External Objects*

ColdFusion can connect to various types of external objects via the `CFOBJECT` tag. `CFOBJECT` allows you to use ColdFusion to access third-party components or back-end systems written in other languages without having to deal with the underlying code or complexity of the object. The types of external objects supported by `CFOBJECT` include:

*COM*
: The Component Object Model (COM) is a Microsoft-sponsored specification for creating distributed software components. There are a large number of third-party COM objects, most of which can be used by ColdFusion. COM is currently supported only in the Windows version of ColdFusion.

*CORBA*
: The Common Object Request Broker Architecture (CORBA) is a specification put forth by the Object Management Group (OMG) for creating platform

neutral distributed software objects. CORBA objects can be written using any number of languages and are supported on all ColdFusion platforms except for Linux.

*Java classes*
The `CFOBJECT` tag can connect to Java class files and, by extension, Enterprise JavaBeans (EJBs).

## *Calling COM Objects*

The `CFOBJECT` tag can call COM objects located on the same machine as the ColdFusion server or on other machines connected to the network. `CFOBJECT` can also communicate with objects residing anywhere on the network using Distributed COM (or DCOM). In order to connect to a COM object using ColdFusion, the object must first be registered. You register a COM object using the *regsvr32* command from the Windows command line as in:

```
C:\> regsvr32 myobject.dll
```

Once a COM object is registered, you can connect to it using ColdFusion. To understand how to use the `CFOBJECT` tag to communicate with a COM object, you first need to understand the tag's syntax:

```
<CFOBJECT TYPE="COM"
          NAME="name"
          CLASS="progID"
          ACTION="action"
          CONTEXT="context"
          SERVER="server_name">
```

When connecting to a COM object, the `TYPE` attribute must always be set to `COM`. The `NAME` attribute is required and specifies a name for the object to be used when referencing the object's attributes and methods in your code. `CLASS` is a required attribute and specifies the program ID for the object you want to invoke. If you don't know the program ID for your object, consult the object's documentation. You can also use Microsoft's OLEView program to view any object's program ID, properties, and methods as long as the object is registered on your system. If you don't have OLEView, you can download if for free (along with instructions for use) from *http://www.microsoft.com/com/resources/oleview.asp*.

The `ACTION` attribute is also required and has two possible values, `Create` or `Connect`. `Create` instantiates the COM object (usually a *.dll*) before assigning properties or invoking methods. `Connect` connects to a COM object (usually an *.exe*) that is already running on the server. `CONTEXT` is optional and specifies the context the object is running in. Valid entries are `InProc`, `Local`, or `Remote`. `InProc` specifies an in-process server object (usually a *.dll*) running in the same process space as the ColdFusion server. `Local` specifies an out-of-process server object (usually an *.exe*) that is still running on the same server as ColdFusion, but not in the same process space. Remote specifies an out-of-process server object (usually an *.exe*) that is running on another machine. If Remote is specified, the SERVER attribute is required. When no value is specified, ColdFusion uses the registry setting for the object. The final attribute, SERVER, specifies a valid server.

Once an object has been instantiated, you can access the properties and methods of the object. An object's properties are similar to an HTML or CFML tag's attributes. Properties allow you to pass values to objects that can be referenced as variables inside the object. Methods are similar to CFML functions in the sense that they cause the object to perform an action and return (sometimes) a value that you can reference.

To set a property, you use the following syntax:

```
<CFSET MyObject.MyProperty = "Value">
```

Conversely, you can read a property's value using the following syntax:

```
<CFSET MyValue = MyObject.Property>
```

There are a few ways to invoke a method depending on the number and type of arguments it expects. To invoke a method that doesn't expect any arguments, use the following syntax:

```
<CFSET MyVariable = MyObject.MyMethod()>
```

Methods that require one or more arguments are said to have their arguments passed by value and are invoked like this:

```
<CFSET MyVal = 123>
<CFSET MyVariable = MyObject.MyMethod (MyVal, "Hello World", 1)>
```

Methods can also have their arguments passed by reference. Arguments passed by reference usually have their values changed by the method being called. In this case, MyVal is enclosed in double quotes and passed to MyObject.MyMethod by reference:

```
<CFSET MyVal = 123>
<CFSET MyVariable = MyObject.MyMethod("MyVal", "Hello World")>
```

Outputting the value of MyVal after the method is called generally results in a different value than 123.

You should note that you can't directly access nested objects using ColdFusion. Instead, you must access the outermost object first and work your way to the innermost object. For example, you can't directly access the object TheObject.TheNestedObject.TheProperty. In order to act on MyNestedObject.MyProperty, you need to use syntax like this:

```
<CFSET MyNestedObject = TheObject.TheNestedObject>
<CFSET MyProperty = MyNestedObject.TheProperty>
```

Now that you have a basic understanding of how ColdFusion uses the **CFOBJECT** tag to interact with COM objects, let's look at an example you can test on your server that demonstrates many of the concepts we just covered. Example 23-1 shows how to invoke the Microsoft Word COM object and use its methods and properties to convert a preexisting Word document to HTML. In order for this example to work, you must have Microsoft Word 97 or 2000 installed on the same server as ColdFusion. You don't need to worry about registering any COM objects as that is handled automatically when Microsoft Office is installed.

*Example 23-1. Using CFOBJECT to Call the Microsoft Word COM Object to Convert a Word Document to HTML*

```
<!--- instantiate the COM object --->
<CFOBJECT TYPE="COM" NAME="MyWord" CLASS="Word.Application"
        ACTION="Create" CONTEXT="Local">

<!--- turn off window visibility --->
<CFSET MyWord.Visible = False>

<!--- open the document and convert it to HTML.  You can change the
      path and filename to a document on your server --->
<CFSET OriginalDoc = MyWord.Documents>
<CFSET OriginalDoc.Open("c:\inetsrv\wwwroot\test.doc")>
<CFSET ConvertedDoc = MyWord.ActiveDocument>

<!--- Save the converted HTML file.  Use this line for Word 2000.
      Comment it out and use the line below for Word 97 --->
<CFSET ConvertedDoc.SaveAs("c:\inetsrv\wwwroot\test.htm",Val(8))>

<!--- uncomment this line to use with Word 97
<CFSET ConvertedDoc.SaveAs("c:\inetsrv\wwwroot\test.htm",Val(10))>
--->

<!--- Close the COM connection --->
<CFSET MyWord.Quit()>

Conversion complete...
```

Executing the template in Example 23-1 causes the Microsoft Word COM object to open a Word document called *Test.doc* (you can test this with any Word document on your server), convert it to HTML, and save it back to the server. The same example could easily be written using CFScript instead, as shown in Example 23-2.

*Example 23-2. Calling the Microsoft Word COM Object Using CFScript Notation and the CreateObject Function*

```
<CFSCRIPT>
// Instantiate the COM object
MyWord = CreateObject("COM","Word.Application","Local");

// turn off window visibility
MyWord.Visible = false;

/* open the document and convert it to HTML.  You can change the
 * path and filename to a document on your server
 */
OriginalDoc = MyWord.Documents;
OriginalDoc.Open("c:\inetsrv\wwwroot\test.doc");
ConvertedDoc = MyWord.ActiveDocument;

/* Save the converted HTML file.  Use this line for Word 2000.
 * Comment it out and use the line below for Word 97
 */
ConvertedDoc.SaveAs("c:\inetsrv\wwwroot\test.htm",Val(8));

/* uncomment this line to use with Word 97
 * ConvertedDoc.SaveAs("c:\inetsrv\wwwroot\test.htm",Val(10));
 */

// close the COM connection
MyWord.Quit();
</CFSCRIPT>

Conversion complete...
```

In the case of the CFScript code in Example 23-2, you can't use CFML tags inside a `CFSCRIPT` block, therefore, the `CreateObject()` function instantiates the COM object. For more information on using the `CreateObject()` function, see Appendix B.

## *Calling CORBA Objects*

ColdFusion uses the `CFOBJECT` tag to access CORBA objects via a piece of middleware called an Object Request Broker (ORB). Because an ORB is required to access CORBA objects, ColdFusion comes bundled with the VisiBroker 3.2 ORB for C++ runtime libraries. These libraries are automatically installed and registered when you install ColdFusion. When a request is made to a CORBA object by the `CFOBJECT` tag, ColdFusion uses the VisiBroker libraries to handle every aspect of finding the specified object, passing attributes, invoking methods, and returning results.

To get a better idea of how the `CFOBJECT` tag connects to CORBA objects, let's look at the tag's syntax:

```
<CFOBJECT TYPE="CORBA"
          NAME="name"
          CONTEXT="IOR|NameService"
          CLASS="file_or_naming_service"
          LOCALE="-type_value_pair_1 -type_value_pair_n">
```

When you invoke a CORBA object, the `TYPE` attribute must be set to `CORBA`. `NAME` is a required attribute and is used to specify a name for the object when referencing its attributes and methods. The `CONTEXT` attribute specifies the context to use for accessing the CORBA object. Valid entries include:

`IOR`
: ColdFusion uses the Interoperable Object Reference to access the CORBA object.

`NameService`
: ColdFusion uses the naming service to access the CORBA object.

Depending on the value of `CONTEXT`, the `CLASS` attribute can specify one of two things. If `CONTEXT` is `IOR`, `CLASS` specifies the name of a file that contains the stringified version of the `IOR`. If `CONTEXT` is `NameService`, `CLASS` specifies a period-delimited naming context for the naming service. `CLASS` is a required attribute.

The final attribute, `LOCALE`, specifies type-value pairs of arguments to pass to `init_orb()`. This feature is specific to VisiBroker ORBs and has been tested to work with the 3.2 C++ version only. Note that all type-value pairs must begin with a minus sign (-).

In CORBA, Interface Definition Language (IDL) is used to define the interface to a CORBA object. The interface describes what parameters (properties) and methods are available to the object. The methods for working with these parameters and methods is similar to the methods we used to work with COM objects. One notable difference is the ability to pass structures and arrays to parameters and methods in CORBA.

Because there is no easy way to create a CORBA object for demonstration purposes, the complexities of creating specific examples using `CFOBJECT` with CORBA are beyond the scope of this book. For more information on using `CFOBJECT` to call CORBA objects, refer to Chapter 19 in the *Developing Web Applications with ColdFusion* book included with the ColdFusion documentation.

## *Calling Java Objects*

As of ColdFusion 4.5, you have the ability to call Java class files, and by extension, Enterprise JavaBeans (EJBs), using the `CFOBJECT` tag. With the explosive growth of Java, this opens up a completely new realm of possibilities for your

ColdFusion applications. To call a Java class file or EJB using the **CFOBJECT** tag, you need to use the following syntax:

```
<CFOBJECT TYPE="Java"
          ACTION="Create"
          CLASS="Java_class"
          NAME="object_name">
```

The **TYPE** attribute specifies the type of object to call. To call a Java object or EJB, **TYPE** must be set to **Java**. **ACTION** currently accepts only one value, **Create**. This creates the connection to the Java object or the EJB environment. The **CLASS** attribute is required and specifies the Java class or EJB environment to create. In the case of Java class files, any Java class listed in the Class Path area of the Java section within the ColdFusion Administrator may be specified. For EJBs, **CLASS** specifies the path to the environment for the EJB. In order to use **CFOBJECT** to connect to EJBs, you must have an EJB server such as Ejipt (bundled with JRun) or WebLogic installed.* The EJB server can reside on the same server as your ColdFusion server or on any other server accessible via the network. The path to the EJB JAR file must be registered in the Class Path area of the Java section in the ColdFusion Administrator. Additionally, the EJB you wish to invoke must be deployed appropriately. The final attribute, **NAME**, is also required and specifies the name to use to reference the Java object in subsequent operations. Using the **CFOBJECT** tag to call a Java object loads the class, but doesn't automatically create an instance of the object. Once you have created the Java object with the **CFOBJECT** tag, you can access any static methods in the object. Additionally, you can make an explicit call to the constructor using the `init()` method like this:

```
<CFSET MyVar=MyObject.init(argument1, argument2)>
```

Calling a public method within an object without first calling the `init()` method results in an implicit call to the default constructor. Arguments and return values may be of any valid Java datatype. ColdFusion handles the conversion of strings automatically when they are passed as arguments or as return values. In addition, methods may be overloaded as long as the number of arguments used differs. The `JavaCast()` function may cast a ColdFusion variable before it's passed to an overloaded method. For more information on the `JavaCast()` function, see Appendix B.

In order to demonstrate the `CreateObject()` function, you need a Java object you can call. Example 23-3 can be compiled using the Java compiler of your choice. It is important that the resulting class file be placed in your Class Path,

---

* For additional information on setting up ColdFusion to work with Java objects, see the release notes for your particular installation of ColdFusion.

specifiable within the Java section of the ColdFusion Administrator. You should compile the file as *HelloWorld.class.*

*Example 23-3. Java Code to Compile to the HelloWorld.class File*

```
class HelloWorld {
        public String getString() {
         // returns a string
            return("Hello World!");
    }
}
```

Once you have compiled the code, you are ready to connect to the object. Example 23-4 shows how to call the Java object you just created using `CFOBJECT`.

*Example 23-4. Calling a Java Object Using CFOBJECT*

```
<!--- call the Java class HelloWorld --->
<CFOBJECT TYPE="Java" ACTION="Create" NAME="MyObject" CLASS="HelloWorld">

<!--- Set MyObject equal to MyObject.MyString --->
<CFSET MyOutput = MyObject.getString()>

<!--- output the value of MyOutput --->
<CFOUTPUT>
#MyOutput#
</CFOUTPUT>
```

Example 23-5 shows the same example written using CFScript.

*Example 23-5. Calling a Java Object Using CFScript*

```
<CFSCRIPT>
MyObject = CreateObject("Java","HelloWorld");
MyOutput = MyObject.getString();
</CFSCRIPT>

<CFOUTPUT>
#MyOutput#
</CFOUTPUT>
```

In this case, the `CreateObject()` function calls the Java class file from within the `CFSCRIPT` block. `CreateObject()` works identically to the `CFOBJECT` tag except it isn't necessary to specify an `ACTION` attribute as you would using `CFOBJECT`.

In ColdFusion 5.0, a new `GetException()` function is available that can be used in conjunction with `CFTRY/CFCATCH` tags to deal with exceptions thrown within Java objects. The function takes a single argument specifying the name of the Java object to retrieve the exception information from.

The following code calls a hypothetical Java object called `MyObject`. If an exception is thrown within the class, the `CFCATCH` tag catches the exception.

```
<CFOBJECT TYPE="Java" ACTION="Create" CLASS="MyClass" NAME="MyObject">

<CFTRY>
<CFSET Test = MyObject.CauseError() >

<CFCATCH TYPE="Any">
   <CFSET MyException = GetException(MyObject)>
   <!--- call the GetErrCode and GerErrMsg methods within the exception
         object --->
   <CFSET ErrorCode = MyException.GetErrCode()
   <CFSET ErrorMessage = MyException.GetErrMsg()>

   <CFOUTPUT>
     Error Code: #ErrorCode#<BR>
     Error Message: #ErrorMessage#
   </CFOUTPUT>
</CFCATCH>
</CFTRY>
```

Within the CFCATCH block, the `GetException()` function retrieves the Java exception object from `MyObject` and assigns it to a variable called `MyException`. Next, two methods in the object are called, `MyException.GetErrCode()` and `MyException.GetErrMssg()`. Each method returns a string (the error code and an error message, respectively), which is then output to the browser.

# *Executing Programs*

As of ColdFusion 4.5, you can execute command-line programs residing on the same machine as the ColdFusion Application Server, using the `CFEXECUTE` tag. This tag allows you to call external programs such as batch utilities from within your ColdFusion application. The following syntax calls an external program using `CFEXECUTE`:

```
<CFEXECUTE NAME="path_to_program_to_execute"
           ARGUMENTS="argument_string"
           OUTPUTFILE="path_to_output_file"
           TIMEOUT="timeout_in_seconds">
</CFEXECUTE>
```

The `NAME` attribute is required and specifies the full path, including filename to the file you want to execute. Depending on the program you are attempting to execute, you may be able to specify just the program name without the full path. `ARGUMENTS` allows you to specify any optional arguments you want to pass to the external program. `ARGUMENTS` can be either strings or arrays and adhere to the following conventions:

`Strings`
: On Windows platforms, the entire string is passed to the Windows process control subsystem for processing.

On Unix and Linux systems, the string is tokenized into an array of strings, delimited by spaces. If spaces occur in the array elements, they are escaped by double quotes.

`Arrays`

On Windows platforms, the elements of the array are concatenated into a space-delimited string of tokens, which is then passed to the Windows process control subsystem for processing.

On Unix and Linux systems, the elements of the array are copied into an array of `exec()` arguments.

The next attribute, `OUTPUTFILE`, is optional and specifies the path to an output file where any text output by the external program is written. If the `OUTPUTFILE` attribute is omitted, the output is returned to the browser. The final attribute, `TIMEOUT`, is also optional and specifies the time in seconds ColdFusion should wait before timing out the call to the external program. Setting the `TIMEOUT` attribute to `0` equates to a nonblocking execution mode. This causes ColdFusion to spawn a thread for the process and immediately return without waiting for the process to end. By contrast, setting the `TIMEOUT` attribute to an arbitrarily high value equates to a blocking execution mode. The default value for `TIMEOUT` is `0`.

You should note that there shouldn't be any HTML or CFML appearing between the start and end of the `CFEXECUTE` tags. As a result, you can refer to the `CFEXECUTE` tag using the following shorthand notation instead of having to include an explicit end tag:

```
<CFEXECUTE NAME="c:\example.exe"/>
```

If for some reason an exception is thrown while attempting to execute the `CFEXECUTE` tag, the following rules apply:

- If the application specified in the `NAME` attribute can't be found, an "Application File Not Found" exception is thrown.
- If the ColdFusion user executing the application doesn't have permission to do so, a security exception is thrown.
- If a value is specified for `OUTPUTFILE` and the file can't be opened, an Output File Cannot be Opened exception is thrown.

Example 23-6 demonstrates how to use the `CFEXECUTE` tag to run the *ipconfig.exe* program on a Windows NT server.

*Example 23-6. Using CFEXECUTE to Run IPCONFIG.EXE*

```
<!--- execute the windows IPCONFIG.EXE program.  Write the results to a
      text file called ipconig.txt in c:\winnt\temp --->
<CFTRY>
<CFEXECUTE NAME="ipconfig.exe" ARGUMENTS="/all"
```

*Example 23-6. Using CFEXECUTE to Run IPCONFIG.EXE (continued)*

```
          OUTPUTFILE="c:\winnt\temp\ipconfig.txt" TIMEOUT="30"/>

<CFCATCH TYPE="Any">
There was an error trying to execute the program specified in the
CFEXECUTE tag.  Details follow:
<P>
<CFOUTPUT>
Type: #CFCATCH.Type#<BR>
Message: #CFCATCH.Message#<BR>
Details: #CFCATCH.Detail#
</CFOUTPUT>
<CFABORT>
</CFCATCH>
</CFTRY>

<!--- check to see if the output file exists.  If so, read it in using
      CFFILE and output the contents to the browser.  If it doesn't
      exist, output a message to the browser asking the user to try
      again --->
<CFTRY>
<CFIF FileExists("c:\winnt\temp\ipconfig.txt")>
    <CFFILE ACTION="READ"
            FILE="c:\winnt\temp\ipconfig.txt"
            VARIABLE="IpConfig">
    <CFOUTPUT>
    <PRE>#IpConfig#</PRE>
    </CFOUTPUT>
<CFELSE>
    The file was not written to the server in time to be included.
    Please hit your browser's Reload button and try again.
</CFIF>

<CFCATCH TYPE="Any">
There was an error trying to access the IpConfig.txt file. Details
follow:
<P>
<CFOUTPUT>
Type: #CFCATCH.Type#<BR>
Message: #CFCATCH.Message#<BR>
Details: #CFCATCH.Detail#
</CFOUTPUT>
<CFABORT>
</CFCATCH>
</CFTRY>
```

Example 23-6 uses the `CFEXECUTE` tag to execute the *ipconfig.exe* utility on a Windows NT system. The `/All` switch is passed along with the request using the `ARGUMENTS` attribute. The output generated by the *ipconfig* program is written to a text file named *ipconfig.txt* and saved to the Windows *TEMP* directory. Once the file has been written, it is read into a variable called `IPConfig` using the `CFFILE` tag. (`CFFILE` is covered in detail in Chapter 12.) Once the contents of the *ipconfig.txt* file are stored in a variable, they are output using the CFOUTPUT tag. The HTML PRE tags preserve whitespace formatting for the output.

If any errors or exceptions are thrown during the execution of either the CFEXECUTE tag or the CFFILE tag, they are caught using the CFTRY/CFCATCH tags in the code. Executing the code in Example 23-6 results in output similar to that shown in Figure 23-1.

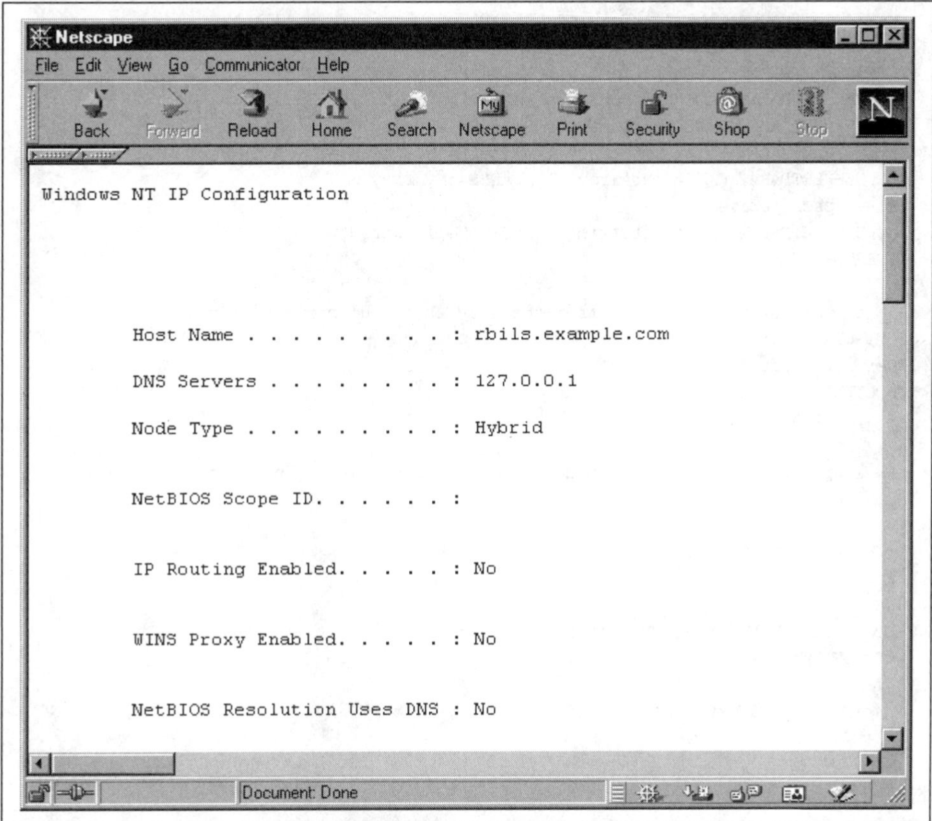


*Figure 23-1. Executing the ipconfig.exe utility using CFEXECUTE*

# *Invoking Java Servlets*

The CFSERVLET tag can invoke a Java servlet from within a ColdFusion template. The CFSERVLET tag requires Allaire's JRun software be installed in order to work. For more information on JRun, see Allaire's web site at *http://www.allaire.com.*

Assuming you already have JRun installed, invoking a servlet is a matter of calling the CFSERVLET tag in your template. Attributes and parameters can be passed to the Java servlet by nesting CFSERVLETPARAM tags within the CFSERVLET tag. Example 23-7 shows the syntax for calling a servlet and passing it parameters.

*Example 23-7. Invoking a Java Servlet with CFSERVLET*

```
<CFSERVLET JRUNPROXY="127.0.0.1:51000" CODE="MyServlet" TIMEOUT="90"
           DEBUG="Yes" WRITEOUTPUT="No">
   <!--- pass attributes.  Each VARIABLE represents a variable created in
         ColdFusion --->
   <CFSERVLETPARAM NAME="parString" VARIABLE="MyString" TYPE="STRING">
   <CFSERVLETPARAM NAME="parDouble" VARIABLE="MyReal" TYPE="REAL">
   <CFSERVLETPARAM NAME="parDate" VARIABLE="MyDate" TYPE="DATE">
   <CFSERVLETPARAM NAME="parInt" VARIABLE="MyInt" TYPE="INT">
   <CFSERVLETPARAM NAME="parBool" VARIABLE="MyBool" TYPE="BOOL">
   <CFSERVLETPARAM NAME="parQuery" VARIABLE="MyQuery">
   <CFSERVLETPARAM NAME="parStruct" VARIABLE="MyStruct">
   <CFSERVLETPARAM NAME="parArray" VARIABLE="MyArray">
   <!--- pass parameter --->
   <CFSERVLETPARAM NAME="attString" VALUE="Hello World">
</CFSERVLET>

<!--- output the text returned from the servlet to the browser --->
<CFOUTPUT>
#CFServlet.Output#
</CFOUTPUT>

<HR>
<!--- loop over the CFSERVLET structure and output any response headers --->
<TABLE>
<TR>
   <TH>Key</TH><TH>Value</TH>
</TR>

<CFLOOP COLLECTION="#CFSERVLET#" ITEM="Key">
   <CFOUTPUT>
   <TR>
     <TD>#Key#</TD><TD>#StructFind(CFSERVLET,Key)#</TD>
   </TR>
   </CFOUTPUT>
</CFLOOP>

</TABLE>
```

In this example, the CFSERVLET tag invokes a servlet named MyServlet. The name of the servlet is specified using the CODE attribute. JRUNPROXY is a required attribute that specifies the hostname or IP address and the port where the JRun engine is located (for JRun 3.x servers). The attribute is optional for JRun 2.3.3 servers as the engine is assumed to be on the same machine as the ColdFusion application server and listening on port 8081. The TIMEOUT attribute allows us to specify the number of seconds ColdFusion should wait while processing a CFSERVLET request before timing out the operation. We set TIMEOUT to 90 seconds (default is 60 seconds). DEBUG is an optional Yes/No attribute that indicates whether to write additional information about the JRun connection status and other activity to the JRun error log file. The final attribute is `WRITEOUTPUT`. This attribute is optional and indicates whether or not output from the servlet should be inline text or stored in a variable. If `Yes`, ColdFusion outputs the text to the browser. If `No`, ColdFusion writes the text to the variable `CFServlet.Output`. The default for `WRITEOUTPUT` is `Yes`.

The `CFSERVLETPARAM` tags are used as child tags of the `CFSERVLET` tag to pass parameters and attributes to the servlet specified by the `CFSERVLET` tag. As you can see in the example, multiple `CFSERVLETPARAM` tags can pass multiple parameters/attributes to the servlet. Both simple and complex datatypes such as arrays, queries, and structures can be passed to servlets via `CFSERVLETPARAM` tags. Data can be passed to a servlet in two ways: by value and by reference. To pass data by value (as a parameter), use the `NAME` and `VALUE` attributes. Data passed by value is only modified within the servlet. To pass data by reference (as an attribute), use the `NAME`, `VARIABLE`, and optionally the `TYPE` attribute. If the servlet modifies data passed by reference, the data in the corresponding ColdFusion variable is also changed. Each of these attributes is described as follows:

`NAME="parameter_name"`
: The name of the parameter or attribute to pass to the `CFSERVLET` tag. Required.

`VALUE="parameter_value"`
: The value of the parameter to pass to the `CFSERVLET` tag. Required when `NAME` is a parameter.

`VARIABLE="CF_variable_name"`
: The name (not the value) of the ColdFusion variable to pass to the `CFSERVLET` tag. Required when `NAME` is an attribute. Using the `VARIABLE` attribute allows you to pass complex ColdFusion datatypes, such as arrays, queries, and structures to Java servlets.

`TYPE="Bool|Date|Int|Real|String"`
: The datatype of the ColdFusion variable being passed to the servlet. Options are `Bool`, `Date`, `Int`, `Real`, and `String`. Optional. The default is `String`. To see how various ColdFusion datatypes map to Java equivalents, see Table 23-1.

*Table 23-1. ColdFusion Datatypes and Java Equivalents*

| ColdFusion Datatype | TYPE Attribute | Java Equivalent |
|---|---|---|
| `Boolean` | `Bool` | *java.lang.Bool* |
| `Date` | `Date` | *java.util.Date* |
| `Numeric` (integer) | `Int` | *java.lang.Integer* |
| `Numeric` (real) | `Real` | *java.lang.Double* |

*Table 23-1. ColdFusion Datatypes and Java Equivalents (continued)*

| ColdFusion Datatype | TYPE Attribute | Java Equivalent |
|---|---|---|
| String | String | *java.lang.String* |
| Array | N/A; omit TYPE | *java.util.Vector* |
| Structure | N/A; omit TYPE | *java.util.Hashtable* |
| Query | N/A; omit TYPE | *com.allaire.util.RecordSet* |

In our example, the first five CFSERVLETPARAM tags pass values contained in ColdFusion variables as attributes, with the datatype explicitly stated in the TYPE attribute. The next three CFSERVLETPARAM tags also pass their values as attributes. This time, however, the values are complex datatypes (a query object, structure, and array). The TYPE attribute is not used in this case. The final CFSERVLETPARAM tag passes a parameter named attString to the servlet. The parameter contains the value "Hello World!".

The last part of the template uses the CFOUTPUT tag to output the contents of the CFServlet.Output variable created because the WRITEOUTPUT attribute of the CFSERVLET tag is set to No. Additionally, if any response headers are returned by the servlet, they are available in a special structure called CFSERVLET. Each response header is accessible by specifying its name as a key in the CFSERVLET structure. In our example, it is possible to output all response headers by looping over the CFSERVLET structure using a collection loop.

If you don't have access to a JRun server, you can still call Java servlets using the CFHTTP tag. The drawback to this method is performance. Calling servlets via the CFSERVLET tag provides a performance edge as connections to the JRun server are pooled, meaning a new connection to the server doesn't have to be made for each subsequent request after the initial connection. For more information on using CFHTTP, see Chapter 14.

*In this chapter:*
- *Creating a Simple Graph*
- *Graphing Query Results*
- *Drilling Down on Graph Data*

# 24 Graphing and Charting

ColdFusion 5.0 provides you with a new way of looking at data, literally, in the form of a server-side graphing engine comprised of Macromedia's JRun and Generator servers.* These servers, combined with the new CFGRAPH and CFGRAPHDATA tags allow you to add new charting and graphing capabilities to your ColdFusion applications.

Five types of graphs and charts are supported with this release of ColdFusion. They are bar and horizontal bar charts, line and area graphs, and pie charts. The CFGRAPH tag can generate graphs in Macromedia's popular Flash format, as PNG images or as JPEG images. You can use the CFGRAPH and CFGRAPHDATA tags to graph static values, query data, or a combination of the two.

## Creating a Simple Graph

Regardless of the type of graph you want to create, all graphing is handled via the CFGRAPH tag. The CFGRAPH tag is a paired tag, meaning it must always have opening and closing tags. To create a graph of any type from static data, you need to include one or more CFGRAPHDATA tags between your beginning and ending CFGRAPH tags. Example 24-1 shows how to generate a bar chart from static data.

* Because CFGRAPH support requires the installation of Macromedia's JRun and Generator servers, when installing ColdFusion 5.0, you are given the option of skipping the installation of graphing and charting services. The version of Generator that is included is multithreaded but is configured to process only requests originating from ColdFusion. Additionally, you should note that the CFGRAPH tag isn't supported when running ColdFusion on Windows 95/98.

*Example 24-1. Simple Graphs*

```
<CFGRAPH TYPE="Bar" FILEFORMAT="Flash" GRAPHHEIGHT="300" GRAPHWIDTH="400"
         BACKGROUNDCOLOR="White" BORDERWIDTH="1" BORDERCOLOR="Black" DEPTH="10"
         TITLE="Employee Salaries" TITLEFONT="Arial">
  <CFGRAPHDATA ITEM="Greg" VALUE="96000" COLOR="Red"
               URL="http://www.example.com/index.cfm?ID=1">
  <CFGRAPHDATA ITEM="Nick" VALUE="54000" COLOR="Orange"
               URL="http://www.example.com/index.cfm?ID=2">
  <CFGRAPHDATA ITEM="Jen" VALUE="41000" COLOR="Yellow"
               URL="http://www.example.com/index.cfm?ID=3">
  <CFGRAPHDATA ITEM="Christine" VALUE="80000" COLOR="Green"
               URL="http://www.example.com/index.cfm?ID=4">
</CFGRAPH>
```

The `CFGRAPH` tag has over 30 attributes you can use in various combinations depending on the type of graph you want and how you want it to look. In Example 24-1, I use 10 of the 13 attributes common to all the graph formats. The other three are for generating graphs from dynamic data, which we'll cover later in the chapter.

The only attribute required by the `CFGRAPH` tag is `TYPE`. `TYPE` specifies the type of graph you want to create. Options are `Bar`, `HorizontalBar`, `Line`, and `Pie`. In this case, we are creating a `Bar` chart. You can just as easily change `TYPE` to `HorizontalBar`, `Pie`, or `Line` to see how the various graphs are rendered from the same data points. Additionally, you can create an area graph by setting the `TYPE` attribute to `Line` and specifying `Yes` for an additional attribute called `FILL`. An area graph is actually a line graph with the area below the line filled with the same color used to draw the line.

Figure 24-1 shows a collage of the various graph types generated from the code in Example 24-1. The `FILEFORMAT` attribute determines what format to use when sending the graph to the browser. You can choose `Flash` (*.swf*), `PNG` (*.png*), or `JPG` (*.jpg*). The default format and the one we use in this example is `Flash`. `GRAPHHEIGHT` and `GRAPHWIDTH` specify the height and width for the graph in pixels. The default height is `240` pixels while the default width is `320` pixels. Although you can adjust the size of the graph, the `CFGRAPH` tag maintains a height/width aspect ratio of 3:4 over the graph itself. Significantly adjusting one aspect of the graph's size without the other may result in an undesirable amount of whitespace in the margin of the graph. You can specify a background color for the graph using the `BACKGROUNDCOLOR` attribute. Colors may be specified by name or hex code in the form `##FFFFCC`. The double pound signs are necessary to keep ColdFusion from throwing an error.

You can give your graph a border by specifying the thickness of the border in pixels for the `BORDER` attribute. To specify no border, use `0`. The default is `1`. You can specify the color for the border using the `BORDERCOLOR` attribute. The same

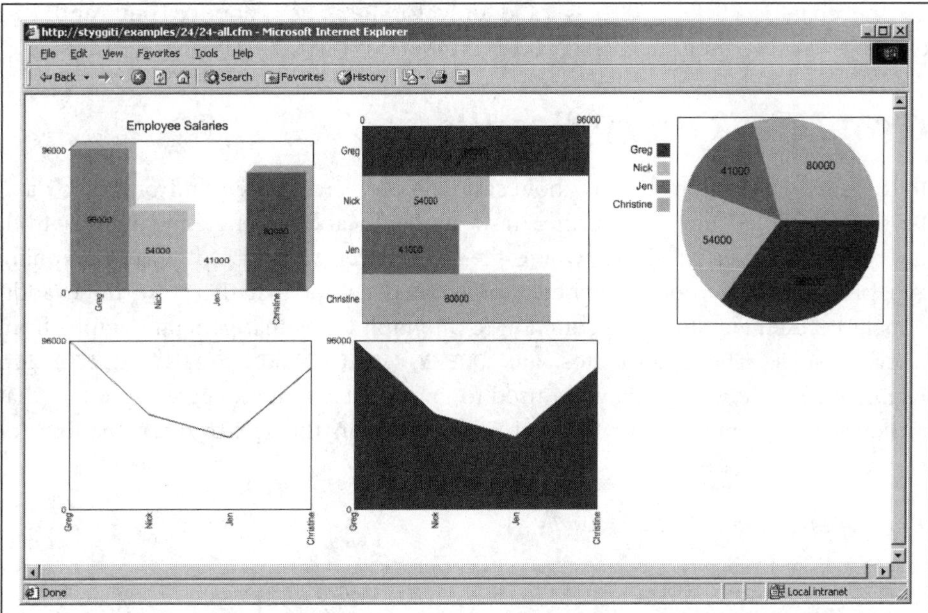


*Figure 24-1. Generating various charts from the same static data*

rules apply for this attribute as for `BACKGROUNDCOLOR`. The default color is `Black`. If you want to give your graph a three-dimensional appearance, you can do so by specifying the depth of the graph in pixels using the `DEPTH` attribute. The default depth is 0 (i.e., not three-dimensional). In this example, we set `DEPTH` to 10.

The final two attributes, `TITLE` and `TITLEFONT` do just what their names imply. The title is displayed centered above the graph unless a legend is present above the graph, in which case the title is displayed centered below the graph. For the title font, you may specify `Arial` (the default), `Courier`, or `Times`.

The actual data for the graph is supplied by the `CFGRAPHDATA` tags. `CFGRAPHDATA` is a child tag of `CFGRAPH` and defines a single data point to graph. The `ITEM` attribute is optional and specifies the label to use for the data point while `VALUE`, a required attribute specifies the numeric value to graph. `COLOR` is optional and associates a specific color with the data point. `COLOR` follows the same rules as the other color attributes in the `CFGRAPH` tag. By default, `CFGRAPHDATA` tag takes the color for the data point from the `COLORLIST` attribute (We'll cover this later on in the chapter) specified in the `CFGRAPH` tag. If no `COLORLIST` is present, `CFGRAPHDATA` uses a color from ColdFusion's default list of colors. If `COLOR` is used with a Line graph, the line assumes the color specified in the first `CFGRAPHDATA` tag encountered. The final attribute, `URL`, is also optional and specifies a URL, including any relevant URL parameters, to link to when the data point on the chart is clicked. `URL` is valid only for `Bar`, `HorizonatalBar`, and `Pie` charts, and only when the `FILEFORMAT` attribute of the `CFGRAPH` tag is `Flash`.

# *Graphing Query Results*

In the previous section, we saw how simple it is to create a graph from static data. Let's take things one step further now and talk about generating graphs from query results. After all, this is where the real power of the ColdFusion's graphing capabilities lies. If you remember, I mentioned earlier that there are three additional `CFGRAPH` tag attributes common to all graph types that generate graphs from query results. These attributes are `QUERY`, `VALUECOLUMN`, and `ITEMCOLUMN`. Example 24-2 show how they are used to graph data from an aggregate query that retrieves the average salary for each department in the `EmployeeDirectory` of our sample database.

*Example 24-2. Graphing Query Results*

```
<CFQUERY NAME="GetSalary" DATASOURCE="ProgrammingCF">
  SELECT Department, AVG(Salary) AS AvgSalary FROM EmployeeDirectory
  GROUP BY Department
</CFQUERY>

<CFGRAPH TYPE="HorizontalBar" QUERY="GetSalary" VALUECOLUMN="AvgSalary"
         ITEMCOLUMN="Department" FILEFORMAT="Flash" GRAPHHEIGHT="360"
         GRAPHWIDTH="480" BACKGROUNDCOLOR="White" BORDERWIDTH="1"
         BORDERCOLOR="Black" DEPTH="10" TITLE="Average Salary by Department"
         TITLEFONT="Arial">
</CFGRAPH>
```

The query in this example retrieves the average salary for each department in the `EmployeeDirectory` table using the `AVG` aggregate function. Two columns of data are returned, the department name, and the average salary for that department. This time, the graph is a `HorizontalBar` chart. The `QUERY` attribute is required for dynamic graphs and specifies the name of the query we want to pull the data from to populate the graph. The name of the query column containing the data to graph is specified in `VALUECOLUMN`. The `VALUECOLUMN` is required when no `CFGRAPHDATA` tags are specified. `ITEMCOLUMN` is optional and accepts the name of a query column containing item labels that correspond to the data points from the query column specified in `VALUECOLUMN`. For `Bar` and `Line` charts, item labels are displayed on the horizontal axis. For `HorizontalBar` charts, the labels appear on the vertical axis. `Pie` charts display item labels in an optional legend. Executing this template results in the output shown in Figure 24-2.

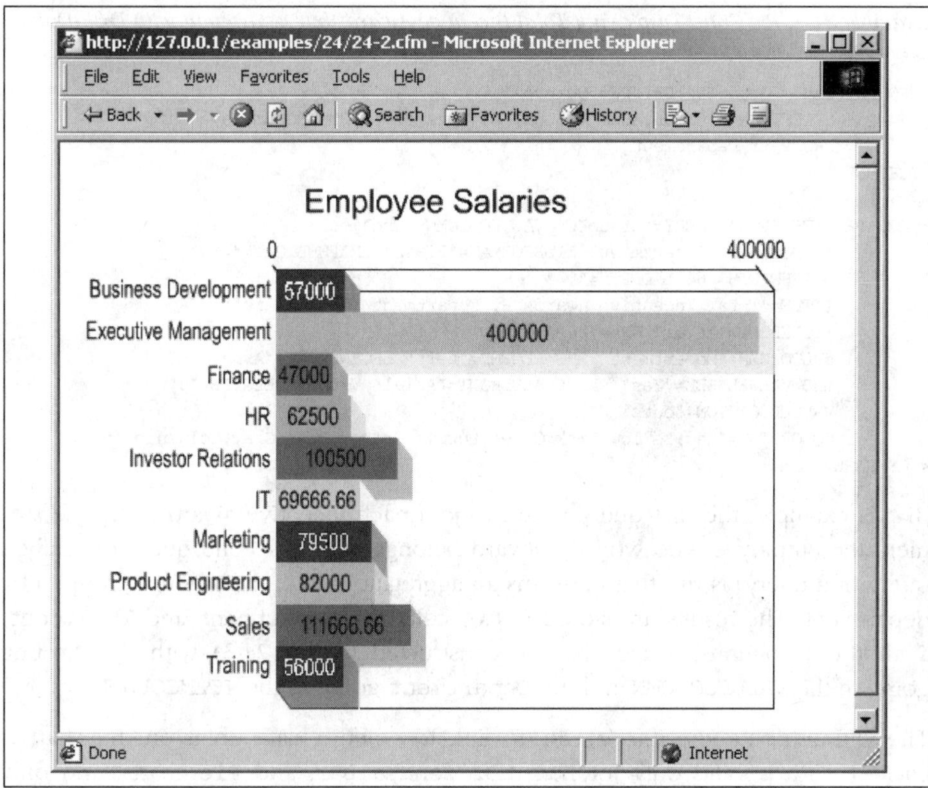


*Figure 24-2. Generating a horizontal bar graph from query results*

# Drilling Down on Graph Data

Another useful feature of the CFGRAPH tag is the ability to create graphs with clickable data points that can link to other templates. This allows you to implement drill-down functionality as we did in Chapter 11, using a graph instead of an HTML table. In order to create a clickable graph, you have to set the FILEFORMAT to Flash. Examples 24-3 and 24-4 demonstrate how to create a pie chart with drill-down capabilities. The pie chart displays the total amount of incentive award dollars given out per department.

*Example 24-3. Pie Chart Displaying Total Incentive Awards by Department with Drill-Down Capability*

```
<CFQUERY NAME="GetEmployeeInfo" DATASOURCE="ProgrammingCF">
        SELECT EmployeeDirectory.Department, IncentiveAwards.Amount
        FROM EmployeeDirectory, IncentiveAwards
        WHERE EmployeeDirectory.ID = IncentiveAwards.ID
</CFQUERY>
```

*Example 24-3. Pie Chart Displaying Total Incentive Awards by Department with Drill-Down Capability (continued)*

```
<CFQUERY NAME="GroupIt" DBTYPE="Query">
         SELECT Department, Sum(Amount) AS TheAmount FROM GetEmployeeInfo
         GROUP BY Department
</CFQUERY>

<CFGRAPH TYPE="Pie" QUERY="GroupIt" VALUECOLUMN="TheAmount"
         ITEMCOLUMN="Department" FILEFORMAT="Flash" GRAPHHEIGHT="480"
         GRAPHWIDTH="640" DEPTH="10"
         TITLE="Total Incentive Awards By Department (In Dollars)"
         TITLEFONT="Arial" URL="24-4.cfm"
         URLCOLUMN="Department" SHOWLEGEND="Left" LEGENDFONT="Arial"
         SHOWVALUELABEL="Yes" VALUELABELFONT="Arial" VALUELABELSIZE="8"
         VALUELOCATION="outside"
         COLORLIST="Red,Yellow,Pink,Green,Purple,Orange,Blue,Gray,Goldenrod">
</CFGRAPH>
```

In this example, the first query is run to join each incentive award to the department the employee who won the award belongs two. A second query (actually a query of a query) is run that performs an aggregate `SUM` of the amount grouped by department. The results are stored in two columns, `Department` and `TheAmount`. With these columns, a Pie chart is constructed (Figure 24-3) with the `Amount` going in the `VALUECOLUMN` and the `Department` going in the `ITEMCOLUMN`.

The URL attribute specifies a URL to link to when a data point on the chart is clicked. URL is valid only for `Bar`, `HorizonatalBar`, and `Pie` charts, and only when `FILEFORMAT` is `Flash`. The URL column is used in conjunction with the `URLCOLUMN` attribute to pass a value associated with a data point to another page for processing. In our example, the URL points to the template in Example 24-4 (*24-4.cfm*). Note the `?Department=` parameter appended to the end of the URL. The `URLCOLUMN` lets us specify a query column containing a value to append to the end of the URL specified in `URL` attribute. This allows us to pass a value associated with a particular data point as a URL parameter to the template in Example 24-4 for processing. Query columns whose values contain spaces and other special characters are automatically URL-encoded before being appended to the URL string.

`SHOWLEGEND` is an optional attribute that determines the position of the legend associated with a `Pie` chart. Choices are `Above` (horizontal layout centered above the chart), `Below` (horizontal layout centered below the chart), `Left` (vertical layout to the left of the chart), `Right` (vertical layout to the right of the chart), and `None`. The default is `Left`. You can set the font for the legend text using the `LEGENDFONT` attribute. Valid fonts are `Arial` (the default), `Courier`, and `Times`.

The `SHOWVALUELABEL` attribute is optional and indicates whether to display the value associated with each data point for `Bar`, `HorizontalBar`, and `Pie` charts.

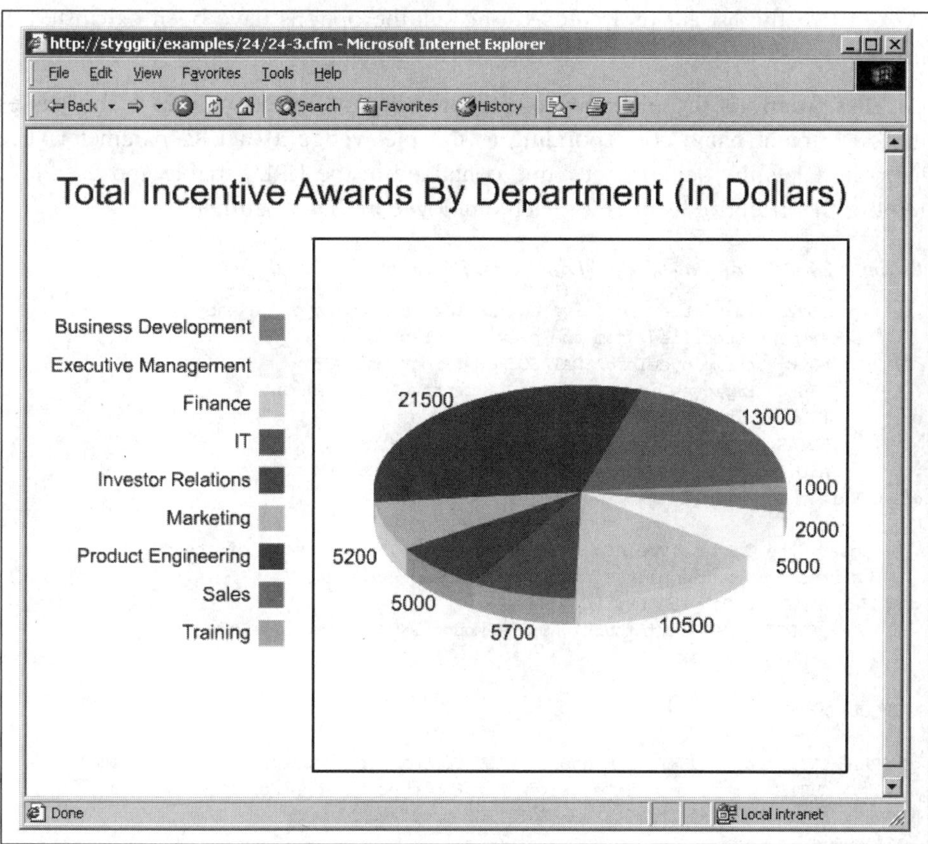


*Figure 24-3. Drilling down on a pie chart*

You have three options: `Rollover`, `Yes`, and `No`. `Rollover` works only when `FILEFORMAT` is `Flash` and indicates that the value be displayed when the user moves her mouse over the data point. The default value is `No`. `VALUELABELFONT` and `VALUELABELSIZE` control the font and font size of the value label. Font options are `Arial` (the default), `Courier`, and `Times`. The font size is expressed in points. The default font size is 12. The `VALUELOCATON` attribute is optional and indicates where value labels should be placed on a `Bar`, `HorizontalBar`, and `Pie` chart. For `Pie` charts, options are `Inside` (the default), indicating that values display inside each segment of the pie chart, or `Outside`, indicating that they display outside the slice of the pie. For a `Bar` or `HorizontalBar` chart, options are `OnBar` (the default), indicating that values should be displayed on the bar itself, or `OverBar`, indicating that values should be displayed over the bar. `COLORLIST` accepts a comma-delimited list of colors to use for the data points in `Bar`, `HorizontalBar`, and `Pie` charts. Color names follow the same rules as in the `BACKGROUNDCOLOR` attribute. If there are more data points than colors specified in

COLORLIST, the list is simply reused once all the options have been exhausted. If no COLORLIST is specified, ColdFusion uses a default list of colors.

Clicking on any of the pie wedges calls the template in Example 24-4 and passes the department name corresponding to the pie wedge as a URL parameter. The template takes the department name contained in the URL variable and uses it to retrieve the incentive awards for each employee in the department.

*Example 24-4. Detail Page for the Drill-down Pie Chart*

```
<!--- retrieve all of the incentive awards for each employee in the
      department specified from the previous graph --->
<CFQUERY NAME="GetEmployeeInfo" DATASOURCE="ProgrammingCF">
         SELECT EmployeeDirectory.Name, IncentiveAwards.Amount
         FROM EmployeeDirectory, IncentiveAwards
         WHERE EmployeeDirectory.ID = IncentiveAwards.ID
         AND EmployeeDirectory.Department = '#URL.Department#'
</CFQUERY>

<!--- query the GetEmployeeInfo query and sum the total amount of incentive
      awards for each employee in the department --->
<CFQUERY NAME="SumPeople" DBTYPE="Query">
         SELECT Name, Sum(Amount) AS TheAmount FROM GetEmployeeInfo
         GROUP BY Name

</CFQUERY>

<CFGRAPH TYPE="bar" QUERY="SumPeople" VALUECOLUMN="TheAmount" ITEMCOLUMN="Name"
         TITLE="Total Incentive Awards Per Employee in #URL.Department#"
         GRIDLINES="5" ITEMLABELORIENTATION="horizontal">
</CFGRAPH>
```

A second query is then run against the first query to sum the incentive awards for each employee. The resulting data is returned in two columns, Name and TheAmount. A Bar graph is then generated based on the values in the TheAmount query column. The GRIDLINES attribute causes grid lines to display between the top and bottom lines on a Bar, HorizontalBar, or Line chart. When grid lines are displayed, a corresponding value is displayed along side the line. This example displays five grid lines. The final attribute for the graph is ITEMLABELORIENTATION. It indicates whether item labels should be displayed horizontally or vertically and is valid only if item labels are displayed (which they are). For Bar and Line charts, the default is Vertical. For HorizontalBar charts, the default is Horizontal. Figure 24-4 shows the graph generated by this example.

For the complete list of attributes for the CFGRAPH and CFGRAPHDATA tags, see Appendix A.

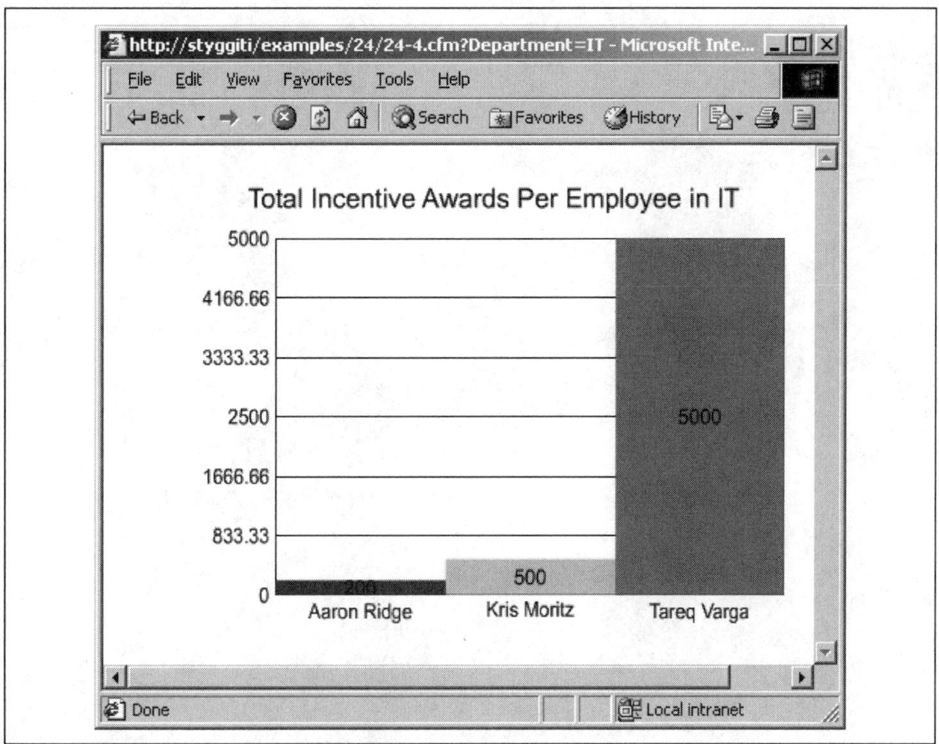


*Figure 24-4. Detail page for drill-down chart*

# Tag Reference

ColdFusion tags are the core components of the CFML language. They take what would otherwise be considered low-level programming tasks, such as making an ODBC or SMTP connection, and abstract them, providing a simple way to program complex functionality. ColdFusion contains over 80 tags that allow you to perform all sorts of tasks, from querying databases to sending and receiving email. This appendix contains reference material on all ColdFusion tags through Version 5.0.

## Tags by Type

The following sections group the CFML tags by their functionality.

### Custom Tag Tags

| | | |
|---|---|---|
| CFASSOCIATE | CFEXIT | CFMODULE |

### Database Tags

| | | |
|---|---|---|
| CFINSERT | CFPROCPARAM | CFPROCRESULT |
| CFQUERY | CFQUERYPARAM | CFSTOREDPROC |
| CFTRANSACTION | CFUPDATE | |

### Error and Exception-Handling Tags

| | | |
|---|---|---|
| CFCATCH | CFERROR | CFLOG |
| CFTHROW | CFTRY | CFRETHROW |

## Extensibility Tags

| | | |
|---|---|---|
| CFGRAPH | CFGRAPHDATA | CFINCLUDE |
| CFMODULE | CFOBJECT | CFSERVLET |
| CFSERVLETPARAM | CFWDDX | |

## Filesystem Tags

| | |
|---|---|
| CFDIRECTORY | CFFILE |

## Flow Control Tags

| | | |
|---|---|---|
| CFABORT | CFBREAK | CFEXIT |
| CFIF | CFINCLUDE | CFLOCATION |
| CFLOOP | CFMODULE | CFSWITCH |

## Form Tags

| | | |
|---|---|---|
| CFAPPLET | CFFORM | CFGRID |
| CFGRIDCOLUMN | CFGRIDROW | CFGRIDUPDATE |
| CFINPUT | CFSELECT | CFSLIDER |
| CFTEXTINPUT | CFTREE | CFTREEITEM |

## Miscellaneous Tags

| | |
|---|---|
| CFAPPLICATION | CFCACHE |
| CFSCHEDULE | CFSCRIPT |

## Output Tags

| | | |
|---|---|---|
| CFCOL | CFCONTENT | CFFLUSHCFHEADER |
| CFHTMLHEAD | CFOUTPUT | CFPROCESSINGDIRECTIVE |
| CFREPORT | CFSAVECONTENT | CFSETTING |
| CFSILENT | CFTABLE | |

## *Protocol Tags*

| | | |
|---|---|---|
| CFFTP | CFHTTP | CFHTTPPARAM |
| CFLDAP | CFMAIL | CFMAILPARAM |
| CFPOP | | |

## *Security Tags*

| | |
|---|---|
| CFADMINSECURITY | CFAUTHENTICATE |
| CFIMPERSONATE | CFNEWINTERNALADMINSECURITY |

## *System Tags*

| | | |
|---|---|---|
| CFEXECUTE | CFNEWINTERNALREGISTRY | CFREGISTRY |

## *Undocumented Tags*

| | | |
|---|---|---|
| CFADMINSECURITY | CFINTERNALDEBUG | CFNEWINTERNALADMINSECURITY |
| CFNEWINTERNALREGISTRY | CFOBJECTCACHE | |

## *Variable Manipulation Tags*

| | |
|---|---|
| CFCOOKIE | CFLOCK |
| CFPARAM | CFSET |

## *Verity Search Engine Tags*

| | | |
|---|---|---|
| CFCOLLECTION | CFINDEX | CFSEARCH |

# *Alphabetical List of Tags*

This section lists all the CFML tags alphabetically, with detailed descriptions of their attributes and proper syntax. Version information is included for many tags; if no version information is listed, the tag is available in ColdFusion 4.0 and later.

---

### CFABORT

<CFABORT>

Halts processing of the CFML template at the tag position.

### *Attributes*

SHOWERROR="*text_message*"

A message to display when the CFABORT tag is executed. Optional.

## CFADMINSECURITY

Enhanced in ColdFusion 5.0

<CFADMINSECURITY>
<CFNEWINTERNALADMINSECURITY>

This undocumented tag handles administrative tasks related to ColdFusion's Advanced Security services. Because of the complexity of this tag and the fact that no documentation exists on its usage, the following information provided may be incomplete.

### *Attributes*

ACTION="*action*"
: Specifies the action the tag should perform. Possible actions include the following: AddHost, AddPolicy, AddRule, AddRuleToPolicy, AddSecurityContext, AddSecurityRealm, AddUserDirectory, AddUserDirectoryToContext, AddUserToPolicy, CreateODBCQueryScheme, DeleteHost, DeleteODBCQueryScheme, DeletePolicy, DeleteRule, DeleteSecurityContext, DeleteSecurityRealm, DeleteUserDirectory, FlushCache, GenerateRule, GetHost, GetODBCQueryScheme, GetPolicy, GetResourceInfo, GetRule, GetRuleForPolicy, GetSecurityContext, GetSecurityRealm, GetUserDirectory, GetUserDirectoryForContext, GetUserPolicy, GetUserForUserDirectory, RemoveRuleFromPolicy, RemoveUserDirectoryFromContext, and RemoveUserFromPolicy.

AUTHTYPE="Basic|X509"
: The authentication protocol to use. The default value is Basic. This attribute is optional and used only when ACTION is set to AddSecurityRealm.

CACHETYPE="Basic|X509"
: The type of security cache to flush. Required when ACTION is FlushCache. New in ColdFusion 5.0.

DESCRIPTION="*text*"
: A description for the object being referenced.

DIRECTORY="*directory_name*"
: The name of the security context being referenced.

IP="*IP_address*"
: The IP address of the ColdFusion Application Server. Used when ACTION is AddHost. Currently, this attribute must be set to 127.0.0.1.

NAME="*name*"
: The name of the object being referenced.

OUTPUT="*variable_name*"
: The name of a ColdFusion variable that holds the results when ACTION is GenerateRule or GetResourceInfo. The data is returned as a ColdFusion structure.

POLICY="*policy_name*"
: The name of the security policy being referenced.

PROTECTALL="Yes|No"
: Whether or not to protect all resources for a given security context. This attribute is optional and used only when ACTION is set to AddSecurityRealm. The default is No.

QUERY="*query_name*"
: The name to use for the query object returned when ACTION is set to GetODBCQueryScheme, GetHost, GetPolicy, GetRule, GetRuleForPolicy, GetSecurityContext, GetSecurityRealm, GetUserDirectory, GetUserDirectoryForContext, GetUserPolicy, or GetUserForUserDirectory. Required for the aforementioned ACTION values.

RESOURCE="*resource_name*"
: The name of the resource when adding or generating a rule.

RESOURCEACTION="*resource_action*"
: The action to associate with a resource when ACTION is set to AddRule or GenerateRule.

RESPONSE=""
: Optional; is available only when ACTION is set to AddRuleToPolicy. RESPONSE should be set to " ".

RESULTS="*integer*"
: The maximum number of results to return when searching an LDAP directory. Optional; used only when ACTION is set to AddUserDirectory.

ROOT="*search_root*"
: The search root for the LDAP server when adding a user directory. Usually, the search root is set to "organization" (o) or "organizational unit" (ou). Optional; used only when ACTION is set to AddUserDirectory.

SCOPE="*search_scope*"
: The scope for the LDAP search. Possible entries are One Level or Subtree. Optional; used only when ACTION is set to AddUserDirectory.

SEARCHEND="*search_end*"
: The value to use when constructing the uid (uid=) part of the DN string for an LDAP query. Optional; used only when ACTION is set to AddUserDirectory.

SEARCHSTART="*search_start*"
: The value to use when constructing the rest of the DN string (after the UID) for an LDAP query. Optional; used only when ACTION is set to AddUserDirectory.

SECRET="*string*"
: A string to be used in generating the encryption key used by advanced security services. Used only when ACTION is set to AddHost.

SERVER="CFSM"
: The name of the ColdFusion security server. The default SERVER used by ColdFusion is "CFSM". You shouldn't use a value other than CFSM unless you manually modify the Site Minder security database. Used only when ACTION is set to AddSecurityRealm or AddUserDirectory.

SQLAUTHUSER="*SQL_statement*"
: Specifies the SQL statement to use for the Authenticate User field when using an ODBC data source to store security profile tables. Required when ACTION is CreateODBCQueryScheme. New in ColdFusion 5.0.

SQLENUM="*SQL_statement*"
Specifies the SQL statement to use for the Enumerate field when using an ODBC data source to store security profile tables. Required when ACTION is CreateODBCQueryScheme. New in ColdFusion 5.0.

SQLGETGROUPPROP="*SQL_statement*"
Specifies the SQL statement to use for the Get Group Property field when using an ODBC data source to store security profile tables. Required when ACTION is CreateODBCQueryScheme. New in ColdFusion 5.0.

SQLGETGROUPPROPS="*SQL_statement*"
Specifies the SQL statement to use for the Get Group Properties field when using an ODBC data source to store security profile tables. Required when ACTION is CreateODBCQueryScheme. New in ColdFusion 5.0.

SQLGETGROUPS="*SQL_statement*"
Specifies the SQL statement to use for the Get Groups field when using an ODBC data source to store security profile tables. Required when ACTION is CreateODBCQueryScheme. New in ColdFusion 5.0.

SQLGETOBJINFO="*SQL_statement*"
Specifies the SQL statement to use for the Get User/Group Info field when using an ODBC data source to store security profile tables. Required when ACTION is CreateODBCQueryScheme. New in ColdFusion 5.0.

SQLGETUSERPROP="*SQL_statement*"
Specifies the SQL statement to use for the Get User Property field when using an ODBC data source to store security profile tables. Required when ACTION is CreateODBCQueryScheme. New in ColdFusion 5.0.

SQLGETUSERPROPS="*SQL_statement*"
Specifies the SQL statement to use for the Get User Properties field when using an ODBC data source to store security profile tables. Required when ACTION is CreateODBCQueryScheme. New in ColdFusion 5.0.

SQLINITUSER="*SQL_statement*"
Specifies the SQL statement to use for the Init User field when using an ODBC data source to store security profile tables. Required when ACTION is CreateODBCQueryScheme. New in ColdFusion 5.0.

SQLISGROUPMEMBER="*SQL_statement*"
Specifies the SQL statement to use for the Is Group Member field when using an ODBC data source to store security profile tables. Required when ACTION is CreateODBCQueryScheme. New in ColdFusion 5.0.

SQLLOOKUP="*SQL_statement*"
Specifies the SQL statement to use for the Lookup field when using an ODBC data source to store security profile tables. Required when ACTION is CreateODBCQueryScheme. New in ColdFusion 5.0.

SQLLOOKUPGROUP="*SQL_statement*"
Specifies the SQL statement to use for the Lookup Groups field when using an ODBC data source to store security profile tables. Required when ACTION is CreateODBCQueryScheme. New in ColdFusion 5.0.

SQLLOOKUPUSER="*SQL_statement*"
: Specifies the SQL statement to use for the Lookup Users field when using an ODBC data source to store security profile tables. Required when ACTION is CreateODBCQueryScheme. New in ColdFusion 5.0.

SQLSETGROUPPROP="*SQL_statement*"
: Specifies the SQL statement to use for the Set Group Property field when using an ODBC data source to store security profile tables. Required when ACTION is CreateODBCQueryScheme. New in ColdFusion 5.0.

SQLSETUSERPROP="*SQL_statement*"
: Specifies the SQL statement to use for the Set Group Properties field when using an ODBC data source to store security profile tables. Required when ACTION is CreateODBCQueryScheme. New in ColdFusion 5.0.

TIMEOUT="*seconds*"
: The time in seconds that ColdFusion should wait before timing out an LDAP directory search. Optional; used only when ACTION is set to AddUserDirectory.

TYPE="*object_type_or_namespace*"
: The object type to be protected within a given security context when ACTION is Addrule, DeleteRule, or GenerateRule. Possible entries are Application, CFML, Collection, Component, Custom Tag, Data Source, File, Function, UserObject, and User. When ACTION is set to AddSecurityContext, the TYPE attribute specifies the namespace for the user directory, either Windows NT, LDAP, or ODBC.

UPDATE="Yes|No"
: Whether or not the data being written to the security database should be added (No) or updated (Yes). Optional. The default value is No.

USER="*user*"
: The name of a user within a valid user directory. Used only when ACTION is set to AddUserToPolicy, GetUserPolicy, and RemoveUserFromPolicy.

USERCREDENTIALS="Yes|No"
: Whether or not to pass login credentials to the LDAP server. Should be set to Yes only when used in conjunction with a USERNAME. Used only when ACTION is set to AddUserDirectory.

USERNAME="*username*"
: A username to use if required by the domain, LDAP directory, or database. You can leave this attribute blank if ColdFusion is running as Administrator. Used only when ACTION is set to AddUserDirectory.

USERPWD="*password*"
: A password to use if required by the domain, LDAP directory, or database. You can leave this attribute blank if ColdFusion is running as Administrator. Used only when ACTION is set to AddUserDirectory.

USERSECURECONNECT=Yes|No"
: Whether or not to encrypt authentication information during transmission between the ColdFusion server and an LDAP server. This attribute must be enabled when connecting to an LDAP server using SSL. Optional; used only when ACTION is set to AddUserDirectory. The default is No.

## CFAPPLET

<CFAPPLET>

References a previously registered Java applet within an instance of CFFORM. Applet registration is handled via the ColdFusion Administrator.

### Attributes

APPLETSOURCE="*registered_applet_name*"
The actual name of the Java applet. Required.

NAME="*form_field_name*"
What to call the Java applet within the context of CFFORM. Required.

ALIGN="*alignment*"
Alignment of the applet. Optional. Valid entries are: Left, Right, Top, TextTopt, Bottom, AbsBottom, Middle, AbsMiddle, Baseline.

HEIGHT="*height_in_pixels*"
Height of the applet in pixels. Optional.

WIDTH="*width_in_pixels*"
Width of the applet in pixels. Optional.

HSPACE="*horizontal_spacing_in_pixels*"
Horizontal space in pixels along each side of the applet. Optional.

VSPACE="*vertical_spacing_in_pixels*"
Vertical space in pixels along the top and bottom of the applet. Optional.

NOTSUPPORTED="*text_messsage*"
Text to appear if Java isn't supported by the user's browser. Optional.

PARAM*n*="*parameter_value*"
Additional user-defined parameters to pass to the applet. Optional.

## CFAPPLICATION

<CFAPPLICATION>

Names a ColdFusion application and controls various application settings, such as the availability of client, session, and application variables, and length of various timeouts.

### Attributes

NAME="*application_name*"
The name of the ColdFusion application. May contain up to 64 characters. Required.

CLIENTMANAGEMENT="Yes|No"
Enables client management for the application. Optional. Default is No.

CLIENTSTORAGE="*client_storage_type*"
The client storage type for the application. Valid entries are Datasourcename (enter the data-source name), Registry, and Cookie. Optional. Default is Registry.

SESSIONMANAGEMENT="Yes|No"
Enables session management for the application. Optional. Default is No.

SESSIONTIMEOUT="#CreateTimeSpan(*days, hours, minutes, seconds*)#"
: The timeout value for session variables in the application. Specified as an interval using the CreateTimeSpan() function. Optional. The default value is specified in the Variables section of the ColdFusion Administrator.

APPLICATIONTIMEOUT="#CreateTimeSpan(*days, hours, minutes, seconds*)#"
: The timeout value for application variables. Specified as an interval using the CreateTimeSpan() function. Optional. The default value is specified in the Variables section of the ColdFusion Administrator.

SETCLIENTCOOKIES="Yes|No"
: Enables client cookies. If cookies are disabled, the values for CFID and CFTOKEN must be passed manually from template to template in the URL. Optional. The default is Yes.

SETDOMAINCOOKIES="Yes|No"
: Indicates whether or not to set client cookies at the domain level, which is useful when you need to share client variables in a clustered environment. If set to Yes, ColdFusion creates a new variable at the domain level called CFMAGIC. CFMAGIC tells ColdFusion that cookies have been set at the domain level and contains the values of the CFID and CFTOKEN cookies. Existing host-level cookies are compared automatically to the values stored in CFMAGIC and migrated to domain-level cookies if the values don't match. Optional. The default is No.

## CFASSOCIATE

<CFASSOCIATE>

Associate a subtag with a base tag (child tag with a parent tag) by saving all the subtag's attributes to a special structure that is available to the base tag. This tag is for use only within custom tags.

### *Attributes*

BASETAG="*tag_name*"
: The name of the base tag. Required.

DATACOLLECTION="*collection_name*"
: The name of the structure that contains subtag data. Optional. By default, ColdFusion saves all subtag attributes in a structure called AssocAttribs.

## CFAUTHENTICATE

<CFAUTHENTICATE>

Authenticates a user within a given security context.

### *Attributes*

SECURITYCONTEXT="*security_context*"
: The name of the security context to authenticate the user within. Required. Security contexts are defined in the ColdFusion Administrator.

USERNAME="*username*"
: The name of the user being authenticated. Required.

PASSWORD="*password*"
The password of the user being authenticated. Required.

SETCOOKIE="Yes|No"
If set to Yes, ColdFusion sets an encrypted cookie on the user's browser that contains the username, security context, browser's remote address, and HTTP user agent. Optional. The default is Yes.

THROWONFAILURE="Yes|No"
Determines if ColdFusion should throw an exception if authentication fails. Optional. The default is Yes.

## CFBREAK

<CFBREAK>

Breaks out of a CFLOOP. The CFBREAK tag has no additional attributes.

### *Example*

```
<CFLOOP INDEX="i" FROM="10" TO="100" STEP="10">
  <CFIF i EQ 50>
    <CFBREAK>
  </CFIF>
```

## CFCACHE

<CFCACHE>

Caches a ColdFusion page for faster access by writing a temporary static HTML version of the page to disk (either server-side or in the client's browser cache). To cache a ColdFusion template, just add the CFCACHE tag to the top of the page.

When the CFCACHE tag caches a page, two files are actually written to the server. First, a temporary file (with a *.tmp* extension) is created that contains the HTML necessary to generate the static version of the page. A mapping file (written as *cfcache.map*) contains the mapping to the temp file, as well as a timestamp that determines when to expire the cached file. When using the CFCACHE tag, there are a few additional points that should be considered:

- Templates that generate errors don't get cached.
- By default, the CFCACHE tag suppresses all debugging information for a ColdFusion template. To use debugging within a cached page, you must explicitly turn it on for the template using the CFSETTING tag.
- Simultaneous Requests in the ColdFusion Administrator must be set to a minimum of 2 for the CFCACHE tag to work.

### *Attributes*

ACTION="cache|clientcache|flush|optimal
The action to be performed by the CFCACHE tag. Optional. The default is Cache, which caches the page. ClientCache caches the page in the client's browser, Flush refreshes the cached page, and Optimal caches the page using both server-side and browser caching.

`PROTOCOL="protocol_name"`
: The protocol to use when creating the pages from the cache. Options are `HTTP://` and `HTTPS://`. Optional. The default is `HTTP://`.

`PORT="port_number"`
: Port number on the web server where the file being cached resides. Optional. The default is 80.

`TIMEOUT="timeout"`
: A date/time value that specifies the oldest acceptable page to pull from the cache. If the cached page is older than the timeout value, ColdFusion refreshes the cached page. Optional.

`DIRECTORY="directory_name"`
: The full path of the directory containing the *cfcache.map* file used by the `CFCACHE` tag. Optional when `ACTION="Flush"`; ignored otherwise. The default value is the directory of the current page.

`CACHEDIRECTORY="directory_name"`
: The full path of a directory where the page should be cached. By default, pages are cached in the directory of the currently executing template. Optional.

`EXPIREURL="wildcarded_URL"`
: A wildcarded URL reference used by ColdFusion to match mappings in the *cfcache.map* file when `ACTION="Flush"`; ignored otherwise. Optional. The default flushes all mappings.

`USERNAME="username"`
: A username to use if required by the page being cached. Optional.

`PASSWORD="password"`
: A password to use if required by the page being cached. Optional.

## CFCASE

See CFSWITCH.

## CFCATCH

See CFTRY.

## CFCOL

```
<CFTABLE>
  [<CFCOL>]
  [<CFCOL>]
  ...
</CFTABLE>
```

Used within a `CFTABLE` block to define the column header, including alignment, width, and text.

### *Attributes*

HEADER="*header_text*"
The text to use for the column's header.

ALIGN="*alignment_position*"
The alignment for the `HEADER` text. Valid entries are: `Left`, `Right`, and `Center`.

WIDTH="*width_in_characters*"
The width in characters for the column; a longer heading is truncated. The default width is 20 characters.

TEXT="*text*"
The text to display in the column. The `TEXT` attribute can contain plain text, HTML, and CFML variables.

## CFCOLLECTION

<CFCOLLECTION>

Creates and manages Verity collections. The `CFCOLLECTION` tag provides a programmatic interface to many of the administrative functions of the ColdFusion Administrator.

### *Attributes*

ACTION="*action*"
The action to perform on the specified Verity collection. Valid entries are `Create`, `Repair`, `Delete`, `Optimize`, and `Map`. Required.

COLLECTION="*collection_name*"
The name of the Verity collection to perform the specified `ACTION` on. Required.

PATH="*directory*"
The path to a Verity collection. Required when `ACTION` is `Create` or `Map`.

LANGUAGE="*language*"
The language to be used when creating the collection. To specify a language other than U.S. English (the default), you must purchase the ColdFusion International Search Pack from Allaire. Optional.

## CFCONTENT

<CFCONTENT>

Sends content of the specified media type to the browser. Content may be dynamically generated by ColdFusion or come from a file. The `CFCONTENT` tag is often used to send files stored above the web root directory to the browser or to generate content for other non-HTML clients, such as wireless devices (cell phones, PDAs, etc.).

### *Attributes*

TYPE="*media_type*"
The media type of the content to be sent to the browser. Required.

FILE="*filename*"
The name of the file being sent to the browser. Optional.

`RESET="Yes|No"`
Whether or not to suppress any output preceding the call to the `CFCONTENT` tag. The `RESET` attribute is ignored if a value is specified for `FILE`. The default is `Yes`.

`DELETEFILE="Yes|No"`
Whether or not to delete the file after it has been sent to the browser. Valid only if a file was specified in the `FILE` attribute. Optional. The default is `No`.

## CFCOOKIE

`<CFCOOKIE>`

Writes a cookie to the user's browser.

### *Attributes*

`NAME="`*`cookie_name`*`"`
Name of the cookie to write. Required.

`VALUE="`*`value_of_cookie`*`"`
The value to assign the cookie. Required.

`PATH="`*`URLs`*`"`
The URLs in `DOMAIN` that the cookie applies to. Multiple entries can be separated by semicolons. Optional.

`DOMAIN="`*`domains`*`"`
The domain for which the cookie can be read and written. Entries must always start with a dot. For example, `DOMAIN=".oreilly.com"` is a valid entry. Multiple entries may be separated by semicolons. Optional.

`EXPIRES="`*`time_period`*`"`
The cookie's expiration date. May be specified as a date, number of days, `Now`, or `Never`. Optional.

`SECURE="Yes|No"`
Whether the cookie must be transmitted securely via SSL. Optional. The default is `No`.

## CFDEFAULTCASE

See `CFSWITCH`.

## CFDIRECTORY

`<CFDIRECTORY>`

The `CFDIRECTORY` tag lists directory contents, as well as creates, renames, and deletes directories on the ColdFusion application server.

### *Attributes*

`ACTION="`*`action`*`"`
The action to perform on the specified `DIRECTORY`. Valid options are `Create`, `Delete`, `List`, and `Rename`. Required. The default value is `List`.

DIRECTORY="*directory_name*"
: The name of the directory to perform the ACTION on. Required.

NAME="*query_name*"
: The name to assign the query object containing the directory listing when ACTION is List. Required for this action; ignored otherwise.

FILTER="*file_extension*"
: A file extension to filter the results returned when ACTION is List. Optional for this action; ignored otherwise. Only one file extension can be used with the FILTER attribute.

MODE="*permissions*"
: Allows you to set permissions the way you would with the Unix *chmod* command. For example, setting the MODE="777" assigns read, write, and execute permissions to the directory for everyone. Optional when ACTION is Create; ignored otherwise.

SORT="*sort_criteria*"
: How to sort each query column returned when ACTION is List. Optional for this action; ignored otherwise. The SORT attribute can take a single query column or a comma-separated list. The actual direction for the sort is specified as ASC for ascending and DESC for descending.

NEWDIRECTORY="*new_directory_name*"
: The name of the new directory to be created when ACTION is Rename. Required when ACTION is Rename; ignored otherwise.

### *Returned Query Columns*

The following values are returned when ACTION is List:

*queryname*.Attributes
: The attributes, if any, for the given object.

*queryname*.DateLastModified
: The time/date stamp that the object was last modified.

*queryname*.Mode
: This column applies only to the Unix versions of ColdFusion and specifies the permissions set for the file or directory. The Mode is the same as the permissions set by the Unix *chmod* command.

*queryname*.Name
: The name of the directory or file.

*queryname*.Size
: The size in bytes of the directory or file.

*queryname*.Type
: Dir if the object is a directory or File if it is a file.

---

## CFDUMP

New in ColdFusion 5.0

<CFDUMP>

Displays the value of a variable in an HTML-formatted table. CFDUMP is useful in debugging situations where you need to display a variable's contents, especially for arrays and structures. The `CFDUMP` tag can output the contents of simple datatypes, arrays, queries, structures, and WDDX packets.

### *Attributes*

`VAR="#`*`variable_name`*`#"`
: The name of the variable you want to display the value(s) for. Note that it is necessary to surround the variable name with pound signs.

## CFELSE

See `CFIF`.

## CFELSEIF

See `CFIF`.

## CFERROR

`<CFERROR>`

Displays a custom error page when an error occurs in a ColdFusion application. The `CFERROR` tag is most often included within an application's *Application.cfm* template.

### *Attributes*

`TYPE="`*`error_type`*`"`
: Specifies the error type to watch for. Required. The default is `Request`, which handles all errors that occur during a page request. `Exception` handles exceptions, `Monitor` sets up an exception monitor, and `Validation` handles form validation errors that occur when a form is submitted (useful only in an *Application.cfm* template).

`TEMPLATE="`*`path`*`"`
: The relative path to the custom error template. Required.

  When TYPE is `Exception`, any ColdFusion tags can be used in the exception handling template. Exception handling templates may also be invoked by specifying a Site-wide Error Handler within the Server Settings section of the ColdFusion Administrator.

  When `TYPE` is `Monitor`, ColdFusion invokes the specified error handling template before processing any `CFTRY/CFCATCH` error handling that may be in the executing template.

  When `TYPE` is `Request`, a number of variables are available in the error-handling template (listed in "Return Variables"), but no other CFML tags can be used. These variables are also available when `TYPE` is `Exception` or `Monitor`.

  When `TYPE` is `Validation`, a number of variables are available to the validation error-handling template (listed next in "Return Variables"), but no other CFML tags may be used in the template.

`EXCEPTION="`*`exception_type`*`"`
: The type of exception to watch for. Required when `TYPE` is `Exception` or `Monitor`. Possible values are: `Any` (the default), `Application`, *`CustomTag`*, `Database`,

`Expression`, `Lock`, `MissingInclude`, `Object`, `Security`, and `Template`. For more details on these types, see `CFTRY`. ColdFusion also supports a number of additional structured exception types, as listed under `CFTRY`.

`MAILTO="`*`email_address`*`"`
: The email address of the person who should be notified if an error occurs. Optional.

### *Returned Variables*

When `TYPE` is `Exception`, `Monitor`, or `Request`, the following variables are made available to the template specified in the `TEMPLATE` attribute and can be referenced within a `CFOUTPUT` block:*

`Error.Browser`
: The browser in use when the error occurred

`Error.DateTime`
: The date and time when the error occurred

`Error.Diagnostics`
: A detailed error message provided by the ColdFusion server

`Error.GeneratedContent`
: The content generated by the failed request

`Error.HTTPReferer`
: The page containing the link to the template where the error occurred

`Error.MailTo`
: The email address specified in the `MAILTO` attribute of the `CFERROR` tag

`Error.RemoteAddress`
: Specifies the IP address of the remote client

`Error.QueryString`
: The URL query string, if any, from the client's request

`Error.Template`
: The page that was in the process of executing when the error occurred

Additionally, if `TYPE` is set to `Monitor` or `Exception`, you can use any `CFCATCH` return variables available to the exception specified in the `EXCEPTION` attribute of the `CFERROR` tag. These variables are listed under `CFTRY`.

When `TYPE` is `Validation`, the following variables are available:

`Error.ValidationHeader`
: Header text for the validation error page

`Error.InvalidFields`
: An HTML unordered (`<UL>`) list of validation errors

`Error.ValidationFooter`
: Footer text for the validation error page

`Error.MailTo`
: The email address specified in the `MAILTO` attribute of the `CFERROR` tag

---

* You can use `CFError` instead of the `Error` prefix if you have `TYPE` set to `Monitor` or `Exception`, as in `CFrror.Browser` or `CFError.Template`. Just like `Error` variables, `CFError` variables can be referenced individually or as key/value pairs within a ColdFusion structure named `CFError`.

## CFEXECUTE

New as of ColdFusion 4.5

`<CFEXECUTE> ... </CFEXECUTE>`

Executes a command-line program on the server. No HTML or CFML should appear between the start and end of the CFEXECUTE tags, and CFEXECUTE tags can't be nested. If for some reason an exception is thrown while attempting to execute the CFEXECUTE tag, the following rules apply:

- If the application specified in the NAME attribute can't be found, an "Application File Not Found" exception is thrown.
- If the ColdFusion user executing the application doesn't have permission to do so, a security exception is thrown.
- If a value is specified for OUTPUTFILE, and the file can't be opened, an "Output File Cannot be Opened" exception is thrown.

### *Attributes*

NAME="*command*"

The full path to the program you want to execute. Required.

ARGUMENTS="*argument_string*"

Arguments to pass to the external program being called. Optional. Arguments can be either strings or arrays. On Windows platforms, a string is passed to the Windows process control subsystem for processing. On Unix and Linux systems, a string is tokenized into an array of strings, delimited by spaces. If spaces occur in the array elements, they are escaped by double quotes. On Windows platforms, the elements of an array are concatenated into a space-delimited string of tokens, which is then passed to the Windows process control subsystem for processing. On Unix and Linux systems, the elements of an array are copied into an array of exec() arguments.

OUTPUTFILE="*output_file*"

The path to an output file where any text output by the external program is written. If omitted, the output is returned to the browser. Optional.

TIMEOUT="*seconds*"

The time in seconds that ColdFusion should wait before timing out the call to the external program. Setting the TIMEOUT attribute to 0 equates to a nonblocking execution mode. This causes ColdFusion to spawn a thread for the process and immediately return without waiting for the process to end. By contrast, setting the TIMEOUT attribute to an arbitrarily high value equates to a blocking execution mode. Optional. The default timeout is 0.

## CFEXIT

`<CFEXIT>`

Aborts processing of a custom tag and returns control to the calling template or parent custom tag (in the case of nested tags). The CFEXIT tag is similar in functionality to the CFABORT tag, except it is intended for use within custom tags. If the CFEXIT tag is used outside of a custom tag, it acts exactly like the CFABORT tag.

### *Attribute*

METHOD="*method*"

The method used to exit the custom tag. Each method produces different results, depending on the location of CFEXIT within the custom tag.

The default method is ExitTag, which simply halts processing of the custom tag and returns control to the calling template. If placed within a block of code where ThisTag.ExecutionMode is Start or End, processing continues after the end tag.

ExitTemplate halts processing and returns control to the calling template. If placed within a block of code where ThisTag.ExecutionMode is Start, processing continues from the first child tag of the calling tag. If ThisTag.ExecutionMode is End, processing continues after the end tag.

Loop reexecutes a block of code in the currently executing custom tag (emulating a CFLOOP). This method can be used only when ThisTag.ExecutionMode is End. Using it in any other location results in an error.

---

## CFFILE

<CFFILE>

Operates on files on the ColdFusion server. The action taken depends on the ACTION attribute. Append appends additional text to the end of a file. Copy copies a file from one location to another. Delete deletes a file from the server. Move moves a file from one location to another. Read reads a text file and stores the contents in a variable. ReadBinary reads a binary file and stores the object in a variable. Rename renames a file on the server. Upload uploads a file from a form submission. Write writes a text or binary file to the server.

### *Attributes*

ACTION="*action*"

The action to be performed by the CFFILE tag. Required. Possible actions are: Append, Copy, Delete, Move, Read, ReadBinary, Rename, Upload, and Write.

FILE="*filename*"

The full path to the file to be operated on. Required for Append, Delete, Read, ReadBinary, and Write.

FILEFIELD="*form_field*"

The name of the submitted form-field (without pound signs) that contains the selected file. Required for Upload.

SOURCE="*filename*"

The full path to the current location of the file. Required for Copy, Move, and Rename.

DESTINATION="*filename*"

The full path to the new location of the file. Required for Copy, Move, Rename, and Upload. If you don't include a filename, you must use a trailing slash. On Windows servers, use the backslash (\). On Unix servers, use the forward slash (/).

OUTPUT="*content*"

The text to be appended to the file for Append or the content to store in the file for Write. Required for these two actions.

ADDNEWLINE="Yes|No"

If set to Yes, a newline character is added to the end of the file. Optional for Append and Write; ignored otherwise. The default is Yes.

VARIABLE="*variable_name*"

Variable where the file contents is stored. Required for Read and ReadBinary.

ATTRIBUTES="*attributes*"

Comma-delimited list of attributes to be applied to the file. Valid choices are Archive, Hidden, Normal, ReadOnly, System, and Temporary. Optional. If no value is specified, the file's original attributes are maintained. If Normal is specified along with other attributes, Normal is ignored.

ACCEPT="*media_types*"

A comma-separated list of media types that the ColdFusion server should be allowed to accept for upload. Optional for Upload; ignored otherwise. The default is to accept all media types.

NAMECONFLICT="error|makeunique|overwrite"

How ColdFusion should behave if the file being uploaded has the same name as a file already existing in the destination directory. Optional for Upload; ignored otherwise. The default is Error, which means that the file isn't saved to the server, and ColdFusion halts processing with an error. MakeUnique assigns the file a unique name and saves it to the server, Overwrite overwrites the existing file, and Skip aborts uploading of the file and returns control to the ColdFusion application without throwing an error.

MODE="*mode*"

Allows you to set permissions the way you would with the Unix *chmod* command. For example, setting the MODE="777" assigns read, write, and execute permissions to the directory for everyone. Optional for Upload and Write; ignored otherwise.

### *Returned Values*

With an Upload action, once the CFFILE tag has executed, a number of ColdFusion variables are created to hold information about the transaction. These variables are read-only and can be referenced using the file scope, as in CFFILE.*VariableName*.* The following list describes all the variables available within the file scope:

CFFILE.AttemptedServerFile

The filename that ColdFusion first attempted to save the uploaded file as.

CFFILE.ClientDirectory

The directory location on the client's machine where the uploaded file came from.

CFFILE.ClientFile

The name of the file uploaded from the client's machine.

CFFILE.ClientFileExt

The file extension of the file uploaded from the client's machine (without an initial period).

CFFILE.ClientFileName

The filename without the extension of the file uploaded from the client's machine.

---

* Prior to Version 4.5, the file scope was prefixed using the File prefix. While this prefix is still supported in ColdFusion 5.0, it has been deprecated.

`CFFILE.ContentSubType`
The media subtype of the uploaded file.

`CFFILE.ContentType`
The media type of the uploaded file.

`CFFILE.DateLastAccessed`
The time and date that the uploaded file was last accessed.

`CFFILE.FileExisted`
`Yes` or `No` depending upon whether the uploaded file already existed.

`CFFILE.FileSize`
The file size of the uploaded file.

`CFFILE.FileWasAppended`
`Yes` or `No` depending upon whether the uploaded file was appended to a file already existing on the server.

`CFFILE.FileWasOverwritten`
`Yes` or `No` depending upon whether a file already on the server was overwritten by the uploaded file.

`CFFILE.FileWasRenamed`
`Yes` or `No` depending upon whether the uploaded file was renamed to resolve a name conflict.

`CFFILE.FileWasSaved`
`Yes` or `No` depending upon whether the uploaded file was saved to the server.

`CFFILE.OldFileSize`
If a file on the server was overwritten, the file size of the file that was overwritten.

`CFFILE.ServerDirectory`
The directory on the server that contains the newly saved file.

`CFFILE.ServerFile`
The filename (filename and extension) of the file saved on the server.

`CFFILE.ServerFileExt`
The file extension (without the initial period) of the file saved on the server.

`CFFILE.ServerFileName`
The filename without the extension of the file saved on the server.

`CFFILE.TimeCreated`
The time the uploaded file was created.

`CFFILE.TimeLastModified`
The time and date the uploaded file was last modified.

---

## CFFLUSH

New in ColdFusion 5.0

<CFFLUSH>

Flushes all currently available content to the client. `CFFLUSH` is typically used within loops or output queries to send results back to the client in incremental chunks. The first time a `CFFLUSH` tag is encountered on a page, it sends all the HTTP headers for the request along with any generated content up to the position in the template where the tag is encountered. Successive `CFFLUSH` tags return any content generated since the previous flush. Once a `CFFLUSH` tag has been used in a template, you can't use any other CFML tags that write to the HTTP header; doing so causes ColdFusion to throw an error because the header has already been sent to the browser. These tags include `CFCONTENT`, `CFCOOKIE`, `CFFORM`, `CFHEADER`, and `CFHTMLHEAD`. In addition, attempting to set a variable in the cookie scope with the `CFSET` tag results in an error because cookies are passed from the server to the browser in the HTTP header.

### *Attribute*

`INTERVAL="`*`integer`*`"`
: The minimum number of bytes that should be returned by the server before the output buffer is flushed. Optional.

---

## CFFORM

Enhanced in ColdFusion 5.0

`<CFFORM> ... </CFFORM>`

Creates a form capable of using controls including HTML input types such as input boxes, drop-down boxes, and radio buttons, as well as a number of specialized Java applets, such as tree, grid, and slider controls.

### *Attributes*

`NAME="`*`name`*`"`
: A name for the form. You should specify a value for `NAME` if you plan to reference the form later in your application. Optional.

`ACTION="`*`form_action`*`"`
: Where the form should be submitted upon completion. Required.

`TARGET="`*`window_name`*`"`
: The name of a frame or window where the target template specified in the `ACTION` attribute should be opened. Optional.

`ENCTYPE="`*`MIME_type`*`"`
: The MIME type for data being submitted via the `POST` method. Optional. The default is "application/x-www-form-urlencoded". If, however, you plan to allow file uploads via your form, you must specify "multipart/form-data".

`ONSUBMIT="`*`javascript_function`*`"`
: A JavaScript function that should be executed after validation occurs but before the form is submitted. Optional.

`ENABLECAB="Yes|No"`
: Whether or not Java controls associated with other `CFFORM` elements should be made available to Microsoft Internet Explorer users as Microsoft cabinet files. Optional. This attribute is deprecated and no longer functional as of ColdFusion 5.0

`CODEBASE="`*`URL`*`"`
: Specifies the URL to a downloadable JRE plugin for MS Internet Explorer. Optional. The default URL is */CFIDE/classes/cf-j2re-win.cab*. New as of ColdFusion 5.0.

`ARCHIVE="`*`URL`*`"`
: Specifies the URL to a downloadable Java archive file containing Java-based CFFORM controls. Optional. The default URL is */CFIDE/classes/CFJava2.jar*. New as of ColdFusion 5.0.

PASSTHROUGH="*HTML_attributes*"
: Any additional HTML attributes you want to specify that aren't directly supported by the CFFORM tag. Optional.

PRESERVEDATA="Yes|No"
: Whether or not to retain and display data submitted from a CFINPUT (excluding radio button and checkbox controls), CFTEXTINPUT, CFSLIDER, or CFTREE control when a form is submitted to itself or to another page with like-named CFFORM controls. This allows you to display the data entered by the user for CFINPUT and CFTEXTINPUT controls without any additional coding. For CFSLIDER controls, the slider is set automatically to the position from the previous form post. For CFTREE controls, the tree expands automatically to the previously selected item. For PRESERVEDATA to work with a tree control, the COMPLETEPATH attribute of the CFTREE tag must be set to Yes. Optional. The default is No. New as of ColdFusion 5.0.

---

## CFFTP

<CFFTP>

Allows a ColdFusion program to communicate with an FTP server. The action taken depends on the ACTION attribute. Open opens an FTP connection between the ColdFusion server and a remote FTP server, while Close closes a connection to an FTP server. The rest of the actions perform various file and directory operations.

### *Attributes*

ACTION="*action*"
: The action to be performed by the CFFTP tag. Required. Possible actions are: Close, ChangeDir, CreateDir, Exists, ExistsDir, ExistsFile, GetCurrentDir, GetCurrentURL, GetFile, ListDir, Open, PutFile, Remove, RemoveDir, and Rename. RemoveDir is new as of ColdFusion 5.0.

USERNAME="*username*"
: The username to send to the FTP server. If none is required, convention dictates that you pass "anonymous" as the username. Required for Open. Also required for all file and directory operations unless using a cached connection.

PASSWORD="*password*"
: Password to send to the FTP server in conjunction with USERNAME. If none is required, convention dictates that you pass the email address of the user as the password. Required for Open. Also required for all file and directory operations unless using a cached connection.

NAME="*query_name*"
: The name of a query to hold the directory listing when ACTION is ListDir. Required for this action.

SERVER="*FTP_server*"
: Hostname or IP address of the FTP server you want to connect to. Required for Open. Also required for all file and directory operations unless using a cached connection.

PORT="*port_number*"
: Port on the FTP server that listens for incoming FTP requests. Optional. The default FTP port is 21.

TIMEOUT="*seconds*"
: The length in seconds that an operation has to execute before the request is timed out. Optional. The default is 30.

CONNECTION="*connection_name*"
: For Open, the name to assign a cached FTP connection so that batch operations can be performed without having to reestablish a new connection for each task. For file and directory operations, can be used to refer to an existing cached FTP session. For Close, the name of the FTP connection to close. If session variables are used to cache the connection, it is important to make sure that you lock access to the session variables during read/write via the CFLOCK tag or from within the ColdFusion Administrator. Optional.

AGENTNAME="*agent_name*"
: A name for the application or entity making the FTP connection. Optional.

ASCIITEXTEXTENSIONLIST="*extensions*"
: A semicolon-delimited list of file extensions that force the transfer mode to ASCII when the TRANSFERMODE attribute is set to Auto. Optional. The default extension list is "txt;htm;html;cfm;cfml;shtm;shtml;css;asp;asa".

TRANSFERMODE="ASCII|Binary|Auto"
: The FTP transfer mode to use when uploading and downloading files. Possible options are ASCII, Binary, and Auto. Optional. The default value is Auto.

FAILIFEXISTS="Yes|No"
: Whether or not a GetFile action fails if a local file with the same name as the file being downloaded already exists. Optional. The default is Yes.

DIRECTORY="*directory_name*"
: The directory on which to perform an FTP operation. Required when ACTION is ChangeDir, CreateDir, ExistsDir, ListDir, or RemoveDir.

LOCALFILE="*filename*"
: The name of the file on the local system. Required when ACTION is GetFile or PutFile.

REMOTEFILE="*filename*"
: The name of the file on the remote FTP server. Required when ACTION is ExistsFile, GetFile, or PutFile.

ATTRIBUTES="*file_attributes*"
: A comma-delimited list of attributes to be applied to the file being downloaded when ACTION is set to GetFile. Valid choices are Archive, Compressed, Directory, Hidden, Normal, ReadOnly, System, and Temporary. Optional. The default value is Normal. File attributes vary depending on the operating systems involved in the file transfer.

ITEM="*file_or_directory_name*"
: The file, directory, or object to act on when ACTION is Exists or Remove. Required for these actions.

EXISTING="*file_or_directory_name*"
: The current name of the file or directory being renamed on the FTP server. Required when ACTION is Rename.

NEW="*file_or_directory_name*"
: The new name for the file or directory being renamed on the FTP server. Required when ACTION is Rename.

PROXYSERVER="*proxy_server*"
: The IP address or hostname of a proxy server or servers if required. If this attribute is NULL, ColdFusion attempts to obtain proxy server information from the registry. Optional.

PROXYBYPASS="*proxy_bypass*"
: A list of IP addresses or hostnames that don't need to be routed through the proxy server. Optional.

RETRYCOUNT="*number*"
: The number of times the FTP operation should be attempted before an error is reported. Optional. The default number of retries is 1.

STOPONERROR="Yes|No"
: If set to Yes, ColdFusion throws an exception and halts processing if an error occurs. Optional. The default is No, which allows ColdFusion to continue processing the page after an error has occurred.

PASSIVE="Yes|No"
: Whether or not to use passive transfer mode. Optional. The default is No.

### *Returned Variables*

When STOPONERROR is set to No, the CFFTP tag returns three variables that contain information related to the error:

CFFTP.Succeeded
: Yes if the FTP connection was closed successfully and No if it was not.

CFFTP.ErrorCode
: An error number corresponding to a value in CFFTP.ErrorText. If no error occurred, returns 0.

CFFTP.ErrorText
: A text message describing the error.

Several of the file and directory operations performed by the CFFTP tag also return a variable called CFFTP.ReturnValue. The following table lists the actions that return this variable as well as a description of the returned value:

| ACTION Value | Returned Value |
|---|---|
| GetCurrentDir | Current directory |
| GetCurrentURL | Current URL |
| Exists | Yes or No |
| ExistsDir | Yes or No |
| ExistsFile | Yes or No |

### *Returned Query Columns*

Query objects created by the `CFFTP` tag when `ACTION` is `ListDir` contain the following query columns:

*queryname*`.Attributes`
: The attributes, if any, for the given object.

*queryname*`.IsDirectory`
: `TRUE` if the object is a directory, `FALSE` if it isn't.

*queryname*`.LastModified`
: The date that the file or directory was last modified.

*queryname*`.Length`
: The length in bytes of the file or directory.

*queryname*`.Mode`
: This column applies only to the Unix versions of ColdFusion and specifies the permissions set for the file or directory. The `Mode` is the same as the permissions set by the Unix *chmod* command.

*queryname*`.Name`
: The name of the file or directory.

*queryname*`.Path`
: The path without drive letter designation to the file or directory.

*queryname*`.URL`
: The URL for the file or directory.

## CFGRAPH

New in ColdFusion 5.0

```
<CFGRAPH>
  [<CFGRAPHDATA>]
  ...
</CFGRAPH>
```

Draws a bar, horizontal bar, line, or pie chart from query and/or static data. The `CFGRAPH` tag uses Macromedia Generator and JRun, both installed when you install ColdFusion, to handle the graphing. Because the `CFGRAPH` tag can graph only numeric data, you must convert any date, time, and formatted numeric data to integers or real numbers. The `CFGRAPH` tag can render graphs in Flash, PNG, and JPEG formats. Although you can adjust the size of the graph, the `CFGRAPH` tag currently maintains a height/width aspect ratio of 3: 4. Changing one aspect without changing the other accordingly can result in an excess border around your graph. It should be noted that the CFGRAPH tag isn't supported when running ColdFusion on Windows 95/98.

### *Attributes*

`TYPE="Bar|HorizontalBar|Line|Pie"`
: The type of graph to create. Required.

`QUERY="`*query_name*`"`
: The name of an available query containing the data you want to graph. Required if no `CFGRAPHDATA` tags are specified.

VALUECOLUMN="*query_column*"
: The name of the query column containing the data you want to graph. CFGRAPH can be used only to graph numeric data. Required if no CFGRAPHDATA tags are specified.

ITEMCOLUMN="*query_column*"
: The name of a query column containing item labels that correspond to the data points from the query column specified in VALUECOLUMN. For Bar and Line charts, item labels are displayed on the horizontal axis. For HorizontalBar charts, the labels appear on the vertical axis. Pie charts display item labels in an optional legend. Optional.

FILEFORMAT="Flash|PNG|JPG"
: The file type to use when displaying the graph. Optional. The default is Flash.

GRAPHHEIGHT="*height_in_pixels*"
: Height in pixels for the graph. Optional. The default is 240.

GRAPHWIDTH="*width_in_pixels*"
: Width in pixels for the graph. Optional. The default is 320.

BACKGROUNDCOLOR="*color*"
: Background color for the graph. Colors may be specified by name or hex code in the form BGCOLOR="##FFFFCC". The double pound signs are necessary to keep ColdFusion from throwing an error. Optional. The default is White.

BORDERWIDTH="width_in_pixels"
: Thickness of the border in pixels. To specify no border, use 0; the default is 1. Optional.

BORDERCOLOR="color"
: Color for the border if a border is present. Colors are specified using the same rules as the BACKGROUNDCOLOR attribute. Optional. The default color is Black.

DEPTH="depth_in_pixels"
: Depth of the graph in pixels. Specifying a depth gives the graph a three-dimensional look. Optional. The default is 0 (i.e., not three-dimensional).

TITLE="text"
: The title to display for the graph. The title is displayed centered above the graph unless a legend is present above the graph, in which case the title is displayed centered and below the graph. Optional.

TITLEFONT="Arial|Courier|Times"
: The font to use for the graph title. Optional. The default is Arial.

URL="*URL*"
: A URL to link to when a data point on the chart is clicked. URL is valid only for Bar, HorizonatalBar, and Pie charts, and only when FILEFORMAT is Flash. URL is typically used in conjunction with the URLCOLUMN attribute, to pass a value associated with a data point to another page for processing. For example, a typical value for URL might look like one of the following:

```
URL="MyPage.cfm?MyVar="
URL="http://www.example.com/graph.cfm?MyVar="
```

The actual value assigned to the URL variable you create is populated by the URLCOLUMN attribute. Optional.

`URLCOLUMN="`*`query_column`*`"`
: Query column containing a value to append to the URL specified in `URL`. The `URLCOLUMN` attribute lets you build dynamic drill-down capabilities into your graphs by providing a way to pass a value associated with a particular data point as a URL parameter to another template for processing. Query columns whose values contain spaces and other special characters are automatically URL-encoded before being appended to the URL string. `URLCOLUMN` is valid only when `FILEFORMAT` is set to `Flash`. Optional.

`SHOWVALUELABEL="Yes|No|Rollover"`
: Whether or not to display the value associated with each data point for `Bar`, `HorizontalBar`, and `Pie` charts. `Rollover` works only when `FILEFORMAT` is `Flash` and indicates that the value be displayed when the user moves her mouse over the data point. Optional. The default it `No`.

`VALUELABELFONT="Arial|Courier|Times"`
: The font to use for the value labels for `Bar`, `HorizontalBar`, and `Pie` charts. Optional. The default is `Arial`.

`VALUELABELSIZE="`*`integer`*`"`
: The font size to use for the value labels for `Bar`, `HorizontalBar`, and `Pie` charts. Optional. The default is `12`.

`VALUELOCATION="OnBar|OverBar|Inside|Outside"`
: Indicates where values should be placed on a `Bar`, `HorizontalBar`, and `Pie` chart. For a `Bar` or `HorizontalBar` chart, options are `OnBar` (the default), indicating that values should be displayed on the bar itself, or `OverBar`, indicating that values should be displayed over the bar. For `Pie` charts, options are `Inside` (the default), indicating that values display inside each segment of the pie chart, or `Outside`, indicating that they display outside the slice of the pie. Optional.

`SCALEFROM="`*`integer`*`"`
: The minimum value to place on the value axis of the graph (vertical axis for `Bar` and `Line` charts, horizontal axis for `HorizontalBar` charts). Optional. The default is `0`.

`SCALETO="`*`integer`*`"`
: The maximum value to place on the value axis of the graph (vertical axis for `Bar` and `Line` charts, horizontal axis for `HorizontalBar` charts). Optional. The default is the maximum value in the set of data points.

`SHOWITEMLABEL="Yes|No"`
: Whether or not to display item labels on `Bar`, `HorizontalBar`, and `Line` charts. For `Line` and `Bar` charts, the item labels are displayed along the horizontal axis. For `HorizontalBar` charts, they are displayed along the vertical axis. Optional. The default is `Yes`.

`ITEMLABELFONT="Arial|Courier|Times"`
: The font to use for the item labels on `Bar`, `HorizontalBar`, and `Line` charts. Optional. The default is `Arial`.

`ITEMLABELSIZE="`*`integer`*`"`
: The font size to use for the item labels for `Bar`, `HorizontalBar`, and `Pie` charts. Optional. The default is `12`.

ITEMLABELORIENTATION="Horizontal|Vertical"
Whether item labels should be displayed horizontally or vertically. Valid only if item labels are displayed. Optional. For Bar and Line charts, the default is Vertical. For HorizontalBar charts, the default is Horizontal.

BARSPACING="*spacing_in_pixels*"
Spacing in pixels between bars in a Bar or HorizontalBar chart. Optional. The default is 0 (no spacing).

COLORLIST="*color*"
A comma-delimited list of colors to use for the data points in Bar, HorizontalBar, and Pie charts. Color names follow the same rules as in the BACKGROUNDCOLOR attribute. If there are more data points than colors specified in COLORLIST, the list is simply reused once all the options have been exhausted. Optional. If no COLORLIST is specified, ColdFusion uses a default list of colors.

LINECOLOR="*color*"
Color used to draw the line in a Line graph. Colors are specified using the same rules as the BACKGROUNDCOLOR attribute. Optional. The default color is Blue.

LINEWIDTH="*width_in_pixels*"
The width in pixels of the line in a Line graph. Optional. The default is 1.

FILL="Yes|No"
Whether or not to fill the area below the line in a Line graph with the same color used for the line, effectively creating an area graph. Optional. The default is No.

GRIDLINES="*integer*"
Number of grid lines to display between the top and bottom lines on a Bar, HorizontalBar, or Line chart. When grid lines are displayed, a corresponding value is displayed alongside the line. Optional. The default is 0.

SHOWLEGEND="Above|Below|Left|Right|None"
The position of the legend associated with a Pie chart. Choices are Above (horizontal layout centered above the chart), Below (horizontal layout centered below the chart), Left (vertical layout to the left of the chart), Right (vertical layout to the right of the chart), and None. Optional. The default is Left.

LEGENDFONT="Arial|Courier|Times"
The font to use for items displayed in the legend. Optional. The default is Arial.

## CFGRAPHDATA

New in ColdFusion 5.0

```
<CFGRAPH>
  [<CFGRAPHDATA>]
  ...
</CFGRAPH>
```

Used as a child tag of CFGRAPH to define a single data point to graph. CFGRAPHDATA tags may be used alone within a CFGRAPH tag block or in combination with data from a query.

### *Attributes*

VALUE="*data_point_value*"
The data point value to be graphed. Required.

ITEM="*data_point_label*"

Label for the data point to be graphed. Optional.

COLOR="*color*"

Color associated with the data point. Colors may be specified by name or hex code in the form COLOR="##FFFFCC". The double pound signs keep ColdFusion from throwing an error. Optional. By default, the CFGRAPHDATA tag takes the color for the data point from the COLORLIST attribute specified in the CFGRAPH tag. If no COLORLIST is present, CFGRAPHDATA uses a color from ColdFusion's default list of colors.

URL="*URL*"

A URL (including any relevant URL parameters) to link to when a data point on the chart is clicked. URL is valid only for Bar, HorizonatalBar, and Pie charts, and only when the FILEFORMAT attribute of the CFGRAPH tag is Flash. Optional.

## CFGRID

```
<CFFORM>
  <CFGRID>
    [<CFGRIDCOLUMN>]
    [<CFGRIDROW>]
    ...
  </CFGRID>
  ...
</CFFORM>
```

Provides a Java-based grid control for displaying and editing tabular data. Used within a CFFORM block.

### *Attributes*

NAME="*name*"

The form-field name for the grid control. Required.

HEIGHT="*height_in_pixels*"

Height in pixels for the grid's display area. Optional.

WIDTH="*width_in_pixels*"

Width in pixels for the grid's display area. Optional.

AUTOWIDTH="Yes|No"

Whether or not the grid should adjust the width of each column automatically so that all columns appear within the grid without having to scroll. Optional. The default is Yes. New as of ColdFusion 5.0.

VSPACE="*vertical_spacing_in_pixels*"

Height in pixels for the padding above and below the grid control. Optional.

HSPACE="*horizontal_spacing_in_pixels*"

Width in pixels for the padding to the left and right of the grid. Optional.

ALIGN="*alignment*"

Alignment for the grid control. Valid entries are Left, Right, Top, TextTop, Bottom, AbsBottom, Baseline, Middle, and AbsMiddle. Optional.

QUERY="*query_name*"

The name of a query to associate with the grid control. Optional.

INSERT="Yes|No"
: Whether or not to allow users to insert new data into the grid. Optional. The default is No.

DELETE="Yes|No"
: Whether or not to allow users to delete data from the grid. Optional. The default is No.

SORT="Yes|No"
: Whether or not to allow users to sort data in the grid using a simple text sort. Optional. The default is No.

FONT="*font_name*"
: The font name used for all data in the grid. Optional.

FONTSIZE="*integer*"
: The font size for all data in the grid. Optional.

ITALIC="Yes|No"
: If Yes, displays all grid data in italic. Optional. The default is No.

BOLD="Yes|No"
: If Yes, displays all grid data in bold. Optional. The default is No.

TEXTCOLOR
: The text color for all data in the grid. Colors may be specified by name (Black, Blue, Cyan, Darkgray, Gray, Lightgray, Magenta, Orange, Pink, Red, White, Yellow) or hex code in the form TEXTCOLOR="##FFFFCC". The double pound signs are necessary to keep ColdFusion from throwing a syntax error, or you may omit the pound signs altogether. By using the appropriate hex code, you may specify colors that can't be specified by name. Optional. The default is Black. New as of ColdFusion 5.0.

HREF="*URL*"
: A URL to associate with the grid item or the name of a query column containing HREF values. The URL may be relative or absolute. Optional.

HREFKEY="*column_name*"
: The name of a query column to use as the Key when a query is used to populate the grid. Optional.

TARGET="*URL_target*"
: The name of a frame or window that the template specified in the HREF attribute should be opened in. Optional.

APPENDKEY="Yes|No"
: Whether or not to pass the CFGRIDKEY variable along with the value of the selected grid item in the URL to the template specified in the CFFORM tag. Optional. The default is Yes.

HIGHLIGHTHREF="Yes|No"
: Whether or not to highlight links associated with the grid control and defined within the HREF attribute. Optional. The default is Yes.

ONVALIDATE="*javascript_function*"
: A JavaScript validation function that should be executed before the form is submitted. Optional.

ONERROR="*function_name*"
: The name of a JavaScript function that should be executed if validation fails for any reason. Optional.

GRIDDATAALIGN="*alignment*"
: Alignment for the grid data. Valid entries are: `Left`, `Right`, and `Center`. Optional. The default is `Left`.

GRIDLINES="Yes|No"
: Whether or not to add row and column lines to the grid. Optional. The default is `Yes`.

ROWHEIGHT="*height_in_pixels*"
: The number of pixels for the minimum row height of the grid control. Optional.

ROWHEADERS="Yes|No"
: Whether or not to display row headers on the grid. Optional. The default is `Yes`.

ROWHEADERALIGN="*alignment*"
: Alignment for the row headers. Valid entries are: `Left`, `Right`, and `Center`. Optional. The default is `Left`.

ROWHEADERFONT="*font_name*"
: The font to use for the row headers. Optional.

ROWHEADERFONTSIZE="*integer*"
: The font size to use for the row headers. Optional.

ROWHEADERITALIC="Yes|No"
: Whether or not to display the row header text in italic. Optional. The default is `No`.

ROWHEADERBOLD="Yes|No"
: Whether or not to display the row header text in italic. Optional. The default is `No`.

ROWHEADERTEXTCOLOR="*color*"
: The text color for row headers in the grid. For color choices, see the `TEXTCOLOR` attribute. Optional. The default is `Black`. New as of ColdFusion Version 5.0.

ROWHEADERWIDTH="*width_in_pixels*"
: The width in pixels of the row header. Optional.

COLHEADERS="Yes|No"
: Whether or not to display column headers on the grid. Optional. The default is `Yes`.

COLHEADERALIGN="*alignment*"
: Alignment for the column headers. Valid entries are: `Left`, `Right`, and `Center`. Optional. The default is `Left`.

COLHEADERFONT="*font_name*"
: The font to use for the column headers. Optional.

COLHEADERFONTSIZE="*integer*"
: The font size to use for the column headers. Optional.

COLHEADERITALIC="Yes|No"
: Whether or not to display the column header text in italic. Optional. The default is `No`.

COLHEADERBOLD="Yes|No"
: Whether or not to display the column header text in bold. Optional. The default is `No`.

COLHEADERTEXTCOLOR="*color*"
: The text color for column headers in the grid. For color choices, see the `TEXTCOLOR` attribute. Optional. The default is `Black`. New as of ColdFusion 5.0.

COLHEADERWIDTH="*width_in_pixels*"
: The width in pixels of the column header. Optional.

BGCOLOR="*color*"
: Background color for the grid control. For color choices, see the TEXTCOLOR attribute. Optional. The default is White.

SELECTCOLOR="*color*"
: The background color for an item that has been selected. For color choices, see the BGCOLOR attribute. Optional.

SELECTMODE="*mode*"
: The selection mode to use for items in the grid. Optional. The default value is Browse, which allows browsing of data only. Edit allows editing of data, Single confines selections to a single cell, Column causes a selection to automatically include the entire column, and Row causes a selection to automatically include the entire row.

MAXROWS="*integer*"
: Maximum number of rows to display in the grid. Optional.

NOTSUPPORTED="*text_message*"
: A text message to display if the user's browser doesn't support Java or Java is disabled. Optional. If no message is specified, ColdFusion displays a default message.

PICTUREBAR="Yes|No"
: Yes displays images for the Insert, Delete, and Sort buttons, while No displays text buttons. Optional. The default is No.

INSERTBUTTON="*text*"
: The text to use on the insert button. Optional. The default is "Insert".

DELETEBUTTON="*text*"
: The text to use on the delete button. Optional. The default is "Delete".

SORTASCENDINGBUTTON="*text*"
: The text to use on the ascending sort button. Optional. The default is "A → Z".

SORTDESCENDINGBUTTON="*text*"
: The text to use on the descending sort button. Optional. The default is "Z → A".

### *Returned Variables*

Depending on the value of SELECTMODE, the CFGRID tag returns several variables on submission. For Browse, no variables are returned. When SELECTMODE is Edit, three one-dimensional arrays are returned containing information about the changes to the data:

form.*gridname*.*columnname*[*RowIndex*]
: The new value of an edited grid cell

form.*gridname*.original.*columnname*[*RowIndex*]
: The original value of the edited grid cell

form.*gridname*.RowStatus.Action[*RowIndex*]
: The type of edit made to the grid cell: I for insert, U for update, and D for delete

When SELECTMODE is Single, there is one variable:

form.*gridname*.*selectedname*
: The value of the selected cell from the grid

When SELECTMODE is Column, grid data is returned as a comma-delimited list of values for the selected column.

When SELECTMODE is Row, there is one variable:

form.*gridname*.*columnname*
: The column data for the selected row

## CFGRIDCOLUMN

```
<CFGRID>
  [<CFGRIDCOLUMN>]
  [<CFGRIDROW>]
  ...
</CFGRID>
```

Specifies individual column data and formatting information within a CFGRID. Values specified for a CFGRIDCOLUMN override any attributes set in the CFGRID tag.

### *Attributes*

NAME="*column_name*"
: A name for the grid column. If the grid column is populated by a query, NAME must be the name of an available query column. Required.

HEADER="*header*"
: The text to use for the column's header. Optional. If no value for HEADER is specified, ColdFusion uses the same value as NAME.

WIDTH="*width_in_pixels*"
: The width of the column in pixels. Optional. The default column width is determined by the longest column value.

FONT="*font_name*"
: The font name for the data in the column. Optional.

FONTSIZE="*integer*"
: The font size for the data in the column. Optional.

ITALIC="Yes|No"
: Whether or not to display the column data in italic. Optional. The default is No.

BOLD="Yes|No"
: Whether or not to display the column data in bold. Optional. The default is No.

TEXTCOLOR="*color*|*expression*"
: The text color for all data in the grid. Colors may be specified by name (Black, Blue, Cyan, Darkgray, Gray, Lightgray, Magenta, Orange, Pink, Red, White, Yellow) or hex code in the form TEXTCOLOR="##FFFFCC". The double pound signs are necessary to keep ColdFusion from throwing a syntax error, or you may omit the pound signs altogether. By using the appropriate hex code, you may specify colors that can't be specified by name. Optional. The default is Black. New as of ColdFusion 5.0.

  You can dynamically specify the text color for a cell based on its value or that of another column in the same row using a special expression as the value of TEXTCOLOR. The expression uses the following format:

```
( CX|Cn GT|LT|EQ string ? color_true : color_false )
```

  CX represents the current column, while C*n* specifies a specific column where *n* is the index position of the column (only displayed columns are available). The operator can be GT, LT, or EQ for both string and numeric comparisons. The ? separates the expression from the values you wish to return. *color_true* is the color to return in the event the expression evaluates True, while *color_false* is the color to return if the expression evaluates False. Colors are specified using a color name or hex code (without the pound signs). The two return values are separated with a colon. Note that whitespace is ignored within the expression except for within *string*.

For example, to specify that text in a certain column of data be blue if the value of the data is greater than 21 or black if it isn't, you can use the following code:

```
TEXTCOLOR="(CX GT 21 ? blue : black)"
```

Likewise, if the first column of data in your grid contains department names, and you want to highlight the names of employees (in gray) in another column who are part of the marketing department, you can code it like this:

```
TEXTCOLOR="(C1 EQ Marketing ? C0C0C0 : 000000)"
```

BGCOLOR="*color*|*expression*"
A background color for all the cells in the column or an expression that returns a color based on its evaluation. For color choices, see the TEXTCOLOR attribute. BGCOLOR also supports the expression syntax listed for TEXTCOLOR. Optional. The default is White. New as of ColdFusion 5.0.

HREF="*URL*"
A URL to associate with the grid item. The URL may be relative or absolute. Optional.

HREFKEY="*column_name*"
The name of a query column to use as the Key when a query is used to populate the grid. Optional.

TARGET="*URL_target*"
The name of a frame or window that the template specified in the HREF attribute should be opened in. Optional.

SELECT="Yes|No"
Whether or not to allow users to select column data to be edited. SELECT is ignored when the SELECTMODE attribute of the CFGRID tag is set to Row or Browse. Optional. The default is Yes.

DISPLAY="Yes|No"
Whether or not to display the column in the grid. Optional. The default is Yes.

TYPE="*type*"
The type of column data to display. Valid entries are Image, Numeric, String_NoCase, and Boolean. Optional.

Image
Specifies an image corresponding to the column value to display. You may specify a path to your own image or use one of the images supplied with ColdFusion by referencing the image name. Valid options are CD, Computer, Document, Element, Folder, Floppy, Fixed, and Remote. If the image is larger than the cell it is being displayed in, the image is automatically cropped to fit within the cell.

Numeric
Allows data in the grid to be sorted by the user as numeric data rather than as text.

String_NoCase
Allows data in the grid to be sorted by the user as case-insensitive text rather than the case-sensitive default.

`Boolean`
: Places a checkbox in the grid column. Useful in situations where you want to represent Boolean data in a grid column. If the grid column containing the checkbox is editable, the checkbox may be checked and unchecked; otherwise it is read-only. New as of ColdFusion 5.0.

`VALUES="`*`list`*`|`*`range`*`|Off"`
: Creates a drop-down box of values for each cell in the grid column. You may specify a delimited list of values, a range of numeric values, or `Off`. For a delimited list of values, the default delimiter is the comma. To specify a range of numeric values, use the format *n-m* where *n* is the minimum value in the range, and *m* is the maximum value. Optional. The default is `Off`. New as of ColdFusion 5.0.

`VALUESDISPLAY="`*`list`*`|`*`range`*`|Off"`
: Used in conjunction with the `VALUES` attribute. `VALUESDISPLAY` allows you to provide a delimited list or range of values to display in lieu of the values in the `VALUES` attribute. This works like the HTML `SELECT` control in that it allows you to display one set of values in the drop-down box while associating them with different values behind the scenes. Optional. The default is `Off`. New as of ColdFusion 5.0.

`VALUESDELIMITER="`*`delimiter`*`"`
: An optional delimiter that separates items in the `VALUES` and `VALUESDISPLAY` attributes. Optional. The default is the comma (`,`). New as of ColdFusion 5.0.

`HEADERFONT="`*`font_name`*`"`
: The font to use for the column headers. Optional.

`HEADERFONTSIZE="`*`integer`*`"`
: The font size to use for the column headers. Optional.

`HEADERITALIC="Yes|No"`
: Whether or not to display the column header text in italic. Optional. The default is `No`.

`HEADERBOLD="Yes|No"`
: Whether or not to display the column header text in bold. Optional. The default is `No`.

`HEADERTEXTCOLOR="`*`color`*`"`
: Specifies the text color for the column header. For color choices, see the `TEXTCOLOR` attribute. The default is `Black`.

`DATAALIGN="`*`alignment`*`"`
: Alignment for the column data. Valid entries are: `Left`, `Right`, and `Center`. Optional. The default is `Left`.

`HEADERALIGN="`*`alignment`*`"`
: Alignment for the column headers. Valid entries are: `Left`, `Right`, and `Center`. Optional. The default is `Left`.

`NUMBERFORMAT="`*`format`*`"`
: A mask to use for formatting numeric column data. For valid options, see the `NumberFormat` function in the Function Reference. Optional.

## CFGRIDROW

```
<CFGRID>
   [<CFGRIDCOLUMN>]
   [<CFGRIDROW>]
   ...
</CFGRID>
```

Populates a `CFGRID` row with data.

### *Attribute*

`DATA="col1, col2, ... coln">`
: A comma-delimited list of column values. Required.

## CFGRIDUPDATE

```
<CFGRIDUPDATE>
```

Updates records in a database using values passed from a `CFGRID` control.

### *Attributes*

`GRID="grid_name"`
: Name of the grid control containing the data to be updated. Required.

`DATASOURCE="data_source_name"`
: The name of the data source to connect to when performing the update. Required.

`DBTYPE="database_type"`
: The type of database driver to use. Optional. Possible choices are:

`ODBC` *(the default)*
: Connect to the data source using an ODBC driver.

`OLEDB`
: Make the connection using an OLEDB driver.

`Oracle73`
: Connect using the Oracle 7.3 native driver. This requires the 7.3.4.0.0 or later client libraries be installed on the ColdFusion server.

`Oracle80`
: Connect using the Oracle 8 native driver. This requires the 8.0 or later client libraries be installed on the ColdFusion server.

`Sybase11`
: Connect using the Sybase 11 native driver. This requires the 11.1.1 or later client libraries be installed on the ColdFusion server.

`DB2`
: Connect using the DB2 5.2 native driver.

`Informix73`
: Connect using the Informix 7.3 native driver. This requires the Informix SDK 2.5 or later or Informix-Connect 2.5 (or later) for Windows.

`Query`
: Specifies the query should use an already existing query as the data source. If this option is used, you don't need to specify a value for `DATASOURCE`. New as of ColdFusion 5.0.

`Dynamic`
: Allows ColdFusion to make an ODBC connection to a data source without having to have the data source registered in the ColdFusion Administrator. When making a dynamic connection, all information normally provided in the ColdFusion Administrator for the connection must be specified in the `CONNECTSTRING` attribute. New as of ColdFusion 5.0.

`DBSERVER="`*`database_server`*`"`
The name of the database server to connect to when using native drivers. Specifying a `DBSERVER` overrides any value set for `DATASOURCE`. Optional.

`DBNAME="`*`database_name`*`"`
The database name. For the Sybase System 11 native driver and `SQLOLEDB` provider only. Optional. Overrides any value set for `DATASOURCE`.

`TABLENAME="`*`table_name`*`"`
The name of the table to insert the data into. Required. Note that Oracle database drivers require the table name to be in all uppercase. In addition, Sybase database drivers use a case-sensitive table name.

`USERNAME="`*`username`*`"`
Username to pass to the data source if one is required. Optional. If a username is specified, it overrides the value set in the ColdFusion Administrator.

`PASSWORD="`*`password`*`"`
Password associated with `USERNAME`. Optional. If a password is specified, it overrides the value set in the ColdFusion Administrator.

`TABLEOWNER="`*`table_owner`*`"`
The name of the table owner for databases that support this feature (e.g., Oracle, SQL Server, and SQL Anywhere). Optional.

`TABLEQUALIFIER="`*`qualifier`*`"`
The table qualifier for databases that support the feature (e.g., Oracle and SQL Server). Optional.

`PROVIDER="`*`COM_provider`*`"`
COM provider for OLE DB connections. Optional.

`PROVIDERDSN=`*`data_source`*`"`
COM provider's data-source name for OLE DB. Optional.

`CONNECTSTRING="`*`connection_string`*`"`
Passes additional connection information to an ODBC data source that can't be passed via the ColdFusion Administrator. `CONNECTSTRING` can also override connection information set for a data source already registered in the ColdFusion Administrator. When making a dynamic data source connection (when `DBTYPE` is `Dynamic`), `CONNECTSTRING` specifies all the information required to connect to the data source. For specific connection-string options, you should consult the documentation for your particular database. New as of ColdFusion 5.0.

KEYONLY=Yes|No"
: If Yes, the WHERE clause of the SQL update contains only the key values. If No, the WHERE clause contains the original values of any changed grid cells as well as the key values. Optional. The default is Yes.

---

## CFHEADER

<CFHEADER>

Generates a custom HTTP header that contains either a custom name/value pair or an HTTP status code and optional text message. Only one name/value pair or status code can be specified per CFHEADER tag. Name/value attributes can't be mixed with status code attributes within the same CFHEADER tag. Multiple CFHEADER tags can be used to set multiple header values as long as they are declared separately.

### *Attributes*

NAME="*header_name*"
: The name of the header element. Required when using the CFHEADER tag to pass a name/value pair.

VALUE="*header_value*"
: The value of the header element. Required when using the CFHEADER tag to pass a name/value pair.

STATUSCODE="*status_code*"
: The HTTP status code to pass in the HTTP header. Required when using the CFHEADER tag to pass status code information.

STATUSTEXT="*status_text*"
: A text message to accompany an HTTP status code. The STATUSTEXT attribute can be used only in conjunction with the STATUSCODE attribute. Optional.

---

## CFHTMLHEAD

<CFHTMLHEAD>

Writes output within the HEAD section of a page.

### *Attribute*

TEXT="*text*"
: The text to add inside of the HTML <HEAD>...</HEAD> tags. Required.

---

## CFHTTP

```
<CFHTTP>
  [<CFHTTPPARAM>]
  ...
</CFHTTP>
```

Performs HTTP and HTTPS GET and POST operations on remote web servers.

### *Attributes*

METHOD="GET|POST"

Specifies whether CFHTTP uses the HTTP GET or POST method. Required.

URL="*URL*"

The full URL of the remote web page to GET or POST to. If you are trying to resolve a URL that doesn't end in a filename (such as *http://www.myserver.com*), and you set the RESOLVEURL attribute to Yes, you need to supply a trailing forward slash (*http://www.myserver.com/*) for this attribute in order for certain URLs (such as those in IMG tags) to resolve properly. Additionally, a port number may be appended to the URL. (*http://www.myserver.com:8080/*). If a port number is appended to the URL, it overrides any value set with the PORT attribute. Required.

RESOLVEURL="Yes|No"

Yes causes any partial or relative URLs embedded in the retrieved document to be fully resolved, so that all links in the document remain valid. Optional. The default is No.

REDIRECT="Yes|No"

Whether or not to allow a CFHTTP request to be automatically redirected. If set to No, the CFHTTP request fails upon encountering a redirect. If the THROWONERROR attribute is set to Yes, an error code and message are written to the CFHTTP.Status_Code return variable. You can see where a request would have been redirected by referencing the LOCATION key in the CFHTTP.ResponseHeader structure. The CFHTTP tag can follow up to five redirections per request. If the limit is exceeded, ColdFusion treats the next redirect as if the REDIRECT attribute is set to No. Optional. The default is Yes.

PORT="*port_number*"

Port number on the remote server where the file being retrieved resides. If used in conjunction with the RESOLVEURL attribute, the port number is automatically appended to all resolved URLs. The PORT attribute is ignored if a port is specified in the URL attribute. Optional. The default is 80.

USERNAME="*username*"

A username when one is required by the remote server. Optional.

PASSWORD="*password*"

A password when one is required by the remote server. Optional.

NAME="*query_name*"

Name of the query to be returned if one is created from a retrieved file. Optional.

COLUMNS="*query_columns*"

A comma-delimited list of column names if they are different from the column names listed in the first row of data from the retrieved file.

PATH="*path*"

The path to a directory where the retrieved file should be saved. Optional.

FILE="*filename*"

The filename to use when saving the retrieved file. Required when METHOD="POST" if PATH is specified. Defaults to the filename in the URL when METHOD="GET".

DELIMITER="*delimiter*"

The delimiter to use when using CFHTTP to create a query. Valid entries are a comma (,) or a tab. Required if creating a query. The default delimiter is a comma.

TEXTQUALIFIER="*character*"
: The character used to mark the beginning and end of a column. Optional.

PROXYSERVER="*proxy_server*"
: The hostname or IP address of a proxy server which CFHTTP must pass through. Optional.

PROXYPORT="*port_number*"
: A port number on the proxy server where the object is being retrieved from. Used in conjunction with the RESOLVEURL attribute, PROXYPORT allows you to preserve links within a template that resolve to a port other than 80. Optional. The default is 80.

TIMEOUT="*seconds*"
: A timeout in seconds for the CFHTTP operation. If a URL timeout parameter is used in conjunction with the template employing the CFHTTP tag, and the TIMEOUT attribute of the CFHTTP tag is used, ColdFusion uses the lesser of the two values. If, however, no URL timeout value is passed, the TIMEOUT attribute isn't used, and no default timeout value is set in the ColdFusion Administrator, ColdFusion will wait indefinitely for the CFHTTP tag to process. This can have serious performance consequences, as each instance of the CFHTTP tag being processed requires a thread of its own. Depending on your server and ColdFusion configuration, the potential to hang the server exists if the CFHTTP tag utilizes all available threads on the system. Optional.

USERAGENT="*user_agent*"
: The user agent to pass in the HTTP request header when CFHTTP makes a request to a remote web server. The default user agent is "ColdFusion". Optional.

THROWONERROR="Yes|No"
: Whether or not to throw an exception that can be caught using a CFTRY/CFCATCH block if an error occurs. Optional. The default is No.

### *Returned Variables*

The following variables are returned when the CFHTTP tag successfully completes a GET or POST operation:

CFHTTP.FileContent
: The contents of the retrieved file. Doesn't apply if a PATH is specified when METHOD is POST.

CFHTTP.MimeType
: The media type of the downloaded file when METHOD is GET.

CFHTTP.Header
: A string that contains the complete HTTP header.

CFHTTP.ResponseHeader["*http_header_key*"]
: A ColdFusion structure that contains the names and values from the HTTP response header. If a particular key appears only once in the header, it is stored as a simple value within the structure. If a key appears more than once, it is stored as an array within the structure.

If the THROWONERROR attribute is set to Yes, ColdFusion returns a variable that contains status information about the CFHTTP operation:

CFHTTP.Status_Code
: Returns the HTTP status code and associated message relating to the status of the CFHTTP operation.

## CFHTTPPARAM

```
<CFHTTP>
  [<CFHTTPPARAM>]
  ...
</CFHTTP>
```

Used in conjunction with the CFHTTP tag to post CGI, cookie, file, form-field, and URL variables to remote web servers.

### *Attributes*

NAME="*name*"
: The name of the parameter to pass. Required

TYPE="*type*"
: The parameter type to pass. Valid entries are CGI, Cookie, File, Formfield, and URL. Required.

VALUE="*value*"
: The value of the CGI, Cookie, Formfield, or URL being passed. Required for all types except File.

FILE="*filename*"
: The name (including path) of the file to post. Required when TYPE is File.

## CFIF

```
<CFIF expression>
  HTML and CFML
<CFELSEIF expression>
  HTML and CFML
<CFELSE>
  HTML and CFML
</CFIF>
```

Performs if-then-else processing of expressions. CFIF/CFELSEIF/CFELSE statements can be nested, and multiple CFELSEIF statements may be used within a single CFIF block. CFIF statements can contain more than one expression to evaluate, as in:

```
<CFIF IsDefined('MyVar') AND MyVar IS "a">
```

Compound CFIF statements that contain multiple expressions separated by operators, such as AND and OR, are processed using short-circuit Boolean evaluation. This means that ColdFusion stops processing the CFIF statement once an expression evaluates to TRUE. Consider using CFSWITCH when you have many cases, as it is generally faster than CFIF.

## CFIMPERSONATE

New as of ColdFusion 4.5

```
<CFIMPERSONATE> ... </CFIMPERSONATE>
```

Allows you to impersonate a user within a security context previously set up within the ColdFusion Administrator.

### Attributes

SECURITYCONTEXT="*security_context*"
: The name of the security context to authenticate the user within. Required. Security contexts are defined in the ColdFusion Administrator.

USERNAME="*username*"
: The name of the user you want to impersonate for authentication. Required.

PASSWORD="*password*"
: The password of the user you want to impersonate. Required.

TYPE="CF|OS"
: The type of impersonation to use. `CF` specifies impersonation at the application level; `OS` specifies impersonation at the operating system, where the user specified is a valid user on the system. `OS` is available only with the Windows NT version of ColdFusion. The operating system user being impersonated must be assigned the user right to "Logon as a Batch Job". While `OS` impersonation processes faster than `CF` impersonation, it is limited in the types of resources the operating system can grant or deny access to. Required.

## CFINCLUDE

```
<CFINCLUDE>
```

Embeds a reference to another template within the current ColdFusion template.

### Attributes

TEMPLATE="*template_name*"
: Path to the template to be included. The path must be relative to the current directory or mapped in the ColdFusion Administrator. Required.

## CFINDEX

```
<CFINDEX>
```

Creates an index to use with ColdFusion's embedded Verity search engine.

### Attributes

ACTION="*action*"
: Specifies the action for the `CFINDEX` tag to take. Optional. The default value is `Update`, which updates the index of the specified collection and adds the key if it doesn't already exist. `Delete` deletes the key from the specified collection, `Purge` purges the specified collection of data and leaves it ready to be repopulated with new data, and

Refresh clears the specified collection of all data and then repopulates it with new data. Optimize optimizes the specified collection, but this action has been superseded by the CFCOLLECTION tag.

COLLECTION="*collection_name*"
: The name of the Verity collection to perform the action on. If the collection being indexed is external, you must specify the full path to the collection. Required.

TYPE="*type*"
: The type of index to create. Optional. Custom indexes the contents of a ColdFusion query, File indexes a specific file, and Path indexes all files in the specified PATH with extensions specified in EXTENSIONS.

TITLE="*title*"
: The column name containing the title for each individual record being indexed. Required when TYPE is Custom.

KEY="*ID*"
: A unique identifier for each record in the index. Optional. An entry for KEY should specify one of the following: the document filename when TYPE is File, the full path when TYPE is Path, or a unique identifier such as the table's primary key column when TYPE is Custom.

BODY="*body*"
: The actual text to index or a comma-delimited list of query column names containing text to index. Required when TYPE is Custom; Ignored otherwise.

CUSTOM1="*custom_value*"
: Custom field that can store additional data for the collection. Optional.

CUSTOM2="*custom_value*"
: Custom field that can store additional data for the collection. Optional.

URLPATH="*URL*"
: The base URL path to be used when TYPE is File or Directory. The value specified in URLPATH is automatically prepended to the URL variable returned by a CFSEARCH operation. Optional.

EXTENSIONS="*file_extensions*"
: A comma-delimited list of file extensions to use when TYPE is set to Path. The default is "HTM, HTML, CFM, CFML, DBM, DBML". An asterisk (*) may be used as a wildcard such that EXTENSIONS="*." returns all files with no extensions. Optional.

QUERY="*query_name*"
: The name of the query object containing the data being indexed. Optional.

RECURSE="Yes|No"
: Whether or not the directories below the path specified in KEY should be included in the indexing process. Optional when TYPE is Path; ignored otherwise.

EXTERNAL="Yes|No"
: Whether or not the Verity collection specified in COLLECTION was created with a version of Verity other than the one bundled with ColdFusion. Optional. The default is No.

LANGUAGE="*language*"
: The language to be used when indexing the collection. To specify a language other than U.S. English (the default), you must purchase the ColdFusion International Search Pack from Allaire. Optional.

## CFINPUT

Enhanced in ColdFusion 5.0

<CFINPUT>

Creates text and password input controls, as well as checkboxes and radio buttons, within a CFFORM.

### Attributes

NAME="*name*"
: The form-field name for the input control. Required.

TYPE="*type*"
: Type of input control to create. Valid entries are Checkbox, Password, Radio, and Text. Optional. The default value is Text.

VALUE="*initial_value*"
: The initial value for the input control. Optional.

SIZE="*integer*"
: The size of the input control. Optional. Ignored when ACTION is Checkbox or Radio.

MAXLENGTH="*integer*"
: The maximum number of characters to accept for a Password or Text input control. Optional.

CHECKED="Yes|No"
: Whether or not a checkbox or radio button input control should be checked. Optional. The default is No.

REQUIRED="Yes|No"
: Whether or not the input control requires a value before being submitted. Optional. The default is No.

RANGE="*min_value, max_value*"
: A range of acceptable numeric values for the form-field. Optional.

VALIDATE="*data_type*"
: Validates the contents of the form-field before it is submitted, using one of the following criteria:

  CreditCard
  : Validates the form-field data using the mod10 algorithm. A credit-card number can be entered as a single value or with dashes or spaces. ColdFusion automatically strips dashes and spaces before validating.

  Date
  : Requires the form-field value to be in the U.S. date format, *mm/dd/yyyy*.

  EuroDate
  : Requires the form-field value to be in the European date format, *dd/mm/yyyy*.

  Float
  : Requires the form-field value to be a floating-point number.

  Integer
  : Requires the form-field value to be an integer.

`Social_Security_Number`
: Requires the form-field value to be a U.S. social-security number in the format *xxx-xx-xxxx* or *xxx xx xxxx*.

`Telephone`
: Requires the form-field value to be a U.S. telephone number formatted either *xxx-xxx-xxxx* or *xxx xxx xxxx*. The area code and exchange are required to begin with a number in the range of 1–9.

`Time`
: Requires that the form-field value be entered as a valid time using the format *hh:mm:ss*.

`ZipCode`
: Requires that the form-field value be entered as either a five- or nine-digit U.S. ZIP code number using the format *xxxxx*, *xxxxx-xxxx*, or *xxxxx xxxx*.

`Regular_Expression`
: Validates the form-field data against a JavaScript regular expression specified in the `PATTERN` attribute.

`PATTERN="`*`javascript_regular_expression`*`"`
: JavaScript regular expression that matches form input when `VALIDATE` is `Regular_Expression`. `PATTERN` may contain ColdFusion variables and expressions as they are evaluated prior to the execution of the regular expression. Optional. New as of ColdFusion 5.0.

`ONVALIDATE="`*`javascript_function`*`"`
: A JavaScript validation function that should be executed before the form is submitted. Specifying a value for `ONVALIDATE` overrides any values set in the `VALIDATE` attribute. Optional.

`MESSAGE="`*`validation_message`*`"`
: Text to appear if validation fails. Optional.

`ONERROR="`*`function_name`*`"`
: The name of a JavaScript function that should be executed if validation fails for any reason. Optional.

`PASSTHROUGH="`*`HTML_attribute`*`"`
: Any additional HTML attributes you need to pass that aren't directly supported by the `CFINPUT` tag. Optional.

---

## CFINSERT

`<CFINSERT>`

Inserts new records into a data source. The `CFINSERT` tag provides a way to insert data into a data source without having to wrap the SQL in a `CFQUERY`.

### *Attributes*

`DATASOURCE="`*`datasource_name`*`"`
: The name of the data source to connect to when performing the insert. Required.

DBTYPE="*database_type*"

The type of database driver to use. Optional. Possible choices are:

ODBC *(the default)*

Connect to the data source using an ODBC driver.

OLEDB

Connect using an OLEDB driver.

Oracle73

Connect using the Oracle 7.3 native driver. This requires the 7.3.4.0.0 or later client libraries be installed on the ColdFusion server.

Oracle80

Connect using the Oracle 8 native driver. This requires the 8.0 or later client libraries be installed on the ColdFusion server.

Sybase11

Connect using the Sybase 11 native driver. This requires the 11.1.1 or later client libraries be installed on the ColdFusion server.

DB2

Connect using the DB2 5.2 native driver.

Informix73

Connect using the Informix 7.3 native driver. This requires the Informix SDK 2.5 or later or Informix-Connect 2.5 (or later) for Windows.

Query

Specifies the query should use an already existing query as the data source. If this option is used, you don't need to specify a value for DATASOURCE. New as of ColdFusion 5.0.

Dynamic

Allows ColdFusion to make an ODBC connection to a data source without having to have the data source registered in the ColdFusion Administrator. When making a dynamic connection, all information normally provided in the ColdFusion Administrator for the connection must be specified in the CONNECTSTRING attribute. New as of ColdFusion 5.0.

DBSERVER="*database_server*"

The name of the database server to connect to when using native drivers. Specifying a DBSERVER overrides any value set for DATASOURCE. Optional.

DBNAME="*database_name*"

The database name. For the Sybase System 11 native driver and SQLOLEDB provider only. Optional. Overrides any value set for DATASOURCE.

TABLENAME="*table_name*"

The name of the table to insert the data into. Required. Note that Oracle database drivers require the table name to be in all uppercase. In addition, Sybase database drivers use a case-sensitive table name.

TABLEOWNER="*table_owner*"

The name of the table owner for databases that support this feature (e.g., Oracle, SQL Server, and SQL Anywhere). Optional.

TABLEQUALIFIER="*table_qualifier*"

The table qualifier for databases that support the feature (e.g., Oracle and SQL Server). Optional.

`USERNAME="`*`username`*`"`
Username to pass to the data source if one is required. Optional. If a username is specified, it overrides the value set in the ColdFusion Administrator.

`PASSWORD="`*`password`*`"`
Password associated with `USERNAME`. Optional. If a password is specified, it overrides the value set in the ColdFusion Administrator.

`PROVIDER="`*`COM_provider`*`"`
COM provider for OLE DB connections. Optional.

`PROVIDERDSN="`*`provider_datasource`*`"`
COM provider's data source name for OLE DB. Optional.

`CONNECTSTRING="`*`connection_string`*`"`
Passes additional connection information to an ODBC data source that can't be passed via the ColdFusion Administrator. `CONNECTSTRING` can also be used to override connection information set for a data source already registered in the ColdFusion Administrator. When making a dynamic data source connection (when `DBTYPE` is `Dynamic`), `CONNECTSTRING` specifies all the information required to connect to the data source. For specific connection string options, you should consult the documentation for your particular database. New as of ColdFusion 5.0.

`FORMFIELDS="`*`formfield1, formfield2, ...`*`"`
A comma-delimited list of form fields to insert. Optional. If no form fields are supplied, ColdFusion uses all the form fields passed from the form.

---

## CFINTERNALDEBUG

`<CFINTERNALDEBUG>`

This undocumented tag is used by the product development group at Allaire for internal debugging purposes. The tag can also compile ColdFusion templates without executing them. The CFML Syntax Checker that comes with ColdFusion 4.x uses this tag.

### *Attributes*

`ACTION="`*`action`*`"`
Specifies the action for the tag to take. Optional. The default action is `Break`, which forces a break-point exception in the execution of a template. `Leak` causes the ColdFusion server to leak memory. The amount of memory to be leaked is specified in the `LEAKSIZE` attribute. These two actions are used by the Allaire product development group for internal debugging. `PCode` compiles the ColdFusion template specified in `TEMPLATEPATH` into p-code without executing it.

`OUTVAR="`*`variable`*`"`
The name of the variable that holds any error messages generated when compiling a template. If no errors are generated, an empty string is saved to the variable. Required when `ACTION` is `PCode`.

`TEMPLATEPATH="`*`path`*`"`
Full path including filename of the ColdFusion template you want to compile. Required when `ACTION` is `PCode`.

`LEAKSIZE="`*`integer`*`"`
The amount of memory to leak. Must be a value greater than 1. Required when `ACTION` is `Leak`.

## CFLDAP

<CFLDAP>

Provides ColdFusion with an interface to Lightweight Directory Access Protocol (LDAP) servers.

### *Attributes*

SERVER="*ldap_server*"
: The server name or IP address of the LDAP server you want to connect to. Required.

PORT="*port_number*"
: The port that the LDAP server listens for requests on. Optional. The default LDAP port is 389.

USERNAME="*username*"
: Username required for the LDAP connection. Optional. If no username is specified, the LDAP connection is anonymous.

PASSWORD="*password*"
: Password to accompany USERNAME. Optional.

ACTION="*action*"
: Specifies the LDAP action to perform. Optional. The default value is Query, which returns entry information from the LDAP server, and requires the ATTRIBUTES, NAME, and START attributes. Add adds entries to the LDAP server and requires the ATTRIBUTES attribute. Delete deletes entries from the LDAP server and requires the DN attribute. Modify modifies entries on the LDAP server except for the distinguished name and requires the ATTRIBUTES and DN attributes. ModifyDN modifies distinguished name entries on the LDAP server and requires the ATTRIBUTES and DN attributes.

NAME="*query_name*"
: The name to assign to the LDAP query. Required when ACTION is Query.

TIMEOUT="*seconds*"
: The maximum amount of time in seconds ColdFusion should wait when processing an LDAP action. Optional. The default is 60.

MAXROWS="*integer*"
: The maximum number of results to be returned for an LDAP query. Optional.

START="*distinguished_name*"
: The distinguished name to use as the start of a search. Required when ACTION is Query.

SCOPE="*scope*"
: The scope of the search in relation to the value specified in START. Optional when ACTION is Query. The default value is OneLevel, which searches one level below the entry specified in the START attribute. Base searches just the entry specified in START, and Subtree searches the entry specified in START and all the entries below it.

ATTRIBUTES="*attribute1, attribute2, ...*"
: When ACTION is Query, specifies a comma-delimited list of attributes to be returned by the query. Specifying a wildcard (*) returns all attributes associated with a query. When ACTION is Add, specifies the list of update columns to be used when adding an

entry. When ACTION is Modify, specifies the list of update columns to be used when modifying an entry. When ACTION is ModifyDN, specifies a comma-delimited list of attributes to be passed to the LDAP server without any syntax checking. In all cases, multiple attributes should be separated with a semicolon (;). Required for all these actions.

DELIMITER="*delimiter*"
: The delimiter to use when separating more than one name/value attribute pair when multiple attributes are specified in ATTRIBUTES. DELIMITER can be used when the ACTION attribute is set to Query, Add, or Modify. Optional. The default is the semicolon (;).

SEPARATOR="*separator*"
: The delimiter to use when separating attribute values in multivalue attributes. The SEPARATOR is used when the ACTION attribute is set to Query, Add, and Modify, as well as for outputting multivalue attributes. Optional. The default is the comma (,).

FILTER="*filter*"
: The search criteria to use when ACTION is set to Query. FILTER entries are referenced as (*attribute operator value*) as in (c=US). Optional. The default is (objectclass=*). ColdFusion supports the following operators within the FILTER attribute: =, ~= (approximately equals), <=, >=, * (wildcard), & (AND), | (OR), and ! (NOT).

FILTERFILE="*filename, stanza*"
: The name of a valid LDAP filter file and the stanza tag within that filter file that contains an LDAP filter string. The FILTERFILE attribute accepts either the full path to the filter file or simply the filename provided it resides in the default ColdFusion LDAP directory (*c:\cfusion\ldap*).

MODIFYTYPE="Add|Replace|Delete"
: Whether to add, replace, or delete an attribute or set of attributes within a multivalue list of attributes. Optional. The default is Replace.

REBIND="Yes|No"
: Whether or not to attempt to rebind the referral callback and reissue the query using the original credentials. If No, referrals bindings are anonymous. Optional. The default is No.

REFERRAL="*number*"
: The maximum number of hops allowed in a referral. Any positive integer may be used. If REFERRAL is set to 0, no data is returned for entries that are referrals. Optional.

SECURE="*cf_security_type_ID*[, *additional_fields*]"
: The type of security to use when authenticating with the LDAP server. Possible options are CFSSL_BASIC and CFSSL_CLIENT_AUTH. Both options require additional parameters as follows:

CFSSL_BASIC
: Uses V2 SSL to provide encryption and server authentication. The USERNAME and PASSWORD attributes are required when using CFSSL_BASIC security. The correct syntax for using CFSSL_BASIC is:

SECURE="CFSSL_BASIC, *certificate_database*"
: *certificate_database* is the name of the certificate database file to use. The filename can be either the full path to the database file or simply the

filename provided it resides in the default ColdFusion LDAP directory (*c:\cfusion\ldap*).

CFSSL_CLIENT_AUTH

Uses V3 SSL to provide encryption, server authentication, and certificate-based client authentication. No USERNAME and PASSWORD attributes are required as authentication is handled via client certificates. The correct syntax for using CFSSL_CLIENT_AUTH is:

SECURE="CFSSL_CLIENT_AUTH, *certificate_database*, *certificate_name*, *key_database*, *key_password*"

*certificate_database* is the name of the certificate database file to use. *certificate_name* specifies the name of the client certificate to use. *key_database* specifies the keyword database file that holds the public/private key pair. *key_password* is the password used by the keyword database. The filenames can be either the full path to the database file or simply the filenames themselves provided they resides in the default ColdFusion LDAP directory (*c:\cfusion\ldap*).

SORT="*attributes*"

The attribute or comma-delimited list of attributes to use when sorting query results. Optional.

SORTCONTROL="Nocase+|asc|desc"

Specifies how results should be sorted. If you wish to perform a case-insensitive sort, SORTCONTROL should be set to Nocase. Additionally, sort order may be specified as ASC (ascending, the default) or DESC (descending). Case sensitivity and sort order may be combined as in SORTCONTROL="Nocase, ASC". Optional. sorting is case-sensitive by default.

DN="*distinguished_name*"

The distinguished name to use for updates to the LDAP server. Required when ACTION is Add, Delete, Modify, or ModifyDN.

STARTROW="*row_number*"

The row to begin outputting LDAP entries from. Optional.

### *Returned Variables*

If the ACTION attribute is set to Query, the CFLDAP tag returns the following variables:

*queryname*.ColumnList

Comma-delimited list of the query column names from the database

*queryname*.CurrentRow

The current row of the query that is being processed by CFOUTPUT

*queryname*.RecordCount

The total number of records returned by the query

## CFLOCATION

<CFLOCATION>

Redirects the user's browser to a new location. Due to the way ColdFusion assembles dynamic pages, you shouldn't attempt to use the CFLOCATION tag within a template after a cookie variable has been set. Setting a cookie variable and using CFLOCATION afterward results in the cookie not being set. If you need to redirect to a different template after setting a cookie, consider using the `CFHEADER` tag instead as in:

```
<CFCOOKIE NAME="MyCookie" VALUE="Hey, look at me!">
<CFHEADER NAME="Refresh" VALUE="0; URL=http://www.example.com/mytemplate.cfm">
```

### *Attributes*

`URL="`*`URL`*`"`
: The URL to redirect the user's browser to. Required.

`ADDTOKEN="Yes|No"`
: Whether or not to append client variable information to the end of the URL specified in the `URL` attribute. In order to use the `ADDTOKEN` attribute, `CLIENTMANAGEMENT` must be turned on in the *Application.cfm* file. Optional. The default is `Yes`.

## CFLOCK

```
<CFLOCK>
CFML and HTML to be locked
</CFLOCK>
```

Provides single-threaded access to code within the `<CFLOCK>`/`</CFLOCK>` tags. `CFLOCK` should be used when reading and writing persistent variables (application, session, and server variables) within your ColdFusion applications, to eliminate the potential for data corruption caused by colliding read/writes. `CFLOCK` can also lock access to non thread-safe CFX tags and to file-manipulation operations that can result in multiple threads attempting to access an already open file.

As of ColdFusion 4.5, additional locking options are available via the ColdFusion Administrator under the Server section. These options allow you to determine how ColdFusion treats locking for all applications across the server. Performance can be significantly affected depending on the options you choose. The following choices are available:

*Single Threaded Sessions (Session Scope)*
: ColdFusion single-threads access to each session by session ID for the duration of a request. While this eliminates all potential variable corruption and conflict within a session, it can have a dramatic effect on performance.

*No Automatic Checking or Locking (Session, Application, and Server Scope)*
: ColdFusion performs no automatic checking or locking of persistent variables. All variables must be locked explicitly using the `CFLOCK` tag. No exceptions are thrown when nonlocked variables are encountered. This method is how ColdFusion handled locking prior to Version 4.5. This option offers the best overall performance.

*Full Checking (Session, Application, and Server Scope)*
: ColdFusion checks to make sure locks are placed around all reads/writes of the variable type specified. If an unlocked variable is encountered, an exception is thrown. This option is useful in debug mode for locating unlocked persistent variables and should be used with care as it can have a negative impact on performance.

*Automatic Read Checking (Session, Application, and Server Scope)*
: If this option is checked, ColdFusion automatically locks reading of the variable scope specified. All writes to the variable scope must be explicitly locked using `CFLOCK`. If a

write occurs to an unlocked variable, an exception is thrown. This option should also be used with careful planning as it can have a negative impact on performance.

### Attributes

`NAME="`*`lock_name`*`"`
: The name to associate with a particular instance of `CFLOCK`. If no `NAME` is specified, ColdFusion assigns a random name to the lock. In order to ensure synchronization across sessions and applications using locks, `Session.SessionID` and `Application.ApplicationName` should be used for the `NAME` attribute when locking access to session and application variables, respectively. The `NAME` attribute works only if the "No automatic checking or locking" option is set in the ColdFusion Administrator's Locking section for the variable scope you are attempting to lock. If a value is supplied for the `SCOPE` attribute, `NAME` can't be used. Optional.

`SCOPE="Application|Server|Session"`
: The scope of the variable you are attempting to lock access to. The `SCOPE` attribute is used when variable locking has been set to "Full Checking" or "Automatic Read Locking" within the ColdFusion Administrator's Locking section. If a value is supplied for the `NAME` attribute, `SCOPE` can't be used. Optional.

`TYPE="ReadOnly|Exclusive"`
: The type of lock to employ. Optional. The default value is `Exclusive`, which allows only one request at a time to access the block of code within the `CFLOCK` tag. This option should be used when writing data to persistent variables. `ReadOnly` allows more than one request at a time to access the block of code within the `CFLOCK` tag. This option should be used when reading persistent variables. This is the faster of the two options.

`TIMEOUT="`*`seconds`*`"`
: The time in seconds that ColdFusion should wait when attempting to obtain an exclusive lock before timing out. Required.

`THROWONTIMEOUT="Yes|No"`
: How ColdFusion should behave in the event that a `CFLOCK` request times out. If set to `Yes`, and a timeout occurs, ColdFusion throws an error that can be caught with `CFTRY/CATCH`. If `No`, the template continues execution after skipping the code within the `CFLOCK` tag. Optional. The default is `Yes`.

---

## CFLOG

New as of ColdFusion 5.0

`<CFLOG>`

Logs messages to the *Application.log* file, the *Scheduler.log* file, or to a custom log file. The log files generated by `CFLOG` follow a standard format. The first line of each log file contains a comma-delimited list of column headers qualified with double quotes that looks like this:

```
"Severity","ThreadID","Date","Time","Application","Message"
```

When an entry is made to the log file, the values that are written to each column are also qualified with double quotes and delimited with commas.

### *Attributes*

`TEXT="`*`message`*`"`
: Text you want to appear in the log entry. Required.

`LOG="`*`log_type`*`"`
: The standard ColdFusion log file to write the entry to. Valid options are:

  `Application`
  : The entry is written to the *Application.log* file. This file is automatically created by ColdFusion and logs application-specific messages.

  `Scheduler`
  : The entry is written to the *Scheduler.log* file. This file is used by ColdFusion to log execution information concerning scheduled tasks.

  If you wish to write to a custom log file, omit the `LOG` attribute and use `FILE` instead. Optional.

`FILE="`*`filename`*`"`
: The name of the log file to write the log entry to. You must specify the name of a file with a *.log* extension. When specifying the filename, leave off the extension. If the file doesn't exist, ColdFusion automatically creates it in the default log file directory specified in the ColdFusion Administrator. Optional. If you specify a value for `FILE`, you must omit the `LOG` attribute.

`TYPE="`*`severity`*`"`
: The severity you wish to assign to the log entry. Possible entries are `Information` (the default), `Warning`, `Error`, and `Fatal`.

`THREAD="Yes|No"`
: Whether or not to include the ID of the service thread responsible for logging the message in the log entry. Service threads typically handle a particular page request from request through completion before moving to the next queued request. Logging thread IDs can be useful (especially to Allaire technical support) for identifying server activity patterns. Optional. The default is `Yes`.

`DATE="Yes|No"`
: Whether or not to include the system date in the log entry. Optional. The default is `Yes`.

`TIME="Yes|No"`
: Whether or not to include the system time in the log entry. Optional. The default is `Yes`.

`APPLICATION="Yes|No"`
: Whether or not to include the application name if one is specified in a `CFAPPLICATION` tag for the application. Optional. The default is `Yes`.

---

## CFLOOP

```
<CFLOOP>
HTML and CFML
</CFLOOP>
```

A looping construct that can implement different kinds of looping, depending on the attributes specified.

### *Attributes*

CONDITION="*expression*"
: Using the CONDITION attribute creates a while loop that repeats while a specified expression is True. In order to work, the expression being tested must change with each iteration until the condition evaluates to False. Can't be used with any other attributes.

COLLECTION="*COM_object_or_CF_structure*"
: The COLLECTION attribute loops over a COM collection object or a ColdFusion structure. Requires the ITEM attribute and can't be used with any other attributes.

ITEM="*collection_or_key*"
: The variable name for the collection (COM object) or key (ColdFusion structure) referenced in a COLLECTION loop. Required with COLLECTION.

INDEX="*index_name*"
: Using the INDEX attribute creates a for loop. This loop either repeats a specified number of times, when used with the FROM, TO, and STEP attributes; or loops through a list, with the LIST and DELIMITERS attributes. INDEX specifies a variable that can access the current value of the index loop. When used with the FROM, TO, and STEP attributes, the INDEX value is set to the FROM value (required) and incremented by the STEP value (optional) for each iteration of the loop until the TO value (required) is reached. When used with the LIST (required) and DELIMITERS (optional) attributes, INDEX is a place holder for the current list item. Can't be used with any other attributes.

FROM="*integer*"
: Number specifying the beginning value for the loop. Required when INDEX is used to loop through a range of values.

TO="*integer*"
: Number specifying the ending value for the loop. Required when INDEX is used to loop through a range of values.

STEP="*integer*"
: The value by which the index loop is incremented after each iteration. Optional. The default is 1.

LIST="*list_items*"
: Delimited list of items or variable containing a delimited list of items. Required when INDEX is used to loop through a list.

DELIMITERS="*delimiter*"
: The character used to separate items in the list. Optional. The default delimiter is a comma.

QUERY="*query_name*"
: Using the QUERY attribute creates a loop over the contents of a query object. QUERY specifies the name of the query to loop over. Can be used with the STARTROW and ENDROW attributes, but no others.

STARTROW="*row_number*"
: Row number to begin looping from. Optional. By default, ColdFusion begins the loop with the first row of the query.

ENDROW="*row_number*"
: Row to stop looping. Optional. By default, ColdFusion continues the loop until it reaches the end of the record set.

## CFMAIL

```
<CFMAIL>
  [<CFMAILPARAM>]
Message body
</CFMAIL>
```

Generates an email message and sends it through a designated SMTP server.

### *Attributes*

FROM="*sender*"
: Sender's email address. Required.

TO="*recipient*"
: Recipient's email address. Separate multiple recipients with commas. Required.

CC="*copy_to*"
: A list of recipients to send copies of the email. Separate multiple recipients with commas. Optional.

BCC="*blind_copy_to*"
: A list of recipients to send blind copies of the email. BCC recipients aren't shown in the email header. Separate multiple recipients with commas. Optional.

SUBJECT="*subject*"
: The subject of the email. Required.

TYPE="*message_type*"
: The extended mail type of the message. The only option currently supported is HTML. HTML mail allows you to control the formatting of your messages by embedding HTML within the message body. Optional.

QUERY="*query_name*"
: The name of a query to use for pulling data to populate messages or to send messages to multiple recipients. Optional.

GROUP="*query_column*"
: The query column that should be used to group data. Grouping data results in the elimination of duplicate output. Grouping is case-sensitive unless the GROUPCASESENSITIVE attribute is set to No. Optional.

GROUPCASESENSITIVE="Yes|No"
: Whether grouping should be case-insensitive or case-insensitive. Optional. The default is Yes. This attribute works only if the record set has already been grouped appropriately. CFMAIL can't reorder or resort the record set on its own.

MAXROWS="*integer*"
: The maximum number of emails to send from a query-based mailing. Optional.

STARTROW="*row_number*"
: The query row to begin emailing from. Optional.

SERVER="*SMTP_server*"
: The server name or IP address of the mail server ColdFusion should use to send SMTP mail. Specifying a value here overrides any values set in the ColdFusion Administrator. Optional.

PORT="*port_number*"
The port used by the mail server to listen for SMTP requests. The default SMTP port is 25. Specifying a value here overrides any values set in the ColdFusion Administrator. Optional.

MAILERID="*header_ID*"
A mailer ID to pass along in the X-Mailer SMTP header. The X-Mailer header identifies the program generating the SMTP message. Optional. The default is "Allaire ColdFusion Application Server".

MIMEATTACH="*attachment_path*"
The full path to a file to be MIME-encoded and attached to the email message. MIMEATTACH performs the same function as the CFMAILPARAM tag but allows only a single file to be attached to the mail message. Using the CFMAILPARAM tag is the preferred method for attaching files to your email messages. Optional.

TIMEOUT="*seconds*"
The number of seconds the ColdFusion server should wait before timing out the connection to the SMTP server. Optional.

## CFMAILPARAM

New as of ColdFusion 4.5

```
<CFMAIL>
  [<CFMAILPARAM>]
Message body
</CFMAIL>
```

Used within a CFMAIL block to send file attachments and custom header information. Multiple CFMAILPARAM tags may be nested within a CFMAIL block. Only one file attachment or custom header can be specified per CFMAILPARAM tag.

### Attributes

FILE="*filename*"
The full path to the file you wish to attach to your email message. Multiple CFMAILPARAM tags may be used to attach more than one file. Can't be used with any other attributes. Required when attaching a file.

NAME="*name*"
The name of the header entry to write. Multiple header entries may be written using a CFMAILPARAM tag for each entry. Can be used only with the VALUE attribute. Required when including custom header information.

VALUE="*value*"
The value to be written for the header entry. Can be used only with the NAME attribute. Required when including custom header information.

## CFMODULE

```
<CFMODULE>
```

Provides an alternative method for calling CFML custom tags.

### *Attributes*

`TEMPLATE="`*`template_path`*`"`

The path to the ColdFusion template to use as a custom tag. Relative paths are automatically expanded from the current page, while absolute paths are expanded using the mappings defined in the ColdFusion Administrator. Optional. If a value is specified for `TEMPLATE`, the `NAME` attribute isn't used.

`NAME="`*`name`*`"`

The name of the custom tag you want to use. The default location for custom-tag storage is *c:\cfusion\customtags*. Custom tags residing in this location may be referenced with dotted notation. For example, a custom tag called `MyCustomTag` (*MyCustomTag.cfm*) residing in the default custom tags directory is referenced as `MyCustomTag`. The same tag residing under a subdirectory of the *customtags* directory called *SpecialTags* is referenced as `SpecialTags.MyCustomTag`. This dotted notation can reference custom tags residing in or any number of levels below the default *customtags* directory. Optional. If a value is specified for `NAME`, the `TEMPLATE` attribute isn't used.

`ATTRIBUTECOLLECTION="`*`attribute_structure`*`"`

The name of a ColdFusion structure containing attribute names and their associated values. Optional.

`ATTRIBUTE`*`n`*`="`*`value`*`"`

Additional attributes and their associated values as required by the custom tag. Optional.

## CFNEWINTERNALADMINSECURITY

This tag is the same as the `CFADMINSECURITY` tag, except it functions even if the `CFADMINSECURITY` tag is disabled in the Basic Security area of the ColdFusion Administrator. For syntax and attributes, see `CFADMINSECURITY`.

## CFNEWINTERNALREGISTRY

This tag is the same as the `CFREGISTRY` tag, except it functions even if the `CFREGISTRY` tag is disabled in the Basic Security area of the ColdFusion Administrator. For syntax and attributes, see `CFREGISTRY`. This tag is deprecated and nonfunctional as of ColdFusion 4.5.

## CFOBJECT

`<CFOBJECT>`

Allows ColdFusion to create and use COM, CORBA, and Java objects. COM objects aren't currently supported for Unix versions of ColdFusion. The `CFOBJECT` tag can be disabled in the Basic Security section of the ColdFusion Administrator.

Using the `CFOBJECT` tag to call a Java object loads the class, but doesn't create an instance of the object. Constructors can be explicitly called using the `init()` method:

```
<CFSET MyVar=MyObject.init(argument1, argument2)>
```

Calling a public method within an object without first calling the `init()` method results in an implicit call to the default constructor. Arguments and return values may be of any valid Java datatype. ColdFusion handles the conversion of strings automatically when they are passed as arguments or as return values. In addition, methods may be overloaded as long as the number of arguments used differ. The `JavaCast()` function may be used to cast a ColdFusion variable before it is passed to an overloaded method.

### Attributes

`TYPE="COM|CORBA|Java"`
: The type of object to create. Required.

`NAME="`*`name`*`"`
: A name for the object to be used by your application when referencing the object's attributes and methods. Required.

`CLASS="`*`object_class`*`"`
: For a COM object, the component program ID for the object to be invoked. For a CORBA object, if `CONTEXT` is `IOR`, `CLASS` specifies the name of a file that contains the stringified version of the `IOR`. If `CONTEXT` is `NameService`, `CLASS` specifies a period-delimited naming context for the naming service. For a Java object, the Java class. Required.

`ACTION="Create|Connect"`
: With a COM object, `Create` instantiates the object (usually a *.dll*), while `Connect` connects to a COM object (usually an *.exe*) that is already running on the server. With a Java object, `Create` is the only valid action. Required for these objects; ignored otherwise.

`CONTEXT="`*`context`*`"`
: For a COM object, valid entries are `InProc`, `Local`, or `Remote`, and the attribute is optional. `InProc` specifies an in-process server object (usually a *.dll*) running in the same process space as the ColdFusion server. `Local` specifies an out-of-process server object (usually a *.exe*) that's running on the same server as ColdFusion, but not in the same process space. `Remote` specifies an out-of-process server object (usually an *.exe*) that's running on another machine. If `Remote` is specified, the `SERVER` attribute is required. When no value is specified, ColdFusion uses the registry setting for the object.

: For a CORBA object, valid entries are `IOR`, which causes ColdFusion to use the Interoperable Object Reference to access the object, and `NameService`, which causes ColdFusion to use the naming service to access the object. Required for CORBA objects.

: Not used with Java objects.

`SERVER="`*`server_name`*`"`
: With COM objects, a valid server name using Universal Naming Convention (UNC) or Domain Name Server (DNS) conventions. Required when `CONTEXT` is `Remote`; ignored otherwise.

`LOCALE="`*`-type_value_pair1, -type_value_pair2, ...`*`"`
: For CORBA objects, type/value pairs of arguments to pass to `init_orb()`. This feature is specific to VisiBroker orbs and has been tested to work with the 3.2 C++ version only. Note that all type/value pairs must begin with a minus sign (-).

## CFOBJECTCACHE

<CFOBJECTCACHE>

Clears the ColdFusion query cache. This tag is an undocumented ColdFusion tag.

### Attribute

`ACTION="Clear"`
: Specifies the action to be taken by the `CFOBJECTCACHE` tag. The only `ACTION` currently supported is `Clear`. Required.

## CFOUTPUT

<CFOUTPUT>
*HTML and CFML*
</CFOUTPUT>

Displays the results of a query or other ColdFusion operation.

### Attributes

`QUERY="`*`query_name`*`"`
: The name of the query from which to pull the data to be output. Optional.

`GROUP="`*`parameter`*`"`
: The parameter that should group data. Grouping data results in the elimination of duplicate output. Optional.

`GROUPCASESENSITIVE="Yes|No"`
: Whether or not grouping should be case-insensitive or case-insensitive. Optional. The default is `Yes`. This attribute works only if the record set has already been grouped appropriately. `CFOUTPUT` can't reorder or resort the record set on its own.

`STARTROW="`*`row_number`*`"`
: The query row to begin outputting from. Optional.

`MAXROWS="`*`integer`*`"`
: The maximum number of rows to output. Optional.

## CFPARAM

<CFPARAM>

Defines a parameter and sets a default value. Can also be used to test for the existence of a parameter and its datatype.

### Attributes

`NAME="`*`parameter_name`*`"`
: Name of the parameter to create. Required.

`TYPE="`*`data_type`*`"`
: The required parameter type. Valid entries are `Any`, `Array`, `Boolean`, `Date`, `Numeric`, `Query`, `String`, `Struct`, `UUID`, and `VariableName` (name of the variable). Optional. The default is `Any`.

DEFAULT="*value*"
: Default value to assign to the variable if it doesn't exist or has no value already assigned.

## CFPOP

<CFPOP>

Retrieves mail, including file attachments, from a POP server.

### *Attributes*

ACTION="*action*"
: Specifies the action for the `CFPOP` tag to take. Optional. The default value is `GetHeaderOnly`, which returns the message header only. `GetAll` returns the message header and message body, plus file attachments if a value is specified for ATTACHMENTPATH. `Delete` deletes messages from the server.

SERVER="*POP_server*"
: Hostname or IP address of the POP server you want to retrieve mail from. Required.

PORT="*port_number*"
: Port on the POP server to use. Optional. The default is 110.

USERNAME="*username*"
: A username to use when logging into the POP server. Optional. If no username is specified, the tag defaults to anonymous access.

PASSWORD="*password*"
: A password to use in order to log into the POP server. Optional.

NAME="*query_name*"
: The name to assign the query object created when `ACTION` is `Get` or `GetAll`. Optional.

MESSAGENUMBER="*message_number*"
: The message number or comma-delimited list of message numbers to perform the specified `ACTION` on. Optional.

UID="*UID*"
: The unique identifier (UID) assigned to a mail message or comma-delimited list of UIDs, to perform the specified `ACTION` on. `UID` may be used in place of the MESSAGENUMBER attribute in cases where the specified POP server doesn't support message numbers (as in the case of the Mercury POP server). Optional. New as of ColdFusion 4.5.1 SP2.

ATTACHMENTPATH="*path*"
: The full path to use to store file attachments when `ACTION` is `GetAll`. Optional.

GENERATEUNIQUEFILENAMES="Yes|No"
: Whether or not to automatically generate unique filenames for file attachments so that name conflicts can be avoided. Generated names are guaranteed to be unique within the specified directory. Optional. The default is No.

MAXROWS="*integer*"
: The maximum number of messages to be retrieved for the query. Optional. This attribute is ignored if a value is given for MESSAGENUMBER.

`STARTROW="`*`row_number`*`"`
The starting row for the message query. Optional. The default is `1`. This attribute is ignored if a value is given for `MESSAGENUMBER`.

`TIMEOUT="`*`seconds`*`"`
The maximum amount of time in seconds that ColdFusion should wait while performing a mail operation before timing out. Optional. The default is `60`.

### *Returned Variables*

The `CFPOP` tag returns several variables depending on the value of the `ACTION` attribute. When `ACTION` is `GetHeaderOnly` or `GetAll`, `CFPOP` returns the following variables:

*`queryname`*`.ColumnList`
A comma-delimited list of the query column names.

*`queryname`*`.CurrentRow`
The current row of the query being processed.

*`queryname`*`.RecordCount`
The total number of messages returned by the query.

*`queryname`*`.Date`
Date and time the message was sent. POP dates can be converted to GMT (Greenwich Mean Time) using the `ParseDateTime()` function.

*`queryname`*`.MessageNumber`
The message number of the current message.

*`queryname`*`.UID`
The UID of the current message. New as of ColdFusion 4.5.1 SP2.

*`queryname`*`.From`
The email address of the sender of the message.

*`queryname`*`.To`
The email address or comma-delimited email addresses of the message recipient(s).

*`queryname`*`.CC`
Email address or comma-delimited list of email addresses that received copies of the message.

*`queryname`*`.BCC`
Email address or comma-delimited list of email addresses that received blind copies of the message.

*`queryname`*`.ReplyTo`
Email address specified as the reply-to address.

*`queryname`*`.Subject`
The subject of the message.

*`queryname`*`.Header`
Returns the complete SMTP message header.

When `ACTION` is `GetAll`, there is an additional variable:

*`queryname`*`.Body`
The content of the message body.

If `ACTION` is set to `GetAll` and the `ATTACHMENTPATH` attribute is set, ColdFusion returns two additional variables containing information about any file attachments included with the message:

`queryname.Attachments`
: A tab-delimited list of the original filenames of all attached files.

`queryname.AttachmentFiles`
: A tab-delimited list of the names of the attachment files as they were written to the directory specified in `ATTACHMENTPATH`.

---

## CFPROCESSINGDIRECTIVE

New as of ColdFusion 4.5

```
<CFPROCESSINGDIRECTIVE>
CFML
</CFPROCESSINGDIRECTIVE>
```

Specifies a p-code compiler processing option to suppress all whitespace produced by the ColdFusion within an executing CFML template. `CFPROCESSINGDIRECTIVE` tags must always occur in matched pairs and may be nested. `CFPROCESSINGDIRECTIVE` settings don't apply to templates called via `CFINCLUDE` or `CFMODULE` or as custom tags.

### *Attribute*

`SUPPRESSWHITESPACE="Yes|No"`
: Whether or not ColdFusion should suppress all whitespace between `CFPROCESSING-DIRECTIVE` tag pairs.

---

## CFPROCPARAM

```
<CFSTOREDPROC>
  [<CFPROCPARAM>]
  [<CFPROCRESULT>]
  ...
</CFSTOREDPROC>
```

Specifies parameter information to send to a stored procedure. `CFPROCPARAM` tags are nested within a `CFSTOREDPROC` tag.

### *Attributes*

`TYPE="In|Out|InOut"`
: Whether the variable being passed is an input, output, or input/output variable. Optional. Default is `In`.

`VARIABLE="variable_name"`
: The name of the ColdFusion variable that references the value returned by the output parameter after the stored procedure is called. Required when `TYPE` is `Out` or `InOut`.

`DBVARNAME="database_variable_name"`
: The name of the parameter within the stored procedure. Required if named notation is used.

`VALUE="parameter_value"`
: The value to pass to the stored procedure. Required when `TYPE` is `In` or `InOut`.

CFSQLTYPE="*parameter_data_type*"

The SQL type of the parameter being passed to the stored procedure. Required. The default is CF_SQL_CHAR. Possible values are: CF_SQL_BIGINT, CF_SQL_BIT, CF_SQL_CHAR, CF_SQL_DATE, CF_SQL_DECIMAL, CF_SQL_DOUBLE, CF_SQL_FLOAT, CF_SQL_IDSTAMP, CF_SQL_INTEGER, CF_SQL_LONGVARCHAR, CF_SQL_MONEY, CF_SQL_MONEY4, CF_SQL_NUMERIC, CF_SQL_REAL, CF_SQL_REFCURSOR (Oracle only), CF_SQL_SMALLINT, CF_SQL_TIME, CF_SQL_TIMESTAMP, CF_SQL_TINYINT, and CF_SQL_VARCHAR.

MAXLENGTH="*length*"

The maximum length of the parameter. Optional.

SCALE="*decimal_places*"

The number of decimal places of the parameter. Optional.

NULL="Yes|No"

Whether or not the value passed is a NULL. If Yes, ColdFusion ignores the VALUE attribute. Optional. The default it No.

## CFPROCRESULT

```
<CFSTOREDPROC>
  [<CFPROCPARAM>]
  [<CFPROCRESULT>]
  ...
</CFSTOREDPROC>
```

Specifies the name for a result set returned by the CFSTOREDPROC tag. This allows other ColdFusion tags to reference the result set. The CFPROCRESULT tag must be nested within the CFSTOREDPROC tag.

### *Attributes*

NAME="query_name"

A name for the query result set returned by the stored procedure. Required.

RESULTSET="integer"

The result set to use if the stored procedure returns more than one result set. Optional. The default value is 1.

MAXROWS="row_number"

The maximum number of rows to return with the result set. Optional. By default, all rows are returned.

## CFQUERY

```
<CFQUERY>
  [<CFQUERYPARAM>]
SQL statements
</CFQUERY>
```

Performs SQL operations against a data source or existing query object.

### Attributes

NAME="*query_name*"

Name to assign to the query. Valid query names must begin with a letter and can contain only letters, numbers, and underscore characters. Required when passing an SQL SELECT statement; optional for all other SQL operations. Although the NAME attribute is required only for SQL SELECT statements, you may wish to use it in all your queries. It makes debugging easier, especially for templates that contain multiple queries because it allows you to identify each query by name in the debugging output.

DATASOURCE="*datasource_name*"

The name of the data source to connect to when executing the query. Required except when DBTYPE is Query or Dynamic.

DBTYPE="*database_type*"

The type of database driver to use. Optional. Possible choices are:

ODBC *(the default)*

Connect to the data source using an ODBC driver.

OLEDB

Connect using an OLEDB driver.

Oracle73

Connect using the Oracle 7.3 native driver. This requires the 7.3.4.0.0 or later client libraries be installed on the ColdFusion server.

Oracle80

Connect using the Oracle 8 native driver. This requires the 8.0 or later client libraries be installed on the ColdFusion server.

Sybase11

Connect using the Sybase 11 native driver. This requires the 11.1.1 or later client libraries be installed on the ColdFusion server.

DB2

Connect using the DB2 5.2 native driver.

Informix73

Connect using the Informix 7.3 native driver. This requires the Informix SDK 2.5 or later or Informix-Connect 2.5 (or later) for Windows.

Query

Specifies the query should use an already existing query as the data source. If this option is used, you don't need to specify a value for DATASOURCE. New as of ColdFusion 5.0.

Dynamic

Allows ColdFusion to make an ODBC connection to a data source without having to have the data source registered in the ColdFusion Administrator. When making a dynamic connection, all information normally provided in the ColdFusion Administrator for the connection must be specified in the CONNECTSTRING attribute. New as of ColdFusion 5.0.

DBSERVER="*database_server*"

The name of the database server to connect to when using native drivers. Specifying a DBSERVER overrides any value set for DATASOURCE. Optional.

`DBNAME="`*`database_name`*`"`
: Specifies the database name. For the Sybase System 11 native driver and `SQLOLEDB` provider only. Optional. Overrides any value set for `DATASOURCE`.

`USERNAME="`*`username`*`"`
: Username to pass to the data source if one is required. Optional. If a username is specified, it overrides the value set in the ColdFusion Administrator.

`PASSWORD="`*`password`*`"`
: Password associated with `USERNAME`. Optional. If a password is specified, it overrides the value set in the ColdFusion Administrator.

`CONNECTSTRING="`*`connection_string`*`"`
: Passes additional connection information to an ODBC data source that can't be passed via the ColdFusion Administrator. `CONNECTSTRING` can also override connection information set for a data source already registered in the ColdFusion Administrator. When making a dynamic data source connection (when `DBTYPE` is `Dynamic`), `CONNECTSTRING` specifies all the information required to connect to the data source. For specific connection string options, you should consult the documentation for your particular database. New as of ColdFusion 5.0.

`MAXROWS="`*`row_number`*`"`
: Maximum number of rows to return in a record set. Optional.

`BLOCKFACTOR="`*`block_size`*`"`
: The maximum number of rows to retrieve from the server at a time. Optional. The range is from `1` to `100`; `1` is the default. Note that some drivers may reduce the block factor automatically.

`TIMEOUT="`*`seconds`*`"`
: Number of seconds to allow the query to execute before timing out. Support for this attribute varies by driver. Optional.

`CACHEDAFTER="`*`date`*`"`
: A date for using cached query data. Cached query data is used only if the date of the original query is after the date specified in `CACHEDAFTER`. To use cached query data, this feature must be enabled in the ColdFusion Administrator. Optional.

`CACHEDWITHIN="`*`time_span`*`"`
: A time span (created using the `CreateTimeSpan()` function) for using cached query data. To use cached query data, this feature must be enabled in the ColdFusion Administrator. Optional.

`PROVIDER="`*`COM_provider`*`"`
: COM provider for OLE DB connections. Optional.

`PROVIDERDSN="`*`datasource`*`"`
: COM provider's data-source name for OLE DB. Optional.

`DEBUG`
: Specifying `DEBUG` results in the output of debugging information, which includes the actual SQL passed to the data source as well as the number of records returned by the query. Optional.

### *Returned Variables*

When the CFQUERY tag selects records from a data source, four variables are returned:

CFQUERY.ExecutionTime
: The amount of time in milliseconds it took the query to execute; note the CFQUERY prefix

*queryname*.ColumnList
: A comma-delimited list of the query column names from the database

*queryname*.CurrentRow
: The current row of the query being processed

*queryname*.RecordCount
: The total number of records returned by the query

## CFQUERYPARAM

New as of ColdFusion 4.5

```
<CFQUERY>
SQL statements
  [<CFQUERYPARAM>]
</CFQUERY>
```

Checks the datatype and optionally validates a query parameter within the SQL statement of a CFQUERY tag. Multiple CFQUERYPARAM tags may be used with a single CFQUERY tag.

The SQL that is generated by the CFQUERYPARAM tag is dependent on the database used. If the database being used doesn't support bind parameters, validation is still performed with the validated parameter being written back to the string. If for any reason validation fails, ColdFusion throws an exception. The following rules determine the validation performed:

- CF_SQL_SMALLINT, CF_SQL_INTEGER, CF_SQL_REAL, CF_SQL_FLOAT, CF_SQL_DOUBLE, CF_SQL_TINYINT, CF_SQL_MONEY, CF_SQL_MONEY4, CF_SQL_DECIMAL, CF_SQL_NUMERIC, and CF_SQL_BIGINT can be converted to numbers.
- CF_SQL_DATE, CF_SQL_TIME and CF_SQL_TIMESTAMP can be converted to a valid date format.

The ColdFusion Sybase 11 native driver doesn't currently support the binding of SQL parameters. If the MAXLENGTH attribute is used, the length of the value for the specified parameter can't exceed the specified length.

### *Attributes*

VALUE="*parameter_value*"
: The value that ColdFusion should pass to the right of the comparison operator in the WHERE clause. Required.

CFSQLTYPE="*parameter_data_type*"
: The SQL type that the parameter is bound to. Required. The default is CF_SQL_CHAR. Possible values are: CF_SQL_BIGINT, CF_SQL_BIT, CF_SQL_CHAR, CF_SQL_DATE, CF_SQL_DECIMAL, CF_SQL_DOUBLE, CF_SQL_FLOAT, CF_SQL_IDSTAMP, CF_SQL_INTEGER, CF_SQL_LONGVARCHAR, CF_SQL_MONEY, CF_SQL_MONEY4, CF_SQL_NUMERIC, CF_SQL_REFCURSOR (Oracle only), CF_SQL_REAL, CF_SQL_SMALLINT, CF_SQL_TIME, CF_SQL_TIMESTAMP, CF_SQL_TINYINT, and CF_SQL_VARCHAR.

LIST="Yes|No"
: Whether or not the VALUE attribute of the CFQUERYPARAM tag should be treated as a list of values separated by the character specified in the SEPARATOR attribute. If set to Yes, an SQL parameter is generated for each value in the list. Each list item is validated separately. If a value is specified for the MAXLENGTH attribute, the MAXLENGTH applies to each item in the list as opposed to the list as a whole. If the value passed is NULL, it is treated as a single NULL value. Optional. The default is No.

SEPARATOR="*separator_character*"
: The character that delimits the list of values when LIST attribute is Yes. Optional. The default is the comma (,).

MAXLENGTH="*length*"
: The maximum length of the parameter. Optional.

SCALE="*decimal_places*"
: The number of decimal places of the parameter. Optional.

NULL="Yes|No"
: Whether or not the value passed is a NULL. If Yes, ColdFusion ignores the VALUE attribute. Optional. The default it No.

---

## CFREGISTRY

<CFREGISTRY>

Performs a registry operation, based on the value of the ACTION attribute.

### *Attributes*

ACTION="*action*"
: The action for the CFREGISTRY tag to take. Required. Get retrieves a value from the registry and stores it in a variable. GetAll retrieves all the registry keys and values for a specified registry branch and stores them in a query object. Delete deletes a key or value from the registry. Set adds or updates a registry key or value.

BRANCH="*branch*"
: For Get, GetAll, and Set, the name of the registry branch containing the value to be accessed or set. For Delete, specifies either the name of the registry key to be deleted (don't specify an ENTRY) or the name of the registry branch that contains the value to be deleted (specify a value for ENTRY). Required.

ENTRY="*key_or_value*"
: The value in the registry to be operated on. Required for all actions except GetAll and certain Delete operations.

TYPE="*type*"
: The type of registry data to be operated on. Valid entries are Key, DWord, and String (the default). Optional.

VARIABLE="*variable*"
: The name of a ColdFusion variable to hold the data returned by CFREGISTRY. Required for Get; ignored otherwise.

NAME="*query_name*"
: The name of a query object to hold the keys and values returned by CFREGISTRY. Required for GetAll; ignored otherwise.

SORT="*sort_criteria*"
The sort order for the result set obtained by the CFREGISTRY action. Results may be ordered by Entry, Type, and Value. Multiple sort criteria can be entered as a comma-delimited list. In addition, the sort type may be specified after each column name as either ASC (ascending) or DESC (descending). Optional for GetAll; ignored otherwise.

VALUE="*string_or_value*"
The value you want to set. Optional for Set; ignored otherwise. If no VALUE is specified, ColdFusion automatically sets a default value based on TYPE. If TYPE is DWord, VALUE is set to zero. If TYPE is String, VALUE is set to an empty string ("").

### *Returned Variables*

The following query columns are returned when ACTION is GetAll. The name of the query object is set in the NAME attribute:

*queryname*.Entry
The name of the registry entry

*queryname*.Type
The type of registry entry returned

*queryname*.Value
The value of the registry entry if TYPE is set to String or DWord

---

## CFREPORT

<CFREPORT> ... </CFREPORT>

Executes a predefined Crystal Reports report and populates it with data from a ColdFusion template. In order to use this tag, you must have Crystal Reports installed on your ColdFusion server.

### *Attributes*

REPORT="*report_path*"
The full path to the Crystal Report file to be executed. Required.

ORDERBY="*result_order*"
Orders results according to your specifications. Optional.

USERNAME="*username*"
A username for the database providing data for the report. Optional. If a username is specified, it overrides the value set in the ColdFusion Administrator.

PASSWORD="*password*"
Password associated with USERNAME. Optional. If a password is specified, it overrides the value set in the ColdFusion Administrator.

FORMULA="*formula*"
One or more named formulas within the report. Separate formula parameters with semicolons. If the formula contains a semicolon, it should be escaped by doubling it up. Optional.

TYPE="*report_type*"
The type of HTML that should be used to generate the report. Options are Standard, Netscape, and Microsoft; they refer to the web browser the report is destined for.

This attribute can be dynamically set by first determining the browser in use with the CGI variable `HTTP_USER_AGENT`. The `TYPE` attribute isn't documented in the Allaire documentation and was designed to overcome a problem using `CFREPORT` with Crystal Reports 8.x. When using the `CFREPORT` tag in versions of ColdFusion prior to 5.0 to generate a report in Crystal Reports 8.x, you must set the `TYPE` attribute to `Netscape` or `Microsoft`. Optional. The default value is `Standard` (don't use the default if using Crystal Reports 8.x). This issue has been fixed in ColdFusion 5.0. As of ColdFusion 5.0, you no longer need to use the `TYPE` attribute to avoid an error.

`DATASOURCE="`*`datasource_name`*`"`

The name of the ODBC data source to obtain data for the report from. If no `DATASOURCE` is provided, the data source specified when the report was created is used. `DATASOURCE` is a previously undocumented attribute of the `CFREPORT` tag. Optional. New as of ColdFusion 4.5.1 SP2.

`TIMEOUT`

Time in seconds ColdFusion should wait before timing out a connection to the Crystal Reports engine. Optional.

---

## CFRETHROW

New as of ColdFusion 4.5

```
<CFTRY>
  CFML
<CFCATCH TYPE="exception_type">
  HTML and CFML
  <CFTRY>
    CFML
    <CFCATCH TYPE="exception_type">
      HTML and CFML
      <CFRETHROW>
    </CFCATCH>
</CFCATCH>

<CFCATCH TYPE="Any">
HTML and CFML
</CFCATCH>
</CFTRY>
```

Used within a `CFCATCH` block to rethrow the active exception while preserving the `CFCATCH.Type` and `CFCATCH.TagContext` return variables. This tag takes no additional attributes.

---

## CFSAVECONTENT

New in ColdFusion 5.0

```
<CFSAVECONTENT>
HTML and CFML
</CFSAVECONTENT>
```

Saves all generated content between tag pairs in a variable. `CFSAVECONTENT` is useful in situations where you want to reuse the content generated by a specific block of code.

### *Attribute*

VARIABLE="*variable_name*"

A variable name for storing the content generated by code between the CFSAVECONTENT tag pairs.

## CFSCHEDULE

<CFSCHEDULE>

Schedules execution of a ColdFusion template.

### *Attributes*

ACTION="*action*"

Action you want the scheduler to perform. Valid entries are Delete, Run, and Update. Required.

TASK="*task_name*"

The name of the task to delete, run, or update. Required.

OPERATION="HTTPRequest"

The operation the scheduler should perform. Required when ACTION is Update. The only OPERATION currently supported is HTTPRequest.

FILE="*filename*"

Filename to use for the static file being published. Required when PUBLISH is Yes.

PATH="*path*"

The path to the location where the static file should be written. Required when PUBLISH is Yes.

STARTDATE="*date*"

Start date for the scheduled task. Required when ACTION is Update.

STARTTIME="*time*"

Start time for the scheduled task. Required when ACTION is Update.

URL="*URL*"

Absolute URL to the template to be executed when the scheduled task runs. Required when ACTION is Update.

PORT="*port_number*"

Port number on the server where the template being executed resides. Optional. The default is 80.

PUBLISH="Yes|No"

Whether or not the output of the scheduled task should be saved as a static file. Optional. The default is No.

ENDDATE="*date*"

End date for the scheduled task. Optional.

ENDTIME="*time*"

End time for the scheduled task. Optional.

INTERVAL="*seconds*"

The interval the scheduler should use when scheduling tasks for execution. Intervals can be set in seconds or as Once, Daily, Weekly, or Monthly. Required when ACTION is `Update`. The default interval is one hour. The minimum interval allowed is 60 seconds.

`REQUESTTIMEOUT="`*`seconds`*`"`
: A value for the `REQUESTTIMEOUT` URL parameter. This attribute can extend the time allowed for execution beyond the default set in the ColdFusion Administrator. Optional.

`USERNAME="`*`username`*`"`
: Specifies the username to use for protected URLs. Optional.

`PASSWORD="`*`password`*`"`
: Specifies the password to use for protected URLs. Optional.

`RESOLVEURL="Yes|No"`
: Whether or not to resolve relative links in the retrieved template to absolute URLs. Optional. The default is `No`.

`PROXYSERVER="`*`proxy_server`*`"`
: Hostname or IP address of your proxy server. Optional.

`PROXYPORT="`*`port_number`*`"`
: Specifies a port number on the proxy server where the template is being executed. Used in conjunction with the `RESOLVEURL` attribute, `PROXYPORT` allows you to preserve links within a template that resolve to a port other than 80. Optional. The default is `80`.

## CFSCRIPT

```
<CFSCRIPT>
Script code
</CFSCRIPT>
```

Tells ColdFusion to process the content between `<CFSCRIPT>/</CFSCRIPT>` as CFScript code.

## CFSEARCH

`<CFSEARCH>`

Performs search operations on data contained in Verity collections.

### *Attributes*

`NAME="`*`search_name`*`"`
: Name for the query containing the search results. Required.

`COLLECTION="`*`collection_name|collection_path`*`"`
: The name of the collection you wish to search, or in the case of externally generated collections, the full path to the collection directory. Multiple collections may be searched provided the collection names or paths are separated by commas. When specifying multiple collections, you can't mix internal and external collections in the same search operation. Required.

`TYPE="Simple|Explicit"`
: Type of search to be performed. Optional. The default is `Simple`, which allows you to use single words, comma-delimited lists of words, and phrases as the `CRITERIA` for a search. Simple searches treat the comma as a Boolean `OR`. phrases can also be used as the `CRITERIA` by surrounding them in quotation marks. By default, `Simple` searches employ the `STEM` operator and the `MANY` modifier. `Explicit` searches treat each search term as a literal, so operators must be used explicitly.

`CRITERIA="`*`search_criteria`*`"`
: The criteria for the search. Optional.

`MAXROWS="`*`integer`*`"`
: Maximum number of records to return for a given search. Optional.

`STARTROW="`*`row_number`*`"`
: The first record number in the query results from which to retrieve data. Optional.

`EXTERNAL="Yes|No"`
: Whether or not the Verity collection being searched was created with a version of Verity other than the one bundled with ColdFusion. Optional. The default is `No`.

`LANGUAGE="`*`language`*`"`
: The language to be used when searching the collection. To specify a language other than U.S. English (the default), you must purchase the ColdFusion International Search Pack from Allaire. Optional.

### *Returned Variables*

*`queryname`*`.ColumnList`
: Comma-delimited list of the query column names from the search result set.

*`queryname`*`.CurrentRow`
: The current row of the query that is being processed by `CFOUTPUT`.

*`queryname`*`.Custom1` *and* *`queryname`*`.Custom2`
: Whatever values were placed in the custom fields during the `CFINDEX` process.

*`queryname`*`.Key`
: The value placed in the `KEY` attribute during the `CFINDEX` operation.

*`queryname`*`.RecordCount`
: The number of records in the Verity collection that match the search criteria provided.

*`queryname`*`.RecordsSearched`
: Returns the total number of records from the collection searched by Verity.

*`queryname`*`.Score`
: A measure of how relevant a particular record in the Verity collection is in relation to the search criteria provided.

*`queryname`*`.Summary`
: The contents of the summary that the Verity engine automatically creates for each record in the collection. The summary is made up of the top three sentences from each record and has a 500-character limit.

*`queryname`*`.Title`
: The value placed in the `TITLE` attribute during the `CFINDEX` operation. For collections containing HTML files, the value inside the `<TITLE> </TITLE>` tags is returned. For PDF and Microsoft Office documents, the title assigned by the application is returned.

*queryname*.URL

The value specified in the URLPATH during the CFINDEX operation. This variable is always empty when the TYPE attribute is set to Custom during the CFINDEX operation.

## CFSELECT

```
<CFFORM>
  <CFSELECT>
  ...
</CFFORM>
```

Creates a Java select box control to use in a CFFORM block.

### *Attributes*

NAME="*name*"

The form-field name for the select box control. Required.

REQUIRED="Yes|No"

Whether or not the select box control requires a value before being submitted. Optional. The default is No.

MESSAGE="*text*"

Text to appear if validation fails. Optional.

ONERROR="*function_name*"

The name of a JavaScript function that should be executed if validation fails for any reason. Optional.

SIZE="*integer*"

The size of the drop-down box in terms of number of entries. Optional.

MULTIPLE="Yes|No"

Whether or not multiple item selections should be allowed. Optional. The default is No.

QUERY="*query_name*"

A query to use for populating the drop-down box. Optional.

SELECTED="*column_value*"

A value that matches at least one VALUE that is automatically selected when the template is called. Optional.

VALUE="*text*"

The field from QUERY to use to fill in the option values of the select box. Optional.

DISPLAY="*text*"

An alternate field from the query (other than VALUE) to display in the select box. Optional. The default is VALUE.

PASSTHROUGH="*HTML_attributes*"

Any additional HTML attributes you want to pass that aren't directly supported by the CFSELECT tag. Optional.

## CFSERVLET

New as of ColdFusion 4.5

```
<CFSERVLET>
  [<CFSERVLETPARAM>]
  ...
</CFSERVLET>
```

Invokes a Java servlet from a ColdFusion template. The **CFSERVLET** tag requires Allaire's JRun software in order to work. Attributes and parameters may be passed to the Java servlet by nesting **CFSERVLETPARAM** tags within the **CFSERVLET** tag.

### *Attributes*

CODE="*servlet_name*"
: The name of the Java servlet that you want to execute. Required.

JRUNPROXY="*server:port*"
: The hostname or IP address and the port where the JRun engine is located. Required when connecting to a JRun 3.x server. Optional when connecting to a JRun 2.3.3 server, as the JRun engine is assumed to be on the same machine as the ColdFusion application server and listening on port 8081.

TIMEOUT="*seconds*"
: The number of seconds ColdFusion waits while processing a **CFSERVLET** request before timing out the operation. Optional. The default is **60**.

WRITEOUTPUT="Yes|No"
: Whether or not to write output from the servlet as inline text or if it should be stored in a variable. If **Yes**, ColdFusion outputs the text to the screen. If **No**, ColdFusion writes the text to the variable **CFSERVLET.OUTPUT**. Optional. The default is **Yes**.

DEBUG="Yes|No"
: Whether or not to write additional information about the JRun connection status and other activity to the JRun error log file. For JRun 2.3.3, the error log is located in *jrunhomedir/jsm-default/logs/stderr.log*. For JRun 3.0, the error log is found in *jrunhomedir/logs/jrunservername_event.log*. Note that **jrunservername** can be specified as **default**, **admin**, or the name of another JRun server that you are running.

### *Returned Variables*

The **CFSERVLET** tag can return two output variables depending on how the tag is called:

CFSERVLET.Output
: Returns the text output by the **CFSERVLET** tag. This variable is returned only if the **WRITEOUTPUT** attribute is set to **No**.

CFSERVLET.*ServletResponseHeader*
: If any response headers are returned by the servlet, they are available in a special structure called **CFSERVLET**. Each response header is accessed by specifying its name as a key in the **CFSERVLET** structure.

## CFSERVLETPARAM

New as of ColdFusion 4.5

```
<CFSERVLET>
  [<CFSERVLETPARAM>]
  ...
</CFSERVLET>
```

Used as a child tag of the `CFSERVLET` tag to pass parameters and attributes to a Java servlet. Multiple `CFSERVLETPARAM` tags may pass multiple parameters/attributes. Both simple and complex datatypes such as arrays, queries, and structures can be passed to servlets via `CFSERVLETPARAM` tags.

Data can be passed to a servlet in two ways: by value and by reference. To pass data by value (as a parameter), use the `NAME` and `VALUE` attributes. Data passed by value is modified only within the servlet. To pass data by reference (as an attribute), use the `NAME`, `VARIABLE`, and optionally the `TYPE` attribute. If the servlet modifies data passed by reference, the data in the corresponding ColdFusion variable is also changed.

### *Attributes*

`NAME="`*`parameter_name`*`"`
: The name of the parameter to pass to the `CFSERVLET` tag when `VALUE` is also specified. If `VARIABLE` is used in lieu of `VALUE`, specifies the name of the Java attribute to associate with the ColdFusion variable specified in `VARIABLE`. Required.

`TYPE="Bool|Date|Int|Real|String"`
: The datatype of the ColdFusion variable being passed to the servlet.Options are `Bool`, `Date`, `Int`, `Real`, and `String`. Optional. The default is `String`. To see how various ColdFusion datatypes map to Java equivalents, see Table A-1.

*Table A-1. ColdFusion Datatypes and Java Equivalents*

| ColdFusion Datatype | TYPE Attribute | Java Equivalent |
|---|---|---|
| `Boolean` | `Bool` | *java.lang.Bool* |
| `Date` | `Date` | *java.util.Date* |
| `Numeric` (integer) | `Int` | *java.lang.Integer* |
| `Numeric` (real) | `Real` | *java.lang.Double* |
| `String` | String | *java.lang.String* |
| `Array` | N/A, omit `TYPE` | *java.util.Vector* |
| `Structure` | N/A, omit `TYPE` | *java.util.Hashtable* |
| `Query` | N/A, omit `TYPE` | *com.allaire.util.RecordSet* |

`VALUE="`*`parameter_value`*`"`
: The value of the parameter to pass to the `CFSERVLET` tag. Required when `NAME` is a parameter.

`VARIABLE="`*`CF_variable_name`*`"`
: The name (not the value) of the ColdFusion variable to pass to the `CFSERVLET` tag. Required when `NAME` is an attribute. Using the `VARIABLE` attribute allows you to pass

complex ColdFusion datatypes, such as arrays, queries, and structures to Java servlets. To see how various ColdFusion datatypes map to Java datatypes, see Table A-1.

## CFSET

```
<CFSET scope.varname=expression>
```

Sets the value of a ColdFusion variable.

## CFSETTING

```
<CFSETTING ENABLECFOUTPUTONLY="Yes"
           SHOWDEBUGOUTPUT="Yes|No">
           CATCHEXCEPTIONSBYPATTERN="Yes|No">
CFML
<CFSETTING ENABLECFOUTPUTONLY="No"
           SHOWDEBUGOUTPUT="Yes|No">
           CATCHEXCEPTIONSBYPATTERN="Yes|No">
```

Controls whitespace, debugging output, and exception handling within ColdFusion templates.

When the `ENABLECFOUTPUTONLY` attribute is used, `CFSETTING` tags must occur in matched pairs where both a `<CFSETTING ENABLECFOUTPUTONLY="Yes">` and a `<CFSETTING ENABLECFOUTPUTONLY="No">` are present. `CFSETTING` tags may be nested any number of levels as long as there are always matching tag pairs. You don't need to use paired `CFSETTING` tags with either the `SHOWDEBUGOUTPUT` or `CATCHEXCEPTIONBYPATTERN` attribute unless it is used in combination with an `ENABLECFOUTPUTONLY` attribute.

### *Attributes*

`ENABLECFOUTPUTONLY="Yes|No"`
: Specifying `Yes` results in the suppression of all HTML output (including whitespace) between `CFSETTING` tags. Optional. The default is `No`.

`SHOWDEBUGOUTPUT="Yes|No"`
: Whether or not to suppress debugging information normally output to ColdFusion templates when debugging is turned on in the ColdFusion Administrator. Optional. The default is `Yes`.

`CATCHEXCEPTIONSBYPATTERN=="Yes|No"`
: Whether or not to override structured exception handling. This attribute was introduced in ColdFusion 4.5 to handle incompatibility issues arising from changes to ColdFusion's structured exception handling in Version 4.5. In Version 4.0.x of ColdFusion, exceptions caught with `CFTRY/CATCH` were handled by the first `CFCATCH` block capable of dealing with the type of exception generated. In ColdFusion 4.5 and later, exceptions are handled by the `CFCATCH` block that's best able to deal with the exception. Optional. The default is `No`.

## CFSILENT

New as of ColdFusion 4.5

```
<CFSILENT> ... </CFSILENT>
```

Suppresses all output produced between the `CFSILENT` tags. `CFSILENT` partially supersedes the `CFSETTING` tag by using a more structured format. `CFSILENT` can suppress generated whitespace in instances where your template does a lot of looping but doesn't produce any output.

## CFSLIDER

Enhanced in ColdFusion 5.0

```
<CFFORM>
  <CFSLIDER>
  ...
</CFFORM>
```

Creates a Java slider control for use within a `CFFORM` block.

### *Attributes*

`NAME="`*`name`*`"`
: The form-field name for the slider control. Required.

`LABEL="`*`text`*`"`
: Text to appear with the slider control. Additionally, `%value%` may be used within the label text to insert the current slider value. If `%value%` is omitted, the current slider value is output to the right of the label text. Optional.

`REFRESHLABEL="Yes|No"`
: Whether or not the label should be refreshed when the slider moves. Default is `Yes`.

`IMG="`*`filename`*`"`
: The filename of an image to appear in the slider groove. Optional.

`IMGSTYLE="`*`style`*`"`
: The style to use for the image provided in `IMG`. Valid entries are `Centered`, `Tiled`, and `Scaled`. Optional. The default is `Scaled`. This attribute is deprecated and no longer functional as of ColdFusion 5.0.

`RANGE="`*`min_value, max_value`*`"`
: The beginning and ending values (numeric only) for the slider control. Optional. The default is "0,100".

`SCALE="`*`integer`*`"`
: The incremental value to use between the values provided by `RANGE`. Optional. The default is 1.

`VALUE="`*`integer`*`"`
: The default slider value. Optional. The default is the bottom number in `RANGE`.

`ONVALIDATE="`*`javascript_function`*`"`
: A JavaScript validation function that should be executed before the form is submitted. Optional.

`MESSAGE="`*`text`*`"`
: Text to appear if validation fails. Optional.

ONERROR="*function_name*"

The name of a JavaScript function that should be executed if validation fails for any reason. Optional.

HEIGHT="*height_in_pixels*"

Height in pixels for the slider. Optional.

WIDTH="*width_in_pixels*"

Width in pixels for the slider. Optional.

VSPACE="*vertical_spacing_in_pixels*"

Height in pixels for the padding above and below the slider control. Optional.

HSPACE="*horizonal_spacing_in_pixels*"

Width in pixels for the padding to the left and right of the slider control. Optional.

ALIGN="*alignment*"

Alignment for the slider control. Valid entries are Left, Right, Top, TextTop, Bottom, AbsBottom, Baseline, Middle, and AbsMiddle. Optional.

GROOVECOLOR="*color*"

The text color for all data in the grid. Colors may be specified by name (Black, Blue, Cyan, Darkgray, Gray, Lightgray, Magenta, Orange, Pink, Red, White, Yellow) or hex code in the form TEXTCOLOR="##FFFFCC". The double pound signs are necessary to keep ColdFusion from throwing a syntax error, or you may omit the pound signs altogether. By using the appropriate hex code, you can specify colors that can't be specified by name. Optional. The default is White. This attribute is deprecated and no longer functional as of ColdFusion 5.0.

BGCOLOR="*color*"

Background color for the slider control. Follows the same rules as GROOVECOLOR. Optional.

TEXTCOLOR="*color*"

Color to use for the LABEL text. Follows the same rules as GROOVECOLOR. Optional.

FONT="*font_name*"

A font name for the LABEL text. Optional.

FONTSIZE="*integer*"

A font size for the LABEL text. Optional.

ITALIC="Yes|No"

Whether or not to display the LABEL text in italic. Optional. The default is No.

BOLD="Yes|No"

Whether or not to display the LABEL text in bold. Optional. The default is No.

TICKMARKMAJOR="Yes|No"

Whether or not to display tick marks at every increment value along the axis of the slider control. For example, if the range for the slider is between 0 and 100 with an increment of 10, a major tick mark is displayed every 10 values, at 0, 10, 20, etc. The default is No. New as of ColdFusion 5.0.

TICKMARKMINOR="Yes|No"

Whether or not to display tick mark between every increment value along the axis of the slider control. For example, if the range for the slider is between 0 and 100 with an increment of 10, a minor tick mark is displayed every 10 values, between the major tick marks, at 5, 15, 25, etc. The default is No. New as of ColdFusion 5.0.

`TICKMARKIMAGES="`*`URL`*`"`
A URL or comma-delimited list of URLs (relative or absolute) to images you wish to use as tick marks for the slider control. The default is no images. New as of ColdFusion 5.0.

`TICKMARKLABELS="Yes|No|`*`String`*`"`
Whether or not to display labels next to each major tick mark. If `Yes`, the numeric value corresponding to the tick mark is displayed. Instead of numeric values, you may choose to display string values instead, by specifying a string or comma-delimited list of string values, one for each major tick mark between the minimum value and the maximum value for the slider. If you don't provide enough tick mark strings, the `CFSLIDER` control repeats the last value until enough have been displayed. Optional. The default is `No`. New as of ColdFusion 5.0.

`LOOKANDFEEL="Windows|Motif|Metal"`
Specifies a theme governing the look and feel of the slider control. Options are `Windows`, `Motif`, and `Metal`. If no value is specified, ColdFusion first tries `Windows`, then uses the platform default. New as of ColdFusion 5.0

`VERTICAL="Yes|No"`
Indicates whether the slider control should be vertical, with the slider moving up and down. The default is `No`. New as of ColdFusion 5.0

`NOTSUPPORTED="`*`text`*`"`
A text message to display if the user's browser doesn't support Java or Java is disabled Optional. If no message is specified, ColdFusion displays a default message.

## CFSTOREDPROC

```
<CFSTOREDPROC>
  [<CFPROCPARAM>]
  [<CFPROCRESULT>]
  ...
</CFSTOREDPROC>
```

Executes a stored procedure on a data source.

### *Attributes*

`PROCEDURE="`*`procedure_name`*`"`
The name of the stored procedure on the database server that you want to call. Required.

`DATASOURCE="`*`datasource_name`*`"`
The data source that contains the stored procedure. Required.

`DBTYPE="`*`database_type`*`"`
The type of database driver to use. Optional. Possible choices are:

`ODBC` *(the default)*
Connect to the data source using an ODBC driver.

`OLEDB`
Connect using an OLEDB driver.

`Oracle73`
Connect using the Oracle 7.3 native driver. This requires the 7.3.4.0.0 or later client libraries be installed on the ColdFusion server.

`Oracle80`
: Connect using the Oracle 8 native driver. This requires the 8.0 or later client libraries be installed on the ColdFusion server.

`Sybase11`
: Connect using the Sybase 11 native driver. This requires the 11.1.1 or later client libraries be installed on the ColdFusion server.

`DB2`
: Connect using the DB2 5.2 native driver.

`Informix73`
: Connect using the Informix 7.3 native driver. This requires the Informix SDK 2.5 or later or Informix-Connect 2.5 (or later) for Windows.

`Query`
: Specifies the query should use an already existing query as the data source. If this option is used, you don't need to specify a value for `DATASOURCE`. New as of ColdFusion 5.0.

`Dynamic`
: Allows ColdFusion to make an ODBC connection to a data source without having to have the data source registered in the ColdFusion Administrator. When making a dynamic connection, all information normally provided in the ColdFusion Administrator for the connection must be specified in the `CONNECTSTRING` attribute. New as of ColdFusion 5.0.

`USERNAME="`*`username`*`"`
: Username to pass to the data source if one is required. Optional. If a username is specified, it overrides the value set in the ColdFusion Administrator.

`PASSWORD="`*`password`*`"`
: Password associated with `USERNAME`. Optional. If a password is specified, it overrides the value set in the ColdFusion Administrator.

`DBSERVER="`*`database_server`*`"`
: The name of the database server to connect to when using native drivers. Specifying a `DBSERVER` overrides any value set for `DATASOURCE`. Optional.

`DBNAME="`*`database_name`*`"`
: Specifies the database name. For the Sybase System 11 native driver and `SQLOLEDB` provider only. Optional. Overrides any value set for `DATASOURCE`.

`BLOCKFACTOR="`*`block_size`*`"`
: The maximum number of rows to retrieve from the server at a time. Optional. The range is from `1` to `100`. `1` is the default. Note that some drivers may reduce the block factor automatically.

`PROVIDER="`*`COM_provider`*`"`
: COM provider for OLE DB connections. Optional.

`PROVIDERDSN="`*`datasource`*`"`
: COM provider's data-source name for OLE DB. Optional.

`CONNECTSTRING="`*`connection_string`*`"`
: Passes additional connection information to an ODBC data source that can't be passed via the ColdFusion Administrator. `CONNECTSTRING` can also override connection information set for a data source already registered in the ColdFusion Administrator. When making a dynamic data-source connection (when `DBTYPE` is `Dynamic`),

CONNECTSTRING specifies all the information required to connect to the data source. For specific connection string options, you should consult the documentation for your particular database. New as of ColdFusion 5.0.

DEBUG="Yes|No"
: Whether or not debugging information is to be output. Optional. The default is No.

RETURNCODE="Yes|No"
: If set to Yes, populates FSTOREDPROC.STATUSCODE with the status code returned by the stored procedure. Optional. The default is No.

### *Returned Variables*

FSTOREDPROC.STATUSCODE
: Returned when RETURNCODE is set to Yes. Contains the status code returned by the stored procedure.

CFSTOREDPROC.EXECUTIONTIME
: The number of milliseconds it takes the stored procedure to execute.

---

## CFSWITCH

```
<CFSWITCH EXPRESSION="expression">
  <CFCASE VALUE="value" DELIMITERS="delimiter">
  HTML and CFML
  </CFCASE>
  <CFCASE VALUE="value" DELIMITERS="delimiter">
  HTML and CFML
  </CFCASE>
  ...
  <CFDEFAULTCASE>
  HTML and CFML
  </CFDEFAULTCASE>
</CFSWITCH>
```

Evaluates an expression against multiple values until a match is made. Once a match has been made, CFSWITCH passes control to the appropriate CFCASE tag where additional action can take place. If no VALUE matches EXPRESSION, the code between the CFDEFAULTCASE tags is executed.

CFSWITCH/CFCASE/CFDEFAULTCASE is similar in function to CFIF/CFELSEIF/CFELSE. CFSWITCH is significantly faster than using multiple CFIF statements however, because the CFCASE statements are evaluated when the ColdFusion language parser compiles the template into p-code. This means that there is no difference in execution time between a CFSWITCH statement with one CFCASE statement or 1,000 CFCASE statements. CFIF statements on the other hand are evaluated one by one at execution time until one statement evaluates True.

### *Attributes*

EXPRESSION="*expression*"
: Any ColdFusion expression that evaluates to a simple value (string, number, Boolean, date/time). Required.

VALUE="*value*"

A value or delimited list of values CFSWITCH uses to perform a case-insensitive comparison against the specified EXPRESSION. If a value listed in VALUE matches EXPRESSION, the code between the CFCASE tags is executed. Required.

DELIMITERS="*delimiter*"

Specifies the character that separates multiple entries in the VALUE attribute. Optional. The default is a comma.

## CFTABLE

Builds an HTML table from a query result set.

```
<CFTABLE>
[<CFCOL>]
[<CFCOL>]
...
</CFTABLE>
```

### Attributes

QUERY="*query_name*"

The name of the query from which to pull the data used to populate the table. Required.

MAXROWS="*integer*"

The maximum number of rows to output. Optional.

STARTROW="*row_number*"

The query row to begin outputting from. Optional.

COLSPACING="*integer*"

The number of spaces to insert between columns in the table. Optional. The default is 2.

HEADERLINES="*integer*"

Displays headers for each column as specified in the CFCOL tag. Optional.

COLHEADERS="*integer*"

Displays the header for each column as specified in the HEADER attribute of the CFCOL tag. Optional.

HTMLTABLE

Creates the table as an HTML 3.0 table. Optional.

BORDER

Used in conjunction with the HTMLTABLE attribute. Adds a border to the table. Optional.

## CFTEXTINPUT

```
<CFFORM>
  <CFSLIDER>
  ...
</CFFORM>
```

Creates a Java-based text input control for use within a `CFFORM`. Provides data validation as well as customizable display characteristics.

### *Attributes*

`NAME="`*`name`*`"`

The form-field name for the text input control. Required.

`VALUE="`*`text`*`"`

The initial value for the text input control. Optional.

`REQUIRED="Yes|No"`

Whether or not the text input control requires a value before being submitted. Optional. The default is `No`.

`RANGE="`*`min_value, max_value`*`"`

A range of acceptable numeric values for the form-field. Optional.

`VALIDATE="`*`validation_type`*`"`

Validates the contents of the form-field before they are submitted using one of the following criteria; optional:

`CreditCard`

Validates the form-field data using the mod10 algorithm. A credit-card number can be entered as a single value or with dashes or spaces. ColdFusion automatically strips dashes and spaces before validating.

`Date`

Requires the form-field value to be in the U.S. date format, *`mm/dd/yyyy`*.

`EuroDate`

Requires the form-field value to be in the European date format, *`dd/mm/yyyy`*.

`Float`

Requires the form-field value to be a floating-point number.

`Integer`

Requires the form-field value to be an integer.

`Social_Security_Number`

Requires the form-field value to be a U.S. social-security number in the format *`xxx-xx-xxxx`* or *`xxx xx xxxx`*.

`Telephone`

Requires the form-field value to be a U.S. telephone number formatted either *`xxx-xxx-xxxx`* or *`xxx xxx xxxx`*. The area code and exchange are required to begin with a number in the range of 1–9.

`Time`

Requires that the form-field value be entered as a valid time using the format *`hh:mm:ss`*.

ZipCode
: Requires that the form-field value be entered as either a five- or nine-digit U.S. ZIP code number using the format *xxxxx*, *xxxxx-xxxx*, or *xxxxx xxxx*.

Regular_Expression
: Validates the form-field data against a JavaScript regular expression specified in the PATTERN attribute.

PATTERN="*javascript_regular_expression*"
: JavaScript regular expression used to match form input when VALIDATE is Regular_Expression. PATTERN may contain ColdFusion variables and expressions as they are evaluated prior to the execution of the regular expression. Optional. New as of ColdFusion 5.0.

ONVALIDATE="*javascript_function*"
: A JavaScript validation function that should be executed before the form is submitted. Specifying a value for ONVALIDATE overrides any values set in the VALIDATE attribute. Optional.

MESSAGE="*text*"
: Text to appear if validation fails. Optional.

ONERROR="*function_name*"
: The name of a JavaScript function that should be executed if validation fails for any reason. Optional.

SIZE="*integer*"
: The number of characters to display before a horizontal scroll bar appears. Optional.

FONT="*font_name*"
: The font face to use for text displayed in the text input control.

FONTSIZE="*integer*"
: The font size for text displayed in the text input control.

ITALIC="Yes|No"
: If Yes, displays text in italic. Optional. The default is No.

BOLD="Yes|No"
: If Yes, displays text in bold. Optional. The default is No.

HEIGHT="*height_in_pixels*"
: Height of the text input control in pixels. Optional.

WIDTH="*width_in_pixels*"
: Width of the text input control in pixels. Optional.

VSPACE="*vertical_spacing_in_pixels*"
: Height in pixels for the padding above and below the text input control. Optional.

HSPACE="*horizontal_spacing_in_pixels*"
: Width in pixels for the padding to the left and right of the text input control. Optional.

ALIGN="*alignment*"
: Alignment of the text input control. Optional. Valid entries are: Left, Right, Top, TextTopt, Bottom, AbsBottom, Middle, AbsMiddle, and Baseline.

BGCOLOR="*color*"
: Background color for the text input control. Colors may be specified by name (Black, Blue, Cyan, Darkgray, Gray, LightGray, Magenta, Orange, Pink, Red, White, Yellow) or hex code in the form BGCOLOR="##FFFFCC". The double pound signs are

necessary to keep ColdFusion from throwing a syntax error, or you may omit the pound signs altogether. Optional.

TEXTCOLOR="*color*"
: Color to use for text entered in the text input control. Follows the same rules as BGCOLOR. Optional.

MAXLENGTH="*integer*"
: The maximum number of characters to accept in the text input control. Optional.

NOTSUPPORTED="*text*"
: A text message to display if the user's browser doesn't support Java or Java is disabled Optional. If no message is specified, ColdFusion displays a default message.

---

## CFTHROW

<CFTHROW>

Creates a custom exception type that can be caught by the CFTRY/CFCATCH tags when the TYPE attribute of the CFCATCH tag is set to Application, Any, or the custom type you specify in the CFTHROW tag.

As of ColdFusion 4.5.x, you can name custom exception types in a hierarchical manor so that you can reference groups of custom exception types with a single CFCATCH tag. Consider the following CFTHROW tag:

```
<CFTHROW TYPE="MyApp.RequiredParameters.MyVar">
```

Any of the three following CFCATCH tags can be used to catch the exception:

```
<CFCATCH TYPE="MyApp.RequiredParameters.MyVar ">
<CFCATCH TYPE="MyApp.RequiredParameters">
<CFCATCH TYPE="MyApp">
```

Note that this new behavior in CF 4.5.x results in a potential backward compatibility problem with Version 4.01 of ColdFusion. In Version 4.01, a custom exception coded as:

```
<CFTHROW TYPE="MyApp.RequiredParameters.MyVar">
```

can only be caught by an identically named CFCATCH tag, as in:

```
<CFCATCH TYPE="MyApp.RequiredParameters.MyVar">
```

but not by these:

```
<CFCATCH TYPE="MyApp.RequiredParameters">
<CFCATCH TYPE="MyApp">
```

This behavior can be manually overridden by including the CFSETTING tag in your *Application.cfm* template with the CATCHEXCEPTIONSBYPATTERN attribute set to No as in:

```
<!--- this is the Application.cfm template --->
<CFAPPLICATION NAME="MyApplication">
<CFSETTING CATCHEXCEPTIONSBYPATTERN="No">
```

### *Attributes*

TYPE="*exception_type*"
: A name for the exception type. You may give the exception type a custom name or use the predefined types Application or Any. Optional. The default is Application.

MESSAGE="*error_message*"
: Message describing the event that triggered the exception. Optional.

DETAIL="*event_description*"
: Additional information to append to the detailed error information supplied by ColdFusion. Optional.

ERRORCODE="*error_code*"
: A custom error code you want to make available. Optional.

EXTENDEDINFO="*extended_information*"
: Additional information regarding the error that you want to make available. Optional.

### *Returned Variables*

When CFTHROW is used in conjunction with the CFTRY and CFCATCH tags, the following variables are available when an exception is thrown:

CFCATCH.Type
: The exception type specified in the TYPE attribute of the CFCATCH tag.

CFCATCH.Message
: The error message generated by the exception, if any.

CFCATCH.Detail
: A detailed error message generated by the CFML interpreter.

CFCATCH.TagContext
: The name and position of each tag in the tag stack as well as the full pathnames of the files containing the tags. CFML Stack Trace must be enabled in the Debugging section of the ColdFusion Administrator in order to populate this variable.

CFCATCH.ErrorCode
: The contents of the ErrorCode attribute, if any, from the CFTHROW tag.

CFCATCH.ExtendedInfo
: The contents of the ExtendedInfo attribute, if any, from the CFTHROW tag.

---

## CFTRANSACTION

<CFTRANSACTION>
*CFML code*
</CFTRANSACTION>

Treats all query operations between <CFTRANSACTION>/</CFTRANSACTION> tags as a single transaction. Changes to the database aren't committed until all queries in the transaction have executed successfully. In the event that a query within the transaction fails, all previous queries are automatically rolled back.

CFTRANSACTION tags may be nested to allow portions of the transaction to be committed or rolled back within the main CFTRANSACTION block. More than one database may be written to within a single CFTRANSACTION block if each transaction is committed or rolled back prior to writing a query to the next database. Exception handling using CFTRY/CFCATCH gives you full control over how queries are committed and rolled back within CFTRANSACTION blocks.

### *Attributes*

ACTION="*action*"
: The action to take. Optional. The default value is `Begin`, which specifies the beginning of a block of code to execute as a transaction. `Commit` commits a pending transaction, and `Rollback` rolls back a pending transaction.

ISOLATION="*ODBC_lock_type*"
: The ODBC lock type to use for the transaction. The following ODBC lock types are supported: `Read_Uncommitted`, `Read_Committed`, `Repeatable_Read`, and `Serializable`.

---

## CFTREE

Enhanced in ColdFusion 5.0

```
<CFFORM>
  <CFTREE>
    [<CFTREEITEM>]
    ...
  </CFTREE>
  ...
</CFFORM>
```

Creates a Java tree control within a `CFFORM` block.

### *Attributes*

NAME="*name*"
: The form-field name for the tree control. Required.

LOOKANDFEEL="Windows|Motif|Metal"
: Specifies a theme governing the look and feel of the tree control. Optional. If no value is specified, ColdFusion first tries `Windows`, then uses the platform default. New as of ColdFusion 5.0.

REQUIRED="Yes|No"
: Whether or not the tree control requires a value before being submitted. Optional. The default is `No`.

DELIMITER="*delimiter*"
: The delimiter to use to separate the segments of returned in the `Path` form variable (`Form.TreeName.Path`). Optional. The default is the backslash (\).

COMPLETEPATH="Yes|No"
: Whether or not to pass the root level of the `Path` form variable (`Form.`*TreeName*`.Path`) when the `CFFORM` containing the `CFTREE` is submitted. If `No`, the root level of the form isn't passed. Optional. The default is `No`.

APPENDKEY="Yes|No"
: Whether or not to append the `CFTREEITEMKEY` variable to the end of the value of a selected `CFTREEITEM`. Optional. The default is `Yes`.

HIGHLIGHTHREF="Yes|No"
: Whether or not to highlight links specified in the `HREF` attribute of associated `CFTREEITEM` tags. Optional. The default is `Yes`.

`ONVALIDATE="javascript_function"`
: A JavaScript validation function that should be executed before the form is submitted. Optional.

`MESSAGE="text"`
: Text to appear if validation fails. Optional.

`ONERROR="function_name"`
: The name of a JavaScript function that should be executed if validation fails for any reason. Optional.

`FONT="font_name"`
: Font face to use for text appearing in the tree control. Optional.

`FONTSIZE="integer"`
: Font size to use for text appearing in the tree control. Optional.

`ITALIC="Yes|No"`
: If `Yes`, displays text in italic. Optional. The default is `No`.

`BOLD="Yes|No"`
: If `Yes`, displays text in bold. Optional. The default is `No`.

`HEIGHT="height_in_pixels"`
: Height in pixels for the tree control's display area. Optional.

`WIDTH="width_in_pixels"`
: Width in pixels for the tree control's display area. Optional.

`VSPACE="vertical_spacing_in_pixels"`
: Height in pixels for the padding above and below the tree control. Optional.

`HSPACE="horizontal_spacing_in_pixels"`
: Width in pixels for the padding to the left and right of the tree control. Optional.

`ALIGN="alignment"`
: Alignment for the tree control. Valid entries are `Left`, `Right`, `Top`, `TextTop`, `Bottom`, `AbsBottom`, `Baseline`, `Middle`, and `AbsMiddle`. Optional.

`BORDER="Yes|No"`
: Whether or not to add a border around the tree control. Optional. The default is `No`.

`HSCROLL="Yes|No"`
: Whether or not to allow horizontal scrolling. Optional. The default is `Yes`.

`VSCROLL="Yes|No"`
: Whether or not to allow vertical scrolling. Optional. The default is `Yes`.

`NOTSUPPORTED="text"`
: A text message to display if the user's browser doesn't support Java or Java is disabled Optional. If no message is specified, ColdFusion displays a default message.

### Returned Variables

When you submit a `CFFORM` containing a `CFTREE` control, two variables are made available to the template being posted to:

`Form.TreeName.Node`
: The node selected by the user from the tree.

`Form.`*`TreeName`*`.Path`

If the `COMPLETEPATH` attribute is set to `Yes`, `Form.`*`TreeName`*`.Path` returns the user's selection specified as "root\node1\noden\value". Otherwise, `Form.`*`TreeName`*`.Path` returns the path from the first node. The delimiter can be changed by specifying a value for the `DELIMITER` attribute.

## CFTREEITEM

```
<CFTREE>
  [<CFTREEITEM>]
  ...
</CFTREE>
```

Used in conjunction with `CFTREE` to populate a Java tree control.

### *Attributes*

`VALUE="`*`text`*`"`

The value to pass when submitting the `CFFORM`. If populating the tree from a query, multiple column names should be specified in a comma-delimited list. Required.

`DISPLAY="`*`text`*`"`

The label to use for the tree item. Label names are specified in a comma-delimited list when populating a tree from a query. Optional. The default is `VALUE`.

`PARENT="`*`parent_name`*`"`

The `VALUE` of the tree item's parent. Optional.

`IMG="`*`filename`*`"`

The image to use with the tree item. You may specify a path to your own image or use one of the images supplied with ColdFusion by referencing the image name. Multiple images may be assigned to recursive levels of the tree by entering them in a comma-separated list. Valid options for `IMG` are `CD`, `Computer`, `Document`, `Element`, `Folder`, `Floppy`, `Fixed`, and `Remote`. Optional. The default image is `Folder`. If you choose to use your own image, you should try to limit the size to 20 pixels by 20 pixels.

`IMGOPEN="`*`filename`*`"`

Image to display when a tree branch is opened. You may use the same images as the `IMG` tag or supply your own. Optional.

`HREF="`*`URL`*`"`

A URL to associate with the tree item or the name of a query column (from a query used to populate the tree) containing `HREF` values. If the tree is being populated from a query, `HREF` URLs can be specified in a comma-delimited list. The URLs may be relative or absolute. Optional.

`TARGET="`*`URL_target`*`"`

The name of a frame or window that the template specified in the `HREF` attribute should be opened in. Optional.

`QUERY="`*`query_name`*`"`

Name of the query that generates data for the tree control. Optional.

`QUERYASROOT="Yes|No|`*`title`*`"`

Defines the specified `QUERY` as the root level of the tree control. This prevents having to code an additional parent `CFTREEITEM` for the root level. Optional. The default is

No. Although the Allaire documentation on the QUERYASROOT attribute states that it accepts Yes or No as possible values, this isn't entirely true. Besides Yes|No, QUERYASROOT also allows you to specify any title you want to be used as the query root.

EXPAND="Yes|No"
: Whether or not a given branch should be expanded to show its children branches by default. Optional. The default is Yes. Although undocumented, the EXPAND attribute can accept a comma-delimited list of Yes|No values indicating whether or not to expand additional sublevels in the tree.

---

## CFTRY

```
<CFTRY>
CFML
<CFCATCH TYPE="exception_type">
HTML and CFML
</CFCATCH>

<CFCATCH TYPE="exception_type">
HTML and CFML
</CFCATCH>
...
</CFTRY>
```

Traps and processes predefined and developer-specified exceptions within ColdFusion templates. The CFTRY/CFCATCH tags allow you to handle exceptions in your templates gracefully, without having to abort processing. Exceptions occurring within CFCATCH blocks can't be handled by the same CFTRY block governing the CFCATCH block. At least one CFCATCH block must be nested within a CFTRY block. CFCATCH tags are processed in the order in which they are coded within a template.

### *Attributes*

TYPE="*exception_type*"
: Specifies the type of exception to trap. Valid entries are:

Application
: Catches application-level exceptions defined using the Application type in the CFTHROW tag.

Any *(default)*
: Catches unexpected exceptions. This exception type should be coded as the last CFCATCH within a CFTRY block.

*CustomType*
: Catches developer-specified exceptions as defined with the CFTHROW tag.

Database
: Catches exceptions raised when interacting with data sources.

Expression
: Catches exceptions that occur when an expression's evaluation results in an error.

`Lock`
: Catches exceptions associated with the `CFLOCK` tag such as timeouts, etc.

`MissingInclude`
: Catches exceptions that occur when an included template isn't found. This exception type covers exceptions thrown by the `CFINCLUDE`, `CFMODULE`, and `CFERROR` tags.

`Object`
: Catches exceptions associated with external objects such as COM/DCOM, CORBA, and Java.

`Security`
: Catches exceptions that result when authentication fails within the ColdFusion security framework.

`Template`
: Catches general application errors associated with ColdFusion templates.

Besides the values already listed for the `TYPE` attribute, ColdFusion also supports a number of additional structured exception types. These exception types are generated by very specific conditions such as request timeouts or by exceptions encountered as the result of a call to various ColdFusion tags. These exception types are as follows:

```
COM.Allaire.ColdFusion.HTTPConnectionTimeout
COM.Allaire.ColdFusion.HTTPFailure
COM.Allaire.ColdFusion.HTTPAuthFailure
COM.Allaire.ColdFusion.HTTPFileNotFound
COM.Allaire.ColdFusion.HTTPFileNotPassed
COM.Allaire.ColdFusion.HTTPUrlValueNotPassed
COM.Allaire.ColdFusion.HTTPCGIValueNotPassed
COM.Allaire.ColdFusion.HTTPCookieValueNotPassed
COM.Allaire.ColdFusion.HTTPFileNotRenderable
COM.Allaire.ColdFusion.HTTPFileInvalidPath
COM.Allaire.ColdFusion.HTTPContinue
COM.Allaire.ColdFusion.HTTPSwitchingProtocols
COM.Allaire.ColdFusion.HTTPCreated
COM.Allaire.ColdFusion.HTTPAccepted
COM.Allaire.ColdFusion.HTTPNonAuthoritativeInfo
COM.Allaire.ColdFusion.HTTPNoContent
COM.Allaire.ColdFusion.HTTPResetContent
COM.Allaire.ColdFusion.HTTPPartialContent
COM.Allaire.ColdFusion.HTTPMultipleChoices
COM.Allaire.ColdFusion.HTTPMovedPermanently
COM.Allaire.ColdFusion.HTTPMovedTemporarily
COM.Allaire.ColdFusion.HTTPSeeOther
COM.Allaire.ColdFusion.HTTPNotModified
COM.Allaire.ColdFusion.HTTPUseProxy
COM.Allaire.ColdFusion.HTTPBadRequest
COM.Allaire.ColdFusion.HTTPPaymentRequired
COM.Allaire.ColdFusion.HTTPForbidden
COM.Allaire.ColdFusion.HTTPNotFound
COM.Allaire.ColdFusion.HTTPMethodNotAllowed
COM.Allaire.ColdFusion.HTTPNotAcceptable
COM.Allaire.ColdFusion.HTTPProxyAuthenticationRequired
COM.Allaire.ColdFusion.HTTPConflict
```

```
COM.Allaire.ColdFusion.HTTPGone
COM.Allaire.ColdFusion.HTTPContentLengthRequired
COM.Allaire.ColdFusion.HTTPPreconditionFailed
COM.Allaire.ColdFusion.HTTPCFHTTPRequestEntityTooLarge
COM.Allaire.ColdFusion.HTTPRequestURLTooLarge
COM.Allaire.ColdFusion.HTTPUnsupportedMediaType
COM.Allaire.ColdFusion.HTTPServerError
COM.Allaire.ColdFusion.HTTPNotImplemented
COM.Allaire.ColdFusion.HTTPBadGateway
COM.Allaire.ColdFusion.HTTPServiceUnavailable
COM.Allaire.ColdFusion.HTTPGatewayTimeout
COM.Allaire.ColdFusion.HTTPVersionNotSupported
COM.Allaire.ColdFusion.POPConnectionFailure
COM.Allaire.ColdFusion.POPAuthFailure
COM.Allaire.ColdFusion.POPDeleteError
COM.Allaire.ColdFusion.SERVLETJRunError
COM.Allaire.ColdFusion.Request.Timeout
COM.Allaire.ColdFusion.CFEXECUTE.Timeout
COM.Allaire.ColdFusion.CFEXECUTE.OutputError
COM.Allaire.ColdFusion.FileException
```

### *Returned Variables*

The following variables are available regardless of the exception type raised:

`CFCATCH.Type`
: The exception type specified in the `TYPE` attribute of the `CFCATCH` tag.

`CFCATCH.Message`
: The error message generated by the exception, if any.

`CFCATCH.Detail`
: A detailed error message generated by the CFML interpreter.

`CFCATCH.TagContext`
: The name and position of each tag in the tag stack as well as the full pathnames of the files containing the tags as an array of structures. Each structure in the `TagContext` array contains the following elements: `ID`, which holds the name of the tag within the stack; `TEMPLATE`, which holds the full path to the template containing the tag; `LINE`, which holds the line number within the template where the tag was found; and `COLUMN`, which holds the column number within the template where the tag was found.

: CFML Stack Trace must be enabled in the Debugging section of the ColdFusion Administrator in order to populate this variable. If this option isn't enabled, ColdFusion returns a zero-length array for `CFCATCH.TagContext`.

`CFCATCH.ErrorCode`
: The contents of the `ErrorCode` attribute, if any, as passed from the `CFTHROW` tag when `TYPE` is `Application` or `Custom`. Returns the same value as `SQLState` when `TYPE` is `Database`. Returns an empty string for all other `TYPE` values.

The remaining variables are all specific to the exception type specified in the `TYPE` attribute of the `CFCATCH` tag:

`CFCATCH.NativeErrorCode` *(TYPE is* `Database`*)*
: The native error code supplied by the database driver for the particular exception. If no error code is provided, ColdFusion returns a value of `-1`.

`CFCATCH.SQLState` *(TYPE is* `Database`*)*
: The SQLState supplied by the database driver for the particular exception. If no SQL-State is returned, ColdFusion returns a value of `-1`.

`CFCATCH.ErrNumber` *(TYPE is* `Expression`*)*
: An internal error number associated with the expression.

`CFCATCH.LockName` *(TYPE is* `Lock`*)*
: The name of the lock affected by the exception. If the lock is unnamed, returns `anonymous`.

`CFCATCH.LockOperation` *(TYPE is* `Lock`*)*
: The operation that caused the exception. Valid return values are `Timeout`, `MuteEx`, and `Unknown`.

`CFCATCH.MissingFileName` *(TYPE is* `MissingInclude`*)*
: The name of the missing include file.

`CFCATCH.ExtendedInfo` *(TYPE is* `Application` *or* `Custom`*)*
: The contents of the `ExtendedInfo` attribute, if any, from the `CFTHROW` tag.

---

## CFUPDATE

<CFUPDATE>

Updates records in a database. The `CFUPDATE` tag provides a way to update database records without having to wrap the SQL in a `CFQUERY`.

### *Attributes*

`DATASOURCE="`*`datasource_name`*`"`
: The name of the data source to connect to when performing the update. Required.

`DBTYPE="`*`database_type`*`"`
: The type of database driver to use. Optional. Possible choices are:

  `ODBC` *(the default)*
  : Connect to the data source using an ODBC driver.

  `OLEDB`
  : Connect using an OLEDB driver.

  `Oracle73`
  : Connect using the Oracle 7.3 native driver. This requires the 7.3.4.0.0 or later client libraries be installed on the ColdFusion server.

  `Oracle80`
  : Connect using the Oracle 8 native driver. This requires the 8.0 or later client libraries be installed on the ColdFusion server.

  `Sybase11`
  : Connect using the Sybase 11 native driver. This requires the 11.1.1 or later client libraries be installed on the ColdFusion server.

  `DB2`
  : Connect using the DB2 5.2 native driver.

`Informix73`
: Connect using the Informix 7.3 native driver. This requires the Informix SDK 2.5 or later or Informix-Connect 2.5 (or later) for Windows.

`Query`
: Specifies the query should use an already existing query as the data source. If this option is used, you don't need to specify a value for `DATASOURCE`. New as of ColdFusion 5.0.

`Dynamic`
: Allows ColdFusion to make an ODBC connection to a data source without having to have the data source registered in the ColdFusion Administrator. When making a dynamic connection, all information normally provided in the ColdFusion Administrator for the connection must be specified in the `CONNECTSTRING` attribute. New as of ColdFusion 5.0.

`DBSERVER="`*`database_server`*`"`
: The name of the database server to connect to when using native drivers. Specifying a `DBSERVER` overrides any value set for `DATASOURCE`. Optional.

`DBNAME="`*`database_name`*`"`
: The database name. For the Sybase System 11 native driver and `SQLOLEDB` provider only. Optional. Overrides any value set for `DATASOURCE`.

`TABLENAME="`*`table_name`*`"`
: The name of the table to perform the update on. Required. Note that Oracle database drivers require the table name to be in all uppercase. In addition, Sybase database drivers use a case-sensitive table name.

`TABLEOWNER="`*`table_owner`*`"`
: The name of the table owner for databases that support this feature (e.g., Oracle, SQL Server, and SQL Anywhere). Optional.

`TABLEQUALIFIER="`*`qualifier`*`"`
: The table qualifier for databases that support the feature (e.g., Oracle and SQL Server). Optional.

`USERNAME="`*`username`*`"`
: Username to pass to the data source if one is required. Optional. If a username is specified, it overrides the value set in the ColdFusion Administrator.

`PASSWORD="`*`password`*`"`
: Password associated with `USERNAME`. Optional. If a password is specified, it overrides the value set in the ColdFusion Administrator.

`PROVIDER="`*`COM_provider`*`"`
: COM provider for OLE DB connections. Optional.

`PROVIDERDSN="`*`datasource`*`"`
: COM provider's data-source name for OLE DB. Optional.

`CONNECTSTRING="`*`connection_string`*`"`
: Passes additional connection information to an ODBC data source that can't be passed via the ColdFusion Administrator. `CONNECTSTRING` can also override connection information set for a data source already registered in the ColdFusion Administrator. When making a dynamic data source connection (when `DBTYPE` is `Dynamic`), `CONNECTSTRING` specifies all the information required to connect to the data source.

For specific connection string options, you should consult the documentation for your particular database. New as of ColdFusion 5.0.

`FORMFIELDS="field_names"`
A comma-delimited list of form fields to update. Optional. If no form fields are supplied, ColdFusion attempts to update the database using all the form fields passed from the form.

---

## CFWDDX

<CFWDDX>

Serializes and deserializes data according to the WDDX XML DTD. The `CFWDDX` tag can also create JavaScript statements that instantiate equivalent JavaScript objects. The `CFWDDX` tag can serialize/deserialize binary data. Binary data is automatically base64-encoded before being serialized. This capability allows you to send binary files in WDDX packets. More information on WDDX can be found at *www.openwddx.org*.

### *Attributes*

`ACTION="action"`
The action to be performed by the `CFWDDX` tag. Required. Possible actions are `CFML2WDDX`, which serializes CFML to WDDX; `WDDX2CFML`, which deserializes WDDX to CFML; `CFML2JS`, which serializes CFML to JavaScript; and `WDDX2JS`, which deserializes WDDX to JavaScript.

`INPUT="data"`
The data to be serialized/deserialized. Required.

`OUTPUT="variable_name"`
A variable to hold the data after it has been serialized/deserialized. Required when `ACTION` is `WDDX2CFML`. For all other actions, if no value is specified for `OUTPUT`, the processing results are outputted in the HTML stream.

`TOPLEVELVARIABLE="variable_name"`
The name of the top-level JavaScript object created when deserialization occurs. Required when `ACTION` is set to `CFML2JS` or `WDDX2JS`.

`USETIMEZONEINFO="Yes|No"`
Whether or not to use time-zone information when serializing CFML to WDDX. If this attribute is set to `Yes`, ColdFusion calculates the hour/minute offset for all date/time objects in the WDDX packet. If set to `No`, local time is used for all date/time objects. Optional. The default is `Yes`.

`VALIDATE="Yes|No"`
Whether or not to use a validating XML parser with the WDDX DTD to determine whether the value specified in `INPUT` is a well-formed WDDX packet when `ACTION` is `WDDX2CFML` or `WDDDX2JS`. If the value is a well-formed WDDX packet, deserialization takes place. If the value isn't well-formed WDDX, an exception is thrown. The `VALIDATE` parameter performs the same job as the `IsWDDX()` function.

# B

# *Function Reference*

ColdFusion functions are an integral part of the CFML coding environment. ColdFusion contains over 255 functions that allow you to manipulate data and format it to suit your specific requirements. Functions can be used for everything from performing mathematical calculations to formatting time and date values. This appendix contains reference material on all the ColdFusion functions through Version 5.0, along with proper syntax, a detailed description, and a working example where possible.

## *Array Functions*

`ArrayAppend()`
`ArrayAvg()`
`ArrayClear()`
`ArrayDeleteAt()`
`ArrayInsertAt()`
`ArrayIsEmpty()`
`ArrayLen()`
`ArrayMax()`
`ArrayMin()`
`ArrayNew()`
`ArrayPrepend()`
`ArrayResize()`
`ArraySet()`
`ArraySort()`
`ArraySum()`
`ArraySwap()`
`ArrayToList()`
`IsArray()`
`ListToArray()`

## *Date/Time Functions*

`CreateDate()`
`CreateDateTime()`
`CreateODBCDate()`
`CreateODBCDateTime()`
`CreateODBCTime()`
`CreateTime()`

CreateTimeSpan()
DateAdd()
DateCompare()
DateConvert()
DateDiff()
DateFormat()
DatePart()
Day()
DayOfWeek()
DayOfWeekAsString()
DayOfYear()
DaysInMonth()
DaysInYear()
FirstDayOfMonth()
GetHTTPTimeString()
GetTickCount()
GetTimeZoneInfo()
Hour()
IsDate()
IsLeapYear()
IsNumericDate()
LSDateFormat()
LSParseDateTime()
Minute()
Month()
MonthAsString()
Now()
ParseDateTime()
Quarter()
Second()
TimeFormat()
Week()
Year()

## *Decision/Evaluation Functions*

CF_IsColdFusionDataSource()
DE()
DirectoryExists()
Evaluate()
FileExists()
IIf()
IsArray()
IsAthenticated()
IsAuthorized()
IsBinary()
IsBoolean()
IsCustomFunction()
IsDate()
IsDebugMode()
IsDefined()
IsK2ServerDocCountExceeded()
IsLeapYear()
IsNumeric()
IsNumericDate()
IsProtected()
IsQuery()
IsSimpleValue()
IsStruct()
IsWDDX()
LSIsCurrency()
LSIsDate()
LSIsNumeric()
ParameterExists()
SetVariable()

## Encoding/Encryption Functions

CFusion_Decrypt()
CFusion_Encrypt()
Decrypt()
Encrypt()
Hash()
ToBase64()
ToBinary()
ToString()
URLDecode()
URLEncodedFormat()

## File/Directory Functions

DirectoryExists()
ExpandPath()
FileExists()
GetBaseTemplatePath()
GetCurrentTemplatePath()
GetDirectoryFromPath()
GetFileFromPath()
GetTempDirectory()
GetTempFile()
GetTemplatePath()

## Formatting Functions

DateFormat()
DecimalFormat()
DollarFormat()
FormatBaseN()
HTMLCodeFormat()
HTMLEditFormat()
JSStringFormat()
Lcase()
LSCurrencyFormat()
LSDateFormat()
LSEuroCurrencyFormat()
LSNumberFormat()
LSTimeFormat()
NumberFormat()
ParagraphFormat()
TimeFormat()
Ucase()
XMLFormat()
YesNoFormat()

## International Functions

GetLocale()
LSCurrencyFormat()
LSDateFormat()
LSEuroCurrencyFormat()
LSIsCurrency()
LSIsDate()
LSIsNumeric()
LSNumberFormat()
LSParseCurrency()
LSParseDateTime()
LSParseEuroCurrency()
LSParseNumber()
LSTimeFormat()
SetLocale()

## *List Functions*

```
ArrayToList()              ListAppend()
ListChangeDelims()         ListContains()
ListContainsNoCase()       ListDeleteAt()
ListFind()                 ListFindNoCase()
ListFirst()                ListGetAt()
ListInsertAt()             ListLast()
ListLen()                  ListPrepend()
ListQualify()              ListRest()
ListSetAt()                ListSort()
ListToArray()              ListValueCount()
ListValueCountNoCase()     QuotedValueList()
ReplaceList()              ValueList()
```

## *Mathematical Functions*

```
Abs()                      ACos()
ASin()                     Atn()
BitAnd()                   BitMaskClear()
BitMaskRead()              BitMaskSet()
BitNot()                   BitOr()
BitSHLN()                  BitSHRN()
BitXor()                   Ceiling()
Cos()                      DecrementValue()
Exp()                      Fix()
IncrementValue()           InputBaseN()
Int()                      Log()
Log10()                    Max()
Min()                      Pi()
Rand()                     Randomize()
RandRange()                Round()
Sgn()                      Sin()
Sqr()                      Tan()
```

## Miscellaneous Functions

CreateObject()
CreateUUID()
DeleteClientVariable()
GetBaseTagData()
GetBaseTagList()
GetClientVariablesList()
GetException()
GetFunctionList()
GetHTTPRequestData()
GetK2ServerCollections()
GetK2ServerDocCount()
GetK2ServerDocCountLimit()
GetMetricData()
GetProfileString()
IsK2ServerDocCountExceeded()
JavaCast()
SetProfileString()
WriteOutput()

## Query Functions

Duplicate()
IsQuery()
PreserveSingleQuotes()
QueryAddColumn()
QueryAddRow()
QueryNew()
QuerySetCell()
QuotedValueList()
ValueList()

## Security Functions

AuthenticatedContext()
AuthenticatedUser()
IsAuthenticated()
IsAuthorized()
IsProtected()

## String Functions

Asc()
Chr()
CJustify()
Compare()
CompareNoCase()
Find()
FindNoCase()
FindOneOf()
FormatBaseN()
GetToken()
Insert()
Lcase()
Left()
Len()
LJustify()
LTrim()
Mid()
REFind()
REFindNoCase()
RemoveChars()
RepeatString()
Replace()

`ReplaceList()`
`ReplaceNoCase()`
`REReplace()`
`REReplaceNoCase()`
`Reverse()`
`Right()`
`RJustify()`
`RTrim()`
`SpanExcluding()`
`SpanIncluding()`
`StripCR()`
`ToBase64()`
`Trim()`
`Ucase()`
`Val()`

## *Structure Functions*

`Duplicate()`
`IsStruct()`
`StructAppend()`
`StructClear()`
`StructCopy()`
`StructCount()`
`StructDelete()`
`StructFind()`
`StructFindKey()`
`StructFindValue()`
`StructGet()`
`StructInsert()`
`StructIsEmpty()`
`StructKeyArray()`
`StructKeyExists()`
`StructKeyList()`
`StructNew()`
`StructSort()`
`StructUpdate()`

## *Undocumented Functions*

`CF_GetDataSourceUserName()`
`CF_IsColdFusionDataSource()`
`CF_SetDataSourcePassword()`
`CF_SetDataSourceUserName()`
`CFusion_DBConnections_Flush()`
`CFusion_Decrypt()`
`CFusion_Disable_DBConnections()`
`CFusion_Encrypt()`
`CFusion_GetODBCDSN()`
`CFusion_GetODBCINI()`
`CFusion_SetODBCINI()`
`CFusion_Settings_Refresh()`
`CFusion_VerifyMail()`

# *Alphabetical List of Functions*

This section lists all the ColdFusion functions alphabetically, with proper syntax, a detailed description, and a working example where possible. Version information is included for many of the functions; if no version information is listed, the function is available in ColdFusion 4.0 and later.

## Abs

`Abs (number)`

Returns the absolute value of a number. Example:

```
The absolute value of -33 is <CFOUTPUT>#Abs(-33)#</CFOUTPUT>
```

## ACos

New as of ColdFusion 4.01

`ACos (number)`

Returns the arccosine of a number expressed in radians. The value of `number` must be between –1 and 1. Example:

```
The arccosine of -1 is <CFOUTPUT>#ACos(-1)#</CFOUTPUT>
```

## ArrayAppend

`ArrayAppend(array, value)`

Appends an element to the end of an array. Upon successful completion, `ArrayAppend()` returns a value of `TRUE`. Here's an example of appending a new element to a one-dimensional array:

```
<CFSET Grades = ArrayNew(1)>
<CFSET Grades[1] = 95>
<CFSET Grades[2] = 93>
<CFSET Grades[3] = 87>
<CFSET Grades[4] = 100>
<CFSET Grades[5] = 74>

<B>Original Array:</B><BR>
<CFLOOP INDEX="Element" FROM="1" TO="#ArrayLen(Grades)#">
  <CFOUTPUT>Grade #Element#: #Grades[Element]#<BR></CFOUTPUT>
</CFLOOP>

<P>Append the value 66 to the array:<BR>
<CFSET ArrayAppend(Grades, "66")>

<P><B>New Array:</B><BR>
<CFLOOP INDEX="Element" FROM="1" TO="#ArrayLen(Grades)#">
  <CFOUTPUT>Grade #Element#: #Grades[Element]#<BR></CFOUTPUT>
</CFLOOP>
```

## ArrayAvg

`ArrayAvg(array)`

Returns the average (mean) of the values in the array. The following example returns the average of the values contained in the one-dimensional array `Grades`:

```
<CFSET Grades = ArrayNew(1)>
<CFSET Grades[1] = 95>
```

```
<CFSET Grades[2] = 93>
<CFSET Grades[3] = 87>
<CFSET Grades[4] = 100>
<CFSET Grades[5] = 74>

<CFLOOP INDEX="Element" FROM="1" TO="#ArrayLen(Grades)#">
  <CFOUTPUT>Grade #Element#: #Grades[Element]#<BR></CFOUTPUT>
</CFLOOP>

<P><CFOUTPUT>The average grade is #ArrayAvg(Grades)#%</CFOUTPUT>
```

## ArrayClear

`ArrayClear(`*`array`*`)`

Removes all data from the specified array. Upon successful completion, `ArrayClear()` returns a value of `TRUE`. Here's an example of clearing all the data from the array `Grades`:

```
<CFSET Grades = ArrayNew(1)>
<CFSET Grades[1] = 95>
<CFSET Grades[2] = 93>
<CFSET Grades[3] = 87>
<CFSET Grades[4] = 100>
<CFSET Grades[5] = 74>

<CFIF ArrayIsEmpty(Grades)>
  The array <B>Grades</B> is empty.
<CFELSE>
  The array <B>Grades</B> contains data.
</CFIF>

<P>Clearing the array...
<CFSET ArrayClear(Grades)>

<P><CFIF ArrayIsEmpty(Grades)>
  The array <B>Grades</B> is empty.
<CFELSE>
  The array <B>Grades</B> contains data.
</CFIF>
```

## ArrayDeleteAt

`ArrayDeleteAt(`*`array, position`*`)`

Deletes data from the designated array at the specified position. Returns a value of `TRUE` upon successful completion. The following example deletes the third element from the one-dimensional array `Grades`:

```
<CFSET Grades = ArrayNew(1)>
<CFSET Grades[1] = 95>
<CFSET Grades[2] = 93>
<CFSET Grades[3] = 87>
<CFSET Grades[4] = 100>
<CFSET Grades[5] = 74>
```

```
<B>Original Array:</B><BR>
<CFLOOP INDEX="Element" FROM="1" TO="#ArrayLen(Grades)#">
  <CFOUTPUT>Grade #Element#: #Grades[Element]#<BR></CFOUTPUT>
</CFLOOP>

<P>Delete Element 4:
<CFSET ArrayDeleteAt(Grades, 4)>

<P><B>New, Array</B><BR>
<CFLOOP INDEX="Element" FROM="1" TO="#ArrayLen(Grades)#">
  <CFOUTPUT>Grade #Element#: #Grades[Element]#<BR></CFOUTPUT>
</CFLOOP>
```

## ArrayInsertAt

`ArrayInsertAt(`*`array, value, position`*`)`

Inserts *`value`* into the designated *`array`* at the specified *`position`*. Values having an index position greater than the inserted data are shifted right by one. Using `ArrayInsertAt()` increases the size of the array by 1 and returns a value of `True` upon successful completion. Here's an example of inserting an element into the third position of a one-dimensional array called `Grades`:

```
<CFSET Grades = ArrayNew(1)>
<CFSET Grades[1] = 95>
<CFSET Grades[2] = 93>
<CFSET Grades[3] = 87>
<CFSET Grades[4] = 100>
<CFSET Grades[5] = 74>

<B>Original Array:</B><BR>
<CFLOOP INDEX="Element" FROM="1" TO="#ArrayLen(Grades)#">
  <CFOUTPUT>Grade #Element#: #Grades[Element]#<BR></CFOUTPUT>
</CFLOOP>

<P>Insert 65 into Element 3:
<CFSET ArrayInsertAt(Grades, 3, 65)>

<P><B>New Array</B><BR>
<CFLOOP INDEX="Element" FROM="1" TO="#ArrayLen(Grades)#">
  <CFOUTPUT>Grade #Element#: #Grades[Element]#<BR></CFOUTPUT>
</CFLOOP>
```

## ArrayIsEmpty

`ArrayIsEmpty(`*`array`*`)`

Returns `TRUE` if the specified array contains no data or `FALSE` if it does contain data. Example:

```
<CFIF ArrayIsEmpty(Scores)>
     There are no scores available for this game!
<CFELSE>
     There are scores available for this game!
</CFIF>
```

## ArrayLen

`ArrayLen(array)`

Determines the length of the specified array. The following example returns the number of elements in the one-dimensional array **Grades**:

```
<CFSET Grades = ArrayNew(1)>
<CFSET Grades[1] = 95>
<CFSET Grades[2] = 93>
<CFSET Grades[3] = 87>
<CFSET Grades[4] = 100>
<CFSET Grades[5] = 74>

<CFOUTPUT>The array <B>Grades</B> contains #ArrayLen(Grades)# elements.</CFOUTPUT>
```

## ArrayMax

`ArrayMax(array)`

Returns the largest numeric value contained in the array. Useful only for arrays containing numeric values. Here's an example that returns the highest grade in the array **Grades**:

```
<CFSET Grades = ArrayNew(1)>
<CFSET Grades[1] = 95>
<CFSET Grades[2] = 93>
<CFSET Grades[3] = 87>
<CFSET Grades[4] = 100>
<CFSET Grades[5] = 74>

<CFOUTPUT>The highest grade is #ArrayMax(Grades)#%.</CFOUTPUT>
```

## ArrayMin

`ArrayMin(array)`

Returns the smallest numeric value contained in the array. Useful only for arrays containing numeric values. Here's an example that returns the lowest grade in the array **Grades**:

```
<CFSET Grades = ArrayNew(1)>
<CFSET Grades[1] = 95>
<CFSET Grades[2] = 93>
<CFSET Grades[3] = 87>
<CFSET Grades[4] = 100>
<CFSET Grades[5] = 74>

<CFOUTPUT>The lowest grade is #ArrayMin(Grades)#%.</CFOUTPUT>
```

## ArrayNew

`ArrayNew(dimension)`

Creates an array of between 1 and 3 dimensions where the value of *dimension* is an integer between 1 and 3. Examples:

```
<CFSET PartNumbers = ArrayNew(1)>
<CFSET Samples = ArrayNew(2)>
<CFSET Colors = ArrayNew(3)>
```

## ArrayPrepend

`ArrayPrepend(array, value)`

Adds a value to the beginning of an array. A value of `True` is returned upon successful completion. The following example adds an element to the beginning of an array:

```
<CFSET Grades = ArrayNew(1)>
<CFSET Grades[1] = 95>
<CFSET Grades[2] = 93>
<CFSET Grades[3] = 87>
<CFSET Grades[4] = 100>
<CFSET Grades[5] = 74>

<B>Original Array:</B><BR>
<CFLOOP INDEX="Element" FROM="1" TO="#ArrayLen(Grades)#">
  <CFOUTPUT>Grade #Element#: #Grades[Element]#<BR></CFOUTPUT>
</CFLOOP>

<P>Prepend the value 80 to the array:<BR>
<CFSET ArrayPrepend(Grades, "80")>

<P><B>New Array:</B><BR>
<CFLOOP INDEX="Element" FROM="1" TO="#ArrayLen(Grades)#">
  <CFOUTPUT>Grade #Element#: #Grades[Element]#<BR></CFOUTPUT>
</CFLOOP>
```

## ArrayResize

`ArrayResize(array, size)`

Resizes the designated array to a size as specified by the size parameter. For performance gains, this function is usually used immediately after creating an array with the `ArrayNew()` function to resize the array to its estimated size. Upon successful completion, `ArrayResize()` returns a value of `True`. Here's an example that creates an array called `Grades` and then resizes it to 50 elements:

```
<CFSET Grades = ArrayNew(1)>

<CFOUTPUT>Grades contains #ArrayLen(Grades)# elements.</CFOUTPUT>
```

```
<P>Resize the array...<BR>
<CFSET ArrayResize(Grades, 50)>

<P><CFOUTPUT>Grades now contains #ArrayLen(Grades)# elements.</CFOUTPUT>
```

## ArraySet

`ArraySet(`*`array, start, end, value`*`)`

Initializes one or more elements in a one-dimensional array, where *start* is the starting position, *end* is the ending position, and *value* is the value to use. The following example creates a one-dimensional array and populates the first five elements with the string "Place holder":

```
<CFSET MyArray = ArrayNew(1)>
<CFSET temp = ArraySet(MyArray, 1, 5, "Place holder")>

<CFLOOP INDEX="Element" FROM="1" TO="#ArrayLen(MyArray)#">
  <CFOUTPUT>Element #Element#:  #MyArray[Element]#<BR></CFOUTPUT>
</CFLOOP>
```

## ArraySort

`ArraySort(`*`array, type`*` [, `*`order`*`])`

Sorts an array based on the sort *type* (`numeric`, `text`, or `textnocase`) and optionally, the sort *order* (`asc`, the default, or `desc`). Here's an example that sorts the values in an array called `Grades` from highest grade to lowest grade in descending order:

```
<CFSET Grades = ArrayNew(1)>
<CFSET Grades[1] = "95">
<CFSET Grades[2] = "93">
<CFSET Grades[3] = "87">
<CFSET Grades[4] = "100">
<CFSET Grades[5] = "74">

<B>Original Array:</B><BR>
<CFLOOP INDEX="Element" FROM="1" TO="#ArrayLen(Grades)#">
  <CFOUTPUT>Grade #Element#: #Grades[Element]#<BR></CFOUTPUT>
</CFLOOP>

<P>Sort Array...
<CFSET ArraySort(Grades, "Numeric", "Desc")>

<P><B>Sorted Array:</B><BR>
<CFLOOP INDEX="Element" FROM="1" TO="#ArrayLen(Grades)#">
  <CFOUTPUT>Grade #Element#: #Grades[Element]#<BR></CFOUTPUT>
</CFLOOP>
```

## ArraySum

`ArraySum(array)`

Calculates the sum of the values in the specified array. The following example calculates the sum of all the values contained in an array called **Grades**:

```
<CFSET Grades = ArrayNew(1)>
<CFSET Grades[1] = "95">
<CFSET Grades[2] = "93">
<CFSET Grades[3] = "87">
<CFSET Grades[4] = "100">
<CFSET Grades[5] = "74">

<B>Original Array</B><BR>
<CFLOOP INDEX="Element" FROM="1" TO="#ArrayLen(Grades)#">
  <CFOUTPUT>Grade #Element#: #Grades[Element]#<BR></CFOUTPUT>
</CFLOOP>

<P><CFOUTPUT>The sum of all of the grades is #ArraySum(Grades)#.</CFOUTPUT>
```

## ArraySwap

`ArraySwap(array, position1, position2)`

Swaps the values stored in the positions specified in *position1* and *position2*. Here's an example that takes an array and swaps the values contained in elements 5 and 2:

```
<CFSET Grades = ArrayNew(1)>
<CFSET Grades[1] = 95>
<CFSET Grades[2] = 93>
<CFSET Grades[3] = 87>
<CFSET Grades[4] = 100>
<CFSET Grades[5] = 74>

<B>Original Array</B><BR>
<CFLOOP Index="Element" FROM="1" TO="#ArrayLen(Grades)#">
  <CFOUTPUT>Grade #Element#: #Grades[Element]#<BR></CFOUTPUT>
</CFLOOP>

<P>Swap 5th and 2nd array elements...
<CFSET ArraySwap(Grades, 5, 2)>

<P><B>Array after ArraySwap</B><BR>
<CFLOOP Index="Element" FROM="1" TO="#ArrayLen(Grades)#">
  <CFOUTPUT>Grade #Element#: #Grades[Element]#<BR></CFOUTPUT>
</CFLOOP>
```

## ArrayToList

`ArrayToList(`*`array`*` [, `*`delimiter`*`])`

Converts the specified one-dimensional array to a ColdFusion list. An optional *`delimiter`* may be specified (a comma is the default delimiter). The following example converts an array to a comma-delimited list:

```
<CFSET Grades = ArrayNew(1)>
<CFSET Grades[1] = 95>
<CFSET Grades[2] = 93>
<CFSET Grades[3] = 87>
<CFSET Grades[4] = 100>
<CFSET Grades[5] = 74>

<B>Original Array</B><BR>
<CFLOOP Index="Element" FROM="1" TO="#ArrayLen(Grades)#">
  <CFOUTPUT>Grade #Element#: #Grades[Element]#<BR></CFOUTPUT>
</CFLOOP>

<P>Convert Array to List...
<CFSET GradeList = ArrayToList(Grades)>

<P><B>New List</B><BR>
<CFOUTPUT>GradeList = #GradeList#</CFOUTPUT>
```

## Asc

`Asc(`*`character`*`)`

Returns the ASCII character code (number) for a given character. Here's an example that generates a chart of the printable ASCII character codes:

```
<TABLE BORDER="1">
  <TR><TH>Character</TH><TH>ASCII Code</TH></TR>

<CFLOOP INDEX="Character" FROM="33" TO="255">
  <CFOUTPUT>
    <TR><TD>#Chr(Character)#</TD><TD>#Asc(Chr(Character))#</TD></TR>
  </CFOUTPUT>
</CFLOOP>
</TABLE>
```

## Asin

`ASin(`*`number`*`)`

Returns the arcsine of a number expressed in radians. The value of *`number`* must be between –1 and 1. Example:

```
The arcsine of -1 is <CFOUTPUT>#ASin(-1)#</CFOUTPUT>
```

## Atn

`Atn(number)`

Returns the arctangent of a number expressed in radians. Example:

```
The arctangent of 1 is <CFOUTPUT>#Atn(1)#</CFOUTPUT>
```

## AuthenticatedContext

New as of ColdFusion 4.01

`AuthenticatedContext()`

Returns the name of the security context for a given application. Example:

```
The current security context is <CFOUTPUT>#AuthenticatedContext()#</CFOUTPUT>.
```

## AuthenticatedUser

New as of ColdFusion 4.01

`AuthenticatedUser()`

Returns the name of the authenticated user within an application. Example:

```
The authenticated user is <CFOUTPUT>#AuthenticatedUser()#</CFOUTPUT>.
```

## BitAnd

`BitAnd(number1, number2)`

Returns the bitwise AND of two 32-bit integers. Examples:

```
<CFOUTPUT>
BitAnd(1,1): #BitAnd(1,1)#<BR>
BitAnd(2,10): #BitAnd(2,10)#<BR>
BitAnd(3,45): #BitAnd(3,45)#<BR>
BitAnd(128,256): #BitAnd(128,256)#<BR>
BitAnd(1024,32): #BitAnd(1024,32)#
</CFOUTPUT>
```

## BitMaskClear

`BitMaskClear(number, startbit, length)`

Returns *`number`* bitwise cleared with *`length`* bits beginning at the bit specified by *`startbit`*. Both *`startbit`* and *`length`* must be integers between 0 and 31. Examples:

```
<CFOUTPUT>
BitMaskClear(127,0,1): #BitMaskClear(127,0,1)#<BR>
BitMaskClear(255,3,3): #BitMaskClear(255,3,3)#<BR>
BitMaskClear(511,2,4): #BitMaskClear(511,2,4)#<BR>
BitMaskClear(1023,4,25): #BitMaskClear(1023,4,25)#<BR>
BitMaskClear(2047,7,4): #BitMaskClear(2047,7,4)#
</CFOUTPUT>
```

## BitMaskRead

`BitMaskRead(number, startbit, length)`

Returns the integer from *length* bits of *number* beginning from the bit specified by *startbit*. Examples:

```
<CFOUTPUT>
BitMaskRead(127,0,1): #BitMaskRead(127,0,1)#<BR>
BitMaskRead(255,3,3): #BitMaskRead(255,3,3)#<BR>
BitMaskRead(511,2,4): #BitMaskRead(511,2,4)#<BR>
BitMaskRead(1023,4,25): #BitMaskRead(1023,4,25)#<BR>
BitMaskRead(2047,7,4): #BitMaskRead(2047,7,4)#
</CFOUTPUT>
```

## BitMaskSet

`BitMaskSet(number, mask, startbit, length)`

Returns *number* bitwise masked with *length* bits of *mask* beginning at the bit specified by *startbit*. Examples:

```
<CFOUTPUT>
BitMaskSet(127,12,0,1): #BitMaskSet(127,12,0,1)#<BR>
BitMaskSet(255,3,3,3): #BitMaskSet(255,3,3,3)#<BR>
BitMaskSet(511,4,2,4): #BitMaskSet(511,4,2,4)#<BR>
BitMaskSet(1023,0,4,25): #BitMaskSet(1023,0,4,25)#<BR>
BitMaskSet(2047,247,7,4): #BitMaskSet(2047,247,7,4)#
</CFOUTPUT>
```

## BitNot

`BitNot(number)`

Returns the bitwise NOT of a 32-bit integer. Examples:

```
<CFOUTPUT>
BitNot(0): #BitNot(0)#<BR>
BitNot(1): #BitNot(1)#<BR>
BitNot(10): #BitNot(10)#<BR>
BitNot(128): #BitNot(128)#<BR>
BitNot(1024): #BitNot(1024)#
</CFOUTPUT>
```

## BitOr

`BitOr(number1, number2)`

Returns the bitwise OR of two 32-bit integers. Examples:

```
<CFOUTPUT>
BitOr(1,1): #BitOr(1,1)#<BR>
BitOr(2,10): #BitOr(2,10)#<BR>
BitOr(3,45): #BitOr(3,45)#<BR>
```

```
BitOr(128,256): #BitOr(128,256)#<BR>
BitOr(1024,32): #BitOr(1024,32)#
</CFOUTPUT>
```

## BitSHLN

`BitSHLN(number, count)`

Bitwise shifts *number* to the left (wthout rotation) *count* bits where *count* is an integer between 0 and 31. Examples:

```
<CFOUTPUT>
BitSHLN(0,1): #BitSHLN(0,1)#<BR>
BitSHLN(1,5): #BitSHLN(1,5)#<BR>
BitSHLN(10,9): #BitSHLN(10,9)#<BR>
BitSHLN(128,23): #BitSHLN(128,23)#<BR>
BitSHLN(1024, 31): #BitSHLN(1024,31)#
</CFOUTPUT>
```

## BitSHRN

`BitSHRN(number, count)`

Bitwise shifts *number* to the right (without rotation) *count* bits where *count* is an integer between 0 and 31. Examples:

```
<CFOUTPUT>
BitSHRN(0,1): #BitSHRN(0,1)#<BR>
BitSHRN(90000,5): #BitSHRN(90000,5)#<BR>
BitSHRN(256,3): #BitSHRN(256,3)#<BR>
BitSHRN(128,1): #BitSHRN(128,1)#<BR>
BitSHRN(1024, 2): #BitSHRN(1024,2)#
</CFOUTPUT>
```

## BitXor

`BitXor(number1, number2)`

Returns the bitwise XOR of two 32-bit integers. Examples:

```
<CFOUTPUT>
BitXor(1,1): #BitXor(1,1)#<BR>
BitXor(2,10): #BitXor(2,10)#<BR>
BitXor(3,45): #BitXor(3,45)#<BR>
BitXor(128,256): #BitXor(128,256)#<BR>
BitXor(1024,32): #BitXor(1024,32)#
</CFOUTPUT>
```

## Ceiling

`Ceiling(number)`

Returns the closest integer greater than the number specified. Examples:

```
<CFOUTPUT>
-2.5: #Ceiling(-2.5)#<BR>
-1: #Ceiling(-1)#<BR>
-1.123: #Ceiling(-1.123)#<BR>
-0.123: #Ceiling(-0.123)#<BR>
0: #Ceiling(0)#<BR>
0.123: #Ceiling(0.123)#<BR>
1: #Ceiling(1)#<BR>
1.123: #Ceiling(1.123)#<BR>
2.5: #Ceiling(2.5)#
</CFOUTPUT>
```

## CFusion_DBConnections_Flush

`CFusion_DBConnections_Flush()`

Drops any existing connections (including database locks) with ColdFusion data sources. This is an undocumented function used by the ColdFusion Administrator. Example:

```
<CFSET temp = CFusion_DBConnections_Flush()>
All ColdFusion database connections have been dropped...
```

## CFusion_Decrypt

`CFusion_Decrypt(encryptedstring, key)`

Decrypts *encryptedstring* using *key*. This is an undocumented function used by the ColdFusion Administrator; it was introduce in the 3.x version of ColdFusion. `CFusion_Decrypt()` is similar to the `Decrypt()` function except it works only with strings encrypted using the `CFusion_Encrypt()` function. Example:

```
<CFSET x=CFusion_Encrypt("this is a message", 12345)>
<CFSET ux=CFusion_Decrypt(x, 12345)>

<CFOUTPUT>
Original String: this is a message<BR>
Encrypted:  #x#<BR>
Decrypted:  #ux#
</CFOUTPUT>
```

## CFusion_Disable_DBConnections

`CFusion_Disable_DBConnections(datasource, Yes|No)`

If set to `Yes`, *datasource* is disabled as a ColdFusion data source. Specifying `No` enables a previously disabled data source. This is an undocumented function used by the ColdFusion Administrator. Example:

```
<CFSET temp = CFusion_Disable_DBConnections('CFExamples', 'Yes')>
The ColdFusion examples database has been disabled...
```

## CFusion_Encrypt

`CFusion_Encrypt(string, key)`

Encrypts *string* using *key*. This is an undocumented function used by the ColdFusion Administrator; it was introduced in the 3.x version of ColdFusion. `Cfusion_Encrypt()` is similar to the `Encrypt()` function but results in a 32-character hexidecimal string, making it more useful than the `CFEncrypt()` function. Example:

```
<CFSET x=CFusion_Encrypt("this is a message", 12345)>
<CFSET ux=CFusion_Decrypt(x, 12345)>

<CFOUTPUT>
Original String: this is a message<BR>
Encrypted:  #x#<BR>
Decrypted:  #ux#
</CFOUTPUT>
```

## CFusion_GetODBCDSN

`CFusion_GetODBCDSN()`

Used in place of the `CFREGISTRY` tag on Unix-based ColdFusion servers to return the names of ODBC data sources stored in the "registry." This is an undocumented function used by the ColdFusion Administrator. Example:

```
<CFSET TheDataSourceNames = CFusion_GetODBCDSN()>

<TABLE>
  <TR><TH>Name</TH><TH>Description</TH><TR>

<CFOUTPUT QUERY="TheDataSourceNames">
  <TR><TD>#Name#</TD><TD>#Description#</TD></TR>
</CFOUTPUT>
</TABLE>
```

## CFusion_GetODBCINI

`CFusion_GetODBCINI("ODBC Data Sources"|datasource_name, entry, value)`

Used in place of the `CFREGISTRY` tag on Unix-based ColdFusion servers to return ODBC data-source information stored in *odbc.ini*. This is an undocumented function used by the ColdFusion Administrator. Example:

```
<CFSET WorkstationID = CFusion_GetODBCIni("ProgrammingCF", "WorkstationID", "")>

<CFOUTPUT>Output: #WorkstationID#</CFOUTPUT>
```

## CFusion_SetODBCINI

`CFusion_SetODBCINI("ODBC Data Sources"_or_datasource_name, entry, value)`

Used in place of the `CFREGISTRY` tag on Unix-based ColdFusion servers to write ODBC data-source information to *odbc.ini*. This is an undocumented function used by the ColdFusion Administrator. Example:

```
<CFSET temp = CFusion_SetODBCINI("Employees", "Description",
  "This is the employee master database")>
```

## CFusion_Settings_Refresh

`CFusion_Settings_Refresh()`

Refreshes ColdFusion server settings that don't require a server restart in order to take effect. This is an undocumented function used by the ColdFusion Administrator. Example:

```
<CFSET temp = CFusion_Settings_Refresh()>
ColdFusion Administrator settings not requiring a server restart have been
refreshed...
```

## CFusion_VerifyMail

`CFusion_VerifyMail(server, port, timeout)`

Verifies that a connection can be made to the SMTP mail server specified in `server`. `port` specifies the port that the SMTP server is using. The default SMTP port is 25. `timeout` specifies an amount of time in seconds ColdFusion should wait before timing out the verification attempt. If a connection can't be made, a diagnostic error message is returned. This is an undocumented function used by the ColdFusion Administrator. Example:

```
<CFSET Verify = Cfusion_VerifyMail('127.0.0.1',25,60)>

<CFIF Verify IS NOT "">
  <CFOUTPUT>#Verify#</CFOUTPUT>
<CFELSE>
  Connection verified!
</CFIF>
```

## CF_GetDataSourceUserName

CF_GetDataSourceUserName(*datasource*)

Returns the username registered under *datasource* within the ColdFusion Administrator. This is an undocumented function used by the ColdFusion Administrator. Example:

```
<CFOUTPUT>
The username regstered with the CFExamples datasource is:
#CF_GetDataSourceUserName('cfexamples')#
</CFOUTPUT>
```

## CF_IsColdFusionDataSource

CF_IsColdFusionDataSource(*datasource*)

Returns `True` if *datasource* is a valid ColdFusion data source or `False` if it isn't. This is an undocumented function used by the ColdFusion Administrator. Example:

```
<CFOUTPUT>
CFExamples: #CF_IsColdFusionDataSource('cfexamples')#<BR>
CFSnippets: #CF_IsColdFusionDataSource('cfsnippets')#<BR>
Cheese: #CF_IsColdFusionDataSource('cheese')#<BR>
</CFOUTPUT>
```

## CF_SetDataSourcePassword

CF_SetDataSourcePassword(*datasource*, *password*)

Sets the ColdFusion login password for the data source specified in *datasource*. This is an undocumented function used by the ColdFusion Administrator. Example:

```
<CFSET temp = CF_SetDataSourcePassword('CFExamples', 'admin')>
The CFExamples data source password has been changed...
```

## CF_SetDataSourceUserName

CF_SetDataSourceUserName(*datasource*, *username*)

Sets the ColdFusion login username for the data source specified in *datasource*. This is an undocumented function used by the ColdFusion Administrator. Example:

```
<CFSET temp = CF_SetDataSourceUserName('CFExamples', 'admin')>
The CFExamples data source username has been changed...
```

## Chr

Chr(*number*)

Returns the character equivalent of the ASCII character code. The following example generates a chart of all the printable ASCII characters:

```
<TABLE BORDER="1">
  <TR><TH>Character</TH><TH>ASCII Code</TH>/TR>
```

```
<CFLOOP INDEX="Character" FROM="33" TO="255">
  <CFOUTPUT>
    <TR><TD>#Chr(Character)#</TD><TD>#Asc(Chr(Character))#</TD></TR>
  </CFOUTPUT>
</CFLOOP>
</TABLE>
```

## CJustify

`CJustify(string, length)`

Center-justifies ***string*** within a field of ***length*** characters. Example:

```
<CFSET OriginalString = "ColdFusion">

<CFOUTPUT>
<B>Original String (quoted):</B> "#OriginalString#"<BR>
<B>Center-justified String (quoted):</B> "#CJustify("ColdFusion", 20)#"
</CFOUTPUT>
```

## Compare

`Compare(string1, string2)`

Performs a case-sensitive comparison of two strings based on their ASCII values. If ***string1*** is less than ***string2***, returns –1. If ***string1*** and ***string2*** are equal, returns 0. If ***string1*** is greater than ***string2***, returns 1. Examples:

```
<CFOUTPUT>
Compare('Apples', 'apples'): #Compare('Apples', 'apples')#<BR>
Compare('oranges', 'oranges'): #Compare('oranges', 'oranges')#<BR>
Compare('apples', 'Oranges'): #Compare('apples', 'Oranges')#<BR>
Compare('oranges', 'Apples'): #Compare('oranges', 'Apples')#<BR>
</CFOUTPUT>
```

## CompareNoCase

`CompareNoCase(string1, string2)`

Performs a case-insensitive comparison of two strings based on their ASCII values. If ***string1*** is less than ***string2***, returns –1. If ***string1*** and ***string2*** are equal, returns 0. If ***string1*** is greater than ***string2***, returns 1. Examples:

```
<CFOUTPUT>
CompareNoCase('Apples', 'apples'): #CompareNoCase('Apples', 'apples')#<BR>
CompareNoCase('oranges', 'oranges'): #CompareNoCase('oranges', 'oranges')#<BR>
CompareNoCase('apples', 'Oranges'): #CompareNoCase('apples', 'Oranges')#<BR>
CompareNoCase('oranges', 'Apples'): #CompareNoCase('oranges', 'Apples')#<BR>
</CFOUTPUT>
```

## Cos

Cos(*number*)

Returns the cosine of an angle expressed in radians. Example:

```
The cosine of 45 is <CFOUTPUT>#Cos(45)#</CFOUTPUT>
```

## CreateDate

CreateDate(*year*, *month*, *day*)

Returns a date/time object for the given date. The time value is set to 00:00:00. Example:

```
August 15, 1998 looks like
<CFOUTPUT>#CreateDate(1998, 08, 15)#</CFOUTPUT>
as a date/time object.
```

## CreateDateTime

CreateDateTime(*year*, *month*, *day*, *hour*, *minute*, *second*)

Returns a date/time object for the given date and time. Example:

```
7 p.m. on August 15, 1998 looks like
<CFOUTPUT>#CreateDateTime(1998, 08, 15, 19, 0, 0)#</CFOUTPUT>
as a date/time object.
```

## CreateObject

New as of ColdFusion 4.5

CreateObject("COM", *class*, *context*, *server*)
CreateObject("CORBA", *class*, *context*, [*locale*])
CreateObject("Java", *class*)

Allows ColdFusion to call different kinds of objects from within CFSCRIPT blocks. This function has the same functionality as the CFOBJECT tag.

When the first argument is "COM", the function supports instantiating and using COM objects on local and remote machines. COM objects aren't currently supported for Unix versions of ColdFusion. In this case, *class* specifies the program ID for the object, and *context* specifies the context the object is running in (InProc, Local, or Remote). *server* is required when context is Remote; it specifies a valid server name using Universal Naming Convention (UNC) or Domain Name Server (DNS) conventions. Example:

```
<CFSCRIPT>
MyWord = CreateObject("COM","Word.Application","Local");
</CFSCRIPT>
```

When the first argument is "CORBA", the function supports calling methods in CORBA objects from within CFSCRIPT blocks. In this case, *context* specifies the context for accessing the CORBA object (IOR or NameService). If *context* is IOR, *class* specifies the name of a file that contains the stringified version of the Interoperable Object Reference (IOR). If *context* is NameService, *class* specifies a period-delimited naming context for the naming service. *locale* specifies type/value pairs of arguments (which must begin with a minus sign) to pass to `init_orb()` (which is specific to VisiBroker orbs and has been tested to work with the 3.2 C++ version only). Example:

```
<CFSCRIPT>
MyCORBAObject = CreateObject("CORBA","C:\myobject.ior","IOR");
</CFSCRIPT>
```

When the first argument is `"Java"`, the function supports calling Java objects and Enterprise JavaBeans (EJBs) from within a `CFSCRIPT` block. In this case, *`class`* refers to the Java class to call. Any Java class listed in the class path area of the Java section within the ColdFusion Administrator may be specified. Example:

```
<CFSCRIPT>
MyObject = CreateObject("Java","HelloWorld");
</CFSCRIPT>
```

## CreateODBCDate

`CreateODBCDate(`*`date`*`)`

Returns the date in ODBC date format. Example:

```
08/15/1998 looks like
<CFOUTPUT>#CreateODBCDate('08/15/1998')#</CFOUTPUT>
in ODBC date format.
```

## CreateODBCDateTime

`CreateODBCDateTime(`*`date`*`)`

Returns the date and time in ODBC format. Example:

```
7pm on 08/15/1998 looks like
<CFOUTPUT>#CreateODBCDateTime('08/15/1998 19:00:00')#</CFOUTPUT>
in ODBC timestamp format.
```

## CreateODBCTime

`CreateODBCTime(`*`date`*`)`

Returns the time in ODBC time format. Example:

```
7:00pm looks like
<CFOUTPUT>#CreateODBCTime('19:00:00')#</CFOUTPUT>
in ODBC time format.
```

## CreateTime

`CreateTime(`*`hour, minute, second`*`)`

Returns a date/time object for the given time. The date value is set to December 30, 1899. Example:

```
7:00pm looks like
<CFOUTPUT>#CreateTime(19,00,00)#</CFOUTPUT>
as a date/time object.
```

## CreateTimeSpan

`CreateTimeSpan(days, hours, minutes, seconds)`

Creates a date/time object for adding to and subtracting from other date/time objects. Here's an example that creates a date/time object for one hour and thirty minutes and adds it to the current time:

```
<CFSET CurrentTime = Now()>
<CFSET TimeToAdd = CreateTimeSpan(0,1,30,0)>
<CFSET NewTime = CurrentTime + TimeToAdd>

<CFOUTPUT>
Current Time: #TimeFormat(CurrentTime, 'hh:mm tt')#<BR>
Time Span:  #TimeFormat(TimeToAdd, 'hh:mm')#<BR>
Current Time + Time Span: #TimeFormat(NewTime, 'hh:mm tt')#
</CFOUTPUT>
```

## CreateUUID

New as of ColdFusion 4.01

`CreateUUID()`

Creates a universally unique identifier (UUID). UUIDs are 35-character representations of 128-bit strings, where each character is a hexadecimal value in the range 0–9 and A–F. UUIDs are used when you need to create a unique identifier (such as a user ID or primary key value). Example:

```
Here is your UUID:  <CFOUTPUT>#CreateUUID()#</CFOUTPUT>.
```

## DateAdd

`DateAdd(datepart, number, date)`

Adds *number* to the *datepart* of the specified *date*. To subtract, make *number* negative. Valid entries for *datepart* are: `s` (second), `n` (minute), `h` (hour), `ww` (week), `w` (weekday), `d` (day), `y` (day of year), `m` (month), `q` (quarter), and `yyyy` (year). Examples:

```
<CFSET MyDateTime=Now()>

<CFOUTPUT>The original time and date is
#TimeFormat(MyDateTime,'hh:mm:ss tt')#, #DateFormat(MyDateTime,'mmmm dd, yyyy')#

<P><B>Add 30 Seconds:</B>
#TimeFormat(DateAdd('s', 30, MyDateTime),'hh:mm:ss tt')#
<BR><B>Subtract 10 minutes:</B>
#TimeFormat(DateAdd('n', -10, MyDateTime),'hh:mm:ss tt')#
<BR><B>Add 2 hours:</B>
#TimeFormat(DateAdd('h', 2, MyDateTime),'hh:mm:ss tt')#
<BR><B>Add 9 weeks:</B>
#DateFormat(DateAdd('ww', 9, MyDateTime),'mmmm dd, yyyy')#
<BR><B>Add 3 weekdays:</B>
#DateFormat(DateAdd('w', 3, MyDateTime),'mmmm dd, yyyy')#
<BR><B>Subtract 67 days:</B>
#DateFormat(DateAdd('d', -67, MyDateTime),'mmmm dd, yyyy')#
```

```
<BR><B>Add 45 days of the year:</B>
#DateFormat(DateAdd('y', 45, MyDateTime),'mmmm dd, yyyy')#
<BR><B>Add 7 months:</B>
#DateFormat(DateAdd('m', 7, MyDateTime),'mmmm dd, yyyy')#
<BR><B>Add 2 quarters:</B>
#DateFormat(DateAdd('q', 2, MyDateTime),'mmmm dd, yyyy')#
<BR><B>Add 5 years:</B>
#DateFormat(DateAdd('yyyy', 5, MyDateTime),'mmmm dd, yyyy')#
</CFOUTPUT>
```

## DateCompare

`DateCompare(date1, date2 [, datepart])`

Compares two date/time objects. Returns –1 if ***date1*** is less than ***date2***, 0 if both date/time objects are equal, or 1 if ***date1*** is greater than ***date2***. The comparison may be limited to a specific part of the date/time object by specifying a value for the optional ***datepart*** parameter. Valid attributes for ***datepart*** are: `s` (second), `n` (minute), `h` (hour), `d` (day), `m` (month), and `yyyy` (year). Examples:

```
<CFOUTPUT>
Compare 08/15/99 and 08/15/99: #DateCompare('08/15/99', '08/15/99')#<BR>
Compare 08/15/99 and 08/15/1999: #DateCompare('08/15/99', '08/15/1999')#<BR>
Compare 15 Aug 1998 and 8/15/98: #DateCompare('15 Aug 1998', '8/15/98')#<BR>
Compare August 15, 1998 and July 4, 1997: 
#DateCompare('August 15, 1998', 'July 4, 1997')#<BR>
Compare 19:00:00 and 7pm: #DateCompare('19:00:00', '7pm')#<BR>
Compare 6:00 and 7:00: #DateCompare('6:00', '7:00')#<BR>
Compare 8/15/1998 and Jan 3, 1999 by year:
#DateCompare('8/15/1998', 'Jan 3, 1999', 'yyyy')#<BR>
Compare 6:59 and 7:38 by minute: #DateCompare('6:59', '7:38', 'n')#
</CFOUTPUT>
```

## DateConvert

New as of ColdFusion 4.01

`DateConvert(type, date)`

Converts ***date*** to Universal Coordinated Time (UTC) or UTC to local time based on ***type*** (`local2UTC` or `UTC2Local`). The following example converts local time to UTC time:

```
<CFSET TheTimeDate = Now()>
<CFSET UCT = DateConvert('local2UTC', TheTimeDate)>

<CFOUTPUT>
<B>Current time/date:</B> #TimeFormat(TheTimeDate,'hh:mm:ss tt')#,
#DateFormat(TheTimeDate,'mmmm dd, yyyy')#
<P><B>UCT:</B> #UCT#
</CFOUTPUT>
```

## DateDiff

`DateDiff(datepart, date1, date2)`

Returns the interval in *datepart* units by which *date2* is greater than *date1*. Valid entries for *datepart* are: `s` (second), `n` (minute), `h` (hour), `ww` (week), `w` (weekday), `d` (day), `y` (day of year), `m` (month), `q` (quarter), and `yyyy` (year). If *date1* is greater than *date2*, a negative number is returned. Examples:

```
<CFSET FirstDate = DateFormat(Now(),'mm/dd/yyyy')>
<CFSET SecondDate = "01/01/2000">

<CFOUTPUT>
FirstDate: #FirstDate#<BR>
SecondDate: #SecondDate#
<P>
There are #DateDiff("s", FirstDate, SecondDate)# seconds between
#FirstDate# and #SecondDate#.<BR>
There are #DateDiff("n", FirstDate, SecondDate)# minutes between
#FirstDate# and #SecondDate#.<BR>
There are #DateDiff("h", FirstDate, SecondDate)# hours between
#FirstDate# and #SecondDate#.<BR>
There are #DateDiff("d", FirstDate, SecondDate)# days between
#FirstDate# and #SecondDate#.<BR>
There are #DateDiff("ww", FirstDate, SecondDate)# weeks between
#FirstDate# and #SecondDate#.<BR>
There are #DateDiff("m", FirstDate, SecondDate)# months between
#FirstDate# and #SecondDate#.<BR>
There are #DateDiff("yyyy", FirstDate, SecondDate)# years between
#FirstDate# and #SecondDate#.<BR>
</CFOUTPUT>
```

## DateFormat

`DateFormat(date [, mask])`

Returns *date* formatted according to *mask*. If no value is specified for *mask*, `DateFormat()` uses the default `dd-mmm-yy`. Valid entries for *mask* are:

| Mask | Description |
|---|---|
| d | Day of the month as a number with no leading zero for single-digit days |
| dd | Day of the month as a number with a leading zero for single-digit days |
| ddd | Three-letter abbreviation for day of the week |
| dddd | Full name of the day of the week |
| gg | Period/era; currently ignored |
| m | Month as a number with no leading zero for single-digit months |
| mm | Month as a number with a leading zero for single-digit months |
| mmm | Three-letter abbreviation for the month |
| mmmm | Full name of the month |

| Mask | Description |
|---|---|
| y | Last two digits of year with no leading zero for years less than 10 |
| yy | Last two digits of year with a leading zero for years less than 10 |
| yyyy | Four-digit year |

Note that `DateFormat()` supports U.S. date formats only. To use locale-specific date formats, see the `LSDateFormat()` function. Examples:

```
<CFSET TheDate = Now()>

<CFOUTPUT>
TheDate = #DateFormat(TheDate, 'mm/dd/yyyy')#
<P>
m/d/yy: #DateFormat(TheDate, 'm/d/yy')#<BR>
mm/dd/yy: #DateFormat(TheDate, 'mm/dd/yy')#<BR>
mm/dd/yyyy: #DateFormat(TheDate, 'mm/dd/yyyy')#<BR>
dd/mm/yyyy: #DateFormat(TheDate, 'dd/mm/yyyy')#<BR>
dd mmm yy: #DateFormat(TheDate, 'dd mmm yy')#<BR>
dddd mmmm dd, yyyy: #DateFormat(TheDate, 'dddd mmmm dd, yyyy')#<BR>
</CFOUTPUT>
```

## DatePart

`DatePart(`*`datepart, date`*`)`

Returns the specified part of a valid date/time object. Valid values for the *`datepart`* parameter are: `s` (second), `n` (minute), `h` (hour), `ww` (week), `w` (weekday), `d` (day), `y` (day of year), `m` (month), `q` (quarter), and `yyyy` (year). If *`date1`* is greater than *`date2`*, a negative number is returned. Examples:

```
<CFOUTPUT>
The current time and date  is
#TimeFormat(Now(),'hh:mm:ss tt')#, #DateFormat(Now(),'mmmm dd, yyyy')#
<P>

<B>Second:</B> #DatePart('s', Now())#<BR>
<B>Minute:</B> #DatePart('n', Now())#<BR>
<B>Hour:</B> #DatePart('h', Now())#<BR>
<B>Week:</B> #DatePart('ww', Now())#<BR>
<B>Weekday:</B> #DatePart('w', Now())#<BR>
<B>Day:</B> #DatePart('d', Now())#<BR>
<B>Day of year:</B> #DatePart('y', Now())#<BR>
<B>Month:</B> #DatePart('m', Now())#<BR>
<B>Quarter:</B> #DatePart('q', Now())#<BR>
<B>Year:</B> #DatePart('yyyy', Now())#
</CFOUTPUT>
```

## Day

`Day(date)`

Returns the day of the month for a given date as a number between 1 and 31. Example:

```
<CFOUTPUT>#Day(Now())#</CFOUTPUT>
```

## DayOfWeek

`DayOfWeek(date)`

Returns the day of the week for a given date as a number between 1 (Sunday) and 7 (Saturday). Example:

```
<CFOUTPUT>#DayOfWeek(Now())#</CFOUTPUT>
```

## DayOfWeekAsString

`DayOfWeekAsString(number)`

Returns the name of the day of the week for a given day's number between 1 (Sunday) and 7 (Saturday). Example:

```
Today is <CFOUTPUT>#DayOfWeekAsString(DayOfWeek(Now()))#</CFOUTPUT>.
```

## DayOfYear

`DayOfYear(date)`

Returns the day of the year as a number between 1 and 365 (366 for leap years). Example:

```
<CFOUTPUT>#DayOfYear(Now())#</CFOUTPUT>
```

## DaysInMonth

`DaysInMonth(date)`

Returns the number of days in the given month. Example:

```
There are <CFOUTPUT>#DaysInMonth(Now())#</CFOUTPUT> days in the current month.
```

## DaysInYear

`DaysInYear(date)`

Returns the number of days in the specified year. Example:

```
There are <CFOUTPUT>#DaysInYear(Now())#</CFOUTPUT> days this year.
```

## DE

DE(*string*)

DE() (for delay evaluation) is used with the **Evaluate()** and **IIF()** functions to allow you to pass a string without having it evaluated. DE() returns ***string*** enclosed within double quotation marks. The following example shows the DE() function used in conjunction with the Evaluate() function:

```
<CFSET MyVar = "3 * 3">

<CFOUTPUT>
MyVar = #MyVar#
<P>
DE(MyVar): #DE(MyVar)#<BR>
Evaluate(MyVar): #Evaluate(MyVar)#<BR>
Evaluate(DE(MyVar)): #Evaluate(DE(MyVar))#
<P>
All together:<BR>
#Evaluate(DE(MyVar))# is #Evaluate(MyVar)#
</CFOUTPUT>
```

## DecimalFormat

DecimalFormat(*number*)

Returns ***number*** as a string formatted to two decimal places with thousands separators. Examples:

```
<CFOUTPUT>
1:  #DecimalFormat(1)#<BR>
10: #DecimalFormat(10)#<BR>
100: #DecimalFormat(100)#<BR>
1000: #DecimalFormat(1000)#<BR>
10000: #DecimalFormat(10000)#<BR>
100000: #DecimalFormat(100000)#<BR>
1000000: #DecimalFormat(1000000)#<BR>
</CFOUTPUT>
```

## DecrementValue

DecrementValue(*number*)

Decrements the integer part of a given number by 1. Examples:

```
<CFOUTPUT>
-1: #DecrementValue(-1)#<BR>
-1.123: #DecrementValue(-1.123)#<BR>
-0.123: #DecrementValue(-0.123)#<BR>
0: #DecrementValue(0)#<BR>
0.123: #DecrementValue(0.123)#<BR>
1: #DecrementValue(1)#<BR>
1.123: #DecrementValue(1.123)#
</CFOUTPUT>
```

## Decrypt

`Decrypt(encryptedstring, key)`

Decrypts *encryptedstring* using *key*. The following example takes an encrypted string and decrypts it:

```
<CFSET MyString = "This is the secret message.">
<CFSET MyKey = "1a2">
<CFSET EncryptedString = Encrypt(MyString, MyKey)>
<CFSET DecryptedString = Decrypt(EncryptedString, MyKey)>

<CFOUTPUT>
<B>Original String:</B> #MyString#<BR>
<B>Key:</B> #MyKey#
<P><B>Encrypted String:</B> #EncryptedString#<BR>
<B>Decrypted String:</B> #DecryptedString#
</CFOUTPUT>
```

## DeleteClientVariable

`DeleteClientVariable("variable")`

Deletes the specified client variable (where the variable name is in double quotes). Returns `True` if successful. The following example creates a client variable, attempts to delete it, and reports whether it was successful (the example assumes you have client variables turned on in the ColdFusion Administrator and that a valid *Application.cfm* file exists in the directory containing the example):

```
<CFSET Client.MyVar="This is a client variable">

<CFOUTPUT>#Client.MyVar#</CFOUTPUT>

<CFSET DeleteClientVariable("MyVar")>

<P><CFIF IsDefined('Client.MyVar')>
Couldn't delete the client variable.
<CFELSE>
Client variable deleted.
</CFIF>
```

## DirectoryExists

`DirectoryExists(path)`

Returns `Yes` if the specified directory exists or `No` if it doesn't. The absolute path to the directory being evaluated must be provided. Example:

```
<CFIF DirectoryExists('c:\cfusion')>
  Directory exists!
<CFELSE>
  Directory doesn't exist!
</CFIF>
```

## DollarFormat

`DollarFormat(number)`

Returns ***number*** as a string formatted to two decimal places with a dollar sign and thousands separators. If ***number*** is negative, it is returned in parenthesis. Examples:

```
<CFOUTPUT>
-1000: #DollarFormat(-1000)#<BR>
-100: #DollarFormat(-100)#<BR>
-10: #DollarFormat(-10)#<BR>
-1: #DollarFormat(-1)#<BR>
1:  #DollarFormat(1)#<BR>
10: #DollarFormat(10)#<BR>
100: #DollarFormat(100)#<BR>
1000: #DollarFormat(1000)#<BR>
10000: #DollarFormat(10000)#<BR>
100000: #DollarFormat(100000)#<BR>
1000000: #DollarFormat(1000000)#<BR>
</CFOUTPUT>
```

## Duplicate

New as of ColdFusion 4.51

`Duplicate(variable)`

Creates a duplicate copy of ***variable*** without any references to the original. ***variable*** can be any ColdFusion datatype with the exception of component objects (COM, CORBA, and Java). `Duplicate()` overcomes problems associated with copying structures and queries. Generally, when copying a structure or query, any future change to the original object results in a change to the copy. `Duplicate()` eliminates this by making an independent copy of the original object. The duplicate copy isn't affected by changes to the original. The `Duplicate()` function is especially useful for copying nested structures and should be used in place of the `StructCopy()` function. The following example illustrates the difference between copying and duplicating query objects:

```
<!--- create a query object --->
<CFSET Products = QueryNew("ProductName, Color")>
<CFSET NewRows  = QueryAddRow(Products, 1)>
<CFSET QuerySetCell(Products, "ProductName", "Widget", 1)>
<CFSET QuerySetCell(Products, "Color", "Silver", 1)>

<!--- create a copy and a duplicate of the query --->
<CFSET CopyProducts = Products>
<CFSET DuplicateProducts = Duplicate(Products)>

<CFOUTPUT>
<B>Original:</B> You selected a #Products.Color# #Products.ProductName#.<BR>
<CFSET QuerySetCell(Products, "Color", "Black", 1)>
<B>Copy:</B> You selected a #CopyProducts.Color# #CopyProducts.ProductName#.<BR>
<B>Duplicate:</B> You selected a #DuplicateProducts.Color#
#DuplicateProducts.ProductName#.
</CFOUTPUT>
```

And here's an example with nested structures:

```
<!--- create a nested structure --->
<CFSET Stock = StructNew()>
<CFSET Stock.Quotes = StructNew()>
<CFSET Stock.Quotes.Ticker = "ALLR">
<CFSET Stock.Quotes.Price = "77">

<!--- create a copy and a duplicate of the structure --->
<CFSET StockCopy = StructCopy(Stock)>
<CFSET StockDuplicate = Duplicate(Stock)>

<CFOUTPUT>
<B>Ticker:</B> #Stock.Quotes.Ticker#<BR>
<B>Original Price:</B> #Stock.Quotes.Price#<BR>
<CFSET Stock.Quotes.Price = "100">
<B>Copied Price:</B> #StockCopy.Quotes.Price#<BR>
<B>Duplicate Price:</B> #StockDuplicate.Quotes.Price#
</CFOUTPUT>
```

## Encrypt

`Encrypt(`*`string, key`*`)`

Encrypts *string* using the specified *key*. `Encrypt()` uses the value of *key* as a seed to generate a random 32-bit key for use in an XOR-based encryption algorithm. The resulting string is then uuencoded and may be as much as three times the size of the original string. The following example takes a string and encrypts it:

```
<CFSET MyString = "This is the secret message.">
<CFSET MyKey = "1a2">
<CFSET EncryptedString = Encrypt(MyString, MyKey)>
<CFSET DecryptedString = Decrypt(EncryptedString, MyKey)>

<CFOUTPUT>
<B>Original String:</B> #MyString#<BR>
<B>Key:</B> #MyKey#
<P><B>Encrypted String:</B> #EncryptedString#<BR>
<B>Decrypted String:</B> #DecryptedString#
</CFOUTPUT>
```

## Evaluate

`Evaluate(`*`string1`*` [,`*`string2`*`] [,`*`stringN`*`])`

Evaluates string expressions from left to right and returns the result from the rightmost expression. `Evaluate()` is useful when you need to evaluate multiple expressions at one time. Examples:

```
<CFSET x=1>
<CFSET y=2>
<CFSET z=3>
<CFSET Form.Name="Jim">
```

```
x=1<BR>
y=2<BR>
z=3<BR>
Form.Name=Jim
<P><CFOUTPUT>
Evaluate(1+1): #Evaluate(1+1)#<BR>
Evaluate(3 MOD 2): #Evaluate(3 MOD 2)#<BR>
Evaluate(x*y*z): #Evaluate(x*y*z)#<BR>
Evaluate(sin(1)): #Evaluate(sin(1))#<BR>
Evaluate((x+y+z)/3): #Evaluate((x+y+z)/3)#<BR>
Evaluate('Form.Name'): #Evaluate('Form.Name')#<BR>
Evaluate(7+2, 3+5): #Evaluate(7+2, 3+5)#<BR>
Evaluate(7+2, 3+5, 1/4): #Evaluate(7+2, 3+5, 1/4)#<BR>
</CFOUTPUT>
```

## Exp

`Exp(number)`

Returns *e* to the power of ***number***. The constant *e* is the base of the natural logarithm and is equal to 2.71828182845904. Example:

```
<CFOUTPUT>10 to the E power is #Exp(10)#.</CFOUTPUT>
```

## ExpandPath

`ExpandPath(relativepath)`

Returns the platform-appropriate absolute path for the specified ***relativepath***. Example:

```
<CFOUTPUT>#ExpandPath('*.*')#</CFOUTPUT>
```

## FileExists

`FileExists(path)`

Returns `Yes` if the specified file exists or `No` if it doesn't. The absolute path to the file being evaluated must be provided. Example:

```
<CFIF FileExists('c:\cfusion\bin\cfcrypt.exe')>
  File exists!
<CFELSE>
  File doesn't exist!
</CFIF>
```

## Find

`Find(substring, string [, startpos])`

Returns the position of the first occurrence of ***substring*** in ***string***. If ***substring*** isn't found, `Find()` returns 0. An optional starting position for the search can be specified by the ***startpos*** parameter. `Find()` performs a case-sensitive search. Example:

```
<CFSET MyString="This is a case-sensitive example of using the Find function to
find a substring within a string.">
```

```
<CFSET MySubString="find">

<CFOUTPUT>
<B>String:</B> #MyString#<BR>
<B>Substring:</B> #MySubstring#
<P>The first occurrence of <B>#MySubstring#</B> is at position
#Find(MySubstring, MyString)#.
</CFOUTPUT>
```

## FindNoCase

`FindNoCase(`*`substring`*`, `*`string`*` [, `*`startpos`*`])`

Returns the position of the first occurrence of ***substring*** in ***string***. If ***substring*** isn't found, **FindNoCase()** returns 0. An optional starting position for the search can be specifies by the ***startpos*** parameter. **FindNoCase()** performs a case-insensitive search. Example:

```
<CFSET MyString="This is a case-insensitive example of using the FindNoCase
function to find a substring within a string.">
<CFSET MySubString="find">

<CFOUTPUT>
<B>String:</B> #MyString#<BR>
<B>Substring:</B> #MySubstring#
<P>The first occurrence of <B>#MySubstring#</B> is at position
#FindNoCase(MySubstring, MyString)#.
</CFOUTPUT>
```

## FindOneOf

`FindOneOf(`*`set`*`, `*`string`*` [, `*`startpos`*`])`

Returns the position of the first occurrence of any character from ***set*** in ***string***. If no characters from ***set*** are found, **FindOneOf()** returns 0. An optional starting position for the search can be specified by the ***startpos*** parameter. **FindOneOf()** performs a case-sensitive search. Example:

```
<CFSET MyString="This is a case-sensitive example of using the FindOneOf function
to find a character from a set of charcters within a string.">
<CFSET MySet="zFx">

<CFOUTPUT>
<B>String:</B> #MyString#<BR>
<B>Set:</B> #MySet#
<P>The first occurrence of any character from the set <B>#MySet#</B>
is at position #FindOneOf(MySet, MyString)#.
</CFOUTPUT>
```

## FirstDayOfMonth

`FirstDayOfMonth(date)`

Returns the day of the year for the first day in the specified month. Example:

```
<CFOUTPUT>
The first day of this month is day #FirstDayOfMonth(Now())# of this year.
</CFOUTPUT>
```

## Fix

`Fix(number)`

Returns the closest integer less than the specified number if the number is greater than 0. If the specified number is less than zero, the closest integer greater than the number is returned. Examples:

```
<CFOUTPUT>
-2.5: #Fix(-2.5)#<BR>
-1: #Fix(-1)#<BR>
-1.123: #Fix(-1.123)#<BR>
-0.123: #Fix(-0.123)#<BR>
0: #Fix(0)#<BR>
0.123: #Fix(0.123)#<BR>
1: #Fix(1)#<BR>
1.123: #Fix(1.123)#<BR>
2.5: #Fix(2.5)#
</CFOUTPUT>
```

## FormatBaseN

`FormatBaseN(number, radix)`

Converts *number* to a string in the base specified by *radix*. Valid values for *radix* are integers in the range of 2 to 36. Examples:

```
<CFOUTPUT>
FormatBaseN(1,2): #FormatBaseN(1,2)#<BR>
FormatBaseN(10,2): #FormatBaseN(10,2)#<BR>
FormatBaseN(100,2): #FormatBaseN(100,2)#<BR>
FormatBaseN(1,6): #FormatBaseN(1,6)#<BR>
FormatBaseN(10,6): #FormatBaseN(10,6)#<BR>
FormatBaseN(100,6): #FormatBaseN(100,6)#<BR>
</CFOUTPUT>
```

## GetBaseTagData

`GetBaseTagData(tag [, instance])`

Returns an object containing data from the specified ancestor *tag*. An optional *instance* number may be set to specify the number of ancestor tag levels to skip through before returning data. The default value for *instance* is 1. Example:

```
<CFSET BaseTagData = GetBaseTagData("CF_MyCustomTag")>
```

## GetBaseTagList

`GetBaseTagList()`

Returns a comma-delimited list (in uppercase) of ancestor tag names. `GetBaseTagList()` is meant for use in custom CFML tags for intertag data exchange. The first element in the returned list of ancestor tags is always the parent tag. Example:

```
<CFOUTPUT>
The parent tag is: #ListFirst(GetBaseTagList())#
<P>The entire list of ancestor tags: #GetBaseTagList()#
</CFOUTPUT>
```

## GetBaseTemplatePath

New as of ColdFusion 4.01

`GetBaseTemplatePath()`

Returns the full path to the top-level ColdFusion template calling the function. Example:

```
<CFOUTPUT>The base template path is:  #GetBaseTemplatePath()#</CFOUTPUT>
```

## GetClientVariablesList

`GetClientVariablesList()`

Returns a list of nonread-only client variables available to the ColdFusion application. In order to use this function, client variables must be turned on in the application's *Application.cfm* file. The following example returns the list of client variables available to the application (it assumes an *Application.cfm* file exists in the application's root directory and that client variables are enabled):

```
<CFSET Client.Name="Jen">
<CFSET Client.ID=123456>

<CFOUTPUT>
Client Variables available to this application: #GetClientVariablesList()#
</CFOUTPUT>
```

## GetCurrentTemplatePath

New as of ColdFusion 4.01

`GetCurrentTemplatePath()`

Returns the full path to the ColdFusion template that calls the function. This function differs from `GetBaseTemplatePath()` in that it returns the path to an included template if called from a directory other than the parent template. Example:

```
<CFOUTPUT>The full path to the template is: #GetCurrentTemplatePath()#</CFOUTPUT>
```

## GetDirectoryFromPath

GetDirectoryFromPath(*path*)

Returns the directory from a full path. The following example returns the directory in which the current template resides:

```
<CFOUTPUT>This directory is: #GetDirectoryFromPath(GetTemplatePath())#</CFOUTPUT>
```

## GetException

GetException(object_name)

Used in conjunction with the CFTRY/CFCATCH tags, GetException() returns a Java exception object thrown by the specified object.

The following example shows how to use GetException() with an imaginary Java object called MyObject:

```
<CFOBJECT TYPE="Java" ACTION="Create" CLASS="MyClass" NAME="MyObject">

<CFTRY>
<CFSET Test = MyObject.CauseError() >

<CFCATCH TYPE="Any">
   <CFSET MyException = GetException(MyObject)>
   <!--- call the GetErrCode and GerErrMsg methods within the exception
         object --->
   <CFSET ErrorCode = MyException.GetErrCode()
   <CFSET ErrorMessage = MyException.GetErrMsg()>

   <CFOUTPUT>
     Error Code: #ErrorCode#<BR>
     Error Message: #ErrorMessage#
   </CFOUTPUT>
</CFCATCH>
</CFTRY>
```

## GetFileFromPath

GetFileFromPath(*path*)

Returns the filename from a full path. The following example returns the filename of the current ColdFusion template:

```
<CFOUTPUT>This file is: #GetFileFromPath(GetTemplatePath())#</CFOUTPUT>
```

## GetFunctionList

New as of ColdFusion 4.5

`GetFunctionList()`

Returns a ColdFusion structure containing the names of the functions available to ColdFusion. Example:

```
<CFSET MyFunctionList = GetFunctionList()>

<CFOUTPUT>
There are #StructCount(MyFunctionList)# functions available in this version
of ColdFusion for #Server.OS.Name#.
</CFOUTPUT>

<CFLOOP COLLECTION="#MyFunctionList#" ITEM="FunctionName">
  <CFOUTPUT>#FunctionName#<BR></CFOUTPUT>
</CFLOOP>
```

## GetHTTPRequestData

New as of ColdFusion 5.0

`GetHTTPRequestData()`

Returns a structure containing the HTTP request headers and body available to the current page. This function is especially useful for parsing Simple Object Access Protocol (SOAP) requests, which are often passed in the HTTP header. The structure returned by `GetHTTPRequestData()` contains the following keys:

`Headers`
: Structure containing all the HTTP request headers as key/value pairs.

`Content`
: If the current page is accessed via a form post, `Content` contains the raw content (string or binary) of the form post; otherwise it is blank. In order to be considered string content, the value of the `CONTENT_TYPE` request header must be "application/x-www-form-urlencoded" or must begin with "text/". All other content types are automatically stored as binary objects. Because of this, you should first use the `IsBinary()` function when evaluating `Content`. You may also consider using the `ToString()` function to convert binary data stored in `Content` to a string value that can then be displayed.

`Method`
: The value contained in the `Request_Method` CGI variable.

`Protocol`
: The value contained in the `Server_Protocol` CGI variable.

The following example demonstrates the use of the `GetHTTPRequestData()` function (try calling the template directly and via a form post to see how the `Content` key is populated differently):

```
<CFSET RequestHeader = GetHttpRequestData()>
<!--- use the CFDUMP (CF 5.0) tag to automatically generate a nice table
      that shows the contents of the RequestHeader structure --->
<CFDUMP VAR = "#RequestHeader#">
```

## GetHTTPTimeString

New as of ColdFusion 4.5

`GetHTTPTimeString([date_time_object])`

Returns *`date_time_object`* formatted according to the HTTP protocol put forth in RFC-1123. If no parameter is specified, **`GetHTTPTimeString()`** returns the current date/time (on the ColdFusion server). Times are output as GMT time. Example:

```
<CFSET x = GetHTTPTimeString()>

<CFOUTPUT>
The current date/time (formatted according to RFC 1123) is: #x#
</CFOUTPUT>
```

## GetK2ServerCollections

New as of ColdFusion 5.0

`GetK2ServerCollections()`

Returns a comma-delimited list of collection aliases for collections used by the K2 server. The K2 server engine must be started in order

for this function to return any results. The following example loops through the list of available K2 server collections, displaying the collection aliases:

```
<H3>K2 server collections:</H3>
<CFLOOP LIST="#GetK2ServerCollections()#" INDEX="CollectionName">
   <CFOUTPUT>#CollectionName#</CFOUTPUT><BR>
</CFLOOP>
```

## GetK2ServerDocCount

New as of ColdFusion 5.0

`GetK2ServerDocCount()`

Returns the total number of documents in all collections accessible by the Verity K2 engine.

The following example displays the total number of documents in all collections available to the K2 server.

```
<CFOUTPUT>
There are currently #GetK2ServerDocCount()# documents available for
searching by
the K2 server.
</CFOUTPUT>
```

## GetK2ServerDocCountLimit

New as of ColdFusion 5.0

`GetK2ServerDocCountLimit()`

Returns the maximum number of documents searchable by the Verity K2 server. For ColdFusion Professional, the document limit is 125,000. ColdFusion Enterprise has a 250,000-document limit. Sites running Allaire Spectra have a limit of 750,000 documents.

The following example outputs the K2 server document limit for your ColdFusion server:

```
<CFOUTPUT>
The K2 server can search a maximum of #GetK2ServerDocCountLimit()#
documents on
this ColdFusion server.
</CFOUTPUT>
```

## GetLocale

`GetLocale()`

Returns the current locale for your server. The server's locale determines display and formatting options for currency, date, number, and time values and is determined by the server's operating system. At startup, ColdFusion sets a variable, **Server.ColdFusion.SupportedLocales**, that contains a comma-separated list containing all supported locales for your ColdFusion server. The following example lists all supported locales for your server, with the current locale in bold:

```
Supported Locales with Current Locale in <B>Bold</B>:
<P><CFLOOP INDEX="Locale" LIST="#Server.ColdFusion.SupportedLocales#">
  <CFOUTPUT>
    <CFIF Locale IS GetLocale()>
      <B>#Locale#</B><BR>
    <CFELSE>
      #Locale#<BR>
    </CFIF>
  </CFOUTPUT>
</CFLOOP>
```

## GetMetricData

New as of ColdFusion 4.5

`GetMetricData(`*`mode`*`)`

Depending on *mode*, returns data representing information about the performance of the ColdFusion server. The following modes may be used by **GetMetricData()**:

`Perf_Monitor`
: Returns a ColdFusion structure containing Performance Monitor data (Windows NT) or CFSTAT data (on Unix/Linux). For this mode to work on Windows NT systems, the Enable Performance Monitoring option must be checked in the Debugging section of the ColdFusion Administrator.

`Simple_Load`
: Returns a number representing the load on the server. This number is produced by an internal algorithm based on ColdFusion queue depths.

`Prev_Req_Time`
: Returns a number representing the previous request time in milliseconds. This metric can calculate server load using the formula:

Load (as a percentage) = Prev_Req_Time / Max_Allowable_Response_Time_In_Milliseconds * 100

`Avg_Req_Time`
: Returns a number representing the average request time in milliseconds. This metric can calculate load using the formula:

  Load (as a percentage) = Avg_Req_Time / Max_Allowable_Response_Time_In_Milliseconds * 100

---

The following example demonstrates the four modes available to the `GetMetricData()` function:

```
<CFSET PerformanceMonitoring = GetMetricData("Perf_monitor")>
<CFSET Load = GetMetricData("Simple_Load")>
<CFSET PreviousRequestTime = GetMetricData("Prev_Req_Time")>
<CFSET AverageRequestTime = GetMetricData("Avg_Req_Time")>

<CFOUTPUT>
Load: #Load#<BR>
Previous Request Time: #PreviousRequestTime#<BR>
Average Request Time: #AverageRequestTime#<BR>
</CFOUTPUT>

<CFSET MyKeyArray = StructKeyArray(PerformanceMonitoring)>

<TABLE>
  <TR><TH>Key #</TH><TH>Name</TH><TH>Value</TH></TR>
  <CFLOOP index="position" from="1" to="#ArrayLen(MyKeyArray)#">
    <CFOUTPUT>
      <TR><TD>#position#:</TD><TD>#MyKeyArray[position]#</TD>
        <TD>#PerformanceMonitoring[MyKeyArray[position]]#</TD></TR>
    </CFOUTPUT>
  </CFLOOP>
</TABLE>
```

---

## GetProfileString

New as of ColdFusion 4.01

`GetProfileString(`*`inipath`*`, `*`section`*`, `*`entry`*`)`

Returns *`entry`* from *`section`* of the initialization file specified in *`inipath`*. Initialization files are used to set operating-system and application-specific variables during system boot or application launch. Initialization files can be identified by their *.ini* file extension. Here's an example that returns a profile string from one of ColdFusion's initialization files:

```
<CFSET MyPath = "C:\cfusion\bin\cf40e.ini">
<CFSET MySection = "Program">
<CFSET MyEntry = "Company">

<CFOUTPUT>
<B>Path:</B> #MyPath#<BR>
<B>Section:</B> #MySection#<BR>
<B>Entry:</B> #MyEntry#<BR>
<P><B>Profile String:</B> #GetProfileString(MyPath, MySection, MyEntry)#
</CFOUTPUT>
```

## GetTempDirectory

`GetTempDirectory()`

Returns the absolute path, including trailing backslash, of the temporary directory used by ColdFusion. Example:

```
<CFOUTPUT>
The temporary directory being used by ColdFusion is: #GetTempDirectory()#
</CFOUTPUT>
```

## GetTempFile

`GetTempFile(`*`directory, filenameprefix`*`)`

Returns the full path to a uniquely named temporary file that ColdFusion creates and saves in *`directory`*. The filename is assigned by taking up to the first three characters of *`filenameprefix`*, appending a unique string to them, and tacking on a *.tmp* extension. The following example creates a temporary file that begins with "tmp_" and saves it to the current directory:

```
<CFSET MyTempFile = GetTempFile(GetDirectoryFromPath(GetTemplatePath()), "tmp_")>

<CFOUTPUT>
<B>Temporary file:</B> #GetFileFromPath(MyTempFile)#<BR>
<B>Path:</B> #GetDirectoryFromPath(MyTempFile)#
</CFOUTPUT>
```

## GetTemplatePath

Deprecated as of ColdFusion 4.0

`GetTemplatePath(`*`path`*`)`

Returns the full path to the top-level ColdFusion template calling the function. This function has been made obsolete by the **`GetBaseTemplatePath()`** function but is still included to ensure backward compatibility. Future code should make use of the `GetBaseTemplatePath()` function. Example:

```
<CFOUTPUT>The top-level template path is: #GetTemplatePath()#</CFOUTPUT>
```

## GetTickCount

`GetTickCount()`

Returns a counter in milliseconds. `GetTickCount()` is useful for reporting the amount of time it takes to process specific parts of CFML code. The following example counts the time (in milliseconds) it takes to process a loop with 10,000 iterations:

```
<CFSET Start = GetTickCount()>

<CFOUTPUT><B>Start TickCount:</B> #Start#</CFOUTPUT>

<P>Looping from 1 to 10000

<CFSET Timer="0">
```

```
<CFLOOP INDEX="counter" FROM="1" TO="10000">
  <CFSET Timer=Timer+1>
</CFLOOP>
<CFSET End = GetTickCount()>

<P>
<CFOUTPUT><B>End TickCount:</B> #End#</CFOUTPUT>

<CFSET TotalTime = (Evaluate(End - Start))>
<P>
<CFOUTPUT><B>Total processing time:</B> #TotalTime# milliseconds</CFOUTPUT>
```

## GetTimeZoneInfo

New as of ColdFusion 4.01

`GetTimeZoneInfo()`

Returns a structure containing time-zone information for the host server calling the function. The following structure keys are returned by calling `GetTimeZoneInfo()`:

`UTCTotalOffset`
: Returns the local offset time in minutes from Universal Coordinated Time (UTC). UTC is coordinated on the prime meridian (running through Greenwich, U.K.). Positive offset values represent time zones west of the prime meridian, while negative offsets represent time zones east of the prime meridian.

`UTCHourOffset`
: Returns the local offset time from UTC in hours.

`UTCMinuteOffset`
: Returns the local offset time in minutes after `UTCHourOffset` is applied. The value for `UTCHourOffset` can range from 0 to 60 depending on where a particular time zone falls in relation to the nearest hour offset. All North American time zones return 0 for `UTCMinuteOffset`.

`IsDSTOn`
: Returns `True` if daylight savings time (DST) is turned on for the host machine and `False` if it isn't.

Example:

```
<CFSET MyTimeZoneInfo = GetTimeZoneInfo()>

<CFOUTPUT>
Local time is offset #MyTimeZoneInfo.utcTotalOffset# minutes from UTC.<BR>
Local time is offset #MyTimeZoneInfo.utcHourOffset# hours and
#MyTimeZoneInfo.utcMinuteOffset# minutes from UTC.<BR>
Daylight Saving Time is <CFIF #MyTimeZoneInfo.isDSTOn#><B>on</B>
<CFELSE><B>off</B></CFIF> for the host.
</CFOUTPUT>
```

## GetToken

`GetToken(string, index [, delimiters ])`

Returns the token from *string* occupying the specified *index* position. An optional set of *delimiters* may be specified. If no *delimiters* are specified, ColdFusion uses the default of spaces, tabs, and newline characters. If *index* is greater than the total number of tokens in *string*, `GetToken()` returns an empty string. `GetToken()` is similar in function to the `ListGetAt()` function but is more versatile because it uses multiple sets of *delimiters*. Note that the `GetToken()` function currently treats successive instances of the same delimiter as a single delimiter. Here's an example of this function:

```
<CFSET MyString="999-99-9999">

<CFOUTPUT>
<B>String:</B> #MyString#
<P>GetToken(MyString, 3, "-"): #GetToken(MyString, 3, "-")#
</CFOUTPUT>
```

## Hash

New as of ColdFusion 4.5

`Hash(string)`

One-way encrypts *string* using the MD5 hash algorithm. The resulting string is a 32-character hexidecimal representation of the original string. Because the MD5 algorithm is a one-way hash, there is no way to decrypt the encrypted string. The `Hash()` function is often used to hash passwords before storing them in a database. This allows you to store passwords in a database without being able to see the actual password. When building an application that uses hashed passwords for authentication, the password entered by the user should be hashed, then compared to the hashed value stored in the database. If they match, you know the user entered a valid password. Here's an example using the `Hash()` function:

```
<CFSET MyHash = Hash('This is a test')>

<CFOUTPUT>#MyHash#</CFOUTPUT>
```

## Hour

`Hour(date)`

Returns the hour portion of a time/date object as a number between 0 and 23. Example:

```
The current hour is<CFOUTPUT>#Hour(Now())#</CFOUTPUT>.
```

## HTMLCodeFormat

`HTMLCodeFormat(string [, htmlversion])`

Returns *string* enclosed in `<PRE>` and `</PRE>` tags with all carriage returns removed and special characters (<, >, ", and &) escaped. The HTML version to use for character-escape sequences can be specified using the optional ***htmlversion*** parameter. Valid entries are `-1` (current HTML version), `2.0` (HTML 2.0, default), and `3.2` (HTML 3.0). Example:

```
<CFSET MyString="<H3>This is an example of the HTMLCodeFormat function.</H3>
View the source of this document to see the escaping of the HTML characters.">

<CFOUTPUT>#HTMLCodeFormat(MyString)#</CFOUTPUT>
```

## HTMLEditFormat

`HTMLEditFormat(`*`string`*` [, `*`htmlversion`*`])`

Returns *`string`* with all carriage returns removed and special characters (<, >, ", and &) escaped. The HTML version to use for character-escape sequences can be specified using the optional ***htmlversion*** parameter. Valid entries are: `-1` (current HTML version), `2.0` (HTML 2.0, default), and `3.2` (HTML 3.0). Example:

```
<CFSET MyString="<H3>This is an example of the HTMLEditFormat function.</H3>
View the source of this document to see the escaping of the HTML characters.">

<CFOUTPUT>#HTMLEditFormat(MyString)#</CFOUTPUT>
```

## IIf

`IIf(`*`condition, expression1, expression2`*`)`

Evaluates *`condition`* as Boolean. If *`condition`* is `True`, `IIf()` then evaluates *`expression1`*. If *`condition`* is `False`, `IIf()` evaluates *`expression2`*. Examples:

```
<CFOUTPUT>
<B>IIF(1+2 IS 3, DE("Yes"), DE("No")):</B><BR>
#IIF(1+2 IS 3, DE("Yes"), DE("No"))#
<P><B>IIF(DayOfWeek(Now()) IS 4, DE("Today is <B>Wednesday</B>!"),
DE("Today is #DayOfWeekAsString(DayOfWeek(Now()))#")):</B><BR>
#IIF(DayOfWeek(Now()) IS 4, DE("Today is <B>Wednesday</B>!"),
DE("Today is #DayOfWeekAsString(DayOfWeek(Now()))#"))#
</CFOUTPUT>
```

## IncrementValue

`IncrementValue(`*`number`*`)`

Increments the integer part of a given number by 1. Examples:

```
<CFOUTPUT>
-1: #IncrementValue(-1)#<BR>
-1.123: #IncrementValue(-1.123)#<BR>
-0.123: #IncrementValue(-0.123)#<BR>
0: #IncrementValue(0)#<BR>
0.123: #IncrementValue(0.123)#<BR>
1: #IncrementValue(1)#<BR>
1.123: #IncrementValue(1.123)#
</CFOUTPUT>
```

## InputBaseN

`InputBaseN(string, radix)`

Converts *string* to the base specified by *radix*. *radix* must be an integer between 2 and 36. Example:

```
<CFLOOP INDEX="radix" FROM="2" TO="36">
  <CFOUTPUT>InputBaseN(128, #radix#): #InputBaseN(128, radix)#<BR></CFOUTPUT>
</CFLOOP>
```

## Insert

`Insert(substring, string, position)`

Inserts *substring* into *string* after *position*. Example:

```
<CFSET MyString="This is how the cookie crumbles.">

<CFOUTPUT>#Insert("chocolate chip ", MyString, 16)#</CFOUTPUT>
```

## Int

`Int(number)`

Returns the closest integer smaller than the given number. Examples:

```
<CFOUTPUT>
-1: #Int(-1)#<BR>
-1.123: #Int(-1.123)#<BR>
-0.123: #Int(-0.123)#<BR>
0: #Int(0)#<BR>
0.123: #Int(0.123)#<BR>
1: #Int(1)#<BR>
1.123: #Int(1.123)#
</CFOUTPUT>
```

## IsArray

`IsArray(value [, dimension])`

Returns `True` if the *value* specified is an array. In addition, `IsArray()` can check to see if the array is a specified *dimension* (1, 2, or 3). Examples:

```
<CFSET Form.MyFormVar = "This is a form variable">
<CFSET URL.MyURLVar = "This is a URL variable">
<CFSET Grades = ArrayNew(1)>
<CFSET Grades[1] = 95>
<CFSET Grades[2] = 93>
<CFSET Grades[3] = 87>
<CFSET Grades[4] = 100>
<CFSET Grades[5] = 74>

<CFIF IsArray(Form.MyFormVar)>
```

```
  Form.MyFormVar is an array!
<CFELSEIF IsArray(URL.MyURLVar)>
  URL.MyURLVar is an array!
<CFELSEIF IsArray(Grades)>
  Grades is an array!
<CFELSE>
  No variables are arrays!
</CFIF>
```

## IsAuthenticated

`IsAuthenticated([`*`securitycontext`*`])`

Returns `True` if the user has been authenticated for the given *`securitycontext`* using `CFAUTHENTICATE`. ColdFusion returns `True` if the user has been authenticated or `False` if they haven't. If no *`securitycontext`* is given, ColdFusion returns `True` if the user has been authenticated for any security context. The `IsAuthenticated()` function is commonly used within an *Application.cfm* file. In order to use the `IsAuthenticated()` function, Advanced Security needs to be enabled within the ColdFusion Administrator, and a valid security context must already be defined. The following example uses `IsAuthenticated()` to determine if a user is authenticated for a security context called `Administrator`:

```
<CFIF NOT IsAuthenticated("Administrator")>
  <CFAUTHENTICATE SECURITYCONTEXT="Administrator"
                  USERNAME="#Form.username#"  PASSWORD="#Form.password#">
</CFIF>
```

## IsAuthorized

`IsAuthorized(`*`resourcetype`*`, `*`resourcename`*` [, `*`action`*`])`

Returns `True` if the user is authorized to perform the *`action`* specified against a particular ColdFusion resource. The parameter *`resourcetype`* specifies the type of resource to check, while *`resourcename`* specifies the actual name of the resource. Possible resource types include `Application`, `CFML`, `Collection`, `Component`, `CustomTag`, `Datasource`, `File`, `Function`, `User`, and `UserObject`. *`action`* is required for all resource types except `Component`, `CustomTag`, `Function`, and `User` and specifies the action to check authorization for. The following table lists each resource type with possible values for *`action`*:

| Resource Type | Possible Values for Action |
|---|---|
| `Application` | `All`, `UseClientVariables` |
| `CFML` | Any valid action of the CFML tag specified in *`resourcetype`* |
| `Collection` | `Delete`, `Optimize`, `Purge`, `Search`, `Update` |
| `Component` | N/A |
| `CustomTag` | N/A |
| `Datasource` | `All`, `Connect`, `Delete`, `Insert`, `Select`, `SP` (stored procedure), `Update` |
| `File` | `Read`, `Write` |

| Resource Type | Possible Values for Action |
|---|---|
| `Function` | N/A |
| `User` | N/A |
| `UserObject` | *`action`* as specified in the ColdFusion Administrator |

To use the `IsAuthorized()` function, Advanced Security needs to be enabled within the ColdFusion Administrator, and a valid security context must already be defined. The following example uses the `IsAuthorized()` function to determine if a user is authorized to use the `CFFILE` tag to perform a file upload:

```
<CFIF IsAuthorized('CFML', 'CFFILE', 'Upload')>
  perform file upload...
<CFELSE>
  You are not authorized to upload files!
</CFIF>
```

## IsBinary

New as of ColdFusion 4.5

`IsBinary(`*`value`*`)`

Returns `True` if the specified value is binary or `False` if it isn't. Examples:

```
<CFSET GifImage=ToBinary("R01GODlhAQABAPcAAAAAAAAAAAAAAAAAAAAAAAAAAAAAAAAAAAAAAAAAAAAAA
AAAAAAAAAAAAAAAAAAAAAAAAAAAAAAAAAAAAAAAAAAAAAAAAAAAAAAAAAAAAAAAAAAAAAAAAAAAAAAAAA
AAAAAAAAAAAAAAAAAAAAAAAAAAAAAAAAAAAAAAAAAAAAAAAAAAAAAAAAAAAAAAAAAAAAAAAAAAAAAAAAA
AAAAAAAAAAAAAAAAAAAAAAAAAAAAAAAAAAAAAAAAAAAAAAAAAAAAAAAAAAAAAAAAAAAAAAAAAAAAAAAAA
AAAAAAAAAAAAAAAAAAAAAAAAAAAAAAAAAAAAAAAAAAAAAAAAAAAAAAAAAAAAAAAAAAAAAAAAAAAAAAAAA
AAAAAAAAAAAAAAAAAAAAAAAAAAAAAAAAAAAAAAAAAAAAAAAAAAAAAAAAAAAAAAAAAAAAAAAAAAAAAAAAA
AAAAAAAAAAAAAAAAAAAAAAAAAAAAAAAAAAAAAAAAAAAAAAAAAAAAAAAAAAAAAAAAAAAAAAAAAAAAAAAAA
AAAAAAAAAAAAAAAAAAAAAAAAAAAAAAAAAAAAAAAAAAAAAAAAAAAAAAAAAAAAAAAAAAAAAAAAAAAAAAAAA
AAAAAAAAAAAAAAAAAAAAAAAAAAAAAAAAAAAAAAAAAAAAAAAAAAAAAAAAAAAAAAAAAAAAAAAAAAAAAAAAA
AAAAAAAAAAAAAAAAAAAAAAAAAAAAAAAAAAAAAAAAAAAAAAAAAAAAAAAAAAAAAAAAAAAAAAAAAAAAAAAAA
AAAAAAAAAAAAAAAAAAAAAAAAAAAAAAAAAAAAAAAAAAAAAAAAAAAAAAAAAAAAAAAAAAAAAAAAAAAAAAAAA
AAAAAAAAAAAAAAAAAAAAAAAAAAAAAAAAAAAAAAAAAAAAAAAAAAAAAAAAAAAAAAAAAAAAAAAAAAAAAAAAA
AAAAAAAAAAAAAAAAAAAAAAAAAAAAAAAAAAAAAAAAAAAAAAAAAAAAAAAAAAAAAAAAAAAAAAAAAAAAAAAAA
AAAAAAAAAAAAACwAAAAAAQABAAAIBAABBAQAOw==")>

<CFOUTPUT>
12:  #IsBinary(12)#<BR>
abc:  #IsBinary("abc")#<BR>
GifImage:  #IsBinary(GifImage)#<BR>
</CFOUTPUT>
```

## IsBoolean

`IsBoolean(`*`value`*`)`

Returns `True` if the specified value can be converted to a Boolean or `False` if it can't. Examples:

```
<CFOUTPUT>
-1: #IsBoolean(-1)#<BR>
0: #IsBoolean(0)#<BR>
```

```
1234: #IsBoolean(1234)#<BR>
abcdef: #IsBoolean('abcdef')#<BR>
true: #IsBoolean(true)#<BR>
false: #IsBoolean(false)#<BR>
yes: #IsBoolean('yes')#<BR>
no: #IsBoolean('no')#<BR>
as45sd-1: #IsBoolean('as45sd')#<BR>
!@$%^: #IsBoolean('!@$%^')#
</CFOUTPUT>
```

## IsCustomFunction

New as of ColdFusion 5.0

`IsCustomFunction()`

Returns `True` if the specified `Name` is that of a user-defined function.

The following example uses `IsCustomFunction()` to determine whether `Mean` is a user-defined function. The `IsDefined()` function makes sure the name exists before testing it with `IsCustomFunction()`. If you attempt to evaluate a name that doesn't exist with `IsCustomFunction()`, ColdFusion throws an error.

```
<CFSCRIPT>
if(IsDefined('Mean') AND IsCustomFunction(Mean)){
   WriteOutput("Mean is a custom function!");
   }
else{
   WriteOutput("Mean is not a custom function!");
   }
</CFSCRIPT>
```

## IsDate

`IsDate(string)`

Returns `True` if the specified string can be converted to a valid date/time object or `False` if it can't. Examples:

```
<CFOUTPUT>
Now(): #IsDate(Now())#<BR>
08/15/1998: #IsDate('08/15/1998')#<BR>
15/08/1998: #IsDate('15/08/1998')#<BR>
13/13/1998: #IsDate('13/13/1998')#<BR>
August 15, 1998: #IsDate('August 15, 1998')#<BR>
15 Aug 1998: #IsDate('15 Aug 1998')#<BR>
August fifteenth, nineteen hundred ninety eight : #IsDate('August fifteenth,
nineteen hundred ninety eight')#<BR>
7 p.m.: #IsDate('7 p.m.')#<BR>
7pm: #IsDate('7pm')#<BR>
19:00: #IsDate('19:00')#<BR>
six thirty: #IsDate('six thirty')#
</CFOUTPUT>
```

## IsDebugMode

`IsDebugMode()`

Returns `True` if debugging mode is turned on in the ColdFusion Administrator or `False` if it is turned off. Example:

```
Debugging is currently <CFIF IsDebugMode()><B>on</B><CFELSE><b>off</b></CFIF>
for your ColdFusion server.
```

## IsDefined

`IsDefined('variable_name')`

Determines if the specified variable exists. Returns `True` if the specified variable exists or `False` if it doesn't. Note that `IsDefined()` replaces the deprecated `ParameterExists()` function. Examples:

```
<CFSET MyVar="Variable">
<CFSET Form.MyFormVar="Form Variable">

<CFOUTPUT>
<CFIF IsDefined('MyVar')>
  Variable MyVar exists:<BR> MyVar = #MyVar#
<CFELSE>
  No variable called MyVar exists.
</CFIF>
<P><CFIF IsDefined('MyFormVar')>
  Variable MyFormVar exists:<BR> MyFormVar = #MyFormVar#
<CFELSE>
  No variable called MyFormVar exists.
</CFIF>
<P><CFIF IsDefined('Queryname.field')>
  Variable Queryname.Field exists:<BR> QueryName.Field = #Queryname.Field#
<CFELSE>
  No variable called Queryname.Field exists.
</CFIF>
</CFOUTPUT>
```

## IsK2ServerDocCountExceeded

New as of ColdFusion 5.0

`IsK2ServerDocCountExceeded()`

Returns `True` if the number of documents contained in collections accessible by the K2 server exceeds the document limit for the server or `False` if it doesn't. For more information on the document limit, see the `GetK2ServerDocCountLimit()` function.

The following example determines whether the K2 server document limit is exceeded:

```
Is the K2 server document limit exceeded?
<CFOUTPUT>#IsK2ServerDocCountExceeded()#</CFOUTPUT>
```

## IsLeapYear

`IsLeapYear(year)`

Returns `True` if the specified year is a leap year or `False` if it isn't. It is important to note that `IsLeapYear()` expects a year (e.g., 2000) as opposed to a date. Example:

```
<CFOUTPUT>
#Year(Now())# <CFIF IsLeapYear(Year(Now()))><B>is</B><CFELSE><B>isn't</B></CFIF>
a leap year.
</CFOUTPUT>
```

## IsNumeric

`IsNumeric(string)`

Returns `True` if the specified string can be converted to a number or `False` if it can't. Examples:

```
<CFOUTPUT>
-1: #IsNumeric(-1)#<BR>
0: #IsNumeric(0)#<BR>
1234: #IsNumeric(1234)#<BR>
1,234,567,890: #IsNumeric('1,234,567,890')#<BR>
$1234.99: #IsNumeric('$1234.99')#<BR>
08/15/1999: #IsNumeric('08/15/1999')#<BR>
7pm: #IsNumeric('7pm')#<BR>
abcdef: #IsNumeric('abcdef')#<BR>
true: #IsNumeric(true)#<BR>
false: #IsNumeric(false)#<BR>
yes: #IsNumeric('yes')#<BR>
no: #IsNumeric('no')#<BR>
as45sd-1: #IsNumeric('as45sd')#<BR>
!@$%^: #IsNumeric('!@$%^')#<BR>
1234abcd: #IsNumeric('1234abcd')#
</CFOUTPUT>
```

## IsNumericDate

`IsNumericDate(realnumber)`

Returns `Yes` if ***realnumber*** can be converted to a numeric date and `No` if it can't. Examples:

```
<CFOUTPUT>
IsNumericDate(Now()): #IsNumericDate(Now())#<BR>
IsNumericDate('1998-08-15 19:00:00'): #IsNumericDate('1998-08-15 19:00:00')#<BR>
</CFOUTPUT>
```

## IsProtected

New as of ColdFusion 4.5

`IsProtected(resourcetype, resourcename [, action])`

Returns `True` if the specified resource is protected by a rule within the security context of the currently authenticated user. The parameter ***resourcetype*** specifies the type of resource to check while *resourcename* specifies the actual name of the resource. Possible resource types include `Application`, `CFML`, `Collection`, `Component`, `CustomTag`, `Datasource`, `File`, `Function`, `User`, and `UserObject`. *action* is required for all resource types except `Component`, `CustomTag`, `Function`, and `User` and specifies the action of the resource to check. The following table lists each resource type along with possible values for *action*:

| Resource Type | Possible Values for Action |
|---|---|
| `Application` | `All`, `UseClientVariables` |
| `CFML` | Any valid action of the CFML tag specified in *resourcetype* |
| `Collection` | `Delete`, `Optimize`, `Purge`, `Search`, `Update` |
| `Component` | N/A |
| `CustomTag` | N/A |
| `Datasource` | `All`, `Connect`, `Delete`, `Insert`, `Select`, `SP` (stored procedure), `Update` |
| `File` | `Read`, `Write` |
| `Function` | N/A |
| `User` | N/A |
| `UserObject` | *action* as specified in the ColdFusion Administrator |

In order to use the `IsProtected()` function, Advanced Security needs to be enabled within the ColdFusion Administrator, and a valid security context must already be defined. The following example uses the `IsProtected()` function to determine if file uploading via `CFFILE` is a protected resource:

```
<CFIF IsProtected('CFML', 'CFFILE', 'Upload')>
  File uploading using CFFILE is a protected resource!
<CFELSE>
  File uploading using CFFILE isn't a protected resource!
</CFIF>
```

## IsQuery

`IsQuery(`*value*`)`

Returns `True` if the specified `value` is a valid ColdFusion query or `False` if it isn't. Examples:

```
<CFSET Form.MyFormVar = "This is a form variable">
<CFSET URL.MyURLVar = "This is a URL variable">
<CFSET Grades = ArrayNew(1)>
<CFSET Grades[1] = 95>
<CFSET Grades[2] = 93>
<CFSET Grades[3] = 87>
<CFSET Grades[4] = 100>
<CFSET Grades[5] = 74>

<CFIF IsQuery(Form.MyFormVar)>
  Form.MyFormVar is a query!
```

```
<CFELSEIF IsQuery(URL.MyURLVar)>
  URL.MyURLVar is a query!
<CFELSEIF IsQuery(Grades)>
  Grades is a query!
<CFELSE>
  No variables are queries!
</CFIF>
```

## IsSimpleValue

`IsSimpleValue(`*`value`*`)`

Returns `True` if the specified value is a number, string, Boolean, or date/time object or `False` if it isn't. Examples:

```
<CFSET MyArray = ArrayNew(1)>
<CFSET MyArray[1]="George">
<CFSET MyArray[2]="Jeff">

<CFOUTPUT>
IsSimpleValue(123): #IsSimpleValue(123)#<BR>
IsSimpleValue('abc'): #IsSimpleValue('abc')#<BR>
IsSimpleValue('123,abc,456,def'): #IsSimpleValue('123,abc,456,def')#<BR>
IsSimpleValue(MyArray): #IsSimpleValue(MyArray)#<BR>
IsSimpleValue(True): #IsSimpleValue(True)#<BR>
IsSimpleValue(11/11/99): #IsSimpleValue(11/11/99)#<BR>
</CFOUTPUT>
```

## IsStruct

`IsStruct(`*`variable`*`)`

Returns `True` if the specified variable is a ColdFusion structure or `False` if it isn't. Examples:

```
<CFSET Stock = StructNew()>

<CFSET StructInsert(Stock, "company", "Allaire")>
<CFSET StructInsert(Stock, "ticker", "ALLR")>
<CFSET StructInsert(Stock, "exchange", "NASDAQ")>
<CFSET StructInsert(Stock, "price", "66.25")>
<CFSET StructInsert(Stock, "change", "+0.375")>
<CFSET StructInsert(Stock, "lasttradetime", "10:17AM")>
<CFSET StructInsert(Stock, "lasttradedate", "05/17/1999")>
<CFSET StructInsert(Stock, "volume", "8300")>

<CFSET MyList = "Allaire, ALLR, NASDAQ, 66.25, +0.375, 10:17AM, 05/17/1999, 8300">

<CFIF IsStruct(Stock)>
  <B>Stock</B> is a structure.
<CFELSE>
  <B>Stock</B> isn't a structure.
</CFIF>
<P>
```

```
<CFIF IsStruct(MyList)>
  <B>MyList</B> is a structure.
<CFELSE>
  <B>MyList</B> isn't a structure.
</CFIF>
```

## IsWDDX

New as of ColdFusion 4.51 SP2

`IsWDDX(value)`

Uses a validating XML parser with the WDDX DTD to determine whether a specified value is a well-formed WDDX packet. Returns `True` if the specified value is a well-formed WDDX packet or `False` if it isn't. The following example shows how to use the `IsWDDX()` function to detect if a value is a well-formed WDDX packet:

```
<!--- serialize a string into a WDDX packet --->
<CFWDDX ACTION="CFML2WDDX" INPUT="I am a string!" OUTPUT="MyWDDXPacket1">

<CFSET MyWDDXPacket2 = "I am a string too!">

<CFOUTPUT>#HTMLEditFormat(MyWDDXPacket1)#<BR></CFOUTPUT><P>

<!--- check if MyWDDXPacket1 contains a well-formed WDDX packet --->
<CFIF IsWDDX(MyWDDXPacket1)>
  <B>Is</B> a well-formed WDDX packet!
<CFELSE>
  <B>Is not</B> a well-formed WDDX packet!
</CFIF>

<CFOUTPUT>#HTMLEditFormat(MyWDDXPacket2)#<BR></CFOUTPUT><P>

<!--- check if MyWDDXPacket2 contains a well-formed WDDX packet --->
<CFIF IsWDDX(MyWDDXPacket2)>
  <B>Is</B> a well-formed WDDX packet!
<CFELSE>
  <B>Is not</B> a well-formed WDDX packet!
</CFIF>
```

## JavaCast

New as of ColdFusion 4.5

`JavaCast(type, variable)`

Casts a ColdFusion variable before being passed to an overloaded Java method. Possible entries for `type` include `bool`, `int`, `long`, `double`, or `string`. The `JavaCast()` function can't cast complex objects, such as query objects, arrays, and structures, nor can it cast to a super-class. The following example demonstrates how to explicitly cast a ColdFusion variable before passing it to an overloaded method within a Java object:

```
<CFOBJECT TYPE="Java" ACTION="Create" CLASS="MyClass" NAME="MyObject">

<CFSET x=10>

<!--- cast x to a string --->
<CFSET MyString = JavaCast("string",x)>
```

```
<CFSET void = MyMethod(MyString)>

<!--- cast x to an integer --->
<CFSET MyInteger = JavaCast("int",x)>
<CFSET void = MyMethod(MyInteger)>
```

## JSStringFormat

New as of ColdFusion 4.5

`JSStringFormat(`*`string`*`)`

Returns *string* with special characters escaped so that it is safe to use in JavaScript statements. Example:

```
<CFSET MyString="""Escape double quotes"".  Escape the \ character. 'Escape
single quotes'">

<CFSET SafeString=JSStringFormat(MyString)>

<CFOUTPUT>
<B>Original String:</B> #MyString#<BR>
<B>JavaScript Safe String:</B> #SafeString#
</CFOUTPUT>
```

## Lcase

`Lcase(`*`string`*`)`

Converts *string* to lowercase. Example:

```
<CFSET MyString="I WANT THIS STRING TO APPEAR IN ALL LOWERCASE.">

<CFOUTPUT>#Lcase(MyString)#</CFOUTPUT>
```

## Left

`Left(`*`string, count`*`)`

Returns the number of characters specified by *count*, beginning at the leftmost position of *string*. The following example returns the 13 leftmost characters of a string:

```
<CFSET MyString="(555)555-5555 x5555">
<CFSET BasePhoneNumber = Left(MyString, 13)>

<CFOUTPUT>
<B>String:</B> #MyString#<BR>
<B>Base Phone Number:</B> #BasePhoneNumber#
</CFOUTPUT>
```

## Len

`Len(string)`

Returns the length of a string as a number. If *string* is binary, `Len()` returns the length of the binary buffer. Example:

```
<CFSET MyString="This is my string.">

<CFOUTPUT>
String:  #MyString#<BR>
MyString is #Len(MyString)# characters long.
</CFOUTPUT>
```

## ListAppend

`ListAppend(list, element [, delimiters])`

Appends *element* to the end of *list*. An optional delimiter can be specified if the list is delimited with a character other than the comma (the default). Here's an example that appends an element to the end of a list:

```
<CFSET MyList = "Monday,Tuesday,Wednesday,Thursday,Friday,Saturday">
<CFSET MyAppendedList = ListAppend(MyList, 'Sunday')>

<CFOUTPUT>
<B>List:</B>  #MyList#<BR>
<B>Appended List:</B> #MyAppendedList#
</CFOUTPUT>
```

## ListChangeDelims

`ListChangeDelims(list, new_delimiter [, delimiters])`

Changes the delimiters used in the list to the specified new delimiters. The following example changes the delimiters in the list from commas to pipes (|):

```
<CFSET MyList = "Monday,Tuesday,Wednesday,Thursday,Friday,Saturday,Sunday">
<CFSET NewList = ListChangeDelims(MyList, '|', ',')>

<CFOUTPUT>
<B>Old Delimiters:</B> #MyList#<BR>
<B>New Delimiters:</B> #NewList#
</CFOUTPUT>
```

## ListContains

`ListContains(list, substring [, delimiters])`

Returns the index of the first element in the list that contains the specified substring as part of the element. If the substring isn't found, 0 is returned. The search is case-sensitive. An optional delimiter can be specified if the list is delimited with a character other than the comma (the default). Here's an example that returns the index of the first element in a list that contains wed:

```
<CFSET MyList = "Monday,Tuesday,Wednesday,Thursday,Friday,Saturday,Sunday">
<CFSET TheSubstring = "wed">
<CFSET TheIndex = ListContains(MyList, TheSubstring)>

<CFOUTPUT>
<B>List:</B> #MyList#
<P><CFIF TheIndex IS 0>
  The substring (#TheSubstring#) could not be found in the list!
<CFELSE>
  The substring (#TheSubstring#) was found in element
  #TheIndex# (#ListGetAt(MyList, TheIndex)#).
</CFIF>
</CFOUTPUT>
```

## ListContainsNoCase

`ListContainsNoCase(`*`list`*`, `*`substring`*` [, `*`delimiters`*`])`

Returns the index of the first element in the list that contains the specified substring as part of the element. If the substring isn't found, 0 is returned. The search is case-insensitive. An optional delimiter can be specified if the list is delimited with a character other than the comma (the default). The following example returns the index of the first element in a list that contains wed:

```
<CFSET MyList = "Monday,Tuesday,Wednesday,Thursday,Friday,Saturday,Sunday">
<CFSET TheSubstring = "wed">
<CFSET TheIndex = ListContainsNoCase(MyList, TheSubstring)>

<CFOUTPUT>
<B>List:</B> #MyList#
<P><CFIF TheIndex IS 0>
  The substring (#TheSubstring#) could not be found in the list!
<CFELSE>
  The substring (#TheSubstring#) was found in element #TheIndex#
  (#ListGetAt(MyList, TheIndex)#).
</CFIF>
</CFOUTPUT>
```

## ListDeleteAt

`ListDeleteAt(`*`list`*`, `*`position`*` [, `*`delimiters`*` ])`

Deletes an element from a list occupying the specified *`position`*. An optional delimiter can be specified if the list is delimited with a character other than the comma (the default). Here's an example that deletes the list element occupying the fifth position in the list:

```
<CFSET MyList = "Monday,Tuesday,Wednesday,Thursday,Friday,Saturday,Sunday">
<CFSET NewList = ListDeleteAt(MyList, 5)>

<CFOUTPUT>
<B>Original List:</B> #MyList#<BR>
```

```
<B>New List:</B> #NewList#
</CFOUTPUT>
```

## ListFind

`ListFind(list, value [, delimiters])`

Returns the index of the first occurrence of value in the specified list. The search is case-sensitive. If no matches are found, 0 is returned. An optional delimiter can be specified if the list is delimited with a character other than the comma (the default). The following example returns the index of the first element in a list that matches **saturday**:

```
<CFSET MyList = "Monday,Tuesday,Wednesday,Thursday,Friday,Saturday,Sunday">
<CFSET TheValue = "saturday">
<CFSET TheIndex = ListFind(MyList, TheValue)>

<CFOUTPUT>
<B>List:</B> #MyList#
<P><CFIF TheIndex IS 0>
  The value (#TheValue#) could not be found in the list!
<CFELSE>
  The Value (#TheValue#) was found in element #TheIndex#
  (#ListGetAt(MyList, TheIndex)#).
</CFIF>
</CFOUTPUT>
```

## ListFindNoCase

`ListFindNoCase(list, value [, delimiters])`

Returns the index of the first occurrence of value in the specified list. The search is case-insensitive. If no matches are found, 0 is returned. An optional delimiter can be specified if the list is delimited with a character other than the comma (the default). Here's an example that returns the index of the first element in a list that matches **saturday**:

```
<CFSET MyList = "Monday,Tuesday,Wednesday,Thursday,Friday,Saturday,Sunday">
<CFSET TheValue = "saturday">
<CFSET TheIndex = ListFindNoCase(MyList, TheValue)>

<CFOUTPUT>
<B>List:</B> #MyList#
<P><CFIF TheIndex IS 0>
  The value (#TheValue#) could not be found in the list!
<CFELSE>
  The Value (#TheValue#) was found in element #TheIndex#
  (#ListGetAt(MyList, TheIndex)#).
</CFIF>
</CFOUTPUT>
```

## ListFirst

`ListFirst(list [, delimiters])`

Returns the first element in the specified list. An optional delimiter can be specified if the list is delimited with a character other than the comma (the default). Example:

```
<CFSET MyList = "Monday,Tuesday,Wednesday,Thursday,Friday,Saturday,Sunday">

<CFOUTPUT>
<B>List:</B> #MyList#<BR>
<B>First Element:</B> #ListFirst(MyList)#
</CFOUTPUT>
```

## ListGetAt

`ListGetAt(list, position [, delimiters])`

Returns the list element specified by *position*. An optional delimiter can be specified if the list is delimited with a character other than the comma (the default). Note that the `ListGetAt()` function currently treats successive instances of the same delimiter as a single delimiter. Here's an example that retrieves the third element of the list:

```
<CFSET MyList = "Monday,Tuesday,Wednesday,Thursday,Friday,Saturday,Sunday">

<CFOUTPUT>
<B>List:</B> #MyList#<BR>
<B>Third Element:</B> #ListGetAt(MyList, 3)#
</CFOUTPUT>
```

## ListInsertAt

`ListInsertAt(list, position, value [, delimiters])`

Inserts *value* into list at the specified position. An optional delimiter can be specified if the list is delimited with a character other than the comma (the default). The following example inserts a value into a list:

```
<CFSET MyList = "Monday,Tuesday,Thursday,Friday,Saturday,Sunday">
<CFSET MyNewList = ListInsertAt(MyList, 3, "Wednesday")>

<CFOUTPUT>
<B>Original List:</B> #MyList#<BR>
<B>New List:</B> #MyNewList#
</CFOUTPUT>
```

## ListLast

`ListLast(list [, delimiters])`

Returns the last element in the specified list. An optional delimiter can be specified if the list is delimited with a character other than the comma (the default). Example:

```
<CFSET MyList = "Monday,Tuesday,Wednesday,Thursday,Friday,Saturday,Sunday">

<CFOUTPUT>
<B>List:</B> #MyList#<BR>
<B>Last Element:</B> #ListLast(MyList)#
</CFOUTPUT>
```

## ListLen

`ListLen(list [, delimiters])`

Returns the number of elements in the specified list. An optional delimiter can be specified if the list is delimited with a character other than the comma (the default). Example:

```
<CFSET MyList = "Monday,Tuesday,Wednesday,Thursday,Friday,Saturday,Sunday">

<CFOUTPUT>
<B>List:</B> #MyList#<BR>
<B>Number of elements:</B> #ListLen(MyList)#
</CFOUTPUT>
```

## ListPrepend

`ListPrepend(list, element [, delimiters])`

Prepends *element* to the beginning of *list*. An optional delimiter can be specified if the list is delimited with a character other than the comma (the default). The following example appends an element to the beginning of a list:

```
<CFSET MyList = "Tuesday,Wednesday,Thursday,Friday,Saturday,Sunday">
<CFSET MyprependedList = ListPrepend(MyList, 'Monday')>

<CFOUTPUT>
<B>List:</B> #MyList#<BR>
<B>Prepended List:</B> #MyPrependedList#
</CFOUTPUT>
```

## ListQualify

New as of ColdFusion 4.01

`ListQualify(list, qualifier [, delimiters] [, elements])`

Places qualifiers (such as single or double quotes) around elements of *list*. An optional delimiter can be specified if the list is delimited with a character other than the comma (the default). Elements accepts `All` or `Char` and specifies whether the function qualifies all elements in the list (the default) or only list items made up of alphabetic characters. Examples:

```
<CFSET MyAlphaList = "Monday,Tuesday,Wednesday,Thursday,Friday,Saturday,Sunday">
<CFSET MyAlphaNumericList =
"1,Monday,2,Tuesday,3,Wednesday,4,Thursday,5,Friday,6,Saturday,7,Sunday">

<CFSET MyQualifiedAlphaList = ListQualify(MyAlphaList, """")>
<CFSET MyQualifiedAlphaNumericList =
  ListQualify(MyAlphaNumericList, """", ',', 'CHAR')>
<CFOUTPUT>
<B>Original Alpha List:</B> #MyAlphaList#<BR>
<B>Original AlphaNumeric List:</B> #MyAlphaNumericList#<BR>
<P><B>Qualified Alpha List:</B> #MyQualifiedAlphaList#<BR>
<B>Qualified AlphaNumeric List:</B> #MyQualifiedAlphaNumericList#<BR>
</CFOUTPUT>
```

## ListRest

`ListRest(`*`list`*` [, `*`delimiters`*`])`

Returns all the elements in the specified list excluding the first element. An optional delimiter can be specified if the list is delimited with a character other than the comma (the default). The following example returns all the elements in the list except for the first element:

```
<CFSET MyList = "Monday,Tuesday,Wednesday,Thursday,Friday,Saturday,Sunday">

<CFOUTPUT>
<B>List:</B> #MyList#<BR>
<B>All Elements Excluding First:</B> #ListRest(MyList)#
</CFOUTPUT>
```

## ListSetAt

`ListSetAt(`*`list`*`, `*`position`*`, `*`value`*` [, `*`delimiters`*`])`

Sets *`value`* at specified *`position`*, overwriting the element already occupying that space. An optional delimiter can be specified if the list is delimited with a character other than the comma (the default). Here's an example that replaces the value in the third element of the list with a new value:

```
<CFSET MyList = "Monday,Tuesday,Wednesday,Thursday,Friday,Saturday,Sunday">
<CFSET MyNewList = ListSetAt(MyList, 3, "Humpday")>

<CFOUTPUT>
<B>Original List:</B> #MyList#<BR>
<B>New List:</B> #MyNewList#
</CFOUTPUT>
```

## ListSort

New as of ColdFusion 4.01

`ListSort(list, sort_type [, order] [, delimiters])`

Sorts a list based on the *sort_type* (`numeric`, `text`, or `textnocase`) and optionally, the sort *order* (`asc`, the default, or `desc`). An optional delimiter can be specified if the list is delimited with a character other than the comma (the default). The following example sorts a list by alphabetical order:

```
<CFSET MyList = "Monday,Tuesday,Wednesday,Thursday,Friday,Saturday,Sunday">

<CFOUTPUT>
<B>List:</B> #MyList#<BR>
<B>Sorted by Alphabetical Order:</B> #ListSort(MyList, 'text')#
</CFOUTPUT>
```

## ListToArray

`ListToArray(list [, delimiters])`

Converts a ColdFusion list to a one-dimensional array. An optional delimiter can be specified if the list is delimited with a character other than the comma (the default). Here's an example that converts a list containing the days of the week to a one-dimensional array:

```
<CFSET MyList = "Monday,Tuesday,Wednesday,Thursday,Friday,Saturday,Sunday">
<CFSET MyArray = ListToArray(MyList)>

<CFLOOP INDEX="Element" FROM="1" TO="#ArrayLen(MyArray)#">
  <CFOUTPUT>Element #Element#: #MyArray[Element]#<BR></CFOUTPUT>
</CFLOOP>
```

## ListValueCount

New as of ColdFusion 4.01

`ListValueCount(list, value [, delimiters])`

Counts the number of times *value* appears in the specified list. The search performed is case-sensitive. An optional delimiter can be specified if the list is delimited with a character other than the comma (the default). The following example counts the number of times each unique value appears in the list and outputs the results for each item:

```
<CFSET MyList = "Apple,orange,apple,Orange,Peach,pear,apple,pear,peach,Pear,
Apple,Peach,orange,apple">
<CFSET UniqueList = "">

<CFLOOP INDEX="Element" LIST="#MyList#">
  <CFIF ListFind(UniqueList, Element) IS "No">
    <CFSET UniqueList = ListAppend(UniqueList, Element)>
  </CFIF>
</CFLOOP>

<CFOUTPUT><B>Original List:</B> #MyList#</CFOUTPUT>
<P><CFLOOP INDEX="Element" LIST="#UniqueList#">
  <CFOUTPUT>
```

```
    #Element# appears: #ListValueCount(MyList, Element)# times.<BR>
  </CFOUTPUT>
</CFLOOP>
```

## ListValueCountNoCase

New as of ColdFusion 4.01

`ListValueCountNoCase(`*`list, value`*` [, `*`delimiters`*`])`

Counts the number of times *value* appears in the specified list. The search performed is case-insensitive. An optional delimiter can be specified if the list is delimited with a character other than the comma (the default). Here's an example that counts the number of times each unique value appears in the list and outputs the results for each item:

```
<CFSET MyList = "Apple,orange,apple,Orange,Peach,pear,apple,pear,peach,Pear,
Apple,Peach,orange,apple">
<CFSET UniqueList = "">

<CFLOOP INDEX="Element" LIST="#MyList#">
  <CFIF ListFindNoCase(UniqueList, Element) IS "No">
    <CFSET UniqueList = ListAppend(UniqueList, Element)>
  </CFIF>
</CFLOOP>

<CFOUTPUT><B>Original List:</B> #MyList#</CFOUTPUT>
<P><CFLOOP INDEX="Element" LIST="#UniqueList#">
  <CFOUTPUT>
    #Element# appears: #ListValueCountNoCase(MyList, Element)# times
    regardless of case.<BR>
  </CFOUTPUT>
</CFLOOP>
```

## LJustify

`LJustify(`*`string, length`*`)`

Left-justifies *string* within a field of *length* characters. Example:

```
<CFSET OriginalString = "ColdFusion">

<CFOUTPUT>
<B>Original String (quoted):</B> "#OriginalString#"<BR>
<B>Left-justified String (quoted):</B> "#LJustify("ColdFusion", 20)#"
</CFOUTPUT>
```

## Log

`Log(`*`number`*`)`

Returns the natural logarithm of a number. *number* must be a positive number greater than zero. Examples:

```
<CFOUTPUT>
Log(0.01) = #Log(0.01)#<BR>
Log(1) = #Log(1)#<BR>
```

```
Log(10) = #Log(10)#<BR>
Log(100) = #Log(100)#<BR>
Log(1000) = #Log(1000)#<BR>
Log(1000.234) = #Log(1000.234)#
</CFOUTPUT>
```

## Log10

`Log10(number)`

Returns the base 10 logarithm of a number. Examples:

```
<CFOUTPUT>
Log10(0.01) = #Log10(0.01)#<BR>
Log10(1) = #Log10(1)#<BR>
Log10(10) = #Log10(10)#<BR>
Log10(100) = #Log10(100)#<BR>
Log10(1000) = #Log10(1000)#<BR>
Log10(1000.234) = #Log10(1000.234)#
</CFOUTPUT>
```

## LSCurrencyFormat

`LSCurrencyFormat(number [, type])`

Returns a locale-specific currency format where ***number*** is the currency amount, and ***type*** is the locale-specific convention. Valid entries for ***type*** are `None` (the amount), `Local` (the amount with locale-specific currency formatting; the default), and `International` (the amount with its corresponding three-letter international currency prefix). The following example displays currency formats for each locale:

```
<CFLOOP INDEX="locale" LIST="#Server.Coldfusion.SupportedLocales#">
  <CFSET temp = SetLocale(locale)>
  <CFOUTPUT>
    <P><B>#locale#</B><BR>
    None: #LSCurrencyFormat(1000000.99, "None")#<BR>
    Local: #LSCurrencyFormat(1000000.99, "Local")#<BR>
    International: #LSCurrencyFormat(1000000.99, "International")#<BR>
  </CFOUTPUT>
</CFLOOP>
```

## LSDateFormat

`LSDateFormat(date [, mask])`

Returns a locale-specific date format according to ***mask***. If no value is specified for ***mask***, `LSDateFormat()` uses the locale-specific default. Valid entries for ***mask*** are:

| Mask | Description |
|---|---|
| d | Day of the month as a number with no leading zero for single-digit days |
| dd | Day of the month as a number with a leading zero for single-digit days |
| ddd | Three-letter abbreviation for day of the week |

| Mask | Description |
|---|---|
| dddd | Full name of the day of the week |
| gg | Period/era; currently ignored |
| m | Month as a number with no leading zero for single-digit months |
| mm | Month as a number with a leading zero for single-digit months |
| mmm | Three-letter abbreviation for the month |
| mmmm | Full name of the month |
| y | Last two digits of year with no leading zero for years less than 10 |
| yy | Last two digits of year with a leading zero for years less than 10 |
| yyyy | Four digit year |

The following example applies the `LSDateFormat()` function to each locale:

```
<CFLOOP INDEX="locale" LIST="#Server.Coldfusion.SupportedLocales#">
  <CFSET temp = SetLocale(locale)>
  <CFOUTPUT>
    <P><B>#locale#</B><BR>
    #LSDateFormat(Now())#<BR>
    #LSDateFormat(Now(), "d/m/yy")#<BR>
    #LSDateFormat(Now(), "d-mmm-yyyy")#<BR>
    #LSDateFormat(Now(), 'dd mmm yy')#<BR>
    #LSDateFormat(Now(), 'dddd, mmmm dd, yyyy')#<BR>
    #LSDateFormat(Now(), "mm/dd/yyyy")#<BR>
    #LSDateFormat(Now(), "mmmm d, yyyy")#<BR>
    #LSDateFormat(Now(), "mmm-dd-yyyy")#<BR>
  </CFOUTPUT>
</CFLOOP>
```

## LSEuroCurrencyFormat

New as of ColdFusion 4.01

`LSEuroCurrencyFormat(`*`amount`*` [, `*`type`*`])`

Returns a locale-specific currency format with the Euro as the symbol where ***number*** is the currency amount and ***type*** is the locale-specific convention. Valid entries for ***type*** are `None` (the amount), `Local` (the amount with locale-specific currency formatting; the default), and `International` (the amount with its corresponding three-letter international currency prefix). The following example displays Euro currency formats for each locale:

```
<CFLOOP INDEX="locale" LIST="#Server.Coldfusion.SupportedLocales#">
  <CFSET temp = SetLocale(locale)>
  <CFOUTPUT>
    <P>
    <B>#locale#</B><BR>
    None: #LSEuroCurrencyFormat(1000000.99, "None")#<BR>
    Local: #LSEuroCurrencyFormat(1000000.99, "Local")#<BR>
    International: #LSEuroCurrencyFormat(1000000.99, "International")#<BR>
  </CFOUTPUT>
</CFLOOP>
```

## LSIsCurrency

`LSIsCurrency(string)`

Returns `True` if *`string`* is a locale-specific currency string and `False` if it isn't. Here's an example that determines whether the given strings are locale-specific currency values for each locale:

```
<CFLOOP INDEX="locale" LIST="#Server.Coldfusion.SupportedLocales#">
  <CFSET temp = SetLocale(locale)>
  <CFOUTPUT>
    <P><B>#locale#</B><BR>
    99.99: #LSIsCurrency('99.99')#<BR>
    $1234: #LSIsCurrency('$1234')#<BR>
    $1,234,567,890: #LSIsCurrency('$1,234,567,890')#<BR>
    $1234.99: #LSIsCurrency('$1234.99')#<BR>
  </CFOUTPUT>
</CFLOOP>
```

## LSIsDate

`LSIsDate(date)`

Functions identically to the `IsDate()` function within the context of the current locale. Returns `True` if *`date`* can be converted to a date/time object in the current locale or `False` if it can't. The following example determines whether the supplied values are valid date/time objects for each locale:

```
<CFLOOP INDEX="locale" LIST="#Server.Coldfusion.SupportedLocales#">
  <CFSET temp = SetLocale(locale)>
  <CFOUTPUT>
    <P><B>#locale#</B><BR>
    08/15/1998: #LSIsDate('08/15/1998')#<BR>
    15/08/1998: #LSIsDate('15/08/1998')#<BR>
    13/13/1998: #LSIsDate('13/13/1998')#<BR>
    August 15, 1998: #LSIsDate('August 15, 1998')#<BR>
    15 Aug 1998: #LSIsDate('15 Aug 1998')#<BR>
    7 p.m.: #LSIsDate('7 p.m.')#<BR>
    7pm: #LSIsDate('7pm')#<BR>
    19:00: #LSIsDate('19:00')#<BR>
    six thirty: #LSIsDate('six thirty')#
  </CFOUTPUT>
</CFLOOP>
```

## LSIsNumeric

`LSIsNumeric(string)`

Functions identically to the `IsNumeric()` function within the context of the current locale. Returns `True` if *`string`* can be converted to a number in the current locale or `False` if it can't. Here's an example that determines whether the supplied values are valid numbers for each locale:

```
<CFLOOP INDEX="locale" LIST="#Server.Coldfusion.SupportedLocales#">
  <CFSET temp = SetLocale(locale)>
  <CFOUTPUT>
    <P><B>#locale#</B><BR>
    -1: #LSIsNumeric(-1)#<BR>
    0: #LSIsNumeric(0)#<BR>
    1234: #LSIsNumeric(1234)#<BR>
    1,234,567,890: #LSIsNumeric('1,234,567,890')#<BR>
    $1234.99: #LSIsNumeric('$1234.99')#<BR>
    08/15/1999: #LSIsNumeric('08/15/1999')#<BR>
    7pm: #LSIsNumeric('7pm')#<BR>
    abcdef: #LSIsNumeric('abcdef')#<BR>
    true: #LSIsNumeric(true)#<BR>
    false: #LSIsNumeric(false)#<BR>
    yes: #LSIsNumeric('yes')#<BR>
    no: #LSIsNumeric('no')#<BR>
  </CFOUTPUT>
</CFLOOP>
```

## LSNumberFormat

`LSNumberFormat(`*`number`*` [, `*`mask`*`])`

Returns *number* formatted according to *mask* using the locale convention. If no value is specified for *mask*, `LSNumberFormat()` returns *number* as an integer. Valid entries for *mask* are the same as for `NumberFormat()`. The following example applies the function to various numbers for each locale:

```
<CFLOOP INDEX="locale" LIST="#Server.Coldfusion.SupportedLocales#">
  <CFSET temp = SetLocale(locale)>
  <CFOUTPUT>
    <P><B>#locale#</B><BR>
    LSNumberFormat(1000.99, '____'): #LSNumberFormat(1000.99, '____')#<BR>
    LSNumberFormat(1000.99, '9999.99'): #LSNumberFormat(1000.99, '9999.99')#<BR>
    LSNumberFormat(1000.99, '09999.9900'):
      #LSNumberFormat(1000.99, '09999.9900')#<BR>
    LSNumberFormat(-1000.99, '(9999.99)'):
      #LSNumberFormat(-1000.99, '(9999.99)')#<BR>
    LSNumberFormat(1000.99, '+9999.99'):
      #LSNumberFormat(1000.99, '+9999.99')#<BR>
    LSNumberFormat(-1000.99, '+9999.99'):
      #LSNumberFormat(-1000.99, '+9999.99')#<BR>
    LSNumberFormat(1000.99, '-9999.99'):
      #LSNumberFormat(1000.99, '-9999.99')#<BR>
    LSNumberFormat(-1000.99, '-9999.99'):
      #LSNumberFormat(-1000.99, '-9999.99')#<BR>
    LSNumberFormat(1000.99, '$9,999.99'):
      #LSNumberFormat(1000.99, '$9,999.99')#<BR>
    LSNumberFormat(1000.99, 'L999,999.99'):
      #LSNumberFormat(1000.99, 'L999,999.99')#<BR>
    LSNumberFormat(1000.99, 'C999,999.99'):
```

```
    #LSNumberFormat(1000.99, 'C999,999.99')#<BR>
   LSNumberFormat(1000.99, 'C_____(^___)'):
    #LSNumberFormat(1000.99, 'C_____(^___)')#<BR>
  </CFOUTPUT>
</CFLOOP>
```

## LSParseCurrency

`LSParseCurrency(`*`string`*`)`

Returns the numeric value of ***string*** where ***string*** is a locale-specific currency amount. `LSParseCurrency()` can be converted from any of the locale-specific currency formats (None, `Local`, `International`). The following example demonstrates for each locale:

```
<CFLOOP INDEX="locale" LIST="#Server.Coldfusion.SupportedLocales#">
  <CFSET temp = SetLocale(locale)>
  <CFOUTPUT>
    <P><B>#locale#</B><BR>
    Local: #LSCurrencyFormat(1000000.99, "local")#<BR>
    LSParseCurrency: #LSParseCurrency(LSCurrencyFormat(1000000.99, "local"))#<BR>
  </CFOUTPUT>
</CFLOOP>
```

## LSParseDateTime

`LSParseDateTime(`*`datestring`*`)`

Returns a locale-specific ColdFusion date/time object from ***datestring***. `LSParseDateTime()` is similar to the `ParseDateTime()` function except it doesn't handle POP dates. Example:

```
<CFLOOP INDEX="locale" LIST="#Server.Coldfusion.SupportedLocales#">
  <CFSET temp = SetLocale(locale)>
  <CFOUTPUT>
    <P><B>#locale#</B><BR>
    #LSParseDateTime("#LSDateFormat(Now())# #LSTimeFormat(Now())#")#<BR>
  </CFOUTPUT>
</CFLOOP>
```

## LSParseEuroCurrency

New as of ColdFusion 4.01

`LSParseEuroCurrency(`*`string`*`)`

Returns the numeric value of ***string*** where ***string*** is a locale-specific currency amount that contains the Euro symbol. `LSParseEuroCurrency()` can be converted from any of the locale-specific Euro currency formats (None, `Local`, `International`). The following example demonstrates for each locale:

```
<CFLOOP INDEX="locale" LIST="#Server.Coldfusion.SupportedLocales#">
  <CFSET temp = SetLocale(locale)>
  <CFOUTPUT>
    <P><B>#locale#</B><BR>
    Local: #LSEuroCurrencyFormat(1000000.99, "local")#<BR>
```

```
  LSParseCurrency: #LSParseEuroCurrency(LSCurrencyFormat(1000000.99,
"local"))#<BR>
  </CFOUTPUT>
</CFLOOP>
```

## LSParseNumber

`LSParseNumber(`*`string`*`)`

Converts *string* to a locale-specific numeric value. Here's an example that applies the function to each locale:

```
<CFLOOP INDEX="locale" LIST="#Server.Coldfusion.SupportedLocales#">
  <CFSET temp = SetLocale(locale)>
  <CFOUTPUT>
    <P><B>#locale#</B><BR>
    Local: #LSNumberFormat(1000000.99)#<BR>
    LSParseNumber: #LSParseNumber(LSNumberFormat(1000000.99))#<BR>
  </CFOUTPUT>
</CFLOOP>
```

## LSTimeFormat

`LSTimeFormat(`*`time`*` [, `*`mask`*`])`

Returns locale-specific *time* formatted according to *mask*. If no value is specified for *mask*, `LSTimeFormat()` uses the default locale's format. Valid entries for *mask* are the same as for `TimeFormat()`. The following example demonstrates for each locale:

```
<CFSET TheTime = Now()>

<CFLOOP INDEX="locale" LIST="#Server.Coldfusion.SupportedLocales#">
  <CFSET temp = SetLocale(locale)>
  <CFOUTPUT>
    <P><B>#locale#</B><BR>
    TheTime = #LSTimeFormat(TheTime)#<BR>
    LSTimeFormat(TheTime, 'h:m:s'): #LSTimeFormat(TheTime, 'h:m:s')#<BR>
    LSTimeFormat(TheTime, 'h:m:s t'): #LSTimeFormat(TheTime, 'h:m:s t')#<BR>
    LSTimeFormat(TheTime, 'hh:mm:ss'): #LSTimeFormat(TheTime, 'hh:mm:ss')#<BR>
    LSTimeFormat(TheTime, 'hh:mm:ss tt'):
      #LSTimeFormat(TheTime, 'hh:mm:ss tt')#<BR>
    LSTimeFormat(TheTime, 'H:M:ss'): #LSTimeFormat(TheTime, 'H:M:s')#<BR>
    LSTimeFormat(TheTime, 'HH:MM:ss'): #LSTimeFormat(TheTime, 'HH:MM:ss')#<BR>
  </CFOUTPUT>
</CFLOOP>
```

## LTrim

`LTrim(string)`

Removes leading spaces from the specified string. Example:

```
<CFSET OriginalString = "      ColdFusion">

<CFOUTPUT>
<B>Original String (quoted):</B> "#OriginalString#"<BR>
<B>Left-trimmed String (quoted):</B> "#LTrim(OriginalString)#"
</CFOUTPUT>
```

## Max

`Max(number1, number2)`

Returns the higher value of two specified numbers. Example:

```
<CFSET x=10>
<CFSET y=20>

<CFOUTPUT>#Max(x,y)# is a larger number than #Min(x,y)#.</CFOUTPUT>
```

## Mid

`Mid(string, startpos, count)`

Returns *count* number of characters from the *string* beginning at the position specified by *startpos*. Example:

```
<CFSET MyString="(555)555-5555 x5555">
<CFSET AreaCode = Mid(MyString, 2, 3)>

<CFOUTPUT>
<B>String:</B> #MyString#<BR>
<B>Area Code:</B> #AreaCode#
</CFOUTPUT>
```

## Min

`Min(number1, number2)`

Returns the lower value of two specified numbers. Example:

```
<CFSET x=10>
<CFSET y=20>

<CFOUTPUT>#Min(x,y)# is a smaller number than #Max(x,y)#.</CFOUTPUT>
```

## Minute

`Minute(date)`

Returns the minute for a valid date/time object as a number between 1 and 59. Example:

```
It is currently <CFOUTPUT>#Minute(Now())#</CFOUTPUT> minute(s) past the hour.
```

## Month

`Month(date)`

Returns the month of the year for a given date as a number between 1 and 12. Example:

```
The current month is month <CFOUTPUT>#Month(Now())#</CFOUTPUT>.
```

## MonthAsString

`MonthAsString(number)`

Returns the name of the month for a given month's number between 1 and 12. Example:

```
The current month is <CFOUTPUT>#MonthAsString(Month(Now()))#</CFOUTPUT>.
```

## Now

`Now()`

Returns the current server time and date as a time/date object in the format `{ts 'yyyy-mm-dd HH:MM:SS'}`. Example:

```
<CFOUTPUT>
Today is #DateFormat(Now(),'dddd mmmm dd, yyyy')#.<BR>
It is currently #TimeFormat(Now(),'hh:mm tt')#.
</CFOUTPUT>
```

## NumberFormat

`NumberFormat(number [, mask])`

Returns *number* formatted according to *mask*. If no value is specified for *mask*, `NumberFormat` returns *number* as an integer formatted with thousands separators. Valid entries for *mask* are:

| Mask | Description |
|---|---|
| _ | Optional digit placeholder |
| 9 | Optional digit placeholder; same as _ but better for showing decimal places |
| . | Decimal point location |
| 0 | Forces padding with zeros |
| ( ) | Surrounds negative numbers in parentheses |

| Mask | Description |
|---|---|
| + | Places a plus sign in front of positive numbers and a minus sign in front of negative numbers |
| - | Places a space in front of positive numbers and a minus sign in front of negative numbers |
| , | Separates thousands with commas |
| L | Left-justifies the number within the width of the mask |
| C | Centers the number within the width of the mask |
| $ | Places a dollar sign in front of the number |
| ^ | Separates left from right formatting |

Examples:

```
<CFSET MyNumber = 1000.99>

<CFOUTPUT>
<B>MyNumber = #MyNumber#</B>
<P>
NumberFormat(MyNumber, '____'): #NumberFormat(MyNumber, '____')#<BR>
NumberFormat(MyNumber, '9999.99'): #NumberFormat(MyNumber, '9999.99')#<BR>
NumberFormat(MyNumber, '09999.9900'): #NumberFormat(MyNumber, '09999.9900')#<BR>
NumberFormat(-MyNumber, '(9999.99)'): #NumberFormat(-MyNumber, '(9999.99)')#<BR>
NumberFormat(MyNumber, '+9999.99'): #NumberFormat(MyNumber, '+9999.99')#<BR>
NumberFormat(-MyNumber, '+9999.99'): #NumberFormat(-MyNumber, '+9999.99')#<BR>
NumberFormat(MyNumber, '-9999.99'): #NumberFormat(MyNumber, '-9999.99')#<BR>
NumberFormat(-MyNumber, '-9999.99'): #NumberFormat(-MyNumber, '-9999.99')#<BR>
NumberFormat(MyNumber, '$9,999.99'): #NumberFormat(MyNumber, '$9,999.99')#<BR>
NumberFormat(MyNumber, 'L999,999.99'): #NumberFormat(MyNumber, 'L999,999.99')#<BR>
NumberFormat(MyNumber, 'C999,999.99'): #NumberFormat(MyNumber, 'C999,999.99')#<BR>
NumberFormat(MyNumber, 'C_____(^___)'):
  #NumberFormat(MyNumber, 'C_____(^___)')#<BR>
</CFOUTPUT>
```

## ParagraphFormat

`ParagraphFormat(string)`

Returns *string* formatted so that single newline characters are replaced with a space character, and double newline characters are replaced with HTML <P> tags. `ParagraphFormat()` is most often used to format text that has been entered in a `Textarea` HTML form field. Example:

```
<CFSET MyText="This is my block of text.
It has both single newline characters in it like this paragraph, and double
newline characters like in the next paragraph.

This is the paragraph with the double newline characters.">

<FORM ACTION="" METHOD="Post">
  <CFOUTPUT>
  <TEXTAREA COLS=50 ROWS=10 NAME="TheText"
```

```
          WRAP="virtual">#ParagraphFormat(MyText)#</TEXTAREA>
  </CFOUTPUT>
</FORM>
```

## ParameterExists

Deprecated as of ColdFusion 3.0

`ParameterExists(`*`parameter`*`)`

Determines if the specified parameter exists. Returns **`True`** if the parameter exists or **`False`** if it doesn't. Note that **`IsDefined()`** should be used instead of **`ParameterExists()`**, as this function has been deprecated. Example:

```
<CFSET MyVar="Variable">
<CFSET Form.MyFormVar="Form Variable">

<CFOUTPUT>
<CFIF ParameterExists(MyVar)>
  Parameter MyVar exists:<BR>
  MyVar = #MyVar#
<CFELSE>
  No variable called MyVar exists.
</CFIF>
<P>
<CFIF ParameterExists(MyFormVar)>
  Parameter MyFormVar exists:<BR>
  MyFormVar = #MyFormVar#
<CFELSE>
  No variable called MyFormVar exists.
</CFIF>
<P>
<CFIF ParameterExists(Queryname.Field)>
  Variable Queryname.Field exists:<BR>
  QueryName.Field = #Queryname.Field#
<CFELSE>
  No variable called Queryname.Field exists.
</CFIF>
</CFOUTPUT>
```

## ParseDateTime

`ParseDateTime(`*`datestring`*` [, `*`conversiontype`*`])`

Returns a valid ColdFusion date/time object from *`datestring`*. An optional *`conversiontype`* may be specified. Valid entries for *`conversiontype`* are `POP` and `Standard` (the default). If `POP` is specified, *`datestring`* is converted to GMT (Greenwich Mean Time) using the English (U.S.) locale. If `Standard` is specified, no conversion is performed. Examples:

```
<CFOUTPUT>
<B>ParseDateTime("Sat, 15 Aug 1998 19:00:00 +0400", "POP"):</B>
#ParseDateTime("Sat, 15 Aug 1998 19:00:00 +0400", "POP")#<BR>
<B>ParseDateTime("Sat, 15 Aug 1998 19:00:00 +0400 (EDT)", "POP"):</B>
#ParseDateTime("Sat, 15 Aug 1998 19:00:00 +0400 (EDT)", "POP")#<BR>
<B>ParseDateTime("Sat, 15 Aug 1998 19:00:00 +0400"):</B>
```

```
#ParseDateTime("Sat, 15 Aug 1998 19:00:00 +0400")#<BR>
<B>ParseDateTime("Sat, 15 Aug 1998 19:00:00 +0400 (EDT):</B>
#ParseDateTime("Sat, 15 Aug 1998 19:00:00 +0400 (EDT)", "Standard")#<BR>
</CFOUTPUT>
```

## Pi

`Pi()`

Returns the value of π accurate to 15 digits (3.14159265358979). The following example uses `Pi()` to calculate the circumference of a circle with a radius of 12 inches:

```
<CFSET r=12>
<CFSET Circumference = 2*Pi()*r>

<CFOUTPUT>
The circumference of a circle with a radius of 12 inches is
#Circumference# inches.
</CFOUTPUT>
```

## PreserveSingleQuotes

`PreserveSingleQuotes(`*`variable`*`)`

Returns *`variable`* without escaping single quotation marks. **`PreserveSingleQuotes()`** keeps ColdFusion from automatically escaping single quotation marks within dynamically set variables. The **`PreserveSingleQuotes()`** function is most often used with SQL statements when it is necessary to pass dynamically generated values. Example:

```
<CFSET Names = "'Pere Money','Mark Edward','Marcel Haney'">

<CFQUERY NAME="GetRecords" DATASOURCE="ProgrammingCF">
        SELECT * FROM EmployeeDirectory
        WHERE Name IN (#PreserveSingleQuotes(Names)#)
</CFQUERY>

<CFOUTPUT>#GetRecords.RecordCount# record(s) found.</CFOUTPUT>
```

## Quarter

`Quarter(`*`date`*`)`

Returns the quarter as a number for the given date. Example:

```
<CFOUTPUT>The current quarter is: #Quarter(Now())#</CFOUTPUT>
```

## QueryAddColumn

New as of ColdFusion 4.01

`QueryAddColumn(`*`query, columnname, arrayname`*`)`

Adds a new column called *`columnname`* to *`query`* and populates its rows with data from a one-dimensional array specified by *`arrayname`*. The following example adds a new column to a query and populates it with data from an array:

```
<CFSET Products = QueryNew("ProductName, Color, Price, Qty")>
<CFSET NewRows = QueryAddRow(Products, 3)>

<CFSET temp = QuerySetCell(Products, "ProductName", "Widget", 1)>
<CFSET temp = QuerySetCell(Products, "Color", "Silver", 1)>
<CFSET temp = QuerySetCell(Products, "Price", "19.99", 1)>
<CFSET temp = QuerySetCell(Products, "Qty", "46", 1)>

<CFSET temp = QuerySetCell(Products, "ProductName", "Thingy", 2)>
<CFSET temp = QuerySetCell(Products, "Color", "Red", 2)>
<CFSET temp = QuerySetCell(Products, "Price", "34.99", 2)>
<CFSET temp = QuerySetCell(Products, "Qty", "12", 2)>

<CFSET temp = QuerySetCell(Products, "ProductName", "Sprocket", 3)>
<CFSET temp = QuerySetCell(Products, "Color", "Blue", 3)>
<CFSET temp = QuerySetCell(Products, "Price", "1.50", 3)>
<CFSET temp = QuerySetCell(Products, "Qty", "460", 3)>

<CFSET ShippingArray = ArrayNew(1)>
<CFSET ShippingArray[1] = "1.99">
<CFSET ShippingArray[2] = "3.48">
<CFSET ShippingArray[3] = "5.00">

<CFSET MyNewColumn = QueryAddColumn(Products, "Shipping", ShippingArray)>

<TABLE>
<TR>
  <TH>Product</TH><TH>Color</TH><TH>Price</TH><TH>Quantity</TH><TH>Shipping</TH>
</TR>
<CFOUTPUT QUERY="Products">
<TR>
  <TD>#ProductName#</TD><TD>#Color#</TD><TD>#Price#</TD><TD>#Qty#</TD>
  <TD>#DollarFormat(Shipping)#</TD>
</TR>
</CFOUTPUT>
</TABLE>
```

## QueryAddRow

`QueryAddRow(`*`query`*` [, `*`number`*`])`

Adds *number* empty rows to *query*. If *number* is omitted, a single blank row is added. Here's an example that creates a blank query and adds three empty rows to it:

```
<CFSET Products = QueryNew("ProductName, Color, Price, Qty")>
<CFSET NewRows = QueryAddRow(Products, 3)>

<CFOUTPUT>
There are now #NewRows# total rows in the query named Products.
</CFOUTPUT>
```

## QueryNew

`QueryNew(columnlist)`

Creates an empty ColdFusion query object with column names as specified by *columnlist*. *columnlist* can be a comma delimited list of column names or a blank string (" "). The following example creates a query called **Products** with four column names:

```
<CFSET Products = QueryNew("ProductName, Color, Price, Qty")>
```

## QuerySetCell

`QuerySetCell(query, columnname, value [, row])`

Sets the cell in *columnname* to *value* for the specified *query*. An optional *row* number may be set, specifying the row for the cell to be set in. If no *row* number is specified, the cell in the last row of the query is set. `QuerySetCell()` returns `True` upon successful completion. Here's an example that adds data to an empty query:

```
<CFSET Products = QueryNew("ProductName, Color, Price, Qty")>
<CFSET NewRows  = QueryAddRow(Products, 3)>

<CFSET temp = QuerySetCell(Products, "ProductName", "Widget", 1)>
<CFSET temp = QuerySetCell(Products, "Color", "Silver", 1)>
<CFSET temp = QuerySetCell(Products, "Price", "19.99", 1)>
<CFSET temp = QuerySetCell(Products, "Qty", "46", 1)>

<CFSET temp = QuerySetCell(Products, "ProductName", "Thingy", 2)>
<CFSET temp = QuerySetCell(Products, "Color", "Red", 2)>
<CFSET temp = QuerySetCell(Products, "Price", "34.99", 2)>
<CFSET temp = QuerySetCell(Products, "Qty", "12", 2)>

<CFSET temp = QuerySetCell(Products, "ProductName", "Sprocket", 3)>
<CFSET temp = QuerySetCell(Products, "Color", "Blue", 3)>
<CFSET temp = QuerySetCell(Products, "Price", "1.50", 3)>
<CFSET temp = QuerySetCell(Products, "Qty", "460", 3)>

<TABLE>
  <TR><TH>Product</TH><TH>Color</TH><TH>Price</TH><TH>Quantity</TH></TR>
<CFOUTPUT QUERY="Products">
  <TR><TD>#ProductName#</TD><TD>#Color#</TD><TD>#Price#</TD><TD>#Qty#</TD></TR>
</CFOUTPUT>
</TABLE>
```

## QuotedValueList

`QuotedValueList(queryname.column [,delimiter])`

Returns a comma-separated list of values for the previously executed query column specified in `queryname.column`. Each element in the list is qualified with a single quote character. An optional delimiter can be specified if the list is to be delimited with a character other than the comma (the default). The following example creates a quoted value list from a ColdFusion query:

```
<CFQUERY NAME="MyQuery" DATASOURCE="ProgrammingCF">
        SELECT * FROM EmployeeDirectory
</CFQUERY>

<CFOUTPUT>
<B>The query column Name contains the following values:</B>
#QuotedValueList(MyQuery.Name)#
</CFOUTPUT>
```

## Rand

`Rand()`

Returns a random number between 0 and 1. Here's an example that returns a random number between 0 and 100:

```
<CFOUTPUT>The random number is: #int(100*Rand())#</CFOUTPUT>
```

## Randomize

`Randomize(`*`number`*`)`

Seeds ColdFusion's random number generator with the integer part of ***number***. This allows the **`Rand()`** function to generate numbers with a higher degree of randomness. Note that the number returned by the **`Randomize()`** function isn't random. The following example uses the **`Randomize()`** function to seed ColdFusion's random number generator before creating random numbers with the **`Rand()`** function:

```
<CFSET temp = Randomize(Second(Now()))>

Here are 10 random numbers:<P>
<CFLOOP INDEX="counter" FROM="1" TO="10">
  <CFOUTPUT>#Rand()#<BR></CFOUTPUT>
</CFLOOP>
```

## RandRange

`RandRange(`*`number1`*`, `*`number2`*`)`

Generates a random integer in the range between two numbers, where ***number1*** and ***number2*** are integers less that 100,000,000. Here's an example that generates a random integer between 1 and 100:

```
<CFOUTPUT>
The following random number should be between 1 and 100: #RandRange(1,100)#
</CFOUTPUT>
```

## REFind

`REFind(regex, string [, startpos] [, returnsubexpressions])`

Returns the position of the first occurrence of *regex* in *string*. *regex* can be any valid ColdFusion regular expression. An optional starting position for the search can be specified by *startpos*. If *returnsubexpressions* is set to `True` (`False` is the default), `REFind()` returns a CFML structure containing two keys, `pos` and `len`, that represents the position and length, respectively, of the matched regular expression. If `REFind()` is unable to find a match for the regular expression, 0 is returned. `REFind()` performs a case-sensitive search. The following example demonstrates the use of the `REFind()` function with the *returnsubexpressions* parameter set to `True`:

```
<CFSET MyString="The name of the bank robber is Rob.">
<CFSET matches= ReFind("Rob", MyString, 1, "TRUE")>

<CFOUTPUT>
<B>String:</B>  #MyString#<BR>
<B>Regex:</B>  Refind(&quot;cat&quot;, MyString, 1, &quot;TRUE&quot;)<BR>
<B>Position:</B> #matches.pos[1]#<BR>
<B>Length:</B> #matches.len[1]#
</CFOUTPUT>
```

## REFindNoCase

`REFindNoCase(regex, string [, startpos] [, returnsubexpressions])`

Returns the position of the first occurrence of *regex* in *string*. *regex* can be any valid ColdFusion regular expression. An optional starting position for the search can be specified by *startpos*. If *returnsubexpressions* is set to `True` (`False` is the default), `REFindNoCase()` returns a CFML structure containing two keys, `pos` and `len`, that represent the position and length, respectively, of the matched regular expression. If `REFindNoCase()` is unable to find a match for the regular expression, 0 is returned. `REFindNoCase()` performs a case-insensitive search. Here's an example that demonstrates the use of the `REFindNoCase()` function with the *returnsubexpressions* parameter set to `True`:

```
<CFSET MyString="The name of the bank robber is Rob.">
<CFSET matches= ReFindNoCase("Rob", MyString, 1, "TRUE")>

<CFOUTPUT>
<B>String:</B>  #MyString#<BR>
<B>Regex:</B>  RefindNoCase(&quot;cat&quot;, MyString, 1, &quot;TRUE&quot;)<BR>
<B>Position:</B> #matches.pos[1]#<BR>
<B>Length:</B> #matches.len[1]#
</CFOUTPUT>
```

## RemoveChars

RemoveChars(*string*, *startpos*, *count*)

Removes *count* characters from *string* beginning at the position specified by *startpos*. If no characters are removed, 0 is returned. Example:

```
<CFSET MyString="cosdafol">

<CFOUTPUT>
<B>Original String:</B> #MyString#<BR>
<B>RemoveChars(MyString, 3, 4):</B> #RemoveChars(MyString, 3, 4)#
</CFOUTPUT>
```

## RepeatString

RepeatString(*string*, *count*)

Returns a string consisting of *string* repeated *count* times. Example:

```
<CFSET MyString="I love ColdFusion!<BR>">

<CFOUTPUT>#RepeatString(MyString, 10)#</CFOUTPUT>
```

## Replace

Replace(*string*, *substring1*, *substring2* [, *scope*])

Returns *string* with *substring1* replaced by *substring2* according to *scope*. *scope* may be set as either One or All, where One results in the replacement of the first occurrence of *substring1*, and All results in the replacement of all occurrences of *substring1*. The default *scope* is One. Replace() performs a case-sensitive search. The following example demonstrates this function:

```
<CFSET MyString="This is a case-sensitive example of using the Replace
function to replace a substring within a string.">
<CFSET MySubstring1="Replace">
<CFSET MySubstring2="<B>Replace</B>">

<CFOUTPUT>
<B>String:</B> #MyString#<BR>
<B>Replace:</B> #MySubstring1# with #MySubstring2#
<P>#Replace(MyString, MySubstring1, MySubstring2)#
</CFOUTPUT>
```

## ReplaceList

`ReplaceList(string, list1, list2)`

Returns *string* with all the elements from *list1* replaced by the corresponding elements from *list2*. `ReplaceList()` performs a case-sensitive search. Here's an example that shows how to use this function:

```
<CFSET MyString="This is my string.">
<CFSET List1=" is,my,string">
<CFSET List2=" function,is,cool">

<CFOUTPUT>
<B>Original String:</B> #MyString#<BR>
<B>List1:</B> #List1#<BR>
<B>List2:</B> #List2#<P>
<B>ReplaceList(MyString, List1, List2):</B> #ReplaceList(MyString, List1, List2)#
</CFOUTPUT>
```

## ReplaceNoCase

`ReplaceNoCase(string, substring1, substring2 [, scope])`

Returns *string* with *substring1* replaced by *substring2* according to *scope*. *scope* may be set as either `One` or `All`, where `One` results in the replacement of the first occurrence of *substring1*, and `All` results in the replacement of all occurrences of *substring1*. The default *scope* is `One`. `ReplaceNoCase()` performs a case-insensitive search. The following example demonstrates the use of this function:

```
<CFSET MyString="This is a case-insensitive example of using the ReplaceNoCase
function to replace a substring within a string.">
<CFSET MySubstring1="Replace">
<CFSET MySubstring2="<B>Replace</B>">

<CFOUTPUT>
<B>String:</B> #MyString#<BR>
<B>Replace:</B> #MySubstring1# with #MySubstring2#
<P>#ReplaceNoCase(MyString, MySubstring1, MySubstring2, "All")#
</CFOUTPUT>
```

## REReplace

`REReplace(string, regex, substring [, scope])`

Returns *string* with *regex* replaced by *substring* for the specified *scope*. *regex* can be any valid ColdFusion regular expression. *scope* may be set as either `One` or `All`, where `One` results in the replacement of the first occurrence of the regular expression, and `All` results in the replacement of all occurrences of the regular expression. The default *scope* is

One. `REReplace()` performs a case-sensitive search. Here's an examples that demonstrates the use of this function:

```
<CFSET OriginalString="T8h3i53s 8a3 t3e2s9t.">

<CFSET NewString = REReplace("T8h3i53s 8a3 t3e2s9t.", "[[:digit:]]", "", "ALL")>

<CFOUTPUT>
Original String:  #OriginalString#<BR>
New String:  #NewString#
</CFOUTPUT>
```

## REReplaceNoCase

`REReplaceNoCase(`*`string`*`, `*`regex`*`, `*`substring`*` [, `*`scope`*`])`

Returns *`string`* with *`regex`* replaced by *`substring`* for the specified *`scope`*. *`regex`* can be any valid ColdFusion regular expression. *`scope`* may be set as either `One` or `All`, where `One` results in the replacement of the first occurrence of the regular expression, and `All` results in the replacement of all occurrences of the regular expression. The default *`scope`* is `One`. `REReplaceNoCase()` performs a case-insensitive search. The following example uses the `REReplaceNoCase()` function to remove doubled words from a string:

```
<CFSET MyString = "I want to go to to the park.">
<CFSET NewString = ReReplaceNoCase(MyString, "([A-Z]+)[ ]+\1", "\1", "All")>

<CFOUTPUT>
<B>Original String:</B> #MyString#
<P>
<B>New String:</B> #NewString#
</CFOUTPUT>
```

## Reverse

`Reverse(`*`string`*`)`

Returns *`string`* with all the characters in reverse order. Example:

```
<CFSET MyString="0123456789">

<CFOUTPUT>
<B>String:</B> #MyString#<BR>
<B>Reversed:</B> #Reverse(MyString)#
</CFOUTPUT>
```

## Right

`Right(`*`string`*`, `*`count`*`)`

Returns the number of characters specified by *`count`*, beginning at the rightmost position of *`string`*. The following example returns the five rightmost characters of a string:

```
<CFSET MyString="(555)555-5555 x5555">
<CFSET Extension = Right(MyString, 5)>
```

```
<CFOUTPUT>
<B>String:</B> #MyString#<BR>
<B>Extension:</B> #Extension#
</CFOUTPUT>
```

## RJustify

`RJustify(string, length)`

Right-justifies *string* within a field of *length* characters. Example:

```
<CFSET OriginalString = "ColdFusion">

<CFOUTPUT>
<B>Original String (quoted):</B> "#OriginalString#"<BR>
<B>Right-justified String (quoted):</B> "#RJustify("ColdFusion", 20)#"
</CFOUTPUT>
```

## Round

`Round(number)`

Rounds off a number to the nearest integer. Examples:

```
<CFOUTPUT>
-2.5: #Round(-2.5)#<BR>
-1: #Round(-1)#<BR>
-1.123: #Round(-1.123)#<BR>
-0.123: #Round(-0.123)#<BR>
0: #Round(0)#<BR>
0.123: #Round(0.123)#<BR>
1: #Round(1)#<BR>
1.123: #Round(1.123)#<BR>
2.5: #Round(2.5)#
</CFOUTPUT>
```

## RTrim

`RTrim(string)`

Removes trailing spaces from the specified string. Example:

```
<CFSET OriginalString = "ColdFusion      ">

<CFOUTPUT>
<B>Original String (quoted):</B> "#OriginalString#"<BR>
<B>Right-trimmed String (quoted):</B> "#RTrim(OriginalString)#"
</CFOUTPUT>
```

## Second

`Second(date)`

Returns the seconds for a valid date/time object as a number between 0 and 59. Example:

```
<CFOUTPUT>
It is currently #Minute(Now())# minute(s) and #Second(Now())# second(s) past the
hour.
</CFOUTPUT>
```

## SetLocale

`SetLocale(newlocale)`

Changes the current locale used by ColdFusion to ***newlocale*** for the duration of the current session. Returns the old locale so that it can be used again if necessary. Valid entries for ***newlocale*** include the following:

| | | |
|---|---|---|
| Dutch (Belgian) | French (Canadian) | Norwegian (Bokmal) |
| Dutch (Standard) | French (Standard) | Norwegian (Nynorsk) |
| English (Australian) | French (Swiss) | Portuguese (Brazilian) |
| English (Canadian) | German (Austrian) | Portuguese (Standard) |
| English (New Zealand) | German (Standard) | Spanish (Mexican) |
| English (United Kingdom) | German (Swiss) | Spanish (Modern) |
| English (United States) | Italian (Standard) | Spanish (Standard) |
| French (Belgian) | Italian (Swiss) | Swedish |

The following example changes the current locale to Swedish:

```
<CFOUTPUT>
Default Locale: #GetLocale()#

<P>Changing locale to Swedish...
<CFSET OldLocale = SetLocale("Swedish")>

<P>New Locale: #GetLocale()#<BR>
Old Locale: #OldLocale#
</CFOUTPUT>
```

## SetProfileString

New as of ColdFusion 4.01

`SetProfileString(inipath, section, entry, value)`

Sets the *value* of a profile string *entry* in *section* of the initialization file specified by *inipath*. If the operation is successful, an empty string is returned. If not, an exception is thrown. Here's an example that changes a profile string entry in one of ColdFusion's initialization files:

```
<CFSET MyPath = "C:\cfusion\bin\cf40e.ini">
<CFSET MySection = "User">
<CFSET MyEntry = "UserCompany">
<CFSET MyValue = "My Company Name">
<CFSET MyProfileString = SetProfileString(MyPath, MySection, MyEntry, MyValue)>
<CFOUTPUT>
<B>Path:</B> #MyPath#<BR>
<B>Section:</B> #MySection#<BR>
<B>Entry:</B> #MyEntry#<BR>
<P><B>Profile String:</B> #MyValue#
</CFOUTPUT>
```

## SetVariable

`SetVariable(variablename, value)`

Assigns *`value`* to *`variablename`* where *`value`* is any passed value. `SetVariable()` is useful when you want to create dynamically named variables. The following example uses `SetVariable()` to assign values to several dynamically created variables:

```
<CFLOOP INDEX="index" FROM="1" TO="10">
  <CFSET ValueOfVariable = SetVariable("MyVar#index#", #Index#)>
</CFLOOP>

<CFLOOP INDEX="pos" FROM="1" TO="10">
  <CFOUTPUT>MyVar#pos# = #Evaluate("MyVar"&"#pos#")#<BR></CFOUTPUT>
</CFLOOP>
```

## Sgn

`Sgn(number)`

Returns 1 if the specified number is positive, 0 if the specified number is 0, or –1 if the number is negative. Examples:

```
<CFOUTPUT>
-1: #Sgn(-1)#<BR>
-1.123: #Sgn(-1.123)#<BR>
-0.123: #Sgn(-0.123)#<BR>
0: #Sgn(0)#<BR>
0.123: #Sgn(0.123)#<BR>
1: #Sgn(1)#<BR>
1.123: #Sgn(1.123)#
</CFOUTPUT>
```

## Sin

`Sin(`*`number`*`)`

Returns the sine of an angle expressed in radians. Example:

```
The sine of 45 is <CFOUTPUT>#Sin(45)#</CFOUTPUT>
```

## SpanExcluding

`SpanExcluding(`*`string, set`*`)`

Returns all the characters contained in *string* until any character from *set* is encountered. `SpanExcluding()` performs a case-sensitive search. Example:

```
<CFSET MyString="I like ColdFusion alot">

<CFOUTPUT>
<B>Original String:</B>  #MyString#
<P><B>SpanExcluding(MyString, "ab"):</B> #SpanExcluding(MyString, "ab")#
</CFOUTPUT>
```

## SpanIncluding

`SpanIncluding(`*`string, set`*`)`

Returns all the characters contained in *string* until any character not in *set* is encountered. `SpanIncluding()` performs a case-sensitive search. Example:

```
<CFSET MyString="I like ColdFusion alot">

<CFOUTPUT>
<B>Original String:</B>  #MyString#
<P><B>SpanIncluding(MyString, "I like"):</B> #SpanIncluding(MyString, "I like")#
</CFOUTPUT>
```

## Sqr

`Sqr(`*`number`*`)`

Returns the positive square root of a number. Examples:

```
<CFOUTPUT>
0: #Sqr(0)#<BR>
1: #Sqr(1)#<BR>
10: #Sqr(10)#<BR>
100: #Sqr(100)#
</CFOUTPUT>
```

## StripCR

`StripCR(string)`

Returns *string* with all carriage returns removed. Example:

```
<CFSET MyString="This is a paragraph of text with carriage returns hardcoded.
#Chr(10)##Chr(13)#As you can see, this is a new line.
#Chr(10)##Chr(13)#This is a new line too.">

<CFOUTPUT>
<B>Original String with Carriage Returns:</B><BR>
<PRE>
#MyString#
</PRE>
<P>
<B>String with Carriage Returns Removed:</B><BR>
<PRE>
#StripCR(MyString)#
</PRE>
</CFOUTPUT>
```

## StructAppend

New as of ColdFusion 4.5.1 SP2

`StructAppend(structure1, structure2, [,overwrite])`

Appends the contents of *structure2* to *structure1*. After completion, *structure1* contains the newly appended structure while *structure2* remains unchanged. Setting the optional *overwrite* parameter to `Yes` allows overwriting of existing keys/values within the appended structure. The default value for *overwrite* is `Yes`. The following example demonstrates the `StructAppend()` function:

```
<!--- create the Stock structure --->
<CFSET Stock = StructNew()>
<CFSET Stock.Company = "Allaire">
<CFSET Stock.Ticker = "ALLR">
<CFSET Stock.Exchange = "NASDAQ">

<!--- create the TradeInfo structure --->
<CFSET TradeInfo = StructNew()>
<CFSET TradeInfo.Price = "66.25">
<CFSET TradeInfo.Change = "+0.375">
<CFSET TradeInfo.LastTradeTime = "10:17AM">
<CFSET TradeInfo.LastTradeDate = "05/17/1999">
<CFSET TradeInfo.Volume = "8300">

<!--- output the contents of the Stock structure --->
<CFSET MyKeyArray = StructKeyArray(Stock)>
<H2>Stock Structure</H2>
<TABLE>
  <TR><TH>Key</TH><TH>Value</TH></TR>
<CFLOOP index="position" from="1" to="#ArrayLen(MyKeyArray)#">
<CFOUTPUT>
  <TR><TD>#MyKeyArray[position]#</TD><TD>#Stock[MyKeyArray[position]]#</TD></TR>
```

```
</CFOUTPUT>
</CFLOOP>
</TABLE>

<!--- output the contents of the TradeInfo structure --->
<CFSET MyKeyArray = StructKeyArray(TradeInfo)>
<H2>TradeInfo Structure</H2>
<TABLE>
  <TR><TH>Key</TH><TH>Value</TH></TR>
<CFLOOP index="position" from="1" to="#ArrayLen(MyKeyArray)#">
<CFOUTPUT>
  <TR>
    <TD>#MyKeyArray[position]#</TD><TD>#TradeInfo[MyKeyArray[position]]#</TD>
  </TR>
</CFOUTPUT>
</CFLOOP>
</TABLE>

<!--- append the TradeInfo structure to the Stock structure --->
<CFSET Temp = StructAppend(Stock, TradeInfo, "No")>

<!--- output the contents of the Appended Stock structure --->
<CFSET MyKeyArray = StructKeyArray(Stock)>
<H2>Appended Stock Structure</H2>
<TABLE>
  <TR><TH>Key</TH><TH>Value</TH></TR>
<CFLOOP index="position" from="1" to="#ArrayLen(MyKeyArray)#">
<CFOUTPUT>
  <TR><TD>#MyKeyArray[position]#</TD><TD>#Stock[MyKeyArray[position]]#</TD></TR>
</CFOUTPUT>
</CFLOOP>
</TABLE>
```

## StructClear

StructClear(*structure*)

Removes all data from the specified structure. Here's an example that removes all data from a structure then tests to see whether the structure is empty:

```
<CFSET Stock = StructNew()>
<CFSET Stock.Company = "Allaire">
<CFSET Stock.Ticker = "ALLR">
<CFSET Stock.Exchange = "NASDAQ">
<CFSET Stock.Price = "66.25">
<CFSET Stock.Change = "+0.375">
<CFSET Stock.LastTradeTime = "10:17AM">
<CFSET Stock.LastTradeDate = "05/17/1999">
<CFSET Stock.Volume = "8300">

<CFSET StructClear(Stock)>

<CFIF StructIsEmpty(Stock)>
  The structure <B>Stock</B> is empty!
```

```
<CFELSE>
  The structure <B>Stock</B> contains key/value pairs.
</CFIF>
```

## StructCopy

`StructCopy(structure)`

Makes an exact copy of the specified structure. This copy isn't by reference, meaning that any changes made to the original structure aren't reflected in the copy. You should note that the `StructCopy()` function shouldn't be used to copy deeply nested structures. If you need to copy nested structures, use the `Duplicate()` function instead. The following example demonstrates the use of the `StructCopy()` function:

```
<CFSET Stock = StructNew()>
<CFSET Stock.Company = "Allaire">
<CFSET Stock.Ticker = "ALLR">
<CFSET Stock.Exchange = "NASDAQ">
<CFSET Stock.Price = "66.25">
<CFSET Stock.Change = "+0.375">
<CFSET Stock.LastTradeTime = "10:17AM">
<CFSET Stock.LastTradeDate = "05/17/1999">
<CFSET Stock.Volume = "8300">

<CFSET StockCopy = StructCopy(Stock)>

<CFOUTPUT>
<B>Company:</B> #StockCopy.company#<BR>
<B>Ticker:</B> #StockCopy.ticker#<BR>
<B>Exchange:</B> #StockCopy.exchange#<BR>
<B>Price:</B> #StockCopy.price#<BR>
<B>Change:</B> #StockCopy.change#<BR>
<B>Last Trade Time:</B> #StockCopy.lasttradetime#<BR>
<B>Last Trade Date:</B> #StockCopy.lasttradedate#<BR>
<B>Volume:</B> #StockCopy.volume#
</CFOUTPUT>
```

## StructCount

`StructCount(structure)`

Returns a count for the number of key/value pairs contained in the specified structure. Here's an example that returns the number of name/value pairs contained in the structure `Stock`:

```
<CFSET Stock = StructNew()>
<CFSET Stock.Company = "Allaire">
<CFSET Stock.Ticker = "ALLR">
<CFSET Stock.Exchange = "NASDAQ">
<CFSET Stock.Price = "66.25">
<CFSET Stock.Change = "+0.375">
<CFSET Stock.LastTradeTime = "10:17AM">
<CFSET Stock.LastTradeDate = "05/17/1999">
<CFSET Stock.Volume = "8300">
```

```
<CFOUTPUT>
There are #StructCount(Stock)# key/value pairs in the structure Stock.
</CFOUTPUT>
```

## StructDelete

`StructDelete(`*`structure`*`, `*`key`*` [, `*`indicatenotexisting`*`])`

Deletes *key* (and its value) from *structure*. Returns `True` regardless of success or failure unless the optional *indicatenotexisting* parameter is set to `True`. The following example deletes several keys from a structure named `Stock`:

```
<CFSET Stock = StructNew()>
<CFSET Stock.Company = "Allaire">
<CFSET Stock.Ticker = "ALLR">
<CFSET Stock.Exchange = "NASDAQ">
<CFSET Stock.Price = "66.25">
<CFSET Stock.Change = "+0.375">
<CFSET Stock.LastTradeTime = "10:17AM">
<CFSET Stock.LastTradeDate = "05/17/1999">
<CFSET Stock.Volume = "8300">

<CFSET StructDelete(Stock, "lasttradetime")>
<CFSET StructDelete(Stock, "lasttradedate")>

The following keys are in the structure <B>Stock</B>:<P>
<CFOUTPUT>#StructKeyList(Stock)#</CFOUTPUT>
```

## StructFind

`StructFind(`*`structure`*`, `*`key`*`)`

Searches structure and returns the value for the specified key. Here's an example that searches the structure `Stock` for various keys:

```
<CFSET Stock = StructNew()>
<CFSET Stock.Company = "Allaire">
<CFSET Stock.Ticker = "ALLR">
<CFSET Stock.Exchange = "NASDAQ">
<CFSET Stock.Price = "66.25">
<CFSET Stock.Change = "+0.375">
<CFSET Stock.LastTradeTime = "10:17AM">
<CFSET Stock.LastTradeDate = "05/17/1999">
<CFSET Stock.Volume = "8300">

<CFOUTPUT>
Find the value of the key <B>company</B>: #StructFind(Stock, "company")#<BR>
Find the value of the key <B>Ticker</B>: #StructFind(Stock, "ticker")#<BR>
Find the value of the key <B>exchange</B>: #StructFind(Stock, "exchange")#<BR>
Find the value of the key <B>price</B>: #StructFind(Stock, "price")#<BR>
Find the value of the key <B>change</B>: #StructFind(Stock, "change")#<BR>
Find the value of the key <B>lasttradetime</B>:
  #StructFind(Stock, "lasttradetime")#<BR>
Find the value of the key <B>lasttradedate</B>:
```

```
  #StructFind(Stock, "lasttradedate")#<BR>
Find the value of the key <B>volume</B>: #StructFind(Stock, "volume")#
</CFOUTPUT>
```

## StructFindKey

New as of ColdFusion 4.5.1 SP2

`StructFindKey(top, key [, scope])`

Searches complex structures for keys matching the *key* parameter. *top* specifies the starting point to begin the search. *key* specifies the key you want to perform the search for. *scope* is optional and may be set as either `One` or `All`, specifying the number of matching keys that should be returned. The default *scope* is `One`. `StructFindKey()` returns an array that contains one structure for each key matched by the search. Each structure contains the following keys:

`Value`
: The value held by the found key

`Path`
: A string that can be used with other functions to reference the found key

`Owner`
: The parent object containing the found key

The following examples demonstrates the use of this function on an array of nested structures:

```
<!--- create a structure of nested arrays containing nested structures. --->
<CFSET TEMP = STRUCTGET("Stock")>
<CFSET TEMP.COMPANY = "Allaire">
<CFSET TEMP.TICKER = "ALLR">

<CFSET TEMP = STRUCTGET("Stock.TradeInfo[1]")>
<CFSET TEMP.PRICE = 60>
<CFSET TEMP.TRADEDATE = "6/11/99">
<CFSET TEMP.VOLUME = 750000>
<CFSET TEMP.DAY.HIGH.PRICE = 62>
<CFSET TEMP.DAY.LOW.PRICE = 59>

<CFSET TEMP = STRUCTGET("Stock.TradeInfo[2]")>
<CFSET TEMP.PRICE = 63>
<CFSET TEMP.TRADEDATE = "6/12/99">
<CFSET TEMP.VOLUME = 737000>
<CFSET TEMP.DAY.HIGH.PRICE = 66>
<CFSET TEMP.DAY.LOW.PRICE = 60>

<CFSET TEMP = STRUCTGET("Stock.TradeInfo[3]")>
<CFSET TEMP.PRICE = 67>
<CFSET TEMP.TRADEDATE = "6/13/99">
<CFSET TEMP.VOLUME = 1220000>
<CFSET TEMP.DAY.HIGH.PRICE = 67>
<CFSET TEMP.DAY.LOW.PRICE = 66>

<!--- change the value of KeyToFind to see how different values work --->
<CFSET KeyToFind = "Price">
```

```
<CFSET FINDTHEKEY = StructFindKey(Stock, KeyToFind, "All")>

<CFOUTPUT>
There are  #ArrayLen(FindTheKey)# keys (returned as structures) matching your
key search for &quot;<B>#KeyTofind#</B>&quot;:<P>
<!--- Loop over the array of structures returned by the search --->
<CFLOOP INDEX="i" FROM="1" TO="#ArrayLen(FindTheKey)#">
    <CFSET TheStructures = FindTheKey[#i#]>
    <B>Structure #i# has the following key/value pairs:</B><BR>
    <!---- Display all of the key/value pairs from each structure in array --->
    <TABLE BORDER="1">
    <CFLOOP COLLECTION="#TheStructures#" ITEM="key" >
        <CFSET Value = StructFind(TheStructures, #key#)>



        <TR><TD>#key#:</TD>
          <CFIF IsSimpleValue(Value)><TD>#Value#</TD>
          <CFELSEIF IsStruct(Value)><TD>This key's owner is a  structure</TD>
          <CFELSEIF IsArray(Value)><TD>This key's owner is an array</TD>
          <CFELSE><TD>This key's owner is of an undetermined data type</TD><BR>
          </CFIF>
        </TR>
    </CFLOOP>
    </TABLE>
<P></CFLOOP>
</CFOUTPUT>
```

---

## StructFindValue

New as of ColdFusion 4.5.1 SP2

`StructFindValue(top, value [, scope])`

Searches complex structures for values matching the *`value`* parameter. *`top`* specifies the starting point to begin the search. *`value`* specifies the actual value you want to search for. *`scope`* is optional and may be set as either `One` or `All`, specifying the number of matches that should be returned. The default *`scope`* is `One`. `StructFindValue()` returns an array containing one structure for each value matched by the search. Each structure contains the following keys:

`Key`
: The key holding the found value

`Path`
: A string that can be used with other functions to reference the found value

`Owner`
: The parent object containing the found value

Here's an example that demonstrates this function:

```
<!--- create a structure of nested arrays containing nested structures. --->
<CFSET TEMP = STRUCTGET("Stock")>
<CFSET TEMP.COMPANY = "Allaire">
<CFSET TEMP.TICKER = "ALLR">
```

```
<CFSET TEMP = STRUCTGET("Stock.TradeInfo[1]")>
<CFSET TEMP.PRICE = 60>
<CFSET TEMP.TRADEDATE = "6/11/99">
<CFSET TEMP.VOLUME = 750000>
<CFSET TEMP.DAY.HIGH.PRICE = 62>
<CFSET TEMP.DAY.LOW.PRICE = 59>

<CFSET TEMP = STRUCTGET("Stock.TradeInfo[2]")>
<CFSET TEMP.PRICE = 63>
<CFSET TEMP.TRADEDATE = "6/12/99">
<CFSET TEMP.VOLUME = 737000>
<CFSET TEMP.DAY.HIGH.PRICE = 66>
<CFSET TEMP.DAY.LOW.PRICE = 60>

<CFSET TEMP = STRUCTGET("Stock.TradeInfo[3]")>
<CFSET TEMP.PRICE = 67>
<CFSET TEMP.TRADEDATE = "6/13/99">
<CFSET TEMP.VOLUME = 1220000>
<CFSET TEMP.DAY.HIGH.PRICE = 67>
<CFSET TEMP.DAY.LOW.PRICE = 66>

<!--- change the value of ValueToFind to see how different values work --->
<CFSET ValueToFind = 60>
<CFSET FindTheValue = StructFindValue(Stock, ValueToFind, "All")>

<CFOUTPUT>
There are  #ArrayLen(FindTheValue)# keys (returned as structures) matching your
key search for &quot;<B>#ValueTofind#</B>&quot;:
<P>
<!--- Loop over the array of structures returned by the search --->
<CFLOOP INDEX="i" FROM="1" TO="#ArrayLen(FindTheValue)#">
    <CFSET TheStructures = FindTheValue[#i#]>
    <B>Structure #i# has the following key/value pairs:</B><BR>
    <!---- Display all of the key/value pairs from each structures in array --->
    <TABLE BORDER="1">
    <CFLOOP COLLECTION="#TheStructures#" ITEM="key" >
        <CFSET Value = StructFind(TheStructures, #key#)>
        <TR><TD>#key#:</TD>
          <CFIF IsSimpleValue(Value)><TD>#Value#</TD>
          <CFELSEIF IsStruct(Value)><TD>This key's owner is a  structure</TD>
          <CFELSEIF IsArray(Value)><TD>This key's owner is an array</TD>
          <CFELSE><TD>This key's owner is of an undetermined data type</TD><BR>
          </CFIF>
        </TR>
    </CFLOOP>
    </TABLE>
<P></CFLOOP>
</CFOUTPUT>
```

## StructGet

New as of ColdFusion 4.5.1 SP2

`StructGet("path")`

Allows you to create nested structures without the need for multiple `StructNew()` calls. `StructGet()` takes a single argument, *path*, that specifies the path to the nested structure. `StructGet()` returns a pointer to the substructure specified as the last element in *path*. The `StructGet()` function automatically creates all the necessary structures and substructures specified in *path*. The `StructGet()` function can also be used to create nested one-dimensional arrays. The following example demonstrates the use of this function:

```
<!--- create the Grades.Mary structure --->
<CFSET temp1 = StructGet("Grades.Mary")>
<CFSET temp1.Test1 = 98>
<CFSET temp1.Test2 = 92>
<CFSET temp1.Test3 = 100>
<CFSET temp1.Test4 = 90>

<!--- create the Grades.Tom structure --->
<CFSET temp2 = StructGet("Grades.Tom")>
<CFSET temp2.Test1 = 96>
<CFSET temp2.Test2 = 88>
<CFSET temp2.Test3 = 94>
<CFSET temp2.Test4 = 90>

<!--- create the Scores array --->
<CFSET test = StructGet("Scores[1].Mary")>
<CFSET test.Test = 100>

<CFOUTPUT>
Is Temp1 a Struct? #IsStruct(Temp1)#<BR>Keys: #StructKeyList(Temp1)#<BR>
Is Temp2 a Struct? #IsStruct(Temp2)#<BR>Keys: #StructKeyList(Temp2)#<BR>
<HR NOSHADE>
Is Grades a Structure: #IsStruct(Grades)#<BR>Keys: #StructKeyList(Grades)#<BR>
Is Grades.Mary a Structure: #IsStruct(Grades.Mary)#<BR>
Keys: #StructKeyList(Grades.Mary)#<BR>
Is Grades.Tom a Structure: #IsStruct(Grades.Tom)#<BR>
Keys: #StructKeyList(Grades.Tom)#<BR>
<HR NOSHADE>
Is Scores an Array: #IsArray(Scores)#
</CFOUTPUT>
```

## StructInsert

`StructInsert(structure, key, value [, allowoverwrite])`

Inserts *key* and *value* into *structure*. Returns `Yes` if the operation is successful and `No` if it isn't. Setting the optional *allowoverwrite* parameter to `True` allows overwriting of existing keys. The default is False. Here's an example that inserts key/value pairs into a structure called Stock:

```
<CFSET Stock = StructNew()>

<CFSET StructInsert(Stock, "company", "Allaire")>
<CFSET StructInsert(Stock, "ticker", "ALLR")>
<CFSET StructInsert(Stock, "exchange", "NASDAQ")>
<CFSET StructInsert(Stock, "price", "66.25")>
<CFSET StructInsert(Stock, "change", "+0.375")>
<CFSET StructInsert(Stock, "lasttradetime", "10:17AM")>
<CFSET StructInsert(Stock, "lasttradedate", "05/17/1999")>
<CFSET StructInsert(Stock, "volume", "8300")>

<CFOUTPUT>
<B>Company:</B> #Stock.company#<BR>
<B>Ticker:</B> #Stock.ticker#<BR>
<B>Exchange:</B> #Stock.exchange#<BR>
<B>Price:</B> #Stock.price#<BR>
<B>Change:</B> #Stock.change#<BR>
<B>Last Trade Time:</B> #Stock.lasttradetime#<BR>
<B>Last Trade Date:</B> #Stock.lasttradedate#<BR>
<B>Volume:</B> #Stock.volume#
</CFOUTPUT>
```

## StructIsEmpty

StructIsEmpty(*structure*)

Returns True if the specified structure contains no data or False if it contains data. The following example checks to see if the structure Stock is empty:

```
<CFSET Stock = StructNew()>
<CFSET Stock.Company = "Allaire">
<CFSET Stock.Ticker = "ALLR">
<CFSET Stock.Exchange = "NASDAQ">
<CFSET Stock.Price = "66.25">
<CFSET Stock.Change = "+0.375">
<CFSET Stock.LastTradeTime = "10:17AM">
<CFSET Stock.LastTradeDate = "05/17/1999">
<CFSET Stock.Volume = "8300">

<CFIF StructIsEmpty(Stock)>
  The structure <B>Stock</B> is empty!
<CFELSE>
  The structure <B>Stock</B> contains key/value pairs.
</CFIF>
```

## StructKeyArray

New as of ColdFusion 4.01

`StructKeyArray(structure)`

Returns an array containing all the keys in ***structure***. Here's an example that lists all the keys contained in a structure called `Stock`:

```
<CFSET Stock = StructNew()>
<CFSET Stock.Company = "Allaire">
<CFSET Stock.Ticker = "ALLR">
<CFSET Stock.Exchange = "NASDAQ">
<CFSET Stock.Price = "66.25">
<CFSET Stock.Change = "+0.375">
<CFSET Stock.LastTradeTime = "10:17AM">
<CFSET Stock.LastTradeDate = "05/17/1999">
<CFSET Stock.Volume = "8300">

<CFSET MyKeyArray = StructKeyArray(Stock)>

<TABLE>
  <TR><TH>Key #</TH><TH>Name</TH><TH>Value</TH></TR>
<CFLOOP index="position" from="1" to="#ArrayLen(MyKeyArray)#">
<CFOUTPUT>
  <TR><TD>#position#:</TD><TD>#MyKeyArray[position]#</TD>
    <TD>#Stock[MyKeyArray[position]]#</TD></TR>
</CFOUTPUT>
</CFLOOP>
</TABLE>
```

## StructKeyExists

`StructKeyExists(structure, key)`

Checks for the existence of key in the specified `structure`. Returns `True` if the key exists or `False` if it doesn't. The following example checks for the existence of different keys in a structure called `Stock`:

```
<CFSET Stock = StructNew()>
<CFSET Stock.Company = "Allaire">
<CFSET Stock.Ticker = "ALLR">
<CFSET Stock.Exchange = "NASDAQ">
<CFSET Stock.Price = "66.25">
<CFSET Stock.Change = "+0.375">
<CFSET Stock.LastTradeTime = "10:17AM">
<CFSET Stock.LastTradeDate = "05/17/1999">
<CFSET Stock.Volume = "8300">

<CFIF StructKeyExists(Stock, "company")>
  The key <B>company</b> exists in the structure called <B>Stock</B>.
<CFELSE>
  The key <B>company</b> doesn't exist in the structure called <B>Stock</B>.
</CFIF>
<P>
<CFIF StructKeyExists(Stock, "address")>
```

```
  The key <B>address</b> exists in the structure called <B>Stock</B>.
<CFELSE>
  The key <B>address</b> doesn't exist in the structure called <B>Stock</B>.
</CFIF>
```

## StructKeyList

New as of ColdFusion 4.01

`StructKeyList(`*`structure`*`)`

Returns a comma-delimited list containing the names of all the keys contained in *`structure`*. The key names are returned in all uppercase. Here's an example that returns a list containing the names of the keys in a structure called `Stock`:

```
<CFSET Stock = StructNew()>
<CFSET Stock.Company = "Allaire">
<CFSET Stock.Ticker = "ALLR">
<CFSET Stock.Exchange = "NASDAQ">
<CFSET Stock.Price = "66.25">
<CFSET Stock.Change = "+0.375">
<CFSET Stock.LastTradeTime = "10:17AM">
<CFSET Stock.LastTradeDate = "05/17/1999">
<CFSET Stock.Volume = "8300">

The following keys are in the structure <B>Stock</B>:
<P><CFOUTPUT>#StructKeyList(Stock)#</CFOUTPUT>
```

## StructNew

`StructNew()`

Creates a new structure. The following example creates a new structure called `Stock`:

```
<CFSET Stock = StructNew()>
```

## StructSort

New as of ColdFusion 4.5.1 SP2

`StructSort(`*`base`*` [,`*`sorttype`*`, `*`sortorder`*`, `*`pathtosubelement`*`])`

Returns an array of structures with the top-level key names sorted by the subelement specified by *`pathtosubelement`*. *`base`* is a required parameter and specifies the name of the top-level structure containing the element you want to sort. *`sorttype`* is an optional parameter and specifies the type of sort to perform (`numeric`, `text`, or `textnocase`). *`sortorder`* is also optional and specifies the sort order for the operation (`asc`, for ascending (the default), or `desc`, for descending). *`pathtosubelement`* is optional and specifies the path (using dot notation) from the *`base`* to the subelement you wish to sort on. Leaving *`pathtosubelement`* blank results in the sort being performed on the top-level structure specified in *`base`*. Only substructures of structures may be specified in *`pathtosubelement`*. Here's an example that demonstrates the use of this function:

```
<CFSET Quotes = StructNew()>
<CFSET Stocks = StructNew()>
```

```
<!--- populate both structures --->
<CFLOOP INDEX="i" FROM="1" TO="5">
  <CFSET Price = NumberFormat((rand()*100),'99.99')>
  <CFSET Quotes["Stock#i#"] = Price>
  <CFSET Stock = StructNew()>
  <CFSET Stock.Price = Price>
  <CFSET Stocks["Stock#i#"] = Stock>
</CFLOOP>

<CFOUTPUT>
<H2>Quote Structure</H2>
Sort Stock Name by Price (No parameters): #ArrayToList(StructSort(Quotes))#<BR>
Sort Stock Name by Price (Text, Desc):
  #ArrayToList(StructSort(Quotes, "Text", "Desc"))#<P>
Sort Stock Name by Price(Numeric, Asc):
  #ArrayToList(StructSort(Quotes, "Numeric", "Asc"))#

<H2>Stocks Structure</H2>
Sort Stock Name by Price (numeric, Desc, Price):
  #ArrayToList(StructSort(Stocks, "Numeric", "Desc", "Price"))#<BR>
</CFOUTPUT>
```

## StructUpdate

`StructUpdate(structure, key, value)`

Updates the specified *key* in *structure* by overwriting the existing data with *value*. The following example uses this function to update a key/value in a structure:

```
<CFSET Stock = StructNew()>
<CFSET Stock.Company = "Allaire">
<CFSET Stock.Ticker = "ALLR">
<CFSET Stock.Exchange = "NASDAQ">
<CFSET Stock.Price = "66.25">
<CFSET Stock.Change = "+0.375">
<CFSET Stock.LastTradeTime = "10:17AM">
<CFSET Stock.LastTradeDate = "05/17/1999">
<CFSET Stock.Volume = "8300">

<CFSET StructUpdate(Stock, "company", "Allaire Corp.")>

<CFOUTPUT>
<B>Company:</B> #Stock.company#<BR>
<B>Ticker:</B> #Stock.ticker#<BR>
<B>Exchange:</B> #Stock.exchange#<BR>
<B>Price:</B> #Stock.price#<BR>
<B>Change:</B> #Stock.change#<BR>
<B>Last Trade Time:</B> #Stock.lasttradetime#<BR>
<B>Last Trade Date:</B> #Stock.lasttradedate#<BR>
<B>Volume:</B> #Stock.volume#
</CFOUTPUT>
```

## Tan

`Tan(number)`

Returns the tangent of an angle expressed in radians. Example:

```
The tangent of 45 is <CFOUTPUT>#Tan(45)#</CFOUTPUT>
```

## TimeFormat

`TimeFormat(time [, mask])`

Returns *time* formatted according to *mask*. If no value is specified for *mask*, `TimeFormat()` uses the default `hh:mm tt`. Valid entries for *mask* are:

| Mask | Description |
|---|---|
| h | Hours based on a 12-hour clock with no leading zeros for single-digit hours |
| hh | Hours based on a 12-hour clock with leading zeros for single-digit hours |
| H | Hours based on a 24-hour clock with no leading zeros for single-digit hours |
| HH | Hours based on a 24-hour clock with leading zeros for single-digit hours |
| m | Minutes with no leading zero for single-digit minutes |
| mm | Minutes with a leading zero for single-digit minutes |
| s | Seconds with no leading zero for single-digit seconds |
| ss | Seconds with a leading zero for single-digit seconds |
| t | Single-character meridian, either A or P |
| tt | Multicharacter meridian, either AM or PM |

Examples:

```
<CFSET TheTime = Now()>

<CFOUTPUT>
TheTime = #TimeFormat(TheTime,'hh:mm:ss tt')#<P>

TimeFormat(TheTime, 'h:m:s'): #TimeFormat(TheTime, 'h:m:s')#<BR>
TimeFormat(TheTime, 'h:m:s t'): #TimeFormat(TheTime, 'h:m:s t')#<BR>
TimeFormat(TheTime, 'hh:mm:ss'): #TimeFormat(TheTime, 'hh:mm:ss')#<BR>
TimeFormat(TheTime, 'hh:mm:ss tt'): #TimeFormat(TheTime, 'hh:mm:ss tt')#<BR>
TimeFormat(TheTime, 'H:M:ss'): #TimeFormat(TheTime, 'H:M:s')#<BR>
TimeFormat(TheTime, 'HH:MM:ss'): #TimeFormat(TheTime, 'HH:MM:ss')#<BR>
</CFOUTPUT>
```

## ToBase64

New as of ColdFusion 4.5

`ToBase64(value)`

Base64 encodes a binary object or string. Base64 is an encoding scheme that uses printable characters to represent binary data. Base64 is typically used to encode binary data before it is sent via email or stored in a database. Here's an example that reads in a binary file using **CFFILE** and encodes it using **ToBase64()**:

```
<CFFILE ACTION="ReadBinary" FILE="D:/mydir/myfile.exe" VARIABLE="MyBinaryFile">

<CFSET MyBase64 = ToBase64(MyBinaryFile)>

<CFOUTPUT>Base64: #MyBase64#</CFOUTPUT>
```

## ToBinary

New as of ColdFusion 4.5

`ToBinary(value)`

Converts a base64-encoded string to its binary form. The following example take a base64-encoded string (in this case a GIF image of the letter R), converts it to a binary object using `ToBinary()`, writes the object out to a file, and then displays it using **CFCONTENT**:

```
<CFSET MyBase64="R0lGODlhGQAZAPcAAP////v7+/Pz8+7u7uLi4t3d3dnZ2dXV1cTExLe3t6qqqp6e
npGRkYmJiYiIiH9/f3t7e25ubmZmZllZWVZWV1FRUURERDw8PDQ0NC8vLyIiIhUVFREREQwMDAQEBAAAA
AAAAAAAAAAAAAAAAAAAAAAAAAAAAAAAAAAAAAAAAAAAAAAAAAAAAAAAAAAAAAAAAAAAAAAAAAAAAAA
AAAAAAAAAAAAAAAAAAAAAAAAAAAAAAAAAAAAAAAAAAAAAAAAAAAAAAAAAAAAAAAAAAAAAAAAAAAAAA
AAAAAAAAAAAAAAAAAAAAAAAAAAAAAAAAAAAAAAAAAAAAAAAAAAAAAAAAAAAAAAAAAAAAAAAAAAAAAA
AAAAAAAAAAAAAAAAAAAAAAAAAAAAAAAAAAAAAAAAAAAAAAAAAAAAAAAAAAAAAAAAAAAAAAAAAAAAAA
AAAAAAAAAAAAAAAAAAAAAAAAAAAAAAAAAAAAAAAAAAAAAAAAAAAAAAAAAAAAAAAAAAAAAAAAAAAAAA
AAAAAAAAAAAAAAAAAAAAAAAAAAAAAAAAAAAAAAAAAAAAAAAAAAAAAAAAAAAAAAAAAAAAAAAAAAAAAA
AAAAAAAAAAAAAAAAAAAAAAAAAAAAAAAAAAAAAAAAAAAAAAAAAAAAAAAAAAAAAAAAAAAAAAAAAAAAAA
AAAAAAAAAAAAAAAAAAAAAAAAAAAAAAAAAAAAAAAAAAAAAAAAAAAAAAAAAAAAAAAAAAAAAAAAAAAAAA
AAAAAAAAAAAAAAAAAAAAAAAAAAAAAAAAAAAAAAAAAAAAAAAAAAAAAAAAAAAAAAAAAAAAAAAAAAAAAA
AAAAAAAAAAAAAAAAAAAAAAAAAAAAAAAAAAAAAAAAAAAAAAAAAAAAAAAAAAAAAAAAAAAAAAAAAAAAAA
AAAAAAAAAAAAAAAAAAAAAAAAAAAAAAAAAAAAAAAAAAAAAAAAAAAAAAAAAAAAAAAAAAAAAAAAAAAAAA
AAAAACwAAAAAGQAZAEcIiwABCBxIsKDBgwQffPigAIHDBh4+YEBoUOGHAgMlLHRAsaPHjyApWlxI8sMEA
SFTqlwpkIGGlzAxUECQ0iLGgRc+cAhpE4CBDR86HKi58KbABQsrsFzKtKlTkCNLfvCQgGdRghUWWv0Q4c
EDCBYWRthaoQKHoFWJXhSYYGGGAFuNDgDagcDTu3gpBgQAOw==">

<CFSET MyBinary=ToBinary(MyBase64)>

<CFFILE ACTION="write" FILE="d:\inetsrv\cf\e\mybinary.gif" OUTPUT=#MyBinary#>

<CFCONTENT TYPE="image/gif" FILE="D:\inetsrv\CF\E\mybinary.gif" DELETEFILE="Yes">
```

## ToString

New as of ColdFusion 4.5

`ToString()`

Converts any datatype, including binary, to a string. If *value* can't be converted, an exception is thrown. Example:

```
<CFSET MyString="Have a nice day!">
<CFSET Base64String = ToBase64(MyString)>
<CFSET BinaryString = ToBinary(Base64String)>
<CFSET BackToString = ToString(BinaryString)>
```

```
<CFOUTPUT>
MyString: #MyString#<BR>
Base64String: #Base64String#<BR>
BackToString: #BackToString#<BR>
</CFOUTPUT>
```

## Trim

`Trim(string)`

Removes all leading and trailing spaces from a string. Example:

```
<CFSET OriginalString = "     ColdFusion     ">

<CFOUTPUT>
<B>Original String (quoted):</B> "#OriginalString#"<BR>
<B>Trimmed String (quoted):</B> "#Trim(OriginalString)#"
</CFOUTPUT>
```

## Ucase

`Ucase(string)`

Converts a string to uppercase. Example:

```
<CFSET MyString="i want this string to appear in all uppercase.">

<CFOUTPUT>#Ucase(MyString)#</CFOUTPUT>
```

## URLDecode

New as of ColdFusion 4.5

`URLDecode(URLEncodedString)`

Decodes a URL-encoded string. URL-encoded strings have all non-alphanumeric characters, replaced characters with their equivalent hexadecimal escape sequences. Here's an example that takes a URL-encoded string and decodes it:

```
<CFSET MyString="Why is the sky blue?">
<CFSET EncodedString=URLEncodedFormat(MyString)>
<CFSET DecodedString=URLDecode(EncodedString)>

<CFOUTPUT>
Original String: #MyString#<BR>
URL Encoded: #EncodedString#<BR>
Decoded: #DecodedString#
</CFOUTPUT>
```

## URLEncodedFormat

`URLEncodedFormat(`*`string`*`)`

Encodes strings that otherwise cause errors when passed as URLs. `URLEncodedFormat()` replaces nonalphanumeric characters with their equivalent hexadecimal escape sequences. ColdFusion automatically decodes any URL-escaped strings it encounters. The following example creates a URL-encoded hyperlink from a string containing spaces and nonalphanumeric characters:

```
<CFSET TheDate = "08/15/1998">
<CFSET ItemID = "123456">
<CFSET Customer = "Caroline Smith">

Click on the link below to check-out:<BR>
<P><CFOUTPUT>
<A HREF="http://www.myserver.com/index.cfm?TheDate=#UrlEncodedFormat(TheDate)#&
ItemID=#UrlEncodedFormat(ItemID)#&Customer=#UrlEncodedFormat(Customer)#">Check-out
</A>
</CFOUTPUT>
```

## Val

`Val(`*`string`*`)`

Returns a number that the beginning of the specified string can be converted to. If conversion isn't possible, returns 0. Examples:

```
<CFOUTPUT>
Val(123): #Val(123)#<BR>
Val('abc'): #Val('abc')#<BR>
Val('1a2b3c'): #Val('1a2b3c')#<BR>
Val(True): #Val(True)#<BR>
Val(11/11/99): #Val(11/11/99)#<BR>
</CFOUTPUT>
```

## ValueList

`ValueList(`*`queryname.column`*` [,`*`delimiter`*`])`

Returns a comma-separated list of values for the previously executed query column specified in `queryname.column`. An optional delimiter can be specified if the list is to be delimited with a character other than the comma (the default). The following example creates a value list from a ColdFusion query:

```
<CFQUERY NAME="MyQuery" DATASOURCE="ProgrammingCF">
         SELECT * FROM EmployeeDirectory
</CFQUERY>

<CFOUTPUT>
<B>The query column Name contains the following values:</B>
#ValueList(MyQuery.Name)#
</CFOUTPUT>
```

## Week

`Week(`*`date`*`)`

Returns the week of the year for a given date as a number between 1 and 53. Example:

```
The current week is week <CFOUTPUT>#Week(Now())#</CFOUTPUT>.
```

## WriteOutput

New as of ColdFusion 4.5

`WriteOutput(`*`string`*`)`

Writes text to the page output stream. `WriteOutput()` is meant to be used inside `CFSCRIPT` blocks but can also be used inside `CFOUTPUT` sections. Examples:

```
<CFSCRIPT>
WriteOutput('The WriteOutput function works best inside CFSCRIPT blocks<BR>');
</CFSCRIPT>

<CFOUTPUT>
#WriteOutput('Although you can use it in CFOUTPUT spaces, why would you?')#
</CFOUTPUT>
```

## XMLFormat

New as of ColdFusion 4.5

`XMLFormat(`*`string`*`)`

Returns *`string`* in a format that is safe to use with XML by escaping the following special characters: ampersands (&), double quotes ("), greater than signs (>), less than signs (<), and single quotes('). Example:

```
<CFSET MyString="Here is an example of the XMLFormat function: 5+5<20">

<CFOUTPUT>#XMLFormat(MyString)#</CFOUTPUT>

<P><I>View the page source to see the escaped text.</I>
```

## Year

`Year(`*`date`*`)`

Returns the year as a number for the given date. Example:

```
The current year is <CFOUTPUT>#Year(Now())#</CFOUTPUT>.
```

## YesNoFormat

`YesNoFormat(`*`value`*`)`

Returns all non-zero values as `Yes` and zero values as `No`. Also returns a Boolean `True` as `Yes` and a Boolean `False` as `No`. Note that Version 4.01 of ColdFusion contains a bug in the `YesNoFormat()` function that causes certain negative decimal values to evaluate incorrectly. This behavior was fixed in ColdFusion 4.5. Here are some examples of the function applied to different values:

```
<CFOUTPUT>
-1: #YesNoFormat(-1)#<BR>
-1.123: #YesNoFormat(-1.123)#<BR>
-0.123: #YesNoFormat(-0.123)#<BR>
0: #YesNoFormat(0)#<BR>
0.123: #YesNoFormat(0.123)#<BR>
1: #YesNoFormat(1)#<BR>
1.123: #YesNoFormat(1.123)#<BR>
True: #YesNoFormat(True)#<BR>
False: #YesNoFormat(False)#
</CFOUTPUT>
```

# C

# *Example Database Tables*

The examples used throughout this book reference several database tables. The schemas and data for these tables are listed in this appendix. Because of its low cost, wide availability, and ease of use, all tables were designed using Microsoft Access. Because Access is a desktop database, I don't recommend using it in production environments, especially where many concurrent users are expected to use the database. Access isn't designed for heavy concurrent use and may experience scalability and performance issues if placed under load. Additionally, there are limits on the amount of data that can reliably be stored in an Access database.

For production applications, I recommend you use an enterprise-level database, such as MS SQL Server, Oracle, DB2, Informix, or Sybase. These databases provide advanced features and functionality, such as stored procedures and triggers, and are specially tuned for handling multiple concurrent requests and massive amounts of data.

Table C-1 lists the schema for the `EmployeeDirectory` table that is used throughout the book, while Table C-2 lists the actual data.

*Table C-1. EmployeeDirectory Table Schema*

| Field Name | Field Type | Max Length |
| --- | --- | --- |
| ID (primary key) | AutoNumber | N/A |
| Name | Text | 255 |
| Title | Text | 255 |
| Department | Memo | N/A |
| Email | Date/Time | N/A |

*Table C-1. EmployeeDirectory Table Schema (continued)*

| Field Name | Field Type | Max Length |
|---|---|---|
| PhoneExt | Number (long int) | N/A |
| Salary | Number (double, two decimal places) | N/A |
| Picture | Memo | N/A |

*Table C-2. EmployeeDirectory Table Data*

| ID | Name | Title | Department | Email | Phone-Ext | Salary |
|---|---|---|---|---|---|---|
| 1 | Pere Money | President | Executive Mgmt | *pere@example.com* | 1234 | 400K |
| 2 | Greg Corcoran | Director | Marketing | *greg@example.com* | 1237 | 96K |
| 3 | Mark Edward | VP | Sales | *mark@example.com* | 1208 | 155K |
| 4 | Marcel Haney | Engineer I | Product Engineering | *marcel@example.com* | 1296 | 86K |
| 5 | Brian Christopher | Junior Accountant | Finance | *brian@example.com* | 1211 | 40K |
| 6 | Nick Gosnell | Risk Mgmt Analyst | Finance | *nick@example.com* | 1223 | 54K |
| 7 | Hugo Keane | Sr. Account Manager | Sales | *hugo@example.com* | 1214 | 100K |
| 8 | Chaz Maxwell | Engineer II | Product Engineering | *chaz@example.com* | 1287 | 78K |
| 9 | Kris Moritz | Network Manager | IT | *kris@example.com* | 1254 | 65K |
| 10 | Aaron Ridge | Analyst | IT | *aaron@example.com* | 1233 | 68K |
| 11 | Tareq Varga | Sr. Analyst | IT | *tareq@example.com* | 1278 | 76K |
| 12 | Jeff Shields | Marcom Manager | Marketing | *jeff@example.com* | 1282 | 63K |
| 13 | Martin Grant | Manager | Business Develop. | *martin@example.com* | 1215 | 57K |
| 14 | Curt Bond | VP | Investor Relations | *curt@example.com* | 1256 | 125K |
| 15 | Ray Roy | Instructor | Training | *ray@example.com* | 1276 | 42K |
| 16 | Rob Tyler | Manager | Training | *rob@example.com* | 1290 | 70K |
| 17 | Andie Moore | Director | HR | *andie@example.com* | 1241 | 84K |

*Table C-2. EmployeeDirectory Table Data (continued)*

| ID | Name | Title | Department | Email | Phone-Ext | Salary |
|---|---|---|---|---|---|---|
| 18 | Jen Newton | Benefits Coordinator | HR | *jen@example.com* | 1283 | 41K |
| 19 | David Holmes | Market Analyst | Investor Relations | *david@example.com* | 1225 | 76K |
| 20 | Christine Booker | Account Manager | Sales | *christine@example.com* | 1262 | 80K |

Table C-3 lists the schema for the `IncentiveAwards` table that is used in Chapter 11, while Table C-4 lists the actual data.

*Table C-3. IncentiveAwards Table Schema*

| Field Name | Field Type | Max Length |
|---|---|---|
| ID (foreign key) | Number (long int) | N/A |
| DateAwarded | Date | N/A |
| Category | Text | 255 |
| Amount | Number (double, two decimal places) | N/A |

*Table C-4. IncentiveAwards Table Data*

| ID | Date Awarded | Category | Amount ($) |
|---|---|---|---|
| 1 | 2/15/98 | Referral | 5000 |
| 2 | 7/12/98 | Referral | 5000 |
| 3 | 4/3/98 | Sales goal | 3000 |
| 3 | 7/12/98 | Sales goal | 3000 |
| 3 | 10/3/98 | Sales goal | 3000 |
| 4 | 6/23/98 | Patent award | 8000 |
| 4 | 2/4/99 | Referral | 5000 |
| 5 | 3/17/98 | Referral | 5000 |
| 5 | 1/10/99 | Perfect attendance | 500 |
| 6 | 9/14/98 | Referral | 5000 |
| 7 | 12/19/98 | Account growth | 4000 |
| 8 | 4/29/98 | Leadership achievement | 500 |
| 8 | 1/5/99 | Patent award | 8000 |
| 9 | 8/1/98 | Employee contest | 500 |
| 10 | 11/4/98 | Anniversary | 200 |
| 11 | 3/29/99 | Referral | 5000 |
| 12 | 5/7/00 | Anniversary | 200 |

*Table C-4. IncentiveAwards Table Data (continued)*

| ID | Date Awarded | Category | Amount ($) |
|---|---|---|---|
| 13 | 2/4/00 | Account growth | 2000 |
| 14 | 7/8/99 | Referral | 5000 |
| 15 | 11/17/99 | Leadership achievement | 500 |
| 16 | 1/10/00 | Perfect attendance | 500 |

Table C-5 lists the schema for the `Links` table that is used in Chapter 10, while Table C-6 lists the actual data.

*Table C-5. Links Table Schema*

| Field Name | Field Type | Max Length |
|---|---|---|
| ItemID (primary key) | AutoNumber | N/A |
| ParentItemID | Numeric | N/A |
| ItemName | Text | 255 |
| LinkURL | Text | 255 |

*Table C-6. Links Table Data*

| ItemID | ParentItemID | ItemName | LinkURL |
|---|---|---|---|
| 1 | 0 | Financial | |
| 2 | 1 | Brokers | |
| 3 | 2 | E*Trade | *http://www.etrade.com* |
| 4 | 2 | Ameritrade | *http://www.ameritrade.com* |
| 5 | 1 | Banks | |
| 6 | 5 | PNC Bank | *http://www.pncbank.com* |
| 7 | 5 | Wingspan Bank | *http://www.wingspanbank.com* |
| 8 | 0 | Computers | |
| 9 | 8 | Software | |
| 10 | 8 | Hardware | |
| 11 | 9 | Allaire | *http://www.allaire.com* |
| 12 | 9 | Microsoft | *http://www.microsoft.com* |
| 13 | 9 | IBM | *http://www.ibm.com* |
| 14 | 9 | Sun Microsystems | *http://www.sun.com* |
| 15 | 10 | Cisco | *http://www.cisco.com* |
| 16 | 10 | Intel | *http://www.intel.com* |
| 17 | 10 | Compaq | *http://www.compaq.com* |

# D

# ColdFusion Resources

This appendix lists sources of additional information about ColdFusion. One of the great things about ColdFusion is the wide variety of available information, from official Allaire resources to community-related material. The majority of resources listed in this appendix are available free of charge and were created by developers for developers.

## Official Allaire Resources

The following table lists the ColdFusion web sites that are maintained by Allaire. These sites should be among your first stops when searching for information on ColdFusion.

| | |
|---|---|
| Allaire Corporation web site | *http://www.allaire.com* |
| Allaire Alive | *http://alive.allaire.com/* |
| Beta site | *http://beta.allaire.com* |
| Certification program | *http://www.allaire.com/certification/* |
| ColdFusion DevCenter | *http://www.allaire.com/developer/referenceDesk/index.cfm* |
| ColdFusion online documentation | *http://www.allaire.com/Documents/cf4docs.cfm* |
| ColdFusion support forum | *http://forums.allaire.com/devconf/* |
| Developer conference information | *http://www.allaire.com/conference* |
| Developer's exchange | *http://devex.allaire.com/developer/gallery/index.cfm* |
| Developer's exchange support forum | *http://forums.allaire.com/taggalleryconf/* |

| | |
|---|---|
| Knowledge Base | *http://www.allaire.com/Support/KnowledgeBase/SearchForm.cfm* |
| Macromedia web site | *http://www.macromedia.com/* |

# *Magazines*

Several quality magazines dedicated to ColdFusion, both online and print, have popped up over the last few years. The following table lists the more popular.

| | |
|---|---|
| *CF Advisor* | *http://www.cfadvisor.com/* |
| *CF Masters* | *http://www.cfmasters.com/* |
| *ColdFusion Developer's Journal* | *http://www.sys-con.com/coldfusion/* |
| *Defusion* | *http://www.defusion.com/* |
| *The Fusion Authority* | *http://www.fusionauthority.com/* |

# *Community Resources*

The sites listed in the following table contain a vast array of ColdFusion-related resources. Many sites provide free code samples, custom tags, tips and tricks, newsletters, and mailing lists. All resources are free and supported by ColdFusion developers.

| | |
|---|---|
| BlackBox | *http://www.black-box.org/* |
| CFBugTraq | *http://www.cfbugtraq.com/* |
| CFMCentral.com | *http://www.cfmcentral.com/* |
| CFM-Resources | *http://www.cfm-resources.com/* |
| CFNewbie | *http://www.cfnewbie.com/* |
| cfObjects | *http://www.cfobjects.com/* |
| CFScripts.com | *http://www.cfscripts.com/* |
| CFSpot! | *http://www.cfspot.com/* |
| CFVault.com | *http://www.cfvault.com/* |
| CodeBits | *http://www.codebits.com/select.cfm?LanguageID=10* |
| ColdCuts | *http://www.teratech.com/coldcuts/* |
| ColdFusion Tips-N-Tricks | *http://www.earthquake.nxs.net/CF_tipsNtricks/* |
| CoolFusion | *http://www.coolfusion.com/* |
| Common Function Library Project | h*ttp://www.cflib.org/* |
| Follett Software | *http://www.fsc.follett.com/cf/* |
| Forta.com | *http://www.forta.com/* |
| Fusebox | *http://www.fusebox.org/* |
| House of Fusion | *http://www.houseoffusion.com/* |

| | |
|---|---|
| Intrafoundation Software | *http://www.intrafoundation.com/freeware.html* |
| TeamAllaire | *http://www.teamallaire.com/* |
| OpenWDDX.org | *http://www.openwddx.org/* |
| WebTricks | *http://www.webtricks.com/* |

# User Groups

ColdFusion user groups (CFUGs) are a great way to learn more about ColdFusion and to share your experiences with other developers. CFUGs are officially sanctioned by Allaire and provide a forum for learning about the latest ColdFusion-related technologies and techniques. New CFUGs are forming all the time, and as of this writing, there are over 200 worldwide. For the most up-to-date information on CFUGs, see Allaire's web site at *http://devex.allaire.com/developer/usergroups/*.

# Index

## Symbols



## A



We'd like to hear your suggestions for improving our indexes. Send email to *index@oreilly.com.*

## B



## C

## D

## G

## *M*

## *N*

## *O*

## P

## *Q*

## R

## S

## T

## V

## *W*

## X



## Y



## Z

## *About the Author*

**Rob Brooks-Bilson** is a freelance writer and the manager of web technologies at Amkor Technology. He has been working with ColdFusion since Version 1.5. Rob has written several freeware custom tags for ColdFusion, including CF_Stockgrabber, which was a winner in Allaire's "Coolest Tags of 1997" contest. Additionally, Rob serves as a coordinator for several open source function libraries at the Common Function Library Project at *http://www.cflib.org/*. He is a member of Team Allaire and a frequent speaker at ColdFusion user groups and industry conferences, including Allaire Developer Conferences. He has written several articles on ColdFusion for *Intranet Design Magazine*, *CFAdvisor*, and CNET's Builder.com.

Rob lives with his lovely and talented wife in Wilmington, Delaware. In his free time (what little of it there is), he enjoys running, rock climbing, mountain biking, and traveling.

## *Colophon*

Our look is the result of reader comments, our own experimentation, and feedback from distribution channels. Distinctive covers complement our distinctive approach to technical topics, breathing personality and life into potentially dry subjects.

The animal on the cover of *Programming ColdFusion* is an Arctic tern. Arctic terns (*Sterna paradisaea*) are small birds, about 12 to 15 inches long, that make the longest migration of any avian on Earth. They breed in the Arctic tundra but fly to the edge of the Antarctic ice pack during the winter. An Arctic tern flies over 21,750 miles each year; it spends most of its life, about 20 years, flying.

The Arctic tern has webbed feet, the tail is long and forked, the legs are short and red, and the head is rounded and white with a black cap and a bright orange beak. Research has shown that Arctic terns don't swim well and will do everything possible to stay out of the water. Even though their feet are webbed, they are small, so the birds swoop down, catch a fish, and eat it while flying.

During the breeding or courtship time male terns fly a "fish flight." A male takes a small fish in its bill and passes as low as it can over a female on the ground. If she notices, she'll join him in the fish flight, and they soon mate.

In Arctic breeding grounds, females lay one or two cream-colored eggs with brown speckles (1.6 inches long). The eggs are laid in a grassy area for protection from their predators and because there are no trees in the Arctic. Both parents care for the eggs and feed the hatchlings.

Native humans watch to see where Arctic terns are feeding. By monitoring where the terns hunt, they can find large schools of fish and increase their catch.

Mary Anne Weeks Mayo was the production editor and copyeditor for *Programming ColdFusion*. Ann Schirmer and Jane Ellin provided quality control. Edie Shapiro, Matt Hutchinson, Sada Preisch, and Molly Shangraw provided production assistance. Nancy Crumpton wrote the index.

Hanna Dyer designed the cover of this book, based on a series design by Edie Freedman. The cover image is an original illustration created by Lorrie LeJeune. Emma Colby produced the cover layout with QuarkXPress 4.1 using Adobe's ITC Garamond font.

Melanie Wang designed the interior layout based on a series design by Nancy Priest. Anne-Marie Vaduva converted the files from Microsoft Word to FrameMaker 5.5.6 using tools created by Mike Sierra. The text and heading fonts are ITC Garamond Light and Garamond Book; the code font is Constant Willison. The illustrations for this book were created by Robert Romano and Jessamyn Read using Macromedia Freehand 9 and Adobe Photoshop 6. This colophon was compiled by Mary Anne Weeks Mayo.

Whenever possible, our books use a durable and flexible lay-flat binding. If the page count exceeds this binding's limit, perfect binding is used.

## U

# How to stay in touch with O'Reilly

## 1. Visit Our Award-Winning Web Site

**http://www.oreilly.com/**

★"Top 100 Sites on the Web" —*PC Magazine*
★"Top 5% Web sites" —*Point Communications*
★"3-Star site" —*The McKinley Group*

Our web site contains a library of comprehensive product information (including book excerpts and tables of contents), downloadable software, background articles, interviews with technology leaders, links to relevant sites, book cover art, and more. File us in your Bookmarks or Hotlist!

## 2. Join Our Email Mailing Lists

### New Product Releases

To receive automatic email with brief descriptions of all new O'Reilly products as they are released, send email to:
**ora-news-subscribe@lists.oreilly.com**
Put the following information in the first line of your message (*not* in the Subject field):
**subscribe ora-news**

### O'Reilly Events

If you'd also like us to send information about trade show events, special promotions, and other O'Reilly events, send email to:
**ora-news-subscribe@lists.oreilly.com**
Put the following information in the first line of your message (*not* in the Subject field):
**subscribe ora-events**

## 3. Get Examples from Our Books via FTP

There are two ways to access an archive of example files from our books:

### Regular FTP

- ftp to:
  **ftp.oreilly.com**
  (login: anonymous
  password: your email address)
- Point your web browser to:
  **ftp://ftp.oreilly.com/**

### FTPMAIL

- Send an email message to:
  **ftpmail@online.oreilly.com**
  (Write "help" in the message body)

## 4. Contact Us via Email

**order@oreilly.com**
To place a book or software order online. Good for North American and international customers.

**subscriptions@oreilly.com**
To place an order for any of our newsletters or periodicals.

**books@oreilly.com**
General questions about any of our books.

**software@oreilly.com**
For general questions and product information about our software. Check out O'Reilly Software Online at **http://software.oreilly.com/** for software and technical support information. Registered O'Reilly software users send your questions to: **website-support@oreilly.com**

**cs@oreilly.com**
For answers to problems regarding your order or our products.

**booktech@oreilly.com**
For book content technical questions or corrections.

**proposals@oreilly.com**
To submit new book or software proposals to our editors and product managers.

**international@oreilly.com**
For information about our international distributors or translation queries. For a list of our distributors outside of North America check out:
**http://www.oreilly.com/distributors.html**

## 5. Work with Us

Check out our website for current employment opportunites:
**http://jobs.oreilly.com/**


O'Reilly & Associates, Inc.
101 Morris Street, Sebastopol, CA 95472 USA
TEL 707-829-0515 or 800-998-9938
(6am to 5pm PST)
FAX 707-829-0104

# International Distributors

http://international.oreilly.com/distributors.html

## UK, Europe, Middle East and Africa (except France, Germany, Austria, Switzerland, Luxembourg, and Liechtenstein)

**INQUIRIES**

O'Reilly UK Limited
4 Castle Street
Farnham
Surrey, GU9 7HS
United Kingdom
Telephone: 44-1252-711776
Fax: 44-1252-734211
Email: information@oreilly.co.uk

**ORDERS**

Wiley Distribution Services Ltd.
1 Oldlands Way
Bognor Regis
West Sussex PO22 9SA
United Kingdom
Telephone: 44-1243-843294
UK Freephone: 0800-243207
Fax: 44-1243-843302 (Europe/EU orders)
or 44-1243-843274 (Middle East/Africa)
Email: cs-books@wiley.co.uk

## France

**INQUIRIES & ORDERS**

Éditions O'Reilly
18 rue Séguier
75006 Paris, France
Tel: 1-40-51-71-89
Fax: 1-40-51-72-26
Email: france@oreilly.fr

## Germany, Switzerland, Austria, Luxembourg, and Liechtenstein

**INQUIRIES & ORDERS**

O'Reilly Verlag
Balthasarstr. 81
D-50670 Köln, Germany
Telephone: 49-221-973160-91
Fax: 49-221-973160-8
Email: anfragen@oreilly.de (inquiries)
Email: order@oreilly.de (orders)

## Canada (French language books)

Les Éditions Flammarion ltée
375, Avenue Laurier Ouest
Montréal (Québec) H2V 2K3
Tel: 00-1-514-277-8807
Fax: 00-1-514-278-2085
Email: info@flammarion.qc.ca

## Hong Kong

City Discount Subscription Service, Ltd.
Unit A, 6th Floor, Yan's Tower
27 Wong Chuk Hang Road
Aberdeen, Hong Kong
Tel: 852-2580-3539
Fax: 852-2580-6463
Email: citydis@ppn.com.hk

## Korea

Hanbit Media, Inc.
Chungmu Bldg. 210
Yonnam-dong 568-33
Mapo-gu
Seoul, Korea
Tel: 822-325-0397
Fax: 822-325-9697
Email: hant93@chollian.dacom.co.kr

## Philippines

Global Publishing
G/F Benavides Garden
1186 Benavides Street
Manila, Philippines
Tel: 632-254-8949/632-252-2582
Fax: 632-734-5060/632-252-2733
Email: globalp@pacific.net.ph

## Taiwan

O'Reilly Taiwan
1st Floor, No. 21, Lane 295
Section 1, Fu-Shing South Road
Taipei, 106 Taiwan
Tel: 886-2-27099669
Fax: 886-2-27038802
Email: mori@oreilly.com

## India

Shroff Publishers & Distributors Pvt. Ltd.
12, "Roseland", 2nd Floor
180, Waterfield Road, Bandra (West)
Mumbai 400 050
Tel: 91-22-641-1800/643-9910
Fax: 91-22-643-2422
Email: spd@vsnl.com

## China

O'Reilly Beijing
SIGMA Building, Suite B809
No. 49 Zhichun Road
Haidian District
Beijing, China PR 100080
Tel: 86-10-8809-7475
Fax: 86-10-8809-7463
Email: beijing@oreilly.com

## Japan

O'Reilly Japan, Inc.
Yotsuya Y's Building
7 Banch 6, Honshio-cho
Shinjuku-ku
Tokyo 160-0003 Japan
Tel: 81-3-3356-5227
Fax: 81-3-3356-5261
Email: japan@oreilly.com

## Singapore, Indonesia, Malaysia and Thailand

TransQuest Publishers Pte Ltd
30 Old Toh Tuck Road #05-02
Sembawang Kimtrans Logistics Centre
Singapore 597654
Tel: 65-4623112
Fax: 65-4625761
Email: wendiw@transquest.com.sg

## All Other Asian Countries

O'Reilly & Associates, Inc.
101 Morris Street
Sebastopol, CA 95472 USA
Tel: 707-829-0515
Fax: 707-829-0104
Email: order@oreilly.com

## Australia

Woodslane Pty., Ltd.
7/5 Vuko Place
Warriewood NSW 2102
Australia
Tel: 61-2-9970-5111
Fax: 61-2-9970-5002
Email: info@woodslane.com.au

## New Zealand

Woodslane New Zealand, Ltd.
21 Cooks Street (P.O. Box 575)
Waganui, New Zealand
Tel: 64-6-347-6543
Fax: 64-6-345-4840
Email: info@woodslane.com.au

## Argentina

Distribuidora Cuspide
Suipacha 764
1008 Buenos Aires
Argentina
Phone: 5411-4322-8868
Fax: 5411-4322-3456
Email: libros@cuspide.com

## U



## V

## W



## Y